HANDBOOK OF
AGRICULTURAL ECONOMICS

VOLUME 4

HANDBOOKS IN ECONOMICS

18

Series Editors

KENNETH J. ARROW
MICHAEL D. INTRILIGATOR

HANDBOOK OF AGRICULTURAL ECONOMICS

VOLUME *4*

Edited by

PRABHU PINGALI

Deputy Director, Agriculture Development, Bill and Melinda Gates Foundation, Seattle, WA, USA

ROBERT EVENSON

Professor of Economics, Yale University, New Haven, CT, USA

Amsterdam • Boston • Heidelberg • London • New York • Oxford
Paris • San Diego • San Francisco • Singapore • Sydney • Tokyo

North-Holland is an imprint of Elsevier
The Boulevard, Langford Lane, Kidlington, Oxford OX5 1GB, UK
Radarweg 29, PO Box 211, 1000 AE Amsterdam, The Netherlands

© 2010 ELSEVIER BV. All rights reserved.
Chapter 61: © 2010 Eugenio Diaz-Bonilla. Published by Elsevier BV. All rights reserved.
Chapter 68: © 2010 Science Council of the CGIAR. Published by Elsevier BV. All rights reserved.

No part of this publication may be reproduced or transmitted in any form or by any means, electronic or mechanical, including photocopying, recording, or any information storage and retrieval system, without permission in writing from the publisher. Details on how to seek permission, further information about the Publisher's permissions policies and our arrangements with organizations such as the Copyright Clearance Center and the Copyright Licensing Agency, can be found at our website: www.elsevier.com/permissions.

This book and the individual contributions contained in it are protected under copyright by the Publisher (other than as may be noted herein).

Notices
Knowledge and best practice in this field are constantly changing. As new research and experience broaden our understanding, changes in research methods, professional practices, or medical treatment may become necessary. Practitioners and researchers must always rely on their own experience and knowledge in evaluating and using any information, methods, compounds, or experiments described herein. In using such information or methods they should be mindful of their own safety and the safety of others, including parties for whom they have a professional responsibility.

To the fullest extent of the law, neither the Publisher nor the authors, contributors, or editors, assume any liability for any injury and/or damage to persons or property as a matter of products liability, negligence or otherwise, or from any use or operation of any methods, products, instructions, or ideas contained in the material herein.

British Library Cataloguing in Publication Data
A catalogue record for this book is available from the British Library

Library of Congress Cataloging-in-Publication Data
A catalog record for this book is available from the Library of Congress

ISBN: 978-0-444-51874-3

For information on all North-Holland publications
visit our website at books.elsevier.com

Printed and bound in the United States of America
09   10   11   12   13   10 9 8 7 6 5 4 3 2 1

The aim of the *Handbooks in Economics* series is to produce Handbooks for various branches of economics, each of which is a definitive source, reference, and teaching supplement for use by professional researchers and advanced graduate students. Each Handbook provides self-contained surveys of the current state of a branch of economics in the form of chapters prepared by leading specialists on various aspects of this branch of economics. These surveys summarize not only received results but also newer developments, from recent journal articles and discussion papers. Some original material is also included, but the main goal is to provide comprehensive and accessible surveys. The Handbooks are intended to provide not only useful reference volumes for professional collections but also possible supplementary readings for advanced courses for graduate students in economics.

Kenneth J. Arrow
Michael D. Intriligator

CONTENTS OF THE HANDBOOK

CONTENTS OF VOLUME 4

PART 2   Regional Perspectives in Agricultural Development

CHAPTER 66   Production, Productivity, and Public Investment in East Asian Agriculture   3401

Shenggen Fan *and* Joanna Brzeska

PART One

Policies for Agriculture Development

CHAPTER 61

Macroeconomics, Macrosectoral Policies, and Agriculture in Developing Countries

Eugenio Diaz-Bonilla

Inter American Development Bank

Sherman Robinson
University of Sussex

Contents

Handbook of Agricultural Economics, Volume 4   doi: 10.1016/S1574-0072(09)04061-4

Abstract

This handbook devotes most of its chapters to reviewing sectoral policies related to agriculture. This chapter moves to a macroeconomic and macrosectoral view of the policy framework and its possible interaction with the agricultural sector. A previous handbook (Gordon Rausser and Bruce Gardner, eds., 2002) devoted a whole section with several chapters to economywide policies.[1] Since then, there have been nontrivial changes in macroeconomic trends and policy debates, not only regarding domestic aspects but also, and perhaps more relevant for developing countries, at the level of the global economy. In the spirit of Schuh (1986) this chapter attempts to review and update some of the world macroeconomic issues relevant for agriculture, while at the same time covering domestic macroeconomic development affecting the sector, in both cases taking mostly the perspective of developing countries.

The rest of this chapter is organized as follows. In Section 1, we define the main macroeconomic topics that we will cover and their links to agriculture. Section 2 presents a brief characterization of differentiated structural issues in developing countries economy in general and the agricultural sector in particular as a background for a more detailed analysis of *world* macroeconomic conditions and trends (Section 3) and of *domestic* macroeconomic policies (Section 4). Section 5 concludes by trying to weave a narrative with the performance of the agricultural sector in developing countries during the last half-century in light of world and domestic macroeconomic issues analyzed in the previous two sections and to present some speculative thoughts about the future evolution of the sector in those countries.

JEL classification: E000, Macroeconomics and Monetary Economics: General; F000, International Economics: General; O110, Macroeconomic Analyses of Economic Development; Q180, Agricultural Policy; Food Policy

Keywords

macroeconomics
developing countries
economic crisis
macroprices

1. MACROECONOMIC AND MACROSECTORAL POLICIES: SOME PRECISIONS AND CONCEPTUAL ISSUES

1.1 What are the macroeconomic problems and issues considered?

The distinction between growth (with policies acting on the aggregate supply, mainly in the medium to long term) and stabilization of cycles (with policies directed at aggregate demand, basically in the short run, to smooth out expansions and recessions) seems, at first, a natural way to organize the discussion about macroeconomic issues. If that dichotomy were accepted, the macroeconomic policy problem could be simply defined as the stabilization of the aggregate demand around the (independently determined) growth trend of the aggregate supply to avoid either unemployment (if there is a lack of aggregate demand compared to potential aggregate supply) or inflation and balance-of-payment problems (in case of excess of aggregate demand over supply). We could call the alignment of aggregate demand with aggregate supply the first macroeconomic problem.

However, as Stock and Watson (1988) have argued, this dichotomy between trend growth and cycles around it could be misleading if there are important interactions between those two aspects. Thus, it is not adequate to define the macroeconomic problem as merely a question of how to align aggregate demand with an independently evolving aggregate supply. The interactions between trend growth and the cycle must be also considered.[2] Those interactions come from several factors, including the influence of macroprices—such as the terms of trade, exchange rate, interest rate, and average wages—on stabilization of the cycle and on growth trends.

The exchange rate plays a central role both in the nominal aspects related to the short-run management of the aggregate demand and in the real aspects affecting aggregate supply in the longer run. The dual role of the exchange rate is reflected in the two approaches to exchange rate policy that have been applied in developing countries. First, the "real exchange rate" approach emphasizes the influence of the exchange rate on production and trade (see Balassa, 1977, 1985). Second, the "nominal anchor" approach highlights the role of the exchange rate in the inflationary process and its relationship with interest rates, capital flows, and asset accumulation. The duality of the exchange rate has been at the core of several problems of inconsistency in economic programs in many countries (see Corden, 1990). Interest rates have a dual role as well. They not only influence aggregate demand in the short run but also affect the choices between savings and investment and, possibly, between technological options, thereby determining long-term growth prospects. Similarly, wages can affect aggregate demand over the cycle, but they also have an effect on the capital/labor ratios, technological alternatives, and the decision to invest in human capital, among other things, all of which define aggregate supply trends. Finally, trends and volatility in the terms of trade have short-term effects on aggregate demand as well as longer-term effects on investment and growth.

Therefore, in addition to the alignment of aggregate demand with aggregate supply, a second macroeconomic policy issue is how "to get macroprices right" (to the extent that can be influenced by policy), avoiding misalignments (variously defined) and reducing volatility and uncertainty.

Economic crises, with their several fiscal, financial, trade, and social components, are particularly dramatic manifestations of imbalances between aggregate demand and aggregate supply (the first macroeconomic policy problem) and/or of misalignments in macroprices (the second macroeconomic policy problem). Crises tend to affect long-term growth prospects and increase poverty through various channels. For instance, higher unemployment and its persistence over time deteriorate human capital; crises also destroy installed capital and their recurrence increases uncertainty, reducing investment and therefore future capital. They also tend to leave a legacy of public and private debt, weakening fiscal accounts and financial systems. Crises also have important negative effects on the poor, who might find their limited human and productive capital compromised if, for instance, children have to be withdrawn from school or if assets, such as small farmers' livestock, are sold to face negative economic shocks. Therefore, crisis avoidance—and when things go wrong, crisis management—can be considered a third macroeconomic issue in its own right.

There are also other efficiency, distributive, and growth effects resulting from some micro aspects of macro policies, such as the structure of tax and public expenditures (and not only the aggregate level), more specific financial and regulatory policies within the general macro framework of a monetary program, and so on. These microeconomic implications of macroeconomic policies are a fourth aspect to be considered.

In summary, macroeconomic policies have implications for smoothing the business cycle, for medium- to long-term growth, and for distributive issues, and in their analysis it is important to consider all four issues: (1) the proper alignment of aggregate demand and aggregate supply; (2) the level, stability, and sustainability of macroprices; (3) microeconomic implications; and (4) avoidance of economic crises.

1.2 Macroeconomic accounts

Building consistent and complete macroeconomic models requires, among other things, that they utilize a definition of flows and stocks that follows double-entry conventions of accounting with regard to the income statement and the balance sheets of the economic agents (Christ, 1987). In fact, it has been said that macroeconomics is a collection of accounting equations plus "opinions." The latter abound: about macroeconomic causality (or "closure rules"); about the intra- and intertemporal behavior of economic agents; about the structure, functioning, and clearing procedures for markets; about the value of key elasticities and parameters, and so on. But the macroeconomic accounting equations, for all the data collection problems they might have, are subject to the discipline of the double-entry convention and cannot be ignored or violated. Many mistakes in macroeconomic analysis and policy can be traced to not having paid adequate attention to those accounting equations and the relations across variables enforced by double-entry accounting (Christ, 1987). In this chapter we will use those accounting equations as a basic framework to discuss macroeconomic options and policies.

There are four main sets of macroeconomic accounts that record transactions in the economy and provide data and structure for any macroeconomic analysis or policy recommendation:
- National income and product accounts
- Balance of payments
- Monetary accounts
- Public sector accounts

These accounts can be integrated within a *social accounting matrix*, or SAM (see Pyatt and Round, 1985): a tableau that records relevant transactions in an economy utilizing double-entry accounting. After the accounts are defined (representing activities, commodities, factors of production, institutions, etc.), each one of them appears twice in the matrix: first as a buyer from other accounts (transactions that are recorded down the columns) and second as a seller (recorded across the rows). The SAM is then a compact representation of the transactions, and each cell is at the same time an incoming flow for the account in the row and an outgoing flow for the account in the column. Because of the double-entry principle, the sum of the cells down a column for an account must equal the sum of the cells across the corresponding row for that account.

The structure and level of disaggregation of the SAM will depend on the objectives of the analysis. Here we present four main "agents," usually called *institutions*: (1) the private sector (including firms and households), (2) the public sector, (3) the monetary sector, and (4) the rest of the world. The various economic agents and institutions must be assigned in such a way that they belong to one and only one of these sectors.

The balance of payments, monetary accounts, and public sector accounts correspond to the rest of the world, the monetary sector, and the public sector, respectively. The national income and product accounts present the transactions for the whole economy, and, if the accounting system is properly structured, the private sector accounts can be derived by subtracting balance of payments, monetary accounts, and public sector accounts from national income and product accounts.

The sectors identified execute three basic functions: (a) they produce and commercialize, (b) they consume (and complete other transactions in their current account), and (c) they accumulate (save and invest). Combining functions and sectors, we have the simplified matrix in Table 1.

As indicated, transactions recorded down the columns indicate payments made by the institution or sector at the top of the matrix. Reading transactions across the rows indicates payments received by the institution or sector at the left of the matrix.[3] For example, in the Current Account where the column of Government crosses with the row of the Private Sector, it reads: INTR * B + ST. That means that the government is paying the private sector interest over the bonds (the interest rate, INTR, times [symbol *] the stock of outstanding debt B, representing the stock of borrowing by the government from the private sector) plus subsidies and other transfers (ST) and reading from the row perspective, of course, the private sector is receiving that same amount.

Production takes place in Activities and distribution/commercialization is in Commodities. This allows the separation, as is common in computable general equilibrium (CGE) models, between domestically produced and consumed goods (D), exports (EX), and imports (IM). This distinction is important even for a single sector of production, reflecting the fact that at the level of disaggregation at which statistics are collected, it is usual to observe all three goods coexisting. In other words, data for a single

Table 1 Social Accounting Matrix

Expenditures By/Receipt By	Activities	Commodities	Factors		Current Account (Income and Expenditures)				Capital Account (Savings and Investments)			
			Labor	Capital	Private Sector	Government	Monetary	Rest World	Private Sector	Government	Monetary	Rest World
Activities		D										
Commodities	A				C	G		EX	INVp	INVg		
Factors: Labor	YL											
Factors: Capital	YK											
Current Account: Private Sector			YL – TL	YK – TK		INTR*B+ST		OPTNp				
Current Account: Government	Tind	Tm	TL	TK	TY		ProfCB	OTNg				
Current Account: Monetary					INTR*CDp	INTR*CDg						
Current Account: Rest World		IM			INTR*CFp	INTR*CFg						
Capital Account: Private Sector	DEPR				Sp						dCDp	dCFp
Capital Account: Government						Sg			dB		dCDg	dCFg
Capital Account: Monetary							Sm – ProfCB		dMp	dMg		
Capital Account: Rest World								Srw			dNFA	

A — Intermediate Goods: Input-Output Table
YL — Labor Income
YK — Capital Income
D — Domestic Goods (produced and consumed)
C — Consumption
G — Government
EX — Exports
IM — Imports
INVp — Private Investment
INVg — Government Investment
DEPR — Depreciation

Tind — Indirect Taxes
Tm — Trade Taxes
TL — Labor Taxes
TK — Taxes on Capital
TY — Income Taxes
ST — Subsidies and Transfers
ProfCB — Profits (losses) from Central Bank
OPTNp — Other Net Factor Payments and/or Private Transfers from/to Abroad
OTNg — Other Government Transfers Net from/to Abroad

Sp — Private Savings (Current Account)
Sg — Government Savings (Current Account)
Sm — Monetary Sector Savings (Current Account)
Srw — Rest World Savings (Current Account)
INTR — Interest Rate
B — Government Bonds
CDp — Domestic Credit to Private Sector
CDg — Domestic Credit to Government
CFp — Foreign Credit to Private Sector
CFg — Foreign Credit to Government
NFA — Net Foreign Assets of the Monetary Sector

Note: The letter *d* indicates change in stocks from the baseline time to the next period considered. The symbol * is utilized to indicate multiplication.

productive sector normally shows at the same time nontraded, exportable, and importable components, with different levels of substitutability among them (see, for instance, Dervis, de Melo, and Robinson, 1982).

Different from CGE models and in line with aggregate macroeconomic analysis, here there is only one activity (with two components, D and EX) and only one commodity (also with two components, D and IM). However, both the activity and the commodity can be divided into many sectors, as is usually done in CGE models.

The activity of production buys intermediate goods/services (A) from Commodities. Also, it pays to Factors the value added, as wages, salaries, and other labor-related factor incomes (YL), and profits and other nonlabor-related factor incomes (YK). To simplify, it is assumed that Activity pays to the Private Sector all value added, which, in turn, pays factor taxes to Government (TK and TL). The value added (YL + YK) is the Net Domestic Product at factor cost. Activity also pays to the Government indirect taxes (Tind), which later are added to the sales of its products, and pays depreciation, DEPR (to simplify notation, we are assuming that it goes only to the private sector).

Activity sells the domestic good/service D to Commodities, for its commercialization in the domestic market, and to the Rest of the World (ROW) as exports (EX). Commodities buys the domestic goods/services D and imports (IM) from ROW (part of which may be used as intermediate inputs), paying import taxes (Tm). Across the row, Commodities sells to the Private Sector and the Government final goods and (nonfactorial) services for consumption and investment, both private and public (C, G, INVp, and INVg).[4] It is also assumed that the Monetary Sector (which here is simplified to be the Central Bank only) does not perform activities of final consumption and investment.

Factors (Labor and Capital[5] in this simplified setting) transfer their respective income (YK and YL) to the private sector (and pay taxes to Government). In disaggregated CGE models, factors are usually subdivided further (for instance, labor can be subdivided by gender, education, and so on). In this table we consider a single private sector. But, again, in more detailed CGE models the private sector is divided into Households and Firms first, and then there may be additional subdivisions within each one of those categories.

The table shows several important submatrices. First, the block where Activities (down) intersects with Commodities (across) corresponds, in more disaggregated matrices, to the *Input-Output Table* (here there is only an intermediate product A). Second, where Factors transfer their incomes to the Private Sector in disaggregated CGE models there is the *matrix of factoral income distribution*. Finally, the block formed by the intersection of the row and column of the Capital Account corresponds to another important submatrix that is sometimes known as the *flow-of-funds matrix*. The Private Sector, Government, Monetary Sector, and ROW transfer their savings from the Current Account to the Capital Account (Sp, Sg, Sm, and Srw, respectively), which, along with the depreciation allowances, will be utilized to finance physical and financial investments. The intermediation between savings and investments takes place within the flow-of-funds matrix.

If the conceptual, statistical, and numerical aspects of the various transactions have been treated adequately, the vertical sum (column) and the horizontal sum (row) of the same sector, activity, or institution must be equal. Those summations produce different equations of fundamental importance for macroeconomic analysis, as shown immediately.

Combining Activities and Commodities, we have Gross Domestic Product at market prices (GDPmp)[6]:

$$YL + YK + Tind + Tm + DEPR = GDPmp = C + G + INVp + INVg + EX - IM \quad (1)$$

For every Institution there is a current account and a capital account equation.
Private Sector:
Current account:

$$YL - TL + YK - TK + I*B + ST + OPTNp = C + TY + I*CDp + i*CFp + Sp$$

Capital account:

$$DEPR + Sp + dCDp + dCFp = INVp + dB + dMp$$

Government:
Current account:

$$Tind + Tm + TL + TK + TY + OTNg + ProfCB$$
$$= G + INTR*B + ST + INTR*CDg + INTR*CFg + Sg$$

Capital account:

$$Sg + dB + dCDg + dCFg = INVg + dMg$$

Combining both accounts, we have the overall government budget constraint:

$$Tind + Tm + TL + TK + TY + OTNg + ProfCB + dB + dCDg + dCFg$$
$$= G + ST + INTR*B + INTR*CDg + INTR*CFg + INVg + dMg \quad (2)$$

The government collects different types of taxes, such as indirect taxes (Tind), trade taxes (Tm), taxes on factors other than income taxes (TL and TK), and income taxes (TY). The range of taxes can be expanded and disaggregated further. In addition to taxes (Tind + Tm + TL + TK + TY, in Eq. 2), the government receives external

transfers to the government (OTNg) and the surplus from the Central Bank (ProfCB) and utilizes several sources of financing (dB + dCDg + dCFg, where d indicates changes, and therefore they are, respectively, changes in government bonds, in credit from the Central Bank, and credit from abroad). All these incoming cash flows are utilized to pay for Government services (G), public sector investment (INVg), subsidies and transfers to the Private Sector (ST), interest on government debt (which may be debt to the Private Sector, INTR*B, to the Monetary sector, INTR*CDg, and to RWO, INTR*CFg), and for the accumulation of money by the Government (dMg).
Monetary Sector:

Here the Monetary Sector is the Central Bank, and it is assumed that this institution hands over to the Government Sector the profits (or losses) generated.

Current account:

$$i*CDp + i*CDg = ProfCB + (Sm - ProfCB)$$

Capital account:

$$Sm - ProfCB + dMp + dMg = dCDp + dCDg + dNFA \qquad (3)$$

Usually, the capital account in Eq. 3 is more relevant for macroeconomic analysis: It says that accumulation of net foreign assets by the Central Bank (dNFA) and provision of credit to the government (dCDg) and the private sector (dCDp) expand the money supply, which is held by the government and the private sector (dMg and dMp, respectively). There may also be some accumulation of wealth at the Central Bank (Sm - ProfCB). In many analyses, the Monetary Sector is defined in stock terms (the balance sheet of the Central Bank, discussed later).[7]
Rest of World:

Current account:

$$EX + OPTNp + OTNg + Srw = IM + INTR*CFp + INTR*CFg$$

Capital account:

$$dCFp + dCFg = Srw + dNFA$$

Combining current and capital accounts, we have the equation for the balance of payments:

$$(EX - IM) + (OPTNp + OTNg - INTR*CFp - INTR*CFg) + (dCFp + dCFg) = dNFA \qquad (4)$$

where (EX − IM) is the trade balance; adding to that (OPTNp + OTNg − INTR * CFp − INTR * CFg), we have the current account balance, and (dCFp + dCFg) is the capital account. The signs for OPTNp and OTNg assume that those transfers are received by the country and paid by ROW (but the sign can be changed if the transfers are received by ROW); in the case of INTR * CFp and INTR * CFg, it is assumed that the country pays interest to the rest of the world; positive (negative) signs for dCFp and dCFg imply capital flows to (or out from) the country or that the country is borrowing from (or lending to) ROW.

Domestic macroeconomic policies, discussed in the next sections, focus on some of the equations mentioned before. For instance, *fiscal policy* will center on the government budget constraint (Eq. 2), *exchange rate and trade policies* focus mainly but not only on the balance of payment (Eq. 4), and *monetary policy* may use a version of the monetary accounts (Eq. 3), sometimes in stock form, usually expanded to the whole financial system and not only the Central Bank. But whatever component of macroeconomic policy is analyzed, it is clear that the repercussions affect the whole economy (Eq. 1), as suggested by Table 1. In the next sections we use these equations to discuss policy options and possible outcomes.

1.3 Macroeconomic links to agriculture and the rural sector

What are the links of macroeconomic issues and the agricultural sector? The analysis of the connections between macroeconomic policies and agriculture in *developing countries* has emphasized mostly price effects caused by trade protection related to import substitutions industrialization (ISI) and by policies that affect the exchange rate (Krueger, et al., 1988; Valdes and Bautista, 1993). These analyses have focused basically on two indicators: the real exchange rate (an index of relative prices of tradable to nontradable products) and the internal terms of trade between agricultural and nonagricultural sectors. Usually these analyses have assumed that agricultural products are mostly tradable and that they do not have a significant content of imports in their production.

However, the impacts on agriculture from different macroeconomic conditions involve a larger number of variables and channels. This has long been recognized in studies of *industrialized countries*: In addition to the importance of the exchange rate for agriculture (Schuh, 1976), other, broader considerations have been factored in, such as income and demand effects, interest rates, and the impact of other monetary and macroeconomic variables operating directly or indirectly on the agricultural sector (see, for instance, Schultz, 1945; Gardner, 1981; the articles in Paarlberg and Chambers, 1988, especially Robert Thompson's; and Orden, 1986). In this chapter we take this second and broader view of macroeconomic issues and policy options and their impacts on agriculture.

Disaggregating the net income of an agricultural production unit helps better identify the channels through which macroeconomic conditions and policies affect the sector.

Defining agricultural net income (Ya) of a production unit (which in many developing countries is mostly family owned) as;

Ya = Value of agricultural production (VPa) − Costs of agricultural production (CPa)
    + Net Transfers from Government (NTG)

$$Vpa = Pa*Qa$$

where Pa is a vector of agricultural prices multiplied (*) by Qa, which is a vector of agricultural quantities, produced and demanded,[8] with each product properly indexed (indices not shown in what follows).

The determination of Pa (per product) depends on the different degrees of tradability. The price of perfectly tradable and homogeneous products (Pat) at the producer level is determined by (assuming the country is small in world markets):

$$Pat = EXR*Paw*(1 + ta)*(1 − margins)$$

where EXR is the exchange rate (domestic currency per international currency that we will call *dollar*); Paw is the price in world markets of the product; ta can be an import tax or an export subsidy; and margins are different costs from the point in the commercialization chain where the world price was defined and up to the point of sale of the producer.

The price of a pure nontradable is defined by domestic supply (Sant) and demand (Dant), which in turn depend on a series of macroeconomic and other factors:

$$Pant = Sant(...) − Dant(...)$$

Production of Qa is a function of factors of production owned by the productive unit (labor Lfa, capital Kfa, and land Tfa, using *f* to indicate that they are family owned), others hired (Lnfa, Knfa, and Tnfa; *nf* for nonfamily owned), and a variety of inputs.

$$Qa = F (Lfa, Lnfa, Kfa, Knfa, Tfa, Tnfa, Inputs)$$

Total external costs are:

$$CPa = w*Lnfa + Pk*Knfa + Pland*LANDnfa + i*CD + Pins*Inputs + Depreciation$$

where w * Lnfa is the cost of nonfamily labor (salary times the quantity of nonfamily labor hired); Pk * Knfa is the cost of obtaining the nonfamily-owned capital (rental price times rented capital); i * CD is the cost of credit (interest times volume of credit); Pland * LANDnfa is the cost of rented land (rental price time the nonfamily land rented to produce); and Pins * Inputs is the cost of productive inputs (price times quantity).

Here costs include those related to factors of production and inputs that are not owned by the family. In that sense (VPa – CPa) is the return to all factors of production owned by producing unit or the value added controlled by that unit. Note that total value added generated by the agricultural unit exceeds the amount received by the owners of that productive unit.

Finally, agricultural net income (Ya) can include net transfers from the government:

$$NTG = Subsidies - Taxes$$

All the previous channels affect the return to *agricultural activities* and the agricultural component of the incomes of rural families (Ya). However, those activities are part of a broader array of activities in the rural sector. For individuals and families in rural areas, incomes may also come from nonagricultural sources (Yna). In turn, all activities (agricultural or not) may feature exportable (Yax, Ynax), importable (Yam, Ynam), and nontradable (Yant, Ynant) goods and services, as in the following simplified matrix:

	Exportable (x)	Importable (m)	Nontradable (nt)
Agriculture (Ya)	Yax	Yam	Yant
Nonagriculture (Yna)	Ynax	Ynam	Ynant

Livelihood strategies of *rural families* in developing countries tend to combine, in different proportions, more than one of those income cells. Therefore the impact of macroeconomic conditions and policies on those families can be ambiguous. Those events or policies that improve (or reduce) agricultural incomes (Ya) can reduce (or increase) nonagricultural ones (Yna), with a variety of net impacts on rural families. Even within each type of income, macroeconomic policies may have different impact on exportable, importable, or nontradable products.

These families and firms, in turn, through their decisions of production and demand, influence the levels of activity and consumption in other productive sectors and contribute to determine general macroeconomic conditions. If there exists the possibility of transferring productive resources to nonagricultural activities (and in the medium and long term, most factors of production can change to other activities) and nonagricultural rates of return and incomes are more rewarding (after adjusting for risk and other factors) than those in agricultural activities, those families and firms will eventually switch resources toward other sectors.

1.4 In summary

As indicated before, some analysis of the impact of macroeconomic policies on agriculture tend to focus on Pa, usually presented as an aggregate index for the sector, and compare it to Pna, a similar price index of nonagricultural goods and services, to detect the possible sectoral bias of applied policies. From the previous sections it is clear that such indicators, although important, capture only a fraction of the channels through which the macroeconomic conditions and policies affect agriculture. A more complete analysis should also include the following:

- First, it is important to consider the level, composition, and rate of growth of the aggregate demand (domestic and exports) in general and of the demand for agricultural products in particular.
- Another channel operates through the level and expected variations in macroprices (exchange rate, interest rates, and wages) and in the prices of products and inputs included in the previous equations. Through those changes, macroeconomic policies and conditions affect, among other things, the level and composition of investment and the technological bias.
- Macroeconomic conditions also affect the availability of certain inputs (in a broad sense) necessary to obtain the planned levels of agricultural production. For example, credit availability depends in part on monetary policy; provision of productive services and infrastructure (such as research and extension, rural roads, and irrigation) is affected by fiscal policy; availability and prices of inputs and machinery can be influenced by exchange rates and international trade policies; and so on.
- Fiscal and trade policies may also affect the level and change in net transfers from governments.
- World macroeconomic conditions not only affect exports, imports, and world prices of agriculture; they also have an influence on other variables such as world interest rates, capital flows, and terms of trade in general, which in turn affect domestic economic conditions in general and the agricultural sector, in particular.

Besides the influence from macroeconomic conditions and policies on agriculture, in developing countries the reverse causality must also be considered, particularly in those countries where agriculture represents a significant percentage of the GDP, employment, trade, and, perhaps, fiscal receipts linked to exports. In those cases, the performance of the agricultural sector will determine growth, inflation, balance of payment conditions, and fiscal balances (see, for instance, Johnson [1987], on the analysis of the agricultural sector in IMF-supported programs, and Ran, In, and Dillon [1995], for a specific analysis of the effects of agricultural production fluctuations on China's macroeconomic conditions).

In Sections 3 and 4, this chapter focuses on those world and domestic macroeconomic conditions and policies. Before moving to that review, Section 2 discusses some differential structural conditions in developing countries that condition their response to macroeconomic developments.

2. BRIEF CHARACTERIZATION OF MACROECONOMIC AND AGRICULTURAL STRUCTURAL ISSUES IN DEVELOPING COUNTRIES

The impact of changes in macroeconomic conditions on developing countries depends on the policies they follow as well as on the structure of their economies, both in general and in relation to the agricultural sector in particular. This section looks at some structural characteristics in developing countries as a background for the subsequent discussion of world and domestic macroeconomic policies in those countries.

2.1 Heterogeneity of country conditions

The fact that developing countries are different from industrialized countries and that they also differ greatly among themselves is obvious. Since the early debates about long-term development strategies, those differences were invoked to design specific policies for developing countries. That debate also included the need to adjust macroeconomic policies (and not only long-term growth policies) to the specific structural characteristics of those countries.[9] More recently different books have been devoted to the specific needs of development countries in the design and implementation of macroeconomic policies (see for instance Lance Taylor, 1979 and 1984, and Agenor and Montiel, 2006). The general point is that although, in abstract, the general economic principles would apply to developing countries as well as to industrialized countries, the setting where those principles operate is sufficiently different in the former as to merit specific adjustments in the design and implementation of macroeconomic policies. Without trying to produce an exhaustive list (for a more detailed discussion, see the books mentioned before), some issues worth mentioning include the following:

- Aggregate rates of growth for developing countries (although with large variations) tend to be higher than in industrialized countries (Table 1), although incomes per capita show a large disparity (over US$30,000/per capita in developed countries versus about US$1600 in developing countries, on average for the 2000s; WDI [2008]).
- Poverty rates and the extent of the informal economy are far larger in developing countries. Labor markets are also more segmented, a fact discussed since Lewis (1953, 1954; for more recent discussions see Agenor, 1996).
- Primary production, particularly agriculture (see the following), is a larger component of the economy in developing countries (about 11% of the GDP versus less than 2% in developed countries). On the other hand, industrialized countries have a larger proportion of services in their GDP (about 72% on average for the 2000s compared to 54%). The proportion of industrial production is now larger in developing countries as a whole (35% of GDP) compared to developed countries (26%). However, because the combined total GDP of developed countries at market rates is about 2.5 to 3 times larger than total GDP of developing countries, the industrial sector in developed countries continues to be the larger component at the world level.
- Those productive characteristics are, of course, reflected in the structure of trade, where developing countries still have larger percentages of primary products in their exports (29% versus 17% in developed economies), whereas developed countries have more industrial goods (about 80% of exports versus 70% in developing countries as a whole). This imparts larger volatility to the terms of trade of developing countries. Another feature to be noticed, related to the lower relative presence of services in the GDP of developing countries, is that the latter have

larger trade/GDP ratios than developed countries (59% versus 44%, average during the 2000s; WDI [2008]).

- In terms of fiscal parameters, governments are bigger in developed countries, with a larger tax base, and able to fund themselves through debt in local currency markets. Developing countries' governments tend to be smaller, have a narrower and more volatile tax base (in many cases with a nontrivial, although declining, proportion of trade taxes), and an important percentage of public debt is usually denominated in hard foreign currencies.
- Inflation is higher in developing countries (see Table 1) than in developed countries, although with variations across countries. Financial deepening, as measured, for instance, by a broad indicator of liquidity such as M3/GDP, is more advanced in developed countries (a ratio of 109% versus 72%). Also, developed countries have financial systems that operate mostly with their own currency (including the case of monetary unions, such as the European monetary system), differing from developing countries, where hard foreign currency is utilized along the domestic currency (see the discussion of dollarization in Section 4).

All these structural characteristics strongly influence the design and operation of macroeconomic policies in developing countries.

It was also mentioned that within developing countries there is also ample heterogeneity. For instance, the World Bank classifies developing countries into lower income, lower middle income, and upper middle income. The latter tend to be more integrated into global financial markets with a lesser degree of government intervention regarding the various trade and financial transactions in the current and capital account of the balance of payments, whereas the situation for lower-income and lower-middle-income countries is different, usually with less integration and more government interventions in the external transactions. These different degrees of global financial integration have important implications for the conduct of macroeconomic policies and for the transmission of global macroeconomic shocks, as discussed in the following sections.

2.2 Heterogeneity of agricultural conditions: Production and food security

The *2008 World Development Report* from the World Bank, which focuses on agricultural issues, divides developing countries into three groups, depending on the contribution of agriculture to growth and the importance of rural poverty. The groups are called *agriculture-based countries* (where agriculture contributes significantly to growth and the poor are concentrated in rural areas), *transforming countries* (where agriculture contributes less to growth but poverty is still predominantly rural), and *urbanized countries* (in which agriculture is not the main contributor to growth and poverty is mostly urban). Basically, sub-Saharan Africa represents the largest percentage in the first group; South Asia, East Asia, and the Pacific and, to a lesser extent, North Africa and the Middle East belong in the second; and Latin America and the Caribbean, basically, but also Eastern Europe and Central Asia are the main geographical regions for the third group (see Table 1.1, p. 31, in WDR, 2008). In the rest of this chapter much of the data is presented by geographical regions, focusing on those just mentioned (following the World Bank aggregations in the World Development Indicators).[10]

Table 2 shows some indicators of the great variety of structural characteristics in the agricultural sector of developing regions. Agriculture in Latin America and the

Table 2   Regional Agricultural Indicators

	Latin America and Caribbean	Sub-Saharan Africa	Middle East and North Africa	South Asia	East Asia and Pacific	All Developing Countries
Agriculture, value added (% of GDP)	7.9	17.9	13.9	28.3	15.4	13.2
Rural population (% of total population)	26.5	68.4	43.6	73.2	67.7	60.6
Agriculture value added per worker (constant 1995 US$)	2915.5	349.2	2163.6	376.2	418.4	589.8
Agricultural exports (% merchandise trade)	28.3	23.9	4.7	17.9	11.7	15.3
Land use, arable land (hectares per person)	0.27	0.26	0.21	0.16	0.11	0.21
Agricultural machinery, tractors (per 100 hectares of arable land)	118.2	18.0	117.8	80.9	67.9	102.0
Roads (km per squared km of total area)	0.141	0.052	0.062	0.551	0.139	0.123

Caribbean (LAC) is less important as a percentage of the GDP and rural population is smaller compared to total population than in other regions. Sub-Saharan Africa (SSA) and South Asia fall on the other extreme, with agriculture production and rural population having larger incidence in those regions. At the same time, LAC depends more on agricultural exports, and agriculture appears more productive (per unit of labor), uses more capital (using tractors as a proxy), and, after South Asia, is the region better served by roads (the large Amazon area in LAC affects the value of this indicator). Africa and LAC have more available arable land per capita than Asian developing countries, but average holdings are far larger in LAC and land appears to be distributed more unequally in LAC than Asia, with Africa in between. It is important to notice that SSA has an availability of land that is comparable to LAC, but at the same time average holdings are of similar sizes to those in Asia, and the region shows the lowest values for the capital/technology and roads indicators, highlighting some of the opportunities and constraints to expand agricultural production in that region.

Looking at food security conditions, Diaz-Bonilla, Thomas, Robinson, and Cattaneo 2006 use cluster analysis across a world sample of developed and developing countries and show the heterogeneity of conditions among developing countries. They apply the theory of "fuzzy sets" in conjunction with more traditional methods of cluster analysis. This study classifies 167 countries encompassing all levels of income into 12 clusters using five indicators of food security: food production per capita, the ratio of total exports to food imports, calories per capita, protein per capita, and the share of the nonagricultural population share. Developing countries appear scattered across all levels of food security and insecurity, except in the very high food-secure group, whereas developed countries are all in food-secure clusters.

Among food-insecure countries, the profiles also differ: Some are predominantly rural (mostly in Africa and South Asia), whereas for others the urban population is more important (as in many countries in Latin America and the Caribbean and in East Europe). Obviously the same policy (such as maintaining domestic prices high to help producers or the opposite, keeping those prices low to help consumers) will have different impacts in these two types of countries. Also, some countries are food insecure mostly because of low levels of calories and proteins per capita, although they do not use large percentages of their exports to buy food. In the terminology of the study, these countries are *consumption vulnerable* but not *trade stressed*. Other food-insecure countries are a mirror image: They appear trade stressed (using a large percentage of their exports to buy food) but less consumption vulnerable (their current levels of calories and proteins per capita are close to the average for all countries considered). Again, the policy options for these two types of countries are different to the extent that the first group may increase imports to improve availability of calories and proteins, whereas the second group appears more constrained.[11]

2.3 Heterogeneity of agricultural conditions: Trade

Developing countries also differ in the structure of their agricultural trade, which has been also changing over time. In the early 2000s, agricultural trade represented about 7–8% of total world merchandise trade and about 40% of world exports of primary products. If trade within the European Union is not netted out, agricultural trade is mostly dominated by industrialized countries, which collectively account for about ⅔ of exports and imports. But shares are about equal, not counting intra-EU trade (Diaz-Bonilla, Thomas, Robinson, and Yanoma, 2002).

On average, from the mid-1990s to the early 2000s industrialized countries and LAC has had agricultural trade surpluses, supplying the other regions, which are net importers. Developing countries as a whole are net buyers (by about US$8 billion on average during that period). Trends in net trade position over time show some important changes. In particular, Africa (excluding the Republic of South Africa) has moved from a positive to a negative trade balance in agricultural and food products since the mid-1970s and the beginning of the 1980s. A less dramatic but still clear switch from positive to negative net trade in agriculture occurred in the Eastern European economies. Among industrialized countries, the most important change has been the disappearance of the European Union as a net buyer in world markets as a result of the impact of the Common Agricultural Policy (CAP). The EU's net demand for agricultural products from the rest of the world, which amounted to about US$30 billion at the beginning of the 1980s (in current dollars), almost disappeared by the end of the 1990s (Diaz-Bonilla, Thomas, Robinson, and Yanoma, 2002).

Developing countries as a whole export a larger share of agricultural exports to developed countries, but the shares differ by developing region. Africa exports mostly to the EU and other African countries. The export partners of Latin American developing countries are mostly the EU and the United States and Canada, followed by LAC countries, but with large differences from north to south on the continent.[12] Developing countries in Asia, on the other hand, sell mostly to other developing countries in the region and only after that to Japan and the EU.

Looking at products, except for rice, for which a few Asian countries' exports account for 70% of world rice trade, the industrialized countries, especially the United States and Canada, dominates world grain exports. Productions of nongrain crops, such as vegetables and fruits, cotton, sugar, and vegetable oil, have a larger presence of developing countries (Diaz-Bonilla and Reca, 2000).

The composition of agrifood exports from developing countries also showed important changes during the last four decades, notably with the emergence of fruits and vegetables and oilseeds and products as the more dynamic export products, displacing traditional export crops such as sugar and coffee, cacao, and tea. On the other hand, developing countries, as a group, are net importers of cereals. Within that general structure, there are important regional differences.[13] Overall, agricultural exports and imports have also become more diversified in the regional groups (see Diaz-Bonilla, Thomas, Robinson, and Yanoma, 2002, for a more detailed analysis).

McCalla and Valdes (1999) provide further evidence of heterogeneity in developing countries by looking at their individual net trade positions: Among 148 developing countries, they identify 105 countries that are net food importers and 43 that are net food exporters, whereas for agriculture as a whole, 85 appear as net importers against 63 net exporters. Among the most vulnerable economic groups, over one third of UN-defined LDCs are net agricultural exporters, and more than half of the low-income food deficit countries (LIFDC) are net agricultural exporters.

2.4 Country heterogeneity and macroeconomic policies and conditions

It is important to keep in mind this heterogeneity of structures and performances in developing countries when discussing the impacts of various world or domestic macro-economic policies and conditions. For instance, trying to improve the internal terms of trade for agricultural products (say, by a devaluation of the local currency) will have a different production response in Africa, where producers face relatively more constraints in infrastructure, capital, and technology, than in the other two regions (Table 2). In turn, the distributive effect (and therefore the political economy constraints for policies bene-fiting the agricultural sector) will be different in small-farmer agricultural economies of Asia than in dualistic agrarian structures of many LAC countries.

In addition, changes in macroeconomic and agricultural policies in Europe, for instance, could have a relatively greater impact on Africa than in Asia, due to greater trade and financial links between the first two regions. The same can be said in the case of the United States and a number of LAC countries. These differences in structure, performance, productions, and trade must be kept in mind in analyzing the impact of world macroeconomic conditions and specific domestic macroeconomic policies.

3. HALF A CENTURY OF WORLD MACROECONOMIC DEVELOPMENTS: AN OVERVIEW

Changes in the agricultural sector and food markets of developing countries over the last decades, and in fact in their economies in general, have been heavily influenced by major world macroeconomic developments. Schuh (1986) summarized the developments up to the mid-1980s by highlighting four main issues: increased dependence on international trade worldwide, including for many developing countries that were abandoning import-substituting industrialization policies and turning toward an "outward orientation" (Balassa, 1989); the emergence of a well-integrated international market for capital, starting with the emergence of the Eurodollar market; the shift from a system of fixed exchange rates to a system of flexible exchange rates, particularly after

Eugenio Diaz-Bonilla and Sherman Robinson

the second U.S. devaluation by the Nixon Administration in early 1973; and the increase in monetary instability and the ratcheting up of inflation in the 1970s, linked to bouts of tight and loose monetary policy in the United States and the injection of Special Drawing Rights, which increased world liquidity. Schuh (1986), in discussing the impact on developing countries' agriculture, also noted what he called "third country" effects: the fact that gyrations in the value of the U.S. dollar not only affected that country but also other countries (and he mentioned Brazil specifically), which followed exchange rate policies linked to the U.S. dollar. Since Schuh's analysis, some of those macroeconomic trends continued while other new ones emerged.

This section presents an overview of global macroeconomic developments during the last five decades and discusses the possible impacts on agriculture. Those global economic conditions are in good measure defined by the policies of the industrialized countries—particularly the United States, whose business cycle has strongly influenced global economic performance since it emerged as the world's largest economy after World War II. In turn, the impact of those modifications in global conditions on developing countries depends both on the size of the shocks (such as the change in interest rates or in commodity prices) and the structural characteristics and policies of the developing countries.

Table 3 presents a summary of the world macroeconomic conditions over the last decades. The evolution of those key variables is discussed in the following sections, with some considerations about their possible links to agriculture.

Table 3 World macroeconomic indicators, 1960s–2000s

Indicator	1960s	1970s	1980s	1990s	2000s
World					
GDP growth (% per year)	5.4	4	3	2.7	3
GDP per capita growth (% per year)	3.4	2.1	1.3	1.2	1.7
Trade growth (% per year)	7.6	6.4	4.7	6.2	6.7
Trade as a share of GDP (%)	24.5	32.2	37.6	41.3	48.6
Developing countries					
Total growth (% per year)	5.0	5.4	3.3	3.4	5.6
Per capita growth (% per year)	2.7	3.2	1.4	1.8	4.2
Share in recession (%)	28.5	29	40.6	35.8	18.9
Capital inflows (% GDP)	N/A	1.25	1.06	1.44	1.11
Consumption volatility	0.91	0.78	1.03	0.80	0.64
Inflation (% per year)[a]					
Industrialized countries		4.9	8.7	6.2	2.8	2
Developing countries	4.9	16.2	36.7	36.1	5.8

Continued

Table 3 World macroeconomic indicators, 1960s–2000s—Cont'd

Indicator	1960s	1970s	1980s	1990s	2000s
Interest rates (%)					
Nominal[b]	6	8.4	10.6	5.5	3.2
Real[c]	1	−0.3	4.1	2.7	1.1

Notes: Growth is aggregated at market exchange rates. Consumption volatility data represent a median of the five-year rolling average of standard deviation/average growth for developing countries. For the 1960s, data cover various years. For the 2000s, data on GDP, trade growth, interest rates, and inflation are for 2000–2006.
N/A = Not available.
[a]Based on the consumption index.
[b]London Interbank Offered Rate, six-month dollar deposits.
[c]Using industrialized-country inflation rates.
Sources: World Bank (2007); IMF (2007).

3.1 Growth

Average world economic growth has declined since the 1960s, when it reached 5.4% total and 3.4% per capita, but it picked up somewhat in the first half of the 2000s compared with the 1990s (Table 3). In particular, world GDP growth per capita went up in the first half of the 2000s, helped in part by declines in population growth, but without reaching the levels of the 1960s and 1970s for the world as a whole. Figure 1 shows the cycles in world growth over the last half-century.[14]

The sustained growth of the 1960s and early 1970s ended with the first oil crisis of the mid-1970s. Since then, the world economy has had three cycles with strong decelerations at the beginning of the 1980s, the 1990s, and the 2000s. As of this writing, the current growth cycle is turning downwards due to the economic recession in the United States and other industrialized countries.

Developing regions show important heterogeneity in growth patterns across both geographical areas and periods (see Table 4). The high growth rates, total and per capita, that LAC, sub-Saharan Africa (SSA), and the Middle East and North Africa (MENA)[15] had during the 1960s and 1970s decelerated to 1% or less for the period 1980–2005. On the other hand, East and South Asia have experienced accelerations in both total and per capita economic growth since the 1980s. Even when China and India are not included in the totals, those regions have approximately maintained (East Asia) or increased (South Asia) their per capita growth rates from the 1980s through the 2000s, compared with the 1960s and 1970s, and those rates have stayed above the averages of other developing regions.

What is the relationship between growth in industrialized countries and developing countries? Figure 2 separates the trends in total growth of the industrialized countries from those of developing countries, with and without China.[16]

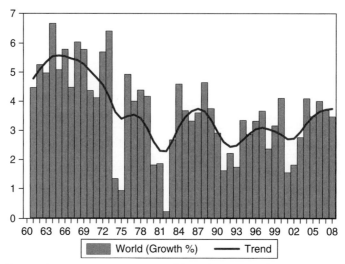

Figure 1 World growth, 1960–2008. Source: World Bank (2007) and IMF estimates for 2008.

Table 4   Growth in GDP, 1960s–2000s

	1960s	1970s	1980s	1990s	2000–2006	1960s–1970s	1980s–2000s
Total							
East Asia and Pacific	3.8	7.2	7.7	8.2	8.3	5.6	8.1
East Asia without China	5.2	7.1	5.4	5.2	5.3	6.2	5.3
Latin America and Caribbean	5.3	5.7	1.8	2.9	3.2	5.5	2.6
Middle East and North Africa	8.8	6.0	2.2	4.3	4.0	6.8	3.5
South Asia	4.2	3.0	5.7	5.4	6.5	3.6	5.8
South Asia without India	4.9	3.2	5.2	4.4	5.2	4.0	4.9
Sub-Saharan Africa	4.6	4.1	2.2	2.0	4.5	4.3	2.7
Developing countries	5.0	5.4	3.3	3.4	5.6	5.2	4.0
Industrialized countries	5.5	3.7	3.0	2.5	2.4	4.5	2.6

Continued

Table 4 Growth in GDP, 1960s–2000s—Cont'd

	1960s	1970s	1980s	1990s	2000–2006	1960s–1970s	1980s–2000s
Per capita							
East Asia and Pacific	1.6	5.0	6.0	6.8	7.4	3.4	6.7
East Asia without China	2.6	4.6	3.4	3.4	3.9	3.7	3.5
Latin America and Caribbean	2.5	3.2	−0.3	1.2	1.8	2.8	0.8
Middle East and North Africa	5.9	3.1	−0.7	2.0	2.2	3.9	1.0
South Asia	1.8	0.6	3.4	3.3	4.7	1.2	3.7
South Asia without India	2.4	0.7	2.8	1.9	2.9	1.5	2.5
Sub-Saharan Africa	2.0	1.2	−0.8	−0.6	2.0	1.6	0.0
Developing countries	2.7	3.2	1.4	1.8	4.2	3.0	2.2
Industrialized countries	4.3	2.9	2.3	1.8	2.4	3.6	2.0

Source: World Bank (2007).

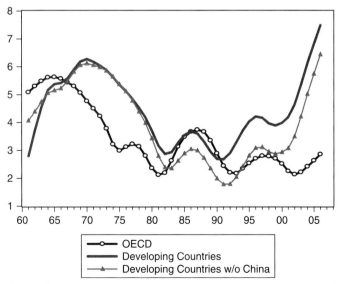

Figure 2 Growth trends, 1960–2008. *Note:* OECD = Organization for Economic Cooperation and Development. Source: World Bank (2007).

This disaggregation shows that the acceleration in world economic growth during the 2000s is clearly the result of the performance of developing countries, where total growth (at 5.6%) is larger than the average in the 1970s (5.4%), whereas growth per capita is at the highest point of the series: 4.2.% in the 2000s (but before the full impact of the recession of late 2000s), compared with 3.2% in the 1970s (see Table 3).

Several points in Figure 2 are worth noting. First, during the 1960s and 1970s, the inflexion in the growth trend for developing countries was preceded by the decline in growth in industrialized countries. In fact, Granger's test of causality shows that growth in industrialized countries led the economic performance of developing countries up to the mid-1990s. Second, the business cycles of industrialized and developing countries appear more synchronized in the world deceleration of the early 1980s and early 1990s; however, the slowdown that occurred at the world level and in industrialized countries in the early 2000s clearly took place after the decline in growth that affected developing countries in the late 1990s, when they suffered a series of financial crises, particularly in Asia and LAC. Unlike in the previous period, Granger's causality tests during the 1990s and 2000s show strong two-way influences between growth in developed and in developing countries (this issue is taken up again later in the section). Third, the trends of developing countries with and without China, which did not differ much in the 1960s and 1970s, began to show a widening gap beginning in the 1980s. Fourth, cycles in industrialized countries during the last three decades took place around a more stationary path; developing countries, on the other hand, although clearly affected by a deceleration in the late 1990s and early 2000s, appear nonetheless on an upward trend, reaching new heights in the second half of the 2000s. As mentioned earlier, this upward path is now negatively affected by the current economic problems in United States and other industrialized countries.

The relationship between growth in industrial and developing countries has been a topic of permanent interest in the development debate. Sir Arthur Lewis, in his Nobel lecture in 1979 (later published in the *American Economic Review*), noted that during the previous hundred years, growth in developing regions depended on the rate of growth in the developed world, and he was concerned about the impact of the evident slowing of the industrialized countries during the late 1970s (see Figure 2). Goldstein and Kahn (1982) analyzed that same period with different statistical approaches and found that growth in industrialized countries was indeed related to growth in developing countries but that additional factors weakened the link, including other developments in the world economy and domestic policies in developing countries. Goldstein and Kahn finished their analysis before the deep economic downturn of the early 1980s, when clearly the recession in the United States and other industrialized countries had extremely negative effects in all developing countries.

During the mid-1990s, Hoffmaister and Samiei (1996) looked mostly at the traditional trade linkages and noted that at least some regions of the developing world, such as many Asian developing countries, have become less influenced by the business cycle in the developed countries. After that paper was written, the issue of linkages across economies gained momentum with the 1997 Asian Crisis and the analysis shifted toward financial aspects.

As an indicative experiment, Figure 3 shows the results of a simple bivariate vector autoregression (VAR) linking growth in industrial production in the main industrialized countries and overall growth in each one of the developing regions for the period 1960–2006.[17]

The impulse-response curves (with 5% confidence bands around them) are shown for LAC and SSA, the only two regions where the impact is statistically significant. It is also clearly positive and economically relevant: Growth of 1% in industrial activity in developed countries leads to growth of about 0.3% for LAC; for SSA growth is somewhat less, at about 0.2%.[18] For the other regions (MENA, SA, and EAP), the impulse–responses are not statistically significant.

The fact that the regions are aggregates of countries certainly mutes the effects that would be more precisely identified at the country level. Also, industrial countries might have different impacts on different regions. For instance, the *2007 IMF World Economic Outlook* uses panel regressions from 1970–2005 to estimate "growth spillovers." The IMF found that U.S. growth has a larger impact on LAC, with 1%

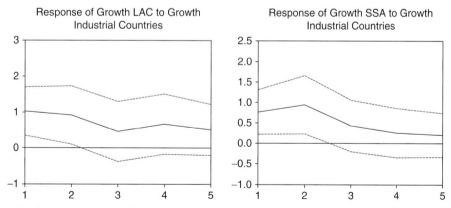

Figure 3 Impulse-response from VARs, 1960–2006. *Notes:* The VARs are run with three lags. The identification uses the Cholesky decomposition, with the ordering starting with the industrial countries. The impulse–response is the result of the impact of a shock of one standard deviation (positive) on the variables of interest, based on the estimated VAR equations. The solid line is the impulse-response and the dotted lines are the confidence intervals. Sources: The index of industrial production is from IMF (2007); growth for the developing regions is from World Bank (2007).

growth in the United States leading to somewhat less than 0.25% for the region, close to the estimate calculated using a simple VAR for all industrialized countries (Figure 3). The European Union affects the economic performance of Africa in particular, with a relationship of 1% to 0.25% (also similar to the simple VAR in Figure 3). Japan does not seem to affect either of those developing regions, and it has only a small influence on Asia. In general, Asia seems to be more influenced by its own internal dynamics, although the United States, Europe, and Japan, in that order, appear to have some influence; however, the coefficients are far smaller than in the case of the United States and LAC or the European Union and Africa (IMF, 2007).

It can also be argued that to the extent that trade and financial integration have been advancing, the impact of industrialized growth on developing countries (and probably vice versa) could be increasing—a point that the IMF also notes (IMF, 2007). In fact, VARs similar to those reported here (not shown; and run by the authors only for the period 1990–2006, without China and India) indicate positive links between growth in industrialized countries and the developing regions. Also, as previously mentioned, Granger's causality tests cannot reject the null of the two-way influence between developing countries and industrialized growth.

The issue of the synchronization of the business cycle across countries is a topic of intense debate (IMF, 2007). Two factors define the nature of the comovements among economies: (1) the clear increase in trade and financial links (e.g., Table 3 shows the increase in the share of trade on GDP; for the increase in financial links, see Prasad et al., 2003), which should lead to increased comovements[19]; and (2) the size of the common shocks—that is, the larger the common shocks, the larger the synchronization. For instance, during the 1960s—a period of lower world shocks and comparatively less economic integration—countries appeared less correlated than during the 1970s and 1980s, when large world shocks were experienced. During the 1990s and 2000s, countries appeared more correlated than in the 1960s because of greater trade and financial integration but less correlated than in the 1970s and 1980s as a result of smaller world shocks (IMF, 2007). The global slowdown of the late 2000s will combine a larger shock with greater integration.

The business cycle of the United States is still at the center of world fluctuations because of the size of the U.S. economy and its openness in trade and financial variables; each one of the world decelerations since 1974–1975 coincided with U.S. recessions (which was not the case in the 1960s, however). Besides world synchronization, regional comovements appear to have increased, particularly within Asia and Latin America.[20]

A more specific question for this chapter is the relationship between world growth and agricultural performance in developing countries. Various authors, mainly in the context of industrialized countries (Schultz, 1953; Thompson, 1988), have argued that total GDP growth influences agricultural growth through income and demand effects. In general, analyses of those links have focused on the implications of domestic growth, not world growth. However, the previous paragraphs have established that there is a nontrivial amount of comovement between world growth, led by industrialized countries (which still represent about 75% of world GDP at market rates; see Díaz-Bonilla, 2008), and developing countries' performance. So, it is valid to take a global view.

A simple VAR with world GDP and agricultural growth can be utilized to explore the links.[21] Figure 4 shows the impulse responses[22]: For the whole sample (1960–2005), changes in GDP growth have a positive impact on agricultural growth on impact in the first year (first panel). However, in the mid-panel that covers the period 1960–1990, there is no

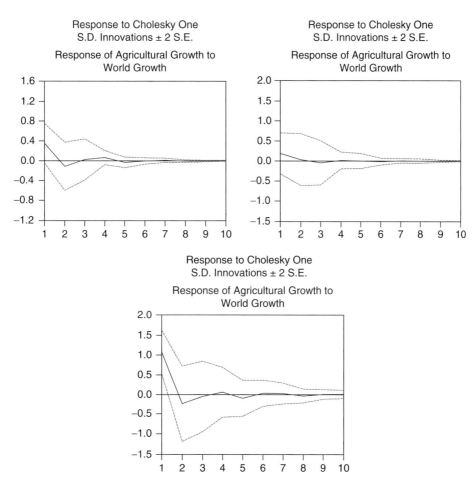

Figure 4 Impact of World Total Growth on World Agricultural Growth.

statistically solid relation between growth in total world GDP and agricultural growth. However, for the period 1990–2005 (third and last panel), the impact of world GDP growth on agricultural growth in the first year increases significantly and is statistically better defined. This suggests that GDP and agricultural performances have become more closely coordinated in the last decades. This greater coordination may be the result of increased integration between domestic and world agricultural markets as a result of the GATT (first) and WTO (later) negotiations and other changes in economic policies in developed and developing countries, making the agricultural sector more responsive to changes in world growth.

3.2 Volatility and crises

Besides average growth performance, volatility of growth may have consequences for agriculture. Table 3 shows the volatility in aggregate consumption for developing countries.[23] Figure 5 shows the proportion of developing countries with zero or negative growth each year from 1961 to 2005, measured in GDP per capita (see also the decade averages in Table 3).

The largest number of developing countries in recession occurred at the time of global slowdowns—in 1975, 1982, and 1992. The exception is 1999, in which a slowdown occurred but the number of developing countries in recession anticipated the world deceleration of 2001–2002 (see Figures 2 and 5). The proportion of developing countries in recession peaked in 1982 and 1992 (the latter still influenced by the breakdown of the Soviet Union) at more than 50%. The proportions in 1975 were just

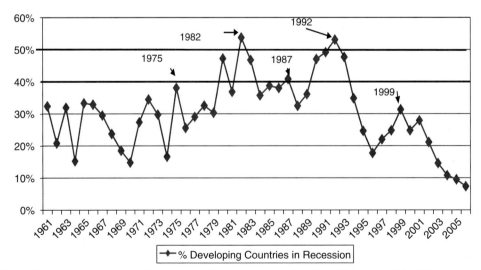

Figure 5　Percentage of developing countries in recession, 1961–2005. Source: Calculations by the author using data from World Bank (2007).

below 40% and in 1999 and 2001 were around 30%. It is interesting to note that 1987, not a year of world deceleration, shows percentages of developing countries in recession above both the years around the mid-1970s and early 2000s; the main reason appears to be the collapse in commodity prices that occurred in the mid-1980s (as discussed later).

It is also important to look at the depth of the recession when discussing the possible impact on agricultural growth (or any other variable). The average growth decline for the countries in recession was about −5.5% in the mid-1970s and −6.7% in the early 1980s. In the early 1990s, influenced by the breakdown of the Soviet Union, it dropped to −8.6%, and finally, the recession of the early 2000s was the mildest in terms of the number of countries involved (see Figure 5), and the average decline was smaller in absolute value at −4.9%.

Clearly, volatility and countries in recession increased during the 1970s, peaking in the recessions of the early 1980s and early 1990s, but they have been declining since then. In fact, during the 2000s, developing countries have experienced the lowest volatility (measured in terms of both consumption volatility and number of countries in recession) for the half-century analyzed here (see Table 3 and Figure 5). This is drastically changing with the deterioration of the economic conditions of the late 2000s.

As was shown, world growth affects the performance of the agricultural sector in developing countries, although the impact depends on the economic structure of the specific country. For "agriculture-based countries" (using the classification of the World Bank, 2008), it is the performance of the agricultural sector that can impart volatility to total domestic growth. In "urbanized countries," on the other hand, the crisis could emanate from other sectors and then affect agriculture. A global crisis reduces growth directly in developing countries (see Figure 5), but the impact can be felt for some time afterwards to the extent that it affects installed capital. Moreover, the recurrence of crises increases uncertainty, reducing investment and therefore the future level of existing capital. In the case of small farmers, crises may also compromise the limited productive capital of the poor if, for instance, assets, such as livestock, must be sold to face negative economic shocks (Lipton and Ravallion, 1995). A crisis also tends to leave a legacy of public and private debt, weakening fiscal accounts and financial systems, which can constrain the provision of public services and credit to the agricultural sector. Crises can also affect human capital due to higher unemployment and its persistence over time, and they can slow or reverse improvements in health, nutrition, and education.

3.3 World Monetary Conditions, Inflation, and Interest Rates

Schuh's analysis pointed to increasing inflation as one of the characteristics of the world economy; since then monetary and macroeconomic policies in general have reversed the trend, in what has been called "the rise and fall of inflation" (IMF, 1996), with a parallel cycle for nominal and real interest rates (see Table 3). Along with the reduction in growth volatility during recent years (which included both developing and industrialized countries), the decline in inflation and interest rates has led some to call the period since the 1990s and until the current economic and financial turmoil the "Great Moderation" (Bernanke, 2004).

In all developing regions, as in the industrialized world, inflationary pressures have abated since the mid- to late 1990s, going back, until the mid-2000s, to levels more comparable to those of the 1960s (see Table 3). There are, however, clear differences across regions, with LAC and Africa showing higher inflationary pressures than Asia and the Middle East (as discussed later in the sections on domestic policies).

World nominal interest rates were also increasing during the 1970s and early 1980s, but in the second half of the 1970s prices were going up faster than nominal interest rates, leading to negative real interest rates (the average for the decade was 8.4% for nominal interest rates but −0.3% in real terms; see Table 3). In the early 1980s, after the second oil shock, several industrialized countries, particularly the United States, turned toward restrictive monetary policies.

Nominal interest rates were raised substantially above inflation rates, leading to high real interest rates (10.6% and 4.1%, respectively, on average for the 1980s, with a peak of about 6–8% in real terms in the early 1980s; Figure 6[24]). This policy change led to the recession of the early 1980s (world growth in 1982 has been the lowest of the five decades considered here[25]; see Figure 1).

Since then, both short- and long-term interest rates have been declining on trend but with the short-term rates showing the cycles influenced by monetary conditions defined mostly by the policy stance of the Federal Reserve. In addition to the clear case

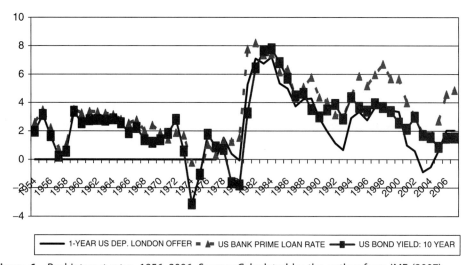

Figure 6   Real interest rates, 1956–2006. Source: Calculated by the author from IMF (2007).

of the 1980s, subsequent events of monetary tightening have usually generated negative financial and growth repercussions in developing countries (as discussed later in this section). During the early 2000s U.S. monetary policy was strongly expansionary (leading to negative short-term rates during that period). These policies were reversed in 2004: Real short-term interest rates increased again to about 2% in real terms, whereas the real U.S. prime rate jumped to about 4% (see Figure 6). This tightening of monetary policy and monetary conditions affected the housing sector in the United States and started the financial crisis that is at the heart of the strong current decline in U.S. growth. Clear signs of financial distress in mid-2007 led to a strong change in monetary policy by the Federal Reserve toward a more expansionary stance. The large price increases of commodities since the second half of 2007 appear to have been influenced by such monetary easing.

There are several channels through which world monetary conditions, interest rates, and inflation trends could affect the performance of agriculture in development countries.

It is usually recognized that world interest rates have direct effects on the business cycle, growth, and crises in developing countries (Calvo et al., 1993; Uribe and Yue, 2003). High real and nominal rates tend to depress growth, and changes in monetary policy conditions that lead to sudden upward adjustments in interest rates in industrialized countries have been at the root of many of the financial crises that afflicted developing countries during recent decades. As has been already indicated, world growth and economic crises also have repercussions for developing countries and their agricultural sectors.

A specific channel that has been discussed is the impact of a monetary contraction that raises the real interest rate (which may happen due to an increase in the nominal interest rate and/or a decline in expected inflation) on real commodity prices. Jeffrey Frankel (1984, 1986) has argued that, in such case, real prices must fall, and in addition, they should overshoot downward. The reason, similar to Dornbusch's theory of exchange rate overshooting (Dornbusch, 1976), is that commodity prices, being flexible to adjust while other prices adjust slowly, must drop enough so that the expectation of future increases is sufficient to compensate for the higher interest rate plus the costs of carrying inventories. So, until all variables return to their equilibrium values, a monetary contraction and increases in real interest rates should have a noticeable negative impact on agricultural prices.

A simple VAR considering world growth rates (World Bank database), changes in world real interest rate (change in the LIBOR, six months, deflated by inflation in industrial countries; IMF), and changes in world real agricultural prices (IMF indices of food, agricultural raw materials, and beverages, deflated by export unit values of industrialized countries) shows that there are important interactions among these variables. The VAR covers the period 1960–2005 and includes a dummy variable for

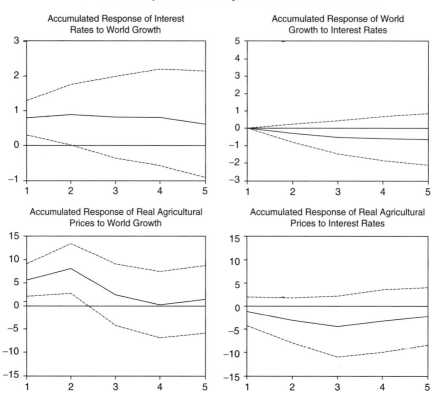

Figure 7 Interaction among world growth, agricultural growth, and interest rates.

El Niño events.[26] The accumulated impulse–response graphs for the key relationships are shown in Figure 7.

It seems that acceleration of world growth is linked to both increases in interest rates (upper-left panel) and higher agricultural prices (lower-left panel). At the same time, increases in interest rates depress both world growth (upper-right panel) and real agricultural prices, with a lag (lower-right panel) (although the coefficients are less well defined). The VAR results (including the nonaccumulated impulse-response, not shown here) are consistent with a commonly accepted view that higher growth is associated with increases in the price for agricultural products. These developments, reflecting generalized inflationary pressures, lead to contractive monetary policies and increases in interest rates, which, in turn, then depress both agricultural prices and world growth.

Another related development that must be noted is that nominal agricultural prices that showed a simple average inflation of about 0.8% in the 1960s jumped to double-digit inflation in the 1970s (about 12.5%), then showed persistent deflation at a rate of −0.9% per year in the 1980s and −1.5% in the 1990s, and then jumped to positive inflation of about 7% during the 2000s. This implies that there have been somewhat larger changes of world agricultural prices in both the upswing and the downswing compared to the prices measured in the CPI of industrialized countries, which is consistent with the notion of agricultural prices being more flexible than other goods and services and therefore absorbing larger adjustments according to the flex-price/fix-price setting discussed previously. If, as some have argued over the years (D. Gale Johnson, 1947; Schultz, 1954), price volatility is more important than average prices in explaining agricultural supply (see also Boussard, 1985, 1999; Timmer, 1991; among others), agriculture may benefit from a more stable non-inflationary environment,[27] which does not force excessive adjustments in goods with flexible prices. In fact, it has been argued that the best that monetary policy can do to stabilize the agricultural sector is to maintain low and steady inflation (see Klieson and Poole, 2000).

Therefore, the reductions in inflation and interest rates (on average for the 2000s, nominal interest rates have been 3.2% and real interest rates 1.1%, with inflation lower than in the 1960s for the industrialized countries; see Table 3) can be considered to have been positive for growth and for the performance of agriculture in the first half of the 2000s.

3.4 Commodity prices

Commodity world prices experienced important changes over the past five decades (see Figures 8 and 9, for real[28] and nominal prices, respectively). During the 1960s and 1970s, prices of agricultural products (particularly food and beverages) stayed high in real terms. Oil prices jumped significantly during the mid- to late 1970s. As

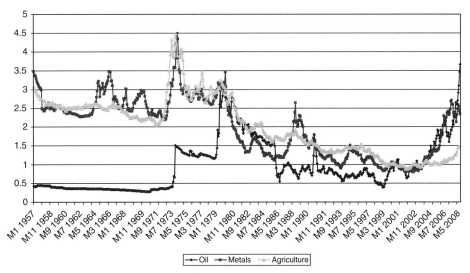

Figure 8 World real prices for commodities, 1957–2008. Source: IMF (2008).

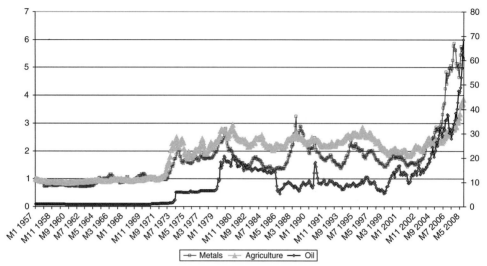

Figure 9 World agricultural prices, nominal indices (monthly: January 1957–February 2008). Source: IMF (2008).

previously mentioned, in the early 1980s the world macroeconomic environment changed markedly: There was a switch from expansionary to contractive monetary policies in key industrialized countries, leading to a sharp decline in world growth.

In the case of agriculture, declines in world prices during the 1980s were associated with slumping world growth but also with other factors such as expanded public support of agricultural production, mostly in industrialized countries, particularly the European Union through the Common Agricultural Policy[29]; changes in the U.S. Farm Bill of 1985; the 1980s debt crises in developing countries; the agricultural transformation in China; the expansion of the Green Revolution in many developing countries; and the breakup of the Soviet Union. All these developments added to the supply side and/or weakened the demand side of agricultural markets, leading to the collapse of agricultural prices in the mid-1980s (see Borensztein et al., 1994; Díaz-Bonilla, 1999).

The decline in the prices of commodities did not happen immediately with the deceleration of the world economy in the early 1980s, for two different reasons, one related to agricultural commodities and the other to oil.

Regarding agricultural commodities, the U.S. Farm Bill of 1980, expecting levels of inflation that later did not materialize, established high nominal values of domestic support prices. Because of the way the U.S. Department of Agriculture managed and accumulated stocks, it actually acted as a global demand buffer, providing support to world real prices. That was modified significantly in the 1985 Farm Bill, which began the process of unloading onto world markets the stocks previously accumulated and started an export subsidy trade war, supposedly aimed at the European Union, but in fact depressing many agricultural world prices.

In the case of oil, from early 1982 to late 1985 OPEC had implemented supply restrictions, with Saudi Arabia acting as a supply buffer. That arrangement broke down by early 1986 because of increased production in countries outside OPEC, which exacerbated the problems of lack of discipline among the members of the cartel (Kilian, 2006).

When, in the mid-1980s, the United States stopped acting as a demand buffer for agricultural products and Saudi Arabia decided not to be a supply buffer for oil, the result was a generalized decline of commodity prices. Countries that had borrowed against expectations of high commodity prices during the 1970s, mainly in LAC and Africa, were first hit by changes in macroeconomic conditions early in the decade and then by the collapse of commodity prices in the mid-1980s. Those countries entered a phase of debt distress and economic crises during that period.

In the 1990s real prices of many commodities were about half the levels of the 1960s and 1970s or less, and they remained on that lower plateau for much of the 1990s and early 2000s. Once the world resumed growth after the deceleration in the early 2000s, nominal prices of various commodities began to climb. Some commodities, such as metals and oil, experienced both nominal and real gains, surpassing the peaks achieved in the 1970s (Figures 8 and 9).

For agricultural goods, however, the story has been somewhat different. Although in the second half of 2007 and early 2008 *nominal* prices had increased significantly (Figure 9), the prices in *real* terms had stayed clearly below the 1970s highs (see Figure 8). Besides the resumption of world growth and greater demand from developing countries in the first half of the 2000s (see Section 3.1), higher nominal prices for food and agricultural items have been also influenced by competition with crops oriented to energy use (which in addition are subsidized in main industrial countries), weather patterns, and financial speculation (Von Braun, 2007). In late 2007 and early 2008 there have been further increases in the U.S. dollar price of several agricultural prices, linked in part to changes in U.S. monetary policy, which led to further declines in the value of its currency, investments by commodity funds seeking short-term gains and hedges against inflation, and changes in trade policies of several key producers that restricted exports to maintain the supply for their domestic markets. Still, most real prices of agricultural products have remained, so far, below 1970s levels. As of this writing, the deepening global slowdown in the late 2000s is bringing nominal prices down, too.

The issue of the trend and volatility of world commodity prices and their impact on developing countries has a long history in development theory, from the Prebisch–Singer theory of the declining terms of trade (Prebisch, 1950; Singer, 1950) through the price stabilization schemes of the 1970s to the current debates about whether higher or lower commodity prices are good for poverty alleviation. Of course, the main issue in any exercise that tries to link changes in prices to variations in development variables is to differentiate commodities, countries, and social groups.

The drop in agricultural prices in the 1980s had important implications for rural development in many developing countries. Depressed world prices of agricultural and food products during part of the 1980s and the 1990s appear to have discouraged investments in the rural sectors of many developing countries. As a result, those countries became dependent on cheap subsidized food from abroad, and many of them, including various SSA countries, changed from net food exporters into net importers by discouraging the domestic production of staples and close substitutes. Low food prices may have also pushed several developing countries into a more extreme specialization in tropical products, increasing their external vulnerability and reinforcing a net food import position that could have been avoided or mitigated under a different set of relative prices. The lack of rural dynamism also contributed to an increase in rural migration to the cities and fostered premature or excessive urbanization in many developing countries. The World Bank and other development banks cut the amounts they would loan to agricultural and rural development projects, a move that was apparently influenced in part by low world agricultural prices that reduced the expected returns of future projects and depressed the actual results of evaluated projects (Lipton and Paarlberg, 1990).[30]

But the behavior of world agricultural prices cannot be separated from the behavior of other commodity prices. Those prices had moved together during the sudden increases of the 1970s and in the price collapse of the mid-1980s and appear to have gone up again in a relatively synchronized manner in the 2000s, especially in late 2007 and early 2008 (see Díaz-Bonilla, forthcoming).

Therefore, an analysis of the impacts of the changes in world commodity prices on developing countries should consider them together. In this regard there are several points to be noticed. First, although primary commodities represent an important component of production, employment, and trade in many developing countries, the percentage has been constantly declining. In the 1960s and 1970s, food, agricultural raw materials, ores and metals, and fuels represented 80–90% of total exports in the aggregate for all developing countries, but by the early 2000s manufactured products accounted for about two thirds of the total exports of developing countries as a whole (UNCTAD, 2004). Primary products, however, still represented about 60–70% of exports in some developing regions, such as Africa, in the early 2000s.

Second, the structure of trade in commodities (considering exports, imports, and net trade) differs greatly among developing countries. For instance, LAC as a whole has positive net trade in agricultural products, minerals, and fuels; Africa shows positive net trade in fuels and minerals but negative net trade in agricultural products, similar to the former republics of the Soviet Union; the Middle East displays negative net trade in agricultural products and minerals but positive net trade in fuels; and Asia has negative trade balances in all three categories (WTO, 2007). Of course, regional aggregates conceal important differences across countries.

Third, although, as indicated, there is comovement across prices of commodities, the correlation between the prices of products varies. For instance, the perception during the 2000s of a generalized commodity boom benefiting developing countries has to be qualified: The increases in prices of metals and oil have clearly been more pronounced than those for agricultural products, for which real prices have stayed, in the aggregate, below the higher levels of the 1960s and 1970s (see Figures 8 and 9).

Fourth, the macroeconomic cross-effects of increases in prices must be considered; current high prices of metals and energy may have contributed to the appreciation of the real exchange rates in several countries, affecting other tradable commodities, including agricultural products, as apparently happened in the 1970s in SSA during another period of high commodity prices (Díaz-Bonilla and Reca, 2000).

Finally, regarding agricultural commodities, the extent to which agricultural production is able to spread income-generation opportunities across large numbers of people (say, by numerous family farms as opposed to concentrated and highly mechanized plantations) changes with the commodities produced and the prevalent production structures.[31] Furthermore, some agricultural products (such as cereals and dairy products) can affect not only incomes and employment but also consumption for the poor, whereas others (coffee or sugar) would mainly affect incomes and employment but would not have a high incidence in the consumption basket. Therefore, the net effect on poverty can vary by product.

Simply as an indicative exercise, Table 5 shows the results of a VAR with growth rates for each region and the five nominal price indices for oil, metals, food, beverages, and agricultural raw materials for the period 1960–2006. The results presented

Table 5 Results of VAR with growth rates and prices, 1960–2006

	Oil	Metals	Food	Beverages	Agricultural Raw Materials
East Asia and Pacific	0	+	0	−	+
Latin America and Caribbean	+	+	+	+	+
Middle East and North Africa	+	0	−	0	−
South Asia	0	+	−	−	−
Sub-Saharan Africa	+	+	0	+	−

Note: Shaded areas significant at 5%.
Source: Calculations by the author based on data from World Bank (2007) and IMF (2007).

correspond to the impulse-response from prices (one standard positive shock) to growth, with the direction of the direct impact indicated by a positive or negative sign or zero. This simple exercise, done at the level of regions as defined by the World Bank, hides significant heterogeneity within them (and partly explains the low statistical significance). In addition, the length of the period covered could obscure relations that emerge in more disaggregated analysis by subperiods. Nonetheless, the results suggest some patterns.

Table 5 clearly shows the variety of experiences among the developing regions, with LAC benefiting across the board from increases in prices, although only two results are significant, at 5%. The only other significant impulse-response is the negative impact of the price of agricultural raw materials on MENA. That region has a positive response to increases in oil prices (although the t statistic is only 1.6 for the impact year). After LAC, the largest number of positives is in SSA, which benefits from increases in the prices of oil, metals, and beverages; growth is not affected by changes in food prices and appears somewhat negatively impacted by increases in prices of agricultural raw materials. EAP is positively influenced by the prices of metals and agricultural raw materials. SA appears negatively affected by increases in prices of agricultural products, but the results are not statistically significant, and the numerical values of the impulse-responses (not shown) appear small.[32]

In a disaggregated study using a country-based export price for the specific basket of commodities exported, Deaton and Miller (1995) found positive impacts on growth and investments in a sample of 32 SSA countries. In their estimation, about 20% of the growth decline in those countries from 1970–1975 to 1980–1985 can be attributed to the fall in world prices. Looking at a subset of commodities in a sample of 56 developing countries during the period 1970–1993, Collier (2005) calculated substantial losses in growth from falls in world agricultural prices. The price declines reduced GDP growth by around 1.4% per year over the period, output at the end of the period was around 5.6% lower than before the price shock, and the total loss of output as a percentage of initial annual income was around 14%. Collier also argues that because of the negative multiplier effects and the types of activities affected, including those in the nontradable sector, agricultural export price shocks are likely to be substantially borne by groups at high risk for poverty. The World Bank (2000a), in an analysis of the declining commodity price trend of the 1990s that separated oil and nonoil exporters in SSA, found that growth in the nonoil-exporting countries of sub-Saharan Africa has not been affected. The primary reason cited for that finding was that even if the prices of SSA exports declined, the loss was partly offset by lower import prices of energy and other products.

Another study by Birdsall and Hamoudi (2002) show that the positive correlation found by Dollar and Kraay (2001) between growth and "globalizing" economies is related to the fact that the countries performing worse were commodity dependent, and the collapse in prices reduced both growth and the value of the variable interpreted as a proxy for openness, creating a misleading correlation.[33] Birdsall and Hamoudi recalculated the growth equation developed by Dollar and Kraay, using a dummy for commodity-dependent countries to show that the estimated growth effect of the "openness" variable becomes statistically insignificant (with a value of the coefficient that is less than half the original estimate).

Another approach to analyzing the relationship between prices and development rather than focusing on commodities looks at the evolution of the terms of trade, which combines commodity prices and other goods and services, as exports and imports. Figure 10 shows the median of the net barter terms of trade for a sample of countries in LAC, SSA, and Asia.[34]

The influence of the decline in commodity prices in the 1980s, particularly since the mid-1980s, is more pronounced in the median terms of trade of LAC, followed by SSA. Asia's terms of trade were more stable during the 1980s and 1990s. The recovery in commodity prices after the lows that coincided with the recession of the early 2000s are reflected more in the increases in the terms of trade of SSA and less in those of LAC. The terms of trade in Asia appear to have been affected negatively rather than positively by the recent increases in commodity prices. This is in line with Asia as a region being a net importer of commodities and an exporter of manufactured goods, whereas SSA remains a significant producer of commodities and has a larger percentage of metals and oil in its basket of exports. LAC is in an intermediate position, with more

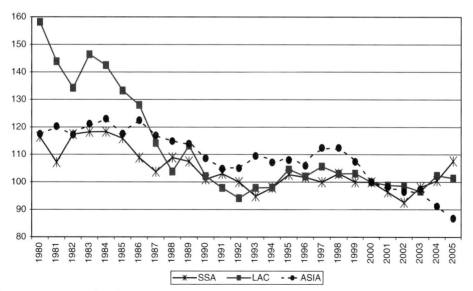

Figure 10 Terms of trade, 1980–2005. *Note:* It corresponds to the median values for 39 countries for SSA, 17 for LAC, and 11 for Asia. Source: World Bank (2007).

agricultural products than SSA (which, at least until 2005, the year of the last data available for terms of trade, had not benefited from the increases that happened later) and fewer manufactured goods than Asia.

Finally, another characteristic of commodity prices is volatility. This affects consumption and investment decisions of economic agents, with potential negative effects on welfare and growth. It also tends to complicate public sector macroeconomic management in many developing countries that depend on taxes on commodities, directly or indirectly, to finance significant percentages of public revenues. Table 6 shows changes in volatility using monthly data for the nominal indices calculated by the IMF for oil, metals, food, agricultural raw materials, and beverages.

The table shows that price volatility increased sharply in the 1970s and then declined in the 1980s and 1990s, but prices never again reached the stability of the 1960s. During the 2000s (as can be inferred from Figures 8, 9, and 10) an important increase has occurred in the volatility of oil and metals prices. This is not generally the case for all agricultural products; basically, the index of nominal prices for *food* products is the one that has increased in level and volatility. Transmitting better prices to producers in rural areas could spur rural investment and overall growth in developing countries; at the same time, however, sudden increases in the prices of basic staples could hurt the poor, who are net food buyers and have occupations that might not immediately benefit from the employment and growth multiplier effects of higher prices.

3.5 Exchange rates of key currencies

Another important aspect of global macroeconomics is the behavior of the U.S. dollar relative to other currencies. With the end of the Bretton Woods system of fixed exchange rates in the first half of the 1970s, volatility of nominal and real exchange

Table 6 Price volatility (monthly), 1960s–2000s

Decade	Oil	Metals	Agricultural Raw Materials	Beverages	Food
1960s	1.3	15.6	2.8	6.0	5.5
1970s	84.9	28.1	36.4	46.6	30.4
1980s	31.5	23.2	18.8	17.4	11.2
1990s	21.5	13.0	11.7	25.3	9.2
2000s	43.5	53.3	10.2	19.2	15.9

Note: Volatility is the standard deviation over the average for a decade times 100. The decade of the 2000s covers until 2007.
Source: IMF (2007).

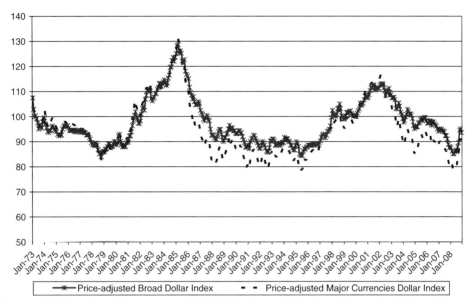

Figure 11 U.S. real exchange rates, 1973–2008. *Notes:* This chart shows the index of the real effective exchange rate calculated by the Federal Reserve for major world currencies and for a broader basket of currencies. The index is calculated such that an increase (decrease) is an appreciation (depreciation) of the dollar in relation to a set of other currencies. Source: U.S. Federal Reserve Database (2008).

rates in major countries increased. In particular, the U.S. dollar underwent two long cycles of appreciation and depreciation (Figure 11), while the behavior of the euro was the opposite (not shown).[35]

After several years of declining value during the 1970s, the U.S. dollar started a cycle of appreciation in the late 1970s that peaked in March 1985 and then declined until the late 1990s. Along the upward trend, various developing countries linked to the dollar could not sustain the peg and had to devalue (the "third country effect" noted by Schuh, 1986). This increased the burden of the U.S. dollar-denominated external debt that had accumulated during the previous period of lower inflation rates and higher commodity prices of the late 1970s. That burden, along with the decline in growth and the increase in real interest rates, led to the 1980s debt crisis that affected mostly Latin American and African developing countries.

The second cycle of appreciation of the U.S. dollar started in early 1996 and continued up to the first quarter of 2002, when a downturn began. Along the upward trend, that pattern was repeated, with various developing countries that had exchange rates tied to the U.S. dollar abandoning their pegs in a sequence of financial crises: Mexico in 1995, several East Asian countries in 1997, Russia in 1998, Brazil in 1999, and Argentina in 2001. The devaluations in Asia led to the contraction of demand for agricultural products in world markets, whereas those in Brazil and Argentina expanded world supplies, leading to the decline of world agricultural prices at the end of the 1990s and beginning of the 2000s (USDA, 2000; IMF, 1999).

The debate now is how much the dollar will have to decline, and against what currencies, to close the U.S. current account deficit. From peak to bottom in the 1980s, the decline in the real exchange rate (against major currencies) was about 40% (measured from the peak), and by the first quarter of 2008 the decline had been about 32%, but it recovered somewhat afterward, for a decline of about 25% by the end of 2008. The U.S. current account deficit in the 1980s, however, was a smaller percentage of both its own GDP and that of the world (see section 3.7). Therefore, the downward adjustment might have some way to go. A study from the McKinsey Global Institute (Farrell et al., 2007) projects that an additional depreciation of 30% from the January 2007 levels would be needed to close the current account by 2012. (This estimate assumes that growth continues on trend; if growth declines, the exchange rate correction required to close the external gap would be smaller.) In addition, Obstfeld and Rogoff (2004) argue that the dollar decline might end up resembling the collapse of the 1970s, when the United States abandoned the Bretton Woods system, rather than the more orderly decline of the 1980s.

The currencies against which the devaluation occurs also matter, given that several developing countries, mostly in Asia, and many oil-producing countries appear to have been defending specific targets for their nominal or real bilateral U.S. exchange rates. Such behavior would slow the overall process of adjustment and put additional pressure on currencies that float more freely. The gap between the real exchange rate index against major currencies (which has a larger percentage of floaters in its composition) and the broad index (which includes more U.S. partners, several of which actively manage their bilateral exchange rates instead of letting them float more freely) reflects those differences in policies by U.S. trade partners.

Besides the question of the "third country effect" and the link between the cycles of the dollar and financial crises in developing countries, another issue is whether the cycle of the dollar against other currencies is related to variations in the dollar prices of commodities. Mundell (2002) has argued that there seems to be a clear association of those cycles, with nominal dollar commodity prices (not only agriculture) declining with the strength of the dollar, and vice versa. He identifies three concurrent cycles: From the mid-1960s to the early 1980s, commodity prices went up and the U.S. dollar depreciated; then from 1980 to 1985 commodity prices fell, coinciding with the sharp strengthening of the dollar; after 1985, United States policy shifted to try to bring the dollar down while commodity prices increased from the 1986 lows peaking in 1995. However, Mundell notes that from 1995 onward the link between those cycles does not seem to hold.

Although Mundell's observations relate to commodities in general, the case of agricultural commodities is shown in Figure 12. It shows a VAR analysis between the

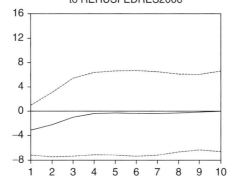

Figure 12 Relationship between real agricultural prices and the U.S. real exchange rate.

Price-Adjusted Broad Dollar Index of the U.S. Federal Reserve Index and an index of nominal world agricultural prices based on the IMF indices of world prices for food and agricultural raw materials.

The VAR shows that there is a persistent negative impact on nominal agricultural prices from the strengthening of the U.S. dollar in real terms, although the impact (looking at the position of the +/−2 SE bands) is not well determined statistically after the first year. The relation between the U.S. dollar and commodity prices may reflect other common factors that affect both variables. As already mentioned, Frankel (1984, 2006) has argued about the negative correlation between real interest rates and commodity prices. In fact, U.S. monetary policies affect both real interest rates and the exchange rate; an expansive monetary policy, as happened in the late 1970s and early 1990s, depreciated the dollar against foreign currencies and turned real interest negative, favoring high prices for commodities. A somewhat similar configuration has taken place in the early 2000s. Conversely, with the monetary tightening of the early 1980s, real interest rates increased significantly, the U.S. dollar appreciated, and dollar commodities prices declined. A qualitatively similar, but quantitatively less pronounced, cycle happened in the second half of the 1990s.

3.6 Capital flows and debt

To better understand the implications of changes in financial flows, it is important to remember the basic equation of the balance of payments:

$$(EX - IM) + (OPTNp + OTNg - INTR^*CFp - INTR^*CFg) + (dCFp + dCFg) = dNFA \tag{4}$$

This can be simplified to:

Current account (CA) + Capital account (KA) = Change in official reserves (dNFA) where CA consists of the trade balance (EX − IM); payments related to capital, such as interests and profits (INTR * CFp, INTR * CFg); payments related to labor (such as remittances); and other transfers to or from a country, such as donations (OPTNp, OTNg). KA includes various types of lending, borrowing, and net investment (dCFp + dCFg); and dNFA is the change in value of official reserves held, in the case presented in Table 1, by the monetary authority.

As an accounting identity this equation always holds, although the balancing can happen in various ways. In fact, the configuration of CA, KA, and dNFA has shown significant variation across countries and over time. First, a country can have a negative CA for several reasons. For instance, a trade deficit might not be compensated by other components of the CA (which is the case in the United States); a country could have high interest payments on its debt, even though it has a trade surplus (as was the case in many developing countries during the debt crisis of the 1980s); highly concessionary foreign aid and/or remittances from abroad may help finance (or create) trade deficits and/or also cover interest payments on external debt (which may be the case for many low-income countries now); and so on, for several other possible combinations of the various components of the CA. The examples just mentioned have very different implications for the world economy. For example, in the first case, the United States, through the trade deficit, is contributing to aggregate demand for the rest of the world. In the second example (debt crises), developing countries are adding to world aggregate supply; in the third case (remittances), they increase aggregate demand (although the magnitude of such effects may be marginal).

Second, a country with a negative CA (for whatever reason) might simultaneously have inflows of capital (a positive KA; i.e., the country is borrowing from the rest of the world) and declines in NFA (i.e., the country is using accumulated assets to finance the negative CA). At the other extreme, a country might have positive CA and KA, which means that NFA is increasing. (For example, China has increased reserves from below US$200 billion in the early 2000s to an estimated US$1500 billion by 2007.) That accumulation of NFA is usually held in assets denominated in U.S. dollars (such as U.S. government bonds) or other global currencies, which means that the increases in NFA in a country imply the financing of the CA of the country that issues the assets in which the reserves are invested, and, therefore, puts downward pressure on the interest rates in those assets.

Another implication of the balance of payment and monetary accounts is that increases in NFA, usually held by central banks or similar institutions, normally lead to the expansion of the domestic money supply. The value of net monetary expansion depends on the use (or not) of parallel sterilization policies that could absorb part of the increases in money supply through measures such as issuing domestic bonds or similar instruments (which implies a financial cost for the central bank) or by increasing reserve requirements at the banking system (which is a financial cost for the banks that can be

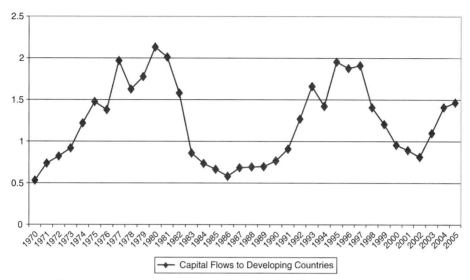

Figure 13 Capital flows to developing countries (% GDP), 1970–2005. *Note:* The chart includes public and private debt, foreign direct investment, and portfolio flows measured as a percentage of GDP. Source: IMF (2007, Box 4.2).

passed on to the depositors and/or borrowers). These issues are discussed further in the sections on domestic policies.

It is important to keep those possible effects in mind in discussing global cycles in capital flows. Figure 13 shows IMF data on capital flows to developing countries since 1970, measured as a percentage of developing countries' GDP.[36]

The first cycle peaked in the early 1980s at more that 2% of the combined GDP for developing countries; it then declined during the debt crisis of the 1980s to a minimum of 0.6% of their combined GDP in 1986. The boom and bust in capital flows were more marked for LAC and SSA during these decades (Díaz–Bonilla, 2008). The second cycle began in the early 1990s, peaked in 1995 at about 2%, and dropped again during the sequence of developing-country crises of the late 1990s and early 2000s, reaching a low of 0.8% of GDP in 2002. During this second cycle, the regions more affected were EAP and LAC. In the early 2000s capital flows to developing countries began to increase again. It remains to be seen how the latest cycle will play out over the next years, particularly in the context of the late 2000s global economic decline.

A relevant question is the reason for those cycles in capital flows, with different views about whether they are driven by internal factors in developing countries, or, rather, they are just the result of global forces mostly unrelated to what developing may be doing. During the 1980s Albert Fishlow, writing about that period's debt crisis, argued that the United States in the 20th century, like the United Kingdom in the 19th century, has had cycles of absorbing from and releasing savings to the rest of the world, in line with its own expansionary and recessionary periods, respectively. During the

1990s Calvo et al, 1993 showed that, at least in the case of LAC, the inflows of capital flows were to a great extent explained by external common factors (the financial conditions in the United States) rather than the internal situation of the countries in the region.

Whatever the causes, the ebb and flow of capital flows to developing countries have been associated with financial crises in developing countries, first during the 1980s and again in the 1990s, when expanded capital flows led to a more volatile world economic environment (as reflected in the already mentioned crises in Mexico, Asia, Russia, Brazil, and Argentina during the second part of the 1990s and in the early 2000s).

The behavior of capital flows has several implications for the economy in general and the agricultural sector in particular. Those capital flows can accelerate growth and help finance additional investments, but they also tend to expand domestic money supply and increase the price of nontradables, appreciating the domestic currency compared to the case without the flows. Consequently, capital inflows could have a positive growth and investment effect on agriculture in general, including particularly those products, such as livestock and dairy, that in many countries are more linked to the evolution of income and demand in the domestic market. On the other hand, the overvaluation of the domestic currency will hurt tradable sectors, including the agricultural exportable and import-competing products. For instance, Reca and Parellada (2001) show the important boom in dairy products in Argentina during the early 1990s, fueled by strong domestic growth, linked to capital inflows, whereas at the same time crop production stagnated due to the appreciation of the Argentine peso (and lower world prices during that period). In the case of several LAC countries that reduced tariffs and other trade barriers protecting import-substitution products during the 1990s (again including several agricultural products), the appreciation of the domestic currency due to capital flows added to the pressure of trade liberalization on the domestic producers.

A source of debate is whether different classes of capital flows have different impacts on growth and crises (see, for instance, Prasad et al., 2003, who try to differentiate foreign direct investment from portfolio investments of different types). Also it is important to determine whether the capital flows end up financing consumption or investment (see Calvo et al 1993).

An additional factor to consider is that capital flows can experience sudden stops and even reversals, which might lead to depreciation of the domestic currency, banking and fiscal crises (particularly when the economy shows an important presence of domestic private and public debt in dollars), and sharp declines in growth (Calvo, 2003; Calvo et al., 2005).

Table 7 shows the large magnitude of some of those episodes of sudden stops and reversals in the 1980s and 1990s.[37]

Table 7 Episodes of sudden stops by country, 1982–1997

Country	Years	GDP (%)
Argentina	1982–1983	20
Argentina	1994–1995	4
Chile	1981–1983	7
Chile	1990–1991	8
Ecuador	1995–1996	19
Hungary	1995–1996	7
Indonesia	1996–1997	5
Malaysia	1993–1994	15
Mexico	1981–1983	12
Mexico	1993–1995	6
Philippines	1996–1997	7
Venezuela	1992–1994	9
Korea	1996–1997	11
Thailand	1996–1997	26
Turkey	1993–1994	10
Average		11.1
Mean		9

Source: Calvo (2003).

As argued before, although the devaluation associated with the capital outflow improves relative prices for tradable products such as agriculture, declines in economic activity affect products that depend on domestic market incomes, and banking and fiscal crises can negatively impact the supply side of various products (through credit constraints and cuts in public investments) and consumer demand. Moreover, domestic production could be affected by increases in prices of imported inputs.

For instance, capital outflows and devaluations during the 1980s debt crises in LAC and the correlated strong decline in overall growth during what has been called the "lost decade" affected production of livestock and dairy products and of raw materials for nonfood manufacturing products, whereas food crop production (which tend to be more tradable) fared relatively better (López-Cordovez, 1987). Another example already mentioned is the sequence of financial crises since the mid-1990s, which disrupted the economies of many Asian and South American countries. Shane and Liefert (2000) analyzed the impacts in countries affected by the crises as well as in nonaffected countries. For many, but not all, of the agricultural producers in crisis countries, currency depreciation improved their terms of trade. For some, however, they worsened, especially those that imported a large share of inputs for production and whose prices rose more than prices for output, such as poultry farmers who imported the bulk of their feed in Indonesia (also the soybean-processing industry in Korea). Capital flight raised interest rates in crisis countries, which reduced the availability of credit, lowered capital investment in agriculture, and raised input costs if producers had to borrow to finance input purchases. Besides the price effects, the decline of incomes resulting from the crisis negatively affected products with higher income elasticity, such as beef or fresh fruits, while others with less elastic demand were not affected and, in some cases, the income decline appears to have increased the demand for inferior good staples. Also, Bresciani et al. (2002) studied the impact of the East Asian financial crisis on farmers in Indonesia and Thailand using household surveys and found differentiated impacts on farmers' incomes and distribution, even though shocks to both countries looked roughly similar. For instance, poor farmers in Thailand were more affected by the crisis than were those in Indonesia, in part because Thai farmers relied more on urban activities to supplement their incomes and because those activities suffered more from the financial crisis.[38] On the other hand, farmers in both countries who specialized in export crops benefited from the currency devaluation.

Financial crises have also had important effects on world commodity markets. The 1997 devaluations in Asia led to the contraction of demand for agricultural products in world markets, whereas devaluations in Brazil and Argentina expanded world supplies, leading to the decline of world agricultural prices at the end of the 1990s and the beginning of the 2000s (IMF, 1999; see also Langley, 1999; Langley et al., 2000; and Shane and Liefert, 2000). The impact was not limited to commodity markets. Most of the capital flowing out of crisis countries largely went to developed countries, mainly the United States. Capital inflows likely placed downward pressures on U.S. interest rates, which stimulated investment demand and growth in U.S. capital stock (see Diao and Roe, 2000). But at the same time that capital inflow appreciated the dollar, affecting U.S. agriculture through a different channel. The world is still trying to correct the imbalances associated with those capital flows, as discussed in the next section.

3.7 Current Accounts and External Imbalances

The previous section looked at capital flows and developing countries. Those flows are part of larger global imbalances. The origin and use of the funds at the world level can be seen from changes in current accounts in different countries and regions (Figure 14).

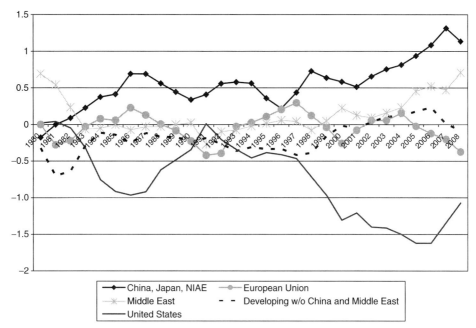

Figure 14 Current account imbalances (% world GDP). *Notes:* Because of lack of complete data in international transactions the numbers do not necessarily add up at the world level. NIAE = newly industrialized Asian economies. Source: IMF (2008).

During the late 1970s and early 1980s, the Middle East (a proxy for oil producers) had a positive current account (CA) and was financing, through the recycling of petrodollars, the rest of the regions that had negative CA, except the United States, which was in equilibrium. The largest negative CA as percentage of the GDP was for developing countries (excluding China and the Middle East[39]). In the 1980s the United States began to increase its CA deficit, financed mostly by Japan and, to a smaller degree, Europe.[40] The largest component of the CA deficit of the United States has been the trade deficit, and the implication is that, as noted before, this country has been imparting positive impulses to world growth through expanded aggregate demand. Developing countries (excluding China and the Middle East) reduced their deficits in CA significantly during the second part of the 1980s: Countries in LAC and Africa were forced to adjust the external accounts to cope with the debt crisis, whereas the decline in real prices of oil reduced or eliminated much of the CA surplus of oil-producing countries.

During the first half of the 1990s, both developing countries (excluding China and the Middle East) and the United States were absorbing capital, mostly from Japan and Europe. The reversal of capital flows and the corresponding adjustment of the CA in developing countries were associated with the sequence of financial crises during the second half of the 1990s. By the end of the 1990s and since, the United States has been receiving flows from Asia (Japan, China, and the newly industrialized Asian economies) and oil exporters while the rest of the developing countries and the European Union have been basically moving up or down around balance.

In 2006 the U.S. CA deficit reached somewhat more than 1.6% of the world GDP, a level unprecedented in modern history. To analyze this event, it is useful to remember the traditional framework to discuss any program aimed at restoring equilibrium in the external accounts of a country, based on the concepts of expenditure reduction, expenditure switching, and external financing. Given some level of external financing, an economic program aimed at restoring some balance in external accounts would include policies that try to adjust down aggregate demand to the level of aggregate supply (expenditure reduction), and other policies, usually linked to the exchange rate, that change the composition of GDP toward the production of more tradable goods and services (expenditure switching; see, for instance, Helmers and Dornbusch, 1988).

During the previous cycle of high CA deficits, the U.S. imbalance peaked at 1% of world GDP in the mid-1980s. The recessions in the early 1980s and early 1990s, along with adjustments in the real exchange rate, were crucial in restoring balance in the CA for the United States (i.e., there were both expenditure reducing and expenditure switching, with little external financing). However, during the recession of the early 2000s, the U.S. imbalance in the CA did not disappear. The reasons why the adjustment did not happen were that the recession of the early 2000s in the United States was milder than previous ones (i.e. little or no expenditure reduction occurred), and that it coincided with a strong real appreciation of the U.S. currency (i.e. no expenditure switching took place). However, this would miss another factor: the increase in external financing toward the United States, as suggested by the larger CA surpluses in the Asian group (Japan, China, and NIAE) and Middle East and the reduction in the CA deficit in developing countries. The availability of external financing to the United States helped keep the dollar strong (no expenditure switching) and reduced the need for expenditure reduction. The recent debate over how to close those imbalances centers on who created the problem in the first place; some point to problems in the U.S. policies, others argue that the countries with CA surpluses are the main culprits.

To approach that question, it is important to start by recognizing that the recent evolution of global imbalances has reflected important changes in economic conditions in both developed countries (particularly the United States) and developing countries. Before the last cycle, low real interest rates in industrialized countries usually meant that capital was flowing toward the developing countries. However, in the 2000s capital flows have been going from China, oil exporters, and some other developing countries toward industrialized countries (excluding Japan), mainly the United States. This is very different from the behavior of capital flows that led to the debt crises of the 1980s and 1990s. In the environment of high commodity prices of the 1970s many developing countries borrowed in expectation of sustained export incomes, but in the 2000s those countries have been improving their fiscal and external accounts, reducing their debts and increasing the availability of savings for the rest of the world. For instance, the East Asian countries that experienced the collapse of 1997 did not go back to the high investment levels that existed before the Asian crisis, when investments were financed by negative current accounts. Rather, they decreased investments and turned to positive current accounts, adding to the world's excess net savings (IMF, 2005). The accumulation of foreign exchange reserves associated with positive current accounts in China and other developing countries, including oil exporters, has also led to expansionary domestic monetary policies in those countries, which sustained their own growth performance.

What led to these changes in the origins and destinations of flows and of the resulting imbalances? A diversity of reasons have been suggested. Bracke et al. (2008) analyze several explanations, which they divide into two general categories: structural and cyclical explanations. Roubini (2006) lists 10 possible explanations. This discussion can be simplified using the definition of the national accounts, where a deficit in the current account of the balance of payments is an excess of domestic investment over domestic savings. Then we have four general explanations of the imbalances (and combinations thereof): the United States has decreased savings; the United States has increased investments; the surplus countries have increased savings; and/or the surplus countries have reduced investments.

The decline in U.S. savings might have resulted from a policy decision. The tax cuts introduced in 2001 switched the nation's fiscal position from a surplus of 2.5% of GDP in 2000 to a deficit of 3.5% of GDP in 2004, a reversal of 6% points of GDP, and would have certainly affected the CA (Roubini, 2006). This is the "twin deficit argument," which links the current account deficit to the public deficit, assuming that private net savings remain stable. But private U.S. savings have also declined. Among the reasons suggested are (1) that the period of the "Great Moderation" gave U.S. consumers a sense of stability and reduced uncertainty, which required less savings on their part (Fogli and Perri, 2006); and (2) that the perception of higher wealth resulting from the appreciation (or bubbles) in the U.S. housing and stock markets, and perhaps lower labor income generation, have led consumers to borrow from those assets to finance consumption. On the investment side, the United States has gone through a process of overinvestment in housing.

The hypotheses regarding increased savings in surplus economies are different depending on the type of country considered. In Japan the increase in savings may be related to the point where the country is in its demographic cycle, which leads to more private savings, whereas in developing countries that are not oil exporters, the cause may be the lack of social security systems (which forces people to save individually) or the structure of financial systems that do not provide adequate domestic vehicles for savings (and therefore a percentage is invested abroad).

There is also a public sector counterpart in increased savings, linked to the desire by governments to insure against the kinds of financial crises that occurred in the second part of the 1990s. This requires accumulation of official reserves. For instance, Aizenman and Lee (2005) tested the importance of this type of self-insurance against economic crises generated by sudden stops and capital flight versus mercantilist objectives in the accumulation of reserves, and they found evidence in support of the first interpretation.[41] A more mercantilist interpretation is the notion that developing countries (particularly in Asia) have kept the exchange rate undervalued as a development strategy (as in the Bretton Woods II hypothesis advanced by Dooley et al., 2003), which has led also to accumulation of foreign reserves (i.e., increasing savings that are invested in international assets). In the case of oil-producing countries, the public and private sectors might have been surprised by income growth and have not yet adjusted expenditures patterns, or they are considering those increases in income temporary and are therefore saving them.

Other explanations may be separate from the overall balance of savings and investment and are linked to its composition. Some argue that financial globalization has allowed some investors to diversify their portfolios and invest abroad; this is particularly true for the United States, which has been usually considered the main supplier of "safe" assets (see IMF, 2005; Roubini, 2006; and Bracke et al., 2008).

All these developments kept world real interest rates low, even though the United States and other industrialized countries turned to relatively more restrictive monetary policies since mid-2004 and until mid-2007. This has been called the "Greenspan conundrum": Although the Federal Reserve was increasing short-term interest rates, long-term rates were holding steady or even falling. Low real interest rates fueled the housing cycle, now in a sharply declining phase in the United States and other industrialized countries, and they contributed to the expansion of leveraged financial operations, mostly in vehicles and instruments that were assumed to be off the balance sheet of the normal banking system. The painful downturn in the housing cycle and its repercussions in financial markets (including the deleveraging of those parallel operations) have ended the current expansion.

The implications of these developments for agriculture are multiple, due to significant potential impacts on growth, inflation, interest rates, commodity prices, and capital flows, all of which will depend on the appropriate management of the unwinding of those imbalances, which requires a proper interpretation and prioritization of causes. As of this writing the potential for a disorderly adjustment, due to the lack of an adequately coordinated policy framework, appears high.

3.8 World trade

World trade grew between 7% and 8% annually during the 1960s and 1970s, declined to somewhat more than 3% in the 1980s but recovered to about 7% in the 1990s and beginning of the 2000s. Those rates were larger than GDP growth in all periods, increasing continuously the ratio of trade to GDP from about a quarter in the 1960s

Table 8 World trade (% of GDP)

	1960s	1970s	1980s	1990s	2000–2005
East Asia and Pacific	NA	20.9	36.5	56.0	71.6
Latin America and Caribbean	20.3	23.5	28.2	35.6	45.3
Middle East and North Africa	NA	67.4	49.5	56.2	60.5
South Asia	13.8	15.3	18.5	24.9	33.0
Sub-Saharan Africa	48.7	53.7	54.5	57.0	64.6
World	24.2	31.9	37.4	41.3	48.1

Source: WDI, World Bank (2006).

to almost half the world GDP in the 2000s (Table 8).[42] Projections for the late 2000s indicate a sharp slowdown in trade growth, affected by the financial turmoil and deepening global economic slowdown.

Although all developing regions increased their levels of integration in trade flows, the rhythm differed across them. East Asia and sub-Saharan Africa appear substantially more integrated in world trade than Latin America and South Asia, as measured by the trade/GDP ratio (Table 8). At least from these indicators there does not seem to be a clear link between the level of trade integration and growth, with high (East Asia) and low (SSA) growth performers in the high trade integration category (similar observation can be made for South Asia [high growth] and LAC [lower growth] as regions with lower trade to GDP ratios).[43]

Although those trends correspond to goods and services in general, a separate question is whether agriculture has become more integrated in world markets. Table 9 shows the ratios of imports and exports over production for all agricultural products since 1961 to the early 2000s for different developing groupings. All variables are measured in world prices of 1989–1991.

Several points deserve mention. First, domestic production for domestic use constitutes the largest component of agriculture in developing countries as a whole. Second, the levels and trends of the import and export ratios for the developing regions differ among them. Sub-Saharan Africa had the largest export/production percentage during the 1960s (28.5%), but it has been declining since then, standing in the 2000s at less than half the initial value (13.. The import/production percentage, on the other hand, climbed from 8% at the beginning of the period to almost 14% in the 2000s. Asia has the lowest export and import ratios, and both have been trending upward but very slowly. LAC has become, by the indicators used here, the more integrated region in world markets, surpassing SSA on both the export and import ratios. In summary, although agricultural integration in world market

Table 9   Agriculture trade ratios (%), 1960s–early 2000s

	1960s	1970s	1980s	1990s	Early 2000s
Export/production					
LAC	23.6	24.7	24.5	26.7	31.4
SSA[a]	28.5	23.0	17.2	15.3	13.2
Asia, developing [b]	5.4	5.7	6.4	6.4	6.4
All three regions	12.1	11.8	11.3	11.0	11.6
Import/production					
LAC	6.7	8.6	11.2	14.0	15.7
SSA[a]	8.1	9.4	12.6	12.3	13.5
Asia, developing [b]	7.1	7.7	9.2	8.9	8.8
All three regions	7.1	8.0	10.0	10.1	10.5

[a]Does not include South Africa.
[b]Does not include China.
Source: FAOSTAT.

(at least measured by these simple trade ratios) appears to have increased on the whole since the 1960s, domestic production for domestic utilization is the dominant characteristic for the agricultural sector of developing countries as a whole. In addition, such integration does not appear to have a uniform trend upward in all regions, with SSA showing lower export ratios now than in the past, and Asia showing lower import ratios in the 1990s and beginning of the 2000s compared to the 1980s.

Moreover, those import and export ratios differ by product: Agricultural products tend to have larger trade ratios than livestock products (see Table 10, which shows the ratio of imports and exports over production; all variables measured in tons from

Table 10   Developing countries: Export and imports over production (metric tons)

		1960s	1970s	1980s	1990s	Early 2000s
Meat	Imports	1.4	2.4	4.1	4.1	5.4
	Exports	4.9	4.6	3.8	3.7	4.4
Milk (no butter)	Imports	7.7	11.1	15.1	11.5	10.2
	Exports	0.3	0.6	0.5	1.2	1.9
Cereals	Imports	9.3	10.5	14.2	14.7	17.3
	Exports	4.7	4	4.3	4.7	6.1
Vegetable oils	Imports	11.4	16.8	27.4	32	33.9
	Exports	20.4	25	33.2	40.1	46.1

Source: FAO STAT.

FAOSTAT). Meat products, for which imports and exports represent only about 4% of production, appear less integrated with world markets than cereals and, particularly, vegetable oils.[44] In the case of meat and milk products' shelf life, sanitary measures and trade protection tend to isolate domestic markets in many countries, making these products behave more like nontradables. The different levels of integration in world trade have implications for the assumptions about the tradability of agricultural products. Many analyses of price biases and price distortions have focused on crops (which are more tradable, in general) rather than livestock products (which tend to be less so). These distinctions are important for a proper analysis of the impacts of various macroeconomic conditions and policies.

4. MACROECONOMIC POLICIES IN DEVELOPING COUNTRIES AND AGRICULTURE

Along with the world trends described before, there have also been important changes in macroeconomic policies and conditions in developing countries. In what follows we discuss various aspects of fiscal, monetary, exchange rates, and trade policies and their implications for agriculture.[45] Before that, we briefly cover the earlier debates about macroeconomic and development policies and agriculture.

4.1 A brief overview of early macroeconomic policy issues in developing countries

4.1.1 Macroeconomic and development policies in developing countries, circa 1950s and 1960s

Macroeconomic analysis in developed countries has been mostly concerned with stabilization issues, usually in the context of a closed economy. Policy analysis and debate have mainly focused on the need of, and means to, managing aggregate demand, with a view to stabilizing price and employment at levels considered adequate for the proper operation of the economy. The economy of the developed countries was supposed to function at a relatively acceptable level of micro-efficiency, and it was also assumed that the forces shaping the long-run prospects for economic growth (the aggregate supply of the economy) could work through the normal operation of the markets, if aggregate demand was sustained at an appropriate level. As to the international influences on macroeconomic performance, it was considered that the regime of floating exchange rates, emerging after the collapse of the Bretton Woods system, could delink the domestic management of the economy from the external forces. Although increasingly since the 1980s this focus has been extended to include the supply-side aspects of macroeconomics and the repercussions of various macro policies on the external accounts, it could be argued that the stabilization of a closed economy remained the basic paradigm (Clarida, 2008).

For developing countries, on the other hand, the analysis and debate of macroeconomic policies followed a different path. The discussion centered on supply-side, long-run issues related to economic growth.[46] The original post-World War development approach, which coalesced around the notion that came to be called *import substitution industrialization* (ISI), was based on the following central themes:

The need to accumulate capital, increasing investment and savings rates   For example, Lewis (1954, 1955) argued that the central problem of underdevelopment was how to go from a situation where domestic economic agents save 4–5% of GDP to one with savings around 15–20%. Investment and capital accumulation, it was argued, would not only solve the internal productive imbalance that were considered the leading cause of inflationary pressures but was thought to also solve the external imbalance, which caused recurrent balance-of-payments crises.

The importance of industrialization in the process of development   This process could advance in a more or less balanced fashion (although for some, like Rosenstein-Rodan, 1943, this would focus basically on light industry; for others, like Mahalanobis, 1955, heavy industry should be incorporated) or instead could be propelled by the fundamental tensions of market disequilibria that created opportunities for investment, as argued by Hirschman (1958).

After World War II, many leaders and intellectuals in the developing world saw industrialization as intrinsically related to nation building. For newly independent countries during the 19th and 20th centuries, the policy approach began with the desire to break free from direct political and economic control by the colonial powers. In this line of analysis, dependency was embedded in the productive structure of the developing countries: They produced primary products and sold them to the colonial powers, from which poor countries, lacking a domestic industrial base, had to import manufactures. It was argued that this international power architecture was also reflected in the social fabric of the developing countries through the presence of landowners and representatives of foreign capital (the latter tied directly or indirectly to agricultural production) and in the structure of land tenancy, where large estates and plantations occupied the dominant position. From this perspective, deemphasizing the role of the agricultural sector in development was part of a double process of economic independence and political sovereignty on one hand and of a transition to a more equitable internal distribution of income.

Even in Latin American countries, which had become independent mostly in the 19th century and which after World War II had a relatively developed industrial base compared to other regions, the argument of unequal external relations had strong resonance.[47] Rather than the more obvious issue of direct political control, the argument, as elaborated by Prebisch (1950, 1968) and Singer (1950), was an economic one, based on the empirical observation at that point in time of declining terms of trade of countries exporting agricultural products (or primary products, in general) compared to countries exporting industrial goods. Singer's arguments were based on the characteristics of agricultural goods (such as supply and demand elasticities); Prebisch contrasted market structures in developed countries (characterized by industrial oligopolies and strong unions) with those of developing countries (characterized by smaller firms and surplus labor) and argued that the former could retain the benefits of technical progress while the latter surrendered gains from productivity through falling prices of their primary exports (hence the decline in the terms of trade).

Besides nation building and economic and political independence, industrialization was also associated with (and, in the stronger version, would cause) social modernization.

Rural populations were supposed to lack entrepreneurial spirit and appeared bound by traditional culture and organization. So, when pioneering firms started in the urban centers, the creation of nonfarm jobs would reduce the sway of agrarian classes. Urbanization was itself linked to modernization of the society; progressive attitudes would result from it. This process was supposed to lead to an open and mobile society, eliminating the assignment of occupations by traditional criteria (gender, ethnicity, family status). Increasing levels of general education for all citizens would generate a more active, pluralistic, and participatory political and social life (the most complete presentation of these arguments is probably Kerr et al., 1964). Although the left did not necessarily share this benign view of modernization, some Marxist arguments emphasized the need to move beyond feudalism (which was associated with the agricultural sector) to capitalism (identified with industrialization and the development of the urban proletariat; Mitrany, 1951).

Yet for all the arguments regarding the military, political, and social externalities of industrialization, the bulk of the public policy discussion was conducted in economic terms. The main objectives of industrialization were growth, employment, and elimination of poverty (see, for instance, Bhagwati, 1993, on the sequence of Indian Plans). The economic externalities of industrialization, which were at the center of what has been called *high development theory* (Krugman, 1994), involved a different set of issues: the interaction of economies of scale, pecuniary external economies, technological spillovers, backward and forward linkages, and strategic complementarities. The combination of these elements suggested the existence of multiple equilibria and the need for some form of coordination, probably, but not only, through government intervention, to move from lower to higher levels of economic activity (Chenery, Robinson, Syrquin, 1986).

The general case is as follows. In any preindustrial economy, pioneering firms are subject to considerable startup costs. Without an industrial base (of skilled labor, supplier networks, experienced capital markets, etc.), each new industry is at much higher survival risk than it would be had it started in an already industrialized country.

Survival risks are attributable to the structural factors noted previously and to the fact that demand for industrial goods would initially be weak: Without an industrial system producing many goods by many wage earners, the first industry is in a highly contingent position, whereas the hundredth is much less so (Rosenstein-Rodan, 1943; Murphy, Shleifer, and Vishny, 1989). At the same time, each new industry would contribute technological spillovers and the development of a skilled labor force to the society as a whole; learning by doing would contribute to the hiring firm's bottom line (for which the firm is compensated) but also to the viability of the industrial sector overall (for which the firm is not compensated).

Another issue was macroeconomic stability. Although not specified as an externality, it was also clear that policymakers considered that industrialization was going to make the economy less vulnerable to external shocks, thus avoiding macroeconomic crises. It was assumed that, as the number of industrial firms increased, dependence on revenue from primary products would gradually be reduced, which was supposed to insulate the economy from external shocks and to protect against the losses implied by the postulated decline in the terms of trade (CEPAL, 1969).

In summary, the positive impact of industrialization appeared substantial: nation building, political and economic independence, national security, modernization, development, technological advance, protection from external shocks, and so on.[48]

A focus on the internal market Rather than expand exports, the approach was to reduce imports through domestic production. The process of import substitution, which focused basically on industrial products, would move "backward" from consumer goods to basic industries, replacing domestically produced goods for imported ones. In the end it was thought that the (small) remnant of nonsubstitutable imports could be financed through the (also reduced) level of exports. The feasibility of expanding the volume of exports was considered small because they would come from the primary sector, in particular the agricultural production, which was supposed to have a low price elasticity of supply and because, in any case, the international demand for those primary products was also deemed to be relatively price inelastic (Little, 1982, provides a review of this debate).

The belief that markets and the price system would not adequately guide the necessary process of investment and capital accumulation This was to be led by government intervention, usually through a development plan with instruments such as trade protection and subsidies for manufactures, taxes on agriculture, and a heavy involvement of the state in the economy (see the accounts by Hirschman, 1982; Sen, 1983).

According to the post-war development strategy, the role of agriculture was subordinated to the needs of the industrialization process   Various arguments were utilized to support this view. Quantitative historical analysis (for instance, Kuznets, 1966) showed that agriculture declined in importance with the advance of economic development. This fact appeared related to Engel's Law, which argued that the percentage of food expenditures declined as incomes increased. Also, and especially in Latin America, various authors argued that (1) agricultural production was inelastic to domestic prices, (2) international demand was also inelastic with respect to international prices, and (3) the international terms of trade were moving against agriculture (Cepal, 1969). It was said that increasing the prices of agricultural products would not increase production but would add to inflationary pressures. If domestic production and international demand were inelastic, the imposition of taxes on agricultural products would not significantly diminish domestic production, and much of the tax would be paid by importing countries in the form of higher prices. It was also argued that even if domestic production and exports were increased, that might not result in greater incomes for the countries following that approach, because of deterioration in the terms of trade. Therefore, over the medium to long term, policymakers pursued the diversification of the productive structure through industrialization.

Consequently, during the 1950s and 1960s, the prevailing idea was to transfer resources from agriculture (considered a low-productivity sector) to industry (where it was assumed that resources would have higher productivity). The role of agriculture in development (see Johnston and Mellor, 1961) was one of transferring surpluses for higher economic growth: (a) the transfer of labor surpluses; workers supposedly unemployed in the agricultural would be transferred to industry (see especially Lewis, 1954); (b) agriculture would provide food (wage goods) and raw materials to the industrial sector; (c) savings in the agricultural sector would be taxed away to sustain the process of investment in the industrial sector and for the development of public infrastructure; and (d) the agricultural sector had to generate surpluses of foreign currency to pay for the importation of capital goods and industrial inputs (Johnston and Mellor, 1961).

Inflation was considered an unwanted yet inevitable result of the growth process in the context of nonintegrated and unbalanced economies   Inflation was considered a lesser evil that must be endured in order to foster economic development. Inflationary pressures were not necessarily attributed to excess aggregate demand; rather, it was thought that relatively "normal" levels of aggregate demand could generate inflationary pressures because the productive sector of the economy was fragmented, with key sectors operating at full capacity or showing rigidities to increase the level of operation while other sectors experienced higher levels of unemployment and unused capacity. Consequently, inflationary pressures were supposed to fade away once the investment process would integrate and balance the productive structure of the economy, making the production bottlenecks disappear. This process was believed to be basically the development and expansion of the industrial sector and related infrastructure. In other cases, inflation was thought to be an expedient way of generating forced savings through the "inflationary tax" administered by the government, which in turn sustained the process of capital accumulation (a discussion of views on inflation and development can be found in Johnson, 1984).

4.1.2 Reassessment of macroeconomic and development policies in the 1970s

By the mid-1960s several concerns began to be voiced about the adequacy of this development strategy. Protection and subsidies to the industrial sector were damaging other sectors, such as agriculture. Schultz (1964), in an influential book, argued that the farmers in the developing countries were "poor but efficient," reacting with economic rationality to changes in prices and incentives. If the agricultural resources were efficiently utilized, there were not gains to be made by the economy from transferring labor and savings to other sectors. The suggestion was to support the agricultural sector through technological development and human capital formation in rural areas. The dispute, between Fei and Ranis (1966) on one hand and Jorgenson (1967) on the other, over the operation of "dual economies" also centered, at a macro level, over whether there were efficiency gains to be made by moving labor from agriculture to industry. Jorgenson's neoclassical position emphasized that labor was paid the value of its marginal productivity and that there was not a labor surplus in agriculture to be transferred to the industrial sector. The key variables in its development model were the rate of population growth and, again, technological change in agriculture. In general, the participation of the state in this process was considered crucial (complementing the traditional vision of the role of the public sector in infrastructure). The Green Revolution of the 1970s and afterward was based on the idea that there could be a technological solution to the rural problem.

Different studies during the 1970s (Little, Scitovsky and Scott, 1970; Balassa, 1971; Krueger, 1978) also criticized the strategy of development based on inward-oriented, import-substituting industrialization in terms of both long-run growth and efficiency aspects. They pointed to the supply-side constraints generated by the structure of macro prices (i.e., the relative price of tradables/nontradables, of industrial/agricultural products, the exchange rate, the interest rate, the wage level) established through governmental policies. According to these studies the policies analyzed had a triply damaging effect: (a) they made the economy operate inside the production possibility frontier (PPF), (b) they did not allow the economy to place itself on the most adequate point on the multidimensional PPF that would allow the country to benefit from international trade, and (c) they slowed the outward movement of the PPF.

Criticisms mounted about the basic assumptions, the policies followed, and the consequences of the ISI strategy. Some argued that the strategy of forced industrialization was a misapplication of historical lessons from English development: Transfers of capital and labor from agriculture to the rest of the economy should take place naturally, not through policies highly discriminatory against the agricultural sector (World Bank, 1986). The obvious realization that the poor in developing countries were concentrated mainly in rural areas led to the conclusion that if poverty alleviation were to be an important objective of economic policy, greater attention should be given to agricultural and rural development (Chenery et al., 1974; Lipton, 1977).

Others pointed out that the supply of agricultural products was reasonably elastic, as was international demand. The terms of trade between industrial and agricultural products —after adjusting for quality and other factors—would not have deteriorated (for an overview of those debates, see Balassa, 1986b). Discrimination against exports and the exclusively inward orientation was criticized because it failed to take advantage of the commercial opportunities offered by the international economy. The costs of inefficiency and lack of competitive incentives to productivity growth due to protection were higher than the possible ones (such as volatility) associated with a greater integration in international trade. Protected industries appeared to require (and strongly lobbied for) protection long after the intended period of "infancy."

It was also said that pervasive state intervention into capital markets made investment funds available only to the large, favored firms and discouraged technical advance in other sectors. On the other hand, developing countries following an export-oriented strategy would benefit from greater flexibility, efficient allocation of resources, technological development, economies of scale, and dynamic effects that could not be attained through reliance on the internal market alone (Balassa, 1986b). It was also argued that industrialization fostered through protectionism had generated an industrial structure more capital intensive than the resource endowment of developing countries required. Therefore poverty alleviation was impaired by policies that protected capital-intensive industrialization and discriminated against agriculture, generating less employment and a distribution of income less equal than what outward development strategies would have allowed. This process of inward industrialization was criticized for appearing to have been accompanied by an uncontrolled process of urbanization and the continuation and even deepening of poverty in rural areas.

At the macroeconomic level, it was argued that import-substitution protectionism had increased inflationary pressures (Krueger, 1981, 1984) and fostered unsustainable fiscal deficits associated with state interventions, leading to recurrent macroeconomic crises. After experiencing the vagaries of world markets for commodities during the 19th and early 20th centuries, many developing countries turned to inward-oriented policies, with the objective, among others, of reducing external vulnerability. However, and contrary to expectations, the countries following inward-oriented policies appeared more vulnerable to external shocks and more prone to balance-of-payments crises, which, when they occurred, tended to have a stronger negative impact on the economy (Balassa, 1984, 1986a). An important reason for such economic instability seems to have been that the ISI strategy created a stop/go dynamic in economic activity; the acceleration of the economy usually led to fewer exports (because a larger percentage of the goods was consumed internally due to growing incomes) and more imported inputs and capital goods (demanded by the expanding industry), generating balance-of-payment crises when official external reserves reached very low levels. In addition, compressing imports through import substitution meant that, because of general equilibrium effects, exports also declined. The result was that those economies ended up with very little diversification on the export side (i.e., the country ended up selling a small range of goods) and was also very dependent on the import side, buying a narrow group of nonsubstitutable imports that were crucial for the operation of the economy. All this, it was argued, appeared to increase the vulnerability of the economy to any external shock on the export, import, or financial side. On the other hand, those countries following outward-orientation policies were considered to show better results terms of not only efficiency but also flexibility and adaptability to external events (Balassa, 1986).

Import substitution was even criticized in noneconomic terms. In India and South Asia, industrialization took place with domestic firms, but in much of Latin America it was related to the expansion of multinational corporations. Critics from the left decried the increasing power of the international capital and attributed different economic and social problems to the dominance of those international corporations (Frank, 1969, among others). From a very different perspective, those holding views of what was called *neoclassical political economy* began to debate the notion of government as a benign planner interested in aggregate national welfare (the implicit view of much of the proposals for state-led development). They pointed out the rent-seeking behavior of actors, which a state-led environment allowed to flourish, with virtually any intervention creating an opportunity for privileges, waste, and fraud (Bauer, 1972; Bhagwati, 1982; Krueger, 1974). Resources were misallocated because decisions were influenced by those rent-seeking activities, which, in addition, themselves consumed resources from the private sector that could have been applied to more productive ends.

But it appeared that the woes of the ISI strategy did not end there: Developing countries seemed plagued by political problems, instability, military coups, and human rights abuses. Industrialization was obviously creating a labor class and urban sectors that began to claim a larger share of economic benefits and more political participation. Public and private sector wage increases related to industrialization and modernization strategies encouraged faster migration from farms to towns, demanding jobs and public services and causing social unrest. When the economic limits of the ISI strategy (high levels of inflation, balance-of-payment crises) converged with social unrest, many developing countries suffered military coups against civilian governments accused of being too corrupt or too weak to control the economic and social crisis; the need to reestablish order was the reason generally given to try to justify the breakdown of the democratic process (see, for instance, Diaz-Bonilla and Schamis, 2001, on Argentina). As Hirschman (1982) noticed, faith in the development consensus was badly damaged by a series of political disasters, from civil wars to the establishment of unsavory authoritarian regimes that trampled civil and human rights, all of which was thought to be somehow connected with the social strains related to development and modernization.

The accumulation of all these (true or alleged) negative impacts on society of the excess support for industry led to a reevaluation of the development and macroeconomic strategy in many developing countries. It was considered that those countries would benefit by adopting a more decentralized focus, with better use of the price mechanism and less protection and fewer controls (Little et al., 1970). The development strategy had to be refocused by taking advantage of opportunities in international trade, eliminating the distortions created by extreme government intervention, allowing the price system to operate more freely, making sure that technology and investment reflected the endowment of human and other resources (thus avoiding the emphasis on capital-intensive enterprises), and positively reappraising the role of agriculture in the economy (see Balassa, 1971; Little et al., 1970; Krueger, 1978). Countries in Asia and some in Latin America, building on previous ISI stages, turned toward export-led strategies that generated many of the success stories of the last decades in terms of growth, industrialization, employment, and poverty reduction.

Although those criticisms focused mainly on the real aspects of development strategy, another line of thought looked at monetary and financial issues. For instance, McKinnon (1973) emphasized the need to liberalize the financial markets, ending the "financial repression" generated basically by unrealistic interest rates set by the government. The administered interest rates tended to become negative either because of the delays in their adjustment in an inflationary context or because of theories that argued for subsidized interest rates to accelerate investment and growth. Besides the negative impact on the capitalization of financial entities, their medium-term sustainability, and the fiscal accounts (due to recurrent bailouts of public banks), there were concerns about the impact on growth. In McKinnon's analysis the government established very low interest rates (passive and active) for the formal banking sector, and this discouraged savings (at least in the "formal" financial system) and generated excess demand for credit. Then the banking system rationed the credit available among customers, through means that would not necessarily direct funds to the most efficient economic alternatives. And the (latent) demand for financial assets by the public would be satisfied through the accumulation of physical assets (gold, land, livestock in agrarian societies, some durable goods), beyond the requirements of efficiency in production. The result would be that the financial market could not perform adequately its task of intermediating between the different types of potential savers and prospective investors and the economy would operate inefficiently. The subsequent debate on these issues focused on the liberalization of interest rates and its impact on growth and stability (Lanyi and Saracoglu, 1983).[49]

While those advocating changes in the import substitution strategy through the liberalization of the real side and the financial side of the economy were addressing issues of aggregate supply growth, economists in the monetarist tradition found the import substitution strategy at fault in another respect: the management of aggregate demand. Inflation and balance-of-payment crises were the reflection of levels of absorption that exceeded domestic output. Appropriate monetary and fiscal policies (through "expenditure reduction") and adjustments in the exchange rate (through "expenditure switching") would align domestic absorption with production. This analysis focused basically on the demand side and monetary aspects that have been the main components of the IMF stabilization programs (see, for instance, Frenkel and Johnson, 1976).

But if the supply-side policies followed by developing countries would have slowed growth and impaired efficiency while the management of aggregate demand (or lack thereof) would have led to inflation and balance of payments problems, the crossed influences also needed to be discussed. The debate included considerations about the impact and effects of growth-oriented real policies on stabilization objectives and of the stability-oriented monetary and fiscal policies on economic growth.

In the line of argument that goes from supply-side policies to stabilization, it has been mentioned that the advocates of the import substitution strategy thought it would solve, through growth, the problem of inflation and external crises. As noted, its critics pointed out that not only was growth less than expected but that it exacerbated the problems of stabilization, increasing inflationary pressures (Krueger, 1981) and making the countries following inward-oriented policies more prone to balance-of-payments crises (Balassa, 1984, 1986).

As to the impact of demand-side policies on growth, the import substitution approach argued that some level of inflation was unavoidable in (or even needed for) the process of economic development. The opposite position, although recognizing that the "inflationary tax" may help to raise funds needed for economic development, considered that the uncertainties generated by inflation and the utilization of resources needed to hedge against them, more than offset the possibly positive effects. Consequently it was argued that stability rather than high and variable inflation advanced growth in the medium to long run (see the early discussion in Johnson, 1984; this issue is revisited again in the context of current economic debates). The monetary and fiscal policies needed to align domestic absorption with total aggregate production (i.e., domestic production plus net trade financed in a sustainable manner), when implemented, were usually part of IMF stabilization programs. With the accumulation of experience in the application of those programs in the 1960s, 1970s, and 1980s, the debate shifted to the relationship between short-run stabilization and long-run growth (and, eventually, the impact on income distribution and equity). In particular, this generated a relatively abundant literature on the debate about the "stagflationary" impacts of the two main components of the stabilization programs, that is, restrictive monetary policy and devaluation of the exchange rate.

4.1.3 Macroeconomic debates and crises in the 1980s and early 1990s

Part of the criticisms of the restrictive monetary policy came from the structuralist tradition, which has always maintained that inflation and balance-of-payments problems are caused by nonmonetary forces, and therefore monetary policies would be, in the best of circumstances, ineffective. But another line of criticism (which came from both structuralist and nonstructuralist economists) argued that monetary policies would not only restrain demand but also shift supply downward through the effect of rising interest rates on production costs, basically those associated with working capital. In this framework, perverse "stagflationary" effects of a restrictive monetary policy could not be ruled out.

As to the policy of exchange rate devaluation, those arguing the "stagflationary" effects of such policy resorted to a combination of demand- and supply-side effects. On the demand side, the distribution of income resulting from the devaluation would be against workers—who would have salaries relatively fixed in nominal terms—and in favor of other social groups with smaller marginal propensities to consume. On the supply side, it was argued that developing countries depended on a certain amount of nonsubstitutable imports that were a necessary part of production costs; devaluation would lead to higher costs and, in the context of oligopolistic markup policies followed by the industrial sector, to higher prices (Taylor, 1979, 1984; Krugman and Taylor, 1978; Buffie, 1986; opposite views can be found in Cline and Weintraub, 1981, and Hanson, 1983). The combination of all these effects could add up to recession with inflation, at least in the short run.

As the criticisms against the import substitution approach and related macroeconomic policies mounted and some of its flaws were apparent while at the same time traditional IMF programs were also under attack, alternative approaches began to be considered in developing countries. In the second half of the 1970s several Latin American countries implemented programs that tried (at least on paper) to make the transition from statist and protectionist policies (with their possible companion of lax fiscal and monetary policies) to the liberalization of the economy in its internal and external aspects, coupled with what was considered a more adequate management of aggregate demand. These programs established predetermined rates of devaluation of the exchange rate ("tablitas") that were expected to act as restrictions to the discretionary management of monetary policy by the government (a proxy for a monetary rule). They illustrated the problem of inconsistencies between the two approaches to the exchange rate already mentioned: the "real approach," with the exchange rate as allocator of resources, and the "nominal anchor approach," with the exchange rate operating to control inflation (Corden, 1990; this issue is analyzed later in greater detail). Most of those programs collapsed at the beginning of the 1980s, generating a lively debate on the policy causes of their failure (see, among others, Edwards, 1984; Balassa, 1985; and the special issues of *World Development*, edited by Corbo and de Melo, 1985, and *Economic Development and Cultural Change*, edited by Edwards and Teitel, 1986).

Although the previous section on the world economy shows that *international* conditions related to the ebb and flow of financial capital were critical to understand those collapses, most of this literature focused on *domestic* policies. The main explanations about the causes of failure from the perspective of domestic policies can be separated in two groups. One line has emphasized problems in the sequence of liberalization of the external accounts: The capital market would have been liberalized prematurely, when the proper sequence would have been to open up first the goods market and only then to reduce the restrictions on external capital flows (Edwards, 1984).

Another line of analysis focused on inconsistencies in managing the exchange rate that would have become misaligned with the fiscal policy (as in Argentina) or with the wage policy (as in Chile). Inadequate macroeconomic policies would have contributed to massive inflow of foreign capital (facilitated by the liberalization of the capital account), which in turn contributed to the overvaluation of the exchange rate and generated the debt problem of the 1980s. On the other hand, overvaluation coupled with trade liberalization negatively affected domestic producers, including efficient firms and sectors that could have operated adequately with a more adequate exchange rate. Finally, when the overvaluation was too obvious, the use of the exchange rate as monetary anchor lost its credibility, a massive outflow of capital (anticipating the expected devaluation) took place, and the economic programs collapsed.

4.1.4 Macroeconomic policies and the agricultural sector

During the 1960s and 1970s, while still within the framework of development and macroeconomic policies shaped by the import-substitution industrialization, the agricultural sector began to receive greater attention. Sectoral policies included investments in technology (the Green Revolution), land reform, settlement programs, and community development, along with specific price, marketing, and credit schemes. In the 1970s, under the auspices of various international organizations, the main approach called for increased investment in agriculture, mainly through integrated programs in rural areas specially targeted to reach low-income groups (see Chenery et al., 1974). However, the 1970s studies already mentioned that criticized the strategy of development based on inward-oriented, import-substituting industrialization (Little, Scitovsky, and Scott, 1970; Balassa, 1971; Krueger, 1978) suggested a change in the general approach rather than just focusing investments within a framework that was considered to discriminate against agriculture.

This message was reinforced by a variety of studies (mostly covering the period from the 1960s to the mid-1980s) that analyzed the direct and indirect effects of trade, exchange rate, and other macroeconomic policies on price incentives for agriculture (Krueger, Schiff, and Valdés, 1988; Schiff and Valdés, 1992; Bautista and Valdés, 1993).[50] The analysis was based on a selection of agricultural products that included mostly tradable crops and the use of partial equilibrium measures of trade and exchange rate policies. They focused on price indicators (the real exchange rate and the relative price between agricultural and nonagricultural sectors) to analyze the incentives provided to specific agricultural products by the policies implemented. This literature argued that relative prices imparted a bias against agriculture that affected incentives and performance of the sector. Eliminating this price bias was one of the goals of policy reform strategies, including structural adjustment programs, supported by the World Bank and others, and many countries undertook such reforms in the 1990s. This price bias is different from the more general "urban bias" discussed by Lipton (1977), which also included public investment and expenditures and other policies.

In particular, Krueger, Schiff, and Valdés (KSV, 1988) looked at a representative group of 18 developing countries over the period 1975–1984 and distinguished between direct and indirect trade policy measures affecting agricultural price incentives. Direct trade policy measures were defined to include all measures that directly affected the wedge between agricultural producer and border prices. These measures typically included domestic agricultural taxes and subsidies, export taxes on cash crops, and import tariffs on food crops. In contrast, indirect trade policy measures were defined as economywide measures that affected the difference between relative agricultural producer and border prices. Indirect measures came under two main headings: industrial protection policies and overvaluation of the exchange rate. The former group of industrial protection measures typically included industrial import tariffs and quotas as well as domestic industrial taxes and subsidies. The overvaluation of the exchange rate was measured by the depreciation required to eliminate the nonsustainable part of the current account deficit in addition to the exchange rate impact of other trade policy interventions.

The quantification of direct and indirect effects of domestic tax and trade policies on agricultural price incentives was primarily based on the computation of nominal protection rates (NPRs). The total NPR for a given traded agricultural product was defined as the proportional difference between (1) the ratio of the agricultural producer price and a nonagricultural producer price index and (2) the ratio between the agricultural border price and a nonagricultural border price index, both measured at the equilibrium exchange rate. Subsequently, the total NPR was additively decomposed into (1) a direct NPR measuring the impact on relative prices of differences between agricultural producer and border prices measured at the current exchange rate and (2) an indirect NPR measuring the impact on relative prices of differences between nonagricultural producer and border prices and the impact of exchange rate overvaluation.

The study by KSV presented NPRs for one agricultural tradable from each of the 18 countries in their sample. Using simple averages, KSV found that agricultural export goods suffered from a negative direct NPR of –11%, whereas import-competing agricultural goods benefited from a positive direct NPR of around 20%. Nevertheless, KSV also found that the direct NPRs were swamped by the economywide indirect NPRs, averaging –27%. Accordingly, the KSV study concluded that indirect effects dominated direct effects and that total nominal protection was, on average, negative for all types of traded agricultural goods. KSV used nominal protection as their measure of relative price distortion, but they acknowledged that a more appropriate measure would be the so-called effective rate of protection (ERP), which also takes distortions in input prices into account. However, due to what the authors considered data inadequacy, the study by KSV contains no results on ERP.

Schiff and Valdés (SV, 1992) covered the same sample of 18 countries but extended the period of coverage to 1960–1984 and generalized the results by extending the coverage of agricultural goods to four to six agricultural commodities that the authors considered typically represented between 40% and 80% of net agricultural product. SV reported average agricultural NPRs, and their results were qualitatively similar to those of KSV. They calculated that agricultural exports and imports faced NPRs of respectively –13% and 14%, on average, and that these direct effects were dominated by indirect NPRs, averaging –22%. The SV study also argued that the nominal disprotection of traded agricultural goods increased over time and that industrial protection has penalized agriculture more than overvaluation of the exchange rate in two thirds of the countries examined.

Based on the assumption that all agricultural goods are traded, KSV and SV argued that their results (for the chosen set of goods) were representative for the overall agricultural sector. The SV study did recognize that traded products have nontradable components, including some distribution and marketing costs, but these were not included in the analysis. Furthermore, by assuming perfect substitution between domestic and world market goods, the possibility of nontradable components of domestic agricultural production was not considered. Another important issue that drives the results is the use of estimated "equilibrium exchange rates," a difficult undertaking in a partial equilibrium setting such as the one utilized by those studies. In addition, general equilibrium income and employment effects from the existing policies and the suggested change in development strategy were not considered (see Jensen, Robinson, and Tarp, 2002).

The work by Mundlak and coauthors, particularly on Argentina (Mundlak, Cavallo, and Domenech, 1989), has been mentioned as general equilibrium work looking at the incentive bias against agriculture (Schiff and Valdés, 2002). However, this work can be more appropriately interpreted as a partial macroeconomic model in which general policies related to trade liberalization, monetary stability, fiscal discipline, a competitive and more stable real exchange rate, and, in general, avoidance of macroeconomic instability and crises facilitate a stronger growth performance for the *whole* economy, not only agriculture. The model considers three sectors: agriculture, nonagriculture without government, and government, and two relative prices: agriculture/government and nonagriculture/government. The simulated counterfactual policies appear to improve *both* relative prices against the government and stabilize incentives, which in the historical baseline are very volatile. Investments in the nongovernment sectors, which depend both on relative prices but also on the inverse of their volatility, increase, as does productivity. Real wages and employment of basic labor decline in the absence of compensatory policies. One interpretation, then, is that less government and less macroeconomic volatility would lead to more growth in the nongovernment sectors, both agriculture and non-agriculture. This is very different from the "bias against agriculture" argument.[51] Even this interpretation of the model and the simulations must be taken with caution because, as noted by Schiff (1997), many of the macroeconomic equations are reduced forms of more complex relationships and therefore are subject to the Lucas Critique: When there are important changes in policy regimes that may affect the coefficients of the equations, it is incorrect to take them as invariant in the simulations. Also, because the paper does not appear to have as full a framework of macroeconomic identities as the one presented in Table 1 to ensure consistency of the simulations, it is not clear whether the variables add up to properly specified and consistent accounting identities—the type of pitfall in macroeconomic model building stressed by Christ (1987).

   In any case, the general work on import substitution in the 1970s already mentioned, along with the more agricultural focused studies mentioned here, led to a shift of emphasis in policy advice, focusing now on the need for changes in the framework of development and macroeconomic policies. The argument was that the development pattern (with its emphasis on import substitution industrialization) and the macroeconomic policies (which led to the overvaluation of the exchange rate and what was considered excessive taxation of agriculture) discriminated against the agricultural sector and denied the economy the beneficial results that could be generated from investment programs in that sector. Moreover, even with specific sectoral policies to increase investments in agriculture, this type of analysis suggested that the results may be disappointing due a general framework of distorting policies that hampered the development of the agricultural sector and the economy in general. Therefore, the policy recommendation was to eliminate inefficient industrial protectionism, to avoid the overvaluation of the exchange rate, and to phase out export taxes on agriculture. At the same time sectoral interventions that supported and subsidized agriculture should also be substantially revamped and scaled down, given that overall incentives would shift in favor of agriculture with the change in the general macroeconomic and trade framework (World Bank, 1986).

This was the general consensus regarding macroeconomic policies and the agricultural sector circa the late 1980s and early 1990s. The sections that follow try to update the discussion, considering fiscal, monetary, exchange rate, and trade policies and looking at more general equilibrium effects and not only relative prices, as explained in Section 1.

4.2 Fiscal policies
4.2.1 Background

Fiscal policies have general macroeconomic effects on aggregate demand expansion as well as impacts on aggregate supply through the influence on macroprices (price level and inflation, interest rate, real exchange rate, and sometimes wage levels in the economy) and microeconomic effects linked to specific taxes, subsidies, and expenditures. It has been argued that high levels of government expenditures and overall taxes, as well as persistent deficits, affect growth negatively (Barro and Sala-i-Martin, 1995). But also the composition of expenditures could have growth effects—for instance, comparing consumption expenditures versus investments in infrastructure or human capital. There is a relatively large literature analyzing the impact of public investment on growth, cost reduction, and increases in productivity, and a majority but certainly not all of the studies tend to find positive results (IMF, 2004). A separate issue is that government expenditures tend to have a larger nontradable component and its expansion may appreciate the RER. There also microeconomic effects of fiscal policy and the tax code—for instance, if agriculture receives less direct taxation acting as a tax shelter.

A starting point for that analysis is a basic equation of national accounts that indicates that the sum of net saving of the private sector (NSp), of the government (NSg), and from the rest of the world to the domestic economy (NSrw) must add up to zero.

$$(NSp) + (NSg) + (NSrw) = 0$$

We can use Eq. 5 to present in greater detail NSg.

$$\begin{aligned} &\text{Tind} + \text{Tm} + \text{TL} + \text{TK} + \text{TY} + \text{OTNg} + \text{ProfCB} + \text{dB} + \text{dCDg} + \text{dCFg} \\ &= \text{G} + \text{ST} + \text{INTR*B} + \text{INTR*CDg} + \text{INTR*CFg} + \text{INVg} + \text{dMg} \end{aligned} \quad (5)$$

If we call Taxes and Domestic Transfers (TT) to:

$$(\text{Tind} + \text{Tm} + \text{TL} + \text{TK} + \text{TY} + \text{ProfCB}) - \text{ST}$$

Then we have:

$$(TT + OTNg) - (G + INVg + INTR*B + INTR*CDg + INTR*CFg)$$
$$= dMg - (dB + dCDg + dCFg)$$

where NSg is the left hand side of the equation $(TT + OTNg) - (G + INVg + INTR * B + INTR * CDg + INTR * CFg)$, and therefore:

$$NSg = dMg - (dB + dCDg + dCFg)$$

A deficit of the public sector (NSg < 0) can be financed in different ways: by using government's cash balances (dMg), by borrowing from the central bank (dCDg), by issuing domestic public debt (dB), or by issuing external public debt (dCFg). On the other hand, a fiscal surplus leads to accumulation of cash balances or the paying off of the three components of public debt.

Each one of these ways of financing the deficit will have different macroeconomic effects: Borrowing from the central bank to cover the deficit expands money supply, and if this exceeds money demand, the result may be inflation in goods, services, and/or assets (including, among the latter, hard foreign currency, which can lead to "currency substitution"[52]) or to increased imports; issuing domestic debt will put pressure on the internal real interest rate, which could bring in capital flows and appreciate the exchange rate; issuing external debt may increase the risk premium (and the country-specific interest rate) paid by the country and tend to appreciate the exchange rate in the short run while capital is flowing in but could force a depreciation later to generate the trade surplus needed to service the debt.

Monetizing the deficit or issuing domestic debt are ways of capturing savings from the private sector (NSp), whereas issuing external debt, obviously, brings savings from the rest of the world (NSrw). However, the government cannot extract from the private sector or the rest of the world a greater level of savings than economic agents are willing to allocate to buying that country's public debt. The attempts to absorb more private savings (external or internal) than the available ones have led in several countries to fast increases of inflation, very high real interest rates, and capital flight (which is a form of placing savings outside government's control). If the deficit of the projected public sector is greater than the sum of the internal private saving and the external saving available, a fiscal adjustment is required.

That adjustment can be achieved in several ways, with different effects in the components of NSg. But those changes can also affect the components of NSp and NSrw, which could reinforce or dampen the initial fiscal adjustment. For example, the deficit of the public sector can be reduced by increasing taxes (TT), decreasing public consumption (G), reducing public investment (INVg), or reducing payment of net interests on public debt (INTR * B + INTR * CDg + INTR * CFg) through, for example, a rescheduling or reduction of the external debt. But each one of those approaches can affect the other components of savings, perhaps forcing further adjustments in NSg. An obvious example is increases in taxes, which can affect GDP, private consumption, and private investment in such a way that the initial improvement in the net public position could be compensated for by a fall in the private net saving (NSp).

On the other hand, if public expenditures are cut, the short-term impact will depend on, among other things, the nature of the goods for which aggregate demand has decreased as a result of the fiscal contraction. If the affected goods are tradable, the smaller internal demand (resulting from the fiscal restriction) can lead to greater exports (if there are no restrictions in international demand) or fewer imports, which would lead to an improvement of the external accounts. If the decrease in public expenditures falls on nontradable goods, the impact in the short term can be reflected in the unemployment of the productive factors dedicated to those activities and a fall of the GDP, which, in turn, would affect net private savings, again forcing other adjustments in the full equation. To compensate for the decrease in the demand for nontradable goods and services and maintain overall economic activity, the real exchange rate has to adjust to favor the production of tradable goods and services, and factor markets must be sufficiently flexible to ensure the channeling of labor and capital toward those activities. In any case, both raising taxes and cutting public expenditures can have recessive effects, at least in the short run, which should be considered. But if the fiscal adjustment reduces the overall level of the interest rate for the economy, it could end up having an expansionary impact through expansion of consumption and investments by the private sector.

In addition to the considerations of short-term adjustments mentioned so far, there are also dynamic and intertemporal aspects of the program of fiscal adjustment that must be taken into account. An obvious trade-off is the decline of public investment dedicated to the formation of human capital and the support of science and technology. These cuts may contribute in the short term to attaining a balance of the public accounts compatible with the availability of internal and external net savings, but they can also decrease the growth rate of the GDP in the future and in such way worsen future fiscal balances.

Another dynamic element is the evolution of the various financial assets and liabilities as a result of the level of the public deficit and its financing. Each of the three methods of financing (monetization, issuing of domestic debt, and issuing of external debt) implies modifications in the stock of a financial asset that, when interacting with the demand of those assets, can produce changes in key macroeconomic variables (as discussed before). But these effects are, in several cases, only the first round of macroeconomic adjustments that can lead to additional modifications in the levels of production, saving, and investment of the economy with their impact on the current account of the balance of payments. Some of those effects may occur not only because the supply and demand of financial assets should be balanced in a moment in time but because there are also intertemporal balances that must be maintained. For instance, economic agents who also consider the future may forecast violations of the intertemporal budget constraint of the government, indicating solvency problems in the future, but then they will react now, with possible repercussions on inflationary expectations, current interest rates, and capital flight.

Taking those general concepts as background, the following discussion presents the evolution of some fiscal variables in developing countries.[53]

4.2.2 Fiscal trends in developing countries[54]

There is a general debate about whether increased integration in the world economy ("globalization") is eroding the tax base of many countries, particularly developing ones (see a review of this debate in Díaz-Bonilla, 2008). This can happen both directly (for example, due to tax competition at the world level reducing the sources of revenues, or due to the international mobility of capital and high-income individuals who do not want to be taxed) and, indirectly, through the impact of globalization on the rate and quality of growth and, therefore, on tax collection. In turn, the level of government revenues affects the possibility of implementing transfer policies (such as food subsidies) and of financing public services and investments in agriculture.

In particular, trade liberalization may reduce government revenues from trade taxes, although the net result depends on the form in which the liberalization is implemented and the reaction from trade flows; if trade liberalization represents a shift from quantitative barriers to tariffs (or from prohibitive tariffs with no trade to lower tariffs that allow some trade), revenues may increase. Trade taxes (both imports and exports) as percentages of current revenues seem to have declined in most developing countries. According to the World Development Indicators (WDI) database (World Bank, 2007), the percentage of trade taxes in revenues fell in East Asia and the Pacific region, from 12.8% in the 1990s to 6.1% in the first half of the 2000s. Comparable figures for Latin America and the Caribbean are 11.7% and 6.2%; South Asia, from 22.6% to 16.2%; lower-middle income, from 13.1% to 7.5%; and upper-middle income, from 8.3% to 3.3% (both categories include developing countries). There is no data for low-income countries (the bottom tier of developing countries), including sub-Saharan Africa.

But these data may simply reflect the fact that the tax structure is changing its composition toward other taxes. Therefore, it would be more relevant to see whether taxes in general (not only trade taxes) have declined. Data again are scarce, but from the 55 developing countries that have data over the last two decades, tax revenues as percentages of the GDP were about the same in the 1990s and the first half of the 2000s, at 14.6% and 14.5%, respectively (the medians were 13.9% and 13.2% and the modes were 12% and 15.5%). This stability contrasts with the upward trend in taxes in the

Table 11   General government final consumption expenditure, 1960s–early 2000s (% of GDP)

	1960s	1970s	1980s	1990s	Early 2000s
East Asia and Pacific	8.2	9.6	13.0	11.4	11.0
Latin America and Caribbean	9.6	10.5	10.3	13.2	14.9
South Asia	8.9	9.6	10.7	10.9	10.8
Sub-Saharan Africa	11.3	14.1	16.2	16.4	16.8
Developing countries	9.5	11.0	12.2	13.4	13.8
High-income OECD countries	15.2	16.7	17.8	17.2	17.4

Source: WDI, World Bank 2005.

industrialized countries that are members of the Organization for Economic Coopera-tion and Development (OECD; WDI, World Bank, 2007).

Moving to the spending side, it has been argued that integration in the global economy forces cuts in government expenditures to maintain competitiveness. Table 11 shows the size of the general government in the economy (not counting local governments), measured by public consumption.[55] It has been increasing in general for all developing regions since the 1960s, as happened in the high-income countries. SSA and Latin America and the Caribbean (LAC) have larger participation of government than developing Asian regions do (between 3 and 6 percentage points above).

It is difficult to generalize from those figures, but taxes seem to have been stable as percentage of GDP, whereas government consumption appears to have increased some-what. However, there are no consistent data on other sources of incomes (such as income from assets, government activities, or grants) and other possible outlays (such as public investments). If the trend toward more consumption with stable taxes were true, there would be a growing gap that needs to be filled with other sources of income, cuts in nonconsumption expenditures, money financing (seignorage tax), or increases in debt.

Regarding the latter, debt service of public and publicly guaranteed debt (see Table 12) was lower in the 1970s for all developing regions than in subsequent decades. Debt service peaked in the 1980s for SSA and LAC and declined in the 1990s. For LAC, however, it increased again in the early 2000s to close to the levels of the 1980s, or about double the levels in Asian countries.

The overall fiscal position of developing (and industrial) countries deteriorated mostly during the 1980s (SSA fiscal problems occurred earlier in the 1970s), but it has improved since then: The average government fiscal deficit was 6% of the GDP among developing countries in the first half of the 1980s but declined to around 2%

Table 12 Public and publicly guaranteed debt service, 1970s–2004 (% of gross national income)

	1970s	1980s	1990s	2000–2004
East Asia and Pacific	n/a	2.6	2.8	1.9
Latin America and Caribbean	2.2	4.4	3.2	4.1
Middle East and North Africa	2.1	3.7	6.5	3.8
South Asia	0.9	1.2	2.5	2.2
Sub-Saharan Africa	1.6	n/a	3.1	2.6
Low- and middle-income countries	1.8	3.5	3.2	3.0

Source: World Bank, 2005.

by the end of the 1990s, with a similar decline in industrialized countries (see Tytell and Wei, 2004).

The general picture from these figures is that fiscal accounts in developing countries became more restricted in the 1980s and 1990s, but that the conditions in public accounts have improved during the 2000s, probably helped by the previous fiscal adjustment, the resumption of growth after the crises of the 1980s and 1990s, and a decline in world interest rates. The global economic slowdown of the late 2000s will be a strong test for the resilience of the fiscal position in developing countries.

4.2.3 Fiscal issues and agriculture

Expenditures Deteriorating public sector finances, along with the decline in world agricultural prices in the mid-1980s, led to fiscal adjustments and pressures to reduce support for agriculture in many countries. For instance, at the beginning of the 1980s several countries in South America, such as Brazil and Chile, embarked on accelerated programs to expand production of wheat (and other cereals) due to concerns about shortages heightened by high prices in the second half of the 1970s. When prices collapsed in the mid-1980s, these programs represented a high cost for the government, and support for those crops was substantially diminished (Díaz-Bonilla, 1999). More generally, van Blarcom, Knudsen, and Nash (1993) found that during the period of structural adjustment programs in the 1980s, agricultural expenditures declined as share of total spending. In fact, the structural adjustment programs that unilaterally or as a condition of loans reduced support for agriculture in many developing countries during the 1980s and 1990s, but also the discussions surrounding the U.S. Farm Bills in the 1980s and 1990s and the adjustments in the Common Agricultural Policy in the 1990s, can all be seen as part of the same effort to confront deteriorated fiscal positions in the context of weak world commodity markets.

Data to assess trends in agricultural expenditures are scarce. The estimates by Fan and Pardey (1998) of public sector agricultural expenditures in Asia (measured in purchasing power parity values)[56] show that although they were growing on average at 4.6% annually in 1972–1993, the pattern was a declining one: During the 1970s they grew at 9.5%, they slowed to 3.5% during the 1980s, and they had a negligible increase of less than 0.5% from 1990–1993. Kheralla et al. (2000) also report diminished expenditures in subsidies and public sector enterprises in SSA. In LAC, data from FAO (2006) show (see Figure 15) that agricultural expenditures in constant currency and in per capita terms for an unweighted average of 18 countries[57] declined from the mid-1980s to the mid-1990s but have recovered since then, to about the values at the beginning of the series. If, instead of the average, the unweighted median is utilized, there seems to have been an increase in the early 2000s above historical values.

Allcott, Lederman, and López (2006) divide those public agricultural expenditures in LAC into "nonsocial subsidies," or "private goods" (export subsidies, forestry subsidies, targeted rural production subsidies, and so on) and "public goods" (such as investment in R&D, plant and animal disease control, and environmental protection) and document the decline in the share of expenditures devoted to nonsocial subsidies over the period, moving from 40–45% in the late 1980s to 30% in 2001, while the average rural public expenditures per capita (as shown in Figure 15, which comes from the same database) increased over the period. Besides documenting those trends, they examine the effects of the size and composition of rural expenditures on agricultural GDP in 15 Latin American countries during the period 1985–2001. Their more

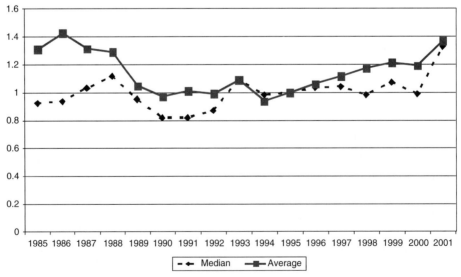

Figure 15   Index of agricultural expenditure in LAC per capita (constant local currency), 1995–2001.

general result is the positive (negative) impact of the public ("nonsocial subsidies" or private) goods on per capita agricultural GDP. Another result is that trade openness leads to more agricultural spending in general (but the coefficient is not statistically significant) and within that, the share of private goods increases (which is significant). There seems to be a "compensation" effect to more trade openness via subsidies (which reduces agricultural GDP per capita), but since all expenditures appear to also increase with more trade, the overall impact of openness on agricultural GDP is not clear (it appears positive in some of their regressions and negative in others).

Taxes   The tax side of agriculture includes (1) direct taxes income, persons and personal wealth or property, and (2) indirect taxes such as sales taxes, excises, stamp taxes, and import and export taxes.[58] Those explicit taxes have different general equilibrium implications. Direct taxes are considered to generate revenues with fewer intersectoral or interpersonal resource transfers than indirect taxes. But that also depends on whether sectors are treated equally or not for taxation purposes. Khan (2001) notes that there are serious data problems to determine the level of explicit direct and indirect taxes paid by farmers in developing countries, among other things, because national tax data are not classified by source or sector and do not include taxes collected by state and local governments. Khan points to some facts and trends on agricultural taxation in recent years. First, taxes on land and agricultural income are not major contributors to overall tax revenues, representing 20% of the total or less; rather, the bulk of agricultural tax revenue comes from taxes and duties on marketed agricultural products in domestic and foreign markets (but usually food items are exempted from sales taxes). Second, the explicit tax burden on farmers has been lower than for other groups.[59] Third, taxes on exported and imported products have traditionally been a major source of government revenues in many poor developing countries, but, as noted, the contribution of export taxes in most developing countries has fallen significantly since the mid-1980s, particularly in Latin America and Asian developing countries. However, they are still high in several countries in sub-Saharan Africa. Fourth, the explicit tax burden on agriculture has fallen significantly in the past 20 years, due mostly to reduction in indirect taxes (such as export taxes) but also to declines in direct taxes on income and land (Kahn, 2001).

Among fiscal issues in agriculture, taxation of exports has received particular attention (see, among others, Krueger, Schiff, and Valdés, 1988). Production taxes have been criticized (other things being equal) for reducing output and exports of the taxed products (which, *ceteris paribus*, is generally true) but also for reducing overall welfare (which is a less obvious result that must be analyzed in a general equilibrium setting). For instance, Cicowiez et al. (2008) analyze the potential elimination of export taxes in Argentina, which were imposed after the strong devaluation of 2002 in that country. Their conclusion, using a CGE model with a labor market specification that allows for unemployment, is that such elimination seems to negatively affect GDP and employment. To understand the negative results on production and employment, one needs to look at the sectoral composition of export taxes and the supply-side response. In terms of sectoral composition, the largest agricultural export taxes are on primary production of grains and oilseeds. The elimination of these taxes increases the supply of sectors that are less labor intensive than other activities, are inputs to other productions, and for which the outward orientation of their sales increases significantly without export taxes. The consequences of the three factors are less employment in general through different and cumulative channels. In the case of agriculture particularly, land is shifted away from other products that tend to be more labor intensive and toward grains and oilseeds, which are less so. This negative employment effect at the primary level is reinforced by the fact that, since the commodities from these sectors are inputs into other production activities, the increase in their prices also affects those other activities, which tends to shrink in production and employment because of higher prices of inputs. Primary products that before were transformed locally are now exported as raw materials and the domestic industry declines. Finally, the outward orientation of the expanding activities appreciates the real exchange rate, affecting the rest of the tradables.

They also find a negative fiscal impact that could be even bigger than the initial collection of export taxes due to the negative production and employment effects. In terms of poverty effects, which are the focus of their paper, the elimination of agricultural export taxes increases the domestic price of food (and therefore the poverty line). This price effect and the decline of employment increase poverty. The authors caution that the results also need to be analyzed in a dynamic setting to better understand the potential for growth and employment of the differential development paths with and without export taxes, assuming that, given enough time, labor could be reconverted and move across activities.

Another angle to the debate on export taxes on primary agricultural products is that when applied to an agricultural primary product that is an input to a processing industry but not to the processed product (e.g., wheat with regard to flour milling, or green coffee to roasted coffee), the reduced domestic price compared to the world price could help the development of the industry in the country imposing the export tax. The empirical evidence on this effect is mixed (see the discussion on differential export taxes in Section 4.5, on trade).

Whatever the general equilibrium results of export taxes, including their revenue generation ability, it has already been mentioned that those taxes have been declining over recent decades. The decline in taxation of agricultural exports in many developing countries since the mid-1980s was related to the strong decline in real agricultural prices since then, as well as the "structural adjustment programs" negotiated with the IMF and the World Bank. Before these adjustments, high prices of commodities in the 1970s appear to have led some countries to tax what was considered permanent "windfall" profits from primary products. The increase in fiscal resources led to expansionary fiscal policies that later proved unsustainable. For instance, Schuknecht (1999) argues that the experience of the mid-1990s coffee boom in Africa shows that countries that liberalized and left a large share of the "windfall" with the private sector and that committed themselves to fiscal austerity via adjustment programs have shown better results in terms of fiscal stability, private sector responses, and economic growth than countries that did not reform. In the period of improved commodity prices during the 2000s, developing countries (although with exceptions) seemed to have reacted differently, treating increased revenues more as a temporary windfall that was utilized to reduce public debt or to accumulate reserves and not to large expansions of public expenditures.

Conclusion   An overall conclusion of this fiscal review is that developing countries suffered some fiscal retrenchment in the 1980s and 1990s, which seems to have affected agricultural expenditures during those years. The fiscal position appears to have improved somewhat in the 2000s and, at least for the LAC countries for which there are more complete data, agricultural expenditures have recovered. At the same time, government expenditures for the sector seem to have been changing relatively toward public goods, whereas on the tax side, trade taxes, particularly export taxes, have declined. Although it is difficult to assess in general terms whether expenditure and taxation *levels* related to agriculture in developing countries are adequate, it seems that at least the *composition* of both components of the fiscal equation has been moving toward configurations somewhat more supportive of agricultural growth. In addition, developing countries appeared to have managed more prudently the fiscal implications of the last period of improved commodity prices, although it will be seen whether that is enough to help them through the current global economic difficulties.

4.3 Monetary and financial policies
4.3.1 Background
Monetary conditions affect growth, employment, inflation, exchange rates, interest rates, the operation of the banking and financial systems, and the probability of crises. Here only a brief discussion of the multiple topics involved can be sketched.

The relationship among money, growth, and inflation has been long debated. In monetary theory there are a variety of results: Inflation has been argued to have no effect on growth (money is super-neutral; Sidrauski, 1967); positive (Tobin, 1965, who assumed that money was a substitute for capital); and negative (Stockman, 1981, using a cash-in-advance model in which money was complementary to capital). With theory being inconclusive, the issue has been analyzed empirically in both industrialized and developing countries. In industrialized countries the discussion has focused on the slope and (the possibly nonlinear) shape of the Phillips curve, linking unemployment and inflation in the short run. This debate has been centered mostly on industrialized countries and it is not reviewed here,[60] although it could become more relevant in the advanced middle-income countries that have moved to inflation targeting (see the discussion that follows).

In the case of developing countries, the early debates were briefly sketched in Section 4.1. In the 1950s and 1960s inflation was considered an unwanted side effect of growth in the context of fragmented economic structures. However, to the extent that inflation began to get increasingly out of control in the 1970s and 1980s in many developing countries, especially in LAC and to a lesser extent in SSA, the focus shifted to the potential negative impact of inflation on growth. Empirical studies, such as Fischer (1993), found a negative correlation between inflation and growth, but it was shown that the results depended mostly on outliers and thus were not robust (Levine and Zervos, 1993).

Other authors have argued that those weak results were the consequence of a nonlinear relationship, with different interactions between inflation and growth at different levels of those variables. Therefore, several studies have attempted to estimate the relationship between inflation and growth using nonlinear specifications, asking whether (1) there are "threshold" effects (e.g., that inflation must reach some minimum before the negative impact on growth becomes serious) and/or (2) there is a "kink" in the relationship (i.e., a variable that might be positively related to growth up to some levels of inflation where the relationship changes sign).

For instance, Dornbusch and Fischer (1991) argued, before the generalized period of disinflation in the second half of the 1990s, that the negative impact of inflation on growth happened at relatively high levels of inflation (a "threshold" effect) that they estimated to be above the range of 15–30%, the limit of what they called "moderate inflation." With more formal methods, Fisher (1993) found other thresholds: Below 15% the impact of inflation on growth was negative but small; from 15–40% there was a strong negative effect of inflation on growth; and over 40% the impact was negative but again tended to be small because the main damage to growth happened in the previous threshold.

Other studies have found a different nonlinear relationship characterized by a period in which growth and inflation are *positively* correlated, then an inflection point is reached (a "kink"), and afterward the relationship turns negative (Figure 16 shows a possible shape for this hypothetical correlation).

Several analyses offer a range of estimates of the levels of growth and inflation where the inflection in the curve takes place (Point B). The estimates usually go from 2.5–19%, with most estimates between 5% and 15% (see Bruno and Easterly, 1995; Sarel, 1996; Ghosh and Phillips, 1998; Burdekin et al., 2000; Khan and Senhadji, 2001; Drukker et al., 2005; Pollin and Zhu, 2005; and Li, 2006). Countries growing "too fast" (such as Point A) will eventually go back to the curve, but it would make a difference which side of Point B the economy will eventually tend to. Policymakers may affect growth by

Figure 16 Growth and inflation.

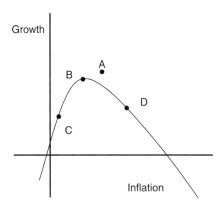

generating monetary conditions that lead to high inflation (as in Point D). However, if the policy target for inflation is set too low (such as Point C), the country would also be paying a price in reduced growth, affecting the agricultural sector as well.

Monetary policies also have strong impacts on the external accounts and the probability of crises. Some of the policy issues can be illustrated starting with a simplified balance sheet of a hypothetical central bank:

Assets	Liabilities
Net foreign assets in "dollars" (NFA$) * Exchange rate (ER)	Monetary base (MB)[a]
Credit to government (CDg)	
Credit to private sector (CDp)	Net worth (NW)[b]

[a]Currency in circulation plus bank's deposits in the central bank.
[b]If positive.

We can write the balance sheet of the Central Bank in domestic currency in equation form (Eq. 3a, which is a slightly modified version of Eq. 3):

$$ER*NFA\$ + CDg + CDg = MB + NW \qquad (3a)$$

We also need the balance-of-payments equation to look at alternative scenarios. Eq. 4a is a simplified version in *dollars* of Eq. 4 (which was expressed before in *domestic currency*):

$$X\$ - IM\$ - INT\$ + dCF\$ = dNFA\$ \qquad (4a)$$

The balance-of-payments equation measured in dollars includes exports (X$), imports (IM$), interest payments and other current account transactions (INT$), capital flows (dCF\$), and changes in net foreign assets (dNFA\$). It can be converted into domestic currency, multiplying all terms of Eq. 4. by the exchange rate (ER).

Finally, we need to consider the money market:

$$MB = L = (1/v)*P*GDP \qquad (5)$$

This is an equilibrium condition in domestic currency where money supply (MB)[61] equals money demand (L); L, in turn, is a function of the inverse velocity $(1/v)$, prices (P), and real gross domestic product (GDP). Money velocity (v), which is an indicator of the desire of holding domestic currency, may also depend on various factors such as real interest rates, expectations of inflation, and expectations of changes in the nominal exchange rate (ER).

If the central bank is buying foreign assets (dNFA\$) because of a positive trade balance or capital inflows or is extending credit to the government (dCDg, probably financing the fiscal deficit) or is providing credit to the private sector (dCDp, perhaps through rediscounts to the banking sector that are on-lent for other activities, such as agriculture), the monetary base (dMB) is expanding (assuming dNW = 0). But this is only the first-round effect. If this expansion in money supply exceeds the demand for domestic currency (L), there are different possible adjustments, depending on the type of goods, services, or assets the unwanted excess supply of money will be spilling onto. Further effects will depend on whether velocity (v) and GDP remain constant or not and what the sources of money creation are. In the latter case, there can be external sources (dNFA\$), and within this, the monetary expansion may come from the current account (most likely a trade surplus, X\$ – IM\$ > 0) or from the capital account (dCF\$ > 0); the source of money creation may also be internal, and it also matters if this comes from credit expansion to the government (dCDg > 0) or the private sector (dCDp > 0).

If there is idle productive capacity and unutilized labor force, credit expansion could lead to increases in GDP. This in turn would increase money demand and perhaps a new equilibrium will be reached, with more economic activity. But if both v and GDP are fixed (at least in the short run), the increase in money supply would push up prices (P) and would appreciate the real exchange rate (if the nominal exchange rate is not adjusted). The appreciation of the RER, in turn, would eventually lead to a decline in the trade balance (X\$ – IM\$).

If the original source of money creation is a positive trade balance, this process could eliminate the trade surplus and close the source of money creation.[62] If the creation of money is due to internal sources, such as a fiscal deficit that was financed through credit by the central bank, and with GDP close to full employment, there will be an impact on prices. Depending on the price level at which the money market may equilibrate and with a nominal ER unchanged, there could be a continuous deterioration in the trade balance that, with INT\$ and dCF\$ fixed, would imply a loss in reserves (–dNFA$). When reserves are low compared to imports or payments of external debts, a devaluation can follow (and in developing countries, usually accompanied by an IMF stabilization program). An alternative policy to try to restore equilibrium to the money market and the trade balance would be a restriction in credit, which reduces money supply, forces prices and/or GDP down, and, through price and income effects, restores the trade balance. This approach has been called the *monetary approach to the balance of payments* and has provided the underpinnings for most of the IMF programs aimed at restoring balance in the external accounts (see, for instance, Frenkel and Johnson, 1976).

This description corresponds mostly to the period of capital controls and prohibitions to hold and circulate "dollars" in the domestic economy during the 1950s, 1960s, and part of the 1970s. Then the process leading to devaluations comprised comparatively slow-motion events, fueled by the deterioration of the trade balance. Since the late 1970s and increasingly during the 1980s and 1990s, but mostly in the category of "urbanized economies" identified by the World Bank (2008), the liberalization and opening up of the transactions of the current and capital account of the balance of payments and the increasing use of hard foreign currencies in the domestic economy of developing countries (a phenomenon that has been called *dollarization*; see the following discussion) transformed the nature of the adjustment to an increase in (unwanted) money supply. Now the impact can be through capital flight (–dCF$) that may happen when economic agents see an important deterioration of the ratio of official reserves to domestic liquidity (in these equations, ER * NFA$/MB, which declines when expansion in CD leads to increases in MB and, possibly, losses in NFA$). In these cases, the exchange rate crises resemble Krugman's model (1979), where imbalances between supply and demand of domestic currency—for instance, fueled by fiscal deficits that are monetized—could lead to sudden attacks on the foreign reserves held by the monetary authority. In Eq. 3a. the increase in CD would lead to an immediate decline in NFA$ through capital flight.

With the opening up of the capital account, the limits of what was called the "impossible trinity" began to be recognized: A country could not have a fixed exchange rate, an open capital account, and an independent monetary policy at the same time but could select only two out of those three policies. This has been an issue mainly for "urbanized economies," because the "agriculture-based" and "transition" economies, in the categorization of the World Bank (2008), tended to maintain more controls on the capital account. But in "urbanized economies," considering the tendency to try to maintain exchange rates stables and with a capital account open, a consequence appears to have been more constrained monetary policies. The approach of the "developmental state" of the 1950s and 1960s that provided ample credit for production, including agriculture, through the central bank became seriously constrained once the current and capital accounts were liberalized.

In summary, a monetary expansion will affect prices, GDP, the exchange rate, and external accounts, but the distribution of the impacts will depend on a variety of reasons, including the structure of the economy as discussed in Section 2. In the following discussion, we look further into some of the monetary trends and policy issues in developing countries.

4.3.2 Trends in monetary conditions

In all developing regions, as in the industrialized world, inflation decreased since the mid-1990s, although the performance has varied over time and across regions (see Table 13).

Asia experienced only mild increases, more in line with inflationary developments in the industrialized world, converging during the 2000s to rates below 3% annually. Inflation peaked during the early 1990s in LAC and Africa; the highest rate was 460% in 1990 in LAC (with cases of hyperinflation in some countries) and about 32% in 1992 in Africa. As a result, the whole decade of the 1990s showed the highest inflation rates, with 130.5% in LAC and 25.9% in Africa. In Asia, however, the highest inflation occurred during the 1970s (10.3%), with a peak in 1974 of about 30%, linked to the oil and food price shocks of that period.

There is now a lively debate about the links between globalization (i.e., a larger integration in trade and financial world markets) and lower inflation. Rogoff (2004), Romer (1993), and Frankcl (2006) have argued that globalization has reduced inflation through different channels, including expanded competition from low-cost economies. Tytell and Wei (2004), for instance, find that their measures of financial integration (in which they try to isolate the component of capital flows that is external to the countries) appear associated with that decline in inflation, concluding that financial globalization could have induced countries to pursue low-inflation monetary policies. Furthermore, they find that increases in trade openness are associated with lower inflation rates. Others, particularly in industrialized countries, have argued that better monetary policies have led to this outcome (Young, 2008).

Table 13   Inflation in developing countries (%), 1960s–2005

	1960s	1970s	1980s	1990s	2000–2005
Africa	5.1	12.6	17.2	25.9	8.3
Asia	3.6	10.3	9.0	8.1	2.7
Latin America and Caribbean	6.6	31.5	91.1	130.5	7.9
Middle East	3.7	10.6	18.7	11.9	5.7

Source: IMF (2007).

Table 14   Money and quasi-money (M2) (% of GDP), 1960s–early 2000s

	1960s	1970s	1980s	1990s	Early 2000s
East Asia and Pacific	NA	25.2	41.7	81.6	129.5
Latin America and Caribbean	15.8	17.5	19.1	24.3	26.7
South Asia	22.2	25.7	35.4	41.0	52.2
Sub-Saharan Africa	29.0	29.3	32.8	33.9	35.7
Low and middle income	19.4	22.6	32.8	43.7	62.6
High income: OECD	61.7	60.3	67.0	71.0	80.6
World	53.3	52.8	60.4	68.8	78.1

It has been already argued (Section 3.3) that lower inflation rates are associated with less price volatility and that if price volatility is more important than average prices in explaining agricultural supply (see Johnson, 1947; Schultz, 1954; and Timmer, 1991, among others), agriculture might have benefited from the more stable inflationary environment since the 1990s.[63]

Another development is that financial deepening of the developing countries' economies measured as money and quasi-money over GDP (Table 14) has increased over time, particularly in East Asia. High-inflation economies such as those of LAC and, to a lesser degree, SSA, although also showing greater monetization of their economies over time, are clearly below the average for developing countries and the world. This monetization has increased while financial integration in world markets has advanced, although it is not clear what the links may be between world financial integration and greater domestic financial deepening. The counterpart of expanding money and quasi-money has been more credit availability. Higher levels of financial deepening have been associated with higher growth rates (see Barro and Sala-i-Martin, 1995).

But the context of that monetization has also changed, depending on the financial and capital controls on external flows. Although with closed capital accounts the level of foreign reserves was related to the need to finance a certain amount of imports and/ or the payment of external debt, with open capital accounts the ratio of reserves of foreign exchange to money became more important as an insurance against financial crises, as discussed elsewhere in this chapter. The concern was the possibility that the excess of domestic liquidity was suddenly swapped into "dollars" (which, without current account or capital controls, can be done freely in open markets), triggering a currency crisis. The ratio of reserves of hard currency to domestic money (or vice

Table 15   Money and quasi-money (M2) to gross international reserves ratio, 1970s–early 2000s

	1970s	1980s	1990s	Early 2000s
East Asia and Pacific	2.8	5.0	4.2	3.3
Latin America and Caribbean	3.6	3.5	3.4	2.0
South Asia	8.2	7.6	5.8	3.1
Sub-Saharan Africa	4.1	6.2	3.2	5.4
Low and middle income	4.0	5.4	3.5	2.8

Note: Median from sample of countries.

versa) became an important indicator of the potential occurrence of such crises. Table 15 shows the ratio of a broad indicator of domestic liquidity to gross international reserves for various developing regions.[64]

With capital accounts mostly closed, the quantity of domestic currency per unit of international reserves was increasing in the 1970s and 1980s, but it declined clearly for most of the regions and for developing countries as a whole in the 1990s, a tendency that continued in the early 2000s (except for SSA). The decline indicates either more restrained expansion of domestic credit (public and/or private) or the need to retain larger levels of international reserves as a cushion against lack of confidence in the domestic currency (with the corresponding costs of maintaining such liquidity with low financial returns). Another impact of that accumulation of reserves is that, because they have been invested in dollar instruments (or the equivalent for other industrialized countries), interest rates in the United States (and other developed countries) have been kept lower than would have otherwise been the case, fueling the overinvestment cycle and global imbalances that are being unwound in the late 2000s. Paradoxically, this financial prudence on the part of developing countries (which tried to insure themselves by increasing reserves) has contributed to global imbalances that are at the core of the late 2000s world financial crisis.

4.3.3 Dollarization
While governments were trying to insure the economies from currency crises by accumulating larger reserves of hard currency to back up domestic circulation of local currency, economic agents, particularly in those countries with a history of inflation and currency crises, have been adopting at different speeds the direct use of foreign currency in many daily transactions and using their own money less. In some instances, countries have abandoned their own currencies, such as Panama and, more recently,

Ecuador and El Salvador, without becoming members of a monetary union, as is the case of the European Union system. Leaving aside the issue of monetary unions, here we focus on a trend in monetary, financial, and fiscal conditions particularly since the 1980s that has been called *dollarization*.[65] This term covers different definitions, from countries that, as mentioned, have unilaterally abandoned their own currencies to different degrees of currency substitution, domestic asset and liability dollarization, and external indebtedness in dollars.

In general, in several developing countries, mostly but not only within the "urbanized" group, an important percentage of both deposits and loans in the banking system are denominated in dollars. Although this seemingly takes care of the currency mismatch from the point of view of the banks, that problem is not significantly resolved if debtors have their incomes in domestic currency and would be forced to default in case of a large adjustment in the exchange rate. In turn, banks might not have enough foreign exchange reserves (neither the domestic economic authorities) to finance large withdrawals of foreign currency deposits from economic agents that see the deterioration of the banks' asset side and want out. Also, governments and private sectors that are increasingly indebted abroad and for which their tax receipts and sales, respectively, are denominated in local currency will also be affected by large devaluations. For a government with dollarized public debt, the devaluation would result in a fiscal crisis as well, through different channels: First, the increase in pesos of the payments of the public debt is not matched by tax receipts that remain in pesos; second, the likely banking crisis may require intervention by the public sector with public funds; and third, the recession caused by the banking crisis would reduce tax receipts. In summary, dollarization creates a strong constituency for exchange rate stability.

Although the reasons for dollarization appeared linked originally to high inflation in those countries, the phenomenon has persisted and even intensified, even when inflation declined, leading to the consideration of other causes such as volatility of domestic inflation vis-à-vis volatility of the real exchange rate, possibly linked to lack of a credible monetary policy and imperfections in financial markets and regulations that offered implicit advantages to holdings of dollars (such as the perceived implicit guarantee of government intervention to bail out banks in case of a large devaluation). Whatever the reasons, dollarization under different definitions appeared to increase in several developing countries up to the early 2000s. Reinhart and Roggoff (2003) utilize multivariate criteria to identify various types of dollarization, depending on whether the phenomenon affects assets and liabilities domestically or externally, and whether the private sector participation in the dollarization process is significant. Under three indicators (foreign currency deposits over total deposits, external debt as percentage of GDP, and private sector participation in that debt; see Table 16), dollarization has gone up in all regions, but it is clearly more advanced in LAC, particularly the Southern Cone, and in the Transition Economies. These measures, however, do not include,

Table 16 Dollarization by region, 1980–2001

	1980–1985 # of Countries	Foreign Currency Deposits to Broad Money (%)	Total External Debt to GDP (%)	Share of Private Debt in Total External Debt (%)	1988–1993 # of Countries	Foreign Currency Deposits to Broad Money (%)	Total External Debt to GDP (%)	Share of Private Debt in Total External Debt (%)	1996–2001 # of Countries	Foreign Currency Deposits to Broad Money (%)	Total External Debt to GDP (%)	Share of Private Debt in Total External Debt (%)
Africa	43	0	67	3	46	2	114	2	48	7	126	3
Emerging Asia	23	3	53	8	26	8	88	7	26	11	91	13
Middle East	13	11	38	4	14	20	66	11	14	21	60	19
Transition Economies	0	0	33	0	22	17	37	3	26	29	50	19
Western Hemisphere of which	29	5	60	10	29	13	106	4	29	23	62	11
South America	11	10	58	20	11	23	61	8	11	35	47	27
Total	108				137				143			

Source: Reinhart, Rogoff, and Savastano, *Addicted to Dollars*. Working Paper 10015, NBER Working Paper Series. National Bureau of Economic Research.

for lack of reliable data, in-country cash holdings of foreign currency and offshore deposits, which may be important for the Middle East (cash holdings) and for Africa (offshore accounts). It should also be noted that dollarization appears to have declined somewhat after peaking in the early 2000s in several developing regions, such as LAC. It is still too early to determine whether this is sustained reversal in the previous upward trend in dollarization.

The main policy issues are (1) whether dollarization could be limiting the possibility of adequate policy responses using monetary, financial, fiscal, and exchange rate instruments and, related to that, (2) whether the rigidities imposed by dollarization could lead to more frequent and/or deeper economic crises. The key conclusions from recent empirical studies are that monetary policy in dollarized economies may be affected by a more unstable demand; also, those economies show lower and more volatile growth, and dollarization appears to have heightened the possibility of banking crises (Levy Yeyati, 2005). De Nicoló et al. (2003) also find that dollarization affects negatively solvency and liquidity indicators of the banking system.

On the other hand, dollarization may have helped to increase financial deepening in high-inflation economies (i.e., it would have been very difficult in those countries to expand the domestic banking system without allowing dollar deposits). But the cost seems to have been a greater likelihood of financial crises.

However, this changed monetary context is not equally present in all developing countries: Large countries such as India and China maintain controls on the current and capital accounts of the balance of payments and do not show important levels of dollarization. Asia in general, which historically has experienced lower inflation rates, is less dollarized than LAC or SSA. In addition, Latin American countries also have very open current and capital accounts. Therefore, the possibility of resorting to direct agricultural credit financed by money creation is very different among those countries.

4.3.4 Inflation targeting

Another recent development in monetary policies in developing countries (basically of the "urbanized" group) has been "inflation targeting" (IT). The factors affecting inflation can also be presented using the following equation (see, for instance, Fortin, 2003):

$$I = a + b1*(Lg)I(-1) + b2*Iexp + b3*(Lg)X + b4*(Lg)Z + e \qquad (6)$$

where current inflation (I) depends on five components: I(−1) lagged inflation, a backward-looking variable (with Lg indicating the number of lags); Iexp, expected inflation, a forward-looking variable; X a measure of excess demand, such as the output gap, unemployment, or capacity utilization; Z indicates different shocks, such as changes in world prices for food or oil; a is the intercept; b1, b2, b3, and b4 are the coefficients of the equation; and e is an error term.

First, policies may try to avoid the setting in of inflationary inertia (the backward component, b1 * (Lg) I (−1)). Second, there may be policies aimed at managing expectations (the forward component, b2*Iexp). Third, there are different policies (fiscal, monetary, and others) that try to align aggregate demand and potential output (one of the aspects of the output gap present in b3 * (Lg)X). Fourth, other measures may focus on the expansion of potential output (another part of the output gap considered in b3 * (Lg)X) by increasing investments in physical capital, human capital, infrastructure, and technology. Fifth, all this has to take into account different exogenous shocks, such as sudden increases in food and oil prices (b4 * (Lg)Z).

Several industrialized countries began in the early 1990s[66] to adopt inflation targeting as a monetary framework for their central banks. This approach has focused mostly on b2 * Iexp and b3 * (Lg)X, and it was based on the notion that the central banks should announce numerical inflation targets (usually a relatively narrow band in single digits over some horizon). These targets would be pursued in the medium term through transparent interest rate policy: Central banks are supposed to increase (decrease) interest rates when the actual or, more likely, forecast inflation is above (below) the announced range. In the process, central banks should maintain clear communication of forecasts and intentions with the public. Although central banks would have some flexibility to reach targets when facing unexpected shocks, they would be held accountable for those results, which also required that they were granted the independence to follow the policies they saw as conducive to reaching the announced inflation target. Bernanke and Woodford (2004, p 10) argued that "inflation targeting offers a number of the basic elements of a successful monetary policy framework, including a clearly defined nominal anchor, a coherent approach to decision making, the flexibility to respond to unanticipated shocks, and a strategy for communicating with the public and financial markets. However, as in any other framework, making good policy requires sensitivity to the specific economic and institutional environment in which policymakers find themselves, as well as the technical capability to modify and adapt the framework as needed."

In the case of developing countries, they seem to have stronger inertia in inflation (b1*(Lg)I(−1)), and the size of the exogenous shocks (b4*(Lg)Z) is usually larger than in industrialized countries. Until the IT approach, the main alternatives to control inflation in developing countries have been (1) the utilization of the exchange rate in fixed, preannounced, or heavily managed pegs and (2) the implementation of targets for some of the main money supply aggregates. Various middle-income countries suffered important economic, banking, and debt crises in the 1980s and 1990s after using exchange rate-based stabilization schemes (see overview in Calvo and Vegh, 1999.). On the other hand, the approach based on targeting money supply has been criticized because, given the variability in money demand and in the money and credit multipliers, it is not clear that controlling those monetary aggregates would control inflation (Batini and Laxton, 2006).

Therefore, toward the end of the 1990s or early 2000s, several middle- to higher-income developing countries began to adopt IT schemes, in several cases after collapses of exchange-based stabilization approaches. The international financial institutions also began to promote the IT framework as "best practice" for developing countries. The policy recipe has been to establish an IT regime for the central banks and let the exchange rate float, discouraging the use of heavy intervention in currencies markets, common in the past and that many saw as the main culprit in the 1980s and 1990s economic crises. By 2005, 21 industrial and developing countries had adopted full-fledged inflation targeting[67] (Batini and Laxton, 2006; Mishkin and Schmidt-Hebbel, 2007).

There are diverse views regarding whether the IT approach helps maintain an adequate macroeconomic performance, considering not only inflation but also other variables such as growth and employment, both levels and volatility (Bernanke and Woodford, 2004). This debate, which is part of the more general topic of optimal monetary policies (see, for instance, Woodford, 2003 and 2006), includes comparisons with the other possible approaches, including targeting the exchange rate, different monetary aggregates, or some other variables (such as wages; see Blanchard, 2003).

On the positive side, it has been argued that IT anchors expectations faster, in part because it focuses directly on the variable of interest (i.e., inflation) rather than using intermediate variables (i.e., the exchange rate or monetary aggregates)[68] and that allows greater flexibility in adjusting to circumstances. Defenders also argue that inflation targeting involves a lower economic cost if a policy failure occurs, particularly compared with exchange rate approaches (Batini and Laxton, 2006).

On the negative side, others believe that IT would lead to worsening performance in other macroeconomic objectives, such as growth or employment (Blanchard, 2003; Michael Kumhof, 2001). In addition, external vulnerability in the face of volatile capital flows may well depend on how flexible (or state-contingent) is the target and the price index targeted (see Caballero and Krishnamurthy, 2004). More generally, Calvo (2006) argues that it is inappropriate to discuss IT without considering the two distinguishing characteristics of emerging markets (i.e., middle- to higher-income developing, incipiently integrated in world financial markets), namely, the possibility of "sudden stops" in capital flows and the extensive presence of domestic debt denominated in foreign exchange ("domestic liability dollarization"). Calvo argues that interest rates for IT may be weak instruments in those countries, especially during periods of high volatility, when it might be advisable to switch temporarily to more robust instruments (such as an exchange rate peg), which could require important levels of reserves in the central bank. In Calvo (2008) it is further argued that not only in crises but also in tranquil times, if credibility is limited, IT can lead to problems not unlike those of exchange rate pegs and other stabilization schemes. He shows in a theoretical model that, while exchange rate stabilization programs under imperfect credibility lead to overheating (i.e. higher growth than what can be sustained) and current account deficits, under IT, using the interest rate, the result is underutilization of capacity (i.e. lower growth than possible) and current account surplus. Both approaches, however, appear to lead to real currency appreciation, at least during the initial stages of the noncredible stabilization experiment. When the experiment ends, endogenously or because of external shocks, the strong adjustment in the exchange rate under IT may be as damaging as under full-fledged exchange rate stabilization schemes.

In consequence, Calvo concludes that because nominal anchors are seriously challenged in economies suffering from imperfect credibility due to domestic factors (such as persistent fiscal deficits) or external shocks (for instance, sudden stops in capital flows or sharp terms-of-trade deterioration), usually governments have had to resort to additional schemes to help whatever nominal anchors they were utilizing.

What is the empirical evidence on IT? Most of the evaluations have been related to the experience of industrialized countries. An exception is Batini and Laxton (2006). The authors look at 13 emerging market inflation targeters and compare them against the remaining 22 emerging market countries that are in the JP Morgan Emerging Markets Bond Index, plus seven additional countries that are classified similarly.[69] These two groups have different behavior pre- and post- the dates utilized as a cut-off for the analysis (see Table 17).

Inflation targeters before IT had lower growth with larger variability, and larger inflation but with lower variability, than not targeters. After IT they still had lower growth (by more than 100 bps) with larger variability, but now inflation and its volatility were lower. Although this is simply descriptive, Battini and Laxton use more formal methods to compare the performance of inflation targeters before and after

Table 17   Comparison of performance of targeters and nontargeters

	Average		Median		Difference	
	Pre-	Post-	Pre-	Post-	Average	Median
Inflation targeters						
Growth	3.3	3.5	2.8	3.5	0.3	0.8
Volatility	1.9	1.1	1.8	1.2	−0.8	−0.6
Inflation	15.8	4.2	15.1	3.8	−11.6	−11.3
Volatility	2.5	1.1	1.9	1.0	v1.5	−1.0
Not inflation targeters						
Growth	4.7	4.6	4.2	4.6	−0.1	0.3
Volatility	1.6	0.9	1.2	0.7	−0.7	−0.5
Inflation	13.2	6.2	11.4	3.9	−7.1	−7.5
Volatility	3.2	1.7	2.7	1.0	−1.5	−1.7

Source: IMF (2005).

adopting inflation targeting relative to the performance of nontargeters, using as a base-line for the "break date" for nontargeters the average adoption date for inflation targe-ters (4Q1999; they experiment with other partitions). Although all countries reduced inflation, they find a comparatively larger decline in inflation and volatility of inflation in targeters compared to nontargeters. They do not report growth in levels, only the volatility, concluding that the improvements in inflation have not been achieved at the cost of destabilizing output. They also argue that economic performance along other dimensions such as inflationary expectations and volatility of interest rates, of exchange rates, and of international reserves has been favorable. The authors also study whether successful adoption of IT regimes requires a demanding set of institutional, technical, and economic preconditions and conclude that it does not seem the case.

However, they caution that the time elapsed since these countries adopted inflation targeting, and therefore the sample for their econometric analysis, is short. In fact, it ends before the spreading global crisis of the late 2000s, which will be the real test for IT or any approach to stabilizing developing economies. In particular, given that many targeters saw important appreciations in their exchange rates, it remains to be seen whether the sudden stop in capitals and the needed adjustments in RER would trigger problems not substantially different in economic costs to those experienced in the previous round of crises of the late 1990s and early 2000s.

4.3.5 Monetary and financial issues linked to agriculture

What are some of the possible implications of the trends and policies discussed previ-ously for the agricultural sector? For those countries with open capital accounts and dollarization (mostly in the "urbanized" category), the different monetary conditions changed the possibilities for resorting to the traditional approach of directed credit. As mentioned, one of the characteristics of the "developmental state" in many devel-oping countries until the market liberalization reforms starting in the late 1970s and going through the 1980s and 1990s was the granting of preferential loans through sec-torally specialized institutions (industrial as well as agricultural and rural banks). For instance, in Brazil during the second half of the 1970s, agricultural credit represented about 100% of agricultural GDP, with interest subsidies that in some years amounted to some 5% of the GDP (World Bank, 1986). The expansion of credit was commonly financed through rediscounts from the central bank or similar institutions. In the context of closed capital accounts, the creation of excess liquidity through agricultural subsidies added to inflationary pressures and/or fueled trade deficits, but the countries retained some level of independence in the conduct of their monetary policies. With open capital accounts, on the other hand, excess liquidity would lead to currency substitution, exchange rate and banking crises, and increased dollarization.

In any case, the approach in many developing countries of directed credit to agri-culture, subsidizing interest rates and the use of certain inputs (such as fertilizers) through public banks and public agencies, began to find limits because of problems in the operation of those intermediaries, even before the changes in overall monetary conditions mentioned before could generate additional constraints. The review by Adams et al. (1984) argued that directed agricultural credit programs undermined the banking system through low collection rates or unsustainable subsidies, did not allow for proper mobilization of rural savings, benefited mostly large farmers, did not ensure that funds were not diverted to other uses, and did not have a clear impact on a sustained expansion of new agricultural technologies.

Consequently, interest in agricultural credit programs declined among multilateral financial institutions: For instance, the volume of agricultural lending by the World Bank in the 1990s declined to only one third the level of 10 years earlier (FAO/GTZ, 1998). But also the IMF, World Bank, and other international organizations, as part of the structural adjustment and stabilization programs of the mid-1980s and 1990s, supported financial sector reforms, including the elimination or scaling down of the public sector agricultural agencies and agricultural banks and parastatal companies that, among other things, provided credit to farmers in African countries (FAO/GTZ, 1998; Kherallah et al., 2003). De Janvry, Key, and Sadoulet (1997) also show reforms in LAC that led to restructuring or closing of agricultural financial institutions and/or upward adjustment in interest rates charged in Colombia (Caja Agraria), Ecuador (Banco Nacional de Fomento), Haiti (BNDAI), Mexico (Banrural), Nicaragua (Banco Nacional de Desarrollo), and Peru (Agrarian Bank, BAP).[70]

Those developments in the agricultural financial systems could have led to declines in agricultural credit through this channel, even without factoring the changes in monetary conditions discussed. Table 18 (from Wenner and Proenza, 1999) shows that the unweighted average ratio of agricultural credit over total credit and as a percentage of agricultural GDP for a number of LAC countries has declined, with potential negative impact on agricultural supply (see, for instance, Reca, 1969 and 1980, for an econometric analysis of agricultural supply with credit as an input to production).

Another study suggests that there were declines in the supply of rural credit in China in the second part of the 1990s, with negative consequences for nonfarm rural enterprises (Enjiang Cheng and Zhong Xu, 2004). However, in regions such as East Asia, where monetization and total credit as percentage of the GDP have increased significantly more than in LAC (see Table 14), it should be expected that agriculture has received more lending as well.

Another development has been the increase in real interest rates (Table 19 for a sample of countries in each region) in the 1990s, particularly in SSA and LAC, where real rates appear very high.[71] Patrick Honohan (2000) found that as financial liberalization progressed, the general level of real interest rates increased more in developing countries than it did in industrial countries, and volatility of interest rates also increased in most liberalizing countries. In developed countries it has been recognized that

Table 18   1984–1986 Agricultural Credit Indicators in LAC

	Agricultural Credit (% Total)			Agricultural Credit (% GDP Agropecuario)		
	1984–1986	1990–1992	1994–1996	1984–1986	1990–1992	1994–1996
Bolivia	NA	18.8	12.2	NA	36	40.4
Brazil	NA	11.3	10.7	NA	60.5	40.5
Costa Rica	NA	23.4	20	NA	20.9	18.9
El Salvador	11.1	18	12.1	21.4	42.9	28.4
Guatemala	17.2	14.2	10.2	42.6	19.8	28.5
Honduras	26.5	22.9	17.9	45.7	36.6	23.1
Jamaica	15.1	9.2	5.3	66.1	31.5	14.2
Mexico	15.3	9.5	7.7	47.2	37	53.8
Perú	27	NA	5.6	28.9	NA	8.3
Dominican Rep.	12.7	13.8	10.8	19.4	15.5	18.4
Unweighted average	*17.8*	*15.7*	*11.3*	*38.8*	*33.4*	*27.5*

Source: Wenner and Proenza (1999).

Table 19   Real interest rate, 1970s–2000s (%)

	1970s	1980s	1990s	2000s
East Asia and Pacific	2.3	4.4	5.8	5.4
Latin America and Caribbean	NA	5.2	8.5	10.4
South Asia	5.0	3.6	6.4	7.1
Sub-Saharan Africa	−0.7	4.8	9.7	12.5
Low and middle income	1.2	4.2	7.4	9.5

Note: Median across sample of countries in each region.
Source: WDI (2004).

interest rates affect agriculture, which tends to be more capital intensive than other sectors in the economy (Thompson, 1988). However, the literature on the links between interest rates and agriculture in developing countries tends to be far more limited. In general it focuses on the need to have interest rates high enough to ensure the viability of rural financial institutions, helping mobilize local savings and allocating credit to the more efficient uses (Adams, Graham, and von Pischke, 1984). Desai and Mellor (1993) argued that, although for a financial institution to remain viable interest rates must cover transaction costs and keep up with inflation, if the interest rate is too high farmers will borrow less, which will reduce the use of fertilizers and other inputs and adversely affect agricultural productivity. They also made the case that in developing countries, accessibility, liquidity, and safety affect rural borrowing, savings, and deposits more than the interest rate and that a high geographical coverage of local offices of financial institutions is critical.

Changes in monetary and financial conditions open a series of questions regarding the conditions for agricultural institutions and agricultural credit going forward. The past approach of financing agriculture by resorting to generous rediscounts from the central bank to be channeled through specialized institutions seems restricted by both the general monetary conditions in countries with open capital accounts and the failures of those intermediaries in the past. On the other hand, the decline in inflation and increased monetization or financial deepening of the economies, as in East Asia, can lead to increases in agricultural credit as part of the general expansion in private credit. However, if prevalent market conditions discriminate against agricultural credit or some type of farmers due to risk conditions or other reasons, specialized institutions could be required. But they will need better management and incentives than in the past and must be framed within a sustainable monetary program that does not lead to inflation or exchange rate crises.

At the same time, increased financial globalization appears to have been accompanied by higher interest rates and an increased likelihood of bank crises, at least in the "urbanized" type of countries. But it could have also led to lower and less volatile inflation, and the exchange rate regimes in many developing countries might have moved away (with the exception of the "dollarizers") from rigid pegs.

With regard to those countries following IT regimes, there have not been specific analyses of those approaches on agricultural performance, although there have been some theoretical arguments about the possible negative impact on agriculture (and, in general, commodity-producing sectors or sectors with greater price flexibility) of trying to force down inflation as measured by a general price index, which would also include goods and services with prices that are sticky, at least in the short run. Also, the issue of the appreciation of the exchange rate in (potentially noncredible) IT frameworks may have affected tradable agricultural products. More generally, given the recent decline in inflation in developing countries, the current debate should also include the potential impact on growth and employment of domestic anti-inflationary policies. The question is whether the domestic macroeconomic policies used to reduce inflation are simultaneously slowing growth and increasing unemployment in a way that could more than compensate for the positive impact of lower inflation on agriculture.

Therefore, monetary policies in developing countries not only have to consider the usual objectives of lower inflation and maintaining growth but might have to include considerations about the exchange rate, the level of official reserves, and the possibility of banking crises, with a variety of impacts on the agricultural sector of developing countries, depending on the specific configuration of the various factors, including the structural aspects discussed in Section 2.

4.4 Exchange rate policies

The exchange rate is one of the most important macroprices. The level and changes (both actual and expected) of the exchange rate have wide influence through the economy, affecting and being affected by the demand and supply of tradable and nontradable products, the demand and supply of money and monetary assets denominated in local currency in comparison with assets denominated in other currencies, the inflow or outflow of capital, and the public budget, among other things. The importance of the real exchange rate and exchange rate policies to the performance of the agricultural sector, particularly the tradable sectors, in both developed and developing countries has been long recognized (Schuh, 1974; Orden, 1986; Balassa, 1988, Krueger, Schiff, and Valdés, 1988; Bautista and Valdés, 1993).

4.4.1 Background

Nominal rates   Except where indicated otherwise, nominal exchange rates (ER) are defined in units of domestic currency per unit of foreign currency (usually the U.S. dollar). Appreciation (depreciation) of a currency means that the amount of that currency paid for one unit of foreign currency decreases (increases). A strong (weak) currency is one that has appreciated (depreciated) vis-à-vis others.

The effective exchange rate (EER1) *for a product* is the nominal rate corrected by taxes or subsidies that may correspond to that product:

$$EER1 = ER*(1 + subsidy\ rate);\ or\ EER1 = ER*(1 - tax\ rate)$$

Also, the concept of effective nominal exchange rate is used *in general*—not for a specific product—to highlight the fact that a country has different exchange rates with different currencies; for example, x pesos per dollar, y pesos per euro, z pesos per yen, and so on. The effective rate (EER2) in this context would be an average of all those rates weighed by the percentage of international trade of a country in each one of those currency areas. It is usually calculated as a geometric average, as follows:

$$EER2 = \Pi_j(ER_j)^{\alpha j} \text{ from } j \text{ to } n; \quad \sum \alpha j = 1$$

where ER_j is the bilateral nominal exchange rate with country j, and αj is an appropriate country weight (usually based on trade variables).[72]

Real exchange rates   A more important concept is the _real_ exchange rate (RER), which is also used in two main conceptual ways. The first one, in the case of a single partner country, is the bilateral nominal exchange rate of the home country with the foreign country corrected by an index of domestic prices and another index of prices in the partner country:

$$RER1 = ER*PI/PD$$

where PI is the price index of the partner country and PD is the local price index.[73] It can be generalized, as in the nominal effective exchange rate (EER2), by calculating a geometrical average of bilateral real exchange rates, weighted as before.

Another definition of real exchange rate is the price of tradable products divided by the price of nontradable ones:

$$RER2 = Pt/Pnt$$

In both definitions, when the nominal amount of local currency paid per foreign currency unit decreases (increases), this ratio also declines (increases), at least initially, and it is usually said that the RER has appreciated (depreciated).[74]

The relationship between RER1 and RER2 can be seen by taking logs of the first equation (indicated by lowercase letters) and defining, also in logs, the price indices for both the domestic and the partner country as a function of the prices of their own tradable and nontradable goods and services (PIt and PInt for the partner country and PDt and PDnt for the home country; see, for instance, Edwards, 1989, and Chinn, 2005):

$$rer1 = er + pi - pd$$
$$pi = \beta*pint + (1 - \beta)*pit$$
$$pd = \delta*pdnt + (1 - \delta)*pdt$$

that can be rearranged as:

$$rer1 = (er + pit - pdt) - \delta*(pdnt - pdt) + \beta*(pint - pit)$$

Then the first version of the real exchange rate (RER1) can be expressed as the sum of three components (Chinn, 2005): (1) the relative price of tradables, a form of the terms of trade in domestic currency; (2) the inverse of RER2 for the home country, weighted by the share of nontradables in the domestic price index; and (3), similarly, the inverse of the RER2 for the foreign country, weighted by the share of nontradables in the price index of the partner country. Assuming that the "law of one price" for tradables applies, the first parenthesis is zero. But if the tradables produced by the home country and the foreign country are not perfectly substitutable, the first parenthesis is another channel influencing RER1.

To understand the implications for agriculture, it is useful to disaggregate the second definition (RER2) in the tradable and nontradable components. The price of the tradables as a whole is an aggregate index of different prices (Pxa and Pma, prices of exports and imports of agricultural products, respectively; Pxna and Pmna, prices of exports and imports of nonagricultural products, respectively); and the price of nontradables is an index that includes Pnta and Pntna, the prices of nontradables from the agricultural and nonagricultural sectors. Defining RER2 as functions of the respective prices, we get:

$$\text{Pt} = f(\text{Pxa}, \text{Pma}, \text{Pxna}, \text{Pmna}) \text{ y } \text{Pnt} = g(\text{Pnta}, \text{Pntna})$$

Then the real exchange rate is equal to:

$$\text{RER} = \text{Pt}/\text{Pnt} = f(\text{Pxa}, \text{Pma}, \text{Pxna}, \text{Pmna})/g(\text{Pnta}, \text{Pntna})$$

$$= \frac{f[\text{Pwxa}^*\text{ER}^*(1+\text{txa}), \text{Pwma}^*\text{ER}^*(1+\text{tma}), \text{Pwxna}^*\text{ER}^*(1+\text{txna}), \text{Pwmna}^*\text{ER}^*(1+\text{tmna})]}{g\{h1[\text{Qnta}(\ldots), \text{Dnta}(\ldots)], h2[\text{Qntna}(\ldots), \text{Dntna}(\ldots)]\}}$$

which indicates that the index of the price of tradables is a function (f) of world prices, the nominal exchange rate, and taxes on (subsidies to) exports and imports; and the index of nontradable products depend on Pnta and Pntna, which in turn are functions (h1 and h2, respectively) of the internal supply and demand Qnta(...), Dnta(...), Qntna(...), and Dntna(...).[75]

Several aspects must be noted. First, although the government could manage the nominal exchange rate ER (particularly with a closed capital account), the real exchange rate is an endogenous variable that depends on how the whole economy adapts to macroeconomic changes and, in particular, on how supplies and demands of the nontradable goods adjust. If the government devalues the domestic currency, the real exchange rate is going to turn more favorable to the tradables only if the impact of the devaluation on the supply and demand of nontradables is such that the change in the prices of those goods (and the index g) is smaller than the increase in the prices of the tradables (reflected in the index f).

Second, looking at the impact of macroeconomic measures on the agricultural sector, it is clear that the concept of the real exchange rate RER (Pt/Pnt) is different from the domestic terms of trade between the agricultural and nonagricultural sectors that could be defined as

$$\text{Pa}/\text{Pna} = u(\text{Pxa}, \text{Pma}, \text{Pnta})/v(\text{Pxna}, \text{Pmna}, \text{Pntna}),$$

where u and v are functions that generate agricultural and nonagricultural price indexes. Therefore, improvements on the RER do not translate one to one to improvements of the relative profitability of the agricultural sector. Furthermore (as discussed in Section 1), changes in the real exchange rate or in the internal terms of trade between agriculture and nonagriculture are only proxy indicators of the possible profitability of the agricultural sector in relation to other sectors; it is also necessary to analyze how different macroeconomic variables affect the costs of the sector, the availability of inputs, the levels of activity and demand, and the productive response of the agricultural sector.

Third, a real devaluation—that is, a nominal devaluation not negated by compensatory increases of the prices of the nontradables—favors not only exports but also activities that substitute imports, which can be of agricultural origin, but also from other sectors such as industry. In this sense, the dichotomy agriculture versus industry, sometimes interpreted simply as the discrimination against exportable agricultural products (affected by taxes) and the support of the industrial activities that substitute imports (benefited with protective tariffs), although valid in some countries, must be subject to important caveats, since there are agricultural activities that substitute imports and are protected by tariffs (and other restrictions to international trade; see Section 4.5 on trade policies), and the industrial sector could have activities that are important net exporters.

Finally, the definitions show that the RER depends on world prices and trade and exchange rate policies but also on any other macroeconomic or sectoral policy that affects supply and demand of tradables and nontradables.

In consequence, for all the reasons indicated, the effect of changes in the nominal exchange rate will also depend on the whole implemented economic program and the general equilibrium rebalancing of the entire economy.

Financial aspects So far we have talked about ER as a policy variable that the government controls, affecting the real side of the economy. But in the monetary section we mentioned the "impossible trinity" that links monetary aspects, capital flows, and the exchange rate. This principle says that if a government has decided to eliminate restrictions in current and capital account financial transactions (first policy choice), it can have only one independent policy decision between the level of the exchange rate (second policy choice) and a separate monetary policy (third policy choice) at the same time.

This can be seen with the following (simplified)[76] arbitrage condition for capital flows under perfect mobility of capital when there are no restrictions in the capital account:

$$\text{INTd} = \text{INTw} + \text{Expected devaluation (in percentage terms)}$$
$$+ \text{Country risk (in percentage terms)}$$

where INTd is the domestic interest rate for the time period considered in domestic currency financial instruments; INTw is the world interest rate in financial instruments in foreign currency; devaluation at $t + 1$ expected at t in percentages is $(ER_{t+1} - ER_t)$ / ER_t; and the country risk is also expressed in percentage terms.

If we assume the country is small in financial markets, INTw is exogenous; ER_t is predetermined (already known at t); country risk is also exogenously given at t.[77] Therefore economic authorities cannot independently define INTd and ER_{t+1}. Capital will flow in (out) depending on whether INTd is greater (smaller) than the right side of the equation, forcing adjustments in INTd and the exchange rate.

More generally, the exchange rate will play a role in both the current account (mostly but not only on the trade balance) and the capital account, affecting the net foreign position of the country as a creditor or a debtor (i.e., that country's external assets minus external liabilities). This has led to the so-called *external sustainability approach* to the determination of exchange rates (IMF, 2006; Isard, 2007). In its simplest way, this approach merely looks at the net foreign liabilities (NFL) position considered appropriate (measured as a ratio to the GDP) and calculates the current account balance that would stabilize the NFL position of the country at that level, using the formula:

$$(CA/GDP) = \{(INT - Growth\ rate)/(1 + Growth\ rate)\}*(NFL/GDP)$$

where CA/GDP is the current account as ratio to the GDP, and INT is the nominal interest on the NFL. The formula includes the expected medium-term growth rate of the economy and the desired ratio of NFL to GDP.

Given some projected and/or desired values for the variables in the right side of the equation, the level of CA/GDP needed to stabilize NFL/GDP at the benchmark (desired) value is determined. The estimated value of the CA is compared with the *current* value of the CA, and the devaluation/revaluation of the domestic currency required to move from the current value to the sustainable CA can be calculated.

A related analysis is called the *macroeconomic balance approach* (IMF, 2006), which calculates the difference between the current account balance projected over the medium term at existing exchange rates and an econometrically estimated equilibrium current account balance. As before, the exchange rate adjustment that would move the existing CA to the equilibrium CA over the medium term can be estimated from econometrically estimated responses of the trade balance to the real exchange rate.

Equilibrium exchange rates   As suggested in the previous paragraphs, the ER is a variable that affects the way that all four macroeconomic identities are fulfilled in its real and nominal aspects. Even with strict controls on capital and current accounts, which could allow the government to use the ER as a policy instrument, the value determined by the economic authorities may generate imbalances in one or several of the macro accounts. Therefore, the ER defined as policy instrument could be different from the equilibrium exchange rate, which is the one that balances the real and nominal aspects of the economy, consistent with its medium-term fundamentals and macroeconomic stability. The equilibrium real exchange rate (ERER) has been defined as the one that attains both internal equilibrium (meaning that nontradable markets clear in the current period and are expected to do so in the future) and external equilibrium (that is, when current accounts balances, now and in the future, are compatible with long-run sustainable capital inflows; see, for instance, Edwards, 1989; Isard, 2007).

Empirical estimations of ERER vary significantly. Isard (2007) identifies six different approaches that have been utilized: purchasing power parity; purchasing power parity adjusted for productivity effects (Balassa-Samuelson); variants of the sustainability of the current account (as discussed elsewhere in this chapter); assessments of the competitiveness of the tradable goods sector; estimates based on a single equation econometrically estimated of the equilibrium exchange rate; and assessments based on general equilibrium models.

Of the six approaches identified by Isard (2007), most empirical analyses in developing countries apply the econometric estimation of a single equation, where both fundamentals and policy variables are considered along with adjustment issues. Box 1, from Chudik and Mongardini (2007), who analyze equilibrium exchange rates in SSA, shows some of the main determinants in those estimations.

The real exchange rate is estimated as a function of fundamentals (such as terms of trade, productivity), and policy variables (other variables in Box 1) that can differ from

---

Box 1   ERER Determinants for Developing Countries

- *The external terms of trade*, defined as the ratio of the price of a country's exports over the price of its imports. Most African countries mainly export primary commodities, such as oil, lumber, metals, and diamonds, and/or agricultural products (e.g., coffee and cocoa). The price for these primary commodities is determined in world commodity markets and subject to significant volatility affecting the terms of trade. An improvement in the terms of trade will positively affect the trade balance and thus lead the ERER to appreciate.
- *Productivity relative to foreign trading partners*, proxied by total factor productivity, where available, or relative per capita real GDP. Developments in relative productivity capture well-known Balassa-Samuelson effects. Countries with higher productivity growth in the tradables sector (where such growth tends to concentrate) can sustain an ERER appreciation without losing competitiveness.

Continued

Box 1 ERER Determinants for Developing Countries—Cont'd

- *Government consumption as a share of GDP* relative to that of foreign trading partners. An increase in government consumption biased toward nontradables creates higher demand for nontradables (relative to the tradable sector). This greater demand boosts the relative prices of nontradable goods, causing the equilibrium real exchange rate to appreciate. However, if the increase in overall government consumption is biased toward the tradable sector, an increase in spending will cause the ERER to depreciate.
- *The severity of trade restrictions*, proxied by openness to trade. *Openness to trade* is defined as the sum of exports plus imports as a share of GDP. Protection of domestically produced goods via restrictions on cross-border trade (e.g., import tariffs and nontariff barriers) leads to higher domestic prices and thus ERER appreciation. Consequently, lifting existing trade restrictions (proxied by an increase in openness to trade) should cause the ERER to depreciate.
- *The ratio of investments to GDP* relative to that of foreign trading partners. Investments in low- and middle-income countries have high import content and thus a direct negative impact on the trade balance. Because this variable may capture technological progress, its overall impact on the ERER is ambiguous.
- *Debt service as a share of exports.* An increase in debt service payments leads the external balance to deteriorate; thus subsequent price adjustments should restore equilibrium. Higher debt service payments should therefore cause the ERER to depreciate.
- *Net foreign assets as a share of GDP*, a proxy for the country's net external position. An increase in capital inflows from abroad implies higher demand for domestic currency, thus causing the ERER to appreciate.
- *Aid flows as a share of exports.* Similar to debt service payments, aid flows can represent a significant fraction of GDP in low-income countries. An increase in aid flows improves the external balance and thus causes the ERER to appreciate.
- *Controls over capital flows.* Similarly to tightening restrictions on the movement of goods across borders, easing controls on capital flows could impact the ERER. The direction of this impact depends on (1) how much the real interest rate in the domestic economy differs with those of its foreign trading partners and (2) the country's risk profile.
- *Fiscal and monetary policy.* In Edwards' model, both fiscal and monetary policies affect the real exchange rate. However, it is not clear whether changes in macroeconomic policies have a long-run impact on the ERER.

From: Chudik and Mongardini (2007).

the levels that could lead to internal and external equilibrium. These equations can be estimated individually (which, for developing countries, are usually not very robust) or in a panel of countries (Chudik and Mongardini, 2007). There are different options depending on how the policy variables are treated for the projection of the equilibrium exchange rate and how transitory and long-term effects are modeled (see Di Bella, Lewis, and Martin, 2007, who identify five alternatives[78]).

When the actual RER does not satisfy the internal and/or external equilibrium, it is said that there is a misalignment of the exchange rate. These problems are usually related to the dual policy role of ER, already mentioned, as a real price in the *real exchange rate approach* (see Balassa, 1977, 1985, which emphasizes the balance between tradable and nontradable goods and the influence on production, trade, and employment) and as a financial variable in the *nominal anchor approach* (which highlights the role of the exchange rate in the inflationary process and its relationship with interest rates and capital flows; Corden, 1990). This dual role has implications for the consistency of the whole economic program and for the political economy of exchange rate adjustments.

With regard to consistency, pursuing a real exchange rate approach without a separate monetary anchor could lead to higher inflation and create macroeconomic problems through this channel for the expected production, trade, and employment objectives. The nominal anchor approach, in turn, without strong fiscal and monetary policies, could lead to appreciation of the RER and create an unsustainable trade and current account position, forcing a devaluation, which feeds into higher inflation and defeats the purpose of the followed approach. Many of the failed economic programs in developing countries have revolved around this issue of the dual objectives of a single policy variable in inconsistent economic programs.

Regarding the political economy aspects, producers of tradables generally prefer a devalued exchange rate (depending on the import content of their products), whereas producers of nontradables may benefit from a strong currency. However, the expansion of assets and liabilities in dollars adds, both technically and in terms of political economy, a new complexity to the decision to devalue the domestic currency. Debtors in domestic currency can be helped by devaluations that increase inflation and reduce the real cost of servicing their debt, but the situation is reversed in dollarized countries, where debtors could have their liabilities denominated in foreign currency.

The analyses of the exchange rate and the possible impacts on the agricultural sector up to the late 1980s have usually been done within the framework of the real exchange rate approach, with some crucially simplifying assumptions about capital flows and the nominal issues raised by the nominal anchor approach (see, for instance, Krueger et al., 1988). Since then the importance of capital flows and the increase in world financial integration, particularly in urbanized economies, require a careful consideration of real and nominal aspects in the determination of internal and external equilibriums and the possible impact on agriculture. Also, in agriculture-based and several transition economies, the issues related to flows of foreign aid and/or remittances pose specific challenges to the integration of real and nominal aspects of that analysis.

4.4.2 Evolution of the exchange rates in developing countries

Wood (1988) analyzed the evolution of the RER in developing countries from the 1960s to the 1980s. He shows that the RER[79] has been depreciating in most developing countries (except oil exporters) during that period (his data end in the mid-1980s). He reports that the ratio of the 1980–1984 to the 1960–1964 RERs was 0.61 for low-income developing countries (not counting India and China, which had ratios of 0.62 and 0.4, respectively) and 0.85 for middle-income, oil-importing developing countries (Table 1 in Wood, 1988). Certainly, the oil shocks and the debt crises of the 1980s in many developing countries forced devaluations in their RERs.[80]

Covering a more recent period, Cashin et al. (2002) calculate the real effective exchange rate[81] for various countries during the period from January 1980 to March 2002 (see Table 20).

It shows that most countries in LAC, Asia, and Africa had devalued their currencies and the REER had declined in value substantially by early 2000s compared to the early 1980s, when most of those regions were still benefiting from the late 1970s increases in capital inflows and high commodity prices in world markets. REERs in LAC were on average below the early 1980s values by 15–20%, in Asia by about 40% below, and in Africa by between 45% and 55%. Still, by late 2001 five countries in LAC and one in Asia showed REERs more appreciated than in the first half of the 1980s.[82] However, the pattern of decline is not uniform. LAC countries adjusted down their REERs in the second half of the 1980s, mostly after the onset of the debt crises with the Mexican default of 1982 and due to the collapse of commodity prices after 1986. But in the mid-1990s they started a process of appreciation that continued until the end of the data in early 2002, although as indicated the REER never reached the levels of the early 1980s. The average and median REER for the sample of countries in Africa and Asia, on the other hand, had declined more or less continuously over the period, although different countries show some appreciations during the mid-1990s.

Overall, it is clear that at least for the countries included, the levels of the REER in the early 2000s were below the levels of the late 1970s and the first half of the 1980s. More recent IMF data (until 2007) but with a smaller country coverage (not shown) suggest that the same observation is valid for the 2000s, with developing countries in LAC, SSA, and Asia maintaining depreciated real exchange rates compared to the 1970s and 1980s and about in line with the levels of the second half of the 1990s.

4.4.3 Exchange rate regimes, policies, and outcomes

A first point to be noticed is the decline in the number of countries with dual or parallel foreign exchange markets, from about 30–50% of the countries in the 1970s and 1980s to about 10% of all countries (developed and developing) by the 2000s (see Rogoff et al., 2003). This suggests the prevalence of a more orderly macroeconomic framework and less distorted relative prices. Yet for some developing regions, such as

3140 Eugenio Diaz-Bonilla and Sherman Robinson

Table 20 Real effective exchange rates, 1980–2001

	1980–1984	1985–1989	1990–1994	1995–1999	2000–2001		1980–1984	1985–1989	1990–1994	1995–99	2000–2001
LAC						**Africa**					
Argentina	119.3	72.0	128.0	148.8	153.8	Burundi	139.4	117.0	83.0	96.7	85.0
Bolivia	145.4	132.1	67.9	69.3	74.4	Cameroon	88.5	105.9	94.1	72.5	69.7
Brazil	104.5	87.1	112.9	119.0	87.1	Central African Rep.	116.7	113.3	86.7	63.4	60.7
Chile	180.8	103.1	96.9	116.8	110.2	Cote d'Ivoire	93.4	101.8	98.2	77.2	74.8
Colombia	174.4	108.8	91.2	118.5	106.8	Ethiopia	109.7	112.3	87.7	46.7	41.3
Costa Rica	111.5	103.4	96.6	102.9	110.2	Ghana	716.4	124.3	75.7	73.4	52.3
Dominica	97.6	103.1	96.9	96.5	105.8	Kenya	126.6	108.1	91.9	108.8	111.1
Ecuador	184.8	110.8	89.2	101.6	93.3	Madagascar	180.9	116.7	83.3	81.9	94.4
Guatemala	155.9	108.7	91.3	112.4	117.6	Malawi	113.5	102.5	97.5	77.6	73.5
Honduras	117.2	129.9	70.1	74.3	95.4	Mali	123.2	111.1	88.9	63.8	59.4
México	114.9	88.1	111.9	100.1	136.1	Mauritania	134.9	110.8	89.2	67.5	58.1
Paraguay	161.1	110.0	90.0	98.9	90.6	Mauritius	118.8	102.0	98.0	96.1	102.6
Peru	53.2	70.3	129.7	134.6	135.1	Morocco	130.7	102.5	97.5	108.2	111.7
Suriname	218.5	114.5	85.5	129.2	147.9	Mozambique	110.1	147.2	52.8	49.3	46.8
Uruguay	134.0	93.2	106.8	144.0	152.4	Niger	157.3	118.0	82.0	61.8	59.4
Venezuela	185.8	114.1	85.9	128.6	183.8	Nigeria	238.4	149.7	50.3	77.1	55.6
Simple average	*141.2*	*103.1*	*96.9*	*112.2*	*118.8*	South Africa	136.3	96.7	103.3	91.1	74.2
Median	*139.7*	*106.0*	*94.0*	*114.6*	*110.2*	Senegal	99.5	109.9	90.1	65.4	61.2
						Sudan	72.1	78.4	121.6	48.2	55.5

Asia					
Bangladesh	109.6	105.6	94.4	97.5	100.0
India	161.6	125.9	74.1	65.9	69.7
Indonesia	187.0	112.5	87.5	72.1	57.7
Malaysia	128.9	108.4	91.6	86.9	82.1
Pakistan	155.2	112.7	87.3	82.6	76.4
Philippines	133.4	104.9	95.1	106.0	92.4
Papua New Guinea	115.4	104.0	96.0	79.5	72.1
Sri Lanka	108.0	101.9	98.1	108.7	113.3
Syria	105.2	142.0	58.0	53.5	53.5
Thailand	128.3	102.3	97.7	92.5	81.4
Simple average	*133.3*	*112.0*	*88.0*	*84.5*	*79.9*
Median	*128.6*	*107.0*	*93.0*	*84.7*	*78.9*

Tanzania	203.2	145.1	54.9	74.2	84.2
Togo	123.2	107.8	92.2	77.6	74.5
Tunisia	135.7	106.6	93.4	95.7	94.4
Uganda	321.1	137.6	62.4	67.2	66.8
Zambia	147.2	97.4	102.6	110.8	117.6
Zimbabwe	153.7	120.7	79.3	71.8	111.1
Simple average	*163.6*	*113.7*	*86.3*	*77.0*	*75.8*
Median	*130.7*	*110.8*	*89.2*	*74.2*	*73.5*

Source: Cashin, Cespedes, and Sahay, "Keynes, Cocoa, and Copper: In Search of Commodity Currencies," IMF Working Paper No. 02/223 (2002).

Africa (excluding the Franc zone) and the Middle East, dual/parallel systems persisted into the 1990s, with average ratios of parallel to official values of the exchange rates of about 2 or 3 to 1. Dual/parallel regimes, which usually indicate troubled macroeconomic and balance-of-payments conditions, tend to be associated with worse growth and inflationary performance: Unified regimes appear to have about one eighth of the annual inflationary rates and about three times the growth rates of dual/parallel regimes (Rogoff et al., 2003). A second fact is that developing countries, as well as industrialized countries, have been changing their exchange rate regimes away from the fixed pegs of the 1950s and 1960s (see Reinhart and Rogoff, 2002). The collapse of the Bretton Woods system in the first half of the 1970s meant that not only industrialized countries but also a variety of developing countries moved away from hard pegs in the second part of the 1970s and the 1980s (see Table 21).[83] Third, and contrary to the view prevalent in the 1990s that developing countries were moving to the polar extremes, either hard pegs (including dollarization and currency boards) or free floats (the "hollowing middle hypothesis"), the *de facto* classification of Reinhart and Rogoff (2002) shows a movement toward the middle of variously managed floats.

The macroeconomic problems of the 1980s and 1990s have also led to an increase in the "free-falling" category for some developing countries. This is a category of rapidly devaluating currencies, usually associated with extensive macroeconomic turmoil reflected in very high inflation and low growth, which Reinhart and Rogoff distinguish from freely floating, in which the float is not linked to rapid devaluation but can move in either direction.

An economically meaningful identification of the exchange rate regime is important in considering whether some exchange rate arrangements are associated with better

Table 21   Developing countries in various exchange rate regimes (%), 1950s–2001

	1950s	1960s	1970s	1980s	1990s	2000–2001
Peg	55.4	57.5	44.3	27.6	30.2	35.8
Limited flexibility	3.3	5.7	10.3	16.0	25.0	27.2
Managed float	13.1	10.2	16.7	20.9	17.1	22.0
Freely floating	0.0	0.0	0.1	1.7	2.7	5.2
Freely falling	2.4	1.4	4.7	11.3	18.8	4.3
No data	25.8	25.3	23.8	22.4	6.3	5.6
Total	100	100	100	100	100	100

Source: Reinhart and Rogoff (2002).

economic performance. The theoretical arguments about whether fixed or flexible regimes are more adequate for a country do not show conclusive results, depending not only on what economic dimension is selected to define "adequate" behavior (say, growth versus inflation) but also on the nature of possible shocks the economy faces, production and trade structural issues, and the flexibility of other nominal variables in the economy, among other things. In fact, Frankel (1999) has argued that there is no exchange regime that can be considered the most adequate all the time, even for the same country; rather, different regimes may perform best at different times of a country's history. Table 22 from Rogoff et al. (2003) summarizes possible effects of flexible and fixed regimes on four economic dimensions: growth, inflation, volatility, and crises.

But, as mentioned earlier, there is an increasing number of countries with regimes in the intermediate categories. Therefore, the assessment of economic performance requires an empirical analysis of the whole range of regimes, acknowledging that different classifications would yield different results. Using the "natural" classification of Reinhart and Rogoff (2002), which is now also approximated by the IMF "de facto" classification, Rogoff et al. analyze the impact of various exchange regimes on three categories of countries: they distinguish developing countries between what they call

Table 22 Economic performance across exchange rate regimes

	Inflation	Growth	Volatility	Crisis
Fixed	May enhance monetary policy credibility and lower inflation. Emerging markets are less likely to be able to import credibility. Moreover, inflation may be "bottled up" under weak macroeconomic management.	May reduce transactions costs, raise trade and growth. May also reduce interest rates and uncertainty, also raising investment and growth.	May increase volatility in the presence of real shocks and nominal rigidities.	Higher risk of speculative attacks against currency, especially when exposed to volatile capital flows. Susceptibility to banking sector distress.
Flexible	The importance of "imported" credibility declines with stronger institutions and financial sectors.	Higher growth due to shock absorbers and fewer distortions following real shocks.	Real exchange rate volatility may spill over into real activity.	Lower risk of currency and banking crises.

"emerging markets" (which using the categories of agricultural countries discussed earlier, would correspond mostly to "urbanized" and some "transition" countries) and the "rest of developing countries" (basically, "agriculture-based" and "transition" countries according to the World Bank); they also consider a third group of industrialized countries.[84] The study controls for other factors affecting the four analyzed dimensions (growth, inflation, volatility, and crises).

The same exchange rate regimes seem to have different effects in each one of those three different categories of countries, depending on their level of integration with private international financial markets and the quality of the domestic institutions and policies, particularly those related to monetary and fiscal issues and to the domestic financial system. The nonemerging developing countries (i.e., "agriculture-based" and "transition" countries), with less linkage to the private international financial markets due to capital controls or because of lack of interest among private investors,[85] appear to have a larger incidence of fixed pegs. This seems to have helped them to achieve lower inflation rates without resigning growth or increasing volatility and the recurrence of crises. Those countries (whose more conspicuous cases are China and India) did not suffer currency or banking crises, as the countries in the emerging markets category did.

Emerging markets ("urbanized" countries), in turn, appear more integrated with private international capital markets than the other developing countries, but at the same time they suffer from different monetary, fiscal, and financial weaknesses that, although perhaps not different from the rest of the developing economies, when combined with international financial integration yield different results in terms of the impact of exchange rate regimes. For instance, pegs appear associated with less growth, more inflation, and more crises than managed floats. In both types of economies freely floating regimes appear to yield worse results in terms of inflation and growth than the other, more fixed regimes. Only for advanced economies does floating seem to function best, due to their stronger policy and institutional settings.

To the extent that higher general growth and low inflation help agriculture, in low-income developing countries with controlled capital accounts the exchange rate arrangement that may benefit agricultural development would be a fixed peg, provided it is not allowed to get overvalued. In the case of more advanced developing countries with greater openness in the capital accounts and deeper integration with world financial markets, both fixed and freely floating regimes seem not to help with either growth or price stability, and therefore agricultural development might benefit from a managed float.

4.4.4 Exchange rates and agricultural growth

The impact of the level and changes in the real exchange rate on the net trade of tradable goods and services has been amply documented (Balassa, 1988; Orden, 1986).[86] A different question involves the impact of the level and changes of the real exchange rate on the rate of growth of the economy in general and of the agricultural sector in particular. Various studies have shown that the overvaluation of the real exchange tends to depress economic growth in general. Even more, it appears that somewhat undervalued exchange rates are associated with higher growth (see for instance Dollar, 1992). Moving from levels to changes in levels, Section 4.1 briefly mentioned the earlier debates about whether the devaluation of the exchange rates might have, or not, "stagflationary" effects. However, the short-term effect must be differentiated from the medium-term consequences.

Focusing on the agricultural sector, the usual presumption is that it is mainly tradable and therefore it should benefit from a more competitive real exchange rate, assuming that it does not have a strong component of imports in the production function (see Krueger et al., 1988). However, this assumption does not necessarily apply uniformly across the whole agricultural sector in developing countries.

To motivate the following debate and as a first (and admittedly simplistic) approximation, Figure 17 shows a scatter diagram of the level of the real exchange rate and agricultural growth by five-year averages for the countries included in Table 20.

Instead of levels, Figure 18 shows, for the same countries, agricultural growth as a function of the devaluation of the real effective exchange rate (defined as the change in levels in the current five-year average compared to those of the previous half decade).

Both figures suggest that the correlation between the real exchange rate (in levels or changes) and agricultural growth is very weak (or nonexistent). Of course, this analysis cannot be conducted on a bivariate basis and needs to consider other factors. The results mentioned in regard to overvaluation (undervaluation) of the exchange rate

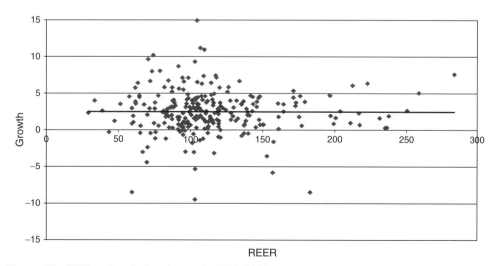

Figure 17   REER and agricultural growth, 1980–2002.

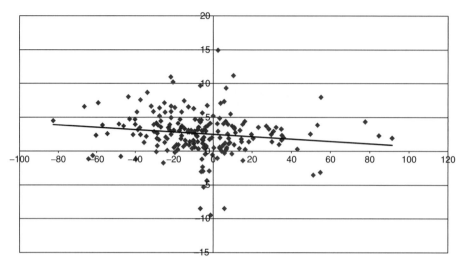

Figure 18   Devaluation of REER and agricultural growth.

leading to less (more) growth for the economy as a whole emerge only after controlling for other influences. But the figures help motivate the following discussion that tries to show the complexities involved.

Let's consider the agricultural margin per unit of product:

$$\text{Net margin (nominal)} = \text{Pag} - \text{Unitary costs}$$

where Pag is the agricultural price of a specific product at the farm level and unitary costs include both fixed and variable costs per unit of product.

In real terms, deflated by an appropriate domestic index PD:

$$\text{Net margin (real)} = \text{Pag/PD} - \text{Unitary costs/PD}$$

We can decompose Pag/PD in the following way (considering the product a tradable one, and abstracting from commercialization margins and other costs between farm level and world price at the border to simplify notation):

$$\text{Pag/PD} = (\text{Pag/PD})*[(\text{ER}*\text{Pagw})/(\text{ER}*\text{Pagw})]*(\text{PI/PI})$$
$$= [\text{Pag}/(\text{ER}*\text{Pagw})]*[(\text{ER}*\text{PI})/\text{PD}]*(\text{Pagw/PI})$$

where [Pag / (ER*Pagw)] is the coefficient of nominal protection (if the domestic price Pag is larger than the world price, Pagw, converted into domestic currency through the multiplication by the nominal exchange rate ER) or of taxation (if Pag < ER*Pagw); (ER*PI) / PD is the first definition of the real exchange rate, RER1, where PI is the price index of the foreign country. Finally, Pagw/PI is the world real price of the agricultural product.

A devaluation in the RER interact with and can be even more than compensated by adjustments in the coefficient of nominal protection/taxation; in PD (as discussed before); and by changes in world prices (which, if the country is a significant exporter, can be affected by the devaluation). Also, the devaluation can change unitary costs in both nominal and real terms, including the effect of more or less production on the average fixed costs per unit of product (for instance, if the devaluation reduces demand, as in the "stagflationary" scenarios, fixed costs may have to be dispersed over a smaller marketed amount, increasing the fixed unitary cost of sold production). Finally, devaluations could affect the commercialization costs and margins that were assumed away here.

Given the complexity of the general equilibrium effects, it is therefore not surprising that different studies offer diverging views on the relationship between the level and change of the RER and agricultural growth. Here only some of the literature is discussed as we try to show a sampling of analytical approaches and different countries.

Devaluations   Jensen, Robinson, and Tarp (2002), utilizing simulation techniques with computable general equilibrium models for a number of developing countries, found that modifications in RERs have diverse effects on relative agricultural price incentives, depending on specific country circumstances. In their simulations exchange rate depreciations improve agricultural price incentives significantly in five countries (Argentina, Brazil, Costa Rica, Malawi, and Zimbabwe), which have relatively large agricultural trade shares, whereas the same adjustment worsens relative agricultural price incentives in five other countries with very small agricultural trade shares, including poorer southern African countries with underdeveloped agricultural sectors (Mozambique, Tanzania, and Zambia) as well as Indonesia and Tunisia. For two other countries (Morocco and Mexico), relative agricultural price incentives appear to have been little affected. The differing relative impacts depend on relative trade shares of agriculture versus nonagricultural sectors, the import composition of those sectors, and relative elasticities of import demand and export supply. An exchange rate appreciation (i.e., a decline in Pt/Pnt) generally leads to (1) lower internal terms–of–trade for export goods, (2) lower protection for import-competing goods, and (3) lower input costs for production sectors using imported inputs. In most of the countries in this study, the combined impact of the terms-of-trade and protection channels dominated the input cost channel. This implies that exchange rate appreciation generally worsens relative price incentives for the most intensively traded sector, whereas exchange rate depreciation generally improves relative price incentives for the most intensively traded sector, which might or might not be agriculture, depending on the country. Bilginsoy

(1997) also finds, in a two-sector model of terms-of-trade determination for Turkey, that devaluation turns the terms of trade against the agricultural sector mainly because of cost-push factors in the industrial sector.

Diaz-Bonilla and Schamis (2001) analyze the differential contractive effects of devaluations in the case of Argentina before and after 1978, when the capital account was open, using VAR analyses for the period 1955–1997. During the period before 1978, with the capital account closed, the government maintained a fixed exchange regime, and the parity was adjusted from time to time through devaluations. VARs covering 1955–1977 (the traditional period of import substitution industrialization) show that devaluations had a small and statistically not significant negative impact on total GDP growth, a negative impact on industrial production (for up about two or three years), and a positive impact on agriculture. However, VARs since 1978 suggest that the recessionary impacts of devaluations on the GDP and industry are larger and statistically significant after 1978, also affecting the agricultural sector, which shows statistically significant declines the first year. It appears that during the period before 1978, devaluations could be utilized to restore relative prices, and that after the initial negative impact the economy began to grow again. But after opening the capital account in 1978, the responses to devaluations have been deeper and longer declines in economic activity, also affecting agriculture.

The authors discuss several reasons for the different behavior in both periods: Devaluations cut real wages before 1978, whereas after that year, real wages appear to have become more rigid, limiting the positive supply-side impact that upward adjustments of the nominal exchange rate might have had on external competitiveness. Then only the negative impact of devaluations on GDP growth through other channels were left, such as the increase in costs of imported intermediate inputs (affecting agricultural supply) and/or a banking crisis, leading to sharp declines in deposits and credit (which would affect both aggregate supply and demand total and for agriculture). The conclusion was that with the capital account open, devaluations, although improving the incentives for the tradable agricultural sector (exports and import substitutes), also have affected overall GDP growth and domestic real wages and incomes (at least in the short run), depressing demand for agricultural goods in general but especially nontradables, also constraining agricultural supply.

However, Figures 17 and 18 consider five-year averages, and therefore the contractionary short-term effects should be less relevant.[87] Also, the paper was written before the 2001–2002 crisis in Argentina, when, after several years of price stability in the 1990s and a long recession that began in 1998, Argentina's economy appear to have reacted the 2002 devaluation with a combination of pre- and post-1978 behaviors, showing a deep recession that affected all sectors but also reductions in real wages and a sharp growth rebound for all tradable activities, including agriculture (Cicowiez et al, 2008).

RER in levels   So far we have discussed devaluations, which usually take place in a short period of time. Other studies analyze appreciations, misalignments, and other issues of the RER in levels, which can require more time to develop. For instance, Homem de Melo (1999), in the case of Brazil, finds that the appreciation of the exchange rate during the period 1989–1997, particularly during the Real Plan, decreased relative prices received by the producers but that despite this fact, total production increased somewhat and the reduction in the per capita production was not significant, because other factors compensated for the negative impact of the overvaluation of the exchange rate, such as increases in international prices of primary products during 1994–1997, reductions in the prices of inputs used in the agricultural sector (in part related to the appreciation of the Brazilian currency), and considerable improvements in productivity.[88] Mendoza Bellido (1994) finds, more conventionally, that Perú's stabilization program under the Fujimori Administration, which, among other things led to the appreciation of the real exchange rate and declines in real wages, explain, to a great extent, the crisis of Peruvian agriculture at that time. Lamb (2000), in a panel estimation of supply functions for 14 African countries during the period 1975–1990, finds that the level of the (log) RER (defined as PD / (ER * PI), and therefore an increase is an appreciation) is inversely correlated with the log of total agricultural output (i.e., it is not growth but the total quantity), after controlling for other factors such as rainfall. The coefficients, which are statistically significant, suggest that each 1% of appreciation in the RER is associated with *total* output decreases of between 0.17% and 0.29%.

Other influences   The decomposition of Pag / PD has shown the influence of world prices on farmers' incentives and, therefore, on agricultural growth in developing countries (see, for instance, the results for Brazil in Homem de Melo, 1999). However, the simple scattered diagrams in Figures 17 and 18 do not consider the evolution of world agricultural prices. We have already shown that world agricultural prices declined significantly in real terms during the 1980s, which in several countries might have compensated for the improvements in incentives for the agricultural sector that devaluations in the RER generated. In fact, if only the 1990s are considered, when real world agricultural prices settle at a lower level (see Figure 8), the link between RERs and growth strengthens somewhat (see Figure 19).

Regional differences   There are also clear differences between regions, with LAC's agricultural growth appearing more responsive to the level of the RER than Africa's or Asia's. Taking a simple linear regression between agricultural growth and the level of RERs for the period 1990–2002 in each region and evaluating the respective elasticities at the average of the samples give values of approximately −1.4 for LAC, −0.7 for Africa, and −0.2 for Asia.[89] It is mentioned elsewhere in this chapter that LAC shows greater integration in world agricultural markets, whereas Asia's agricultural ratios of

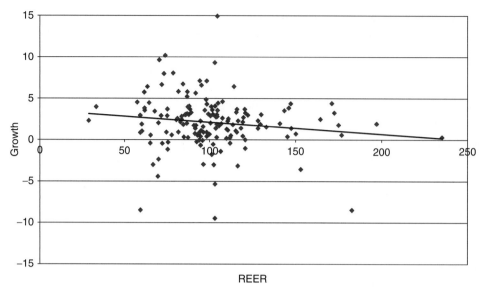

Figure 19   REER and agricultural growth, 1990–2002.

exports and imports over production are smaller than other regions, making them less affected by world prices. Also, several Asian countries seem to apply other policies of support and protection for the agricultural sector that can separate its performance from the evolution of the RERs.

Equilibrium exchange rates and misalignments   Figure 17 and estimates of agricultural output against actual RERs in levels operate as though there were "appropriate" values for such RER that do not change across countries and over time. A different approach is to ask what would be the equilibrium exchange rate and to evaluate the impact of the difference with the actual ER (the degree of misalignment) on agriculture.

An application of the concept of misalignment and its impacts on agricultural supply is shown in Thiele (2002b). The study utilizes two measures of misalignment: first, the ratio between the parallel market exchange rate and the official exchange rate, and second, an estimate using pooled times-series and cross-section data for 35 SSA countries over the period 1975–1998. Both indicators suggest reductions in misalignments over the period (Thiele, 2002a). Those indicators are used in single-country equations where the (log of) agricultural production is the dependent variable, and in the LHS there are several variables, including the real domestic price of agriculture (the deflator of value added in agriculture divided by the consumer price index), the border price of aggregate tradable agriculture, the share of irrigated land in the total devoted to annual and permanent crops, the coefficient of nominal protection, the actual RER and the measures of misalignment mentioned. If the variables are nonstationary, cointegration equations are estimated. One or both measures of misalignment appear cointegrated with (log of) agricultural production in Cameroon, Ghana, Kenya, Malawi, and Tanzania. The regression for Kenya is not reported, and the sign of one of the misalignment indicators (the one estimated econometrically) has the wrong sign for Malawi (i.e., the increase in the misalignment appears to increase agricultural production). However, the black-market premium, the other misalignment indicator for Malawi, shows the right sign.[90] Furthermore, the equations for Cameroon, Ghana, and Tanzania show that reductions in the misalignment, in one or both definitions, increase agricultural production. On the other hand, there are countries for which the indicators of misalignment do not appear cointegrated with agricultural production.

"Commodity currencies"   So far we have been discussing the impact of exchange rate regimes, policy actions, and trends on the agricultural sector. A different line of inquiry relates to the impact of world prices of commodities, which affect the terms of trade of developing countries, and the behavior of the real exchange rate in those countries. During the 1980s there were some studies on the terms of trade and the real exchange rate in Latin America (Edwards, 1989) and, more recently, on commodity-exporting developed countries such as Australia, Canada, and New Zealand. Cashin, Cespedes, and Sahay (2002) extended the analysis to 58 commodity-exporting countries (including five industrial countries) for the period January 1980 to March 2002. These countries (including the industrialized ones) depend on commodity exports for more than 50% (and in several developing countries, particularly those in SSA, the share exceeds 80%), and, in many cases, a single product dominates those exports. They asked two main questions: first, whether real commodity prices and real exchange rates move together, and second, whether the exchange regime affects a country's ability to cope with commodity price swings.

Cashin et al. (2002) found a stable, long-run relationship between a country's real exchange rate and the real price of its commodity exports (i.e., both variables were cointegrated) in 22 of the 58 countries, with SSA countries representing half of them. For those countries with "commodity currencies," more than 80% of the variation in the real exchange rate is explained, on average, by changes in real commodity prices. The elasticity of the real exchange rates to commodity prices ranged between 0.2 and 0.4, with a median of 0.38 (i.e., a 10% drop in the real price of the exported commodity was associated with a 3.8% depreciation of the real exchange rate of the country considered).

Furthermore, Cashin et al. (2002) found that for the commodity-currency countries the variability of the real exchange rate was similar across the various nominal exchange rate regimes (which they categorized using the Reinhart-Rogoff classification and the IMF *de jure* classification). In other words, it was the nature of real shocks to the economy that determined the behavior of real exchange rates, not the type of nominal exchange rate regime, whether more rigid pegs, limited flexibility or managed regimes, or flexible floats.

Therefore, they recommend that commodity-exporting developing countries should analyze the effects of commodity price movements on exchange rates and use that information as a guide for the conduct of monetary and exchange rate policies. This means considering commodity prices in both the design of inflation-targeting arrangements and evaluating whether exchange rates have deviated excessively from their equilibrium value.

In this last regard Frankel (2005) has gone further than acknowledging the link between RER and commodity prices, and suggested, as normative policy, that countries specializing in a mineral or agricultural export commodity (or commodities) should peg their currency to the prices of that commodity (or commodities). He calls the policy "pegging to the export price index" (PEPI), and it would target a representative basket of export commodities for that country (which is different from a generic world commodity standard). That approach would provide both adjustment to trade shocks and a nominal anchor. Frankel argues that this nominal anchor has benefits over others such as the CPI utilized in inflation targeting. The argument is that when export prices fall, the local currency should depreciate against the dollar, and PEPI achieves that result, whereas CPI targeting does not. If import prices rise, Frankel argues that CPI inflation targeting leads to a tightening of monetary policy, which would appreciate the currency. This seems to be the wrong reaction to a deterioration of the terms of trade and most likely would exacerbate movements in trade and output. PEPI would not lead to the necessary devaluation, but it would avoid the counterproductive appreciation. He argues that monetary policy should tighten when export prices go up (as PEPI would do) and not when import prices increase (as would be the case under CPI inflation targeting).

Volatility in ER   So far we have discussed the link between levels of exchange rate and growth. A related issue is the impact of exchange rate variability. Various studies have shown the negative impact of exchange rate variability on production and exports in general. For instance, Bleaney and Greenaway (2001) analyze the impact on investment and growth of the level and volatility of the terms of trade and the real effective exchange rate in a panel of 14 sub-Saharan African countries over 1980–1995. Growth is negatively affected by terms of trade instability, and investment by real exchange rate instability. More specifically in the case of agriculture, Cho, Sheldon, and McCorriston (2002) utilize a sample of bilateral trade flows across 10 developed countries between 1974 and 1995 and, using a gravity model, find that after controlling for other factors, real exchange rate uncertainty has had a significant negative effect on agricultural trade over this period and that the negative impact of uncertainty has been more significant for agricultural trade than for other sectors.

Table 23 Volatility of REER, 1980–early 2000s

	Average	Median
1980–1984	0.14	0.08
1985–1989	0.25	0.15
1990–1994	0.14	0.12
1995–1999	0.09	0.08
Early 2000s	0.06	0.04

Source: Calculated by the authors from Cashin et al. (2002).

Table 23 shows the change in volatility over five-year periods for the 57 developing countries reported in Cashin et al. (2002; measured as the standard deviation for the period divided by the average for the same period). After increasing in the late 1980s and early 1990s, it seems to have decreased visibly in the late 1990s and early 2000s. This should have been positive for agricultural production.

4.4.5 Dutch Disease

There is a great deal of literature on the so-called *Dutch disease*, beginning with Corden and Neary (1982). Initially it was linked to developments in the Netherlands during the 1960s and 1970s, where the discovery in 1959 of large deposits of gas led to increased energy exports that put upward pressure on the guilder and the wage rate and appeared to lead to declines in other tradable sectors, particularly industry. Later the idea was generalized to refer to the general phenomenon of a booming productive sector that leads to larger exports and appreciated domestic currencies, which negatively affects other tradable sectors and, eventually, the whole economy if the contracting sectors were important sources of productivity growth (perhaps through learning by doing, as in van Wijnbergen, 1984) and the expanding one was mainly a resource-based activity with limited spillover effects. Cases of Dutch disease in agriculture have been documented as in the examples of oil in Indonesia (Timmer, 1994) or copper in Zambia (Lofgren, Robinson and Thurlow, 2002). The booming sector associated with Dutch disease, although in many cases has been mineral or energy production, could be anything, including a subsector of the agricultural sector, as in the case of coffee in Colombia studied by Kamas (1986). By extension, the concept has also been utilized to refer to the effect of various capital inflows (such as official aid, foreign direct investment, remittances, and others) on the appreciation of the real exchange rate and the decline of tradable sectors (see, for instance, IMF, 2005).

The policy issues have also been extensively discussed. The main distinction is whether the boom is considered temporary or permanent. If it is temporary, the best approach is to try to stabilize incomes and the exchange rate through a public stabilization fund created through some form of taxation of excess revenues. If the boom is permanent, governments would have to help manage the structural transformation—for example, by investing part of the additional revenues in various productivity-enhancing measures such as investments in infrastructure, technology, and human capital. It is clear that, over time, different countries managed differently the episodes of their newly acquired wealth, with different impacts on agriculture. For instance, Usui (1997) argued that there have been important differences between Indonesia and Mexico in their policy adjustments to the oil boom of the 1970s, especially in their fiscal, foreign debt, and exchange rate policies, as well as in the use of oil revenues to invest in strengthening the affected tradable sectors. Indonesia appears to have managed its wealth more conservatively and invested more heavily in nonbooming tradable sectors, avoiding the "resource curse" better than Mexico. If the newly acquired riches are managed properly, the notion of additional wealth as a "disease" does not seem appropriate.

Raju and Melo (2003), focusing on Colombia, show, using a vector error correction (VEC) model, that coffee price shocks have exerted an important influence on money growth, inflation, and real exchange rates, in line with the predictions of traditional Dutch disease models, but also, and differing from other hypotheses, coffee booms resulted in positive long-run output effects, which reduce both current account and government deficits. They conclude that the term *Dutch disease* is a misnomer and that, at least in the case of Colombia, coffee booms helped strengthen internal and external balances.

At least as relevant for low-income developing countries as the management of potential commodity booms is the issue of foreign aid and remittances. Rajan and Subramanian (2006) find that foreign aid is associated with overvaluation of the real exchange rate in their sample of developing countries, with negative effects on the growth rate of exporting industries, particularly labor intensive. Remittances, on the other hand, do not seem to lead to the same effects (they conjecture that this is so in part because of the nature of the goods and factors on which remittances are spent and, in part, because countries that *already* have appreciated exchange rates appear to receive less flows of remittances). In "agriculture-based" and "transition" countries, which receive the largest amounts of foreign aid as percentages of their GDPs, it is then crucial to ensure that those flows are invested in programs that raise the productivity of tradable sectors, such as transportation, communication, and productive infrastructure, technology, and human capital, so as to outweigh the negative impact of the potential overvaluation (IMF, 2005).

4.5 Trade policies
4.5.1 Background
International trade policies, through measures such as taxes and subsidies to exports and imports, the establishment of quotas and prohibitions to import or to export, and other measures that affect the level and composition of the international

transactions, obviously have a very important impact on the macroeconomic conditions of a country and on the operation of the agricultural sector. For the analysis of these and other policy measures, a perspective of general macroeconomic balances must always be adopted. Using a simplified version of Eq. 1 from national accounts and rearranging terms, the absorption equation can be utilized to highlight some general aspects of macroeconomic balances:

$$GDP - (C + I + G) = GDP - A = X - IM$$

where (C + I + G) is called *domestic absorption* (A).

Attempts to substitute imports by, say, protecting the industrial sector (such as raising import taxes, imposing quotas, and similar measures) diminish imports (IM), which is the desired effect. But this policy will be successful only if it changes the balance between GDP and domestic absorption, which would most likely require additional policies. If that balance does not change, that means that X must diminish to fulfill the accounting equation *ex-post*. If the exportable products are basically agricultural products, they would be the component of the economy that suffers the impact of the policy of substitution of industrial imports. This is the usual argument in the literature related to the "bias against agriculture," which is normally presented in a partial equilibrium setting. But it is also simple to show in a more general framework using the preceding equation.

The main point is that any attempt to correct the balance between X and IM by means of a reduction of IM, without adjusting the balance between the GDP and A, is going to leave the balance between X and IM unchanged but at lower levels of international trade (the country becomes more closed). Vice versa, if the goal is to improve the balance of external payments, the way to do it is to increase the internal production (through capital accumulation and the utilization of idle factors of production) or to reduce domestic absorption, or a combination of both.

The accounting equation also serves to consider other measures such as, for example, a proposal to lower the taxes to agricultural exports as a way to increase production and exports of the sector. As mentioned, the final impact will depend on how the rest of the macro variables adjust. One aspect is the effect of the decrease in taxes on the public budget: the fiscal deficit could diminish, stay the same, or increase, depending on the answer of the agricultural production and exports. And if the reduction of export taxes turns out to be a net loss of fiscal income, the final impact of the measure will depend on how that budget gap is covered: with other taxes, with cuts in expenses, with monetary emission, or with greater public indebtedness. Another aspect is how the tax cut may affect consumption (C) and investment (I). The net effect on additional exports (total, and not only the agricultural exports for which taxes were reduced) will depend on the general equilibrium balance indicated in the absorption equation (see Cicowiez et al., 2008).

4.5.2 Trends in trade policies

Over recent decades, developing countries have been opening up their economies, reducing the levels of tariffs and reducing or eliminating other measures that limit trade, including, as discussed before, export taxes (see the discussion in the fiscal section).

Looking at the import side, Table 24 shows unweighted tariffs for a sample of countries.[91] Except for Middle East and North Africa, which have somewhat increased the levels of protection, for the rest of the regions the tariffs in the early 2000s are 40% to 70% lower than during the 1980s. LAC and East Asia and Pacific show the smaller tariff levels (around 10%). The largest cut has been in South Asia, which reduced tariffs from 60–70% to somewhat less than 20%.

A more precise way of gauging this decline in protection is to look at the import tax revenues as percentages of total imports. Table 25 presents WTO data on those percentages for some individual countries. It is clear that except for Brazil, the collection of import duties as a percentage of total imports has declined significantly in those countries. In the case of India, although the percentage has been reduced by more than half, it is still far higher than the rest of the countries in Table 23.

Table 24   Unweighted tariffs (median for a sample of countries), 1980s–early 2000s

	1980s	1990s	Early 2000s
SSA			
Average	28.3	21.5	16.4
Median	29.5	21.3	15.6
LAC			
Average	25.5	13.5	10.3
Median	20.4	13.3	11.2
East Asia Pacific			
Average	27.0	19.5	10.2
Median	29.2	17.8	8.6
South Asia			
Average	62.3	34.8	19.1
Median	72.2	37.8	18.6
MENA			
Average	24.5	25.5	25.7
Median	23.5	28.3	27.5

Source: World Bank, WITS.

Table 25   Ratio of import duties collected as percentage of total imports by selected developing countries, 1985–2000

	1985–1989	1990–1994	1995–2000
China	10.3	4.7	3.2
Mexico	5.2	5.7	2.0
Republic of Korea	8.0	5.3	3.6
Chinese Taipei	7.1	4.9	3.5
Malaysia	6.4	4.0	2.3
Thailand	11.3	9.0	5.0
Brazil	8.2	8.1	8.0
India	54.8	38.4	24.5
Indonesia	5.2	5.0	2.4
South Africa	6.6	4.4	3.8

Source: WTO from IMF, government finance statistics, and various issues and national statistics.

4.5.3 Trade and agricultural goods: Trends in protection

Tables 24 and 25 show averages for all goods. But what is the situation for agricultural products? The conventional wisdom circa late 1980s was that industrial protection in developing countries was larger than for agricultural products, imparting an anti-agricultural bias to overall incentives (World Bank, 1986; Krueger, Schiff, and Valdés, 1988; Bautista and Valdés, 1993). More recent data, however (see Table 26), do not show that pattern. Rather, the opposite holds: Agriculture (considering both primary and processed) seems, on average, more protected than industry (including textiles and apparels) in developing countries.

The imbalances are particularly large in MENA, with important levels of protection for agriculture.

In line with these results, recent estimates of the nominal rate of assistance (NRA) for agriculture in developing countries presented in Anderson and Valenzuela (2008)[92] show that such assistance has been growing in developing countries, turning positive since the mid-1990s. The improvements in NRA in those countries have been both the result of more protection for importables (i.e., a growing $NRA > 0$) and less taxation for exportables (a decline in the absolute value of the tax, as $NRA < 0$; see Figure 20).

Table 26   Average protection applied by various importing regions (%)

Product	Asian NICs	China	South Asia	Transition Economies	Sub-Saharan Africa	Middle East and North Africa	Latin America	Western Europe	North America	Japan	Rest of the World
Natural resources	2.3	1.9	14.1	1.3	4.9	4	4.9	0	0.2	0	4.5
Primary agriculture	37.7	15.5	20.6	12.6	16.3	48.7	12.4	12.1	8.5	30	6.3
Processed agriculture	20.2	15.4	29.4	19.7	26.9	57.8	16.5	20.9	10	46	12.5
Textiles and apparel	8	12.9	27.5	13.5	20.5	13.4	14.7	5.1	10.3	6	14.2
Other manufactures	4.8	6.1	23.8	8.8	10.9	8	10.7	1.9	1.3	0.3	9.2

Source: UNCTAD (2002).

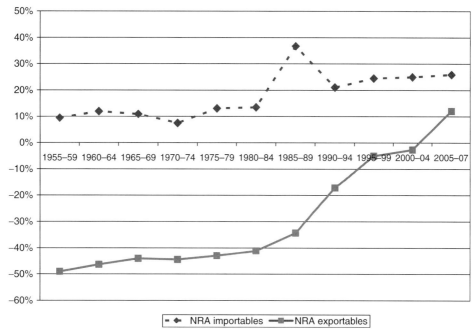

Figure 20 NRA for importables and exportables in developing countries, 1955–2004. Source: Anderson and Valenzuela, 2008.

4.5.4 Agricultural protection, poverty, and food security

The current debate in several developing countries and civil society in the context of the ongoing Doha trade negotiations is whether increased protection will help reduce poverty and increase food security in developing countries. Some proposals implicitly or explicitly suggest taxing consumers in developing countries through higher levels of border protection, to support agricultural producers as a way of reducing poverty and promoting food security. Sometimes this suggestion is accompanied by the argument that such protection "does not cost money" and is easier to implement in poor countries than options considered in the Green Box, such as agricultural research and extension. Both arguments are debatable. First, protection costs money. Contrary to the common perception of protection as a tax paid by foreigners and collected by governments, much of the (implicit) tax is paid by domestic consumers and collected privately by producers in the form of higher prices. This tax on food has an obvious negative impact on poor households, which in many developing countries spend more than half their incomes on food (FAO, 1993), and is mainly received by bigger agricultural producers with larger quantities of products to sell. Landless rural workers, poor urban households, and many poor small farmers tend to be net buyers of food (see

FAO, 1999). At the same time, it is also important to note the steady shift in the locus of poverty in developing countries, where food insecurity and malnutrition are moving from rural to urban areas (Ruel, Haddad, and Garrett, 1999; Haddad, Ruel, and Garrett, 1999; and Garrett and Ruel, 2000). Urbanization in developing countries is posing new questions regarding economic and social policies in general and in relation to the impact of trade and trade policies on poverty and food security.

Certainly a government may try to compensate consumers through food subsidies, but they can become a heavy budgetary burden.[93] For instance, during the second half of the 1990s Morocco has been spending about 1.7–2.4% of the GDP in food subsidies (IMF, 2001), in part trying to compensate for the higher prices generated by trade protection. At the same time, simulations of alternative uses of water in Morocco showed that protection of certain crops was drawing the use of that scarce resource toward protected products while the value of agricultural production measured at world prices would increase if protection were reduced and water were reallocated to other crops (Diao, Roe, and Doukkali, 2002). Moreover, concentration of production in some protected crops seems to have increased the vulnerability of the agriculture to droughts and made the whole economy more volatile (World Bank, 2001). Finally, more expensive food may be putting upward pressure on wages, affecting various manufacturing sectors in which Morocco may otherwise have had comparative advantages. If the dynamic export sector is manufactures, the maintenance of competitiveness in the latter without reducing real wages may require a reduction, and not an increase, in the cost of food. However, this should be achieved through investments in agriculture and not forcing the terms of trade against agriculture.

Special and differential treatment in the form of protection at the level of staple crops considered relevant for food security, or for other reasons, is not necessarily the most effective and equitable way to address problems of poverty and hunger. Instead, poor countries need adequate policies that operate at the household and individual levels. Investments should be targeted to the poor and vulnerable rather than to protect and subsidize crops in general, which usually benefits larger farmers. More generally, to the extent that protection is a "privatized" tax, there is always the question of whether those funds can be collected explicitly by the government and put to better uses. For instance, Diaz-Bonilla, Diao, and Robinson (2004) simulate those two alternatives in a world model. In the first scenario there is an arbitrary increase in protection on food security crops (assumed to be grains in the simulations) only in those countries that supported the concept of a development or food security box. In the second scenario, the governments in those countries collect, through an explicit tax, the equivalent of the implicit consumption tax privately collected through protection and then invest that amount in agricultural research and development (R&D). The increase in agricultural protection results for those countries in a negative effect on GDP and employment, and there is less consumption of food products, suggesting that food security declines with increased protection. An increase in investment in agricultural

R&D financed by an equivalent tax calculated from the first scenario shows increases in GDP, employment, agricultural production, and consumption, including, particularly, food items. Also, agricultural trade among developing countries, including those applying the higher levels of protection, declines in this simulation, suggesting that such policies may hurt South/South agricultural trade.

Although high and permanent agricultural protection is not the answer for addressing poverty and hunger concerns in developing countries, there are other aspects that must be considered in analyzing the liberalization of agricultural and trade policies in those countries. One is the presence of high levels of protection and subsidization in industrialized countries that survived changes during the Uruguay Round. There are certainly imbalances in the AoA, because industrialized countries have been able to secure exemptions for some of their policies (such as the Blue Box) and were allowed to continue using significant amounts of expenditures for domestic support and export subsidies. Under some proposals by WTO members, those asymmetries may continue even after the Doha Round. Developing countries, though pressing for a substantial reduction of those subsidies and protection in rich countries, are also rightly requesting some trade instruments to defend themselves during the transition period to a less asymmetric situation. In addition, food-insecure and vulnerable countries need (1) longer transition times that must be utilized to implement adequate rural development and poverty alleviation strategies and (2) simplified and streamlined instruments to confront import surges that could irreparably damage the livelihoods of small farmers. The latter point is linked to the fact that the poor are more vulnerable to crises. Long-lasting damage to their already low levels of human and physical capital may occur; crises may force poor families to sell productive assets, increase the possibility of illness, or have their children drop out of school (see, for instance, Addison and Demery, 1989, Lipton and Ravallion, 1995). Therefore, the concerns raised by developing countries regarding the presence of significant distortions in world markets and the need to protect vulnerable groups from negative shocks are important issues that need to be addressed.

4.5.5 Production and import tax differentials

Within the WTO and some regional trade agreements such as NAFTA there has been some debate over whether the "export tax differential" should be considered a subsidy and therefore subject to disciplines. The argument is that to the extent that this trade intervention reduces the domestic price of the primary product below the world price, it acts as a subsidy to the industry that uses that product as an input. As usual, the impact must be analyzed in a general equilibrium context. For instance, Hudson and Ethridge (1999) argue that Pakistan's export tax on raw cotton from 1988–1995 (aimed at benefiting the domestic yarn industry) had a negative impact on the growth rate in the cotton sector while not increasing the growth rate of yarn production above what would have occurred naturally.

Countries using export taxes have also argued that the "export tax differential" is only a defense to counter the mirror image of the "import tax differential" or tariff escalation by which countries that do not produce the primary product tax the processed imported product at a higher rate to favor industrialization in their own territory.

The practice of imposing high import taxes on processed goods and low or no tariffs on primary products places agroindustrial production in the primary producing countries (PPCs) at considerable disadvantage, strongly tilting their export profile toward raw materials (Balassa and Michalopoulos, 1986). As an example, assume, for instance, that PPCs can sell raw material or processed products at world exogenous prices. Assume also that the cost structure for the agroindustry is such that the raw material amounts to 60% of the total value of the processed good, another 20% is spent in other cost items except factors of production, and 20% is value added. Assume then that the raw material, produced by a primary producing country, is imported by a nonproducer with zero tariffs but that the processed product faces an import tariff of 10%, and transport costs add 5% to the world price of the raw material. Finally, assume that the agroindustry in the nonproducing country has the same basic cost structure except for trade taxes and transport costs. Then nonproducing countries, even though the basic technology is the same and they have to absorb transport costs, still have a value-added margin 35% larger than the PPCs (27 cents on the dollar for nonproducing against 20 cents in PPCs).[94] This implies that the factors of production in the PPCs will be paid less, probably discouraging the processing of the raw material in those developing countries.

Golub and Finger (1979), in one of the early studies that quantitatively analyzed the issue of tariff escalation for some manufactured products, including only coffee and cocoa from the food sector, found that the removal of such escalation would lead to the reallocation of some processing of agricultural products from industrialized to developing countries and that there were nontrivial increases in export revenues from processed cocoa and coffee exports. Although this characteristic of the tariff structure has diminished somewhat after the Uruguay Round, significant levels of tariff escalation still remain after the implementation of the Uruguay Round (Lindland, 1997; OECD, 1997). The fact that even in the 2000s, industrialized countries dominate or are important players in world trade of cocoa and coffee processed products (when they do not produce the raw material) is a testament to the impact of tariff escalation.

4.6 Where have all the biases gone?

The previous sections discussed different general equilibrium implications of macroeconomic policies, including but going beyond the issue of *relative prices* between agriculture and nonagricultural sectors, which was the focus of much of the early work on macroeconomics and agriculture. As discussed in previous sections, this chapter has also tried to consider "quantity" issues (such as aggregate demand), other important macroprices, and the impact of macroeconomic policies on inputs to agricultural production, to determine *relative profitability* across sectors.

Still, the issue of relative prices and incentives is an important one and deserves a separate discussion. Schultz (1964) showed that, as their counterpart in rich countries, farmers in developing countries react to price incentives within the constraints they face. Also, it has been long recognized that *individual* agricultural products react to relative prices, whereas a more debated issue has been the *aggregate* supply response to price incentives. There are very different estimates of the price elasticity of aggregate supply, depending on the time horizon considered (with short-term elasticities being obviously smaller), the variables included as conditioning factors in the equation, the methodologies utilized, and so on (see reviews in Mamingi, 1996; Schiff and Montenegro, 1997; Mundlak, Larson and Butzer, 1997 and 2008). We are not going to review the debate here. It suffices to note that, in general, the consensus is, in line with Schultz's main contention, that agricultural supply is responsive to relative prices[95] within the constraints faced by the producer (such as access to infrastructure, ownership of physical and human capital, land and natural resource base, access to credit, available technology, marketing structures, governance institutions, and weather conditions) and that the price elasticity of supply increases when longer horizons are taken.

Here we briefly review the evolution of relative prices for agriculture, taking as a starting point the already mentioned studies (mostly covering the period from the 1960s to the mid-1980s) that analyzed the direct and indirect effects of trade, exchange rate, and other macroeconomic policies on price incentives for agriculture (Krueger, Schiff, and Valdés, 1988; Schiff and Valdés, 1992a and 1992b). The focus was basically on the relative price between agricultural and nonagricultural sectors (or agriculture versus industry) in the whole economy. As discussed before, those studies argued that there was a price bias against agriculture (which was even referred to as the "plundering" of agriculture in developing countries (Schiff and Valdés, 1992b), mainly as a consequence of the trade and exchange rate policies followed by many developing countries, in particular those that privileged industrialization over agricultural development.

More recently this literature has been criticized for probably overstating the calculated bias for several reasons (Jensen, Robinson, and Tarp, 2002): (1) the studies relied on a partial equilibrium modeling methodology that misses intersectoral linkages and feedback effects from changes in incomes and relative prices as well the determination of the nominal and real exchange rates; (2) the reliance on *nominal* protection rates ignored potentially important relative price incentive effects due to differences in relative input cost structures between agricultural and nonagricultural production; and (3) they assumed that domestic agricultural products and world market goods are perfect substitutes and that essentially all agricultural goods are traded.

Jensen et al. (2002) ran simulations to measure the level of agricultural bias in a similar sample of countries. In contrast with KSV and SV, their work considers imperfect substitutions between domestic and world market goods as well as general equilibrium effects. The computable general equilibrium framework allows the direct computation of *value-added* prices under various policy scenarios, which measure resource pulls in factor markets and provide a theoretically appropriate measure of *effective* rates of protection (as opposed to nominal ones). They also consider marketing margins in a general equilibrium perspective. Their simulations measure the impact of tax and tariff structures (including stylized versions of an import substitution industrialization, or ISI, strategy) as well as the impact of eliminating current account deficits and surpluses and the resulting appreciation/depreciation of the exchange rate. The impact on relative price incentives is measured by the proportional difference between (1) an agricultural value-added price index and (2) a nonagricultural value-added price index.

An important issue of the simulations in a general equilibrium context is to specify the macroeconomic closure rules, an issue that cannot be addressed in partial equilibrium models. The simulations in Jensen et al. (2002) are carried out using a macro closure that assumes no major swings in macro aggregates in response to external shocks.[96]

In contrast to earlier findings that policies in many developing countries imparted a major incentive bias against agriculture, Jensen et al. find that in their sample during the 1990s, the economywide system of indirect taxes, including tariffs and export taxes, significantly discriminated against agriculture in only one country, was largely neutral in five, provided a moderate subsidy to agriculture in four, and strongly favored agriculture in five. Earlier work found that overvaluation of the exchange rate would generally hurt agriculture, which was assumed to be largely tradable. In a general equilibrium setting, the impact of changes in the exchange rate on relative agriculture/nonagriculture incentives depends crucially on relative trade shares. If a current account deficit of 3% of absorption is considered to be the proper level of sustainability,[97] the combination of exchange rate and tax policy generated a significant bias against agriculture bias in only two sample countries (Malawi and Zimbabwe), whereas seven showed significant agricultural protection. The net effect in the remaining six was small. Although the issue of determining a sustainable current account is controversial, the previous analysis indicates that tax and exchange rate policies during the 1990s had more complex impacts than those assumed in partial equilibrium analysis.

The sample included six countries that were also part of the comparative World Bank study led by Krueger, Schiff, and Valdés (1988): Argentina, Brazil, Egypt, Korea, Morocco, and Zambia. The results indicate that there are very limited signs of anti-agricultural bias in these countries in the 1990s. Whereas the estimated level of agricultural protection in Korea in the Bank studies resembles results in Jensen et al. (2002), findings of strong levels of anti-agricultural bias in Argentina, Brazil, Egypt, Morocco, and Zambia are not borne out by the general equilibrium analysis.

The second part of the simulations by Jensen et al. (2002) indicates that traditional ISI-type policies, including nonagricultural import tariffs, agricultural export taxes, and overvalued exchange rates, can affect relative price incentives in strongly divergent directions, depending on country-specific characteristics. The impact of agricultural export taxes on relative overall agricultural price incentives depends strongly on agricultural export shares and rarely exceeds 2% for the majority of countries for which agricultural export shares are small. In contrast, the impact of nonagricultural import tariffs was found to depend strongly on relative agricultural trade shares and the impact of real exchange rate appreciation induced by the introduction of pervasive tariffs.

In sum, Jensen et al. (2002) argue that the partial-equilibrium measures used in earlier studies tended to overstate the price bias against agriculture. Their analysis, however, can also be interpreted as suggesting that whatever *price bias* there was to begin with, was reduced or eliminated during the 1990s, through all the changes in exchange rate, fiscal, monetary, and trade policies documented in previous sections (including structural adjustment programs with international organizations). It must be noted again that there may be other biases, such as the general *urban bias* in investments suggested by Lipton, 1977.

In what follows, we look at two indicators of possible price biases: one uses nominal protection data (in the spirit of earlier studies) and another utilizes value added deflators (as in Jensen et al., 2002).

The data presented in Anderson and Valenzuela (2008) show that the nominal rate of assistance (NRA) for agriculture has been growing in developing countries while NRA for nonagricultural goods has been declining, with the relative rate of assistance (RRA)[98] showing a significant bias against agriculture during the 1960s, 1970s, and early 1980s but moving since then in favor of the agricultural sector and turning positive in the late 1990s and early 2000s (Figure 21).

Another possible indicator of relative prices is the ratio of the value added deflator for the agricultural sector and the equivalent deflator for the rest of the economy. In principle, national accounts measure outputs at basic prices or producer prices and

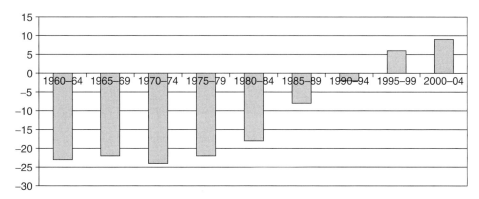

Figure 21   Relative rate of assistance in developing countries, 1960–2004.

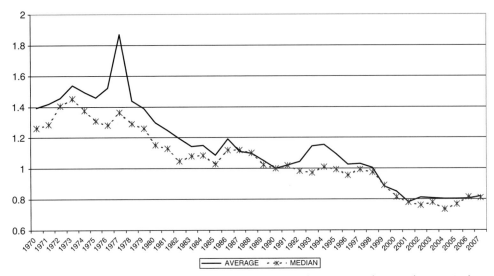

Figure 22   Latin America and the Caribbean ratio of price deflators: Agriculture and nonagriculture, 1970–2007.

measure inputs at purchaser prices, and therefore the ratio of value added deflators should reflect the proper incentives for a sector.[99] Figures 22, 23, and 24 show such ratio for countries in LAC, SSA, and Asia that have had national accounts since the 1970s from which to derive the indicators.[100] The calculation of the deflators was done in local currency units, dividing the value added in current values by the constant ones.

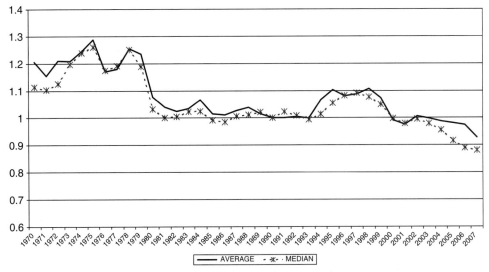

Figure 23   Asia ratio of price deflators: Agriculture and nonagriculture, 1970–2007.

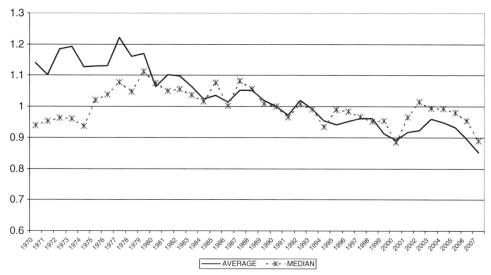

Figure 24   Sub-Saharan Africa ratio of price deflators: Agriculture and nonagriculture, 1970–2007.

Value added in the nonagricultural sector (constant and current) was calculated by subtracting agricultural valued added from total GDP. The figures show the annual average and the median for the countries in each region, from 1970 to 2007.

The figures show that the price of the value added in the agricultural sector was higher in relation to the rest of the economy during the period considered to show a bias against agriculture, and the ratio was declining during the subsequent decades, when that bias should have declined given the changes in policies. However, this trend can be seen simply as another manifestation of "Baumol's effect," with increasing costs in low-productivity activities, mostly in services and including government, which make up a good percentage of the nonagricultural sectors (see, for instance, Baumol and Towse, 1997).

Another way to look at relative prices is between agriculture and industry, which is also in line with the idea of "plundering" the former to help the latter. Figures 25, 26, and 27 show this perspective.

For LAC and SSA the pattern of the deflators of agricultural value added over industrial value added does not show a bias against agriculture during the 1970s when compared to subsequent decades. In the case of Asia, the ratio shows two cycles, but they do not seem to support the view of low relative prices for agriculture to favor import substitution industrialization in the 1970s. Figure 28 shows the same ratio for selected countries that have been considered representatives of the strategy of import substitution industrialization.[101] Again, at least considering the relative prices from value added, agriculture had a more favorable ratio during the 1970s than afterward.

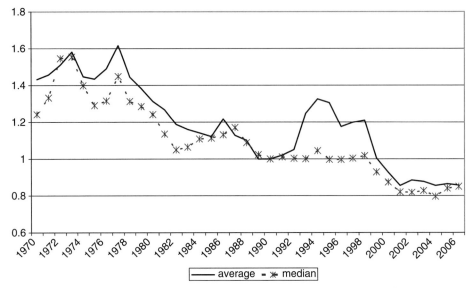

Figure 25   Latin America and the Caribbean ratio of deflators: Agriculture over industry, 1970–2007.

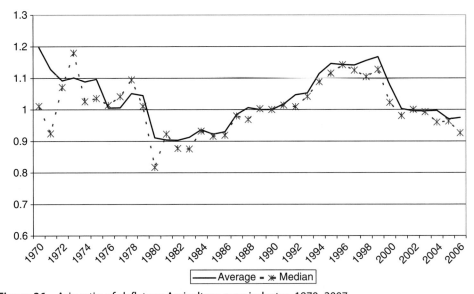

Figure 26   Asia ratio of deflators: Agriculture over industry, 1970–2007.

A possible interpretation is that, even if macroeconomic and trade policies favored industry in the 1970s, high world real prices for agricultural commodities during those years and sectoral policies that kept costs low for agriculture[102] resulted in relative prices for agriculture that were more favorable than in subsequent decades, when world prices declined and many of the favorable sectoral policies for the sector were

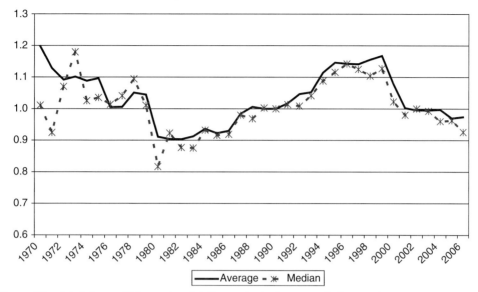

Figure 27   Sub-Saharan Africa: ratio of deflators: Agriculture over industry, 1970–2007.

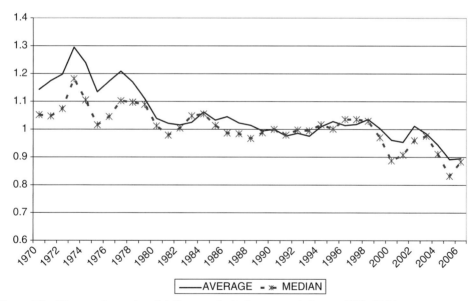

Figure 28   ISI countries, ratio of deflectors: Agriculture over industry, 1970–2006.

eliminated. In this context, ISI policies may be seen as a way of capturing part of those high world prices to support other sectors in the economy but in a context in which agriculture was also being benefitted by direct policies. Then, during the 1980s, with the start of the debt crisis and the decline in the world prices of commodities, many developing countries had to modify both ISI policies and agricultural policies in a way that, combined with the fall in world prices, led to declines in the relative price of agriculture (as measured by the deflators).

Another possible explanation (not necessarily incompatible with the previous comments) is that productivity change in the agricultural sector as a whole has been higher than in industry in developing countries during recent decades (Martin and Mitra, 1999).

In any case, given that the trends in the ratios of valued added do not seem to coincide with the trends in relative rates of protection discussed before, it should be important to determine empirically which one captures better the relative incentives to produce. In that exercise it should be recognized that, as it was discussed mainly in Section 1 and 3, besides relative prices, for agricultural production it also matters how the rest of the domestic economy is doing, what are the costs of inputs, the evolution of the world economy (for tradable agricultural goods), and so on. Analyzing only biases (measured by relative prices) may leave out important determinants of the performance of the agricultural sector in developing countries.

5. AGRICULTURAL PERFORMANCE AND MACROECONOMIC DEVELOPMENTS: OVERVIEW AND CONCLUSIONS

The previous sections discussed the significant changes in global macroeconomic conditions and domestic policies during recent decades. How were those changes reflected in the performance of agricultural production in developing countries? Here we take a brief look at this issue as a conclusion to the chapter. The approach is mostly descriptive, which we hope provides some overall perspectives that can be later analyzed in greater detail by interested researchers.

5.1 Production trends

Agricultural and food production, both total and per capita, have been steadily increasing in developing countries since the 1960s (see Tables 27 and 28). Total agricultural and food production more than tripled between early 1960s and early 2000s for developing countries as a whole, whereas, measured in per capita terms, the 2000s production levels are about 60% over the average of the 1960s. This has been in good measure the result of rapid technological change linked to the Green Revolution and capital investments (mainly irrigation). Agricultural area utilized, on the other hand, has not increased much (only about 10% between early 1960s and late 2000s). The main exception to this trend of production increases that outpaced population growth is Africa, particularly sub-Saharan Africa, where the levels of agricultural and food production per capita are below the 1960s levels.[103] The African decline in per capita production took place in the 1980s and has rebounded somewhat since then.[104]

Table 27 Indices of agricultural production (net), base, 1960s–2000s

	1960s	1970s	1980s	1990s	2000/04	Ratio 2000s/ 1960s	Ratio 2000s/ 1980s
Total							
Africa, developing	41.3	51.0	59.9	85.5	103.3	2.50	1.73
Africa, south of Sahara	42.3	52.3	60.4	85.4	102.8	2.43	1.70
Asia, developing	28.9	38.2	54.1	82.0	106.0	3.67	1.96
East and South East Asia	32.0	44.0	62.8	85.9	106.7	3.33	1.70
of which China	22.7	30.5	45.9	77.3	108.6	4.79	2.37
South Asia	35.2	44.6	59.6	85.2	101.9	2.90	1.71
Latin America and Caribbean	37.5	49.1	64.8	84.5	106.3	2.83	1.64
Developing countries	31.8	41.5	56.7	82.8	105.7	3.32	1.86
Developed countries Per capita	68.8	83.2	94.6	97.5	100.7	1.46	1.06
Africa, developing	105.2	101.6	90.8	97.4	98.7	0.94	1.09
Africa, south of Sahara	111.2	107.1	93.6	98.1	97.9	0.88	1.05
Asia, developing	56.8	60.0	70.7	88.6	103.2	1.82	1.46
East and South East Asia	64.2	70.2	82.4	93.2	103.8	1.62	1.26
of which China	39.3	42.5	55.2	81.0	107.0	2.72	1.94
South Asia	74.6	76.0	82.3	94.3	98.4	1.32	1.19
Latin America and Caribbean	77.8	80.1	85.6	91.9	103.2	1.33	1.21
Developing countries	65.3	67.9	75.8	90.3	102.5	1.57	1.35
Developed countries	88.1	97.5	103.4	99.8	100.0	1.14	0.97

Source: FAOSTAT.

While Tables 27 and 28 show levels, Table 29 shows the average and median growth rates for the three main regions of developing countries, which broadly coincide, as discussed, with the three types of agricultural situations identified by the World Bank (2008).[105]

Table 28   Indices of food production, 1960s–2004 (net), base, 1960s–2000s

	1960s	1970s	1980s	1990s	2000–2004	Ratio 2000s/ 1960s	Ratio 2000s/ 1980s
Total							
Africa, developing	40.3	49.9	59.1	85.1	103.6	2.57	1.75
Africa, south of Sahara	41.8	51.7	60.1	85.1	103.0	2.46	1.72
Asia, developing	28.2	37.4	53.0	81.1	106.1	3.76	2.00
East and Southeast Asia	31.4	43.3	62.5	85.9	106.7	3.40	1.71
of which China	22.3	29.8	44.1	75.9	108.6	4.88	2.46
South Asia	34.3	43.8	58.9	84.5	101.9	2.97	1.73
Latin America and Caribbean	34.7	46.8	62.8	83.8	106.2	3.06	1.69
Developing countries	30.8	40.5	55.5	82.0	105.8	3.44	1.91
Developed countries	67.7	82.3	94.1	97.2	100.8	1.49	1.07
Per capita							
Africa, developing	102.7	99.4	89.6	96.9	98.8	0.96	1.10
Africa, south of Sahara	110.0	105.8	93.1	97.8	98.1	0.89	1.05
Asia, developing	55.5	58.8	69.2	87.6	103.2	1.86	1.49
East and Southeast Asia	62.9	69.0	81.9	93.1	103.8	1.65	1.27
of which China	38.6	41.5	53.1	79.6	107.0	2.77	2.02
South Asia	72.8	74.7	81.4	93.5	98.5	1.35	1.21
Latin America and Caribbean	72.0	76.3	83.0	91.2	103.1	1.43	1.24
Developing countries	63.1	66.1	74.1	89.4	102.6	1.63	1.38
Developed countries	86.7	96.5	102.7	99.5	100.2	1.16	0.97

Source: FAOSTAT.

The behavior of growth rates differs significantly across developing regions, depending on whether aggregates or country indicators are utilized as well as on whether total or per capita growth rates are considered. For Africa the best decades, both in the aggregate and for country indicators and total and per capita, have been

Table 29   Agricultural growth, 1960s–2005

		1960s	1970s	1980s	1990s	2000–2005	Average
Africa							
Total	*Aggregate*	*3.3*	*1.3*	*3.0*	*3.4*	*1.8*	*2.6*
Total	Average	3.1	1.9	3.0	3.1	1.9	2.7
Total	Median	3.3	2.0	2.4	3.2	1.9	2.6
Per capita	*Aggregate*	*0.8*	*−1.5*	*0.1*	*0.8*	*−0.5*	*0.0*
Per capita	Average	0.6	−0.8	0.1	0.6	−0.4	0.1
Per capita	Median	0.5	−0.6	−0.3	0.6	−0.5	0.0
Asia							
Total	*Aggregate*	*3.0*	*3.1*	*4.1*	*4.1*	*2.9*	*3.5*
Total	Average	3.4	3.8	4.2	3.5	2.7	3.6
Total	Median	3.0	3.2	3.4	3.0	2.8	3.1
Per capita	*Aggregate*	*0.6*	*0.9*	*2.1*	*2.4*	*1.6*	*1.5*
Per capita	Average	0.1	0.7	1.3	1.4	0.8	0.9
Per capita	Median	0.1	0.5	0.9	0.8	1.0	0.6
LAC							
Total	*Aggregate*	*3.1*	*3.1*	*2.5*	*3.1*	*3.2*	*3.0*
Total	Average	3.4	2.4	1.5	2.1	2.0	2.3
Total	Median	3.2	2.5	1.7	2.2	1.4	2.3
Per capita	*Aggregate*	*0.4*	*0.6*	*0.4*	*1.4*	*1.8*	*0.8*
Per capita	Average	0.9	0.4	−0.2	0.5	0.6	0.4
Per capita	Median	0.5	0.4	−0.3	0.3	0.0	0.2

Source: FAOSTAT.

the 1960s and the 1990s; the worst performances for the region have taken place in the 1970s and then in the first half of the 2000s.

In the case of LAC, the best country indicators clearly happened in the 1960s and 1970s, whereas aggregate indicators are equally good for most of the other periods, except the 1980s; the difference in behavior of indicators at the regional aggregate and by country suggests that what was good for the larger economies might not have been equally favorable for the rest of smaller countries. In terms of per capita growth, the difference is more marked, with the early 2000s being the best period at the aggregate level, but using country averages and medians, clearly the 1960s had the highest growth rates in per capita production. On the other hand, the 1980s were the worst decade by most indicators.

Finally, Asia had the best decades in the aggregate and by country indicators, considering both total and per capita growth, during the 1980s and 1990s. On the other hand, the weakest period differs when we use total growth (the early 2000s) or per

Table 30   Livestock production over total value of agricultural production (%), 1960s–2003

	1960s	1970s	1980s	1990s	2000–2003
Developing	26.3	26.8	29.0	32.7	35.1
Developing minus China	29.4	29.6	31.0	32.3	33.4
Africa, developing	26.2	27.0	29.8	27.7	27.8
Sub-Sahara	26.6	27.0	29.7	26.5	25.9
Latin America and Caribbean	43.3	43.3	43.5	45.7	45.8
Asia, developing	19.6	20.5	23.8	29.6	33.0
South Asia	20.9	21.1	23.7	26.2	29.1
East Southeast Asia	17.0	17.7	19.2	22.7	23.5
China	15.8	18.5	23.8	33.6	38.0

Source: FAOSTAT.

capita growth (the 1960s), but Asia still has the best performance of all regions, considering that even during the slowest periods the region has not had any period with negative per capita production.

An important aspect of the agricultural sector in developing countries is the growth of livestock production (Delgado et al., 1999), which has been growing faster than crops; therefore, it has been increasing its share in the total value of the sector in all developing regions except SSA (see Table 30[106]). The increase in share compared to crops has been particularly noticeable in Asia (pushed by China), although the largest absolute share is in LAC.

Moreover, the growth rates of these two components of agricultural production do not appear correlated with each other in developing countries (see Figure 29, which shows yearly growth rates from crops and livestock, 1962–2005, for the three regions of Asia, Africa, and LAC as aggregates). This change in composition is important to keep in mind in trying to explain the impact of world and domestic macroeconomic conditions on the agricultural sector as a whole.

One of the possible reasons for this lack of correlation (other than the fact that with limited land both productions may compete for its use) is their different levels of tradability, which makes them react differently to changes in world and domestic macroeconomic conditions. For instance, in both LAC and East Asia during the period of capital flows in the late 1970s and early 1990s, respectively, which preceded the debt crises of the early 1980s in LAC and the late 1990s in East Asia, crops appear to have had lackluster performance (about 2% total growth per year, on average), whereas livestock grew faster (at about 5%). Capital inflows, as noted, might have appreciated the

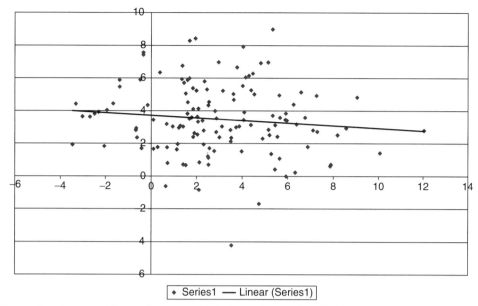

Figure 29 Crops and livestock growth, 1962–2005. Source: FAOSTAT.

real exchange rate, affecting crops (which tend to include more tradable products), but fast income growth (linked to the capital inflows) translated into increased domestic demand for livestock products (which are relatively less tradable, considering the nature of the products and trade restrictions). The opposite occurred during the early 1980s in LAC and the late 1990s in East Asia, when strong exchange rate adjustments related to the debt and financial crises helped crops, but income declines (and the higher cost of tradable feed products) negatively affected the dynamism of livestock products. Therefore, the distinction between crops and livestock appears important in trying to analyze the impact of world and domestic macroeconomic conditions on the agricultural sector as a whole.

5.2 A chronological narrative
5.2.1 The 1960s and the 1970s
As discussed in Section 3, the 1960s were years of high growth (in both developed and developing countries), moderate inflation, low (and even negative) real interest rates, accelerated expansion of trade, and high real prices of commodities (see Table 3). The economic buoyancy of those years was based on expansionary Keynesian macro-economic policies in industrialized and developing countries. Stable exchange rates among main industrialized countries under the Bretton Woods system, coupled with the liberalization and increase of world trade as a result of the success of the sequence of GATT rounds of trade negotiations, also supported world growth. LAC, Africa, and

the Middle East were the fastest-growing regions in the 1960s, and they continued to grow strongly during the 1970s, although East Asia began to overtake all developing regions in that decade. Rents from natural resources (including agriculture) financed, in various degrees, the development of the industrial sector and the expansion of the welfare state in many developing countries.

Synchronized and high growth across a variety of industrialized and developing economies sustained global demand for commodities. Within this supportive economic environment, agriculture showed strong growth rates in the three developing regions of Asia, Africa, and LAC during the 1960s.

In the early 1970s those expansionary policies led to accelerating inflation. The United States abandoned the Bretton Woods system of fixed exchange rates in the first half of the 1970s, and nominal and real exchange rates in major countries turned volatile. In particular, the U.S. dollar underwent a cycle of depreciation in the 1970s. A depreciating dollar also contributed to higher commodity prices (see Section 3).

Besides high growth, a depreciating dollar, and expanding inflationary pressures, the jump in agricultural prices was also related to poor weather conditions in many parts of the world (a cyclone in Bangladesh, 1970; a long drought in sub-Saharan Africa; partial failure of the Soviet cereal crop in 1972; floods in India) and a hike in fertilizer prices, partly due to problems with Morocco's industry.

Agricultural prices jumped over 70% in 1973 (food, about 80%), but other commodity prices also increased significantly. In the case of oil, it happened in 1974 (the year *after* the sudden increase in agricultural prices), and it was also related to geopolitical developments in the Middle East and the Yom Kippur War.

In 1974 and 1975 the global economy suffered a significant slowdown, with many industrialized economies posting negative growth and close to 40% of the developing countries also in recession.

After the first oil crisis, developed countries tried to fight the slowdown with expansionary fiscal and monetary policies. The 1978 Bonn Summit reiterated the intention of industrialized countries to maintain global pro-growth policies. This approach only exacerbated inflationary pressures and eventually led to a more drastic monetary tightening in the 1980s. In the case of the developing countries, the notion of recycling petrodollars was promoted by the international community as part of the general effort to maintain world aggregate demand, which allowed many developing countries to borrow against ample export revenues supported by high commodity prices. All these policies contributed to world growth and inflation in the latter part of the 1970s and set the stage for the dramatic changes in the monetary policies of the industrialized countries and the developing counties' debt crises of the 1980s.

The story of the interaction of world macroeconomic conditions and agricultural production differs by developing regions during the 1970s. LAC, as mentioned before, had the best agricultural performance during the 1960s, and although declining, it also did well in the 1970s. High world prices fueled the expansion of exportable and import-substitution agricultural products while strong domestic demand sustained those products that (for policy reasons or due to intrinsic characteristics) were non-traded goods, and the expansion of the industry provided demand for agricultural raw materials. It is true that the whole economy grew faster than agriculture during this period, but this sector's growth was significant nonetheless and stood above growth rates achieved in subsequent years. It appears that even accepting the argument that the overall policy strategy was biased toward the industrial sector, supportive world markets and domestic income growth helped generate comparatively higher growth rates in the agricultural sector of LAC in that period. Of course, advances in agricultural technology, linked to the expansion of the Green Revolution and supported by the creation of national institutes of agricultural technology in the 1960s and 1970s in the region, and the expansion of public and private infrastructure provided the material basis for that rapid growth.

In SSA, growth declined during the 1970s, mostly as a result of collapse in crops, while livestock production increased significantly. Overall, in SSA comparatively poorer production performance has been associated with macroeconomic imbalances, antitrade biases, war and civil conflict, lack of investment in agriculture, and high incidence of disease in rural areas. But the importance of these factors changed during various decades. For some African countries the emergence of mineral exports appreciated exchange rates during the 1970s, which had a Dutch-disease effect on agriculture and agroindustry. Also, Africa's economic growth and exports began to decline during the difficult transition from colonial rule to independence in the 1960s. The commodity boom facilitated increases in public and private indebtedness that, like LAC, ended up in the debt crisis of the 1980s in several countries.

Asia, however, continued growing, mostly determined by domestic conditions and internal economic growth during the 1960s and 1970s. In general, the density of the population and the mostly small-farm basis of production have made agriculture basically a domestic affair: Neither on the export nor the import side have the ratios of trade to domestic production gone beyond the 10–15% range. As in LAC and even probably to a larger extent advances in agricultural technology, irrigation, and infrastructure in general provided the material underpinnings for that fast growth.

5.2.2 The 1980s

After the second oil crisis at the end of the 1970s, inflation jumped to two digits in industrialized countries, and a series of elections brought new governments that changed the focus of policies from trying to sustain growth through Keynesian policies to fighting inflation using monetarist approaches. Nominal interest rates were raised substantially above inflation rates, leading to high real interest rates (10.6% and 4.1%, respectively, on average for the 1980s, with a peak of about 6–8% in real terms in the early 1980s; see Section 3). This policy change led to the global recession of the early 1980s, with world growth in 1982 being the lowest of the last five decades until the current downturn.

The deceleration of the world economy in the early 1980s did not cause an immediate decline in the prices of commodities because the United States acted as a demand buffer for agricultural products (due to the Farm Bill of 1980), and Saudi Arabia functioned as a supply buffer for oil. With the new U.S. Farm Bill of 1985 and the breakup of discipline in OPEC, plus the important changes in supply and demand discussed in Section 3.4, the result was a generalized decline of commodity prices in the mid-1980s.

The impact of these changes in world and domestic macroeconomic conditions on the agricultural sector differed by region. In LAC the accumulation of external debt during the period of high commodity prices led to the debt crisis of the 1980s. Devaluations of the exchange rates and the progressive advance of trade liberalization were supposed to remove the policy bias against agriculture that may have existed. Real exchange rates depreciated as many countries in the region favored export and import substitution agricultural productions. However, reductions in government expenditures in infrastructure and technology as well as the elimination of marketing and price support programs that were benefiting specific crop and livestock production in several countries tended to negatively affect supply. Furthermore, the higher cost of imported inputs (as a result of the devaluations) and the reduction of credit to agriculture by the public and private banking sectors (partially linked to structural-adjustment programs) had a negative impact on agricultural production. The slowdown in domestic demand affected livestock and dairy productions, which usually have an important component of domestic consumption; the crisis of the industrial sector carried over to some agricultural raw materials; and the weakness in world markets hit hard exportable agricultural goods and made it difficult for LAC governments (already fiscally constrained by the debt crisis) to continue the support of some import-substitution products, such as wheat in Brazil and Chile (Diaz-Bonilla, 1999). As a result of this combination of positive and negative circumstances, agriculture in LAC, although it continued to grow in the 1980s and performed better than the rest of the economy (particularly industry) during that harsh decade, the overall performance of the sector was worse than in the 1960s and the 1970s. The fact that during these earlier decades, when it was argued that agriculture suffered from a negative policy bias in incentives, agricultural growth was clearly higher than in the 1980s (when the bias was being removed) points to the importance of considering other income, demand, technological and cost factors when evaluating the performance of the sector.

In Africa, the impact of the debt crises was also felt in adjustments in exchange rate and fiscal policies. At the same time, competition from other regions, including the transformation of the European Union from a net agricultural importer during the 1960s and 1970s into a net exporter in the 1980s, affected agriculture in Africa.

The low prices of the 1980s also discouraged investments in the rural sector of many developing countries that came to depend on cheap and subsidized food from abroad and contributed to turning many of them, including a number of countries in sub-Saharan Africa, from net food exporters into net importers. Also during the 1980s there were disruptions related to the expansion of the Cold War to that continent. The East/West conflict appears to have hit Africa particularly hard, reinforcing and militarizing ethnic divisions.[107]

In summary, both Africa and LAC suffered more than Asia from the change in world macroeconomic conditions in the 1980s after the second oil crisis. That crisis, along with changes in agricultural and trade policies in developed countries, led to the worldwide collapse in agricultural commodity prices during the second half of the 1980s. The heterogeneous performances were in part related to the different policy reactions, with Asia adjusting earlier and more efficiently to the economic shocks (Balassa, 1989). But the decline in world export shares by Africa and LAC also reflected the fact that these regions were more dependent on developed countries' markets for their exports than was Asia and that sectoral and trade agricultural policies in rich countries were changing during the 1980s in ways that undermined agricultural and agroindustrial production and exports from developing countries. The negative impact of industrialized countries' agricultural policies on the agricultural sector of developing countries has been amply documented (see, among others, Diao, Díaz-Bonilla, and Robinson, 2003).[108]

On the other hand, Asia, as already mentioned, followed a different path, mostly determined by domestic conditions. In addition, as being mostly a net importer of primary agricultural products, the decline in international prices of commodities during the 1980s might have even benefitted Asia. At the same time, capital flows to Asia were smaller in the 1970s than those entering Africa and LAC. The adjustment to changed global macroeconomic conditions (with very high real interest rates) did not affect Asia as much as LAC and several countries in Africa, which had also to absorb larger reversals in capital flows. Having avoided the crises of the 1980s, the good overall economic performance of the region generated growing internal markets that supported the expansion of primary agriculture and agroindustry.

5.2.3 The 1990s

After the early 1980s recession, the world moved to a lower rate of economic growth compared to the 1960s and 1970s—a shift that in part can be attributed to the economic consequences of the previous period of high growth and inflationary pressures in both developed and developing countries—and most commodities entered the decade of the 1980s with expanded supply capabilities created by both market forces and policy decisions reacting to high prices. The consequence was that real prices of commodities continued declining into the 1990s. In the case of agricultural products, industrial countries' programs of protection and subsidization continued while in many developing countries they were dismantled as part of stabilization and structural adjustment programs supported by the IMF and the World Bank.

From early 1994 to mid-1995, the U.S. monetary authorities initiated a period of tightening, increasing the federal funds rate about 300 basis points. The dollar, which had weakened in the previous years during the period of slow growth and low returns to assets, changed course and began to appreciate. Various middle-income countries that have currencies pegged to the dollar, particularly in LAC and Asia, began to lose external competitiveness. However, resorting to devaluation to restore competitiveness was not that simple, given the level of indebtedness in hard currency and the impact that such devaluation would have on the balance sheets of debtors and on the financial sector that had intermediated those hard-currency loans. The main difference from the crises of the 1980s (when international banks intermediated petrodollars, mainly to the public sector) was that in the 1990s an increasing component of external debt was held by the private sector. Devaluations were eventually forced by the reversal of capital flows to developing countries, and, as noted in Section 3, a second wave of debt crises erupted in developing countries, first in Mexico in 1995 and then in East Asia (1997), Russia (1998), Brazil (1999), and Argentina (2001).

In LAC trade and economic liberalization (including the accelerated pace of regional economic integration), the return of capital flows and the resumption of total domestic growth supported agricultural production. The latter was further helped by better international conditions once the world recovered from the mild recession at the beginning of the 1990s and agricultural trade wars between the EU and the United States declined in intensity.

In Africa, macroeconomic imbalances and antitrade policies began to be corrected during the 1990s in several countries, and agricultural growth recovered significantly.

In Asia, aggregate growth continued strong, even though the cycle of high inflow of capitals during the first part of the decade, followed by sharp reductions after the financial crises of 1997, appeared to have somewhat affected some of the East Asian countries. South Asia, on the other hand, experienced during the 1990s the best agricultural growth, along with the decade of the 1960s.

5.2.4 The 2000s

The sequence of financial crises in developing countries in the late 1990s and early 2000s eroded the demand side of many commodities, and devaluations in producing countries, such as Brazil and Argentina, expanded the supply of several of them. The unraveling of the technology boom in the United States and other industrialized countries and the events of September 11, 2001, led to the slowdown in the early 2000s in the U.S. and world economies. These supply and demand changes, combined with an appreciating dollar that reached its peak in the early 2000s, forced commodity prices, in general, to the lowest nominal levels in decades and to the absolute lowest real values for the whole history of data on them.

However, there were several developments at the global level that, incipiently since the mid-1990s and with full force once the early 2000s world slowdown was over, began to impart an increasingly expansionary tilt to macroeconomic policies worldwide. The millions of workers incorporated in the global economy due to the policy changes in China and the end of the Cold War put downward pressure on salaries and prices of manufactured goods, helping reduce inflationary trends. This, in turn, allowed central banks in industrialized countries to pursue more expansionary monetary policies. In the case of the United States, the easing of monetary conditions that started due to concerns about the impact of the change of the year 2000 on computer networks was reinforced after the "dot-com" collapse and the terrorist attacks of September 11. Until 2004 nominal rates were kept at very low levels not seen since the 1950s, and even then interest rates were held down for shorter periods.[109] This strong (and, some have argued, exaggerated) monetary impulse eventually led to the economic acceleration that the United States and the world have experienced in the 2000s until recently, and it contributed to the subsequent sharp decline later in this decade.

That expansionary monetary policy was further reinforced by significant increases in private leverage (i.e., the amount of credit and debt built over a given level of incomes and capital). This increase in leverage was based on a lower perception of risk, fostered by (1) the relatively low volatility and high growth that the world had experienced since the mid-1990s, which some have dubbed the "Great Moderation" (see, among others, Bernanke, 2004), and (2) technological innovations in credit instruments that seemed to reduce risk (such as credit default swaps) or disperse it in a more manageable way (such as securitization and tranching of asset-backed instruments). A related development was the emergence, during the last decade, of a parallel banking and financial structure (which some have called the "shadow banking system") that has been borrowing short term and lending long term using securitized financial vehicles on both ends (Hamilton, 2007).

Monetary policies were also expansionary in developing countries. China maintained a semifixed exchange rate regime with the U.S. dollar, which generated current account surpluses and accumulation of reserves, expanding its own domestic money supply and accelerating growth. The Chinese reserves were invested in dollar-denominated instruments, mostly U.S. public bonds, contributing to the reduction of long-term interest rates. This arrangement was dubbed Bretton Woods II by some (see Dooley et al., 2003). Similar mechanisms operated in various Asian and Latin American countries that, to avoid the disruptions caused by the financial crises of the 1990s, accumulated reserves in their central banks, expanding their money supply, and invested those reserves outside their countries, in many cases in dollar-denominated assets, also putting downward pressure on global interest rates. Oil producers (and, to a lesser extent, other producers of commodities), benefiting from the increase in the prices of their products, also accumulated reserves, with similar internal and external monetary consequences. By keeping longer-term interest rates low, these capital flows contributed to the housing and stock market bubbles.

Developing and emerging countries became net exporters of capital, which, along with traditional surpluses from Japan, went mostly toward the United States, and the current account of this country that had briefly gone back into equilibrium during the recession of early 1990s started a sustained process of growing external deficits since the mid-1990s, until it reached the record of more than 6% of the U.S. GDP (Farrell et al., 2007). The continuous expansion of the U.S. trade deficit (reflected in the widening current account deficit) and low interest rates supported global growth. This, in turn, began to push up nominal and real prices of several commodities, particularly metals and energy. The devaluation of the U.S. dollar since the early 2000s also added pressure to the prices of commodities.

For agricultural goods, besides the resumption of world growth and greater demand from developing countries, higher nominal prices have been also influenced by competition with crops oriented to energy use (which, in addition, are subsidized in main industrial countries) and weather patterns (Von Braun, 2007).

The very accommodative U.S. monetary policy began to be reverted by mid-2004, putting in motion the events that led to the housing and related credit events of 2007 in several industrialized countries: The housing market peaked in early 2006 and started to decline sharply, whereas the stock market peaked in late 2007 and turned downward.

Clear signs of financial distress in mid-2007 led to a strong change in monetary policy by the Federal Reserve toward a more expansionary stance. The large price increases of commodities in the second half of 2007 and early 2008 appear to have been influenced by such monetary easing, which at that time led to fears of inflation and the decline in the U.S. dollar, prompting investors to turn to commodities as inflation hedges in a context where alternative investments in stocks and other assets did not show good returns (Frankel, 2006). This was combined with declining inventories in a series of commodities to generate the large price increases. Other factors such as world growth, supply conditions, or biofuel laws (although part of the structural reasons for strengthening prices), did not change in the second half of 2007 and first half of 2008 so as to explain the sudden increase. Changes in trade policies of several key countries also contributed to the run-up. Still, most real prices, as mentioned in Section 3, stayed below 1970s levels.

By mid-2008 financial stress was evolving into a full-blown financial crisis. As of this writing, a serious economic downturn is still unfolding.

All the changes in the world macroeconomic scenario during the current decade appeared to have contributed to a general slowdown of agricultural growth in developing countries during the first part of the 2000s, but this set the stage for the explosion in prices in the second half of 2007 and early 2008. Going forward, a strong world deceleration in 2009, extending possibly to 2010, appears unavoidable. Once the current recession is over the main question will revolve around the medium-term trend for commodity prices and agricultural growth in general and in developing countries in particular. This analysis requires characterizing both the current global recession and the potential paths out of it, topics that largely exceed the coverage of this chapter (see Díaz Bonilla, 2008 and forthcoming). It is clear, however, that future trends for agricultural growth and prices will depend (in addition to the usual impact of population growth, urbanization, and related consumption patterns) on the complex links of energy, agriculture, the resource base, climate change, and the environment (see Figure 30; from Díaz-Bonilla, 2008).

Regarding primary agricultural prices and agricultural growth, during the 1970s energy prices affected these issues mostly through the costs of production (through inputs such as fertilizers and gas/oil) while consumer prices were also influenced by transportation and processing costs. Now the energy-agriculture equation is more complex: In addition to the same production, transportation, and processing links, we have two other channels. First is the competition for land, water, labor, capital, and inputs in the production of biofuels. Second is the impact on climate change of the energy matrix. Though the previous episode of high oil prices led to additional oil discoveries, such as in the North Sea, now simply following a fossil-based growth strategy based on new sources (such as Canada's oil shale) is not feasible, given the climate-change constraints.

Therefore, projections of agricultural prices and growth on any forecasting horizon are more linked to energy prices and sources. After the current down cycle is over and even with milder world growth in the medium term, potential imbalances in world energy markets for the next few years are looming (International Energy Agency,

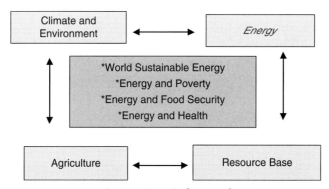

Figure 30   Links among energy, environment, agriculture and poverty.

Table 31   Energy, population, and GDP, 1950–2050

	1950–1960	2004	2050
Population (M)	2500	6400	9000/10,000
GDP (US$M, 1990)	5300	36,000	105,000/115,000
Nonfood energy (exajoules)	90	460	800/900
Food energy (exajoules)	10	28	39/43

Source: Calculations by author based on World Bank data (2006).

2007). In the longer term, the requirements are even more daunting. Table 31 shows the evolution of population, GDP, and nonfood and food energy requirements from the 1950s–1960s to 2004, with long-term projections for 2050 under some variations of current trends. The three data points are separated by about half a century.

In terms of energy sources, the supply of coal is more than adequate to meet the world's requirements, but of course there is the problem of greenhouse emissions, and as yet there are no viable energy alternatives for transportation, which is projected to increase with more population and economic activity. Over time, the implications of energy consumption for climate change may carry significant consequences for the evolution of agricultural production in developing countries, and more generally, for their societies. The combination of issues surrounding energy use, economic development, poverty alleviation, and climate change is affected by a market coordination failure of global proportions (Stern, 2006) and, similarly to the shorter-term macroeconomic imbalances discussed mostly in Section 3, they are problems for which there are no widely accepted international mechanism for their resolution.

5.3 Some Concluding Words

This chapter has tried to document both some crucial *world* macroeconomic developments,and the important changes in *domestic* macroeconomic policies in developing countries, all of which have had visible effects on the agricultural sector of the various developing regions. Exchange rates have been unified in many of those countries, regimes appear to have moved toward managed floats, and there have been clear movements toward devaluation of the RERs. All this should imply less frequency of exchange rate crises, after the spate of traumatic episodes of the mid- to late 1990s. However, a question mark is the behavior of countries with inflation targeting regimes that might have led to the appreciation of exchange rates during the period of bonanza and now have had to absorb important devaluations.

Fiscal policies appear more constrained, in no minor measure because of the lingering effects of the debt crises of the 1980s and 1990s. Although the levels of expenditures may be less than what would be needed to develop a dynamic agriculture, it seems, at the same time, that the composition expenditures in agriculture appear to have moved somewhat toward more efficient uses, with a relatively greater focalization on public goods.

Developing economies have been operating in a less inflationary environment, and monetization or financial deepening of the economies seems to have been increasing, which could lead to further expansion of agricultural credit as part of the general increase in private credit. Still, monetary policies also appear constrained by the opening of capital accounts and the spreading of dollarization in several developing countries, and interest rates appear relatively high in real terms in many developing countries. In any case, the past approach of financing agriculture by resorting to generous rediscounts from the central bank to be channeled through specialized institutions seems restricted by both the general monetary conditions and the problems of those intermediaries in the past. However, the agricultural sector in many developing countries still requires differentiated credit approaches, which would have to be framed by an appropriate general monetary program and managed by sustainable institutions.

Developing countries have been reducing overall trade protection, and now in some cases agriculture may be more protected that industry. Overall, all these adjustments in exchange rates, trade and other macro policies, appear to have eliminated or at least reduced the "policy bias" against agriculture, if it ever existed properly measured.

Agriculture in developing countries should benefit, in general, from this improved domestic policy setting. Those advances, however, must be set against an international economy in which protectionism and subsidies, mostly in industrialized countries, continues, where capital flows have generated recurrent financial crises, and where financial liberalization (in the context of weak financial institutions) appear to maintain high real interest rates. The current global recession is another negative condition that works against the advances in macroeconomic domestic policies in many developing countries, which, although with some dispersion, have clearly improved during the last decade. For instance, developing countries have in general tried (1) to strengthen the fiscal position of the public sector, reducing public sector debt ratios and even using additional resources from high commodity prices to create countercyclical funds (a stronger fiscal position of the public sector will be needed to set up safety nets for the poor and vulnerable during the coming slowdown); (2) to avoid rigid and appreciated real exchange rates that could lead to trade imbalances and excessive accumulation of external debt; and (3) to maintain relatively higher levels of reserves in central banks than in the past, as a precaution against possible global turbulence that could lead to declines in growth and commodity prices and could stop or revert capital flows to developing countries.

In analyzing the links of these world and domestic macroeconomic changes to agriculture, it seems important to remember that not all agricultural products function as pure tradables and that, among the latter, there are export-oriented and import-competing products, all of which may be affected differently by specific macroeconomic policies. In this regard, it is also relevant to notice the differences between agricultural products (such as feed grains) that are inputs to other activities (such as beef and poultry production), and the potential differing impacts of the same macroeconomic event (see for instance, the already mentioned work by Shane and Liefert (2000) on the impact of the Asian crisis on different agricultural products in the cases of Indonesia and Korea). At the same time, however, liberalization of trade policies, improvements in infrastructure and logistics, and more uniform and science-based sanitary and phytosanitary policies may be increasing the tradability of all agricultural products. Also, whatever happens to agricultural products, incomes of agricultural families in various developing countries will still show different compositions of rural/urban and tradable/nontradable activities, with a potential variety of effects on employment, poverty, and food security.

Once the current recession is over, it could be argued that with a more stable world and domestic macroeconomic environment and if the important policy-induced imbalances in world agricultural and financial markets are diminished, the evolution of agriculture in developing countries will return to being determined more by the internal dynamics of the sector, defined by increasingly market-oriented sectoral policies and the traditional interplay of technology, population, weather, and natural resources. The main question is for how long the cycle of technological change, spurred by the Green Revolution, can continue and be adapted to the daunting challenges presented by the interface of energy supply, climate change, management of natural resources, and agricultural and food production.

Agriculture in developing countries, and the welfare of the whole world, will depend on how industrialized and developing countries resolve the two big coordination problems humanity is confronting: first, the resolution of the macroeconomic imbalances in the short term, and second, how to solve the market and institutional failures associated with energy and climate issues, which over time will become ever more relevant for poverty trends in developing countries. Building a world economy that is macroeconomically stable, based on sustainable energy, and capable of ensuring the benefits of progress to everyone requires that humankind properly address those two crucial issues of global governance.

End Notes

1. This is particularly the case of Chapter 29: "Agriculture and the Macroeconomy, with Emphasis on Developing Countries," by Maurice Shiff and Alberto Valdes; Chapter 30: "Agriculture and the Macroeconomy," by Pier Gorgio Ardeni and John Freebairne; and Chapter 34: "Agriculture in the Macroeconomy: Theory and Measurement," by Alex McCalla and Phil Abbot. Other relevant chapters in that handbook include Chapter 28: "Applied General Equilibrium Analysis of Agricultural and Resource Policies," by Thomas Hertel; Chapter 31: "Agriculture and Economic Development," by Peter Timmer; Chapter 32: "The Rural Sector in Transition Economies," by John Nash and Karen Brooks; and Chapter 33: "Rural Development and Rural Policy," by Elisabeth Sadoulet, Alain DeJanvry, and Rinku Murgai.

2. The argument of Stock and Watson refers mainly to the U.S. economy. Similarly, Aguiar and Gopinath (2004) argue that for developing countries, "the cycle is the trend."

3. The way these transactions are placed in the table assumes a specific direction of payments and receipts (i.e., who is paying and who is receiving). These transactions can be changed from cell to cell to represent a different direction of the flows, or they can be kept in the same cell with the sign reversed.

4. The accounting conventions of the System of National Accounts distinguish an activity sector "Government" producing public sector services (through the purchase of goods and services from the different productive branches and the purchase of factorial services) and "Government" as an institutional sector buying those services at the cost of production. Here we show only Government as institution; the other conception of "Government" is aggregated in the single Activity/Commodity. The value of G is financed through taxes and other means in the Current and Capital accounts of the Government as an institution (see the following discussion).

5. Capital can be broadly defined to include land in agriculture and other nonlabor factors.

6. GDP at factor cost is $YL + YK + DEPR = C + G + INVp + INVg + EX - IM - (Tint + Tm)$. Net Domestic Product is obtained by subtracting DEPR from both sides, and it can be expressed at factor costs or market prices.

7. The treatment of financial intermediaries is the subject of some controversy within national accounting. The discussion centers around what is the output of the banks and how to treat the difference in interest paid and received by the banks (this, of course, also includes the case in which banks may be receiving, but not paying, interest, as when the Central Bank extends credit through the creation of fiat money and when commercial banks provide credit based on deposits in checking accounts on which they do not pay interest). The solutions suggested have been to treat that difference as either a "factor-type service," in which case interest payments are always part of the value added generated in the sector using the financial capital, or a "commodity-type service," in which case interest payments are treated as intermediate consumption of, and are from income generated in, the sector using the financial capital but give rise to income in the owning sector (Mamalakis, 1987, p. 171). This broadly coincides with the economic specification of money in the production function or money in the utility function (see, for instance, Blanchard and Fischer, 1989, Chapter 4).

8. Quantities are net of losses but may include agricultural production for self-consumption and own-production that is utilized as intermediate inputs to other agricultural production in the same unit (in the latter case they must then be included in costs, or they may be netted out from production and costs in the equation).

9. For instance, Prebisch, 1950 noted that although cycles in industrialized countries were mainly related to movements in domestic aggregate demand, in developing countries economic oscillations were linked to exports. From that observation, he derived policy observations regarding macroeconomic management in developing countries as different from industrialized ones.

10. Several comments are in order. First, this chapter only tries to give a sense of the macroeconomic policies in different settings, not to conduct an exhaustive and differentiated analysis by region. Because the data on the countries emerging from the former Soviet Union is scarcer than for other regions and/or covers only the last decade or so, in several of the comparative analyses presented in the text, that region might not appear prominently. Second, it must be noted that sometimes the aggregate data is for the region as a whole (in which case the numbers are dominated by the largest countries in that region) and sometimes may be the average (or the median) for all countries in that region, without weighting by size of the economy. Each one of those two different ways of characterizing the situation in a region or group of developing countries has its advantages and disadvantages, depending on the objective of the analysis. The text will try to clarify what indicator is being used in the specific context.

11. Besides the general policy implications, the paper focuses on the issue of classifications for trade negotiations, particularly with respect to their food security status under current WTO rules and

3188 Eugenio Diaz-Bonilla and Sherman Robinson

ongoing negotiations, such as developing countries, least-developed countries (LDCs), net food-importing developing countries (NFIDCs), and the issue of food security within the "multifunctionality" approach suggested by some developed countries. Díaz-Bonilla et al. conclude that (1) there does not seem any basis for the claims advanced by several developed countries regarding food security as part of the "multifunctionality" of agriculture, and the discussion of food security should be limited to the vulnerability of some developing countries; (2) however, granting food security exceptions to developing countries as a whole fails to discriminate among them; (3) being a NFIDC appears to be only a weak indicator of food vulnerability; (4) LDCs, on the other hand, include mostly countries suffering from food insecurity, and (5) some developing countries that appear in food-insecure categories are neither LDCs nor NFIDCs; therefore, limiting the special and differential treatment related to food security problems only to LDCs or food-insecure NFIDCs would leave them out.

12. For instance, about ¾ of Mexico's agricultural exports are oriented to the United States and Canada; on the other hand, for Argentina and Uruguay only about a third of their exports go to developed countries.

13. African agricultural exports are still dominated by coffee/tea/cocoa and have a larger incidence (about 10%) of textile fibers in total exports. Compared to other regions, Asia has a larger incidence of cereal exports, with about 13% of total exports. All three regions are net exporters of fruits and vegetables and coffee/tea/cocoa, but LACs have a stronger net export position than the other regions in those products. Of the three developing regions, LACs have the larger incidence of meat exports, with around 6% in total exports (Diaz-Bonilla Thomas, Robinson, and Yanoma, 2002).

14. The trend is calculated using the Hodrick-Prescott filter (power 4; smoothing parameter 6.25). The aggregation is at market exchange rates. The IMF also calculates a world growth variable, aggregated using PPP exchange rates as weights. The world growth variable calculated with PPP weights shows higher world growth rates than at market exchange rates because it gives more weight to fast-growing developing countries such as China. Here market exchange rates are utilized, considering that growth impulses from trade and financial flows are transmitted at market, not PPP, rates.

15. This chapter primarily follows the country aggregates defined in the World Development Indicators of the World Bank. The other developing regions are East Asia and the Pacific (EAP) and South Asia (SA). The category of "low- and middle-income countries" is taken here to represent all developing countries. The world total is completed with the category "high-income countries" (which, in World Bank aggregations, is divided into the high-income countries of the Organization for Economic Cooperation and Development and the rest).

16. Excluding India also does not make much of a difference because its growth, contrary to China's, has stayed close to the average for all developing countries.

17. It is customary to use *industrial* growth in developed countries (which is supposed to have a stronger linkage with developing countries through tradables) instead of *total* growth in those countries (which mixes growth of tradables and nontradables) to run causality analyses. For developing countries, on the other hand, total growth is used.

18. These numbers come from comparing the value of one standard deviation in industrial production (about 3 percentage points) with the impact coefficients shown in Figure 3.

19. It has been argued that not all trade increases comovements equally: Intraindustry trade increases synchronization more significantly than does interindustry trade.

20. In Díaz Bonilla (2008), there is a brief analysis of the correlation of growth across developing regions. It is noted that LAC, SSA, and MENA, which are commodity-producing regions, were more correlated in the 1960s to 1980s, when prices of commodities also had strong comovements (see the following discussion on commodity prices). During the 1990s and 2000s, the correlation in growth was

stronger between LAC and EAP, which benefited from capital flows and then suffered from their withdrawal (capital flows are also analyzed later).

21. The VAR includes a dummy for El Niño/La Niña events (due to the impact of weather on agriculture) and a constant. The Akaike and Schwarz criteria are utilized to define the length of the lags.

22. The ordering utilized here is total world GDP and agricultural GDP. Changing the ordering does not modify the results.

23. Volatility of GDP, or consumption growth, is calculated as the five-year moving average of the standard deviation of growth of the respective variable divided by the five-year moving average of its mean. This is done for every developing country. Then the median over all developing countries is calculated for every year, and averages are taken for the decade.

24. Figure 6 shows the evolution of short- and long-term real interest rates, represented respectively by the one-year U.S. dollar London Interbank Offered Rate (LIBOR) and the 10-year U.S. bond rate. The chart also includes the U.S. prime rate in real terms. The deflator is inflation measured by the U.S. Consumer Price Index.

25. IMF projections for 2009 point to world growth rates (at market exchange rates) lower than in 1982, indicating a very deep downturn.

26. The ordering utilized, based on Granger causality tests, is world growth, changes in interest rates, and changes in real world agricultural prices.

27. High (low) inflation is usually associated to high (low) volatility (see, for instance, Fischer, 1993).

28. Data in the charts are deflated by the U.S. Consumer Price Index, which would indicate the capacity of those commodities to buy the consumption basket of the United States. Another common deflator is the export unit value of industrialized countries. The resulting index can then be interpreted as the capacity of the commodities considered to buy the bundle of export goods from developed countries. Using either deflator the story is broadly the same.

29. For some products, such as cereals, beef, and sugar, the EU moved from being a net importer to becoming a net exporter. In the 1960s and 1970s the current countries of the European Union imported, per year, an average of about 21 million metric tons (MT) of cereals, 550,000 MT of beef, and 2 million MT of sugar; since the 1980s, however, and until the 1990s, those countries became net exporters of 18 million MT, around 500,000 MT, and almost 3.5 million MT for the same products, on average, per year (Diaz-Bonilla and Reca, 2000).

30. The World Bank sharply curtailed its agricultural lending, including for integrated rural development, as the decade of the 1980s progressed; it declined (in constant 2001 U.S. dollars) from about $5 billion and some 30% of total World Bank lending in the late 1970s and first half of the 1980s to $3 billion and 10–15% of total lending in the second part of the 1980s. By the early 2000s agricultural lending had declined further, to about $1.5 billion and 7% of total World Bank loans. Similar trends occurred in other multilateral institutions and individual donors (Lipton and Paarlberg, 1990).

31. It has also been noted that the positive social impact of growth based on ores and metals or energy products seems to be lower than for other commodities (Sachs and Warner, 1995; Tsangarides et al., 2000). However, these general effects also depend on specific country effects. For instance, ores and metals represent a high share of merchandise exports in Chile (46%) and Peru (41%). But during the 2000s Chile has shown a better growth and poverty reduction performance than Peru: 4.4% growth and 2% of poverty headcount (using the World Bank measure of US$1/day) in the case of Chile, compared to 4% and 14%, respectively, for Peru.

32. A possible reason for that correlation is that negative global weather effects, which affected agricultural and total growth in South Asia, also led to high world prices for food products, particularly in the 1960s and 1970s.

33. In Dollar and Kraay (2001) the numerator of the trade/GDP variable is defined as exports (X) plus imports (M), and GDP is defined as domestic absorption (D) plus exports minus imports. Then the variable is $(X + M) / (D + X − M)$. Countries hit by declines in the prices of their main exports are also forced to cut imports (given a certain level of sustainable financing of the trade deficit), which reduces the value of the numerator. If, as usually happens, financing of the trade deficit also dries up because lenders see the decline in export values that is the implicit collateral, then the trade deficit declines, which means that the value of $(X − M)$ increases, pushing the value of the denominator up. Decline in exports and import contraction also affect D negatively, but usually the absolute value of the changes in X, M, and the trade deficit are bigger than the decline in D, forcing the trade/GDP variable down. Therefore, the collapse in export prices has caused declines or stagnation in the "globalization" variable and in the growth rate, generating the misleading correlation.

34. Terms of trade are defined as price of exports divided by price of imports, calculated from national accounts.

35. References to the euro before it was created correspond to the previous equivalent basket of currencies.

36. It must be noted, however, that the largest values of capital flows in the last decades have been among industrialized countries (not shown here).

37. The percentage reported is the absolute value of the reversal in the current account of the balance of payment relative to the GDP of the country; for instance, if the country had a deficit in the current account of 5% of the GDP before the crisis and after that event had a surplus of 3%, the reversal was 8% of GDP.

38. A greater impact on those rural populations that were more dependent on urban employment was also observed in the 1980s crisis in LAC, where migration toward the cities was stopped and even reversed in several countries.

39. Developing countries in Figure 14 do not include China and Middle East. Also, Hong Kong, Singapore, Korea, and Taiwan, labeled the newly industrialized Asian economies (NIAE), are considered separately.

40. In Figure 14 Japan is combined with China and the NIAE. During that period it was basically Japan that generated the surpluses. Large surpluses in the CA of China and the NIAE happened later, since the late 1990s and early 2000s.

41. Although the variables associated with the mercantilist motive are statistically significant, Aizenman and Lee found that the economic impact in accounting for reserve accumulation is minimal compared with the precautionary motive.

42. Trade is the sum of exports and imports of goods and services measured as a share of gross domestic product.

43. The conclusions of the analysis may vary depending on what indicators are being utilized. For instance, the high ratios for SSA have been presented as evidence that "excessive" globalization leads to poor economic performance (Mazur, 2000). But, with higher levels of openness East Asian developed countries have done better. On the other hand, a commonly quoted study in support of globalization by Dollar and Kraay (2001) has compared *changes* in openness rather than absolute *levels* and concluded that those more globalized (in changes) have done better. Yet, looking at levels instead of changes in levels, either of trade/GDP ratios, or import tariffs, countries labeled as "non-globalizers" by Dollar and Kray have larger ratios of trade to GDP and lower tariffs than the countries labeled as "globalizers" (see Figures 1 and 2 in Dollar and Kraay, 2001).

44. For a comparison of export and import ratios for developed and developing countries and various products, see Diaz–Bonilla (2001).

45. Another component of macroeconomic policies relate to labor market issues. This is a vast topic in itself that is not addressed here (see, for instance, Agenor, 1996).

46. More recently, macroeconomic books have focused on long-term growth issues; see, for instance, Romer, 1996 and 2001.

47. Latin American industry had emerged in good measure as a result of growing demand in the region and the natural protection offered by the breakdown of trade and finances during the Great Depression and the two World Wars.

48. Borrowing from the current debate that focuses on agriculture (see OECD, 2001), the "multifunctionality" of industry appeared substantial for policymakers in the 1950s and 1960s. Díaz-Bonilla and Tin (2006), on which part of this section is based, present a more detailed comparison of the current debate on multifunctionality in agriculture with the older one on industry. Among other things, they note that though the early development literature appeared to assign zero marginal value to labor in the agricultural sector, or at least a value far smaller than in alternative uses (Lewis, 1954), now the multifunctional approach to agriculture seems to assign a higher value to employment in agriculture than to alternative uses, at least in industrialized countries. Of course, in both cases, the issue is not only the postulated "multifunctional" effects of a sector but the general equilibrium impacts of the policies followed, which may deny the beneficial contribution of other sectors that would shrink due to the excessive expansion of the favored sector. Diaz-Bonilla and Tin also note that given some world demand conditions, expanding the agricultural supply in industrial countries on account of its multifunctionality there will most certainly lead to the displacement of agricultural production in developing countries, denying the latter the postulated multifunctional effects of their agriculture.

49. Alternative scenarios discussed at that time suggested that the flow of savings not captured by, and the demand for credit rationed out of, the formal sector may spill over to the informal or "curb" market (Van Wijnbergen, 1983). Instead of savings being locked into unproductive or inefficient alternatives, they would flow through the operation of the informal sector. Then, increasing interest rates in the formal sector would only divert funds out of the "curb" market, and if for some reason the latter is more efficient in the process of financial intermediation, the impact of that policy recommendation over growth, prices, and economic efficiency might be negative. Another element of the debate was whether the liberalization of the interest rate could have stagflationary effects (at least in the short run) through the channel that links aggregate supply to the interest rate via production costs related to working capital (see, among others, McKinnon, 1973, and Kalpur, 1976).

50. The next paragraphs are based on Jensen, Robinson, and Tarp, 2002.

51. The simulations also beg the question why those more stable macroeconomic policies were not followed in Argentina during the period analyzed, and the answer has to be looked at in terms of political economy considerations. For instance, Diaz-Bonilla and Schamis (2002) discuss the political economy of macroeconomic instability in Argentina, focusing on the exchange rate. A more general study by the World Bank notes the important income inequalities and the political clashes leading to the interruption in democracy in Argentina because the proper institutions for inclusion were not created by the elites during the golden age, from the 1870s to the 1920s (see World Bank Development Report 2006 Box 6.2, p. 113).

52. *Currency substitution* usually refers to the behavior of domestic agents who abandon local currency in favor of foreign currencies considered to be better stores of value.

53. Fiscal policies also have had important effects on agriculture in developed countries. For instance, O'Mara et al. (1999) argue that fiscal policy in Australia had destabilizing effects on interest rates and the real exchange rate from the mid-1970s to the mid-1980s, but since then it helped stabilize those variables, which was important to increase supply.

54. Fiscal data is from the World Development Indicators of the World Bank. It provides a general view, but it does not cover all expenditure categories or levels of government involved.

55. This is a limited indicator of the size of the public sector to the extent that it does not include public investments and transfers, among other things.

56. The countries included in the study were Bangladesh, China, India, Indonesia, Republic of Korea, Malaysia, Myanmar, Nepal, Pakistan, Philippines, Sri Lanka, and Thailand.

57. The countries are Argentina, Bolivia, Brazil, Chile, Colombia, Costa Rica, Ecuador, Guatemala, Honduras, Jamaica, Mexico, Nicaragua, Panama, Paraguay, Peru, Dominican Republic, Uruguay, and Venezuela.

58. Those are explicit taxes. It has been already mentioned that some studies argued that implicit taxes such as overvalued exchange rates, nontariff barriers, import tariffs, and procurement programs (monopoly marketing) affecting output prices have been more important in defining the level of taxation of agriculture (see, for instance, Krueger, Shiff, and Valdes, 1988). The issues raised by those interventions are discussed elsewhere in this chapter.

59. In general, it has been shown that the overall tax/GDP ratio is inversely related to the share of agricultural production in the economy due to the fact that it is more difficult and costly to collect explicit taxes on a disperse population, which, additionally, in many developing countries operates in the informal sector (see Ghura, 1998, for the case of SSA).

60. Several macroeconomic texts have a good treatment of the issues involved; see, for instance, Romer (2001).

61. The monetary base (MB, also called *high-powered money*) includes currency in circulation plus bank deposits in the central bank. The MB is amplified into larger monetary aggregates through the money multiplier of the banking system, which depends on, among other things, the ratio of liquid reserves to total credit that the banking or financial system maintains and on the fraction the public wants to keep in cash. For the basic policy points to be illustrated in the text, we can ignore these additional issues.

62. This is the so-called *price-specie-flow mechanism* attributed to David Hume in his criticism of the mercantilists regarding the nonsustainability of their proposal to try to maintain permanent trade surpluses.

63. Lower inflation tends to also benefit the poor: Easterly and Fischer (2000), using household data for 38 countries, find that in both their perception (the poor are more likely to mention inflation as a concern) and reality (several measures of welfare of the poor are negatively correlated with inflation in general, and high inflation lowers the share of the bottom quintile and the real minimum wage and increases poverty), inflation is a real problem for the poor.

64. The countries included are Argentina, Bolivia, Brazil, Chile, Colombia, Costa Rica, Dominican Republic, Ecuador, El Salvador, Guatemala, Haiti, Honduras, Jamaica, Mexico, Nicaragua, Panama, Paraguay, Peru, Trinidad and Tobago, Uruguay, and Venezuela in LAC; China, Indonesia, Malaysia, Philippines, Thailand, and Vietnam in East Asia and Pacific; Bangladesh, India, Nepal, Pakistan, and Sri Lanka in South Asia; And Benin, Botswana, Burkina, Faso, Burundi, Cameroon, Cape Verde, Central African Republic, Chad, Congo, Cote d'Ivoire, Ethiopia, Gabon, The Gambia, Ghana, Kenya, Liberia, Madagascar, Malawi, Mali, Mauritania, Mauritius, Niger, Nigeria, Rwanda, Senegal, Sierra Leone, South Africa, Sudan, Swaziland, Tanzania, Togo, Uganda, Zambia, and Zimbabwe in SSA.

65. This is a simplified way to refer to the increase use of a foreign currency, usually (but not only) the U.S. dollar, to perform one or several of the monetary functions of medium of exchange, store of value, and unit of account.

66. The initial countries were New Zealand (1990), Canada (1991), and United Kingdom (1992).

67. Industrial countries: New Zealand 1990, Canada 1991, United Kingdom 1992, Australia 1993, Sweden 1993, Israel 1997, Switzerland 2000, Iceland 2001, and Norway 2001. Emerging markets and developing countries: Czech Rep. 1998, Korea, Rep. 1998, Poland 1999, Brazil 1999, Chile

1999, Colombia 1999, South Africa 2000, Thailand 2000, Hungary 2001, Mexico 2002, Peru 2002, and Philippines 2002.

68. It should be noted that this distinction is not completely correct, because it can be argued that the IT has the interest rate as an instrument, the same way that the money-supply and exchange rate approaches have monetary aggregates and the exchange rate, and that the latter approaches also indicated their inflation preferences. The only difference would then be in the degree of emphasis in the announcement and communication of the target.

69. Inflation targeters: Brazil, Chile, Colombia, Czech Republic, Hungary, Israel, Republic of Korea, Mexico, Peru, Philippines, Poland, South Africa, Thailand. Nontargeters in the JP Morgan Emerging Markets Bond Index: Argentina, Belize, Bulgaria, China, Cote d'Ivoire, Dominican Republic, Ecuador, Egypt, El Salvador, Indonesia, Iraq, Kazakhstan, Lebanon, Malaysia, Pakistan, Panama, Russia, Serbia, Trinidad and Tobago, Tunisia, Turkey, Ukraine, Uruguay, Venezuela, and Vietnam. Nontargeters not in the JP Morgan Emerging Markets Bond Index: Botswana, Costa Rica, Ghana, Guatemala, India, Jordan, and Tanzania.

70. According to de Janvry et al. (1997), in Colombia reform of the rural financial sector in 1990–1994 raised real interest rates and restructured and recapitalized the rural development bank, the Caja Agraria. In Ecuador, subsidies to the Banco Nacional de Fomento were lowered starting in 1991, and interest rate ceilings on deposit accounts were removed in 1993. Haiti closed BNDAI, the national bank for agricultural and industrial development, in 1989. In Mexico, Banrural closed about 60% its branches and cut staff by more than half in 1992. Interest rate subsidies were reduced, leading to positive real interest rates. Government transfers to development banks were decreased and agricultural credit declined from 22% of all credit in 1983 to 8% in 1992. In Nicaragua, the Banco Nacional de Desarrollo has raised real interest rates significantly since 1992. In Peru, preferential interest rates to agriculture were eliminated. The Agrarian Bank, BAP, was declared bankrupt in 1992.

71. The countries included are Bangladesh, India, Nepal, Sri Lanka, in South Asia; China, Indonesia, Malaysia, Myanmar, Philippines, and Thailand in East Asia and Pacific; Bolivia, Chile, Colombia, Costa Rica, Ecuador, El Salvador, Guatemala, Guyana, Honduras, Jamaica, Nicaragua, Panama, Peru, Trinidad and Tobago, Uruguay, and Venezuela in LAC; and Burundi, Cameroon, Central African Republic, Chad, Congo, Gabon, Gambia, Kenya, Nigeria, Sierra Leone, South Africa, Swaziland, Zambia, and Zimbabwe in SSA. All the low- and middle-income countries include additional countries from North Africa, Middle East, and Transition Economies.

72. See Chinn (2005) for the complexities in defining appropriate weights.

73. See also Chinn (2005) for the various price indices that can be utilized (such as consumer price indices, wholesale price indices, producer price indices, GDP deflators, and so on) and their advantages and disadvantages.

74. In both definitions the ratio *decreases* when the RER *appreciates* (which may generate confusion) in several applications the ratios are inverted (i.e. PD/ER* PI and Pnt/Pt), so they increase (decrease) when the RER appreciates (depreciate). In this way, the normal meaning of the word and the value of the ratios point in the same direction. These alternative definitions are a source of confusion. In the following discussion, the text will clarify the definition that is being utilized.

75. As before, we are assuming that the country is "small" in terms of the exportable and the importable products and that the domestic product and the world product are homogeneous. The price of the nontradables is determined by internal supply and demand. Of course, if there are no pure tradables or pure nontradables, the equations must be adjusted accordingly. But the points made in the text would be even more valid with those adjustments.

76. Disregarding second-order interactions between variables.

77. Although the country could affect the country risk in the future through policy changes. At time t, however, it is predetermined.

78. They distinguish the following approaches: the Behavioral Equilibrium Exchange Rate (BEER, which estimates the long-run relationship between the RER and its fundamentals), the Permanent Equilibrium Exchange Rate (PEER, similar to BEER but that distinguishes transitory and permanent components), the Fundamental Equilibrium Exchange Rate (FEER, which considers sustainable policy paths that ensure internal and external equilibrium), the Desired Equilibrium Exchange Rate (DEER, which considers desired, rather than only sustainable, policy paths that ensure internal and external equilibrium), and Natural Real Exchange Rate (NATREX, which considers both a short-term and a long-term equilibrium exchange rate and the transition path from the current level of capital stock and foreign debt, which support the short term estimate, to the capital stock and foreign debt stabilized at their steady-state levels, which are behind the long-term equilibrium exchange rate estimates; Di Bella, Lewis, and Martin, 2007).

79. Wood uses Pnt/Pt, the ratio of nontraded to traded goods (the inverse of the definitions presented before in the text), such that an increase (decrease) is an appreciation (depreciation) of the real exchange rate and implies a decline (increase) in external competitiveness.

80. Wood also argued that the downward adjustment in developing countries was related to a substantial appreciation of the ratio of nontraded/traded goods in industrialized countries due to a combination of faster technical progress in traded goods, increased trade openness, and an increase in the wage-rental ratios because of overall productivity and real wage growth.

81. It is also defined as the inverse of the definitions in the text. Therefore, a higher value of the index indicates an appreciation of the domestic currency.

82. Since then, in early 2002, Argentina underwent a large nominal and real devaluation. The index in Cashin et al. stands at 80.2 in March 2002, or about half the average for 2000–2001.

83. Reinhart and Rogoff (2002) calculated using a special algorithm what would be the de facto exchange rate regime, in opposition to the declared or *de jure* system registered by the IMF. They identify 15 detailed groups that are later aggregated into five more general categories, which are the ones utilized in Table 21. Countries for which data are missing and cannot be classified are included in "No data." Table 21 is based on data for 116 developing countries.

84. Emerging markets include Argentina, Brazil, Chile, China, Colombia, Czech Republic, Egypt, Hungary, India, Indonesia, Israel, Jordan, Korea, Malaysia, Mexico, Morocco, Pakistan, Peru, the Philippines, Poland, Russia, South Africa, Thailand, Turkey, and Venezuela. The rest of developing countries include all those under the low- and middle-income categories of the World Bank. All other countries are considered advanced.

85. The high ratio of capital flows to GDP in Africa is mostly related to public sector flows and therefore cannot be interpreted as a high integration with private financial markets.

86. However, Barret (1999) has argued, based on estimations for several commodities in Madagascar, that the expansionary effects on tradables of real exchange rate depreciations do not hold universally, but only for importables that remain imported and nontradables that become exportable. On the other hand, Lamb (2000), in a panel of 14 African countries, finds a positive impact of devaluations on export crop production.

87. For instance, Kamin and Klau (1998), along with others, found that devaluations have contractionary effects on total GDP in the short run, although they do not find such effects in the long run, after controlling for other influences.

88. It is interesting to note that Schuh (1974), in his seminal work on exchange rates and agriculture in the United States, argued that the overvaluation of the RER would *increase* production because the reduced profit margins forced farmers to innovate and increase productivity to survive (a variation of the "treadmill effect"). This response was facilitated by the fact that there were productivity-enhancement technologies available. Of course, in other institutional, social, and economic settings,

the response could well be to abandon production and migrate out of the rural areas, as happens in some developing countries.

89. Just as an example, assuming for LAC a value of RER = 100 and average agricultural growth of 3%, an increase or appreciation of the RER by 10% reduces agricultural growth by 14% of 3% (0.42% points), which, subtracted from 3%, gives 2.58%.

90. It should be noted that only one misalignment indicator appears in each cointegrated equation.

91. East Asia Pacific includes China, Indonesia, Korea, Malaysia, Papua New Guinea, Philippines, Thailand. South Asia includes Bangladesh, India, Nepal, Pakistan, Sri Lanka. Middle East and North Africa (MENA), includes Algeria, Egypt, Iran, Jordan, Morocco, Syria, Tunisia, Yemen. Latin America and the Caribbean includes Argentina, Belize, Bolivia, Brazil, Chile, Colombia, Costa Rica, Dominican Republic, Ecuador, El Salvador, Guatemala, Guyana, Haití, Jamaica, México, Nicaragua, Paraguay, Peru, Suriname, Trinidad and Tobago, Uruguay, Venezuela. Sub-Saharan Africa includes Benin, Burkina Faso, Burundi, Cameroon, Central Africa Rep, Congo DR, Congo, Rep., Cote d'Ivoire, Ethiopia, Ghana, Guinea, Kenya, Madagascar, Malawi, Mauritania, Mauritius, Mozambique, Nigeria, Rwanda, Senegal, Sierra Leone, Somalia, South Africa, Sudan, Tanzania, Uganda, Zambia, and Zimbabwe.

92. The NRA includes border trade measures but other subsidies and estimates of the impact of exchange rates. The study covers 75 countries, 55 of which are developing countries. According to the authors, those countries represent 90% of the population, 92% of agricultural value added, and 95% of GDP at the world level (Anderson and Valenzuela, 2008).

93. Only a fraction of total consumption of food products is imported in developing countries (typically not more than 10–20%). But border restrictions increase prices for the total amount of the commodities consumed domestically, of which 80–90% are produced domestically. Thus, through border protection, there is an implicit transfer from domestic consumers to producers. This same fact also limits the use of the receipts from import taxes to subsidize food consumption of the poor, as suggested by some. To the extent that the volume of taxed commodities is only a fraction of total domestic consumption and that the poor population may represent, as a whole, even though not necessarily per capita, a sizable percentage of that domestic consumption, government revenues from taxing imported commodities would typically not be enough to compensate poor consumers. The case of developed countries, where the incidence of poverty is smaller and which have additional fiscal resources, is different. They can tax consumers in general with border protection for food, but then, at the same time, are able to subsidize poor consumers through different targeted policies financed by general revenues.

94. Assuming ER = 1, the profit equation in the importing country is 110 (world price plus 10% import tax) − 60 (cost of raw material, with same technology as the exporting country) − 3 (5% of transport costs over the total cost of raw material) − 20 (same other costs) = 27.

95. Mamingi (1996) notes that there are several definitions of the appropriate deflator for the relative price, such as the consumer price, a price index for inputs, and the price of alternative productions.

96. In particular, the assumptions are as follows. First, to maintain investment as a fixed share of nominal absorption, household savings rates were assumed to vary proportionately. Second, in line with the public finance literature, all simulations were carried out using a revenue-neutral specification of the government budget. To fix government revenue, household tax rates, which are treated as lump-sum taxes in the model, were also allowed to vary proportionately. Third, the factor market closure specifies full employment of available factor supplies. Fourth, all simulations were carried out specifying a flexible real exchange rate and fixed foreign savings, except for the set of exchange rate simulations for which the impact of preset exchange rate appreciation and depreciation are analyzed. To analyze specific policies, there is no alternative to postulating some macroeconomic closure rule (or rules). The mark of good analysis is to make those assumptions

explicit and justify them in terms of the type of analysis performed and the structure of the economy considered.

97. The assessment of overvalued exchange rates has to be based on some measure of the "sustainability" of the current account (see Section 4.4 on exchange rate policies). Obviously, different assumptions about the proper level of current account sustainability will generate different results for the simulations.

98. Where RRA = (1 + NRA agriculture) / (1 + NRA nonagriculture) − 1. Therefore, anti-agricultural bias (pro-agricultural bias) would be RRA < 0 (RRA > 0).

99. According to the United Nations, the system of national accounts utilizes two kinds of output prices, namely, basic prices and producers' prices: "(a) The basic price is the amount receivable by the producer from the purchaser for a unit of a good or service produced as output minus any tax payable, and plus any subsidy receivable, on that unit as a consequence of its production or sale. It excludes any transport charges invoiced separately by the producer; (b) The producer's price is the amount receivable by the producer from the purchaser for a unit of a good or service produced as output minus any VAT, or similar deductible tax, invoiced to the purchaser. It excludes any transport charges invoiced separately by the producer." For inputs it uses purchasers' prices: they are "the amount paid by the purchaser, excluding any deductible VAT or similar deductible tax, in order to take delivery of a unit of a good or service at the time and place required by the purchaser. The purchaser's price of a good includes any transport charges paid separately by the purchaser to take delivery at the required time and place." See http://unstats.un.org/unsd/sna1993/tocLev8.asp?L1=6&L2=10.

100. The countries in LAC are Argentina, Bolivia, Brazil, Chile, Colombia, Costa Rica, Dominican Republic, Ecuador, El Salvador, Guatemala, Guyana, Honduras, Mexico, Paraguay, Peru, and Venezuela. In Asia, the countries are China, Indonesia, Korea, Malaysia, Papua New Guinea, Philippines, Thailand, Bangladesh, India, Nepal, Pakistan, and Sri Lanka. In SSA, the countries are Benin, Botswana, Burkina Faso, Burundi, Cameroon, Central African Republic, Chad, Congo, Dem. Rep., Cote d'Ivoire, Gambia, Ghana, Guinea-Bissau, Kenya, Lesotho, Madagascar, Malawi, Mali, Mauritania, Niger, Rwanda, Senegal, South Africa, Togo, Zambia, and Zimbabwe.

101. Argentina, Brazil, Egypt, India, Korea, Mexico, Morocco, Philippines, Pakistan, and South Africa.

102. It should be remembered that the figures show deflators for the value added of the sectors.

103. The same can be said from the former republics of the Soviet Union (not shown), which suffered a collapse in production during the 1990s.

104. Although *food* production per capita declined in SSA, the levels of *consumption* of calories and proteins per capita in the region has remained stable, with the decline in domestic production compensated by increased imports.

105. Aggregate agricultural growth rates in Table 29 are for each region as a whole, and, therefore, bigger countries define the behavior of that variable (as is the case in Tables 27 and 28). On the other hand, the lines reporting average and median values in Table 29 are calculated from the performance of *individual* countries in each region, and the average is a non-weighted one, to give a better sense of the performance at the country level. Another issue to be noted is that FAOSTAT data are the value of production using average *world prices* for the *same base period*. This is different from World Bank data, which are *value added*, calculated at *local base prices utilized in national accounts*, which differ from country to country. These differences should be kept in mind when looking at indicators of agricultural growth from both data sources.

106. This table is for aggregate regions, from FAOSTAT. Because the share is measured in prices of a benchmark period, the increase in share reflects only changes in quantity produced.

107. Several developing countries, particularly in Africa but not only there, have been hurt further by armed conflict that affected agricultural production and increased poverty and hunger. According to some estimates, conflict in Africa resulted in lost agricultural production of more than US$120

billion during the last three decades of the 20th century (FAO, 2004). That conflict has sometimes been the result of competition over scarce natural resources, including land and water. See, for instance, Messer, Cohen, and D'Costa (1998).

108. Some have argued that even though agricultural production in developing countries would expand with agricultural liberalization in industrialized countries, there could be aggregate negative welfare impacts for some developing countries that are net food importers and/or have preferential access to protected markets in rich countries. The possible negative result of agricultural trade liberalization for some developing countries was highlighted early in trade studies (see, for instance, Koester and Bale, 1984) and has received some attention lately (see Panagariya, 2004). The arguments related to net food importers are usually based on static analyses that do not include employment multipliers (by assuming full employment in the trade simulations) and/or do not allow for capital accumulation, land expansion, or technological change as a result of the elimination of agricultural protectionism and subsidies in industrialized countries. In regard to erosion of preferences, a first-best option is to directly compensate poor countries for preferences lost instead of maintaining distorted regimes in industrialized countries.

109. The effective federal funds rate was about 1.4% (nominal) for the period from December 2001–December 2004, similar to the nominal rates from mid-1954 to the second half of 1955 and again during part of 1958. However, in the 2000s, rates were kept low for about three years, whereas in 1954–1955 they lasted only about 15 months and, in 1958, just 10 months.

Bibliography

Abbott, P., & McCalla, A. (2002). Agriculture in the macroeconomy: Theory and measurement. In: B. L. Gardner & G. C. Rausser (Eds.), *Handbook of agricultural economics 2A* (pp. 1660–1686). Amsterdam: Elsevier.

Abimanyu, A. (2000). Impact of agriculture trade and subsidy policy on the macroeconomy, distribution, and environment in Indonesia: A strategy for future industrial development. *Developing Economies*, *38*(4), 547–571.

Adams, D. W., Graham, D. H., & von Pischke, J. (1984). *Undermining rural development with cheap credit.* Boulder, CO: Westview Press.

Addison, T., & Demery, L. (1989). The economics of rural poverty alleviation. In S. Commander (Ed.), *Structural adjustment and agriculture: Theory and practice in Africa and Latin America.*

Adserà, A., & Boix, C. (2002). Trade, democracy, and the size of the public sector: The political underpinnings of openness. *International Organization*, *56*(2), 229–262.

Aguiar, M., & Gopinath, G. (2004). *Emerging market business cycles: The cycle is the trend.* NBER Working Paper No. 10734, Cambridge, MA: National Bureau of Economic Research.

Ahmed, A. U., Hill, R. V., Smith, L. C., Wiesmann, D. M., & Frankenberger, T. (2007). *The world's most deprived characteristics and causes of extreme poverty and hunger.* IFPRI 2020 Discussion Paper No. 43, Washington, DC: International Food Policy Research Institute.

Aizenman, J., & Jinjarak, Y. (2006). *Globalization and developing countries—A shrinking tax base?* NBER Working Paper No. 11933.

Aizenman, J., & Lee, J. (2005). *International reserves: Precautionary versus mercantilist views, theory and evidence.* NBER Working Paper No. 11366. Cambridge, MA: National Bureau of Economic Research.

Allcott, H., Lederman, D., & López, R. (2006). *Political Institutions, Inequality, and Agricultural Growth: The Public Expenditure Connection.* World Bank Policy Research Working Paper 3902.

Amsden, A. H., & Hikino, T. (2000). The bark is worse than the bite: New WTO law and late industrialization. *Annals of the American Academy of Political and Social Science*, *570*(1), 104–114.

Anderson, K., & Valenzuela, E. (2008). *Estimates of global distortions to agricultural incentives, 1955 to 2007.* Washington DC: World Bank. Available at www.worldbank.org/agdistortions.

Asseery & Peel, D. A. (1991). The effects of exchange rate volatility on exports. *Economic Letters*, *37*, 173–177.

Athukorala, P. C., & Sen, K. (1998). Processed food exports from developing countries: Patterns and determinants. *Food Policy, 23*(1), 41–54.

Australian Bureau of Agricultural and Resource Economics (ABARE). (1999). *Multifunctionality: A pretext for protection? Current Issues, 99*(3).

Balassa, B. (1989). Outward orientation. In H. Chenery, & T. Srinivasan (Eds.), *Handbook of development economics* (Vol. 2, Chapter 31). New York: North-Holland.

Balassa, B. (1989). *New directions in the world economy.* The Macmillan Press Inc.

Balassa, B. (1986). *Economic incentives and agricultural exports in developing countries.* Background Papers World Development Report 1986. World Bank.

Balassa, B., & Michalopoulos, C. (1986). The extent and the cost of protection in developed-developing country trade. *The Journal of World Trade Law, 20*(1), 3–28.

Balassa, B. (1986). Policy responses to external shocks in developing countries. *American Economic Review.*

Balassa, B. (1985). *Change and challenge in the world economy.* New York: St. Martin's Press.

Balassa, B. (1984). Adjustment policies in developing countries: A reassessment. *World Development.*

Balassa, B., & Associates. (1982). *Development strategies in semi-industrial economies.* Baltimore: Johns Hopkins University Press.

Balassa, B. (1980). The process of industrial development and alternative development strategies. *Essays in International Finance, 140.* Princeton: Princeton University.

Balassa, B. (1977). *Policy reform in developing countries.* Oxford: Pergamon Press.

Balassa, B. (1977). Revealed comparative advantage revisited: An analysis of relative export shares of the industrial countries, 1953–1971. *Manchester School of Economics and Social Studies, 45,* 327–344.

Balassa & Associates. (1971). *The structure of protection in developing countries.* Baltimore: The Johns Hopkins University Press.

Baldwin, R. (1969). The case against infant industry protection. *Journal of Political Economy, 77,* 295–305.

Barret, C. (1999). The effects of real exchange rate depreciation on stochastic producer prices in low-income agriculture. *Agricultural Economics, 20*(3), 215–230.

Batini, N., & Laxton, D. (2006). *Under what conditions can inflation targeting be adopted? The experience of emerging markets.* Central Bank of Chile. Working Papers N 406.

Baumol, W. J., & Towse, R. (Eds.). (1997). *Baumol's cost disease: The arts and other victims.* UK: Edward Elgar.

Bautista, & Valdés. (1993). Agricultural incentives in developing countries: Measuring the effects of sectorial and economy wide policies. *World Bank Economic Review, 2*(3), 255–271.

Bautista, R., & Valdes, A. (1993). *The relevance of trade and macroeconomic policies for agriculture.* In R. Batista, & A. Valdes (Eds.), *The bias against agriculture: Trade and macroeconomic policies in developing countries.* San Francisco: ICS Press.

Barro, R. J., & Sala-i-Martin, X. (1995). *Economic Growth.* New York: McGraw-Hill.

Bauer, P. T. (1972). *Dissent on development.* Cambridge, MA: Harvard University Press.

Becker, G., Philipson, T. J., & Soares, R. R. (2003). *The quantity and quality of life and the evolution of world inequality.* NBER Working Papers 9765. Cambridge, MA: National Bureau of Economic Research.

Bernanke, B. S. (2004). *The great moderation. Remarks at the meetings of the Eastern Economic Association.* Washington, DC. www.federalreserve.gov/BOARDDOCS/SPEECHES/2004/20040220/default. htm#f2

Bernanke, B., & Woodford, M. (Eds.). (2004). *The inflation-targeting debate.* University of Chicago Press in NBER Book Series Studies in Business Cycles.

Bhagwati, J. N. (1982). Directly unproductive profit seeking (DUP) activities. *Journal of Political Economy, 90*(5), 988–1002.

Bhagwati, J. (1971). The generalized theory of distortions and welfare. In Bhagwati, et al. (Eds.), *Trade balance of payments and growth: Papers in international economics in honor of Charles Kindleberger.* Amsterdam: North-Holland.

Bhagwati, J. (1993). *India in transition: Freeing the economy.* London: Oxford University Press.

Bhalla, S. (2002). *Imagine there's no country: Poverty, inequality and growth in the era of globalization.* Washington, DC: Institute for International Economics.

Bilginsoy, C. (1997). A macroeconomic analysis of agricultural terms of trade in Turkey, 1952–1990. *The Journal of Development Studies, 33*(6), 797.

Birdsall, N., & Hamoudi, A. (2002). *Commodity dependence, trade, and growth: When "openness" is not enough.* Working Paper No. 7. Washington, DC: Center for Global Development.

Blanchard, O., & Fischer, S. (1989). *Lectures on macroeconomics.* Cambridge, MA: The MIT Press.

Blarrcom, V. B., Knudsen, O., & Nash, J. (1993). *The role of public expenditures for Agriculture.* World Bank Discussion Paper #216. Washington, DC: World Bank.

Bleaney, M., & Greenaway, D. (2001). The impact of terms of trade and real exchange rate volatility on investment and growth in sub-saharan Africa. *Journal of Development Economics, 65*(2), 491–500.

Bordo, M. (2006). *Sudden stops, financial crises, and original sin in emerging countries: Déjà vu?.* NBER Working Paper No. 12393. Cambridge, MA: National Bureau of Economic Research.

Borensztein, E., Khan, M. S., Wickham, P., & Reinhart, C. (1994). *The behavior of non-oil commodity prices.* Occasional Paper No. 112, September 15, 1994. Washington, DC: International Monetary Fund.

Bourguignon, F. (2004). *The poverty-growth-inequality triangle.* Paper presented at the Indian Council for Research on International Economic Relations. World Bank. http://povlibrary.worldbank.org/files/15185_ICRIER_paper-final.pdf

Bourguignon, F. (2002). The growth elasticity of poverty reduction: Explaining heterogeneity across countries and time periods. In T. S. Eicher, & S. J. Turnovski (Eds.), *Inequality and growth theory and policy implications.* Cambridge, MA: MIT Press.

Bracke, T., Bussière, M., Fidora, M., & Straub, R. (2008). *A framework for assessing global imbalances.* Occasional Paper No. 78. Frankfurt, Germany: European Central Bank.

Bresciani, F., Feder, G., Gilligan, D. O., Onchan, T., & Jacoby, H. G. (2002). Weathering the storm: The impact of the East Asian crisis on farm households in Indonesia and Thailand. *World Bank Observer, 17* (1), 1–20.

Bruce, N., & Purvis, D. (1984). The specification of goods and factor markets in open economy macroeconomic models. In R. Jones, & P. Kenen (Eds.), *Handbook of International Economics* (Chapter 16). North-Holland.

Bruno, M., & Easterly, W. (1995). *Inflation crises and long-run growth.* NBER Working Paper No. 5209. Cambridge, MA: National Bureau of Economic Research.

Bruno, M., & Sachs, J. (1985). *Economics of worldwide stagflation.* Cambridge, MA: Harvard University Press.

Bruno, M., & Sachs, J. (1982). Energy and resource allocation: A dynamic model of the 'Dutch Disease.' *Review of Economic Studies, 49*(5), 845–859.

Bruton, H. (1998). A reconsideration of import substitution. *Journal of Economic Literature, 36,* 903–936.

Bruton, H. (1989). Import substitution, handbook of development economics. In H. Chenery, & T. N. Srinivasan (Eds.), *Handbook of development economics* (1st ed., Vol. 2, Chap. 30, pp. 1601–1644). Elsevier.

Buffie, E. (1986). Devaluation, investment and growth in LDCs. *Journal of Development Economics, 20.*

Buffie, E. (1984). The macroeconomics of trade liberalization. *Journal of International Economics.*

Buiter W. (1990). *Principles of budgetary and financial policy.* MIT University Press.

Buiter, W. (1986). *Structural and stabilization aspects of fiscal and financial policy in the dependent economy. Part I.* World Bank. Discussion Paper DRD 180 September 1986.

Burdekin, R., Denzau, A., Keil, M., Sitthiyot, T., & Willett, T. (2000). *When does inflation hurt economic growth? Different nonlinearities for different economies.* Working Paper No. 2000-22. Claremont, CA: Claremont McKenna College. http://econ.claremontmckenna.edu/papers/2000-22.pdf

Caballero, R., & Krishnamurthy, A. (2004). Inflation targeting and sudden stops chapter 10. In B. Bernanke, & M. Woodford (Eds.), *The inflation-targeting Debate.* University of Chicago Press in NBER Book Series Studies in Business Cycles.

Calvo G. (2006). *Monetary policy challenges in emerging markets: Sudden stop, liability dollarization, and lender of last resort.* Inter-American Development Bank. Research Department. Working Paper #596, December 2006.

Calvo, G. A., Izquierdo, A., & Mejia, L. F. (2004). *On the empirics of sudden stops: The relevance of balance-sheet effects.* NBER Working Papers 10520. National Bureau of Economic Research, Inc.

Calvo, G. (2003). *Explaining sudden stop, growth collapse, and BOP crisis: The case of distortionary output taxes.* Special issue, IMF Staff Papers 50: 1–20.

Calvo, G. A., & Reinhart, C. M. (2002). Fear of floating. *Quarterly Journal of Economics, 117*(2), 379–408.

Calvo, G., Leiderman, L., & Reinhart, C. M. (1993). Capital *inflows to Latin America: The role of external factors.* IMF Staff Papers 40 (March): 108–151.

Calvo, G. A., & Vegh, C. A. (1999). Inflation stabilization and balance of payment crises in developing countries. In J. B. Taylor, & M. Woodford (Eds.), *Handbook of Macroeconomics* (1st ed., Vol. 1, Chap. 24, pp. 1531–1614). Elsevier.

Calvo, G. (1987). Balance of payments crises in a cash in advance economy. *Journal of Money, Credit and Banking.*

Calvo, G. (1978). On the time consistency of optimal policy in a monetary economy. *Econometrica.*

Cardoso, E. (1992). *Inflation and poverty.* NBER Working Paper No. 4006. Cambridge, MA: National Bureau of Economic Research.

Cardoso, F. H., & Faletto, E. (1979). *Dependency and development in Latin America.* Berkeley: University of California Press.

Cashin, P. A., Cespedes, L. F., & Sahay, R. (2002). *Keynes, cocoa, and copper: In search of commodity currencies.* IMF Working Paper No. 02/223. December 1, 2002.

CEPAL. (1969). *América Latina. El Pensamiento de la CEPAL.* Santiago de Chile: Editorial Sudamericana.

Chen, S., & Ravallion, M. (2004). *How have the world's poorest fared since the early 1980s?* Policy Research Working Paper No. 3341. Washington, DC: World Bank.

Chenery H., Robinson, S., & Syrquin, M. (1986). *Industrialization and growth: A comparative study.* A World Bank Research Publication. Oxford University Press.

Chenery, H., Ahluwalia, M., Bell, C., Dulloy, J., & Jolly, R. (1974). *Redistribution with growth.* World Bank, Oxford University Press.

Chenery, H., & Srinivasan T. N. (Eds.). *Handbook of development economics.* Elsevier Science Publishers B.V.

Cheng, E., & Zhong X. (2004). Rates of interest, credit supply and China's rural development. *Savings and Development Quarterly Review,* 2.

Chinn, M. D. (2005). *A primer on real effective exchange rates: Determinants, overvaluation, trade flows and competitive devaluation.* National Bureau of Economic Research Working Paper 11521. Cambridge, MA. www.nber.org/papers/w11521

Cho, G., Sheldon, I. M., & McCorriston, S. (2002). Exchange rate uncertainty and agricultural trade. *American Journal of Agricultural Economics,* 84(4), 931–942.

Chowdhury, A. (1993). Does exchange rate volatility depress trade flows? Evidence from error- correction model. *The Review of Economics and Statistics,* 75, 700–706.

Christ, C. (1987). *Pitfalls in macroeconomic model building.* The Johns Hopkins University (mimeo).

Christ, C. (1979). On fiscal and monetary policies and the government budget restraint. *American Economic Review.*

Christ, C. (1978). Some dynamic theory of macroeconomic policy: Effects on income and prices under the government budget restraint. *Journal of Monetary Economics.*

Chudik, A., & Mongardini, J. (2007). In search of equilibrium: Estimating equilibrium real exchange rates in sub-saharan African countries. IMF Working Paper 07/90. Washington, DC: International Monetary Fund.

Cicowiez, M., Díaz-Bonilla, C., & Díaz-Bonilla, E. (2008). The impact of global and domestic trade liberalization on poverty and inequality in Argentina. GTAP Eleventh Annual Conference, Helsinki. In K. Anderson, & W. Martin (Eds.), To be published in World Bank book.

Collier, P. (2005). The macroeconomic repercussions of agricultural shocks and their implications for insurance. In S. Dercon (Ed.). *Insurance against poverty* (Chap. 7). Oxford, UK: Oxford University Press.

Collier, P., & Gunning, J. W. (1999). Explaining african economic performance. *Journal of Economic Literature,* XXXVII, 64–111.

Collier, P., & Hoeffer, A. E. (1998). On the economic causes of civil war. *Oxford Economic Papers,* 50(4), 563–573.

Cooper, R. (1980). *The economics of interdependence.* Council on Foreign Relations Series. New York: Columbia University Press.

Corbo, V., & de Melo, J. (1987). *External shocks and policy reforms in the Southern cone: A reassessment.* Development Research Department Discussion Paper No. 241.

Corbo, V., & de Melo, J. (Eds.). (1985). Liberalization with stabilization in the Southern cone of Latin America. Special issue of *World Development.*

Corden, W. M., & Neary, J. P. (1982). Booming sector and de-industrialisation in a small open economy. *The Economic Journal*, *92*(368), 825–848.

Corden, W. M. (1990). *Exchange rate policy in developing countries*. Policy Research Working Paper No. 412, April 1990.Washington, DC: World Bank. www-wds.worldbank.org/external/default/WDSContent-Server/WDSP/IB/1990/04/01/000009265_3961001165700/Rendered/PDF/multi0page.pdf

Corden, W. M. (1984). The normative theory of international trade. In R. Jones, & P. Kenen (Eds.), *Handbook of international economics* (Chap. 2). North-Holland.

Corden, W. M. (1974). *Trade policy and economic welfare*. Oxford University Press.

Corden, W. M. (1971). *The theory of protection*. Oxford University Press.

Crafts, N. (2000). *Globalization and growth in the twentieth century*. IMF Working Paper No. 00/44. Washington, DC: International Monetary Fund.

Cushman, D. O. (1988). U.S. bilateral trade flows and exchange rate risk during the floating period. *Journal of International Economics*, *24*, 317–330.

De Janvry A., Key, N., & Sadoulet, E. (1997). Agricultural and rural development policy in Latin America. New directions and new challenges. *FAO Agricultural Policy and Economic Development Series – 2*. Rome: FAO.

De Janvry, A., Marsh, R., Runsten, D., Sadoulet, E., & Zabin, C. (1989). *Rural development in Latin America: An evaluation and a proposal*. San José (Costa Rica): IICA.

De Nicolo, G., Honohan, P., & Ize, A. (2003). Dollarization of the banking system: good or bad? *World Bank Policy Research Working Paper*, No. 3116.

Deaton, A. (2001). Counting the world's poor: Problems and possible solutions. *World Bank Research Observer*, *16*(2), 125–147.

Deaton, A., & Miller, R. (1995). International commodity prices, macroeconomic performance and politics in Sub-Saharan Africa. *Princeton Studies in International Economics*, *79*.

Delgado, C. J., Hopkins, J., Kelly, V. A., Hazell, P., McKenna, A. A., Gruhn, P., et al. (1998). *Agricultural growth linkages in Sub-Saharan Africa*. IFPRI Research Report No. 107. Washington, DC: International Food Policy Research Institute.

Delgado, C., Rosegrant, M., Steinfeld, H., Ehui S., & Courbois, C. (1999). *Live stock to 2020: The next food revolution*. Food, Agriculture, and the Environment Discussion Paper 28. Washington, DC: International Food Policy Re search Institute.

Dercon, S. (Ed.). (2005). *Insurance against poverty*. Oxford, UK: Oxford University Press.

Dercon, S., & Hoddinott, J. (2005). Health, shocks, and poverty persistence. In Part III of S. Dercon (Ed.), *Against poverty insurance*. Oxford, UK: Oxford University Press.

Dervis, K., de Melo, J., & Robinson, S. (1982). *General equilibrium models for development policy*. Cambridge University Press.

Desai, B., & Mellor, J. W. (1993). *Institutional finance for agricultural development: An analytical survey of critical issues*.

Diao, X., Diaz–Bonilla, E., & Robinson, S. (2003). Poor countries would gain from open agricultural markets. In *Agriculture in the Global Economy. Hunger 2003*. 13th Annual Report on the State of World Hunger. Washington, DC: Bread for the World.

Diao, X., Díaz-Bonilla, E., & Robinson, S. (2003). *How much does it hurt? The impact of agricultural trade policies on developing countries*. Issue Brief. Washington, DC: International Food Policy Research Institute.

Diao, X., Roe, T., & Doukkali, R. (2002). *Economy-wide benefits from establishing water user-right markets in a spatially heterogeneous agricultural economy*. Trade and Macroeconomics discussion paper 103. Washington, DC: International Food Policy Research Institute.

Diao, X., & Roe, T. (2000). How the financial crisis affected world agriculture: A general equilibrium perspective. *American Journal of Agricultural Economics*, *82*, 688–694.

Diaz-Bonilla, E. (2008). *Global macroeconomic developments and poverty*. IFPRI Discussion Paper No. 00766. Markets, Trade and Institutions Division. Washington, DC: The International Food Policy Research Institute (IFPRI).

Diaz-Bonilla, E., Frandsen, S. E., & Robinson, S. (Eds.). (2006). WTO *negotiations and agricultural trade liberalization : the effect of developed countries' policies on developing countries*. Wallingford Oxfordshire, UK: CABI.

Díaz-Bonilla, E., Thomas, M., Robinson, S., & Cattaneo, A. (2006). Food security and the world trade organization: A typology of countries. In E. Diaz-Bonilla, S. E. Frandsen, & S. Robinson (Eds.), *WTO negotiations and agricultural trade liberalization : The effect of developed countries' policies on developing countries* (Chap. 8, pp. 162–183). Wallingford Oxfordshire, UK: CABI.

Díaz-Bonilla, E., & Tin, J. That was then but this is now : multifunctionality in industry and agriculture. In E. Diaz-Bonilla, S. E. Frandsen, & S. Robinson(Eds.), *WTO negotiations and agricultural trade liberalization : The effect of developed countries' policies on developing countries* (Chap. 11, pp. 235–260). Wallingford Oxfordshire, UK: CABI.

Diaz-Bonilla, E., Robinson, S., Thomas, M., & Yanoma, Y. (2002). *WTO, agriculture and developing countries: A survey of issues.* Washington, DC: International Food Policy Research Institute.

Diaz-Bonilla, E. (2001). Globalization, poverty, and food security. In *Putting globalization to work for the poor.* Panel discussion at Sustainable Food Security for All by 2020, 2020 Vision Conference, September 4–6, Bonn, Germany. www.ifpri.org/2020conference/PDF/summary_diaz-bonilla.pdf.

Diaz-Bonilla, E. (2001). Globalization and agriculture: Some facts, interpretations, and policy issues. In O. Solbrig, R. Paarlberg, & F. Di Castri, (Eds.), *Globalization and the Rural Environment* (Chap. 17). Cambridge, MA: USA, The David Rockefeller Center for Latin American Studies and Harvard University Press.

Diaz-Bonilla, E. (2001). *Globalization, poverty, and food security in sustainable food security for all by 2020.* Proceedings of an international conference, September 4–6, 2001, Bonn, Germany. 2002. International Food Policy Research Institute. www.ifpri.org/2020conference/PDF/summary_diaz-bonilla.pdf

Diaz-Bonilla, E., & Robinson, S. (2001). *Shaping globalization for poverty alleviation and food security.* 2020 Vision Focus No. 8. Washington, DC: International Food Policy Research Institute.

Diaz-Bonilla, E., & Schamis, H. (2001). From redistribution to stability: The evolution of exchange rate policies in Argentina, 1950–1998. In J. Frieden, & E. Stein (Eds.), *The currency game: Exchange rate politics in Latin America* (Chap. 3). Washington, DC: The Johns Hopkins University Press and Inter-American Development Bank.

Díaz-Bonilla, E., & Reca, L. (2000). Trade and agroindustrialization in developing countries: Trends and policy impacts. *Agricultural Economics, 23*(3), 219–229.

Diaz-Bonilla, M. T., Robinson, S., & Cattaneo, A. (2000). *Food security and trade negotiations in the world trade organization: a cluster analysis of country groups.* Trade and Macroeconomics Working Paper Number 59. IFPRI.

Diaz-Bonilla, E. (1999). South American wheat markets and MERCOSUR. In J. M. Antle, & V. H. Smith (Eds.), *The economics of world wheat markets.* Oxfordshire, UK; Cambridge, MA: CABI.

Díaz-Bonilla, E. (1989). *Los programas de ajuste sectorial agropecuario. Reflexiones sobre algunas experiencias en América del Sur.* Instituto de Desarrollo Económico del Banco Mundial. Documentos de Trabajo. World Bank.

Díaz-Bonilla, E. (forthcoming). Globalisation of agriculture and the food crises: then and now. In B. Karapinar, & C. Haberli (Eds.), *The end of cheap food* (Chap. 2). Cambridge University Press.

Di Bella, G., Lewis, M., & Martin, A. (2007). *Assessing competitiveness and real exchange rate misalignment in low-income countries.* IMF Working Paper 07/201. Washington, DC: International Monetary Fund.

Dollar, D. (1992). *Outward-oriented developing economies really do grow more rapidly: Evidence from 95 LDCs, 1976-1985. Economic Development and Cultural Change, 40*(3), 523–544.

Dollar, D., & Kraay, A. (2001). *Growth is good for the poor.* Working Paper No. 2587. Washington, DC: World Bank Development Research Group.

Dooley, M., Folkerts-Landau, D., & Garber, P. (2003). *An essay on the revived Bretton Woods system.* NBER Working Paper No. 9971. Cambridge, MA: National Bureau of Economic Research.

Dornbusch, R., & Fischer, S. (1993). *Moderate inflation.* NBER Working Paper No. 3896, Cambridge, MA: National Bureau of Economic Research.

Dornbusch, R. (1976). Expectations and exchange rate dynamics. *Journal of Political Economy, 84*(6), 1161–1176.

Dornbusch, R. (1973). Money, devaluation and non-traded goods. *American Economic Review, 63.*

Dorosh, P. A., & Sahn, D. E. (2000). A general equilibrium analysis of the effect of macroeconomic adjustment on poverty in Africa. *Journal of Policy Modeling, 22*(6), 753–776.

Dos Santos, T. (1970). The structure of dependence. *The American Economic Review, 16*, 231–236.

Dreher A., Sturm, J. E., & Ursprung, H. W. (2006). *The impact of globalization on the composition of government expenditures: Evidence from panel data.* CESIFO Working Paper No. 1755.

Drukker, D., Gomis-Porqueras, P., & Hernandez-Verme, P. (2005). *Threshold effects in the relationship between inflation and growth: A new panel-data approach.* http://gemini.econ.umd.edu/cgi-bin/conference/download.cgi?db_name=MWM2005&paper_id=54

Easterly, W. (2005). *What did structural adjustment adjust? The association of policies and growth with repeated IMF and World Bank adjustment loans.* Center for Global Development Working Paper 11. Washington, DC. www.cgdev.org/content/publications/detail/2779

Easterly, W. (2003). IMF and World Bank structural adjustment programs and poverty. In M. P. Dooley, & J. Frankel (Eds.), *Managing currency crises in emerging markets* (Chap. 11). The University of Chicago Press.

Easterly W., Islam, R., & Stiglitz, J. E. (2000). Shaken and stirred: Explaining growth volatility. In *Annual World Bank conference on development economics* (pp. 191–211).

Easterly, W., & Fischer, S. (2000). *Inflation and the poor.* World Bank Policy Research Working Paper No. 2335.

Eastwood, R., & Lipton, M. (2001). *Pro-poor growth and pro-growth poverty reduction: What do they mean? What does the evidence mean? What can policymakers do?* Paper presented at the Asia and Pacific Forum on Poverty. Manila, Philippines.

Edwards, S. (1989). *Real exchange rates, devaluation and adjustment: Exchange rate policy in developing countries.* Cambridge, MA: MIT Press.

Edwards, S., & Teitel, S. (Eds.). (1986). Growth, reform, and adjustment: Latin America's trade and macroeconomic policies in the 1970s and 1980s. Special issue of *Economic Development and Cultural Change.*

Edwards, S. (1984). *The order of liberalization of the balance of payments.* World Bank Staff Working Papers Number 710.

Epaulard, A. (2003). *Macroeconomic performance and poverty reduction.* IMF Working Paper No. 03/72. Washington, DC: International Monetary Fund.

Fallon, P., & Lucas, R. (2002). The impact of financial crises on labor markets, household incomes, and poverty: A review of evidence. *World Bank Research Observer, 17*(1), 21–45.

Fan, S., & Pardey, P. (1998). Government spending on Asian agriculture: Trends and production consequences. In *Agricultural public finance policy in Asia.* Tokyo: Asian Productivity Organization.

FAOSTAT. http://faostat.fao.org/default.htm.

FAO. (2006). *Base de datos de estadísticas e indicadores de gasto publico agrícola y rural.* Santiago, Chile: Regional Office for Latin America and the Caribbean of the Food and Agriculture Organization of the United Nations.

FAO (Food and Agriculture Organization of the United Nations). (1999). *Agriculture, trade and food security: Issues and options in the WTO negotiations from the perspective of developing countries.* (Vol. 1). Rome: Commodities and Trade Division, Food and Agriculture Organization of the United Nations.

FAO/GTZ. 1998. *Agricultural finance revisited: Why? Food and Agriculture Organization (FAO) and German Agency for Technical Cooperation (GTZ).* Africa Series No. 1. Rome.

Farrell, D., Lund, S., Maasry, A., & Roemer, S. (2007). *The U.S. imbalancing act: Can the current account deficit continue?.* McKinsey Global Institute.

Feenstra, R. (1986). Functional equivalence between liquidity costs and the utility of money. *Journal of Monetary Economics, 17.*

Fei, J., & Ranis, G. (1966). Agrarianism, dualism and economic development. In I. Adelman, & E. Thorbecke (Eds.), *Theory and design of economic development* (Chap. 4). Baltimore: Johns Hopkins Press.

Felix, D. (1965). Monetarists, structuralists, and import-substituting industrialization: A critical appraisal. *Journal Studies in Comparative International Development, 1*(10), 137–153.

Finger, J. M., & Shuler, P. (1999). Implementation of the Uruguay Round commitments: The development challenge. Presented at the World Bank Conference on Agriculture and the New Trade Agenda: Interests and Options in the WTO 2000 Negotiations, Geneva. October 1–2.

Fischer, S. (1993). The role of macroeconomic factors in growth. *Journal of Monetary Economics, 32*, 485–512.

Fischer, S. (1990). *The economics of budget deficits.* World Bank (mimeo).

Fischer, S. (1974). Money in the production function. *Economic Inquiry, 12*(4), 518–533.

Fishlow, A. (1985). Lessons from the past: Capital markets during the 19th century and the interwar periods. *International Organization, 39*, 383–439.

Fogli, A., & Perri, F. (2006). *The "Great Moderation" and the U.S. external imbalance.* CEPR Discussion Paper 6010, London: Centre for Economic Policy Research.

Fortin, P. (2003). The bank of canada and the inflation-unemployment trade-off. In *Macroeconomics, monetary policy, and financial stability: A festschrift in honour of charles freedman* (pp. 3–24). Proceedings of a conference held by the Bank of Canada. Ottawa: Bank of Canada.

Frank, A. G. (1969). *Capitalism and Underdevelopment in Latin America.* New York: Monthly Review Press.

Frankel, J. (2006). *What do economists mean by globalization? Implications for inflation and monetary policy.* Written for Academic Consultants Meeting, September 28, 2006 Board of Governors of the Federal Reserve System1. http://ksghome.harvard.edu/~jfrankel/FRB-Globalzn&InflOct4.pdf

Frankel, J. (2006). *The effect of monetary policy on real commodity prices.* NBER Working Paper No. 12713, Cambridge, MA.

Frankel, J. (2005). Peg the export price index: A proposed monetary regime for small countries. *Journal of Policy Modeling, 27*(4), 495–508.

Frankel, J. (1999). *No single currency regime is right for all countries or at all times.* Working Paper 7338. Cambridge, MA: National Bureau Of Economic Research. http://www.nber.org/papers/w7338

Frankel, J. (1986). Expectations and commodity price dynamics: The overshooting model. *American Journal of Agricultural Economics, 68*(2), 344–348.

Frankel, J. (1984). Commodity prices and money: Lessons from international finance. *American Journal of Agricultural Economics, 66*(5), 560–566.

Frenkel, J. (1983). *Panel discussion on southern cone.* Special issue of IMF Staff Papers.

Frenkel, J. A., & Johnson, H. G. (Eds.). (1976). *The monetary approach to the balance of payments.* London: George Allen & Unwin.

Gardner, B. (1981). On the power of Macroeconomic Linkages to Explain Events in U.S. Agriculture. *American Journal of Agricultural Economics,* 871–878.

Gardner, B., & Rausser, G. (Eds.). *Handbook of agricultural economics.* Elsevier Science. Vols. 1A and 1B, 2001, Vols. 2A and 2B, 2002.

Garrett, J. L., & Ruel, M. (Eds.). (2000). *Achieving urban food and nutrition security in the developing world.* IFPRI 2020 Focus 3, August. Washington, DC: International Food Policy Research Institute. Available online at www.ifpri.org/2020/focus/focus03/focus03.pdf

Ghosh, A., & Phillips, S. (1998). *Inflation, disinflation, and growth.* IMF Working Paper 98/68, Washington, DC: International Monetary Fund.

Ghura, D. *Tax revenue in sub-saharan africa: effects of economic policies and corruption.* IMF Working Paper: WP/98/135. Washington, DC.

Giavazzi, F., & Tabellini, G. (2005). Economic and political liberalizations. *Journal of Monetary Economics, 52,* 1297–1330.

Goldberg, R. A. (1988). A holistic macroeconomics of agriculture. *Research in domestic and international agribusiness management, 9,* 127–144.

Goldin, I., & Winters, L. A. (1992). *Open economies: Structural adjustment and agriculture.* Cambridge University Press.

Goldin, I., & Knudsen, O. (Eds.). (1990). *Agricultural trade liberalization: Implications for developing countries.* Paris: Organization for Economic Co-operation and Development. Washington, DC: World Bank.

Goldstein, M., & Kahn, M. (1982). *Effects of slowdown in industrial countries on growth in non-oil developing countries.* IMF Occasional Paper No. 12. Washington, DC: International Monetary Fund.

Golub, S., & Finger, J. (1979). The processing of primary commodities: Effects of developed-country tariff escalation and developing-country export taxes. *Journal of Political Economy, 87*(3), 559–577.

Hamilton, J. (2007). Borrowing short and lending long. *Econbrowser, Analysis of Economic Conditions and Policy.* www.econbrowser.com/archives/2007/09/borrowing_short.html

Hanson, J. (1983). Contractionary devaluation, substitution in production and consumption and the role of the labor market. *Journal of International Economics.*

Helmers F. L. C. H., & Dornbusch, R. (1988). *The open economy: Tools for policy makers in developing countries.* EDI Series in Economic Development. World Bank. Oxford University Press.

Hirschman, A. (1982). The rise and decline of development economics. In M. Gersowitz, C. Díaz-Alejandro, G. Ranis, & M. Rosenzweig (Eds.), *The theory and experience of economic development*. London: George Allen and Unwin.

Hirschman, A. (1968). The political economy of import-substituting industrialization in Latin America. *The Quarterly Journal of Economics*.

Hirschman, A. (1958). *The strategy of economic development*. New Haven, CT: Yale University Press.

Hoffmaister, A. W., & Samiei, H. (1996). *Have north-south growth linkages changed?*. IMF Working Paper No. 96/54. Washington, DC: International Monetary Fund.

Homem de Melo, F. (1999). Os Efeitos Negativos da Politica Cambial sobre a Agricultura Brasileira. (The Negative Effects of the Exchange Rate Policy on the Brazilian Agriculture). *Economia Aplicada/Brazilian Journal of Applied Economics*, *3*, Special Issue March 1999: 35–46.

Honohan, P. (2000). *How interest rates changed under financial liberalization: A cross-country review*. Working Paper No. 2313. Washington, DC: World Bank.

Hudson, D., & Ethridge, D. (1999). Production taxes and sectoral economic growth evidence form cotton and yarn markets in Pakistan. *Agricultural Economics*, *20*(3), 263–276.

IMF (International Monetary Fund). (2007). *World economic outlook (WEO): Spillovers and Cycles in the Global Economy*. Washington, D.C.

IMF (International Monetary Fund). (2005). *World economic outlook (WEO): Building Institutions*. Washington, DC.

IMF (International Monetary Fund). (2001). Morocco: 2001 Article IV Consultation—Staff Report; Public Information Notice; and Statement by the Executive Director for Morocco. IMF Country Report No 01/205.

IMF (International Monetary Fund). (1999). *World economic outlook (WEO): International financial contagion*. Washington, DC.

Insel, B. (1985). A world awash in grain. *Foreign Affairs*, *63*(4).

Inter-American Development Bank. (1995). *Informe del progreso económico y social en Latinoamérica y el Caribe*. Washington, DC.

Intergovernmental Panel on Climate Change (IPCC). (2007). *Climate change 2007: Impacts, adaptation and vulnerability*. Working group II contribution to the intergovernmental panel on climate change fourth assessment report. Summary for policymakers, approved at the 8th Session of Working Group II of the IPCC, Brussels.

International Energy Agency. (2007). *Medium-term oil market report*. Paris, France.

International Energy Agency. (2004). *World energy outlook*. Paris, France.

International Monetary Fund (IMF). (2007). *International financial statistics*. www.imfstatistics.org/imf/. Database accessed through subscription.

International Monetary Fund (IMF). (2005). *The macroeconomics of managing increased aid inflows: experiences of low-income countries and policy implications*. Prepared by the Policy Development and Review Department (in consultation with the Area, Fiscal, Monetary and Financial Systems, and Research Departments). August 8, 2005. www.imf.org/external/np/pp/eng/2005/080805a.pdf

International Monetary Fund (IMF). (2004). *Public investment and fiscal policy*. Prepared by the Fiscal Affairs Department and the Policy Development and Review Department (in consultation with other departments and in cooperation with the World Bank and the Inter-American Development Bank). Approved by Teresa Ter-Minassian and Mark Allen. March 12, 2004).

International Monetary Fund. (1977). *The monetary approach to the balance of payments*. Washington, DC: IMF.

International Monetary Fund (IMF). (1996, 1999, 2005, 2007). *World economic outlook*. Washington, DC.

Isard, P. (2007). *Equilibrium exchange rates: Assessment methodologies*. IMF Working Paper 07/296. Washington, DC.www.imf.org/external/pubs/ft/wp/2007/wp07296.pdf

Jaramillo, C. (2001). Liberalization, crisis, and change: Colombian agriculture in the 1990s. *Economic Development and Cultural Change*, *49*(4); 821–846.

Jensen, H. T., Robinson, S., & Tarp, F. (2002). *General equilibrium measures of agricultural policy bias in fifteen developing countries*. TMD discussion papers 105. International Food Policy Research Institute (IFPRI).

Johnson, D., & Gale, J. (1947). *Forward prices for agriculture*. Chicago: University of Chicago Press.

Johnson, O. (1987). *The agricultural sector and adjustment programs supported by IMF stand-by arrangements.* IMF Working Paper No. 87/57. Washington, DC.

Johnson, O. (1984). On growth and inflation in developing countries. *Staff Papers, International Monetary Fund, 31*(4), 636–660.

Johnston, B., & Mellor J. (1961). The role of agriculture in economic development. *American Economic Review, 51*(4).

Jorgenson, D. (1967). Surplus agricultural labor and the development of a dual economy. *Oxford Economic Papers.*

Kamanou, G., & Morduch, J. (2005). Measuring vulnerability to poverty. In S. Dercon (Ed.), *Insurance against poverty* (Chap. 8). Oxford, UK: Oxford University Press.

Kamas, L. (1986). Dutch disease economics and the colombian export boom. *World Development, 14*, 1177–1198.

Kamin & Klau. (1998). *Some multi-country evidence on the effects of real exchange rates on output.* Federal Reserve Board International Finance Discussion Paper No. 611.

Kanbur, R. (2001). *Economic policy, distribution and poverty: The nature of disagreements.* Rome: International Fund for Agricultural Development. www.ifad.org/poverty/lecture.pdf

Kaufmann, D., Kraay, A., & Zoido-Lobatón, P. (1999). *Governance matters.* Policy Research Working Paper No. 2196. Washington, DC: World Bank.

Kehoe, T. J. (2000). The international financial crisis: macroeconomic linkages to agriculture: Discussion. *American Journal of Agricultural Economics, 82*(3), 703–706 (4 p.).

Keohane, R., & Nye, J. (1977). *Power and interdependence: World politics in transition.* Boston: Scott Foresman and Company.

Kerr, C., Dunlop, J. T., Harbison, F., & Myers, C. A. (1964). *Industrialism and Industrial Man.* New York: Oxford University Press.

Khan, M. H. (2001). Agricultural taxation in developing countries: a survey of issues and policy. *Agricultural Economics, 24*, 315–328.

Khan, M., & Senhadji, A. (2001). Threshold effects in the relationship between inflation and growth. *IMF Staff Papers, 48*(1), 1–21.

Kherallah, M., Delgado, C., Gabre-Madhin, E., Minot, N., & Johnson, M. (2000). *The road half-travelled: Agricultural market reform in sub-Saharan Africa.* Washington, DC: Food Policy Report. International Food Policy Research Institute.

Kherallah, M., Lofgren, H., Gruhn, P., & Reeder, M. M. (2000). *Wheat policy reform in Egypt: Adjustment of local markets and options for the future.* Washington, DC: IFPRI.

Kilian, L. (2006). *Not all oil price shocks are alike: Disentangling demand and supply shocks in the crude oil market.* CEPR Discussion Paper No. 5994. London, UK.: Centre for Economic Policy Research.

Klieson, K. L., & Poole, W. (Federal Reserve Bank of St Louis). (2000). Agriculture outcomes and monetary policy actions: Kissin' cousins? *Federal Reserve Bank of St. Louis Review, 82*(3), 1–12.

Koe, M. A., Prasad, E. S., & Terrones, M. E. (2005). Growth and volatility in an era of globalization. *IMF Staff Papers, 52*, 31–63.

Koester, U., & Bale, M. D. (1990). The common agricultural policy: A review of its operation and effects on developing countries. *World Bank Research Observer, 5*(1), 95–121.

Kose, M. A., Prasad, E. S., Rogoff, K. S., & Wei, S. J. (2006). *Financial globalization: A reappraisal.* NBER Working Paper No. 12484.

Kose, M., Ayhan, E. P., & Terrones, M. (2005). Growth and volatility in an era of globalization. Special issue, *IMF Staff Papers, 52*, 31–63.

Krueger, O. (1992). *The political economy of agricultural pricing policy.* Baltimore: Johns Hopkins University Press.

Krueger, A. O., Schiff, M., & Valdes, A. (1988). Agricultural incentives in developing countries: measuring the effects of sectorial and economy wide policies. *World Bank Economic Review, 2*(3), 255–271.

Krueger, A. (1984). Trade policies in developing countries. In *Handbook of international economics* (Chap. 11). North Holland.

Krueger, A. (1981). Interactions between inflation and trade regime objectives in stabilization programs. In Cline & Weintraub (Eds.), *Economic stabilization policy in developing countries.*

Krueger, A. (1978). *Liberalization attempts and consequences*. National Bureau of Economic Research.

Krueger, A. O. (1974). The political economy of the rent-seeking society. *American Economic Review, 64* (3), 291–303.

Krugman, P. (1997). *Development, geography, and economic theory* (3rd ed.). Cambridge: MIT Press.

Krugman, P. (1994). *The fall and rise of development economics*. In Rodwin & Schon (Eds.), *Rethinking the development experience*. Washington, DC: Brookings Institution Press.

Krugman, P., & Taylor, L. (1978). Contractionary effects of devaluation. *Journal of International Economics, 8*(3), 446–454.

Kumhof, M. (2001). *A critical view of inflation targeting: Crises, limited sustainability, and aggregate shocks*. Central Bank of Chile. Working Papers N° 127.

Kuznets, S. (1966). *Modern economic growth*. New Haven, CT: Yale University Press.

Kydland, F., & Prescott, E. (1977). Rules rather than discretion: The inconsistency of optimal plans. *Journal of Political Economy, 85*(3), 473–492.

Lamb, R. (2000). Food crops, exports, and the short-run policy response of agriculture in Africa. *Agricultural Economics, 22,* 271–298.

Langley, S. (Ed.). (2000). *International agriculture and trade reports: International financial crises and agriculture*. Washington, DC: U.S. Department of Agriculture, Economic Research Services.

Langley, S., Giugalc, M., Meyers, W., & Hallahan, C. (2000). International financial volatility and agricultural commodity trade: A primer. *American Journal of Agricultural Economics, 82,* 695–700.

Lanyi, A., & Saracoglu, P. (1983). *Interest rate policy in developing countries*. IMF Occasional Paper 22.

Leetmaa, S., & Ackerman, K. (1999). Production subsidies. In *the Uruguay Round Agreement on Agriculture (URAA) issues series*, Economic Research Service, U.S. Department of Agriculture, Updated 3 January 2001, available online at www.ers.usda.gov/briefing/WTO/Production.htm.

Levine, R., & Zervos, S. (1993). *Looking at the facts: What we know about policy and growth from cross-country analysis*. Policy Research Working Paper No. 1115. Washington, DC: World Bank.

Levy Yeyati, E. (2005). *Financial dollarisation: Evaluating the consequences*. Business School Working Papers 03/2005. Universidad Torcuato Di Tella. www.utdt.edu/Upload/CIF_wp/wpcif-032005.pdf

Levy Yeyati, E., & Sturzenegger, F. (2003). To float or to fix: Evidence on the impact of exchange rate regimes on growth. *American Economic Review, 93*(4), 1173–1193.

Lewis, A. W. (1980). The slowing down of the engine of growth. *American Economic Review, 70*(4), 555–564.

Lewis W. A. (1954). Economic development with unlimited supplies of labour. *Manchester School of Economic and Social Studies, 22.*

Lewis, W. A. (1955). *The theory of economic growth*. London: George Allen & Unwin.

Li, M. (2006). *Inflation and economic growth: Threshold effects and transmission mechanisms*. Paper presented at the Midwest Macroeconomics Meetings, Iowa City. http://economics.ca/2006/papers/0176.pdf

Li, Q., & Reuveny, R. (2003). Economic globalization and democracy: An empirical analysis. *British Journal of Political Science, 33,* 29–54.

Lindland, J. (1997). The impact of the Uruguay Round on tariff escalation in agricultural products. *Food Policy, 22*(6), 487–500.

Lipset, S. M. (1960). *Political man. The social bases of politics*. Garden City, NY: Anchor Books. Doubleday and Company Inc.

Lipton, M., & Ravallion, M. (1995). Poverty and policy. In J. Behrman, & T. N. Srinivasan (Eds.), *Handbook of development economics* (Vol. 3). Amsterdam: North-Holland.

Lipton, M., & Paarlberg, R. (1990). *The role of the World Bank in agricultural development in the 1990s*. Washington, DC: International Food Policy Research Institute.

Little, I. (1982). *Economic development: Theory, policy and international relations*. Basic Books.

Little, I., Scitovsky, T., & Scott, M. (1970). *Industry and trade in some developing countries*. Organization for Economic Co-operation and Development. Paris: Oxford University Press.

Löfgren, H., Robinson, S., & Thurlow, J. (2002). *Macro and micro effects of recent and potential shocks to copper mining in Zambia*. TMD discussion papers 99. International Food Policy Research Institute (IFPRI).

Lopez, R. (2004). *Effect of the Structure of Rural Public Expenditures on Agricultural Growth and Rural Poverty in Latin America*. Rural Development Unit, Sustainable Development Department, Inter.-American Development Bank.

López, R. (2005). Under-investing in public goods: evidence, causes, and consequences for agricultural development, equity, and the environment. *Agricultural Economics.*, *32*(1), 211–224.

López-Cordova, J. E., & Meissner, C. M. (2005). *Globalization and democracy 1870–2000.* Working Paper No. 11117. Cambridge MA: National Bureau of Economic Research.

López-Cordova, L. (1987). Crisis, políticas de ajuste y agricultura. In *Revista de la CEPAL* (No. *33*). Santiago de Chile, Chile: Naciones Unidas.

Lustig, N. C. (2000). *Crises and the poor: Socially responsible macroeconomics.* Working Paper No. 108. Washington, DC: Inter-American Development Bank, Sustainable Development Department, Poverty and Inequality Advisory Unit.

Luther, G. T. (1980). Macroeconomics in crisis: Agriculture in an underachieving economy. *American Journal of Agricultural Economics*, *62*(5), 853–865.

Mahalanobis, P. C. (1955). The approach of operational research to planning in India Sankhya. *The Indian Journal of Statistics*, *16.*

Mamalakis, M. (1987). The treatment of interest and financial intermediaries in the national accounts: The old 'Bundle' versus the new 'Unbundle' approach. *Review of Income and Wealth Series*, *33*(2).

Marshall, M., & Gurr, T. R. (2005). *Peace and conflict 2005: A global survey of armed conflicts, self-determination movements, and democracy.* College Park, MD: Center for International Development and Conflict Management, University of Maryland. www.cidcm.umd.edu/inscr/PC05print.pdf

Martin, W., & Mitra, D. (1999). *Productivity growth and convergence in agriculture and manufacturing.* World Bank Policy Research Working Paper No. 2171. Washington DC.

McKinnon, R. (1981). Comments. In W. Cline, & S. Weintraub (Eds.), *Economic stabilization policy in developing countries.*

McKinnon, R. (1973). *Money and capital in economic development.* Washington, DC: The Brookings Institution.

McKenzie, M. D. (1999). The impact of exchange rate volatility on international trade. *J Econ Sur*, *13*, 71–106.

Mendoza Bellido, W. (1994). Agricultura e estabilizacao macroeconomica no Peru—1990/93. *Pesquisa e Planejamento Economico*, *24*(3), 519–551.

Messer, E., Cohen, M., & D'Costa, J. (1998). *Food from peace: Breaking the links between conflict and hunger.* 2020 Vision Discussion Paper No. 24. Washington DC: International Food Policy Research Institute.

Mitrany, D. (1951). *Marx against the peasant: A study in social dogmatism.* London: George Weidenfeld & Nicolson Ltd.

Modigliani, F., & Ando, A. (1976). Impacts of fiscal actions on aggregate income and the monetarist controversy: Theory and evidence. In J. Stein (Ed.), *Monetarism.*

Mody, A., & Pattillo, C. (Eds.). (2006). *Macroeconomic policies and poverty reduction.* New York: Routledge.

Moore, M., Leavy, J., Houtzager, P., & White, H. (1999). *Polity qualities: How governance affects poverty.* Working Paper No. 99. Brighton, UK: Institute for Development Studies, University of Sussex.

Mundell, R. (2002). *Commodity prices, exchange rates and the international monetary system.* Presentation by Robert Mundell at the Consultation on Agricultural Commodity Price Problems, Commodities and Trade Division, Food and Agriculture Organization of the United Nations, Rome, 25–26 March 2002. www.fao.org/docrep/006/Y4344E/y4344e04.htm

Mundell, R. (1999). A pro-growth fiscal system. In *The rising tide: The leading minds of business and economics chart a course toward higher growth and prosperity.* New York: John Wiley and Sons.

Mundlak, Y. (1997). The dynamics of agriculture. In *Proceedings of the XII international conference of agricultural economics,* Sacramento, California, August 10–16, 1997.

Mundlak, Y., Larson, D., & Butzer, R. (1997). *The determinants of agricultural production: A cross-country analysis.* Policy Research Working Paper Series 1827. the World Bank.

Mundlak, Y., Larson, D., & Butzer, R. (2008). *Heterogeneous technology and panel data: the case of the agricultural production function.* Policy Research Working Paper Series 4536. The World Bank.

Mundlak, Y., Cavallo, D., & Domenech, R. (1989). *Agriculture and economic growth in Argentina, 1913–84.* Research Report 76. Washington DC: International Food Policy Research Institute.

Murphy, K., Shleifer, A., & Vishny, R. (1989). Industrialization and the Big Push. *Journal of Political Economy*, *97.*

Nash, J., & Brooks, K. (2002). The rural sector in transition economies. In B. Gardner, & G. Rausser (Eds.), *Handbook of agricultural economics* (Vol. 2A, pp. 1547–1592). Amsterdam: North-Holland.

Ng, F., & Yeats, A. (1997). Open economies work better! Did Africa's protectionist policies cause its marginalization in world trade? *World Development.*

Nkrumah, K. (1965). *Neo-Colonialism: The last stage of imperialism.* International Publishers Co., Inc., 1966.

Obstfeld, M., & Rogoff, K. (2004). *The unsustainable U.S. current account position revisited.* NBER Working Paper No. 10869. Cambridge, MA.: National Bureau of Economic Research.

Obstfeld, M. (1985). The capital inflows problem revisited: A stylized model of Southern cone disinflation. *Review of Economic Studies.*

OECD-FAO. (2008). *Agricultural outlook 2008–2017.* www.agri-outlook.org/pages/0,2987, en_36774715_36775671_1_1_1_1_1,00.html

OECD. (2001). *Multifunctionality towards an analytical framework.* Paris: OECD Publications.

OECD. (1997). *The uruguay round agreement on agriculture and processed agricultural products.* France: OECD Publications.

O'Mara, L. P., Bartley, S. W., Ferry, R. N., Wright, R. S., Calder, M. F., & Douglas, J. (1999). Some issues affecting the macroeconomic environment for the agricultural and resource sectors: the case of fiscal policy. *The Australian Journal of Agricultural and Resource Economics., 43*(2).

Orden, D., & Diaz Bonilla, E. (2006). Holograms and ghosts: New and old ideas for agricultural policy. In K. Anderson, & W. Martin (Eds.), *Agricultural trade reform & the doha development agenda.* Copublication of the World Bank and Palgrave Macmillan.

Orden, D. (1986). Agriculture, trade and macroeconomics: The U.S. case. *Journal of Policy Modeling, 8*(1), 27–51.

OXFAM. (1987). *Common ground. How changes in the common agricultural policy affect the third world poor.* Prepared by Adrian Moyes. UK: OXFAM.

Oyejide, T. A. (1993). The oil boom, macroeconomic policies and Nigerian agriculture: Analysis of a 'Dutch disease' phenomenon. In R. M. Bautista, & A. Valdes (Eds.), *The bias against agriculture: trade and macroeconomic policies in developing countries.* Washington, DC: ICEG and IFPRI.

Paarlberg, P., & Chambers, R. (1988). Macroeconomics. In R. (Ed.), *Agriculture and exchange rates* (pp. 219–226). Boulder, CO: Westview Press.

Paarlberg P., Shiff, M., & Valdes, A. (2002). Agriculture and the macro economy. *Handbook of agricultural economics* (p. 1443). Elsevier Science.

Pan, A. Y., & Lau, L. J. (1974). On modeling the agricultural sector in developing economies: An integrated approach of micro and macroeconomics. *Journal of Developing Economics, 1*(2); 105–127.

Pardey, P., Wright, B. D., & Nottenburg, C. (2002). *Are intellectual property rights stifling agricultural biotechnology in developing countries?* The 2000–2001 Annual Report. Washington, DC: International Food Policy Research Institute.

Paxson, C., & Schady N. (2004). *Child health and the 1988–1992 Economic crisis in peru.* Policy Research Working Paper No.3260. Washington, DC: The World Bank.

Pollin, R., & Zhu, A. (2005). *Inflation and economic growth: A cross-country non-linear analysis.* Working Paper Number 109. Amherst, MA.: Political Economy Research Institute, University of Massachusetts.

Powers, E. T. (1995). Inflation, unemployment, and poverty revisited. *Economic Review of the Federal Reserve Bank of Cleveland, 2,* 2–13. http://clevelandfed.org/Research/Review/1995/95-q3-powers.pdf

Prasad, E., Rogoff, K., Wei j, S., & Ayhan Kose, M. (2003). *Effects of financial globalization on developing countries: Some new evidence.* IMF Occasional Paper No. 220. Washington, DC: International Monetary Fund.

Ping, H. (1998). On primary commodity prices: The impact of macroeconomic/monetary shocks. *Journal of Policy Modeling, 20*(6), 797–90.

Prebisch, R. (1968). Development problems of the peripheral countries and the terms of trade. In J. D. Theberge (Ed.), *Economics of trade and development.* New York: John Wiley and Sons Inc.

Prebisch, R. (1961). *Economic development or monetary stability: A false dilemma. Economic bulletin for Latin America, 6*(1), 1–25.

Prebisch, R. (1950). *The economic development of Latin America and its principal problems.* New York: United Nations.

Pyatt, G., & Round, J. (Eds.). (1985). *Social accounting matrices: A basis for planning*. Washington, DC: The World Bank.

Ravallion, M. (2004). *Pro-poor growth: A primer*. Policy Research Working Paper No. 3242. Washington, DC: World Bank. http://siteresources.worldbank.org/INTPGI/Resources/15174_Ravallion_PPG_Primer.pdf

Ravallion, M. (2003a). *The debate on globalization, poverty and inequality: Why measurement matters*. Working Paper No. 3038. Washington, DC: World Bank Development Research Group.

Ravallion, M. (2003b). Measuring aggregate welfare in developing countries: How well do national accounts and surveys agree? *Review of Economics and Statistics, 85*(3), 645–652.

Ravallion, M. (2001). Growth, inequality and poverty: Looking beyond averages. *World Development, 29* (11), 1803–1815.

Ran, G., In, F., & Dillon, J. L. (1995). Effects of agricultural production fluctuations on the Chinese macroeconomy. *Agricultural Economics, 12*(1), 69–78.

Rajan, R. G., & Subramanian, A. (2006). *What undermines aid's impact on growth?* Paper presented at the Trade and Growth Conference, Research Department Hosted by the International Monetary Fund, Washington, DC. www.imf.org/external/np/res/seminars/2006/trade/pdf/rajan.pdf

Raju, S. S., & Melo, A. (2003). Money, real output, and deficit effects of coffee booms in Colombia. *Journal of Policy Modeling, 25*(9), 963–983.

Reca, L. (1969). Determinantes de la Oferta Agropecuaria en el Argentina. In *Estudios Sobre la Economía Argentina* (No. 5, pp. 57–65). Buenos Aires, Argentina.

Reca, L. (1980). *Argentina: Country case study of agricultural prices and subsidies*. World Bank Staff Working Paper 386. Washington, DC.

Reca, L., & Parellada, G. H. (2001). La agricultura argentina a comienzos del milenio: Logros y desafíos. *Desarrollo Economico, 40*(160), 707–737.

Reinhart, C., & Rogoff, K. (2002). *The modern history of exchange rate arrangements: A reinterpretation*. NBER Working Paper No. 8963.

Reinhart, C. M., Rogoff, K. S., & Savastano, M. A. (2003). *Addicted to dollars*. NBER Working Paper No. 10015.

Rigobon, R., & Rodrik, D. (2004). *Rule of law, democracy, openness and income: Estimating the interrelationships*. Working Paper No. 10750. Cambridge, MA: National Bureau of Economic Research.

Robinson, S., & Tyson, L. (1984). Modeling structural adjustment: Micro and macro elements in a general equilibrium framework. In H. Scarf, & J. Shoven (Eds.), *Applied general equilibrium analysis*. Cambridge University Press.

Rodriguez, C. A. (1989). *The external effects of public sector deficits*. World Bank Working Papers.

Rodriguez, C. A. (1989). *Macroeconomic policies for structural adjustment*. World Bank PPR Working Papers 247.

Rogoff, K., Husain, A. M., Mody, A., Brooks, R. J., & Oomes, N. (2004). *Evolution and performance of exchange rate regimes*. IMF Occasional Paper 229. Washington, DC: International Monetary Fund.

Rogoff, K. (2004). Globalization and global disinflation. In *Federal reserve bank of kansas city, monetary policy and uncertainty: Adapting to a changing economy*.

Rogoff, K., Husain, A., Mody, A., Brooks, R., & Oomes, N. (2003). *Evolution and performance of exchange rate regimes*. IMF Working Paper WP/03/243.

Romer, D. (1993). Openness and inflation: Theory and evidence. *Quarterly Journal of Economics, 108*(4), 869–903.

Romer, D. (1996). *Advanced Macroeconomics*. McGraw Hill/Irwin.

Romer, D. (2001). *Advanced Macroeconomics*. McGraw Hill/Irwin.

Romstad, E., Vatn, A., Rorstad, P. K., & Soyland, V. (2000). *Multifunctional agriculture: implications for policy design*. Oslo: Agricultural University of Norway.

Roubini, N. (2006). *My latest paper on global imbalances. Words into action delegate publication: Singapore 2006*. London: Faircount. www.rgemonitor.com/blog/roubini/146183

Royal Ministry of Agriculture (Norway). (1998). *Non-trade concerns in a multifunctional agriculture—Implications for agricultural policy and the multilateral trading system*. Paper presented by Norway to the WTO. www.landbruk.dep.no/landbruksdepartementet/multifunctionality/assets/images/NTC_paper.doc, Accessed June 8, 2000.

Ruel, M., Garrett, J. L., Morris, S. S., Maxwell, D., Oshaug, A., & Engle, P., et al. (1998). *Urban challenges to food and nutrition security: a review of food security, health, and caregiving in the cities.* Food Consumption and Nutrition Division discussion paper 51. Washington, DC: International Food Policy Research Institute.

Ruel, M., Haddad, L., & Garrett, J. L. (1999). *Some urban facts of life.* Food Consumption and Nutrition Division discussion paper 64. Washington, DC: International Food Policy Research Institute.

Sachs, J., & Warner, A. M. (1995). *Natural resource abundance and economic growth.* NBER Working Paper No. 5398, Cambridge, MA: National Bureau of Economic Research.

Sachs, J., & Warner, A. (1995). Economic reform and the process of global integration. *Brookings Papers in Economic Activity, 1,* 1–118.

Sachs, J. (1980). *Energy and growth under flexible exchange rates: A simulation study.* NBER Working Paper 582.

Sachs, J., & Lipton, D. (1980). *Accumulation and growth in a two-country model: A simulation approach.* NBER Working Papers 572.

Sadoulet, E., de Janvry, A., & Murgai, R. (1999). *Rural development and rural policy.* University of California at Berkeley and the World Bank.

Sala-i-Martin, X. (2002a). *The disturbing "rise" of global income inequality.* NBER Working Paper No. 8904. Cambridge, MA: National Bureau of Economic Research.

Sala-i-Martin, X. (2002b). *The world distribution of income (estimated from individual country distributions).* NBER Working Paper. No. 8933. Cambridge, MA: National Bureau of Economic Research.

Sala-i-Martin, X. (1997). I just ran two million regressions. *American Economic Review, 87*(2), 178–183.

Sarel, M. (1996). *Nonlinear effects of inflation on economic growth.* IMF Staff Papers, *43*(1); 199–215.

Sargent, T., & Wallace, N. (1981). Some unpleasant monetarist arithmetic. *Federal Reserve Bank of Minneapolis Quarterly Review,* Fall.

Sarris, A. H. (1991). European agriculture, international markets and LDC growth and food security. *European Review of Agricultural Economics, 18*(3–4), 289–310.

Scarf, H., & Shoven, J. (Eds.). (1984). *Applied general equilibrium analysis.* Cambridge University Press.

Schady, N. (2004). Do macroeconomic crisis always slow human capital accumulation? *The World Bank Economic Review, 18*(2).

Schamis, H. (1999). Distributional coalitions and the politics of economic reform in Latin America. *World Politics, 51,* 236–268.

Schiff, M., & Valdes, A. (1992a). The political economy of agricultural pricing policy. In *A synthesis of the economics in developing countries* (Vol. 4). Baltimore: Johns Hopkins Press.

Schiff, M., & Valdes A. (1992b). *The plundering of agriculture in developing countries.* Washington, DC: World Bank.

Schuh, G. E. (1986). *The united states and the developing countries: An economic perspective.* Washington, DC: The National Planning Association.

Schuh, G. E. (1976). The new macroeconomics of agriculture. *American Journal of Agricultural Economics, 58*(5), 802–811.

Schuh, G. E. (1974). The exchange rate and U.S. agriculture. *American Journal of Agricultural Economics, 56,* 1–13.

Schuknecht, L. (1999). Tying government's hands in commodity taxation. *Journal of African Economies, 8*(2).

Schultz, T. W. (1964). *Transforming traditional agriculture.* New Haven, CT: Yael University Press

Schultz, T. W. (1953). *The economic organization of agriculture.* McGraw-Hill.

Schultz, T. W. (1954). The instability of farm prices reconsidered. *Journal of Farm Economics, 36*(5).

Schultz, T. W. (1945). *Agriculture in an unstable economy.* New York: McGraw-Hill.

Schulze, G. G., & Ursprung, H. W. (1999). Globalisation of the economy and the nation state. *World Economy,* 03785920. *22*(3).

Seers, D. (1962). A theory of inflation and growth in under-developed economies based on the experience of Latin America. *Oxford Economic Papers, 14,* 173–195.

Sen, A. (1984). *Resources, values, and development.* Cambridge, MA: Harvard University Press.

Sen, A. K. (1983). Development: Which way now? *The Economic Journal,* December.

Servan-Schreiber, J. J. (1968). *The American challenge.* New York: Atheneum.

Shane, M., & Liefert, W. (2000). The international financial crisis: Macroeconomic linkages to agriculture. *American Journal of Agricultural Economics, 82,* 682–687.

Sharma R., Konandreas, P., & Greenfield, J. (1996). An overview of the assessments of the impact of the uruguay round on agricultural prices and incomes. *Food Policy, 21*(4–5), 351–363.

Sidrauski, M. (1967). Rational choice and patterns of growth in a monetary economy. *American Economic Review, 57*, 534–544.

Singer, H. (1950). The distribution of gains between investing and borrowing countries. *American Economic Review, 40*, 473–485.

Smith, L., & Haddad, L. (2000). *Explaining child malnutrition in developing countries: A cross country analysis.* Research Report No.111. Washington, DC: International Food Policy Research Institute.

Stern, N. (2006). *Stern review on the economics of climate change.* www.hm-treasury.gov.uk/independent_reviews/stern_review_economics_climate_change/stern_review_report.cfm

Stiglitz, J. (2002). *Globalization and its discontents.* New York: W.W. Norton and Company.

Stiglitz, J. E. (1987). Some theoretical aspects of agricultural policies. *The World Bank Research Observer, 2*(1), 43–60.

Stock, J. S., & Watson, M. (1988). Variable trends in economic time series. *Journal of Economic Perspectives, 2*(3), 147–174.

Stockman, A. C. (1981). Anticipated inflation and the capital stock in a cash-in-advance economy. *Journal of Monetary Economics, 8*, 387–393.

Sunkel, O. (1958). La inflación chilena: un enfoque heterodoxo. *El Trimestre Económico. Mexico, 25*(4), 570–599.

Swinbank, A., & Ritson, C. (1995). The impact of the GATT agreement on EU fruit and vegetable policy. *Food Policy, 20*(4), 339–357.

Taylor, J. (2007). Housing and monetary policy. Paper presented at the Federal Reserve Bank of Kansas City's economic symposium, Jackson Hole, Wyoming. www.stanford.edu/~johntayl/Housing%20and%20Monetary%20Policy–Taylor–Jackson%20Hole%202007.pdf.

Taylor, L. (1984). *Structuralist macroeconomics: Applicable models for the third world.* Basic Books.

Taylor, L. (1979). *Macroeconomic models for developing countries.* McGraw-Hill.

Thomas, V., Dailami, M., Dhareshwar, A., Kaufmann, D., Kishor, N., López, R., et al. (2000). *The quality of growth.* Oxford, UK; Washington, DC: Oxford University Press/World Bank.

Timmer, C. P. (1994). *Dutch Disease and Agriculture in Indonesia: The Policy Approach.* Papers 490. Harvard Institute for International Development. Harvard University.

Timmer, P. (1991). Food price stabilization: rationale, design, and implementation. In D. H. Perkins, & M. Roemer (Eds.), *Reforming economic systems* (pp. 219–259). Cambridge, MA: Harvard Institute for International Development, Harvard University.

Tobin, J. (1969). A general equilibrium approach to monetary theory. *Journal of Money, Credit and Banking.*

Tobin, J. (1965). Money and economic growth. *Econometrica, 33*(4), 671–684.

Thompson, R. (1988). U.S. macroeconomic policy and agriculture. In P. Paarlberg, & R. Chambers (Eds.), *Macroeconomics, agriculture and exchange rates* (pp. 219–226). Boulder, CO: Westview Press.

Truman, E. M. (2003). Comment to william easterly. In M. P. Dooley, & J. A. Frankel (Eds.), *Managing currency crises in emerging markets* (Chap. 11). Chicago: University of Chicago Press.

Tsangarides, C. G., Ghura, D., & Leite, C. A. (2000). *Is growth enough? Macroeconomic policy and poverty reduction.* IMF Working Paper No. 02/118. Washington, DC: International Monetary Fund.

Tytell, I., & Wei, S. J. (2004). *Does financial globalization induce better macroeconomic policies?* IMF Working Paper 2004 International Monetary Fund WP/04/84 IMF Institute and Research Department.

United Nations Conference on Trade and Development (UNCTAD). (2004). *UNCTAD handbook of statistics, 2004.* Geneva, Switzerland.

United Nations Development Program. (2007/2008). *Human Development Report.* New York. Data from Table: http://hdrstats.undp.org/indicators/10.html

United Nations Development Program. (1999). *Human development report 1999: Globalization with a human face.* New York.

Uribe, M., & Yue, V. Z. (2003). *Country spreads and emerging countries: Who Drives whom?* NBER Working Paper No. 10018. Cambridge, MA: National Bureau of Economic Research.

Usui, N. (1997). Dutch disease and policy adjustments to the oil boom: a comparative study of Indonesia and Mexico. *Resource Policy, 23*(4), 151–162.

U. S. Federal Reserve. (2008). *Exchange Rates Database.* www.federalreserve.gov/releases/H10/summary/

Valdés, A., & Zietz, J. A. (1980). *Agricultural protection in OECD countries: Its costs to less-developed countries.* IFPRI Research Report Series, No. 21. Washington, DC: International Food Policy Research Institute.

Valdés, A. (1988). Agricultural incentives in developing countries: Measuring the effects of sectorial and economy wide policies. *World Bank Economic Review, 2*(3), 255–271.

Van Blarcom, B., Knudsen, O., & Nash, J. (1993). *The reform of public expenditures for agriculture.* World Bank Discussion Paper 216. Washington, DC: World Bank.

Van Wijnbergen. (1984). The 'Dutch disease': a disease after all? *Economic Journal, 94,* 41–55.

Van Wijnbergen, S. (1983). Interest rate management in LDCs. *Journal of Monetary Economics, 12*(3), 433–452.

Vernon, R. (1971). *Sovereignty at bay: The multinational spread of U.S. enterprises.* New York: Basic Books.

Von Braun, J. (2007). *The world food situation: New driving forces and required actions.* IFPRI Food Policy Report No. 18. Washington, DC: International Food Policy Research Institute.

Von Braun, J., Teklu, T., & Webb, P. (1999). *Famine in Africa: Causes, responses, and prevention.* Baltimore: Johns Hopkins University Press.

Wade, R. H. (2004). Is globalization reducing poverty and inequality? *World Development, 32*(4), 567–589.

Wei, S. J. (2000). *Natural openness and good government.* Working Paper No. 7765. Cambridge, MA: National Bureau Of Economic Research.

Wenner, M. D., & Proenza, F. (1999). *Rural finance in Latin America and the Caribbean: Challenges and opportunities.* Sustainable Development Department, Microenterprise Unit Working Paper. Washington, DC: Inter-American Development Bank.

Woodford, M. (2003). *Interest and prices: Foundations of a theory of monetary policy.* Princeton University Press.

Woordford, M. (2006). *Rules for monetary policy.* NBER Reporter: Research Summary Spring 2006. http://www.nber.org/reporter/spring06/woodford.html

World Bank. (2001). Memorandum of the President of the International Bank for Reconstruction and Development and the International Finance Corporation to the Executive Directors on a Country Assistance Strategy of the World Bank Group for The Kingdom of Morocco. World Bank Document Report No. 2115-MOR.

World Bank. (2000a). *Global economic prospects.* Washington, DC.

World Bank. (1999). *Voices of the poor.* http://web.worldbank.org/WBSITE/EXTERNAL/TOPICS/EXTPOVERTY/0,contentMDK:20622514~menuPK:336998~pagePK:148956~piPK:216618~theSitePK:336992,00.html

World Bank. (2000b). *World development report.* Washington, DC.

World Bank. (2007). *World development indicators.* Washington, DC. Database accessed through subscription.

World Bank. (2005). *World development indicators 2005.* Washington, DC: World Bank.

World Bank. (2004). *World development indicators 2004.* Washington, DC: World Bank.

World Bank. (1990). *World Development Report.* Washington, DC.

World Bank. (1987). *World Development Report.* New York: Oxford University Press.

World Bank. (1986). *World development report 1986.* New York: Oxford University Press.

World Trade Organization (WTO). (2007). *International trade statistics.* http://www.wto.org/english/news_e/news07_e/its_nov07_e.htm.

Xinshen, D., & Roe, T. (2000). How the financial crisis affected world agriculture: A general equilibrium perspective. *American Journal of Agricultural Economics, 82,* 688–694.

Yeats, A. J. (1974). Effective tariff protection in the United States, the European economic community, and Japan. *The Quarterly Review of Economics and Business, 14,* 41–50.

Young, G. (2008). *On the sources of macroeconomic stability.* Bank of England Quarterly Bulletin 2008 Q2 U.K. http://www.bankofengland.co.uk/publications/quarterlybulletin/qb080204.pdf

International Trade Policies Affecting Agricultural Incentives in Developing Countries

Kym Anderson
University of Adelaide

Contents

This chapter is a product of a World Bank research project on distortions to agricultural incentives (www.worldbank.org/agdistortions). The author is grateful for helpful comments from various workshop participants; for the efforts of nearly 100 authors who provided the country case studies for the Agricultural Distortions project; for computational assistance from a team of assistants led by Ernesto Valenzuela that brought together the global Agricultural Distortions database; and for funding from various World Bank Trust Funds, particularly those provided by the governments of the Netherlands (BNPP) and the United Kingdom (DfID). Views expressed are the author's alone and not necessarily those of the World Bank or its executive directors.

Handbook of Agricultural Economics, Volume 4   doi: 10.1016/S1574-0072(09)04062-6

Abstract

For decades, earnings from farming in many developing countries have been depressed by a pro-urban bias in own-country policies as well as by governments of richer countries favoring their farmers with import barriers and subsidies. Both sets of policies reduce national and global economic welfare and inhibit economic growth. In particular, they add to inequality and poverty in developing countries, since three quarters of the world's billion poorest people depend directly or indirectly on farming for their livelihood. During the past two decades, however, numerous developing-country governments have reduced their sectoral and trade policy distortions, while some high-income countries have also begun reforming their protectionist farm policies.

This chapter surveys the changing extent of policy distortions to prices faced by developing-country farmers. After outlining the basic measurement theory, the chapter provides a brief history of policies of advanced and developing economies and then surveys empirical studies that document the changing extent of price distortions over the past half century. It reviews the economic effects of policy reforms since the early 1980s and of interventions remaining in the early part of the present century, according to global economywide modeling results. The chapter concludes by pointing to the scope and prospects for further pro-poor policy reform at home and abroad.

JEL classification: F13, F14, Q17, Q18

Keywords

Distorted incentives
Agricultural
trade policy reforms

1. INTRODUCTION

International trade—which has been going on ever since societies began seeking to improve well-being through specialization in production and exchange—began with agricultural products. Trade between nation states, in both basic and luxury foods, dates back several millennia. The first major intercontinental trade also began with agricultural products, along the Silk Road that linked Europe and Asia. Likewise, agricultural products (spices from South and Southeast Asia) formed the basis of the first truly global trade, which began with the early expeditions of European mariners to the Americas, the Far East, and Australasia in the late 1400s. Trade in farm products has since been stimulated by technological changes in transport, such as the coming of railways and canals, the replacement of wooden sailing boats with steel-hulled ships propelled by fossil fuels, refrigeration on ships, and the advent of bulk carriers and air freight. And changes in information and communication technologies have added to the scope for farm product trade, beginning with the telegraph in the 19th century and boosted hugely in the late 20th century by the Internet, email, and mobile telephony.

Even though the benefits from specialization in production and exchange have been recognized for millennia, governments have nonetheless intervened to restrict international trade, including in agricultural goods. Sometimes it would be export taxes to raise revenue for the government or rulers. An early example was the tax on wine exports: from the Greek island of Thasos in the second century B.C. (Robinson, 1994, p. 465) and from France and Germany in the Dark Ages.[1] At other times it took the form of import duties or bans (often as part of gyrations in international relations). Wine trade between France and Britain again provides a stark example, where import restrictions caused huge fluctuations in bilateral trade in the 1700s and 1800s.[2] The practice was so pervasive that wine was used as the example of British imports in the first treatise on the theory of comparative advantage (Ricardo, 1817).

For advanced economies, the most common reason for farm trade restrictions in the past two centuries has been to protect domestic producers from import competition as they come under competitive pressure to shed labor in the course of economic development. But in the process, those protective measures hurt not only domestic consumers and exporters but also foreign producers and traders of farm products, and they reduce national and global economic welfare. For many decades agricultural protection and subsidies in high-income (and some middle-income) countries have been depressing international prices of farm products, which lowers the earnings of farmers and associated rural businesses in developing countries. It therefore adds to inequality and poverty, since three quarters of the world's poorest people depend directly or indirectly on agriculture for their main income (World Bank, 2007).[3]

But in addition to this external policy influence on rural poverty, the governments of many (especially newly independent) developing countries have directly taxed their farmers over the past half-century. A well-known example is the taxing of exports of plantation crops in post-colonial Africa (Bates, 1981). The use of multiple exchange rates also introduced an anti-trade bias. Furthermore, most developing countries chose to also pursue an import-substituting industrialization strategy, predominantly by restricting imports of manufactures. This policy indirectly taxed other tradable sectors in those developing economies, including agriculture.

This disarray in world agriculture, as D. Gale Johnson (1991) described it in the title of his seminal book, means that there has been overproduction of farm products in high-income countries and underproduction in more needy developing countries. It also means there has been less international trade in farm products than would be the case under free trade, thereby thinning markets for these weather-dependent products and thus making them more volatile. Using a stochastic model of world food markets, Tyers and Anderson (1992, Table 6.14) found that instability of international food prices in the early 1980s was three times greater than it would have been under free trade in those products.

Thus the price incentives facing developing-country farmers—especially those producing exportables—have been depressed by both own-country and other countries' international trade (including multiple exchange rate) policies while the insulating aspect of those policies has made international food prices more volatile. During the past quarter-century, however, numerous countries have begun to reform their agricultural price and trade policies, which raises the question as to how far the world has come in reducing market distortions relative to how far it still has to go before they are free.

The chapter begins with a brief survey of the methodology required to measure the extent of own-country distortions to farmer incentives. It then surveys analyses of the effects of those trade policies on incentives over time, focusing on the worsening of that situation between the 1950s and the mid-1980s and the progress that has been made over the subsequent 25 years. In doing so it provides estimates of the contributions of policies at the national border versus domestic measures to the overall level of farm price distortions in a country.

Notwithstanding recent reforms, many price distortions remain in the agricultural sector of both developing and high-income countries. The second part of the chapter draws on new economywide computable general equilibrium modeling results as they affect developing countries to examine the market, welfare, and net farm income effects of distortions as of 2004 compared with (1) distortions in the early 1980s and (2) a world free of agricultural price and trade policies. The chapter concludes by drawing on what we understand about the political economy of those policies, to assess the prospects for reducing remaining distortions. Particular attention is given to the roles international institutions, especially the World Trade Organization (WTO), can play to help phase out remaining welfare-reducing distortions in the wake of ever-evolving suggestions as to why governments should continue to intervene.

2. NATIONAL DISTORTIONS TO INCENTIVES: BASIC THEORY[4]

Bhagwati (1971) and Corden (1997) define the concept of a market policy distortion as something that governments impose to create a gap between the marginal social return to a seller and the marginal social cost to a buyer in a transaction. Such a distortion creates an economic cost to society that can be estimated using welfare techniques such as those pioneered by Harberger (1971). As Harberger notes, this focus allows a great simplification in evaluating the marginal costs of a set of distortions: Changes in economic costs can be evaluated, taking into account the changes in volumes directly affected by such distortions, ignoring all other changes in prices. In the absence of divergences such as externalities, the measure of a distortion is the gap between the price paid and the price received, irrespective of whether the level of these prices is affected by the distortion.

Other developments that change incentives facing producers and consumers can include flow-on consequences of the distortion, but these should not be confused with the direct price distortion that needs to be estimated. If, for instance, a country is large in world trade for a given commodity, imposition of an export tax may raise the price in international markets, reducing the adverse impact of the distortion on producers in the taxing country. Another flow-on consequence is the effect of trade distortions on the real exchange rate, which is the price of traded goods relative to nontraded goods. Neither of these flow-on effects are of immediate concern, however, because if the direct distortions are accurately estimated, they can be incorporated as price wedges into an appropriate country or global economywide computable general equilibrium (CGE) model, which in turn will be able to capture the full general equilibrium impacts (inclusive of terms of trade and real exchange rate effects) of the various direct distortions to producer and consumer prices.

It is important to note that the total effect of distortions on the agricultural sector will depend not just on the size of the direct agricultural policy measures but also on the magnitude of distortions generated by direct policy measures altering incentives in nonagricultural sectors. It is relative prices and hence relative rates of government assistance that affect producers' incentives. In a two-sector model, an import tax has the same effect on the export sector as an export tax: the Lerner (1936) Symmetry Theorem. This carries over to a model that has many sectors and is unaffected if there is imperfect competition domestically or internationally or if some of those sectors produce only nontradables (Vousden, 1990, pp. 46–47). The symmetry theorem is therefore also relevant for considering distortions *within* the agricultural sector. In particular, if import-competing farm industries are protected—for example, via import tariffs—this has similar effects on incentives to produce exportables, as does an explicit tax on agricultural exports; if both measures are in place, this is a double imposition on farm exporters.

In the following discussion, we begin by focusing first on direct distortions to agricultural incentives before turning to those affecting the sector indirectly via non-agricultural policies.

2.1 Direct agricultural distortions

Consider a small, open, perfectly competitive national economy with many firms producing a homogeneous farm product with just primary factors. In the absence of externalities, processing, producer-to-consumer wholesale plus retail marketing margins, exchange rate distortions, and domestic and international trading costs, that country would maximize national economic welfare by allowing both the domestic farm product price and the consumer price of that product to equal E times P, where E is the domestic currency price of foreign exchange and P is the foreign currency price of this identical product in the international market. That is, any government-imposed diversion from that equality, in the absence of any market failures or externalities, would be welfare reducing for that small economy.

2.1.1 Price-distorting trade measures at the national border

The most common distortion is an *ad valorem* tax on competing imports (usually called a *tariff*), t_m. Such a tariff on an imported product that is a perfect substitute for the domestically produced good is the equivalent of a production subsidy and a consumption tax, both at rate t_m. If that tariff on the imported primary agricultural product is the only distortion, its effect on producer incentives can be measured as the nominal rate of assistance to farm output conferred by border price support *(NRA$_{BS}$)*, which is the unit value of production at the distorted price less its value at the undistorted free market price expressed as a fraction of the undistorted price:[5]

$$NRA_{BS} = \frac{E \times P(1 + t_m) - E \times P}{E \times P} = t_m \tag{1}$$

The effect of that import tariff on consumer incentives in this simple economy is to generate a consumer tax equivalent (CTE) on the agricultural product for final consumers:

$$CTE = t_m \tag{2}$$

The effects of an import subsidy are identical to those in Eqs. 1 and 2 for an import tax, but t_m in that case would have a negative value.

Governments sometimes also intervene with an export subsidy s_x (or an export tax, in which case s_x would be negative). If that were the only intervention:

$$NRA_{BS} = CTE = s_x \tag{3}$$

If any of these trade taxes or subsidies were specific rather than *ad valorem* (e.g., \$y/kg rather than z percent), its *ad valorem* equivalent can be calculated using slight modifications of Eqs. 1, 2, and 3.

2.1.2 Domestic producer and consumer price-distorting measures

Governments sometimes intervene with a direct production subsidy for farmers, s_f (or production tax, in which case s_f is negative, including via informal taxes in kind by local and provincial governments). In that case, if only this distortion is present, the effect on producer incentives can be measured as the nominal rate of assistance to farm output conferred by domestic price support *(NRA$_{DS}$)*, which is as above except s_f replaces t_m or s_x, but the CTE in that case is zero. Similarly, if the government just imposes a consumption tax c_c on this product (or a consumption subsidy, in which case c_c is negative), the CTE is as above except c_c replaces t_m or s_x, but the *NRA$_{DS}$* in that case is zero.

The combination of domestic and border price support provides the total rate of assistance to output, NRA_o.

$$NRA_o = NRA_{BS} + NRA_{DS} \qquad (4)$$

2.1.3 What if the exchange rate system is also distorting prices?

Should a multitier foreign exchange rate regime be in place, then another policy-induced price wedge exists. A simple two-tier exchange rate system creates a gap between the price received by all exporters and the price paid by all importers for foreign currency, changing both the exchange rate received by exporters and that paid by importers from the equilibrium rate E that would prevail without this distortion in the domestic market for foreign currency (Bhagwati, 1978).

Exchange rate overvaluation of the type considered here requires controls by the government on current account transfers. A common requirement is that exporters surrender their foreign currency earnings to the central bank for changing to local currency at a low official rate. This is equivalent to a tax on exports to the extent that the official rate is below what the exchange rate would be in a market without government intervention. That implicit tax on exporters reduces their incentive to export and hence the supply of foreign currency flowing into the country. With less foreign currency, demanders are willing to bid up its purchase price. That provides a potential rent for the government, which can be realized by auctioning off the limited supply of foreign currency extracted from exporters or creating a legal secondary market. Either mechanism will create a gap between the official and parallel rates.

Such a dual exchange rate system is depicted in Figure 1, in which is it assumed that the overall domestic price level is fixed, perhaps by holding the money supply constant (Dervis, de Melo, and Robinson 1981). The supply of foreign exchange is given by

Figure 1 A distorted domestic market for foreign currency. Source: Martin (1993). See also Dervis, de Melo, and Robinson (1981).

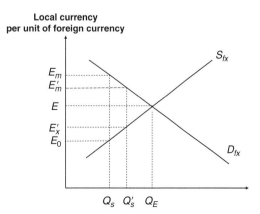

the upward sloping schedule, S_{fx}, and demand by D_{fx}, where the official exchange rate facing exporters is E_0 and the secondary market rate facing importers is E_m. At the low rate E_0, only Q_S units of foreign currency are available domestically, instead of the equilibrium volume Q_E that would result if exporters were able to exchange at the "equilibrium rate" E units of local currency per unit of foreign currency.[6] The gap between the official and the secondary market exchange rates is an indication of the magnitude of the tax imposed on trade by the two-tier exchange rate: Relative to the equilibrium rate E, the price of importables is raised by $e_m \times E$, which is equal to $(E_m - E)$, whereas the price of exportables is reduced by $e_x \times E$, which is equal to $(E - E_0)$, where e_m and e_x are the fractions by which the two-tier exchange rate system raises the domestic price of importables and lowers the domestic price of exportables, respectively. The estimated division of the total foreign exchange distortion between an implicit export tax, e_x, and an implicit import tax, e_m, will depend on the estimated elasticities of supply of exports and of demand for imports.[7] If the demand and supply curves in Figure 1 had the same slope, $e_m = e_x$ and $(e_m + e_x)$ is the secondary market premium or proportional rent extracted by the government or its agents.[8]

If the government chooses to allocate the limited foreign currency to different groups of importers at different rates, that is called a *multiple exchange rate system*. Some lucky importers may even be able to purchase it at the low official rate. The more that is allocated and sold to demanders whose marginal valuation is below E_m, the greater the unsatisfied excess demand at E_m and hence the stronger the incentive for an illegal or "black" market to form and for less unscrupulous exporters to lobby the government to legalize the secondary market for foreign exchange and to allow exporters to retain some fraction of their exchange rate earnings for sale in the secondary market. Such a right to exporters to retain and sell a portion of foreign exchange receipts would increase their incentives to export and thereby reduce the shortage of foreign exchange and hence the secondary market exchange rate (Tarr, 1990). In terms of Figure 1, the available supply increases from Q_S to Q_S', bringing down the secondary rate from E_m to E_m' such that the weighted average of the official rate and E_m' received by exporters is E_x' (the weights being the retention rate r and $(1 - r)$). Again, if the demand and supply curves in Figure 1 had the same slope, the implicit export and import taxes resulting from this regime would each be equal to half the secondary market premium.

In the absence of a secondary market and with multiple rates for importers below E_m and for exporters below E_0, a black market often emerges. Its rate for buyers will be above E the more the government sells its foreign currency to demanders whose marginal valuation is below E_m and the more active is the government in catching and punishing exporters selling in that illegal market. If the black market was allowed to operate "frictionlessly," there would be no foreign currency sales to the government at the official rate, and the black market rate would fall to the equilibrium rate E.

So, even though in the latter case the observed premium would be positive (equal to the proportion by which E is above nominal official rate E_0), there would be no distortion. For present purposes, since the black market is not likely to be completely "frictionless," it can be thought of as similar to the system involving a retention scheme. In terms of Figure 1, E'_m would be the black market rate for a proportion of sales and the weighted average of that and E_0 would be the exporters' return. Calculating E'_x in this case (and hence being able to estimate the implicit export and import taxes associated with this regime) by using the same approach as in the case with no illegal market thus requires not only knowing E_0 and the black market premium but also guessing the proportion, r, of sales in that black market.

In short, where a country has distortions in its domestic market for foreign currency, the exchange rate relevant for calculating the NRA_o or the CTE for a particular tradable product depends, in the case of a dual exchange rate system, on whether the product is an importable or an exportable, whereas in the case of multiple exchange rates it depends on the specific rate applying to that product each year.

2.1.4 What if trade costs are sufficiently high for the product to be not traded internationally?

Suppose the transport costs of trading are sufficient to make it unprofitable for a product to be traded internationally, such that the domestic price fluctuates over time within the band created by the CIF import price and the FOB export price. Then any trade policy measure (t_m or s_x) or the product-specific exchange rate distortion (e.g., e_m or e_x) is redundant. In that case, in the absence of other distortions, $NRA_o = 0$, and the $CTE = 0$. However, in the presence of any domestic producer or consumer tax or subsidy (s_f or t_c), the domestic prices faced by both producers *and* consumers will be affected. The extent of the impact depends on the price elasticities of domestic demand and supply for the nontradable (the standard closed-economy tax incidence issue).

To give a specific example, suppose that just a production tax is imposed on farmers producing a particular nontradable, so $s_f < 0$ and $t_c = 0$. In that case:

$$NRA_{DS} = \frac{s_f}{1 + \frac{\varepsilon}{\eta}} \tag{5}$$

and

$$CTE = \frac{-s_f}{1 + \frac{\eta}{\varepsilon}} \tag{6}$$

where ε is the price elasticity of supply and η is the (negative of the) price elasticity of demand.[9]

2.1.5 What if farm production involves not just primary factors but also intermediate inputs?

Where intermediate inputs are used in farm production, any taxes or subsidies on their production, consumption, or trade would alter farm value added and thereby also affect farmer incentives. Sometimes a government will have directly offsetting measures in place, such as a domestic subsidy for fertilizer use by farmers but also a tariff on fertilizer imports. In other situations there will be farm input subsidies but an export tax on the final product.[10] In principle all these items could be brought together to calculate an effective rate of direct assistance to farm value added (ERA). The nominal rate of direct assistance to farm output, NRA_o, is a component of that, as is the sum of the nominal rates of direct assistance to all farm inputs—call it NRA_i. In principle, all three rates can be positive or negative. Where there are significant distortions to input costs, their *ad valorem* equivalent can be accounted for by summing each input's NRA times its input/output coefficient to obtain the combined NRA_i, and adding that to the farm industry's nominal rate of direct assistance to farm output, NRA_o, to get the total nominal rate of assistance to farm production—call it simply NRA.[11]

$$NRA = NRA_o + NRA_i \qquad (7)$$

2.1.6 What about post-farm-gate costs?

If a state trading corporation is charging excessively for its marketing services and thereby lowering the farm-gate price of a product—for example, as a way of raising government revenue in place of an explicit tax—the extent of that excess should be treated as though it is an explicit tax.

Some farm products, including some that are not internationally traded, are inputs into a processing industry that may also be subject to government interventions. In that case the effect of those interventions on the price received by farmers for the primary product also needs to be taken into account.

2.2 The mean of agricultural NRAs

When it comes to averaging across countries, each polity is an observation of interest, so a simple average is meaningful for the purpose of political economy analysis. But if one wants a sense of how distorted is agriculture in a whole region, a weighted average is needed. The weighted average NRA for covered primary agriculture can be generated by multiplying each primary industry's value share of production (valued at the farm-gate equivalent undistorted prices) by its corresponding NRA and adding across industries.[12] The overall sectoral rate, $NRAag$, could also include actual or assumed information for the noncovered commodities and, where it exists, the aggregate value of nonproduct-specific assistance to agriculture.

A weighted average can be similarly generated for the tradables part of agriculture—including those industries producing products such as milk and sugar that require only light processing before they can be traded—by assuming that its share of nonproduct-specific assistance equals its weight in the total. Call that $NRAag^t$.

2.3 The dispersion of agricultural NRAs

In addition to the mean, it is important to provide a measure of the dispersion or variability of the NRA estimates across the covered products. The costs of government policy distortions to incentives in terms of resource misallocation tend to be greater the greater the degree of substitution in production (Lloyd, 1974). In the case of agriculture, which involves the use of farmland that is sector-specific but transferable among farm activities, the greater the variation of *NRAs* across industries within the sector, the higher will be the welfare cost of those market interventions. A simple indicator of dispersion is the standard deviation of industry *NRAs* within agriculture.

Anderson and Neary (2005) show that it is possible to develop a single index that captures the extent to which the mean and standard deviation of protection together contribute to the welfare cost of distortionary policies. That index recognizes that the welfare cost of a government-imposed price distortion is related to the square of the price wedge and so is larger than the mean and is positive regardless of whether the government's agricultural policy is favoring or hurting farmers. In the case where it is only import restrictions that are distorting agricultural prices, the index provides a percentage tariff equivalent that, if applied uniformly to all imports, would generate the same welfare cost as the actual intrasectoral structure of protection from import competition. Lloyd, Croser, and Anderson (2009) show that once *NRAs* and *CTEs* have been calculated, they can be used to generate such an index, even in the more complex situation where there might be domestic producer or consumer taxes or subsidies in addition to trade taxes or subsidies or quantitative restrictions. They call it a Welfare Reduction Index. They also show that, if one is willing to assume that domestic price elasticities of supply (demand) are equal across farm commodities, the only information needed to generate the index, in addition to the *NRAs* and *CTEs,* is the share of each commodity in the domestic value of farm production (consumption) at undistorted prices.

2.4 Trade bias in agricultural assistance

A trade bias index also is needed to indicate the changing extent to which a country's policy regime has an antitrade bias within the agricultural sector. This is important because, as mentioned, the Lerner (1936) Symmetry Theorem demonstrates that a tariff assisting import-competing farm industries has the same effect on farmers' incentives as though there was a tax on agricultural exports; if both measures are in place, this is a double imposition on farm exports. A dual exchange rate system adds further to the antitrade bias. The higher the nominal rate of assistance to import-competing agricultural production ($NRAag_m$) relative to that for exportable farm activities ($NRAag_x$), the more incentive producers in that subsector will have to bid for mobile resources that would otherwise have been employed in export agriculture, other things being equal.

Once each farm industry is classified as either import-competing, as a producer of exportables, or as producing a nontradable (its status could change over time), it is possible to generate for each year the weighted average $NRAs$ for the two different groups of tradable farm industries. They can then be used to generate an agricultural trade bias index defined as:

$$TBI = \left[\frac{1 + NRAag_x}{1 + NRAag_m} - 1 \right] \qquad (8)$$

where $NRAag_m$ and $NRAag_x$ are the average $NRAs$ for the import-competing and exportable parts of the agricultural sector (their weighted average being $NRAag^t$). This index has a value of zero when the import-competing and export subsectors are equally assisted, and its lower bound approaches -1 in the most extreme case of an antitrade policy bias.

Anderson and Neary (2005) also show that it is possible to develop a single index that captures the extent to which import protection reduces the volume of trade. Once $NRAs$ and $CTEs$ have been calculated, they can be used to generate a more general trade reduction index that allows for the trade effects of domestic price-distorting policies, regardless of whether they (or the trade measures) are positive or negative (Lloyd, Croser, and Anderson, 2009). Such a measure provides a percentage trade tax equivalent that, if applied uniformly to all agricultural tradables, would generate the same reduction in trade volume as the actual intrasectoral structure of distortions to domestic prices of farm goods. They also show that, if the domestic price elasticities of supply (demand) are equal across farm commodities, again, the only information needed in addition to the $NRAs$ and $CTEs$ is the share of each commodity in the domestic value of farm production (consumption) at undistorted prices.

2.5 Indirect agricultural assistance/taxation via nonagricultural distortions

In addition to direct assistance to or taxation of farmers, the Lerner (1936) Symmetry Theorem demonstrates that their incentives are also affected indirectly by government assistance to nonagricultural production in the national economy. The higher the nominal rate of assistance to nonagricultural tradables production ($NRAnonag^t$), the more incentive producers in other tradable sectors will have to bid up the value of mobile resources that would otherwise have been employed in agriculture, other things being equal. If $NRAag^t$ is below $NRAnonag^t$, one might expect there to be fewer resources in agriculture than there would be under free market conditions in the country, notwithstanding any positive direct assistance to farmers, and conversely.

One way to capture this idea is to calculate a relative rate of assistance, *RRA*, defined as:

$$RRA = \left[\frac{1 + NRAag^t}{1 + NRAnonag^t} - 1 \right] \qquad (9)$$

Since an *NRA* cannot be less than −1 if producers are to earn anything, neither can an *RRA*. This measure is a useful indicator for providing international comparisons over time of the extent to which a country's policy regime has an anti- or pro-agricultural bias.

3. NATIONAL DISTORTIONS TO FARMER INCENTIVES: THE EVOLUTION OF POLICIES

Before turning to the contemporary (post-World War II) situation, it is insightful to briefly examine the long history of government intervention in international markets for farm products by today's advanced economies, since similar political economy forces may influence policy choices in later-developing countries. Attention then turns to the price-distorting policies of developing countries since the 1950s as they became independent from their colonial masters.

3.1 The long history in high-income countries

Long-distance trade between nation-states arises whenever the domestic price differs from that of a similar foreign product by more than the costs of making a sale. Price differentials for agricultural products arise from time to time for a range of reasons. The most common is seasonality. Crops ripen at different times in places with different climates, which can give rise to fresh fruit and vegetable imports in the off-season. Also, weather variations cause cereal harvests to vary from year to year so that even countries that are normally food self-sufficient may import following an especially poor season, or export following a bumper harvest.

In addition to seasonality, price differences that affect international trade in farm products can arise through technological changes, particularly in transport and communication services. For example, following the American Civil War the rapid spread of the U.S. rail network in the 1870s and 1880s made it possible to transport wheat to tidewater areas more cheaply than the canal system. Railroad construction from the Ukrainian wheat fields to Crimean ports had a similar effect. Coupled with the shift from wooden to iron ships, these developments lowered very substantially the cost of getting wheat to Western Europe. So, in the 1880s, when weather patterns generated low yields in Western Europe, wheat farmers there did not enjoy the compensation of an increase in wheat prices. On the contrary, with less natural (transport cost) protection from import competition and coincidentally high yields in America, they faced real wheat price declines of around 15% between 1873 and 1896 (Kindleberger, 1951).

This chapter, however, is concerned with international price differences that result not from natural phenomena but from governmental taxes and subsidies, particularly those at a country's border. Although much government intervention in agricultural trade over the centuries has been aimed at stabilizing domestic food prices and supplies, there has been a general tendency for poor agrarian economies to tax agriculture relative to other sectors. Then, as nations industrialize, their policy regimes have tended to gradually change from negatively to positively assisting farmers relative to other producers (and conversely, from subsidizing to taxing food consumers).

Consider Britain, the first country to undergo an industrial revolution. Prior to that revolution—from the late 1100s to the 1660s—Britain used export taxes and licenses to prevent domestic food prices from rising excessively. But from 1660–1690 a series of Acts gradually raised food import duties (making imports prohibitive under most circumstances) and reduced export restrictions on grain (Stuart, 1992). These provisions were made even more protective of British farmers by the Corn Laws of 1815. True, the famous repeal of the Corn Laws in the mid-1840s heralded a period of relatively unrestricted food trade for Britain, but then agricultural protection returned in the 1930s and steadily increased over the next five decades.

Similar tendencies have been observed in many other Western European countries, although on the Continent the period of free trade in the 19th century was considerably shorter and agricultural protection levels during the past century were somewhat higher on average than in Britain. Kindleberger (1975) describes how the 19th century free-trade movements in Europe reflected the national economic, political, and sociological conditions of the time. Agricultural trade reform was less difficult for countries such as Britain, with overseas territories that could provide the metropole with a ready supply of farm products. The fall in the price of grain imports from America in the 1870s and 1880s provided a challenge for all, however. Denmark coped well by moving more into livestock production to take advantage of cheaper grain. Italians coped by sending many of their relatives to the New World. Farmers in France and Germany successfully sought protection from imports, however, and so began the post-industrial revolution growth of agricultural protectionism in densely populated countries. Meanwhile, tariffs on West European imports of manufactures were progressively reduced after the GATT came into force in the late 1940s, thereby adding to the encouragement of agricultural relative to manufacturing production (Lindert, 1991; Anderson, 1995).

Japan provides an even more striking example of the tendency to switch from taxing to increasingly assisting agriculture relative to other industries. Its industrialization began later than in Europe after the opening up of the economy following the Meiji

Restoration in 1868. By 1900 Japan had switched from being a small net exporter of food to becoming increasingly dependent on imports of rice (its main staple food and responsible for more than half the value of domestic food production). This was followed by calls from farmers and their supporters for rice import controls. Their calls were matched by equally vigorous calls from manufacturing and commercial groups for unrestricted food trade, since the price of rice at that time was a major determinant of real wages in the nonfarm sector. The heated debates were not unlike those that had led to the repeal of the Corn Laws in Britain six decades earlier. In Japan, however, the forces of protection triumphed, and a tariff was imposed on rice imports from 1904. That tariff then gradually rose over time, raising the domestic price of rice to more than 30% above the import price during World War I. Even when there were food riots because of shortages and high rice prices just after that war, the Japanese government's response was not to reduce protection but instead to extend it to its colonies and to shift from a national to an imperial rice self-sufficiency policy. That involved accelerated investments in agricultural development in the colonies of Korea and Taiwan behind an ever-higher external tariff wall that by the latter 1930s had driven imperial rice prices to more than 60% above prices in international markets (Anderson and Tyers, 1992). After the Pacific War ended and Japan lost its colonies, its agricultural protection growth resumed and spread from rice to an ever-wider range of farm products.

The other high-income countries were settled by Europeans relatively recently and are far less densely populated. They therefore have had a strong comparative advantage in farm products for most of their history following Caucasian settlement and so have felt less need to protect their farmers than Europe or Northeast Asia. Indeed, Australia and New Zealand, until the present decade, have tended—like developing countries—to have adopted policies that discriminated against their farmers (Anderson, Lloyd, and MacLaren, 2007).[13]

3.2 Developing countries since the 1950s

In South Korea and Taiwan in the 1950s, as in many newly independent developing countries, an import-substituting industrialization strategy was initially adopted, which harmed agriculture. But in those two economies—unlike in most other developing countries—that policy was replaced in the early 1960s with a more neutral trade policy that resulted in their very rapid export-oriented industrialization. That development strategy in those densely populated economies imposed competitive pressure on the farm sector, which, just as in Japan in earlier decades, prompted farmers to lobby (successfully, as it happened) for ever-higher levels of protection from import protection (Anderson, Hayami, and others, 1986, Ch. 2).

Many less advanced and less rapidly growing developing countries not only adopted import-substituting industrialization strategies in the late 1950s and early 1960s (Little

Scitovsky and Scott, 1970; Balassa, 1971); they also imposed direct taxes on their exports of farm products. It was common in the 1950s and 1960s, and in some cases through to the 1980s, to use dual or multiple exchange rates so as to indirectly tax both exporters and importers (Bhagwati, 1978; Krueger, 1978). This added to the antitrade bias of developing countries' trade policies. Certainly within the agricultural sector of each country, import-competing industries tended to enjoy more government support than those that were more competitive internationally (Krueger, Schiff, and Valdés, 1988, 1991; Herrmann et al., 1992; Thiele, 2004). The Krueger et al. study also reveals, at least up to the mid-1980s, that direct disincentives for farmers, such as agricultural export taxes, were less important than indirect disincentives in the form of import protection for the manufacturing sector or overvalued exchange rates, both of which attracted resources away from agricultural industries producing tradable products.

In short, historically countries have tended to gradually change from taxing to subsidizing agriculture increasingly relative to other sectors in the course of their economic development, although less so, and at a later stage of development, the stronger is a country's comparative advantage in agriculture (Anderson, Hayami, and others, 1986; Lindert, 1991). Hence at any time farmers in poor countries tended to face depressed terms of trade relative to product prices in international markets, whereas the opposite is true for farmers in rich countries (Anderson, 1995). Again, the exceptions have been rich countries with an extreme comparative advantage in agriculture (Australia, New Zealand).

That policy history of developing countries is now well known and has been documented extensively in previous surveys (e.g., Krueger, 1984), but less well known is the extent to which many emerging economies have belatedly followed the example of South Korea and Taiwan in abandoning import substitution and opening their economies. Some (e.g., Chile) started in the 1970s; others (e.g., India) did not do so in a sustained way until the 1990s. Some have adopted a very gradual pace of reform, with occasional reversals; others have moved rapidly to open markets. And some have adopted the rhetoric of reform but in practice have done little to free up their economies. To get a clear sense of the overall impact of these reform attempts, there is no substitute for empirical analysis that quantifies over time the types of indicators raised in the preceding theory section, to which we now turn. Again it is helpful to begin with analyses of the more advanced economies, not least because they were completed before systematic time series studies covering developing countries.

4. NATIONAL DISTORTIONS TO FARMER INCENTIVES: EMPIRICAL ESTIMATES SINCE THE 1950s

After post-war reconstruction, Japan continued to raise its agricultural protection, just as had been happening in Western Europe, but to even higher levels. Domestic prices exceeded international market prices for grains and livestock products by less than 40%

in both Japan and the European Community in the 1950s.[14] By the early 1980s the difference was more than 80% for Japan but was still around 40% for the EC—and was still close to zero for the agricultural-exporting rich countries of Australasia and North America (Anderson, Hayami, and others, 1986, Table 2.5). Virtually all that assistance to Japanese and European farmers in that period was due to restrictions on imports of farm products rather than domestic producer subsidies.

Since 1986 the OECD Secretariat has been computing annual producer and consumer support estimates (PSEs and CSEs) by member countries. For the OECD as a whole, the PSE rose between 1986–1988 and 2005–2007 in U.S. dollar terms (from $239 to $263 billion) but has come down when expressed as a share of support-inclusive returns to farmers (from 37% to 26%). Because of some switching of support instruments, including to measures that are based on noncurrent production or on long-term resource retirement, the share of that assistance provided via market price support measures has fallen from three quarters to one half. When the PSE payment is expressed as a percentage of undistorted prices to make it an NRA so as to be comparable with the definition in Eq. 7, the NRA fall is from 59% to 35% between 1986–1988 and 2005–2007 (OECD, 2008a). This indicator suggests OECD policies have become considerably less trade distorting, at least in proportional terms, even though farmer support in high-income countries has continued to grow in dollar terms because of growth in the value of their farm output.

As for developing countries outside Northeast Asia, the main comprehensive set of pertinent estimates over time is for the period just prior to when reforms became widespread. They were generated as part of a major study of 18 developing countries for the 1960s to the mid-1980s by Krueger, Schiff, and Valdés (1988, 1991). That study by the World Bank, whose estimates are summarized in Schiff and Valdés (1992), shows that the depression of incentives facing farmers has been due only partly to various forms of agricultural price and trade policies, including subsidies to food imports. Much more important in many cases have been those developing countries' nonagricultural policies that hurt their farmers indirectly. The two key ones have been manufacturing protectionism (which attracts resources from agriculture to the industrial sector) and overvalued exchange rates (which attracts resources to sectors producing nontradables, such as services). That indirect impact was negative for all four groups of countries shown in Table 1, whereas the impact of direct agricultural policies was negative only for the two lowest-income country groups. In addition to the total assistance being more negative for the poorer the country group, Table 1 also reveals that it is lower for producers of exportables than for the subsector focused on import-competing farm products, suggesting a strong antitrade bias for the sector as a whole.

Since there were no comprehensive multicountry, multiregion studies of the Krueger/Schiff/Valdés type for developing countries that monitored progress over the reform period,[15] a new study was launched by the World Bank in 2006 aimed at

Table 1   Direct and indirect nominal rates of assistance to farmers in eighteen developing countries, 1960–mid-1980s (%)

Country Group	Direct Assistance	Indirect Assistance	Total Assistance[a]	Assistance to Agricultural Export Subsector[a]	Assistance to agric. import-competing subsector[a]
Very low income	−23	−29	−52	−49	−11
Low income	−12	−24	−36	−40	−13
Lower middle income	0	−16	−16	−14	−2
Upper middle income	24	−14	10	−1	15
Unweighted sample average	**−8**	**−22**	**−30**	**−35**	**−9**

[a]Total assistance is the weighted average of assistance to the agricultural subsectors producing exportables, importables, and nontradables (the latter not shown). Source: Schiff and Valdés (1992, Tables 2–1 and 2–2).

filling this lacuna. The new study covers not only 41 developing countries but also 14 European transition economies as well as 20 high-income countries. The results from that study[16] do indeed reveal that there has been a substantial reduction in distortions to agricultural incentives in developing countries over the past two to three decades. They also reveal that progress has not been uniform across countries and regions, and that—contrary to some earlier claims (e.g., from Jensen, Robinson, and Tarp, 2002)—the reform process is far from complete. In particular, many countries still have a strong anti-trade bias in the structure of assistance within their agricultural sector; and some countries have 'overshot' in the sense that they have moved from having a relative rate of assistance to farmers that was negative to one that is positive, rather than stopping at the welfare-maximizing rate of zero. Moreover, the variance in rates of assistance across commodities within each country, and in aggregate rates across countries, remains substantial; and the begger-thy-neighbor practice of insulating domestic markets from international food price fluctuations continues, thereby exacerbating that volatility.

The global summary of those new results is provided in Figure 2. It reveals that the nominal rate of assistance (NRA) to farmers in high-income countries rose steadily over the post-World War II period through to the end of the 1980s, apart from a small

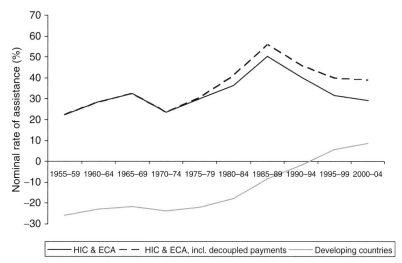

Figure 2 Nominal rates of assistance to agriculture in high-income and European transition economies and in developing countries, 1955-2004 (%, weighted averages, with "decoupled" payments included in the dashed HIC line).

dip when international food prices spiked around 1973–1974. After peaking at more than 50% in the mid-1980s, that average NRA for high-income countries has fallen a little, depending on the extent to which one believes some new farm programs are "decoupled" in the sense of no longer influencing production decisions. For developing countries, too, the average NRA for agriculture has been rising, but from a level of around –25% during the period from the mid-1950s to the early 1980s to a level of nearly 10% in the first half of the present decade. Thus the global gross subsidy equivalent of those rates of assistance has risen very substantially in constant (2000) U.S. dollar terms, from close to zero up to the mid-1970s to more than $200 billion per year at the farm gate since the mid-1990s (Figure 3).

When expressed on a per-farmer basis, the gross subsidy equivalent (GSE) varies enormously between high-income and developing countries. In 1980–1984 the GSE in high-income countries was already around $8000, and by 2000–2004 it had risen to $10,000 on average (and $25,000 in Norway, Switzerland, and Japan), or $13,500 when "decoupled" payments are included. By contrast, the GSE in developing economies was –$140 per farmer in the first half of the 1980s, which is a nontrivial tax when one recalls that at that time the majority of these people's households were surviving on less than $1 a day per capita. By 2000–2004 they received on average around $50 per farmer (Anderson, 2009, Ch. 1). Although this represents a major improvement, it is less than 1% of the support received by the average farmer in high-income countries.

The developing economies of Asia—including Korea and Taiwan, which were both very poor at the start of the period—have experienced the fastest transition from

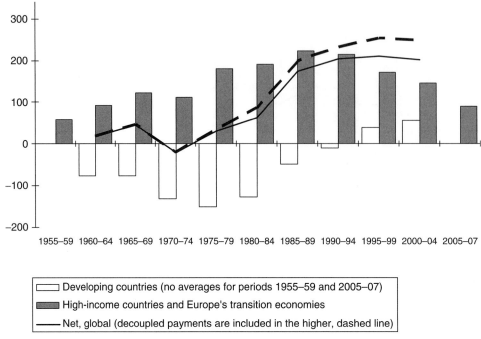

Figure 3   Gross subsidy equivalent of NRAs in high-income and European transition economies and in developing countries, 1960–2007 (constant 2000 US$B). Source: Anderson (2009).

negative to positive agricultural NRAs. Latin American economies first increased their taxation of farmers but gradually moved during the mid-1970s to the mid-2000s from around −20% to 5%. Africa's NRAs were similar, though slightly less negative than those of Latin America until the latter 1980s, before they fell back to −7% (implying a gross tax equivalent per farmer of $6). In Europe's transition economies farmer assistance fell to almost zero at the start of their transition from socialism in the early 1990s; but since then, in preparation for EU accession or because of booms in exports of energy raw materials, assistance has gradually increased to nearly 20%, or $550 per farmer (Anderson, 2009, Ch. 1).

The developing-country average NRA also conceals the fact that the exporting and import-competing subsectors of agriculture have very different NRAs. Figure 4 reveals that though the average NRA for exporters has been negative throughout (going from −20% to −30% before coming back up to almost zero in 2000–2004), the NRA for import-competing farmers in developing countries has fluctuated between 20% and 30% (and even reached 40% in the low-priced years in the mid-1980s). Having increased in the 1960s and 1970s, the antitrade bias within agriculture for developing countries has diminished considerably since the mid-1980s,[17] but the NRA gap between the two subsectors still averages around 20 percentage points.

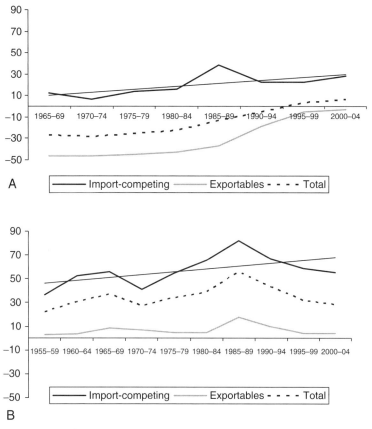

Figure 4 Nominal rates of assistance to exportable, import-competing, and all covered agricultural products,[a] high-income and developing countries, 1955–2007 (%). (a) Developing countries. (b) High-income countries plus Europe's transition economies. Source: Anderson (2009).
[a]Covered products only. The total also includes nontradable.

A further decomposition of the developing countries' NRAs worth commenting on is the contribution to them from trade policy measures at each country's border, as distinct from domestic output or input subsidies or taxes. Often political attention is focused much more on direct domestic subsidies or taxes than on trade measures, because those fiscal measures are made so transparent though the annual budgetary scrutiny process, whereas trade measures are reviewed only infrequently and are far less transparent, especially if they are not in the simple form of *ad valorem* tariffs. That attention would appear to be misplaced, however, because between 80% and 90% of the NRA for developing-country agriculture (not including nonproduct-specific support, which is very minor) comes from border measures such as import tariffs or export taxes (Anderson, 2009, Ch. 1).

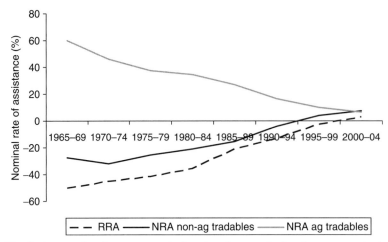

Figure 5   Nominal rates of assistance to agricultural and nonagricultural sectors and relative rate of assistance,[a] developing countries, 1965[b]–2004 (%, weighted averages).

Finally, the improvement in farmers' incentives in developing countries is understated by the preceding NRAag estimates because those countries have also reduced their assistance to producers of nonagricultural tradable goods, most notably manufactures. The decline in the weighted average NRA for the latter, depicted in Figure 5, was clearly much greater than the increase in the average NRA for tradable agricultural sectors for the period to the mid-1980s, consistent with the finding of Krueger, Schiff, and Valdés (1988, 1991). For the period since the mid-1980s, changes in both sectors' NRAs have contributed almost equally to the improvement in farmer incentives. The relative rate of assistance, captured in Eq. 5, provides a useful indicator of relative price change: The RRA for developing countries as a group went from −46% in the second half of the 1970s to 1% in the first half of the present decade. This increase (from a coefficient of 0.54 to 1.01) is equivalent to an almost doubling in the relative price of farm products, which is a huge change in the fortunes of developing-country farmers in just a generation. This is mostly because of the changes in Asia, but even for Latin America that relative price hike is one half, whereas for Africa that indicator improves by only one eighth (Figure 6).

With this as background, attention now turns to the market and welfare effects of the distortions to agricultural incentives in both high-income and poorer countries. This is done using first the simple partial equilibrium index approach outlined in the methodology and then using a global economywide modeling approach with the model calibrated to 2004. That provides a helpful benchmark against which to compare reforms since the 1980s as well as prospects for liberalizing global markets for agricultural and other products.

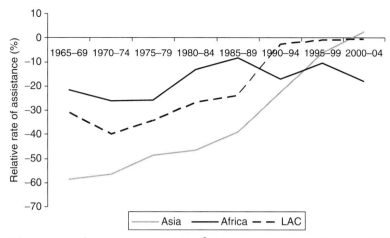

Figure 6 Relative rates of assistance to tradables,[a] Asia, Africa, and Latin America, 1965–2004 (%).

5. NEW INDEXES OF AGRICULTURAL PRICE DISTORTIONS

To capture distortions imposed by each country's border and domestic policies on its economic welfare and its trade volume, Lloyd, Croser, and Anderson (2009) define a Welfare Reduction Index (WRI) and a Trade Reduction Index (TRI) and estimate them for 75 countries since 1960, taking into account that the NRA differs from the CTE for some products. As their names suggest, these two indexes respectively capture in a single indicator the direct welfare- or trade-reducing effects of distortions to consumer and producer prices of covered farm products from all agricultural and food policy measures in place (while ignoring noncovered farm products and indirect effects of sectoral and trade policy measures directed at nonagricultural sectors). The WRI measure reflects the true welfare cost of agricultural price-distorting policies better than the NRA because it captures the disproportionately higher welfare costs of peak levels of assistance or taxation. In addition, the WRI and TRI measures are comparable across time and place. They thus go somewhat closer to what a computable general equilibrium (CGE) can provide in the way of estimates of the trade and welfare (and other) effects of the price distortions captured by the product NRA and CTE estimates, and they have the advantage over CGE models of being able to provide an annual time series.

The WRI five-year results in Figure 7 indicate a slightly rising tendency for covered products' policies to reduce welfare from the 1960s to the mid-1980s, but a substantial decline in the 1990s. This pattern is generated by different policy regimes in the various country groups, though: In high-income countries, covered products were assisted throughout the period, although less so after the 1980s, whereas covered products in

	1960-64	1965-69	1970-74	1975-79	1980-84	1985-89	1990-94	1995-99	2000-04
Africa	51	51	52	49	50	80	52	37	36
Asia	32	45	44	45	50	51	33	23	21
Latin America	37	26	36	35	42	37	39	18	22

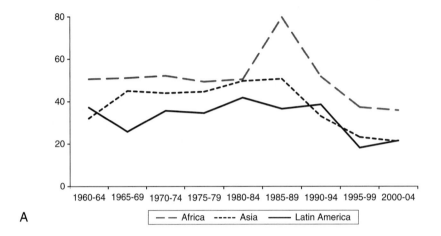

A

	1960-64	1965-69	1970-74	1975-79	1980-84	1985-89	1990-94	1995-99	2000-04	2005-07
Developing countries	41	43	44	43	48	51	36	23	22	
Europe's transition econs.							47	40	40	44
High-income countries	55	66	54	73	77	95	77	60	58	33

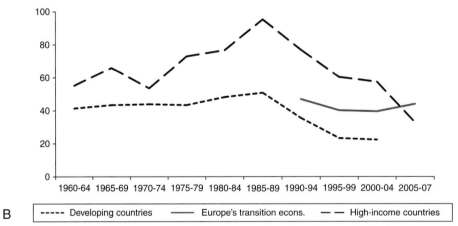

B

Figure 7   Welfare reduction indexes for covered tradable farm products by region, 1960–2007 (%). (a) Africa, Asia, and Latin America. (b) Developing countries, high-income countries, and Europe's transition economies. Source: Lloyd, Croser, and Anderson (2009), based on NRAs and CTEs in Anderson and Valenzuela (2008).

developing countries were disprotected until the most recent years. That is, the WRI has the desirable property of correctly identifying the welfare consequences that result from both positive and negative assistance regimes, because it captures the dispersion of NRAs among covered products: The larger the variance in assistance levels, the greater the potential for resources to be used in activities that do not maximize economic welfare. One consequence is that the WRI values are much higher than the NRAs for high-income countries. Another consequence is that the WRI for Africa spikes in the mid-1980s in contrast to the NRA, which moves close to zero. The reason is that although Africa was still taxing exportables, it had moved (temporarily) from low to very high positive levels of protection for import-competing farm products. At the aggregate level, African farmers received almost no government assistance then (NRA close to zero), but the welfare cost of its mixture of agricultural policies as a whole was at its highest then, according to the WRI. A third consequence is that for developing countries its average WRI in the years 1995–2004 is around 20%, even though its average NRA for covered products in those years is close to zero, again reflecting the high dispersion across product NRAs—particularly between exportables and import-competing goods—in each country.

For developing countries as a group, the trade restrictiveness of agricultural policy was rising until the late 1980s, and thereafter it declined, especially for Asia and Africa, according to the five-year average TRI estimates (Figure 8). For high-income countries the TRI time path was similar, but the decline began a few years later. The aggregate results for developing countries are being driven by the exportables

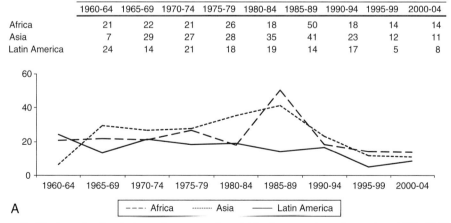

	1960-64	1965-69	1970-74	1975-79	1980-84	1985-89	1990-94	1995-99	2000-04
Africa	21	22	21	26	18	50	18	14	14
Asia	7	29	27	28	35	41	23	12	11
Latin America	24	14	21	18	19	14	17	5	8

A

Figure 8   Trade reduction indexes for covered tradable farm products by region, 1960–2007 (%). (a) Africa, Asia, and Latin America.

(Continued)

	1960-64	1965-69	1970-74	1975-79	1980-84	1985-89	1990-94	1995-99	2000-04	2005-07
Developing countries	17	26	24	26	31	38	22	11	11	
Europe's transition econs.							8	14	14	6
High-income countries	30	33	23	32	40	45	39	33	29	15

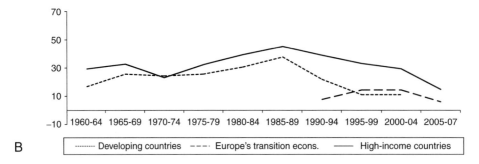

B

------- Developing countries   ---- Europe's transition econs.   —— High-income countries

Figure 8—Cont'd (b) Developing countries, high-income countries, and Europe's transition economies. Source: Lloyd, Croser, and Anderson (2009), based on NRAs and CTEs in Anderson and Valenzuela (2008).

subsector, which is being taxed, and the import-competing subsector, which is being protected (albeit by less than in high-income countries). For high-income countries, policies have supported both exporting and import-competing agricultural products and, even though they favor the latter much more heavily, the assistance to exporters has offset somewhat the antitrade bias from the protection of import-competing producers in terms of their impacts on those countries' aggregate volume of trade in farm products. Thus up to the early 1990s the TRI for high-income countries was below that for developing countries; and, to use again the example of Africa, in 1985–1989 when the NRA was closest to zero the TRI peaked, correctly identifying the trade-reducing effect of positive protection to the import-competing farmers and disprotection to producers of exportables.

6. ECONOMYWIDE EFFECTS OF PAST REFORMS AND REMAINING POLICIES

It is clear from the previous discussion that over the past quarter of a century there has been a great deal of change in policy distortions to agricultural incentives throughout the world: The antiagricultural and antitrade biases of policies of many developing countries have been reduced, export subsidies of high-income countries have been cut, and some reinstrumentation toward less inefficient and less trade-distorting forms of support, particularly in Western Europe, has begun. However, protection from agricultural import competition has continued to be on an upward trend in both rich and poor countries, notwithstanding the Uruguay Round Agreement on Agriculture that aimed to bind and reduce farm tariffs.

What, then, have been the net economic effects of agricultural price and trade policy changes around the world since the early 1980s? And how do those effects on global markets, farm incomes, and economic welfare compare with the effects of policy distortions still in place as of 2004? Valenzuela, van der Mensbrugghe, and Anderson (2009) use a global economywide model known as Linkage (van der Mensbrugghe, 2005) to provide a combined retrospective and prospective analysis that seeks to assess how far the world has come and how far it still has to go in removing the disarray in world agriculture. It quantifies the impacts of both past reforms and current policies by comparing the effects of the project's distortion estimates for the period 1980–1984 with those of 2004.

Several key findings from that economywide modeling study are worth emphasizing. First, the policy reforms from the early 1980s to the mid-2000s improved global economic welfare by $233 billion per year, and removing the distortions remaining as of 2004 would add another $168 billion per year (in 2004 U.S. dollars). This suggests that in a global welfare sense the world had moved three fifths of the way toward global free trade in goods over that quarter-century.

Second, developing economies benefited proportionately more than high-income economies (1.0% compared with 0.7% of national income) from those past policy reforms and would gain nearly twice as much as high-income countries if all countries were to complete that reform process (an average increase of 0.9% compared with 0.5% for high-income countries). Of those prospective welfare gains from global liberalization, 60% would come from agriculture and food policy reform. This is a striking result given that the shares of agriculture and food in global GDP and global merchandise trade are less than 9%. The contribution of farm and food policy reform to the prospective welfare gain for just developing countries is even greater, at 83%.

Third, the share of global farm production exported (excluding intra-EU trade) in 2004 was slightly smaller as a result of those reforms since 1980–1984, because of fewer farm export subsidies. Agriculture's 8% share in 2004 contrasts with the 31% share for other primary products and the 25% for all other goods—a "thinness" that is an important contributor to the volatility of international prices for weather-dependent farm products. If the policies distorting goods trade in 2004 were removed, the share of global production of farm products that is exported would rise from 8% to 13%, thereby reducing instability of prices and quantities of those products traded.

Fourth, the developing countries' share of the world's primary agricultural exports rose from 43% to 55% and its farm output share from 58% to 62% because of the reforms since the early 1980s, with rises in nearly all agricultural industries except rice and sugar. Removing remaining goods market distortions would boost their export and output shares even further, to 64% and 65%, respectively.

Fifth, the average real price in international markets for agricultural and food products would have been 13% lower had policies not changed over the past quarter-century. Evidently the impact of the RRA fall in high-income countries (including the cuts in farm export subsidies) in raising international food prices more than offset the opposite impact of the RRA rise (including the cuts in agricultural export taxes) in developing countries over that period. By contrast, removing remaining distortions as of 2004 is projected to raise the international price of agricultural and food products by less than 1% on average. This is contrary to earlier modeling results based on the GTAP protection database. (For example, Anderson, Martin, and van der Mensbrugghe, 2006, estimated they would rise 3.1% or, for just primary agriculture, 5.5%). The lesser impact in these new results is because export taxes in developing countries based on the above NRA estimates for 2004 are included in the new database (most notably for Argentina) and their removal would offset the international price-raising effect of eliminating import protection and farm subsidies elsewhere.

Sixth, for developing countries as a group, net farm income (value added in agriculture) is estimated to be 4.9% higher than it would have been without the reforms of the past quarter-century, which is more than 10 times the proportional gain for nonagriculture. If policies remaining in 2004 were removed, net farm incomes in developing countries would rise a further 5.6%, compared with just 1.9% for nonagricultural value added. Furthermore, returns to unskilled workers in developing countries—the majority of whom work on farms—would rise more than returns to other productive factors from that liberalization. Together, these findings suggest that both inequality and poverty could be alleviated by such reform, given that three quarters of the world's poor are farmers in developing countries (Chen and Ravallion, 2008).

Finally, removal of agricultural price-supporting policies in high-income countries would undoubtedly lead to painful reductions in income and wealth for farmers there if they were not compensated—although it should be kept in mind that the majority of farm household income in high-income countries comes from off-farm sources (OECD, 2008b). But the gainers in the rest of their societies could readily afford to compensate them fiscally from the benefits of freeing trade.

7. PROSPECTS FOR FURTHER REDUCTIONS IN DISTORTIONS

It is not obvious how future policies might develop. A quick glance at the preceding policy indicators could lead one to view developments from the early 1960s to the mid-1980s as an aberrant period of welfare-reducing policy divergence (negative and declining RRAs in low-income countries, positive and rising RRAs in most high-income countries) that has given way to welfare-improving and poverty-reducing reforms during which the two country groups' RRAs are converging. But on inspection of the NRAs for exporting and import-competing subsectors of agriculture (Figure 4), it is clear that the convergence of NRAs to near zero is mainly with respect to the exporting subsector, whereas NRAs for import-competing farmers are positive and trending upward over time at the same rate in both developing and high-income countries—notwithstanding the Uruguay Round Agreement on Agriculture, which was aimed at tariffying and reducing import protection. True, applied tariffs have been lowered or suspended as a way of dealing with the international food price spike in 2008, but this, and the food export taxes or quantitative restrictions imposed that year by numerous food-exporting developing countries, may be only until international prices return to trend (as happened after the price hike of 1973–1974 and the price dip of 1986–1987).

The indications are very mixed as to why some countries appear to have reformed their price-distorting agricultural and trade policies more than others in recent decades and why some have stubbornly resisted reform. Some reforming countries have acted unilaterally, apparently having become convinced that it is in their own national interest to do so. China is but the most dramatic and significant example of the past three decades among developing countries, whereas among the high-income countries only Australia and New Zealand are in that category. Others might have done so partly to secure bigger and better loans from international financial institutions and then, having taken that first step, they have continued the process, even if somewhat intermittently. India is one example, but there are also numerous examples in Africa and Latin America. Few have gone backward in terms of increasing their anti-agricultural bias, but Zimbabwe and perhaps Argentina qualify during the present decade—and numerous others joined them in 2008, at least temporarily, in response to the sudden upward spike in international food prices. And some have reduced their agricultural subsidies and import barriers at least partly in response to the GATT's multilateral Uruguay Round Agreement on Agriculture, the European Union being the most important example (helped by its desire for otherwise costly preferential trade agreements, including its recent expansion eastward).

The EU reforms suggest that agricultural protection growth can be slowed and even reversed if accompanied by reinstrumentation away from price supports to decoupled measures or more direct forms of farm income support. The starker examples of Australia and New Zealand show that one-off buyouts can bring faster and even complete reform.[18] But in the developing countries where levels of agricultural protection are generally below high-income levels, there are fewer signs of a slowdown of the upward trend in agricultural protection from import competition over the past half-century.

Indeed, there are numerous signs that developing country governments want to keep open their options to raise agricultural NRAs in the future, particularly via import restrictions. One indicator is the high tariff bindings developing countries committed themselves to following the Uruguay Round: As of 2001, actual applied tariffs on agricultural products averaged less than half the corresponding bound tariffs for developing countries of 48% and less than one sixth in the case of least-developed countries (Anderson and Martin, 2006, Table 1.2).

Another indicator of agricultural trade reform reluctance is the unwillingness of many developing countries to agree to major cuts in bound agricultural tariffs in the

WTO's ongoing Doha round of multilateral trade negotiations. Indeed, many of them believe high-income countries should commit to reducing their remaining farm tariffs and subsidies before developing countries should offer further reform commitments of their own. Yet modeling results reported in Valenzuela, van der Mensbrugghe, and Anderson (2009) suggest that if high-income countries alone were to liberalize their agricultural markets, such a subglobal reform would provide less than two-thirds of the potential gains to developing countries that could come from global agricultural policy reform.

More than that, the current negotiations have brought to prominence a new proposal for agricultural protectionism in developing countries. This is based on the notion that agricultural protection is helpful and needed for food security, livelihood security, and rural development. This view has succeeded in bringing "Special Products" and a "Special Safeguard Mechanism" into the multilateral trading system's agricultural negotiations, despite the fact that such policies, which would raise domestic food prices in developing countries, could worsen poverty and the food security of the poor (Ivanic and Martin, 2008).

To wait for high-income country reform before liberalizing the farm trade of developing countries is unwise as a poverty-alleviating strategy, not least because the past history revealed in the NRAs summarized previously suggests that such reform will be at best slow in coming. In the United States, for example, the most recent two five-year farm bills were steps backward from the previous regime, which at least sought to reinstrument protection toward less trade-distorting measures (Gardner, 2009). Nor have the world's large number of new regional integration agreements of recent years been very successful in reducing farm protection. Furthermore, for developing countries to postpone their own reform would be to forego a major opportunity to boost theirs and (given the size and growth in South/South trade of late) their neighbors' economies. It would be doubly wasteful if, by being willing to commit to reform in that way, they would be able to convince high-income countries to reciprocate by signing on to a more ambitious Doha agreement, the potential global benefits from which are very considerable.[19]

Developing countries that continue to free up domestic markets and practice good macroeconomic governance will keep growing, and typically the growth will be more rapid in manufacturing and service activities than in agriculture, especially in the more densely populated countries where agricultural comparative advantage is likely to decline. Whether such economies become more dependent on imports of farm products depends, however, on what happens to their relative rates of assistance (RRA). The first wave of Asian industrializers (Japan, and then Korea and Taiwan) chose to slow the growth of food import dependence by raising their NRA for agriculture even as they were bringing down their NRA for nonfarm tradables, such that their RRA became increasingly above the neutral zero level. A key question is: Will later

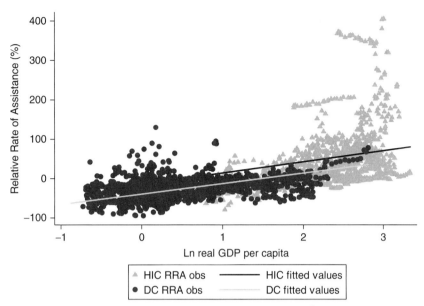

Figure 9 Relationships between real GDP per capita and RRA,[a] all focus countries, 1955–2007. Source: Anderson (2009), using country fixed effects and the RRA estimates in Anderson and Valenzuela (2008).

	Coefficient	Standard Error	R^2
DCs	0.26	0.02	0.17
HICs	0.28	0.03	0.14

industrializers follow suit, given the past close association of RRAs with rising per capita income and falling agricultural comparative advantage? Figure 9 suggests developing countries' RRA trends of the past three decades have been on the same upward trajectory as the high-income countries prior to the 1990s. So, unless new forces affect their polities, the governments of later industrializing economies could well follow suit.

One new force is disciplines on farm subsidies and protection policies of WTO member countries following the Uruguay Round. Earlier industrializers were not bound under GATT to keep down their agricultural protection. Had there been strict disciplines on farm trade measures at the time Japan and Korea joined GATT in 1955 and 1967, respectively, their NRAs could have been halted at less than 20% (Anderson, 2009, Figure 1.12). At the time of China's accession to the WTO in December 2001, its NRA was less than 5%, according to Huang et al. (2009), or 7.3% for just import-competing agriculture. Its average bound import tariff commitment was about twice that (16% in 2005), but what matters most is China's out-of-quota bindings on the items for which imports are restricted by tariff rate quotas. The latter tariff bindings as of 2005 were 65% for grains, 50% for sugar, and 40% for cotton (Anderson, Martin, and Valenzuela, 2009). Clearly, the legal commitments even China made on acceding to WTO are a long way from current levels of support for its farmers and so are unlikely to constrain the government very much in the next decade or so. And the legal constraints on developing countries that joined the WTO earlier are even less constraining. For India, Pakistan, and Bangladesh, for example, their estimated NRAs for agricultural importables in 2000–2004 are 34%, 4%, and 6%, respectively, whereas the average bound tariffs on their agricultural imports are 114%, 96%, and 189%, respectively (WTO, ITC, and UNCTAD, 2007). Also, like other developing countries, they have high bindings on product-specific domestic supports of 10% and another 10% for nonproduct specific assistance, a total of 20 more percentage points of NRA (17%, in China's case) that legally could come from domestic support measures, compared with, currently, 10% in India and less than 3% in the rest of South Asia.

Hopefully, developing countries will choose not to make use of the legal wiggle room they have allowed themselves in their WTO bindings to follow Japan, Korea, and Taiwan into high agricultural protection. A much more efficient and equitable strategy would be to instead treat agriculture in the same way they have been treating nonfarm tradable sectors. That would involve opening the sector to international competition and relying on more efficient domestic policy measures for raising government revenue (e.g., income and consumption or value-added taxes) and to assist farm families (e.g., public investment in rural education and health, rural infrastructure, and agricultural research and development). According to Table 2, investments in public agricultural R&D in developing countries as a group are currently equivalent to less than 1% of the gross value of farm

Table 2 Intensity of public agricultural R&D expenditure, high-income and developing country regions, 1971–2004 (% of gross value of agricultural production at undistorted prices)

	1970s	1980s	1990s	2000–2004
All high-income countries	2.2	2.2	1.9	1.6
All developing countries	0.4	0.6	0.75	0.9
Asia	0.3	0.6	0.7	0.9
Latin America	0.2	0.4	0.45	0.6
Sub-Saharan Africa	1.2	1.1	1.2	1.1

Source: Anderson and Valenzuela (2008), based on R&D data from the CGIAR's Agricultural Science and Technology Indicators website at www.asti.cgiar.org (see Pardey et al., 2006).

production (about half the intensity of high-income countries). Given the extremely high rates of return at the margin for such investments (see, e.g., Fan, 2008), expenditure on that would be far wiser than providing price supports to appease demands from agribusiness vested interests as middle-income economies develop.

As for high-income countries, the previously described distortion estimates show that they have all lowered the price supports for their farmers since the 1980s. In some countries, that has been partly replaced by assistance that is at least somewhat decoupled from production. If that trend continues at the pace of the past quarter-century and if there is no growth of agricultural protection in developing countries, before the middle of this century most of the disarray in world food markets will have been removed. However, if the WTO's Doha Development Agenda collapses and governments thereby find it more difficult to ward off agricultural protection lobbies, it is all the more likely that developing countries will follow the same agricultural protection path this century as that which was taken by high-income countries last century. One way to encourage developing countries to follow a more liberal policy path could be to extend the Integrated Framework's Diagnostic Trade Integration Study (DTIS) process to a broader range of low-income countries. That process, which provides action plans for policy and institutional reform and lists investment and technical assistance needs, could be expanded to include the "aid for trade reform" proposal that has been discussed in the context of the Doha round (Hoekman, 2005), regardless of the fate of that round.

End Notes

1. Taxes on Bordeaux exports were so high that when they were lowered in 1203, tax revenue actually increased and allowed consumption in Britain to rise to 4.5 litres of claret per capita by 1308 (Johnson, 1989, p. 142) —the same volume as in the early 1970s. Along the Rhine River in the 14th century, there were no fewer than 62 customs points. With such implicit subsidizing of local consumption (and because drinking water was unsafe), the volume of wine consumed per capita by the 15th century in Germany is estimated to have exceeded 120 litres (Johnson, 1989, p. 120), or five times today's per capita consumption.
2. French exports to Britain fell from around 10 Ml in the 17th century to just 1 Ml from 1690 to 1850, when Portugese exports grew from 0 to 12 Ml and Spain's from 4 to 6 Ml per year (Francis, 1972, Appendix). See also Nye (2007).
3. Currently fewer than 15 million relatively wealthy farmers in developed countries, with an average of almost 80 hectares per worker, are being helped at the expense of not only consumers and taxpayers in those rich countries but also the majority of the 1.3 billion relatively impoverished farmers and their large families in developing countries who, on average, have to earn a living from just 2.5 hectares per worker.
4. This section draws heavily on Anderson, Kurzweil, Martin, Sandri, and Valenzuela (2008).
5. The NRA_{BS} thus differs from the producer support estimate (PSE), as calculated by the OECD, in that the PSE is expressed as a fraction of the distorted value. It is thus $t_m/(1+t_m)$, and so for a positive t_m the PSE is smaller than the NRA_{BS} and is necessarily less than 100 percent.
6. *Equilibrium* in this sense refers to what would prevail without this distortion in the domestic market for foreign currency. In the diagram and in the discussion that follows, the equilibrium exchange rate E exactly balances the domestic supply and demand for foreign currency. Taken literally, this implies a

zero balance on the current account. The approach here can readily be generalized to accommodate exogenous capital flows and transfers, which would shift the location of Q_E. With constant-elasticity supply and demand curves, all the results would carry through, and any exogenous change in those capital flows or transfers would imply a shift in the D_{fx} or S_{fx} curves.

7. From the viewpoint of wanting to use the NRA_o and CTE estimates later as parameters in a CGE model, it does not matter what assumptions are made here about these elasticities, since the CGE model's results for real variables will not be affected. What matters for real impacts is the magnitude of the total distortion, not its allocation between an export tax and an import tax: the traditional incidence result from tax theory that also applies to trade taxes (Lerner, 1936). For an excellent general equilibrium treatment using an early version of the World Bank's 1-2-3 Model, see de Melo and Robinson (1989). There the distinction is made between traded and nontraded goods (using the Armington (1969) assumption of differentiation between products sold on domestic as distinct from international markets), in contrast to the distinction between tradable and nontradable products made below.

8. Note that this same type of adjustment could be made where the government forces exporters to surrender all foreign currency earnings to the domestic commercial banking system and importers to buy all foreign currency needs from that banking system where that system is allowed by regulation to charge excessive fees. This apparently occurs in, for example, Brazil, where the spread early this decade was reputedly 12%. If actual costs in a nondistorted competitive system are only 2% (as they are in the less distorted Chilean economy), the difference of 10 points could be treated as the equivalent of a 5% export tax and a 5% import tax applying to all tradables (but, as with nontariff barriers, there would be no government tariff revenue but rather rent, in this case accruing to commercial banks rather than to the central bank). This is an illustration of the point made by Rajan and Zingales (2004) of the power of financial market reform in expanding opportunities.

9. As in the two-tier exchange rate case, the elasticities are used merely to identify the incidence of these measures: As long as both the NRA_o and the CTE are included in any economic model used to assess the impact of the production tax, the real impacts will depend only on the magnitude of the total distortion, s_f, not on the estimated NRA and CTE.

10. On this general phenomenon of offsetting distortions for outputs and inputs (and even direct payments or taxes), see Rausser (1982).

11. Bear in mind that a fertilizer plant or livestock feed-mix plant might be enjoying import tariff protection that raises the domestic price of fertilizer or feed mix to farmers by more than any consumption subsidy (as had been the case for fertilizer in Korea; Anderson, 1983), in which case the net contribution of this set of input distortions to the total NRA for agriculture would be negative.

12. Corden (1971) proposed that free-trade volume be used as weights, but since they are not observable (and an economywide model is needed to estimate them) the common practice is to compromise by using actual distorted volumes but undistorted unit values or, equivalently, distorted values divided by $(1 + NRA)$. If estimates of own- and cross-price elasticities of demand and supply are available, a partial equilibrium estimate of the quantity at undistorted could be generated, but if those estimated elasticities are unreliable this can introduce more error than it seeks to correct.

13. In an early attempt to compile a global set of NRA estimates for agriculture for use in a 30-region model of world food markets calibrated to 1980–1982, Tyers and Anderson (1986, 1992, p. 76) estimated the following OLS regression relationship between those NRAs and data on the log of per capita income relative to the global average (YPC) and an index of agricultural comparative advantage (CA, the food self-sufficiency ratio under free farm trade as generated by their model):
NRA = 0.22 + 0.11YPC − 0.51CA adjusted R^2 = 0.83, n = 30
(8.7) (5.6) (−10.7)

14. Gulbrandsen and Lindbeck (1973, p. 38) estimate that the average nominal rate of agricultural protection in Western Europe increased from less than 30% in the 1930s and early 1950s to around 40% in the latter 1950s and 60% by the latter 1960s.

15. Exceptions include a pair of follow-on studies by Valdés (1996, 2000) for a sample of Latin American and European transition economies and a recent study of four Asian countries by Orden et al. (2007).

16. A global overview of the results is provided in Anderson (2009), and the detailed country case studies are reported in four regional volumes covering Africa (Anderson and Masters, 2009), Asia (Anderson and Martin, 2009), Latin America (Anderson and Valdés, 2008), and Europe's transition economies (Anderson and Swinnen, 2008).

17. The weighted average antitrade bias index, defined in Eq. 8, fell during 1980–1984 and 2000–2004, from −0.38 to −0.15 for Africa, from −0.49 to −0.15 for Asia, and from −0.32 to −0.19 for Latin America (Anderson, 2009, Ch. 1).

18. For a detailed analysis of the buyout option versus the slower and less complete cashout option (moving to direct payments), as well as the uncompensated gradual squeeze-out or sudden cutout options, see Orden and Diaz-Bonilla (2006).

19. On the size of those potential net benefits compared with those from other opportunities that could address the world's most important challenges as conceived by the Copenhagen Consensus project (whose expert panel ranked trade reform as having the second highest payoff among those dozens of opportunities), see www.copenhagenconsensus.org, including the trade paper by Anderson and Winters (2009).

References

Anderson, J., & Neary, P. (2005). *Measuring the Restrictiveness of International Trade Policy*. Cambridge MA: MIT Press.

Anderson, K. (1983). Fertilizer Policy in Korea. *Journal of Rural Development*, *6*(1), 43–57, June.

Anderson, K. (1995). Lobbying Incentives and the Pattern of Protection in Rich and Poor Countries. *Economic Development and Cultural Change*, *43*(2), 401–423, January.

Anderson, K. (Ed.). (2009). *Distortions to Agricultural Incentives: A Global Perspective, 1955–2007*. London: Palgrave Macmillan and Washington, DC: World Bank.

Anderson, K., Hayami, Y., & Others. (1986). *The Political Economy of Agricultural Protection*. Boston, London and Sydney: Allen and Unwin.

Anderson, K., Kurzweil, M., Martin, W., Sandri, D., & Valenzuela, E. (2008). Measuring Distortions to Agricultural Incentives, Revisited. *World Trade Review*, 7(4), 675–704, October.

Anderson, K., Lloyd, P. J., & MacLaren, D. (2007). Distortions to Agricultural Incentives in Australia Since World War II. *The Economic Record*, *83*(263), 461–482, December.

Anderson, K., & Martin, W. (Eds.). (2006). *Agricultural Trade Reform and the Doha Development Agenda*. London: Palgrave Macmillan and Washington, DC: World Bank.

Anderson, K., & Martin, W. (Eds.). (2009). *Distortions to Agricultural Incentives in Asia*. Washington, DC: World Bank.

Anderson, K., Martin, W., & Valenzuela, E. (2009). Long-Run Implications of WTO Accession for Agriculture in China. In C. Carter, & I. Sheldon (Eds.), *China's Agricultural Trade: Issues and Prospects*. London: CABI (forthcoming).

Anderson, K., Martin, W., & van der Mensbrugghe, D. (2006). Distortions to World Trade: Impacts on Agricultural Markets and Farm Incomes. *Review of Agricultural Economics*, *28*(2), 168–194, Summer.

Anderson, K., & Masters, W. (Eds.). (2009). *Distortions to Agricultural Incentives in Africa*. Washington, DC: World Bank.

Anderson, K., & Swinnen, J. (Eds.). (2008). *Distortions to Agricultural Incentives in Europe's Transition Economies*. Washington, DC: World Bank.

Anderson, K., & Tyers, R. (1992). Japanese Rice Policy in the Interwar Period: Some Consequences of Imperial Self Sufficiency. *Japan and the World Economy, 4*(2), 103–127, September.

Anderson, K., & Valdés, A. (Eds.). (2008). *Distortions to Agricultural Incentives in Latin America*. Washington, DC: World Bank.

Anderson, K., & Valenzuela, E. (2008). *Estimates of Distortions to Agricultural Incentives, 1955 to 2007*. Washington, DC: World Bank, downloadable at www.worldbank.org/agdistortions

Anderson, K., & Winters, L. A. (2009). The Challenge of Reducing International Trade and Migration Barriers. In B. Lomborg (Ed.), *Global Crises, Global Solutions* (2nd ed.). Cambridge and New York: Cambridge University Press (forthcoming).

Armington, P. (1969). "A Theory of Demand for Products Distinguished by Place of Production" *IMF Staff Papers* 16:159–78.

Balassa, B., & Associates. (1971). *The Structure of Protection in Developing Countries*. Baltimore: Johns Hopkins University Press.

Bates, R. H. (1981). *Market and States in Tropical Africa: The Political Basis of Agricultural Policies*. Berkeley: University of California Press.

Bhagwati, J. N. (1971). The Generalized Theory of Distortions and Welfare. In J. N. Bhagwati, et al. (Ed.), *Trade, Balance of Payments and Growth*. Amsterdam: North-Holland.

Bhagwati, J. N. (1978). *Foreign Trade Regimes and Economic Development: Anatomy and Consequences of Exchange Control Regimes*. Cambridge, MA: Ballinger.

Chen, S., & Ravallion, M. (2008). *The Developing World is Poorer Than We Thought, But No Less Successful in the Fight Against Poverty*. Policy Research Working Paper 4703. Washington, DC: World Bank, August.

Corden, W. M. (1971). *The Theory of Protection*. Oxford: Clarendon Press.

Corden, W. M. (1997). *Trade Policy and Economic Welfare (second edition)*. Oxford: Clarendon Press.

de Melo, J., & Robinson, S. (1989). Product Differentiation and the Treatment of Foreign Trade in Computable General Equilibrium Models of Small Economies. *Journal of International Economics, 27*, 47–67.

Dervis, K., de Melo, J., & Robinson, S. (1981). A General Equilibrium Analysis of Foreign Exchange Shortages in a Developing Country. *Economic Journal, 91*, 891–906.

Fan, S. (2008). *Public Expenditures, Growth and Poverty in Developing Countries: Issues, Methods and Findings*. Baltimore: Johns Hopkins University Press.

Francis, A. D. (1972). *The Wine Trade*. London: Adams and Charles Black.

Gardner, B. (2009). United States and Canada. In K. Anderson (Ed.), *Distortions to Agricultural Incentives: A Global Perspective, 1955–2007* (Ch. 4). London: Palgrave Macmillan and Washington, DC: World Bank.

Gulbrandsen, O., & Lindbeck, A. (1973). *The Economics of the Agricultural Sector*. Uppsala: Almquist and Wicksell.

Harberger, A. (1971). Three Basic Postulates for Applied Welfare Economics: An Interpretative Essay. *Journal of Economic Literature, 9*(3), 785–797, September.

Herrmann, R., Schenck, P., Thiele, R., & Wiebelt, M. (1992). *Discrimination Against Agriculture in Developing Countries?* Tubingen: J. C. B. Mohr.

Hoekman, B. (2005). Making the WTO More Supportive of Development. *Finance and Development*, 14–18, March.

Huang, J., Rozelle, S., Martin, W., & Liu, Y. (2009). China. In K. Anderson, & W. Martin (Eds.), *Distortions to Agricultural Incentives in Asia* (Ch. 3). Washington, DC: World Bank.

Ivanic, M., & Martin, W. (2008). *Implications of Higher Global Food Prices for Poverty in Low-Income Countries*. Policy Research Working Paper 4594. Washington, DC: World Bank, April.

Jensen, H. T., Robinson, S., & Tarp, F. (2002). *General Equilibrium Measures of Agricultural Policy Bias in Fifteen Developing Countries*. TMD Discussion Paper No. 105. Washington, DC: IFPRI, October.

Johnson, D. G. (1991). *World Agriculture in Disarray (revised edition)*. London: St. Martin's Press.

Johnson, H. (1989). *The Story of Wine*. London: Mitchell Beasley.

Kindleberger, C. P. (1951). Group Behaviour and International Trade. *Journal of Political Economy, 59*(1), 30–47, February.

Kindleberger, C. P. (1975). The Rise of Free Trade in Western Europe, 1820–1875. *Journal of Economic History, 35*(1): 20–55, March.

Krueger, A. O. (1978). *Foreign Trade Regimes and Economic Development: Liberalization Attempts and Consequences.* Cambridge, MA: Ballinger.

Krueger, A. O. (1984). Trade Policies in Developing Countries. In R. W. Jones, & P. B. Kenen (Eds.), *Handbook of International Economics, Vol. 1: International Trade* (Ch. 11). Amsterdam: North-Holland.

Krueger, A. O., Schiff, M., & Valdés, A. (1988). Agricultural Incentives in Developing Countries: Measuring the Effect of Sectoral and Economy-wide Policies. *World Bank Economic Review, 2*(3), 255–272, September.

Krueger, A. O., Schiff, M., & Valdés, A. (1991). *The Political Economy of Agricultural Pricing Policy, Volume 1: Latin America, Volume 2: Asia, and Volume 3: Africa and the Mediterranean.* Baltimore: Johns Hopkins University Press for the World Bank.

Lerner, A. (1936). The Symmetry Between Import and Export Taxes. *Economica, 3*(11), 306–313, August.

Lindert, P. (1991). Historical Patterns of Agricultural Protection. In P. Timmer (Ed.), *Agriculture and the State.* Ithaca: Cornell University Press.

Little, I. M. D., Scitovsky, T., & Scott, M. (1970). *Industry and Trade in Some Developing Countries: A Comparative Study.* London: Oxford University Press.

Lloyd, P. J. (1974). A More General Theory of Price Distortions in an Open Economy. *Journal of International Economics, 4*(4), 365–386, November.

Lloyd, P. J., Croser, J., & Anderson, K. (2009). Welfare- and Trade-based Indicators of National Distortions. In K. Anderson (Ed.), *Distortions to Agricultural Incentives: A Global Perspective, 1955–2007* (Ch. 11). London: Palgrave Macmillan and Washington, DC: World Bank.

Martin, W. (1993). Modeling the Post-Reform Chinese Economy. *Journal of Policy Modeling, 15*(5&6), 545–579.

Nye, J. V. C. (2007). *War, Wine, and Taxes: The Political Economy of Anglo-French Trade 1689–1900.* Princeton, NJ: Princeton University Press.

OECD. (2008a). Producer and Consumer Support Estimates (online database accessed at www.oecd.org

OECD. (2008b). *The Role of Farm Households and the Agro-Food Sector in the Economy of Rural Areas: Evidence and Policy Implications,* TAD/CA/APM/WP(2008)25. Paris: Organization for Economic Co-operation and Development, 18 September.

Orden, D., Cheng, F., Nguyen, H., Grote, U., Thomas, M., Mullen, K., et al. (2007). *Agricultural Producer Support Estimates for Developing Countries: Measurement Issues and Evidence from India, Indonesia, China and Vietnam,* IFPRI Research Report 152. Washington, DC: International Food Policy Research Institute.

Orden, D., & Diaz-Bonilla, E. (2006). Holograms and Ghosts: New and Old Ideas for Reforming Agricultural Policies. In K. Anderson, & W. Martin (Ed.), *Agricultural Trade Reform and the Doha Development Agenda* (Ch. 11). London: Palgrave Macmillan and Washington, DC: World Bank.

Pardey, P., Beintima, N. M., Dehmer, S., & Wood, S. (2006). *Agricultural Research: A Growing Global Divide?* Food Policy Report 17. Washington, DC: International Food Policy Research Institute.

Rajan, R., & Zingales. (2004). *Saving Capitalism from the Capitalists: Unleashing the Power of Financial Markets to Create Wealth and Spread Opportunity.* Princeton: Princeton University Press.

Rausser, G. C. (1982). Political Economic Markets: PERTs and PESTs in Food and Agriculture. *American Journal of Agricultural Economics, 64*(5), 821–833, December.

Ricardo, D. (1817). *On the Principles of Political Economy and Taxation.* London: John Murray.

Robinson, J. (1994). *The Oxford Companion to Wine.* London: Oxford University Press.

Schiff, M., & Valdés, A. (1992). *The Political Economy of Agricultural Pricing Policy, Volume 4: A Synthesis of the Economics in Developing Countries.* Baltimore: Johns Hopkins University Press for the World Bank.

Stuart, C. (1992). *Corn Laws and Modern Agricultural Trade Policy.* Seminar Paper 524. Institute for International Economic Studies, University of Stockholm.

Tarr, D. (1990). Second-Best Foreign Exchange Policy in the Presence of Domestic Price Controls and Export Subsidies. *World Bank Economic Review, 4*(2), 175–193, May.

Thiele, R. (2004). The Bias Against Agriculture in Sub-Saharan Africa: Has it Survived 20 Years of Structural Adjustment Programs? *Quarterly Journal of International Agriculture, 42*(1), 5–20.

Tyers, R., & Anderson, K. (1992). *Disarray in World Food Markets: A Quantitative Assessment.* Cambridge and New York: Cambridge University Press.

Valdés, A. (1996). *Surveillance of Agricultural Price and Trade Policy in Latin America During Major Policy Reforms*. World Bank Discussion Paper No. 349. Washington, DC, November.

Valdés, A. (Ed.). (2000). *Agricultural Support Policies in Transition Economies*. World Bank Technical Paper No. 470. Washington, DC, May.

Valenzuela, E., van der Mensbrugghe, D., & Anderson, K. (2009). General Equilibrium Effects of Price Distortions on Global Markets, Farm Incomes and Welfare. In K. Anderson (Ed.), *Distortions to Agricultural Incentives: A Global Perspective, 1955–2007* (Ch. 13). London: Palgrave Macmillan and Washington, DC: World Bank.

van der Mensbrugghe, D. (2005, January). LINKAGE Technical Reference Document: Version 6.0. Unpublished, World Bank, Washington, DC. Accessible at www.worldbank.org/prospects/linkagemodel

Vousden, N. (1990). *The Economics of Trade Protection*. Cambridge: Cambridge University Press.

World Bank (2007). *World Development Report 2008: Agriculture for Development*. Washington, DC: World Bank.

WTO, I. T. C., & UNCTAD. (2007). *Tariff Profiles 2006*. Geneva: World Trade Organization.

CHAPTER *63*

Development Aid and Agriculture

Robert W. Herdt

International Professor of Applied Economics and Management, Adjunct, Cornell University

Contents

Handbook of Agricultural Economics, Volume 4
© 2010 Elsevier BV. All rights reserved.

doi: 10.1016/S1574-0072(09)04063-8

Abstract

This chapter is motivated by the question of whether development assistance directed at agriculture ("agricultural aid") is effective. It argues that development assistance is continually changing as the ascendant visions of strong global leaders interact with theories of economic growth and evidence on the impact of past aid, and that agricultural aid has reflected similar continual changes in its composition and mode of delivery.

The chapter briefly summarizes evidence on the contribution of aid to overall economic growth, then reviews the evidence of whether agricultural aid accelerates agricultural or economic development. It reviews evaluations of projects and sets of projects related to agricultural credit, integrated rural development, irrigation, research, extension, and higher education. However, except for the World Bank's Operations Evaluation Department (OED) work, most studies of agricultural aid fail to estimate economic rates of return or contributions to incomes of farmers or national economies. It is impossible to conclude, from the evaluation literature, whether agricultural aid accelerates economic development or not.

The chapter shows that donors change the object of their assistance with great frequency. Economic growth takes time, and donors have not stayed committed to key activities for a sufficiently long time to achieve results. Aid to agriculture from nearly all donors fell precipitously beginning in the mid-1980s despite clear evidence that there was a continuing need for broad, long-term support for agriculture in sub-Sahara Africa.

This review suggests that those with responsibility for allocating assistance across sectors do not understand the crucial importance of agriculture at the early stages of development, because the urge to fund new approaches dominates decisions rather than judgment of what is needed and what is likely to be effective. However, one may also understand the unwillingness of aid decision makers to place too much credence in the results of impact evaluation studies because there are few consistent results, whether on national economic growth or agricultural growth, and most studies stress the difficulty of attributing agricultural production growth to development assistance.

JEL classifications: O130, O190, O220, O470, Q000

Keywords

development effectiveness
impact evaluation
aid impact
agricultural aid
economic growth

1. INTRODUCTION

The United States devoted substantial amounts of its development assistance funds to agriculture in low-income countries between 1960 and 2005. At its peak in the 1980s, "annual United States Agency for International Development (USAID) investments in agriculture exceeded $1 billion" a year (McClelland, 1996, p. 3). Assistance for "food production and nutrition" made up 55% of total development assistance from

1975 through 1985 but then decreased to less than 50% in 1985 and, in 1990, to less than 40%. Beginning in 2004, the United States provided aid through a new government-funded organization, the Millennium Challenge Corporation (MCC), which was envisioned to take a substantial role. By the end of 2006 the MCC had, in its first three years of operation, committed about $3 billion, a good part of which was for agricultural activities. Although foreign aid has long been provided through a number of government agencies, USAID has dominated, managing by far the largest amount.[1] In the wake of the events of September 11, 2001, and the wars in Iraq and Afghanistan, the share of development assistance managed by the U.S. Department of Defense increased to 22% in 2005 while USAID's share fell below 40% (Development Assistance Committee OECD, 2006). The United States is also an important supporter of the World Bank, other multilateral banks, the United Nations Development Program (UNDP), and other multilateral development agencies, all of which provided loans and grants for agricultural development.

Aid is motivated by a number of concerns—humanitarian, national security, economic, and the self-interest of companies contracting to provide products. These have changed little over the past 50 years, although their relative strength in the public consciousness varies. Nonetheless, every 10 to 20 years the overarching vision used by leaders to mobilize political and public support for aid does change. A national or international leader becomes convinced of the truth of a particular approach to fostering development based on his or her understanding of history, political reality, human nature, past experience, and perceived inadequacies of earlier assistance activities. That articulation of how development assistance ought to be delivered takes over the discussions held at the highest levels of global development organizations and reshapes the modes by which development aid is delivered. Harry Truman, John Kennedy, and Robert McNamara, each in his own time, articulated a vision that became widely accepted. This "ascendant vision" pervades the rhetoric in which aid is discussed and the modes by which it is delivered, often changing the shape of the entire enterprise. In 1999 Kofi Annan raised global consciousness of the importance of achieving significant improvements in such areas as education, health, poverty alleviation, nutrition, and child survival, leading to the Millennium Development Goals, which became the ascendant vision for the discussion and evolution of development activities for virtually all agencies in the new century.

Sometimes world events, such as the oil shocks of the 1970s or the events of September 11, 2001, play a similar role. After the destruction of the World Trade Towers, President George W. Bush made development aid the "third pillar" in his national security strategy, together with diplomacy and defense. In addition to delivering aid through the Defense Department, his vision was to transform aid through creation of a new instrumentality as an alternative to USAID, the Millennium Development Corporation, intended to reward actions seen as consistent with U.S. interests and using the market as an instrument for development assistance. These changes in the ascendant vision of leaders get conflated with other forces and generate an ever-changing stream of development assistance approaches, activities, and attitudes. The hypothesis explored in this chapter is that the frequent changes in programs and approaches, together with the short-run horizon of donor political power and the bureaucracy implementing assistance programs, are important factors limiting the contribution of development assistance to development.

2. DEVELOPMENT AID AND NATIONAL ECONOMIC GROWTH

Development is a complex concept. I use it as a shorthand to indicate moving to a state of greater self-determination or freedom to determine the actions to be taken. It can apply to an individual, family, group, or nation. Many things contribute to development. The passage of time is necessary for an individual to pass from being utterly dependent on his mother through childhood and into independent adulthood. Some consider interdependence a more mature stage. Nations also can be dependent on others or independent, although in reality all are interdependent. Income contributes to development, but unlike the passage of time in an individual's life, income is an instrument to obtain the things that lead to self-determination: education, health, food, shelter, and freedom from domination by others. Though there are alternative useful indicators of the state of development, the rate of growth of income is still the most widely used and arguably the best proxy indicator for development. In any case, I use it as an indicator of the wider concept of development briefly introduced here.

Serious research on the effects of aid on national economic growth began in the 1970s and continues. Three fundamental issues have limited the conclusiveness of research to measure the impact of aid on economic growth: (1) inconsistent definitions and poor quality of data on aid; (2) the lack of a clear, agreed understanding of the causes of economic growth; (3) and the lack of models that capture the economic mechanisms involved (White, 1992).

There has also been a failure to recognize the difference between the results of analyses and critiques of the methodologies used. Hansen and Tarp reviewed dozens of empirical analyses of the impact of aid on economic growth. They reached three strong conclusions: (1) there was "overwhelming evidence" that aid increased savings and thus, according to economic growth theory, ought to accelerate economic growth; (2) among the empirical estimates of the direct effect of aid on growth, 56% were positive and significant, whereas 43% showed no significant relationship (one study had a significant *harmful* effect of aid on growth); (3) "When all the studies are considered as a group, the positive effect is convincing ... The unresolved issue in assessing aid effectiveness is not whether aid works, but how and whether we can make the different kinds of aid instruments at hand work better in varying country circumstances" (Hansen and Tarp, 2000, p. 124). But their rather forceful conclusions have neither quieted the controversy nor slowed research into the matter, as reflected in work by Burnside and Dollar (2000), Easterly, Levine, et al. (2003), Clements, Radelet, et al. (2004), Headley, Rao et al. (2004), and Roodman (2004).

On balance, the reviewer believes that the evidence supports the position that development assistance in many but not all cases accelerates national economic growth in recipient countries. Unfortunately, the factors responsible for its partial effectiveness are not well established. One interesting analysis distinguishes three categories: emergency and humanitarian; aid to health, education, environment, and democracy; and aid for productive purposes such as agriculture and industry, so called "short-impact" aid (Clements, Radelet et al., 2004). The authors find that "even at a conservatively high discount rate, at the mean a $1 increase in short-impact aid raises output (and income) by $8 in the typical country." However, few studies consider whether aid to one or another sector is more or less productive than to other sectors.

This chapter reviews the literature evaluating the effectiveness of aid directed at agriculture. Section 3 gives an overview of my understanding of the process of agricultural development and a summary of empirical analyses of agricultural growth; Section 4 summarizes the trends and subsectoral composition of aid to agriculture; Section 5 examines evaluations of aid directed to projects in the major subsectors of agriculture; and Section 6 concludes. The chapter focuses on aid provided by the United States and the World Bank, occasionally referring to other agencies.

3. AID'S CONTRIBUTION TO AGRICULTURAL GROWTH

Agriculture in each of the developing world regions grew by two and half times or more since 1960 (Table 1), with developing Asia increasing its output almost fourfold. With the exception of sub-Sahara Africa, output grew more rapidly than population, with the per capita index of production at 185 in Asia in 2001–2004 compared to 100 in 1961–1965, 134 in Latin America, and 111 in the Mideast. At the same time, although incomes grew rapidly in Asia and food demand grew faster than population, food production more than kept pace with demand and consequently there was downward pressure on grain prices. Global trends were similar: The global supply of grain stayed ahead of demand and world grain prices fell in real terms. Sub-Sahara Africa stands out as the one region where agriculture failed to keep pace with population growth.

Development aid could have contributed to agricultural growth in several ways: Aid might provide *inputs* to be used in agricultural production free or at a subsidized cost; aid might help improve production *efficiency* by improving marketing and information flow; and aid might have helped to create technology with higher inherent *productivity* so that available inputs produce more output. In production function terms, the first corresponds to moving along a production function, the second to shifting a production function, and the third to creating a completely new, higher production

Table 1 Index of agricultural production by region (= 100), 1961–1965

	1961–1965	1966–1970	1971–1975	1976–1980	1981–1985	1986–1990	1991–1995	1996–2000	2001–2004
Africa, south of Sahara	100	116.52	129.02	135.44	146.18	171.29	203.16	238.86	260.35
Asia, developing	100	116.84	133.83	156.2	193.43	231.68	282.64	346.31	396.69
Developed countries	100	112.81	123.28	135.94	144.36	150.55	147.24	151.35	154.3
Latin America and Caribbean	100	115.93	130.5	156.58	179.48	200.68	227.72	265.87	305.84
Mideast	100	116.45	134.96	157.67	180.78	210.61	243.99	287.97	309.92

Source: FAOSTAT.

function. Hayami and Ruttan conceived of the "meta" production function to expand the conceptual space to make room for the third possibility (Hayami and Ruttan, 1985), whereas other analysts focus on factors that shift the production function or increase the efficiency of production (Evenson and Kislev, 1975; Antle, 1983; Lau and Yotopolous, 1989; Fulginiti and Perrin, 1997).

The key to moving out of subsistence is generating a surplus over subsistence needs. Then farmers can purchase goods such as soap, matches, soft drinks, education, and health care from the nonagricultural sector while the nonagricultural sector buys food and labor from agriculture. For agriculture to generate the surplus, it must produce a growing amount of output per person; typically this has taken the form of first using more land and labor, then using inputs such as fertilizer and machinery that are made outside agriculture and then through new technology. Development aid has contributed to all these.

3.1 Agriculture in low-income countries

There is, of course, almost an infinite variety of ways in which aid can be given, but to be most effective it must be tailored to the existing conditions of agriculture in the recipient country. Recognizing that everyone does not clearly understand those conditions, the *1992 World Bank Annual Review of Evaluation Results* provided a useful summary of characteristics of agricultural development. The statement has elements consistent with views of many development specialists, and so lengthy quotation is useful:

> **Agriculture has unique characteristics that profoundly condition its development. In developing countries, it is usually a small-scale, private-sector activity. It is heterogeneous and site-specific, involves a complex sequence of cultural operations during the production process, and is subject to high risks, e.g., in production (disease, pests, and weather) and in marketing (price, input supply). In situations where rapid development is possible, e.g., knowledge of a profitable but under-exploited technique, management has to be highly adaptive, and the complexity of decisions involved requires the kind of incentive that only private ownership can provide. Because of these characteristics, growth usually requires simultaneous satisfaction of many conditions: large numbers of farms with access to markets for inputs and outputs; new or improved technologies available to increase yields; and economic incentives sufficient to encourage farm families to invest in education and training, land (irrigation and conservation), or directly in increased production. (World Bank Operations Evaluation Department, 1993, p. 62).**

The report goes on to note the overriding importance of the enabling environment of well-functioning markets for inputs and outputs; the importance of favorable input/output prices; the fallacy of the public production model using centralized management of farms; the importance of technological change and hence agricultural research; the danger of promoting "poorly adapted" technical packages; the importance of rural roads; and the complementarities of education and roads to more direct agricultural inputs. A comparison of these points with those enunciated 30 years earlier by Arthur Mosher as the keys to getting agriculture moving would show a remarkable degree of agreement (Mosher, 1966).

4. AGRICULTUREWIDE REVIEWS

Development assistance is sometimes explained by economists as ways of augmenting national savings or foreign exchange, but the dominant mode by which most development assistance is provided is the project—discreet, time-bound, goal-oriented, and conducted by operating units of recipient governments. Most evaluations therefore concentrate on the performance of projects, but from time to time, some donors review the whole set of projects directed at a sector such as agriculture. Beginning in the early 1990s USAID's Center for Development and Information undertook a systematic review of the agency's portfolio of agricultural projects. Background papers were commissioned covering subcategories defined as: policy reform and planning; technology development and diffusion; rural infrastructure; agricultural services; asset distribution and access. An earlier review had covered sustainable agriculture and natural resources. A synthesis report provides a summary of findings and recommendations to USAID management (McClelland, 1996).

The report did not list projects by subsector or provide their estimated rates of return—impossible because the evaluations on which it was based provided little economic return information. It was, rather, largely a narrative, but it did provide valuable, concisely stated insights.[2] It identified "the country's predisposition to agriculture" as a key factor conditioning success, and initiatives most likely to alleviate the bottlenecks to agricultural growth as "policy reform, technology development, and rural infrastructure," with agricultural services and asset distribution generally less critical. The report strongly supported USAID investment in "the development of new agricultural technologies" and in new rural infrastructure and the maintenance of existing infrastructure. It recognized that "nonproject assistance can help governments of low-income developing countries create an economic policy environment designed to help agricultural markets work," but only when governments were genuinely committed to such policies. It stated unequivocally that "[t]he private sector is best equipped to provide agricultural inputs and services that can be sold for a profit. The public sector has an important role in helping markets work better ..." It recognized the important political and distributional effect of land distribution but concluded that "most investments in this area are best left to the indigenous public sector." The study did not venture into a judgment about the contribution of USAID agricultural projects to agricultural output growth or to general economic growth in the recipient countries.

The World Bank, on the other hand, has a highly developed system of evaluation conducted by its Operations Evaluation Department (OED) that in many cases estimates internal rates of return after project completion. It classes projects with internal rates of return below 10% as unsatisfactory, over 15% as satisfactory, and those between as marginal. From time to time the *Annual Review* of the OED focuses on particular issues or sectors. The 1992 and 2001 reports included summaries of agricultural lending and its performance.

Over two thirds of World Bank agriculture lending from 1961–1965 went for irrigation and flood control, with mechanization a substantial but much smaller fraction. Smallholders, poor farmers, or limited-resource farmers were seldom mentioned in Bank documents prior to the 1970s. The McNamara presidency brought a dramatic shift of lending toward poverty reduction, the "social sectors" of health and education, as well as a big increase in agricultural lending (McNamara, 1973). In 1970–1972 annual World Bank lending for agriculture was roughly $1.2 billion (in 1990 dollars); it grew rapidly thereafter, reaching nearly $6 billion a year in 1978. Rural areas, where poverty is overly concentrated, became the object of concern, with agriculture lending reaching 30 percent of all Bank lending by 1978. Area development projects, also called "integrated rural development," became a "basic element in the Bank's strategy to eliminate rural poverty," especially in Latin America and Africa; in Asia irrigation continued to be the most important subsector in the Bank's agricultural lending (World Bank Operations Evaluation Department, 1993, p. 64).

From 1970–1973, about 75% of World Bank agricultural loans were rated as satisfactory in routine *ex post* evaluation by OED. By the mid-1980s the "satisfactory" rating for agricultural projects was about 65%, well below the average of 80% for all bank loans. Lending for agriculture fluctuated between $5 and $6 billion between 1978 and 1986 and then stabilized around $4 billion a year from 1987 to 1991. Irrigation, farm credit, integrated area development, and plantation crops projects together comprised 75% of the Bank's agricultural portfolio. The sets of loans for irrigation, credit, and plantation crops each had satisfactory performance, above the average for agriculture loans, whereas 49% of integrated rural development projects were satisfactory (World Bank Operations Evaluation Department, 1993, p. 77). The OED reported that, overall, "it was clear that agricultural lending was in trouble" (p. 65).

A decade later the performance of loans approved in the early 1990s had improved and the World Bank review of its agriculture portfolio reflected a brighter picture. The OED review attributed this to a change in Bank policies away from funding public-production-and-control projects to greater reliance on liberal policies and markets. In fact, however, the data on project effectiveness showed that 67% of the agricultural sector loans completed in the 1996–1999 fiscal years gave satisfactory outcomes, compared to 71% of all Bank loans, and for 2000–2001 fiscal years 81% of completed agricultural loans had satisfactory performance compared to 78% of all Bank loans (Battaile, 2002,

p. 65). There had been some improvement in agriculture and some deterioration in the rest of the portfolio.[3] Given that it takes five to eight years to complete loans, those completed in 2000–2001 were mainly prepared following the earlier review and likely had been subjected to more rigorous standards. Thus, by 2000 the Bank had focused its agricultural lending on activities that, on average, performed at a par with all other lending. But agricultural projects comprised about 6% of lending in 1999–2001, down from about 10% in 1990–1992 and much lower than the 30% of all Bank lending that had been typical in the 1970s.

4.1 Aid to Africa's agriculture

Reviews of project performance in many subsectors by both USAID and World Bank suggest that aid was less effective in Africa than in other regions. To help understand these phenomena, the World Bank, with the collaboration of other major donors, undertook a massive study on aid to African agriculture during the 1960s to the 1980s. Called the MADIA project, for "Managing Agricultural Development in Africa," it was carried out with the help of seven other donors[4] and governments of six African countries: "The purpose of the study was to determine the sources of agricultural growth in selected African countries in the period after independence; the extent to which domestic policies, the external environment, and donor assistance contributed to this growth; the effect of the growth on incomes, employment and consumption; and the potential sources of future growth" (Lele and Jain, 1991). The report reads more like a process evaluation than an impact evaluation, however.

The MADIA study countries—Kenya, Malawi, and Tanzania in East Africa and Nigeria, Cameroon, and Senegal in West Africa—accounted for 40% of the population of sub-Saharan Africa and over half its gross economic product. The donor agencies that participated in the study together accounted for nearly 60% of the aid going to Africa. Each agency conducted analyses of its operations in the study countries, helped design the comparative analytical framework for the study, and facilitated entrée to key actors in recipient agencies and countries. The authors of individual chapters in the book drew on documentation of the donors and depended on their assistance in gaining access to aid recipients, but they were for the most part independent professionals, not members of the donor agency's staff.

The study reports many successes and failures among the hundreds of aid projects considered but did not generalize any economic rate of return on projects or quantify the average contribution to economic growth. However, the following summary statements reflect some typical findings:

> **The flow of goods and services from the capital created by Swedish aid has not been impressive. In the programs surveyed, the physical capital stock is declining and the capacity utilization is low ... Whether the aid resources have been productively spent is impossible to answer with any degree of certainty. The fact that construction was slow and the capacity utilization**

low in the four large programs surveyed suggests that the cost–benefit ratio was substantially below the level (whether assessed or not) that led the planners to go ahead with the projects. (Radetzki, 1991)

Regarding aid from the European Community:

The success of the Northeast Benoue Settlement Project may be attributable to the relatively modest targets, the geographic concentration, and the rather undistorted economic conditions in Cameroon by comparison with Tanzania. The lack of success in eastern Senegal demonstrates the importance of involving local communities in basic decisions (for example, on the cropping pattern). (Kennes, 1991)

By the beginning of the 1990s it was clear that African agriculture was not the engine of economic growth it had been in much of Asia in the 1970s and 1980s, but rather that agriculture's stagnation was holding back economic growth. Some blamed the donors, arguing that aid to African agriculture fell during the 1990s while most countries in the region had not yet achieved the preconditions for growth or at the least were at a very early stage, when agriculture is most needed and has the greatest potential to contribute to development. Carl Eicher and his colleague find that although overall aid to Africa increased from $5 billion in 1971 to $16 billion in 2001 (in constant dollars), the percentage of aid going to agriculture was halved, from 11% to 6% (Kane and Eicher, 2004).

Though clearly sympathetic toward Africa's needs, they report that "the high failure rate of agricultural projects and programs during Africa's first 25 years of independence (1960–1985) contributed to donor skepticism about African agriculture." In addition, aid to agriculture in Africa was lower than it perhaps should have been because at independence, leaders of most African countries had great reluctance to invest in agriculture, ignoring the ideas of leading agricultural development thinkers (Johnston and Mellor, 1961; Schultz, 1964; Lewis, 1988) in their "fervent belief in industrialization as the engine of development." Africa faced no food shortages during the decade of independence, and when shortages did appear, food aid helped fill the gaps and allowed ministers of finance to avoid or postpone capacity-building agricultural investments. Even in the face of the horrendous Ethiopia famine of 1984–1985, world opinion was mobilized behind food aid but not behind agricultural development assistance.

5. TRENDS AND ALLOCATIONS TO SUBSECTORS

Assistance to agriculture from all OECD donors (in 2002 dollars) grew from $4.7 billion a year in 1973 to over $12 billion a year in 1983–1987 and since then has fallen back to about the 1973–1977 levels (Table 2). U.S. aid to agriculture followed the same general pattern over time making up between 9% and 14% of the OECD total. The sharp fall in aid to agriculture after 1992 is difficult to explain in terms of needs.

Table 2 Agriculture ODA from all donors to all developing countries' agriculture subsectors, five-year annual averages (constant 2002 US$M), 1973–2002

	1973–1977	1978–1982	1983–1987	1988–1992	1993–1997	1998–2002
Agricultural policy and administration	421	359	857	1468	562	1614
Agricultural water resources	1097	2207	2114	1699	1061	660
Integrated rural development and general	735	1251	2307	1188	1081	647
Forestry, not research	149	369	613	880	468	354
Crop production, not research	331	1173	1028	724	388	258
Fisheries, not research	192	471	400	408	285	235
Research on crops, fish, forestry	63	275	456	375	184	201
Agricultural inputs	313	684	552	317	309	186
Agricultural land resources	204	253	795	417	271	178
Agricultural finance and crops	425	1127	1549	895	209	132
Extension	104	235	514	230	77	99
Livestock production and vet services	274	379	331	312	124	94
Agricultural services	426	544	1035	840	167	71
Agrarian reform	0	38	31	440	143	63
Total agriculture	4735	9371	12596	10201	5353	4813
Food aid (not included above)	2681	2858	3000	1502	524	1383

Source: Extracted from OECD Corporate Data Environment, deflated by the total DAC deflator. See www1.oecd.org/scripts/cde/members/DACAuthenticate.asp.

True, there was evidence of vigorous agricultural growth in Asia by the 1980s, but the opposite held in Africa. Development theory would have supported a continuation of donor aid to agriculture with an increase in the proportion to Africa, but instead there was reduction in aid to agriculture from the late 1980s on.

Irrigation and drainage projects received the largest share of agricultural aid. These big projects absorbed large amounts of capital consistent with filling the foreign exchange and government budget gaps. Agricultural credit and integrated rural development each went through periods of increase and decline over the period. Assistance for "agricultural sector policy, planning and programs; aid to agricultural ministries; institution capacity building and advice; unspecified agriculture," shown as agricultural policy and administration in the table, underwent two waves of expansion: the first in the late 1980s and a second, more dramatic increase from the late 1990s to the 2000s, when they comprised one third of all agricultural aid.

For comparison, food aid is shown in the final line in the table. Food aid was 25% to 50% as large as agriculture development assistance in the 1970s and declined to 10% in the early 1990s. However, by the end of the 1990s it had again grown to nearly one third as large as development aid to agriculture.[5] Although there are some differences of opinion about the net contribution of food aid, many analysts hold that it contributes much like a direct income transfer, raising consumption levels, not like an investment that generates a continuing flow of income over time. Most would not compare it to other categories of development assistance, and it is not included in the OECD definition of "agricultural aid."

Aid for agricultural research has been fairly stable since the mid-1980s at around 4%, but the accounting of aid to agricultural research in Table 3 reports aid to developing countries research and does not include resources provided to the CGIAR centers, which alone total nearly $400 million annually in recent decades. The CGIAR is considered a multilateral institution in OECD CRS/DAC reporting, and donor' contributions to the CGIAR are therefore excluded from the CRS database and this table. Although they are included in DAC multilateral ODA figures, mixed with other multilateral contributions, they are not separately shown.

The pattern of U.S. support shows similar variations as OECD aid (Table 3). Aid for agricultural policy and management dominated U.S. assistance over the entire period, and integrated rural development was the second most important subsector in four of the six periods. Water resource and agricultural services projects were third or fourth most important in most periods. Research generally received 3% to 4% of the total but was nearly 10% in 1976–1987. Aid to provide fertilizer and other inputs was important in the 1970s but not afterward. The finance and cooperatives sectors were strongly supported in the early 1970s but then faded. Agrarian reform received relatively more support in the final period than any other time throughout the period.

Table 3   U.S. agricultural development aid (average/year, constant 2002 $M), 1973–2002

	1973–1977	1978–1982	1983–1987	1988–1992	1993–1997	1998–2002
Agricultural policy, management	142.31	29.44	206.90	130.55	74.19	231.66
Integrated rural development	40.93	124.29	195.63	77.73	27.82	46.66
Crop, livestock, forestry research	12.62	68.19	133.35	78.67	13.41	16.79
Agrarian reform	0.00	7.04	25.58	13.94	12.81	15.95
Crop production, post-harvest	22.75	31.46	21.57	15.48	26.94	8.19
Agricultural services	45.29	99.90	160.72	90.67	26.47	3.98
Water resources	69.49	107.17	161.17	67.77	4.75	3.97
Land resources	0.00	35.07	24.00	5.07	5.28	1.51
Livestock production, vet services	9.96	8.33	20.64	2.79	3.57	1.04
Finance and cooperatives	24.43	5.64	2.72	4.52	3.50	0.91
Forestry production	0.00	23.14	18.25	14.04	1.57	0.83
Fisheries production	0.00	11.77	2.52	11.95	5.39	0.34
Ag education, extension	16.03	38.03	63.97	14.99	6.38	0.28
Fertilizer and other inputs	31.87	93.59	18.49	18.47	0.98	0.14
Total	415.67	720.06	1410.28	1311.27	740.88	411.08

Source: Extracted from OECD Corporate Data Environment, deflated by the total DAC deflator. See www1.oecd.org/scripts/cde/members/DACAuthenticate.asp.

5.1 Agricultural project effectiveness

The "logical framework" or "log-frame" often used in development assistance project preparation posits that aid provides *financial* resources for activities that generate *inputs*; the inputs produce *outputs* as a direct result; the outputs in turn lead to *impact*, which are improvements in the lives of poor people, the ultimate objective of development assistance. Unfortunately, too many "evaluations" are light on quantitative indicators of output and even lighter on estimated impact, but they often provide copious assertions of the *importance* for development of the particular focus of the evaluation. Such narratives may provide valuable insights, but not on the question of effectiveness. In contrast, many evaluations by the World Bank *do* estimate economic benefits as a rate of return. Though these sometimes require heroic assumptions, the advantage is they reflect more of the conditions necessary for effectiveness than do nonquantitative evaluations.

One inherent challenge to understanding the contribution of projects is the integrated nature of agricultural production: Growing improved varieties with irrigation is more productive than growing them without, but it is near impossible to separate the contribution of irrigation from new varieties. Likewise, crops will bring a higher price in areas with improved roads, and livestock health projects will have greater payoff where crop productivity improvements have increased available livestock feed. Despite the inherent interrelationships, project assessments generally attempt to identify only the narrowly defined direct effect of the project under examination.

Equally challenging is the problem of attribution: So many factors contribute to most situations that attributing any observed change, positive or negative, to development assistance is challenging. Where more than one donor contributes to a development project—often the case—estimating the contribution of any single donor's inputs is impossible. Hence, one has a good deal of sympathy with evaluators who fail to quantify the impact of the projects they evaluate.

6. IRRIGATION AND WATER MANAGEMENT

From the 1960s through the 1990s irrigation was one of the most important agricultural development assistance subsectors. The cumulative investments from the 1960s onward as reported by one reviewer are impressive (Steinberg, Clapp-Wincek, et al., 1983). USAID invested between $3 billion and $4 billion in irrigation through the 1970s; the World Bank loaned more than $10.4 billion for irrigation projects through 1982; borrowing governments complemented that investment with another $15 billion. Through 1982 the Asian and Inter-American development banks provided over $1.5 billion for irrigation projects that irrigated or improved the irrigation on some 2.2 million hectares; over the period the African Development Bank invested $273 million in irrigation projects.

In the 1950s and 1960s irrigation investments were primarily for water delivery systems. In the 1970s there was increased awareness of the importance of drainage, and it was more frequently included as part of irrigation investment. In the 1980s the need for industrial water and for domestic water (drinking, washing, sanitation) in rural as well as urban areas was increasingly recognized by development donors.

In the 1990s "global water crisis" became the watchword in the wake of analyses showing that in the early part of the 21st century many countries would need to make substantial investments to meet their needs for industrial, domestic, and agricultural water uses.

When designed primarily to provide irrigation, aid projects might be properly evaluated for their contribution to increased agricultural output and income. When domestic uses become important, a much broader set of criteria become relevant, complicating the evaluation task. Even when focused on agriculture, irrigation, like other aid investments, is expected to reduce poverty, not simply increase aggregate output, but its contribution to agricultural output depends on the agronomic, climatic, and socioeconomic conditions prevailing in project areas and is not easy to measure. The analytical, methodological, and policy issues crucial for understanding and promoting poverty alleviation through irrigation have been discussed by several analysts (Berry, Ford, et al., 1980; Barker and Molle, 2004; Saleth, Nemara, et al., 2003). However, the systems that provide irrigation are so complex that their economic evaluation has proven challenging, even to world-class organizations.[6]

6.1 USAID

U.S. assistance for irrigation made up about 15% of total U.S. assistance to agriculture from the mid-1970s until the mid-1980s.[7] That fell to 5% of U.S. agricultural assistance in the 1988–1992 period and thereafter fell to below 2%. Because total U.S. agricultural assistance was also declining, the absolute reduction in aid for irrigation was even more dramatic—from around $100 million a year in the mid-1980s to below $5 million a year in the 1990s.

Around the time of the peak of investments in the 1970s, USAID's Office of Evaluation initiated a comprehensive look at its irrigation assistance experience. An important element was a commissioned study to outline "issues that should be examined in any comprehensive evaluation of irrigation projects," which concluded that it is necessary to consider economic viability, efficiency of resource use, effectiveness of water delivery systems, environmental quality, and social soundness (Berry, Ford, et al., 1980).

A second important element in the review was a 1983 conference to consider the agency's 30-year experience, drawing on analytical work supported by the agency and on evaluations of USAID's irrigation projects in Sudan, Senegal, Egypt, Morocco, Turkey, Pakistan, Korea, the Philippines, and Indonesia. The summary paper that followed provides valuable insight into the thinking of the day, although it contains no generalizations about rates of return to the aid investments (Steinberg, Clapp-Wincek, et al., 1983). Instead it draws attention to factors that affect the translation of yield gains into income and other factors that affect farmers' incomes, such as tenancy, energy costs, and debt. It also provides valuable insights into mistakes that can be made in project preparation that can lead to overoptimistic expectations from irrigation investments, noting that:

> In spite of continued optimism demonstrated by vast investments by host governments and foreign donors, multilateral and bilateral donor-supported irrigation projects have failed to realize their potential. Although the causes are varied, the major impediments seem to be poor water management. The donor experience in irrigation, however, has been generally positive to some degree even if the goals have been inflated. (Steinberg, Clapp-Wincek, et al., 1983, p. i)

6.2 World Bank

Irrigation has long been an important objective of the World Bank's activities. The organization made six loans for irrigation in the 1950s, 41 in the 1960s, and over 250 each decade of the 1970s and 1980s. Lending for irrigation averaged $37 million a year in the 1950s, $343 million a year in the 1960s, $1120 million a year in the 1970s, $1273 million a year in the 1980s, and $1032 million a year in the 1990s (in constant 1991 U.S. dollars; World Bank Operations Evaluation Department, 1995). In total, from 1950–1993, the World Bank lent about $31 billion for 614 irrigation projects. This continued funding of irrigation by the Bank contrasted to USAID, which largely ceased funding irrigation projects in the mid-1980s.

A 1995 review of World Bank irrigation focused on the returns "in the broadest sense of the term" on irrigation investments. The findings were optimistic, indicating that benefits of most irrigation investments have reached the poor and reporting that 67% of irrigation projects performed in a satisfactory way. This was "better than the average for all Bank-supported agriculture projects (65%) but worse than the figure for all Bank projects (76%)" (World Bank Operations Evaluation Department, 1995, p. 3).

However, in 1993, two years before the 1995 report was published, the Bank had proclaimed a new operational policy on water resources management that took a far broader perspective on water investments. Designed to be comprehensive, the 1993 policy paper included domestic water, pollution control, navigation, and flood control. It stressed irrigation system rehabilitation over new construction, larger watershed areas over smaller ones, strengthened legal and institutional frameworks for water resource management, cost sharing by water users, and agricultural services to complement irrigation investments (World Bank, 1993). But the momentum of earlier directions was hard to change, and a 1998 outside review of selected "new style" irrigation projects reported that "systematic monitoring of the impact of rehabilitation/modernization components has been rare, making it difficult to determine whether there has been significant impact on water services, equity or reliability" (Easter, Plusquellec, et al., 1998). A 2002 review of the new water resources policy, unlike the 1995 review, was pessimistic, reflecting concern about mismanagement of water resources and poor service delivery, particularly for the poor. It reported the overall performance of water projects completed in 1988–1999 was below the Bank average, based on their outcome, their institutional development contribution, and the likely sustainability of project benefits (Pitman, 2002).

The World Bank's 1993 water strategy was a radical change from a largely pro-ductivity-enhancing irrigation and drainage program to one concerned with the environment, households, transport, and urban use. Reinforcing that new direction, the 2002 review suggested that productivity gains of domestic water supply and sanitation would come through a healthier population working in the general economy, not an easy effect to evaluate. In the 1993 strategy water is seen as a human right, and the purpose of water-related development assistance from the World Bank is to:

> **maximize the contribution of water to countries' economic, social and environmental development while ensuring that resource and water services are managed sustainable; to help countries establish comprehensive and analytical frameworks to foster informed and transparent decision making, with an emphasis on demand management; and to promote decentralized implementation processes and market forces to guide the appropriate mix of public and private sector provision of water services. (Pitman, 2002)**

However, the use of water for directly productive purposes continued to be a priority for many borrowing countries, and a new World Bank strategy emerged a decade later. In that, the 2004 Water Resources Sector Strategy seemed to make a return to the earlier productivity emphasis. That strategy seemed to reflect greater domination of an engineering perspective, in contrast to the social emphasis of the 1993 strategy. The 2004 strategy, while recognizing that progress had been made in many areas of water resource management, chose to focus on a number of "difficult and contentious issues where World Bank practice needs to improve" (Water Resources Management Group, 2004, p. 2). In particular the 2004 strategy stressed the growth and poverty reduction contribution of dams, interbasin transfers, and irrigation and declared that "the World Bank will reengage with high-reward-high-risk hydraulic infrastructure" (p. 3).

6.3 Africa irrigation

Some discussions of irrigation projects in sub-Sahara Africa suggest that irrigation there is inordinately expensive and, indeed, in the mid-1980s, the average cost of World Bank irrigation projects in sub-Sahara Africa was estimated at $18,000 per hectare compared to $4800 per hectare for all Bank irrigation projects (Operations Evaluation Department, 1994). The cost difference was one reason for low economic returns in sub-Saharan Africa relative to other regions (FAO, 1986; Brown and Nooter, 1992). Other factors contributed as well: a natural environment with limited water available for irrigation; unfavorable operational policies; macroeconomic climates that give overvalued exchange rates and suppressed farm prices; and deficit-induced constraints on capital and operating budgets. Unfavorable policies have delayed construction and hampered crucial maintenance; producers have been discouraged from intensifying cropping and marketing, and consequently farm incomes have not increases as envisioned.

The differences between the generally water-plentiful environments of tropical Asia and much of sub-Sahara Africa mean that there will be differences in the most appropriate kinds of irrigation. Flood irrigation was suitable in many places in Asia during the 20th century, but water availability and cost factors could make small-scale, low-cost, drip irrigation suitable for places in Africa in the 21st (Chigerwe, Manjengwa, et al., 2004). Small-scale projects are no panacea, however, as illustrated by a study reviewing 202 small-scale irrigation projects in South Africa, which found that:

> **With the exception of sugarcane and limited areas of other crops, efficiency of production was disappointingly low, with many farmers carrying heavy debt loads. Many projects are in dire need of rehabilitation, including diagnostic analysis, amended water legislation, land reform, increased responsibility of participants, appropriate technology, farmer selection and integration in rural development, all factors in which agricultural extension has an important role to play. (Bembridge, 1997, p. 71)**

There has been proportionately less irrigation investment and a higher proportion of "failed projects" in Africa than in Asia, but despite that, about 75 percent of World Bank sub-Sahara irrigation projects have achieved or exceeded their expected rate of economic return (Olivareas, 1990). A comprehensive analysis of 314 World Bank irrigation projects from sub-Sahara Africa (45), Middle-East/North Africa (51), Latin America (41), South Asia (91), Southeast Asia (68), and East Asia (18) showed that there is no difference in irrigation project costs per hectare between sub-Sahara Africa and other regions once a half-dozen clearly "failed projects" are excluded and one takes into account the factors identified by Olivareas (Kikuchi, Inocencio, et al., 2007; Kikuchi, Inocencio, et al., 2005, p. 20). The challenge is to prevent the project failures that lead to huge cost overruns and apply approaches that are suitable for African conditions (Inocencio, Sally, et al., 2003). Some successful irrigation projects will be private or small-scale, and others may be public, but government's job, with suitable development assistance, is to create the institutional environment that will enable farmers to reap the benefits of well-designed irrigation systems.

6.4 The impact of irrigation aid

Data from evaluations conducted by the World Bank show that irrigation projects were, over the long run, as effective as any other group of bank projects. The average economic rate of return on irrigation investment in the 1995 review, estimated after project completion and weighted by size of area served, was 25 percent, varying with size of the irrigated area, output price, crop yield, and cost of irrigation per hectare. The evaluation observed that over time there had been a secular decline in the price of the farm products produced on irrigated land and "ironically, these declines, which have significantly lowered evaluation rates of return for irrigation, have probably been caused in part by irrigation investments, especially in the case of rice. But lower food and fiber prices have been an immense benefit to the poor" (World Bank Operations Evaluation Department, 1995, p. 4). Unfortunately, irrigation evaluations have not quantified such benefits.

Aggregate analyses of agricultural output consistently identify irrigation as one of the primary factors associated with output growth. For example, in India irrigation investment generated total factor productivity "growth over and above the contribution to output growth that irrigation makes as a "conventional" input" (Evenson, Pray, et al., 1999). Cross-country analyses give similar conclusions (Hayami and Ruttan, 1985; Suhariyanyto, Lusigi, et al., 2001; Coelli and Rao, 2003). Analysis of productivity growth in 41 sub-Sahara African countries confirmed that irrigation increased the efficiency of production, although irrigation is fairly rare (Fulginiti, Perrin, et al., 2004). Successful irrigation projects contribute to the acceleration of agricultural growth and, where they encourage adoption of improved technology, contribute to increasing productivity. Where this happens, it is likely that irrigation is one of the factors moving agricultural supply ahead of demand, leading to lower food prices and thereby to consumer benefits that are of immense benefit to the poor. To the extent that irrigation allows farmers to produce output at lower per-unit cost, farmers also benefit. If irrigation investment were to be evaluated for economic benefits to producers and consumers using the same analytical framework used in evaluations of agricultural research, greater light would be shed on its total impact, complementing the results from project evaluations. Together, these might reinforce the willingness of donors to invest in appropriately designed irrigation systems for Africa, where agricultural growth is clearly needed to propel economic development.

7. CREDIT AND RURAL FINANCE

Aid intended to help provide farmers with credit to purchase inputs has been an important part of development assistance for decades. The rationale for such programs is straightforward: productivity gains come from adoption of new technology; use of technology often entails purchased inputs; this requires cash or credit; poor farmers are short of cash and have to pay high prices for credit; therefore programs to make low-cost credit available seem appropriate. Since the 1960s three approaches have flourished: subsidized farm credit, credit guarantees, and microcredit.

7.1 Subsidized farm credit

Subsidized credit was a part of India's intensive agricultural development program in the 1960s and was a common policy in many countries in the 1970s. In the Philippines banks were required to allocate 25% of their lending as low-interest loans to the agriculture sector, financed by low interest paid on deposits. Banks in India faced similar limits; in Mexico, a compulsorily government-owned credit insurer provided an explicit subsidy to rural financial institutions (Besley, 1998).

Despite the low interest rates, a high incidence of nonrepayment plagued most of these programs because farmers treated them as government handouts. By the mid-1970s development assistance for agricultural credit came under intensive scrutiny. Research found little evidence that the credit had a positive impact on small farm productivity or income, and this led to a series of other questions: How is the subsidized credit allocated among all farmers? Does it stimulate competition from "informal" sources so that total agricultural credit is increased and its cost lowered? How are the subsidies financed and what are the opportunity costs of alternative uses? What are the moral hazards to repaying government-backed credit in democratic countries? (Donald, 1976). Examination of these and related questions culminated in an influential body of work by Dale Adams, Gordon Donald, J. D. von Pischke, and their associates in the early 1980s, with one of the studies concluding as follows:

> **Despite the optimistic expectations of their sponsors, the results of these programs have been disappointing. Loan-default problems are often serious. Most poor farmers are still unable to obtain formal loans, and those who succeed in using such credit are often unnecessarily and inequitably subsidized. Many agricultural banks and other specialized formal lenders serving rural areas are floundering, and as a result they often severely limit the range of services they provide. Few aggressively offer savings-deposit facilities, for example. Their medium- and long-term loan portfolios are supported almost entirely by resources provided by government and development assistance agencies rather than by resources mobilized directly from savers and investors. ... These problems persist after three decades of development assistance. They endure in spite of the fact that some governments have nationalized their banks in efforts to expand credit access, while others have piled regulation on regulation in an attempt to improve the performance of rural financial markets. Despite institutional and cultural diversity, similar problems fester in a large number of countries. Credit programs tend to self-destruct and policymakers are largely resigned to recurring institutional problems and poor financial results from rural credit programs. (Adams, Graham, et al., 1984)**

Clearly, the results of these programs were disappointing. Subsidies were inequitable and default problems serious. Most poor farmers were unable to obtain program loans; those who got loans were often the wealthier. Excessive defaults led agricultural banks and other specialized formal lenders serving rural areas to founder, and they began to limit the range of financial services provided. These problems persisted in spite of considerable government and donor assistance. The negative evaluations (probably along with falling resources) greatly reduced USAID rural finance assistance. Others continued providing aid for credit programs, but the problems persisted. In 2001 the Asian Development Bank found that fewer than 60% of its rural credit projects were successful. Although they had increased the availability of credit in rural areas and improved the quality of loan portfolios, longer-term financial viability was seen as less certain, given the more or less regular infusions of government capital into the credit institutions (Asian Development Bank Operations Evaluation Office, 2001).

7.2 Credit guarantees

In the 1990s, credit guarantee projects were suggested as ways to offset the risk perceived as discouraging formal credit institutions from extending credit to poor farmers. It was expected that lenders would make more loans to farmers if protected from excessive losses, enabling farmers to increase their borrowing and productivity. Evaluations found no evidence that guarantee programs were any more effective than subsidies, although the available base of evidence was weak. Researchers argued that more analysis was needed to determine whether guarantees really produce the results that their designers expect and whether the benefits obtained justify the costs and subsidies involved (Meyer and Nagarajan, 1996). Others had similar reactions: "As one unpacks each argument, the realization grows that, given the current state of empirical evidence on many relevant questions, it is impossible to categorically assert that an intervention in the credit markets is justified" (Besley, 1998).

7.3 Microcredit

As pioneered in Bangladesh, microcredit provides very small amounts of credit (exclusively to women in the early years of the Grameen Bank) who join small, mutual-support groups of neighbors, pledge to uphold a set of prescribed behaviors, and learn good business practices. Borrowers are not subsidized—they pay market rates of interest. Since 1990, many organizations have created programs similar to Grameen, the donor community has become quite supportive, and microcredit has become the subject of much interest (Morduch, 1999; Brown, 2004). The broad interest led donors to establish the Consultative Group to Assist the Poor (CGAP) as a global umbrella organization for consultation on microfinance; the United Nations proclaimed 2005 the International Year of Microcredit,[8] and in 2006 the founder of Grameen, Dr. Mohammed Yunus, was awarded the Nobel Peace Prize.

CGAP began an ambitious evaluation of microcredit in 2002 with financial support from the International Fund for Agricultural Development. An initial list of 80 promising agricultural microcredit projects was identified and reviewed based on available information. The review found that "While many on the long list proved to be fundamentally unsustainable, or lacked the potential to achieve scale, about 30 were sufficiently promising to merit further research."[9] Of that resulting short list, five case studies were selected for wider dissemination in a series of brief publications.

Two leading members of CGAP, the World Bank and UNDP, undertook in-depth evaluations of their microcredit portfolios in 2002, each examining the effectiveness of nearly 70 of their own projects. Projects were graded on the extent to which they resulted or appeared likely to result in sustainable levels of loan repayment and cost recovery. Less than one quarter of the projects was found to be successful, with 45% of World Bank projects unacceptable and 43% of UNDP projects unacceptable and the remainder of about 30% being graded as "weak" (Rosenberg, 2006).

IFPRI research on rural finance programs for the poor in 11 African and Asian countries found that, in contrast to earlier agricultural credit projects, microcredit projects were generally successful in delivering credit to the poor and in raising incomes of the poor. They found that interest rate subsidies are unnecessary because poor people are willing and able to borrow at market rates and the programs addressed the primary constraint facing the poor: access to loans. IFPRI concluded that governments can provide moderate subsidies to support the development of financial institutions and lower the costs of processing small loans, but interest and transaction costs should be borne by the customer; and, more credit should be focused on agriculture because farmers with access to credit use improved farming technologies (IFPRI, 1997). Still, the experiences of the World Bank and UNDP suggest pessimistic answers to larger questions about the longer-term financial viability of microfinance systems. Microcredit may be an effective way to deliver charity, but not effective *development aid* investments.

8. INTEGRATED RURAL DEVELOPMENT

Integrated rural development was the third largest subsector of OECD agricultural development assistance, for many years absorbing 13–20% of agricultural aid. It was the second or third largest subsector of U.S. agricultural assistance as well. Known variously as "area development," "rural development," and "integrated rural development," this subsector includes support to projects designed to improve the conditions of poor people in rural areas through better health, more education, paved roads, and increased agricultural productivity in fairly small, well-defined geographic regions. Such projects provide a range of agricultural services that may include credit, irrigation, extension advice, fertilizer sales, soil analysis, marketing, livestock disease control, and market access roads. Many include construction of rural roads, schools, and health clinics. The extent to which such projects attempt to bring together distinctly different elements into integrated projects or programs is highly variable, and some entities use the "integrated" term while others do not. The degree of success varied across the hundreds of projects and provide a pool of experience from which to sample (Morss and Gow, 1984).

One of the first efforts at area-based agricultural development was India's Intensive Agricultural District Program (IADP), beginning in 1961 with assistance from the Ford Foundation and following principles articulated in a widely circulated report on India's food crisis (Ford Foundation Agricultural Production Team, 1959). The government of India selected seven districts (each roughly equivalent to a U.S. county) and financed provision of farm inputs, staff, and credit. The Ford Foundation provided advisors and some financial support. Ironically, most of the advisors came from the United States, where they had never been involved in such a combined approach. Each advisor brought the experience he or she had accumulated as extension worker, professor, rural banker, or engineer, but that experience was obtained in a multiorganization system where individual firms or organizations each provided a single component. IADP was implemented as an integrated project in which all aspects were brought together under a district project director who, in turn, reported to the highest government authority in the district, the district commissioner. In the initial phase, farmers opted into the program by having project staff prepare a farm plan; their soil was tested and fertilizer application rates recommended on the basis of the test; the necessary fertilizer and seed was obtained on credit provided through the program. Appropriate "packages of practices" of technology were demonstrated to inform farmers and encourage them to use the technology. Initially the program was intended to guarantee minimum product prices, although this was impossible to implement.

8.1 USAID

In the early 1970s, rural development received a great deal of attention in development literature, national plans, and political platforms. The concept of integrated rural development was enthusiastically embraced by USAID and other donor agencies. Four premises were crucial: There are multiple constraints to development (e.g., health, education, agriculture, transport) that cannot be overcome in isolation; expenditures on health, education, and nutrition should be regarded as investments; the benefits of economic growth do not necessarily trickle down to the poor, and when they do they take a long time to get there; and participation of the local population is essential for generating long-term, self-sustaining growth (Kumar, 1987).

Integrated rural development projects promised to address the needs of the poor in a participatory way that was almost irresistible. USAID supported over 100 such projects between 1970 and 1987, in all regions where AID was active. Most combined social services such as education, health care, and nutrition with agricultural productivity enhancement through fertilizer, seeds, and credit. Academics were left to puzzle exactly what the paradigm was and why it was being embraced so energetically, but rural development projects clearly were a growth area (Ruttan, 1974–1975; Belshaw, 1977; Livingston, 1979; Ruttan, 1984). A decade after the big acceleration in projects a number of evaluations had been started and donors began asking questions about implementation and effectiveness (Brinkerhoff, 1981; Crawford, 1981).

USAID's Center for Development Information and Evaluation prepared a summary of the agency's 15 years of experience with integrated rural development projects in 1987. It found that the projects had contributed to increases in agricultural production and productivity, to a greater extent in Asia and South America than in Africa. Where agricultural production had increased, the incomes of participating farmers had also increased, but the main beneficiaries seemed to be the wealthier farmers who could take advantage of the opportunities afforded by the projects because of their privileged position in society. On the positive side, the social services entailed in most projects— health care, housing, drinking water and education—did reach the poor. But when projects faced financial constraints or administrative difficulties and funding was cut, there was a general tendency to cut the social services.

In practice it proved difficult to coordinate multiple ministries and agencies. Plans required extensive coordination, money flowed slowly, and project staff on deputation from various units had divided loyalties. The projects largely depended on public organizations—bureaucracies—to implement their complex programs: lack of individual accountability, lack of adequate controls despite complex procedures, and low levels of compensation all contributed to poor implementation. Many evaluations found modest income gains but difficulty with the organizational structure established to manage the projects (Clapp-Wincek, 1985; USAID, 1986). Many of the units created to manage the integrated development projects were inappropriately located or didn't have the power to carry out their mandates. A review of experience was deemed useful so the agency could "learn from its experience and apply the lessons to future programs." The summary reported that such projects were "no longer encouraged" and "projects that involved activity components across several sectors were "considered inappropriate" (Kumar, 1987, p. v).

8.2 World Bank

The Lilongwe Development Project in Malawi and the Wolamo Area Development Project in Ethiopia were among early integrated rural development projects of the World Bank. Like India's IADP, they were large, multifunctional efforts focused on specified geographic areas that employed a relatively large number of expatriates in technical management positions. The Funtua, Gasau, and Gombe projects in the north of Nigeria followed a similar pattern (Maddock and Wilson, 1994). Project "authorities" were created to implement virtually all area development projects and given responsibility for tasks normally carried out by regular government ministries because those ministries were seen as unsuitable for the multifunctional management task involved in area development. It was deemed necessary to create something new that usually took over a range of activities that were already the responsibility of several existing government departments.

Some observers believe that these multidimensional projects appealed to the World Bank and other donors because they promised to address the plight of the rural poor. "Until the emergence of the IRD approach much of the foreign aided investment in rural areas (concentrating on input supply, technical services, advice and in places, credit), had appeared to mainly benefit the larger producers rather than small farmers, tenants and landless" (Maddock and Wilson, 1994). Following the 1973 policy speech in which World Bank President Robert McNamara declared the new focus of the World Bank on meeting "basic human needs" and fighting poverty (McNamara, 1973), the Bank issued the Rural Development Sector Policy Paper outlining its position: Rural development "is a strategy designed to improve the economic and social life of a specific group of people—the rural poor. It involves extending the benefits of development to the poorest among those who seek a livelihood in the rural area. The group includes small-scale farmers, tenants and the landless" (World Bank, 1975). Most were multidimensional, but some commodity-oriented projects were considered as rural development—for example, tea in Kenya, cotton in Mali, or coffee in Papua New Guinea (World Bank Operations Evaluation Department, 1988).

In the three-year period 1971–1973, before the World Bank embraced the rural development approach, it had funded five area development projects a year. This more than tripled to 17 a year in the next three-year period and increased further to 24 a year in 1977–1979. In Nigeria alone, by 1982 a total of nine area development projects had been established covering over 75,000 sq. km. and 555,000 farm families, with a planned investment cost of over $600 million (Maddock and Wilson, 1994). Between 1965 and 1986 the Bank dedicated about half its agricultural lending to rural development: total bank lending over the period was $157.2 billion; agricultural sector lending was $41.7 billion in 1162 loans; rural development lending was just about half that, with 574 loans for $19.8 billion; and, of the rural development lending, area development and irrigation made up over $14 billion. Annually, lending for area development increased from $8 million annually to $730 million over the period. It was estimated that the intended direct beneficiaries included some 13 million families at a project cost of $18.8 billion, or $1120 per family (World Bank Operations Evaluation Department, 1988).

But questions raised through the period of rapid growth led to the inevitable slowdown of support. From an average of 24 new projects a year in 1977–1979, the number declined to 21 per year in 1980–1982 and 18 per year in 1983–1985 (World Bank Operations Evaluation Department, 1988). A 1992 OED review indicated that 49% of area development projects performed satisfactorily, compared to a 65% overall success rate for agriculture projects. On average the area development projects generated a 10.4% economic rate of return, with just over half giving an economic rate of return over 10% (the others were characterized as "failures" because they produced an estimated economic rate of return below the Bank cut-off of 10%). Failures were most frequent in Eastern and Southern Africa, where 12 out of 15 area development projects failed, the only exceptions being one in Mauritius and two in Malawi. In the other four subregions of Africa the record was better, with 17 out of a total of 25 area development projects approved in 1974–1979 found to be successful (World Bank Operations Evaluation Department, 1988).

Disillusionment was evident: "There have been many studies of IRD and the general conclusion is that performance has been disappointing. In the majority of cases economic rates of return have been below those projected at the appraisal stage and also below levels achieved by other forms of project initiatives" (Maddock and Wilson, 1994). "That form of area development project that came to be known as "integrated rural development" (that is, a multicomponent project involving two or more agencies) performed so poorly as to raise questions about the utility of that approach in many situations" (World Bank Operations Evaluation Department, 1988). Among the reasons identified for these failures were the use of independent project management units instead of the normal government administration, financing at a higher level than normally available, indifferent government agencies, lack of appropriate farm technology, difficulty fulfilling training functions, and an inability of many countries to manage such complex projects.

9. AGRICULTURAL RESEARCH

The development and adoption of improved agricultural technology have been major driving forces in the transformation from agrarian to high-income industrial and post-industrial societies between 1800 and the end of the 20th century (Hayami and Ruttan, 1985). However, in 1950 food-crop agriculture in the tropics was quite traditional and failed to increase output at more than 1% or 2% a year—far too slow to allow the shift of population and investment resources into other productive sectors that is needed to produce rapid economic growth. Early United States development assistance efforts included substantial efforts to transfer US agricultural technology to developing countries but met with disappointment. The crop varieties and animal breeds that had driven the American transformation simply didn't perform in the tropics, and biologists soon pointed out that agricultural climate, soil, and pest conditions in the United States and the tropics were so different that research to develop appropriate technology would have to be done in the tropics.

The Rockefeller Foundation started helping Mexico develop its own improved agricultural technology in 1943 and in the late 1950s, together with the Ford Foundation, conceived of an international research center focused on rice. At the invitation of the government of the Philippines, they created the International Rice Research Institute (IRRI) in 1960 to create new rice technology that would raise yields and incomes of Asian rice farmers. That began a new era of international agricultural research. In the late 1960s the existing Rockefeller-supported program in Mexico was split into an international maize and wheat research program that became CIMMYT and a national program in support of Mexican agricultural research. By 1970 the Ford and Rockefeller foundations were supporting international agricultural research centers in Nigeria (IITA) and Colombia (CIAT) as well as those in Mexico and the Philippines (Baum, 1986).

By the mid-1970s the semi-dwarf varieties of rice from IRRI and wheat from CIMMYT had been widely released and had spread to 30 million hectares with such unprecedented speed that the phenomenon was dubbed the Green Revolution (Dalrymple, 1975). Bilateral donors and the World Bank had joined with the foundations to establish the Consultative Group on International Agricultural Research (CGIAR), and by 1976 over $62 million was being made available annually by 26 donor organizations (Baum, 1986). In 1985, 16 centers were being supported. Development assistance for agricultural research grew through the 1970s and 1980s as the donors sought to build both the international centers and national research systems to take the international products and further adapt them to local conditions. But although the growth in support for agricultural research was rapid, the amount of aid going to research never got very large in absolute terms, never reaching even 5% of total aid to agriculture through 2002.

9.1 Research evaluation

In the early 1980s the World Bank commissioned a team of 10 distinguished international agricultural research experts to review the accomplishments of 128 research and extension projects in Brazil, India, Indonesia, Kenya, Mali, Morocco, Nigeria, Sudan, Thailand, and Turkey. Their review covered the period between 1970 and 1980, when the World Bank committed $745 million in 27 full-scale research or extension projects in 13 countries and $419 million additional for research or extension components in hundreds of agriculture and rural development projects; in addition, the Bank committed another $55 million for support of the CGIAR (World Bank Operations Evaluation Department, 1985). In 1999 the Bank reported on another review of its experience with supporting national agricultural research in the early 1980s and 1990s, a period when Bank support for agricultural research reached an annual commitment of $200 million in 32 countries in addition to its annual support to the international agricultural research system. That review refers to a "virtual absence of quantitative data" in *ex post* evaluations of Bank-supported agricultural research projects but pointed to the "generally very favorable economic benefits" reported in empirical studies on agricultural research (World Bank Operations Evaluation Department, 1999).

Agricultural research investments made a key contribution to China's agricultural productivity growth over the past 40 years. China's agricultural research system generated new crop varieties with yield potentials that grew between 1% and 2.5% a year between 1980 and 1995 (Rozelle, Jin, et al., 2003; Fan, Zhang, et al., 2002). Likewise, in India agricultural output and incomes accelerated as the products of agricultural research were adopted by farmers. Between 1967 and 2003 about 300 modern varieties (MVs) of rice and 2000 modern varieties of wheat, sorghum, and other crops were released. From 1970 to 2000 India's food grain production doubled from about 100 million to about 200 million tons (Janaiah and Hossain, 2002). The agricultural growth was primarily a result of massive public investments in agricultural research and extension, along with investment in rural roads (Fan, Hazell, et al., 1999).

There is an inherent difficulty in separating the contributions of research and extension. Conceptually, the first produces new technology while the second enables farmers to access it and put it to use, but without the latter the former can have little effect. Some analysts recognize this; others ignore it and focus on one or the other. To the extent that one examines the relative efficiency of alternative forms of research or extension, preoccupation with one to the exclusion of the other is justified (Picciotto and Anderson, 1997), but a combined approach that recognizes the contribution (and cost) of both might be a better option in most cases (Anderson and Feder, 2004).

9.2 Returns to research

Numerous studies have quantified the economic contributions of research using the relatively straightforward model developed to investigate the returns to hybrid corn research in the United States (Griliches, 1957). Research generates technical change, which enables producers to use fewer units of inputs for each unit of output. The input savings mean that under competitive market conditions more output will be supplied to the market at any given price. The savings are shared between consumers and suppliers of the product, the proportion to each depending on the nature of demand and the production technology. Economists have made over 300 studies of the benefits and costs of agricultural research in countries throughout the world using the Griliches methodology and refinements of it.

Alston and colleagues conducted a systematic meta-analysis of the literature, evaluating returns to investment in agricultural research between 1953 and 1998 (2000). The studies reported over 1880 rates of return, with a median internal rate of return of 48% per year for all the studies combined; for all studies of extension alone it was 63% per year, and for all studies of research and extension combined it was 37% per year.

The authors concluded the rate of return to research varies according to problem focus in ways that make intuitive sense; however, there was no evidence that the rate of return to research has declined over time. Because each technology builds on earlier technologies and most technologies use research findings from several different institutions, it is difficult to know what results to attribute to what research and is a challenge to fully to account for all the costs. Efforts to disentangle these various effects support the conclusion that returns to research investment in Brazil were approximately 40% (Pardey, Alston, et al., 2003).

More challenging are questions about the possibility of selection bias—analysis focused on the more successful research projects. Studies that evaluate the returns to all research or all research and extension in a country over a period of time help to overcome the selection bias problem (Anderson and Feder, 2002). An analysis of research and extension in India between 1956 and 1987 concluded that "the returns to public agricultural research were greater than 50%. The rates of return to extension, private research and development, and imported modern varieties generated mainly by the IARCs were also high" (Evenson, Pray, et al., 1999).

9.3 International Agricultural Research

The international agricultural research centers supported through the CGIAR have been a significant source of agricultural technology used in developing countries since the 1960s. The first comprehensive study of the impact of CGIAR research investment was undertaken in the mid-1980s (Anderson, Herdt, et al., 1988) and since then there have been numerous studies to estimate the impact of the research conducted by the centers, with recent efforts coordinated by the Standing Panel on Impact Assessment (SPIA) of the CGIAR. One compilation of work in this vein was prepared for a 2002 conference, tellingly entitled "Why Has Impact Assessment Research Not Made More of a Difference?" Over 75 studies related to assessing the impact of the CGIAR were reported to the conference (SPIA/CIMMYT, 2002).

SPIA commissioned a set of studies to assess the crop genetic improvement research of the CGIAR (Evenson and Gollin, 2003). Unlike national research funded by an individual country, CGIAR work is designed to provide benefits to all developing countries. Achieving those benefits depends on how well the international agricultural research centers (IARCs) are able to target conditions they are intended to serve in the developing countries. Often, the best use of CGIAR gene products is as raw material for national plant-breeding programs, although in some cases national authorities test and release center-developed varieties suitable for their conditions.

The SPIA study is built around lists of crop varieties released by agricultural authorities in the national programs cooperating with the international agricultural research centers from 1965–1998. The crop studies carried out by national and CGIAR economists enumerate the releases of new varieties of rice, wheat, maize, sorghum, millets, barley, lentils, beans, cassava, and potato.[10] Approximately 8000 varieties of these crops were released over the study period. About 160 new varieties of these crops were released annually in the late 1970s—almost double the rate of the late 1960s. Varietal production continued to accelerate so that by the late 1990s about 350 new varieties were being released annually. "Further, the data indicate that 36% of the approximately 8000 released varieties were crossed in an IARC program." National program varietal releases (the remaining 64%) "can be further classified according to whether one or both parents in the cross were an IARC parent. For all NARS-crossed varieties, roughly 17% had at least one IARC parent," while the remaining 47% had no identified CGIAR parent (Evenson and Gollin, 2003).

New varieties spread most rapidly in Asia. By the 1980s nearly half the area's wheat and rice was planted to modern varieties, and by the end of the 1990s over 85% of the wheat area and 65% of the rice area were in modern varieties. Other crops showed similar trends in Asia. By contrast, in sub-Sahara Africa adoption of new varieties was low for all crops, even through the 1990s, when new varieties of maize, the region's most widely used cereal crop, had not reached 20%. In Latin America and the Middle East adoption rates were generally slower than in Asia. By the middle of the 1990s, modern varieties of maize covered about 30% of the Latin America crop and modern varieties of wheat covered nearly 40% of the Middle East.

New agricultural technology is an important source of agricultural growth, but estimates of its productivity impact and benefits are not straightforward. From 1965 to 2000 massive numbers of farmers adopted new crop varieties that led to higher production throughout much of the developing world. What would have been the situation if this had not happened? An attempt to answer this question using a "counterfactual" modeling approach that includes the global market for all staple foods and the respective demand characteristics in each country suggests that staple grains prices would have been from 35% to 66% higher (Evenson and Rosegrant, 2003, p. 485). Consumers, especially the poor, derived significant benefits from these low food prices. Farmers who adopted the new varieties benefited because their real costs of production were reduced by more than enough to offset the price declines.

9.4 USAID CRSP

The Collaborative Research Support Programs (CRSPs), initiated in 1975 by USAID, took a somewhat different approach from that of the international agricultural research centers. The CRSPs were intended to generate solutions to agricultural problems of developing countries through research and to strengthen research capacities of developing countries through complementary educational programs, but each CRSP was focused on a specific commodity, production system, or resource and drew on the scientific and managerial resources of U.S. universities. The programs have been intensively evaluated,[11] with farm-level impact assessments conducted. A 1995 evaluation focused on seven individual CRSPs (for sorghum and millet, small ruminants, soil management, pond dynamics and aquaculture, peanuts, and fisheries stock management) reported significant accomplishments in both research and education from this $200 million, 20-year program (Swindale, Barrett, et al., 1995).

Some of the contributions from research came as byproducts of advanced degree training in the U.S. universities. About 450 developing country nationals obtained Ph.D. degrees and about 650 obtained Master's degrees in association with various CRSPs. Over the years those who were trained advanced their careers, with many achieving positions of responsibility. The evaluation concluded that the CRSPs had:

largely achieved their stated objectives. They have educated many scientists from the United States, host countries, and other developing countries. They have produced a massive quantity of research results and information, improved crop cultivars that were released for farmer use, and made substantial contribution to the body of knowledge concerning tropical soils, agriculture, and fisheries. New methods have been developed to identify, and in some cases to control, a wide variety of pests and diseases of crops and animals. (Swindale, Barrett, et al., 1995)

10. EDUCATION AND AGRICULTURAL DEVELOPMENT

The obvious difference in education levels between poor and wealthy countries pointed to education as a target from the first days of development assistance, and the deep involvement of academics at the Ford and Rockefeller foundations in the discussions of agriculture development gave them a prominent role in designing U.S. assistance to higher education. Like U.S. hybrid corn, grain combines, and credit systems, to them the value of the U.S. system of agricultural higher education was a given: What poor countries needed were universities staffed by faculty with Ph.D. degrees who taught resident students, conducted cutting-edge research, and took the results of that research to farmers with the help of an extension system—the tripartite "land-grant university model."

Exactly how aid to education was to contribute to agricultural growth was not made completely clear. One line of argument is that education makes people better able to understand change and adapt to it—for example, by adopting new institutions or technology that facilitate faster growth. Another is that like any other part of the economy, agriculture will grow more quickly with more educated people and therefore aid to agricultural education should increase agricultural growth. Still a third argument is that aid to agricultural universities increases their capacity to invent, adapt, and extend new technology to farmers, thereby increasing the rate of agricultural growth. Together these and other arguments provided adequate rational for supporting agricultural higher education.

The classical tangible factors of production—land, labor, and capital—play an obvious role in economic activity. They can be seen and measured. But labor is not a homogeneous input, and the differences generated in labor by education could be less visible than differences among various types of land and capital. To the extent that education embodied in human beings increases productivity and requires the person being educated to refrain from consumption of some of his or her potential earnings while "accumulating" education, it is similar to physical capital. The level of education is often identified as the level of human capital; it would logically seem to be important in economic growth, and indeed, the idea that expansion of education leads to more rapid economic growth is a central tenet of human capital theory.[12]

In the 1920s and 1930s, long before human capital theory or development assistance from national governments, the Carnegie and Rockefeller foundations supported university-level education in British colonial Africa, China, and over 60 other countries around the world (Nielsen, 1984). Rockefeller funding in China helped establish the Peking Union Medical College and helped develop the agricultural economics department at Nanjing University, where John Lossing Buck, husband of the novelist Pearl Buck (*The Good Earth*), worked with colleagues from Cornell.

World War II brought overseas foundation funding almost to a halt, but after the war the foundations turned with renewed attention to the emerging nations. Largely staffed by former university professors, the foundations believed deeply in higher education as a means to development. The Kellogg Foundation started a program of fellowships in Latin America; the Ford Foundation initiated overseas work in 1950 with a prominent role for fellowships and to help develop universities in the Philippines and Peru; the Rockefeller Foundation supported medical, business, and agricultural higher education in Thailand, Kenya, Brazil, and elsewhere (Coleman and Court, 1993).

However, empirically measuring the contribution of education, whether primary, secondary, or higher, has proven elusive, with some much-noted studies finding little association between education and economic growth (Todaro, 1989; Benhabib and Spiegel, 1994). Empirical analysis took two quite different approaches (Krueger and Lindahl, 2001). One, in the tradition of macroeconomic growth models, tries to estimate a numerical association between rates of economic growth and variables reflecting education (Mankiw, Romer, et al., 1992) (Solow, 2001); the other compares the earnings of groups with different levels of education within countries, to estimate benefit/cost ratios for educational investment (Psacharopoulos, 1994).

Inconsistent results and considerable differences in the apparent contribution of education in high- compared to low-income countries (Serrano, 2003) plagued macroeconomic analyses. These were attributed to poor data and poor analytical techniques (Krueger and Lindahl, 2001), and no robust estimate of the effect of education had been agreed on in the macroeconomic literature on growth through the 1990s (Appleton, Bigsten, et al., 1999). Subsequent research giving rigorous attention to comparability of data and the application of sophisticated econometric techniques generated results that show the expected positive relationship between higher education and economic growth rates (Cohen and Soto, 2001). But for decades even those arguing for funding for higher education had little empirical basis for their case and projected some ambivalence about such investments (World Bank Operations Evaluation Department, 1994).

The second approach, on the other hand, used a much more understandable analytical method and generated copious results that strongly influenced assistance to education.

Comparisons of the earnings of individuals at different levels of education, the so-called human capital earnings function of labor economics, consistently show high private and social rates of return to investment in education (Rosen, 1977; Psacharopoulos, 1994; Tansel, 1995; Card, 1999). Unfortunately, it seems that at least one aspect of that work generated confusion: Estimates of the relative benefits and costs of primary, secondary, and tertiary education suggested that returns were highest to primary education. An influential set of such studies by World Bank staff achieved wide acceptance in the World Bank and among borrowing nations in the late 1980s and was revisited in the mid-1990s (Psacharopoulos, 1994; Tansel, 1995), resulting in the aforementioned internal World Bank ambivalence about funding higher education.

10.1 Agricultural higher education

For many years U.S. development assistance authorities, like foundation leaders, simply assumed that higher education was critically important and made support of agricultural universities a central element in U.S. aid. American land grant universities were contracted to take the responsibility for implementing that aspect of U.S. assistance to developing countries. In the early 1960s there was a virtual explosion of investment in higher education by the foundations, government aid organizations, and the multilateral development banks. Between 1964 and 1990 the World Bank assisted 68 agricultural higher education institutions in 25 countries, and USAID assisted 70 institutions in 40 countries. Ten institutions receive help from both (World Bank Operations Evaluation Department, 1992). As with the foundations in the 1950s, the agencies simply assumed that such aid was a good investment. The World Bank provided loans for education projects but did not estimate expected rates of return or contribution to economic growth prior to approval, as a matter of policy (Vawda, Moock, et al., 1999; Berk, 2002).

USAID assistance created the basis for agricultural universities in India, Pakistan, Bangladesh, Sri Lanka, South Korea, Indonesia, Thailand, Kenya, Nigeria, Ethiopia, Malawi, Morocco, Uganda, Tanzania, Sierra Leone, Brazil, Colombia, Costa Rica, Peru, Ecuador, Chile, and elsewhere.[13] In addition to over a dozen agricultural universities in India, these efforts led to some of the developing world's leading agricultural universities, including Indonesia's Bogor Agricultural University, Thailand's Kasetsart, Kenya's Egerton, Malawi's Bunda College, several Nigerian universities, Uganda's Makerere University, and others. Between 1964 and 1990 the Bank assisted 68 agricultural universities or colleges through 41 education projects in 25 countries, through loans amounting to $715 million (World Bank Operations Evaluation Department, 1992).

In designing the program to help create agricultural universities in India, USAID recognized the federal responsibilities of the Indian Council of Agricultural Research (ICAR) and engaged it in the design of what are known in India as the "state agricultural universities." The ICAR drew on advice from a former Dean of agriculture of the

University of Illinois who developed a Model Act for the establishment of agricultural universities in India (Busch, 1988) and the leadership of Dr. Ralph W. Cummings, Sr., the director of the Rockefeller Foundation's Indian agricultural program (Lele and Goldsmith, 1989). However, though local authorities were involved to some extent, the dominant approach was to transfer the land grant university model with heavy emphasis on giving the new universities responsibility for research and extension as well as teaching.

But despite enthusiasm for education among some development agencies, evaluations that estimate the impact of aid to higher education on economic and agricultural growth were scarce. The contribution of higher education to agricultural productivity growth was neither well documented nor agreed in the development community in the 1970s and 1980s. As the ascendant vision for aid became direct aid to the "poorest of the poor," second thoughts about higher education set in. By 1974, USAID had reduced the number of universities it was assisting from 74 to 18, and by 1978 USAID was supporting no more than 10 developing country universities: "From the early 1960s to the early 1970s, one witnessed the astonishing spectacle of a meteoric expansion in external funding of Third World university development during the first half, when this was considered the favored remedy, and, after cresting in the late 1960s, an equally precipitate plunge to virtual abandonment during the second half" (Coleman and Court, 1993).

By the mid-1980s many of the original agricultural university projects had been completed and a series of Project Impact Evaluations was conducted to review the experience with agricultural universities. The India evaluation reported that over 300 U.S. faculty members had been assigned to posts in India and more than 1000 Indians received M.Sc. and/or Ph.D. degrees from the cooperating U.S. universities. The Indian universities had gained the capacity to train students through the Ph.D. level, helping build the world's second largest agricultural scientific establishment and providing technical support to the various state extension services. Expanded opportunities for women and a series of research innovations were enumerated (Busch, 1988). Evaluations of the experience in other countries confirmed that in most cases the new universities had achieved significant teaching capacity (Welsch, Flora, et al., 1987; Ericksen, Compton, et al., 1988; Ericksen, Busch, et al., 1987; Price and Evans, 1989; Gamble, Blumberg, et al., 1988). However, the same reports noted that the new institutions generally did not have responsibility for extension and were conducting limited amounts of research.

A 1989 summary of the findings from evaluations of USAID assistance for university development noted both positive and negative results. On the positive side, it said:

> **[...] most of the U.S.-trained host-country faculty returned to their home universities and emerged as the primary leaders in expanding and moving their institutions to a position of educational prominence. Their**

undergraduate programs have greatly expanded the supply of trained agriculturalists, and many institutions are now able to support training at the graduate level. In addition, many of these universities have led the research and development of new production technologies for the agricultural sector.

On the negative side:

Despite their past accomplishments, the future growth of many of these universities likely will be constrained by declining budgetary sources, faculty "inbreeding," excessive government regulation, and a lack of access to state-of-the art advances in international science and education. To maintain the universities' leadership in research and education, new forms of international collaboration are needed to address larger issues of renewing and sustaining university vitality. (Hansen, 1989)

In 1992 the World Bank undertook an evaluation of its experience with higher education in agriculture based on eight "case study audits" supplemented by desk studies of 33 other projects. Most higher education subprojects identified institution building, manpower needs, and strengthening the agricultural higher education systems of countries as objectives; few made any attempt at developing agricultural extension. Most also identified an increase in agricultural production as an objective, although the pathway by which agricultural university strengthening would help achieve production increases was usually not spelled out. The projects had "generally satisfactory results," but their longer-term effectiveness was questioned and was subject to the same skeptical view of higher education prevailing in the Bank at that time. For example, the report stated:

[H]igher education in general was becoming a more controversial subsector, as universities were increasingly plagued by problems of quality and relevance of programs and output, inequitable access, and heavy reliance on public coffers that seemed to many disproportionate to the social benefits generated. (World Bank Operations Evaluation Department, 1992)

Ten years later the Bank's report on tertiary education had just the opposite tone, stressing the importance of higher education in the emerging global "knowledge economy"; identifying contributions to poverty reduction through economic growth, redistribution, and employment; and highlighting externalities beyond the individuals who received the higher levels of education. It reviewed the importance of higher education for growth and social development; discussed how countries should position themselves to take advantage of the potentials offered by tertiary education; reviewed the justification for continuing public support for tertiary education and the appropriate role of the state in it; and discussed how the Bank and other development agencies could assist countries in building their capacity (World Bank, 2002).

10.2 Institutional misdesign?

Despite the positive accomplishments of many new universities, the evaluations reflect an undercurrent of concern about the rapidly changing nature of agriculture and the ability of the new universities to adjust to changing circumstances and to muster the political support needed to maintain adequate funding. Many also lacked systems by which they could continuously review their "programs, projects, and mission"; they seemed isolated from other universities, whether in the same country, neighboring countries, or in the world scientific community; faculty quality was compromised; there were inadequate diffusion of new findings, inadequate representation of women, understaffing of the social sciences and consequent overemphasis of the technical science capacity, inadequate library resources, and outdated or nonfunctional research facilities.

In India, important institutional differences between India and the United States seemed to have been overlooked in the design of the state agricultural universities, despite the involvement of the Indian Council of Agricultural Research. In the United States, national legislation had given the land-grant universities responsibility for research, extension, and teaching, with states and counties linked to their respective university extension activities. In India, the responsibility for research rested with the ICAR, a semiautonomous body linked to the Ministry of Agriculture; the responsibility for extension rested with the Ministry of Community Development and Cooperation and the responsibility for education rested with the Ministry of Education.

The Model Act for state agricultural universities, designed by ICAR and the U.S. advisors and more or less followed by India's state legislatures, incorporated responsibilities for teaching, research, and extension in the new institutions. But in reality these mandates were limited and the larger institutional landscape was too powerful to overcome. Five years after the effort started, one acute observer put it directly:

> **The U.S. universities may have assumed too much from the start that they knew what was needed and they knew how to do it. The "land-grant" banner was carried high and too literally; it was not recognized that the task was more than a simple "transplant" job. ... The many difficulties and possibilities of error in trying to transplant our ideas or to establish new patterns in a culture so different from ours were not anticipated. Now, in looking back, the universities wonder why so much was assumed. (Kiel, 1967)**

Two decades later, an evaluation of India's experience reflected the same basic concern: that the new universities seemed to have accepted too wholeheartedly the land grant doctrine without truly understanding it. There was much conflict over such superficial issues as the trimester system (which turned out to be a temporary phase in U.S. universities), disciplinary specialization, internal evaluations, and multiple examinations throughout the academic year. More serious was a basic misunderstanding of the land-grant mission of addressing matters of practical relevance to the mass of the population through research and extension. As one study put it: "Discussions of these issues are usually framed in terms of the 'U.S. system.' Often, these debates appear to focus on conformity with an abstract U.S. model, rather than assessing the costs and benefits to Indian students of pursuing various approaches" (Busch, 1988).

Many of the evaluators of individual agricultural universities projects reflected this mode of thinking, comparing the new universities to the land-grant model rather than identifying their educational contributions in their local institutional settings (Theisen, Armstrong, et al., 1989). For example, the evaluation of the Nigeria experience highlighted research accomplishments—crop varieties, production economics, livestock nutrition, and animal health—but disappointment with limited success in establishing the land-grant model as well.

> **Efforts to transfer the tripartite land grant model (teaching, research and extension) to the three Nigerian universities have had mixed success. Amadu Bello University comes closest to the model in practice. Staff at the other two universities understand and appreciate the concept but have been limited in their ability to practice it. All three universities adopted the teaching component of the model. However, of the three, only Amado Bello, because of its incorporation of established Nigerian research institutes at the time of its founding, has produced a significant amount of locally relevant research and has been able to mount more than a minimal extension effort to reach local farmers. (Gamble, Blumberg, et al., 1988).**

11. SUMMARY

The post-World War II ascendant vision of a liberal global economic system, induced by the perception that the economic autarchy and political repression that followed World War I in Europe were major sources of the Great Depression and World War II, motivated the creation of the United Nations, the World Bank, the International Monetary Fund, and the specialized U.N. agencies. That vision of the need for foreign aid was overtaken by a second,[14] stated in "point four" of President Harry S. Truman's 1949 inaugural speech: to make "the benefits of scientific advances and industrial progress available for the improvement and growth of underdeveloped areas." President John F. Kennedy's vision that a more prosperous world would be a more secure world motivated the personal commitments of Peace Corps volunteers but also large financial transfers through USAID. As president of the World Bank, Robert McNamara articulated a focus on basic human needs and human rights of the poor majority in the poorest countries. That vision was dominant well into the 1980s. The fifth was the "doctrine of closer linkage between economic and security assistance"; the sixth, intergenerational equity and sustainable development; and the seventh was reflected in the second Bush administration's vision of a foreign policy grounded in diplomacy, defense, and development.

These visions shaped aid programs by identifying various critically important issues: capital shortage, unlimited supplies of labor, institutional development, human capital, scientific and technological change, basic human needs, market failures, the environment, poverty alleviation, market fundamentalism, market failure, and government failure. Reflecting these issues, the nature, sectoral composition, and delivery mode for U.S. development assistance varied over time. In the post-World War II period, European relief and recovery and the creation of the World Bank and the IMF dominated. By the 1950s U.S. assistance efforts entailed the direct transfer of U.S. scientific advances and industrial products and, not incidentally, encouragement of poor nations to choose capitalism and democracy over communism. In the 1960s large financial transfers and costly infrastructure projects were expected to propel nations into growth by filling the "two gaps" of widely accepted economic growth models. In the 1970s, McNamara's vision focused aid on basic human needs, but the oil "crises" soon led donors to abandon that vision and focus more on sustainability and intergenerational equity. The 1980s brought a reliance on market mechanisms and the "Washington Consensus." In the 1990s participation and decentralization of decision making, including "democracy," came to dominate development assistance discussions in USAID and the World Bank. The Millennium Development Goals of the 21st century saw a return to a concern with directly addressing the health, education, housing, water, and other components of human poverty alleviation. The United States turned away from its Agency for International Development, created (but underfunded) the Millennium Challenge Corporation, and managed much of its reconstruction aid in Iraq and Afghanistan largely through the Defense Department.[15]

Empirical macroeconomic studies of the relationship of development assistance to economic growth in recipient countries have become increasingly sophisticated over time as econometrics and measurement have improved. Efforts to identify the effects of factors such as exchange rate policy, openness to international trade, government economic operations, natural resource endowments, exposure to risk from economic and natural fluctuations, or other factors that might condition the effectiveness of aid give different results in the hands of different analysts. A meta-analysis of 72 macroeconomic analyses concluded that 41 showed significant positive relationships between aid and growth, whereas 30 relationships were not significantly different from zero. One line of analysis argues that development assistance is effective in countries that follow "good policies," whereas another argues that countries chronically subjected to shocks from external natural or economic events fail to make effective use of development assistance but should not be penalized for those external shocks by donor' withholding assistance.

The agricultural sector receives a small fraction of total development assistance—about 20% in the 1970s, declining to about 8% in 2002–2005. Although there have been a few efforts to understand the contributions of agricultural aid as whole, assessments of the effectiveness of agriculture aid have largely been conducted through evaluations of individual projects or sets of projects directed at subsectors of agriculture. The relationship between project performance and sectoral or econo-mywide performance has not been resolved, but, given that decisions about assistance actually come down to decisions about resources for specific projects, learning as much as possible about which projects in which subsectors are "successful" and which are not would seem to be useful.

Table 4 presents this reviewer's summary of the findings discussed above and his judgment on the cost effectiveness of development assistance to each sub-sector. There "cost-effective" is similar to the World Bank's "economic success" rating – where aid investments generally have rates of return in excess of 10%. The Table also provides a judgment about the sustainability of such investments. In "Sustainable" subsectors, after donor assistance is complete funding generally continues from other sources. On the other hand, "Not sustainable" indicates that investment in the activities supported by donor assistance generally ceased within 3–5 years after the development assistance funding ended.

Projects to provide agricultural credit and build agricultural cooperatives to serve resource-poor farmers comprised the third largest fraction of development assistance to agriculture, over 10% of the total in the 1970s and 1980s. Evaluations of many credit programs led to the conclusion that the results of such programs were disappointing, loan-default problems were often serious, most poor farmers were not able to obtain loans through the programs and the specialized banks established to provide such credit could not be sustained over the longer term. Credit projects lost favor in the late 1980s and 1990s and currently make up less than 3% of the agricultural assistance portfolio. Micro-credit programs, however, which are more recent and have received much less aid, seem to be more effective in reaching the poor but also seem unlikely to be sustainable over the long term without continued capital infusions.

Integrated rural development projects and their precursors, including general development and crop and livestock production, comprised the second largest investment in agricultural development assistance in the 1960s and 1970s and increased rapidly in the portfolios of USAID and the World Bank for 10 years, through the early 1980s. Initially they were roughly as successful in World Bank evaluations as irrigation projects. However, by the late 1980s their complexity had led to high rates of failure and disillusionment within the Bank and USAID. A 1992 Bank review of such area development projects indicated an overall success rate of only 49%. On average they generated a 10.4% economic rate of return, with just over half giving a "successful" economic rate of return over 10% (the other half were characterized as "failures" because they produced below 10%). Moreover, in most cases countries failed to continue supporting such projects after external funding ceased.

Irrigation and drainage was the largest subsector of agricultural development assistance from the World Bank, the United States, and other donors through the

Table 4 Patterns of support and effectiveness of agricultural development assistance by subsector

Subsector	Pattern of Support	Success Rate	Experience	Cost-Effective? Sustainable?
Subsidized credit	Widespread in 1960s and 1970s but largely abandoned by USAID and the World Bank in the 1980s	Impossible to maintain programs more than five years in most cases	Credit reaches mainly larger farmers; repayment poor; rural credit suppliers collapse	*Not* cost-effective *Not* sustainable
Microcredit	Embraced by donors in 1990s, created Consultative Group to Assist the Poor	Evaluation began in 2002; few case studies of success in agriculture	Credit reaches poor farmers; repayment sustained; microfinance suppliers need donor subsidies	Cost-effective *Not* sustainable
Integrated rural development	USAID >100 projects in 1970s, "no longer encouraged" in 1985; World Bank projects: 1971–1973: 5/yr 1974–1976: 17/yr 1977–1979: 24/yr 1980–1982: 21/yr 1983–1985: 18/yr	Fewer than 50% successful, in a 1992 World Bank review	"That form of area development project that came to be known as 'integrated rural development' (that is, a multi-component project involving two or more agencies) performed so poorly as to raise questions about the utility of that approach in many situations"	*Not* cost-effective *Not* sustainable

Continued

Table 4 Patterns of support and effectiveness of agricultural development assistance by subsector—Cont'd

Subsector	Pattern of Support	Success Rate	Experience	Cost-Effective? Sustainable?
Irrigation and drainage	USAID agriculture: 15%, 1970s–1980s 5%, 1988–1992 < 2% thereafter World Bank: $1120/yr, 1970s $1273/yr, 1980s $1032/yr, 1990s	World Bank: 1995: 67% of 208 projects successful; 2002: 336 projects, success rates "below Bank average"	World Bank: Continued large lending despite pessimistic tone in 1993 and 2002 reports; reaffirmation of importance of "hydraulic infrastructure" in 2004	Cost-effective Sustainable
Research and extension	3–5% of agricultural support	Hundreds of studies: median rates of return, 40–50%	Wide recognition of the need to get technology to farmers, no agreement on optimal mode of extension	Cost-effective *Marginally* Sustainable
Higher education	USAID: 1960–1970: 74 projects 1974: 18 projects 1978: 10 projects World Bank: 1964–1990: 68 universities 1992: Reluctant 2002: Encouraging	No estimates of economic rates of return or success rates	New universities successfully established teaching programs, many through the Ph.D. level; unsuccessful in gaining responsibility and funding for research and extension	Cost-effective *Marginally* Sustainable

mid–1980s. The World Bank lent about \$31 billion for irrigation from 1950 to 1993; 67% of those projects were rated as satisfactory, generating an average rate of return of 15%. USAID was largely out of irrigation projects by the late 1980s, instead providing small amounts of funding for improving the management of irrigation and water. In the mid–1990s one can detect a reluctant tone in Bank documents about irrigation, and water projects had been transformed from investments intended to generate additional income into social support projects enhancing the contribution of water to country economic, social, and environmental development while ensuring that resource and water services were managed sustainably. By 2004, however, a water resources management group within the Bank had reasserted the importance of "hydraulic infrastructure" that seemed to herald a return to the "hardware" (concrete) side of irrigation system development. Irrigation projects tend to continue to receive national or farmer support after the initial funding is completed although not at the level required to maintain systems at their maximum design operating level. Often the benefits are concentrated among more powerful groups or those nearest the source of water so disadvantaged groups do not benefit as intended. Still, irrigation is so productive in most cases that someone finds it profitable to maintain.

Assistance to agricultural research has been relatively stable, around 4% of agricultural development assistance, over the past 25 years. Many studies of the economic rates of return to agricultural research have been conducted and, contrary to the overwhelming conclusion reached for other kinds of agricultural assistance, over 95% of the studies show substantial positive economic returns. Overall, the median rate of return to agricultural research investments is nearly 50% and the median rate of return to research and extension combined is nearly 40%. Careful examination of nearly 300 studies reporting over 1800 individual rates of return indicate no support for the idea that returns have fallen over time, but there is support for the idea that returns vary in other ways that make intuitive sense. In particular, research on commodities with longer production cycles, such as livestock, and more diffuse effects such as natural resource management have lower rates of return.

Agricultural higher education is a small fraction of either aid to education or aid to agriculture but had a high profile in the U.S. development assistance community. USAID and the World Bank both sought to transfer the institutional model of the U.S. agricultural university having responsibility for teaching, research, and extension into countries where responsibilities for all education rested with one national ministry, agricultural research in a second ministry, and, in some cases, extension in a third. This basic institutional difference was not recognized by most of those charged with higher education assistance. Where it was recognized, the efforts made to reallocate responsibilities generally fell short of being effective, and two decades later evaluations of the assistance identified this as a basic shortcoming. However, aid for higher education helped build hundreds of universities in developing countries that are educating the farm credit staff, businesspeople, researchers, and extension workers who are making agricultural development a success in many countries.

Despite the considerable evidence for the cost effectiveness of investments in agricultural research and extension, it has proven difficult to sustain financial support at the levels envisioned by project designers after development assistance projects end. Ironically, this may be because these activities generate public goods which are precisely the kinds of benefits for which public funding is most appropriate. But because it is so difficult to demonstrate the benefits of public goods to any particular individual or group it is difficult to mobilize the political support that public funding requires. Although there is limited evidence for high *social* rates of return to higher education, the private benefits to those receiving higher degrees is clear and to some degree has led to ambivalence in government support for higher education. Hence research, extension and higher education are called marginally sustainable because they receive continued funding from national sources, but at sub-optimal levels.

Sub-Sahara Africa remains the largest challenge for development assistance. Not only is it the poorest region, with the least educated people, the poorest health conditions, and the most pervasive food problems of any major region, it is the only one where per capita income actually declined during 1980–2000. Its population is still 60–90% dependent on agriculture, and aid has done little to build alternative economic activity or to redress the basic human problems. Every category of project has been least effective in Africa. A small number of irrigation projects have been costly and abject failures and as a result the average cost per irrigated acre in Africa has been high. Not only that, but throughout Africa irrigation is subject to highly variable climate, making production highly variable. Integrated rural development projects of great complexity had inadequate managerial capacity in locations with inadequate roads and consequent difficult market access. Agricultural production in many countries has failed to keep pace with demand, a situation especially disappointing because development professionals have reached substantial agreement on the priorities for agricultural development, including the critical role of technology, human capital, and institutions. Both African governments and donors bear responsibility.

Only when governments themselves have a commitment to agricultural growth and back that commitment with appropriate policies is agricultural aid effective. Such commitment has been lacking in many African countries. But donors also bear a heavy responsibility for the general ineffectiveness of aid to African agriculture. There has been declining understanding within the donor community of the role of agriculture in development at early stages and of the importance of technical know-how about agriculture. This lack of expertise has contributed to the inadequate grasp in donor agencies of the complex, location-specific nature of agriculture. Donors have paid inadequate attention to identifying those investments most needed for promoting smallholder agriculture at particular times and places and have not developed long-term, strategic, balanced approaches to supporting Africa's agriculture.

Donors have not given priority to the investments to develop the human, institutional, and technological capital needed to modernize traditional agriculture and the need for broad, long-term support for developing capacity within Africa to develop that capital. Donors have leaned toward the achievement of short-run results by investing large sums in urban-biased physical and social infrastructure. Donors have embraced rural education and health care but have not recognized that rural people themselves must have remunerative employment within a dynamic economy to sustain those social services over the long run.

Perhaps most damaging, donors have not stayed committed to the key requirements for a sufficiently long time to achieve the needed results. Eicher blames "changing whims." Lele speaks of support that has swung between one extreme and another— "food security and export crops," "growth and equity," crop productivity and industrialization"—and pleads for a balance between "structural adjustment assistance and project assistance." It seems that the urge to replace existing work with new approaches dominates decisions rather than being driven by a deep understanding of what is needed and what is likely to be effective.

12. CONCLUSION

Accelerating agricultural production to grow faster than subsistence needs is key to generating a surplus to support the nonagricultural sector and hence stimulate general economic growth. Development aid, when effective, helps countries accelerate their economic growth driving independence and self-direction by providing more income to pay for basic health, basic education, basic housing, and basic food. Faster economic growth is *not* always better for a society, but for people in extreme poverty in nations of extreme poverty, faster economic growth *is* necessary if people are to gain lives reasonably free of hunger, disease, and ignorance. To the extent that agricultural development assistance contributes to accelerating agricultural production, it contributes to development and the ability to pay for health, education, housing, and food and over the longer run to pay for secondary and higher education, more health care, art, music, and even in some cases intangibles such as serenity, wisdom, and knowledge.

The shape of development assistance is constantly changing, as reflected in the ascendant vision of those who promote it, pay for it, deliver it, receive it, and evaluate it. Within the changing vision, four forces interact in determining the size and configuration of development assistance projects: politics, theory, practice, and evaluation. National politics is perhaps most important in determining the allocation of assistance across recipients, but it also enters into decisions about which sectors are emphasized within recipient countries. Development theory provides an articulated understanding of the role of aid in the development process. Practitioners, especially those with high-level responsibilities within aid organizations, exert a good deal of influence by translating the ascendant vision into operations. Individuals on the firing line of assistance organizations can modify the dominant forces and keep a particular kind of project alive long after it would have otherwise died, or close down work that might otherwise have been kept alive. Evaluations play two roles: often they are used to justify decisions that have been made on other grounds; less cynically viewed, they build a body of knowledge that informs all concerned with development assistance. Over the longer run this knowledge contributes to theory, practice, and the evolution of the next ascendant vision, but such influence is not quickly manifested.

Those with responsibility for allocating assistance across sectors apparently do not understand the crucial importance of agriculture at the early stages of development, as evidenced by the declining aid to African agriculture. It has been treated like Asia and Latin America where, one can argue, agricultural growth is now relatively less important. Those of us responsible for informing those who make the allocations have apparently failed to make a convincing case for agricultural investments in Africa. True, there has been an outpouring of information on the returns to investment in agricultural research, but much less on how to make investments in research pay off. There is lots of information on the payoff to new crop varieties but little on managing the biological, physical, and chemical dimensions of soil to achieve healthy soils in the tropics. Likewise, there is much on the importance of agricultural technology but little on the importance of the complementary requirements such as effective markets, roads, price information systems, and input availability, and even less on how development assistance can help provide these.

Development aid decision makers may be correct in not placing too much credence in the results of impact studies. There are few consistent sets of results, whether on national economic growth or agriculture. Studies correctly stress the difficulty of attributing production or growth results to assistance projects or programs because of inherent time lags, diversity of influencing factors, and multiplicity of projects. Even the strong evidence supporting the productivity of agricultural research cannot be used to simply argue for more agricultural research aid, whether to specific countries or internationally. Agricultural growth requires precisely the right combination of conditions – what is most needed in a particular place at a particular time must be specifically identified. Where it is technology, research might be needed. But those pleading for more agricultural assistance have to do a better job of identifying what is needed in specific countries at specific times and insist on that—not simply clothing their favorite agricultural activity in rhetoric that matches the latest donor whim.

End Notes

1. The diversity of agencies providing some kind of foreign aid is recounted in Lancaster (2000), *Transforming foreign aid: United States assistance in the 21ˢᵗ century*, Washington, D.C., Institute for International Economics, and Brown, Siddiqi, et al. (2006), U.S. Development Aid and the Millennium Challenge Account: Emerging Trends in Appropriations, Washington, D.C., Center for Global Development.

2. Chapter 7 of the report gives much fuller discussions of factors associated with success; the quotations here are from the Management Recommendations in Chapter 8 of McClelland (1996), *Investments in Agriculture: A synthesis of the Evaluation Literature*, Washington, D.C., Center for Development Information and Evaluation, USAID: 47 + appendices.

3. Data from p. 66 of Battaile (2002), *2001 Annual Review of Development Effectiveness: Making Choices*, Washington, D.C., World Bank Operations Evaluation Division.

4. The United States, the United Kingdom, Sweden, Germany, France, Denmark, and the European Community (the European Commission).

5. Emergency food relief is in addition to the aid amounts shown, as was made clear in reference to Table 2.

6. For example, the "Comprehensive Assessment of Water Management" project of the International Water Management Institute says, "an overarching picture on the water-food-livelihoods-environment nexus is missing, leaving uncertainties about where to invest in order to address both human and environmental water needs." See the website www.iwmi.cgiar.org/assessment/index.asp?nc=5771&id=1272&msid=93.

7. The aid flows summarized in this paragraph were generated from data in OECD Development Assistance Committee (2003).

8. See www.yearofmicrocredit.org/pages/reslib/reslib_recreading.asp.

9. www.cgap.org/docs/AMCaseStudy_01.pdf.

10. For example, one of the studies that Evenson and Gollin drew on reported studies of adoption of improved varieties of sorghum, millet, chickpea, and pigeonpea in 10 Indian provinces and five other countries (Bantilan and Joshi, eds. (1998), *Assessing Joint Research Impacts,* Patancheru, India, International Center for Research in the Semi-Arid Tropics).

11. See, for example, Gapasin, Cherry, et al. (2005), *The Peanut Collaborative Research Support Program (CRSP): 2005 External Evaluation Report,* Griffin, University of Georgia; Stovall, Herdt, et al. (2006), *External Evaluation Panel Five-Year Technical Review (2002–07) of the Bean/Cowpea Collaborative Research Support Program (CRSP),* East Lansing, Michigan State University and USAID: 93.

12. Human capital theory developed from the work of T. W. Schultz, with significant contributions by others at the University of Chicago. See Schultz (1964), *Transforming Traditional Agriculture,* Yale University Press; Becker (1993), *Human Capital: A Theoretical and Empirical Analysis, With Special Reference to Education,* University of Chicago Press; Schultz (1995), *Investment in Women's Capital,* University of Chicago Press. Also see Ranis, Stewart, et al. (2000), "Economic growth and human development," *World Development* **28**(2): 197–219.

13. For an outstanding review of the work of U.S. universities in this area, see Price (2006), *Thirty Years of Title XII: Presentation to BIFAD,* October 18, 2006, Texas A&M University.

14. Vernon Ruttan articulated overarching motivations for aid (and many other extremely valuable insights about aid) in Ruttan (1996), *United States Development Assistance Policy: The Domestic Politics of Foreign Economic Development*, Johns Hopkins University Press.

15. "Since the Millennium Challenge Corporation (MCC)—the entity charged with administering the MCA—has become operational, the original vision of $5 billion in aid increases for MCA eligible countries has not come to fruition. For FY 2007, the president requested $3 billion and Congress appropriated only $2 billion to the MCC, the highest allocation yet, but still far below the original vision" (Brown, Siddiqi, et al. (2006), *U.S. Development Aid and the Millennium Challenge Account: Emerging Trends in Appropriations,* Washington, D.C., Center for Global Development: 10, p. 2).

References

Adams, D. W., Graham, D. H., et al. (Eds.). (1984). *Undermining Rural Development with Cheap Credit.* Boulder, CO: Westview Press.

Anderson, J. R., & Feder, G. (2002). Rural extension services. In *Handbook of Agricultural Economics* (Vol. 3), Amsterdam: Elsevier.

Anderson, J. R., & Feder, G. (2004). Agricultural extension: Good intentions and hard realities. *The World Bank Research Observer, 19*(1), 41–60.

Anderson, J. R., Herdt, R. W., et al. (1988). *Science and Food: The CGIAR and its Partners.* Washington DC: The World Bank.

Antle, J. (1983). Infrastructure and aggregate agricultural productivity: International evidence. *Economic Development and Cultural Change, 31*(April), 609–619.

Appleton, S., Bigsten, A., et al. (1999). *Educational expansion and economic decline: returns to education in Kenya, 1978–1995.* Oxford: Center for the Study of African Economies, University of Oxford.

Asian Development Bank Operations Evaluation Office. (2001). *Impact Evaluation Study on ADB's Rural Credit Assistance in Bangladesh, People's Republic of China, Indonesia, Nepal, Philippines, Sri Lanka, and Thailand.* Manila: Asian Development Bank.

Bantilan, M. C. S., & Joshi, P. K. (Eds.). (1998). *Assessing Joint Research Impacts.* Patancheru, India: International Center for Research in the Semi-Arid Tropics.

Barker, R., & Molle, F. (2004). *Evolution of irrigation in South and Southeast Asia.* Colombo, Sri Lanka: Comprehensive Assessment Secretariat.

Battaile, W. (2002). *2001 Annual Review of Development Effectiveness: Making Choices.* Washington, DC: World Bank Operations Evaluation Division.

Baum, W. C. (1986). *Partners Against Hunger: The Consultative Group on International Agricultural Research.* Washington, DC: The World Bank.

Becker, G. S. (1993). *Human Capital: A Theoretical and Empirical Analysis, With Special Reference to Education.* Chicago: University of Chicago.

Belshaw, D. R. G. (1977). Rural development planning: Concepts and techniques. *Journal of Agricultural Economics, 28*, 279–292.

Bembridge, T. J. (1997). Small-scale farmer irrigation in South Africa: Implications for extension. *South African Journal of Agricultural Economics, 26*, 71–81.

Benhabib, J., & Spiegel, M. (1994). The role of human capital in economic development: Evidence from aggregate cross-country data. *Journal of Monetary Economics, 34*, 143–173.

Berk, D. (2002). *Tertiary education: Lessons from a decade of lending, FY 1990–2000.* Washington, DC: The World Bank.

Berry, L., Ford, R., et al. (1980). *The Impact of Irrigation on Development: Issues for a Comprehensive Evaluation Study.* Washington, DC: USAID.

Besley, T. J. (1998). How do market failures justify interventions in rural credit markets? In C. K. Eicher, & J. M. Staatz (Ed.), *International Agricultural Development* (pp. 370–389). Baltimore and London: Johns Hopkins University Press.

Brinkerhoff, D. W. (1981). *The Effectiveness of Integrated Rural Development: A Synthesis of Research and Experience.* Washington, DC: USAID.

Brown, E., & Nooter, R. (1992). *Successful Small-scale Irrigation in the Sahel.* Washington, DC: The World Bank.

Brown, K., Siddiqi, B., et al. (2006). *U.S. Development Aid and the Millennium Challenge Account: Emerging Trends in Appropriations.* Washington, DC: Center for Global Development.

Brown, M. M. (2004). *Aid Effectiveness: Microfinance as a Test Case.* New York: United Nations Development Program.

Burnside, C., & Dollar, D. (2000). Aid, policies and growth. *American Economic Review, 90*, 847–868.

Busch, L. (1988). *Universities for Development: Report of the Joint Indo-US Impact Evaluation of the Indian Agricultural Universities.* Washington, DC: USAID.

Card, D. (1999). The causal effect of schooling on earnings. In O. Ashenfelter, & D. Card (Eds.), *Handbook of Labor Economics.* North Holland: Amsterdam.

Chigerwe, J., Manjengwa, N., et al. (2004). Low head drip irrigation kits and treadle pumps for smallholder farmers in Zimbabwe. *Physics and Chemistry of the Earth*, 1049–1059.

Clapp-Wincek, C. (1985). *Integrated Rural Development Projects: A Review of Impact Evaluations.* Washington, DC: USAID.

Clements, M. A., Radelet, S., et al. (2004). *Counting chickens when they hatch: The short-term effect of aid on growth.* Washington, DC: Center for Global Development.

Coelli, T. J., & Rao, D. S. P. (2003). Total Factor Productivity Growth in Agriculture: A Malmquest Index Analysis of 93 Countries, 1980–2000. St. Lucia, Australia: Center for Efficiency and Productivity Analysis, School of Economics, University of Queensland.

Cohen, D., & Soto, M. (2001). *Growth and Human Capital: Good Data, Good Results.* Paris: OECD Research Program on Human Capital.

Coleman, J. S., & Court, D. (1993). *University Development in the Third World.* New York: Pergamon Press.

Crawford, P. R. (1981). *Implementation Issues in Integrated Rural Development: A Review of 21 USAID projects.* Washington, DC: Development Alternatives, Inc.

Dalrymple, D. G. (1975). *Measuring the Green Revolution: The Impact of Research on Wheat and Rice Production.* Washington, DC: Foreign Development Division, Economic Research Service, U.S. Department of Agriculture.

Development Assistance Committee OECD. (2006). United States (2006) DAC Peer Review: Review of the Development Co-operation Policies and Programmes of the United States. Retrieved January 29, 2007.

Donald, G. (1976). *Credit for Small Farmers in Developing Countries.* Boulder, Colorado: Westview Press.

Easter, W., Plusquellec, H., et al. (1998). *Irrigation Improvement Strategy Review.* Washington, DC: World Bank Water Resources Thematic Group.

Easterly, W., Levine, R., et al. (2003). *New Data, New Doubts: Revisiting Aid, Policies, and Growth.* Washington, DC: Center for Global Development.

Ericksen, J., Busch, L., et al. (1987). *The Hassan II Institute of Agriculture and Veterinary Medicine in Morocco: Institutional Development and International Partnership.* Washington, DC: USAID.

Ericksen, J. H., Compton, J. L., et al. (1988). *Kasetsart University in Thailand: An Analysis of Institutional Evolution and Development Impact.* Washington, DC: USAID.

Evenson, R., & Kislev, Y. (1975). *Agricultural Research and Productivity.* New Haven, CT: Yale University Press.

Evenson, R., Pray, C., et al. (1999). *Agricultural Research and Productivity Growth in India.* Washington, DC: International Food Policy Research Institute.

Evenson, R. E., & Gollin, D. (Eds.). (2003). *Crop Variety Improvement and its Effects on Productivity: The Impact of International Agricultural Research.* Wallingford, United Kingdom: CABI Publishing.

Evenson, R. E., & Rosegrant, M. (2003). The Economic Consequences of Crop Genetic Improvement Programmes. In R. E. Evenson, & D. Gollin (Eds.), *Crop Variety Improvement and its Effect on Productivity.* Wallingford, UK: CAB International.

Fan, S., Hazell, P., et al. (1999). *Linkages Between Government Spending, Growth, and Poverty in India.* Washington, DC: International Food Policy Research Institute.

Fan, S., Zhang, L., et al. (2002). *Growth, Inequality, and Poverty in Rural China.* Washington, DC: International Food Policy Research Institute.

FAO. (1986). *Irrigation in Africa South of the Sahara.* Rome: Food and Agriculture Organization.

Ford Foundation Agricultural Production Team. (1959). *Report on India's Food Crisis & Steps to Meet it.* New Delhi: Government of India, Ministry of Food and Agriculture and Ministry of Community Development and Cooperation.

Fulginiti, L. E., & Perrin, R. K. (1997, August). LDC agriculture: Nonparametric Malmquist productivity indexes. *Journal of Development Economics, 53,* 373–390.

Fulginiti, L. E., Perrin, R. K., et al. (2004). Institutions and agricultural productivity in sub-Saharan Africa. *Agricultural Economics, 31,* 169–180.

Gamble, W. K., Blumberg, R. L., et al. (1988). *Three Nigerian Universities and their Role in Agricultural Development.* Washington, DC: USAID.

Gapasin, D., Cherry, J., et al. (2005). *The Peanut Collaborative Research Support Program (CRSP): 2005 External Evaluation Report.* Griffin, Georgia, USA: University of Georgia.

Griliches, Z. (1957). Hybrid corn: An exploration in the economics of technical change. *Econometrica*.

Hansen, G. (1989). *The Impact of Investments in Agricultural Education*. Washington, DC: USAID.

Hansen, H., & Tarp, F. (2000). Aid effectiveness disputed. In F. Tarp, & P. Hjertholm (Ed.), *Foreign Aid and Development: Lessons Learnt and Directions for the Future* (pp. 103–128). London and New York: Routledge.

Hayami, Y., & Ruttan, V. (1985). *Agricultural Development: An International Perspective*. Baltimore and London: The Johns Hopkins University Press.

Headley, D. D., Rao, D. S. P., et al. (2004). *All the conditions of effective foreign aid*. St. Lucia, Queensland, Australia: Center for Efficiency and Productivity Analysis, School of Economics, University of Queensland.

IFPRI. (1997). *Commentary: Making Rural Microcredit Work for the Poor*. Washington, DC: International Food Policy Research Institute.

Inocencio, A., Sally, H., et al. (2003). *Innovative Approaches to Agricultural Water Use for Improving Food Security in sub-Saharan Africa*. Colombo, Sri Lanka: International Water Management Institute.

Janaiah, A., & Hossain, M. (2002). *The productivity impact of the green revolution: The Indian experience*. Workshop on Green Revolution in Asia and its Applicability to Africa. Tokyo, Japan: Foundation for advanced studies on international development.

Johnston, B., & Mellor, J. (1961). The Role of Agriculture in Economic Development. *American Economic Review*, *51*(4), 566–593.

Kane, S., & Eicher, C. K. (2004). *Foreign aid and the African farmer*. East Lansing, Michigan: Department of Agricultural Economics, Michigan State University.

Kennes, W. (1991). European Communities assistance for agricultural development in Cameroon, Senegal, and Tanzania, 1960–87. In U. Lele. (Ed.), *Aid to African Agriculture: Lessons from Two Decades of Donor's Experience*. Baltimore and London: The Johns Hopkins University Press.

Kiel, E. (1967). *The Objectives of the Indian Agricultural Universities*. The 11th Campus Coordinators' Conference: Agricultural Universities Development in India. Urbana, Illinois: University of Illinois.

Kikuchi, M., Inocencio, A., et al. (2005). Costs of Irrigation Projects: A comparison of sub-Sahara Africa and other developing regions and finding options to reduce costs.

Kikuchi, M., Inocencio, A., et al. (2007). *Costs and Performance of Irrigation Projects: A comparison of sub-Sahara Africa and other developing regions*. Colombo, Sri Lanka: International Water Management Institute.

Krueger, A. B., & Lindahl, M. (2001). Education for growth: Why and for whom. *Journal of Economic Literature*, *39*(4), 1101–1136.

Kumar, K. (1987). *AID's Experience with integrated rural development projects*. Washington DC: USAID.

Lancaster, C. (2000). *Transforming Foreign Aid: United States Assistance in the 21st Century*. Washington, DC: Institute for International Economics.

Lau, L., & Yotopolous, P. (1989). The meta-production function approach to technological change in world agriculture. *Journal of Development Economics*, *31*, 241–269.

Lele, U., & Goldsmith, A. A. (1989). The development of national agricultural research capacity: India's experience with the Rockefeller Foundation and Its significance for Africa. *Economic Development and Cultural Change*, *37*(2), 305–343.

Lele, U., & Jain, R. (1991). Aid to African Agriculture: Lessons from two decades of donor's experience. In U. Lele (Ed.), *Aid to African Agriculture: Lessons from two Decades of Donor's Experience* (pp. 574–612). Baltimore and London: The Johns Hopkins University Press.

Lewis, J. P. (1988). Strengthening the poor: Some lessons for the international community. In J. P. Lewis (Ed.), *Strengthening the Poor: What Have We Learned?* (pp. 3–26). New Brunswick and Oxford: Transaction Books.

Livingston, I. (1979). On the concept of integrated rural development planning in LDCs. *Journal of Agricultural Economics*, *30*, 49–53.

Maddock, N., & Wilson, F. A. (1994). Agricultural projects and institutional sustainability: A review of integrated approaches to project interventions in the agricultural sector. In N. Maddock, & F. A. Wilson (Eds.), *Project Design for Agricultural Development*. Aldershot, U.K., and Brookfield, VT: Avebury.

Mankiw, G., Romer, R., et al. (1992). A contribution to the empirics of economic growth. *Quarterly Journal of Economics*, *107*(2), 407–437.

McClelland, D. G. (1996). *Investments in Agriculture: A synthesis of the Evaluation Literature*. Washington, DC: Center for Development Information and Evaluation, USAID.

McNamara, R. S. (1973). *Address to the Board of Governors*. Washington, DC: The World Bank.

Meyer, R. L., & Nagarajan, G. (1996). *Evaluating credit guarantee programs in developing countries*. Columbus, Ohio: Department of Agricultural Economics and Rural Sociology, Ohio State University.

Morduch, J. (1999). The microfinance promise. *Journal of Economic Literature, 37*, 1569–1614.

Morss, E. R., & Gow, D. D. (1984). *Implementing Rural Development Projects: Lessons from AID and World Bank Experience*. Boulder, CO: Westview Press.

Mosher, A. (1966). *Getting Agriculture Moving*. New York: Praeger.

Nielsen, W. (1984). *The Golden Donors*. New York: Truman Talley.

Olivareas, J. (1990). *Chapter 2: The potential for irrigation development in sub-Sahara Africa; in Shawki Barghouti and Guy Le Moigne, Irrigation in sub-Sahara Africa: The development of public and private systems*. Washington, DC: The World Bank.

Operations Evaluation Department. (1994). *Rural Finance: Time for a Policy Change?* Washington, DC: World Bank.

Pardey, P. G., Alston, J. M., et al. (2003). International and institutional R&D spillovers: Attribution of benefits among sources for Brazil's New Crop Varieties. Submitted to AJAE.

Picciotto, R., & Anderson, J. R. (1997). Reconsidering agricultural extension. *The World Bank Research Observer, 12*(2), 249–259.

Pitman, G. K. (2002). *Bridging Troubled Waters: Assessing the World Bank Water Resources Strategy*. Washington, DC: The World Bank, OED.

Price, E., & Evans, C. (1989). *Alemaya University of Agriculture*. Washington, DC: USAID.

Price, E. C. (2006). *Thirty Years of Title XII: Presentation to BIFAD, October 18, 2006*. Texas: A&M University.

Psacharopoulos, G. (1994). Returns to investment in education: A global update. *World Development, 22*(9), 1325–1343.

Radetzki, M. (1991). Swedish aid to Kenya and Tanzania: Its effect on rural development. In U. Lele (Ed.), *Aid to African Agriculture: Lessons from Two Decades of Donor's Experience* (pp. 232–277). Baltimore and London: The Johns Hopkins University Press.

Ranis, G., Stewart, F., et al. (2000). Economic growth and human development. *World Development, 28*(2), 197–219.

Roodman, D. (2004). *The anarchy of numbers: Aid, development and cross-country empirics*. Washington, DC: Center for Global Development.

Rosen, S. (1977). Human capital: A survey of empirical research. In R. Ehernberg (Ed.), *Research in Labor Economics*. Greenwich, CT: JAI Press.

Rosenberg, R. (2006). *Aid Effectiveness in Microfinance: Evaluating Microcredit Projects of the World Bank and the United Nations Development Programme*. Washington, DC: Consultative Group to Assist the Poor.

Rozelle, S., Jin, S., et al. (2003). Chapter 18. The impact of investments in agricultural research on total factor productivity in China. In R. E. Evenson, & D. Gollin (Ed.), *Crop Variety Improvement and its Effects on Productivity: The Impact of International Agricultural Research*. Wallingford, UK: CABI Publishers.

Ruttan, V. W. (1974–1975). Integrated rural development programs: A skeptical perspective. *International Development Review, XVII*(4), S1–S16.

Ruttan, V. W. (1984). Integrated rural development programs: A historical perspective. *World Development, 12*.

Ruttan, W. (1996). *United States Development Assistance Policy: The Domestic Politics of Foreign Economic Development*. Baltimore and London: The Johns Hopkins University Press.

Saleth, R. M., Nemara, R. E., et al. (2003). Dynamics of irrigation-poverty linkages in rural India: Analytical framework and empirical analysis. *Water Policy, 5*(5/6), 459–473.

Schultz, T. P. (1995). *Investment in Women's Capital*. Chicago: University of Chicago Press.

Schultz, T. W. (1964). *Transforming Traditional Agriculture*. New Haven: Yale University Press.

Serrano, L. (2003). Measurement error in schooling data: The OECD case. *Applied Economics Letters, 10*(2), 73–75.

Solow, R. M. (2001). Applying growth theory across countries. *The World Bank Economic Review, 15*(2), 283–289.

SPIA/CIMMYT. (2002). *Why has impact assessment not made more of a difference? International Conference on Impact of Agricultural Research and Development*. San Jose, Costa Rica: CIMMYT.

Steinberg, D. I., Clapp-Wincek, C., et al. (1983). *Irrigation and AID's Experience: A consideration based on evaluations*. Washington, DC: USAID.

Stovall, J., Herdt, R., et al. (2006). *External Evaluation Panel Five Year Technical review (2002–2007) of the Bean/Cowpea Collaborative Research Support Program (CRSP)*. East Lansing, MI: Michigan State University and USAID.

Suhariyanyto, K., Lusigi, A., et al. (2001). *Productivity growth and convergence in Asian and African agriculture*. In P. Lawrence, & C. Thirtle (Eds.), *Asia and Africa in Comparative Economic Perspective* (pp. 258–274). London: Palgrave.

Swindale, L., Barrett, I., et al. (1995). An Evaluation of the USAID and Universities Collaborative Research Support Programs. Washington DC: USAID.

Tansel, A. (1995). Return to investment in education in Middle Eastern and North Africa Countries. *Forum, 2*(2).

Theisen, G., Armstrong, G., et al. (1989). *Indonesia: The Bogor Institute of Agriculture*. Washington, DC: USAID.

Todaro, M. P. (1989). *Economic development in the Third World*. New York: Longman.

USAID. (1986). *Development Management in Africa: Context and Strategy: A Synthesis of Six Agricultural Projects*. Washington, DC: USAID.

Vawda, A., Moock, P., et al. (1999). *Economic Analysis of World Bank Education Projects and Project Outcomes*. Washington, DC: The World Bank.

Water Resources Management Group. (2004). *Water Resources Sector Strategy*. Washington, DC: The World Bank.

Welsch, D., Flora, J., et al. (1987). *Malawi: Bunda Agriculture College*. Washington, DC: USAID.

White, H. (1992). *The Macroeconomic Impact of Development Aid*. Washington, DC: The World Bank.

World Bank. (1975). *Rural Development Sector Policy Paper*. Washington, DC.

World Bank. (1993). *Water Resources Management: A World Bank Policy Paper*. Washington, DC: The World Bank.

World Bank. (2002). *Constructing Knowledge Societies: New Challenge for Tertiary Education*. Washington, DC: The World Bank.

World Bank Operations Evaluation Department. (1985). *Agricultural Research and Extension: An Evaluation of the World Bank's experience*. Washington, DC: The World Bank.

World Bank Operations Evaluation Department. (1988). *Rural Development: World Bank Experience, 1965–1986*. Washington, DC: The World Bank.

World Bank Operations Evaluation Department. (1992). *Agricultural Higher Education*. The World Bank.

World Bank Operations Evaluation Department. (1993). *Annual Review of Evaluation Results 1992*. Washington, DC: The World Bank.

World Bank Operations Evaluation Department. (1994). *Higher Education: The Lessons of Experience*. Washington, DC: The World Bank.

World Bank Operations Evaluation Department. (1995). *The World Bank and Irrigation*. Washington, DC: The World Bank.

World Bank Operations Evaluation Department. (1999). *Achievements and Problems in Development of National Agricultural Research*. Washington, DC: The World Bank.

CHAPTER 64

Plantations Agriculture[1]

Yujiro Hayami

National Graduate Institute of Policy Studies (GRIPS)

Contents

Abstract

Large plantations producing tropical cash crops based on hired labor represent a sharp contrast with small family farms, popularly called "peasants" in developing economies. The family farm is an old institution that has existed since time immemorial, but the plantation is a new institution introduced by Western colonialism for extracting tropical cash crops for export to home countries.

Large-scale operation of the plantation was necessary for internalizing gains from investment in infrastructure needed for opening vast tracts of unused lands. However, where the communities of indigenous smallholders had already been established, family farms proved to be equally or more efficient producers of tropical export crops using the family labor of low supervision costs, relative to plantations based on hired labor. This advantage of family farms rose as population density increased and rural infrastructure improved, whereas not only economic but also social drawbacks of the plantation system loomed. However, reforms aimed to break down plantations to the operation of smallholders by a government's coercive power could be disruptive and inefficient. A better approach might be to support the initiative of the private sector to reorganize the plantation system into a more decentralized system, such as the contract farming system in which an agribusiness enterprise manages the processing/marketing process and contracts with small growers on the assured supply of farm-produced raw materials.

JFL classification: D23, O13, P42, N50, Q13

Handbook of Agricultural Economics, Volume 4
doi: 10.1016/S1574-0072(09)04064-X

Keywords

Plantations versus peasants
colonialism
trade
vent for surplus
contract farming

1. INTRODUCTION

Plantations in the tropics, employing a large number of laborers under the command of centralized management hierarchy for the production of tropical cash crops for commercial sales, represent a unique organization in agriculture. They are unique in contrast with small farms based mainly on family labor, which are the common form of agricultural production in the world, including both temperate and tropical areas, with respect to subsistence crops such as rice, wheat, and maize. How has this organization emerged in the tropics? What roles has it played until present and might it play in the future? These are the questions addressed in this chapter.

According to a broad definition by William Jones (1968, p. 154), the plantation is "an economic unit producing agricultural commodities (field crops or horticultural products, but not livestock) for sale and employing a relatively large number off unskilled laborers whose activities are closely supervised." This definition can include estate farms based on forced labor, such as slavery, corvee, and serf, instead of free wage labor and may also be called plantations. These estates based on forced labor were established typically before the onset of the industrial revolution in Europe and North America, having major impacts on the southern United States and Latin America, including the Caribbean as well as Eastern Europe (such as the Junker estates in Prussia). Despite their great historical interests, these estate farms based on forced labor are not included in this review. The plantations dealt with in this chapter are those based on free wage labor, which were typically established in tropical Asia and Africa after the mid-19th century. From the beginning their operation was based on wage laborers, though many laborers were imported from densely populated economies such as China and India under long-term contracts, often tied by credit, akin to debt peonage.

Following this introduction, Section 2 outlines advantages of family farms under the specific environmental and technical conditions specific to agricultural production, to understand why plantations remain rather an exceptional organization in agriculture relative to family farms. Section 3 explains the unique advantage of the plantation system at the stage of opening new lands for cultivation of crops corresponding to the sudden expansion of external demand. Section 4 specifies the tendency of the plantation system to lose its advantage in the process of closing land frontiers, increasing population density, and improving rural infrastructure. Finally, Section 5 tries to identify the direction of reorganizing plantations to better serve the purpose of rural development in tropical developing economies.

2. FAMILY FARMS VERSUS PLANTATIONS

The nature and the role of plantations can best be understood through comparisons with family farms. The family farm is defined here as the farm production unit operated mainly by the operator's and his or her family members' labor. This characteristic makes the actual tillers of soil the "residual claimants" in family farms, whereas laborers tilling the soil of plantations usually have no claim on the residual profit that is defined as output minus paid-out costs. The family farm in this definition can be very large in terms of its operational land holding in high-income economies, since a farm of several hundred hectares can easily be cultivated by one or two family members with the use of modern labor-saving machinery. However, family farms in low-income economies in the tropics, where plantations are commonly observed, are typically small—on the order of a few hectares to even less than 1 hectare—corresponding to the low market wage rate that represents the major determinant of the farm operator's reservation utility. Their production is usually oriented toward subsistence of family members, being characterized by low marketable surplus ratios.

A traditional paradigm, developed under colonialism, was to identify the plantations as modern enclaves geared for the international market, with family farms, or "peasants," dominated by subsistence orientation and irresponsive to profit incentives created by changes in market demands and technology (Furnivall, 1944; Boeke, 1953). This stereotyped view was demolished by three great development economists, Theodore W. Schultz (1964), Hla Myint (1965), and W. Arthur Lewis (1970). Schultz convincingly argued that small farmers in traditional agriculture are rational and efficient in resource allocation and that they remain poor not because they are irresponsive to economic incentives but because only limited technical and market opportunities are available to which they can respond. Myint, drawing on the experience of Southeast Asia, demonstrated how they responded vigorously to market incentives in opening new lands for the production of export cash crops. Lewis found this observation for Southeast Asia to be no exception in tropical development worldwide from the late 19th to the early 20th centuries.

The modern theory of economic organization and contract (e.g., Hayami and Otsuka, 1993) dictates that the advantage of family farms lies in their predominant reliance on family workers who have the strong incentive to elicit conscientious work efforts for the sake of their own families' well-being, in contrast to hired wage workers who are inclined to shirk in the absence of supervision. This advantage applies to not only farm but also nonfarm family enterprises, but it is especially pronounced in agricultural production. Agricultural production is characterized by inherent difficulties in enforcing contracts with hired labor. In urban industries, work is standardized and relatively easy to monitor. The biological process of agricultural production, however, is subject to infinite ecological variations. Different ways of handling crops or animals are often required for even slight differences in temperature and soil moisture. The dispersal of agricultural operations over wide areas adds to the difficulty of monitoring. This difficulty multiplies as the farming system becomes more complex, involving more intensive crop care, crop rotations, and crop-livestock combinations:

> **In areas more suitable for multiple enterprise farms, family operations have had the advantage. Increasing the enterprises so multiplies the number of on-the-spot supervisory management decisions per acre that the total acreage which a unit of management can oversee quickly approaches the acreage which an ordinary family can operate. (Brewster, 1950, p. 71)**

In fact, large plantations based on hired labor are limited largely to monoculture.

This constraint of managerial ability and family labor on operational farm size is exacerbated by the danger of reckless use of draft animals and machines by nonfamily operators that results in capital loss. Therefore,

> **a landless person with a family who owns animals and/or machines and possesses some managerial skill will find it more profitable to rent in land than to hire out his endowments separately. Similarly, a large landowner will find it more profitable to rent out land than to manage a large operation because of scale diseconomies arising from the use of hired workers. (Binswanger and Rosenzweig, 1986, p. 524)**

In other words, technological-scale economies arising from the use of indivisible inputs such as managerial ability and animals/machines are counterbalanced by scale diseconomies from the use of hired labor, so the nuclear family farm is usually the most effective, except for some plantation crops that need close coordination with large-scale processing and marketing.

Another major advantage of family farm operations is the ability to utilize the low-opportunity-cost labor of women, children, and aged family members who have little employment opportunity outside their own farms.

These advantages underlie the dominance of family farms in agriculture worldwide. In fact, family farms are the dominant form of agricultural production, not only in developing economies but also in developed economies, including North America and Western Europe (Hayami, 1996). In the United States, for example, the operational holdings of commercial farms are typically as large as several hundreds to thousands of hectares. Still, the majority of them base core farm operations mainly on family labor, though supplemented by hired labor to some extent or another. The farms primarily dependent on teams of hired laborers organized under the command of central management, akin to tropical plantations, are rather exceptional, being limited to such special enterprises as large-scale commercial vegetable production, cattle ranches, and feed-lot operations existing in rather limited areas such as California and Texas.

Superiority of the family farm as a production organization in agriculture has further been attested to by two major developments since World War II. The first was the disastrous failures of collective farming in socialist economies, followed by the experience in China of achieving a major boost in agricultural production by the transition from collective farming under the people's communes to family farming under the so-called household responsibility system (Lin, 1988, 1922). The second saw repeated failures in the attempt to develop large farms as either private or state enterprises (Eicker and Baker, 1992; Johnson and Ruttan, 1994). Concurrently, the high potential of "peasants" to adopt new, profitable technologies and achieve economic growth was amply proven by the successful diffusion of modern, high-yielding varieties and related inputs—the so-called Green Revolution in Asia.

3. CONDITIONS OF THE PLANTATION SYSTEM

Considering the unique advantage of family farms in agricultural production, why has it been necessary to introduce the plantation system?

3.1 Scale economies in production

A conventional explanation for this question is to assume the existence of scale economies inherent in the production of tropical export crops, in contrast to the absence of scale economies in temperate crops such as wheat (Baldwin, 1956). However, the crops subject to sufficiently strong scale economies at the farm production level to make the use of the plantation system necessary are few (Pim 1946; Wickizer 1951, 1960; Lim, 1968; Hayami, Quisumbing, and Adriano, 1990).[2] In fact, one can find an example of every so-called plantation crop being grown successfully by family farms somewhere in the world.

Significant increasing returns emerge only at the levels of processing and marketing activities. The vertical integration of a large estate farm with a large-scale central processing and/or marketing system is called for because of the need to supply farm-produced raw materials in a timely schedule. This need is known to be strong for the processing of such products as palm oil, sisal, and tea. Comparison of processing tea leaves between fermented black tea and unfermented green tea is especially illuminating on this problem. The manufacturing of black tea at a standardized quality for export requires a modern fermentation plant into which fresh leaves must be fed within a few hours after plucking (Wickizer, 1951, 1960). The need for close coordination between farm production and large-scale processing underlies the traditional use of the plantation system for black-tea production. Unfermented green tea, in contrast, remains predominantly the product of family farms in China and Japan.[3]

In the case of bananas for export, harvested fruits must be packed, sent to the wharf, and loaded on a refrigerated boat within a day. One full boat of bananas that can meet the quality standard of foreign buyers must be collected within a few days. Therefore, the whole production process, from planting to harvesting, must be precisely controlled so as to meet the shipment schedule. Thus the plantation system has a decisive advantage for bananas for export, but not for bananas for domestic consumption, so that they are usually produced on family farms.

On the other hand, for the crops for which centralized processing and marketing are not necessary, plantations have no significant advantage over family farms. Typical examples are cocoa and coconuts. The fermentation of cocoa and the drying and smoking of coconuts to make copra can be handled in small lots with no large capital requirement beyond small indigenous tools and facilities. These crops are grown predominantly on family farms.

Sugar is frequently cited as a classic case of scale economies stemming from the need for coordination between farm production and large-scale central processing (Binswanger and Rozenweig, 1986). Efficient operation of a centrifugal sugar mill requires the steady supply of a large amount of cane over time. Coordination of production from planting to harvesting with processing is required. This coordination, however, need not be as stringent as it is for tea and bananas. The rate of sugar extraction decreases as the processing of cane is delayed, but this loss is in no way comparable to the devastating damage to the quality of tea and bananas for export that can result from delayed processing. Sugar cane can be hauled from relatively long distances and stored for several days. Therefore, the need for vertical integration is not as large, and the necessary coordination can be achieved through contracts of a sugar mill with cane growers on the time and the quota of cane delivery. In fact, an efficient sugar industry has developed with smallholders in Australia, Taiwan, and, more recently, in Thailand.

Another explanation for the use of the plantation system is the advantage of large estate farms in accessing capital. For this reason, it has been argued that plantations have an advantage with regard to tree crops characterized by long gestation periods from planting to maturity (Binswanger and Rosenzweig, 1986). However, the opportunity costs of labor and capital applied to formation of the tree capital are not necessarily high for peasants. Typically, they plant the trees in hitherto unused land. If such land is located near their residence, they open new land for planting by means of family labor at low opportunity cost during the idle season for the production of food crops on farmland already in use. When they migrate to frontier areas, a typical process is to slash and burn jungles and to plant subsistence crops such as maize, potatoes, and upland rice, together with tree seedlings (Hayami, 1996b). Such a complex intercropping system is difficult to manage with hired labor in the plantation system due to inherent difficulty in monitoring the work of hired wage laborers over spatially dispersed and ecologically variable farm operations (Brewster, 1950; Binswanger and Rosenzweig, 1986; Hayami and Otsuka, 1993).

3.2 Internalization of investments in infrastructure

Therefore, even in the export boom of tropical cash crops under colonialism from the 19th to the early 20th centuries, the plantation system failed to make inroads in regions where indigenous populations had established family farms (Lewis, 1970, pp. 13–45). Western traders found it more profitable to purchase tropical agricultural commodities from peasant producers in exchange for imported manufactured commodities than to produce the tropical crops themselves by means of the plantation system.

The establishment of plantations in less developed economies became a necessity when the industrialized nations' demand for tropical products continued to rise, whereas the regions physically suited for the production of these products had no significant peasant population that could produce and trade their commodities. Opening frontier land for the production of new crops entailed high capital outlays. Virgin land had to be cleared and developed, and physical infrastructure, such as roads, irrigation systems, bridges, and docking facilities, had to be constructed. Capital, in the form of machinery and equipment, had to be imported and redesigned to adapt to local situations. Laborers were not only imported from the more populous regions but also had to be trained in the production of these crops.

The establishment of plantations thus requires huge initial capital investment. For the investors to internalize gains from investment in infrastructure, the farm size inevitably must be large. Viewed from this perspective, it follows that the plantation system evolved not because it was generally a more efficient mode of productive organization than the peasant mode. Instead, the system was adopted because it was the most effective type of agricultural organization for extracting the economic benefit accruing from the exploitation of sparsely populated virgin areas, typically in the development process based on the exploitation of unused natural resources, which Myint (1965) called "the vent-for-surplus development." From this perspective, it is easy to understand why the same crop is grown mainly by family farms in one place and mainly by plantations in another. For example, for sugar cane production the family farm system is more common in old settled areas of Luzon, and the plantation system predominates in the newly opened Negros, both in the Philippines (Hayami, Quisumbing, and Adriano, 1990, Ch. 5). Usually the share of family farms in the production of export cash crops rises as the initial land-opening stage is over and infrastructure is decently established with increased population density (Booth, 1988, Ch. 6).

3.3 Preemption of frontier lands

Although recognizing the economic advantage of the plantation system at the vent-for-surplus stage, plantations could not have been established unless concessions were granted to planters holding large tracts of virgin land for their exclusive use. Colonial governments gave these concessions to Western planters, typically under British rule in such places as the highlands of Kenya and Sri Lanka. In Indonesia, the Dutch colonial government had traditionally tried to prevent alienation of farmland for rice production from indigenous peasants by regulating against land purchase by foreigners, including ethnic Chinese. However, in the late 19th century, when demands for tropical cash crops rose sharply, by the Agricultural Land Law of 1870 the government granted Dutch planters had long-term contracts to lease wild lands in upland areas, which were *de jure* owned by the government (though *de facto* used by native tribes). This new institutional arrangement should have accelerated the development of "empty land" for cash crop production, but it served as an instrument to preempt land for the elite, closing smallholders' land access (Pelzer, 1945; Hayami and Kikuchi, 1981, 2000). Similar public land-leasing arrangements were also practiced under the U.S. colonial administration in frontier land of the Philippines, especially in Mindanao, which became the basis of large plantations in bananas and pineapples under the management of multinational corporations (Hayami, Quisumbing, and Adriano, 1990, Ch. 6).

3.4 Reinforcing conditions

To reiterate, the plantation system tends to be adopted, despite its high cost of labor management, where: (1) close coordination between farm-level production and large-scale processing/marketing facilities is required for certain crops, (2) basic infrastructure is absent in the land-opening stage so that the large-scale production unit is needed for internalizing the gain from its supply of infrastructure, and (3) concessions on the use of large tracts of virgin land are granted for exclusive use by certain power elite, such as Western planters during the colonial period. Historically, it was common to observe these conditions reinforcing each other to result in the domination of the plantation system in some specific areas for specific crops, outside which the family farm tends to dominate. Absence of one of the three conditions can prevent the plantation system from emerging, even if other conditions are met.

For example, unlike Indonesia, Malaysia, and Vietnam, where rubber plantations were developed under the colonial government policy to grant concessions of frontier lands to white planters, rubber production in independent Thailand has been held solely in the hands of smallholders.

On the other hand, even where land preemption occurred, the plantation system did not necessary emerge. An example can also be found in the history of Thailand. In the late 19th century, when the delta of the Chao Praya River opened for rice production, the government of the Siam Kingdom gave concessions on large tracts of unused land to canal-building companies, resulting in the emergence of large private ownership of rice land. The large landowners in the delta, however, did not attempt to establish rice plantations. Instead, they leased out their land in small parcels to smallholders who migrated from outside the newly opened delta, resulting in the pervasive establishment of small family farms under tenancy (Hayami, 2001a). Why was the family farm, instead of the plantation system, established in the new land-opening stage under the policy of land preemption to wealthy canal builders? The reason could partly be the difficulty of standardizing tasks in rice production and, hence, of monitoring the efforts of farm workers. However, the more decisive reason appears to be that paddies are storable and hence the need of close coordination between farm production and processing/marketing is not necessary, unlike the cases of black tea and bananas for export, as explained before. Although rice milling and marketing for export involved significant scale economies, the operators of this business could secure adequate supply of paddies through ordinary market transactions. As a result, they were dispensed with efforts to vertically integrate farm production with processing and marketing by means of the plantation system. Therefore, it should not be unreasonable to postulate the counterfactual hypothesis that, if the nature of rice milling technology were such as to require close coordination with paddy production, large rice plantations would have been established in the Rangsit area, where canals were extensively built by private companies.

The experience of Thailand—that the preemption of frontier lands by the power elite did not give rise to the plantation system but the traditional family farm system was maintained under tenancy arrangements—was shared in common with the development of the Irrawaddy Delta in Myanmar and the Mekong Delta in Vietnam as well as the inland area of Luzon in the Philippines in the late 19th century.

4. DECLINING ROLES OF PLANTATIONS

The previous section explained that the efficiency of the plantation relative to the family farm system was high in the initial opening-up process of land-abundant and labor-scarce economies. However, several negative aspects of plantations become significant as tropical economies shifted from the land-abundant to the land-scarce stage after the completion of the opening-up process.

4.1 Increasing drawbacks

First, the plantation system tends to substitute capital for labor because of the inherent difficulty in supervising wage laborers in spatially dispersed and ecologically diverse farm operations as well as their relatively easy access to both private credit markets and government's concessional loans. This substitution becomes socially inefficient in many developing economies, when labor becomes more abundant relative to capital.

Second, agricultural land tends to be cultivated less intensively under the plantation system, which employs mainly wage labor and usually practices monoculture. Complicated intercropping and crop-livestock combinations are more difficult to manage in the command system, implying that both labor input and income per hectare are lower in plantations.[4] This is a source of inefficiency in the plantation system, where land becomes scarce relative to labor under the pressure of population growth. In contrast, small family farms tend to cultivate land more intensively.

Third, plantations usually specialize in a single crop. This bias for the practice of monoculture reduces the flexibility of these productive organizations to respond to changing demand by shifting to the production of other crops. Moreover, continual cropping of a single crop tends to result in soil degradation and an increase in pest incidence. Counter-application of fertilizer and chemicals causes serious stress on environment and human health, incurring high social costs.

Fourth, the specialization of plantation workers in specific tasks inhibits the development of their managerial and entrepreneurial capacity (Baldwin, 1956; Myint, 1965; Beckford, 1972, Hayami, 1996a).

Fifth, the plantation system is a source of class conflict between laborers and managers/capitalists. The presence of a plantation enclave in rural economies where the peasant mode of production predominates has often strained relationships in rural communities through such incidents as pollution with pesticides used by a plantation over surrounding smallholders. In terms of the criterion of social stability, therefore, the plantation system is no match for the system of relatively homogeneous small producers owning small assets, however small they might be.

Overall, whether the net contribution of the plantation system is positive or negative depends on the population density of the region, the development of public infrastructure, the nature of the crop produced, and the quality of management employed in plantations. It is, however, inevitable that the negative impacts of the plantation system tend to outweigh its positive contributions as population increases in once sparsely populated regions and as unused lands become scarce.

4.2 Some evidence from Southeast Asia

As an illustration of this declining efficiency of the plantation relative to the family farm system, recent changes in the competitive position in the world market of agriculture in Thailand are compared with those of Indonesia and the Philippines. These three economies in Southeast Asia were traditionally endowed with relatively abundant land resources, which were exploited for export crop production in the late 19th to the early 20th centuries along the so-called "vent-for-surplus theory" put forth by Hla Myint (1965). In this process the plantation system became dominant in the production of export cash crops in colonized Indonesia and the Philippines (as well as neighboring colonized economies), whereas the family farm continued to be dominant in independent Thailand.[5] Thus, changes in the advantage of plantations relative to family farms are likely to reflect the differential performances in the exports of agricultural commodities across these economies.

For properly assessing the effects of production organizations, however, ecological differences must be clearly understood between (1) the continental part of Southeast

Asia, including Thailand, and (2) the insular and peninsular part, including Indonesia and the Philippines. The former was characterized by, among other things, major river deltas and the latter by tropical rain forests. Before the 1860s, when new transportation technology integrated this region with the rapidly industrializing West, major deltas and thick rainforests were then largely unused for agricultural production. When Southeast Asia faced growing demands from the West for tropical products, the deltas were converted into paddy fields for commercial rice production. In contrast, the rainforests were converted to plantations for tropical cash crops, though lowland coastal plains and valleys continued to be cultivated by subsistence-oriented peasants.[6]

In terms of both environmental conditions and relative resource endowments, traditional comparative advantage in agricultural production of Thailand lay in rice and that of Indonesia and the Philippines lay in tropical cash crops. It is, therefore, no surprise to find that Thailand was a major rice exporter (the world's largest today) with its world market share continuing to rise in the past half-century. On the other hand, Indonesia and the Philippines remained net importers. However, it is important to notice that their import margins were significantly reduced, reflecting much faster growth in rice output over domestic consumption, despite rapid increases in population. The high performances in rice production in Southeast Asia reflect the strengthened competitive position of family farms in this region. Their success owed much to public investments in development and diffusion of modern rice varieties, improvements in irrigation systems, and fertilizer supply conditions that together brought about the so-called Green Revolution. This experience represents a strong evidence for the very high production potential of family farms that can be realized with adequate public investments in infrastructure, such as research and irrigation systems.

Surprising is the rise of Thailand as the exporter of several tropical cash crops associated with the decline of Indonesia and, more conspicuously, that of the Philippines. Sugar represents a typical example. Thailand was a net importer of sugar before World War II and was barely self-sufficient in the early 1960s. Nevertheless, Thailand rose to be the third largest exporter in the world next to Brazil and Australia in the 1990s. In contrast, Indonesia and the Philippines, two traditional exporters of sugar in Asia, almost completely lost their significance in the world sugar market. Also, Thailand exceeded Indonesia in the export of rubber and exceeded the Philippines in the export of pineapple products by the 1990s. Note that pineapples for processing are produced by large plantations in the Philippines and a significant share of rubber is produced in plantations in Indonesia. On the other hand, both of these two crops as well as sugar cane are almost exclusively grown on family farms in Thailand. Indonesia was able to achieve a major increase in the world market share of coffee and cocoa, but these crops were predominantly grown by smallholders in Indonesia (Akiyama and Nishio, 1996). These data seem to reflect increases in the advantage of family farms over plantations in the production of cash crops.

Of course, the quality of management greatly matters in terms of the efficiency of plantation operations. Compared with Indonesia and the Philippines, the plantation sector in Malaysia has been able to maintain or even increase the traditional comparative advantage in tree crops, as reflected in the sharp increase in its world market share of palm oil. The rise of Malaysia to become the dominant supplier of palm oil, through efficient conversion of rubber to oil palm estates, has been supported by the high entrepreneurship of private planters in managing their own estates as well as their ability to organize cooperative research on plantation crops since the colonial period. Vital for this success has been the preservation of private ownership and management of plantations, including those based on foreign capital, after Malaysia achieved independence.

In contrast, the plantation sector in post-independence Indonesia that expropriated the estates of Dutch planters seems to have suffered from inefficiency common to state enterprises. Several attempts to cure this problem include the "nuclear estate" scheme by which a state plantation acts as a marketing/processing center with a demonstration farm for technical extension, along which smallholders are organized in a manner similar to contract farming. These attempts have often been marred by the direct application of plantations' technology and practice, without due understanding of smallholders' conditions (Barlow and Tomich, 1991; Hayami, 1996b).

Although a large room should still exist for improving the competitive position of plantations, it seems rather reasonable to hypothesize that Thailand's remarkable success in increasing the world shares of its agricultural product exports in recent years has been based to a significant extent on the rise of efficiency in the family farm over the plantation system, corresponding to increases in population density and improvements in infrastructure. Of course, there were factors other than the production organization that supported agricultural growth in Thailand. Critically important were rapid land opening, especially in the Northeast, associated with major improvements in roads and highways. However, these factors cannot fully explain why Indonesia performed less well than Thailand, despite its large open frontiers in the Outer Islands and remarkable improvements in communication and transportation infrastructure under the Suharto regime. It seems reasonable to interpret that the improvements of infrastructure increased the advantage of the family farm over the plantation system, thereby causing Thailand to surpass Indonesia in the exploitation of available land frontiers for cash crop production.

Also, since the early the 1970s, the Philippines has been losing out in world competition in most of the tropical cash crops, not only because of growing inefficiency of the plantation system but also because of the government's trade monopoly during the regime of President Marcos (Bautista, 1987; Intal and Power, 1989) and of the negative incentive of land reform programs on planters, which is discussed later. In contrast, liberal trade and foreign direct investment policies adopted in Thailand since the 1970s, together with public investment on transportation and communication systems, have resulted in significant improvements in agricultural product and input markets, on which peasants have been able to stand in global competition (Warr, 1993).

5. PROSPECT FOR PLANTATIONS

In view of the increasing disadvantage of plantations relative to family farms as tropical economies shift from the land-abundant to the land-scarce stage, what kind of reorganization might be called for?

5.1 Via redistributive land reform

One possible route could be to apply redistributive land reform to the plantation sector such that the government confiscates private plantations and subdivides each into small units for the cultivation of family farms. Such a reform has had a strong popular appeal in view of plantations becoming the major source of inequality and class conflicts in the rural sector, as discussed in the previous section.

However, apart from the political difficulty of violating private property rights inherent to redistributive land reform of any kind, administrative and technical difficulties involved in its application to the plantation sector are especially large. Despite strong advocacy voiced for land reform since the end of World War II, its success has been very rare, and the rare success cases have been limited to the transfer of land ownership from landlords to tenants (in addition to the reduction of land rents). In the economies where the landlord/tenant relation predominates, it is easy to identify who should be the beneficiaries of land reform—a tenant who used to cultivate a certain land parcel leased from a landlord before reform is unambiguous to receive the ownership of that land parcel. Since this beneficiary had the experience of managing cultivation of the land using his family labor and his own capital (such as farm instruments and draft animals), no major disruption in production is expected to occur from the transfer of ownership.

In contrast, in the case of plantations, it is difficult to identify who should receive the title of which land parcel. Plantation workers typically work by group and by task over the territory of a plantation, and no individual worker continues to cultivate a certain land plot over a crop season, unlike the case of tenant farmers. Moreover, the question would arise: Who among the employees is entitled to share the land ownership? Should beneficiaries be limited to field workers? Is it fair to exclude truck drivers or mechanics in processing plants within the same plantation? How about clerks and accountants? Even if the ownership of a land parcel is transferred to an employee in any category, the time and cost to train him to be a manager of his own farm plus purchase (or lease) the minimum amount of capital goods for his independent operation will be quite large.

Confronted with such obvious difficulties, the application of redistributive land reform to plantations will almost inevitably create major disruptions in production. Indeed, successful application of distributive land reform has been limited mainly to the food-crop sector consisting of family farms in Asia in such economies as Japan, Korea, and Taiwan, where plantations are virtually absent.[7] Attempts in Latin America to apply the redistributive land reform to large estates using workers hired on wages or labor dues for subsistence plots (hacienda) have largely resulted in disastrous consequences (de Janvry and Sadoulet, 1989). It is feared that some attempts in Africa, such as those happening in Zimbabwe, might prove more devastating.

A recent attempt in the Philippines is illustrative of the difficulty of applying redistributive land reform to the plantation sector. Following to the success of land reform in the rice sector in the 1970s, the Philippine government tried to extend the reform to the cash crop sector, including plantations, by the Comprehensive Agrarian Reform Law of 1988. However, this law has not been significantly implemented, obviously because of the difficulties we have mentioned. Nevertheless, fear has prevailed among plantation owners about eventual expropriation of their land. It is only natural that they have stopped investing to improve their land infrastructure, including planting/replanting of trees. Some landowners have even preferred to keep their land idle rather than use it for agricultural production. It should be reasonable to hypothesize that the poor performance of Philippine agriculture in competition for world export markets, as discussed in the previous section, was, to a large extent, rooted in this great uncertainty on the part of the planters of tropical cash crops concerning the future course of land reform.

5.2 Via contract farming

It appears that the reorganization of plantations to a more efficient form could better be induced under the initiative of private entrepreneurs rather than based on the government's coercive measures. The design of a new structure attractive to private business must be based on a clear understanding of the pros and cons of the plantation versus the peasant system. To recapitulate, the advantage of the family farm system is the high work incentive and the low cost of enforcing family labor so that family farms are capable of managing complicated crop rotation and crop-livestock combination by making productive use of low-opportunity-cost labor on scarce land. The advantage of the plantation system consists of (1) the low transaction costs associated with the supply of farm-produced materials to central processing and/or marketing characterized by scale economies, (2) internalization of external effects such as provision of public infrastructure and prevention of contagious pest and disease, and (3) low credit costs.

These advantages of the two systems can be combined in the so-called "contract farming" system in which an agribusiness enterprise manages the processing/marketing process and contracts with small growers on the assured supply of farm-produced raw materials. The contract may include stipulations not only on the time and quantity of material supply but also on prices, credit, and technical extension services.[8]

However, a high degree of entrepreneurship and managerial skill is required to organize and operate an efficient contract farming system, because it is not easy to enforce contracts with a large number of smallholders concerning the quantity, quality, and time of their product delivery to processing plants and/or marketing centers.

Insufficient ability and effort of agribusiness firms in this regard have often resulted in the failure in the operation of contract farming. Thus, the performance of contract farming has so far been mixed, even in Thailand (Siamwalla, 1992). The same applies to other areas, including Africa, where it is reported that contract farming organized by government agencies is usually inefficient (Jaffe and Morton, 1995, pp. 94–107).

A gradual reorganization of the existing plantation system into an efficient contract-farming system should be feasible, though difficult, if the high management capability of agribusiness, including multinational corporations, can be mobilized for this endeavor. Policies are needed to direct plantation management efforts toward such reorganization, which can include: (1) gradual phasing out of special treatments to plantations, such as public land leases at favorable terms and special allocation of import and foreign exchange licenses, (2) more strict enforcement of land taxation on the ownership of large farm estates, and (3) more strict application of labor and environment codes to corporate farms. At the same time, government must invest in education, research, and extension for developing the capability of small growers to operate effectively under the contract-farming scheme.

Another approach might be to encourage the organization of cooperatives for processing and marketing. Inefficiency in organizing farm production by cooperatives has been amply illustrated by the experiments of centrally planned as well as some market economies. On the other hand, examples of successful cooperatives in organizing agricultural product marketing and processing are not rare—for example, horticultural marketing cooperatives in the Netherlands and cooperative creameries in Denmark (Hayami and Ruttan, 1985, pp. 429–32). The best services of marketing and processing will be provided to both consumers and farm producers in an environment in which cooperatives and private marketing agents compete with each other and among themselves. Their services are bound to degenerate if monopoly is granted to the cooperatives, as demonstrated by the Japanese experience (Hayami, 1988).

5.3 Toward revitalization of the plantation sector

Plantations have been and will continue to be an important sector in the tropics; however, rapid agrarian reorganization may proceed. Although negative aspects of plantations have been looming larger over time, government's direct controls on their operations will likely prove damaging to both national economic development and the well-being of rural people. The entrepreneurship and management capability of agribusiness enterprises, including multinational corporations, in the area of agricultural marketing and processing are very valuable inputs that developing economies cannot afford to lose in many years to come. The rational approach, therefore, should be to design an inducement mechanism toward an agrarian organization that might be able to combine the merits of both the family farm and the plantation systems. Also, it must not be forgotten that a large room still exists to increase the efficiency of plantation management through privatization and deregulation as well as improvements in corporate governance. Revitalization of the plantation sector should be incorporated as an indispensable component in the rural development strategy in the tropics, even though its role will likely continue declining relative to the family farm sector.

End Notes

1. This chapter develops a synthesis of my ideas on this theme, which have been advanced in several earlier publications (Hayami, 1994, 1996, 2001a, 2001b, 2002).
2. Absence of scale economies in agriculture in developing economies in general is also attested to by the estimation of aggregate production functions based on intercountry cross-sectional data (Hayami and Ruttan, 1985, Ch. 5).
3. Even for the manufacture of black tea it is not imperative to use the plantation system, as is evident from the case of Taiwan, where smallholders have been used to produce both black and green tea with small-scale equipment. Plantations have used the large fermentation plant as a device for enforcing work schedules and standardizing product quality for the export market. In fact, farm production by smallholders based on the system of "contract farming" (explained in Section 5) has recently been developing in Kenya (Lamb and Muller, 1982).
4. Official statistics often record that yields per hectare of cash crops such as coffee and rubber are higher in plantations than in smallholders. However, these statistics do not take into account various products intercropped with principal cash crops by smallholders, whereas monoculture is the common practice of plantations.
5. Unlike Indonesia and the Philippines, where the large-scale preemption of frontier lands was carried out by the colonial governments, the land preemption in Thailand was relatively minor. Except for certain areas in the Chao Praya Delta, where land concessions were given to canal builders, frontier lands in Thailand were open for native peasants to settle in. The traditional custom—to give every man the right of taking as much as wild land from the state as he and his family could cultivate—was maintained, and the right of receiving title on the land after continued cultivation for three years was maintained even after Thailand opened trade with Western nations (Hayami, 2001a).
6. Agrarian structures are not homogeneous within each of the two major regions in Southeast Asia but differ across various areas within each region, corresponding to different crops with different technological characteristics grown under different ecological conditions as well as different social and political histories (Pelzer, 1945; Furnivall, 1948; Mclennan, 1969; Ingram, 1971; Feeny, 1982; Hayami and Kikuchi, 1981; Hayami, 2001).
7. Of course, factors other than agrarian structures underlay the success of land reform in these three economies in Northeast Asia. Among others, the pressure of the Allied Occupation Forces in Japan, the motivation of Kuomintang to survive in Taiwan, and the confrontation of South Korea against North Korea had decisive influences. For other factors, see Hayami and Yamada (1991, pp. 83–85).
8. Possible incorporation of credit provision in the contract farming system includes not only cash credits but also in-kind credits in the form of supply of inputs to farmers during the crop-growing season before harvest, akin to the "putting-out system" in manufacturing. In this contract the cost of inputs is usually deducted from the payment for the delivery of products. This practice, which is commonly called "credit tying," is often used by traders/processors as a means of enforcing farm producers to fulfill their contractual obligations, such as the timely delivery of products satisfying a certain quality standard, while it increases farmers' access to credits, especially for those possessing no assets usable for collateral. The empirical evidence of this practice being used as an instrument for traders/processors to exploit small farmers is not very strong (Hayami and Kawagoe, 1993).

References

Akiyama, T., & Nishio, A. (1996). *Indonesia's Cocoa Boom: Hands-Off Policy Encourages Smallholder Dynamism*. Washington, DC: Policy Research Working Paper 1580, The World Bank.

Baldwin, R. E. (1956). Patterns of Development in Newly Settled Regions. *Manchester School of Economics and Social Studies*, *24*(May), 161–179.

Bardhan, P. (1993). Symposium on Management of Local Commons. *Journal of Economic Perspectives*, *7*(Autumn), 87–92.

Barlow, C., & Tomich, T. P. (1991). Indonesian Agricultural Development: The Awkward Case of Smallholder Tree Crops. *Bulletin of Indonesian Economic Studies*, *27*(Dec.), 29–53.

Bautista, R. M. (1987). *Production Incentive in Philippine Agriculture: Effects of Trade and Exchange Rate Policies*. Washington, DC: International Food Policy Research Institute.

Beckford, G. L. (1972). *Persistent Poverty: Underdevelopment in Plantation Economies in the Third World*. New York: Oxford University Press.

Binswanger, H. P., & Rosenzweig, M. R. (1986). Behavioral and Material Determinants of Production Relations in Agriculture. *Journal of Development Studies*, *22–23*(April), 503–539.

Boeke, S. (1953). *Economics and Economic Policy of Dual Society as Exemplified by Indonesia*. New York: Institute of Pacific Relations.

Booth, A. (1988). *Agricultural Development in Indonesia*. Sydney: Allen & Unwin.

Brewster, M. (1950). The Machine Process in Agriculture and Industry. *Journal of Farm Economics*, *32*(February), 69–81.

de Janvry, A., & Sadoulet, E. (1989). A Study in Resistance to Institutional Change: The Lost Game of Latin America. *World Development*, *17*, 1397–1407.

Eicker, C., & Baker, D. C. (1992). Research on Agricultural Development in Sub-Saharan Africa: Critical Survey. In L. Martin (Ed.), *Survey of Agricultural Economics Literature, Vol. 4, Agriculture in Economic Development* (pp. 3–328).

Feeny, D. (1982). *The Political Economy of Agricultural Productivity: Thai Agricultural Development, 1880–1975*. Vancouver: University of British Colombia Press.

Furnivall, J. S. (1944). *Netherlands India: A Study of Plural Economy*. Cambridge, UK: Cambridge University Press.

Furnivall, J. S. (1948). *Colonial Policy and Practice: A Comparative Study of Burma and Netherlands India*. Cambridge, UK: Cambridge University Press.

Hayami, Y. (1988). *Japanese Agriculture under Siege*. London: Macmillan.

Hayami, Y. (1994). Peasant and Plantation in Asia. In G. M. Meier (Ed.), *From Classical Economics to Development Economics*. New York: St Martin's Press.

Hayami, Y. (1996a). The Peasant in Economic Modernization. *American Journal of Agricultural Economics*, *78*(December), 1157–1167.

Hayami, Y. (1996b). In Search of Modern Sustainable Agriculture: A View from Upland Agriculture. *Asian Journal of Agricultural Economics*, *2*(August), 1–10.

Hayami, Y. (2001a). Ecology, History, and Development: A perspective from Rural Southeast Asia. *World Bank Observer*, *16*(Fall), 169–198.

Hayami, Y. (2001b). *Development Economics: From the Poverty to the Wealth of Nations* (2nd ed.). Oxford: Oxford University Press.

Hayami, Y. (2002). Family Farms and Plantations in Tropical Development. *Asian Development Review*, *19*(2), 67–89.

Hayami, Y., & Kikuchi, M. (1981). *Asian Village Economy at the Crossroads*. Tokyo: University of Tokyo Press and Baltimore: Johns Hopkins University Press.

Hayami, Y., & Kikuchi, M. (2000). *A Rice Village Saga: Three Decades of Green Revolution in the Philippines*. London: Macmillan; New York: Barnes & Noble; Los Baños, Philippines: International Rice Research Institute.

Hayami, Y., & Otsuka, K. (1993). *The Economics of Contract Choice*. New York: St. Martin's Press.

Hayami, Y., & Ruttan, V. W. (1985). *Agricultural Development: An International Perspective* (Revised ed.). Baltimore: Johns Hopkins University Press.

Hayami, Y., Agnes Quisumbing, M. & Adriano, L. S. (1990). *Toward an Alternative L& Reform Paradigm: A Philippine Perspective*. Quezon City, Philippines: Ateneo de Manila University Press.

Hayami, Y., & Yamada, S. (1991). *The Agricultural Development of Japan: A Century's Perspective*. Tokyo: University Tokyo Press.

Ingram, J. C. (1971). *Economic Change in Thailand, 1850–1970*. Stanford: Stanford University Press.

Intal, P. S., Jr., & Power, J. H. (1989). *Trade, Exchange Rate, and Agricultural Pricing Policies in the Philippines*. Washington, DC: World Bank.

Johnson, N. R., & Ruttan, V. W. (1994). Why Are Farms So Small? *World Development*, *22*(May), 691–706.

Jones, W. O. (1968). Plantations. In *International Encyclopedia of the Social Sciences* (Vol. 12, pp. 154–159). New York: Macmillan and Free Press.

Lamb, G., & Muller, L. (1982). *Control Accountability, and Incentives in a successful Development Institution: The Kenya Tea Development Authority*. Washington, DC: World Bank.

Lewis, W. A. (Ed.). (1970). *Tropical Development, 1880–1913: Studies in Economic Progress*. London: Allen & Unwin.

Lim, Yongil. (1968). Input of Tea Industry on the Growth of the Ceylonese Economy. *Social and Economic Studies*, *17*(December), 453–467.

Lin, J. Y. (1988). The Household Responsibility System in China's Agricultural Reform: A Theoretical and Empirical Study. *Economic Development and Cultural Change*, *36*(April), 199–224.

Lin, J. Y. (1922). Rural Reforms and Economic Development. *American Economic Review*, *82*(March), 14–52.

McLennan, M. S. (1969). Land and Tenancy in the Central Luzon Plain. *Philippine Studies*, *17*(October), 651–682.

Myint, Hla. (1965). *The Economics of Developing Countries*. New York: Praeger.

Pelzer, K. J. (1945). *Pioneer Settlement in the Asiatic Tropics*. New York: American Geographical Society.

Pim, A. (1946). *Colonial Agricultural Production*. London: Royal Institute of International Affairs, and New York: Oxford University Press.

Schultz, T. W. (1964). *Transforming Traditional Agriculture*. New Haven: Yale University Press.

Siamwalla, A. (1992). *Myths, Demons and the Future of Thai Agriculture*. Paper presented at Year-end Conference on Thailand's Economic structure: Toward Balanced Development. Bangkok: Thailand Development Research Institute.

Warr, P. G. (Ed.). (1993). *Thai Economy in Transition*. Cambridge University Press.

Wickizer, V. D. (1951). *Coffee, Tea, and Cocoa: An Economic and Political Analysis*. Stanford, CA: Stanford University Press.

Wickizer, V. D. (1960). The Smallholder in Tropical Export Crop Production. *Food Research Institute Studies*, *1*(February), 49–99.

CHAPTER 65

Farm Size

Robert Eastwood
University of Sussex

Michael Lipton
University of Sussex Poverty Research Unit

Andrew Newell*
University of Sussex

Contents

Abstract

What patterns can be discerned in the distribution of farm sizes across countries and over time? How does the behavior of individual economic agents interact with the natural environment and general economic development to affect farm size? How has concerted human intervention, understood as national and supranational policy actions, altered these outcomes? We find that operated farm size rises with economic development, especially in the 20th century, with marked exceptions: large farms in Latin America and Southern Africa; small farms in parts of Northwest Europe; diminishing farm size in South Asia. Despite increased scale, in many advanced countries the family remains the main source of farm labor. Hired labor supervision costs tend to favor family farming as the equilibrium institution. Theory suggests that the family farm will typically become larger with economic development, but its efficiency advantage over the agroindustrial enterprise will decline.

Handbook of Agricultural Economics, Volume 4
doi: 10.1016/S1574-0072(09)04065-1

Sufficiently land-augmenting technical advances can upset the relationship between development and equilibrium scale, as in the Green Revolution. Concerted intervention can also cause departures from such equilibria. Colonial land grabs have led to inefficiently large farms, with market forces and land reform subsequently reducing average size after decolonization. Greater land rights have thereby raised the rural poor's income, status, and power, but farmland collectivizations, and much farm tenancy reform, have largely failed to achieve this goal. However, classic land reforms, and some decollectivizations, have proved more incentive-compatible and have distributed large land areas among many small family-managed units. Farm size is, in principle, also affected by net taxes on farm production (mostly negative in OECD, mostly positive in developing countries, though reduced), but such effects remain empirically elusive. Globalization and liberalization—effects via relative prices aside—have induced institutional changes that are not neutral with respect to farm size. These include supermarkets' increased role in the supply chain. *JEL classifications*: O130, Q130, Q150

Keywords

farm size
land reform
small farms
family farms

1. INTRODUCTION

This chapter addresses three questions: (1) What patterns can be discerned in the distribution of farm sizes across countries and across time? (2) How does the behavior of individual economic agents interact with the natural environment and general economic development to affect farm size? (3) How has concerted human intervention, understood as national and supranational policy actions, altered these outcomes?

Under Question 1 (Section 2), operated farm size rises with the level of economic development, especially in the 20th century, but there are marked exceptions (large farms in Latin America and Southern Africa; small farms in parts of Northwest Europe; diminishing farm size in South Asia, despite economic growth). Although there is a broad association between smallness and family management, in many advanced countries the family remains the main source of farm labor.

Under Question 2, we begin by asking under what assumptions we would expect agriculture to be dominated by family farming. Transaction costs, especially supervision costs, associated with hired labor are central to the family farm theory. Will family farms get larger as development proceeds? Suppose that development brings a rise in the price of labor and a fall in the price of capital. Theory suggests that the first of these will tend to make family farms bigger, whereas the effect of the second is ambiguous. Will development tend to lead to displacement of the family farm by agroindustrial enterprises? Theory suggests that this could happen, since a rising capital/labor ratio must diminish the relative importance of hired labor supervision costs relative to capital transactions costs, thus eroding the economic rationale for family farming. In sum, the changes in factor prices that accompany development can explain a tendency for a concomitant rise in farm size, whether or not family farming remains the dominant mode of production. Some exceptions to this tendency (e.g., declining farm sizes in South Asia following the Green Revolution) can be traced to the effects of technological progress or to the unwinding of past distortions. Finally, in this section, we consider evidence relating to the assumptions on which the family farm theory is based: Crucial is that scale diseconomies associated with labor use (because of transactions costs associated with *hired* labor) should be more important than scale economies that might arise from production, the use of capital inputs, and the processing and marketing of output. The well-established inverse relationship between farm size and land productivity, to the extent that it reflects a relatively low shadow price of labor on small farms, is an important piece of supporting evidence.

Under Question 3, we distinguish concerted interventions that are aimed directly at changing farm size (colonial land grab and land reform) from those for which farm size effects arise as a byproduct (taxes, subsidies, and trade interventions). In the case of colonial land grab, we ask why it happened where it did (much of Latin America and Southern Africa) and why the resulting highly unequal distribution of land persisted. In the case of land reform we document the effects of the classic Land Authority model of reform as well as alternatives, such as titling, tenancy reforms, and the privatization and decollectivization of state farms. We show that output taxes (subsidies) in a simple family farm model should raise (lower) farm size; though there is evidence that farming has been generally taxed in developing countries and subsidized in advanced countries, we have not found direct evidence of the expected farm size effects. Turning to trade interventions, theory would suggest that liberalization and globalization would in developing countries turn the domestic terms of trade in favor of agriculture and therefore act, like a subsidy, to reduce equilibrium farm size. We end the chapter by assessing the view that liberalization and globalization might have the contrary effect because of institutional aspects, *viz.* the growing role of supermarkets, grades and standards, and export horticulture.

2. PATTERNS OF FARM SIZE ACROSS COUNTRIES AND TIME

This section provides international evidence on the distribution of farm size, its long-term evolution, and the extent to which farmers rely on family labor through the process of economic development. The main sources of information are the FAO Agricultural Censuses of 1960–2000.[1] Countries with higher per capita GDP tend to have larger average farm size and fewer small farms. Also, as GDP per capita grew through the latter part of the 20th century, farms tended to become larger in the advanced countries but smaller in Asia and, perhaps, Africa. Thus mean farm size has diverged internationally. The share of family workers in total farm labor does not vary systematically with GDP per capita; indeed, in many advanced countries the family is still the main source of farm labor. However, in the few low-income African countries with FAO data, little hired labor is recorded. The great international diversity in its record of use may partly reflect issues of measurement. Section 2.1 describes longer-term trends in farm size; Section 2.2 concentrates on its pattern and recent change. Section 2.3 reviews evidence on the balance between family and hired farm labor.

2.1 Longer-term trends in farm size

We first note, but then sidestep, the issue of what measure best summarizes the scale of an agricultural operation. There are many possible dimensions, including land area, value added, output value, output volume, and labor input. There are further subtleties, mostly about quality adjustments. However, discussions of empirical facts are driven by the available comparative data. In the FAO farm censuses, land area of holdings is available for most countries, but no other potential measure of scale is widely available.

FAO data suggest several possible measures of central tendency as well as alternative indicators of the size distribution of farms. Table 1, representing a wide range of continents and income levels, shows that alternative summary statistics on farm size since about 1990 all tend to vary similarly across countries. We shall analyze mainly

Table 1   International correlations among measures of farm size, 1990s

	1.	2.	3.	4.	5.	6.	7.
1. Ln mean	1	0.73	0.70	−0.92	−0.82	−0.91	−0.83
2. Median by holding		1	0.69	−0.74	−0.45	−0.56	−0.46
3. Median by area			1	−0.34	−0.32	−0.54	−0.43
4. Proportion of holdings <2 hectares				1	0.88	0.95	0.84
5. Share of area in holdings <2 hectares					1	0.73	0.89
6. Proportion of holdings <5 hectares						1	0.85
7. Share of area in holdings <5 hectares							1

Note: All coefficients above 0.50 in magnitude are statistically significant at the 1% level.
Source: FAO Statistics division at www.fao.org/es/ess/index_en.asp. The data are all taken from the 1990 round of Agricultural Censuses. Sample sizes vary between 40 and 60, depending on data availability. For a full listing of the countries, see Appendix Table 1.

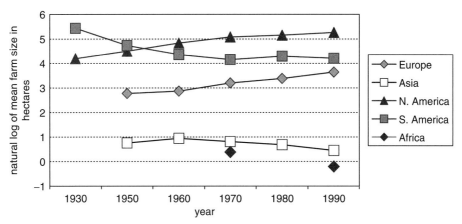

Figure 1 Mean farm size by continent, 1930s–1990s. Source: FAOSTAT at www.fao.org/es/ess/index_en.asp.

(the natural log of) national mean farm size, which is available for more countries than any other measure. It is strongly correlated with other measures, e.g., (negatively) with the proportion of farms below 2 hectares and the share of total agricultural land in such farms (Row 1 of Table 1).[2]

Figure 1 shows the path of average farm size in a sample of countries grouped into continents from 1930 to 1990. In Europe and North America farm sizes have been increasing on average since 1950. In Africa[3] and Asia, by contrast, farm sizes seem to have declined in the 20th century. In South America[4] there is no clear long-run trend.

There seems to be little evidence of farm size growth in the advanced countries before the 20th century. In Western Europe, it is hard to see much general movement between the pre-19th century and the late 19th century (Table 2). The U.S. evidence for 1850–1997 (Figure 2) is that, after the sharp decline following the Homestead Act of 1862 (Sokoloff and Engermann, 2002), average farm size was fairly stable until 1910. It thereafter grew at a rising rate, especially after 1950. Average farm size also rose steadily throughout the 20th century in Canada and, more gradually, in England and Wales.[5] Most advanced countries felt the forces that reshaped agriculture in the Northern United States: mechanical and biological innovations in agriculture, the growth of nonfarm wages, the transportation and communication revolutions (Olmstead and Rhode, 2000: 693–4), and the rise of synthetic substitutes.

We find no evidence of long-term trends in farm size in the Asian historical record. Here are two examples. Figure 3 shows mean cultivated area per rural household in China during periods of private ownership of land from 2 AD to 1600 AD. No trend is

Table 2   Historical data on farm size in Western Europe

	Percentage of holdings less than:					
	1 ha	1.5 ha	2 ha	3 ha	5 ha	20 ha
Pre-19th century						
E. England, c. 1280				32.7		
Savoy, 16th c.	52.4				87.1	
Sainte-Croix, France, 16th c.					38.8	
Bohemia, early 18th c.		35.7			56.7[1]	
Hochberg Germany, 1788	45.0[2]				94.6[2]	
19th century						
Ireland, 1845			23.6			
Norway, 1850					80.0	
England and Wales, 1851						41.5
Germany, 1882			58.0		76.6	94.2
Sweden, 1890			22.5			88.8
France, 1892	39.2				71.3	
Late 20th century						
France, 1989			27.4		38.4	54.8
Germany, 1995			31.6		46.4	64.1
Ireland, 1991			2.6		11.2	53.7
Norway, 1989			13.7		37.3	87.9
Spain, 1989			44.2		65.3	88.0
United Kingdom, 1993			5.6		14.5	41.7

[1]For Bohemia the upper limit is 4.5 hectares.
[2]For Hochberg, the limits are 0.7 and 5.8 hectares, respectively.
Source: For pre-19th century and 19th century data, Grigg (1992), Tables 8.3 and 8.4, pp. 97–99. For late 20th century data, FAOSTAT Statistics division at www.fao.org/es/ess/index_en.asp.

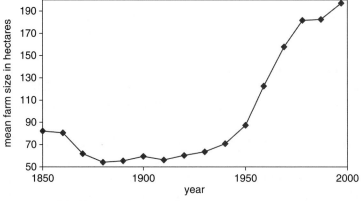

Figure 2   Mean size of holding in the United States since 1850. Source: U.S. Department of Commerce (1975, 2000).

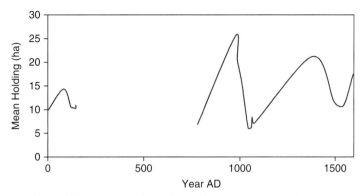

Figure 3 Mean cultivated land per rural household, China, 2–1600 AD. Source: Lee (1921, 436). For much of the period from the Tsin Dynasty to the Yang Yen (Tang), 280–780 AD, there was public land distribution (Lee, 1921).

visible, but there is great variation, for which Lee (1921) offers two important explanations: the effect of wars on population size and the impact of tax regimes on participation in censuses. For India, Fukazawa (1983, 201) offers some fragments of evidence from village surveys in Western India that suggest large falls in average size of land holdings during the 19th century in Maharashtra and gradual falls in average land holdings from the early 20th century to the end of the colonial regime. (Section 4.2.1 gives supporting evidence on farm size inequality trends.)

2.2 Economic development and farm size in the late 20th century

Appendix Table 1 gives a range of measures of farm size distribution from the FAO farm surveys, summarized by continent in Table 3. We begin this subsection by drawing out two major stylized facts. First, average farm size is very small in parts of sub-Saharan Africa and South, Southeast and East Asia, e.g., Bangladesh, China, Democratic Republic of the Congo,[6] Egypt, Indonesia, India, and Korea. In these countries the great majority of farms are less than 2 hectares. Contrast this with, for instance, Western European countries, where the median holding is mostly well above 10 hectares. Second, average farm size and measures of farm size inequality are related. For instance, (log) mean farm size and the Gini coefficient are positively correlated across countries (correlation coefficient = 0.48). This is illustrated in Figure 4.[7]

Why do we find such variation across countries? Economic and technological factors matter (Section 3), but so do exogenous agroecological conditions, partly reflected in the share of land devoted to pasture. The 48 countries with data show a strong correlation[8] between log farm size and the proportion of land devoted to pasture (Figure 5). Many developing countries, especially in South and Central America, Central Asia, North

Table 3   Continental average farm size and dispersion measures, 1990s

Continent		Mean	Gini	% Permanent Pasture	% Holdings < 2 ha.	% Area < 2 ha.
Sub-Saharan Africa	Mean	2.4	0.49	9.0	69.2	32.0
	N	15	11	1	12	8
	SD	1.4	0.1	.	23.1	27.7
Central America and the Caribbean	Mean	10.7	0.75	38.0	62.8	12.4
	N	11	10	9	9	9
	SD	10.2	0.1	27.9	27.0	11.0
South America	Mean	111.6	0.90	74.6	35.7	0.87
	N	10	9	8	4	3
	SD	149.5	0.05	14.5	17.3	1.0
South Asia	Mean	1.4	0.54		77.8	40.1
	N	4	4		3	3
	SD	1.2	1.1		19.1	26.9
East Asia	Mean	1.0	0.50		92.2	59.2
	N	3	2		3	3
	SD	0.3	0.2		3.7	11.9
Southeast Asia	Mean	1.8	0.60	1.4	57.1	23.6
	N	6	6	3	4	4
	SD	1.0	0.1	0.3	16.8	14.5
West Asia and North Africa	Mean	4.9	0.70	7.1	65.0	24.7
	N	11	10	5	9	8
	SD	4.6	0.1	7.1	27.3	23.3
Europe	Mean	32.3	0.60	35.9	29.9	3.8
	N	21	20	18	18	17
	SD	25.7	0.2	21.2	24.6	4.9
Canada		273.4		96.1	6.8	
United States		178.4	0.78	47.9	4.2	0.0
Australia		3601.7	..	96.1	..	..
New Zealand		222.6			6.8	

Source: FAOSTAT at www.fao.org/es/ess/index_en.asp.

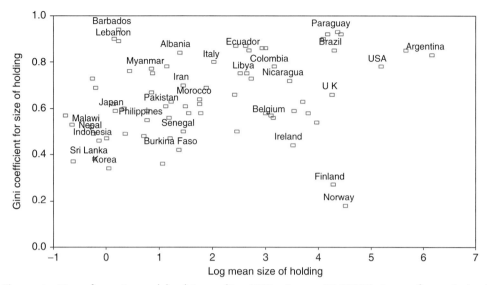

Figure 4 Mean farm size and land inequality, 1990s. Source: FAOSTAT at www.fao.org/es/ess/index_en.asp.

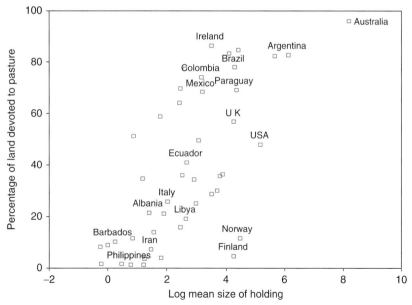

Figure 5 Mean farm size and the pastoral-arable mix of farms, 1990s. Source: FAOSTAT at www.fao.org/es/ess/index_en.asp.

Africa, and the Middle East, have unusually large areas of low-quality land, usable only for grazing, and farmed in large units (see, for instance, the data for Iran, Libya, Morocco, Pakistan, and Turkey). Among advanced countries, we observe large areas of lower-quality, arid land devoted to livestock ranches in Australasia and North America, alongside much higher mean farm sizes than in Europe. An inverse relationship between land quality and equilibrium farm size is consistent with the theory discussed in Section 3. In Section 4 we discuss the impact of concerted human interventions on farm size distributions, including the diverse legacy of colonialism. In much of Asia and West and Central Africa, colonists did not seize a lot of farmland, and plantations remain a small proportion of farm area. In contrast, in much of Latin America, the Caribbean, and Southern and East Africa, colonialism has left a legacy of unequally distributed farms, some very large.

We now turn to the statistical association between farm size and economic development. Figure 6 reveals (for 1990) a broadly positive association between mean farm size and GDP, much but not all of it between continents. Table 4 presents this association in regression form, showing an estimated elasticity of unity. The residuals suggests that temperate countries have larger farms, controlling for GDP *per capita*. This is likely to be related to the global distribution of land quality and climate discussed earlier.

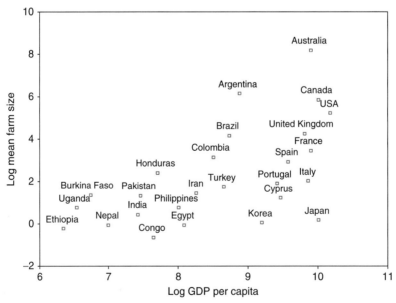

Figure 6   Mean farm size and GDP per capita, selected countries, 1990s. Source: Mean farm size: FAOSTAT at www.fao.org/es/ess/index_en.asp. GDP per capital: Penn World table version 6.1, variable rgdpl: real GDP *per capita* (Laspeyres index), 1990, in 1985 U.S. dollars.

Table 4   The international distribution of farm size

Dependent Variable	In Mean Farm Size
Ln GDP per capita	1.00(4.7)
R^2	0.37
Adjusted R^2	0.35
Sample	50

Note: Weighted least squares regression is weighted by square root of population. Absolute *t*-ratio in parentheses. Results are very similar if continental dummy variables are included. Mean farm size from the *1990 Round of FAO Agricultural Censuses*. GDP per capita from Penn Word Tables, v. 6.1.

Cross-section correlations suggest, but do not imply, corresponding intertemporal correlations for single countries. Using data from countries that have a sequence of FAO surveys, we next investigate whether *changes* in GDP are associated with *changes* in farm size. The divergent trends across continents (Figure 1) do not foreshadow a strong correlation; indeed, changes in GDP per capita are only weakly associated with changes in farm size over the approximately decade-long gaps between surveys (Table 5, Column 1).

Table 5   International changes in mean farm size, 1970–1990

	coef (*t*-ratio)	coef (*t*-ratio)
Constant	−0.01 (1.6)	0.02 (4.2)
Annual average change in ln GDP per capita	0.25 (1.8)	0.20 (2.2)
Annual average population growth rate		−1.41 (8.7)
R^2	0.06	0.60
Adjusted R^2	0.04	0.58
Sample	59	59

Note: Dependent variable is the annual average change in ln mean farm size. Weighted least squares regression is weighted by square root of population. Absolute *t*-ratios in parentheses. Farm size data from the 1970, 1980, and 1990 FAO rounds. Other data are from Penn World Tables, v 6.1. Countries included are as follows: Africa: Ethiopia, Lesotho. Asia: Cyprus, Indonesia, India, Israel, Japan, Korea, Nepal, Pakistan, the Philippines, Thailand, and Turkey. Rest of the world: Austria, Belgium, Brazil, Denmark, Fiji, Finland, France, Germany Greece, Ireland, Italy, Luxembourg, Netherlands, Norway, Panama, Paraguay, Peru, Portugal, Puerto Rico, Spain, Switzerland, the United Kingdom, and the United States.

In Column 2, annual average population growth is added to the regression, and its estimated coefficient is negative, large, and significant. Why? It might seem obvious that more people crowded into the same land area must mean smaller farms, but a simple interpretation along these lines is inadequate, e.g., because of the growth of nonfarm activity (see Section 3.1 for a fuller discussion). Note also that this regression cannot establish cause from population growth to farm size decline. For example, population growth is negatively associated with GDP/capita and may therefore proxy some other factor that depresses mean farm size (Figure 6), e.g., perhaps, the Green Revolution, as we discuss later.

2.3 The mix of family and hired workers and development

Is it true, either over time or across countries, that larger mean farm size is associated with a lower weight of family labor in total farm labor? Data are scarce, but there is some support for the proposition in Table 6, if we exclude the tiny Central American

Table 6   Ratio of permanent hired labor to family labor, circa 1990

Country	Ratio of Permanent Hired Labor to Family Labor	Mean Farm Size in Hectares
Africa		
Egypt	0.02	1.0
Guinea	0.01	2.0
Morocco	0.04	5.8
Central America		
Grenada	0.29	0.8
Guadeloupe	0.59	3.2
Martinique	1.44	2.4
South America		
Brazil	0.32	64.6
French Guiana	0.60	4.6
Paraguay	0.09	77.5
Asia		
Myanmar	0.06	2.4
Pakistan	0.03	3.8
Thailand	0.03	3.4
Europe		
Austria	0.10	26.4
Luxembourg	0.07	33.2
Norway	0.51	10.0
Spain	0.21	18.8

Note: See Section 3 for a discussion of permanent versus temporary hired labor.
Source: FAOSTAT at www.fao.org/es/ess/index_en.asp.

plantation economies. We see more hired labor in the European and Latin American economies than in the African and Asian ones. The FAO surveys do not report employment status data for many countries; for poorer countries, and African countries in particular, data for hired labor are rarely collected.[9]

As for North America, a high share of family labor in the farm workforce may have persisted despite large and growing farm size, in part because of labor-displacing capital accumulation and technical progress (mechanization, crop spraying). From 1900 until the 1970s at least, families provided about three quarters of agricultural labor in the United States (U.S. Department of Commerce, 1975, 467). The Canadian data tell a similar story. Thus the North American answer seems to be, on average, that the importance of the family in agriculture survives to the present.

Data from the International Labor Office (Figure 7) give no clear indication that hired workers loom larger in farming in higher-income countries.[10] However, the five poorest countries shown have very low shares of employees in employment in agriculture, so perhaps if data for more poor countries were available, a positive relationship would emerge.

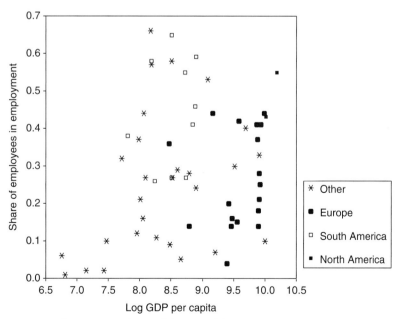

Figure 7   Farm employees as a share of farm workforce, various countries, circa 1990. Sources: Share of hired labor: http://laborsta.ilo.org. GDP per capita. Penn World table version 6.1, variable rgdpl: real GDP per capita (Laspeyres index), 1990, in 1985 U.S. dollars.

Two continental groups stand out. First, European countries tend to have unexpectedly high shares of family labor in total farm labor, given their mean GDP.[11] Second, countries in South America have somewhat higher proportions of employees than most other countries at similar mean GDP levels. These differences are explored in Section 4.

3. SOME ECONOMICS OF FARM SIZE

3.1 The theory of farm size

Section 2 reviewed what is known about variation in the size distribution of farms across time and space. To explain the observed variation, we may appeal to two sorts of influences: those that entail concerted human intervention and the rest.

Two categories of concerted human intervention may perhaps be identified. In the first, one group, typically an invader, establishes a system of discrimination based on some exogenous human characteristic, such as race. In the colonial period in Kenya, for example, the best land (in the "White Highlands") was reserved exclusively for European farmers, and a system of laws and taxes was put in place that gave European farmers further advantages over African farmers (Deininger and Binswanger, 1995). Caribbean sugar plantations in the 19th century, worked first by African slaves and then by indentured Indian labor, are another case in this first category. In the second category we place policy regimes that, although not involving arbitrary discrimination among persons, nevertheless change agrarian structures. Examples in this category are the prohibition or discouragement of land tenancy in some Indian states, land reform schemes, and the EU's Common Agricultural Policy. The distinction between these two types of concerted intervention is not hard and fast, since a policy might appear nondiscriminatory while being discriminatory in practice. For instance, it might be that a law against tenancy has the effect (and, perhaps, the intention) of preventing members of a particular caste from obtaining or retaining all their rights to land.

If we abstract from concerted human intervention (hereafter, *intervention*), we are led to the theory of agricultural development represented by Boserup (1965), Binswanger and Rosenzweig (1986), and Binswanger and McIntyre (1987). In this theory, *population pressure* is a key *exogenous* determinant of changes in agrarian production relations. Starting from an original position of land abundance and forest-fallow agriculture, population growth generates increasing intensification of land use, through bush-fallow and settled agriculture to multicrop intensive farming, and—*pari passu*—an increasing pressure for security of land tenure. According to this theory, transaction costs—especially those associated with the supervision of hired labor—are sufficiently important in relation to (production) scale economies that the optimal production unit is the family farm, and Binswanger and Rosenzweig argue in some detail (see the following discussion) that in the absence of tenancy restrictions (and other interventions), and provided that the *operation* as opposed to the *ownership* of farmland does not confer local political power to a significant degree, even a skewed land *ownership* structure will not prevent the family-*operated* farm from coming to dominate in equilibrium. Size, crop choice, and factor use in the equilibrium farm will be determined by a set of material and economic elements: soil type and agroclimatic conditions; relative factor prices; prices of intermediate inputs; farm-gate output prices; and technology.[12] Note that this theory requires in some circumstances that long-term tenancy is feasible. This applies if (1) efficient operation requires that the land itself, or fixed capital such as irrigation equipment, or trees in the case of long-gestation tree crops, needs significant maintenance, and (2) it is costly to ensure that short-term tenants will undertake such maintenance.

The *family farm theory* of agrarian production relations therefore derives from the view that it is transactions costs, especially the supervision costs of hired labor, rather than technical scale economies that, in the absence of intervention, determine how the "agricultural firm" is organized (Roumasset, 1995). Although the term *family farm* is widespread in the literature, we have not been able to find a precise definition. It is not straightforward to decide who is to count as a family member, and after that is resolved one must specify just how much hired labor (per unit of family labor) is consistent with family farming and whether for these purposes temporary labor (at harvest time, for instance) is to be counted. Whether family members are full-time on the farm may also be relevant because this bears on the amount of labor supervision that they are undertaking. We take it for the purposes of this chapter that *family farming* means that at least a third of permanent labor input is provided by family members.[13] To define transactions costs, we think of there being a *marketplace* in which factors are available, and goods sellable, at given prices: Then transactions costs are any costs associated with the use of factors from, and delivery of goods to, that marketplace.[14] Transactions costs thus defined may be divided into *transport* costs and *information* costs. Information costs are often thought of as the same as *agency* costs, but this is imprecise: Information costs associated with labor arise from search, screening, training, and supervision, only the last of which is of necessity a cost of agency.

Hired labor supervision costs plus constant technical returns to scale in farming by no means lead us to the family farm theory, still less to a simple relation between economic development and "equilibrium" farm size; to the contrary, such assumptions in general tend to imply an agrarian structure in which heterogeneity in household endowments leads to heterogeneity in farm organization and farm size for a given level of development (measured, say, by a constellation of market prices for outputs and inputs plus a given technology). Thus Eswaran and Kotwal (1986), in a model with perfect rental markets in labor and land but household-specific capital endowments (including owned land), together with convex supervision costs for nonfamily labor, show how agriculture will differentiate into four classes according to capital endowments. *Laborer-cultivators*, the least well endowed, employ some land for self-cultivation and also work for others; *self-cultivators*, with more capital, find it optimal to employ more land and to work only for themselves; *small capitalists* employ yet more land and spend part of their time supervising hired workers; *large capitalists* specialize in supervision of hired labor. The exogenous distribution of capital thus generates an equilibrium distribution of operated land and an "inverse relationship" between farm size and land productivity; the land distribution will evolve in the course of development as a result of both capital accumulation and policy interventions, such as land reform.

Suppose, contrary to Eswaran and Kotwal, that heterogeneities in household endowments of land and capital are, given the magnitude of transactions costs in markets for credit and the sale and rental of land, not sufficient to prevent the family farm from emerging as *the* equilibrium institution. Can we then identify a relationship between development and equilibrium farm size? In an idealized case, with homogeneous land and fixed labor input per family (and neglecting seasonality in labor demand), this is equivalent to asking how economic development affects the equilibrium land/labor ratio in farming, a question amenable to attack via standard production theory. Suppose that economic development raises the reservation utility of families, makes capital relatively cheap, and is accompanied by technological progress in agriculture. We now show that higher reservation utility raises farm size, whereas the effects of technological progress and cheaper capital are ambiguous.

Assume, initially:

A1. Production is in family farms, which face no transaction costs; each family provides a fixed and identical amount of labor; hired labor is zero.

A2. Output, Y, depends on land and labor input only and exhibits constant returns to scale and diminishing returns to individual factors.

A3. Land is homogeneous and in fixed supply to farming.

A4. Families are in perfectly elastic supply at reservation utility U in terms of output.

Supposing competitive behavior in the land market, it follows that equilibrium farm size, N, will be such as to maximize rent/hectare, denoted R. Denoting output per hectare by $F(N)$, N must maximize:

$$R = (F(N) - U)/N \tag{1}$$

differentiation of which gives the first-order condition determining equilibrium farm size, N^*:

$$N^* . F'(N^*) = F(N^*) - U \tag{2}$$

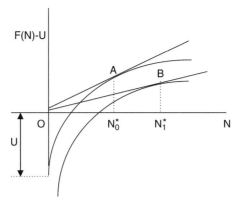

Figure 8   The determination of equilibrium farm size

Figure 8 illustrates how *N* is determined: maximized rent is given by the slope of OA, and ON_0^* is the equilibrium farm size.

Total differentiation of Eq. (2) shows that $dN^*/dU > 0$. So, if development raises the reservation utility of families, as one expects, it both lowers land rents—the demand from families to rent land is reduced because they have better off-farm opportunities—and raises equilibrium farm size, as illustrated by the shift from A to B in the figure. Development, by raising U, has simply shifted the curve down. We can extend the model to examine other development effects such as technological advance in the agricultural sector and change in the cost of capital. The effects of technological change turn out to depend on its nature; we can distinguish three pure types:

1. Neutral technical advance is represented by a production function $Y = \gamma F(N)$, where γ is a technology parameter that grows through time; the effects of a rise in the relative price of agricultural goods, or an output subsidy, have effects equivalent to this type of advance.
2. Labor-augmenting technological advance is represented by a production function $Y = \beta F(N/\beta)$: This represents a case where, as time passes, farm size can rise in proportion to β with no loss in output per hectare (in effect, the amount of "effective" labor possessed by the family is growing).
3. Land-augmenting technological advance is represented by a production function $Y = F(\alpha N)$, where α is the technology parameter: αN is the amount of "effective land." As time passes a family can extract the same output from progressively smaller amounts of land.

It can readily be shown that:

1. (a) Neutral technical advance raises land rent and reduces farm size. (b) An advance that is matched by an equiproportional rise in reservation utility leaves farm size unchanged.

2. (a) Labor-augmenting technological advance raises land rent and raises (lowers) farm size if the elasticity of substitution between land and labor is lower (higher) than the share of land in output. (b) An advance that is matched by an equiproportional rise in reservation utility raises farm size.

3. Land-augmenting technological advance, by attracting more families to farm a fixed total land area, raises land rent and reduces farm size (at the same time raising population density on the land).[15]

Now consider the extension of the model to allow for a third factor of production—capital—first neglecting (as we have with land) the possibility of transaction costs so that the amount of capital as well as the amount of land that a "family" employs will be determined by the usual marginal productivity conditions. The interesting question is: what happens to equilibrium farm size if the (rental) price of capital falls? *A priori*, we cannot tell; the answer depends on factor substitution elasticities. To understand this ambiguity, note that (with the "family" as the unit of labor), farm size equals labor productivity divided by land productivity. Therefore, a given exogenous change will raise equilibrium farm size if labor productivity rises proportionately more than land productivity and will lower it in the opposite case.

Either outcome is a possible consequence of a fall in the price of capital. For example, cheaper capital could make the introduction of combine harvesters profitable, allowing a family to farm a much larger area, but without much effect on output/hectare. Labor productivity rises by much more than land productivity and equilibrium farm size rises. However, the introduction of confined animal-feeding units to livestock farming could have the opposite effect: Land productivity rises, but labor productivity could rise by less or even fall.[16] In sum, we can assume that capital becomes relatively abundant and thus relatively cheap as development proceeds, but we cannot be sure of the effect on the size of the family farm; capital that is complementary to land will tend to raise farm size, and capital that substitutes for land will tend to lower it.[17]

Thus the family farm theory predicts that the rise in the reservation utility of "families" that accompanies development will raise equilibrium farm size but that the effects of both cheaper capital and technological advances can go either way. We must recognize as well that development may undermine the family farm theory itself (see the following discussion).[18] So, should we expect to find a simple relationship between growth in GDP/capita and growth in farm size, as investigated in Section 2? Not necessarily, for two reasons.

First, growth in GDP/capita is a highly imperfect proxy for growth in *marginal* family reservation utility. With population rising rapidly in a predominantly agrarian economy, growth in GDP/head can well coexist with rising population pressure on the land and thus with lower reservation utility and smaller farms.[19] Some sub-

Saharan African countries might fit this case, especially where there is significant land degradation; we have earlier noted declining mean farm size in Lesotho and Malawi. Second, the ambiguities associated with technology and capital cannot be neglected; for example, technological advances in agriculture may in some cases have been fast and land-augmenting enough to account for declining farm size in spite of growing GDP/capita, as with several Asian countries during rapid technological change associated with high-yielding varieties of rice, more fertilizers, and modern irrigation techniques. As noted previously, land-augmenting technological change, with unchanged reservation utility, reduces farm size and raises rents. These effects will be offset if nonfarm labor demand is rising faster than workforce growth so that wages (i.e., reservation utility) are rising. If the offset is partial, we have general economic advance, with *rising* wages accompanying a *rise* in the labor-to-land ratio and a *fall* in farm size.

We now consider relaxing assumptions A3 and A4. Assumption A4, that the supply of "families" is perfectly elastic, is unduly strong and, in fact, unnecessarily so. Since the preceding analysis implies, for fixed total land, a downward-sloping demand curve for families as a function of reservation utility (low reservation utility, *ceteris paribus*, means high rent, thus a high number of intensively worked farms), an upward-sloping supply of families—which shifts left as development proceeds—will link development to increasing farm size. In some cases, this would mischaracterize development. The case of a land frontier, as in the United States in the 19th century, might be thought of as one in which total land is fixed but the supply of families is inelastic, though shifting to the right over time; this leads to cheap land and large farms at the outset, with pressures for rents to rise and farm size to fall as immigration proceeds. Subsequent rises in reservation utility associated with nonagricultural growth would then be expected to raise equilibrium farm size again. This appears consistent with Figure 8.

We may relax assumption A3 to allow for heterogeneous land. Then a cross-section application of preceding results 1–3 suggests that good-quality land will earn a high rent and will be farmed in units the relative size of which depends on the nature of land quality differences. A Ricardian "margin of cultivation" is also created. Then exogenous changes (those associated with development, or in taxes or subsidies; see Section 4) will affect the observed distribution of (family) farm sizes through shifts in the margin as well as in the labor/land ratio on farms that remain in operation. Most simply, rises in U, *ceteris paribus*, will reduce total area farmed as equilibrium rent on marginal lands goes to zero.

Spatial heterogeneity raises complex questions, since both input and output farm-gate prices will depend on remoteness, with diverse effects. If farms are trading, adverse farm-gate prices for outputs and, say, fertilizer inputs will create "price scissors," causing rents to be low and farms large. With increasing remoteness, though, the "scissors" could create a limit at which production for sale generates no economic surplus: Beyond this limit farms will be autarkic and small. Further complexities, pulling in different directions, arise if we take into account the following: (1) variations in household reservation utilities (disadvantaged groups could be driven into remote areas; see Section 4.2.1.), (2) price scissors effects vary across outputs,[20] and (3) "remoteness" is not exogenous and might be associated with low land quality, perhaps related to poor access to water. Some recent evidence from Madagascar and Nepal suggests that remoteness raises farm (or plot) size (Stifel, Minten, and Dorosh, 2004; Fafchamps and Stilpi, 2003).

Instead of assuming the family farm theory, is it possible to obtain it formally from a model in which farm size is chosen to minimize unit transactions costs? The literature does not contain any such model, for good reason: for given factor proportions, total (factor) transaction costs will combine (*inter alia*) a presumably concave capital component with a labor component that is locally convex, where labor input starts to include some hired labor and that might or might not be globally convex (Eswaran and Kotwal, ibid: 496). The possibility of multiple local minima of transaction costs per unit land (one being self-cultivation), though making general results unavailable, does imply that the global minimum *may* jump sharply from self-cultivation to much larger-scale operation using hired labor as the capital/labor ratio in farming rises with development—in effect, because labor transactions costs are becoming less important relative to capital transaction costs.

How is the family farm theory to be assessed empirically? If we could identify a group of countries that had experienced minimal "intervention," it would be expected that agrarian systems in those countries would be dominated by family farming and that operated farm size and crop choice variations within them could be plausibly attributed to exogenous variation in, for instance, rainfall, toposequence, soil type, and market access. Inequality in operational land holdings would be expected to be low.

It is difficult to identify countries that have not experienced significant interventions, but those in East Asia could be closest to the ideal type of the theory, conforming to Otsuka et. al.'s assertion that "... family farms, either owner or tenant operated, have continued to be a more dominant mode of agricultural production organization than large-scale farm firms or plantations based on hired labor" (Otsuka et al., 1992; here large-scale means 10–15 ha and upward). Basing their argument mainly on Asian experience, they find further support for the transaction cost theory in a contrast between East Asia and South Asia, where large farms with attached labor are more common, by tracing this difference to the inhibition of land tenancy in South Asia, especially India (ibid., p. 2003).[21]

For countries where significant "intervention" has led to highly skewed distributions of owned and operated land, proponents of the family farm theory have sought to trace the way interventions have led to the widespread departures from this model that we observe in practice, especially, as far as the developing world is concerned, the prevalence of large commercial farms in Latin America and Eastern and Southern Africa and of plantations in the Caribbean and Sri Lanka. The general argument, surveyed in great detail by Binswanger, Deininger, and Feder (1995, henceforth BDF), is that large farms, even though inefficient, can generate large surpluses for their owners, provided that the reservation utilities of laborers on these farms can be artificially depressed, so that, in particular, these laborers cannot profitably exit to set up family farms of their own. Transportation of labor is a particularly effective way of lowering reservation utility, and—whether or not there exist any plantation crops for which economies of scale are sufficient to nullify the family farm theory—it might be possible to account for the emergence of slave- and indentured-labor plantations in the Caribbean (and, especially, in Sri Lanka, where indentured Indian labor was employed *instead of* available Sri Lankan labor) in these terms.[22]

It should be noted that interventions of the "land reform" type have generally been undertaken to reverse the effects of earlier interventions that have concentrated land. Assessment of the family farm theory might also use evidence from land reforms, in particular to ask whether the more equal agrarian structures thereby created have proved stable. The theory would be called into question if there were evidence of reconcentration of land following reform. The evidence is mixed (Carter, 1987; Carter and Alvarez, 1989; Zevallos, 1989). Reconcentration might be explained by distress selling in the presence of imperfect credit and risk markets. Historically, this "played a major role in the accumulation of land" in China, Japan, Latin America, and the Punjab (BDF, 2709).

The analysis of links from interventions to agrarian relations and structure forms the subject of Section 4. In this section we concentrate on assessing the assumptions of the family farm theory, which are that (1) technical economies of scale, though (perhaps, for some crops or ecosystems) present at very small farm sizes, are generally exhausted before a size incompatible with family farming is reached, and (2) transaction cost relations in factor and output markets are such as to favor the family farm: In particular, unit transaction costs decline for capital as capital use rises and rise for labor as labor use rises.

3.2 Farm size and efficiency

Before embarking on a discussion of the relation between farm size and "efficiency," we must note two caveats. First, in the presence of transactions costs, efficient farm size is not independent of household endowments of labor and capital. If labor supervision costs are sufficiently important that "labor autarky" is optimal, efficient farm size increases with the number of family members of working age. Likewise, in an

Eswaran-Kotwal world, efficient farm size is dependent on the household's working capital endowment. So, strictly speaking, the following discussion is from the point of view of an idealized household with no capital endowment. Second, except where stated, we think of efficiency in terms of the maximum *expected* return to the household, thus neglecting exogenous risk.

The efficient scale of farm operation depends both on narrowly defined scale economies in production (essentially a matter of lumpiness of inputs and specialization of labor) and on scale-related transaction costs in input and output markets, including both information costs and scale economies in transport and marketing. Empirical assessment of scale economies in production is normally approached via the fitting of production functions to farm-level data so as to measure differences in total factor productivity between large and small farms, as reviewed by Mundlak in an earlier volume of this handbook (Mundlak, 2001). According to BDF (p. 2701), proper empirical assessment of efficient scale ideally requires a measure of "profits net of the cost of family labor, per unit of capital invested."[23] Such a measure not only allows for transaction costs and scale economies, it also allows for the possibility that optimal factor proportions vary with scale (which would in general imply that narrowly defined scale economies would vary according to the factor-proportions "ray" along which they were being measured).

3.2.1 Lumpy inputs

Lumpy inputs give rise to economies of scale, so it could be that the mechanization of farming that results from a rise in the price of labor relative to capital would lead to such a large increase in the minimum efficient scale that the family farm would become obsolete. Studies of the United Kingdom and the United States quoted by BDF suggest that the average cost-minimizing scale might be about 50 ha in British mixed farms or as much as 250 ha in cash-grain farms in Illinois, but as is pointed out there, such large-scale farms "are still managed largely by family labor" (p. 2697). Whether lumpy inputs will have a substantial influence on optimal scale in a given case depends on whether a rental market exists in those inputs, which is itself dependent partly on whether processes are, for example, because of climatic homogeneity, synchronized across farms.

In the United States, for instance, there is an active rental market in combine harvesters, which follow the seasons across the country. Transaction costs associated with the care, maintenance, and transport of lumpy inputs may be such as to inhibit renting, with a potential impact not only on optimal scale but also on mode of organization of farming, which could be essentially driven by the accumulation of wealth in the form of these inputs. For example, it has been argued that when conditions have led to the development of land rental markets, it will be families that own draught animals that will rent and operate farmland (Binswanger and Rosenzweig, 1986).[24] Similarly, in a study of rice farming in one area of Andhra Pradesh (Frisvold, 1994) it was suggested that the ownership of "lumpy" irrigation equipment was determining farm size at a level above that of the family farm (there were about six hired workers per family worker on the average farm). An extra element in this case was that the farms were almost all owner-operated, suggesting the absence of secure long-term land rental contracts that might allow tenants to amortize investments in *immobile* lumpy equipment. Yet it could be that choice of technique rather than mode of production will adjust. Examples are the emergence of hand and treadle pumps in Bangladesh and of bamboo tube wells in India, where the initially introduced tubewell and pump technologies had favored larger scale (Howes, 1982; Singh, 2002).

Management skill is another lumpy input that can account for scale economies. Moreover, good farm managers are more likely than poor managers to find it optimal to manage larger farms. To the extent that the availability of new seeds, fertilizers, and pesticides, together with the possibility of obtaining credit to pay for them, has increased, one expects the returns to scarce managerial skill to have risen, which is lent support by evidence that the impact of schooling on agricultural productivity is substantially higher in such modernizing environments than in traditional ones (Haddad et al., 1991). Where this has in fact induced the acquisition of greater skills, one would expect optimal scale to have risen. Against this, some technological advance might favor local knowledge sufficiently that efficiency demands more intensive managerial input, leading to smaller scale.

3.2.2 Specialization of labor

Economies of scale can arise from this source, but the sequential nature of tasks associated with the annual cycle of production limit such economies in agriculture relative to industry (Smith, 1776; van Zyl et al., 1995). The implication is that once scale economies of the lumpy input type have been exhausted, productive efficiency provides few reasons for an increase in farming scale.

3.2.3 Scale economies in processing and marketing

In principle, scale economies in off-farm processing or transportation have no necessary implication, on their own, for the optimal scale of farming.[25] Efficient use of milling machinery implies that it be used year round in the case of storable crops; whether wheat or rice is brought to market by small or large producers makes little difference. For certain plantation crops, such as bananas, rubber, tea, and sugar cane, perishability or specific delivery requirements, together with economies of scale in processing or transport, create a particularly severe coordination problem between harvesting and processing/transport (Binswanger and Rosenzweig, 1986). Whether there is any implication for efficient farm size depends on how the associated contracting costs depend on scale. If such scale dependence is not too great, there might be little to prevent production by small farmers, tenants or otherwise; indeed, according to BDF, this structure is widespread for sugar cane in India and Thailand. In the

1970s the Kenya Tea Development Authority also stimulated factories' provision of competitive leaf-purchasing services to small growers. Bananas for export present an extra difficulty, since they are a long-gestation crop. So, even though in principle contract farming could work in this case, the transaction costs are more severe than for sugar cane in that long-term tenancy is needed unless the distribution of owned land is relatively even. Processing and transport aside, the spread of supermarkets and the related shift in demand toward products meeting stringent grades and standards have potential implications for efficient farm size that are taken up in Section 5 of this chapter.

3.2.4 Capital-related transaction costs

In principle, one expects that both farm size and the value of collateralizable assets possessed by the farmer will influence the terms under which credit is available. A farm size effect will arise in the presence of fixed transaction costs per loan contract (evaluation of the borrower's creditworthiness by the lender, for instance) and on the presumption that larger farms will demand larger loan contracts than small farms. More collateral reduces transaction costs by reducing deadweight costs of default (a formal account is to be found in Romer, 1986, Ch. 8).

Fixed per-loan transaction costs favor a *large-scale operation*, irrespective of the pattern of ownership and could—if large enough—threaten the conclusion that family farming is efficient. In contrast, collateral-related transaction costs favor *owner operation*, when land is the form in which wealth is predominantly held. If land is unequally distributed, the efficiency of family farming is again put in doubt. However, there could be institutional mechanisms that enable the disadvantages of small scale or low wealth to be sidestepped, notably the interlinking of markets. Thus Binswanger and Rosenzweig (ibid.) argue that unequal ownership of land need not prevent an equal distribution of operated land emerging, since large landowners can obtain capital cheaply and pass it on to tenants without incurring substantial transaction costs; there is already a contractual relationship between landlord and tenant and their continuing interdependence is likely to inhibit voluntary default. Moreover, to the extent that equilibrium land prices contain a collateral-value component, would-be family farmers cannot profitably buy land on mortgage, so tenancy rather than land purchase is the equilibrium outcome. A countervailing effect, however, is that (long-term) investment *demand* by tenants could be lower than that of owners if tenancy contracts are relatively short term (see the earlier discussion of Andhra Pradesh rice farming). Landlord/tenant relations aside, there could also be interlinking of credit and output markets, whereby merchants advance credit to farmers with whom they already have trading relationships, obtaining security via the threat of retaining (and causing other merchants to retain) output market receipts and reducing the transaction costs of small farmers (Bell, Srinivasan, and Udry, 1997).[26]

We now consider the empirical literature on the distribution of agricultural credit in developing countries. Generally, big farms borrow formally from lenders whose many branches reduce covariate risk; small farmers borrow informally from local lenders, whose lower costs of credit supervision (reducing adverse selection and moral hazard) and of repayment enforcement are more important, in dealing with poor customers, than is low risk covariance. A key problem for research has been the separation of credit demand and supply; it is well known that small producers are less likely than large producers to obtain formal sector credit, but this could reflect low demand or supply. Thus in a study based on Indian data, Kochar (1997) finds using a univariate probit that 81% of rural households do not obtain formal loans, with both land area and quantity of irrigated land being significantly associated with the loan probability. When demand and supply are separated, the estimated probability of rationing falls to 40%. Moreover, the principal factors determining rationing are regional rather than individual: Regional grain yield, *total* regional bank credit, and length of concrete road matter, whereas the household landholding variables are not significant. In contrast, Barham, Boucher, and Carter (1996) *do* find, in a study of Guatemalan households in which credit demand is measured using a questionnaire (allowing the identification of those who do not apply for credit because they anticipate rejection) that lower household wealth raises the probability of a household being constrained by credit supply. Similarly, Sial and Carter (1996), in a relatively homogeneous sample of peasant grain producers in Pakistan, find that the estimated shadow value of capital is higher for less wealthy households.

Carter and Olinto (2003) consider the interplay of two potential effects of land ownership on investment. As noted earlier, land ownership can increase investment demand at the same time as net land wealth relaxes credit supply constraints because of collateralization. In a panel of 284 Paraguayan farms, in a subset of which title (in effect) was acquired between the two survey dates, these two effects are separated via a distinction between attached and movable capital. Up to 5 ha, the credit supply constraint is biting so that titling causes a *shift* from movable to attached capital; above about 8 ha, titling raises movable capital (along with attached capital) rather than lowering it.[27] It is concluded that below 5 ha, titling does not relax the credit supply constraint (although it does alter the type of investment), whereas above 8 ha the credit constraint is relaxed. The implication of these results for the Binswanger/Rosenzweig view that ownership as such does not matter are therefore mixed for farms under 5 ha; ownership does not affect total credit supply, but it does alter the type of investment, enabling farmers (efficiently, one supposes) to take a longer view.

3.2.5 Labor-related transaction costs

Labor supervision costs in agriculture differ fundamentally from those in industry (van Zyl et al., 1995). Machinery in industry is stationary and so accordingly is the labor that operates it; in agriculture, both machinery and labor move, raising supervision and management costs. Such costs are therefore likely to be particularly significant in agriculture, favoring a structure of family farming in which, for the most part, labor is hired temporarily to meet seasonal bulges in labor demand. If hired labor, when imperfectly supervised, is less productive than family labor and if supervision is in fact optimally imperfect, it might be possible to infer the presence of supervision costs from separate treatment of family labor and hired labor in the production function. Early studies (Bardhan, 1973; Deolalikar/Vijverberg, 1983, 1987) suggested that, if anything, hired labor was *more* productive than family labor, but it is argued by Frisvold (1994, ibid.) that such results may be attributable either to quality differences between hired and family labor (hired labor could, for example, be predominantly female) or to endogeneity (e.g., a farm with a bumper harvest is likely to need to hire more labor at harvest time). Frisvold's own research (1) uses a panel of plot-level ICRISAT rice-farming data, together with time and household dummies (among others), (2) considers only pre-harvest labor inputs, and (3) estimates supervision time directly as family labor employed on the same plot and task simultaneously with hired labor. He finds a significantly positive but small effect of supervision on effective labor input: At sample means, the estimated elasticity of effective labor input to supervision time is 0.07. In spite of this low elasticity, output losses associated with imperfect supervision are estimated to exceed 10% on more than 40% of plots; the level of hired labor is high, for reasons noted earlier, and supervision costs can account for the estimated output losses.[28]

One way of investigating labor transaction costs is via *recursiveness* (Sadoulet et al., 1988). If the opportunity cost of labor to the household is the market wage, it is possible in the absence of other market failures to solve the household problem recursively: production behavior first, and consumption behavior afterward. So, for instance, production behavior should then be found to be independent of household demographic variables such as the number of working-age adults. Labor transaction costs that open up a gap between shadow wages for labor sale and purchase should not destroy recursiveness, provided that sellers and buyers are grouped separately. In an advance on earlier studies that had tested for (and usually rejected) recursiveness globally, Sadoulet et al. split their sample of Mexican *ejidatario* corn producers into labor sellers, labor buyers, and labor nontraders and found that recursiveness held except for the nontraders. For nontraders, on average, the labor transaction costs were found to be very important. For instance, a typical household with three irrigated-equivalent hectares of land would not hire labor unless its number of unskilled male equivalents fell below two, yet would not sell labor unless this number rose to six (ibid., Figure 2). By allowing the shadow wage gap to vary across districts, the authors could also identify some determinants of labor transactions costs, such as the density of organizations for infrastructure, input acquisition, credit, and marketing.

3.2.6 Risk and efficient scale

The extent to which risk affects the behavior of a risk-averse farmer depends both on constraints on consumption smoothing across time and on imperfections in insurance markets. If both are present, farmer decisions will depend not only on expected profit but also its variance (and higher moments in general). Rosenzweig and Binswanger (1993) demonstrate a link from weather risk (especially spatially covariant, so hard to diversify) to portfolio choice in a sample of Indian farmers by showing that (1) household consumption is particularly sensitive to weather shocks and (2) the estimated marginal effects on the mean and variance of profit of increasing the quantity of a given asset are positively correlated. In other words, weather risk is transmitted into consumption risk and, as a result, marginal expected returns on different assets are not equalized. Moreover, weather risk causes poor farmers to favor safe low-return assets, raising the possibility that, as a result, wealth inequality might rise through time: however, this effect is found to act as no more than a partial offset—even at high levels of weather risk—to a strong negative relationship between the rate of return on wealth and wealth itself. Asset choice aside, poor farmers may also mitigate risk exposure by diversifying crops or household labor allocation. To the extent that this raises off-farm work by household members, this effect will tend to lower the size of the family farm.

In sum, spatially covariant risk and wealth can both have important effects in practice on farmer portfolio choice and crop choice as well as on household labor allocation. Wealth will matter either if risk aversion varies with wealth or if access to credit and insurance markets is wealth dependent. Whether there is an implication for equilibrium scale then depends, just as discussed under capital-related transactions costs, on whether contractual arrangements between tenant farmers and landlords and merchants are such as to allow efficient risk spreading.

3.2.7 Accumulation, adoption of new technology, and the dynamics of farm size distribution

Discussions of "the" efficient scale of farming in a particular context must take account of the inconvenient fact that farm size is normally far from equalized within countries. The family farming theory predicts that variation in equilibrium farm size (for given market prices, technology, and household reservation utility) will arise from variations in household size, agroecology, transport costs, and—if land or capital markets are imperfect—household endowments of these factors. Agroecological variation will have its effect partly through choice of crop. So, in advanced countries, where imperfections in land and capital markets as well as transport costs are relatively low—and where, as noted earlier, family farming does for the most part still predominate—much farm size variation could be attributable to agroecological factors, often working through crop choice (large wheat farms in one area and smaller strawberry farms in another, for instance).

In developing countries, however, there is evidence of enduring heterogeneity across households, especially that arising from the endowment of working capital as in Eswaran-Kotwal, that will generate a corresponding heterogeneity in farm size and dynamics that depend, in that case, on the pattern of capital accumulation. Technology represents another potential source of heterogeneity in developing countries if adoption of new technology is scale dependent. This is likely if information acquisition, credit markets, or willingness to take risk exhibit-scale dependence or if, in the case of export crops especially, there are scale economies in processing and marketing. Whether there will be equalization or unequalization of the operated land distribution over time will depend (via feedback from profits to land acquisition and disposal) on the strength of any scale effects together with the effectiveness of institutional mechanisms that might emerge to circumvent them.

The evidence on the uptake of high-yielding varieties of rice in Asia suggests longer lags in uptake by smaller farmers but eventual scale neutrality (Hazell and Ramasamy, 1991).[29] The history of agroexport booms in Central and Latin America suggests, however, that these have been associated in the past with a pattern of adoption and accumulation that has entrenched a dualistic structure.[30] Labor-intensive nontraditional (NT) exports thus present a particularly interesting case, which has been studied using a 1991 agrarian history survey of highland farmers in Guatemala by Barham et al. (1995). This paper finds, on one hand, that small farms had a high probability of participating in NT (73% of farms of 1–2 ha planted some) but also that there was, among small farmers, evidence of a ceiling on the area planted to NT for farms in the range 2–4 ha. This would be consistent with a financial constraint affecting these farmers (rather than a labor supervision constraint, since for farms above 4 ha area planted to NT began to increase with farm size). The authors conclude that "the ability of the Latin American peasantry to participate in agroexport expansion is quite fragile," since "of the various factors likely to favor different operations in the adoption process, only labor supervision diseconomies cut clearly in the direction of small farms" (ibid., p. 106).

3.2.8 Evidence on scale economies and the "inverse relationship"

Here we consider the empirical evidence on production scale economies as well as the inverse relationship (IR) between size and land productivity (and the labor/land ratio) that has been found in many studies of developing countries. What stands out in Mundlak's survey (ibid.) of the cross-farm microeconometric literature on production scale economies is the pervasive difficulty presented by unobserved heterogeneity, especially cross-farm variation in the quality of management. If farmers better endowed with management skills both run a farm of a given size more efficiently than the less well endowed and (as is reasonable, on the transaction cost view) find it optimal to choose to operate larger farms, then cross-farm regressions relating a measure of profit or output to size and other inputs will overstate returns to scale. Such unobserved heterogeneity does not appear to be confined to management skill: In a study of 3000 U.S. districts, the introduction of regional dummies was found to reduce the estimate of the returns to scale parameter from 1.167 to 1.05 (Kislev, 1966, cited in Mundlak ibid.). The suggestion from cross-country studies that in developing countries the returns to scale parameter might be well in excess of 1.0 has been proved vulnerable in just the same way.

Cross-farm studies in developing countries include work on India by Yotopoulos and Lau (1973) and Carter (1984). Neither study can reject constant returns to scale in production overall, but when farms are disaggregated by size in Carter's study, small farms (those of less than 10 acres) are found to be about 15% less efficient than the remainder (based on data for the Punjab for 1969–1971); Carter suggests that the gap could reflect relatively slow take-up of HYV technology on small farms, in line with the evidence cited earlier.

For developing countries and with the exception of plantation crops (sugar cane production in Brazil), a strong "inverse relationship" has been found in the studies just cited and in many others.[31] For example, in a study of the Muda river area of Indonesia, Berry and Cline (1979, Table 4.48) find a sharp decline in the value of farm output/unit of land from the smallest farms (less than 1.5 relong, equivalent to about 0.4 ha) upward, with this measure 2.4 times higher for the smallest farms than for those in the largest group (6–12 ha).

How robust is the IR? It has been suggested that could in part be a spurious artifact of the omission of land quality from regressions of yield on farm size, since better-quality land might tend to be farmed in smaller parcels. Bhalla and Roy (1988) found in a study of Indian agriculture that the IR was weakened by geographical disaggregation, consistent with the idea of a bias arising from cross-district land-quality variation. Such tests are, however, rather indirect, and the use of even more disaggregation (village-level dummies in Carter, 1984, and household-level dummies in Heltberg, 1998) suggests that the IR is immune to the land-quality objection.[32] A recent Uganda study by Nkonya et al. (2004) finds a strong negative effect of *farm* size on *plot* output value after controlling for plot size, labor input, equipment, and a wide range of other factors, including land-quality proxies, suggesting that not only land productivity but also total factor productivity is higher in plots belonging to smaller farms.

Such findings are consistent with the Eswaran-Kotwal analysis discussed earlier, the effect of which is that labor supervision costs are low, both on average and at the margin, on farms with a relatively high ratio of family labor to land—that is, on small farms. Supervision costs are not the only route by which a wedge can be driven between the opportunity costs of family and hired labor. It might be that family labor is more or less "captive" because the probability of off-farm employment is low due to high unemployment rates or because off-farm labor markets do not exist for some categories of labor (Kutcher and Scandizzo, 1981). In this case, however, an inverse relationship for land productivity but not total factor productivity would be expected. Estimates of the "wedge" can be large: Carter (1984) estimates that the shadow wage on small farms is some 35% below the market wage and the estimates of Kutcher and Scandizzo for Northeast Brazil, comparing family and nonfamily farms, are of similar magnitude (ibid., Table 4.6). Clearly, these results are important indirect evidence for the central plank of the family-farm theory, namely the economic distinctness of hired and family labor.

What are the implications of the IR for socially efficient scale? This question is hard to address in the abstract, not only because it will depend on what shadow price is chosen for labor, but also since what is (socially or privately) efficient will depend on what transactions costs have to be borne and that could depend, for instance, on the distribution of ownership. In other words, we cannot separate efficiency from equity in general. Nevertheless, we can put that difficulty to one side and try to estimate social profits per hectare at different scales of operation, using specific assumptions on the shadow price of labor. Berry and Cline's work on Brazil (ibid., Ch. 4.1) estimates "social factor productivity" by taking gross receipts divided by a measure of aggregate input,[33] finding that this is mostly maximized for the second smallest size class (10–50 ha). Rosenzweig and Binswanger (1993), using the ICRISAT panel, find that their measure of profit per unit area is highest in the smaller size groups.

Further support for the proposition that higher scale does not confer efficiency advantages can be found in a study of late 18th century enclosures in England by Allen (1982), using data on 231 farms originally collected by Arthur Young. Allen finds that the enclosure process had little effect on arable husbandry or yields but amounted to an expropriation of farmers' surpluses by landlords, essentially via expropriation of common grazing rights. This partly explains why, in the simple cross-section of enclosed and open farms, rents are *not* higher on the enclosed farms, as one might have expected on an "expropriation" view (the rest of the explanation is that land quality on enclosed farms in the sample was worse than on open farms). As Allen remarks: "... the enclosure movement might be regarded as the first state-sponsored land reform. Like so many since it was justified with efficiency arguments, while its main effect (according to the data analyzed here) was to redistribute income to rich landowners" (ibid., pp. 950–1).

It should be noted that the enclosed and open farms in Allen's sample are of similar average size (about 120 ha); despite this, enclosure is clearly interpretable as a rise in scale of operation.

4. DOES CONCERTED HUMAN ACTION ACCOUNT FOR FARM SIZE?

4.1 The argument of this section

We have argued that equilibrium farm size tends to rise with development. Yet big proportions of land remain in small farms in some developed countries (Europe) and in large farms in some developing countries (Latin America, Southern Africa). In addition, farms in Asia have got smaller during development. Are such anomalies due to concerted human action? Two such actions, colonial land grab (Section 4.2) and land reform (Section 4.3), are intended to affect farm size, and do so via both laws and incentives to avoid laws. Farm size may also be affected by policy interventions *not* mainly intended to change it. Farm production functions are changed by agricultural research and other policies affecting technical progress; impacts on farm size were explored theoretically in Section 3. In Section 4.4, we first demonstrate analogous effects on farm size from policies affecting farm input and output prices—taxes, subsidies, and foreign trade intervention—and then sketch relevant evidence from OECD farm subsidies and developing-country farm taxes.

4.2 Colonial land grab

Some developing countries have very high farmland Ginis (Table 2.3); much land in "underfarmed" giant holdings; yet big impoverished rural populations crowded into "overfarmed" tiny farms. Does these countries' history of enforced colonial land seizure explain these phenomena? This breaks down into several subquestions.

4.2.1 Where did colonial land grabs happen?

In most of West and Central Africa, colonists saw little gain in seizing and farming often low-grade land. In most of Asia, land quality was higher, but land grab would have implied high costs in acquiring and securing formal land rights from, and then controlling or reconciling, farm populations that were often densely settled and with formal land rights. Nor, in these areas, did colonists' efforts to suborn local clients, *compradors* or tax farmers, lead to land grants that greatly raised farm scale; claims that this happened rest partly on a mythology of pre-colonial equality. In particular, British colonialism in India probably had little ultimate effect on land inequality (see, e.g., Kumar, 1983; Stokes, 1983). In these regions, colonial and other plantations typically occupied below 5% of farm area. Today, Ginis of operated land are modest, around 0.3–0.6. Most land is operated in small farms (Table 2.3), compatible with efficient supervision of labor-intensive operations.

In much of Latin America, the Caribbean, and Southern and Eastern Africa and in a few areas of Southeast Asia and India, colonists took over large proportions of land, mainly for commercial farming.[34] Despite their protestations that such land had previously been empty (the pseudo-frontier), usually it had been long used by indigenous people, sometimes via cyclic bush fallowing, hunting/gathering, or grazing. By expelling them, often into tiny holdings on remote, hilly, and inferior marginal land, colonizers of better land created a highly unequal, possibly inefficient large-farm system that survives today.

4.2.2 In such areas, why did colonizers tend to farm large, unequal holdings?

Colonizing nations might have seen land seizures as creating farm options for many of their poor people, affected, perhaps, by domestic population growth or land exhaustion. This would have suggested small-scale, labor-intensive farm colonization, as

3354 Robert Eastwood, Michael Lipton, and Andrew Newell

implied in writing on emigration in 19th century Britain. However, there is no example of such "small-scale egalitarian colonization" in the classical colonial period. Even in our own time, "internal colonialism" (except for Chinese land policies in Tibet in the 1990s) appears soon to have involved highly unequal settlement, for example, on some lands seized by Mengistu's government in Ethiopia and Mugabe's in Zimbabwe.

Why does forced farmland seizure by a colonizing state and its army tend to create large ownership holdings for a few conquerors? First, raising and leading armies is expensive and risky, attracting people with resources and risk-bearing capacity, who will hazard them only in expectation of large rewards. Second, even if it is later colonial arrivals who are the initial farmers, breaking and managing unfamiliar land involve high risks and often long gestation periods. These are likeliest to be accepted by better-off people, perhaps with experience of substantial entrepreneurship.

An exception is the appropriation, for owner-farming, of Native American and Inuit lands in North America. Only in the Southern United States did this conform in some respects (large farms, great land inequality, agrestic servitude) to the Latin American model. Elsewhere, relatively small, not-very-unequal, owner-operated family farms were normal, as the United States absorbed Native American areas soon after Independence—well before codification in the 1862 Homestead Act, which granted newly farmed land in fairly equal and, given land quality and productivity, small homestead units (Barrington Moore, 1996; Sokoloff and Engerman, 2002).

4.2.3 Soon after colonial land seizures, why were operated farms often large?

The spread of large ownership holdings of farmland is easier where there is an extensive margin, land frontier, or pseudo-frontier. This avoids land marketing costs (although perhaps by renewed colonization or theft at the pseudo-frontier). However, even far from a land frontier, one can reconcile large *ownership* holdings with small, efficient *operated* farms. Leasing, sharecropping, or labor tenancy developed in Southern Africa (often illegally), Latin America, and the Southern United States after post-Emancipation land reform was aborted (Herring, 2003). Yet huge, owner-operated farms cover most cropland and private grazing in much of Latin America and Southern Africa. Why? Given the advantages of small-scale farms in early development, if large landowners can internalize some of the gains by selling or leasing land into smaller farms, would agency costs in land or other markets prevent this for long?

The advantages of small farming were muted for some decades after colonization, which often brought brutal consequences—widespread deaths from disease or war (Diamond, 1999) or expulsions—for indigenous peoples, sharply cutting labor/land ratios. Settlers to take their place were initially much fewer. Settler expansion into thinly populated, traditionally farmed areas was enforceable. Also, labor-linked transaction costs could be cut where labor could be denied mobility: enslaved or coerced into agrestic servitude, sometimes with the help of a head tax (Arrighi and Saul, 1973). *Temporarily*, larger farm size paid.

4.2.4 If large and unequal farm size became inefficient in colonized countries, why didn't it adjust?

As population, person/land ratios, and labor mobility grew in Latin America and Southern Africa, why was efficiency not achieved by more land transfers from big owned to smaller operated holdings (sale, lease, sharecropping, contract farming, etc.)—that is, why should the early colonial size-distribution of owned farmland affect that of operated farmland for long afterwards? First, where farm operation (as well as ownership) is inherited, large farmers may prefer perceived "life-style advantages" to profitable sale or lease to more efficient smaller units. Second, efficiency-induced pressures to cut operated farm size are reduced if large-scale owner-operation confers local extra-economic status, power, and income. Third, ethnic barriers could limit local competition. Finally, insecure property rights deter leasing: once admitted, tenants may later keep land at the point of a gun—or a vote.

4.2.5 The special case of plantations

Large proportions of farmland and workforce in the southern states of colonial America, the Caribbean, and southern and eastern Africa—and small proportions elsewhere—were appropriated by colonists for a special case of large-scale farming: plantations. But how did they affect farm size after colonial land grab? Almost always, land-water regimes provided special advantages for export crops (tea, coffee, cocoa, rubber, cane sugar, cotton, tobacco, spices) with high labor/land ratios. These lacked scale economies in production, but needed swift, orderly collection for processing, which did feature them. Nowadays, labor-intensive small-farm production is often combined with large-scale processing. However, initial colonization often drove away, killed, or dispossessed much production labor. Also, many new colonial landowner entrepreneurs chose to be absentees, unable to supervise typical paths to labor-intensive production—small-scale tenancy or sharecropping—without severe agency problems. These were eased by cutting labor's reservation utility via the plantation system (Section 3.2), with various forms of labor tying, repression, serfdom, slavery, or (above all) labor import and indenture. These same features, together with workforce growth, explain both the initial competitiveness of plantations and their later decline (Hayami, this vol.).

4.3 Land reform and farm size

4.3.1 Definition, initial situations,[34a] candidate land reforms

Land reform means legislated interventions in farm size, tenure, or transfer conditions designed to change farm size distribution. The stated motive of most land reform is more equitable distribution of *owned* landholding, but this normally has major effects on our concern in this paper: *operated* farm size. Largely compensatory, gradual, consensual land reforms in many countries have led to big falls in owned and operated farm size (Section 4.3.3), contrary to conventional wisdom. Less controversially, forcible, swift, often noncompensatory reforms have transformed operated farm-size distributions for more than a third of the world's farmers, through either internal revolutionary processes (e.g., Mexico, 1915–1925, 1934–1940; Russia, 1917–1929, 1926–1935) or external action. For example, most of East Asia before 1939 had some big and much tiny farming, very unequal, and semi-feudal or landlord dominated. From this base, (1) China made three *internal revolutionary* transitions: to much less unequal, owner-operated holdings in 1950–1952; to collectivization in 1958–1962; and to egalitarian, quasi-private "household responsibility" farms in 1977–1984;[35] (2) *external (U.S.) action* led to direct transitions to fairly equal, mainly owner-operated holdings (Ladejinsky, 1977) in Japan, 1946–1950 (Dore, 1959; Kawagoe, 2000), Korea, 1950–1955 (Ban et al., 1980), and Taiwan, 1949–1955 (Yager, 1988).

To see how land reforms work (and affect farm size), we distinguish four main pre-reform situations.

In *communal-customary tenure*, an individual (person, household, kin-group), while taking farm decisions and keeping usufruct, has land transfer rights severely limited by "the community." Individual vis-à-vis communal (or chiefly) powers to sell, rent, gift, bequeath, or mortgage land vary (Noronha, 1985). Usually the community shares grazing land, but animals are privately owned; cropland is farmed privately but not transferable outside the commons. Communal tenure covers almost all land in cyclic bush fallowing and much settled farmland: in sub-Saharan Africa, most farmland; in decollectivized land systems, the areas left in "usership" or "lifetime possession"; in Mexico, the privately run 80% of the "vast area" farmed by 3 million *ejido* households (Heath, 1992, 695–6); and substantial areas elsewhere.

Smallholder individual tenure typifies South and East Asia.[36] Over 70% of farms are largely family cultivated. Most (Table 2.3) have less than 1 ha of irrigated land (or 2 ha of rain-fed land). Less than 25% of land is in holdings above 10 times that size. And 5–30% of land is rented.

Latifundia-minifundia systems, in some cases plantation-like, are mostly Latin American. Private landowners with 100–10,000 ha, often absentee yet with local sociopolitical power, are patrons and employers for many families; each usually also farms 0.1–0.5 ha leased out, or transferred in return for labor, by its employer. Land reform and other pressures in 1950–1980 sharply raised the proportion of land in small farms. Later rural emigration and market structure changes (Section 4.4.6) are transforming many remaining largeholders into resident, capital-intensifying farmers (the "Junker path" of Binswanger et al., 1995, and de Janvry, 1981); other rural people move to the nonfarm sector, casual hired farm employment, or smallholding.

State or collective farming, despite reforms, dominated the FSU, and some persists still. It has similarities to colonial farming systems in Southern Africa. A few thousand people—large white farmers, or collective- and state-farm managers—command most farmland. Such farm systems are in transition; we ask which transitions involve "land reform" and the effects on farm size.

In these tenurial environments, there are many candidates for "land reform." We first consider classical Land Authority (LA) reform (Sections 4.3.2–4.3.4) and then a number of alternatives: titling, patrialization, tenancy, laws to restrict or regulate it, consolidation, settlement schemes, collectivization and its reversal, and 'New Wave' land reform.

4.3.2 The distributivist LA model

Here, a date is legislated, by when individuals or households (or, in principle, state or collective farms) must surrender land owned above a *ceiling* to a state LA. By a later target date, the LA divests land to land-poor or other target households. Such reforms, despite much avoidance and evasion, have been widely implemented partially in the latifundia-minifundia systems of Latin America and in the most in unequal parts of the smallholder systems of Asia, and massively in state and collective lands worldwide (4.3.4.vii; on Romania and Bulgaria [Brooks et al., 1991: 158–9]). The farm size effects depend on:

- Whether land is measured in ha or "efficiency units" allowing for soil quality, irrigation, and so on[37]
- Whether land is distributed, or permissibly kept, per household, person,[38] or family worker[39]
- Whether priority for redistribution goes to the landless, the poorest, or those needing least land to bring them to a floor (so the largest number can benefit)
- Whether land is distributed as a set amount (perhaps quality-adjusted) per beneficiary or to increase the holding to a set size (a floor)
- Whether post-redistribution holdings must suffice for a full-time livelihood (however defined)
- Whether high or low ceilings are set (seeking, respectively, fewer losers or more beneficiaries)
- Whether small or large per-beneficiary amounts (or floors, if any) are set

This last choice is crucial. Small amounts enable many people to be helped, if often only a little. It is widely claimed that this creates "unviably small" post-reform holdings, a concept that overlooks the worldwide facts of (1) part-time farming and (2) very small-scale farming where land is scarce, together with (3) the absence of evidence that either of these is inefficient. Moreover, if redistribution created inefficiently small holdings, agglomeration through sale or lease would be expected, so that the improvement in equity would not be at the expense of efficiency. Farm size effects of LA reform also depend crucially on implementation and verification. A key civil servant during the West Bengal reforms of 1969–1971 has analyzed the components required (Bandyopadhyay, 1995, 305, 319–20).

4.3.3 Did LA-led reforms substantially affect farm size distributions?

Absent political support, LA reforms suffer delay in vesting and divesting land, evasion, shortfall, corruption, and disappointment. Yet in many countries they shifted much land from rich to poor. So why did "commitment to redistributive land reforms...wane during the 1980s" (FAO, 1991)?[40] Despite some revival in the 1990s in the FSU and Southern Africa, Rashid and Quibria (1995: 133) "consider ... land reform passé." This reflects doubts that LAs have distributed much land. These doubts sometimes rest on errors of fact; on seeing reforms as failures unless they fully achieve targets; on unrealistic expectations, for example, that land reform alone can end most rural poverty; and on inattention to indirect effects (that much avoidance and evasion of LA reforms still makes farms smaller, and that much avoidance and evasion of LA reforms still makes farms smaller, and that smaller farms help the landless, by using more labor per hectare). Yet the doubters have a case. First, land shortage reduces *supply* of above-ceiling land for distribution: increasingly "the sheer numbers of landless people ... render [distribution of plots large enough to suffice for a livelihood] financially unfeasible and politically unpalatable," tending to "reduce" the LA model to distribution—albeit substantial—of very small field plots (and even more of home garden plots)[41] (Hanstad et al., 2004; cf. Mitchell and Hanstad, 2004) or even of land for dwellings only (Herring, 1983). Second, in Asia, despite big LA-style reforms, *demand* for land reform is uncertain. Land inequalities are usually far less than in pre-reform Latin America. Often, LA reform is alleged to be complete, as in China in 1977–1985,[42] or bogus, as in South Asia. Third, political pressure for land reform can weaken where land shortage causes less poverty than before: The Green Revolution has greatly raised yield on many tiny Asian holdings, and the Asian poor's dependence on land is moderated by education, nonfarm growth, and fertility decline.[43] These trends are weaker in Southern and Eastern Africa. There, land inequality is greater, rich-to-poor LA reforms fewer, and their urgency greater.

4.3.3.i South Asia   In much of Northern India and Bangladesh after independence, "the zamindari system [in which land tax was funneled to the colonial power through] rent-collecting intermediaries ... was abolished ... millions of tenants were made secure on their land and freed from a host of illegal exactions" (Singh, 1990: 293; 278, 285), though beneficiaries were seldom the very poorest. The scale of reform—and in India the compensation, Rs. 6.7b in 1950–1956 prices—was vast. "Statutory landlordism constituted in 1947–1948 ... 57% of the private agricultural land in British India [and more in] princely states ... Over 20m tenants were brought into direct relationship with the State [as owners, paying much] less by way of land revenue" (Saxena, 1990: 116–7).[44]

Was the second, LA phase of land reform—redistribution of land in an intermediary-free system—frustrated in South Asia (Dore, 1959)? "It is conventionally thought that ceiling-redistributive reforms in India have achieved little" (Mearns, 1999) and there *was* widespread evasion of ceilings. In India by 1990, "only" 2.9m ha had been declared surplus, 2.4m possessed, and 1.8m distributed to 4.1m beneficiary households. As with the further 0.9m ha distributed in 1952–1954 in the Bhoodan movement (Section 4.3.4.ix), most land was poor, and the scale of direct distributions was "too small to make an impact on landlessness" overall. Yet LA reform reached beneficiaries, including—with families—12–18m members of scheduled castes and tribes, most of them poor (Saxena, 1990, 124–6). These numbers are not negligible compared to the 163m ha of arable land and 80m agricultural households in 1990 (FAOSTAT, 2004),[45] and especially to the 25m ha of land in 63m holdings below 1 ha (DES, 2004, Table 16.1). Also, substantial indirect land redistribution was caused.[46] Big farmers sought to evade LA ceilings via bad-faith sales and transfers, but transferees began to insist on their rights (Vyas, 1976). Field studies even in notoriously evasive states show substantial reform-induced shedding of surplus lands to poor farmers (Yugandhar et al., 1990, for Bihar). In all, "the threat of ceilings [seems] to have prevented the further expansion of large holdings and . . . redistribution of even very small plots of homestead land has brought substantial benefits to the poor" (Mearns, 1999).

Even tenancy restrictions—though usually counterproductive *without* potentially enforceable LA ceilings (Section 4.3.4.ii)—can get land rights to the poor *with* ceilings, which impede landowners from responding to restrictions by evictions. In Kerala and West Bengal, political activism helped such enforcement, and poor tenants improved their position. In Karnataka (Manor, 1989, 353–60), populist politics led to successive land reforms that benefited castes comprising mainly poor tenants. In India overall, though evictions in the wake of tenancy regulation sharply cut the proportion of land *tenanted*, the proportion of land *farmed in small holdings* rose[47] due to sales to escape ceilings legislation (and to partible inheritance alongside population growth; Vyas, 1976). The proportion of operated land in holdings up to 1 hectare rose from 39% in 1961–1962 through 46% in 1971–1972 and 56% in 1981–1982 to reach 62% in 1995–1956 (Singh, 1990, 66; DES, 2004; Swamy, 1988, 561).[48] India is among several countries in which fragmentation of land among growing farm families, plus a just-plausible threat of ceilings implementation, prevented land concentration: both owned and operated holdings became slightly less unequal (Sanyal, 1988; Singh, 1990, Ch. 3). This pattern appears confined to countries with land reforms—and covers some, such as Pakistan and Sri Lanka, with much evasion.[49]

4.3.3.ii Latin America   Experience with ceilings-based "land authority" reform in Latin America and West Asia is summarized in Table 7. In Latin America, land reforms after the mid-1980s slowed down in part because several countries had largely completed them (Thiesenhusen, ed., 1989), although Ginis remain high (Table 3), especially in the largest countries. In 2006, ceilings reform is back (though ill-planned and confrontational) in Venezuela and Bolivia, while in NE Brazil and Colombia (Deininger, 1999;

Table 7 Land authority (classical) land reforms in Latin America and West Asia

Where	When	Outcomes: Land Transfers	Outcomes: People	Change in Distribution	References
Mexico	1918–1968	64m ha, 65% of 1961 farmland		Farmland Gini still high (.68 1991)	Otero 1989: 27; King 1977: 93
Ecuador	1964–1983	0.8m ha, 9% of farmland	15% of farm families received land	Share of land in holdings > 100 ha fell from 37.1% (1954) to 22.1% (1974)	Carter and Alvarez 1989: 23–43; Carter and Mesbah 1993: 291; Zevallos 1989:50–2
El Salvador	After 1980	Land acquired from holdings above 100 ha	22.7% of rural households received land		Strasma 1989: 409–12; Diskin 1989: 429–43; Powelson 1984: 105
Dominican Republic	Between 1961 and 1981	83,000 ha (2.7% of 1961 farmland) as private parcels and 30,000 ha as collectives	32,275 private parcels created, comprising 13% of peasant holdings		Stanfield 1989: 319–23
Peru	1969–1980	About 8.6m ha, 40–50% of farmland, acquired	375,000 direct beneficiaries, 24% of rural workforce	Land Gini 0.91 (1972), 0.86 (1994)	Carter and Mesbah 1993: 288–9

Chile	Up to 1973	0.9m (basic irrigated) ha acquired (20% of 1973 arable area). 1986: 57% still in reform sector		Land Gini 0.92 in 1996	Jarvis 1989: 245 Thome 1989: 204
Iraq	1958–1982	1958, 1970 reforms affected 60% of arable land by 1984	322,000 (56%) of ag. households got land by 1980	Land Gini 0.90 (1958), 0.39 (1982)	El-Ghonemy 1990: 216–21
Iran	1962–1975, in three stages	53% villages redistributed	1.9m families got land		Amid 1990: 93–9, 102–3

Tendler, 1991) it has been inserted into New Wave reform (Section 4.3.iv.ix). Overall, Table 7 and subsequent events suggest much land redistribution (though even more was targeted, and in some cases, such as Mexico,[50] there might may have been reconcentration). Unduly gloomy is the conventional wisdom that land reform has achieved little:

- It has been claimed that in Mexico "the revolution ... did not modify property relations fundamentally" (Otero, 1989, 277). Yet in 1918–1968 intermittent but at times "truly revolutionary reforms" had redistributed two-thirds of farmland. There remained huge inequalities and many near-landless farm workers (King, 1977, 93), largely *indigenos* whose alienation precipitated violence in Chiapas from 1994.
- Despite the changes in Ecuador reported in the table, with little reconcentration (Zevallos, 1989), Carter and Alvarez (1989) report claims that neither the 1964 nor the 1970 reform brought "major redistribution of land."
- In El Salvador Diskin (1989, 429–43) claims that "a much-vaunted smallholders' reform has accomplished only [sic] half its goals ... 40 per cent or more of the rural [landless] are not statutorily included". Yet "22.7 per cent of rural families benefited," a big achievement, even if less than "a goal of 60%."
- In Chile many stress Pinochet's counter-reforms, yet by 1986 most land acquired before the 1973 coup had stayed in the reform sector under cooperative or individual management (Jarvis, 1989, 245).
- Other Latin American countries have had substantial land reforms, but Colombia exemplifies aborted reform (de Janvry and Sadoulet, 1989). In Argentina and (despite experiments in the NE) Brazil, access to land is largely unreformed, very unequal, and (Kutcher and Scandizzo, 1981) a brake on efficient farming.

4.3.3.iii Other regions

In Iran, farmland went to 92% of families eligible. Yet skeptics stress that landlords kept the best land; many peasants got to own plots "probably less than the holdings they used to cultivate" as pre-reform tenants; and even if "land reform [gave land] to a large majority of the eligible peasants ... most of the remainder lost their rights and joined the landless" (Amid, 1990: 93–9, 102–3).

In East Asia, China in 1977–1985 saw the world's biggest LA reform, but of collective lands (Section 4.3.4.viii), as in Vietnam in 1993. There were radical LA redistributions in Japan, Taiwan, and Korea after 1945. Though nominally tenancy reforms, they included de facto ownership ceilings, which prevented resumption. Before 1990, reforms in the Philippines—although underfulfilled and with some bad side effects— were major; the debate and legislation later turned from tenancy reforms (which fortuitously transferred much land from landlords to middling-poor tenants before the Green Revolution increased economic rents [Bell, 1990]) toward attempts to help even poorer people through effective ceilings legislation that, by reducing farm size, increases employment per hectare (Hayami et al., 1990).

Substantial, rapidly increasing areas of Eastern and Southern Africa have, or are moving towards, individual farming of once communal lands. Kenya experienced much LA redistribution in the 1960s (Hunt, 1984). Ethiopia in the 1980s suffered a terrible detour [fn. 35]; very unequal crown, church, and other privileged lands were partly collectivized under Mengistu and then submerged in conflict, but since his fall in 1991, not-very-unequal family farming has emerged in most provinces. South Africa ended apartheid in 1994 with 60,000 white commercial farms occupying over 85% of farmland while over a million largely part-time African smallholders shared the remainder; the new government's program to redistribute, to these, one third of large private and state-owned farmland has moved at snail's pace and refocused on increasing medium-scale African farming. Zimbabwe, after independence in 1980, was bound by treaty to enforce no land distribution for 10 years; took no action for a further 12 years; but then embarked on a violent, confused transfer of large commercial white-owned farms, in large part to so-called "war veterans," usually ruling-party supporters and often with no farming experience or intent. This caused major crop losses and job losses by farm workers (often from neighboring countries or minority tribes).[51]

In several countries, a good case for reform has been spoiled by assigning lands to political clients. Much of Eastern and Southern Africa will see growing pressure for orderly reform but risks of land grab. The large-farm growth path in Malawi proved increasingly inefficient as land scarcity and labor surplus became the norm (Sahn and Arulpragasam, 1993).[52] In some other countries with similar trends, both poverty reduction and efficient farm growth require redistribution of land rights away from absentee yeoman politicians and their clients (on Kenya, see Hunt, 1984; but cf. Migot-Adholla, et al., 1991, 169).

4.3.4 Alternatives to the LA model: Do they change farm sizes or get land to the poor?

4.3.4.i Titling, registration   Secure titling can affect size by legalizing sale and rental transactions, and/or providing land collateral so small farms can borrow or long-term security so they invest more. However, *enforced* titling has not produced these effects. Farmers with communal *tenure* almost always farm privately. In Africa, they borrowed as readily as comparable farmers with title (Migot-Adholla, et al., 1991, 171). Lack of title constrained borrowing by small farmers in Guatemala (Shearer, 1991, iv, 19) and Thailand (Feder, et al., 1988), but titled tenure is spreading voluntarily there. In four African countries, neither title nor land transfer rights affected farm productivity (Migot-Adholla, et al., 1991; Place and Hazell, 1993).

Where the state or powerful landowners have title but many smallholders do not, titling improves smallholders' security, as in Honduras (Shearer et al., 1991, iv, 9–13) and West Bengal, where landlords had shifted tenants around to stop them establishing the right to buy land under tenancy laws (Bandyopadhyay, 1995). However, under communal tenure, pressure for titling often comes from "big men" seeking to enclose common land as in the English Enclosure Acts of 1760–1830, or to ease their acquisition of formally common, but in fact private though not legally saleable, smallholdings; "titles may offer more advantage to large . . . farmers who have better access to markets" (Shearer et al., 1991, viii). Titling of customary land led to transfer of income and land from small farms to big estate owners in Malawi (Sahn and Arulpragasam, 1993, 308–11), South Africa (Cross, 1996), and Kenya (FAO, 1991, 25; Barrows and Roth, 1989, 4–11). In Uganda, assignment of square-mile freehold title, and later eviction rights, to chiefs and other notables reduced small tenants' security while not inducing investment (ibid: 15). In Latin American communal areas, titling had similar results (Hirschmann, 1984), on Mapuche lands in Chile (Thiesenhusen, 1989, 494).

State support of agreed, voluntary titling in communal lands could accelerate development of land markets. That could increase farm productivity and investment, though the African evidence is weak. Gains seldom accrue mainly to small farms; titling can often be enclosure in disguise. It helps the poor mainly on disputed or state land and when accompanied by other measures to get them land rights through enforcing ceilings on owned land, settlement, or sale of public land, as in urban areas (de Soto, 1989). Otherwise, especially in communal areas, titling could threaten the poor by helping others deprive them of land.

In general, whether stronger state backing for "property rights" advances *smaller* farms or poorer people depends on two things: initial income and power distribution (if equal, secure title protects the weak; if very unequal, it reinforces the strong) and prospective returns to landholding or to investment on land (if and only if they are high, as in peri-urban Colombia [de Soto, 1992], so are gains from title). Hence the impact of secure property rights depends critically on context, including type of rights and type of investment.

In many post-decollectivization agricultures, very small equal farms have been maintained via periodic redistribution from shrinking to growing farm families. This creates, in some areas but not others, tenure insecurity. In Ethiopia the impact . . . varies across types of investment; [for small households only] insecure tenure . . . encourages planting of trees but discourages terracing . . . [E]liminating the risk of future redistribution and resolving conflicts over land with local authorities would increase the propensity to invest in improving terraces by 28%; making land rights fully transferable [would] add . . . 38%. (Adenew et al., 2003)[53] In North Vietnam "land tenure security [strongly] and land titling [weakly] affect investment behavior *additively*," but effects are weak or absent in the South, with its history of less equal but more secure rights (Ngo, 2005).

4.3.4.ii Patrialization
In British ex-colonies of East, Central, and Southern Africa and French ex-colonies of North Africa and Southeast Asia, the return, to patrials, of farmland owned by ex-colonists or descendants is a major theme of recent agrarian change. Transfer of colonially *owned* farms to grant ownership to indigenous tenants is

redistributive but might not cut *operated* farm size. In Vietnam, [i]n 1955 ... 40 per cent of riceland areas in the South were held by 0.25 per cent of the population, most of them French. [F]rom 1971 to 1974 [the state] redistributed over 1.1 million ha ... to about 1 million tenants, [comprising] 44 per cent of total farm area and over 75 per cent of tenanted area. By 1974 agriculture in the South was dominated by small, owner-operated farms [while] per capita growth in rice production and productivity increased. (Prosterman and Hanstad, 1994, 6) Substantial equalization of *operated* farmland, however, followed only after the "family responsibility" reforms in the decollectivisation of 1993.

Where land was not yet scarce (e.g., South Africa, francophone North Africa, Kenya, Zimbabwe), colonists preferred extensive owner-farming, with labor agency costs cut by plantation-style methods instead of tenancy. This made post-colonial patrialization a rougher road to smaller, more equal farms. Laborers have less managerial experience than tenants. Colonist farmers can became nationals, using their power to skew agricultural institutions and markets in their favor and to repress indigenous farming competition. Their descendants, powerful even after independence (or deracialization), contribute substantially, and often efficiently, albeit with subsidies, to farm output and might obtain support from powerful members of majority ethnic groups. If not, in successor nations *without* mass tenant pressure, governments all too readily patrialize to civil servants and politicians, not to small farmers. Relevantly, several African countries have retained colonial Subdivision Laws that forbid new holdings below a given size or subsidies to labor-displacing equipment. In such cases, patrialization can bring little extra land to smallholders.

4.3.4.iii Tenancy as quasi-land-reform?

Tenancy may be the means through which operated farm size becomes efficient, irrespective of the distribution of ownership (Section 3). In most of Latin America and Asia (and some of Africa), tenancy—often concealed—covers 10–25% of farmland.[54] Typically this leads to smaller farms, providing the otherwise landless with returns to enterprise and raising the demand for labor (Singh, 1990; Otsuka et al., 1992). In India, tenancy reduces plot fragmentation (Mearns, 1999). In China, tenancy markets move land to the poor more efficiently than official redistributions from shrinking to growing farm families (Jin and Deininger, 2002). However, in advanced areas of Asian developing agriculture (e.g., Korea, Punjab), "reverse tenancy" grows (reflecting the rise in equilibrium farm size discussed in Section 3), with small farmers renting at fixed rates to big farmers (Otsuka et al., 1992). If, as is often the case, reverse tenancy affects only a part of a small farmer's landholding, the effect is to raise median but not mean operated holding size.

4.3.4.iv Laws to restrict or regulate tenancies

Tenancy, like land reform, normally strengthens the poor's access to land where land access is unequal, as in South Asia— and much of Africa, despite "communal tenure." Yet this often prohibits tenancy

(Noronha, 1985),[55] as do some Indian states (Mearns, 1999). As population mounts, the gains to all parties from reducing farm size via tenancy increase; even when illegal under land apartheid in South Africa, surreptitious "labor tenancies" emerged. Many governments have outlawed or limited sharecropping, given tenants rights to buy at below-market prices, granted near-absolute security of tenure, set maximum rentals, or otherwise controlled contracts to favor tenants.

Such laws (when backed up with a credible threat of enforcement) induce large owners to evict tenants and self-cultivate (Lanjouw and Stern, 1999, for village evidence from India), so are normally not incentive-compatible. They further concentrate land in big farms; reduce employment, efficiency, and equality; and harm those denied tenancy (Otsuka, 1991). Small tenant farmers' security also suffers via laws seeking "to ban tenancy outright ... [which] inevitably [bring] concealed tenancy ... more informal, shorter (increasingly seasonal), and less secure than ... prior to reform" (Mearns, 1999). In much of rural Asia and Latin America, less farmland is rented—especially for sharecropping, where risk sharing best suits the risk profile of the rural poor—than 25–50 years ago or than would be the case if the landlord were not afraid of tenancy restrictions. So, despite gains to some small-farm tenants who enjoy better terms and can retain their rented land, enforced tenancy restrictions have militated against small farms, except where combined with ceilings laws, which (as in Taiwan and South Korea in the 1950s and West Bengal in 1968; Mearns, 1999) stop large owners from evicting for personal cultivation.

4.3.4.v Consolidation Partible inheritance and population growth mean more fragments per farm in developing countries, raising the cost of land in borders and of labor in moving among fragments. This cuts output, deterring intensive farming, and land value. Consolidation[56] seeks remedy by exchange of fragments. The gains rise with the marketed share of output and as more heavy inputs (from tractors to fertilizers) must be got to the fields: that is, as farms develop, specialize, and exchange (Johnson, 1970). Though, absent redistribution, land consolidation benefits large farmers most *absolutely* (Mearns, 1999), it probably raises income proportionately more for small farmers. First, fragments per hectare vary inversely with farm size. Second, on small farms even a given number of fragments per farm can mean tiny plots. Even twenty years ago, in China, "each farm household ... cultivates an average of 0.6 ha divided into nine separate plots" (Bruce and Harrell, 1989, 6). Oldenburg (1990) argues that, since consolidation means greater gain for small farmers, it may achieve the same goals as LA reform but less contentiously.

To assess this, we should ask: Why do farmers seldom "simply agree to consolidate their holdings" (Johnson, 1970, 176), if this benefits everybody, cuts unit cost, and does not challenge the power structure?[57] First, agency costs, including those of creating trust and providing information on others' land, are big. It might be easier for outsiders to facilitate consolidation for a village, but private firms seldom offer such services. A public authority can, as in Maharashtra; but costs remain high.[58] Second, private farmers often want to keep their fragments. Apart from attachment to plots known from long experience, this can raise or smooth a farm's income. Armenian family farms "are fragmented because irrigated, rain–fed, orchards, grasslands and pasture were distributed separately within each village" at decollectivization (Csaki et al., 1995, 34), as in Albania (Stanfield et al., 1992, 9, 12). In Ghana and Rwanda "consolidation [via] restrictions on sales or rentals limits ability of farmers to adjust optimally the fragmentation ... of their holdings over time" (Blarel et al., 1991). Fragments may have different seasonal peaks for labor, water, or food production (hence Farmer, 1960, advised "not controlling subdivision of paddy lands" in Sri Lanka). Fragmentation can also reduce risk. In wet years, when lowland is waterlogged, higher patches can yield at their best; in drought years, low-lying patches may get enough water while upland yields nothing.[59] Finally, consolidation may have an ecological "downside. Farmers [concentrate on] pockets of land [with] better soils and moisture [and so] ... retard the spread of pests and diseases" (Roth and Bruce, 1994, 36).

So consolidation, though raising input and net output most for small family farms, raises risk (to which they are specially vulnerable) and cuts flexibility (one of their major advantages). In addition, although consolidation cuts labor movement costs, that raises incentives to employ labor; if on balance wage-rates rise, that can induce shifts to larger, less labor-using farms (Csaki et al., 1995, 40; Bain, 1993, 129–36), especially if costs of labor-saving capital (e.g., of tractor movements) fall. If consolidation reduces costs of titling, the poor can lose because they lack influence on deciding claims, setting borders, and valuing lands. Even *after* titling, it may harm the poor if big owners unduly influence it. That did not happen in the Indian Punjab mainly because, after partition, the exchange of refugees and migrants between the Pakistani and Indian rural Punjabs led to equalizing land redistribution (Randhawa, 1986, 58). Such special conditions may be required if consolidation is not to shift land from small farms and poor people. Although consolidation of fragments need not raise farm size, in practice it has tended to do so.

4.3.4.vi Settlement schemes   These, like consolidation, seem to redistribute to small farms without confronting the rich. Settlement involves (1) abandoned farmland, such as tea estate land in Sri Lanka in the 1970s; (2) "new" lands, after state-supported development; or (3) state lands. Many governments have tried such schemes (Kenya, Malaysia, Brazil) and some are huge. Transmigration from Java to Indonesia's "outer islands" involved 418,000 persons in state-supported settlement and 604,000 spontaneously in 1950–1972 and a further 377,000 and 221,000, respectively, in 1975–1980

(FAO, 1991, 7–18). After 1980, in Indonesia, Thailand, and North Africa, settlement took increasing priority over direct land redistribution.

Settlement has performed worse than the LA model at cost-effectively getting land to small farms. Most LA beneficiaries had experience nearby; much settled land reached people with remote, or no, farm experience (FAO, 1991; Kinsey and Binswanger, 1993, 13). In Indonesia in 1976, one in three settlers had never owned or managed farms (Oberai, 1988, 52). Whether settled land reaches able small farmers depends on:

- *Whether planners assume "that 'big is beautiful.'"* In Kenya and Zimbabwe, "obstacles to efficient land use and ... employment generation" included "laws against subdivision [, enforcing] large blocks of land"; in Zimbabwe "insistence [in] official settlement ... on large, contiguous areas ... meant that many isolated farms acquired remained unused." In Sudan's Gezira, "settlers became absentee landlords because the land allocated to them initially far exceeded the labor capacity of their families ... [Conversely, i]n Kenya ... the increase in production arising from [an early] shift from large to small units [was] 15–90%" (Kinsey and Binswanger, 1993, 5–9).
- *Whether settlers must move house.*
- *Whether land has to be "developed" through irrigation, fencing, etc.*
- *Whether settlement is (1) supported by low-cost infrastructure, (2) spontaneous, or (3) for individual farming.* (1) For the Settlement Authority to meet many settler needs has high costs (cf. FELDA in Malaysia), but "the finite horizon of the Kenyan task force approach and of the Indonesian handover to local governments has avoided ... perpetual paternalism." Public provision of extension and clean water to initial settlers has advantages, yet "there is no direct evidence ... that higher public costs per beneficiary family are associated ... with success" (Kinsey and Binswanger, 1993). (2) In the 1970s three out of four settlers were spontaneous (World Bank, 1978). Infrastructure for a spontaneously settled 5 ha rice farm in the Philippines cost half as much as in a scheme (Oberai, 1988, 155). (3) Collective farming (usually directed) almost assured settlement failure in Latin America (Nelson, 1973, 265), as elsewhere.
- *Whether poor settlers farm worse.* "Agricultural settlement schemes do not make good welfare programmes." However, of features linked to settler success in farming—being married; more workers per household; age under 45; farm experience and skills; better education—the first three are more common among poorer (and presumably smaller) settlers. Only the last goes with affluence (ibid., 13).
- *Whether pluralist politics pressurizes the authorities to settle the poor and to provide them appropriate public goods such as research.* In Kenya pluralism weakened after 1974, and land reform as well as settlement increasingly favored the less poor (Harbeson, 1984, 157). In Malaysia local leaders favored claims to remote lands for "known troublemakers ... to get rid of them" (Oberai, 1988, 96). Politics can trump economics, so bigger farmers engross the benefits. In Brazil, one in three settlers were "familiar with cropping 25 ha or more"; settlements replicated farm inequality in areas of origin (Oberai, 1988, 337–9).

Though small farmers may gain from a settlement scheme, that outcome is often is costly and uncertain. If the rich retain great power, schemes will not get much good new land to the poor. Historically, schemes have aimed mainly to even out population density and develop "new" lands—not to redistribute land or to cut poverty. Population growth and spontaneous settlement have greatly reduced the scope for such schemes.

4.3.4.vii State and collective farms   Russia's October 1917 Revolution[60] and the 1949 Chinese Revolution were supported partly because they promised small, fairly equal family farms and initially delivered tens of millions of them[61]; but 10–15 years later most (Wolf, 1969; Bruce and Harrell, 1989) were forced into Soviet collective and state farms and Chinese communes and brigades. Huge units, without independent farmers, were ideal foci for state extraction of food and fuel wood by compulsory quotas and "price scissors." After 1945, such policies found analogues in parts of Southeast Asia, East Europe, Africa, and Latin America. After decades of rural misery, the promise of land reform was redeemed again in 1977–1984 in China and in the 1990s in Vietnam, Armenia (Csaki et al., 1995), Albania (Stanfield et al., 1992), and Romania. There, de facto privatization into small, fairly equal family farms is almost complete.

Through force or famine, the "terrible detour" killed thousands in Africa in the 1980s and millions in the Soviet Union in the 1930s and China in 1959–1963. As for productivity, in the U.S.S.R. the tiny proportion of land in private smallholdings achieved many times the TFP of the (large) collective farms (Hanstad, 1998). "[For] vegetables, potatoes, meat and milk, these large farms failed to compete against small, subsidiary land plots . . . privately operated by workers of state and collective farms after work" (Overchuk, 2003). In Zimbabwe in the 1980s, the semicollectivist Model B farms on reform lands did far worse than Model A family farms; this was "typical of experiments in Ethiopia, Tanzania and Mozambique" (Roth and Bruce, 1994, 25–6; cf. Bruce, 1986, 63).

Why was the record so bad? First, collective action and centralized management are especially costly in farming—a geographically extended, micro-location-specific, sequential activity needing swift, hands-on adjustment and personal knowledge of the land. Second, forced surplus extraction, so convenient from big state or collective farms, removed much of whatever incentive remained for them; in their lower output per ha–year (than small family farms) outweighed the higher marketed share of output, *reducing* surplus (Ellman, 1975)! Third, advocacy of huge state/collective farms in the U.S.S.R. (less so in China) ignored the fact that growing labor surpluses and increasing land scarcity favored small *operated* holdings. Later, unsuccessful African and Latin American collective/state farm experiments, though less violent and disruptive (outside Ethiopia), were similar in these respects to U.S.S.R. and Chinese experiences.

4.3.4.viii Privatization and decollectivization   Around 1976, over a billion persons were trapped, often unable to leave legally, in state or collective farms. Yet China had completed the move to near-egalitarian household farming by 1985, and Albania, Armenia, Romania, and Vietnam had done so by 1995.[62] By 2000 most other transitional economies had divested much of the former enforced joint farms to family or middle farmers. Russia made a slow start, and in some of the FSU the move from "forced farming" stalled. In some cases (Poland, Hungary), development has meant rising rural capital/labor ratios so that transaction costs have come to favor, if not giant farms as under collectivism, at least moderately large farm size.[63] Elsewhere, will decollectivization create thriving small family farms? Key issues are:

- Is land _supply_ truly privatized? In Russia[64] most "decollectivized" land was distributed via shares, without demarcation of plots, and with strong pressure on recipients to sell, or even give, shares back to the collective management (Duncan and Ruetschle, 2002). In 2000 (Giovarelli and Bledsoe, 2001) "Western CIS countries [were] ... primarily farming through large collective-style farms" and many remain today. Some attribute this to fear that demarcated small farms, or part-time farms, even if chosen in the market, are "uneconomic" (Overchuk, 2003; Rembold, 2003). The evidence does not justify that fear (Hanstad, 1998).
- Is land _demand_ for post-reform private plots constrained by demographics (e.g., irreversibly aging rural populations) (Wegren and Durgin, 1997)?
- How trammeled are private-property rights? Most joint farmland in transitional economies was divested with usufruct rights for 20–40 years or life but with limited or no rights to sell, mortgage, or rent. Whatever the disadvantages,[65] land thus redistributed into small farms tended to stay that way.
- Is the land restituted or redistributed? Most countries dissolving state and collective farmland (over and above marginal uses to enlarge household plots) redistribute to members of collectives or state farm workers, often in proportion to household size. Armenia, Albania, and Vietnam have almost completed this process. However, Bulgaria, the Czech and Slovak republics, East Germany, and the Baltic FSU restituted to original owners or descendants; Hungary and Romania combined restitution and redistribution (Brooks and Lerman, 1994, 27). They can reach similar results if, as in Bulgaria (Kopeva et al., 1994, 203–4) and Albania, pre-Communist farm ownership had been fairly equal and most rural families had continued to farm locally on state or collective farms. Elsewhere, restitution may impede small farms. In the Czech Republic, land moved back to former aristocrats, "big men" with local monopoly power, and other rich victims of expropriation under Communism. Even if some take the "Junker path" to progressive, albeit labor-displacing, large-scale farming, this is hardly geared to optimal farm size.
- Does change aim to shift state and collective lands toward (1) more or bigger household plots, (2) small commercial farms, or (3) large commercial farms? Household plots helped prevent starvation in the Ukraine in the 1990s. Hanstad (1998) summarizes evidence that "small is efficient" in parts of the FSU. But this cannot apply everywhere (in combine-harvested Russian and Ukrainian wheatlands laid out in

large farms), nor forever, as development brings rural exodus and capital-intensification.

- Where land has moved from state or collective farms into fairly equal family small-holdings (e.g., China, Vietnam, Romania, Armenia, Albania, and Ethiopia), how is any transition to larger farms, which may be indicated as economic growth reduces rural labor/capital ratios, handled to minimize inefficiency and inequity? Alternative models of change in China—where, it should be noted, 5 ha is a large farm—are reviewed in Prosterman et al. [1998], Chen et al. [1998], Zhou [2000], and Ping Li [2003].

4.3.4.ix New Wave land reform (NWLR) NWLR (Bell, 1990; Carter and Mesbah, 1991; de Janvry and Sadoulet et al., 1991; Tendler, 1991; Deininger, 1999; Deininger and Olinto, 2000) seeks to shift farmland from big to small farms by consensual, decentralized, market-assisted transfer. That implies measures to raise the poor's land demand curve, big farmers' land supply curve, and/or the proportion of land sales that are from rich to poor (call this *N-land*); normally, most sales are among big landowners or among small ones (Shearer et al., 1991).[66] In most NWLR, consensus requires subsidies or compensation, and thus taxpayers or donors willing to share land redistribution costs normally borne by those who transact in land.

Demand-led NWLR often is implemented via land vouchers for poor buyers, raising the issues of detail discussed in Section 4.3.2 and with the effect of raising land prices. That, over time, cuts the amount of land obtained for a given subsidy (e.g., voucher fund)—and hence affordability for state or donor—to an extent arithmetically dependent on initial farmland turnover, the supply elasticity of farmland, and the share of N-land.

Supply-led NWLR may be driven by fear that governments will enact LA reforms, implement more forcefully those already enacted, or fail to respond to land seizures, for example, by movements of the landless or small farmers. Then, specifically, rich-to-poor land sales are stimulated. Vinoba Bhave's Bhoodan, or land-gift, movement in India in the 1950s appealed to rich people's moral sense and released several million hectares of land.[67] In Taiwan in 1953, the government induced higher land supply by offering landlords compensation with shares in seized Japanese urban assets. In Africa, derestricting subdivision raises the share of N-land in total supply. States can also make sales to the poor more attractive to the rich; in Brazil's decentralized reforms, local authorities offered large farmers who gave up N-land cheaply access to new irrigation on retained land (Tendler, 1991).[68] This works if someone, taxpayers or (as here) a World Bank loan, pays. Even here, threats as well as promises lay behind the increases in the supply of N-land: rich nonparticipants might be exposed to *Sim Terra* land invasions (*Financial Times*, August 15, 1991; August 11, 1994) or to enforcement of laws, currently ignored, that set land ceilings and restricted the occupation of common lands (Tendler, 1991).

4.4 Market interventions and farm size
4.4.1 Taxes and subsidies and farm size

In this section we consider the relationship between the tax regime (i.e., taxes and sub-sidies on inputs and outputs) facing agriculture and farm size. In principle this relation-ship may be two-way, and the "political economy" effects from farm size to the tax regime may be rather subtle. For instance, in France it may be that large farmers have an interest in keeping small farms in business in order that pressure for farm protection may make appeal to the need to preserve *la France profonde*.

The analysis in Section 3 suggests three general ways in which tax policy and levels can impinge on farm size.[69] We begin with the case where the conditions, discussed in Section 3, for a single equilibrium size of farm are met and restrict attention to propor-tional taxes and subsidies. Tax policy can affect (1) the equilibrium size of the family farm, (2) the equilibrium size of the nonfamily ("commercial") farm, and (3) the rela-tive advantages of family versus commercial farming.

As regards (2), commercial farms, by definition, are large enough that a high pro-portion of labor input is hired, so the lower supervision costs of family labor are not having a significant influence on optimal scale. We do not here explore whether unit supervision costs of hired labor *itself* vary enough to significantly affect equilibrium farm size. We have seen that for such large farms the evidence is consistent with the hypoth-esis of constant returns to scale, and if that is correct equilibrium farm size is indetermi-nate. *A fortiori*, the impact of the tax regime on equilibrium farm size is indeterminate.

As regards (3), we argued in Section 3 that as capital becomes cheaper relative to labor, the advantages of large scale in reducing unit capital-related transactions costs may come to outweigh the advantages of small scale in reducing unit labor-related transaction costs. This shift of advantage may cause an equilibrium shift from family to commercial farming in the course of economic development. Evidently changes in the tax regime that cheapen capital relative to labor could bring about the same shift.

As regards (1), tax policy can affect the equilibrium size of the family farm on land of given quality in two main ways. First, it can affect the equilibrium land/labor ratio; for example, an output subsidy will, as observed in Section 3, raise land rents and lower the land/labor ratio, thus making the family farm smaller for given labor input per farm. Second, tax policy might affect that labor input—and therefore equilibrium farm size—by changing either the amount of hired labor used on the farm or the amount of family labor used off the farm. For instance, if the earnings of temporary migrant strawberry pickers on family-operated U.K. farms should become effectively free of tax, that would raise the incentive for the farms to employ such labor at harvest time and would tend therefore to raise equilibrium farm size.

Allowing for variation in land quality so that there is a Ricardian "margin of culti-vation" is one way to get equilibrium heterogeneity in farm size; therefore tax policy can affect the size distribution of family farms by moving the extensive margin. Thus a tax change that favors agriculture will bring more low-quality land into use, with an effect on average farm size that depends on whether the land/labor ratio is relatively high or low on this marginal land. This might go either way. Low quality in rocky or hilly terrain might mean that extra labor input is needed to extract a given output from a given patch of land; this means that family farms on marginal land will be relatively small. The opposite case would obtain where lands were marginal because they were of low fertility and suitable only for grazing.

The discussion so far has ignored taxes that are explicitly discriminatory across farms of different sizes. Plainly a tax that only applies to farms above X ha will discourage such farms. More subtly, in many circumstances the reach of the tax authorities will not extend to the interior of the farm, so self-consumed product and the employment of family labor and of other own-farm inputs will be exempt. Rises in output or labor taxes in such cases will clearly favor farming for subsistence.

Turning to political economy, larger size is artificially favored because big farms are better placed to have tax laws written or interpreted to their advantage. As for subsidies, except perhaps in efficient autocracies, the biggest farmers need to share gains with others, to create popular backing for farm support despite its costs to consumers and/or taxpayers. A few dozen large French farmers alone cannot alone block the roads with tractors, nor a few dozen large U.S. farmers swing the vote in marginal states; to achieve large distortive subsidy they need support from many others, and it is usually smaller farmers (plus perhaps rural traders dependent on their custom) who can most plausibly be mobilized—but only if their share of subsidies is attractive enough.[70] A dominating coalition, even if not reconciled to much overt land reform, might accept, or advocate, output tax and subsidy reform, increasing incentives to big owners to sell or lease land to smaller and more labor-intensive holdings. In Brazil, removal of fiscal concessions that favor large owners or operators or their typical crops over small farmers has been advocated to level the tax-subsidy treatment of outputs (Thiesenhusen and Melmed-Sanjak, 1990, 408) and inputs (Binswanger and Elgin, 1988). Such processes sit well with liberalization and are sometimes advocated as less contentious than land reform. Both may be impeded by the self-same often powerful potential losers. Fiscal crises make governments readier to reduce deficits by tax-subsidy reform but less ready to spend on land reform. Furthermore, democratic pressures can push small and middle farmers, who might oppose the landless when these sought land reform, to join them in seeking more equitable tax-subsidy treatment (de Janvry and Sadoulet, 1991).[71]

4.4.2 OECD farm support: effect on farm size

In 1995, OECD agricultural subsidies to producers totaled $182 billion, or 40% of production. OECD farm producer prices were 66% above border prices (de Moor, 1996). Subsidies reached $248 billion in 1999–2001 (Ricupero, 2003). This is often stated to help smaller farms (which are relatively labor-intensive) to survive, thereby enabling more people to stay in farming or farm employment—the *peasant outcome*.[72] In fact, OECD farm support has not overcome the tendency of farm size to grow and of farm numbers and employment to decline. Moreover, the (weak) evidence suggests that farm support went with *worse* prospects for the peasant outcome. Between 1986–1990 and 1996–1997, farm employment fell from 7.1% of the workforce to 4.9% and in absolute terms fell 14% in the EU-15, despite massive farm support.[73] The fall was far slower in the two OECD countries with least farm support, New Zealand (10.4–8.8%, an absolute fall of only 5%) and Australia (5.7–5.1%, an absolute *rise* of 2%; Findeis et al., 2001). Between 1989–1990 and 1997, farms with over 40 ha in the EU-12 rose from 6.3% to 8.5% of all farms; if land is standardized by quality, the rise in the "largest" groups' share was more, from 6.8% to 10.5% (Directorate-General for Agriculture, 2002, Ch. 1, Tables 2.3, 2.7). So farm support has not prevented concentration, nor employment decline in agriculture. Part of the reason may be that incidence is not impact. Only about $1 of every $5 of EU net farm support added to *net* farm income; in the early 1990s, "$2.75 is spent [on] additional inputs [and] $1 covers the opportunity cost of diverted household resources" (de Moor, 1996).

Has the part of farm subsidies that stays with farmers benefited mainly big farms? Their pressures on the U.S. Senate/House reconciliation committee blocked the proposal in the 2001 Farm Security Bill to cap (at $275,000) producer support to any single farm. In the EU in 2003, their pressures successfully blocked the Commission's proposal to reform the Common Agricultural Policy by paying out producer supports that declined as farm size rose (van Donkersgoed, 2003). In the EU, the best-off 20% of farmers receive 80% of subsidies; the 15% of French farms receiving over 20,000 euros in subsidies account for 60% of total payments (Ricupero, 2003). In the United States, from 1995–2002 the top 10% of recipients received 71% of all USDA subsidies, whereas the bottom 80% received only 14% (Environmental Working Group, 2003), but such figures can mislead, both because proportions of land and value added are not known and because some apparently large recipients (including the four largest) are cooperatives.[74] More tellingly, at the very top end, the 20 largest recipients of USDA subsidies in 1995–2002 include Tyler Farms ($35 million of commodity support), Pilgrims Pride ($15.1M), Cargill ($10.9M), J. G. Boswell ($10.5M) and Morgan Farms ($9.5M; EWG, 2003). In 1996–2000, although the median farm subsidy was $4675, among Fortune 500 companies Westvaco in 1996–2000 received $269,000, Chevron $260,000, John Hancock $211,000, and du Pont $118,000, and David Rockefeller secured $352,000 of subsidies for his family farm. Of U.S. commodity subsidies, 90% are for five crops; this excludes some 60% of farmers for whose products there is no government program and among whom small farms are overrepresented (Riedel and Frydenlund, 2001, 2003).

In sum, we find an interesting tension among three ideas: (1) that subsidies keep small farms on marginal land afloat, (2) that small farm workforces have fallen fastest in OECD countries with the heaviest farm subsidies, and (3) that manipulable subsidies favor very large size for reasons of political economy.

4.4.3 Forex and other farm price repression in poor countries: Farm-size effects

Agricultural producers in a sample of 18 developing countries faced a *de facto* net output tax rate of 30% from 1960 to 1984, usually less due to *overt* interventions (overt input and output, including export, taxes net of subsidies; quotas) than *implicit* in exchange rate overvaluation and selective industrial protection. Income transfers out of agriculture averaged 46% of agricultural GDP annually between 1960 and 1984. In showing this, Krueger et al. (1995) identify four groups:

- *Extreme taxers.* These are all, and only, the sample countries in sub-Saharan Africa, viz., Ivory Coast, Ghana, and Zambia, with implicit or overt net taxes on agriculture above half its value added. (The proportions have since declined sharply.)
- *Representative taxers.* For example, Argentina, Colombia, Egypt, Morocco, Pakistan, and Thailand: 30–40%.
- *Mild taxers.* From 8–22% (Brazil, Chile, and Malaysia).
- *Protectors.* South Korea and Portugal subsidized agriculture by roughly 10% of value added.

"Graduating" developing countries often become fiercer protectors than long-developed countries; on Mexico in 1982–1986, see (Burger, 1994), and note the trajectories of Portugal and South Korea from 1984 to 2003.

Burger (1994) finds similar results for 1982–1986 and concludes that most developing countries had net production taxes. "There is no hard evidence [that] agriculture is taxed in the 1990s" in developing countries, but—despite liberalization, and as with farm support in the developed world—"many ... policies which previously produced the large taxation [in developing countries] still exist" (de Moor, 1996). This occurs despite large gross subsidies to pesticides (Farah, 1994) and fertilizers (Repetto, 1988), though these have declined since the 1980s as fiscal pressures pushed developing countries, if they liberalized, to do more to curb overt farm input subsidies than (far larger, but usually implicit) output taxes.

As argued in Section 4.4.1, net taxation of agriculture tends in principle to raise equilibrium farm size, except to the extent that small farms are insulated by subsistence. Such insulation declines with developmental and agricultural specialization and progress, as in much of Asia. Moreover, despite their net taxes on agriculture, most developing countries have subsidized inputs, which big farmers have the most power to access. Therefore, even though the size of the effect cannot be quantified, the extractive price regime in most developing countries in the past 50 years appears to have conduced to increasing farm size. Conversely, Nishio and Akiyama (1996), using data from Sulawesi Island, Indonesia, showed that the boom in cocoa prices during 1990–1994 favored small farmers against large ones. Moreover, just as price extraction tends to be especially harmful to small farms, so support for provision of market-undersupplied roads, research, extension, land policy, credit, water, and so on—not just of "pure public goods"—potentially favors them.

4.4.4 Progressive land taxes to affect farm size?

Progressive land taxes, unlike output taxes and subsidies, are *intended* as incentives to land redistribution. However, a prerequisite is a reliable, up-to-date land register; few developing countries have this. Second, "the trick ... of distributing the burden in a manner acceptable to the contending parties" (Bell, 1990, 157) may be no easier than for land redistribution. Third, some claim that land tax, especially if progressive, is costly, evadable, and hard to collect. Fourth, success in stimulating land redistribution implies revenue losses from progressive land tax. However, progressive land tax can be made simple, at some cost to fairness. Especially where land is very unequal, tax can be confined to holdings above a given worth—say, the highest-value 10% of owned holdings. These are almost always titled and registered. A tax of 1% per year on land value *above* that of the 20th highest percentile would achieve rough-and-ready progressiveness. Assuming that farmland value is 10 times the net farm income it generates, this tax would take 10% of net farm income of the top landed quintile—unlikely to engender counterrevolution, especially if it replaced top rates of agricultural income tax.[75] Avoidance of progressive land tax by subdivision (via sale or lease) of large owned holdings is not an objection to, but an object of, such taxation.

There were successes "in Japan and Australia in the 19th and early 20th centuries." In the United States, property or land taxes absorb over 15% of the return on farmland, and in 1994 Sweden introduced a 1.7% tax on land values (see also Dorner and Saliba, 1981). In the Indian states as a whole, land taxes fell from 20–21% of revenue in 1950 and 1960 to 2.6% in 1989–1990, but this is no iron law; in West Bengal, the proportion recovered from 3% in 1970–1971 to 17% by 1989–1990 (Prasad, 1993, 73, 76). Zimbabwe allowed local councils to impose modest but progressive land taxes, and most do (Roth and Bruce, 1994, 55–6). In Meitan County, China, small land taxes for local use were effectively collected (Bruce and Harrell, 1989, 14–15). Chile, Jamaica, and Colombia have significant land taxes (Shearer et al., 1991, 41). So do other Latin American countries, some with progressive elements; low revenue yields indicate lax implementation, but this does "not indicate that land taxes have little potential but the lack of a strong commitment" (Dorner, 1992, 78).

Particular tax-subsidy reforms, such as a shift toward progressive land taxes, can, if feasible, achieve some of the aims of land reform. But tax-subsidy reform can only rarely substitute for land reform. Bell (1990, 158) advocates announcing land reform "only after the effects of tax reform are largely realized." However, progressive inheritance taxes, if these preserve horizontal equity among locations and types of assets, may be complementary with New Wave land reform (Section 4.3.4.ix).

5. LIBERALIZATION AND SMALL FARMS IN POOR COUNTRIES: SUPERMARKETS, GRADES, HORTICULTURE, AND INTERMEDIATION FAILURE

Standard Heckscher-Ohlin models and their modern successors (e.g., Wood, 1994) imply that liberalization and globalization (LG), by reallocating activity within a country toward products for which it has a comparative advantage, favor sectors and types of firms that make intensive use of that country's relatively plentiful factors. Developing countries have plentiful labor, per unit of capital and of skills (and in a growing majority of cases, of land), compared to developed countries. So, LG should, in principle, change GDP structure and hence redistribute national income—within developing countries progressively, toward labor, toward agriculture, and within it toward labor-intensive products (e.g., horticulture) and producers (e.g., small farms); within developed countries regressively, against all these.[76] LG is many-faceted and gradual, and evidence on its distributive impact is incomplete and controversial (Winters et al., 2004; Cornia, ed., 2004). However, it is hard to detect shifts—factor-price-induced or other—toward smaller-scale farming in the slipstream of LG in most developing countries. Small farms in South and East Asia raised their share of land *before* LG. Why, contrary to theory, might LG fail to redistribute activity and income toward small farms in developing countries? First, agricultural LG has proceeded more slowly than for industry in most developing countries and at snail's pace in their OECD customers. Second, where LG *has* affected agriculture in a developing country and its trading partners, that country's gains could go to larger and more capital-intensive farms (despite Heckscher-Ohlin-Wood) for reasons of political economy, time lags, or the path of agrotechnical progress.[77]

Recent narratives suggest that perverse pro-large-farm, anti-labor results of LG in developing countries can be rooted in the interface between LG institutions and those of most developing countries. In that context, Reardon et al. (2001, 2002, 2003, 2005) argue that three linked concomitants of LG—the growing role of *supermarkets, grades and standards*, and *export horticulture*—often tend to favor large farms but that outcomes more favorable to small farms can sometimes be achieved through policy interventions, changed incentives, or collective action by small farmers.

First, LG in the form of greatly expanded foreign direct investment (FDI) is the main factor among many (Reardon et al., 2003) raising the profile of *supermarkets*, "increasingly and overwhelmingly multi-nationalized (foreign-owned) and consolidated," in developing countries. "Latin America [in the 1990s experienced] the same development of supermarket [share at retail as] the USA had experienced in five decades" (ibid., 5). By 2000, the supermarket share of food retail sales for the six largest Latin American countries was 60%; in South Africa, 55%; rising fast in East Africa; and (for processed and packaged foods only) 63% in Korea, Taiwan, and the Philippines; 33% in Malaysia, and Thailand; and increasing fast in China. Due mainly to lower salience of FDI, supermarket expansion has been slower in South Asia and much slower in Central and West Africa (in Nigeria, supermarkets still accounted for only 5% of food at retail; ibid., and Reardon et al., 2002). Supermarket expansion initially concentrates on packaged foods but increasingly affects fruits and vegetables, meat, dairy products, and even food staples. Expansion starts in the main cities but soon spreads, first to smaller towns, then countrywide.

To cut unit acquisition costs, supermarkets have come to rely on fewer and consolidated wholesalers and have otherwise developed procurement methods and supply chains highly favorable to deliveries of standardized products in large quantities. This hampers, or even cuts out, small farmers. Even where their unit production costs are lower, their market share can be imperiled by higher unit transaction costs in the new, supermarket-induced distribution chain (Reardon et al., 2003, 12–16, 18, 20). Rapid, LG-fueled expansion of supermarkets into the hinterland, and recently into horticulture, seems, in some countries, to threaten all small-farm competitiveness, outside a few high-weight/value products for self- or local consumption in remote areas unattractive to supermarkets.

Until nonfarm opportunities expand rapidly, are there policy options to help small farmers and to avoid farm size concentration, with its tendency to reduce the share of labor in agricultural income? Restrictions on supermarket growth or FDI are unlikely, given LG. However, some public or collective actions, or incentives, can make supermarket growth friendlier to small farms. Reardon et al. (2002) emphasize "public support (for investment, retraining, certification, and licensing) to producers and their organizations to allow them direct access to supermarkets; promotion of . . . payments within 30 days by supermarkets; promotion of competition among supermarkets [and alternative retail outlets for small farmers,] including . . . modernization of specialist shops and street fairs." In Zambia and South Africa (Weatherspoon et al., 2003), "where projects can be put in place to 'upgrade' the small farmers to meet the needs of supermarkets, the chains appear to be eager to participate." The "meteoric" growth of supermarkets in China, with average farm size of 0.5 ha and low farmland inequality, has spawned a variety of small-friendly arrangements for outgrowing and procurement, with producers' associations prominent around Shanghai, as in Indonesia (Reardon et al., 2004; and personal communication).

Second, LG accompanies the spread of *grades and standards* (G&S). Public G&S are imposed by state or state-like agencies overseeing health, labor, and environment largely on behalf of cities, developed countries, the EU, and international agencies.

Private G&S—imposed by supermarkets or other retailers or by wholesalers or other intermediaries—may add areas of overview not required by public G&S. Otherwise, private G&S are pointless except to advertise firms' will to enforce public G&S or, more commonly, to be more rigorous than these. Such rigor is partly to satisfy concerned customers or outspoken NGOs—and partly to increase the competitive edge of large buyers. "The role of G&S has shifted from a technical instrument [to cut] transaction costs in homogeneous commodity markets to a strategic instrument of competition in differentiated product markets ... The changes have tended to exclude small firms and farms ... because of the implied investments" (Reardon et al., 2001).[78] Economies of scale in financing and constructing these, and in supervising their application, threaten small farms' competitiveness. The threat is exacerbated because G&S increasingly apply not only to *products* (specifying, for example, fruits' pesticide maxima, size, or color) but also to *processes*. For example, farms supplying formal buyers are increasingly required to abjure child labor. Though small farms have lower unit labor-linked transaction costs and may thus face lower unit costs in *meeting* G&S, that may be outweighed by their higher costs in *validating* G&S, especially process G&S; it is cheaper to monitor and certify absence of child labor or safety of pesticide application on one farm selling 5000 kg of bananas than on 50 farms each selling 100 kg. Many small dairy and poultry farmers in Latin America have gone out of business due to such effects (Reardon et al., 2001; Farina et al., 2000). Small farms risk being confined by G&S to "markets that are purely local and traditional"—unless helped to *upgrade* products (e.g., by the joint work by Technoserve and ICRISAT with smallholder pigeon-peas in India) or to *certify* products already meeting G&S (e.g., by certification companies, such as Mayacert in Guatemala) (Reardon et al., 2001). It is in the interests of buyers to stimulate such small-farm competition in meeting G&S and of smallholders to elicit it, whether through market or political processes. The question is: for what crops, countries and markets is this process fast enough to help smallholders *before* large farms exploit their earlier management of G&S to obtain an unchallengeable niche?

Third, LG have increased the proportion of developing-country farm activity devoted to *export horticulture*. EH products are either climate-specific or only seasonally able to undersell domestic horticulture in developed countries. This has undercut protectionist opposition in the rich world. Also, developing-country EH, as a part of international expansion in farm trade, is favored absolutely by long-term falls in the ratio of transport to production costs and relatively by EH crops' generally high value/weight ratio and income-elastic demand. In several developing countries, EH has recently received most foreign and much large-scale domestic private investment in agriculture. Technical progress in increasing shelf life has enabled developing-country producers, especially those with reliable water and near the equator, to provide a year-round stream of EH products from an almost aseasonal agriculture. EH exports from sub-Saharan Africa grew 150% in 1989–1997, most sold through major Western super-markets. Yet, though EH is usually more labor-intensive than staples farming, small-holders often benefited little, supplying only 18% of export vegetables in Kenya and 6% in Zimbabwe in the late 1990s (Dolan et al., 1999). Incomplete and imperfect credit markets for smallholders (due to asymmetric information) may explain their exclusion from fruit tree crops, which have long gestation periods; in parts of Latin America, such exclusion has eroded or reversed smallholders' gains from earlier land reform (Kydd et al., 2002). However, there are not long gestation periods for pineap-ples, raspberries, or most vegetables. Rather, in a world of spreading G&S and super-market procurement, small farms have been disadvantaged in—even excluded from—EH expansion by demands for product standardization, precisely timed and coordinated delivery, and capacity to negotiate credibly with large buyers. Yet most vegetables and many fruits have traditionally been smallholder products in developing countries. Cooperative marketing enabled them to remain competitive in EH in Gua-temala (von Braun et al., 1989). Private intermediation can also work; in 2001–2003, the well-developed hierarchy of wholesale markets made it easy for tiny farms to export a range of fruits and vegetables to big Indian cities (though seldom for export) in the wake of commercial drip irrigation in Maharashtra (Phansalkar, 2002).

The three challenges to the Heckscher-Ohlin expectation that LG in developing countries would shift activity and income toward small farms—supermarkets, grades and standards, and export horticulture—share a key feature: *intermediation failure*. Inter-mediation is required when an upstream sector, such as farming, minimizes unit pro-duction costs at one (usually a small) size or output level but has to supply to a downstream (e.g., processing) sector in ways that minimize unit delivery costs, which is achieved at a different (usually larger) farm size or scale. The tension can be reduced or reconciled by appropriate intermediation.[79] In many countries, specialized firms have long collected small amounts of rubber, tea, or sugar, intermittently but to a strict schedule, from many small farmers; checked quality and fed back problems to them; and delivered a smooth, large product flow to large processors (Binswanger et al., 1996). The main barrier to the natural small-farm, labor-intensive, and hence redistrib-utive outcome of LG is the failure, in new countries or for new products, of analogous intermediaries to emerge efficiently or rapidly between small farms and supermarkets, horticultural exporters or buyers, or dealers requiring specific G&S. Intermediation failure can arise from market failure (due to lack of information or otherwise) or from high startup costs of intermediation in countries with inadequate information, contract law, or transport. In either case, some initial subsidy to administrative cost of (rather than to prices paid or charged by) intermediaries between small farmers and the emerging LG system may be indicated. Successful intermediaries have included coop-eratives, firms, and (as with AMUL in India) public enterprises, usually with a hard budget constraint.

End Notes

*. We gratefully acknowledge valuable comments from Robert Evenson, help with data from Hiek Som of FAO and Steve Wiggins of ODI, and research assistance from Alvaro Herrera.

1. FAO Agricultural Censuses involve fieldwork by the implementing country—a minority in most continents and a small minority in Africa—to a (more or less) standardized FAO template and with FAO help at any time in the identified decade but most of the time in the first three or four years of the decade, though processing and availability can take another three or four years.

2. Some countries exclude tiny farms. This omission can undermine international comparisons of mean farm size. Since the proportion of farmland in tiny farms is normally itself tiny, "median by area" may be a preferable measure in some circumstances.

3. Just three countries represent Africa here: Ethiopia, Lesotho, and Malawi.

4. Argentina is not included, but comparison of 1914 data (from Diaz-Alejandro, 1970) with the 1988 FAO census shows little change in the size distribution of holdings over the century and certainly no increase. In 1914 the mean holding was 531 ha, compared to 469 ha in 1988. In 1914, 33% of holdings in Argentina were less than 25 ha; in 1988, this proportion was roughly 37%.

5. Canadian farms were around 40 ha on average 1870 to 1880 and increased to an average of around 80 ha in 1920, over 100 ha by 1950, and over 270 ha by 2001. In England and Wales the rise was comparatively slight. The proportion of holdings with more than 121.5 hectares of crop and grass rose from 3.4% in 1875 to 5% in 1966 (MAFF, 1968).

6. In the DR Congo, only the traditional sector is included in the census.

7. The outlying observations for Finland and Norway are intriguing. See also Figure 5.

8. Correlation coefficient 0.68, significant at 1%. Data in Appendix A.

9. The surveys for Benin, Burkina Faso, and the Democratic Republic of the Congo include only holdings in what is defined as the traditional sector, for which collection of data on hired labor may have been judged not worthwhile.

10. These data differ from the FAO data because in censuses and labor force surveys individuals are asked to decide their status in their main job. People who both operate smallholdings and work for other farmers will have to choose which is their main occupation and reply accordingly. By contrast, in a farm survey, these people may legitimately be counted twice. It follows that the reported proportion of hired workers will differ depending on the whether the farm or the individual is the unit of observation. Unfortunately, the difference between the two measures cannot be signed unambiguously. The difference depends upon, among other things, the amount of dual job holding and the probability with which dual jobholders will report themselves as hired or self-employed. A further complication arises as one notes that agricultural contractors who are hired labour from a farm perspective are self-employed from a labour market perspective.

11. In contrast, the United States and Canada have unexpectedly high shares of family labor in total farm labor, given their mean *farm size*.

12. A detailed discussion of how these elements interact in sub-Saharan Africa to determine the geographical pattern of intensification is provided by Pingali, Bigot, and Binswanger (1987), Part 1.

13. It is consistent, therefore, that a big majority of farms in country X are family farms, whereas a big majority of the agricultural population are *not* family farmers, because many of them are peripatetic temporary laborers.

14. If account is to be taken of transaction costs associated with the supervision and training of family members, one may define such costs for hired labor as net of the family labor transaction costs.

15. No neat equivalent to 1(b) and 2(b) exists for this case.

16. In the limit, as in the case of most livestock production in the United States, land could become sufficiently insignificant as a factor of production that the activity is best viewed as industrial rather than agricultural.

17. This discussion has avoided many of the complexities of three-factor production theory, especially much of the interplay between factor prices and factor proportions. A fuller explanatory note is available from the authors.

18. Development has an ambiguous effect on land rent in this model—for example, technological advance and rises in reservation utility pull in opposite directions. Schultz (1964) noted that land rents tended not to rise with development.

19. If labor productivity in nonagriculture sufficiently exceeds that in agriculture, just a rise in the share of the labor force in nonagriculture (small enough not to absorb all the absolute growth in the labor force) can generate such a result. So, it is not even necessary to appeal to differential rates of productivity growth across sectors.

20. Causation is complex; for instance, livestock may predominate in remote areas, both because it is relatively cheap to deliver to market in good condition and, independently, because land is cheap.

21. An exception to the East Asia generalization is the Philippines, where a land reform that prohibited leasing led, in the context of the introduction of high-yielding varieties of rice, to an expansion in contract labor (Hayami and Otsuka, 1993).

22. In Sri Lanka, the gradual extension of citizenship to Indian Tamil laborers after 1971 allowed them to move off plantations, forcing them to raise wages, lose experience, and become uncompetitive; in general, free labor markets normally undermine indenture systems.

23. This criterion, although far superior to crude measures such as yield/hectare, itself appears open to question if capital-related transaction costs should be scale-dependent. Perhaps the best measure, assuming a fixed supply of land, is Ricardian surplus per hectare, i.e., surplus calculated after accounting for all inputs except land.

24. Where there is a rental market in draught animals, those who own their own animal(s) are typically able to rent others on relatively favorable terms.

25. We are avoiding some complexities here, since whether processing occurs on- or off-farm might not be independent of farm size.

26. Interlinked markets are often seen as pressures toward larger farms, being ways for a large landowner to entrap small farmers by pressing them to give him the first—or only—option as a merchant, employer, or (above all) creditor and subsequent forecloser. However, whether interlinking of markets is good or bad for small farmers clearly depends on the alternative, which could be virtual exclusion from ready local access to hired work, output sales, and, above all, collateral-free credit (Bell and Srinivasan, 1989).

27. The authors control for the selectivity bias that arises if titling should be endogenous.

28. See also Taslim (1989), who uses evidence from Bangladesh to suggest that labor supervision costs become important only after the ratio of hired to family labor exceeds a threshold. Among his findings is that the correlation between family labor per hectare and hired labor per hectare is negative for small farms and positive for large farms (above a threshold of 2–3 ha). The idea is that hired labor may be plugging a labor gap on small farms while being used up to a limit associated with the supervisory constraint on larger farms.

29. There is evidence for Bangladesh of more intensive use of fertilizers and seeds on smaller farms (Hossain, 1988). This could be understood in terms of a fixed adoption cost and a relatively low shadow price of labor on small farms. See also Lipton's analysis of Lenin's work on 1890s Russia (Lipton, 1977, p. 115).

30. See, for instance, evidence for Guatemala over 1964–1979 in von Braun et al. (1989)

31. A useful list can be found in Heltberg (1998).

32. We can note another possible cause of an IR: For farmers specializing in staples, production price risk (and the absence of market mechanisms for consumption smoothing), together with risk aversion, may induce small food-deficit farmers to raise production in the direction of self-sufficiency, with large food-surplus farmers reacting analogously by reducing production (Barrett, 1996).

33. Aggregate input equals 0.15 times aggregate capital (capital value plus land value), plus labor input, valued at a number of different shadow wages.

34. The appropriation by colonists, for owner-farming, of Native American and Inuit lands in North America conforms roughly to the Latin American model, but later history, and hence trajectories of land inequality, were very different (Section 4.2.2).

34a. Lipton [2009] provides fuller analysis and evidence on land reform updated to mid-2009.

35. "The path from concentrated individual property rights to [their] fairly egalitarian distribution ... may have entailed an unnecessary ... detour into collectivism" (Bell, 1990). Vietnam (like parts of Latin America [Thiesenhusen, 1988], Ethiopia, and Albania) suffered a similar "terrible detour."

36. These juxtapositions (of land rules and areas) are rough and ready. "Tribal" areas of Thailand, Burma, N.E. India ("jhum" cultivation), and parts of Latin America (e.g., Mapuche areas in Chile, "Indian: areas of Amazonia in Brazil and Ecuador) feature cyclic bush fallowing. Rwanda and much of Kenya are increasingly in individualist mode as person/land ratios grow. Sugar, coconuts, and many fruit crops in the Philippines approximate latifundia-minifundia systems (Hayami et al., 1990).

37. Simple options—for example, X ha of irrigated land, 0.5X of unirrigated land, or a combination, as a ceiling–may be less fair or "efficient" than complex scaling of land quality, but are easier to administer, with fewer prospects for corruption or evasion.

38. Sometimes even with periodic redistribution as family size changed, as in Vietnam and China.

39. Land-per-person ceilings (and rights to reform land) better reflect wealth but ease evasion and bad-faith transfers, and can encourage fertility and discourage farm investment (Prosterman and Hanstad, 1994, 28 and fn, 56).

40. FAO 1991: iv. Iran, Zimbabwe and the Philippines are noted as exceptions. Also in "1984–9, Indonesia transferred 400,000 families from densely populated areas to ... uncultivated [public] lands ... Thailand allocated 650,000 ha to 170,000 households in 1987–1990 ... Morocco reported distributing 320,000 ha to 23,600 beneficiaries ... in Algeria 3139 state farming enterprises [went to] 5677 individual[s] and 22,356 groups [and] 273,000 ha to 66,945 beneficiaries ... Iran ... distributed [564,000 ha]" [ibid.: 17].

41. Studies show that tiny home gardens, "from 10–120 m2 [to] 5000–20,000 square metres in [Zambia and from] 172–500 to 200–1700 square metres in [Java]" can substantially raise household income, security, or labor-market bargaining power (Mitchell and Hanstad, 2004).

42. China is an extreme case of the Bell detour (Section 4.3.4.vii): the reforming of hugely unequal private holdings into much more equal and productive family farms but via wasteful, often cruel, interim collectivization.

43. In Korea, these trends, plus rapid development, have long caused market-led *increases* in farm size and inequality, albeit both from very low post-reform levels. In 1970–1989 farms below 0.5 ha fell from 32.6% to 17.7% of all farms (NACF, 1992).

44. See, however, Stokes 1983, p. 86: "Despite all the revolutions in the revenue-collecting right and proprietary titles ... the upper and middle agricultural castes remained ... hardly altered in their cultivating possession" from "the time when the stillness of the *pax Britannica* first fell upon the land" to the conclusion of zamindari abolition.

45. FAOSTAT gives farmers plus landless laborers 493m *persons*; we assume rural households average 6.

46. In Tamil Nadu ceilings forced big "landlords to sell land and resulted in a more equal distribution"; in Rajoor, West Bengal, "large joint families, in an attempt to evade the land ceilings, separated into smaller [owned] units" (Lanjouw and Stern, 1999). In six semi-arid villages, "the threat of confiscation enhanced the perceived risks [of] land accumulation among large farmers" (Mearns, 1999).

47. Proportions of area *both* in tenanted *and* in large holdings declined in most Indian states between the Agricultural Censuses of 1961–1962, 1971–1972, and 1981–1982 (Singh, 1990; Sanyal, 1988). So other factors outweighed the tendency of reductions in the quantum of tenancies (to avoid the restrictions) to put land

back into larger holdings, now self-cultivated. However, the *period* of tenancies has shortened, and they have become more frequently concealed and/or insecure, harming remaining tenant farmers.

48. The proportion of land in such holdings rose faster, from 7% to 17.2% over 1961–1995 (DES, 2004).

49. The rise in land equality excludes the landless; in India, however, the proportions of rural people who *own* no land, who neither own nor operate, and even—in some states—who *operate* no land, all fell between 1960–1961 and 1970–1971 (Singh, 1990, 72–3).

50. With so much land distributed in 1918–1968, Mexico's still high Gini suggests: much redistribution was counted more than once; much redistributed land got back to large holders; or farmland fell sharply from 1910–1968 (FAOSTAT 2004 shows a fall in 1961–1968).

51. All this was unfortunate and unnecessary. Post-independence smallholders had shown their capacity to gain from removal of past biases; smallness was linked to higher maize productivity (Kinsey, 1999). Tobacco, the main cash crop, is ideal for nucleus-estate, consensual smallholder farming. Aid was available for orderly land redistribution.

52. Dorward's (1999) data, however, show large farms outperforming small ones in Malawi. This is only, we suggest, due to heavy bias in laws and in input, output, research, service, and credit arrangements; cf. Sahn and Arulpragasam (1993).

53. They further cite much evidence of large "investment effects of land title" in Latin America and (contrary to Carey and Faruqee, 1997) parts of Asia, while "in Africa ... many observers have found [that titling is] unimportant in effect on investment and subsequent farm income" or that investment is cause, not effect, of "more secure property rights to land."

54. Much land is tenanted to cut labor-linked agency costs, but some is tenanted for convenient location or timing of farming, e.g., vis-à-vis urban education or employment.

55. The rules vary. Often some tenancy is allowed but restricted to short leases and/or to a particular tribe or clan (Noronha, 1985).

56. The word is sometimes misused to mean "joining small farms to create larger ones."

57. It may have raised output by over 15% in the Indian Punjab (Oldenburg, 1990) and France (Roche, 1956, 541).

58. Even in one village, months of time of a skillful and trusted official are needed to win acceptance for complex land exchanges. Bain (1993, 128–39) shows the high cost of consolidation in Taiwan.

59. In an Indian village, farmers bequeathed strips of land, from top to bottom of slopes, to give each legatee a mix of high and low land, diversifying against risk. Over the generations, this leads to ever-thinner strips that must be ploughed up and down the slope because animals (or tractors) cannot turn in a very narrow space. The result is increasing erosion (Lipton, 1969).

60. It at first speeded up an ongoing process in which poor peasants seized, and farmed privately, land held by big farmers or the community (the *mir*). In 1923–1924, Lenin restituted some of these lands to medium farmers (*kulaks*) (Wolf, 1969).

61. "[I]n the early 1930s less than 10 per cent of the rural population owned ... 70–80 per cent of China's arable land ... [I]n 1949, the government redistributed about 47 m. ha [of China's 100 m. ha] of arable land on an equitable basis to some 50–60 m. rural households" (Bruce and Harrell, 1989, 3).

62. Romania in 1990–1992 transferred the collective 80% of its farmland to fairly equal private holdings, though semivoluntary "associations" continued to offer some of the services—and problems—of the old collectives. As in several other transitional economies, wage-secure state farm workers proved less favorable to reform than farmers in collectives.

63. This can also be induced by post-Communist removal or easing of laws against townward or overseas migration and by the requirements of trade for new EU members.

64. In Russia "12 million people suddenly became legal owners of 119 million ha of prime agricultural land. Most ... never planned or anticipated [it.] ... Early reformers [saw] land shares as a transitional tool that will allow transfer of land [and] believed that ... shares would start to be traded ... and

eventually find their way to more efficient owners. Most land-shares owners have *preferred* to lease their property to large farms... Less than 5 percent of landowners have *decided* to transform their land into real-estate parcels and become independent private farmers... Large [mostly de facto nonprivatised: ML] farms constitute 79% of agricultural land ... *In about 70 percent of cases the land they are using is leased from owners of land shares* ... At the start of the reforms, private family farms were expected to become the main type of business in the agricultural sector. *By 2002 they occupied approximately 9% of agricultural land. They only own 40 percent of the land they occupy*" (Overchuk, 2003, our italics).

65. It cuts incentive to invest (or conserve), the user's family has limited time to enjoy income from improvements, and lack of land collateral can restrict access to credit. This matters most when, as in China, sources of agricultural improvement shift from seeds and fertilizers, giving benefits in the same season to longer-term investments (Prosterman and Hanstad, 1993, 30). However, we lack evidence that 20–40 years' usufruct rights, often renewable and heritable, do less than full ownership to stimulate farm investment or to help poor land users. Ukrainian farmers prefer a regime of lifetime heritable possession, without sale rights, to full rights including sale (Lerman et al., 1994, 49).

66. Mearns (1999), while summarizing longitudinal village-study evidence that both land sale and rent markets improve operated land distribution in India, shows counter-examples precisely where markets were thin and imperfect and hence confined to distress sales. So steps to create or improve such markets—often part of NWLR packages—probably tend to cut median farm size.

67. Although, predictably, mostly bad land, which did not always pass to the poor quickly or at all.

68. The scale of these NWLRs has grown. In Ceara, Brazil, the World Bank's 1996 program had by 2002 placed 15,000 families on over 400,000 ha and was set to expand into four further states (Teofilo and Prado Garcia, 2003).

69. Rural people's decisions affecting farm size have long-run effects and so are normally influenced, not so much by current levels or trends in tax or subsidy on farm inputs and outputs but by the credibility of policymakers' claims that such levels or trends will last– that is, by expectations of *future* price levels, trends, and policies.

70. We recognize that this analysis is inconsistent with a simplistic reading of Olsen (1965).

71. Leveling tax-subsidy treatment between big and small farmers has two advantages over credit policy as a means to enhance the poor's access to land. First, easier credit to buy land raises demand and bids up the price; removing tax-subsidy incentives to big farms raises supply of land to small buyÂers, not just demand. Second, it is hard to identify, for credit, those who are poor, will use it to buy land, and will repay, but lower subsidies on post-reform inputs and ancillary services went with greater success in steering land to the poor—that is, discouraging the rich from incurring costs to capture gains—in Northeast Brazil (Tendler, 1991, 120).

72. This is often claimed to be socially, culturally, or environmentally desirable, for example, to preserve *la France profonde*. It is beyond the scope of this paper to assess this claim, let alone to juxtapose it against the cost of OECD farm support to OECD consumers and taxpayers and to farmers in developing countries.

73. These data understate the decline because they fail to allow for the growing role of part-time labor. Standardizing for part-time versus full-time employment, the agricultural workforce in the EU-15, minus Germany, fell from 11.7 million "annual working units" in 1980 to 6.1 million in 2001 (Directorate General for Agriculture, 2002, Ch. 1, Fig. 3.1).

74. The largest recipient, Riceland Foods Inc., received $426 million of USDA support from 1995–2002 ($110 million, of $12,151 million total USDA support, in 2002 alone; EWG, 2003), but this is a cooperative of some 9000 farmer members (www.riceland.com/about/); a subsidy of $12,222 per farmer is only about double the U.S. mean.

75. This has proved, as in India, to be costly to collect, easy to avoid, and hard to administer—perhaps more so than land tax.

76. In line with Section 3, LG raises agricultural demand and land rent and thereby the labor/land ratio; any resulting general-equilibrium rise in the wage will provide a partial offset.

77. These can be combined; for example, despite a thrust to labor-intensity and small farms from LG in a developing country, its technical progress may be embodied in farm capital or inputs (1) imported from rich countries (where most research is done) and responding to incentives to be labor-saving and pro-large-farm, and/or (2) though generated in developing countries, responding with a lag to pre-LG incentives to generate technology supportive of protected, capital-intensive or large-farm activity.

78. In Brazil especially, refrigeration tanks, to meet milk quality and safety standards, require a minimum scale (Farina et al., 2000). AMUL and its successors in India have succeeded in safely and profitably collecting and safely processing milk from millions of tiny farms.

79. Vertical integration (common in EH) can solve the problem only if the integrated firm intermediates internally and thus harmonizes small-scale optimal production with large-scale optimal delivery. Managerial costs and company norms are not necessarily more likely—perhaps less so—to permit this with vertical integration than without.

References

Adenew, B., Deininger, K., Gebre-Selassie, S., Jin, S., & Nega, B. (2003). *Exploring different types of land-related investment in Ethiopia.* Washington, DC: World Bank.

Allen, R. C. (1982). The efficiency and distributional consequences of eighteenth century enclosures. *Economic Journal, 92,* 937–953.

Amid, M. J. (1990). *Agriculture, poverty and reform in Iran.* London: Routledge.

Arrighi, G., & Saul, J. (1973). *Essays in the political economy of Africa.* New York: Monthly Review.

Bain, J. (1993). *Agricultural reform in Taiwan: From here to modernity?* Hong Kong: Chinese University Press.

Ban, S. H., Moon, P. Y., & Perkins, D. (1980). *Rural development: Studies in the modernization of the republic of Korea: 1945–75* (Ch. 10). Cambridge, MA: Harvard University Press.

Bandyopadhyay, D. (1995). Reflections on land reform in India since independence. In T. V. Sathyamurthy (Ed.), *Industry and agriculture in India since independence.* Delhi: Oxford University Press.

Bardhan, P. (1973). Size, productivity and returns to scale: an analysis of farm-level data in Indian agriculture. *Journal of Political Economy, 81*(6), 1370–1386.

Barham, B., Carter, M., & Sigelko, W. (1995). Agro-export production and peasant land access: examining the dynamic between adoption and accumulation. *Journal of Development Economics, 46,* 85–107.

Barham, B., Boucher, S., & Carter, M. R. (1996). Credit constraints, credit unions, and small-scale producers in Guatemala. *World Development,* 793–806.

Barrett, C. B. (1996). On price risk and the inverse farm size-productivity relationship. *Journal of Development Economics, 51,* 193–215.

Barrows, R., & Roth, M. (1989). *Land tenure and investment in African agriculture: theory and evidence.* Madison: Land Tenure Centre Paper no. 136.

Bell, C., & Srinivasan, T. N. (1989). Interlinked Transactions in Rural Markets: An Empirical Study of Andhra Pradesh, Bihar and Punjab. *Oxford Bulletin of Economics and Statistics, 51,* 73–83.

Bell, C., Srinivasan, T. N., & Udry, C. (1997). Rationing, spillover and interlinking in credit markets: the case of rural Punjab. *Oxford Economic Papers, 49,* 557–585.

Bell, C. (1990, July). Reforming property rights in land and tenancy. *World Bank Research Observer, 5,* 2.

Berry, R. A., & Cline, W. R. (1979). *Agrarian structure and productivity in developing countries.* Baltimore, MD: Johns Hopkins Univ. Press.

Bhalla, S. S., & Roy, P. (1988). Mis-specification in farm productivity analysis: the role of land quality. *Oxford Economic Papers, 40,* 55–73.

Binswanger, H., & McIntyre, J. (1987). Behavioral and material determinants of production Relations in land abundant tropical agriculture. *Economic Development and Cultural Change, 36,* 75–99.

Binswanger, H. P., Deininger, K., & Feder, G. (1995). Power, distortions, revolt and reform in agricultural land relations. In J. Behrman, & T. N. Srinivasan (Eds.), *Handbook of development economics* (Vol. III). Amsterdam: Elsevier Science Publishers.

Binswanger, H. P., & Rosenzweig, M. (1986). Behavioral and material determinants of production relations in agriculture. *Journal of Development Studies, 22*(3), 503–539.

Binswanger, H., & Elgin, M. (1988). *What are the prospects for land reform?* Discussion Paper. Washington, DC: World Bank.

Blarel, B., Hazell, P., Place, F., & Quiggin, J. (1991, September 23). *The economics of farm fragmentation: evidence from Ghana and Rwanda.* Mimeo. Washington, DC: World Bank.

Boserup, E. (1965). *Conditions of agricultural growth.* Chicago: Aldine Publishing Company.

Brooks, K., & Lerman, Z. (1994). *Land reform and farm restructuring in Russia.* Agrarian Inst., Russian Academy of Science and World Bank. World Bank Discussion Paper no. 223. Washington, DC: World Bank.

Brooks, K., Guasch, J., Braverman, A., & Csaki, C. (1991). Agriculture and the transition to the market. *Journal of Economic Perspectives, 5,* 4.

Bruce, J. (1986). *Land tenure issues in project design and strategies for agricultural development in sub-Saharan Africa.* Working Paper No 28. Madison: Land Tenure Centre, University of Wisconsin.

Bruce, J., & Harrell, P. (1989). *Land reform in the People's Republic of China, 1978–1988.* Land Tenure Centre: Research paper no. 500. Madison: University of Wisconsin.

Burger, A. (1994). *The agriculture of the world.* Avebury.

Carter, M., & Alvarez, E. (1989). Changing paths: the decollectivization of agrarian reform agriculture in coastal Peru. In Thiesenhusen (Ed.).

Carter, M., & Mesbah, D. (1991). Land reform and the rural poor in Latin America. In Lipton & van der Gaag (Eds.).

Carter, M., & P. Olinto. (2003). Getting institutions 'right' for whom? Credit constraints and the impact of property rights on the quantity and composition of investment. *American Journal of Agricultural Economics, 85*(1), 173–186.

Carter, M. (1984). Identification of the inverse relationship between farm size and productivity: an empirical analysis of peasant agricultural production. *Oxford Economic Papers, 36,* 131–145.

Carter, M. (1987). Risk sharing and incentives in the decollectivization of agriculture. *Oxford Economic Papers, 39,* 577–595.

Chen, F. U., Wang, L., & Davis, J. (1998). Land reform in rural China since the mid-1980s. *Land Reform, Rural Development and Co-operatives, 2.*

Cornia, G. A. (Ed.). (2004). *Inequality, growth and poverty in an era of liberalisation and globalisation.* UNU-Wider Studies in Development Economics. Oxford: Oxford University Press.

Cross, C. (1996). Making a living under land reform: weighing up the chances in Kwazulu-Natal. In M. Lipton, F. Ellis, & M. Lipton (Eds.), *Land, labour and livelihoods in rural South Africa, Vol. 2: Kwazulu-Natal and Northern Province.* Durban: Indicator Press.

Csaki, C., Brook, E., Lundell, M., Zuschlag, A., Arakelar, R., & Moury, S. (1995). *Armenia: the challenge of reform in the agricultural sector. Based on a mission in May–June 1993.* World Bank Country Studies. Washington, DC: World Bank.

De Janvry, A. (1981). *The Agrarian question and reformism in Latin America.* Baltimore: Johns Hopkins.

De Janvry, A., & Sadoulet, E. (1991). Rural development in Latin America: re-linking poverty reduction to growth. In Lipton & van der Gaag (Eds.).

De Janvry, A., & Sadoulet, E. (1989, June). *Path-dependent policy reforms: from land reform to rural development in Colombia.* Mimeo. World Bank Annapolis Workshop.

De Moor, A. P. G. (1996). *Perverse incentives—subsidies and sustainable development: key issues and reform strategies, Earth Council.*

De Soto, H. (1992). *The other path.* New York: Praeger.

Deininger, K., & Binswanger, H. (1995). Rent seeking and the development of agriculture in Kenya, South Africa and Zimbabwe. *Economic Development and Cultural Change, 43,* 493–522.

Deininger, K. (1999). Making negotiated land reform work: initial experience from Colombia. Brazil and South Africa. *World Development, 27*(4): 651–672.

Deininger, K., & Olinto, P. 2000. *Asset distribution, inequality and growth*. Policy Research Working Paper no. 2375. Washington, DC: World Bank.

Deolalikar, A., & Vijverberg, W. (1983). Heterogeneity of family and hired labor in agricultural production: a test using district-level data from India. *Oxford Bulletin of Economics and Statistics, 49*, 291–305.

Deolalikar, A., & Vijverberg, W. (1987). A test of heterogeneity of family and hired labour in Asian agriculture. *Journal of Economic Development, 8*(2), 45–69.

Diamond, J. (1999). *Guns, germs and steel*. Norton.

Diaz-Alejandro, C. (1970). *Essays on the economic history of the Argentine Republic*. New Haven: Yale Univ. Press.

Directorate General for Agriculture. (2002). *European agriculture entering the 21st century*. Brussels: European Commission.

Directorate of Economics and Statistics. (2004). *Agricultural statistics at a glance—2003*. New Delhi: Govt. of India.

Diskin, M. (1989). El Salvador: reform prevents change. In Thiesenhuesen.

Dolan, C., Humphrey, J., & Harris-Pascal, C. (1999). *Horticulture commodity chains: the impact of the UK market on the African fresh vegetable industry*. Working Paper no. 96. Brighton: Institute of Development Studies.

Dore, R. (1959). *Land reform in Japan*. Oxford: Oxford University Press.

Dorner, P. (1992). *Latin American land reform in theory and practice*. Madison: University of Wisconsin Press.

Dorner, P., & Saliba, B. (1981). *Interventions in land markets to benefit the poor*. Land Tenure Centre: Research paper no. 21. Madison: University of Wisconsin.

Dorward, A. (1999). Farm size and productivity in Malawian smallholder agriculture. *Journal of Development Studies, 35*(5), 141–161.

Duncan, J., & Ruetschle, M. (2002). Agrarian reform and agricultural productivity in the Russian Far East. In Thornton & Ziegler (Eds.), *Russia's Far East: A Region at Risk*. University of Washington Press.

el-Ghonemy, M. R. (1990). *The political economy of rural poverty*. London: Routledge.

Ellman, M. (1975, December). Did the agricultural surplus provide the resources for the increase in investment in the USSR during the First Five Year Plan? *Economic Journal, 85*(4).

Environmental Working Group (EWG) Farm Subsidy Database version 2.0. (2002–2003). www.ewg.org/farm/help/faq.php#housebill, www.ewg.org/farm/concentrationtable.php?fips=00000, and www.ewg.org/farm/top_recips.php?fips=00000&progcode=total&yr=2002

Eswaran, M., & Kotwal, A. (1986). Access to capital and agrarian production organisation. *Economic Journal, 96*, 482–498.

FAO. (2004–2006). *FAOSTAT* at www.fao.org/es/ess/census/default.asp

FAO. (1991). *Third Progress Report on Action Programme of World Conference on Agrarian Reform and Rural Development*. Rome: Mimeo. C91/19.

Fafchamps, M., & Shilpi, F. (2003). The spatial division of labor in Nepal. *Journal of Development Studies, 39*(6), 23–66.

Farah, J. (1994). *Pesticide policies in developing countries: do they encourage excessive use?* Washington, DC: The World. Discussion paper no. 238.

Farina, E., & Reardon, T. (2000, Dec). Agrifood grades and standards in the extended Mercosur: their role in the changing agrifood system. *American Journal of Agricultural Economics*.

Farmer, B. (1960). On not controlling subdivision in paddy lands. *Transactions of the British Institute of Geographers*, 28.

Feder, G., Onchan, T., Chelamwang, Y., & Hongladaran, C. (1988). *Land policies and farm productivity in Thailand*. Baltimore: Johns Hopkins.

Findeis, J., Weiss, C., Saito, K. (University of Tokyo), & Antón, J. (2001). *Agricultural policy reform and farm employment, Working Party on Agricultural Policies and Markets*, AGR/CA/APM 10/(2001). OECD, Directoraste for Agriculture and Fisheries.

Frisvold, G. B. (1994). Does supervision matter? Some hypothesis tests using Indian farm-level data. *Journal of Development Economics, 43*, 217–238.

Fukazawa, H. (1983). *Agrarian relations: Western India*. In *The Cambridge Economic History of India, vol. 2: 1757–1970*. Cambridge: Cambridge University Press.

Giovarelli, R., & Bledsoe, D. (2001, October). Land reform in Eastern Europe: Western CIS, Transcaucusus, Balkans, and EU accession countries. *Land Reform, Rural Development and Co-operatives*.

Grigg, D. (1992). *The transformation of agriculture in the West*. Oxford: Blackwell.

Haddad, W. D., Carnoy, M., Rinaldi, R., & Regel, O. (1991). *Education for development: evidence and for new priorities*. Discussion Paper 95, World Bank.

Hanstad, T. (1998). Are small farms appropriate for former Soviet Republics? *Rural Development Institute: Reports on Foreign Aid & Development*, n. 97.

Hanstad, T., Nielsen, R., & Brown, J. (2004). *Land and livelihoods–making land rights real for India's rural poor*. Seattle: Rural Development Institute.

Harbeson, J. W. (1984). International influences on land reform in Africa. In Montgomery (Ed.).

Hayami, Y., & Otsuka, K. (1993). Kasupong in the Philippine rice bowl: the emergence of new labor institutions after the land reform. In K. Hoff, A. Braverman, & J. Stiglitz (Eds.), *The economics of rural organization : theory, practice and policy*. OUP for the World Bank.

Hayami, Y., Quisumbing, A., & Adriano, L. (1990). *Towards an alternative land reform paradigm: a Philippine perspective*. Manila: Ateneo de Manila University Press.

Hazell, P. B. R., & Ramasamy, C. (1991). *The green revolution reconsidered: the impact of high-yielding rice varieties in South India*. Delhi: Oxford University Press.

Heath, J. (1992). Evaluating the Impact of Mexico's land reform on Agricultural Productivity. *World Development, 20*, 695–711.

Heltberg. (1998). Rural market imperfections and the farm size-productivity relationship: evidence from Pakistan. *World Development, 26*, 1807–1826.

Herring, R. (1983). *Land to the tiller: The political economy of agrarian reform in South Asia*. London: Yale University Press.

Hirschmann, A. O. (1984). *Getting ahead collectively*. New York: Pergamon.

Hossain, M. (1988). *Nature and impact of the green revolution in Bangladesh*, Research Report no. 67. Washington, DC: International Food Policy Research Institute.

Howes, M. (1982). The creation and appropriation of value in irrigated agriculture: a comparison of the deep tubewell and the handpump in rural Bangladesh. In M. Howes, & M. Greeley (Eds.) *Rural technology, rural institutions and the rural poorest*. Dhaka: CIRDAP/IDS.

Hunt, D. (1984). *The impending crisis in Kenya: the case for land reform*. Aldershot: Gower.

ILO. (2004–2006). LABORSTA.

Jarvis, L. S. (1989). The unravelling of Chile's agrarian reform, 1973–1986. In Thiesenhusen (Ed.).

Jin, S., & Deininger, K. (2002). *Land rental markets as an alternative to government reallocation? Equity and efficiency considerations in the Chinese land tenure system*, Policy Research Working Paper Series 2930. Washington, DC: World Bank.

Johnson, O. (1970). A note in the economics of fragmentation. *Nigerian Journal of Economic and Social Studies*, 12.

Kawagoe, T. (2000). *Agricultural land reform in postwar Japan: experiences and issues*. Staff Working Paper no. 2111. Washington, DC: World Bank.

King, R. (1977). *Land reform: a world survey*. Boulder: Westview.

Kinsey, B. (1999). Land reform, growth and equity: emerging evidence from Zimbabwe's resettlement programme. *Journal of Southern African Studies, 25*(2), 173–196.

Kinsey, B., & Binswanger, H. 1993. *Characteristics and performance of settlement programmes*. World Bank Working Paper 1207. Washington, DC: World Bank.

Kislev, Y. (1966). Overestimates of returns to scale in agriculture–a case of synchronized aggregation. *Journal of Farm Economics, 48*(4), 967–983.

Kochar, A. (1997). An empirical investigation of rationing constraints in rural markets in India. *Journal of Development Economics, 53*, 339–372.

Kopeva, D., Mishev, P., & Howe, K. (1994). Land reform and liquidation of collective farm assets in Bulgaria. *Communist Economies and Economic Transformation, 6*(2).

Krueger, A., Schiff, M., & Valdes, A. (1995). Agricultural incentives in developing Countries: measuring the effect of sectoral and economy-wide policies. In G. Peters (Ed.), *Agricultural Economics*. Elgar: Aldershot.

Kumar, D. Agrarian relations: South India. In Kumar & Desai (Eds.).

Kumar, D., & Desai, M. (Ed.). (1983). *The Cambridge economic history of India, Vol. II: c.1757–c.1970*. Cambridge: Cambridge University Press.

Kutcher, G. P., & Scandizzo, P. L. (1981). *The agricultural economy of Northeast Brazil*. Baltimore, MD: World Bank and Johns Hopkins University Press.

Kydd, J., Dorward, A., & Poulton, C. (2002). Institutional dimensions of trade liberalisation and poverty. In *Agricultural trade and poverty: Making policy analysis count*. Paris: OECD.

Lanjouw, P., & Stern, N. (1999). *Economic development in Palanpur over five decades*. Oxford: Oxford University Press.

Ladejinsky, W. (1977). Agrarian reform as unfinished business: the selected papers of Wolf Ladejinsky. In L. Walinsky (Ed.), New York: Oxford University Press.

Lee, M. P. H. (1921). *The economic history of China*. New York: Columbia University.

Lerman, Z., Brooks, K., & Csaki, C. (1994). *Land reform and farm restructuring in the Ukraine*. Discussion paper no. 270. Washington, DC: World Bank.

Lipton, M. (1969). The theory of the optimizing peasant. *Journal of Development Studies, 4*, 327–351.

Lipton, M. (1977). *Why poor people stay poor: urban bias in world development*. London: Temple Smith.

Lipton, M. (2009). *Land reform in developing countries: property rights and property wrongs*. London: Taylor and Francis.

Manor, J. (1989). Karnataka: caste, class, dominance and politics in a cohesive society. In Frankel, F., & Rao, M. (Eds.), *Dominance and state power in India* (Vol. 1). Oxford: Oxford University Press.

McCulloch, N., Winters, A., & Cirera, X. (2001). *Trade liberalization and poverty: a handbook*. London: UK Department for International Development and the Centre for Economic Policy Research. 3 (ML18).

Mearns, R. (1999). *Access to land in rural India: policy issues and options*. World Bank Policy Working Paper. Washington, DC: World Bank.

Migot-Adholla, S., Hazell, P., Blarel, B., & Place, F. (1991). Indigenous land rights systems in sub-Saharan Africa: a constraint on productivity? *World Bank Economic Review, 5*(1).

Ministry of Agriculture, Fisheries and Food. (1968). *A century of agricultural statistics*. London: HMSO.

Mitchell, R., & Hanstad, T. (2004, March). *Small home garden plots & sustainable livelihoods for the poor*. Seattle: Rural Development Institute.

Montgomery, J. D. (Ed.). (1984). *International dimensions of land reform*. Boulder: Westview.

Moore, F. B. (1996). *The social origins of dictatorship and democracy*. London: Peregrine.

Mundlak, Y. (2001). Production and supply. In B. L. Gardner, & G. C. Rausser (Eds.), *Handbook of agricultural economics* (Vol. 1A, Ch. 1). North Holland.

NACF (National Agricultural Co-operative Federation). (1992). *Farm size and structural reform of agriculture I: Korea*. Jung-Ku, Korea: So-Hyun Kim Farm Management Research Division.

Nelson, M. (1973). *The development of tropical lands: policy issues in Latin America*. Baltimore: Johns Hopkins University Press.

Ngo, T. M. P. (2005). *How to grow equitably: land redistribution, agricultural growth, and poverty reduction in Vietnam (1992–1998)*. Ph.D., London School of Economics.

Nishio, A., & Akiyama, T. 1996. *Indonesia's Coca Boom: hands-off policy encourages smallholder dynamism*. Working Paper no. 1580. Washington, DC: World Bank.

Nkonya, E., Pender, J., Jagger, P., Sserunkuuma, D., Kaizzi, C., & Ssali, H. (2004). *Strategies for sustainable land management and poverty reduction in Uganda*. Research Report 133. Washington, DC: International Food Policy Research.

Noronha, R. (1985). *A review of the literature on land tenures systems in sub-Saharan Africa*. Discussion Paper ARU43. Washington, DC: World Bank.

Oberai, A. S. (Ed.). (1988). *Land settlement policies and population redistribution in developing countries*. New York: Praeger.

Oldenburg, P. (1990). Land consolidation as land reform, in India. *World Development, 18*(2).

Olmstead, A. L., & Rhode, P. W. (2000). The transformation of Northern agriculture. In S. Engerman, & R. Gallman (Eds.), *Cambridge economic history of the United States* (Vol. III). Cambridge: Univ. Press.

Olson, M. (1965). *The logic of collective action: public goods and the theory of groups.* Harvard U. P.

Otero, G. (1989). Agrarian reform in Mexico: capitalism and the State. In Thiesenhusen (Ed.).

Otsuka, H. (1991). Determinants and consequences of land reform implementation in the Philippines. *Journal of Development Economics, 35.*

Otsuka, K., Chuma, H., & Hayami, J. (1992). Land and labor contracts in agrarian economies: theories and facts. *Journal of Economic Literature,* XXX, 1965–2018.

Overchuk, A. (2003). Integrated approach to land policy, development of land administration institutions and land market in the Russian Federation. *Land Reform, Rural Development and Co-operatives, 3.*

Phanasalkar, S. J. (2002). *Appropriate drip irrigation technologies promoted by International Development Enterprises India: a socio-economic assessment.* New Delhi: IDE.

Ping, Li. (2003). Rural Land Tenure Reforms in China: Issues, Regulations, and Prospects for Additional Reforms. *Land Reform, Land Settlement and Cooperatives,* 2003/3.

Pingali, P., Bigot, Y., & Binswanger, H. (1987). *Agricultural mechanization and the evolution of farming systems in Sub-Saharan Africa.* World Bank.

Place, F., & Hazell, P. (1993, Feb). Productivity effects of indigenous land tenure systems in sub-Saharan Africa. *American Journal of Agricultural Economics.*

Powelson, J. P. (1984). International public and private agencies. In Montgomery (Ed.).

Prosterman, R., & Hanstad, T. (1994). *Agricultural reform in Vietnam and the 1993 land law.* RDI papers on farm aid and development #13. Seattle: Rural Development Institute.

Prosterman, R., Hanstad, T., & Li, P. (1998). Large-scale farming in China: an appropriate policy? *Journal of Contemporary Asia, 28*(1).

Randhawa, M. S. (1986). *A history of agriculture in India.* New Delhi: Indian Council of Agricultural Research.

Rashid, S., & Quibria, M. G. (1995). Is land reform passé? With special reference to Asian agriculture. In M. G. Quibria (Ed.), *Critical issues in Asian development: theories, experiences and policies* (pp. 127–59). Hong Kong: Oxford University Press.

Reardon, T., Berdegue, J., & Farrington, J. (2002). Supermarkets and farming in Latin America: pointing directions for elsewhere? *Perspectives, 81.* London: Dept for International Development.

Reardon, T., Codron, J. M., Busch, L., Bingen, J., & Harris, C. (2001). Global change in agrifood grades and standards: agribusiness strategic responses in developing countries. *International Food and Agribusiness Management Review, 2*(3).

Reardon, T., Rozelle, S., Timmer, P., & Wang, H. (2004). Emergence of supermarkets with Chinese characteristics. *Development Policy Review,* forthcoming.

Reardon, T., Timmer, P., Barrett, C., & Berdegue, J. (2003). The rise of supermarkets in Africa, Asia and Latin America. *American Journal of Agricultural Economics, 85*(5), 3–20.

Reardon, T., & Timmer, P. (2005). Transformation of markets for agricultural output in developing countries Since 1950: how has thinking changed? In R. Evenson, P. Pingali, & T. P. Schultz (Eds.), *Handbook of agricultural economics. Vol. III: Agricultural development: farmers, farm production & farm markets.*

Rembold, F. (2003). Land fragmentation and its impact in Central and Eastern European countries and CIS. *Land reform, Rural Development and Co-operatives,* 2003/3.

Repetto, R. (1988). *Economic policy for natural resource conservation.* Environment Department Working Paper no. 4. Washington, DC: Environment Department, World Bank.

Ricupero, R. *Report of address to UN (ECOSOC), 30/6/2003.* Third World Network. www.twnside.org.sg/title/twe309a.htm

Riedel, B., & Frydenlund, J. (2003). *Still at the federal trough: farm subsidies for the rich and famous shattered records in 2001, #1542 Apr 30.* www.heritage.org/Research/Agriculture/BG1542.cfm

Riedel, B., & Frydenlund, J. (2001, Nov. 26). *At the federal trough: farm subsidies for the rich and famous.* Heritage Foundation.

Roche, J. (1956). Important aspects of consolidation in France. In K. Parsons, R. Penn, & P. Raup (Eds.), *Land Tenure.* Madison: University of Wisconsin.

Romer, D. (1986). *Advanced macroeconomics.* McGraw-Hill.

Rosenzweig, M. R., & Binswanger, H. (1993). Wealth, weather risk and the composition and profitability of agricultural investments. *Economic Journal, 103*, 56–78.

Roth, M., & Bruce, J. (1994). *Land tenure, agrarian structure and captive land use efficiency in Zimbabwe: options for land tenure reform and land redistribution.* Land Tenure Centre: Research Paper no. 117. Madison: University of Wisconsin.

Roumasset, J. (1995). The nature of the agricultural firm. *Journal of Economic Behaviour and Organization, 26*, 161–177.

Sadoulet, E., de Janvry, A., & Benjamin, C. (1998). Household behavior with imperfect labor markets. *Journal of Industrial Relations, 37*(1), 85–108.

Sahn, D., & Arulpragasam, J. (1993). Land tenure, dualism and poverty in Malawi. In Lipton & van der Gaag (Eds.).

Sanyal, S. K. (1988). Trends in landholding and poverty in rural India. In T. N. Srinivasan, & P. K. Bardhan (Eds.), *Rural development in South Asia.* New York: Columbia.

Saxena, K. B. (1990). Access to land as an instrument of poverty alleviation. *Journal of Rural Development, 9.*

Schultz, T. W. (1964). *Transforming traditional agriculture.* New Haven: Yale University Press.

Shearer, E., Lastarria-Cornhiel, S., & Mestah, D. (1991). *The reform of rural land markets in Latin America and the Caribbean: research, theory and policy implications.* Land Tenure Centre: Paper no. 141. Madison: University of Wisconsin.

Sial, M. H., & Carter, M. R. (1996). Financial market efficiency in an agrarian economy: microeconometric analysis of the Pakistani Punjab. *Journal of Development Studies, 32*, 771–798.

Singh, I. J. (1990). *The great ascent: the rural poor in South Asia.* Baltimore: Johns Hopkins.

Smith, A. (1937). 1776. *The wealth of nations.* New York: Modern Library Edition.

Sokoloff, K., & Engerman, S. (2002). *Factor endowments, inequality, and paths of development among New World economies.* Working Paper 9259. National Bureau for Economic Research.

Stanfield, J. D. (1989). Agrarian reform in the Dominican Republic. In Thiesenhusen (Ed.).

Stanfield, J. D., Lastarria-Cornhiel, S., Bruce, J., & Friedman, E. (1992). *Property rights in Albania's new private farm sector.* Land Tenure Centre: paper no. 146. Madison: University of Wisconsin.

Stifel, D. C., Minten, B., & Dorosh, P. (2003). *Transactions costs and agricultural productivity: implications of isolation for rural poverty in Madagascar. MSSD.* Discussion Paper 56, IFPRI.

Stokes, E. (1983). Agrarian relations: Northern and Central India. In Kumar & Desai (Eds.).

Strasma, J. (1989). Unfinished business: consolidating land reform in El Salvador. In Thiesenhusen (Ed.).

Swamy, D. S. (1988). Agricultural tenancy in the 1970s. *Indian Journal of Agricultural Economics, 43*(4).

Taslim, M. (1989). Supervision problems and the size-productivity relation in Bangladesh agriculture. *Oxford Bulletin of Economics and Statistics, 51.*

Tendler, J. (1991). *New Lessons from old projects: the dynamics of rural development in North-east Brazil.* Operations Evaluation Dept., World Bank.

Teofilo, E., & Prado Garcia, D. (2003). Brazil: land politics, poverty and rural development. *Land Reform, Rural Development and Co-operatives, 3.*

Thiesenhusen, W. C. (Ed.). (1989). *Searching for agrarian reform in Latin America.* Boston: Unwin Hyman.

Thiesenhusen, W. C., & Melmed-Sanjak, J. (1990). Brazil's agrarian structure: changes from 1970 through 1980. *World Development, 18*(3).

Thome, J. R. (1989). Law, conflict and change: Frei's law and Allende's agrarian reform. In Thiesenhusen (Ed.).

U.S. Department of Commerce. (1975). *Historical statistics of the United States: colonial times to 1970.* Washington, DC: Bureau of the Census.

U.S. Department of Commerce. (2000). *Statistical abstract of the United States, 2000.* Washington, DC: Bureau of the Census.

van Zyl, J., Binswanger, H. P., & Thirtle, C. (1995). *The relationship between farm size and efficiency in South African agriculture.* Washington, DC: The World Bank.

von Braun, J., Hotchkiss, D., & Immink, M. (1989). *Nontraditional export crops in Guatemala: effects on production, income, and nutrition.* Research Report 73. Washington, DC: International Food Policy Research Institute in collaboration with the Institute of Nutrition of Central America and Panama.

von Braun, J., Puetz, D., & Webb, P. (1989). *Irrigation technology and commercialization of rice in the Gambia: effects on income and nutrition*. Research Report no. 75. Washington, DC: International Food Policy Research Institute.

Vyas, V. (1976). Some aspects of structural change in Indian. *Indian Journal of Agricultural Economics, 34*.

Weatherspoon, D., & Reardon, T. (2003). The rise of supermarkets in Africa: implications for agrifood systems and the rural poor. *Development Policy Review, 21*(3).

Wegren, S., & Durgin, F. (1997). The political economy of private farming in Russia. *Comparative Economic Studies, 39*(Fall–Winter), 3–4.

Winters, A., McCulloch, N., & McKay, A. (2004). Trade liberalisation and poverty: the evidence so far. *Journal of Economic Literature, XLII*.

Wolf, E. (1969). *Peasant wars in the twentieth century*. London: Faber.

World Bank. (1978). *Agricultural land settlement*. Washington, DC: The World Bank.

Wood, A. (1994). *North-South trade, employment and inequality: changing fortunes in a skill-driven world*. Oxford: Clarendon Press.

Yager, J. (1988). *Transforming agriculture in Taiwan: The experience of the JCRR*. Ithaca: Cornell.

Yotopoulos, P., & L. Lau. (1973). A test for relative efficiency: some further results. *American Economic Review, 63*(1), 214–223.

Yugandhar, B. N., & Gopal Iyer, K. (Eds.). (1990). *Land reforms in India Vol. I: Bihar*. New Delhi: Sage.

Zevallos, J. V. (1989). Agrarian reform and structural change: Ecuador since 1964. In Thiesenhusen (Ed.).

Zhou, J. M. (2000). Principal forms of land consolidation and expansion in China. *Land Reform, Land Settlement and Cooperatives, 1*, 88–107.

APPENDIX

Table 1   Measures of the distribution of farm size from the 1990 and 2000 rounds of FAO farm censuses

	Year	Mean	Gini	% Permanent Pasture	% Holdings < 2 ha.	% Area < 2 ha.	% Holdings < 5 ha.	% Area < 5 ha.
Africa								
North								
Algeria	01	8.26	0.65		16.7	0.44	21.8	0.8
Egypt	99/00	0.83	0.69	..	90.8	47.4	..	..
Libya	87	14.22	0.75	19.2	17.7	..	42.5	..
Morocco	96	5.84	0.64	..	..	..	71.1	23.9
Sub-Saharan								
Botswana	93	3.18	..	..	..	..	..	..
Burkina Faso	93	3.92	0.42	..	32.4	12.9	73.6	61.5
DR Congo	90	0.53	0.37	..	97.1	86	..	..
Ethiopia	01/02	1.01	0.47	9.0	87.1	60.4	99.0	93.1
Gambia	01/02	4.41	..	..	..	..	..	..
Guinea	95	2.03	0.48	..	65.2	32.2	93.2	74
Guinea-Bissau	88	1.14	0.62	..	87.8	..	97.9	..
Lesotho	89/90	1.44	0.49	..	76.8	..	96.5	..
Malawi	93	0.75	0.52	..	95.0	..	..	..
Mozambique	99/00	1.28	..	..	83.4	..	97.3	..
Namibia	96/97	2.89	0.36	..	38.9	15.8	87.8	69.9
Reunion	89	4.42	0.61	..	55.9	11.4	83.5	36.5
Senegal	98/99	4.30	0.50	..	37.5	8.1	70.0	33.3
Togo	96	1.96	..	..	..	..	..	72.7
Uganda	91	2.16	0.59	..	73.4	..	90.8	..
Zambia	90	..	..	..	..	..	92.2	..

Americas

North

	Year							
Canada	01	273.4	::	::	::	::	::	::
United States	02	178.35	0.78	47.9	4.2	0.0	10.1	0.2

Central and Caribbean

	Year							
Bahamas	94	11.55	0.87	15.9	61.2	4.3	::	::
Barbados	89	1.26	0.94	10.2	97.8	13	98.9	15.6
Dominica	95	2.34	0.67	11.6	74.5	23.5	::	::
Grenada	95	0.77	0.73	8.4	92.5	32	::	::
Guadeloupe	89	3.24	0.56	34.7	58.9	17.8	90.4	42.6
Honduras	93	11.17	0.66	64.3	::	::	54.7	7.7
Martinique	89	2.40	0.75	51.3	77.9	16.4	93	36
Mexico (ex ejidos)	91	24.58		68.4	::	::	59	3
Nicaragua	01	31.34	0.72	::	21.3	0.7	::	::
Panama	90	13.75	0.87	77.6	58.1	1.5	71.5	4.2
Puerto Rico	02	15.37	0.73	::	22.9	2.5	50.9	7.0

South

	Year							
Argentina	88	468.97	0.83	82.9	::	::	15.1	0.1
Brazil	96	73.09	0.85	78.0	20.3	0.3	36.8	1.0
Chile	97	83.74	0.92	84.9	::	::	42.5	0.9
Colombia	01	23.90	0.78	74.2	::	::	50.3	3.8
Ecuador	99/00	14.66	0.85	41.2	43.42	2.0	63.5	6.3
French Guiana	00	6.52	::	::	56.3	::	91.1	::
Paraguay	91	77.53	0.93	69.3	::	::	40	1.0
Peru	94	20.15	0.86	::	::	::	::	::
Uruguay	00	287.40	0.85	82.5	::	::	23.4	0.4
Venezuela	97	60.02	0.90	83.4	22.6	0.3	48.4	1.6

Continued

Table 1 Measures of the distribution of farm size from the 1990 and 2000 rounds of FAO farm censuses—Cont'd

	Year	Mean	Gini	% Permanent Pasture	% Holdings < 2 ha.	% Area < 2 ha.	% Holdings < 5 ha.	% Area < 5 ha.
Asia								
Bangladesh	96	0.46	0.57	..	95.5	68.8	..	..
China	97	0.67	..	..	95.8	57.5	99.2	77.3
Cyprus	94	3.41	0.63	3.5	53.9	11.2	..	..
India	95/6/7	1.41	0.60	..	80.3	36.0	95.1	67.5
Indonesia	93	0.87	0.46	..	..	..	..	..
Iran	93	4.29	0.70	7.2	50.5	4.8	71.2	17.1
Israel	95	12.35	..	..	..	..	..	..
Japan	95	1.20	0.59	..	88.5	48.2	97.6	69.9
Jordan	97	3.15	0.78	..	69.9	11.0	86.2	26.2
Korea, Rep. of	90	1.05	0.34	..	92.4	71.8	..	..
Kyrgystan	02	1.16	0.90	..	88.2	14.0	97.2	31.3
Laos	98/99	1.57	0.76	1.7	72.7	42.8	..	..
Lebanon	98	1.27	0.89	..	86.8	34.8	..	..
Myanmar	93	2.35	0.77	..	56.7	20.7	..	..
Nepal	02	0.79	0.49	1.5	92.4	68.7	99.2	92.7
Pakistan	02	3.08	0.61	..	57.6	15.5	85.7	43.4
Philippines	91	2.16	0.55	1.3	65.1	23.4	90.6	56.2
Sri Lanka	02	0.81	0.38	..	..	..	..	..
Thailand	93	3.36	0.47	1.2	33.9	7.6	72.9	43.8
Turkey	01	5.99	0.58	4.1	34.5	5.3	65.4	21.3
Vietnam	94	0.52	0.53	..	..	..	..	..

Europe								
Albania	98	4.05	0.84	21.6	90.0	17.3	..	..
Austria	99/00	34.11	0.59	28.7	14.6	2.2	36.4	7.4
Belgium	99/00	23.12	0.56	..	17.2	0.9	30.8	3.0
Czech Rep.	00	64.50	0.92	..	44.3	0.5	72.5	1.3
Denmark	02	52.75	0.54	..	..	..	..	..
Finland	99/00	72.24	0.27	4.6	3.4	1.1	10.6	3.9
France	99/00	45.04	0.58	35.7	16.8	0.7	29.1	2.0
Germany	99/00	40.47	0.63	30.0	8.0	0.3	24.9	2.5
Greece	99/00	4.74	0.58	14.0	49.0	11.4	76.8	32.0
Ireland	00	33.31	0.44	86.5	2.2	0.1	8.3	0.9
Italy	00	7.57	0.80	25.8	57.2	6.0	77.8	14.5
Latvia	01	19.89	0.58	25.3	6.2	0.4	25.9	3.7
Netherlands	99/00	22.05	0.57	49.8	15.9	1.0	31.3	3.7
Norway	99	89.85	0.18	11.5	8.2	4.2	20.5	10.6
Poland	02	6.59	0.69	21.1	50.9	7.4	72.4	20.0
Portugal	99	12.47	0.75	36.0	54.6	9.2	78.8	19.7
Slovak Rep.	01	48.7	..	36.3	..	..	94.3	..
Slovenia	91	5.83	0.62	59	41.1	..	64.3	..
Spain	89	18.79	0.86	34.3	44.2	1.8	65.3	5.4
Switzerland	90	11.65	0.50	69.8	..	..	37.9	4.8
United Kingdom	99/00	70.86	0.66	56.8	13.9	0.3	23.1	0.8
Oceania								
Australia	90	3601.7	..	96.1	..	..	2.6	..
New Zealand	02	222.64	..	..	6.8	..	17.1	..

Notes: 1. Italicized numbers are linear interpolations from grouped data. 2. Data for Mexico are shares less than 5.1 ha.; data for Myanmar data shares less than 2.02 ha.; data for Thailand are shares less than 1.6 ha and 4.8 ha..

Source: FAOSTAT at www.fao.org/es/ess/census/default.asp.

PART Two

Regional Perspectives in Agricultural Developement

CHAPTER 66

Production, Productivity, and Public Investment in East Asian Agriculture

Shenggen Fan
International Food Policy Research Institute (IFPRI)

Joanna Brzeska
International Food Policy Research Institute

Contents

Abstract

Since the 1950s, agricultural growth in East Asia (China, Mongolia, North Korea, South Korea, and Taiwan) has reduced rural poverty and created a strong base for economic development. To gain a better understanding of the nature of this growth, we examine the sources of change in agricultural production and total factor productivity (TFP) and decompose the measurements into reform-based time periods. We also review studies that link public investments to agricultural growth and

Handbook of Agricultural Economics, Volume 4
doi: 10.1016/S1574-0072(09)04066-3

poverty reduction. We find that formulating growth-inducing and poverty-reducing strategies requires policymakers to understand the relative returns of different types of investments.
JEL classifications: Q12, Q14, Q18, O13, O47

Keywords

total factor productivity
agricultural growth
public expenditures
China
Mongolia
North Korea
South Korea
Taiwan

1. INTRODUCTION

East Asian agriculture has experienced a rapid transformation during the last several decades. On the institutional side, land reforms were successfully implemented in the 1950s. Rural cooperatives in finance, credit, and marketing were set up or strengthened. Market-led reforms were also introduced in former centrally planned economies in the late 1970s and 1980s. On the technology side, the Green Revolution, characterized by the wide adoption of high-yielding varieties and intensive use of chemical fertilizers, pesticides, and irrigation, was initiated in the 1960s and 1970s and has spread to almost every corner of East Asian agriculture. By the1990s, the majority of cropped areas in the region were planted with high-yielding (or improved modern) varieties (Fan and Pardey, 1998).

As a result of these institutional and technological innovations, production, partial productivities, and total factor productivity have grown the most rapidly among all regions. Consequently, rural poverty has been directly reduced. In addition, rapid agricultural growth provided a fundamental base for economic development that led to the regional economic boom of the 1980s and 1990s. Thus, rural poverty also declined through these indirect effects in the region, and the food shortage foreseen by many observers disappeared.

The objective of this chapter is to review the recent literature on the measures of production and productivity growth as well as the sources of this growth, particularly the role of public investment, in East Asian agriculture. The chapter begins with a review of general patterns of agricultural growth in five East Asian countries, including a focus on crop output, yield, and production trends in the individual countries, alongside a decomposition of production growth into area and yield increase components. The next section outlines the conceptual framework of the total factor productivity (TFP) measure, followed by a review of empirical studies on agricultural TFP growth in East Asian agriculture. The last section synthesizes studies of linkages between public investments and agricultural growth and poverty reduction, specifically focusing on the variation in the impact within various regions and types of government expenditure.

2. TRENDS IN AGRICULTURAL AREA, YIELD, AND PRODUCTION

East Asian agriculture has grown rapidly during the last several decades. Yet behind the overall pattern of agricultural growth lies a plethora of temporal and country-specific variability across the individual East Asian countries. This section first examines the trends in area harvested, production, and yield for major crops in five East Asian countries, namely China, Mongolia, North Korea, South Korea, and Taiwan. To gain better insight into these trends across time, the analyses are further divided into five subperiods. Second, the production growth in each country is decomposed into area and yield change, thus allowing us to identify the sources of production change within each country across time.

2.1 China

As a result of major policy changes and reforms, Chinese agriculture has grown rapidly during the past several decades, with most major crops experiencing increased yield, area harvested, and production. Between 1961 and 2004, maize, cotton, wheat, and oilseed production had an average growth rate of 4% per annum, while rice production growth was 2.8% per annum (Table 1). Moreover, crop yields grew at a rate of 2.64–4.81% per annum during the period, while the area under harvest showed much smaller growth rates (0.16–1.28%), with area harvested for wheat experiencing negative growth (−0.38%), that is, the contraction of crop area. A closer examination of the trends indicates that all crops except for oilseeds underwent the most rapid growth in crop area, yield, and production between 1961 and 1980, a period marked by rapid adoption of modern crop varieties and inputs such as chemical fertilizers and pesticides, together with improved irrigation. The period between 1980 and 2000 saw a slowdown in the growth of these indicators, with area harvested showing the largest deceleration, followed by production.

Yield increases were responsible for a majority of the production growth from 1961 to 2004. The most pronounced relationship between yield and production growth was between 1980 and 2000, when the contribution of yield to production growth for rice, cotton, and wheat exceeded 100%, indicating that yield increases offset the negative impact that land contraction had on production levels. These results are in line with the agricultural policies of the 1980s and 1990s, a period in which the Chinese government sought to increase production and productivity through a series of decentralization and marketing reforms aimed at improving production incentives. Area contraction is a reflection of loss of agricultural land due to urbanization and a reduction in cropping index.

2.2 Mongolia

Agriculture has traditionally dominated the Mongolian economy. Although livestock farming is the largest sector in Mongolian agriculture, crop farming nevertheless provides essential elements to the Mongolian diet, with wheat making up a large part of crop production (Bayarsaihan and Coelli, 2003). However, the growth rates for wheat crops in terms of area harvested, yield, and production indicate that the crop has experienced minimal growth of less than 1% per annum between 1961 and 2004 (Table 2). A decomposition of the trends into subperiods shows that the growth decelerated between 1961–1980 and 1980–2000. For example, crop area grew at an annual rate of 2.26% per annum in 1961–1980 but contracted to −4.05% in 1980–2000, only returning to positive levels (13.85% growth) in the most recent subperiod, 2000–2004. Similarly to China, the Mongolian government has recently made a significant departure from its centrally planned economic system and has implemented a number of policies aimed at liberalizing the economy. The deceleration in growth experienced between 1961–1980 and 1980–1990 can be at least partially attributed to the policy changes implemented in the 1990s (Bakey, 1998). More specifically, the Mongolian agricultural sector in the 1990s was characterized by underdeveloped financial systems and the inability of the low-income collective units to adapt to the new market economy, therefore leading to reduced crop production and land underutilization.

A decomposition of the sources of wheat production growth indicates that growth between 1961 and 2004 was primarily driven by yield growth, with modest contributions from crop area. More specifically, between 1961 and 1980, production growth was attributed to virtually equal contributions from yield growth and area expansion. In the subsequent subperiod of 1980–2000, not even the positive yield growth could alleviate the negative effect area contraction had on crop production. However, recent area expansion in 2000–2004 fueled increased production, offsetting the negative effect of the decreasing yields.

2.3 North Korea

Achieving self-sufficiency in food production has been one of the most important objectives of North Korea's economic strategy (Park, 2002). To further self-reliance and overcome the country's unfavorable land conditions, North Korean agricultural policies focused on increasing the mechanization of the agricultural sector and the capital intensiveness of agricultural production, resulting in North Korea having one of the world's most input-intensive agricultural systems (Noland, 2003; Park, 2002). The period between 1961 and 2004 saw minimal growth in area harvested for rice and soybeans and negative growth for maize and wheat (Table 3). On the other hand, yield growth was positive for all crops except rice in 1961–2004, and production growth was positive for all crops during the same period. Yet despite generally positive growth in crop yield and production in 1961–2004, subperiod trends indicate a downturn for most crops between 1961–1980 and 1980–2000, with yield, area harvested, and production growth for wheat, maize, and rice becoming negative in 1980–2000. This decline in agricultural indicators is consistent with the overall economic decline as well as the declining input availability, overuse of chemical fertilizers, and soil depletion plaguing North Korea since the late 1980s (FAO and WFP, 2003; Norton, 2003). With the exception of rice crops, production growth in 1961–2004 was primarily due to an increase in yield, especially in the case of wheat and maize. Increased production of rice, the key crop in North Korea's self-sufficiency development strategy, however, was completely fueled by crop area expansion in 1961–2004 and, more specifically, in the subperiod 1961–1980. Yet data for the subperiods indicate that decreased maize, rice, and wheat production in 1980-2000 was more evenly distributed between yield and area components, while the contribution of yield has had a larger impact on more recent (i.e., 2000–2004) production growth for all crops except soybeans.

2.4 South Korea

Since the early 1960s, South Korea has transformed itself from a low-income agrarian economy into a middle-income industrialized "miracle" (Hayami, 1998), and the agricultural sector in South Korea has not been immune to the tremendous structural change. Agriculture has been declining in importance relative to the manufacturing and service sectors, most notably evidenced by the decline in the agricultural sector's share of GDP from 29.8% in 1972 to 5.6% in 1999. The limited amount of arable land and increasing pressures to industrialize have resulted in negative crop area growth for all crops, whereas yield has increased in 1961–2004 (Table 4). The contraction of area harvested was especially pronounced in 1980-2000 as a result of increased demand for land for industrial-residential purposes (Yoo, 2003). Although the type of intervention has changed over the years, the South Korean government has continually pursued statist agricultural policies, foremost focusing, as with North Korea, on achieving self-sufficiency and increasing production in the rice subsector (Burmeister, 2000; Song, 2003). While crop area growth decreased for all crops between 1961–1980 and 1980–2000, the smallest decline was recorded for rice. Moreover, rice was the only crop to show an increase in yield and production growth rates between the two periods. The "state-rice complex" in South Korea (Burmeister, 2000) has resulted in a mixed pattern of annual production growth between 1961 and 2004, with wheat and soybeans experiencing negative annual rates of growth while maize and rice crops recorded positive growth.

The decomposition of South Korea's production growth shows that, despite land area contraction, maize and rice crops experienced positive production growth in 1961–2004 due to increased yield. Positive yield growth for wheat and soybean crops, on the other hand, could not alleviate the negative effect of area contraction on the production growth of these two crops in 1961–2004, resulting in negative production growth for these crops. It is interesting to note that the decline in production was continually driven by area contraction, whereas increased production was driven primarily by yield change in some cases and by area change in other instances.

2.5 Taiwan

In an environment of poor natural resources and subsequent encroachment of the industrial and services sector on agriculture (Ranis, 1998; Liang and Mei, 2005), Taiwan has experienced negative growth rates of rice, wheat, and oilseed area harvested from 1961 until 2004 (Table 5). Even the land area under maize cultivation, which expanded at a rate of 1.1% per annum from 1961 to 2004, only expanded in 1961–1980 and then shrank in the subsequent decades. Maize was also the only crop to record increased production (4.22% per annum) in 1961–2004, although the most recent subperiod 2000–2004 showed decreased production. In direct contrast to the general decline of production and contraction of crop area, crop yields grew in 1961–2004, although fluctuations between subperiods are evident. Despite this yield growth, area expansion and contraction were the main drivers of production change, with the exception of rice in 1961–1980 and maize in 1961–2004. Although the rates of production fluctuated with crop type and subperiod, most instances of decreasing production were attributed to a contraction in crop area. For example, production growth of maize crops was initially driven by area expansion but in subsequent period was largely due to increased yields.

3. CONCEPTUAL FRAMEWORK: TFP, TECHNICAL CHANGE, EFFICIENCY IMPROVEMENT

3.1 TFP measures

Total factor productivity (TFP) measures the overall efficiency of agricultural production, calculated as a ratio of aggregate output to aggregate input. In other words, productivity is raised when growth in output is more than growth in input. Productivity growth increase without an increase in inputs is the best kind of growth to aim for rather than attaining a certain level of output by increasing inputs, since these inputs are subject to diminishing marginal returns. However, finding a way to measure the total inputs and total output is both conceptually and empirically difficult.

In aggregating total output, prices are often used as weights to add all products together. Many economists have pointed out that using constant prices to aggregate output may result in biased estimate of production growth (Alston et al., 1995). Despite these concerns, many countries and international organizations still report growth in output aggregated using constant prices. This potential bias is illustrated in Figure 1, where Q_0 represents a production possibility curve, which indicates the different combination of products Y_1 and Y_2, using the same amount of inputs.[1] Profit-maximizing producers choose different combinations of Y_1 and Y_2 based on relative prices of the two products. Producers would choose point *a* in the production possibility curve when relative prices are P_1, and *b* when relative prices are P_2. If total output is aggregated using a liner aggregation of the two products weighted by their relative

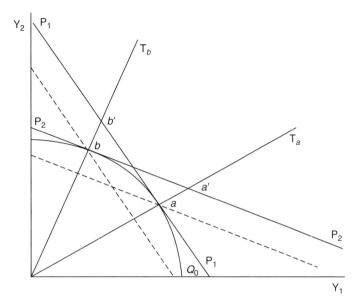

Figure 1 Aggregation bias in output.

prices P_1, aggregate output at *a* (equal to output at *b'*) would be greater than that at *b*. But if P_2 were used in the aggregation, output at *b* (equal to output at *a'*) would be greater than that at *a*. Different output measures are obtained using different price weights, although producers only move along the same production possibility curve.

Figure 2 shows the potential bias that arises from input aggregation, where I_0 represents an isoquant in which the same amount of output is produced using different input combinations, X_1 and X_2. Cost-minimizing producers choose input combination based on relative input prices, W_1 and W_2. If producers face relative prices W_1, the optimal combination of inputs would be at point *c*. If relative prices change to W_2, the optimal combination of inputs would be at *d*. This shift is the producers' response to input price changes (the substitution effect) along the same isoquant. But using different relative prices as weights yields different input aggregates. For example, if relative prices W_1 are used as weights, aggregated input at *d* is greater than that at *c* (equal to output at *d'*). Conversely, if the relative price W_2 is used, aggregate input at *c* is greater than that at *d* (equal to output at *c'*). The resulting productivity index using these biased estimates of aggregate output and input is also biased, even when there has been no change in quantities of either inputs or outputs.

To minimize the potential bias caused by relative price changes, several approaches have been developed in the literature. The most commonly used method is the Divisia index. As Richter (1966) has shown, the Divisia index is desirable because of its invariance property: If nothing real has changed (e.g., the only quantity changes involve movements around an unchanged isoquant), the index itself is unchanged. In practice,

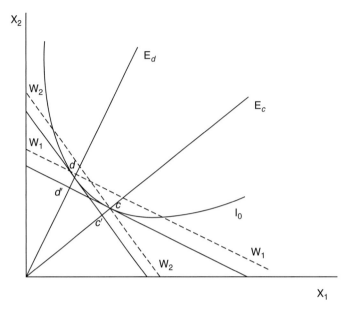

Figure 2 Aggregation bias in input.

the Törnqvist-Theil (TT) index is usually used to approximate the Divisia index. The formula for a TT index of aggregate output is:

$$lnQI_t = \Sigma_i 1/2 * (S_{i,t} + S_{i,t-1}) * \ln(Y_{i,t}/Y_{i,t-1}), \qquad (1)$$

where $lnQI_t$ is the log of the aggregate output index at time t, and $S_{i,t}$ and $S_{i,t-1}$ are output i's share in total production value at time t and $t-1$, respectively. $Y_{i,t}$ and $Y_{i,t-1}$ are quantities of output i at time t and $t-1$, respectively. The advantage of such an index is that rolling weights accommodate any substantial changes in relative prices over time. Diewert (1976) and Lau (1979) proved that the TT index is exact for the more general class of translog aggregator functions. The TT index of aggregated input growth can be expressed in a similar way.

Based on the growth of aggregated output and input, TFP is defined as the difference between these two. Specifically, the TFP index can be written as follows:

$$lnTFP_t = \Sigma_i 1/2 * (S_{i,t} + S_{i,t-1}) * \ln(Y_{i,t}/Y_{i,t-1}) - \Sigma_i 1/2 * (W_{i,t} + W_{i,t-1})$$
$$* \ln(X_{i,t}/X_{i,t-1}) \qquad (2)$$

where $lnTFP_t$ is the log of total factor productivity index, $W_{i,t}$ and $W_{i,t-1}$ are the cost shares of input i in total cost at time t and $t-1$, respectively, and $X_{i,t}$ and $X_{i,t-1}$ are the quantities of input i at time t and $t-1$, respectively.

3.2 Sources of growth
3.2.1 Primal approach

Growth in total output can be decomposed into growth in input and productivity. Often the contribution of TFP to growth is also interpreted as the contribution of technical progress. To perform source accounting, assume that agricultural output in a particular year follows a well-behaved, neoclassical production function:

$$Y_{it} = f(X_{it}, T) + v_{it} \tag{3}$$

where i denotes i^{th} firm or farm and t denotes time. Y_{it} is output and X_{it} is *1xk* rows of inputs, and T is a technology variable.

Taking the first derivative of Eq. (3) with respect to time t *assuming input use and technology are separable (or neutral technological change)*, the growth of production can be decomposed as:

$$\partial Y_{it}/\partial t = \partial X_{it}/\partial t + \partial T/\partial t \tag{4}$$

The first term of Eq. (4) represents the effect of increased input use; the second term measures the effect of technical change or productivity improvement. In many empirical studies, the residual of accounting – the growth in total output net of growth in total inputs – is treated as technical change or productivity improvement (Solow, 1957).

But the preceding approach assumes that farms or firms are equally efficient in using the technology. This assumption might not be realistic. Initiated by Farrell (1957), a frontier production function concept was introduced, and new concepts of technological change and technical efficiency improvement were introduced. Technological change is defined as a shift of the frontier production function; technical efficiency improvement is defined as the decrease in the distance the firm (or farm)'s realized output and potential output (or frontier). Considering the following production function:

$$Y_{it} = f(X_{it}, T) + u_{it} + v_{it}, \tag{5}$$

where i denotes i^{th} firm or farm, and t denotes time. Y_{it} is output and X_{it} is *1xk* rows of inputs, $f(X_{it}, T)$ is potential output, and u_{it} is one-sided distribution, $u_{it} <= 0$, which represents technical inefficiency, *and* v_{it} is a stochastic variable representing the uncontrolled random shocks. The nonpositive disturbance u indicates that output must lie on or below the frontier $f(X_{it}, T)$. Therefore, growth in output can be decomposed into three different components:

$$\partial Y_{it}/\partial t = \partial X_{it}/\partial t + \partial T/\partial t + \partial u_{it}/\partial t. \tag{6}$$

The first term is the effect of the increased input use on production growth, the second term captures technological change, and the third term is the efficiency improvement.

3.2.2 Dual approach

Most of the studies on the sources of growth in East Asian agriculture used the production function approach (Lin, 1992; Fan, 1991; Wen, 1993). However, this approach cannot measure the impact of improvement of allocative efficiency due to changes and reforms. It might be useful to define the different concepts of technical and allocative efficiency.

Technological change and efficiency improvement are important sources of production growth in any economy. *Technological change* is defined as a shift in the frontier production function. Efficiency improvement can be further decomposed into technical and allocative efficiency. The concept of technical efficiency is based on input and output relationships. *Technical inefficiency* arises when actual or observed output from a given input mix is less than the maximum possible. *Allocative inefficiency* arises when the input mix is not consistent with cost minimization. Allocative inefficiency occurs when farmers do not equalize marginal returns with true factor market prices.

Various concepts of efficiency and technological change can be illustrated using Figure 3, with two inputs, X_1 and X_2, and a single product, Y. The two isoquants F_1 and F_2 represent production frontiers for the same physical output at time 1 and time 2, respectively. They are the best-practice technologies used by farmers. However, a producer might not reach the frontier because of technical inefficiency. Points A_1, B_1, A_2, and B_2 are technically efficient, but C_1 and C_2 are not. The price of input X_1 relative to X_2 is represented by P_1 and P_2 for the two time periods, respectively. Allocative efficiency occurs if the inputs are combined so that their marginal products

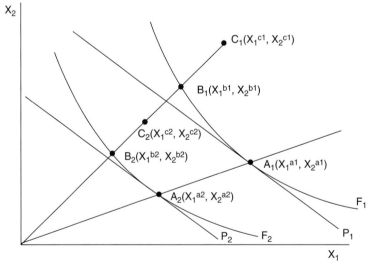

Figure 3   Effects of technological change and efficiency improvement on production.

are in the same ratios as their relative prices. Points A_1 and A_2 are allocatively efficient, but B_1 and B_2 are not. A_1 and A_2 are both technically and allocatively efficient because they are on the production frontiers and are located where the ratios of marginal products are the same as the ratios of relative prices.

In the cost function framework, technological change can be measured as $-[C(X_1^{a2}, X_2^{a2}) - C(X_1^{a1}, X_2^{a1}] / C(X_1^{a1}, X_2^{a1})$; technical efficiency can be measured as $C(X_1^{b1}, X_2^{b1}) / C(X_1^{c1}, X_2^{c1})$ at time 1, and $C(X_1^{b2}, X_2^{b2}) / C(X_1^{c2}, X_2^{c2})$ at time 2, respectively; and allocative efficiency can be measured as $C(X_1^{a1}, X_2^{a1}) / C(X_1^{b1}, X_2^{b1})$ at time 1, and $C(X_1^{a2}, X_2^{a2}) / C(X_1^{b2}, X_2^{b2})$ at time 2, respectively. Economic efficiency is the product of technical efficiency and allocative efficiency. Therefore, economic efficiency is $C(X_1^{a1}, X_2^{a1}) / C(X_1^{c1}, X_2^{c1})$ at time 1, and $C(X_1^{a2}, X_2^{a2}) / C(X_1^{c2}, X_2^{c2})$ at time 2, respectively.

4. EMPIRICAL TFP MEASURES IN EAST ASIAN AGRICULTURE

Over the past 50 years, the countries of East Asia have experienced tremendous institutional and policy changes that have had a large impact on growth and poverty levels in rural areas as well as on agricultural productivity. To have a better understanding of the trends in agricultural productivity, it is therefore important to not only look at general productivity growth information but to also decompose the analysis into reform-based time periods.

4.1 China (1952–1997)

During the period between 1952 and 1978, major land reforms were introduced in the agricultural sector to meet the needs of the industrial and urban sectors (Fan, Zhang, and Zhang, 2002). The government adopted an increasingly collective and large-scale mode of production, encouraging farmers to pool their land and other resources into large production units. Complete control was exercised over production through centrally mandated quotas and procurement prices for agricultural inputs and outputs. The forced collectivization and communization gave farmers little incentive to increase productivity. More specifically, market transactions of most major agricultural products were prohibited outside the procurement system and farmers' incomes were not closely linked to their production efforts. The nature of the communal incentive structure was not conducive to large productivity gains. Consequently, inefficiency was rampant in agricultural production. Using official Chinese statistics with adjustments on livestock and fishery output, Fan and Zhang (2002) constructed a Törnqvist-Theil index of output, input, and TFP growth in Chinese agriculture from 1952 to 1997 (Table 6). According to these data, agricultural output increased at a rate of 2.38% per annum, whereas total factor productivity grew at a 0.12% per annum. The minimal growth in productivity is not surprising, given that one of the main drawbacks of the agricultural control structure during this period was the inadequate level of checks and balances within the production system and the general lack of incentives for farmers to increase agricultural productivity.

In an effort to improve the weak production and incentive structure within the agricultural sector, the Chinese government introduced institutional, marketing, and pricing reforms starting in 1978. One of the first implemented reforms sought to eliminate the free-rider problem inherent within collective systems by linking performance to work efforts. A "two-tiered" land tenure system was introduced, whereby land ownership remained with the communes but land-use rights and production decisions were decentralized to the individual household level. In addition to decentralizing agricultural production, the government also began to scale back the agricultural procurement system and to liberalize factor and output markets, thereby expanding the role of the free market in the allocation of agricultural resources. Further policy changes in the early 1990s were dictated by China's efforts to join the WTO and were characterized by broad-based trade liberalization. The transformation from a command-and-control to a free-market system has had a constructive influence on production levels and productivity. As a result of the decentralization efforts and market reforms, the growth rate of agricultural output nearly doubled to 4.57% per annum compared to the previous period. Even more important, TFP grew at a rate of 3.28% per annum between 1979 and 1997, a significant increase from the growth rate of 0.12% during the preceding period. A recent study by Brümmer, Glauben and Wu (2006) further decomposed productivity growth data from the province Zhejiang into four reform-based subperiods between 1986 and 2000. Although the period 1986–2000 saw moderate productivity growth, the most rapid change, of approximately 11.2% per annum, in TFP was realized during China's second stage of reforms (1986–1989), a period marked by market oriented reforms and deregulation, such as the introduction of agricultural input subsidies and a reduction in procurement quotas.

4.2 South Korea (1971–1998)

In direct contrast to the industrial focus of the 1960s, South Korean policies during the 1970s and 1980s emphasized improved terms of trade for the agricultural sector *vis à vis* the rest of the economy (Moon and Kang, 1991). More specifically, agricultural policies between 1970 and 1980 were aimed at stimulating domestic agricultural production, protecting domestic agricultural markets and upgrading agricultural incomes. Beginning in the early 1970s, government intervention in the agricultural sector became more pervasive, as evidenced by the steady use of domestic price support mechanisms and quantitative import restrictions for many agricultural products and inputs. Using agricultural production and TFP data obtained by Kwon and Kim (2000), we examine the output and production indices for Korean agriculture. The results are summarized in Table 7. In an atmosphere of protective agricultural policies and subsidies between 1971 and 1989, agricultural output grew at an annual rate of 4.1%. Moreover, the increase in output is found to be approximately three times larger than the 1.6% growth in agricultural TFP during the same period. Moon and Kang (1991) note that agricultural productivity was chiefly hampered by the small size of farms and the scarcity of land resources in the country. The divergence between the growth of outputs and TFP is not surprising given the emphasis of agricultural policies during this period on stimulating production rather than productivity.

The period between 1990 and 1998 was marked by a series of bilateral and multilateral negotiations that gradually reduced South Korea's trade barriers and price support mechanisms. Amid the "East Asian Miracle" of the 1970s and 1980s, South Korea increasingly came under pressure from its trade partners to open up and liberalize its markets. Since South Korea no longer suffered a balance of payment deficit, its ability under the GATT to impose quantitative trade barriers was revoked in 1989. Subsequently, the South Korean government began a gradual liberalization of its agricultural markets and the removal of most import quotas. Moreover, the Uruguay Round Agreement on Agriculture negotiations added more fuel to the liberalization process, subsuming and further adding to the removal of agricultural protection (Diao et al., 2002). To prepare for the opening of the agricultural sector and assist in the adjustment of the agricultural sector to the impending trade liberalization, the South Korean government enacted a series of agricultural restructuring and rural development plans aimed at raising agricultural efficiency and competitiveness (Moreddu et al., 1999). In an environment of structural adjustment and increased competition in the agricultural sector, the annual growth rates of agricultural output and productivity were 0.25% and 1.1% per annum, respectively, between 1990 and 1998. Compared to the previous period, the deceleration in output growth was much greater than the contemporaneous deceleration in TFP. The results therefore indicate that the removal of agricultural protection was accompanied by a greater emphasis on efficiency over sheer production gains.

4.3 Taiwan

Using the Törnqvist index method, Liang and Mei (2005) measured the growth of TFP for the economy of Taiwan as a whole and individually for 36 sectors between 1978 and 1999. During the entire 1978–1999 period, the average annual TFP growth rate for agriculture was 1.38%, in comparison to 4.01% for the whole economy. A decomposition of the TFP growth into several subperiods indicates that TFP growth in the agricultural sector was mostly steady, although slight variation over time was evident. More specifically, although always positive, average TFP growth per annum initially increased between the period 1978–1982 and 1982–1986 but then decelerated between 1986–1991 and 1991–1996. The downward trend, however, reversed in the most recent period, 1996–1999. The fluctuations in agricultural productivity mimicked the trends in the whole economy, although the magnitudes of the deceleration and acceleration were different.

4.4 Mongolia

Bayarsaihan and Coelli (2003) examined productivity change in the Mongolian agricultural sector between 1976 and 1990 by focusing on potato and grain crops, which are the principle crops in Mongolia. The results of the study indicate a generally poor performance by Mongolian state farms, which were the main producers of crops in the country, with an average annual TFP change of −1.7% for grain and 0.8% for potatoes. Yet the aggregate data mask an abundance of temporal variability that is directly linked to state agricultural policies during the study period. On the one hand, government policy between 1976 and 1980 emphasized input-based output growth, resulting in declining TFP for grain and potatoes during this period. On the other hand, the authors attribute the annual growth in TFP of approximately 7% for both crops between 1980 and 1989 to the shift in agricultural policy away from increased input usage and towards policies promoting new technology, improved education, greater management autonomy, and improved incentive structures.

4.5 Cross-country studies

There have been many reports on TFP measures in China, but few TFP measures are available for the other East Asian countries, with many authors choosing to focus on the economywide or industrial productivity of the Asian Tigers. Moreover, many past studies of agricultural TFP of East Asian countries have primarily been on a cross-country level, comparing TFP indices across countries and regions. Suhariyanto and Thirtle (2001), for example, measured the agricultural TFP for 18 Asian countries by calculating the Malmquist index using the sequential frontier method. According to the authors, this approach, unlike the contemporaneous frontier technology, is able to overcome the dimensionality methods implicit in studies that have many variables but few observations. The results show that China, South Korea, and Mongolia experienced positive TFP growth between 1965 and 1996, with the highest productivity growth found in South Korea (3.3%), followed by China (0.99%) and Mongolia (0.97%). On the other hand, agricultural TFP in North Korea decreased at an annual rate of −0.3% during the same time period. A division of the TFP growth into subperiods shows that South Korea experienced positive annual growth in each decade since 1961, whereas the productivity growth rate in North Korea was negative during the initial (1965–1970) and most recent periods (1991–1996). Annual TFP growth in Mongolia and China fluctuated between the subperiods, with Mongolia achieving the highest annual growth rate during 1965–1970 and China during 1981–1990.

5. SOURCE OF PRODUCTIVITY GROWTH IN EAST ASIAN AGRICULTURE

In explaining productivity growth in East Asian agriculture, economists originally limited themselves to the role of conventional inputs such as land, labor, and physical capital. For example, Wiens (1982) used a traditional accounting approach to decompose growth in Chinese agriculture into growth in land, labor, fertilizer, and machinery. The author used the accounting residual to represent the technological change and concluded that Chinese agriculture experienced technical regression, with most of growth in agriculture coming from increased use of labor, chemical fertilizer, and machinery during the prereform period.

The outstanding performance of Chinese agriculture after the reforms of the late 1970s triggered numerous studies to analyze the sources of the rapid growth. A number of these studies decomposed productivity change in Chinese agriculture into input and technological change and technical efficiency improvement. According to Fan (1990), 70% of the observed productivity growth in China between 1965 and 1986 was a result of increased input use, with the rest driven equally by efficiency and technical change. In a study by Kalirajan et al. (1996), the authors estimated a varying coefficient production frontier to measure provincial-level agricultural TFP growth in China. During the prereform period of 1970–1978, output growth, which was accompanied by negative TFP growth in a majority of the provinces, came almost exclusively from changes in inputs. On the other hand, the authors attribute a majority of the output growth during the 1979–1983 reform period to the positive productivity growth, which itself was primarily driven by technical efficiency change.

A handful of other studies have attempted to analyze the impact of institutional changes on production growth during the reform period up to the early 1990s, e.g., McMillan, Whalley, and Zhu (1989); Fan (1990); Fan (1991); Lin (1992); Zhang and Carter (1997). McMillan, Whalley, and Zhu (1989) argue that 80% of the productivity growth over 1978–1984 was due to institutional reforms, whereas 20% was due to output price changes. Similarly, Fan (1991) found that institutional reforms accounted for 27% of production growth or 63% of productivity growth, and technical change measured as the residual accounted for only 16% of the production growth or 37% of the productivity growth from 1965 to 1985. Using the percentage of households that adopted the production responsibility system as a proxy for institutional change in his production function, Lin (1992) attributed 94% of the productivity growth from 1978–1984 to institutional and policy reforms.

Huang and Rozelle (1996) extended the traditional approach to include environmental variables such as soil salinity and erosion as another factor in accounting for growth in Chinese agriculture. They found that these environmental factors have severely constrained further growth in Chinese agriculture. The significance of this study is a wake-up call for Chinese agriculture to develop long-term sustainable growth.

Colby et al. (2000) investigated sources of output growth and supply response in rice, wheat, corn, and soybeans in China's grain sector for the period 1978–1997 using growth accounting methodology. They found large contributions from TFP to grain production growth after China's rural economic reform of 1978–1985. The period between 1995 and 1997 saw a drop of 16% per annum in grain productivity growth as greater use of inputs increasingly contributed to overall growth. However, their approach might have ignored the effects of improved allocative efficiency among crops. In addition, cash crops and livestock might have enjoyed higher productivity growth after 1995.

Most of the previously described studies used the production (or supply) function approach. As previously mentioned, this approach cannot measure the impact of improvement of allocative efficiency due to changes and reforms. Therefore, Fan (2000) defined technological change, technical efficiency, and allocative efficiency in a stochastic frontier shadow cost of function framework to estimate the improvement of both technical and allocative efficiency. His results show that the rate of technological change continued to increase over the whole study period, resulting from long-term government investment in technology and rural infrastructure. Moreover, the first phase of rural reforms in China, which decentralized the production system, had a significant impact on technical efficiency but not on allocative efficiency. By contrast, during the second phase of rural reforms, which focused on rural market liberalization, technical efficiency improved very little and allocative efficiency slightly increased. It is important to note that Fan suggests that the large variation among regions in allocative efficiency implies that China still has potential to promote production growth by reducing regional differences in allocative efficiency. Similarly, Carter and Estrin (2001) found that grain self-sufficiency policies and incomplete market reforms in the 1980s and 1990s led to allocative inefficiency within the Chinese agricultural sector, while farmland fragmentation reduced agricultural technical efficiency. Brümmer, Glauben and Wu (2006) identify and measure the sources of productivity change during the 1980s and 1990s, decomposing the traditional index of total factor productivity growth into technical and allocative efficiency, a scale effect and technical change. The authors find that the relatively large increase in TFP during the second reform period (1986-1990) was primarily driven by a high rate of technical change with virtually unchanged technical efficiency. During the subsequent reform phase, TFP grew at a smaller rate than previously and was primarily driven by technical efficiency change, leading the authors to argue that farmers are not able to maintain the high rate of catching up to the frontier during this period, possibly as a result of the deterioration of extension services and land infrastructure that prevents farmers from applying the best practice production techniques. TFP growth continued to stagnate further in the late 1990s, stemming from a modest technical regress that is offset by a small increase in technical efficiency. Moreover, changes in allocative efficiency were negligible during the period under observation, potentially reflecting the tightened supply controls during this period.

Unlike China studies, a large majority of TFP decomposition studies for Taiwan focus on the industrial sector (e.g., Jang et al., 2005), making information regarding the sources of agricultural TFP growth limited. According to Aly and Grabowski (1988), traditional TFP estimates of Taiwanese agricultural growth overstate the importance of technical change because they failed to distinguish between the increase in output from technical change and improvements in technical efficiency. To overcome the technical change bias, the authors constructed a production function that decomposed agricultural output change between 1911 and 1972 into three components: input growth, technical change, and technical efficiency improvement. The results of the study indicate that output growth in Taiwanese agriculture during this period was primarily explained by increased input usage and high levels of technical efficiency, in direct contrast to earlier studies that attributed more importance to technical change. It is worth noting that increased efficiency is an especially important component of the economic growth strategy for resource-scarce countries such as Taiwan.

As in the case of Taiwan, TFP decomposition studies of South Korea are mainly of an economywide or industry focus (e.g., Kim and Han, 2001). In a study of South Korean agriculture, Kwon and Kim (2000) used an estimated aggregate cost function to decompose agricultural productivity change between 1971 and 1998. The authors found that the scale effect was the dominant source of TFP change until the late 1980s. These results accord well with a study by Young (1995), who found that growth in the manufacturing sectors of South Korea, Taiwan, Hong Kong, and Singapore was primarily driven by a scale effect, that is, participation, investment, and education rates, and that technical innovations are adopted no faster than in other countries. However, the analysis by Kwon and Kim also shows that the scale effect has been in decline in more recent years, with productivity change increasingly being dependant on technological developments and change. More recently, Kwon and Lee (2004) focused on the regional and temporal trends of productivity within the South Korean rice-farming sector. Although the main aim of the paper was to compare empirical results of productivity measures using parametric and nonparametric approaches, the study also examined productivity indices and decomposition trends over time and across regions within South Korea. The results indicate that, despite variation among parametric and nonparametric approaches, technical change, that is, a shift in the production frontier, has been a greater and steadier source of productivity growth in the Korean rice sector than technical efficiency, that is, catching up with the frontier. As a further indication of the importance of technological adaptation, the authors found that the regions that exhibited the lowest efficiency in their rice production also experienced the highest productivity growth, with the most efficient regions experiencing the lowest productivity growth. More recently, the East Asian financial crisis has had a negative impact on all sectors of the Korean economy, including the agricultural sector, the productivity of which decreased due to adverse input and output prices (Yu, 2004).

Suhariyanto and Thirtle (2001) decomposed the productivity growth of 18 Asian countries into technical efficiency and technological progress components. Between 1965 and 1996, TFP growth in South Korea was entirely attributable to technical change, that is, innovation, with the agricultural sector considered to be fully efficient in 1965. Moreover, the slowdown in the rate of productivity growth in South Korea during the last period (1991–1996) is entirely due to a deceleration in technical change. In China and Mongolia, increased technological change dominated declining efficiency as the main determinant of increased productivity in the two countries, indicating that the countries are falling further behind the frontier production function (due to increased inefficiency) as technological change shifts the frontier further out (due to increased innovation). Yet during the last two decades, 1981–1990 and 1990–1996, China experienced a steady improvement in the contribution of efficiency change to productivity growth, with efficiency change largely driving the increase in agricultural productivity during the last five years. On the other hand, efficiency loss in North Korea between 1965 and 1978 overshadowed technological improvement, resulting in negative annual productivity growth. Similarly, Bayarsaihan and Coelli (2003) found that the majority of the measured TFP change (both the initial decline and subsequent increase) in Mongolia was due to technical change, though the authors argue that problems with management and incentive structures were behind the changes in productivity, in addition to the lack of improvement in technology during this period.

6. RETURNS TO INVESTMENT

Public investment plays an important role in the economic and social strategies of both developed and developing countries. Although government decisions regarding public investment allocations are imbedded in country-specific circumstances, policy-makers share a set of overarching reasons for implementing these expenditures, namely: (1) the correction of market failures, (2) improvement of equity, and (3) construction of an enabling environment for private sector (Fan, Zhang, and Rao, 2004). Moreover, government expenditures can influence growth and poverty through a number of avenues. Public investment-induced growth in agricultural productivity has the potential to not only benefit the poor directly through increased farm incomes but indirectly through a "trickle-down" process, whereby increased productivity leads to higher agricultural wages, improved nonfarm employment opportunities, and growth in the rural and national nonfarm economy. However, variations in the marginal effects of public investments are large across various types of spending and regions. To realize the full potential of public investments within the framework of poverty alleviation and agricultural growth strategies, it is necessary to understand the different conditions and channels through which public investments operate most efficiently and productively. This section outlines the multidimensional relationship between government spending and both economic growth and poverty reduction, decomposing the impact of public investment according to type of investment and region.

6.1 Productivity and poverty reduction impact

Fan and Pardey (1992) were among the first to point out that omitted variables, such as research and development (R&D) investment, biased estimates of the sources of production growth. To address this concern, they included a research stock variable in the production function to account for the contribution of R&D investment to the rapid production growth in addition to the increased use of inputs and institutional changes. They found that ignoring the R&D variable in the production function estimation led to an overstatement of the effects of institutional change. Later, Huang, Rosegrant, and Rozelle (1997) used a supply function framework to comprehensively account for the sources of growth in grain production in Chinese agriculture. They concluded that public investment (mainly in R&D) accounted for 3% and 11% of rice production growth for the periods 1978–1984 and 1984–1992, respectively. For other grains, public investment accounted for only 6% of the total growth over 1978–1992.

Similarly, in a review of government expenditure trends across 15 Asian countries, Fan and Pardey (1998) used a production-function model to examine the link between government spending and agricultural growth, disaggregating public expenditures into research and nonresearch components. According to the authors, long-term investments in research, extension, rural infrastructure, and irrigation have a large impact on agricultural production. For both China and South Korea, the study revealed that agricultural research contributed substantially more to production growth than nonresearch expenditures and input changes. These results are similar to the findings of Fan and Rao (2003), whose analysis of 43 developing countries showed that agricultural research spending has a much greater impact on productivity than other forms of public (nonresearch) spending. Moreover, Fan and Pardey (1998) added that properly managed public investments could also stimulate private investments, thereby generating further production and productivity growth.

Other studies have shown that the impact of public investment goes beyond rural areas. Fan, Fang, and Zhang (2001) examined the effect of agricultural R&D investments and of subsequent increases in agricultural production on food prices and the incidence of urban poverty in China. According to the study, increased investment in agricultural R&D lowers food prices through increased agricultural production, which, in turn, benefits the urban poor, who spend more than 60% of their income on food. Agricultural research investments are thus an effective tool in helping the urban poor rise above the poverty line, with such investments accounting for

18–30% of the urban poverty reduction between 1992 and 1998. The results show that agricultural research has played an important role in reducing not only rural but also urban poverty in China. Although the impact has weakened in recent years due to increasing incomes and the devolution of food items in most households' budgets, the ongoing urbanization within China makes this price effect a relevant issue. The results of this study are consistent with later findings by Fan (2002), in which agricultural research in India was found to have the largest impact on urban poverty reduction among all the rural investments considered through similar food price channels.

However, agricultural research spending does not always trump other forms of public spending in terms of the largest impact on economic growth and poverty reduction. Fan, Zhang, and Zhang (2004) estimated a simultaneous equations system to calculate the marginal returns in agricultural production and poverty reduction to various government investments, including agricultural R&D, irrigation, education, and rural infrastructure. During 1978–1984, institutional and policy reforms were the dominant factor in promoting both production growth and in reducing rural poverty. However, between 1985 and 2000, public investment became the largest source of production growth and poverty reduction. Government spending on agricultural R&D had the largest impact on agricultural GDP growth. These results are especially significant for China given that increased productivity is essential to meet the growing food demands of an increasingly rich and large population and offers an effective solution to China's long-term food security problems. Moreover, the benefits of agricultural production growth also trickled down to the rural poor, with the poverty-reduction effect of agricultural R&D investment ranking second after investment in rural education. Government expenditure on education also had very high returns to growth in agriculture and the nonfarm sector, as well as to the rural economy as a whole. Public spending on rural infrastructure (electricity, telecommunications, and roads) had a substantial marginal impact on rural poverty reduction. These poverty-reduction effects came mainly from improved nonfarm employment and increased rural wages. Irrigation investment had only modest impact on growth in agricultural production and even less impact on rural poverty reduction, whereas government spending on loans specifically targeted for poverty alleviation had the least impact on rural poverty reduction as well as no obvious productivity effect. These findings are consistent with Fan, Hazell, and Thorat's (2000) study of public expenditure in India, although the ranking of the poverty and productivity effects differed somewhat. More specifically, the Indian study found that public investments on roads and R&D have by far the largest impact on rural poverty and agricultural productivity growth, respectively, in India. A decomposition of the impact of investments showed that road investments reduce poverty not only through productivity growth but also through increased nonagricultural employment and higher wages.

6.2 Regional variation

Given that China is a large country with vast and diverse natural resource endowments and various socioeconomic conditions across regions, a more disaggregated analysis of public investment is required. Fan, Zhang, and Zhang (2002) found sizable regional variations in the marginal returns of government spending, for both growth as well as poverty reduction. Disaggregating the effects of various types of government expenditures into different regions reveals that, in terms of poverty reduction, the highest returns to investments were in the less developed western region, whereas the highest returns in terms of agricultural production growth were in the more developed central region for most types of spending. Investment in agricultural research, for example, had a much greater marginal impact on poverty reduction in the western region than similar investment in the wealthier areas. The authors conclude that decisions regarding the regional targeting of public investments should be based on the overall development priorities of the government. The regional variation of public investment impact is consistent with the findings of Zhang and Fan (2004). The authors found that investments in the less developed western region of China led to the greatest decline in regional disparity for all types of government spending, whereas additional investments in the more developed coastal and central regions worsened existing regional inequalities. Moreover, the magnitude of the impact of various public investments differed, with investments in rural education and agricultural research having had the largest and most favorable impact on reducing regional inequality in the western region.

More recently, Fan and Chan-Kang (2005) examined the impact of public infrastructure on growth in China, paying particular attention to the variation in contribution of different varieties of roads by disaggregating road infrastructure into different classes based on road grade. The study found that low-grade, predominately rural roads in China have a greater impact on national, rural, and urban GDP as well as on poverty alleviation than other types of roads. Yet the authors also found that a significant trade-off exists between growth and poverty reduction when investing in different parts of China. More specifically, the economic impact of road investments is greatest in the central and eastern regions of China whereas their contribution to poverty alleviation is greatest in western China.

The regional variation in the effects of different public investment often impedes many authors from identifying universal public investment strategies. However, Hazell and Haddad (2001) not only outlined the channels through which agricultural research can benefit the poor but also identified the key priorities for a pro-poor agricultural research agenda based on a typology of different agricultural regions. Although the studies reviewed in this section point to different public investment strategies for different cases, the common message is that the purpose to which public investment is put is perhaps more important than the actual quantity of public investment. To minimize trade-offs between agricultural growth and poverty reduction, governments should not blindly raise public investments but should target their investments based on country- and region-specific characteristics, such as income, market access, and infrastructure levels.

7. CONCLUSION

Over the last two decades, there have been tremendous improvements in data, methodology, and understanding of TFP growth and sources of growth in East Asian agriculture. In the 1970s and most of the 1980s, debate focused on data quality, while methodology received little attention. The accounting of sources of growth and the construction of TFP index were largely based on ad hoc assumptions on the weights of inputs and based on output growth aggregated using constant prices. The technical change or TFP growth was treated as residual. As institutional and market reforms were successfully implemented and more reliable official data became available, a large number of literature emerged in the late 1980s and 1990s. This literature has improved in terms of both quality and impact on policy circles and academia. On TFP measures, both the aggregate level and crop levels have been conducted. The methodologies have also been further improved. In accounting for growth, sources have been extended from increased input use and residuals to also include technical change, allocative and technical efficiency, and institutional change. More recently, human and physical capital, in addition to agricultural research and extension and irrigation, have also been included to explain production and productivity growth.

Studies of East Asian agriculture have shown that the sector has experienced a rapid transformation during the last several decades, with institutional and policy reforms alongside changes in technological progress and efficiency contributing to agricultural production and total factor productivity. A detailed examination of specific indicators of agricultural performance (i.e. area harvested, yield and production data for major crops) between 1961 and 2004 points to a plethora of temporal and country-specific variability across the five East Asian countries. Moreover, most of these countries experienced positive TFP growth since the 1970s, although a division of the growth into subperiods also reveals fluctuations that correspond to institutional, marketing and other productivity-enhancing reforms.

Prioritizing different types of investments in less developed regions has been proven to be a critical component of productivity-enhancing (and hence poverty-reducing and growth-inducing) strategies. Given the resource constraints faced by most developing countries, increasing public rural investment significantly is difficult—if not unlikely—so countries must use their public investment resources more efficiently. This requires improved targeting of investments to achieve growth and poverty-alleviation goals, as well as improved efficiency within the agencies that provide public goods and services. Reliable information on the marginal effects of various types of government spending is crucial for governments to be able to make sound investment decisions. Moreover, policymakers need a clear understanding of not only how public investments affect economic growth and poverty levels but, more important, how this impact varies according to type of investment and region.

End Note

1. Alston et al. have also demonstrated the potential bias in aggregation of inputs and outputs when technical change is both present and absent. See Alston, Julian M., George W. Norton, and Philip G. Pardey, *Science Under Scarcity: Principles and Practice for Agricultural Research Evaluation and Priority Setting* (Ithaca: Cornell University Press, 1995).

References

Alston, J. M., Norton, G. W., & Pardey, P. G. (1995). *Science under scarcity: Principles and practice for agricultural research evaluation and priority setting*. Ithaca: Cornell University Press.

Aly, H. Y., & Grabowski, R. (1988). Technical change, technical efficiency, and input usage in Taiwanese Agricultural Growth. *Applied Economics, 20*, 889–899.

Bayarsaihan, T., & Coelli, T. J. (2003). Productivity growth in pre-1990 Mongolian agriculture: Spiralling Disasterdor emerging success. *Agricultural Economics, 28*(2), 121–137.

Bakey, A. (1998). Country Papers: Mongolia. In *Agricultural Public Finance Policy in Asia*. Tokyo: Asian Productivity Organization.

Brümmer, B., Glauben, T., & Lu, W. (2006). Policy reform and productivity change in Chinese agriculture: A distance function approach. *Journal of Development Economics, 81*(1), 61–79.

Burmeister, L. L. (2000). Dismantling statist East Asian agriculture? Global pressures and national responses. *World Development, 28*(3), 443–456.

Carter, C. A., & Estrin, A. J. (2001). Market reforms versus structural reforms in rural China. *Journal of Comparative Economics, 29*, 527–541.

Colby, H., Diao, X., & Somwaru, A. (2000). *Cross-commodity analysis of china's grain sector: Sources of growth and supply response*. Washington, DC: U.S. Department of Agriculture, Economic Research Service.

Diao, X., Dyck, J., Scully, D., Somwaru, A., & Lee, C. (2002). *Structural change and agricultural protection: Costs of Korean agricultural policy, 1975 and 1990*. Agricultural Economic Report No. 809. Washington, DC: USDA.

Diewert, W. E. (1976). Exact and superlative index numbers. *Journal of Econometrics, 4*, 115–145.

Fan, S. (1991). Effects of technological change and institutional reform on production growth in Chinese agriculture. *American Journal of Agricultural Economics, 73*(2), 266–275.

Fan S. (2002). *Agricultural research and urban poverty in India*. EPTD Discussion Paper No. 94. Washington, DC: IFPRI.

Fan, S. (2000). Technological change, technical and allocative efficiency in Chinese agriculture: the case of rice production in Jiangsu. *Journal of International Development, 12*, 1–12.

Fan, S., & Chan-Kang, C. (2005). *Road development, economic growth, and poverty reduction in China*. Research Report No. 138. Washington, DC: International Food Policy Research Institute.

Fan, S., Fang, C., & Zhang, X. (2001). *How agricultural research affects urban poverty in developing countries: The case of China*. EPTD Discussion Paper No. 83. Washington, DC: International Food Policy Research Institute.

Fan, S., Hazell, P., & Thorat, S. (2000). Government spending, growth and poverty in rural India. *American Journal of Agricultural Economics, 82*(4), 1038–1051.

Fan, S., & Pardey, P. G. (1998). Government spending on Asian agriculture: Trends and production consequence. In *Agricultural Public Finance Policy in Asia*. Tokyo: Asian Productivity Organization.

Fan, S., & Pardey, P. G. (1992). *Agricultural research in China: Its institutional development and impact.* The Hague: International Service for National Agricultural Research.

Fan, S., & Rao, N. (2003). *Public spending in developing countries: Trends, determination, and impact. Environment, Production and Technology Division.* Discussion Paper 99. Washington, DC: International Food Policy Research Institute.

Fan, S., & Zhang, X. (2002). Production and productivity growth in Chinese agriculture: new national and regional measures. *Economic Development and Cultural Change, 50*(4), 819–838.

Fan, S., Zhang, X., & Rao, N. (2004). *Public expenditure, growth, and poverty reduction in rural Uganda.* DSGD Discussion Paper No. 4. Washington, DC: International Food Policy Research Institute.

Fan, S., Zhang, L., & Zhang, X. (2004). Reforms, investment, and poverty in rural China. *Economic Development and Cultural Change, 52*(2), 395–422.

Fan, S., Zhang, L., & Zhang, X. (2002). *Growth, inequality, and poverty in rural China: The role of public investment.* Research Report No. 125. Washington, DC: International Food Policy Research Institute.

Fao. (2006). FAOSTAT.

Farrell, M. J. (1957). The measurement of productive efficiency. *Journal of Royal Statistics Society, Ser. A., 120*, 253–281.

Hazell, P., & Haddad, L. (2001). *Agricultural research and poverty reduction.* Food, Agriculture, and the Environment Discussion Paper No. 34. Washington, DC: International Food Policy Research Institute.

Hayami, Y. (1998). Toward an East Asian model of economic development. In Y. Hayami, & M. Aoki (Eds.), *The Institutional Foundations of East Asian Economic Development.* New York: St. Martin's Press.

Huang, J., & Rozelle, S. (1996). Technological change: Rediscovering the engine of productivity growth in China's rural economy. *Journal of Development Economics, 49*, 337–369.

Huang, J., Rosegrant, M., & Rozelle, S. (1997). *Public investment, technological change, and agricultural growth in China.* Working Paper. Stanford, CA: Food Research Institute, Stanford University.

Jang, S. L., Weng, M. H., & Wang, Y. (2005). Industrial diversification and its impact on productivity growth in Taiwan's electronics industry. *Asian Economic Journal, 19*(4), 423–443.

Kalirajan, K. P., Obwona, M. B., & Zhao, S. (1996). A decomposition of total factor productivity growth: the case of Chinese agricultural growth before and after reforms. *American Journal of Agricultural Economics, 78*, 331–338.

Kim, S. H., & Han, G. (2001). A decomposition of total factor productivity growth in Korean manufacturing industries: A stochastic frontier approach. *Journal of Productivity Analysis, 16*(3), 269–281.

Kwon, O. S., & Lee, H. (2004). Productivity improvement in Korean rice farming: Parametric and nonparametric analysis. *Australian Journal of Agricultural and Resource Economics, 48*(2), 323–346.

Kwon, O. S., & Kim, Y. T. (2000). Sources of productivity change in Korean Agriculture. *Korean Journal of Agricultural Economics, 41*(2), 25–48.

Lau, L. J. (1979). On Exact Index Numbers. *The Review of Economics and Statistics, 61*, 73–82.

Liang, C., & Mei, J. (2005). Underpinnings of Taiwan's economic growth: 1978–1999 productivity study. *Economic Modelling, 22*(2), 347–387.

Lin, J. Y. (1992). Rural reforms and agricultural growth in China. *American Economic Review, 82*(1), 34–51.

McMillan, J., Whalley, J., & Zhu, L. G. (1989). The impact of China's economic reforms on agricultural productivity growth. *Journal of Political Economy, 97*, 781–807.

Moon, P. Y., & Kang, B. S. (1991). The Republic of Korea. In A. O. Krueger, M. Schiff, & A. Valdes (Eds.), *The Political Economy of Agricultural Pricing Policy: Asia* (Vol. 2). Baltimore, MD: Johns Hopkins University Press.

Moreddu, C. (1999). *Review of agricultural policies in Korea.* Paris: OECD.

Noland, M. (2003). *Famine and reform in North Korea.* Working Paper 03-05. Institute for International Economics.

Park, P. (2002). *Self-reliance or self-destruction*: Success and failure of the Democratic People's Republic of Korea's development strategy of self-reliance. New York: Routledge.

Ranis, G. (1998). *The comparative development experience of Mexico, the Philippines and Taiwan from a political economy perspective.* Center Paper No. 530. New Haven: Yale University.

Richter, M. K. (1966). Invariance axioms and economic indexes. *Econometrica, 34*, 755–793.

Song, B. (2003). *The rise of the Korean economy.* Oxford: Oxford University Press.

Suhariyanto, K., & Thirtle, C. (2001). Asian agricultural productivity and convergence. *Journal of Agricultural Economics*, *52*(3), 96–110.

Wen, G. J. (1993). Total factor productivity change in China's farming sector: 1952–1989. *Economic Development and Change*, *42*, 1–41.

Wiens, T. (1982). Technical change. In R. Barker, et al. (Eds.), *The Chinese Agricultural Economy*. Boulder: Westview Press.

Yoo, C. H. (2003). Korea's agricultural strategy in the globalization era. In O. Y. Kwon, S. Jwa, & K. Lee (Eds.), *Korea's New Economic Strategy in the Globalization Era*. Northampton, MA: Edward Elgar Publishing, Inc.

Yu, Young-Bong Yu. (2004). Impact of financial crisis on productivity of agriculture: Korean case. In *Financial Crisis and Agricultural Productivity in Asia and the Pacific*, Report of the APO Study Meeting on Effects of Financial Crisis on Productivity of Agriculture, Japan, 6–13 December.

Zhang, B., & Carter, C. (1997). Reforms, the weather, and productivity growth in China's grain sector. *American Journal of Agricultural Economics*, *79*, 1266–1277.

Zhang, X., & Fan, S. (2004). Public investment and regional inequality in rural China. *Agricultural Economics*, *30*(2), 89–100.

APPENDIX

AGRICULTURAL GROWTH RATES AND AREA-YIELD ACCOUNTING, 1961–2004

Table 1   China

	Annual Growth Rate (%)				Decomposition of Change in Production (%)			
	1961–1980	1980–2000	2000–2004	1961–2004	1961–1980	1980–2000	2000–2004	1961–2004
Area harvested								
Maize	1.54	0.63	2.68	1.22	23.03	23.75	48.22	26.01
Rice, paddy	1.35	−0.61	−1.60	0.16	26.28	−40.54	98.53	5.64
Seed cotton	1.27	−0.97	7.52	0.78	19.39	−38.78	81.35	15.95
Wheat	0.70	−0.45	−4.98	−0.38	9.59	−15.06	248.29	−8.47
Oilseeds	−0.09	2.83	0.20	1.28	−2.82	51.41	9.16	30.79
Yield								
Maize	5.16	2.02	2.88	3.48	76.97	76.25	51.78	73.99
Rice, paddy	3.78	2.11	−0.02	2.64	73.72	140.54	1.47	94.36
Seed cotton	5.29	3.49	1.72	4.11	80.61	138.78	18.65	84.05
Wheat	6.64	3.47	2.97	4.81	90.41	115.06	−148.29	108.47
Oilseeds	3.30	2.67	1.98	2.89	102.82	48.59	90.84	69.21
Production								
Maize	6.78	2.67	5.64	4.74	100	100	100	100
Rice, paddy	5.18	1.49	−1.62	2.80	100	100	100	100
Seed cotton	6.63	2.48	9.37	4.92	100	100	100	100
Wheat	7.39	3.00	−2.15	4.41	100	100	100	100
Oilseeds	3.21	5.58	2.18	4.21	100	100	100	100

Source: Calculated by the authors using data from FAO, 2006.

Table 2   Mongolia

	Annual Growth Rate (%)				Decomposition of Change in Production (%)			
	1961–1980	1980–2000	2000–2004	1961–2004	1961–1980	1980–2000	2000–2004	1961–2004
Area harvested (ha)								
Wheat	2.26	−4.05	13.85	0.27	49.99	166.79	405.19	27.60
Yield								
Wheat	2.26	1.62	−10.43	0.71	50.01	−66.79	−305.19	72.40
Production								
Wheat	4.57	−2.49	1.97	0.99	100	100	100	100

Source: Calculated by the authors using data from FAO, 2006.

Table 3 North Korea

	Annual Growth Rate (%)				Decomposition of Change in Production (%)			
	1961–1980	1980–2000	2000–2004	1961–2004	1961–1980	1980–2000	2000–2004	1961–2004
Area harvested								
Maize	1.45	−1.64	−0.05	−0.14	35.17	34.8	−0.37	−17.87
Rice, paddy	2.33	−0.97	2.17	0.77	114.58	43.45	25.01	121.29
Wheat	−3.52	−1.81	4.37	−2.02	−365.5	53.42	12.33	−113.87
Soybeans	—	0.16	0.40	0.11	—	113.1	56.81	6.46
Yield								
Maize	2.67	−3.07	13.55	0.90	64.83	65.20	100.37	117.87
Rice, paddy	−0.30	−1.26	6.51	−0.13	−14.58	56.55	74.99	−21.29
Wheat	4.49	−1.58	31.06	3.79	465.5	46.58	87.67	213.87
Soybeans	3.72	−0.02	0.30	1.64	—	−13.1	43.19	93.54
Production								
Maize	4.16	−4.65	13.49	0.76	100	100	100	100
Rice, paddy	2.02	−2.22	8.82	0.63	100	100	100	100
Wheat	0.81	−3.36	36.78	1.69	100	100	100	100
Soybeans	3.72	0.15	0.71	1.76	—	100	100	100

Source: Calculated by the authors using data from FAO, 2006.

Table 4 South Korea

	Annual Growth Rate (%)				Decomposition of Change in Production (%)			
	1961–1980	1980–2000	2000–2004	1961–2004	1961–1980	1980–2000	2000–2004	1961–2004
Area harvested								
Maize	2.10	−3.94	1.83	−0.78	16.94	91.71	84.22	−22.29
Rice, paddy	0.47	−0.70	−1.71	−0.28	70.26	−45.00	121.76	−31.65
Seed cotton	−8.63	—	—	—	129.98	—	—	—
Wheat	−5.14	−15.68	44.44	−6.62	163.66	92.40	91.37	110.99
Soybeans	−1.64	−4.13	−0.59	−2.71	−71.64	118.18	−16.31	899.79
Yield								
Maize	10.29	−0.36	0.34	4.28	83.06	8.29	15.78	122.29
Rice, paddy	0.20	2.24	0.31	1.15	29.74	145.00	−21.76	131.65
Seed cotton	1.99	—	—	—	−29.98	—	—	—
Wheat	2.00	−1.29	4.20	0.66	−63.66	7.60	8.63	−10.99
Soybeans	3.93	0.63	4.17	2.41	171.64	−18.18	116.31	−799.79
Production								
Maize	12.60	−4.28	2.18	3.47	100	100	100	100
Rice, paddy	0.67	1.53	−1.41	0.87	100	100	100	100
Seed cotton	−6.81	—	—	—	100	—	—	—
Wheat	−3.24	−16.77	50.50	−6.00	100	100	100	100
Soybeans	2.23	−3.52	3.56	−0.37	100	100	100	100

Source: Calculated by the authors using data from FAO, 2006.

Table 5　Taiwan

	Annual Growth Rate (%)				Decomposition of Change in Production (%)			
	1961–1980	1980–2000	2000–2004	1961–2004	1961–1980	1980–2000	2000–2004	1961–2004
Area harvested								
Maize	5.30	−1.41	−5.53	1.10	68.09	−62.28	220.61	26.25
Rice, paddy	−1.06	−3.10	−8.60	−2.73	−128.24	143.61	128.28	212.10
Seed cotton	−11.44	—	—	—	128.07	—	—	—
Wheat	−14.39	−15.86	29.10	−11.77	108.17	112.35	131.10	105.54
Oilseeds	−4.40	−4.23	−4.11	−4.29	236.86	250.45	345.74	250.06
Yield								
Maize	2.48	3.67	3.02	3.08	31.91	162.28	−120.61	73.75
Rice, paddy	1.88	0.94	1.90	1.44	228.24	−43.61	−28.28	−112.10
Seed cotton	2.51	—	—	—	−28.07	—	—	—
Wheat	1.09	1.74	−6.90	0.62	−8.17	−12.35	−31.10	−5.54
Oilseeds	2.54	2.54	2.92	2.58	−136.86	−150.45	−245.74	−150.06
Production								
Maize	7.91	2.21	−2.67	4.22	100	100	100	100
Rice, paddy	0.80	−2.19	−6.87	−1.33	100	100	100	100
Seed cotton	−9.22	—	—	—	100	—	—	—
Wheat	−13.46	−14.39	20.19	−11.22	100	100	100	100
Oilseeds	−1.97	−1.80	−1.31	−1.83	100	100	100	100

Source: Calculated by the authors using data from FAO, 2006.

MEASURES OF OUTPUT, INPUT, AND TFP GROWTH

Table 6   Chinese agriculture, 1952–1997 (1952=100)

Year	Output Index	Input Index	TFP Index
1952	100	100	100
1953	100	103	97
1954	103	106	97
1955	112	108	104
1956	118	112	105
1957	119	116	103
1958	125	107	116
1959	111	104	107
1960	92	106	87
1961	82	111	74
1962	89	116	77
1963	97	122	80
1964	109	128	85
1965	118	132	89
1966	129	139	93
1967	133	141	95
1968	136	140	97
1969	141	144	98
1970	143	150	95
1971	147	157	94
1972	147	160	92
1973	157	164	96
1974	165	165	100
1975	170	168	101
1976	167	169	99

1977	168	171	98
1978	185	179	103
1979	197	185	106
1980	202	187	108
1981	218	187	116
1982	238	191	125
1983	252	192	131
1984	275	192	143
1985	286	190	151
1986	293	193	152
1987	306	196	156
1988	300	199	151
1989	313	205	153
1990	339	210	162
1991	352	214	164
1992	363	215	169
1993	375	216	174
1994	385	218	176
1995	408	223	183
1996	436	227	192
1997	441	232	190
Annual growth rate			
1952–1978	2.38	2.26	0.12
1979–1997	4.57	1.25	3.28
1952–1997	3.35	1.88	1.44

Source: Fan and Zhang, 2002.

Table 7   South Korean agriculture, 1971–1998 (1971=100)

Year	Output Index	Input Index	TFP Index
1971	100.0	100.0	100.0
1972	102.0	97.9	104.2
1973	104.4	105.9	98.6
1974	110.1	95.2	115.6
1975	127.1	99.8	127.4
1976	142.6	104.4	136.6
1977	151.6	106.2	142.8
1978	163.1	109.3	149.2
1979	166.9	113.8	146.7
1980	130.0	110.3	117.8
1981	150.2	114.1	131.7
1982	156.0	111.4	140.1
1983	165.2	120.4	137.2
1984	177.2	121.3	146.1
1985	179.5	120.4	149.0
1986	187.0	122.3	153.0
1987	189.1	121.8	155.3
1988	204.4	122.1	167.4
1989	205.6	122.9	167.4
1990	199.0	118.3	168.2
1991	191.7	115.0	166.7
1992	195.4	115.5	169.2
1993	203.0	116.4	174.4
1994	198.4	116.8	169.9
1995	202.8	114.6	177.0
1996	208.5	113.0	184.6

1997	205.2	111.7	183.7
1998	203.0	110.3	184.0
Annual growth rates			
1971–1989	4.09	1.15	1.65
1990–1998	0.25	−0.87	1.13
1971–1998	2.66	0.36	1.45

Source: Kwon and Kim, 2000.

CHAPTER 67

Rural Poverty and Income Dynamics in Southeast Asia[1]

Jonna P. Estudillo
National Graduate Institute for Policy Studies

Keijiro Otsuka
National Graduate Institute for Policy Studies

Contents

Abstract

Many rural households in Asia have been able to move out of poverty in the presence of increasing scarcity of farmland, initially by increasing rice income through the adoption of modern rice technology and gradually diversifying their income sources away from farm to nonfarm activities. Increased participation in nonfarm employment has been more pronounced among the more educated children, whose education is facilitated by an increase in farm income brought about by the spread of modern rice technology. An important lesson for poverty reduction is to increase agricultural productivity through the development and adoption of modern technology, which subsequently stimulates the development of the nonfarm sector, thereby providing employment opportunities for the rural labor force. This chapter explores the key processes of long-term poverty reduction in Southeast Asia using the Philippines and Thailand as case studies.
JEL classification: O12, O15, O53, Q12, Q15

Keywords

Green Revolution
poverty
nonfarm employment
child schooling

Handbook of Agricultural Economics, Volume 4
doi: 10.1016/S1574-0072(09)04067-5

ACKNOWLEDGMENT

The authors thank Prabhu Pingali for his comments on an earlier draft of this chapter. The usual caveat applies.

1. INTRODUCTION

There was a belief from the 1950s to the 1970s that high population pressure on closed land frontier would result in high incidence of rural poverty, food shortages, and even widespread famine in Southeast Asia and South Asia. High population pressure leads to a decline in the size of farmland and an increase in the incidence of landlessness, even though farmland is a major source of income of rural households in the early stage of development (Estudillo and Otsuka, 1999; Hayami and Kikuchi, 2000; Hazell and Haggblade, 1991; Lanjouw, 2007). Indeed, the incidence of poverty is observed to be higher among the land-poor and landless households than among the farmer households (World Bank, 2008a; Estudillo et al., 2008; Hossain et al., 2009). The direct impacts of the Green Revolution, as exemplified by the adoption of modern rice technology, on employment opportunities for the poor agricultural landless and near-landless population seem to be modest (Lipton and Longhurst, 1989). Demand for agricultural labor is seasonal, and there has been an increasing trend in the adoption of labor-saving technologies (Jayasuriya and Shand, 1986). The major direct impact of the Green Revolution comes mainly through an increase in rice production, attributable to yield increase and the shorter growing period that significantly reduced rice prices, thereby increasing the welfare of the poor as consumers (Barker and Herdt, 1985; David and Otsuka, 1994).

Yet we observe a clear and remarkable movement of rural households out of poverty in Southeast and South Asia in the midst of the unfavorable scenario of increasing scarcity of farmland and declining labor employment opportunities in the farm sector. According to the Asian Development Bank (2008), the proportion of population living on less than the Asian poverty line of US$1.35 per day declined 5.9 percentage points in the Philippines, 7.8 percentage points in Thailand, 21.4 percentage points in Indonesia, and 47.7 percentage points in Vietnam from the early 1990s to the mid-2000s. Interestingly, income growth and, consequently, poverty reduction have become evident in land-scarce regions of sub-Saharan Africa, where land was once considered a relatively abundant resource (Otsuka et al., 2009a). This could indicate that African rural households have been experiencing the same pattern of structural change and tracking similar pathways out of poverty that rural households in tropical Asia have experienced in the past 20–25 years. An important issue is to identify the strategic processes by which rural poverty has been declining in Asia, which serves as a lesson not only to sub-Saharan Africa but to other developing countries as well.

We found that the rise in nonfarm income is the major driver behind poverty reduction, which was facilitated by earlier decision of households to invest in children's schooling, made possible by the increase in farm income brought about by the Green Revolution. This is the first study to our knowledge that examines the structural transformation of rural economies from farm to nonfarm activities by exploring the causal mechanisms that link agricultural productivity growth with human capital investments, the development of the nonfarm sector, and poverty reduction.[2] We selected four countries in Southeast Asia—the Philippines, Thailand, Indonesia, and Vietnam—where poverty reduction has been remarkable; then we focus on dynamic changes in income structure and composition of rural labor force in selected villages in the Philippines and Thailand, where the Green Revolution took place.

This chapter has five remaining sections. Section 2 presents an overview of the structural transformation of the economy away from farming in four countries in Southeast Asia. Section 3 discusses the conceptual framework and postulates basic hypotheses. Section 4 describes the data set in the Philippines and Thailand. Section 5 identifies the determinants of household income, investments in children's schooling, occupational choice of children, and nonfarm income. Finally, Section 6 presents the summary and conclusions.

2. ECONOMIC TRANSFORMATION IN SOUTHEAST ASIA

If the rural labor force increases under the scenario of closed land frontier and stagnant technology, we can expect a decrease in the marginal productivity of labor, which leads to a decrease in income and rise in the incidence of poverty. This is seemingly the case in Southeast Asia, where the land frontier had been closed in the 1960s and 1970s and population grew at an annual growth rate of well more than 2% in the same period. Unexpectedly, however, poverty incidence has declined in these countries, along with the structural shift of the economy away from agriculture to industry and services, as shown by the decline in the proportion of gross domestic product (GDP) coming from agriculture. In Southeast Asian countries, we found that the service sector has been the dominant sector in the Philippines, whereas industry has become important in Thailand, Indonesia, and Vietnam (Table 1).

Vietnam has shown the most dramatic shift of its economic activities toward industry and away from agriculture and service sectors. Simultaneous with the swift transformation is the marked decline in the incidence of poverty, by as much as 48 percentage points from 1993 to 2004. As a result, the incidence of poverty in 2004 became lower in Vietnam compared with that in the Philippines and Indonesia, which started at a

Table 1 Indicators of structural transformation in selected countries in Southeast Asia, 1995 and 2006

	1995	2006
Philippines		
Gross national income per capita (US$)[a]	1050	1390
% agriculture[b]	22	14
% industry (% manufacturing)[b]	32 (23)	32 (23)
% services[b]	46	54
Thailand		
Gross national income per capita (US$)	2740	3050
% agriculture	10	11
% industry (% manufacturing)	41 (30)	45 (35)
% services	50	45
Indonesia		
Gross national income per capita (US$)	980	1420
% agriculture	17	13
% industry (% manufacturing)	42 (24)	47 (28)
% services	41	40
Vietnam		
Gross national income per capita (US$)	240	700
% agriculture	27	20
% industry (% manufacturing)	29 (15)	42 (21)
% services	44	38
% of household below $1.35 per day[c]	Initial year	Final year
Philippines (1994–2006)	32.9	27.0
Thailand (1992–2002)	7.9	0.1
Indonesia (1993–2005)	60.7	39.2
Vietnam (1993–2004)	73.3	25.6

[a]Taken from World Bank (1997, 2008b, Table 1.1). Refers to gross national product in 1995 and gross national income in 2006.
[b]Taken from World Bank (2008b, Tables 4.2 and 6.1).
[c]Taken from Asian Development Bank (2008, Table 6.1). The poverty line is the Asian poverty line, which is the 2005 purchasing power parity based on consumption.

much lower incidence of poverty in the early 1990s. It is by now well known that direct participation in the labor market in the nonfarm sector in industry and services is the most important route to upward income mobility and an escape from poverty for a large majority of the rural poor (Hayami and Kikuchi, 2000; Lanjouw, 2007; Estudillo et al., 2008).

Employment structure in Thailand, Indonesia, and Vietnam shows that agriculture remains the largest employer of both male and female labor. In contrast, females in the Philippines are largely employed in the service sector (i.e., 55% of the female labor force in the early 1990s) and increasingly so in more recent years (i.e., 64% in the mid-2000s), whereas males remain largely in agriculture (Asian Development Bank, 2008). Similarly, in Thailand and Indonesia, females in the labor force have been increasingly flocking to the service sector, whereas males have been moving out of agriculture to industry. According to Momsen (2004), females in the world at large have been moving out of agriculture faster than men to the industry sector, initially from the 1960s to the 1980s and, finally, to the service sector from the 1990s. Increased involvement of Southeast Asian females in the industry coincides with the movement of the production base of labor-intensive, low-technology products away from Taiwan, Korea, and Hong Kong to Southeast Asia, when these East Asian countries shift in a major way to more sophisticated products corresponding to their sharp wage increases in the late 1970s to the early 1980s.

Meanwhile, agricultural productivity in these countries began rising before the structural transformation of the entire economy, as exemplified in rice yield increase, attributed to the development and adoption of modern rice varieties (MVs) in the 1970s and 1980s (Figure 1). In the Philippines, MV adoption and the subsequent yield increase can be observed from the early 1970s to the mid-1980s, during which structural transformation had been only slowly taking place. The same pattern holds true in Indonesia, where rice yield is higher than in the Philippines because of its favorable agroclimatic conditions (largely free from typhoons). A more dramatic transformation in Thailand's economy took place even though the adoption of MVs and rice yield growth are lower. Traditional Thai rice has better grain quality and commands a higher price in the international market, thus it occupies a larger share of the country's rice area. MVs were introduced in Vietnam in the mid-1970s and MV adoption quickly reached 80% of the total rice area in the early 1990s. Dramatic yield increase has been observed since the early 1980s, reaching about 5 tons per hectare in the mid-2000s. Vietnam has become the world's second largest rice exporter, next only to Thailand, and much of the rural populace depends on rice production. It is reasonable to assume that the booming rice sector is one of the major propelling forces in income growth and poverty reduction in rural Vietnam.[3]

Although it is clear that structural transformation in Southeast Asian countries has subsequently led to poverty reduction, the strategic processes by which agricultural growth in earlier years have triggered the subsequent transformation of the rural economies have not been identified. We focus on new technology in the rice sector because rice is largely produced in owner-cultivated farms, which comprise about

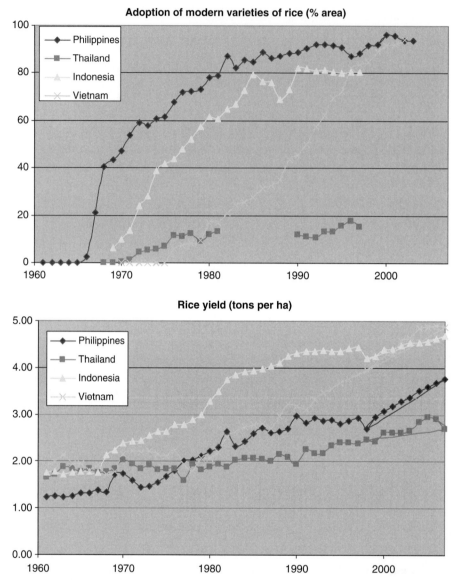

Figure 1 Adoption of modern rice and rice yield in selected Asian countries, 1960–2007. Data source: World Rice Statistics online.

80% of the total number of farms in Asia (Otsuka, 2007).[4] Since the production possibility frontier shifts outward with modern agricultural technology, the development of the nonfarm sector will be stimulated, given the rising income and high income elasticity of demand for nonfarm products. The development of agriculture is likely to stimulate the development of the rural nonfarm sector through the consumption and

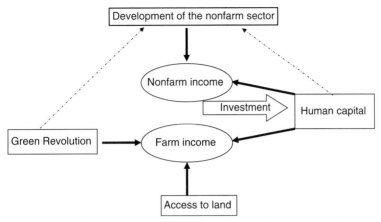

Figure 2 An illustration of the linkages between farm and nonfarm sectors. Source: Otsuka et al. (2009b, Figure 1.1).

production linkages (Haggblade et al., 2007). Empirical evidence on the magnitude of these effects, however, remains scanty. We, therefore, postulate the following sequence of events in the transformation: Green Revolution → higher farm income → larger investments in schooling of children → supply of educated labor force to the nonfarm sector → higher income of children and poverty reduction → further development of the nonfarm sector (Figure 2).

3. CONCEPTUAL FRAMEWORK AND HYPOTHESES

Classic studies on the dual economic model pioneered by Lewis (1954) and developed further by Ranis and Fe (1961), Jorgenson (1961), and Harris and Todaro (1970) focus on the process of labor reallocation away from the low-productivity farm sector to a high-productivity nonfarm sector. They argue that capital investment in the modern urban sector is the leading factor that promotes the development of overall economies, without much regard to the role of technological change in agriculture (Hayami and Godo, 2005). In reality, however, significant technological change has been taking place in Asian agriculture. We argue that the main factor behind the structural transformation is the Green Revolution that increases the marginal products of labor and purchased inputs, such as chemical fertilizer, in agriculture. As illustrated in Figure 1, we hypothesize that the Green Revolution significantly increases farm income through higher rice yield and higher cropping intensity attributed to shorter growing period and nonphotoperiod sensitivity of MVs. Farm household income is determined largely by agricultural technology and household access to farmland, while the contribution of human capital might not be large unless a modern and dynamic technology is successively introduced, which is characterized by a changing and complex optimum input mix and management technique (Schultz, 1975). We postulate the first hypothesis:

> **Hypothesis 1: In the early stage of economic development, when farming is a dominant source of income, access to land and agricultural technology are the major determinants of farm household income.**

As the economy develops, the availability of jobs in the rural nonfarm sector, urban labor markets, and overseas markets increases partly because of the decline in food prices, which are considered wage goods for urban workers (Hayami and Godo, 2005), and partly by the production and consumption linkages brought about by the Green Revolution (Figure 1). Increased demand for labor leads to the rise in returns to both "quality" and "quantity" of human capital, which means that the wages of both the educated and uneducated labor force have risen. Thus, we predict the increasing importance of human capital and the decreasing importance of land as sources of household income for rural households.

> **Hypothesis 2: As the economy develops, the availability of nonfarm jobs increases so as to increase the returns to both the "quality" and "quantity" of human capital. Consequently, the development of the nonfarm sector leads to an increase in nonfarm income of rural households and a major reduction in rural poverty.**

Poverty tends to be higher in areas characterized by unfavorable agricultural conditions susceptible to droughts and flooding with poor access to markets. Increasing availability of nonfarm jobs is the single most important factor in increasing rural household income in such unfavorable areas so long as the nonfarm labor markets are regionally integrated. The landless households, which depended primarily on agricultural labor employment, also benefit from the expanded nonfarm employment opportunities. To the extent that the income of landless households increases faster than that of landed households and the income in unfavorable areas grows faster than in favorable areas, we can reasonably assume that the structural transformation of rural economies is pro-poor.

> **Hypothesis 3: In the early stage of economic development, income was lower and poverty incidence was higher in unfavorable areas, but household income, particularly nonfarm income, grew more rapidly and the incidence of poverty declined more sharply in unfavorable areas than in favorable areas.**

With the development of the nonfarm sector and the subsequent increases in returns to schooling, rural households tend to invest in schooling of children because this can generate increased nonfarm income and remittances in the long run. We expect that farm income is the more important determinant of investments in schooling in the early stage of development because the parents, who are interested in investing in children, earn substantial portion of their income from farming. Thus, we postulate the following hypotheses:

> **Hypothesis 4: In the early stage of economic development, when farming is a dominant source of income, farm income is a major determinant of schooling investments in children of rural households.**

> **Hypothesis 5: Educated workers tend to find lucrative jobs in the nonfarm sector, where returns to schooling are higher.**

If Hypotheses 4 and 5 are empirically supported, in all likelihood the Green Revolution contributed to poverty reduction by inducing investments in children's schooling and increasing the availability of an educated labor force to the nonfarm sector.

4. DESCRIPTION OF THE DATA SETS

To examine the empirical validity of Hypotheses 1–5, we analyze the detailed household panel data collected in the Philippines and Thailand in the last few decades. This section describes the basic characteristics of the data sets.

There are two data sets from the Philippines. The first one comes from a survey of households located along a loop of the national highways in the Central Luzon region (henceforth referred to as "Central Luzon"). The sample set in Central Luzon consists of essentially identical 126 households in both 1979 and 2004, in addition to a survey of 499 grownup children in 2004. This sample set consists of farming households with the exclusion of landless households. Farmer households are those that operate farmland, including owner-cultivators, leasehold tenants, and share tenants. Landless households are those that do not have a farm to operate, including the agricultural workers, who eke out a living on casual farm work, and the nonagricultural households whose livelihood depends purely on nonagricultural work. The sample set in Central Luzon represents the relatively high-income farming households that have easy access to markets and agricultural extension services owing to their proximity to major highways connecting Central Luzon to Metro Manila.

The second data set comes from the surveys of 447 households consisting of both farmer and landless households that were randomly selected in two villages each in Nueva Ecija in the Central Luzon region and Iloilo Province in Panay Island in southern Philippines (henceforth referred to as "Nueva Ecija and Iloilo"), which were interviewed repeatedly in 1985, 1992, 1997, 2001, and 2004. These villages were selected from an extensive survey of 50 villages representing irrigated and rain-fed lowland rice production environments in northern, central, and southern Luzon (David and Otsuka, 1994). This data set in the Philippines captures the intricacies of the land tenure system, including the subtenancy arrangements that emerged because of the regulations of the land reform laws.

In Thailand, 295 households in three villages each in the Central Plain, which is relatively affluent and located near Bangkok, and northeast provinces, which are known to be much poorer and located near the local city of Khon Kaen, were surveyed in 1987 and 2004. One village in each province represents one of the three typical rice production environments in Thailand. Two villages represent the favorable environment owing to the existence of the gravity irrigation system, two villages represent the favorable rain-fed environment, and another two represent the unfavorable environment, including a flood-prone area in the Central Plain and a drought-prone area in the northeast. Note that although MV adoption rates are generally low in Thailand (Figure 1), they are relatively high in our study sites (i.e., 54% of the area planted in the Central Plain and 91% in the northeast in 2004). Landless households were not included in 1987 because there were very few of them, although their share increased to 13% of the total household population in 2004. An interesting phenomenon in these villages is the tendency of households to use pump irrigation for rice farming and to venture into high-value crop production in recent years. More important, households have become increasingly mobile to local cities as well as Bangkok to engage in regular nonfarm work, which became more frequent in 2004.

All the three data sets provided invaluable information on the changing sources of household income and the factors affecting rice, nonrice, and nonfarm income as well as the determinants of households' investments in schooling of children. The Central Luzon and Thai data sets were used further to examine the factors affecting occupational choice of grownup children and their nonfarm income. Because of the panel nature of Nueva Ecija and Iloilo and Thai data sets, which included both farmer and landless households, we measured the extent of landlessness and traced the movements of households in and out of poverty. Overall, these long-term data sets served as the base from which we were able to systematically analyze the long-term processes of poverty reduction in the context of Southeast Asia.

5. HOUSEHOLD INCOME, CHILDREN'S SCHOOLING, AND OCCUPATIONAL CHOICE

To trace the long-term processes of poverty reduction, we describe the changing sources of household income, patterns in progress of children in school, and choice of occupation of children.

5.1 Farm size and landlessness

Table 2 shows a large reduction in the size of operational landholdings of farm households and an increase in the proportion of landless households from the late 1980s to the early 2000s. In the Philippines, the average operational farm size of sample households was 1.0 ha in 1985, but it decreased to 0.76 ha in 2004. The proportion

Table 2 Farm size and sources of household income of sample households in the Philippines and Thailand, late 1980s and early 2000s

	Late 1980s[a]	Early 2000s[a]
Philippines		
Average farm size[b] (ha)	1.00	0.76
Landless households (%)[b]	22	44
Composition of household income[c]		
Favorable areas		
Per capita income (PPP$)	1065	2364
Agricultural wage (%)	13	11
Rice (%)	37	12
Nonrice farm income (%)	5	7
Nonfarm income (%)	45	70
Unfavorable areas		
Per capita income (PPP$)	386	1119
Agricultural wage (%)	30	7
Rice (%)	20	9
Nonrice farm income (%)	13	24
Nonfarm income (%)	36	60
Poverty incidence (head-count ratio)[d]		
Favorable areas	40	23
Unfavorable areas	66	42
Thailand		
Average farm size[e] (ha)	4.24	2.42
Landless households (%)[e]	0	13
Composition of household income[c]		
Favorable areas		
Per capita income (PPP$)	2014	4617
Agricultural wage (%)	4	6
Rice (%)	66	26
Nonrice farm income (%)	21	22
Nonfarm income (%)	10	47
Unfavorable areas		
Per capita income (PPP$)	959	2543
Agricultural wage (%)	12	5
Rice (%)	54	7
Nonrice farm income (%)	13	14
Nonfarm income (%)	21	74
Poverty incidence (head-count ratio)[d]		
Favorable areas	51	12
Unfavorable areas	70	21

[a]*Late 1980s* refers to 1985 in the Philippines and 1987 for Thailand; *early 2000s* refers to 2004.
[b]Taken from Estudillo et al. (2009a, Table 2.1).
[c]Taken from Otsuka et al. (2009b, Table 9.2).
[d]Taken from Otsuka et al. (2009b, Table 9.3).
[e]Taken from Cherdchuchai et al. (2009, Table 4.4).

of landless households rose from 22% to 44% in the same period. A more drastic reduction in farm size was found in Thailand, and the proportion of landless households rose from nil in 1987 to 13% in 2004. Surprisingly, as we show later, there was a movement of households away from poverty in the midst of increasing scarcity of farmland and decline in labor employment opportunities in rice farming due to mechanization and wider adoption of labor-saving direct seeding methods replacing labor-using transplanting (Otsuka, Asano, and Gascon, 1994).

5.2 Household income sources and poverty

We divided the villages into favorable (or irrigated areas) and unfavorable rain-fed areas susceptible to drought or flooding. Unfavorable areas in the mid-1980s are generally characterized by lower income and higher incidence of poverty owing to poor production environment and poor access to markets. Households derive their income from (1) agricultural wages, (2) rice farming, (3) propagation of livestock and poultry and production of nonrice crops, and (4) nonfarm activities, including nonfarm wages, remittances, and gifts, and income from operating their own businesses. We have included the imputed value of home-consumed products in both rice and nonrice income.

We have a few important observations from Table 2, which shows the changing sources of household income in the 1980s and early 2000s. First, the importance of farm income was much higher in the 1980s than in the early 2000s. Rice income was particularly important in favorable areas in the 1980s, yet its contribution declined in later years, notably because of the decline in rice prices coupled with only a modest increase in yield. In the Philippines, rice income composed 37% of the total household income but declined to 12%; in Thailand, it was 66% but declined to 26%. This indicates the decline in the importance of farmland as a source of household income for rural households.

Second, the proportion of income from agricultural wages has declined (except in the favorable areas in Thailand, where its share is relatively small), and the decline was spectacular in the unfavorable areas. This is explained to a large extent by the decline in labor demand in rice farming, brought about by the acceleration in the use of labor-saving technologies, decrease in rice prices, and stagnant productivity. Inasmuch as hired labor was supplied by the landless households and marginal farmers, we can fairly presume that reliance on agricultural labor market alone is not sufficient to promote income growth and poverty reduction (Otsuka and Yamano, 2006).

Third, the contribution of nonrice income has risen in unfavorable areas in the Philippines, indicating that the agricultural systems in these areas have moved away from the dominance of rice production to a more diversified system with increased importance of high-value crops and livestock. Yet the increase in nonrice farm income was hardly the driver of income growth, since it represented a relatively small share of total household income.

Fourth, the share of nonfarm income has increased dramatically in all areas, along with a sharp rise in per capita income. The more drastic change was observed in the unfavorable areas in Thailand, where the nonfarm income share rose from 21% in 1987 to 74% in 2004 and per capita income rose by 2.7 times. This remarkable transformation was facilitated by the availability of nonfarm wage employment in local districts of Bangkok and Khon Kaen. Traditionally, farmers in this region migrate to western regions to engage in low-wage employment in sugar cane cutting but, in more recent years, these low-wage jobs were replaced by high-wage jobs in urban areas. In the Philippines, the increase in nonfarm income share was partly brought about by the influx of domestic and foreign remittances, the income share of which rose from 11% in 1985 to 17% in 2004. Sawada and Estudillo (2008) found that transfer income from abroad serves as an important transmission mechanism through which international emigration positively contributes to poverty reduction. In both the Philippines and Thailand, the nonfarm income accounts for, by far, the largest share of total rural household income in 2004.

Fifth, although per capita income rose in both the favorable and unfavorable areas, the income increase was more dramatic in the latter, where the initial income was lower and poverty incidence was higher (i.e., 66% in the Philippines in 1985 and 70% in Thailand in 1987). This growth of income was generally brought about by the rise in nonfarm income in all areas but more visibly in unfavorable areas, which resulted in a much larger reduction in poverty, thereby supporting Hypothesis 3 on the catch-up of unfavorable areas with favorable areas with respect to income growth and poverty reduction.

A comparison between the group of landless, near-landless (0–1 ha), and small farmer (1–2 ha) households and the group of big farmers (2 ha and above) demonstrates that the former group tends to earn a larger percentage of income from nonfarm sources, particularly those located in unfavorable areas (Otsuka et al., 2009b). A comparison of per capita income within the group of landless, near-landless, and small farmer households showed no considerable differences, even though the per capita income of the large farmer was much higher. Large farmer households include distinctively large farmers and those receiving large remittances from their well-educated children working outside the cities and overseas. Yet the fact remains that the recent development of the nonfarm sector favors the land-poor households, which would otherwise have been much poorer in the midst of low agricultural wages and declining employment opportunities in the farm sector. Otsuka et al. (2009b) found a more remarkable movement out of poverty for the landless poor and a decline in the income gap between the group of landless, near-landless, and small farmer and large farmer households.

Overall, it seems clear that the development of the nonfarm sector and increased access of agricultural households to nonfarm labor markets have proven to be the major driving forces behind the reduction in poverty in rural villages in the Philippines and Thailand. The transformation of rural economies toward nonfarm activities is clearly pro-poor, since it increases the demand for labor, thereby decreasing the incidence of unemployment and underemployment.

5.3 Determinants of household income

It is important to rigorously explore the significant factors affecting sources of household income. We divided household income into three major components: (1) rice, (2) nonrice, and (3) nonfarm income. Rice income includes income from agricultural wages and from rice farming.

We report the important factors affecting household income in the two countries using the regression results reported in Takahashi and Otsuka (2009) in Central Luzon and Estudillo et al. (2009a) in Nueva Ecija and Iloilo in the Philippines, and Cherdchuchai et al. (2009) in Central Plain and northeast Thailand (Tables 3 and 4). There are five important categories of factor: (1) size of cultivated area, shown in terms of owned, leasehold, and share tenant lands; (2) adoption of MVs and availability of irrigation; (3) "quantity" characteristics of human capital, represented by the number of adult household members and number of members falling into different age categories; (4) "quality" characteristics, represented by the ratio of adults with secondary (or lower secondary) and tertiary (or postsecondary) schooling; and (5) market access, represented by village dummies.[5]

The estimation results of reduced-form farm income and rice income functions show that the size of cultivated area, particularly owned and irrigated areas planted with modern rice varieties, was the most important determinant of farm income in the early years, which clearly supports Hypothesis 1 on the importance of access to land and farm technology for farm income. The relative contribution of rice income to total household income, however, has declined, owing to the decline in rice prices and stagnant yield growth. Accordingly, although the size of cultivated area remains a significant factor affecting rice income, its impact on total household income has declined, owing to the declining share of rice income. In Nueva Ecija and Iloilo villages, we found that leasehold land under rain-fed conditions positively and significantly affected nonrice income in the early 2000s, reflecting the diversification of rain-fed agriculture to production of high-value crops, which could have been facilitated by the spread of portable irrigation pumps that allowed the production of a nonrice crops during the dry season. This argument is also supported by the positive and significant coefficient of irrigation ratios in nonrice income function in the early 2000s, which again renders support to Hypothesis 1, which explains the importance of agricultural technology in generating farm income. In the Central Plain of Thailand, households tended to retreat from farm work to get involved more heavily in nonfarm activities by leasing out land.

In Nueva Ecija and Iloilo, the number of household members falling into various age categories had, in general, positive and significant effects on rice and nonrice farm income in the late 1980s, indicating that additional labor resources of households were

Table 3 Determinants of household income in sample villages in the Philippines, late 1970s, late 1980s, and early 2000s

| Variable | Central Luzon[a] | | Nueva Ecija and Iloilo[b] | | | | | |
| | Late 1970s | | Late 1980s | | | Early 2000s | | |
	Farm	Nonfarm	Rice	Nonrice	Nonfarm	Rice	Nonrice	Nonfarm
Owned land (ha)	4.23**	4.42**						
Owned land irrigated (ha)			5.17**	0.63	−3.11**	73.42**	3.04**	−1.74
Owned land rain-fed (ha)			−1.44	−0.05	−1.05	5.85	2.92	−7.29
Leasehold land (ha)	2.52**	−0.75						
Leasehold land irrigated (ha)			0.03	0.17	−0.89	12.05	0.54	−4.16
Leasehold land rain-fed (ha)			1.84	−0.36	−0.65	−0.13	12.65**	−8.64
Share tenant land (ha)	−1.40**	2.17**						
Share tenant land irrigated (ha)						31.0	2.06	−14.97
Share tenant land rain-fed (ha)			−2.94	−1.11	−0.36	7.37	3.67	−8.83
Irrigation ratio	10.50**	0.68	1.26		0.71	2.76	3.49*	
Number of adults	−0.97**	2.76**					13.13*	

Continued

Table 3 Determinants of household income in sample villages in the Philippines, late 1970s, late 1980s, and early 2000s—Cont'd

Variable	Central Luzon[a]		Nueva Ecija and Iloilo[b]					
	Late 1970s		Late 1980s			Early 2000s		
	Farm	Nonfarm	Rice	Nonrice	Nonfarm	Rice	Nonrice	Nonfarm
Number of household members								
22–30 years old			1.58	1.99**	-1.24	8.61	-1.74	-1.56
31–40 years old			3.26**	2.11**	0.18	-5.87	-0.83	10.32**
41–50 years old			4.45**	2.07**	-1.16	-6.14	2.97*	17.85**
51–60 years old			2.31	1.95*	-2.29*	3.56	1.19	25.28**
61 years old or more			4.15**	1.60**	0.78	1.62	1.15	10.43**
Ratio of adults with secondary schooling	0.373	-3.50	2.37	0.57	2.53	-20.54	1.34	36.80**
Ratio of adults with tertiary schooling	-2.27	12.26**	0.40	-1.49	4.53	20.30	12.15**	89.64**

* = Significant at 5% level.
** = Significant at 1% level.
[a]Taken from Takahashi and Otsuka (2009, Table 3.6). *Income* refers to per capita income of parents. *Late 1970s* refers to 1979.
[b]Taken from Estudillo et al. (2009a, Table 2.8). *Income* refers to household income. *Late 1980s* refers to 1985; *early 2000s* refers to 2001.

Table 4 Determinants of household income in sample villages in Thailand,[a] late 1980s and early 2000s

Variable	Rice		Nonrice		Nonfarm	
	Late 1980s	Early 2000s	Late 1980s	Early 2000s	Late 1980s	Early 2000s
Central Plain						
Owned land (ha)	1.58★	0.84	−0.40	1.03	−3.35★	−1.84
Leasehold land (ha)	0.86	3.25★★	0.56	0.42	−0.36	−3.10★★
Share tenant land (ha)	0.56	1.22	0.13	−0.48	−2.36	−3.35
Ratio of irrigation times ratio of area planted with MV[b]	32.36★★	22.20★★	6.09	10.93	5.00	4.76
Ratio of irrigation times ratio of area planted with TV[c]	17.24★★		2.07		9.03	
Number of household members						
Male 23–40 years old	−0.68	−3.61	−4.98	−4.28	3.32	11.37★★
Male 41–60 years old	−0.65	−2.49	9.21	−3.21	6.58	11.94★
Male over 60 years old	−1.65	−5.90	12.12★	1.87	−5.58	3.35
Female 23–40 years old	−0.70	−7.68	−4.12	3.37	7.04	8.50
Female 41–60 years old	−2.24	4.33	−2.81	1.40	−4.18	1.60
Female over 60 years old	−6.75★	4.63	−1.00	0.13	−7.48	−6.38
Ratio of adults with lower secondary schooling	−5.49	7.61	9.49	5.36	9.21	18.15
Ratio of adults with post-lower secondary schooling	−21.06	−0.26	16.40	−9.78	−19.45	23.56★

Continued

Table 4 Determinants of household income in sample villages in Thailand,[a] late 1980s and early 2000s—Cont'd

Variable	Rice		Nonrice		Nonfarm	
	Late 1980s	Early 2000s	Late 1980s	Early 2000s	Late 1980s	Early 2000s
Northeast						
Owned land (ha)	1.18**	1.43*	0.73**	3.31*	1.26	-3.76
Leasehold land (ha)	0.58	-1.53	0.38	1.20	-2.22	-24.76
Share tenant land (ha)	1.21**	0.92*	0.21	0.89	-3.60	-4.45
Ratio of irrigation times ratio of area planted with MV	10.54	-0.39	-0.71	-12.17**	-26.87	-1.24
Ratio of irrigation times ratio of area planted with TV	9.03	7.58	-3.64	0.03	-17.44	3.27
Number of household members						
Male 23–40 years old	0.14	-0.91	-0.49	-2.29	-4.01*	2.62
Male 41–60 years old	-1.63*	-1.65	-0.03	-2.19	0.04	0.26
Male over 60 years old	0.48	-0.53	0.38	1.71	-4.09	-8.45
Female 23–40 years old	-1.01	-1.36	0.14	-3.58	-1.71	-1.80
Female 41–60 years old	-0.43	-0.79	-0.26	-0.24	-6.90*	7.58
Female over 60 years old	-0.14	-1.80*	-0.32	-3.04	-8.72*	-7.10
Ratio of adults with lower secondary schooling	-0.22	-2.97	1.38	-3.20	-18.51*	3.81
Ratio of adults with post-lower secondary schooling	-7.28	-1.47	-3.88	-1.53	23.93	26.01*

* = Significant at 5% level.
** = Significant at 1% level.
[a] Taken from Cherdchuchai et al. (2009, Table 4.8). *Late 1980s* refers to 1987; *early 2000s* refers to 2004. All incomes are calibrated in per capita household income.
[b] Modern varieties of rice.
[c] Traditional varieties of rice.

mainly allocated to farming. Such positive and significant impact disappeared in the early 2000s, indicating a shift of labor resources away from farming to nonfarm activities. Indeed, the coefficients of the four age categories above age 31 were all significantly positive in nonfarm income regression in the early 2000s. This tendency was also confirmed in the Central Plain of Thailand, where males between 23 and 40 years old and between 41 and 60 were actively involved in nonfarm work in the early 2000s. Interestingly, Filipino females tended to be more active than men in nonfarm jobs in earlier years because they have the comparative advantage in nonfarm work due to having more education than males (Quisumbing et al., 2004). Yet in the early 2000s, the expanded labor employment opportunities in the nonfarm sector gave relatively equal employment opportunities for all working members regardless of sex, which was observed in both the Philippines and Thailand. This observation indicates the absence of gender discrimination in the nonfarm labor markets in these countries.

The coefficients of secondary and tertiary schooling variables in the Philippines and postsecondary schooling in the Central Plain and northeast of Thailand were positive and significant in the nonfarm income equation in the early 2000s but not in earlier years, which renders support to Hypothesis 2 on the importance of quality of human capital in nonfarm income. This means that the more educated labor force became more actively involved in nonfarm work in later years, perhaps because returns to education became higher, which supports Hypothesis 5 on educated household members' preference to work in the nonfarm sector. It is also interesting to note that rice income and nonrice farm income, as a whole, were not affected by schooling, which indicates that schooling did not have a significant effect on the efficiency of farm management, at least in the Philippines and Thailand. Foster and Rosenzweig (1996), however, found that the adoption and subsequent profitability of new seeds were highly dependent on schooling of adult members in the early 1970s, when the Green Revolution had just began in India. Indeed, the classic work of Schultz (1975) indicated that schooling increases productivity by enhancing the ability to deal with disequilibria in resource allocation brought about by new agricultural technology, among other things. Since modern rice technology was no longer new in Southeast Asia in the early 1980s, there was no inconsistency between our findings and those of Foster and Rosenzweig (1996).

The estimation results of income functions capture the increasing importance of both the quantity and the quality of human capital and the decreasing importance of farmland in generating rural household income in the course of economic development of rural societies in Asia, rendering support to Hypothesis 2. Estudillo et al. (2008), using the Oaxaca decomposition method, found that the rise in returns to the number of working-age members has accounted for much of the growth of per capita income in rural Philippines. This means that the poor households, which did not invest in schooling because they cannot afford to do so, were able to improve their income position by participating in the nonfarm labor market, where they benefited from the rising wages of uneducated and unskilled labor. Overall, it appears that the development of the nonfarm sector is pro-poor, since the poor households are able to utilize their primary asset, which is unskilled labor.

5.4 Determinants of children's schooling

Table 5 compares the schooling attainment of parents and children in the sample villages. There are a few important observations. First, average schooling attainment of both parents and children was higher in the Philippines than in Thai villages by about three to four years, thanks to an extensive public school system with roots going back the American colonial period in the 1900s. Second, children have attained significantly higher levels of schooling than their parents. Filipino parents completed five to eight years of schooling only, whereas their children completed seven to eleven years of schooling. In Thailand, parents completed three to five years of schooling only, whereas their children completed five to nine years. Investing in children's schooling seems to be the main form of intergenerational transfer of wealth for rural households when the size of farmland has become smaller. And third, the proportion of adult working members with secondary schooling has increased in both countries and, more remarkably in the Philippines, indicating that, in this country, returns to higher levels of schooling have risen particularly rapidly. The highly educated labor force must have been absorbed by the nonfarm sector inasmuch as schooling does not affect farm management efficiency.

We used incremental years in school of adult children in the Philippines and completed years of schooling in Thailand as measures of parental investments in schooling. These adult children are those who were in school age at the time of the base-year surveys.[6] Table 6 shows the estimation results of the determinants of schooling investments. We divided our explanatory variables into the following categories: (1) size of farmland and tenure in the base year, (2) farm and nonfarm incomes in the base year, (3) modern agricultural technology, represented by the adoption of MVs and irrigation ratio, (4) completed years in school of father and mother, (5) characteristics of the child such as age and gender, and (6) supply-side factors such as the availability of schools and roads and their quality, as captured by the village dummies. In Table 6, we show the coefficients of (1), (2), (3), and (4) only; the impacts of (5) and (6) are discussed in the text. Model 1 in Central Luzon has a two-stage procedure that uses predicted values of farm and nonfarm incomes from the first-stage income functions. Model 2 uses reduced-form regression model on the presumption that the impacts of access to land and agricultural technology on total household income come indirectly through their effect on household farm income. Reduced-form regression was also used in Central Plain and northeast Thailand.

Table 5 Schooling attainment of parents and children in sample villages in the Philippines and Thailand, late 1970s, late 1980s, and early 2000s

| | Philippines | | | |
| | Central Luzon[a] | | Nueva Ecija and Iloilo[b] | |
	Late 1970s	Early 2000s	Late 1980s	Early 2000s
Years in schooling				
Parents	7.0	8.1	6.2	7.7
Adult children[c]	9.2	10.7	7.2	9.6
% of adult working members with				
Secondary schooling[d]	25	36	23	37
Tertiary schooling[e]	13	31	8	20

| | Thailand[f] | | | |
| | Central Plain | | Northeast | |
	Late 1980s	Early 2000s	Late 1980s	Early 2000s
Years in schooling				
Parents	3.1	4.6	4.0	4.7
Adult children	5.7	8.9	5.7	9.1
% adult working members with				
Lower secondary schooling[g]	4	9	6	11
Post-lower secondary schooling[h]	4	11	2	11

[a]Calculated from the database of Takahashi and Otsuka (2009). *Late 1970s* refers to 1979; *early 2000s* refers to 2003.
[b]Taken from Estudillo et al. (2009a, Table 2.3). *Late 1980s* refers to 1985; *early 2000s* refers to 2004.
[c]Children who are 22 years old or more.
[d]Refers to 7–10 years of schooling.
[e]Refers to 11 years of schooling or more.
[f]Taken from Cherdchuchai et al. (2009, Table 4.3). *Late 1980s* refers to 1987; *early 2000s* refers to 2004.
[g]Refers to 7–9 years of schooling.
[h]Refers to 10 years of schooling and over.

It is important to mention that a land reform program was implemented in the Philippines, which was the major cause of an income transfer from the landlord to share tenants, thereby allowing the latter to invest in children's schooling. The Philippine land reform consists of two major programs: (1) a tenancy reform

Table 6 Determinants of schooling investments in sample villages in the Philippines and Thailand, 1979–2004

	Philippines				Thailand[c]	
	Central Luzon[a]		Nueva Ecija and Iloilo[b]		Central Plain	Northeast
	1979–2003		1985–1989	2002–2004	2004	
	Model 1	Model 2				
Sized of pawned-out land (ha)			0.19	1.02**		
Farm income in the base year (1985 or 2002)			0.14**	−0.00		
Nonfarm income in the base year (1985 or 2002)			0.05	0.02**		
Predicted farm income in 1979	0.05*					
Predicted nonfarm income 1979	0.04*					
Owned land in 1979 (ha)		1.15**				
Leasehold land in 1979 (ha)		−0.04				
Share tenant land in 1979 (ha)		0.28				
Irrigation ratio in 1979		0.54*				
Cultivated land in 1987 (ha)					−0.03	0.11
Proportion of owned land in 1987					2.81	1.46
Proportion of leasehold land in 1987					4.34	0.16
Ratio of irrigation times ratio of area planted with MV[1]					0.29	−0.43
Ratio of irrigation times ratio of area planted with TV[2]					3.48*	−1.25
Completed years in school of father	0.14*	0.15*	−0.00	0.01	0.23	0.05
Completed years in school of mother	0.10	0.08	0.03**	0.01	0.33*	0.13

** = Significant at 1% level.
* = Significant at 5% level.
[a]Taken from Takahashi and Otsuka (2009, Table 3.7). Dependent variable is incremental years in school between two survey years.
[b]Taken from Estudillo et al. (2009a, Table 2.9). Dependent variable is incremental years in school between two survey years.
[c]Taken from Cherdchuchai (2009, Table 4.9). Dependent variable is completed years in school.
[1]MV means modern variety of rice.
[2]TV means traditional varieties of rice.

(Operation Leasehold), which converts share tenants into leasehold tenants; and (2) a land redistribution program, which converts share tenants into amortizing owners (holders of a Certificate of Land Transfer [CLT]). Leasehold rent and amortization fees were fixed at 25% of the average rice yield for three normal crop years preceding the land reform implementation in 1972. Rice yields rose in the villages because of the diffusion of MVs so that a divergence between the returns to land and fixed leasehold rents and amortization fees prescribed by law was created. This divergence led to the emergence of a subtenancy arrangement in the form of land pawning.

Under the pawning arrangement, the moneylender advances cash to the farmer and takes over the cultivation of the land while the indebted farmer commonly remains in possession of the cultivation right of the land as a sharecropper (Andersen, 1962; McLennan, 1969; Hayami and Kikuchi, 2000). The moneylender pockets the difference (amounting to about 15% of the gross output) between his share of output and the fixed leasehold rent mandated by law. The pawning arrangement enables beneficiaries of land reform, who were former share tenants, to invest in human capital, including schooling and migration of children, and self-employed nonfarm activities.

In Nueva Ecija and Iloilo, the size of pawned-out land has positively affected progression in schooling of children in 2002–2004. This indicates that the development of a pawning market for farmland has enabled households to raise funds for children's schooling. In fact, pawning revenues have also been used to finance overseas migration and to venture into nonagricultural businesses, both of which entail high fixed costs but nonetheless open up opportunities for rural households to step further up the income ladder (Estudillo et al., 2009b).

In Nueva Ecija and Iloilo, we also found that the difference in the progress of children through school, measured as the difference in years of schooling completed in 1985–1989 and 2002–2004, between the landless and farmer households was large in 1985–1989, but then declined in 2002–2004, even for those households with children in tertiary-school age. This implies that landless parents have been able to afford to send their children even to tertiary schools, in recent years, as much as the parents of landed households. Since the landless households did not have pawning revenues, it seems clear that the increasing dominance of nonfarm income was the major force behind the rise in schooling attainment of the children of landless households vis-à-vis the children of farmer households. Inasmuch as secondary and tertiary schooling has positive and significant effects on nonfarm income, we can reasonably conjecture that the improvement in the income position of the landless vis-a-vis the landed households was brought about by the acquisition of higher levels of schooling of their children, who eventually became active participants in the nonfarm labor market.

In Central Luzon, both farm and nonfarm incomes have positive and significant effects on completed years in school of adult children, whereas in Nueva Ecija and Iloilo, farm income appeared to be the single most important source of funds to finance additional years in school in 1985–1989. In Central Luzon, the size of owned land and the irrigation ratio in 1979 and in the Central Plain of Thailand, irrigated area planted with traditional varieties (TVs) have significantly and positively affected completed years in school of adult children. These findings indicate that access to land and agricultural technology was critical in human capital accumulation in earlier years, when farming was a dominant economic activity, rendering support to Hypothesis 4.

Completed years in school of parents, in general, has improved children's schooling attainment because the more educated parents can perceive increases in returns to schooling, so they tend to invest more in schooling of children in anticipation of their children joining the nonfarm labor market upon completing school. It is interesting to note that mother's schooling has a higher impact on children's schooling than the father's in Nueva Ecija and Iloilo and in Central Plain of Thailand, perhaps because women in those areas tend to be more active in nonfarm employment, which is important in light manufacturing industries (Momsen, 2004).

Birth-year dummies showed that schooling investments were made in favor of younger cohorts. The male dummy was negative and significant in the Philippines, even after controlling for other effects, implying that parents tend to favor females when investing in child schooling. This preference was particularly significant for eldest daughters, who are expected to help finance the schooling of her younger siblings on finishing school and entering the job market. In Thailand, the male dummy was not significant, which means that Thai parents invest equally in schooling of children, irrespective of gender.

To summarize, our regression results demonstrate that access to land and agricultural technology, through its positive impact on farm income, are by far the most important factors that have induced investments in schooling of children in the 1980s. In the case of the Philippines, the Green Revolution and land reform implementation stimulated the development of the land-pawning market and, subsequently, investments in schooling of the young generations. It is worth emphasizing that, despite the lack of access to farmland, the Filipino landless households, who were the poorer members of rural societies, were able to invest in children's schooling in the early 2000s as much as the farmer households, most likely because of the increase in their nonfarm income.

The results of our analyses of the Philippines and Thailand are consistent with those in South Asia. In Bangladesh, Hossain et al. (2009) reported that the adoption of improved agricultural technologies, crop diversification, and occupational mobility from farm to nonfarm activities, such as trade, business, and services, are the important pathways out of poverty to a significant proportion of the poor house-holds. The shift in the structure of household income in favor of nonfarm activities has been facilitated by the decision of households to invest in schooling of children, who later joined the nonfarm sector. Farm income and education of adult workers are by far the most important determinants of children's school enrollment, pointing to the importance of the adoption of new rice technology. Higher nonfarm income is the major factor behind the dramatic rise in household income and the reduction in poverty. In Tamil Nadu (India), Kajisa and Palanichamy (2009) reported that children from households with higher farm income are able to attend school beyond the compulsory level, pointing to the important role of new technology in rice, non-rice crops, and livestock production in inducing children's attendance in school. Unlike in the case of the Philippines, nonfarm income is not a significant factor, which, according Kajisa and Palanichamy (2009, p. 138), could be due to the fact that nonfarm earnings of children are not spent to finance schooling investments of their younger siblings.

5.5 Occupational choice and nonfarm income

The main occupation of the household heads, who are predominantly male in Central Luzon, was rice farming, because early surveys were tailored to look closely at economic activities of rice-farming households. In Nueva Ecija and Iloilo, our sample set included households headed by both farmers and landless workers. Because of the decline in inheritable size of farmland and land reform restrictions on land transfer, there was an increase in the number of landless agricultural workers in the children's generation. Clearly, without the increasing availability of nonfarm jobs, the rural low-income population is bound to increase.

While the parents were engaged in agriculture, their adult children occupied highly diversified jobs in the village, local towns, and cities. Occupations in the village and local towns were predominantly unskilled, including jobs in the informal sector in transportation, commerce, domestic work, and skilled artisan work, reflecting the increasing demand for these services in the rural areas. In contrast, manufacturing jobs are seldom available. These observations seem to suggest that the growth linkage effects work for the development of service sectors, whose products are nontradable goods, but not for manufacturing sectors, whose products are tradable. Skilled jobs were held by the more educated children living in the cities and overseas, and many of them were professionals, including nurses, doctors, teachers, and engineers. Professional jobs and overseas work require earlier investments of households in schooling, facilitated by an increase in farm income in earlier years, as shown earlier. We also found an increasing tendency for the international labor market to accept unskilled workers, such as women in domestic and men in construction jobs, in later years. These workers were commonly high school graduates with only 10 years of schooling or even less.

They must have come from the lower income group, yet they were able to venture into the international labor market, partly because job placement fees have become affordable as international labor markets have become more competitive.

In Central Plain, Thailand, urban wage employment is popular because children in this region can easily migrate to work in factories located in Bangkok and nearby industrialized areas. In northeast Thailand, rural nonfarm work consisting of casual and regular salary work and self-employment dominates among young generations. Distribution of children's nonfarm occupations was fairly similar for males and females in the Central Plain. Females in the northeast are more likely to work in rural casual nonfarm jobs; men migrate out to obtain regular nonfarm jobs in Bangkok.

Table 7 shows the determinants of current occupational choice of children, shown as the marginal effects of the regressors evaluated at their means, on the probability of choosing rural nonfarm, urban, and overseas work. Filipino females tended to engage more in rural nonfarm activities than males, reflecting the comparative advantage of females in nonfarm jobs and males in farm jobs (Quisumbing et al., 2004). Filipino females also had higher propensity to venture into overseas migration, reflecting the increasing contribution of females in household income generation as a result of the integration of the rural labor market with the international markets. Education was positively associated with the probability of participation in both rural and urban nonfarm activities, which supports Hypothesis 5 on the relationship between child schooling and occupational choice. The marginal impact of education on out-migration was higher than in participation in rural nonfarm employment in rural areas. Education does not seem to be a significant factor in overseas migration, perhaps because of the large number of overseas workers in unskilled jobs such as domestic and construction work, especially in the Middle East and East Asia.

In both Central Plain and northeast Thailand, we found that the marginal effects of higher education, shown as a dummy for post-lower secondary schooling, suggest a pattern in which the probability of joining the nonfarm labor markets increases at the expense of farm and self-employment as education level goes up. Children with more educated mothers are less likely to be involved in farming and more likely to work in nonfarm jobs in the Central Plain and Bangkok.[7] Agricultural technology, shown as the interaction term between the ratio of irrigation and the ratio of area planted with MVs, increased the probability of farming in the Central Plain, which indicates that farming is profitable with the adoption of modern rice technology. Children with more educated mothers are more likely to participate in nonfarm employment and less likely to be involved in farming in the Central Plain.

To summarize, our regression results reveal that in both the Philippines and Thailand, there is a clear shift of occupational choice away from farm to nonfarm jobs, with the more educated children venturing into the more lucrative nonfarm jobs, in

Table 7 Determinants of current occupational choice of children in sample villages in the Philippines and Thailand (marginal effects), early 2000s

	Central Luzon, Philippines, in early 2000s[a]		
	Rural Nonfarm	Migrate	Abroad
Year of birth	0.01	0.10	0.03
Year of birth squared	0.00	−0.00	0.00
Female dummy	0.15★★	0.10	0.23★★
Education	0.01★★	0.04★★	0.02
Owned land in 1979 (ha)	−0.22	−0.29	0.68
Leasehold land in 1979 (ha)	0.00	−0.21	0.05
Share-tenant land in 1979 (ha)	−0.04	−0.27	−1.14
Irrigation ratio	0.01	0.02	0.08
Father's education (years)	−0.00	0.00	0.00
Mother's education (years)	0.00	−0.01	−0.00

	Central Plain, Thailand, in early 2000s[b]		
	Farm	Nonfarm	Self-Employed
Age (years)	−0.03	−0.13	0.16
Age squared/100	0.04	0.19	−0.24
Female dummy	−0.01	0.03	−0.01
Dummy for lower secondary schooling	−0.02	0.06	−0.04
Dummy for post-lower secondary schooling	−0.21★	0.35★★	−0.14★★
Cultivated area in 1987	0.01	−0.01	0.00
Ratio of owned land in 1987	−0.02	0.00	0.02
Ratio of irrigation times ratio of area under MVs[c]	0.50★	−0.29	−0.21
Ratio of irrigation times ratio of area under TVs[d]	0.48★	−0.31	−0.18
Father's education (years)	0.00	−0.03	0.02
Mother's education (years)	−0.04★	0.05★★	−0.01

	Northeast Thailand in early 2000s[b]		
	Farm	Nonfarm	Self-Employed
Age (years)	−0.09	0.03	0.06
Age squared/100	0.15	−0.07	−0.07
Female dummy	0.03	−0.04	0.02
Dummy for lower secondary schooling	−0.02	−0.09	0.11
Dummy for post-lower secondary schooling	−0.17★★	0.12	0.04
Cultivated area in 1987	0.01	−0.03	0.02
Ratio of owned land in 1987	−0.07	0.16	−0.09
Ratio of irrigation times ratio of area under MVs	−1.00	−1.37	2.37

Continued

Table 7 Determinants of current occupational choice of children in sample villages in the Philippines and Thailand (marginal effects), early 2000s—Cont'd

| | Northeast Thailand in early 2000s[b] | | |
	Farm	Nonfarm	Self-Employed
Ratio of irrigation times ratio of area under TVs	−1.58	0.79	2.37
Father's education (years)	0.02	−0.01	−0.01
Mother's education (years)	−0.03	0.03	0.00

[a]Taken from Takahashi and Otsuka (2009, Table 3.8). *Early 2000s* refers to 2003.
[b]Taken from Cherdchuchai et al. (2009, Table 4.10). *Early 2000s* refers to 2004.
[c]Refers to improved varieties.
[d]Refers to traditional varieties.
**=Significant at 1% level.
*=Significant at 5% level.

which returns to schooling are expected to be higher, rendering support of Hypothesis 5 on the relationship between occupational choice and schooling attainment. An important point of inquiry is to what extent education has affected nonfarm income, since the increase in nonfarm income is expected to be the major driving force behind poverty reduction.

We show statistical results of the determinants of individual nonfarm income drawn from Takahashi and Otsuka (2009) for the Philippines and Cherdchuchai et al. (2009) for Thailand. Table 8 shows a "Mincerian-type income function" using personal characteristics of the worker (i.e., schooling, work experience, age, and gender) as explanatory variables of log farm earnings (i.e., daily labor earnings in the Philippines and annual earnings in Thailand). The Mincerian function was estimated using a two-stage procedure to control for sample selection bias, since only those children who work in rural nonfarm sectors and Manila were included in the sample set; we excluded children working in the farm sector, such as farmers and agricultural workers. Nonetheless, the selectivity correction term was not significant for the two-country regressions.

Education, which is specified both in years of schooling completed and as dummy variables for secondary and tertiary schooling completed, has positively and significantly affected nonfarm income of children in Central Luzon. The average rates of returns of education were substantially higher in Manila than in rural areas, judging from the large difference in the magnitude of the coefficients. Moreover, tertiary schooling (but not secondary schooling) has positively affected rural nonfarm income, whereas both tertiary and secondary schooling were significant factors explaining earnings in Manila. These findings suggest that the disadvantage of having primary schooling only is relatively small in rural nonfarm jobs, where the informal service sector remains

Table 8 Determinants of nonfarm earnings in the sample villages in the Philippines and Thailand, early 2000s

| | Central Luzon, Philippines, in early 2000s[a] | | | |
| | Rural | | Manila | |
	Model 1	Model 2	Model 1	Model 2
Education (years)	0.06★★		0.13★★	
Dummy for secondary schooling		−0.12		0.66★★
Dummy for tertiary schooling		0.43★★		0.73★★
Experience (years)	0.07★★	0.07★★	0.02	0.04
Experience-squared	−0.002★	−0.002★	−0.00	−0.00
Female dummy	0.25	0.27★	0.05	0.28

| | Thailand in early 2000s[b] | | | |
| | Central Plain | | Northeast | |
	Nonfarm	Self-Employed	Nonfarm	Self-Employed
Dummy for lower secondary schooling	0.27	0.00	0.03	0.21
Dummy for post-lower secondary schooling	0.27★	0.53	0.69★★	0.50
Age (years)	0.15	−0.24	0.25★	0.64
Age squared/100	−0.17	0.43	−0.38	−0.97
Female dummy	−0.17	−0.37	−0.12	−0.34

[a]Taken from Takahashi and Otsuka (2009, Table 3.9). *Early 2000s* refers to 2003.
[b]Taken from Cherdchuchai et al. (2009, Table 4.11). *Early 2000s* refers to 2004.

dominant. In other words, the development of the rural nonfarm sector is likely to be especially more pro-poor than that of the urban nonfarm sector.

It is interesting to observe that the coefficients of experience and its squared term are significant only in rural areas but not in Manila, suggesting the importance of accumulation of specific human capital that is specific to the available jobs in rural areas. It implies that even the lowly educated workers can increase their nonfarm earnings in rural areas by simply accumulating work experience. This story does not hold in Manila, where tertiary schooling is particularly important to increase earnings, perhaps because jobs in Manila require general skills, which can be obtained only through formal training in schools.

In Thailand, our regression results also show the significant and positive impact of education on annual earnings, which again supports Hypothesis 5—that the more educated workers tend to obtain employment in the more lucrative nonfarm sector, where they can fully maximize the returns of their schooling. Education did not have an impact on self-employment, which provides mainly informal service, suggesting that formal schooling is not a requisite to increase income in this sector. Thus, rural nonfarm jobs in service sectors tend to provide employment opportunities for the poor, who are less educated than the rich. Nonetheless, this important function of the rural nonfarm labor markets did not receive much attention in the literature on rural nonfarm economies (Haggblade et al., 2007).

In both countries, we found that gender did not affect earnings, except in the rural nonfarm sector in Central Luzon, where presumably domestic work, which is more appropriate for women, is more common among the sample respondents. In the Central Plain of Thailand, children of the more educated parents tended to earn significantly higher income in the nonfarm sector, reflecting the tendency of educated parents to relay information to children on the more lucrative nonfarm jobs. Overall, our regression results show the prime importance of acquiring higher education as a strategy to increase individual income, that neither work experience nor gender affects nonfarm earnings, especially in the city, and that rural nonfarm jobs are particularly pro-poor since they seldom require higher education.

6. SUMMARY AND CONCLUSION

This chapter has explored the strategic processes by which rural households in Southeast Asia were able to change their sources of household income and how poor households were able to move out of poverty using long-term panel data sets in villages in the Philippines and Thailand. Rural households are able to move out of poverty in the presence of increasing scarcity of farmland and declining labor employment opportunities in agriculture, by diversifying their income sources away from rice to nonrice crops and, more important, by engaging in nonfarm activities. The rise in nonfarm income is the most decisive factor directly responsible for poverty reduction in rural Asia.

We observed that the younger and more educated children are those who are more actively involved in nonfarm jobs. The Green Revolution is the major driving force behind the rise in investments in children's schooling through the increase in farm income, thereby contributing to poverty reduction not only in the short run but in the longer run as well. These findings suggest a sequence of long-term changes from the Green Revolution toward increased farm income, increased investment in children's schooling, and the choice of lucrative nonfarm occupations by the younger and educated labor force, which contributed to poverty reduction and the development of the nonfarm sector.

Yet income growth and poverty reduction were observed, even in areas where the Green Revolution did not take place. This was facilitated by the increased availability of nonfarm jobs, even for the unskilled labor, which is the major asset of the poor, who cannot invest in schooling because they cannot afford to do so in the absence of efficient credit markets. In all likelihood, the major driving force behind the movement of the poor out of poverty in areas where the Green Revolution did not take place is the rise in job opportunities brought about by the development of the nonfarm sector, including the urban sector, which would have been partly induced to develop by the Green Revolution.

A major research agenda is to see how the Green Revolution has stimulated the growth of labor-intensive rural industries and services through production and consumption linkages, which have provided greater employment opportunities for unskilled labor. The growth linkage effects, however, do not necessarily work locally. Increased demand for nonfarm tradable commodities may facilitate the development of urban nonfarm sectors, particularly in industrial clusters where agglomeration economies lead to cost and production advantages (Sonobe and Otsuka, 2006).

The major policy implication is that, to stimulate the development of the entire economy, it is sensible to develop agriculture first, when that sector dominates the economy. Thus, it is critically important to develop improved agricultural technologies and to diffuse the production of high-value crops in poor areas where agriculture is the dominant source of rural household income. Agricultural development can trigger a subsequent transformation of rural economies toward increased nonfarm activities by stimulating investments in schooling of younger children, who subsequently contribute to poverty reduction and further development of the nonfarm sector. In this context, another major research agenda is to explore the strategy to develop rural nonfarm sectors with due consideration of market failures that hinder the development of the unskilled and uneducated labor-intensive segment of the economy.

End Notes

1. This chapter is a synthesis of Sawada et al. (2009), Estudillo et al. (2009a), Takahashi and Otsuka (2009), Cherdchuchai et al. (2009), and Otsuka et al. (2009b), which are Chapters 1–4 and 9 of the book *Rural Poverty and Income Dynamics in Asia and Africa* (Otsuka et al., 2009a).

2. At the aggregate level, Rosegrant and Hazell (2000) found that Asian countries that grew the earliest and fastest are those that experienced rapid agricultural growth in the early stages of growth. This growth was broad-based, benefiting both small and medium-sized farms, and was made possible by an equitable distribution of land. Strong agricultural growth in these countries is based on rapid growth on input use and productivity growth. The main sources of productivity growth have been public agricultural research and extension, expansion of irrigated area and rural infrastructure, and improvement in human capital.

3. Household-level surveys in major rice-producing areas in northern and southern Vietnam reveal that modern rice technology significantly increases rice production income and total household income in

areas with well-developed irrigation systems, flood control and drainage, and transportation and communication facilities, since rural infrastructure is a necessary condition for an efficient rice marketing system (Ut et al., 2000)

4. Hayami (2001) traces the trajectories of development performance of Indonesia, the Philippines, and Thailand through the country's ecological conditions and colonial history. In Indonesia, rural communities were bifurcated into rice-farming peasant proprietors and large plantations for tropical export crops based on hired labor during the Dutch colonial period, when large-scale exploitation of tropical rainforests took place. In the Philippines, exploitation of the same resource base under Spanish rule resulted in pervasive landlessness. In Thailand, landowning peasants continued to dominate because the delta plains that formed the resource base for development were mainly suitable for rice production.

5. *Adults* are working-age members between 22 and 65 years old in the Philippines and between 23 and 65 years old in Thailand.

6. In Nueva Ecija and Iloilo villages, our sample was the group of children who were 6–20 years old at the time of the base-year surveys in 1985 and 2002. *Incremental years* means increases in schooling years between 1979 and 2003 in Central Luzon and between 1985 and 1989 and 2002 and 2004 in Nueva Ecija and Iloilo.

7. In study villages in Thailand, *nonfarm activities* refer almost exclusively to urban nonfarm activities in nearby cities, whereas in Philippine villages, nonfarm activities include both rural and urban nonfarm activities.

References

Andersen, J. (1962). Some aspects of land and society in a Pangasinan community. *Philippine Sociological Review, 10*(1), 41–58.

Asian Development Bank. (2008). *Key Indicators for Asia and the Pacific.* Philippines: Manila.

Barker, R., & Herdt, R. (1985). *The Rice Economy of Asia. Resources for the Future.* Washington, DC.

Cherdchuchai, S., Otsuka, K., & Estudillo, J. P. (2009). Income dynamics, schooling investment, and poverty reduction in Philippine villages, 1985–2004. In K. Otsuka, J. P. Estudillo, & Y. Sawada (Eds.), *Rural Poverty and Income Dynamics in Asia and Africa.* London: Routledge.

David, C. C., & Otsuka, K. (1994). *Modern Rice Technology and Income Distribution in Asia.* Boulder, CO: Lynne Rienner.

Estudillo, J. P., & Otsuka, K. (1999). Green revolution, human capital, and off-farm employment: changing sources of income among farm households in Central Luzon, 1966–94. *Economic Development and Cultural Change, 47*(3), 497–523.

Estudillo, J. P., Sawada, Y., & Otsuka, K. (2008). Poverty and income dynamics in Philippine villages, 1985–2004. *Review of Development Economics, 12*(4), 877–890.

Estudillo, J. P., Sawada, Y., & Otsuka, K. (2009a). Income dynamics, schooling investment, and poverty reduction in Philippine villages, 1985–2004. In K. Otsuka, J. P. Estudillo, & Y. Sawada (Eds.), *Rural Poverty and Income Dynamics in Asia and Africa.* London: Routledge.

Estudillo, J. P., Sawada, Y., & Otsuka, K. (2009b). The changing determinants of schooling investments: evidence from villages in the Philippines, 1985–89 and 2002–04. *Journal of Development Studies, 45*(3), 391–411.

Foster, A. D., & Rosenzweig, M. (1996). Technical change and human-capital returns and investments: evidence from the Green Revolution. *American Economics Review, 86*(4), 931–953.

Haggblade, S., Hazell, P., & Reardon, T. (2007). Sectoral growth linkages between agriculture and the rural nonfarm economy. In S. Haggblade, P. Hazell, & T. Reardon (Eds.), *Transforming the Rural Nonfarm Economy: Opportunities and Threats in the Developing World.* Baltimore, MD: The Johns Hopkins University Press.

Harris, J. R., & Todaro, M. P. (1970). Migration, unemployment and development: a two-sector analysis. *American Economic Review, 60*(1), 126–142.

Hayami, Y. (2001). Ecology, history, and development: a perspective from rural Southeast Asia. *The World Bank Research Observer, 16*(2), 169–198.

Hayami, Y., & Godo, Y. (2005). *Development Economics: From the Poverty to the Wealth of Nations* (3rd ed.). Oxford: Oxford University Press.

Hayami, Y., & Kikuchi, M. (2000). *A Rice Village Saga: Three Decade of Green Revolution in the Philippines.* London: Macmillan Press.

Hazell, P., & Haggblade, S. (1991). Rural-urban growth linkages in India. *Indian Journal of Agricultural Economics, 46*(4), 515–529.

Hossain, M., Rahman, M., & Estudillo, J. P. (2009). Income dynamics, schooling investments, and poverty reduction in Bangladesh. In K. Otsuka, J. P. Estudillo, & Y. Sawada (Eds.), *Rural Poverty and Income Dynamics in Asia and Africa.* London: Routledge.

Jayasurija, S. K., & Shand, R. T. (1986). Technical change and labor absorption in Asian agriculture: some emerging trends. *World Development, 14*(3), 415–428.

Jorgenson, D. W. (1961). The development of a dual economy. *Economic Journal, 71*(282), 309–334.

Kajisa, K., & Palanichamy, N. V. (2009). Income dynamics and schooling investments in Tamil Nadu, India, 1971–2003: changing roles of land and human capital. In K. Otsuka, J. P. Estudillo, & Y. Sawada (Eds.), *Rural Poverty and Income Dynamics in Asia and Africa.* London: Routledge.

Lanjouw, P. (2007). Does the rural nonfarm economy contribute to poverty reduction? In S. Haggblade, P. Hazell, & T. Reardon (Eds.), *Transforming the Rural Nonfarm Economy: Opportunities and Threats in the Developing World.* Baltimore, MD: The Johns Hopkins University Press.

Lewis, W. A. (1954). Economic development with unlimited supplies of labor. *Manchester School of Economic and Social Studies, 22*(1), 139–191.

Lipton, M., & Longhurst, R. (1989). *New Seeds and Poor People.* London: Unwin Hyman.

McLennan, M. (1969). Land and tenancy in the Central Luzon plain. *Philippine Studies, 17*(4), 651–682.

Momsen, J. H. (2004). *Gender and Development.* London: Routledge.

Otsuka, K. (2007). Efficiency and equity effects of land markets. In R. Evenson, & P. Pingali (Eds.), *Handbook of Agricultural Economics* (Vol. 3). Amsterdam: Elsevier.

Otsuka, K., Asano, S., & Gascon, F. (1994). 'Second Generation' MVs and the Evolution of the Green Revolution: The Case of Central Luzon, 1966–90. *Agricultural Economics, 10*(3), 283–295.

Otsuka, K., Estudillo, J. P., & Sawada, Y. (2009a). *Rural Poverty and Income Dynamics in Asia and Africa.* London: Routledge.

Otsuka, K., Estudillo, J. P., & Sawada, Y. (2009b). Toward a new paradigm of farm and nonfarm linkages in economic development. In K. Otsuka, J. P. Estudillo, & Y. Sawada (Eds.), *Rural Poverty and Income Dynamics in Asia and Africa.* London: Routledge.

Otsuka, K., & Yamano, T. (2006). Introduction to the special issue on the role of nonfarm income in poverty reduction: evidence from Asia and East Africa. *Agricultural Economics*, Supplement to Issue 35.3.

Quisumbing, A. R., Estudillo, J. P., & Otsuka, K. (2004). *Land and Schooling: Transferring Wealth Across Generations.* Baltimore: Johns Hopkins University Press.

Ranis, G., & Fei, J. C. H. (1961). A theory of economic development. *American Economic Review, 51*(4), 533–558.

Rosegrant, M. W., & Hazell, P. B. (2000). *Transforming the Rural Asian Economy: The Unfinished Revolution.* Oxford: Oxford University Press.

Sawada, Y., Estudillo, J. P., & Otsuka, K. (2009). Introduction: An overview and conceptual framework. In K. Otsuka, J. P. Estudillo, & Y. Sawada (Eds.), *Rural Poverty and Income Dynamics in Asia and Africa.* London: Routledge.

Sawada, Y., & Estudillo, J. P. (2008). Trade, migration and poverty reduction in the globalizing economy: the case of the Philippines. In M. Nissanke, & E. Thorbecke (Eds.), *Globalization and the Poor in Asia: Can Shared Growth Be Sustained?* New York: Palgrave Macmillan.

Schultz, T. W. (1975). The value of the ability to deal with disequilibria. *Journal of Economic Literature, 13*(3), 827–846.

Sonobe, T., & Otsuka, K. (2006). *Cluster-Based Industrial Development: An East Asian Model.* Hampshire, UK: Palgrave Macmillan.

Takahashi, K., & Otsuka, K. (2009). Human capital investment and poverty reduction over generations: a case from the rural Philippines, 1979–2003. In K. Otsuka, J. P. Estudillo, & Y. Sawada (Eds.), *Rural Poverty and Income Dynamics in Asia and Africa.* London: Routledge.

Ut, T., Hossain, M., & Janaiah, A. (2000). Income distribution and poverty in Asia: Insights from village studies. *Economic and Political Weekly, 35*(52–53), 25–42.

World Bank. (2008a). *World Development Report 2008: Agriculture for Development.* Washington, DC.

World Bank. (2008b). *World Development Indicators.* Washington, DC.

World Bank (2009). *World Development Report 2009: Reshaping Economic Geography.* Washington, DC.

CHAPTER 68

An Assessment of the Impact of Agricultural Research in South Asia Since the Green Revolution

Peter B. R. Hazell[1]

Centre for Enviromental Policy, Imperial College, London

Contents

Handbook of Agricultural Economics, Volume 4   doi: 10.1016/S1574-0072(09)04068-7

Abstract

The post-Green Revolution period has seen profound changes in the economic situation in South Asia and evolving challenges for the agricultural R&D system. The priorities have changed from a narrow focus on the productivity of food grains to a need for more work on natural resources management and sustainability issues; increasing the productivity and quality of high-value crops, trees, and livestock; agricultural intensification in many less favored areas; more precise targeting of the problems of the poor, including enhancing the micronutrient content of food staples; and analysis of policy and institutional options for achieving more sustainable and pro-poor outcomes in the rural sector. This study draws on the available literature to assess how successful the agricultural R&D system has been in achieving these new goals in South Asia. Overall, it finds that the R&D system has responded well to these changing needs in terms of both budgetary allocations and the kinds of research that has been undertaken. Moreover, market liberalization has enabled a more diverse set of agents to engage in agricultural R&D, and private firms and NGOs have helped ensure that important research and extension needs have not been overlooked.

Findings on the impact of this evolving research agenda are mixed. The economic returns to crop improvement research have remained high and well in excess of national discount rates. Public investments in crop improvement research have also given higher returns than most other public investments in rural areas. There is little credible evidence to suggest that these rates of return are declining over time. Agricultural R&D has also made important contributions to reducing poverty in South Asia, but it has done less well in reducing interhousehold and interregional inequities. The greatest impact on poverty has been obtained by lowering food prices, but this pathway might be less important in the future now that food prices are aligned more with border prices and food accounts for a smaller share of consumers' budgets. Also, given that agriculture now plays a relatively small part in the livelihoods of many marginal farmers in South Asia, questions arise about the efficacy of continuing to target agricultural R&D to their problems. Agricultural R&D has also been successful in addressing many of the environmental problems associated with agriculture, with a demonstrated potential for favorable impacts in farmers' fields. Yet the uptake of improved technologies and management practices that reduce environmental damage has been disappointing, particularly in intensively farmed areas. Finally, a large amount of policy research has been undertaken in South Asia since the GR, and case studies show favorable returns to policy research, though the conditions under which it leads to policy change are not well understood.

JEL classifications: O13, O47, Q16, Q18

Keywords

agricultural research and development
productivity results
social effects
environmental impacts
policy research

1. INTRODUCTION

The Green Revolution (GR) brought modern science to bear on a widening Asian food crisis in the 1960s. The speed and scale with which it solved the food problem at regional and national levels was remarkable and unprecedented, and it contributed to a substantial reduction in poverty and to launching broader economic growth in Asian countries (Asian Development Bank, 2000).

Although highly successful in achieving its primary food goal, the GR left many poor people and regions behind, an outcome that was aggravated by continuing population growth. And though it saved large areas of forest, wetlands, and fragile lands from agricultural conversion, it did not save all, and it generated environmental problems of its own, especially ones related to the overuse and mismanagement of modern inputs, the unsustainable use of irrigation water, and the loss of bio-diversity within rural landscapes and individual crop species (Asian Development Bank, 2000).

Agricultural research, including the contributions of some of the member institu-tions of the Consultative Group on International Agricultural Research (CGIAR),[2] played a key role in developing the technologies that powered the GR (Tribe, 1994; Rosegrant and Hazell, 2000). As a consequence, agricultural R&D has been criticized for contributing to the poverty and environmental problems that continue to plague the South Asian continent. In recent decades, the national and international R&D sys-tems have tried to address some of these concerns by including the goals of reducing poverty, protecting the environment and enhancing the sustainability of natural resources as part of their research strategy. In an attempt to evaluate how effective these efforts been, this study reviews and assesses a large body of evidence on the impacts of agricultural research by the CGIAR and its partners in South Asia. The study focuses on the post-GR era which, for the purposes of this paper, is broadly defined to have begun in the early 1980s and extends to the present time.

The post-GR period has seen a dramatic economic and social transformation of South Asia that has redefined the context in which the agricultural R&D systems oper-ate. Understanding this changing context is important in assessing how responsive the CGIAR and NARS have been to evolving problems and opportunities as well as eval-uating how effective those responses have been. The chapter begins with a brief review of this transformation in Section 2 and the ways in which national policymakers and agricultural R&D systems have responded.

The following sections then review the evidence on the impact of agricultural R&D since the early 1980s. The review draws almost entirely on peer-reviewed and published studies so as to ensure reasonable standards of evidence and is structured around four key themes.[3] Section 3 assesses the productivity impacts of agricultural R&D; Section 4 assesses social impacts; particularly inequality and poverty impacts; Section 5 assesses environmental impacts; and Section 6 assesses policy impacts. Each section begins with an overview of the main pathways through which impact can occur, which is then followed by a review of the available empirical evidence. Section 7 synthesizes the findings and makes some recommendations for future impact assessment work.

2. THE CHANGING CONTEXT FOR R&D

2.1 An economic and social transformation

The Green Revolution enabled South Asia to move from regional food shortages in the 1960s to food surpluses beyond effective demand within 25 years, despite a 70% increase in population. It also contributed to national economic growth, although the pace of national economic growth only really picked up in the 1990s, after a period of economic reforms and market liberalization (Rosegrant and Hazell, 2000). Recent years have seen significant growth in national per capita incomes, rapid urbanization, and economic diversification, with a sharp drop in agriculture's share in national GDP (Table 1; Rosegrant and Hazell, 2000). Rising incomes and urbanization have led to rapid diversification of national diets, with high growth rates in demand for many high-value foods, particularly livestock products and fruits and vegetables (Joshi et al., 2007; Dorjee et al., 2003). The agricultural sector has continued to grow at respectable rates, as has the sector's total factor productivity growth, but both now lag the manufacturing sector (Krishna, 2006).

Notwithstanding these generally favorable trends, agriculture and the rural sector remain problematic. Despite out-migration, rural populations and agricultural work forces have continued to grow in much of the region, and the share of the total work force engaged in agriculture remains obstinately high (Table 1). This has led to increasing pressure on land, and the total number of farms has continued to increase, leading to a decline in the average farm size and an increase in the number of small farms less than 2 ha (Table 2). Given that agriculture's GDP share is declining much faster than its labor share, the average productivity of the agricultural workforce (measured in GDP/capita) is necessarily falling relative to the productivity of the nonagricultural workforce, leading to widening income gaps between the agricultural and nonagricultural sectors. Poverty, which fell from 59.1% to 43.1% of the population between 1975 and the early 1990s (Asian Development Bank, 2000), remains stubbornly high, especially in rural areas (Table 1).

In this changing context, some of the key challenges that have emerged for agriculture and the rural economy can be summarized as follows:
- The need to diversify agriculture into high-value production to match changing patterns of domestic and export demand. This has required a shift in policy priorities from heavy state intervention in food staples production and national self-sufficiency goals to greater emphasis on high-value market chains and private sector development.
- There are too many small farms of questionable viability and too many workers in agriculture to provide reasonable levels of income parity with the nonagricultural workforce. On the other hand, growth in exit opportunities is still too low (see Bhalla and Hazell, 2003, for an analysis of the situation in India). Most South Asian countries have yet to reach a tipping point where the absolute number of their agricultural workers begins to decline.[4] Until that happens, agriculture's shares in GDP

Table 1   Key economic and social indicators for South Asian countries

	Bangladesh	India	Nepal	Pakistan	Sri Lanka
GNI/capita (US$)					
1980–1985	200	290	170	330	380
2006	450	820	320	800	1310
Average growth rate (%)					
GDP, 2000–2006	5.6	7.4	2.7	5.4	4.8
GDP/capita, 2005–2006	4.9	7.7	−0.1	4.1	6.6
Agric. VA, 1990–2005	3.2	2.5	2.9	3.5	1.4
Agric. GDP share (%)					
1970	54.6	45.2	67.3	36.8	28.3
1990	36.9	31.0	51.6	26.0	26.3
2005–2006	20.0	18.0	35.0	20.0	16.5
Agric. labor share (%)					
1970	83.5	72.6	94.4	64.6	55.3
1990–1992	66.4	68.1	82.3	48.9	44.3
2001–2003	51.7	NA	NA	45.3	34.7
Urban population share (%)					
1970–1985	17.5	24.3	7.8	29.3	21.4
1995–2001	25.6	27.9	12.2	33.4	23.1
Population growth (%)					
Total (2000–2006)	1.9	1.5	2.1	2.4	0.4
Rural (1990–2005)	1.6	1.4	1.8	2.0	1.1
Poverty (%[a])					
Rural	53.0	30.2	34.6	35.9	27.0
Urban	36.6	24.7	9.6	24.2	15.0
National	49.8	28.6	30.9	32.6	25.0
Irrigated land (% cropland)					
1990–1992	33.8	28.3	43.0	78.5	28.0
2001–2003	54.3	32.7	47.2	81.1	34.4
1990–2005 growth rate (%)	3.8	1.4	1.0	0.9	2.2

[a]The latest poverty data years are Bangladesh, 2000; India, 1999–2000; Nepal, 2003–2004; Pakistan, 1998–1999; and Sri Lanka, 1995–1996.
Sources: World Bank Indicators and World Bank (2007).

and employment cannot begin to align, and the income gap between the agricultural and nonagricultural workforces will widen.

• Small farms that cannot diversify into high-value farming have little chance of making an adequate income from farming. At the same time, market chains have

Table 2   Changes in average farm size and number of small farms by country, 1960–2002

Country	Census Year	Average Farm Size (Ha)	Number of Farms < 2 Ha (M)
Bangladesh[a]	1960	1.7	
	1983–1984	0.91	
	1996	0.68	17.8[c]
India[b]	1971	2.3	49.114
	1991	1.6	84.480
	1995–1996	1.4	92.822
Nepal[b]	1992	1.0	2.407
	2002	0.8	3.083
Pakistan[b]	1971–1973	5.3	1.059
	1989	3.8	2.404
	2000	3.1	3.814

Source: [a]Hossain et al. (2007).
[b]Nagayets (2005).
[c]Anriquez and Bonomi (2007).

changed, becoming more competitive and integrated and increasingly consumer-driven through the penetration of supermarkets and other large trading firms. These changes have made it harder for small farmers to participate in new growth opportunities and many have been left behind (Joshi et al., 2007).

• The rural poor have diversified their livelihoods, and agriculture now plays a relatively small and declining role. Many of the agriculturally dependent rural poor are also concentrated in less favored areas where gains in agricultural productivity have been slower than elsewhere.

• There has been an increasing public awareness of the environmental problems associated with agriculture and growing demand for improved environmental services such as clean waterways, protection of forest, biodiversity, and sites of natural beauty. These demands often conflict with current agricultural interests. Increasing water scarcities also pose a growing conflict of interest between farmers and the rest of society.

2.2 National responses

The Indian experience typifies the important policy changes that have occurred in most South Asian countries and is reviewed here.

The national policy response to the changing agricultural situation in India has been slow compared to the speed with which the government embraced the economic liberalization policies of the early 1990s. Progress has been particularly slow in liberalizing food grain markets, including associated agro-industries. This has led many farmers and agro-processing firms to become locked into unprofitable activities, with growing dependence on government price and subsidy supports.

The government has been unable to cut input subsidies for farmers (power, water, fertilizer, credit). The cost has grown to over Rs.450 billion per year, which, unlike in earlier GR days, is now largely a wasted investment in terms of productivity growth (Jha, 2007). Moreover, the high cost of the subsidies has squeezed out productive public investments in rural infrastructure and R&D, and these have shrunk as a share of total public expenditure (World Bank, 2007).

The large input subsidies on power, water, and fertilizer have also contributed to environmental damage (e.g., waterlogging and salinization of irrigated lands, fertilizer runoff, high pesticide use) and to the unsustainable use of ground water and worsening water scarcities. The public institutions that provide power and water remain inefficient and have not been adequately reformed, and they are unresponsive to the changing needs of farmers.

Policies towards the high-value sectors have generally been better, and the private sector has been allowed to operate more freely. In value terms, horticultural and livestock products now account for over half of India's agricultural output, with most going to the domestic market. Government is active in helping to promote high-value exports, and this will be important for future agricultural growth as domestic high-value markets become saturated. A policy challenge for the high-value sector is linking many more small farmers into these increasingly integrated market chains (Joshi et al., 2007).

The national agricultural R&D system has made several important adjustments over the years. Beginning in the 1980s, the private sector, which had already been active in research on pesticides, fertilizer, and agricultural machinery, began to expand into crop improvement research (Evenson et al., 1999). For example, across Asia, the private sector has captured more than 89% of the maize seed market, largely through the production of hybrid rather than open pollinated varieties (Gerpacio, 2003). This activity has been facilitated by a national seed policy, which allows importation of seed materials and majority ownership of seed companies by foreign companies. The government also provides tax breaks for private research expenditures and has strengthened intellectual property rights over research products (Pal and Byerlee, 2006). Some NGOs, such as the M. S. Swaminathan Research Foundation and the Mahyco Research Foundation, have also become actively involved.

These changes have led to a much more diverse set of actors and agendas in agricultural R&D, with more focus today on natural resource management and sustainable agriculture, the problems of less favored areas and poor farmers, and more participatory research approaches. Yet at the same time there has been expansion of research capacity in modern science and biotechnology.

In real terms, South Asian countries nearly tripled their public spending on agricultural R&D between 1981 and 2002 (Table 3). Research has also been diversified over the years

Table 3   Total public agricultural research expenditures (2005 PPP dollars, M), 1981–2002

	Bangladesh	India	Nepal	Pakistan	Sri Lanka	South Asia
1981		396				630
1991	81	746		223	39	1103
1996	82	861	15	188	42	1188
2002	109	1355	26	171	51	1712

Source: Beintema and Stads (2008).

to reflect the growing diversification of the sector and the importance of environmental and social issues. In 1996–1998, about 35% of the research resources of the Indian Council for Agricultural Research (ICAR) were allocated to crops research, 20% to livestock research, 15% to NRM, and 12% to horticulture. Social science received about 2.5% of total expenditure but 10% of the total scientists (Pal and Byerlee, 2006). Private sector research expenditure accounts for small shares of total R&D spending in most South Asian countries other than India (Beintema and Stads, 2008).

2.3 The CGIAR response

The CG centers have maintained a commodity research focus on productivity growth for South Asia but with greater attention to sustaining high yields through improved management techniques in GR systems (e.g., the Rice-Wheat Consortium for the Indo-Gangetic Plains; www.rwc.cgiar.org) and enhancing the nutritional and consumer traits of modern crop varieties (e.g., the Harvest Plus Challenge Program on biofortification; www.harvestplus.org). Additionally, a broader research agenda has evolved that includes work on:

- Poverty, gender, and empowerment
- More general environment and NRM issues, including forest, fish, and biodiversity
- Greater focus on the problems of less favored areas
- Agricultural policy

The CGIAR consistently spends 25–30% of its total budget on Asia, though it does not report a separate breakout for South Asia (CGIAR Annual Reports). Its research in South Asia is dominated by five centers (ICRISAT, IRRI, CIMMYT, IWMI, and IFPRI). Total CGIAR spending in Asia in 2006 was $131 million. Assuming half of this went to South Asia, this would have been about $65 million. This is slightly less than half the combined total budgets of the five centers that do most of the work in the region and about 3% of total public R&D spending in the region (Table 3). The CGIAR has become a relatively small partner in the region.

2.4 Assessing the impact of agricultural R&D

Assessing the impact of agricultural R&D within this rapidly unfolding economic, social, institutional, and policy context is complex, much more so than assessing impact during the GR era. In the first place, there are many more dimensions to impact assessment today, not all of which can easily be measured or quantified. In addition to the usual productivity-based approaches that form the foundation of most benefit/cost and rate-of-return analysis, there are important social (e.g., poverty, inequality, and empowerment) and environmental (e.g., sustainability, ecosystem, and human health) dimensions to consider. There is also a more diverse array of research activity to consider. Crop and livestock improvement work has been the mainstay of most impact assessment work in the past, but much research undertaken since the GR has focused on improved agronomic and natural resources management practices, environmental management, human nutrition, and poverty alleviation. The mix of research players has also changed, leading to more complex interplays between research organizations. Sometimes this leads to collaborative undertakings, sometimes it leads to competition driven by different motives (e.g., private versus public) or conflicting research paradigms (e.g., low or no input versus GR technologies). The resulting "contest" of ideas and interventions can lead to healthy enrichment of the technology options available to farmers and to countervailing checks that prevent any one approach from overreaching. But sometimes it leads to misinformation, confusion, and misdirection of scarce research resources. In this context, evidence-based research that screens and validates competing paradigms and technologies can also have high social value. Assessing these many dimensions of R&D requires a much broader review of different types of research activities than has been conventional in the past literature on impact assessment.

There are also difficult methodological issues to address. Although there are now standard and quantitative indicators for assessing productivity impacts, there is much less consensus on how to measure poverty and environmental impacts and less opportunity for establishing broadly accepted quantitative indicators. Additionally, it is difficult to establish relevant counterfactuals for assessing impacts when dynamic demographic and market forces are also impacting poverty and inequality and adding to pressures on the environment. Given the long lead times inherent in bringing much agricultural research to fruition and in realizing environmental benefits, much agricultural research must be assessed in a long-term framework and against goals and market and social contexts for which it was not necessarily designed. There are also difficult issues to address when the impact of new technologies is to be attributed to specific institutions such as CGIAR centers. Best-practice guidelines need to be followed: use of an adequate counterfactual situation; controlling for other relevant factors besides R&D that are driving change; allowing for the longish lead times characteristic of much agricultural R&D; use of credible impact measures for social and environmental outcomes; and investments evaluated against goals at the time they were initiated as well as against eventual outcomes. Given these kinds of difficulties, the review that follows draws primarily on peer-reviewed publications since their methods are most likely to meet best-practice guidelines.

3. PRODUCTIVITY IMPACTS

3.1 Productivity impact pathways

Given the large populations to be fed in the face of growing resource scarcities, improving agricultural productivity has consistently remained one of the main objectives of agricultural R&D in South Asian countries. The most direct way in which R&D can impact productivity is through yield levels and yield variability. But other pathways are also important. Crop improvement research can shorten crop growing periods and reduce plant sensitivity to day length, both of which enable more crops to be grown on the same land each year. Research into labor-saving technologies such as mechanization and herbicides can increase labor productivity, freeing up labor for other income-generating activities. Research on natural resources management (NRM), including water management, can enhance as well as sustain the productivity of key natural resources.

Productivity growth in agriculture can also have far-reaching impacts on the productivity and growth of regional and national economies. There are several growth linkages that drive this relationship: benefits from lower food prices for workers; more abundant raw materials for agro-industry and export; release of labor and capital (in the form of rural savings and taxes) to the nonfarm sector; and increased rural demands for nonfood consumer goods and services, which in turn support growth in the service and manufacturing sectors.

There is substantial and compelling empirical literature on these productivity impacts, which is reviewed here in descending order from macro to micro impacts. The productivity impacts of improved NRM research are largely taken up in Section 5 because they are also important for environmental sustainability.

3.2 Evidence of economy and sectorwide impacts

The powerful economywide benefits emanating from technologically driven agricultural growth were amply demonstrated during the GR era in South Asia (Mellor, 1976). In India, the fact that nonagriculture's share of total national employment did not change for over a century, until the full force of the Green Revolution was under way in the 1970s, provided strong circumstantial evidence of the importance of agricultural growth as a motor for the Indian economy. This was also confirmed by Rangarajan (1982), who estimated that a one percentage point addition to the agricultural growth rate stimulated a 0.5% addition to the growth rate of industrial output and a 0.7% addition to the growth rate of national income.

Regional growth linkage studies have also shown strong multiplier impacts from agricultural growth to the rural nonfarm economy (Hazell and Haggblade, 1991; Hazell and Ramasamy, 1991). The size of the multipliers varies depending on the method of analysis chosen, and for South Asia they vary between $0.30 and $0.85; i.e., each dollar increase in agricultural income leads to an additional $0.30–0.85 increase in rural nonfarm earnings (Haggblade et al., 2007). The multipliers tend to be larger in GR regions because of better infrastructure and market town development, greater use of purchased farm inputs, and higher per capita incomes and hence consumer spending power (Hazell and Haggblade, 1991).

As South Asian economies have grown and diversified, other important engines of growth have emerged at national and regional levels. In India, for example, national economic growth has accelerated to new highs in recent years, even as agricultural growth has slowed. In many rural areas, the correlation between agricultural growth and growth of nonfarm income and employment has also become weaker (Harriss-White and Janakarajan, 1997; Foster and Rosenzweig, 2004). There is also evidence that the fastest growth in the rural nonfarm economy is occurring in areas linked to major urban centers and transport corridors, regardless of their agricultural base (Bhalla, 1997).

This is not to say that agricultural growth is now unimportant. Agriculture's contribution to national GDP is higher than ever in absolute terms; it is only less important in relative terms. Moreover, large shares of the working population are still primarily engaged in agriculture, as are most of the poor. Continued growth in agricultural productivity is needed to maintain favorable national food balances, meet rising demands for high-value foods, including livestock products, and raise the living standard of those workers and poor people remaining in agriculture and rural areas.

3.2.1 Economic impact of aggregate R&D investments

Several studies have attempted to measure the economic returns that can be attributed to total public investments in agricultural research. These studies invariably estimate changes in total factor productivity (TFP) and the share of that change that can be attributed to agricultural R&D investments. Evenson, Pray, and Rosegrant (1999) identified 10 *ex post* studies of the returns to aggregate research programs in South Asia. Seven of these plus a more recent study by Thirtle et al. (2003) extend into the post-GR era and are summarized in Table 4. Despite some differences in methods of analysis and time periods covered, all the studies show rates of return that are much higher than any reasonable discount rate.

Fan, Hazell, and Thorat (2000) used a simultaneous equations model to estimate the returns to public investments in agricultural R&D in India. In addition to controlling

Table 4 Estimated internal rates of return to agricultural research in South Asia, 1955–1995

Study	Country	Period	Rate of Return (%)
Nagy (1985)	Pakistan	1959–1979	64
Khan and Akbari (1986)	Pakistan	1955–1981	36
Evenson and McKinsey (1991)	India	1958–1983	65
Dey and Evenson (1991)	Bangladesh	1973–1989	143
Azam, Bloom, and Evenson (1991)	Pakistan	1956–1985	58
Evenson and Bloom (1991)	Pakistan	1955–1989	65
Rosegrant and Evenson (1992)	India	1956–1987	62
Evenson, Pray, and Rosegrant (1999)	India	1977–1987	57
Thirtle et al. (2003)	South Asia[a]	Various years, 1985–1995	24

[a]Includes Bangladesh, India, Nepal, Pakistan, and Sri Lanka.

for other types of public investments (necessary to avoid biasing the estimated returns to research), this approach has the added advantage of giving comparative returns between different types of public investment. They find that public investment in agricultural research yielded the highest productivity return in recent decades, with a benefit/cost ratio of 13.5 (Table 5). This is more than double the benefit/cost ratio for the next best public investment—rural roads—and more than 10 times the ratios for education, irrigation, and rural development.

Fan, Hazell, and Thorat (1999) also find that the marginal benefits of R&D investment in India show little sign of diminishing over time, unlike some other public investments. This is confirmed by Evenson, Pray, and Rosegrant (1999) in a study of the determinants of growth in India's agricultural total factor productivity (TFP) from 1956 to 1987.

3.3 Evidence of commodity impacts
3.3.1 Cereals
The spread of modern cereal varieties in recent decades and their enormous contribution to the growth in food production throughout South Asia has been widely documented (Evenson and Gollin, 2003, provide a comprehensive assessment). Adoption rates continue to rise (Tables 6 and 7), and modern varieties are continually being improved and replaced (Lantican et al., 2005; Evenson and Gollin, 2003).

Table 5 Productivity and poverty effects of government investments in rural India, 1993

Expenditure Variable	Productivity Returns in Agriculture in Rupees, Per Rupee Invested	Number of People Lifted Out of Poverty Per Million Rupees Invested
R&D	13.45	84.5
Irrigation	1.36	9.7
Roads	5.31	123.8
Education	1.39	41.0
Power	0.26	3.8
Soil and water	0.96	22.6
Rural development	1.09	17.8
Health	0.84	25.5

Source: Fan, Hazell, and Thorat (2000) but with the productivity returns expressed as benefit-cost ratios as reported in Fan and Rao (2008).

Table 6 Harvested area under modern cereal varieties in South Asia (%), 1965–2000

	Rice	Wheat	Maize
1965	0.0	1.7	0.0
1970	10.2	39.6	17.1
1975	26.6	72.5	26.3
1980	36.3	78.2	34.4
1985	44.2	82.9	42.5
1990	52.6	87.3	47.1
1995	59.0	90.1	48.8
2000	71.0	94.5	53.5

Source: Gollin et al. (2005).

CGIAR-related germplasm continues to be used extensively by national breeding programs in South Asia (Evenson and Gollin, 2003). For example, over 90% of the wheat varieties now grown in South Asia contain CIMMYT-related germplasm (Lantican et al., 2005).

Table 7   Planted area under improved sorghum and millet varieties by country (%), 1966–1998

Country	Year	Share (%)
Sorghum[1]		
India	1966	1.0
	1971	4.1
	1976	15.4
	1981	23.3
	1986	34.5
	1991	54.8
	1998	71.0
Pakistan	1995–1996	21
Millet[2]		
India	1995–1996	65

[1]Deb et al. (2005) and Deb and Bantilan (2003).
[2]Bantilan and Deb (2003).

Yields of wheat and rice have continued to rise on average across South Asia, but despite continuing improvements in crop varieties (e.g., the recent release of hybrid rice), annual growth rates are slowing (Table 8). This is confirmed by more careful, micro-based studies of wheat and rice yields in the Indo-Gangetic Plain (Murgai et al., 2001; Ladha et al., 2003; Cassman and Pingali, 1993; Bhandari et al., 2003) and in India's major irrigated rice-growing states (Janaiah et al., 2005). There are several possible reasons for this slowdown: displacement of cereals on better lands by more profitable crops such as groundnuts (Maheshwari, 1998); diminishing returns to modern varieties when irrigation and fertilizer use are already at high levels; and the fact that food-grain prices have until recently been low relative to input costs, making additional intensification less profitable. But there are concerns that the slowdown also reflects a deteriorating crop-growing environment in intensive monocrop systems. Ali and Byerlee (2002) and Murgai, Ali, and Byerlee (2001), for example, report deteriorating soil and water quality in the rice/wheat system of the Indo-Gangetic Plain, and Pingali et al. (1997) report degradation of soils and buildup of toxins in intensive paddy systems.

These problems are reflected in growing evidence of stagnating or even declining levels of total factor productivity in some of these farming systems (e.g., Janaiah et al., 2005). Ali and Byerlee (2002) have shown that degradation of soil and water are directly implicated in the slowing of TFP growth in the wheat/rice system of the Pakistan Punjab. Ladha et al. (2003) examine long-term yield trials data at multiple sites across South Asia and find stagnating or declining yield trends when input use is held constant. One consequence has been

Table 8   Annual growth rates for crop yields in major producing countries and South Asia (average % per year), 1961–2005

Crop/ country	1961–1970	1971–1980	1981–1990	1991–2000	2001–2005	1961–2005
Rice						
Bangladesh	0.43	2.45	2.67	2.67	2.27	1.97
India	1.14	1.64	3.59	1.08	0.85	1.95
South Asia	1.15	1.78	3.20	1.46	1.17	1.94
Wheat						
India	4.46	1.87	3.11	1.82	−0.98	3.05
Pakistan	3.82	3.49	1.62	2.60	2.64	2.65
South Asia	4.27	2.31	2.67	2.03	−0.22	2.95
Sorghum						
India	0.54	5.09	1.76	−0.05	0.05	1.38
South Asia	0.58	4.90	1.71	−0.05	0.08	1.35
Millet						
India	2.02	1.59	2.00	2.04	6.03	1.90
South Asia	1.94	1.54	1.89	2.01	5.89	1.84
Maize						
India	1.67	1.36	2.52	2.54	1.01	1.73
Pakistan	0.63	1.30	1.29	2.99	15.90	1.63
South Asia	1.69	0.90	2.33	3.51	10.63	2.14
Groundnuts						
India	0.34	0.93	1.20	0.56	4.37	1.10
South Asia	0.46	0.90	1.17	0.57	4.17	1.08
Chickpeas						
India	3.82	−1.38	0.22	0.8	2.90	0.18
Pakistan	1.46	0.34	−0.42	3.88	1.42	1.03
South Asia	−0.80	−4.11	2.28	4.86	2.98	0.14
Potatoes						
India	2.17	3.71	2.21	1.54	−1.52	2.39
Nepal	0.63	−0.73	2.84	0.90	3.62	1.56
Pakistan	2.65	−0.44	−0.37	4.29	2.74	1.35
South Asia	2.78	3.14	1.88	1.56	−0.69	2.23

Source: Calculated from FAOSTAT.

that farmers have had to use increasing amounts of fertilizers to maintain the same yields over time (Pingali et al., 1997). There is also concern that pest and disease resistance to modern pesticides now slows yield growth and that breeders have largely exploited the yield potentials of major GR crops, though sizeable gaps still remain between experiment-plot and average farmer yields. We return to these issues in Section 5.

Growth in sorghum yields has also slowed, but the yields of maize and millets have accelerated in recent years (Table 8). In the case of maize, the rapid spread of hybrids since the 1980s has added significantly to yields. Singh and Morris (2005) estimate that without hybrid maize, India's annual maize production would be about 1 million tons (or 10%) less each year. Growth in millet yields accelerated in recent years because improved varieties were only developed and released in the 1980s and are still spreading (Bantilan and Deb, 2003).

Not all of this progress can be credited to agricultural research. Nevertheless, estimates of the economic value of crop improvement research in South Asia are consistently high (Evenson and Gollin, 2003). Table 9 summarizes the rates of return estimated for a range of commodities in studies published since 1985.

Rates of return range from 20–155% and average 60%. They are also consistent with the high average returns reported in the literature for all Asia; Evenson (2001) reports an average rate of return of 67%, and Alston et al. (2000) report an average rate of 49.6% (median 78.1%). Alston et al. (2000) and Evenson, Pray, and Rosegrant (1999) find no evidence that rates of return are declining over time.

Going beyond rate-of-return calculations, Fan (2007) estimated that India's rice variety improvement work contributes about $3–4 billion per year to national rice production in constant 2000 prices, considerably greater than the total annual cost of the national R&D system (Table 3). Using some plausible and alternative attribution rules, Fan also estimates that IRRI's rice improvement work can be credited with between 12% and 64% of India's $3.6 billion gain in 2000 (i.e., a gain of between $432 million and $2304 million) and with 40–80% of the $3.9 billion gain in 1991 (i.e., a gain of between $1560 million and $3120 million). He notes that IRRI's contribution has diminished since 1991 but is still far more each year than needed to justify the institute's entire research budget. Indeed, in both years it was enough to cover the annual cost of the CGIAR's entire global program!

Lantican et al. (2005) estimate that the additional value of wheat production in developing countries attributable to international wheat improvement research ranges from $2.0–6.1 billion per year (2002 U.S. dollars). They do not provide a regional allocation of these benefits, but assuming that benefits are shared in rough proportion to the share of the world wheat area grown,[5] then South Asia captures about 28% of the benefits, or $560–1710 million per year. Similarly, Morris et al. (2003, p. 156) estimate that the economic benefits to the developing world from using CIMMYT-derived maize germplasm fall in the range of $557–770 million each year. Again, they do not provide a regional allocation of these benefits, but assuming that benefits are

Table 9 Estimated internal rates of return to crop improvement research in South Asia

Study	Country	Commodity	Period	Rate of Return (%)	Benefit/Cost Ratio
Nagy (1985)	Pakistan	Maize	1967–1981	19	
		Wheat		58	
Morris, Dublin, and Pokhrel (1992)	Nepal	Wheat	1966–1990	37–54	
Evenson and McKinsey (1991)	India	Rice	1954–1984	155	
		Wheat		51	
		Jowar (sorghum)		117	
		Bajra (pearl millet)		107	
		Maize		94	
Byerlee (1993)	Pakistan	Wheat	1978–1987	22	
Azam, Bloom, and Evenson (1991)	Pakistan	Wheat	1956–1985	76	
		Rice		84	
		Maize		45	
		Pearl millet		42	
		Sorghum		48	
Collins (1995)	Pakistan	Wheat		60–71	
Iqbal (1991)	Pakistan	Rice	1971–1988	50–57	
Byerlee and Traxler (1995)	South Asia	Wheat (spring bread)		91	
Hossain (1998)	Bangladesh	Rice	1973–1993		16.6

Continued

Table 9 Estimated internal rates of return to crop improvement research in South Asia—Cont'd

Study	Country	Commodity	Period	Rate of Return (%)	Benefit/Cost Ratio
Joshi and Bantilan (1998)	India	Groundnuts (improved variety plus raised bed and furrow)		13.5–25.2	2.1–9.4
Bantilan and Joshi (1996)	India	Pigeonpea (wilt resistance)	1986–2005[a]	61	
Ramasamy et al. (2000)	India	Pearl millet	1970–2000[a]	27	
Mittal and Kumar (2005)	India	Wheat	1976–1980 1986–1990 1991–1995	65.5 67.8 61.1	

[a]Projected beyond historical data.

shared in rough proportion to the world share of the area grown, South Asia captures about 8% of the total benefits, or $45–62 million per year.

3.3.2 Stability of cereal production

Modern cereal varieties were developed to give higher yields in favorable environments, such as irrigated areas with high fertilizer usage. This led to some initial concern that they would be more vulnerable to pest and weather stresses than traditional varieties, increasing the risk of major yield and food production shortfalls in unfavorable years. Early work by Mehra (1981), among others, suggested that yield variability for cereals in India was increasing relative to increases in average yield (higher coefficients of variation) at the national level, raising the specter of a growing risk of national food shortages and high prices some years. Subsequent analysis showed that at the plot level, many modern varieties were no more risky than traditional varieties in terms of downside risk,[6] and that although some crop yields measured at regional and national levels were becoming more variable (a bigger problem for maize and other rain-fed cereals than wheat or rice[7]), this was largely the result of more correlated or synchronized patterns of spatial yield variation across space (Hazell, 1982, 1989). Several scholars suggested that these changes might be attributable to the widespread adoption of more input-intensive production methods that led to larger and more synchronized yield responses to changes in market signals and weather events, shorter planting periods with mechanization, and the planting of large areas to the same or genetically similar crop varieties (e.g., Hazell, 1982; Ray, 1983; Rao et al., 1988). Later studies showed that rice and wheat yields generally became more stable in South Asia in the 1990s, but the patterns for maize and coarse grains were more mixed, especially at country and subregional levels (Sharma et al., 2006; Chand and Raju, 2008; Gollin, 2006; Larson et al., 2004; Deb and Bantilan, 2003; Singh and Byerlee, 1990).

National yield and production variability are less a policy issue today, given that international trade can play a bigger role in stabilizing market supplies and prices. But since large areas of major cereals are still planted to relatively few modern varieties, concern remains about the risk of possible genetic uniformity making crops vulnerable to catastrophic yield losses from changes in pests, diseases, and climate. The famine that was triggered by potato blight in Ireland in the 19th century is often cited as an historical example of society's vulnerability to a narrow genetic base in food crops. As early as 1786, colonial officers in the Asian subcontinent recorded the devastation and hunger caused by epidemics of rust disease in wheat. According to such records, wheat landraces in India, which were planted to millions of hectares, were highly susceptible to rust disease (Howard and Howard, 1909). The hunger and starvation associated with these events were aggravated by the absence of any serious relief efforts at the time and hence would be less likely to occur today. Apart from a few isolated incidents, mostly outside the South Asian continent (e.g., southern corn leaf blight, *Helminthosporium maydis*, in the United States in 1970 and the vulnerability of

IR8 rice to brown plant hopper in Southeast Asia), there has not been a recorded catastrophe in production of major food crops in modern times.

The absence of any catastrophic crop failures is due in large part to extensive behind-the-scenes scientific work to prevent such disasters. Crop genetic uniformity has been counteracted by spending more on conserving genetic resources and making them accessible for breeding purposes, through breeding approaches that broaden the genetic base of varieties supplied to farmers,[8] and by changing varieties more frequently over time to stay ahead of evolving pests, disease, and climate risks (Smale et al., forthcoming). These measures reflect the growing strength of national breeding and genetic conservation programs as well as the backup and support provided by CGIAR centers. For example, the CGIAR centers have contributed to the buildup and characterization of germplasm banks for South Asian crops and have facilitated access to genetic materials from other parts of the world. They also spend significant shares (estimated at between 33% and 50% for the commodity centers) of their budgets on "maintenance" research to provide national systems with new germplasm on a timely basis in response to emerging new pest, disease, and climate risks (Smale et al., forthcoming).[9]

3.3.3 Oilseeds

Demand for vegetable oils has grown rapidly in South Asia since the GR. In India, a growing share of this demand has had to be met by imports because domestic production could not keep pace. Yield growth has accelerated in recent years (Table 8), and the area planted to oilseeds has also increased. In some areas, oilseeds are now more profitable than cereals on irrigated land (e.g., Maheshwari, 1998).

In India, groundnuts are the main oilseed crop, and ICRISAT has worked with the Indian NARS to develop improved varieties that are higher yielding and more disease, pest, and drought resistant. Deb, Bantilan, and Nigam (2005) found that improved varieties have been widely adopted in the main groundnut-producing states of India and that in many cases yields have increased 50–100%. Compared to the best-performing local varieties, the improved varieties also have 20–30% lower per-ton production costs and per-hectare returns that are at least 50% higher. The net economic return to the groundnut improvement research is not calculated.

Joshi and Bantilan (1998) have assessed the economic returns to an ICRISAT-promoted groundnut technology package that involves improved varieties plus improved agronomic practices built around a raised bed and furrow (RBF) concept. This package was widely adopted in the state of Maharashtra during the early 1990s and by 1994 was applied to 47,000 hectares, or about 31% of the total groundnut area. Improved groundnut varieties grown without the full RBF package were also adopted on 83% of the cropped area. The full technology package led to average yield gains of 38%. It also proved profitable, and average net income increased 70% per hectare. Taking into account the full costs of the research program incurred by

ICRISAT and its Indian partners in developing the RBF package, the benefit/cost ratio is estimated at between 2.1 and 9.4 (with internal rates of return between 13.5% and 25.2%) over the period 1974–2005, depending on assumptions about the extent of adoption of key components of the technology package. The lion's share of the economic gains is estimated to be captured by farmers, with less than 20% accruing to consumers through lower groundnut prices.

3.3.4 Pulses

Pulses are an important protein-rich crop grown mostly under unirrigated conditions; they are important to the poor. The area planted to pulses stagnated or declined with the spread of high-yielding cereal technologies, because there were no comparable improvements in pulse technologies at the time. Yields have since increased, but the gains tend to be crop specific. Chickpea yields, for example, have picked up in recent years in South Asia (Table 8), but in India, yields of most other pulses grew by less than 1% per year during the 1990s, and total factor productivity growth fared little better (Joshi and Saxena, 2002). Research targeted at pulses has led to improved varieties (India alone released 92 improved pulse varieties during the eighth plan period; Ramasamy and Selvaraj, 2002), but there has been only modest impact at aggregate levels. Nevertheless, there have been smaller-scale successes.

Joshi, Asokan, and Bantilan (2005) report a more than doubling of chickpea production in Andhra Pradesh between 1980 and 1995 (to 36,000 t), driven by higher yields (up 247%) and a doubling of the crop area. The adoption of improved varieties developed by ICRISAT played an important role in this expansion.

Shiyani et al. (2002) assess the impact of two of ICRISAT's improved chickpea varieties in a poor tribal area in Gujarat, India. The two improved varieties (ICCV2 and ICCV10) were selected from a range of existing ICRISAT varieties using participatory methods. The improved varieties spread quickly and, based on a farm survey, Shiyani et al. (2002) find that they increased yields over the traditional variety by 55% for ICCV10 and 34% for ICCV2. Both varieties reduced unit costs of production, and net returns per hectare increased 84% for ICCV10 and 68% for ICCV2. Both varieties also doubled labor productivity and reduced the variability of yields. An analysis of adoption patterns shows significantly greater adoption among small farmers than large.

Bantilan and Joshi (1996) assess the impact of a wilt resistant variety of pigeonpea (ICP8863) developed by ICRISAT and partners in the 1980s. Wilt is a major problem in Karnataka, considered the pigeonpea granary of India, and nearby growing areas in Andhra Pradesh, Maharashtra, and Madhya Pradesh. Together, these areas grew 1,280,000 ha of pigeon pea in 1990. The improved variety not only provided wilt resistance, it raised yields 57% and reduced production costs per ton 45%. Although released in the late 1980s, it had been adopted on 60% of the crop area by 1992–1993. Taking account of the research costs of ICRISAT and its partners, the IRR was estimated at 61%.

Mungbeans are one of the more important pulses grown in Pakistan, and about 90% of the crop is grown in the Punjab. Improved varieties developed by the NARS and AVRDC are high yielding, pest resistant, fast growing, and have good consumption characteristics. These varieties were released in the early 1980s (Ali et al., 1997). Ali et al. (1997) assessed the economic impact of the improved mungbean varieties based on a farm survey conducted in the Pakistan Punjab in 1994. They reported that adoption was rapid and widespread: Desi, the main traditional variety, was grown by 80% of farmers in 1988 but by only 10% in 1994. At the same time, the area planted to mungbeans increased from about 100,000 ha to 167,900 ha, and their importance in total pulses increased from 3% in 1980 to 11% in 1993–1994. Modern varieties raised yields 45% and per-hectare profit by 240%. Because mungbeans are grown in rotation with wheat each year (two crop seasons), they also had residual impact on wheat yields and reduced the need for N fertilizer by about 45%. Using a consumer and producer surplus approach and taking account of benefit for wheat production, Ali et al. (1997) estimate the net social benefit of the improved varieties to be $20 million, or $119 per hectare of mungbeans grown in 1993–1994. They do not estimate the research costs incurred in developing the varieties.

3.3.5 Potatoes

Growth in potato yields has slowed in recent years for South Asia, mainly because of slowing yield growth in India, the largest producing country in the region (Table 8). CIP-related breeding material has yet to widely penetrate the region and was planted on only 4.1% of the potato area in 2007 (Table 10). This despite an earlier study showing favorable impacts on yields and per-hectare returns (Khatana et al., 1996). Khatana et al. (1996) also calculated a projected rate of return of 33% to CIP's research in India, but this must now be downgraded because of the much slower adoption than projected at the time of the study.

Table 10   Potato adoption area in South Asia (ha), 2007

Country	CIP Distributed, NARS Released	CIP Cross, NARS Selected	NARS Cross, CIP Progenitor	Total CIP-NARS Partnerships	Total Planted Area (%)
Bangladesh		5595		5595	1.47
India			43,016	43,016	3.11
Nepal	35,842			35,842	19.6
Pakistan					0
Total	35,842	5595	43,016	84,453	4.11

Source: CIP.

3.3.6 Other commodities

The rapid growth of high-value agriculture in South Asia in recent years has led to a substantial increase in agricultural research targeted to these commodities. As noted earlier, the private sector has expanded rapidly into these markets, and in 1996–1998 ICAR, the Indian NARS, spent about one third of its total budget on livestock and horticulture research.

The real growth in livestock production in South Asia since 1980 has been in poultry, eggs, and dairy production. The only involvement of the CGIAR centers has been in research on policy and marketing issues and in increasing feed supplies. ILRI, ICRISAT, and the Indian NARS have been working jointly to develop dual-purpose varieties of sorghum and millets that have more nutritious straw for feeding to ruminants. An *ex ante* assessment using GIS to identify potential adoption areas and a feed-animal performance simulation model to estimate production impacts, yielded an estimated present-day value of net benefits over 10 years of $42 million, an expected benefit/cost ratio of 15 and an internal rate of return of 28% (Kristjanson et al., 1999). The research is ongoing and hence has not yet been subjected to an *ex post* assessment.

The CGIAR centers have undertaken some work on vegetables and fruits within the context of nutrition and biodiversity conservation (e.g., Bioversity International's work on *in-situ* conservation), but these are not likely to have had major productivity impacts. The World Vegetable Centre (AVRDC), a more important player in South Asia, has contributed to productivity-enhancing research in Bangladesh. In an assessment of that work, Ali and Hau (2001) show high on-farm returns during the 1990s, improved nutrition outcomes, and an internal rate of return of 42% to the cost of AVRDC's research investment. However, due to the small scale of the work, the net benefits to the country were only about $1 million per year.

WorldFish (ICLARM) has developed genetically improved strains of Nile tilapia for on-farm production and extended these to farmers in six Asian countries, including Bangladesh. An assessment of on-farm trials by Deb and Dey (2006) shows yield gains of 78% in Bangladesh, achieved without any increase in production costs. Using economic surplus methods, Deb and Dey (2006) quantified the benefits from and costs of research and dissemination by WorldFish and its partners in all six countries and obtained an internal rate of return of 70.2%.

4. SOCIAL IMPACTS

4.1 Poverty impact pathways

The primary goal of agricultural research during the GR era was to increase food production. Historically, this led to a focus on food grains in high potential areas where the quickest and highest returns to R&D could be expected. This strategy was extremely successful in achieving its primary goal in South Asia. Additionally, it helped cut poverty in the region during the 1970s and 1980s—from 59.1% of the population in 1975 to 43.1% in the early 1990s (Rosegrant and Hazell, 2000). But it did not eliminate poverty or malnutrition, and today, despite the fact that most South Asian countries now have plentiful national food supplies, poverty is still a major problem. About 450 million South Asians currently live below the $1/day poverty line (about the same as in 1975), and 80% of these are rural and obtain at least part of their livelihood from agriculture and allied activities (World Bank, 2007; Ahmed et al., 2008). The agricultural research systems have responded to this problem by targeting more of their research toward the problems of small farmers and the rural poor, hopefully enhancing poverty-reducing impacts.

Given the complex causes underlying poverty and the diversity of livelihoods found among poor people, the relationship between agricultural research and poverty alleviation is necessarily complex. There are a number of pathways through which improved technologies could potentially benefit the poor (Hazell and Haddad, 2001). Within adopting regions, research could help poor farmers directly through increased own-farm production, providing more food and nutrients for their own consumption and increasing the output of marketed products for greater farm income. Small farmers and landless laborers could gain additional agricultural employment opportunities and higher wages within adopting regions. Research could also empower the poor by increasing their access to decision-making processes, enhancing their capacity for collective action, and reducing their vulnerability to economic shocks via asset accumulation.

Agricultural research could also benefit the poor in less direct ways. Growth in adopting regions could create employment opportunities for migrant workers from other less dynamic regions. It could also stimulate growth in the rural and urban nonfarm economy with benefits for a wide range of rural and urban poor people. Research could lead to lower food prices for all types of poor people. It could also improve poor peoples' access to foods that are high in nutrients and crucial to their well-being—particularly poor women.

But agricultural research could also work against the poor. Some technologies are more suited to larger farms, and some input-intensive technologies that are, in principle, scale-neutral could nevertheless favor large farms because of their better access to irrigation water, fertilizers, seeds, and credit. Some technologies (e.g., mechanization and herbicides) could displace labor, leading to lower earnings for agricultural workers. By favoring some regions or farmers over others, technology could harm nonadopting farmers by lowering their product prices, even though only the adopting farmers benefit from cost reductions.

Given that many of the rural poor are simultaneously farmers, paid agricultural workers, and net buyers of food and earn nonfarm sources of income, the impacts of technological change on their poverty status could be indeterminate, with households experiencing gains in some dimensions and losses in others. For example, the same household might gain from reduced food prices and from higher nonfarm wage earnings but lose from lower farm-gate prices and agricultural wages. Measuring net benefits to the poor requires a full household income analysis of direct and indirect impacts as well as consideration of the impacts on poor households that are not engaged in agriculture and/or who live outside adopting regions. Much of the controversy that exists in the literature about how R&D impacts the poor has arisen because too many studies have taken only a partial view of the problem.

There is a great deal of literature on the impacts of agricultural research on the poor in South Asia but hardly any impact studies that quantify the research costs of reducing poverty. Many studies focus on assessing changes in income distribution or poverty in areas where new technologies have been adopted, but only a few attempt linking changes in inequity or poverty to research expenditures. More recently, measures of poverty have also been expanded to include broader and less quantifiable social impacts such as empowerment and changes in social capital. One consequence is that if we focus only on quantitative studies that evaluate the impact of research investments, this section of this chapter would be very short indeed and would not do justice to the large amount of research that has been done on poverty issues or the large number of studies that shed useful light on how improved technologies can benefit the poor at farm and community levels. Those who invest in agricultural research need to know that relevant work has been undertaken with proven poverty reduction impacts in the field, even if we do not yet have much quantitative evidence to show which types of research give the best poverty impact per dollar invested.

4.2 Evidence on impacts within adopting regions

The initial experience with the Green Revolution in Asia stimulated a huge number of studies into how technological change affects poor farmers and landless workers within adopting regions. A number of village and household studies conducted soon after the release of Green Revolution technologies raised concern that large farms were the main beneficiaries of the technology and poor farmers were either unaffected or made worse off. More recent evidence shows mixed outcomes. Small farmers did lag behind large farmers in adopting GR technologies, yet many of them eventually did so. Many of these small-farm adopters benefited from increased production, greater employment opportunities, and higher wages in the agricultural and nonfarm sectors (Lipton with Longhurst, 1989). In some cases small farmers and landless laborers actually ended up gaining proportionally more income than larger farmers, resulting in a net improvement in the distribution of village income (e.g., Hazell and Ramasamy, 1991; Maheshwari, 1998; Thapa et al., 1992).

Freebairn (1995) reviewed 307 published studies on the Green Revolution and performed a meta-analysis. The primary concern of nearly all the studies that he reviewed was on changes in inequality and income distribution rather than absolute poverty, the latter emerging as a more important issue in the 1990s. Freebairn found that 40% of the studies he reviewed reported that income became more concentrated within adopting regions, 12% reported that it remained unchanged or improved, and 48% offered no conclusion. He also found there were more favorable outcomes in the literature on Asia than elsewhere and that within the Asian literature, Asian authors gave more favorable conclusions than non-Asian authors. Later studies did not report more favorable outcomes than earlier studies, thereby casting some doubt on the proposition that small farmers did adopt but later than large farms. However, it should be noted that Freebairn's analysis did not include repeat studies undertaken at the same sites over time, such as Hazell and Ramasamy (1991) and Jewitt and Baker (2007), both of whom found favorable longer-term impacts on inequality. Freebairn (1995) also found that micro-based case studies reported the most favorable outcomes, whereas macro-based essays reported the worst outcomes.

Walker (2000) argues that reducing inequality is not the same thing as reducing poverty and might be much more difficult to achieve through agricultural R&D. More recent studies focusing directly on poverty confirm that improved technologies do impact favorably on many small farmers, but the gains for the smallest farms and landless agricultural workers can be too small to raise them above poverty thresholds (Hossain et al., 2007; Mendola, 2007). However, the poor can benefit in other ways, too. Hossain et al. (2007) found that in Bangladesh, the spread of HYV rice helped reduce the vulnerability of the poor by stabilizing employment earnings, reducing food prices and their seasonal fluctuations, and enhancing their ability to cope with natural disasters. In India, Bantilan and Padmaja (2008) found that the spread of ICRISAT's groundnut improvement technology, based on a raised bed and furrow concept, helped increase social networking and collective action within adopting villages, and this proved especially helpful to poor farmers and women in accessing farm inputs, credit, and farm implements as well as sharing knowledge. Use of participatory research methods in the selection of improved rice varieties in Uttar Pradesh, India, has been shown to empower women as decision makers in their farming and family roles as well as leading to greater adoption of improved varieties (Paris et al., 2008).

The lessons from many past studies might have less relevance today because of the changing nature of the livelihoods of the rural poor in South Asia. With rapid growth in nonfarm opportunities in much of South Asia and shrinking farm sizes, farming and agricultural employment have become less important in the livelihood strategies of the rural poor (Nargis and Hossain, 2006; Kajisa and Palanichamy, 2006; Lanjouw and Shariff, 2004). Within this new context, many poor people with limited access to land gain more from nonfarm opportunities than from productivity gains or wage earnings in farming, though investments in education and access to capital are often crucial for accessing such opportunities (World Bank, 2007; Nargis and Hossain, 2006; Kajisa and

Palanichamy, 2006; Krishna, 2005). This is not to say that publicly funded agricultural research cannot still usefully be targeted to the problems of poor, part-time farmers. Hazell and Haddad (2001) identify several opportunities, including increasing the productivity of food staples to free up land and labor for other activities, improving the nutrient content of staples, developing new technologies for small-scale home gardening of micronutrient-rich food, and using participatory research methods to enhance the relevance of improved technologies for poor farmers. But questions arise about the efficacy of these kinds of interventions and whether they are cost effective in reducing poverty compared to alternative types of interventions. Answering these questions should be a priority for future impact studies.

4.3 Evidence of economy and sectorwide impacts

There is a large econometric literature that uses cross-country or time-series data to estimate the relationship between agricultural productivity growth and poverty. These studies generally find high poverty reduction elasticities for agricultural productivity growth. Thirtle, Lin, and Piesse (2002) estimate that each 1% increase in crop productivity reduces the number of poor people by 0.48% in Asia. For India, Ravallion and Datt (1996) estimate that a 1% increase in agricultural value added per hectare leads to a 0.4% reduction in poverty in the short run and 1.9% in the long run, the latter arising through the indirect effects of lower food prices and higher wages. Fan, Hazell, and Thorat (2000) estimate that each 1% increase in agricultural production in India reduces the number of rural poor by 0.24%. For South Asia, these poverty elasticities are still much higher for agriculture than for other sectors of the economy (World Bank, 2007; Hasan and Quibria, 2004).

There is some evidence that the poverty elasticity of agricultural growth may be diminishing because the rural poor are becoming less dependent on agriculture. In Pakistan, for example, agricultural growth was associated with rapid reductions in rural poverty in the 1970s and 1980s, but the incidence of rural poverty hardly changed in the 1990s despite continuing agricultural growth (Dorosh, et al. 2003). Dorosh, et al. (2003) show that this is partly because a growing share of the rural poor households (46% by 2001–2002) had become disengaged from agriculture; even small-farm households and landless agricultural worker households received about half their income from nonfarm sources.

Some of the studies reviewed in Section 3 that quantify the productivity impacts of public investments in agricultural R&D also assessed the impacts on poverty reduction and provide comparisons with other types of public investment. Fan et al. (1999) find that agricultural R&D investments in India have not only given the highest productivity returns in recent decades but have also lifted more people out of poverty per unit of expenditure than most other types of public investment (Table 5). Investments in agricultural R&D and rural roads dominate all others in terms of the size of their impacts and can be considered the best "win/win" strategies for achieving growth and poverty alleviation in India.

Fan et al. (2007) have used an econometric model to estimate the impact of rice research in India on poverty reduction, including providing a breakout of an estimate of IRRI's contribution. They find that about 5 million rural poor people have been lifted out of poverty each year as a result of rice improvement research in India. Using plausible attribution rules, they estimate that IRRI's research contribution accounts for significant shares of these annual reductions in the number of rural poor. In 1991, IRRI is attributed with lifting 2.73 million rural poor people out of poverty, but because of the lag structures in their model, the contribution declines over time to only 0.56 million rural poor in 1999. They calculate that the number of persons lifted out of poverty for each $1 million spent by IRRI declined from 59,040 in 1991 to 15,490 persons in 1999. This corresponds to an increase in the cost of raising each person out of poverty from $0.046/day in 1991 to $0.177/day in 1999.

Fan (2007) has also estimated the impact of agricultural research on urban poverty in India. He estimates that in 1970, accumulated agricultural research investments lifted 1.2 million urban poor out of poverty, and this annual reduction increased to 1.7 million by 1995. These numbers correspond to between 2% and 2.5% of the remaining urban poor each year. On a cost basis, 196 urban poor were lifted out of poverty in 1970 for each million rupees spent, and this had declined to 72 urban poor per million rupees by 1995. Since the same investment in research also lifted many rural poor out of poverty (see previous discussion), there is a double dividend that makes research investments especially attractive for reducing poverty.

Lower food prices and growth linkages to the nonfarm economy play a large role in most of the results cited, and these benefit the urban as well as the rural poor. These indirect impacts have sometimes proved more powerful and positive than the direct impacts of R&D on the poor within adopting regions (Hazell and Haddad, 2001). A question arises as to whether the power of these indirect benefits has diminished over time with market liberalization and greater diversification of South Asian economies. In addition, if unit production costs are not falling as in the past (as reflected in stagnating TFP growth), this will constrain future food price reductions. This is an issue that warrants further study.

4.4 Evidence of interregional disparities

Agricultural development in South Asia has not benefited all regions equally, and some of the poorest regions that depend on rain-fed agriculture were slow in benefiting from the GR (Prahladachar, 1983). The widening income gaps that resulted have been buffered to some extent by interregional migration. In India, the Green Revolution led to the seasonal migration of over a million agricultural workers each year from the eastern states to Punjab and Haryana (Oberai and Singh, 1980; Westley, 1986). These numbers were tempered in later years as the GR technology eventually spilled over into eastern India in conjunction with the spread of tube wells. In a study of the impact of the Green Revolution in a sample of Asian villages, David and Otsuka (1994) asked whether regional labor markets were able to spread the benefits between adopting and nonadopting villages and found that seasonal migration did go some way to fulfilling that role. But although migration can buffer widening income differentials between regions, it is rarely sufficient to avoid them. In India, for example, regional inequalities widened during the GR era (Galwani et al., 2007), and the incidence of poverty remains high in many less favored areas (Fan and Hazell, 2000).

4.5 Evidence of nutrition impacts

Agricultural research has been very successful in increasing the supply of food and reducing prices of food staples in South Asia. Making food staples more available and less costly has proved an important way through which poor people benefited from technological change in agriculture (Rosegrant and Hazell, 2000; Fan, Hazell, and Thorat, 1998; Fan, 2007). Several micro-level studies from the Green Revolution era in South Asia found that higher yields typically led to greater calorie and protein intake among rural households within adopting regions. For example, Pinstrup-Andersen and Jaramillo (1991) found that the spread of HYV rice in North Arcot district, South India, led to substantial increases over a 10-year period in the energy and protein consumption for farmers and landless workers. Their analysis showed that, after controlling for changes in nonfarm sources of income and food prices, about one third of the calorie increase could be attributed to increased rice production. Ryan and Asokan (1977) also found complementary net increases in protein and calorie availability as a result of GR wheat in the six major producing states of India, despite some reduction in the area of pulses grown.

More aggregate analysis of the impacts of rising incomes on diets and nutrient intake has proved more complex, particularly as concern has shifted from calorie and protein deficiencies to micro nutrients and broader nutritional well-being. Food price declines are, in general, good for households that purchase more food than they sell, since this amounts to an increase in their real income. Real income increases can be used to increase consumption of important staples and to purchase more diverse and nutritionally rich diets. However, a study of Bangladesh showed that a downward trend in the price of rice over the period 1973–1975 to 1994–1996 was accompanied by upward trends in the real prices of other foods that are richer in micronutrients, making these less accessible to the poor (Bouis, 2000). Similar patterns were observed in India during the 1970s and 1980s, when farmers diverted land away from pulses to wheat and rice, leading to sharp increases in the price of pulses and a drop in their per capita consumption (Kennedy and Bouis, 1993; Kataki, 2002).

Since then there have been substantial changes in food intake patterns in rural India. In particular, the share of cereals in total food expenditure has declined while that of milk, meat, vegetables, and fruits has increased. Per capita consumption of cereals has also fallen in absolute terms (Nasurudeen et al., 2006). It is significant that these substitutions occurred among both the rich and the poor; not only do the top 25% spend relatively greater amounts on milk, meat, and other nutrient-rich foods, the decline in the share of staples is also apparent among the poorest 25% (J. V. Meenakshi, personal communication). However, since deficiencies in iron and the B-vitamins are common among the poor, the increases in micronutrient-rich foods must not always have been high enough to offset the decline from cereals. Other micronutrient deficiencies exist (e.g., vitamins C and D), but these are not related to reductions in cereal consumption.

Agricultural research has been directed at the problem of enhancing the nutritional quality of the diets of the poor. The main research strategies are:
• Improvements in the productivity of fruits, vegetables, livestock, and fish, both in home gardens and ponds for on-farm consumption and more generally to increase the marketed supplies of these nutrient-rich foods
• Promotion of food-crop biodiversity, especially traditional crops and cultivars that are rich in nutrients
• Biofortification of major food staples

Ali and Hau's (2001) assessment of the World Vegetable Centre's program in Bangladesh showed significant improvements in nutrition among participating farm families as well as increased supplies and lower prices of vegetables in the market. However, they also find that, although home gardens can increase incomes as well as improve nutritional intake, they are not sufficient to improve nutrition to desired levels, and there is still need for nutritional education. After reviewing 30 agricultural interventions (including six from South Asia) to improve nutrition among participating families, Berti et al. (2004) also concluded that interventions need to be complemented by investments in nutrition education and health services and targeted in ways that empower women with additional spending power.

Biofortification research is relatively new, and the CGIAR and its national partners are working together on some aspects of this research under the aegis of the Harvest Plus Challenge Program (Bouis et al., 2000). It is rather early to measure any impacts, though one *ex ante* study has been completed (Meenakshi et al., 2007).

5. ENVIRONMENTAL IMPACTS

5.1 Environmental impact pathways

Agricultural growth can impact the environment in many ways, and it is helpful to distinguish between the problems associated with intensive irrigated and high-potential rain-fed areas, where agricultural growth is largely of the land intensification (yield increasing) type, and the problems of less favored or backward areas, where agricultural growth is often of the expansionary (land increasing) type, even though the problems of the two types can sometimes overlap. The drivers of change and the appropriate research and policy responses are quite different in these two environments (Hazell and Wood, 2008).

In less favored areas, crop area expansion is often realized by reductions in the length of fallows and by encroachment into forests and fragile lands (e.g., steep hillsides and watershed protection areas), resulting in land erosion, declining soil fertility, and loss of biodiversity. Expansionary pathways in South Asia are typically associated with areas of poor infrastructure and market access, poverty, and population pressure.

Agricultural intensification in high potential areas helps avoid the kinds of problems prevailing in many less favored areas. By increasing yields, it reduces pressure to expand the cropped area, helping to save forest and other fragile lands from agricultural conversion (Nelson and Maredia, 1999). But intensification often brings its own environmental problems. These include water contamination with nitrates and phosphates from fertilizers and manures, pesticide poisoning of people and wildlife, unsustainable extraction of irrigation water from rivers and groundwater, and loss of biodiversity within agriculture and at landscape levels (Santikarn Kaosa-Ard, Mingsan, and Rerkasem, 2000; Pingali and Rosegrant, 2001). Intensification pathways are associated with the GR and arise mostly in irrigated and high potential rain-fed areas.

Just how serious are the environmental problems associated with agriculture, and are they likely to undermine future production and South Asia's ability to feed itself? Measuring environmental impacts of research and technological change is difficult, and as a result good empirical evidence is fragmentary, often subjective, and sometimes in direct contradiction with the overall trends in agricultural productivity. The evidence that is available tells a mixed story.

Some good news is that despite continued agricultural growth, the total forest area in South Asia has changed little since 1990 (Table 11). Declines in Nepal, Pakistan, and Sri Lanka have been offset by forest expansion in India. There has, however, been a 10% decline in the total area of other woodland, including a 30% reduction in India, which might be a better indicator of the competition between tree cover and agricultural expansion, particularly in less favored areas.

Less encouraging are several international land assessment exercises that have reported widespread degradation of most types of agricultural land in South Asia. The Global Land Assessment of Degradation (GLASOD) mapping exercise of Oldeman, Hakkeling, and Sombroek (1991) found that 43% of South Asia's agricultural land was degraded to some degrees. Young (1993) subsequently revisited these estimates using additional national data and claimed the problem was actually more severe and that nearly three quarters of the agricultural land area was degraded to some extent, with 40% moderately or severely degraded (Table 12). Degradation associated with

Table 11 Change in extent of forest and other wooded land by country (1000 ha), 1990–2005

Country	Forest			Other Wooded Land		
	1990	2000	2005	1990	2000	2005
Bangladesh	882	884	871	44	53	58
Bhutan	3035	3141	3195	566	609	611
India	63,939	67,554	67,701	5894	4732	4110
Nepal	4817	3900	3636	1180	1753	1897
Pakistan	2527	2116	1902	1191	1323	1389
Sri Lanka	2350	2082	1933	0	0	0
Total	77,580	79,677	79,238	8875	8470	8065

Source: FAO (2005).

Table 12 Extent of degradation of agricultural land in South Asia[10]

Type of Degradation	Total That Is Degraded (%)	Total That Is Moderately or Severely Degraded (%)
Water erosion	25	15
Wind erosion	18	13.9
Soil fertility decline	13	1.3
Waterlogging	2	1.5
Salinization	9	6.5
Lowering of water table	6	2.4
Total	73	40.6

Source: Young (1993) as summarized by Scherr (1999).

irrigation accounts for 23% of the total degraded area and for 25% of the moderately or severely degraded area. For India, Sehgal and Abrol (1994) estimated that 64% of the land area is degraded to some extent, with 54% moderately to severely degraded.

Although these data provide a useful warning, they do not tell us much about the causes. Agriculture is only one contributing factor; others include geological processes (especially in the Himalayas), mining, road construction, and urban and industrial encroachment. Even where agriculture is responsible, we need to separate out the land degradation due to agricultural extensification versus agricultural intensification. It is also hard to reconcile some of these estimates with the continuing growth in average yields and land productivity across South Asia. Although there are reports of hotspot areas where degradation is adversely affecting both the productivity and sustainability of land, there must be large areas where agricultural productivity is not adversely affected and where the problems are overstated. Some of the problem areas are intensively farmed irrigated areas, but many are rain-fed farming areas that, especially in the Himalayas and semi-arid areas, are farmed more extensively.

More detailed data are available on the impact of irrigation on the waterlogging and salinization of irrigated land:

- About 4.2 million hectares of irrigated lands (26% total) are affected by salinization in Pakistan (Ghassemi et al., 1995). Chakravorty (1998) claims that one third of the irrigated area in Pakistan is subject to waterlogging and that 14% is saline. Salinity retards plant growth, and he also claims agricultural output is lower by about 25% than it would otherwise be.
- Dogra (1986) estimates that in India nearly 4.5 million hectares of irrigated land are affected by salinization and a further 6 million hectares by waterlogging. India had about 57 million hectares of net irrigated land in the late 1990s. Umali (1993), quoted in CGIAR (2001, page 13), claims that 7 million hectares of arable land have been abandoned in India because of excessive salts.
- In a random sample of 110 farmers from four villages in Uttar Pradesh, Joshi and Jha (1991) found a 50% decline in crop yields over eight years due to salinization and waterlogging in irrigation systems.

Even more worrying for irrigated agriculture is the threat from the growing scarcity of fresh water in much of South Asia. Many countries are approaching the point at which they can no longer afford to allocate two thirds or more of their fresh water supplies to agriculture (Comprehensive Assessment of Water Management in Agriculture, 2007). Most of the major river systems in South Asia are already fully exploited, and the massive expansion of tubewell irrigation in Bangladesh, India, and Pakistan has led to serious overdrawing of groundwater and falling water tables. On the Indian subcontinent, groundwater withdrawals have surged from less than 20 cubic kilometers to more than 250 cubic kilometers per year since the 1950s (Shah et al., 2003). More than a fifth of groundwater aquifers are overexploited in Punjab, Haryana, Rajasthan, and Tamil Nadu, and groundwater levels are falling (World Bank, 2007; Postel, 1993). Even as current water supplies are stretched, the demands for industry, urban household use, and environmental purposes are growing (Comprehensive Assessment of Water Management in Agriculture, 2007; Rosegrant and Hazell, 2000). It would seem that either farmers must learn to use irrigation water more sparingly and more sustainably or the irrigated area will have to contract.

Finally, as discussed in Section 3, there is growing evidence from long-term crop trials and declining TFP of the adverse impact of environmental stress on crop yields in some GR areas. This may be the result of the formation of hard pans in the subsoil, soil toxicity buildups (especially iron), and micronutrient deficiencies (especially zinc; Pingali, Hossain, and Gerpacio, 1997).

5.2 The R&D response

A growing awareness of these environmental problems has led to significant changes in agricultural R&D in South Asia since the early GR years. It has led to the entry of environmentally oriented NGOs, some of which have contested the GR approach and undertaken research and extension activities of their own to broaden the spectrum of technologies and farming practices available to farmers. The national and international R&D systems have also invested heavily in natural resource management research and technologies and management practices for improving water, pest, and soil fertility management.

One of the outcomes of greater NGO involvement has been a lively debate about competing farming paradigms, and "alternative" farming[11] has been offered as a more sustainable and environmentally friendly alternative to the modern input-based approach associated with the Green Revolution. The alternative farming approach includes extremes that eschew use of any modern inputs as a matter of principle (e.g., organic farming) but also includes more eclectic whole-farming systems approaches such as low external input (LEI) farming (Tripp, 2006) and ecoagriculture (McNeely and Scherr, 2003). Kasavan and Swaminathan (2007) provide a useful review of these approaches.

The alternative farming literature provides many successful examples of agricultural intensification, but most of these have arisen in rain-fed farming systems that largely missed out on the GR. We review several of these experiences in Section 5.4 on less favored areas. But by sleight of aggregation, proponents of alternative agriculture frequently mix these kinds of successes with much more modest results obtained in GR areas, giving the impression that productivity levels can be increased significantly across the board by switching to alternative farming approaches. In fact, most alternative farming approaches cannot match the high productivity levels achieved by modern farming methods in Green Revolution areas. Pretty et al. (2007), in a revisit of Pretty et al. (2003), examine yield claims for 286 sustainable agriculture projects disaggregated into eight farming systems categories developed by Dixon et al. (2001) and show that the more sizeable gains nearly all arose within rain-fed farming systems. Moreover, the gains reported for rice and wheat yields, the main GR crops, were modest, sometimes even negative.

Despite significant R&D investments in environmentally oriented research of both paradigms, there are very few impact studies of the value of that work. As with poverty impact assessment, the state of the art in assessing environmental impacts in ways that can be quantified in social cost/benefit calculations is still poorly developed. This is partly because of difficulties in measuring environmental changes over the time spans and levels of scale required as well as because of difficulties in assigning economic values to changes, even when they can be measured (Freeman et al., 2005). The few impact studies that exist either report changes in selected physical indicators or rely on farmers' perceptions of change in resource or environmental conditions. However, these are sufficient to demonstrate that relevant work has been undertaken with proven productivity and environmental impacts in the field, even though we do not yet have calculations of the rates of return to those investments to show which types of institutions or research give the best returns.

In reviewing these developments and their impacts, we continue with the useful distinction between intensively farmed GR areas and extensively farmed less favored areas.

5.3 Evidence of impact in Green Revolution areas

Only a few GR critics argue for a drastic reversal from GR to traditional technologies of the kinds that dominated South Asia before the GR (e.g., Shiva, 1991; Nellithanam et al., 1998). Such authors claim that yield growth rates were already high before the GR but ignore the fact that this was largely the result of the spread of irrigation and fertilizers prior to the introduction of HYVs (Evenson et al., 1999). More generally, R&D has contributed to a broad range of technologies for improving soil, water, and pest management in GR areas that span the spectrum from zero use of modern inputs to high but precision managed use.

5.3.1 Organic farming

Despite widespread publicity to the contrary, organic farming (OF) seems to have little to offer farmers in GR areas who want to continue to grow cereals. A recent study (Halberg et al., 2006, page 40) concludes: "In high yielding regions with near to economic optimal inputs of fertilizers and pesticides the yields of organic farming are between 15–35% lower than present yields when comparing single crops, and possibly at the low end (35%) when including crop failures and the need for green manure in crop rotations."[12] This statement draws heavily on results from temperate countries, and crop losses could be even higher in tropical countries because of greater problems with pest and disease control. The same study concludes that OF has more to offer farmers in less intensively farmed areas, such as many LFAs, or farmers who can benefit from price premiums for organically produced foods. Zundel and Kilcher (2007) report somewhat lower yield losses for OF in temperate and irrigated areas but do not allow for crop failures and diversion of land to produce green manure and other organic matter.

Badgley et al. (2007) reviewed a large number of published studies comparing organic and conventional crops. Although they claim organically grown grains in developing countries have an average yield advantage of 57%, the more detailed results in their Table A1 tell a more nuanced story. Organically grown rice under irrigated conditions in South Asian countries showed little if any yield gain. The best OF yield gains for South Asia were obtained on upland rice and for maize and sorghum grown under rain-fed conditions. These are areas where the conventionally grown crops usually receive limited nutrient inputs of any kind and hence have low yields.

5.3.2 System of rice intensification (SRI)

SRI was developed in the early1980s by Henri de Laulanie, a French missionary priest in Madagascar, as another alternative farming approach to the available GR rice technologies for small farmers. It has since been widely promoted by a number of NGOs and the International Institute for Food, Agriculture, and Development (IIFAD) at Cornell University (http://ciifad.cornell.edu/sri). Not only was SRI initially developed outside the international and public sector research system, but if its claimed benefits proved true, it would render irrelevant much of the research on intensive rice farming that has been conducted in recent decades by the public and international R&D systems. Not surprisingly, SRI has attracted the attention of the scientific and donor communities and sparked a lively debate and research agenda.

The main components of SRI are transplanting of young seedlings (8–15 days instead of three to four weeks) on small hills at much lower plant densities than usual; water management that keeps the soil moist rather than flooded; frequent weeding; and use of high rates of organic compost for fertilizer.

The claimed benefits include high yields, even with traditional rice varieties, a significant savings in seed; little or no artificial fertilizer required; natural pest and disease control, eliminating the need for pesticides; reduced water use; and a flexible management that allows farmers to experiment and adapt the approach to their particular growing conditions. The approach is claimed to be environmentally sustainable and of particular relevance for poorer farmers who cannot afford modern inputs (Uphoff, 2003).

Controversy has arisen because of claims of very high yields, sometimes exceeding the best experiment station yields for modern rice technologies, sometimes even without the use of fertilizer or modern varieties. These high yields defy current understanding of the physiology of rice plant growth (Sheehy et al., 2005). Proponents argue that there are strong synergies between the various management components of SRI that lead to strong root growth and higher yields, although these synergies are not well understood (Mishra et al., 2006).

Few of the yield claims have been verified under controlled experimental conditions. Trials undertaken at IRRI found no significant yield differences between SRI and conventional GR practices (quoted in Namara et al., 2003). McDonald et al. (2006) analyzed 40 sets of field trial results reported in the literature (5 from Madagascar and 35 from 11 Asian countries), which compared SRI with "best management practices" appropriate to each site. Apart from the five Madagascar studies, which consistently showed higher yields with SRI, SRI led to an average yield loss of 11% in the other 35 studies, with a range of −61% to 22%.

Yield gains appear to be better in farm adoption studies. Farmers in Ratnapura and Kurunegala districts in Sri Lanka obtained 44% higher yields, on average, with SRI than with modern rice farming methods (Namara et al., 2003), and the average yield gain was 32% for farmers in the Purila district of West Bengal (Sinha and Talati, 2007). However, in both studies SRI farmers showed considerable variation in the management methods they used, making it rather unclear as to what was being compared in the name of SRI. For example, many SRI farmers used inorganic fertilizer as well as compost, many grew modern as well as traditional rice varieties, and their weeding and water management practices varied considerably.

SRI has yet to be widely adopted in any one country, although it can be found on small scales in many countries, including many parts of South Asia.[13] Some of the reasons for poor uptake include the difficulties of controlling water with sufficient precision in many surface irrigation systems, the need for large amounts of compost, and the high labor demands for transplanting, hand weeding,[14] and generating and distributing compost. This is confirmed by available adoption studies. In Sri Lanka, adoption is positively related to family size (availability of labor) and ownership of animals (availability of manure) and is more common among rain-fed than irrigated rice farmers (Namara et al. 2003). Moser and Barrett (2003) obtained similar results in an adoption study in Madagascar. Moser and Barrett (2003), Namara et al. (2003), and Sinha and Talati (2007) all find that adopters only practice SRI on small parts of their rice area despite higher returns to both land and labor, and they also find high rates of disadoption. This again suggests important constraints, possibly labor or suitability of available irrigation systems, as well as disappointing returns.

5.3.3 Improved nutrient management

More pragmatic approaches to intensive farming seek to increase the efficiency of fertilizer use rather than displace it, thereby reducing production costs and environmental problems. Fertilizer efficiency can be improved through more precise matching of nutrients with plant needs during the growing season and by switching to improved fertilizers such as controlled release fertilizers and deep placement technologies.

Site-specific nutrient management (SSNM) was developed by IRRI and its partners as a way of reducing fertilizer use, raising yields, and avoiding nitrate runoff and greenhouse gas emissions (especially nitrous oxide) from intensive rice paddies (Pampolina et al., 2007). Developed in the mid-1990s, SSNM is a form of precision farming that aims to apply nutrients at optimal rates and times—taking account of other sources of nutrients in the field and the stage of plant growth—to achieve high rice yields and high efficiency of nutrient use by the crop. Farmers apply N several times over the growing period and use leaf color charts to determine how much N to apply at different stages. SSNM has been tested through on-farm trials in several Asian countries, and IRRI has developed practical manuals and a website (http://www.irri.org/irrc/ssnm) to guide application.

Pampolino et al. (2007) provide an economic assessment of SSNM compared to farmers' usual fertilizer practices. They undertook focus group discussions with adopting and nonadopting farmers at sites in India and two sites in Southeast Asia. For India, yields of adopting farmers were found to be 17% higher. Modest savings in fertilizer use were largely offset by higher labor costs, but profit per hectare was 48% higher. There was also a useful reduction in nitrous oxide emissions, a powerful greenhouse gas. In an impact study in West Bengal, India, Islam et al. (2007) found small but not significant increases in yields but 20% savings in nitrogen use and 50% savings in pesticide use, as well as economic benefits of $19–27/ha, depending on the season.

The International Fertilizer Development Center (IFDC) has been pioneering urea deep placement (UDP) technology in rice. This involves the deep placement of urea in the form of supergranules or small briquettes into puddled soil shortly after transplanting the rice (Bowen et al., 2005). The method improves N-use efficiency by keeping most of the urea N in the soil close to the plant roots and out of the floodwater, where it is susceptible to loss. On-farm trials in Bangladesh that compared UDP with standard urea broadcasting practices showed 50–60% savings in urea use and yield increases of about 1 t/ha (Bowen et al., 2005). The briquettes are also simple to make with small pressing machines and can create additional local employment. Adoption data are not available, but the approach appears to be spreading in Bangladesh with the active support of the government.

5.3.4 Low or zero tillage (ZT)

In response to the declining growth in productivity of the rice/wheat farming system in the Indo-Gangetic Plain (IGP), zero tillage (ZT) has been adapted and introduced by the Rice-Wheat Consortium (RWC), a partnership of CGIAR centers and the NARS from Bangladesh, India, Nepal, and Pakistan. The technology involves the direct planting of wheat after rice, without any land preparation. Rice crop residues from the previous season are left on the ground as mulch. The wheat seed is typically inserted together with small amounts of fertilizer into slits made with a special tractor-drawn seed drill. The technology has many claimed advantages over conventional tillage in the rice/wheat system: It saves labor, fertilizer, and energy; minimizes planting delays between crops; conserves soil; reduces irrigation water needs; increases tolerance to drought; and reduces greenhouse gas emissions (Erenstein et al., 2007; World Bank, 2007). However, it often requires some use of herbicides for general weed control. A key ingredient for its success has been the development of an appropriate seed drill for local conditions in the IGP.

In an assessment of the technology based on a sample of farmers in Haryana, India, and Punjab, Pakistan, Erenstein et al. (2007) find that ZT adoption has been rapid. In Haryana, 34.5% of the sampled farmers had adopted ZT in 2003–2004 and 19.4% in the Punjab, even though diffusion of the technology began only around 2000.

Adopting farmers used the technology on large shares of their total wheat areas. Adoption has been highest on larger farms with tractors. The study finds mixed results for yield gains and water savings (more significant in Haryana than the Punjab), but all farms made drastic savings in tractor and fuel costs. There were no observed impacts on the following rice crop. Although the technology is attractive to farmers, the high percentage of nonadopting farmers, together with disadoption rates of 10–15%, suggests continuing constraints on its use. No one factor was clearly identified in the study, but access to tractors and ZT seed drills is important, especially for smaller farms. Rental markets for these machines exist but might not offer farmers sufficient flexibility in the timing of their operations, which is crucial if higher yields are to be obtained. Other ZT assessments from adoption studies, on-farm trials, and focus group discussions confirm the large savings in tractor and fuel costs, and most show significant water savings and yield gains (Laxmi et al., 2007; Laxmi and Mishra, 2007).

It is estimated that about 200,000 ha of wheat were planted under zero tillage in the Pakistan IGP in 2001–2002 and 820,000 ha in the Indian IGP in 2003–2004 (about 8% of the total wheat area). The latter had doubled by 2004–2005 (Laxmi et al., 2007). Based on an estimated ceiling adoption rate of 33%, Laxmi et al. (2007) undertook an economic assessment of the likely returns to the research costs incurred by the RWC partners in developing the technology for India's IGP. Even with conservative assumptions about yield gains and cost savings (6% and 5%, respectively), the estimated benefit/cost ratio is 39 and the internal rate of return is 57%. With more optimistic assumptions (yield gains and cost savings of 10%), the benefit/cost ratio increases to 68 and the IRR to 66%. This analysis does not include any environmental benefits.

5.3.5 Improved water management
Improved water management in South Asian agriculture is essential for redressing growing water scarcities, improving water quality, and halting the degradation of additional irrigated land. This will require significant and complementary changes in policies, institutions, and water management technologies. Agricultural research has been conducted on all three aspects, although little of this research has been subjected to impact analyses.

Technical research has shown the potential to increase yields in irrigated farming with substantial savings in water use (e.g., Mondal et al., 1993; Guerra et al., 1998). Realizing these gains is easiest when farmers have direct control over their water supplies, as with tubewell irrigation or small-scale farmer-managed irrigation schemes. For larger schemes the best hope lies in the devolution of water management to local water user groups or associations, an approach known as *irrigation management transfer* (IMT).

IMT began to be adopted in some South Asian countries during the late 1980s as a response to the disappointing performance of many large-scale irrigation schemes. It was hoped that IMT would increase the accountability of water irrigation services to farmers, encourage greater farmer input into the maintenance of irrigation systems, improve cost recovery, and enable improved control of water at local levels. All this was expected to lead to higher water use efficiency, increased agricultural productivity, better environmental outcomes, and irrigation schemes that were more financially sustainable.

Despite the promise, there was little hard evidence to show that IMT did in fact lead to these realized benefits. IWMI therefore embarked on a set of studies in 1992 to monitor and evaluate the experience with IMT and provide guidelines for its successful implementation in the future. The results from the Asian case studies proved disappointing. Sri Lanka, which began to implement IMT in 1988, is typical of the results obtained. Samad and Vermillion (1999) surveyed irrigation schemes that had been transferred and some that had not, within each of which were schemes that were rehabilitated and some that were not. The findings suggest only modest gains to farmers or the sustainability of irrigation schemes. Farmers in IMT areas did not incur additional water supply costs, nor did they perceive any improvements in the quality of water services they received from their irrigation agency. There were significant gains in yields, land, and water productivity in some IMT areas, but the best results were obtained in schemes that were both rehabilitated and transferred to producer organizations. Simply devolving management without also rehabilitating the irrigation schemes achieved little.

Following these mixed findings, IWMI embarked on a follow-up program of research to identify best-practice approaches from around the developing world. Within South Asia, IWMI subsequently provided policy advice to the governments of Sri Lanka and Nepal in developing national IMT strategies and engaged in action research in Pakistan and Sri Lanka to help improve implementation policies. This led to the development with FAO of a handbook on best practice (Vermillion and Sagardoy, 1999) and to a number of guideline papers on specific implementation issues.

A subsequent assessment of IWMI's work on IMT is provided by Giordano et al. (2007). They claim significant impact on water policies in Nepal and Sri Lanka and some success in affecting the employment of improved techniques in Pakistan and Nepal. They also report high demand for IWMI's guideline publications on IMT.

5.3.6 Integrated pest management (IPM)

Pest problems emerged as an important problem during the early GR era because many of the first released HYVs had poor resistance to some important pests. The problem was compounded by a shift to higher cropping intensities, monocropping, high fertilizer use (which creates dense, lush canopies in which pests can thrive), and the planting of large adjacent areas to similar varieties with a common susceptibility. Control was initially based on prophylactic chemical applications, driven by the calendar rather than incidence of pest attack. This approach disrupted the natural pest/predator balance and led to a resurgence of pest populations that required even more pesticide applications to control. Problems were compounded by the buildup of pest resistance to the commonly used pesticides. As pesticide use increased, so did environmental and health problems. Rola and Pingali (1993) found that the health costs of pesticide use in rice reached the point at which they more than offset the economic benefits of pest control.

As these problems began to emerge, researchers gave greater attention to the development of crop varieties that have good resistance to important pests and biological and ecological pest control methods. This led to the development of integrated pest management (IPM), an approach that integrates pest-resistant varieties, natural control mechanisms, and the judicious use of some pesticides. The CGIAR centers have been important sources of research on IPM, and IRRI has been especially important for IPM in rice in Asia (Waibel, 1999).

Bangladesh has been in the forefront of IPM since 1981, and the government, with assistance from FAO, has aggressively promoted the approach through farmers' training schools. Sabur and Molla (2001) undertook a farm survey in 1997–1998 and found that IPM farmers used less than half the amount of pesticides on rice as non-IPM farmers and had significantly higher gross income per hectare. Similar results were obtained by Susmita et al. (2007) and by Rasul and Thapa (2003). Both studies found that IPM farmers saved significantly on costs (labor and pesticides). None of the studies reports any significant productivity impact from use of IPM, so the main economic benefits arise from lower costs. Farmers perceived fewer health problems with IPM in all three studies, though neither Susmita et al. (2007) or Rasul and Thapa (2003) could find statistical differences between the perceptions of adopting and nonadopting farmers. None of the studies provides any data on environmental impacts.

There is no hard evidence to show that IPM has been widely adopted among South Asian farmers. There are two difficult constraints to overcome. One is farmer training. IPM is knowledge intensive, requiring farmers have the capability to identify harmful and beneficial insects and the ability to flexibly manage their response to pest attacks. Farmer field schools have had some success in providing the required training (Waibel, 1999; Tripp et al. 2006; Van Den Berg and Jiggins, 2007). But this can be a slow and expensive way of training large numbers of farmers, particularly if, as Tripp et al. (2006) found in Sri Lanka, knowledge-intensive methods such as IPM do not easily spread from farmer to farmer. The other constraint is the need for collective action among neighboring farmers. IPM cannot be successfully undertaken at single plot or farm levels but must be adopted at landscape levels. This is difficult to organize without effective community or producer organizations.

5.4 Evidence on impact in less favored areas

Following Pender and Hazell (2000), less favored areas (LFAs) are broadly defined in this paper to include lands that have been neglected by man as well as nature. They include marginal lands that are of low agricultural potential due to low and uncertain rainfall, poor soils, steep slopes or other biophysical constraints, and areas that may

Table 13 Classification of favored and less favored areas

Access to Markets and Infrastructure	Agricultural Potential	
	High	Low (Biophysical Constraints)
High	Favored areas	Marginal areas (LFA)
Low	Remote areas (LFA)	Marginal and remote less favored areas

have higher development potential but that are currently underexploited due to poor infrastructure and market access, low population density, or other socioeconomic constraints. Conceptually they include all the shaded areas in Table 13.

An attempt to operationalize this two-dimensioned concept of LFAs suggests that about one quarter of South Asia's rural population live in LFAs (World Bank, 2007, Chapter 2).

Much of the deforestation, woodland loss, and land degradation (including soil erosion and soil fertility loss) that has occurred in South Asia arose in LFAs that did not benefit much from the GR. This degradation is often driven by insufficient agricultural intensification relative to population growth. As more and more people seek to eke a living out of these areas, they expand cropping in unsustainable and erosive ways and fail to replenish the soil nutrients that they remove. Migration and nonfarm development have important roles to play in reducing pressures on the natural resource base, but more sustainable forms of agricultural growth are needed if the environmental problems in these areas are to be reversed.

LFAs also account for a significant share of the rural poor in South Asia. Precise estimation is difficult because poverty data are reported by administrative units rather than agroecological areas or farming systems. Fan and Hazell (2000) estimate that 41% of India's rural poor (76 million people) lived in LFAs in 1993, and ICRISAT estimates that 40% of India's rural poor live in the semi-arid tropics and another 16% in arid areas and semi-arid temperate areas (Rao et al., 2005). There is some controversy about whether the incidence of poverty is higher among LFA populations than in irrigated and high potential rain-fed areas, but since estimates range from "no significant difference" (Kelley and Rao, 1995) to higher concentrations of poor in LFAs (Fan and Hazell, 2000), this controversy need not detract from the importance of agricultural research for LFAs.

An early and appropriate (at that time) bias during the GR era toward R&D spending on irrigated areas and best rain-fed areas has changed. Pal and Byerlee (2006) found no evidence of any underinvestment (relative to irrigated areas) in rain-fed and marginal lands by 1996–1998. At a commodity level, Byerlee and Morris (1993) did not find any bias for wheat research, but Pandey and Pal (2007) found a modest bias against LFAs in the allocation of research scientists for rice research. These studies calculate desired research shares on the basis of congruency with agricultural or commodity outputs and not on the basis of poverty. An analysis based on poverty might tell a different story, but that would first require resolving the controversy about where the poor are most concentrated and an analysis of the relative merits of the indirect (e.g., food and labor market) benefits from investing in each type of area (Renkow, 2000). An environmental perspective might also justify greater investment in agricultural research in many LFAs.[15]

Most LFAs in South Asia are unsuitable for the kinds of intensive, monocrop farming associated with the GR. A lack of irrigation potential, erratic and often deficient rainfall, poor soils, and often sloped land make crops less responsive to fertilizers, and the fragility of the resource base requires more integrated and mixed farming approaches to avoid degradation. Economically, the remoteness of many LFAs from markets also makes modern inputs expensive relative to the prices farmers receive for their products. In this context, a lot of research has been targeted at improving NRM practices that conserve and efficiently use scarce water, control erosion, and restore soil fertility while using low amounts of external inputs. These kinds of technology improvements can lead to significant gains in productivity and stability while reversing some types of resource degradation. Within this context, there has been considerable convergence between the objectives and approaches of different farming paradigms for LFAs.

The analysis by Pretty et al. (2007) of yield claims for 286 sustainable agriculture projects from around the developing world show that the more sizeable gains nearly all arose within rain-fed farming systems. Some of the most successful projects for these areas included improved crop varieties, water harvesting, soil and water conservation at catchment or watershed levels, and use of organic residues for soil improvement. For South Asia, yield gains of 63% are reported for highland mixed farming systems in India, Nepal, Pakistan, and Sri Lanka, and 79% for rain-fed mixed farming systems in India.

Of 293 yield ratios for organic versus modern crop production methods reviewed by Badgley et al. (2007), only 10 have relevance to LFAs in South Asia. There are five ratios for upland rice (ranging from 1.23 in Pakistan to 3.4 in Nepal) and five for sorghum and millets in India (ranging from 1.65 to 3.5). Organic farming in these locations requires mixed farming, soil and water conservation, and use of organic residues for soil improvement.

Although there are grounds to be skeptical about the high yield levels claimed in some of these studies (Cassman, 2007), they are consistent with the fact that the existing farming systems are low yielding, usually because of low rates of application of fertilizers or organic matter and poor soil and water management. In these circumstances, many improved NRM practices that reverse land degradation, improve soil condition, and provide much-needed water and nutrients for crops can make a large difference, whether motivated by alternative or modern agricultural philosophies. Even so, one recent study undertaken in a backward and hilly area of Himachal Pradesh, India, found that though organically grown wheat and maize were more profitable than their modern production counterparts, this was nearly all due to a price premium of about 100% (Thakur and Sharma, 2005).

Important lines of research in LFAs involving CGIAR centers in South Asia include crop improvement, watershed development, and integrated soil nutrient management.

5.4.1 Crop improvement research

Much plant breeding for LFAs has focused on producing varieties that can withstand drought and poor soil conditions and that have greater pest and disease resistance. Such varieties can raise average yield response and reduce yield instability. They can also contribute to reductions in pesticide use and, by raising the productivity of food crops, help reduce the cropped area needed by subsistence-oriented farmers. This can reduce the pressure on more fragile lands and free up some land and labor for other activities. Most of ICRISAT's crop improvement research is directed at LFAs, and there are spill-in benefits to these areas from the crop improvement work that IRRI (upland rice), CIMMYT (maize), and CIP (potatoes) undertake more broadly in Asia.

At an aggregate level, there is evidence from India that crop improvement research is having favorable productivity and poverty impacts in many LFAs (Fan and Hazell, 2000). Based on an econometric analysis of time series data for three different types of agricultural areas (irrigated, high-potential rain-fed, and low-potential rain-fed), they find more favorable marginal returns (measured as rupees of agricultural production per additional hectare planted to modern varieties) for crop improvement research in low-potential rain-fed areas than in either high-potential rain-fed areas or irrigated areas. Moreover, additional crop research investment in low-potential rain-fed areas lifts more people out of poverty than in the other two types of areas. Fan, Hazell, and Haque (2000) provide a more nuanced set of results for 13 different types of rain-fed zones in India. They find seven zones where the benefit/cost ratio for additional crop-improvement research is greater than five and which also have favorable poverty impacts. Neither of these studies assesses environmental impacts.

The measured impacts of some of the commodity improvement work reviewed in Section 3.2 have arisen in LFAs (e.g., maize, sorghum, and millets), although the cited studies do not separate the impacts in LFAs from GR areas. However, a few examples illustrate the impacts of crop improvement research that was targeted to the specific problems of poor people in LFAs.

As mentioned earlier, Shiyani et al. (2002) found that ICRISAT improved chickpea varieties have been widely adopted in a poor tribal area in Gujarat, India, with favorable impacts on yields, unit production costs, and net returns per hectare.

ICRISAT's package of improved groundnut varieties grown in combination with improved agronomy practices built around a raised bed and furrow concept (see Table 9 and earlier discussion) is another example of a commodity improvement program that has paid off handsomely in a less favored area: in this case, the semi-arid tropical areas of central India. The high internal rate of return of about 25% reported by Joshi and Bantilan (1998) is seemingly robust to within a percentage point or two, even when corrected for possible positive and negative environmental outcomes that affect yield and production costs (Bantilan et al., 2005). This is one of the few available impact studies that attempts to value environmental impacts within a cost/benefit analysis framework.

5.4.2 Watershed development

There have been significant investments in research on watershed development in South Asia in recent decades. India began developing model operational research projects (ORPs) in a number of representative watersheds in the mid-1970s, and these were used to test and validate integrated watershed management approaches before they were scaled up in huge publicly funded schemes across the country. By 1999–2000, India had spent Rs. 35,915 million to develop 37 million ha, or 22% of the problem area (Babu and Dhyani, 2005), and by the late 1990s was spending about $500 million each year on additional watershed development projects (Kerr et al., 2002). The total had exceeded $2 billion by 1999–2000 (Joshi et al., 2004). ICRISAT and IWMI have both undertaken research on watershed development and related soil and water management issues and have been involved in watershed evaluation work.

There have been many evaluations of watershed development projects in India, though seemingly none on the returns to research on watershed development. Joshi et al. (2005) undertook a meta-analysis of 311 evaluation studies spanning a large number of types of projects and agroclimatic conditions. They found that the average benefit/cost ratio was 2.14 with a range of 0.8–7.1, and the average internal rate of return was 22% with a range of 1.4–94%. On average, the projects created additional employment of 181 days/ha/year, increased the irrigated area 34% and the cropping intensity 64%, and slowed soil losses by 0.82 t/ha/year. Among other things, the meta-analysis showed that the benefit/cost ratio was highest in areas with annual rainfall of between 700 and 1100 mm than in areas with low (less than 700 mm) or high (greater than 1100 mm) rainfall; 42% greater in macro watersheds (greater than 1250 ha) than micro; larger when state governments were involved in the planning and execution compared to purely central government projects; and higher when there was active people's participation.

Kerr et al. (2000) surveyed 86 villages in Maharashtra and Andhra Pradesh, some included in watershed projects and some not. Three types of projects were included: government (Ministry of Agriculture) run projects, NGO run projects, and collaboratively run projects between NGOs and state government. The government projects largely focused on technical improvements, NGO projects focused more on social organization, and the collaborative projects tried to draw on the strengths of both approaches. Qualitative and quantitative data were both collected, including data on conditions in the study villages before and after the projects were implemented.

Overall, the participatory NGO projects performed better than their technocratic, government run counterparts. However, participation combined with sound technical input performed best of all. For example, though all projects reduced soil erosion on uncultivated lands in their upper watersheds reasonably well, the NGO and NGO/government collaborative projects had particularly good records in this regard. Greater NGO and community involvement also helped ensure that project investments were maintained over time. Although definitive hydrological data were not available, farmers in villages in NGO and NGO/government projects frequently perceived that the projects' water-harvesting efforts increased the availability of water for irrigation and their net returns to rain-fed farming were higher.

6. POLICY IMPACTS

The economic transformation of South Asia in recent years and the huge success of the GR have necessitated some major changes in agricultural policies. With market liberalization the established roles of the state in marketing, storing, and distributing food, providing farm credit and modern inputs, and regulating international trade and agro-industry have all been challenged. The rapid emergence of high-value agriculture and the seriousness of some of the environmental problems associated with agriculture have also required new policy responses. As governments have sought to navigate these turbulent waters, there has been an important opportunity for policy research to help inform the debate.

A vast policy research literature written during this period in South Asia is testament to the prolific response of the region's own researchers. The CGIAR centers have also been active participants, including through networking endeavors, such as that created by IFPRI, in the Policy Analysis and Advisory Network for South Asia (PAANSA), described in an evaluative manner by Paarlberg (2005) at www.ifpri.org/impact/ia24. pdf. ICRISAT, IRRI, and IWMI, for example, have contributed many policy studies for improving adoption of improved technologies, NRM, and IPM (Pingali et al., 1997; Pingali and Rosegrant, 2001). IWMI has contributed to improved understanding of water policies, from river basin management and management of irrigation schemes to water management in farmers' fields. ICRISAT has worked on policy issues related to mechanization, risk and technology design, herbicides and equity, marketing, credit policies, and watershed management. IFPRI has contributed to many of these issues and to a wide range of other policy issues, including market and trade policy reform, public investment, food subsidies, and environmental issues. Other external agencies such as the World Bank and Asian Development Bank have also made many important analytical contributions.

It is difficult to tease out the impact of all this policy research and even more so to try and attribute any impact to the CGIAR centers. Many of the policy reforms are not yet complete (e.g., the phasing out of key input subsidies and reform of water policies), and some might have been implemented anyway without the benefit of policy research. Fortunately, a few impact assessments have been undertaken that shed some light on the value of policy research in South Asia in recent years.

6.1 Water policy

IWMI's work on irrigation management transfer (IMT) has already been reviewed in Section 5.3. Giordano et al. (2006) show that this work led to significant impact on water policies in Sri Lanka and had some success in affecting the employment of improved techniques in Pakistan and Nepal. They also report high demand for IWMI's guideline publications on IMT.

6.2 Bangladesh: Changing the course of food and agricultural policy

During 1989–1994, IFPRI placed a small team of researchers in Bangladesh to collaborate with the Ministry of Food on a set of research activities to guide aspects of the market liberalization program. The impact of this program is reviewed by Babu (2000). A study of the comparative advantages of various crops guided the development of a new strategy aimed at diversifying agriculture. Studies of rice and wheat markets found that the government could turn grain procurement and sales over to the private sector without harming the food security of the poor. When the government opened the grain markets to private sector participation, it saved $37 million by lowering the official procurement price.

An IFPRI study of the rural food ration program uncovered poor management and substantial leakages. The government had long been aware that the ration program was not effectively reaching its intended beneficiaries—the rural poor—and the study put hard numbers to the government's suspicions. By eliminating the program, the government saved $60 million. Some of these savings were used to increase expenditures on other, better targeted food and nutrition programs, including the innovative Food-for-Education program. Later evaluations found that this program raised school attendance about 30%. Besides these policy changes, the research resulted in other, more effective programs and strategies and saved the government at least $100 million, many times the research cost of less than $5 million (Babu, 2000; Ryan and Meng, 2004). Moreover, the collaboration increased the body of knowledge on food policy in Bangladesh and the number of people equipped to make use of it by producing more than 70 research reports and providing training in food policy analysis to over 200 individuals.

6.3 Pakistan: Examining the effectiveness of subsidies

In collaboration with the Pakistan Institute of Development Economics (PIDE) and the Pakistan Ministry of Food and Agriculture (MINFA), IFPRI's research and policy dialogue were instrumental in changing the direction of food and agricultural policies in Pakistan. The impact of the program is reviewed by Islam and Garrett (1997). From 1986–1994, this collaboration produced a large body of research—over 80 journal articles and research manuscripts—that policymakers drew on as they made policy decisions. IFPRI's research, from 1986–1991, resulted in over $200 million in savings to the government. The total cost of research for the entire period was only about $6 million.

IFPRI's work on the wheat ration shop program provides a clear example of the changes Pakistan made in its food policies. In this program, poor consumers were able to buy subsidized wheat from special shops. By the 1980s the government was spending millions on a program that was, by most accounts, corrupt and ineffective. Policymakers wanted to know whether the program helped the poor or not and what the effects on the poor would be if the program were eliminated. In a national survey, IFPRI-PIDE research showed that well over half the wheat never reached the target population. Only 19% of the population in cities and 5% of the population in rural areas, where most of the poor lived, even used the ration shops. The research put numbers to the program's failure to reach the poor, a finding that was expected but until then had been based mostly on conjecture, anecdotes, and one small study. The research provided solid data to drive the final nail in the coffin of the ration shop system. The government abolished the wheat ration shops in 1987.

7. CONCLUSION

The post–Green Revolution period has seen profound changes in the economic situation in South Asia and evolving challenges for the agricultural R&D system. The priorities have changed from a narrow focus on the productivity of food grains to a need for more work on natural resources management and sustainability issues; increasing the productivity and quality of high-value crops, trees and livestock; agricultural intensification in many less favored areas; more precise targeting of the problems of the poor, including enhancing the micronutrient content of food staples; and analysis of policy and institutional options for achieving more sustainable and pro-poor outcomes in the rural sector.

The available evidence suggests that both the national and international systems have responded well to these changing needs in terms of their budgetary allocations and the kinds of research they have undertaken. Moreover, market liberalization has enabled a more diverse set of agents to engage in agricultural R&D, and private firms and NGOs have helped ensure that important research and extension needs have not been overlooked.

There is also reasonable evidence to show that agricultural R&D has been broadly successful in achieving many of its new goals.

7.1 Productivity impacts

The economic returns to crop improvement research have remained high and well in excess of national discount rates. Public investments in crop improvement research have also given higher returns than most other public investments in rural areas. There is little credible evidence to suggest that these rates of return are declining over time.

Given the patchy nature of the available impact studies and the fact that few have attempted to make any direct attribution to the work of the CGIAR centers, only a few inferences can be offered about the returns to CGIAR investments. One approach is to attribute to CGIAR investments the same rates of return as achieved at national levels for aggregate measures of public research expenditure. This would suggest an annual rate of return of 2550% (Table 4). Assuming a sustained annual investment of around $65 million (see Section 2.3), this leads to an annual average payoff of between $17.5 million and $35 million. But this estimate is much lower than the payoffs suggested for recent years by Fan (2000), Lantican et al. (2005), and Morris et al. (2003). As discussed in Section 3.3, these studies suggest annual payoffs from the CGIAR's research of between $432 million and $2304 million for rice, $560–1710 million for wheat, and $45–62 million for maize research. Even without including the CGIAR's other lines of research, the estimated payoff already exceeds $1 billion each year, which is more than enough to cover the costs of the CGIAR's entire global program, let alone the $65 million or so spent in South Asia each year. These kinds of calculations are at best indicative, but they do suggest that, from a narrow productivity perspective, the CGIAR's research in South Asia continues to be a sound investment, much as Raitzer and Kelley (2008) show at the global level.

7.2 Social impacts

Research has made important contributions to reducing poverty in South Asia, but it has done less well in reducing interhousehold and interregional inequities. Often, favorable poverty impacts arise from the indirect benefits of increases in productivity, such as the reductions in food prices that arise from technologies that reduce farmers' growing costs per ton of output. Indirect growth benefits in the nonfarm economy are another example. Measured at these levels, agricultural research can be a cost-effective way of reducing poverty, both relative to other public investments and in terms of the cost per person raised out of poverty.

Within adopting regions, the impact evidence is more mixed and there is insufficient evidence to conclude whether or not the more deliberate targeting of agricultural research to the problems of poor households and women, including use of participatory research methods, is paying off. This is an area of impact assessment that warrants further attention, especially because the rural poor have diversified their livelihoods and are less easily helped through agricultural productivity growth.

7.3 Environmental impacts

There has been a rich research agenda targeting environmental problems associated with agriculture and a demonstrated potential for favorable impacts in farmers' fields. Many improved technologies and NRM practices are also win/win in that they halt or reverse environmental problems while also increasing yields and/or reducing modern input use and cost. Despite this, there are virtually no impact studies from South Asia that estimate a return to a research investment corrected for environmental costs and benefits. The closest is the Bantilan et al. (2005) study of ICRISAT's groundnut improvement technology for the semi-arid areas of India. The high internal rate of return of about 25% reported by Joshi and Bantilan (1998) in an earlier study is seemingly robust to within a percentage point or two, even when corrected for possible positive and negative environmental outcomes that affect yield and production costs (Bantilan et al., 2005). But many environmental problems cannot be captured through productivity impacts and hence are not so easily quantified. Other studies measure productivity impacts from new technologies but limit their environmental analysis to qualitative statements about environmental impacts. For example, the Kerr et al. (2002) study of watershed development projects in India might be the most that can realistically be hoped for, and if there were greater agreement on the environmental indicators to use, it would be possible to at least allow for research investments to be ranked in different dimensions.

Given the popularity of alternative farming approaches and their competition for R&D funding, more rigorous assessments are needed. Their approaches seem to work well in LFAs, but they have proved disappointing in GR areas. There is no evidence that organic farming or LEI approaches can match current high yields in GR areas, whereas more precise approaches to modern inputs seem to offer significant steps in the right direction.

Another challenge facing researchers in South Asia is farmers' generally poor adoption rates of many improved NRM practices that reduce environmental damage. There are several possible reasons for this, including high levels of knowledge required for their practice, perverse incentives caused by input subsidies, labor constraints and insecure property rights, difficulties of organizing collective action, and externality problems. Additional policy research on these issues might be able to help leverage additional impact from past and future technology research.

7.4 Policy impacts

A vast amount of policy research has been undertaken in South Asia since the GR, and several CGIAR centers have been active participants. Case studies show favorable returns to policy research, though the conditions under which it leads to policy change are not well understood. Additional policy research is needed to identify more practical solutions for overcoming some of the constraints on adoption of more environmentally favorable technologies and NRM practices.

7.5 Emergent issues

A number of issues have arisen in this study that warrant further attention. These include questions of research policy and measurement issues in impact assessment studies.

7.5.1 Reaching marginal farmers

Given that agriculture now plays a relatively small part in the livelihoods of many marginal farmers in South Asia, is it still worthwhile to target agricultural R&D to their problems, or are there less costly approaches? Two aspects to this question need to be considered. First, many more workers will have to exit agriculture in South Asia as the economic transformation proceeds. Agriculture's share in GDP is already much lower than its employment share, implying that the average productivity of agricultural workers is already lower than that of nonagricultural workers. This finding is reflected in widening per capita income gaps between farm and nonfarm workers and between rural and urban areas. Unless South Asia is to become a much larger exporter of agricultural goods, the gap can be reduced only if the number of agricultural workers declines. This exit is a normal part of the economic transformation of a country and is driven by increasing opportunities for workers to move to faster-growing sectors in manufacturing and services. In this context, investments in large numbers of marginal farmers as farmers could simply end up delaying the inevitable, much as happened in Europe during the 20th century.

The second aspect to consider is that, although some types of agricultural research can be targeted to marginal farmers, it would be too expensive to develop technologies that have to be tailored to fit their individual and very diverse livelihood strategies. Further work is needed to identify the kinds of research that can still provide public goods on a sufficiently large scale to justify their cost and that are cost effective compared to alternative ways of assisting marginal farmers. This issue becomes even more pressing as R&D resources are directed at increasing the empowerment and social capital of the poor.

7.5.2 Food price and growth linkage effects

Have market liberalization and economic growth weakened food price effects and growth multipliers to the point where agricultural R&D can no longer make big reductions in poverty? Lower food prices and growth linkages to the nonfarm economy have played a large role in reducing poverty in South Asia in the past but might be less important now that food prices are aligned more with border prices and agriculture is a relatively small motor of national economic growth. There is some evidence for this in the form of declining poverty impacts per dollar spent on agricultural research in India, but this is an issue that warrants further study. A related issue stems from the observed decline in total factor productivity growth for some crops. This implies that unit production costs are unlikely to fall at the same pace as in the past, leaving less room for future price reductions.

7.5.3 Impact assessment issues

Although far from perfect, the literature contains a wealth of empirical studies that link agricultural research investments to productivity outcomes, with established analytical procedures for calculating rates of returns to investment and cost/benefit ratios. What is lacking is a similar body of empirical studies linking agricultural research investments to poverty and environmental outcomes. Apart from needing these kinds of studies to assess the economic value of poverty and environmentally oriented research, they are also needed to better understand the potential tradeoffs and complementarities among productivity, social, and environmental goals in agricultural research and for determining the kinds of research that offer the best win/win/win outcomes.

There are very few impact studies from South Asia that estimate a return to a research investment corrected for environmental costs and benefits or that calculate the research investment cost associated with an observed reduction in the number of poor. Many environmental problems cannot be captured through productivity impacts and hence are not so easily quantified. Other studies measure productivity impacts from new technologies but limit their environmental analysis to qualitative statements about environmental impacts. This might be the most that can realistically be hoped for, and if there were greater agreement on the environmental indicators to use, it would be possible to at least allow research investments to be ranked in different dimensions. Much the same goes for assessing poverty impacts; though in principle it is possible to convert changes in the mean and distribution of income into a single social welfare measure for cost/benefit analysis, it is generally more practical and insightful to work with a broader range of poverty indicators, not all of which need to be quantitative. Again, agreement on a set of indicators would be helpful for more systematic and comparative ranking of research investments in different dimensions.

Finally, very little has been said in this report about regional spillovers and spillins from agricultural research in South Asia, yet these are important issues. IRRI, for example, does work on rice problems that cut across Asian rice systems, and much the same can be said about the commodity work of CIMMYT and ICRISAT. Shiferaw et al. (2004) have characterized some of these spillovers for South Asia, and Maredia and Byerlee (2000) have developed a model for quantifying their impacts, but still missing is a comprehensive analysis of their benefits and implications for calculations of the economic returns to agricultural research in South Asia.

End Notes

1. At the time of undertaking this study, the author was visiting professor at the Centre for Environmental Policy, Imperial College London. The author is grateful to Jock Anderson, Dana Dalrymple, Tim Kelley, Mywish Maredia, and Jim Ryan for helpful comments on earlier drafts and to Nega Wubeneh and Jenny Nasr of the CGIAR Science Council Secretariat for research assistance. The author is

grateful to the Standing Panel on Impact Assessment of the CGIAR Science Council who commissioned this study and gave permission to reprint it.

2. The Consultative Group on International Agricultural Research currently comprises 15 member international agricultural research centers (IARCs); see www.cgiar.org for details. Of these, the International Rice Research Institute (IRRI) and the International Maize and Wheat Improvement Centre (CIMMYT) developed the high-yielding rice and wheat varieties that were the lynchpin of the GR.

3. An exhaustive literature search was conducted of published materials using electronic searches of library and journal databases, CGIAR contact persons, and personal contacts.

4. In India there were 226.8 million workers in agriculture in 1980; this figure had increased to 249.2 million in 1990 and 286.8 million in 2000.

5. This might overstate the benefits to South Asia, since the share of the area planted to wheat varieties with CIMMYT germplasm is lower for all Asia than for the rest of the developing world (Lantican et al., 2005).

6. See relevant case study material in Anderson and Hazell (1989).

7. In contrast to India, Tisdell (1988) found that relative yield and production variability of food grain fell at district and national levels in Bangladesh over a similar time period.

8. Work with molecular markers shows that at the molecular level, the amount of diversity present within CIMMYT-bred wheat materials has risen steadily over time and the newest CIMMYT lines show similar levels of diversity as landraces (Lantican et al., 2005). The steady increments in diversity reflect the increasing use by CIMMYT wheat breeders of varieties and advanced lines derived from multiple landraces and synthetic wheats.

9. Ongoing efforts to contain the spread of Ug99, a new race of stem rust *(Puccinia graminis tritici)* in wheat that emerged in Uganda in 1999 and has spread to wheat-growing areas of Kenya and Sudan and now threatens Asia, is a good example of payoff from genetic conservation and maintenance research (Wanyera et al., 2006).

10. Covers Afghanistan, Bangladesh, Bhutan, India, Iran, Nepal, Pakistan, and Sri Lanka.

11. Sometimes also called *sustainable* or *ecological farming*.

12. Since organic agriculture involves greater generation of plant nutrients and organic matter within the landscape through crop rotations, fallows, green manures, and integration of livestock into cropping systems, each hectare of harvested cropland must be supported by additional land dedicated to these other needs. Although it might well be possible to obtain comparable yields for some crops at the plot level, farm-level productivity can be considerably lower for organic farming. Yet few studies of yield gains with organic farming seem to make this basic correction, leading to results that are inevitably biased in their favor.

13. See http://ciifad.cornell.edu/sri.

14. The combination of wide spacing and reduced flooding creates ideal conditions for weed growth; hence the need for frequent weeding.

15. An attempt to prioritize agricultural R&D on the basis of production, poverty, and environmental goals has been undertaken by Mruthyunjaya, Suresh Pal, and Raka Saxena (2003).

References

Ahmed, U. A., Hill, R. V., Weismann, D. M., & Smith, L. C. (2008). *Reducing Poverty and Hunger in Asia.* Brief 3, 2020 Focus No. 15, Reducing Poverty and Hunger in Asia. Washington, DC: IFPRI.

Ali, M., & Vu Thi Bich Hau. (2001). *Vegetables in Bangladesh: Economic and Nutritional Impact of New Varieties and Technologies. Technical Bulletin* 25. Taiwan: AVRDC.

Ali, M., Malik, L. A., Sabir, H. M., & Ahmad, B. (1997). *The Mungbean Green revolution in Pakistan. Technical Bulletin* No. 24. Taiwan: AVRDC.

Ali, M., & Byerlee, D. (2002). Productivity growth and resource degradation in Pakistan's Punjab: A decomposition analysis. *Economic Development and Cultural Change, 50*(4), 839–863.

Alston, J. M., Chan-Kang, C., Marra, M. C., Pardey, P. G., & Wyatt, T. J. (2000). *A meta-analysis of rates of return to agricultural R&D, Ex Pede Herculem?* Research Report 113. Washington, DC: IFPRI.

Anderson, J. R., & Hazell, P. B. R. (Eds.). *Variability in Grain Yields: Implications for Agricultural Research and Policy in Developing Countries.* Baltimore: Johns Hopkins University Press.

Anriquez, G., & Bonomi, G. (2007). *Long-term farming and rural demographic trends.* Background Paper for the World Development Report 2008. World Bank.

Asian Development Bank. (2000). *Rural Asia: Beyond the Green Revolution.* Manila, Philippines: Asian Development Bank.

Azam, Q. T., Bloom, E. A., & Evenson, R. E. (1991). *Agricultural research productivity in Pakistan.* Economic Growth center Discussion Paper No. 644. New Haven, Connecticut: Economic Growth Center, Yale University.

Babu, S. (2000). *Impact of IFPRI's policy research on resource allocation and food security in Bangladesh.* Impact Assessment Discussion Paper No. 13. Washington, DC: IFPRI.

Babu, R., & Dhyani, B. L. (2005). Impact assessment of watershed technology in India. In P. K. Joshi, Suresh Pal, P. S. Birthal, & M. C. S. Bantilan (Eds.). *Impact of Agricultural Research: Post-Green Revolution Evidence from India.* India: National Centre for Agricultural Economics and Policy Research and ICRISAT.

Badgley, C., Moghtader, J., Quintero, E., Zakem, E., Chappell, M. J., Aviles-Vazquez, K., et al. (2007). Organic agriculture and the global food supply. *Renewable Agriculture and Food Systems, 22*(2), 86–108.

Bantilan, M. C. S., & Padmaja, R. (2008). Empowerment through social capital build-up: Gender dimensions in technology uptake. *Experimental Agriculture, 44,* 61–80.

Bantilan, M. C. S., Anupama, K. V., & Joshi, P. K. (2005). Assessing economic and environmental impacts of NRM technologies: An empirical application using the economic surplus approach. In B. Shiferaw, H. A. Freeman, & S. M. Swinton (Eds.), *Natural Resource Management in Agriculture: Methods for Assessing Economic and Environmental Impacts.* Wallingford, Oxford: CAB International.

Bantilan, M. C. S., & Deb, U. K. (2003). Impacts of genetic enhancement in pearl millet. In R. E. Evenson, & D. Gollin (Eds.), *Crop variety improvement and its effects on productivity.* Wallingford: CABI.

Bantilan, M. C. S., & Joshi, P. K. (1996). *Returns to Research and Diffusion Investments on Wilt Resistance in Pigeonpea.* Impact Series No. 1. Patancheru, Andhra Pradesh: ICRISAT.

Beintema, N. M., & Stads, G.-J. (2008). *Agricultural R&D capacity and investments in the Asia-Pacific region.* Research Brief No. 11, Agricultural Science and Technology Indicators (ASTI) initiative. Washington, DC: IFPRI.

Berti, P. R., Krasevec, J., & FitzGerald, S. (2004). A review of the effectiveness of agriculture interventions in improving nutrition. *Public Health Nutrition, 7*(5), 599–607.

Bhalla, S. (1997). *The Rise and Fall of Workforce Diversification Processes in Rural India: A Regional and Sectoral Analysis.* Centre for Economic Studies and Planning, DSA Working Paper. New Delhi: Jawaharlal Nehru University.

Bhalla, G. S., & Hazell, P. (2003). Rural Employment and Poverty; Strategies to Eliminate Rural Poverty within a Generation. *Economic and Political Weekly, 38*(33), 3473–3484.

Bhandari, A. L., Amin, R., Yadav, C. R., Bhattarai, E. M., Das, S., Aggarwal, H. P., et al. (2003). How extensive are yield declines in long-term rice-wheat experiments in Asia? *Field Crops Research, 81,* 159–180.

Bouis, H. E. (Ed.). (2000). Special issue on improving nutrition through agriculture. *Food and Nutrition Bulletin, 21*(4).

Bouis, H., Graham, R., & Welch, R. (2000). The CGIAR Micronutrients Project: Justification and objectives. *Food and Nutrition Bulletin, 21*(4), 374–381.

Bowen, W. T., Diamond, R. B., Singh, U., & Thompson, T. R. (2005). Urea deep placement increases yield and saves nitrogen fertilizers in farmers' fields in Bangladesh. Session 12. In K. Toriyama, K. L. Heong, & B. Hardy (Eds.), *Rice is life: scientific perspectives for the 21ˢᵗ century.* Proceedings of the World Rice Research

Conference held in Tokyo and Tsukuba, Japan, 4–7 November 2004. Los Banos (Philippines): IRRI and Tsukuba (Japan): Japan International Research Center for Agricultural Science. CD.

Byerlee, D., & Traxler, G. (1995). National and international wheat improvement research in the post-Green Revolution period: evolution and impacts. *American Journal of Agricultural Economics, 77*(2), 268–278.

Byerlee, D., & Morris, M. (1993). Research for marginal environments: Are we underinvested? *Food Policy, 18,* 381–393.

Byerlee, D. (1993). Technical change and returns to wheat breeding research in Pakistan's Punjab in the post-Green Revolution period. *The Pakistan Development Review, 31*(1), 69–86.

Cassman, K. (2007). Editorial response by Kenneth Cassman: Can organic agriculture feed the world—science to the rescue? *Renewable Agriculture and Food Systems, 22*(2), 83–84.

Cassman, K. G., & Pingali, P. (1993). Extrapolating trends from long-term experiments to farmers fields: the case of irrigated rice systems in Asia. In Proceedings of the Working Conference on Measuring Sustainability Using Long-term Experiments, Rothamsted Experimental Station, April 28–30, 1993, funded by the Agricultural Science Division, The Rockefeller Foundation.

Chakravorty, U. (1998). The economic and environmental impacts of irrigation and drainage in developing countries. In E. Lutz (Ed.), *Agriculture and the Environment; Perspectives on Sustainable Rural Development.* A World Bank Symposium (pp. 271–282). Washington, DC: World Bank.

Chand, R., & Raju, S. S. (2008). *Instability in Indian Agriculture during Different Phases of Technology and Policy.* Discussion Paper NPP 01/2008. New Delhi: National Centre for Agricultural Economics and Policy Research, ICAR.

Collins, M. I. (1995). *The economics of productivity maintenance research: A case study of wheat leaf rust resistance breeding in Pakistan.* Ph. D. Dissertation. St. Paul: University of Minnesota.

Comprehensive Assessment of Water Management in Agriculture. (2007). *Water for Food, Water for Life: A Comprehensive Assessment of Water Management in Agriculture.* London: Earthscan, and Colombo: International Water Management Institute.

David, C. C., & Otsuka, K. (1994). *Modern rice technology and income distribution in Asia.* Boulder, CO: Lynne Rienner.

Deb, U. K., Bantilan, M. C. S., & Reddy, B. V. S. (2005). *Impacts of improved sorghum cultivars in India.* In P. K. Joshi, Suresh Pal, P. S. Birthal, & M. C. S. Bantilan (Eds.), *Impact of Agricultural Research: Post-Green Revolution Evidence from India.* India: National Centre for Agricultural Economics and Policy Research and ICRISAT.

Deb, U. K., Bantilan, M. C. S., & Nigam, S. N. (2005). *Impacts of improved groundnut varieties in India.* In P. K. Joshi, Suresh Pal, P. S. Birthal, & M. C. S. Bantilan (Eds.), *Impact of Agricultural Research: Post-Green Revolution Evidence from India.* India: National Centre for Agricultural Economics and Policy Research and ICRISAT.

Deb, U. K., & Bantilan, M. C. S. (2003). Impacts of genetic improvement in sorghum. In R. E. Evenson, & D. Gollin (Eds.), *Crop variety improvement and its effects on productivity.* Wallingford: CABI.

Dey, M. M., & Evenson, R. E. (1991). *The economic impact of rice research in Bangladesh.* Gazipur, Bangladesh: Bangladesh Rice Research Institute; Los Banos, Philippines: IRRI; and Dhaka, Bangladesh: Bangladesh Agricultural Research Council.

Dixon, J., Gulliver, A., & Gibbon, D. (2001). *Farming Systems and Poverty: Improving Farmers' Livelihoods in a Changing World.* Rome and Washington: DC: Food and Agriculture Organization of the United Nations (FAO) and World Bank. Available online at www.fao.org/DOCREP/003/Y1860E/y1860e00.htm

Dogra, B. (1986). The Indian experience with large dams. In E. Goldsmith, & N. Hildyard (Eds.), *The social and environmental effects of large dams* (Vol. 2, pp. 201–208). London: Wadebridge Ecological Centre.

Dorjee, K., Broca, S., & Pingali, P. (2003). *Diversification in South Asian agriculture: Trends and constraints.* ESA Working Paper No. 03-15, Agriculture and Development Division. Rome: FAO; July.

Dorosh, P., Khan, M., & Nazli, H. (2003). Distributional impacts of agricultural growth in Pakistan: a multiplier analysis. *The Pakistan Development Review, 42*(3), 249–275.

Erenstein, O., Farook, U., Malik, R. K., & Sharif, M. (2007). *Adoption and impacts of zero tillage as a resource conserving technology in the irrigated plains of south Asia.* Comprehensive Assessment Research Report 19. Colombo, Sri Lanka: IWMI.

Evenson, R. E., & Gollin, D. (Eds.). (2003). *Crop variety improvement and its effects on productivity.* Wallingford: CABI.

Evenson, R. E. (2001). *Economic impact studies of agricultural research and extension. In: Handbook of Agricultural Economics.* Amsterdam: North Holland Publishing Company.

Evenson, R. E., Pray, C. E., & Rosegrant, M. W. (1999). *Agricultural research and productivity growth in India.* Research Report 109. Washington, DC: IFPRI.

Evenson, R. E., & McKinsey, J. (1991). Research, extension, infrastructure, and productivity change in Indian agriculture. In R. E. Evenson, & C. E. Pray (Eds.), *Research and productivity in Asian agriculture.* Ithaca, NY: Cornell University Press.

Evenson, R. E., & Bloom, E. A. (1991). Research and productivity in Pakistan agriculture. In Haider, Hussain, McConnen, & Malik (Eds.), *Agricultural Strategies in the 1990s: Issues and Policies.* Pakistan Association of Agricultural Social Sciences.

Fan, S., & Rao, N. (2008). Public investment, growth and rural poverty. In S. Fan (Ed.), *Public Expenditures, Growth and Poverty: Lessons from Developing Countries.* Baltimore: Johns Hopkins University Press.

Fan, S., Chan-Kang, C., Qian, K., & Krishnaiah, K. (2007). National and international agricultural research and rural poverty: The case of rice research in India and China. In M. Adato, & R. Meinzen-Dick (Eds.), *Agricultural Research, Livelihoods, and Poverty: Studies of Economic and Social Impacts in Six Countries.* Baltimore: Johns Hopkins University Press.

Fan, S. (2007). Agricultural research and urban poverty in China and India. In M. Adato & R. Meinzen-Dick (Eds.), *Agricultural Research, Livelihoods, and Poverty: Studies of Economic and Social Impacts in Six Countries.* Baltimore: Johns Hopkins University Press.

Fan, S., & Hazell, P. (2000). Returns to Public Investments in the Less-favored Areas of India and China. *American Journal of Agricultural Economics, 83*(5), 1217–1222.

Fan, S., Hazell, P., & Haque, T. (2000). Targeting public investments by agro-ecological zone to achieve growth and poverty alleviation goals in rural India. *Food Policy,* (25), 411–428.

Fan, S., Hazell, P., & Thorat, S. (1999). *Linkages between government spending, growth and poverty in rural India.* Research Report 110. Washington, DC: IFPRI.

Fan, S., Hazell, P., & Thorat, S. (2000). Government Spending, Growth and Poverty in India. *American Journal of Agricultural Economics, 82*(4), 1038–1051.

FAO. (2005). *Global Forest Resources Assessment 2005.* Rome: FAO.

Foster, A. D., & Rosenzweig, M. R. (2004). Agricultural productivity growth, rural economic diversity and economic reforms: India, 1970–2000. *Economic Development and Cultural Change, 52*(3), 509–542.

Freebairn, D. K. (1995). Did the Green Revolution concentrate incomes? A quantitative study of research reports. *World Development, 23*(2), 265–279.

Freeman, H. A., Shiferaw, B., & Swinton, S. M. (2005). Assessing the impacts of natural resource management interventions in agriculture: concepts, issues and challenges. In B. Shiferaw, H. A. Freeman, & S. M. Swinton (Eds.). *Natural Resource Management in Agriculture: Methods for Assessing Economic and Environmental Impacts.* Wallingford, Oxford: CAB International.

Galwani, K., Kanbur, R., & Zhang, X. (2007). *Comparing the evolution of spatial inequality in China and India: a fifty-year perspective.* DSGD Discussion Paper No. 44, IFPRI.

Gerpacio, R. V. (2003). The roles of the public sector versus private sector in R&D and technology generation: The case of maize in Asia. *Agricultural Economics, 29,* 319–330.

Ghassemi, F., Jakeman, A. J., & Nix, H. A. (1995). *Salinization of Land and Water Resources: Human Causes, Extent, Management and Case Studies.* Canberra, Australia: Centre for Resource and Environmental Studies. Australian National University.

Giordano, M. A., Samad, M., & Namara, R. E. (2007). Assessing the outcomes of IWMI's Research and Interventions on Irrigation Management Transfer. In H. Waibel, & D. Zilberman (Eds.). *International Research on Natural Resource Management: Advances in Impact Assessment.* Wallingford, UK: CAB International.

Gollin, D. (2006). *Impacts of international research on intertemporal yield stability in wheat and maize: an economic assessment.* Mexico, DF: CIMMYT.

Gollin, D., Morris, M., & Byerlee, D. (2005). Technology adoption in intensive post-green revolution systems. *Amer. J. Agr. Econ.*, *87*(5): 1310–1316.

Guerra, L. C., Bhuiyan, S. I., Tuong, T. P., & Barker, R. (1998). *Producing More Rice with Less Water from Irrigated Systems*. SWIM Paper 5. Colombo, Sri Lanka: IWMI.

Haggblade, S., Hazell, P. B., & Dorosh, P. A. (2007). Sectoral growth linkages between agriculture and the rural nonfarm economy. In S. Haggblade, P. B. Hazell, & T. Reardon (Eds.), *Transforming the Rural Nonfarm Economy*. Baltimore: Johns Hopkins University Press.

Halberg, N., Sulser, T., Hogh-Hensen, H., Rosegrant, M., & Knudsen, M. T. (2006). In N. Halberg, H. F. Alroe, M. T. Knudsen, & E. S. Kristensen (Eds.), *Global Development of Organic Agriculture: Challenges and Prospects* (pp. 277–322). Wallingford, UK: CABI Publishing.

Harriss-White, B., & Janakarajan, S. (1997). From Green Revolution to rural industrial revolution in south India. *Economic and Political Weekly*, *32*(25), 1469–1477.

Hasan, R., & Quibria, M. G. (2004). Industry matters for poverty: A critique of agricultural fundamentalism. *Kyklos*, *57*(2), 253–264.

Hazell, P., & Wood, S. (2008). Drivers of change in global agriculture. *Philosophical Transactions of the Royal Society B*, *363*(1491), 495–515, 12 February.

Hazell, P., & Haddad, L. (2001). *Agricultural Research and Poverty Reduction*. Food, Agriculture, and the Environment Discussion Paper 34. Washington, DC: International Food Policy Research Institute, August.

Hazell, P. B. R., & Haggblade, S. (1991). Rural-Urban Growth Linkages in India. *Indian Journal of Agricultural Economics*, *46*(4), 515–529.

Hazell, P. B. R. (1982). *Instability in Indian foodgrain production*. Research Report 30. Washington, DC: IFPRI.

Hazell, P. B. R. (1989). Changing patterns of variability in world cereal production. In J. R. Anderson, & P. B. R. Hazell (Eds.). *Variability in Grain Yields: Implications for Agricultural Research and Policy in Developing Countries*. Baltimore: Johns Hopkins University Press.

Hazell, P. B. R., & Ramasamy, C. (1991). *Green Revolution Reconsidered: The Impact of the High Yielding Rice Varieties in South India*. Johns Hopkins University Press and Oxford University Press (India).

Hossain, M., Lewis, D., Bose, M. L., & Chowdhury, A. (2007). Rice research, technological progress, and poverty: The Bangladesh case. In M. Adato, & R. Meinzen-Dick (Eds.), *Agricultural Research, Livelihoods and Poverty: Studies of Economic and Social Impacts in Six Countries*. Baltimore: Johns Hopkins University Press.

Hossain, M. (1998). Rice research, technological progress, and the impact on the rural economy: The Bangladesh case. In P. L. Pingali, & M. Hossain (Eds.). *Impact of Rice Research*, Proceedings of the International Conference on the Impact of Rice Research, 3–5 June 1996, Bangkok, Thailand. Bangkok and Los Banos: Thailand Development Research Institute (TDRI) and IRRI.

Howard, A., & Howard, G. L. C. (1909). *Wheat in India: Its Production, Varieties, and Improvement*. Calcutta, India: Thacker, Spink, and Co., for the Imperial Dept. of Agriculture in India.

Iqbal, M. (1991). Rates of return to investment in agricultural research: The case of rice and cotton in Pakistan. Ph.D. thesis. Columbus: Department of Agricultural Economics and Rural Sociology, Ohio State University.

Islam, Y., & Garrett, J. L. (1997). *IFPRI and the abolition of the wheat flour ration shops in Pakistan: A case-study on policymaking and the use and impact of research*. Impact Assessment Discussion Paper No. 1. Washington, DC: IFPRI.

Islam, Z., Bagchi, B., & Hossain, M. (2007). Adoption of leaf color chart for nitrogen use efficiency in rice: Impact assessment of a farmer-participatory experiment in West Bengal, India. *Field Crops Research*, *103*, 70–75.

Janaiah, A., Otsuka, K., & Hossain, M. (2005). Is the productivity impact of the Green Revolution in rice vanishing? *Economic and Political Weekly*, December 31, 2006, 5596–5600.

Jewitt, S., & Baker, K. (2007). The Green Revolution re-assessed: insider perspectives on agrarian change in Bulandshahr district, Western Uttar Pradesh, India. *Geoforum*, *38*, 73–89.

Jha, R. (2007). *Investments and subsidies in Indian agriculture*. ASARC Working Paper 2007/03. Canberra: Australia South Asia Research Centre, ANU.

Joshi, P. K., Pangare, V., Shifraw, B., Wani, S. P., Bouma, J., & Scott, C. (2004). Watershed development in India: Synthesis of past experiences and needs for future research. *Indian Journal of Agricultural Economics, 59*(3), 303–320.

Joshi, P. K., & Saxena, Raka. (2002). A profile of pulses production in India: Facts, trends and opportunities. *Indian Journal of Agricultural Economics, 57*(3), 326–339.

Joshi, P. K., Jha, A. K., Wani, S. P., Joshi, Laxmi., & Shiyani, R. L. (2005). *Meta-analysis to assess impact of watershed program and people's participation.* Comprehensive Assessment Research Report 8. Colombo, Sri Lanka: IWMI.

Joshi, P. K., & Bantilan, M. C. S. (1998). *Impact assessment of crop and resource management technology: A case of groundnut production technology.* Impact Series no. 2. Patancheru, India: ICRISAT.

Joshi, P. K., & Jha, D. (1991). *Farm-level effects of soil degradation in Sharda Sahayak Irrigation Project.* Working Papers on Future Growth in Indian Agriculture No. 1. New Delhi and Washington, DC: Central Soil salinity Research Institute, Indian Council for Agricultural research and IFPRI.

Joshi, P. K., Gulati, A., & Cummings, R., Jr. (2007). *Agricultural diversification and smallholders in south Asia.* New Delhi, India: Academic Foundation.

Joshi, P. K., Asokan, M., & Bantilan, M. C. S. (2005). Chickpea in Nontraditional Areas: Evidence for Andhra Pradesh. In P. K. Joshi, Suresh Pal, P. S. Birthal, & M. C. S. Bantilan (Eds.), *Impact of Agricultural Research: Post-Green Revolution Evidence from India.* India: National Centre for Agricultural Economics and Policy Research and ICRISAT.

Kajisa, K., & Venkatesa Palanichamy, N. (2006). Income dynamics in Tamil Nadu from 1971 to 2003: changing roles of land and human capital. *Agricultural Economics, 35*(Suppl.), 437–448.

Kasavan, P. C., & Swaminathan, M. S. (2007). Strategies and models for agricultural sustainability in developing Asian countries. *Phil. Trans. R. Soc. B.,* Published online.

Kataki, P. K. (2002). Shifts in cropping system and its effect on human nutrition: case study from India. *Journal of Crop Production, 6*(1–2), 119–144.

Kelley, T. G., & Parthasarathy Rao, P. (1995). Marginal environments and the poor.. *Economic and Political Weekly,* October 7, 24945.

Kennedy, E., & Bouis, H. (1993). *Linkages between agriculture and nutrition: implications for policy and research.* Washington, DC: IFPRI.

Kerr, J., Pangare, G., Pangare, V. L., & George, P. J. (2000). Sustainable agriculture and natural resource management in India's semi-arid tropics. In D. R. Lee, & C. B. Barrett (Eds.), *Tradeoffs or synergies? Agricultural intensification, economic development and the environment.* Wallingford: CABI.

Khan, M. H., & Akbari, A. H. (1986). Impact of agricultural research and extension on crop productivity in Pakistan: A production function approach. *World Development, 14*(6), 757–762.

Khatana, V. S., Updhya, M. D., Chilver, A., & Crissman, C. C. (1996). Economic impact of true potato seed on potato production in Eastern and Northeastern India. In T. S. Walker, & C. C. Crissman (Eds.). *Case studies of the economic impact of CIP-related technologies.* Lima, Peru: International Potato Center.

Krishna, A. (2005). Pathways out of and into poverty in 36 villages of Andhra Pradesh, India. *World Development, 34*(2), 271–288.

Krishna, K. L. (2006). Some aspects of total factor productivity in Indian agriculture. In R. Radhakrishna, S. K. Rao, S. Mahendra Dev, & K. Subbarao (Eds.), *India in a Globalizing World, Essays in Honour of C. H. Hanumantha Rao.* New Delhi: Academic Foundation.

Kristjanson, P. M., Zerbini, E., Rao, K. P. C., Kiresur, V., & Hofs, P. (1999). *Genetic enhancement of sorghum and millet residues fed to ruminants: An ex ante assessment of returns to research.* ILRI Impact Assessment Series 3. Nairobi: ILRI.

Ladha, J. K., Dawe, D., Pathak, H., Padre, A. T., Yadav, R. L., Singh, Bijay., et al. (2003). How extensive are yield declines in long-term rice-wheat experiments in Asia? *Field Crops Research, 81,* 159–180.

Lanjouw, P., & Shariff, A. (2004). Rural non-farm employment in India: Access, incomes and poverty impact. *Economic and Political Weekly, 39*(40), 4429–4446.

Lantican, M. A., Dubin, H. J., & Morris, M. L. (2005). *Impacts of international wheat breeding research in the developing world, 1988–2002.* Mexico, DF: CIMMYT.

Larson, D. W., Jones, E., Pannu, R. S., & Sheok&, R. S. (2004). Instability in Indian agriculture: a challenge to the Green Revolution technology. *Food Policy, 29*(3), 257–273.

Larson, D. W., Jones, E., Pannu, R. S., & Sheokand, R. S. (2004). Instability in Indian agriculture – A challenge to the Green Revolution technology. *Food Policy*, *29*(3), 257–273.

Laxmi, J., Erenstein, O., & Gupta, R. K. (2007). Assessing the impact of natural resource management research: The case of zero tillage in India's rice-wheat systems. In H. Waibel, & D. Zilberman (Eds.), *International Research on Natural Resource Management: Advances in Impact Assessment*. Wallingford, UK: CAB International.

Laxmi, V., & Mishra, V. (2007). Factors affecting the adoption of resource conservation technology: Case of zero tillage in rice-wheat farming systems. *Indian Journal of Agricultural Economics*, *62*(1), 126–138.

Lipton, M., Longhurst, R. (1989). *New seeds and poor people*. Baltimore, MD: Johns Hopkins University Press.

Maheshwari, A. (1998). Green Revolution, market access of small farmers and stagnation of cereals' yield in Karnataka. *Indian Journal of Agricultural Economics*, *53*(1), 27–40.

Maredia, M. K., & Byerlee, D. (2000). Efficiency of research investments in the presence of international spillovers: wheat research in developing countries. *Agricultural Economics*, *22*, 1–16.

McDonald, A. J., Hobbs, P. R., & Riha, S. J. Does the system of rice intensification outperform conventional best management? A synopsis of the empirical record. *Field Crops Research*, *96*, 31–36.

McNeely, J. A., & Scherr, S. J. (2003). *Ecoagriculture: Strategies to Feed the World and Save Wild Biodiversity*. Washington: Island Press.

Meenakshi, J. V., Johnson, N., Manyong, V., De Groote, H., Javelosa, J., Yanggen, D., et al. (2007). *How cost-effective is biofortification in combating micronutrient malnutrition? An ex ante assessment*. HarvestPlus Working Paper No. 2. Washington, DC: c/o IFPRI.

Mehra, S. (1981). *Instability in Indian agriculture in the context of the new technology*. Research Report 25. Washington, DC: IFPRI.

Mellor, J. W. (1976). *The New Economics of Growth: A Strategy for India and the Developing World*. Ithaca, NY: Cornell University Press.

Mendola, M. (2007). Agricultural technology adoption and poverty reduction: A propensity-score matching analysis for rural Bangladesh. *Food Policy*, *32*, 372–393.

Mishra, A., Whitten, M., Ketelaar, J. W., & Salokhe, V. M. (2006). The system of rice intensification (SRI): a challenge for science, and an opportunity for farmer empowerment towards sustainable agriculture. *International Journal of Agricultural Sustainability*, *4*(3), 193–212.

Mittal, S., & Kumar, P. (2005). Total factor productivity and sources of growth in wheat in India. In P. K. Joshi, Suresh Pal, P. S. Birthal, & M. C. S. Bantilan (Eds.), *Impact of Agricultural Research: Post-Green Revolution Evidence from India*. India: National Centre for Agricultural Economics and Policy Research and ICRISAT.

Mondal, M. K., Islam, M. N., Mowla, G., Islam, M. T., & Ghani, M. A. (1993). Impact of on-farm water management research on the performance of a gravity irrigation system in Bangladesh. *Agricultural Water Management*, *23*, 11–22.

Morris, M., Mekuria, M., & Gerpacio, R. (2003). Impacts of CIMMYT maize breeding research. In R. E. Evenson, & D. Gollin (Eds.), *Crop variety improvement and its effects on productivity*. Wallingford: CABI.

Morris, M. L., Dublin, H. J., & Pokhrel, T. (1992). *Returns to wheat research in Nepal*. CIMMYT Economics Program Working Paper 92/04. Mexico, DF: CIMMYT.

Moser, C. M., & Barrett, C. (2003). The disappointing adoption dynamics of a yield-increasing, low external-input technology: the case of SRI in Madagascar. *Agricultural Systems*, *76*, 1085–1100.

Mruthyunjaya, S. P., & Saxena, R. (2003). *Agricultural research priorities for South Asia*. Policy Paper 20. New Delhi: National Centre for Agricultural Economics and Policy research, ICAR.

Murgai, R., Ali, M., & Byerlee, D. (2001). Productivity growth and sustainability in post-green revolution agriculture: the case of the Indian and Pakistan Punjabs. *World Bank Research Observer*, *16*(2), 199–218.

Nagayets, O. (2005). *Small farms: Current status and key trends*. Information brief for the workshop "The future of small farms," organized by the International Food Policy Research Institute, Imperial College London, and the Overseas Development Institute, Wye, England, June 26–29.

Nagy, J. G. (1985). Overall rate of return to agricultural research and extension investments in Pakistan. *Pakistan Journal of Applied Economics*, *4*(Summer), 17–28.

Namara, R. E., Weligamage, P., & Barker, R. (2003). *Prospects for adopting system of rice intensification in Sri Lanka: A socioeconomic assessment*. Research Report 75. Colombo, Sri Lanka: IWMI.

Nargis, N., & Hossain, M. (2006). Income dynamics and pathways out of rural poverty in Bangladesh, 1988–2004. *Agricultural Economics*, *35*(Suppl.), 425–435.

Nasurudeen, P., Kuruvila, A., Sendhil, R., & Chandresekar, V. (2006). The dynamics and inequality of nutrient consumption in India. *Indian Journal of Agricultural Economics*, *61*(3), 363–373.

Nellithanam, R., Jacob, & Sarvodaya Shiksham Samati. (1998). Return of the Native Seeds. *The Ecologist*, *28*(1).

Nelson, M., & Maredia, M. (1999). *Environmental Impacts of the CGIAR: An initial Assessment*. TAC Secretariat Report presented at the International Centers Week 1999, Oct. 25–29, Washington, DC.

Oberai, A., & Singh, H. (1980). Migration flows in Punjab's green revolution belt. *Economic and Political Weekly*, *15*, A2–A12.

Oldeman, L. R., Hakkeling, R. T. A., & Sombroek, W. G. (1991). *World map of the status human-induced soil degradation: An explanatory note*. Wageningen and Nairobi: The International Soil Reference and Information Centre (ISRIC) and United Nations Environmental Programme (UNEP).

Pal, S., & Byerlee, D. (2006). India: The funding and organization of agricultural R&D – evolution and emerging policy issues. Chapter 7. In P. G. Pardey, J. M. Alston, & R. R. Piggot (Eds.), *Agricultural R&D in the developing world, too little, too late?* Washington, DC: IFPRI.

Pampolino, M. F., Manguiat, I. J., Ramanathan, S., Gines, H. C., Tan, P. S., Chi, T. T. N., et al. (2007). Environmental impact and economic benefits of site-specific nutrient management (SSNM) in irrigated rice systems. *Agricultural Systems*, *93*(1-3), 1–24.

Pandey, S., & Pal, S. (2007). Are less-favored environments over-invested? The case of rice research in India. *Food Policy*, *25*(2000).

Paris, T. R., Singh, A., Cueno, A. D., & Singh, V. N. (2008). Assessing the impact of participatory research in rice breeding on women farmers: A case study in Eastern Uttar Pradesh, India. *Experimental Agriculture*, *44*, 97–112.

Paarlberg, R. (2005). *Regional Policy Networks: IFPRI's Experience with Decentralization*. Impact Assessment Discussion paper 24. Washington, DC: IFPRI.

Pender, J., & Hazell, P. (Eds.). (2000). *Promoting sustainable development in less-favored areas*. Focus No. 3, 2020 Policy Briefs. Washington, DC: IFPRI.

Pingali, P. L., Hossain, M., & Gerpacio, R. V. (1997). *Asian rice bowls: The returning crisis*. Wallingford, UK. CAB International.

Pingali, P. L., & Rosegrant, M. W. (2001). Chapter 20. In D. R. Lee, & C. B. Barrett (Eds.), *Tradeoffs or Synergies? Agricultural Intensification, Economic Development and the Environment*. Wallingford, UK: CAB International.

Pinstrup-Andersen, P., & Jaramillo, M. (1991). The impact of technological change in rice production on food consumption and nutrition. In P. B. R. Hazell, & C. Ramasamy (Eds.), *The Green Revolution Reconsidered: The Impact of the High Yielding Rice Varieties in South India*. Johns Hopkins University Press and Oxford University Press (India).

Postel, S. (1993). Water and agriculture. In P. H. Gleick (Ed.). *Water in Crisis: A Guide to the World's Fresh Water Resources*. New York: Oxford University Press.

Prahladachar, M. (1983). Income distribution effects of the green revolution in India: A review of empirical evidence. *World Development*, *11*(11), 927–944.

Pretty, J. N., Noble, A. D., Bossio, D., Dixon, J., Hine, R. E., Penning de Vries, F. W. T., et al. (2007). Resource conserving agriculture increases yields in developing countries. *Environmental Science & Technology*, *40*(4), 1114–1119.

Pretty, J., Morrison, J. I. L., & Hine, R. E. (2003). Reducing food poverty by increasing agricultural sustainability in developing countries. *Agriculture Ecosystems & Environment*, *95*(1), 217–234.

Raitzer, D. A., & Kelley, T. G. (2008). Benefit-cost meta-analysis of investment in the International Agricultural Research Centers of the CGIAR. *Agricultural Systems*, *96*, 108–123.

Rao, C. H. H., Ray, S. K., & Subbarao, K. (1988). *Unstable Agriculture and Droughts: Implications for Policy*. New Delhi: Vikas Publishing House Pvt. Ltd.

Rao, K. P. C., Bantilan, M. C. S., Singh, K., Subrahmanyam, S., Deshinkar, P., Parthasara, P., et al. (2005). *Overcoming poverty in rural India: Focus on rainfed semi-arid tropics*. Patancheru, India: ICRISAT.

Ramasamy, C., Bantilan, M. C. S., Elangovan, S., & Asokan, M. 2000. *Improved cultivars of pearl millet in Tamil Nadu: Adoption, impact and returns to research investment.* Impact Series No. 7, Patancheru, India: ICRISAT.

Ramasamy, C., & Selvaraj, K. N. (2000). Pulses, oilseeds and coarse grains: Why they are slow growth crops? *Indian Journal of Agricultural Economics*, *57*(3), 289–315.

Rangarajan, C. (1982). *Agricultural growth and industrial performance in India.* Research Report 33. Washington, DC: IFPRI.

Rasul, G., & Thapa, G. (2003). Sustainability analysis of ecological and conventional agricultural systems in Bangladesh. *World Development*, *31*, 1721–1741.

Ravallion, M., & Datt, G. (1996). How important to India's poor in the sectoral composition of economic growth? *World Bank Economic Review*, *10*(1), 1–26.

Ray, S. K. (1983). An empirical investigation of the nature and causes for growth and instability in Indian agriculture: 1950–80. *Indian Journal of Agricultural Economics*, *38*(4), 459–474.

Renkow, M. (2000). Poverty, productivity and production environment: A review of the evidence. *Food Policy*, *25*, 463–478.

Rola, A. C., & Pingali, P. L. (1993). *Pesticide, Rice Productivity and Farmer's Health: An Economic Assessment.* Washington, DC: World Resources Institute and Los Banos, Philippines: IRRI.

Rosegrant, M. W., & Hazell, P. B. R. (2000). *Transforming the Rural Asia Economy: The Unfinished Revolution.* Hong Kong: Oxford University Press.

Rosegrant, M. W., & Evenson, R. E. (1992). Agricultural productivity and sources of growth in South Asia. *American Journal of Agricultural Economics*, *74*(August), 757–791.

Ryan, J. G., & Meng, X. (2004). *The contribution of IFPRI research and the impact of the food for education in Bangladesh on school outcomes and earnings.* Impact Assessment Discussion Paper No. 22. Washington, DC: IFPRI.

Ryan, J. G., & Asokan, M. (1977). Effects of Green Revolution in Wheat on Production of Pulses and Nutrients in India. *Indian Journal of Agricultural Economics*, *32*(3), 8–15.

Sabur, S. A., & Molla, A. R. (2001). Pesticide use, its impact on crop production and evaluation of IPM technologies in Bangladesh. *Bangladesh Journal of Agricultural Economics*, *XXIV*(1&2), 21–38.

Samad, M., & Vermillion, D. (1999). *Assessment of participatory management of irrigation schemes in Sri Lanka: Partial reforms, partial benefits.* Research report 34. Colombo, Sri Lanka: IWMI.

Santikarn Kaosa-Ard, M., Khaosa'at Mingsan, & Rerkasem, B. (2000). *The Growth and Sustainability of Agriculture in Asia.* Hong Kong: Oxford University Press for the Asian Development Bank.

Scherr, S. J. (1999). *Soil Degradation: A Threat to Developing Country Food Security by 2020?* Food, Agriculture and the Environment Discussion Paper 27, 2020 Vision Project. Washington, DC: IFPRI.

Sehgal, J., & Abrol, I. P. (1994). *Soil Degradation in India: Status and Impact.* New Delhi: Oxford University Press.

Shah, T., Roy, A. D., Qureshi, A., & Wang, J. (2003). Sustaining Asia's groundwater boom: An overview of issues and evidence. *Natural Resources Forum*, *27*(2), 130–141.

Sharma, H. R., Singh, K., & Kumari, S. (2006). Extent and source of instability in foodgrains production in India. *Indian Journal of Agricultural Economics*, *61*(4), 647–666.

Sheehy, J. E., Sinclair, T. R., & Cassman, K. G. (2005). Curiosities, nonsense, non-science and SRI. *Field Crops Research*, *91*, 355–356.

Shiferaw, B., Bantilan, M. C. S., Gupta, S. C., & Shetty, S. V. R. (2004). *Research spillover benefits and experiences in inter-regional technology transfer: An assessment and synthesis.* Patancheru, India: ICRISAT.

Shiva, V. (1991). The Green Revolution in the Punjab. *The Ecologist*, March/April.

Shiyana, R. L., Joshi, P. K., Asokan, M., & Bantilan, M. C. S. (2002). Adoption of improved chickpea varieties: KRIBHCO experience in tribal region of Gujarat, India. *Agricultural Economics*, *27*, 33–39.

Singh, A. J., & Byerlee, D. (1990). Relative variability in wheat yields across countries and over time. *Journal of Agricultural Economics*, *41*(1), 21–32.

Singh, R. P., & Morris, M. L. (2005). Adoption and impact assessment of hybrid maize seed in India. In Joshi, P. K., Suresh Pal, P. S. Birthal, & M. C. S. Bantilan (Eds.), *Impact of Agricultural Research: Post-Green Revolution Evidence from India*. National Centre for Agricultural Economics and Policy Research and ICRISAT, India.

Sinha, S., & Talati, J. (2007). Productivity impacts of the system of rice intensification (SRI): a case study in West Bengal, India. *Agricultural Water Management*, *87*, 55–60.

Smale, M., Hazell, P., Hodgkin, T., & Fowler, C. (Forthcoming). Do we have an adequate global strategy for securing the biodiversity of major food crops? Forthcoming. In A. K. U. Pascual & M. Smale (Eds.), *Agrobiodiversity and Economic Development*. Routledge.

Susmita, D., Meisner, C., & Wheeler, D. (2007). Is Environmentally Friendly Agriculture Less Profitable for Farmers? Evidence on Integrated Pest Management in Bangladesh. *Review of Agricultural Economics*, *29*(1), 103–118.

Thakur, D. S., & Sharma, K. D. (2005). Organic farming for sustainable agriculture and meeting the challenges of food security in 21st Century: An economic analysis. *Indian Journal of Agricultural Economics*, *60*(2), 205–219.

Thapa, G., Otsuka, K., & Barker, R. (1992). Effect of modern rice varieties and irrigation on household income distribution in Nepalese villages. *Agricultural Economics*, 7(3-4), 245–265.

Thirtle, C., Lin, L., & Piesse, J. (2003). The Impact of Research-Led Agricultural Productivity Growth on Poverty Reduction in Africa, Asia, and Latin America. *World Development*, *31*(12), 1959–1975.

Tisdell, C. (1988). Impact of new agricultural technology on the instability of foodgrain production and yield: Data analysis for Bangladesh and its districts. *Journal of Development Economics*, *29*(2), 199–227.

Tribe, D. (1994). *Feeding and Greening the World; The Role of International Agricultural Research*. Wallingford, Oxford: CAB International.

Tripp, R. (2006). *Self-Sufficient Agriculture: Labour and Knowledge in Small-Scale Farming*. London: Earthscan.

Tripp, R., Wijeratne, M., & Hiroshini Piyadasa, H. (2006). After school: the outcome of farmer field schools in southern Sri Lanka. In: *Self-Sufficient Agriculture: Labour and Knowledge in Small-Scale Farming*. London: Earthscan.

Umali, D. (1993). *Irrigation Induced Salinity: A Growing Problem for Development and the Environment*. World Bank Technical Paper No. 215. Washington, DC: World Bank.

Uphoff, N. (2003). Higher yields with fewer external inputs? The system of rice intensification and potential contributions to agricultural sustainability. *International Journal of Agricultural Sustainability*, *1*(1), 38–50.

Van Den Berg, H., & Jiggins, J. (2007). Investing in farmers: The impacts of farmer field schools in relation to integrated pest management. *World Development*, *35*(4), 663–686.

Vermillion, D. L., & Sagardoy, J. A. (1999). *Transfer of Irrigation Management Services: Guidelines*. FAO Irrigation and Drainage Paper 58. Rome: FAO.

Waibel, H. (1999). *An evaluation of the impact of integrated pest management at international agricultural research centres*. Rome: IAEG Secretariat.

Walker, T. S. (2000). Reasonable expectations on the prospects for determining the impact of agricultural research on poverty in ex-post case studies. *Food Policy*, *25*, 515–530.

Wanyera, R., Kinyua, M. G., Jin, Y., & Singh, R. P. (2006). The spread of stem rust caused by Puccinia graminis f. sp. tritici, with Virulence on Sr31 in wheat in Eastern Africa. *Plant Disease*, *90*(1), 113.

Westley, J. R. (1986). *Agriculture and equitable growth: The case of Punjab-Haryana. Westview Special Studies in Agriculture Science and Policy*. Boulder, CO: Westview Press.

World Bank. (2007). *World Development Report 2008: Agriculture for Development*. Washington, DC: World Bank.

Young, A. (1993). *Land degradation in South Asia: Its severity, causes, and effects upon people. Final report prepared for submission to the Economic and Social Council of the United Nations (ECOSOC)*. Rome: Food and Agriculture Organization of the United Nations, United Nations Development Programme, and United Nations Environment Programme.

Zundel, C., & Kilcher, L. (2007). *Issues Paper: Organic Agriculture and Food Availability*. Paper presented at an international conference on Organic Agriculture and Food Security, 3–5 May. Italy: FAO.

CHAPTER 69

Population Growth and Trends in Food Production and Consumption in the CWANA Region

Kamil H. Shideed, Farouk Shomo, *and* **Aden Aw-Hassan**

International Center for Agricultural Research in the Dry Areas (ICARDA)

Contents

Abstract

Many of the financial and social challenges that face Central and West Asia and North Africa (CWANA) can be addressed through more efficient and sustainable use of arable land and water resources. In recent years improvements in land and water use have come from an agricultural sector that is moving from state to market control, but without greater changes the region will continue to be constrained by environmental degradation, institutional inefficiencies, and persistently high population growth rates. This chapter presents a trend analysis of major cropping groups for the period 1961–2002 and summarizes ways to address the key problems of food security, poverty reduction, and conservation of natural resources throughout the CWANA region. The International Center for Agricultural Research in the Dry Areas (ICARDA) and its partners are presented as a regional knowledge portal through which many of these initiatives can occur.

JEL classifications: Q01, Q13, Q15, Q16, Q17, Q18

Handbook of Agricultural Economics, Volume 4
© 2010 Elsevier BV. All rights reserved.

doi: 10.1016/S1574-0072(09)04069-9

Keywords

agricultural research priorities
integrated natural resource management
food security
policy intervention

SUMMARY

The Central and West Asia and North Africa (CWANA) region is characterized by high population growth; low and erratic rainfall; limited areas of arable land; and severely limited water resources for further development of irrigation. Therefore, methods for more efficient and sustainable use of these limited resources must be found. Cereal production has increased 80% since 1979–1981, especially in Egypt and Morocco, due mainly to increased wheat yield. The modest increase in barley production is the result of area expansion and yield increases. The number of small ruminants has grown greatly throughout the region, resulting in doubling meat production. Regardless of these gains, the food gap is expected to grow 2.9% per year throughout the coming decade.

Past policies in the region, in general, have led to environmental degradation while doing little to improve the livelihoods of the rural poor. Agricultural sectors and rural communities face severe natural resource and institutional constraints. The main natural resource constraints are a fragile land resource base and declining soil fertility, limited water resources and growing water scarcity, and frequent climate shocks (e.g., drought). The institutional constraints include unequal land distribution and insecure land tenure, poor and unstable management of common resources, low public sector investment in physical and social infrastructure in the rural areas, lack of active and effective local institutions, and low adoption rates of improved technologies and practices. In many countries of the region, the agricultural sector is in state of transition, from heavily controlled by the state to largely driven by market forces. However, some socially driven policies, such as consumer food subsidy, subsidized credit and agricultural inputs, and price support measures, are still in place in some countries.

CWANA countries vary greatly in terms of per capita income, living standards, and economic performance. Per capita income, measured by annual gross national product (GNP) per capita, ranges from $230–260 for Somalia, Sudan, and Yemen to about $2900–3300 for Lebanon and Turkey. Egypt, Jordan, and Morocco are in the middle of this range, with an annual GNP per capita of $1100–1500 (IFAD, 2002). Most countries can be classified as "lower-middle-income countries," but their indicators of human development are lower than would be expected, given their income levels.

Among the CWANA region, the Near East and North Africa (NENA) sub-region has been characterized by persistently high population growth rates, averaging 3.1% in the 1980s. Although the population grew slowly in the 1990s at an annual rate of 2.3%, the labor force is still growing at more than 3% annually as a result of previous population growth.

The contribution of the agricultural sector to the national economies is low (about 16%), despite the fact that nearly 36% of the active population is engaged in agriculture.

All countries except Turkey and Syria are experiencing food deficits and thus depend on imports to varying degrees. For the NENEA sub-region as a whole, the proportion of cereal imports to total consumption increased from 15% in the 1970s to 30% in the 1980s.

All countries in CWANA region in general and the WANA region in particular have faced severe challenges in increasing their agricultural production over the last 40 years. This is mainly due to many factors, including a limited natural resource base of arable land and water, low and volatile rainfall with frequent drought, growing population, low rates of productivity growth, increased rural/urban migration, low public and private investments in rain-fed areas, weak extension systems, inappropriate agricultural policies, and low adoption rates of new technologies. Government policies have helped expand agricultural production but at the expense of deteriorating the natural resource base. Most policies have been directed to increase cereal and meat production, which include highly subsidized fuel and credit for machinery and other modern inputs, high support prices for producers, high producer and consumer subsidies, and high tariffs on imported food commodities. To better understand the status of food production in CWANA region, a trend analysis was conducted for major cropping groups using FAO data from 1961–2002.

Growth performance of CWANA's cereal production over the last four decades has been impressive. Results show that CWANA has achieved a 2.9% annual growth rate in cereal production during the 1962–2002 period. Most of the growth is attributed to, first, productivity enhancement and second to area expansion. Cereal yield and area grew 1.5% and 1.3%, respectively, during the same period.

Cereal production performance during the last four decades was particularly strong in Egypt (3%), Iran (3.5%), Kyrgyzstan (3.1%), Pakistan (3.5%), Saudi Arabia (7.6%), Syria (3.7%), Tajikistan (7.7%), Turkmenistan (9%), and Uzbekistan (7.7%). Yield increase has been the major source of cereal growth in most of CWANA countries, including Egypt, Iran, Kyrgyzstan, Pakistan, Saudi Arabia, Syria, and Uzbekistan. Area expansion has been the main contributor to cereal growth in Tajikistan and Turkmenistan.

Grain consumption growth in the CWANA region was most rapid during the 1960s, 1970s, and 1980s. The region had a particularly rapid decline in annual demand growth in the last decade, falling from 4.0% in 1970–1979 to 1.8% in 1990–2002. Grain demand growth declined in most CWANA countries during the 1990s while remaining strong in Egypt, Ethiopia, Lebanon, Sudan, and Tunisia. Grain demand growth from 1980–1989 and 1990–2002 declined the most in Algeria, Iraq,

Kazakhstan, Morocco, and Turkey. Declining population growth rates, saturation of demand, and declining oil revenues helped slow the overall growth of grain demand in CWANA during the 1990s.

WANA had net cereal imports of 45.1 million tons in 1997. Cereal imports increased most rapidly during the 1980s, a period when agricultural production grew at a rate of 3.8% per year as a result of oil-financed investments. Increased oil revenues during this period permitted both large-scale development of local production and large quantities of cereal imports. Exploding domestic demand is expected to increase WANA's cereal net imports to 73.1 million tons by 2020. Wheat imports alone, at 37.8 million tons, will account for 52% of the total cereal net imports in 2020. Thus increasing wheat production can contribute greatly to enhancing food security in WANA and thus save a large amount of hard currency currently used for wheat imports.

Similarly, imports of livestock products are projected to increase substantially during the next two decades. All meat imports are expected to increase from 0.946 million tons in 1997 to 1.767 million tons in 2020, among which beef and poultry account for 42% and 51%, respectively. Net imports of sheep and goat, milk, and eggs are also expected to increase sharply by 2022 as a result of increased demand for livestock products due to population growth, changes in consumers' preferences, and increased per capita income.

The food consumption pattern is expected to change dramatically during the next 20 years in response to increases in population and per capita income and changes in consumer preferences. Meat per capita consumption is projected to increase rapidly, by 29% for poultry and 19% for beef. Per capita consumption of other livestock products will increase as well. Milk and sheep/goat per capita consumption is expected to increase by 14% and 12%, respectively, between 1997 and 2020.

Only the per capita consumption of two major cereal commodities, wheat and maize, is projected to decrease, by 2% and 16%, respectively. This reduction in wheat and maize per capita consumption will only slightly contribute to grain deficit reduction in the CWANA region. Total grain deficit in CWANA is expected to decrease from 46 million tons in 2002 to 35 million tons in 2020. Low growth rates of population, consumption, and yield in WANA could explain the anticipated decrease in grain deficit. The annual demand for cereals is expected to decrease to less than 2% per year by 2020, which is lower than the annual growth rates of the 1980s and 1990s, estimated at 4% and 2.5%, respectively. The rate of increase in production and yields is expected to decrease during the next 20 years. The cereal yields in WANA are expected to increase slightly during the next two decades, but they are still far below those of East Asia.

A significant and important opportunity exists to create a synergistic partnership of ICARDA with diverse research institutions and development agencies to apply science and technology to address the key problems of food security, poverty reduction, and conservation of natural resources in the CWANA region. The previously described trends and constraints facing the development of the agricultural sector in the CWANA region have important research and policy implications. Governments and national and international research centers will adopt strategic approaches of agricultural research to alleviate poverty through:

- Improved technologies that increase productivity, particularly per unit of water, sustain resource use, and are applicable by poor people with few inputs.
- Resource management practices that conserve natural resources without decreasing productivity.
- Diversified farming systems to reduce risk, increase resource-use efficiency, and improve returns to farm labor.
- Improved vertical integration from producer to consumer to add value to products and improve quality of production.
- Knowledge management. Through research continuity, ICARDA and its partners have gathered invaluable research findings. The management and dissemination of this information, coupled also with tacit knowledge, with ICARDA acting as a regional knowledge portal, will increasingly become a major contribution to global public goods. Such information is useful in the temporal dimension to understand aspects of sustainability and in the spatial dimension for geographical generalization from site-specific research.

1. INTRODUCTION

Food demand growth caused by expanding populations and shifting consumption patterns will necessitate future food production increases, but unexploited, available land is limited, placing increased pressure on technologically driven yield improvements (Rosegrant *et al.*, 2001). The need for modern agricultural technologies, however, must be balanced against legitimate concerns about environmental sustainability. Empirical evidence has demonstrated that the negative effects on the environment from inappropriately applied technologies can translate into productivity losses and threaten human health, although assessing the precise extent of these effects is often difficult. Growing urban and industrial demands on existing water supplies and the need for improved water quality further complicate the situation.

Growth rates of world agricultural production and crop yields have slowed in recent years. This, together with weak systems of food distribution, has raised fears that the world might not be able to provide enough food and other commodities to ensure that future populations are adequately fed. In many societies, including the CWANA region, the problem of resource redistribution represents an important part of the problem of poverty and food shortage, both currently and in the long run. However, an FAO study (FAO, 2002) suggests that world agricultural production can grow in line with demand, provided that the necessary national and international policies to promote agriculture are in place. Regional shortages are unlikely, but serious problems that already exist at national and local levels may worsen unless focused efforts are made:

- *Sources of growth in crop production.* There are three main sources of growth in crop production: expanding the land area (horizontal expansion), increasing the frequency with which land is cropped (often through irrigation), and boosting yield (vertical expansion). It has been suggested that the world may be approaching the ceiling of what is possible for all three sources (FAO, 2002). A detailed examination of production potentials does not support this at the global level, although in some countries and sub-regions, serious problems already exist and could deepen.

- *Water.* Irrigation is crucial to the world's food supplies. In 1997–1999, irrigated land made up only about one fifth of the total arable area in developing countries but produced two fifths of all crops and close to three fifths of cereal production. The role of irrigation is expected to increase still further. The developing countries as a whole are likely to expand their irrigated area from 202 million ha in 1997–1999 to 242 million by 2030. Most of this expansion will occur in land-scarce areas where irrigation is already crucial. The net increase in irrigated land is predicated to be less than 40% of that achieved since the early 1960s. There appears to be enough unused irrigable land to meet future needs. FAO studies suggest a total irrigation potential of some 402 million ha in developing countries, of which only half is currently in use. However, water resources will be a major factor constraining expansion in South Asia, which will be using 41% of its renewable freshwater resources by 2030, and in the Near East and North Africa, which will be using 58%. These regions will need to achieve greater efficiency in water use.

- *Yield.* In the past four decades, rising yields accounted for 70% of the increase in crop production in the developing countries. The 1990s experienced a slowdown in the growth of yields. Wheat yields, for example, grew at an average of 3.8% a year between 1961 and 1989 but at only 2% a year between 1989 and 1999. Yield growth continues to be the dominant factor underlying increases in crop production in the future. In developing countries, it will account for about 70% of growth in crop production to 2030. To meet population projections, future yield growth will not need to be as rapid as in the past. For wheat yields, an annual rise of only 1.2% a year is needed over the next 30 years (FAO, 2002). Overall, the FAO estimated that nearly 80% of the future increase in crop production in developing countries will have to come from intensification, higher yields, increased multiple cropping, and shorter fallow periods.

- *Improved technology.* New technology is needed for areas with shortages of land or water or with particular problems of soil or climate. These are frequently areas with a high concentration of poor people, where such technology could play a key role in improving food security.

Agricultural production could probably meet expected demand over the period to 2030 even without major advances in modern technology. However, the new technologies of molecular analysis could give a significant boost to productivity, particularly in areas with special difficulties, thereby improving the incomes of the poor, just as the Green Revolution did in large parts of Asia during the 1960s and 1980s. A second

Green Revolution in agricultural technology is needed for the 21st century. Productivity increases are still vital but must be combined with environmental protection or restoration, while new technologies must be both affordable by and geared to the needs of the poor and undernourished.

- *Livestock.* Diets in developing countries are changing as incomes rise. The share of staples, such as cereals, roots, and tubers, is declining while that of meat, dairy products, and oil crops is increasing. From 1964–1966 and 1997–1999, per capita meat consumption in developing countries increased 150% and that of milk and dairy products by 60%. By 2030, per capita consumption of livestock products could rise 44%. As in the past, poultry consumption will grow fastest.
Productivity improvements are likely to be a major source of growth. Milk yields should improve, whereas breeding and improved management will increase average carcass weights and off-take rates. This will allow increased production with lower growth in animal numbers and thus corresponding slowdown in the growth of environmental damage from grazing or wastes.

- *Environment and climate.* Global warming is not expected to depress food availability at the global level, but at the regional and local levels there could be significant impacts. Current projections suggest that the potential for crop production will increase in temperate and latitudes, whereas in parts of the tropics and subtropics it could decline. This could further deepen the dependence of developing countries on food imports, though at the same time it could improve the ability of temperate exporters to fill the gap. Rising sea levels will threaten crop production and livelihoods in countries such as Bangladesh and Egypt.

CWANA is characterized by high population growth; low and erratic rainfall; limited areas of arable land; and severely limited water resources for further development of irrigation. Therefore, methods for more efficient and sustainable use of these limited resources must be found. Cereal production has increased 80% since 1979–1981, especially in Egypt and Morocco, due mainly to increased wheat yield. The modest increase in barley production is the result of area expansion and yield increases (IFAD, 2002). The number of small ruminants has grown greatly throughout the region, resulting in doubling meat production. Regardless of these gains, the food gap is expected to grow 2.9% per year throughout the coming decade.

Past policies in the region, in general, have led to environmental degradation while doing little to improve the livelihoods of the rural poor. Agricultural sectors and rural communities face severe natural resources and institutional constraints. The main natural resource constraints are a fragile land resource base and declining soil fertility, limited water resources and growing water scarcity, and frequent climate shocks (e.g., drought). The institutional constraints include unequal land distribution and insecure land tenure, poor and unstable management of common resources, low public sector investment in physical and social infrastructure in the rural areas, lack of active and effective local institutions, and low adoption rates of improved technologies and practices. In many countries of the region, the agricultural sector is in a state of transition, from heavily controlled by the state to largely driven by market forces. However, some socially driven policies, such as consumer food subsidy, subsidized credit and agricultural inputs, and price support measures, are still in place in some countries. Farmers are obliged to sell their output to states at fixed prices, which are either higher or lower than market prices.

Economically, the policies of subsidies and market controls has led to market distortion, inefficient allocation of resources, and stagnation of the agricultural economy.

2. ECONOMIC AND POPULATION TRENDS

CWANA countries vary greatly in terms of per capita income, living standards, and economic performance. Per capita income, measured by annual gross national product (GNP) per capita, ranges from $230–260 for Somalia, Sudan, and Yemen to about $2900–3300 for Lebanon and Turkey. Egypt, Jordan, and Morocco are in the middle of this range, with an annual GNP per capita of $1100–1500 (IFAD, 2002). Most countries can be classified as "lower-middle-income countries," but their indicators of human development are lower than would be expected, given their income levels. Morocco's per capita income, for example, in 1999 was close to that of the Philippines and Sri Lanka, but its human development index ranking (124th out of 174 countries) was far behind those of the Philippines and Sri Lanka (77th and 84th, respectively).

Growth rates of GNP in the 1990s varied considerably among countries. Algeria and Morocco experienced the lowest growth rates of 1.6% and 2.3%, respectively, whereas Lebanon and Syria achieved the highest growth rates of 7.7% and 5.7%, respectively. These high growth rates are attributed to postwar reconstruction in Lebanon and to good weather and oil production in Syria. The remaining countries in the region have experienced moderate growth rates in the GNP, ranging from 3.2% in Yemen to 4.6% in Tunisia. Due to high population growth rates of 2.3% during the 1990s, these favorable growth rates resulted in only a small net improvement (IFAD, 2002). The other obstacle is the persistent inequalities in income level and its distribution. The reduced demand for labor in the Gulf States has further worsened the rising unemployment rates and has had a great impact on remittances from migrant workers, especially in Egypt and Yemen (the two countries that supplied much of the Arab casual labor market).

Within the CWANA region, the Near East and North Africa (NENA) subregion has been characterized by persistently high population growth rates, averaging 3.1% in the 1980s. Although the population grew slowly in the 1990s at an annual rate of 2.3%, the labor force is still growing at more than 3% annually as a result of previous population growth (IFAD, 2002). The fertility rate has declined to from 6.6 in the 1970s to 4.9 for many countries, but remains at around 7.0 for other countries such as Somalia and Yemen. Rural population, on average, accounts for about 47% of the sub-region entire population. However, rural population represents nearly 20% of total population in Djibouti and Lebanon and about 66% in Somalia and Sudan.

The contribution of the agricultural sector to the national economies is low (about 16%), despite the fact that nearly 36% of the active population is engaged in agriculture. This low contribution to the national economies is mainly attributed to low productivity and poor integration of rural population with the rest of the economy. The agricultural sector in Jordan contributes only 3% to the national economy, whereas in Sudan the contribution was much higher (40%) before the country started producing oil. In most other countries, the contribution of agriculture to GDP ranges from 10–20% (IFAD, 2002). However, agriculture is a major market for labor in many countries. The proportion of active population engaged in agriculture varies from 4% in Lebanon to over 70% in Somalia, with an average of 30% for other countries.

All countries except Turkey, Syria, and Tunisia are experiencing food deficits and thus depend on imports in varying degrees. For the NENEA sub-region as a whole, the proportion of cereal imports to total consumption increased from 15% in the 1970s to 30% in the 1980s.

Averaging the poor with the rich masks poverty in many WANA countries. Consider Libya, Oman, Saudi Arabia, Kuwait, and the United Arab Emirates as examples of the major oil exporters. We find large disparities between these and the remaining WANA countries. The oil exporters, with only 7% of the region's population, represent the region's highest per capita GNP, averaging just over US$9400, which, even so, is only a quarter of the per capita GNP of industrialized countries. The remaining 93% of WANA's population has a far lower per capita income. The four most economically disadvantaged states of South WANA (Eritrea, Ethiopia, Somalia, and Sudan) have a per capita GNP of only US$88, which is less than 1.2% of the oil exporters with small populations. In fact, 42% of the total population of 239 million people has a per capita GNP of less than US$1.0 per day and are thus in the grip of severe poverty.

There is more absolute poverty and incidence of poverty in rural than urban areas in WANA. Even though infrastructure in the rural sector has improved in the last 20 years, there has not been a proportional increase in employment or poverty alleviation. Economic disparities will continue to fuel migration from rural to urban areas and from poor to rich countries both within and outside the WANA region (El-Beltagy, 1997).

The dry areas of West Asia and North Africa face severe and growing challenges due to the rapidly growing demand for water resources. New sources of water are increasingly expensive to exploit, limiting the potential for expansion of new water supplies. Irrigation accounts for 80% of withdrawals regionwide, but demand is expanding most rapidly in urban areas. Withdrawals in the Libyan Arab Jamahiriya, Saudi Arabia, the Gulf States, and Yemen already exceed renewable supplies, whereas Egypt and Jordan have essentially reached the limit; Algeria and Tunisia face several regional deficits, even if in total they are in surplus (ESCWA and ICARDA, 2000). Improving on-farm water-use efficiency (FWUE) can contribute directly to increased availability of water. Six empirical studies on economic assessment of FWUE in agriculture, jointly conducted by ICARDA and ESCWA, demonstrate the low ratios of water-use efficiency in crop production.

ICARDA research has shown great potential for increasing water productivity through the use of supplementary irrigation, water savings by improving on-farm water use efficiency, water harvesting, deficit irrigation, improved cultural practices, and germplasm improvements. To disseminate these technological advances to farmers, ICARDA has developed and implemented several regional projects using an integrated natural resource management approach (INRM) in cooperation with national programs and full participation and involvement of rural communities. The interventions include a package of technical, institutional, and policy options targeting conserving the scarce water resource and optimizing its use. If policymakers encourage the adoption of appropriate technical as well as incentive packages, water-use efficiency can be improved. In this way, ample water will be available for productive use, leading to increasing water productivity and consequently agricultural production.

According to the Falkenmark Index (expressed as thousands of m^3 per capita per year), CWANA countries were grouped into three groups. The first group, for which the index ranges between 11800 and 1800, contains Tajikistan, Kyrgyzstan, Turkmenistan, Kazakhstan, Sudan, Turkey, Pakistan, Mauritania, Iran, and Ethiopia. The second group includes Syria, Lebanon, Eritrea, Uzbekistan, and Morocco, with a Falkenmark Index range between 1600 and 1100. The last group, with an Index range between 400 and 100, contains Oman, Tunisia, Algeria, Egypt, Yemen, United Arab Emirates, Saudi Arabia, and Jordan (Figure 1).

Available information on the water poverty index (WPI) and its sub-indices (resources, use, access, capacity, and environment) are used to monitor the performance of scarce water in the CWANA region. Although a negative association between resources and use is to be expected *a priori* (the scarcer the resources, the better use is made of them), the positive correlation between these two indicators of 0.30 suggests that water resources are misused in the CWANA region. Similarly, the positive correlation of 0.21 between resources and environment is not consistent with *a priori* expectations of negative association (the scarcer the resources, the more attention is paid to conservation generally), indicating that water resources in the region are not sustainably managed. The negative correlation between resources and access sub-indices also contradicts what one might have expected, suggesting that people in the region do not have adequate access to the available water resources. There is a positive association between the WPI and the human development index (HDI) for CWANA countries. Similar positive correlation is found between WPI and the food security index (FSI). Preliminary results of regression analysis indicate that increasing the WPI by 1% will increase per capita grain production by 4 Kg per year, thus contributing to increased food security (Shideed, 2004).

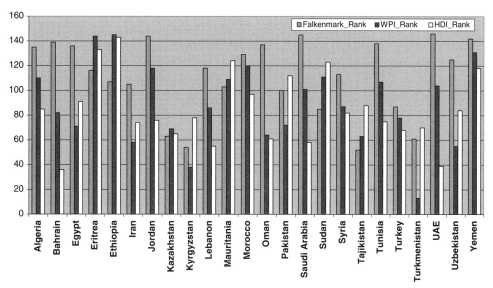

Figure 1   CWANA ranking according to WPI and HDI: Selected countries.

WPI sub-indices reveal that water availability (resources) is the most limiting factor to the development of the water sector in all CWANA countries except Eritrea, Ethiopia, Kazakhstan, Kyrgyzstan, and Sudan. For Eritrea and Ethiopia, improving population access to clean water and sanitation and enhancing access to irrigation would be more productive investments to improve the efficiency of water sector. However, environmental attributes such as water quality, water pollution, regulations, and information capacity are the priority areas for interventions in Kazakhstan, Kyrgyzstan, and Sudan.

Available information indicates that scarce water resources are poorly managed and inefficiently used in the dry areas of the CWANA region. Irrigation accounts for 80–90% of all water consumed in the region; thus, improving FWUE can contribute directly to increased availability of water. Six empirical studies on the economic assessment of FWUE in agriculture, jointly conducted by ICARDA and ESCWA, demonstrate the low ratios of water-use efficiency in crop production. FWUE for wheat, for example, was found to be 0.61 in Radwania (Syria), 0.37 in Rabea (Iraq), 0.65 in Nubaria and Beni Sweif (Egypt), 0.30 in Al Ghor (Jordan), and 0.77 in Nineveh (Iraq). These estimates indicate that farmers over-irrigated wheat by 20–60%. It is, therefore, possible to save an enormous amount of water that can be used to expand the wheat-growing area and thus increase total production, or to produce other crops. Alternatively, farmers can increase the wheat yield considerably under current levels of water use and with improved water and crop management practices. Either option can contribute greatly to food security in the region.

3. MIGRATION

Natural-resource degradation causes a net loss of productivity in the short and long term. Also, small landholdings or lack of land, high production risks, lack of stable employment, low wages, malnutrition, limited access to health and education services, and social and political marginalization compound rural poverty, inducing rural/urban migration. Water scarcity is one of the major factors forcing rural poor to migrate to urban centers. Migration within and outside WANA countries can destabilize the countries' economies, causing social friction and later indigenous resource-management patterns. On the positive side, migration enhances investments through remittances. Remittances subsidize the rural poor by allowing them to remain on the land, but without necessarily providing sufficient means to conserve and improve their limited resource endowments (Rodriguez, 1997).

In Egypt the 1986 census estimated that 2.25 million Egyptian nationals were working outside the country. In 1979 remittance amounted to US$2 billion. Between 1970 and 1985, about 45,000 Egyptians immigrated to the United States. In Iran since 1979, nearly 750,000 educated Iranians migrate to Western Europe or the United States or Turkey. Jordan experienced more than one form of migration, large segments of the labor force worked abroad, and rural/urban migration continued unabated. Government figures for 1987 stated that nearly 350,000 Jordanians were working abroad, a remarkably high number for such a small domestic population. Problems of employment, housing, services, and drought created internal migration in Sudan. In the 1970s nearly 10% of the population moved away from their areas to large cities, particularly Khartoum. The number of migrants escalated greatly in the latter 1980s because of drought and famine and the civil war in the south. In 1991 Sudan was host to about 763,000 refugees from neighboring countries such as Ethiopia and Chad (U.S. Library of Congress, 2004). But remittances may be affected by the formal financial systems not suited to the needs of expatriate population. Migration remains a volatile sector in CWANA because political changes could cause large-scale repatriation, increasing unemployment, and potential political unrest in the countries of origin.

Rural-to-urban migration is not only population flow within a country; quite the contrary! These two examples illustrate that other flows, from town to town, from rural to rural, and even from town to rural, can even be more important. In Ethiopia in 1994, 45% of the urban population was composed of recent or older migrants, but 43% of these came from other towns; in Ghana, 49% of urban people in 1998 were migrants, with 70% coming from other towns. Rural-to-rural migrations are the most important flows in these two countries (which have remained predominantly rural); but even urban-to-rural migration is not negligible (Vercueil, 2004).

Out-migration has, of course, a significant impact on the regions of origin. On one hand, it improves the situation by reducing the pressure on resources, by offering income alternatives and diversification against risk, and by establishing new relations with other areas, a source of information and "social capital." Migration is also a source of income for the rural areas through migrants' remittances, which can be especially important—the example of Morocco or post-work returnees. On the other hand, because usually it is the more able who are leaving, out-migration impoverishes rural areas, creates labor shortages at peak periods, and can lead to a vicious circle of degradation (smaller markets for local activities).

4. FOOD SECURITY AROUND THE GLOBE

Food security indicators of 70 low-income developing countries show slow improvement of their food security over the next decade. A USDA study showed that average per capita food consumption of these countries stagnated in 2002, and the number of people not meeting nutritional requirements was estimated to be higher than in previous years (USDA, 2003). Instability in short-run food production continues to hamper long-run food security progress because poor countries tend to focus their policies and resources toward dealing with emergencies when they are faced with frequent economic shocks. This has raised concerns about the attainability of the 1996 World Food Summit goal to halve the number of hungry people by 2015. In fact, the food security situation for some countries, as in sub-Saharan Africa, has worsened since 1996 (USDA, 2003). In its response to these concerns, the World Food Summit in 2002 called for more resources to battle hunger and food insecurity. Similar efforts were taken by other international forums, such as the WTO meeting in Doha (July 2002) and the Summit on Sustainable Development in Johannesburg (August 2002). The situation is further complicated by food production shortfalls, a global economic slowdown that intensifies foreign exchange constraints and thus reduces purchasing power of consumers and worsens poverty, and grain price increases that limit a country's ability to import food. Theoretically, increases in grain prices should improve production incentives for producers in low-income countries. However, low producers' response to price changes (supply is price inelastic), lack of productive resources, and inefficient markets have limited farmers' ability to take advantage of higher prices.

Economic shocks (natural and manmade conflicts) are major constraints to improve food security in many developing countries. The food needed (in grain equivalent) to maintain per capita food consumption at the 1999–2001 level was estimated at 6.8 million tons in 2002. To meet average nutritional requirements, the food gap is estimated at 17.7 million tons. It increases to 31 million tons to provide food needed to raise consumption in each income group to meet nutritional requirements in the 70 low-income countries. Consequently, the number of hungry people increased from 896 million in 2001 to about 1 billion in 2002. Overcoming short-term instability in the

Table 1 World trade of wheat, barley, and beef and veal (total net imports, M tons), 2002–2013

Year	Wheat	Barley	Beef and Veal
2002–2003	73.37	12.71	3.25
2003–2004	76.99	14.82	3.46
2004–2005	84.18	16.02	3.73
2005–2006	89.43	16.16	3.87
2006–2007	91.85	16.94	3.99
2007–2008	94.30	17.30	4.05
2008–2009	95.99	17.87	4.08
2009–2010	97.92	18.26	4.12
2010–2011	100.13	18.56	4.16
2011–2012	102.17	18.97	4.17
2012–2013	104.18	19.26	4.14

Source: Food and Agricultural Policy Research Institute (FAPRI, 2003). *U.S. and World Agricultural Outlook*. Iowa State University and University of Missouri-Columbia. Staff Report 1–03, ISSN 1534–4533, Ames, Iowa, January 2003.

food supply will result in declining the food gap and the number of hungry people by 2012 (USDA, 2003).[1]

World wheat net trade is projected to increase by 3.6% annually, reaching 104.2 million tons by 2012–2013 (Table 1). Growth in imports from developing Asia and Middle Eastern countries accounts for most of this increase because of rising demand and limited potential to increase production. African and Middle Eastern countries make up more than half the market for wheat imports, and they are the second fastest-growing market for wheat (FAPRI, 2003). Egypt's net imports, for example, will grow 2.4% annually, reaching 7.9 million tons in 2012–2013, because of low prices and higher per capita consumption (see Appendix, Table 1). Similarly, Iran's net imports will increase 3.6% per year, reaching 4.8 million tons in 2012–2013.

World barley demand increases steadily at an annual rate of 4%, fueled by growing demand from China and Saudi Arabia. Beef trade is projected to grow by an annual growth rate of 3.01% in the next decade after a two-year decline in its trade due to BSE and FMD diseases. Beef production is also expected to increase 1.5% annually, reaching 54.71 million tons in 2012. Recovery in major importing countries, such as Mexico and Russia, will slightly reduce growth in trade in the next decade, and the trend ends at 4.14 million tons in 2012 (FAPRI, 2003).

IFPRI projections for production in 2020 suggest that many of the major commodities remain critical for developing countries' access to food. Rising food deficits in the WANA region are important in wheat, rice, maize, and fish. The wheat deficit in WANA is largely associated with rising urban consumption, and alternative sources of supply exist in the international market. The deficit in beef in WANA is predicted to be important. The implication is that maintenance research on productivity of the identified staples and new emphasis on nontraditional exports as sources of foreign exchange earnings would be appropriate. Toward 2030, according to the FAO, the developing countries will become increasingly dependent on cereal imports. The most serious imbalances for cereals will be experienced in wheat and coarse grains in WANA, East Asia, and sub-Saharan Africa, respectively. The primary means through which increased yields will be met is through increased intensification and technological efficiency in reducing yield gaps. New science has an important role to play in meeting these needs. Changes in the commodity composition of food are expected to occur in developing countries with a relative stabilization of per capita consumption of cereals, roots and tubers, and pulses and marked increases in vegetable oils, meat, and milk and dairy products. There will need to be relatively large increases in the production of meet (beef and veal, mutton and lamb, and poultry meat) in developing countries.

5. DRIVING FORCES FOR SLOW PROGRESS IN IMPROVING FOOD SECURITY

The slower-than-expected rate of progress in improving food security in low-income countries has created increased concerns among international organizations, international and national research systems, and policymakers at various levels. Some of the forces that drive food insecurity are (USDA, 2003):

- *Shocks in food supplies.* Conflicts and production shortfalls are two major causes of shocks in food supplies in most of the food-insecure countries. Although a relationship between hunger and poverty and political unrest cannot easily be established, empirical evidence indicates that instability often occurs in poorer countries, where the coping mechanisms are weakest. FAO estimated average agricultural output losses due to political conflicts in developing countries at $4.3 billion annually, a large enough amount to provide nutritionally adequate food for 330 million undernourished people (USDA, 2003). Conflicts combined with food shortfalls accounted for six out of the seven famines occurred in Africa during the last two decades. Both high- and low-income countries are susceptible to economic shocks, but these only affect food security in countries with limited resources, where domestic production is strongly linked to consumption and the agricultural sector is the major employer.
- *High output risk.* Low-income countries are characterized by high output risk because agricultural production largely occurs in rain-fed areas that are subject to severe

weather variations. In addition, population growth contributed to further deterioration of the land, often leading to erosion, deforestation, and depletion of topsoil, which in turn increases susceptibility to drought.

- *Slow growth of the agricultural sector.* Slow growth of the agricultural sector has led to the poor performance of cash crops, which are the main source of exports to finance food imports. Share for sub-Saharan Africa of global agricultural exports, for example, declined from 13% in 1970 to nearly 2% in 2000. If the region had maintained its global market share, the value of its agricultural exports would have been $44 billion higher in 2000, thus increasing its food import capacity and perhaps improving food security.
- *Food and social security.* Food security is the foundation for social security. Therefore, short-run actions to mitigate and prevent food insecurity should be combined with long-run food security strategies. Expanding the use of improved technologies to increase productivity and thus farm income would enhance farmers' capacity to cope with production shocks and instability. In the CWANA region, particularly in WANA, there is huge potential to increase yields for staple crops consumed by the poor and the general public. Actual farm yields of crops in the region are far below their potentials.
- *Investments in rural development.* Rural development requires appropriate investments as long-term strategies to food security. Investments in rural development are critical to increase productivity in the agricultural sector and provide nonfarm employment opportunities for rural communities to diversify their income sources, leading to higher incomes and less risk in both the short and long runs. Currently, rural areas in many CWANA countries face growing unemployment, which could contribute to social instability and food insecurity.
- *Rural markets.* Developing rural markets could create a low-risk environment that is essential for sustaining economic growth and improving food security (USDA, 2003).
- *Safety net.* Efficient safety-net programs for food security have an important role in reducing the negative impact of economic shocks. It is thus essential to review existing safety-net programs in WANA in terms of their efficiency and effectiveness in enhancing food security.

6. FOOD PRODUCTION IN THE CWANA REGION

All countries in the CWANA region in general and the WANA region in particular have faced severe challenges in increasing their agricultural production over the last 40 years. This is due to many factors, including a limited natural resource base of arable land and water, low and volatile rainfall with frequent drought, growing population, low rates of productivity growth, increased rural/urban migration, low public and private investments in rain-fed areas, weak extension systems, inappropriate agricultural policies, and low adoption rates of new technologies. Total land area in the CWANA region is 2.3 billion hectares; the arable land is about 170 million hectares, or 7% of the total area of the region. Irrigated land made up about 35% of the arable land in CWANA in 2002 (FAOSTAT, 2003). In Armenia, Egypt, Kyrgyzstan, Oman, Pakistan, Turkmenistan, and Uzbekistan, irrigated land ranged between 80% and 100% of the arable land. Ethiopia irrigated land was only 2% of the arable land in 2002, which indicates a high potential of increasing crop productivity by increasing irrigated land in the country. Government policies have helped expand agricultural production but at the expense of deteriorating the natural resource base. Most policies have been directed to increasing cereal and meat production, which includes highly subsidized fuel and credit for machinery and other modern inputs, high support prices for producers, high producer and consumer subsidies, and high tariffs on imported food commodities. To better understand the status of food production in the CWANA region, a trend analysis was conducted for major cropping groups using FAO data in 1961–2002. Results are summarized here by commodity groups.

6.1 Cereals

Growth performance of CWANA's cereal production over the last four decades has been impressive. Data in Table 2 show that CWANA achieved a 2.9% annual growth rate in cereal production during the 1962–2002 period. Most of the growth is attributed to, first, productivity enhancement and second to area expansion. Cereal yield and area grew 1.5% and 1.3%, respectively, during the same period. The highest production growth rates occurred in the 1960s (3.4%) and the 1970s (2.7%), mostly attributed to high yield growth rates of 2.1% and 2.5%, respectively. The contribution of yield to the growth of cereal production decreased during the 1980s and 1990s. However, the CWANA region has maintained an annual growth rate in cereal production of 2.1% during the last two decades. This is mainly attributed to substantial investments made by oil-producing countries during the 1980s, which skewed overall regional growth

Table 2 Cereal growth rates in CWANA region, 1961–2002

Period	Growth Rates (%)		
	Area	Yield	Production
1961–1969	1.4	2.1	3.4
1970–1979	0.2	2.5	2.7
1980–1989	0.9	1.1	2.1
1990–2002	0.7	1.1	2.1
1961–2002	1.3	1.5	2.9

Source: Estimates by the authors using the FAO database.

upward. Saudi Arabia, for example, has expanded its cereal production substantially through massive investments in irrigation, using nonrenewable water supplies and heavy application of subsidized fertilizers.

Cereal production performance during the last four decades was particularly strong in Egypt (3%), Iran (3.5%), Kyrgyzstan (3.1%), Pakistan (3.5%), Saudi Arabia (7.6%), Syria (3.7%), Tajikistan (7.7%), Turkmenistan (9%), and Uzbekistan (7.7%). Data in Table 3 clearly demonstrate that the source of cereal production growth varies among countries. Yield increase has been the major source of cereal growth in most CWANA countries, including Azerbaijan, Egypt, Iran, Kyrgyzstan, Pakistan, Saudi Arabia, Syria, and Uzbekistan. Area expansion has been the main contributor to cereal growth in Armenia, Georgia, Tajikistan, and Turkmenistan. Cereal production decreased annually in four countries: Afghanistan (−0.9%), Jordan (−2.3%), Kazakhstan (−4.7%),

Table 3 Cereal growth rates (%) in CWANA countries, 1961–2002

Country	Area	Yield	Production
Afghanistan	−1.4	0.2	−0.9
Algeria	−1.0	1.5	0.5
Armenia	1.69	0.5	2.19
Azerbaijan	1.13	4.4	5.59
Egypt	1.0	2.0	3.0
Ethiopia	0.1	1.5	1.6
Georgia	5.23	−1.36	3.8
Iran	1.1	2.4	3.5
Iraq	1.1	−0.7	0.4
Jordan	−5.3	3.1	−2.3
Kazakhstan*	−6.3	1.6	−4.7
Kyrgyzstan*	0.8	2.2	3.1
Lebanon	−1.8	2.6	0.7
Libya	−1.5	3.0	1.4
Mauritania	−0.6	3.0	2.4
Morocco	0.7	0.3	1.0
Oman	−0.8	2.3	1.4

Continued

Table 3 Cereal growth rates (%) in CWANA countries, 1961–2002—Cont'd

Country	Area	Yield	Production
Pakistan	1.1	2.4	3.5
Saudi Arabia	3.1	4.4	7.6
Somalia	0.6	0.4	1.0
Sudan	4.0	−1.3	2.6
Syria	1.6	2.1	3.7
Tajikistan★	4.7	2.9	7.7
Tunisia	−0.7	1.9	1.2
Turkey	0.2	1.9	2.1
Turkmenistan★	8.2	0.8	9.0
Uzbekistan★	0.5	7.9	7.7
Yemen	−1.8	0.7	−1.1
CWANA region	1.3	1.5	2.9

★1992–2002. Source: Calculated by the authors using the FAO database.

and Yemen (−1.1%). Other countries have achieved moderate growth in cereal production during the last 40 years. Figure 2 shows cereal growth rates in CWANA countries between 1961 and 2002.

ICARDA cereal mandate crops, barley and wheat, showed production growth rates range between 3.77% and −22.92% for barley and between 17.71% and −3.89% for wheat during the 1961–2002 period. The highest production growth rate for barley was recorded in Iran (3.77%) and the lowest in Turkmenistan. In general all Central Asian republics recorded negative growth rates in barley production, which can be attributed to decreases in planted areas as a result of changing the cropping pattern in these countries and shifting to wheat, which recorded high production growth rates. Turkmenistan, Uzbekistan, Tajikistan, and Saudi Arabia reached the highest growth rates in wheat production of 17.71%, 17.70%, 12.73%, and 11.26%, respectively. Armenia, Azerbaijan, Georgia, Kyrgyzstan, and Sudan reached high production growth rates in wheat production between 6.84% and 5.10%. Other countries, such as Egypt, Iran, Libya, Mauritania, Pakistan, Syria, and Yemen, reported wheat production growth rates between 4.33% and 3.42%. Jordan, Kazakhstan, and Oman reported negative wheat production growth rates. In Egypt, Georgia, Iran, Libya, and Mauritania, increasing the productivity of wheat was the main factor of increasing the production

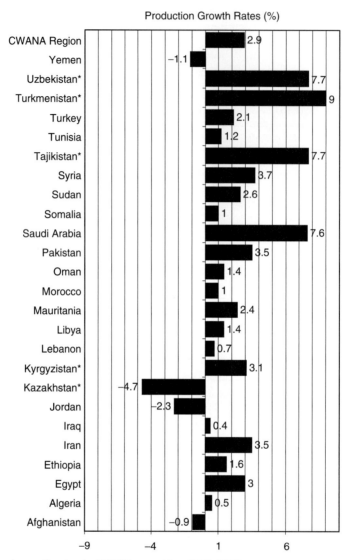

Figure 2 Cereal growth rates in CWANA countries, 1961–2002.

growth, but in other countries such as Saudi Arabia and Sudan, increasing the cultivation areas was the major cause of increasing wheat production. Appendix Table 3 shows barley and wheat production growth rates for all CWANA countries.

6.2 Pulses

Pulses are an important part of the human diet in the CWANA region and constitute the major protein source for the poor. Table 4 indicates that pulse production sustained an annual growth rate of 1.2% during the 1960s and 1970s. This growth rate is totally

Table 4   Pulses growth rates in the CWANA region, 1961–2002

Period	Growth Rates (%)		
	Area	Yield	Production
1961–1969	−0.5	1.6	1.2
1970–1979	1.3	−0.1	1.2
1980–1989	3.7	0.0	3.7
1990–2002	−0.3	−0.1	−0.4
1961–2002	1.3	0.3	1.6

Source: Calculated by the authors using the FAO database.

attributed to yield increase in the 1960s. However, output growth is totally attributed to the expansion of planted area during the 1970s. The CWANA region's highest growth in pulse production, 3.7%, is entirely attributed to the expansion of area by 3.7% annually during the 1990s. The region was able to stop the deterioration in pulses yield in the 1980s but not capable of reversing it. In fact, pulse yield demonstrated a negative growth rate during the 1990s, contributing to production deterioration during the same period. Overall, the CWANA region has achieved growth in pulse production during the last 40 years at an annual rate of 1.6%, which is largely originated from area expansion. Only 20% of growth in pulse production is attributed to yield increase, which mainly occurred in the 1960s.

For individual countries, however, differences in pulse production growth rate and its sources can be extreme (Table 5). Three Central Asian countries achieved the highest growth in pulse production during the 1990s, estimated at 16.3% for Kazakhstan,

Table 5   Pulse growth rates (%) in CWANA countries, 1961–2002

Country	Area	Yield	Production
Afghanistan	1.3	1.0	2.4
Algeria	0.2	−0.1	0.2
Armenia	2.79	−2.42	0.3
Azerbaijan	2.69	−1.06	1.6
Egypt	−0.6	1.0	0.8

Continued

Table 5 Pulse growth rates (%) in CWANA countries, 1961–2002—Cont'd

Country	Area	Yield	Production
Ethiopia	0.4	1.5	0.7
Georgia	−2.16	1.24	−0.95
Iran	4.7	−0.9	3.8
Iraq	−1.6	0.7	−0.9
Jordan	−6.3	1.6	−4.7
Kazakhstan★	−20.2	10.7	16.3
Kyrgyzstan★	41.2	7.7	−0.5
Lebanon	0.2	2.0	2.3
Libya	2.8	3.3	6.1
Mauritania	1.9	0.3	2.2
Morocco	−0.2	−0.6	−0.9
Pakistan	−0.2	0.3	0.1
Saudi Arabia	2.5	0.3	2.8
Somalia	7.1	−0.1	7.0
Sudan	1.8	0.4	2.2
Syria	0.7	0.3	1.0
Tajikistan★	−1.9	1.2	−0.9
Tunisia	0.4	1.7	2.1
Turkey	4.1	−0.5	3.6
Turkmenistan★	−12.2	−1.9	5.2
Uzbekistan★	−3.1	14.7	13.8
Yemen	0.4	1.0	1.4
CWANA Region	1.3	0.3	1.6

★1992–2002. Source: Calculated by the authors using the FAO database.

5.2% for Turkmenistan, and 13.8% for Uzbekistan. Productivity enhancement accounts for 100% of the growth in pulse production in these countries. The other two states in Central Asia, Kyrgyzstan and Tajikistan, have experienced annual declines in pulse production. In Caucus countries, pulse production achieved small or negative growth rates; for Armenia pulse growth rate during 1992–2002 was estimated at 0.3%, 1.6% for Azerbaijan, and −1% for Georgia. Except for Iraq, Jordan, and Morocco, all other CWANA countries have experienced annual growth in pulse production. The annual growth rate of pulse production is 3.5% for Iran, 2.2% for Mauritania and Sudan, 1.0% for Syria, 2.1% for Tunisia, and 3.6% for Turkey.

7. FOOD CONSUMPTION IN THE CWANA REGION

Grain consumption growth in the CWANA region was most rapid during the 1960s, 1970s, and 1980s. Table 6 shows that the region had a particularly rapid decline in annual demand growth in the last decade, falling from 4.0% in 1970–1979 to 1.8% in 1990–2002. Grain demand growth declined in most CWANA countries during

Table 6   Grain consumption growth rates (%) in CWANA countries, 1961–2002

Country	1961–1969	1970–1979	1980–1989	1990–2002	1961–2002
Afghanistan	1.4	1.9	−2.8	−0.2	−0.8
Algeria	2.8	7.4	5.4	1.9	4.4
Armenia	NA	NA	NA	1.0	1.0
Azerbaijan	NA	NA	NA	1.8	1.8
Egypt	2.7	5.7	3.2	3.0	3.6
Ethiopia	2.1	−0.1	−0.6	4.3	1.8
Georgia	NA	NA	NA	1.1	1.1
Iran	5.9	5.8	4.3	2.0	4.5
Iraq	3.7	3.7	4.1	−8.7	1.8
Jordan	−3.7	5.4	4.3	0.4	4.6
Kazakhstan★	NA	NA	NA	−7.8	−7.8
Kyrgyzstan★	NA	NA	NA	0.0	0.0
Lebanon	3.6	−0.3	1.5	3.0	1.8
Libya	7.9	6.6	7.5	0.1	6.1

Continued

Table 6   Grain consumption growth rates (%) in CWANA countries, 1961–2002—Cont'd

Country	1961–1969	1970–1979	1980–1989	1990–2002	1961–2002
Mauritania	2.3	3.4	7.4	4.0	4.0
Morocco	7.5	1.6	5.6	1.3	2.6
Pakistan	4.7	3.9	2.4	1.7	3.1
Saudi Arabia	1.6	13.2	8.9	0.0	8.5
Somalia	−0.1	3.2	3.7	−0.2	2.2
Sudan	1.4	2.7	1.5	3.3	3.0
Syria	−0.1	5.7	−0.1	0.9	4.0
Tajikistan★	NA	NA	NA	−7.5	−7.5
Tunisia	0.5	4.2	1.9	2.2	3.5
Turkey	1.9	3.8	2.1	0.8	2.0
Turkmenistan★	NA	NA	NA	0.4	0.4
Uzbekistan★	NA	NA	NA	−1.6	−1.6
Yemen	1.1	3.7	3.7	2.5	3.1
CWANA region	3.1	4.0	3.1	1.8	3.4

★1992–2002. Source: Calculated by authors using FAO database.

the 1990s while remaining strong in Egypt, Ethiopia, Lebanon, Sudan, and Tunisia. Grain demand growth from 1980–1989 and 1990–2002 declined the most in Algeria, Iraq, Kazakhstan, Morocco, and Turkey. Declining population growth rates, saturation of demand, and declining oil revenues helped slow the overall growth of grain demand in CWANA during the 1990s (FAO, 2000).

WANA had net cereal imports of 45.1 million tons in 1997 (Table 7). Despite the slowing of demand growth, net imports continued to increase in the 1990s. The growth rate of WANA's imports was not strongly related to the performance of the agricultural sector (Rosegrant, 2001). Cereal imports increased most rapidly during the 1980s, a period when agricultural production grew at a rate of 3.8% per year as a result of oil-financed investments (Rosegrant, 2001). Increased oil revenues during this period permitted both large-scale development of local production and large quantities of cereal imports. Exploding domestic demand is expected to increase WANA's cereal net imports to 73.1 million tons by 2020. Wheat imports alone, at 37.8 million tons,

Table 7 Production, consumption, and trade for major commodities in WANA (M tons), 1997 and 2002

Commodity	1997			2020		
	Production	Consumption	Trade	Production	Consumption	Trade
Beef	1.388	1.747	−0.377	2.352	3.095	−0.744
Sheep and goat	1.769	1.845	−0.104	2.990	3.092	−0.102
Poultry	3.151	3.482	−0.459	5.765	6.670	−0.905
All meat	6.368	7.140	−0.946	11.196	12.962	−1.767
Wheat	50.487	75.109	−25.91	73.194	110.967	−37.773
Rice	54.53	8.151	−3.069	8.275	13.418	−5.143
Maize	94.88	18.296	−9.703	13.413	27.777	−14.364
Other course grains	20.025	27.435	−6.400	27.592	43.423	−15.831
All cereals	85.453	128.991	−45.08	122.474	195.585	−73.111
Egg	2.215	2.227	−0.010	3.507	3.574	−0.067
Milk	25.467	30.167	−4.885	41.424	49.289	−7.864

Source: Rosegrant et al. (2001, p. 177, Table D.1).

account for 52% of the total cereal net imports in 2020. Thus increasing wheat production can contribute greatly to enhancing food security in WANA and thus save a large amount of hard currency currently used for wheat imports.

Similarly, imports of livestock products are projected to increase substantially during the next two decades. All meat imports are expected to increase, from 0.946 million tons in 1997 to 1.767 million tons in 2020, among which beef and poultry account for 42% and 51%, respectively. Net imports of sheep and goat, milk, and eggs are also expected to increase sharply by 2022 as a result of increased demand for livestock products due to population growth, changes in consumers' preferences, and increased per capita income.

It is generally accepted that full food self-sufficiency is not attainable in the foreseeable future, if ever. Thus WANA will remain a food and feed deficit region and so depends on international markets to feed its growing population.

Food security in Algeria, Egypt, Morocco, and Tunisia is much better than in the other regions because of higher per capita incomes and consumer price subsidies. With the exception of Egypt, other countries are subject to instability in food production because a major part of their food is produced under rain-fed conditions. During the last two decades NA countries suffered from severe and consequent droughts and thus greatly reduced local food production. However, availability of foreign exchange enables North African countries to increase imports to stabilize food supplies. Production and imports make up almost equal shares of the food supplies in this region (USDA, 2003).

Food supplies in Algeria, Egypt, Morocco, and Tunisia are projected to be sufficient to meet nutritional requirements through 2012. Calorie consumption in these countries averaged 3165 calories per day in 1998–2000, well above the nutritional requirements of 2100 calories per day recommended by FAO (USDA, 2003). Food security in these countries is highly dependent on imports. Production and imports account for an equal share of food supplies in these countries, making them the most import-dependent countries in the region. Food crop production increased 3.5% annually between 1980 and 2001, mainly attributed to substantial growth in yields. Projections indicate a marked slowdown in production growth during the next decade as yield growth rates are expected to be minimal. Egypt's grain yields are the highest, even by world standards, due to the extensive use of irrigated areas. With the limited potential for expanding irrigated areas given increased water scarcity, it is expected that future growth will be slight, since yields have virtually peaked. Historically, imports grew by an annual rate of 2.4%, but this growth is projected to slow due to slow population growth. The population growth rate is expected to decrease from 2.3% in the historical period to 1.5% over the next 10 years.

Among these countries, Tunisia is the most food secure and Algeria is the least. However, consumption in Algeria is projected to exceed minimum nutritional requirements. Although the food security situation is expected to deteriorate during the next decade, consumption will remain above the nutritional target in these countries (USDA, 2003). With the exception of Egypt, most food crop production in these countries is under rain-fed conditions, resulting in large production variability. Therefore, country's commercial imports increase in response to fluctuations in crop production. Morocco, for example, experienced the largest production shortfalls in 1995, resulting in doubling imports. Since imports constitute nearly 45% of food supplies, the state of the economies of these countries and export potential play a major role in the food security outlook.

For Central Asian countries, the demand for both cereal and meat products is expected to rise by 3.37 million tons (31.58% change) and 0.91 million tons (47.7% change), respectively, by the year 2020. It is projected that the per capita food availability will increase 6.1% as a whole for Central Asia, from 2685 calories per day in 1995 to 2850 calories per day in 2020. In spite of the negative economic growth during the 1990s, all the Central Asian countries are expected to see a 3% economic growth rate, at least up to the year 2020 (Pandya-Lorch, 2000). Even with positive economic growth expected, the Central Asian countries will need to import some cereals and double their imports in meats to meet the food demand, which might not meet the quantity and quality of food needed for food security due to low purchasing power (see Appendix Table 4).

8. CHANGES IN THE FOOD CONSUMPTION PATTERN OF THE WANA REGION

The food consumption pattern is expected to change dramatically during the next 20 years in response to increases in population, per capita income, and changes in consumer preferences. Meat per capita consumption is projected to increase rapidly, 29% for poultry and 19% for beef (Per Pinstrup-Andersen, 2002). Per capita consumption of other livestock products will increase as well. Milk and sheep/goat per capita consumption is expected to increase 14% and 12%, respectively, between 1997 and 2020. Figure 3 shows changes in food per capita consumption in WANA for the period 1997 and 2020.

Only the per capita consumption of two major cereal commodities, wheat and maize, is projected to decrease, 2% and 16%, respectively. This reduction in wheat and maize per capita consumption will only slightly contribute to grain deficit reduction in the CWANA region. Total grain deficit in CWANA is expected to decrease from 46 million tons in 2002 to 35 million tons in 2020 (Table 8). Low growth rates of population, consumption, and yield in WANA could explain the anticipated decrease in grain deficit. The annual increase in the demand for cereals is expected to decrease to less than 2% per year by 2020, which is lower than the annual growth

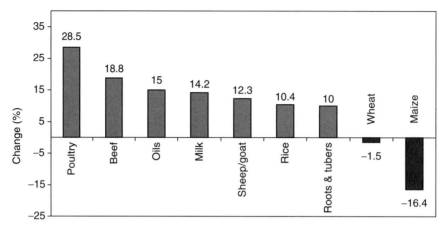

Figure 3 Change in food per capita consumption in WANA, 1997–2020. Source: Per Pinstrup-Andersen (2002).

Table 8 Projections of population and grain deficit in the CWANA region, 2002–2020

Year	Population (M)	Production (M Tons)	Consumption (M Tons)	Deficit (M Tons)
2002	732.71	166.17	212.08	−45.91
2005	777.30	180.81	230.64	−49.83
2010	863.89	208.16	255.57	−47.41
2015	946.23	239.69	281.60	−41.91
2020	1036.02	276.01	310.77	−34.75

Source: Calculated by the authors based on the FAO database.

rates of the 1980s and 1990s, estimated at 4% and 2.5%, respectively (Per Pinstrup-Andersen, 2002). The rates of increase in production and yields are expected to decrease during the next 20 years. The cereal yields in WANA are expected to increase slightly during the next two decades, but they are still far below those of East Asia.

Data in Table 9 show that increases in production fell shorter than increases in demand for cereals during the last 40 years. Annual growth rate of grain consumption in CWANA is estimated at 3.4% during the 1961–2002 period. However, grain production has increased at an annual growth rate of 2.9% during the same period. The increase in the demand for grain is partially explained by a modest population growth rate of 1.4% annually during the last four decades. As a result, net cereal imports in

Table 9 Grain production and consumption growth rates in the CWANA region, 1961–2002

Period	Growth Rates (%)		
	Population	Production	Consumption
1961–1969	1.6	3.4	3.1
1970–1979	1.4	2.7	4.0
1980–1989	1.0	2.1	3.1
1990–2002	1.4	2.1	1.8
1961–2002	1.4	2.9	3.4

Source: Calculated by the authors using the FAO database.

WANA increased from about 6 million tons in 1967 to about 44 million tons in 2002, with a projection to increase to more than 70 million tons by 2020 (Pinstrup-Andersen, 2002). The rapid increase in net cereal imports is more evident for rice, wheat, and maize. Net imports of rice are expected to increase 65% by 2002. Meanwhile, wheat and maize net imports will increase nearly 50% during the same period.

The WANA meat position is not different; the current level of net imports of 1 million tons per year is expected to increase to about 1.8 million tons by year 2020 (Figure 4).

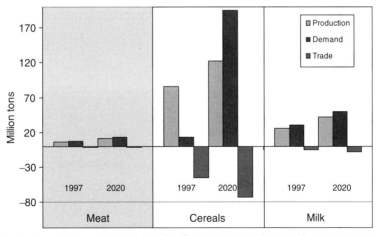

Figure 4 Production, consumption, and trade of major commodities in the WANA region, 1997 and 2020. Source: Per Pinstrup-Andersen, 2002.

9. MAJOR CONSTRAINTS FACING THE CWANA REGION

The CWANA region is facing some limiting and persistent constraints that hinder the region's ability to feed itself. These constraints include the following (IFAD, 2002):

- *Institutions.* Religious and local cultural traditions are the dominant institutions in the CWANA region. New forms of association and other grassroots organizations that would help the rural population interact with political, administrative, and economic institutions are relatively rare and undeveloped. The range and number of civil groups and informal institutions in CWANA countries are very limited. As a result, poor rural people are unable to claim their rights and entitlements, have little leverage in negotiating with more powerful groups, and have a weak voice in local politics.

- *Water.* Water is the single most binding constraint on the development of the agricultural sector and rural communities in the CWANA region. Available water for agriculture is limited, although the region uses more than 80% of its water resources for agriculture, compared with 65% for most other regions. The agricultural sector must therefore produce more food with less water to feed its accelerating population. Pressure from competing industrial and domestic uses is growing steadily, and access to drinking water in the rural areas is a serious problem. Scarcity of water is becoming the most binding constraint on agricultural production in the 21st century (World Bank, 2002). Hence improving water use efficiency and savings in both agricultural and nonagricultural uses is high priority for all countries in the region. Maintenance of irrigation facilities, water pricing, improving efficiency of water use, increasing water productivity, use of improved irrigation technologies such as water harvesting, supplemental and drip irrigation, and crop pricing and production policies are important issues in many WANA countries. Water harvesting and supplemental irrigation show promise for increasing production, improving livelihoods and household food security for many rural communities in the world.

- *Land.* The size and quality of the land available to farmers and pastoralists has a direct influence on food production levels. Growing population, fragmented lands, and traditional/religious inheritance rights have led to small sizes of land holdings. The quality of soil is poor as a result of land degradation, diminishing fertility, overuse, and wind and water erosion. Poor pastoralists, whose livelihood depends mainly on rangeland and common property water resources, have been adversely affected by encroaching urban and rural communities and by previous government policies that encouraged cereal plantation, overgrazing, and mechanization with unsuitable land-preparation implements. Further, rigid rangeland tenure policies and poor social organizations have made it impossible to develop effective common-property management programs that encourage beneficiaries to use and maintain the rangelands in a more sustainable manner.

- *Technology.* The rural areas are constrained by disproportionately low investments in rain-fed technology in relation to the number of households that depend on it. These constraints are reflected in the low adoption rates of improved, drought-tolerant crop varieties, limited application of water-saving technologies, few investments in research, and limited attention to improved rangeland management techniques.

Similarly, improved animal breeds or the technology to produce them are either not available in the poor areas or, due to the high costs involved, are beyond the reach of poor rural populations.

- *Human assets*. Rural areas in the region suffer from clear lack of physical infrastructure such as roads, safe water, sanitation, and communication and information networks, and there is a shortage of social infrastructure, such as schools and clinics. Cuts in public expenditures as a result of structural adjustment programs have further reduced state investments in rural areas. Lack of infrastructure in rural areas in particular has created increased cleavages between people living in rural and urban areas as well as the conflict potentials implied in a further increase of this cleavage. The rural poor have little access to services to improve their human capital, resulting in limited engagement in rewarding economic activities. As a result, the rural poor are often economically, physically, intellectually, and socially isolated from the rest of the country, especially in remote areas such as the mountainous regions of Morocco, Turkey, and Yemen.
- *Financial services*. Public sector institutions, especially with respect to finance for agricultural and other rural-based economic activities, primarily provide financial services. In the past, governments have tended to use state financial institutions in the rural areas to implement national development and planning programs, allocate subsidies, and provide inputs on credit. These institutions' lending policies favored larger farmers and entrepreneurs with physical or financial collateral, thus excluding the rural poor. Low-income rural households have few alternative sources of finance, and informal financial institutions or community-based savings and credit groups are very rare in the CWANA region.
- *Political environment*. Political instability, poor governance, and urban bias in economic and social policies characterize the CWANA region. All these factors increased the vulnerability of the rural poor. War and conflicts create a new category of poor people due to loss of physical or human assets (land, farms, house, productive family members, etc.) or unemployment due to weaker unstable economies.

10. RESEARCH AND POLICY IMPLICATIONS

A significant and important opportunity exists to create a synergistic partnership of ICARDA with diverse research institutions and development agencies to apply science and technology to address the key problems of food security, poverty reduction, and conservation of natural resources in the CWANA region. The previously described trends and constraints facing the development of agricultural sector in the CWANA region have important research and policy implications. These policy issues and research areas, which are in need of action, include the following:

- Identification of research priorities for the CWANA region. ICARDA and national programs in the region have developed priority settings for the region, with full participation of all stakeholders and concerned bodies. Identified regional priorities for the region can be grouped into five main clusters. These include germplasm management (crops—wheat, forages, barley; animals—small ruminants, cattle; fisheries—marine), natural resource management (water and soil), socioeconomic and policy (technology dissemination, markets), cross-cutting issues (human resource development), and methodologies and approaches (regional forums and networking). There is a need to revisit these priorities in line with the newly developed Science Council research priorities of the CGIAR system. This can be done in consultation with NARS and other stakeholders.

- Adoption, by governments and national and international research centers, of strategic approaches to agricultural research to alleviate poverty through the following (Erskine, 2004):
  - Improved technologies that increase productivity, particularly per unit of water; sustain resource use, and be applicable by poor people with few inputs.
  - Resource management practices that conserve natural resources without decreasing productivity.
  - Diversified farming systems to reduce risk, increase resource-use efficiency, and improve returns to farm labor.
  - Improved vertical integration from producer to consumer to add value to products and improve quality of production.
  - Knowledge management. Through research continuity, ICARDA and its partners have gathered invaluable research findings. The management and dissemination of this information, coupled with tacit knowledge, with ICARDA acting as a regional knowledge portal, will increasingly become a major contribution to global public goods. Such information is useful in the temporal dimension to understand aspects of sustainability and in the spatial dimension for geographical generalization from site-specific research.
- Adoption of an integrated natural resource management (INRM) approach for developing the agricultural sector on sustainable basis. The INRM approach integrates research of various types of natural resources into stakeholder-driven processes of adaptive management and innovation to improve livelihoods, agro-ecosystem resilience, agricultural productivity, and environmental services at community, eco-regional, and national levels of intervention and impact.
- Adoption of technical, institutional and policy options to increase water-use efficiency and water productivity. Empirical studies have shown that the scarce water resource is misused and poorly managed in the CWANA region, resulting in a very low ratio of water use efficiency. Farmers in Egypt, Jordan, Iraq, and Syria over-irrigate their crops by as much as 60% for wheat, 30% for cotton, 55% for potato, and 40% for vegetable crops. These figures imply that a great potential for water savings exists if the resource is efficiently used. Use of improved irrigation technologies and application of deficit irrigation, for example, have greatly increased crop and water productivity under rain-fed conditions. Results of a farm survey in Iraq showed that the use of supplemental irrigation has increased wheat grain yield 128% and increased water productivity 30% (ESCWA/ICARDA, 2003). Similarly, the use of water harvesting techniques will significantly increase the productivity of rainwater. Such information reveals that there is great potential to increase crop production from the same amount of water use or produce the same crop production with less water.

- Enhancing crop/livestock integration at the farm level. CWANA is classified as a food and feed deficit region. The quantity and quality of feed resources are far beyond the feed requirements for the region's livestock animals. Such feed shortages, coupled with health problems and water shortages for animal watering, have resulted in low productivity and poor reproductive performance. Expanding forage legume plantation in barley areas, increased use of alternative feed sources such as agro-industrial feed blocks and shrubs, and rangeland rehabilitation and communal management are vital options to enhance crop/livestock integration and thus increase animal productivity.

- Partnerships. The diverse and huge challenges and constraints facing the CWANA region require thematic partnerships with other agencies (donors, NGOs, research institutions, universities, and agricultural authorities)

- Policy dialogue. A continuous policy dialogue between research institutions and development agencies with policymakers is an essential strategy to make real changes in rural communities and realize the intended impacts of research outputs. This calls for a long-term policy dialogue on key areas such as land tenure and property rights issues, empowerment of rural communities, equitable access to resources, pro-poor rural finance schemes, technology adoption, community development, gender mainstreaming, and management of natural resources (water, watersheds, rangelands). Such dialogue should be carried out with full participation and involvement of rural communities because successful institutions have to be grounded on local perceptions.

- Priorities for policy intervention. Priority areas for public sector involvement are community development for management of common resources, promoting appropriate technologies, on-farm long-term investment, rural infrastructure, rural financial institutions and marketing, and micro-enterprise development.

- Given the expectations that WANA will remain a food and feed deficit region and thus depends on international markets to feed its growing population, it is recommended that analysis of alternative resource uses be conducted.

- For effective policies and institutions targeting sustainable food security, nine driving forces, with varying relative importance to CWANA countries, need to be taken into consideration (Per Pinstrup-Andersen, 2002). These driving forces are:

  - *Globalization and trade liberalization.* Continued protection of domestic agriculture and increasing food safety concerns in industrialized countries could limit the market access by developing countries. The main issue here is the way that globalization can be guided to improve food and nutrition security as well as natural resources in low-income countries. Appropriate national and international policies and institutions are required for globalization to favor developing countries. Otherwise, globalization could either bypass or harm many poor people in developing countries. Rapidly changing markets in the context of globalization, the penetration of supermarkets in food distribution, and agro-industrial transformation pose new challenges for small farmers. Best practices need to be identified in setting up a quality context that will help the poor use their resources to escape poverty. Poverty is to a large extent determined by insufficient control over productive assets. For the globalization of the world economy to assist, rather than hinder, the rural poor in finding their way out of poverty, they must be able to maintain or increase access to assets and find opportunities to use these assets productively and competitively.

- *Technological changes.* The very poor tend to be associated with marginal production environments in rural areas. New technologies fit for these marginal and risky environments are still largely missing and constitute an evident priority for the CGIAR (Science Council, 2004). Identifying small farmers' constraints to technology adoption and use continues to be a priority issue for consideration and planning. New technical advances in molecular biology and information communications provide great potential to advance food security and improve the sustainability of natural resources management for poor people. However, there is a serious concern as to whether poor and food-insecure people will have access to such technologies, many of which are currently developed by the private sector and focused primarily on well-off people in industrialized countries. Past investments in public agricultural research in developing countries have effective in enhancing productivity, protecting the environment, and increasing food security. However, rapid changes in the financing management and organization of agricultural research may require new policy interventions to further enhance the benefits obtained by low-income people. Without such policy and institutional changes, the current and potential technological revolutions could leave the poor and food-insecure people further behind.

- *Degradation of natural resources and increasing water scarcity.* Degradation of natural resources is escalating in CWANA region, characterized by fragile soils, low and erratic rainfall, relatively high population growth rates, misuse of scarce resources and modern farming inputs, and stagnant agricultural productivity. Although natural resource degradation is often a consequence of poverty, it also contributes to poverty. Water scarcity is emerging as the most constraining factor for food security in many CWANA countries in the future. Failure to effectively deal with the natural resource issue in the quest to achieve food security will result in increased poverty and nutrition problems. Property rights and collective action play key roles in determining access to natural resources critical to sustaining rural livelihoods and the likelihood that resources will be available to meet future needs. Property determines long-term incentives to invest in and improve resources. Depending on their distribution, property rights shape patterns of quality and inequality with respect to resource access. Natural resources, such as rangeland, forests, and irrigation schemes, can be managed more effectively by groups of people. Collective action by multiple resource users can also enable a more equitable distribution of resource benefits.

- *Accelerating health and nutrition crises.* There have been growing health and nutrition challenges facing many CWANA countries that contribute directly to food and nutrition insecurity in the region. Healthy people and nutritive diets are essential elements for achieving a food-secure region.

- *Rapid urbanization.* Most future population increases will occur in cities and towns of developing countries, including those of the CWANA region. This will create new challenges to provide employment, education, health care, and food. Although current actions must continue to focus on the rural communities, where the majority of the poor and food-insecure reside, future policy and institutional options must pay increasing attention to the growing poverty and food insecurity in urban areas.

- *Structural changes of farming.* Rapidly emerging factors such as aging of the farm population, the feminization of agriculture, labor shortages and depleting asset bases, and the decreasing cost of capital relative to labor will result in escalated changes in the structure of farming in many developing countries. Minimizing the effect of such factors calls for new and innovative approaches to agricultural policies and rural institutions. Small-scale family farms, which traditionally have been considered the backbone of much of developing-country agriculture, are under threat due to labor scarcity caused by out-migration and health problems. This leads us to conclude that the future of small-scale farming is increasingly uncertain. Domestic investment in infrastructure will provide better markets and marketing opportunities for rural communities.

- *Continued conflict.* Social unrest and violent conflicts continue to have a severe impact on food security, nutrition, and natural resource management in developing countries. Policy action is needed to deal with the underlying causes and the resulting consequences on the people because achieving sustainable food security for the whole population is unlikely under continued conflict.

- *Climate change.* To achieve sustainable food security, future policy action must take into consideration the likely consequences of the ongoing climate change and associated fluctuations in weather patterns. Policies and institutions are needed to counter or compensate for negative effects. Future agricultural policies need to focus on ways to accommodate food, agriculture, and natural resources as climate change continues.

- *Increasing the role of community-based organizations.* The decreasing and changing role of national governments in many countries in the region is likely to continue in the future. Local governments, the private sector, and nongovernmental organizations are taking on an increasing number of responsibilities for activities previously undertaken by national governments. Local communities, with the help of community-based nongovernmental organizations, are demanding an increasing voice in policies and programs related to their livelihoods.

End Note

1. Early signs of long-run food security problems in a country include an inability to maintain per capita food consumption levels from year to year and difficulty in meeting average minimum nutritional requirements.

References

Pinstrup-Andersen, P. (2002, May 4). *A 2020 Vision for Food Security in West and North Africa.* Prepared for the 25th Anniversary of ICARDA. IFPRI, FAO. World Agriculture Toward 2015/2030: Summary report. ISBN 92-5-104761-8.

El-Beltagy, A. (1997). *West Asia and North Africa: A Regional Vision.* Paper presented at the Mid-Term Meeting, May 26–30, Cairo.

Erskine, W. (2004). *Dry Area Agriculture Challenges - Setting the Scene: Options for Agriculture in Dry Areas.* Seminars presented at "A World Bank Hub Training/Study Tour". ICARDA, (12-16 June). Jointly organized with the World Bank's (ARD). 40p.

ESCWA/ICARDA. (2003). *Enhancing Agricultural Productivity through On-Farm Water Use Efficiency: An Empirical Case Study of Wheat Production in Iraq.* United Nations, New York, 03-0941.

ESCWA/ICARDA. (2000). *Economic assessment of on-farm water use efficiency in agriculture: methodology and two case studies.* United nations, New York.

FAO (Food and Agriculture Organization of the United Nations) 2002 *World agriculture: towards 2015/2030, summary* See http://www.fao.org/docrep/004/y3557e/y3557e00.HTM

FAOSTAT, 2003. Land Use database. http://faostat.fao.org/site/377/default.aspx#ancor

FAPRI (Food and Agricultural Policy Research Institute). (2003). *US and World Agricultural Outlook.* Ames, Iowa: Iowa State University and University of Missouri-Columbia. Staff Report 1-03, ISSN 1534-4533.

IFAD (International Fund for Agricultural Development). (2002, March). *Regional Strategy Paper: Near East and North Africa.*

Pandya-Lorch, R. (2000). Prospects for global food security: a Central Asian context. In Babu & Tashmatov A. (Ed.), *Food Policy Reforms in Central Asia: Setting the Priorities.* Washington, DC: International Food Policy Research Institute.

Rodriguez, A. (1997). *Rural Poverty and Natural Resources in the Dry Areas: The Context of ICARDA's Research.* Working Paper. Aleppo, Syria: ICARDA.

Rosegrant, M., Paisner, M., Meijer S., & Witcover, J. (2001, August). *Global Food Projections to 2020: Emerging Trends and Alternative Futures.* IFPRI.

Science Council. (2004, October). Revised Summary Report on Developing CGIAR System Priorities for Research. Consultative Group on International Agricultural Research Science Council. Science Council Working Document, Science Council Secretariat, FAO.

Shideed, K. H. (2004). *Implications of water scarcity on agriculture in CWANA region: Limitations and Potentials.* Keynote presentation at the International FORUM on Food Security under water scarcity in the Middle East: problems and solutions. COMO (Italy) November, 24–27, 2004.

USDA, ERS. (2003, February). *Food Security Assessment.* Agriculture and Trade Report No. (GFA14) 88 pp.

U.S. Library of Congress. (2004). http://countrystudies.us/country/49.htm

Vercueil, J. (2004, December 12). *Agriculture and rural-urban migrations in developing countries: facts and policy implications.* Presentation based on an FAO study from the "Roles of Agriculture" Project. National Agricultural Policy Center, Damascus.

World Bank. (2002). *Reaching the Rural Poor: A Rural Development Strategy for the Middle East and North Africa Region.* Rural Development, Water, Environment and Social Group.

APPENDIX

Table 1   Wheat per capita consumption in selected WANA countries (kg per capita), 2002–2013

Year	Algeria	Egypt	Iran	Morocco	Pakistan
2002–2003	197	173	215	193	131
2003–2004	195	175	223	191	133
2004–2005	193	175	224	193	133
2005–2006	193	175	224	193	133
2006–2007	193	175	224	194	133
2007–2008	192	175	224	194	133
2008–2009	191	175	224	194	133
2009–2010	190	176	224	193	133
2010–2011	189	176	223	192	133
2011–2012	188	176	223	191	133
2012–2013	187	176	223	190	133

Source: FAPRI (2003). *U.S. and World Agricultural Outlook*. Iowa State University and University of Missouri-Columbia. Staff Report 1-03, ISSN 1534-4533, Ames, Iowa, January 2003.

Table 2   Total land area, arable and irrigated land in the CWANA region (in 1000 ha), 2002

Country	Total	Arable	Irrigated	% Arable of Total	% Irrigated of Total	% Irrigated of Arable
Afghanistan	65,209	7910	2386	12	4	30
Algeria	238,174	7665	560	3	0.2	7
Armenia	2980	495	280	17	9	57
Azerbaijan	8660	1783	1455	21	17	82
Egypt	100,145	2900	2900	3	3	100
Ethiopia	110,430	9936	190	9	0.2	2
Georgia	6970	799	469	11	7	59

Continued

Table 2 Total land area, arable and irrigated land in the CWANA region (in 1000 ha), 2002—Cont'd

Country	Total	Arable	Irrigated	% Arable of Total	% Irrigated of Total	% Irrigated of Arable
Iran	164,820	15,020	7500	9	5	50
Iraq	43,832	5750	3525	13	8	61
Jordan	8921	295	75	3	1	25
Kazakhstan	272,490	21,535	2350	8	1	11
Kyrgyzstan	19,990	1345	1072	7	5	80
Lebanon	1040	170	104	16	10	61
Libya	175,954	1815	470	1	0.3	26
Mauritania	102,552	488	49	1	0.1	10
Morocco	44,655	8396	1345	19	3	16
Oman	30,950	38	38	0.1	0.1	100
Pakistan	79,610	21,448	17,800	27	22	83
Saudi Arabia	214,969	3600	1,620	2	1	45
Somalia	63,766	1045	200	2	0.3	19
Sudan	250,581	16,233	1950	6	1	12
Syria	18,518	4593	1333	25	7	29
Tajikistan	14,310	930	719	6	5	77
Tunisia	16,361	2771	381	17	2	14
Turkey	77,482	25,938	5215	33	7	20
Turkmenistan	48,810	1850	1800	4	4	97
Uzbekistan	44,740	4484	4281	10	10	95
Yemen	52,797	1538	500	3	1	33
CWANA	**2,279,716**	**170,770**	**60,567**	**7**	**3**	**35**

Source: FAOSTAT (2003).

Table 3 Wheat and barley growth rates in the CWANA region, 1961–2002

Country	Area		Production		Yield	
	Barley	Wheat	Barley	Wheat	Barley	Wheat
Afghanistan	0.98	0.99	0.99	1.00	1.00	1.01
Algeria	−0.57	−1.26	1.05	0.25	1.63	1.54
Armenia	−2.38	5.25	−3.42	5.10	−1.06	−0.14
Azerbaijan	−6.00	2.72	−3.25	6.84	2.92	4.01
Egypt	0.45	1.77	0.43	4.33	−0.02	2.51
Ethiopia	−0.47	−1.97	0.92	0.28	1.40	2.30
Georgia	0.51	4.08	2.43	6.23	1.91	2.07
Iran	1.07	0.99	3.77	3.42	2.66	2.41
Iraq	1.02	1.00	0.02	0.2	−0.3	−0.4
Jordan	−2.50	−6.92	−0.29	−3.89	2.27	3.26
Kazakhstan	−14.69	−2.45	−13.39	−0.75	1.52	1.74
Kyrgyzstan	−13.87	6.07	−12.14	6.67	2.00	0.57
Lebanon	−0.14	−2.23	1.61	0.71	1.75	3.01
Libya	−2.85	−0.07	−1.26	4.06	1.64	4.13
Mauritania	0.86	0.30	3.08	3.85	2.20	3.54
Morocco	0.61	1.38	0.09	2.20	−0.52	0.81
Oman		−3.26		−1.28		2.04
Pakistan	−0.61	1.40	0.72	4.15	1.34	2.72
Saudi Arabia	5.72	7.34	11.96	11.26	5.90	3.66
Somalia						
Sudan		4.33		5.66		1.27
Syria	3.04	0.56	2.26	4.16	−0.75	3.57
Tajikistan	−3.34	7.41	−3.23	12.73	0.11	4.95
Tunisia	0.07	−0.82	1.67	1.15	1.60	1.99
Turkey	0.98	0.44	2.64	2.30	1.64	1.85

Continued

Table 3 Wheat and barley growth rates in the CWANA region, 1961–2002—Cont'd

Country	Area		Production		Yield	
	Barley	Wheat	Barley	Wheat	Barley	Wheat
Turkmenistan	−5.47	13.15	−22.92	17.71	−18.46	3.70
Uzbekistan	−16.17	6.87	−12.43	17.70	4.47	10.13
Yemen	−2.95	3.29	−3.05	4.05	−0.10	0.78
CWANA	1.53	1.74	2.8	3.82	2.54	3.28

Note: The growth rates for Central Asia and Caucus countries are for the period 1992–2002 due to lack of data.
Source: FAOSTAT (2003 database).

Table 4 Demand and imports of cereals and meat in Central Asian countries, 1995 and 2020

Item	1995	2020	Change (1995–2020)
Cereal demand (M tons)	18.06	24.01	5.95
Meat demand (M tons)	1.95	2.86	0.91
Per capita cereal demand (kg)	335	345	10.0
Per capita meat demand (kg)	36	41	5
Imported cereals (M tons)	−0.51	−0.76	0.25
Imported meat (M tons)	−0.16	−0.38	0.22

Source: Pandya-Lorch, 2000.

CHAPTER 70

The Changing Context and Prospects for Agricultural and Rural Development in Africa

Hans Binswanger-Mkhize

Institute for Economic Research of Innovation, Tshwane University of Technology, Pretoria, South Africa

Alex F. McCalla[1,2]

Agricultural and Resource Economics, University of California, Davis

Contents

Handbook of Agricultural Economics, Volume 4
© 2010 Elsevier BV. All rights reserved.

doi: 10.1016/S1574-0072(09)04070-5

Abstract

Over the past decade, economic and agricultural growth in sub-Saharan Africa (SSA) has resumed. The secular downward trend in agricultural prices ended in the early 1990s; growing incomes in Asia and Africa, combined with continued rapid population growth, are fueling food demand, which is expected to lead to a gradual upward trend in international real agricultural prices. For Africa the major agricultural growth opportunities will be in regional and domestic markets for food staples. To seize these opportunities, SSA will have to support economic growth via continued sound macroeconomic policies, further improvements in the investment climate, and investments in infrastructure and institutions. In the agricultural sector SSA will have to (1) remove the remaining agricultural taxation that still disadvantages African farmers relative to all other farmers in the world, (2) improve its services for small farmers, (3) significantly increase its investment in agricultural technology generation and dissemination at national and subregional levels, (4) empower local governments, communities, and farmer organizations for their own development via further administrative and fiscal decentralization and community-driven development, and (5) strengthen the already existing regional agricultural institutions for agricultural trade, biosafety, phytosanitary regulations, seed production, regulation and trade, and technology generation.

1. SUMMARY

We undertook this task in a period of optimism about the prospects for Africa and African agriculture and rural development (ARD). For Africa as a whole, economic growth was well above 5% until 2008, whereas for sub-Saharan Africa (SSA) it was above 5.5% (IMF, 2009). Agricultural growth in SSA has been above 3.5%, well above the population growth rate of about 2%. Armed conflicts are down to 5 from 15 in 2003. Although there are setbacks, such as the recent Kenya and Zimbabwe crises, democracy has advanced significantly. SSA now has faster progress in its business environment than the Middle East and North Africa (MENA) and Latin America (World Bank and IFC, 2006). Africa is in the process of strengthening its regional and subregional institutions. Agriculture returned as a priority on the international development agenda even before the recent food price spike and now more so as a consequence of it. The African Union (AU), in conjunction with the New Partnership for African Development (NEPAD), has developed the Comprehensive Africa Agricultural Development Program (CAADP) and is encouraging countries to allocate more fiscal resources to agricultural development. Although the recent sharp rise in international food prices increased poverty rates and food import bills in the short run, combined with economic growth, it created major short-term opportunities for African farmers in domestic, regional, and international markets.

The purpose of this context and prospects review of African agriculture is to provide a comprehensive evaluation of future challenges for those interested in AADARD. The study (1) identifies major ARD policy, sector, and subsector issues, from an African and a global perspective, and (2) draws on lessons from the past three decades to analyze issues likely to be of relevance for future development assistance to the sector.

This context paper comes at a time when many others have summarized the state of knowledge of food and agriculture, including FAO (2007), IFPRI (2006), Inter-Academy Council (2005), and the World Bank (2007). There are also recent studies on governance failure, conflict, and natural resource dependence (Collier, 2007), governance and regional integration (Economic Commission for Africa (ECA, 2006), and especially the causes and consequences of the recent food price rises (FAO, 2008; OECD-FAO, 2008; IFPRI, 2008). This chapter harvests this rich knowledge.

Section 2 reviews the terrible legacy that past failure to grow and the neglect of agriculture have left behind in terms of poverty and hunger as well as the powerful role that agricultural growth can and has played in dramatically reducing poverty and hunger elsewhere in the world. Section 3 covers the changes that have occurred in the international and institutional landscape that affect the prospects for African ARD. Section 34 analyzes the global winds of change, which have significantly altered the environment for agricultural development, and in particular analyzes the causes and short- and long-run consequences of the recent sharp increases in international food and agricultural prices. Section 5 then turns to developments in Africa itself and analyzes the factors that have inhibited African economic and agricultural growth for so long as well as the change in macroeconomic and other policies that have brought about the recent turnaround and successes. In Section 6 the focus is specifically on the plight of the "bottom billion" countries that remain stuck with low growth rates. Section 7 focuses on the institutional pillars that need to be in place for ARD, including the respective roles of the private sector, communities, local government, and central and subregional institutions. Section 8 covers the new market opportunities for African farmers that arise from the higher future price levels to which international prices are expected to settle after the recent spike, then reviews the challenges that African agriculture faces in consolidating the recent turnaround and seizing new opportunities.

1.1 The legacy of the past failure to grow and of the neglect of agriculture

Except for North Africa and selected countries in SSA that have joined the ranks of middle-income countries, growth in SSA has been the slowest of all regions in the world and is characterized by low investment and slow productivity growth. As a consequence, rather than improving over the past five decades, as in all other regions of the world, poverty and hunger have deepened in Africa. Among Africa's regions, poverty, hunger, and HIV and AIDS are significantly worse in East, Southern, and Central Africa than in North and West Africa. Where growth has recently been improved, it has reduced poverty, although it is only where agricultural growth has also increased that hunger has been reduced.

Landlocked, resource-poor countries have had the slowest growth rates. Slow growth was also caused by the delay in the demographic transition, which led to very high dependency rates. Poor governance, macroeconomic instability, and limited integration into global markets sharply reduced growth until the mid-1990s, when things started to improve significantly. Today these issues constitute less of a negative factor. Instead, it is structural impediments that continue to impede further acceleration of growth: Infrastructure (roads, electricity, water supply) is poor, transport costs are high, and the cost of doing business is much higher than in other parts of the world. Financial markets in general and rural finance in particular are very poorly developed, and savings rates are much too low.

Up to the recent past, agriculture in much of Africa was discriminated against via macroeconomic, trade, and agricultural policies and starved of fiscal resources. Even at the height of donor support for agriculture in the 1980s, apart from often being poorly designed, foreign aid was insufficient to compensate for these negative policies and lack of domestic resources, especially after its dramatic decline in the 1990s and the early years of this century. The combination of these negative factors has prevented agriculture from making its contribution to growth and to the reduction in poverty and hunger that it has so powerfully made in East and South Asia.

1.2 Global winds of change

Global winds of change provide both significant opportunities, as for example from the biotechnology revolution and in the longer run the potential for the production of biofuels, as well as significant impediments and threats—for example, the failure of the Doha Round of trade negotiations to start dismantling OECD agricultural subsidies and trade barriers or the expected negative impact of climate change on agricultural productivity. Although the Bali discussions of climate change provided a promise of support to mitigation and adaptation in poor countries, the actual mechanisms and actual funding remain far away. Dramatic changes are also occurring in the consolidation of private international agribusiness firms and the associated supermarket revolution that so far is driven by African players in SSA. The privatization of much of agricultural research as a consequence of the biotechnology revolution is a similarly dramatic change.

The biggest global shock came from the energy and food price spikes of the past three years. While crude oil prices peaked at around four times their level in the early years of this century, aggregate food prices, including not just grains and oilseeds, peaked at approximately 60% in real terms. Prices of individual commodities rose even more sharply. The food price spike came after decades of continuous decline. Therefore aggregate real food prices peaked at much lower levels than in the early 1980s. At the time of this writing, real prices of meat, milk, and oilseeds are close to the same level as in the early years of this century, whereas real prices of cereals and sugar are around 60% higher.

The spike in food prices was driven by a combination of permanent structural changes in supply and demand conditions. These were exacerbated by weather shocks, the dramatic rise in energy prices, and low interest rates that might have incited additional speculative behavior. On the demand side, rapid growth and rising incomes in emerging economies such as India and China have increased that rate of demand expansion. Urbanization and global growth mean demands for a larger and more varied food supply. At least some of the increase in biofuel demand will be around for a while. On the supply side, the rate of increase supply has slowed over the past decade because of declining rates of productivity growth and increased competition for water and land. Investments in agricultural R&D have declined globally, as has investment in agricultural development. Finally, higher long-run petroleum prices might have permanently increased the costs of agricultural production. As a consequence of all these trends, global grain consumption exceeded global production in six of the last eight years. The result was a drawdown of stocks to critically low levels. Thus when the weather shocks of the past three years combined with the dramatic surge in biofuel production, they caused prices to rise sharply.

At the time of finalization of this chapter, the energy and food price spikes have abated, in part because of the global economic crisis that started in 2007. The question is what will happen when the global economy recovers: Will real food prices settle at levels similar to the early years of this century and perhaps resume their gradual downward trend, or will they settle at higher levels?

The major unknowns here are the future development of food demand: The IMF projects that emerging and developing countries will continue to grow during the global economic downturn at 1.6% in 2009, rebounding to 4% and 6.1%, respectively, in 2010 and 2011. Since their demand for food is more income elastic than that of the high-income countries, this suggests that food demand will resume its rapid growth. It is therefore appropriate to look at projections of longer-term trends that were made before the global economic crisis: The large emerging literature on this topic is reviewed in Section 4. The OECD-FAO (2008) conclusion comes closest to our reading of the literature:

> **World reference prices in nominal terms for almost all agricultural commodities covered in this report are at or above previous record levels. This will not last and prices will gradually come down because of some of the transitory nature of some of the factors that are behind the recent hikes. But there is strong reason to believe that there are now also permanent factors underpinning prices that will work to keep them both at higher average levels than in the past and reduce the long-term decline in real terms. (p. 11)**

Since OECD-FAO's analysis, most prices have fallen from their 300% increase levels to about 40–60% higher than they were before the run-up.

In the short run, the food price spike significantly increased poverty for urban populations and for poor net buyers of food in rural areas, especially in food-importing countries that have only limited ways to prevent international prices to pass through to consumers. Food import bills were expected to rise more than 1% of GDP in most North, East, and Southern African countries and in a few West African countries. Many of these countries at the same time are even harder hit by the rise in global energy prices.

In the longer run, after food prices settle back, food prices with a rising trend could provide major additional opportunities for African farmers, especially in domestic and regional markets that will also grow because of rising incomes. In these markets farmers compete on the basis of import parity prices rather than the lower export parity prices and with fewer quality and phytosanitary barriers. African farmers would have a major opportunity to reconquer markets lost over the past decades. Internationally the changing food demand and supply patterns will lead to more South/South trade, which in the long run will bolster the opportunities arising from domestic and regional markets. Of course, whether they are able to seize these opportunities depends on many factors reviewed in this chapter.

1.3 African growth and agricultural trends

Section 45 analyzes major recent improvements in Africa itself and the opportunities for Africa and its agricultural and rural populations arising from the following favorable trends: Since 2002, the number of armed conflicts has been significantly reduced; better macroeconomic management has combined with accelerating improvements in the business environment and a more appropriate public/private sector division of labor; as a consequence, fiscal deficits and inflation have come down and growth has accelerated. Significant advances in democracy, combined with stronger civil society, community, and farmer's associations, have made governments more accountable to their populations. Africa has built stronger regional and subregional organizations at both the political level as well as for agricultural research; new private and emerging economy donors are providing growing volumes of aid.

The agriculture-specific positive trends include significantly improved price incentives for agricultural producers as a consequence of unified exchange rates, lower industrial protection, and sharply reduced export taxation; somewhat higher international commodity prices that might be here to stay and could create growing opportunities for import substitution and regional agricultural trade; and, finally, African governments, the regional institutions, and development partners, at least in words, are showing increasing commitment for agricultural and rural development. All these positive trends have led to a significant acceleration of per capita economic and agricultural growth and significant reductions in poverty headcount in the fastest-growing countries. Unfortunately, except in North and Western Africa, they have not yet translated into measurable reductions in hunger and malnutrition.

Areas where progress is less satisfactory are the persistent HIV/AIDS crisis; the several stubborn conflicts that have defied resolution; little improvement in governance and decentralization; slow regional integration with a persistence of underfunded regional and subregional organizations; inadequate fiscal commitments to agriculture and rural development by national governments; and slow progress in the infrastructure linking landlocked countries and remote regions of coastal countries to the centers of demand and the harbors.

Widely shared agricultural growth also remains impeded by poor financial markets and rural finance institutions. Development of competitive output and input markets is limited. Services for smallholder agriculture remain poor. Competition for natural resources—soil, water, fisheries, and forests—is increasing, and management of these resources is improving only slowly, if at all. Progress in biotechnology is inadequate and combines with persistent underfunding of agricultural research, agricultural extension, and institutions of higher learning to condemn SSA agriculture to slow and inadequate technical change, thus contributing to a growing technology divide.

The future agenda of all players must focus in particular on widely shared growth that includes rural areas. Ndulu et al. propose a medium–term growth strategy that hinges on taking action in four areas (characterized as the four "Is"): improving the *investment* climate; a big push toward closing the *infrastructure* gap with other regions of the world; a greater focus on *innovation* as the primary motor for productivity growth and enhanced competitiveness; and *institutional* and human capacity.

1.4 Opportunities and constraints

Stagnant volume and quality of aid from the traditional donors combined with only slowly growing financial commitments for ARD from national governments have been persistent constraints to agricultural development. In general, African countries have placed far too much hope on donor support for their ARD programs than is warranted by (1) the past volumes and quality of aid, (2) poor donor specialization and coordination, (3) follow-through on recent aid commitments, and (4) the only modest improvements in donor behavior over the past two decades. The growing fiscal space arising from rapid economic growth is a major opportunity for change.

1.4.1 The new aid architecture

Without falling back to the idea that ARD can be financed via donor support, the proliferation of new donors provides some opportunities to complement domestic resources with donor finance. However, countries will continue to have great difficulties in coordinating all the old and new donors. Nevertheless ways must be found to ensure that other donors and aid recipients conform to national development and sector policies and national strategies and plans. But their entrepreneurial drive and ability to raise and deploy resources without taxing government capacities should be encouraged, as has long been the case with donations from foreign religious institutions of all faiths. The burden of compliance with national policies could be put squarely on the recipient of the funds, combined with *ex-post* "audits," which could verify that policies have been adhered to. This would help reduce the donor coordination burden. Of course, for the larger existing and new government and multilateral donors, the coordination agenda of the Rome and Paris declaration remain fully in place.

1.4.2 Focusing on the "bottom billion"

Focusing on these countries will require donors to relax their rigid lending allocation rules. It will also increase the risk of grant and lending operations. These risks can partially be offset by enhancing supervision resources, and therefore supervision budgets might need to increase in these settings. Finally, all institutions might need to time their operations more carefully, focusing on rapid provision of technical assistance following an incipient turnaround or conflict resolution, followed by a strong shift to investment lending. *Stronger coordination of the capacity-building and investment lending with all major players will also be needed.*

1.4.3 The capacity of agricultural and rural institutions

Compared to 1980, the institutional environment for ARD has significantly improved. The space for the private sector, including producers associations, has dramatically expanded, even though the private sector response has not yet entered input and output markets sufficiently to create a vibrant and competitive environment for small farmers. Communities and civil society organizations have much more opportunity to participate in development and are receiving domestic and foreign support. Though most governments have decentralization initiatives under way, administrative and fiscal decentralization are badly lagging behind political decentralization. The sector institutions that should set and monitor policies and finance or provide service for small farmers remain largely ineffective, however. It is now well understood that these four sets of institutions need to collaborate at the local level as coproducers of local and community development, including agricultural development, in the form of public/ private partnerships. Such collaboration needs to be led and fostered by the central government, which continues to have overall policy and financing responsibilities and needs to drive further decentralization and public sector reform.

Although there are no studies that measure the impact of the improved institutions on agricultural growth, there is little doubt that these improvements, in addition to macroeconomic stability and improved price incentives, are one of the explanatory factors for the recent acceleration of agricultural growth.

Capacity development of agricultural and rural institutions would flourish best in the context of a broader, national capacity development strategy and program. It cannot be done as a top-down provision of capacity development services. Instead it involves learning by doing, in which communities, local governments, farmer's organizations, and private sector actors are given opportunities and resources and can exercise control over their own development. Of course, these actors should be provided with mandatory training, in particular in diagnosis and planning, financial management and reporting, procurement, and monitoring and evaluation. Other training should be provided largely on a demand-driven basis. Capacity development must build on the considerable latent capacities that are found in rural areas all over the world. To do so, rules and regulations for program execution must become much more participatory and empowering and eliminate complex features that destroy latent capacity or hinder its mobilization (Binswanger and Nguyen, 2005). Finally, the broader-sector institutions involved in ARD need to become much more accountable to their clients.

1.4.4 Innovation and scaling up

IFAD argues that innovation should be redefined as "innovation for scaling up of targeted programs for the rural poor." Rather than focusing on individual innovations, this would involve putting packages together using best international practices to reach their target group and improve their incomes and food security, with selective innovations in areas where international best practice is still not satisfactory, such as rural finance. Innovation would then mean to test and perfect the integrated approaches on a sufficiently large scale so that they can be scaled up nationally. Its analytical capacity and work program should also be sharply focused on these tasks, rather than attempting to cover all issues associated with agricultural and rural development.

1.4.5 The remaining challenges of agricultural incentives

A number of issues remain to be resolved: A declining number of countries in the region, including, until recently, Zimbabwe, continue to pursue disastrous macro-economic policies. In other countries inflation remains stubbornly high, leading to high real interest rates that make it difficult for agriculture to compete for investment resources.

In terms of Africa's own agricultural trade policies, five conclusions stand out:

- Although on balance protection rates (or more precisely, nominal rates of assistance to agriculture) are no longer negative, they remain below −10% in Ethiopia, Sudan, Tanzania, Zambia, Côte d'Ivoire, and Zimbabwe.
- Taxation is still concentrated on exportable commodities. However, from taxing them at extremely high rates in the 1970s and 1980s, Africa has steadily improved its incentives regime, and on average it is now less than 10%. However, taxation levels of a number of individual exportable commodities remain alarmingly high.
- Despite the improvements in incentives, African farmers still face the worst agricultural incentives in the world. This is because, first, only Europe has reduced its nominal rates of assistance to agriculture, whereas both the United States and (especially) Japan have increased them. Second, the other developing regions have moved from disprotecting agriculture to protecting their agriculture, in the case of Asia at a level that is now getting closer to the average of the developed world.
- Although many initiatives for subregional integration are progressing in all subregions of SSA, agricultural incentives also still suffer from barriers to interregional trade and poor phytosanitary capacities.
- Though improving, the business climates in most countries still remain far worse than in other developing countries, holding back private sector activities upstream and downstream from the farm.

If countries in SSA want to compete better in domestic, regional, and international markets and benefit from the likely rising trend in international agricultural prices, they must move aggressively to eliminate export taxation of agriculture and remaining barriers to regional trade.

1.4.6 The future of small farmers

As a consequence of the spike in crude oil and food prices, many private and sovereign investors have expressed strong interest in investing in large-scale farming in Africa. Our review of the literature on economies of scale in agriculture and the past experience with large-scale farming suggests that small-scale farmers still are likely to fare better than large-scale farms in seizing the significant opportunities in domestic and regional markets for staple foods and livestock products, since they usually have lower costs of production than large-scale units. Rental markets for farm machinery, provision of agricultural services, joint marketing and input supply arrangements via organizations of their own, and contract farming with agroindustries are ways in which they can overcome disadvantages in mechanization, access to technologies, marketing, and input supply. It is only in the so-called "plantation crops," where highly perishable products have to be processed or packaged and shipped rapidly, including tea, sugar cane, and fruits and vegetables for export, that midsize or large-scale farms appear to become competitive or even have a comparative advantage, and selected success stories across Africa confirm this view. Even there, contract farming with smallholders could sometimes be a more profitable option for entrepreneurs.

1.4.7 Rural finance

Because of the extremely adverse environment for rural finance in most of Africa, it is not surprising that many aid agencies have found it excruciatingly difficult to achieve success in rural finance. But they still put rural finance high on the agenda in their agricultural programs. Instead we believe that the solution to the farm investment issues needs to come from substantially improved agricultural incentives and profitability in general so that farmers can invest profits back into their farms. This can be supported by easily accessible and low-cost savings mechanisms, such as postal savings systems linked to rural savings clubs. A complementary approach would be to finance more agricultural and rural investments via matching grants, with the matches coming from both community contributions in kind as well as individual savings.

1.4.8 Agricultural science and technology

In spite of good returns to agricultural research in Africa, the science and technology divide between SSA agriculture and the rest of the world is growing because of inefficient and underfunded science and technology institutions in SSA and because of rapid changes in the international research environment toward biotechnology and private agricultural research. Borrowing opportunities from other regions and within the continent are constrained by the uniqueness and the heterogeneity of African agricultural environments. Combined with a relatively poor climate and resource base and the large number of stressors on productivity, this will require more, rather than less, research than in other regions. The challenges of natural resource management and of climate change and growing climate risks only add to this imperative.

Fortunately, African leaders have started to respond to this challenge by creating consensus on what needs to be done, improving their national institutions of higher learning and research, building subregional and regional agricultural technology institutions, and developing biotechnology networks and institutions. Pillar 4 of the Comprehensive African Agricultural Development Program provides a vision and an action plan for African agriculture, science, and technology. Unfortunately, the significant institutional responses have not so far been matched by adequate funding from national government and international donors, especially in the areas of biotechnology and science education.

1.5 The imperative of regionalization

Throughout this chapter there have been many critical issues that can be best, or only, solved by regional action, and more are yet to come. Let's recall a sampling:

- Small countries dominate the African scene, often lacking financial capacity for public goods investments.
- Small landlocked countries generally do worse and depend on regional integration to be able to do better.
- Expanded regional trade in agriculture and food products is good for growth and farmer's income and regional food security; the short-run management challenges of the recent food price spike and the long-run opportunities arising from prices that are expected to settle at higher than past levels only add to this imperative.
- Expanded regional trade and food security will be helped by the harmonization of standards and sanitary measures and subregional and regional capacities to implement them.
- Freer borders and internal infrastructure should encourage private sector traders.
- For small countries, regional infrastructure—roads, communications, ports—are critical for access to each others' and external markets.
- Reversing land degradation and desertification and preserving biodiversity require transboundary collective action.
- Managing crucial but under-threat forestry and fisheries resources must be approached on a transnational basis.
- Defense against plant and animal disease epidemics requires collective responses at subregional and regional levels.
- Success in agriculture crucially depends on indigenous scientific capacity to generate new technology; given small and poor countries, this is far better done on a regional or subregional basis: FARA and the SROs are on the right track, but the efforts need to be greatly expanded.
- Biotechnology research is expensive and requires a large critical mass; therefore two or three regional institutes are far superior to 48 or 24 underfunded, under-resourced national institutions.
- Indigenous scientific capacity requires trained people, again better done by regional institutions that have critical mass and necessary financial support.
- Regional approaches to rural financial architecture can increase potential deposits and loanable funds and spread risk.

Hopefully these examples are enough to illustrate that the potential for regional approaches and an overall regional strategy for rural Africa are significant. Yet in most of these areas institutional development programs remain massively underfunded. The main reason for this is that the regional efforts produce regional and subregional public goods, and therefore their financing is subject to the familiar free-rider problem of financing public goods. Except for the largest countries, which have an incentive to supply themselves with these regional public goods, countries will seek to benefit from the investment of others. It is precisely here that a regional development finance institution such as the African Development Bank (AfDB) has a major opportunity to step in, since it can both coordinate as well as contribute to the financing of these essential regional capacities. AfDB has fully recognized this comparative advantage in general and can become much more active in supporting cross-border agricultural collaboration. To effectively exercise a leadership role, it needs to develop analytical and implementation capacities as well as streamlined mechanisms for financing them that are not dependent on individual country borrowing decisions to effectively exercise this leadership role.

2. INTRODUCTION

We undertook this task in a period of optimism about the prospects for Africa and for African agriculture. Much of Africa has started to grow rapidly. It has built more robust and sustainable policies and institutions at local, national, and regional levels and is strengthening their capacity. Democracy has advanced all over the continent: In 2007 Katito claimed that no fewer than 22 African countries held elections that were declared "free and fair" (Katito, 2007). Africa has moved from being the last region in terms of reforms of the business environment, ahead of the Middle East and Latin America (World Bank and IFC, 2006). Although regional and global risks remain high for Africa, the new environment also provides many opportunities.

Agriculture is finally identified as a sector that can both contribute to growth and lead in reducing poverty. Agriculture and rural development have returned as priorities on the international development agenda. African nations, working through the African Union (AU), have identified joint action as critical and have created the New Partnership for Africa's Development (NEPAD). In NEPAD agriculture has a critical role through the AU-NEPAD Comprehensive Africa Agricultural Development Program (CAADP).

Finally, general economic performance is positive, as this quote from the High Level Panel (HLP) indicates:

> **A favorable global economic context, characterized by strong demand for many of Africa's primary commodities, allied to progress by Africa on macroeconomic policy reform and governance are the main drivers behind the Continent's strong performance of the past several years.**

> **Africa's recent progress is striking when compared to the 1990s:**
> **–Real GDP growth is forecast to exceed 6% in 2007 compared to less than 3%.**
> **–Inflation has fallen from nearly 30% to stabilize in the 10% range.**

-Following macro-economic reforms, many African countries have benefited from debt relief, which is reflected in significantly lower external debt-to-GDP ratios.

-While Africa had a fiscal deficit of 3.5% of GDP in 1999, the continent has produced fiscal surpluses since 2004. ("Preliminary Observations of the African Development Bank High Level Panel," May 16, 2007)

As a consequence, though conscious of the remaining serious risks, this review takes a moderately optimistic stance and develops its recommendations based on such a view.

2.1 Our approach

This chapter is being written at a time when many others have summarized the state of knowledge on food and agriculture, what works in agricultural development, and the "Opportunities and Challenges for African Agriculture" in great depth, including FAO (2007), IFPRI (2006), InterAcademy Council (2005), and World Bank (2007). There are also a number of recent studies on governance failure, conflict, and natural resource dependence (Collier, 2007), governance and regional integration (Economic Commission for Africa (ECA, 2006), and other relevant topics. This chapter therefore does no original work on these topics but instead harvests this rich knowledge.

To set the background for the challenges and opportunities, in Section 2, we start by reviewing the great challenge of poverty and hunger that the past failure to grow has left behind. It is in this section that we look at the major contribution that agricultural growth can make to poverty reduction, as long recognized in the literature and analyzed again in the recent WDR. In Section 3 we review the major changes that have occurred in the international and institutional landscape regarding ARD, globally and for Africa, in the period 1980–2007. In Section 4 we discuss global winds of change that have significantly altered the environment for agricultural development in Africa in the same period. We explore their implications for Africa and what Africa can or should do about them.

With this changing global context as background, in Sections 5 and 6 we investigate the African scene, noting, as have many others, that heterogeneity is the operative descriptor—in natural resources, climate, soil and water resources, farming systems, infrastructure, access to markets for inputs and outputs, political stability/instability, governance, and economic performance. Section 5 first reviews the record of economic growth and the factors that have inhibited it for so long but now are starting to contribute to the recent successes. We then turn specifically to agricultural growth and review the specific agricultural policies and factors that have for so long prevented its growth but have also now been turned around. In Section 6 we focus specifically on the plight of the "bottom billion" countries, in the terminology of the recent book by Paul Collier that is reviewed in that section. It holds many important lessons for the future operations of the two institutions.

In Section 7 we turn to the institutional pillars that need to be in place for agricultural and rural development (ARD), including the private sector, communities, local government, and central and subregional institutions. We specifically analyze how they need to assume specific functions and collaborate with each other in a process of "coproduction" of agricultural and rural development. We note that a great deal of progress has been made in improving the institutional environment for ARD, but we also note the remaining strong weaknesses, especially in decentralization and regional integration. Section 8 first reviews the emerging market opportunities of African agriculture. It then reviews the remaining challenges for African agriculture that are primarily under the direct control of African countries and the region (rather than external influences). We divide these challenges into four groups:

- Demographic, social, health, and safety-net issues
- Agro-climate, biophysical resources, and natural resource management
- Enhancing agricultural profits and rural investments
- The ultimate source of growth: Agricultural technology

It is in all these four broad areas that that more progress is needed to consolidate the recovery and to achieve rapid growth and poverty reduction.

2.2 The past failure to grow and the neglect of agriculture have left the troubling challenge of poverty and hunger

Africa is second only to Asia in its size and heterogeneity. Its land mass is larger than that of Brazil, Japan, Australia, Europe, and the continental United States combined. Japan alone could easily fit into Madagascar. Africa's climates include Mediterranean climes in the North and, in South Africa, subtropical and tropical highlands, the largest deserts, and vast stretches of arid, semi-arid, subhumid, and humid tropical areas. Of Africa's 900 million people, about two thirds live in villages and small rural towns. Except for the deserts, rural people live, farm, and raise livestock in all the diverse environments of Africa. They are much more concentrated where agroclimatic conditions are better, such as in areas of Mediterranean climate and subtropical and tropical highlands, leading to sharp variations in population densities across the continent. African countries vary greatly in geographic area and population, but compared to other regions, a higher proportion of countries are very small. Many countries are rich in natural resources; others are resource-poor. A larger proportion of African countries is landlocked than in any other region of the world. There are significant differences in culture and historical backgrounds, education levels, and population trends among the countries. And economic growth has differed widely across countries and over time. These large differences across and within countries imply different development and growth opportunities. They make generalization across the continent difficult. In this chapter we

describe general trends and feasible generalizations, but we pay greater attention
to how these differences have influenced past general and agricultural growth,
performance, and prospects and the elements that have shaped them, such as
conflicts, governance, investment, productivity, trade, and other determinants of
performance.

> **[Sub-Saharan] Africa (SSA) has the highest incidence of poverty of all
> developing regions. It accounts for 10 percent of the world's people, but is
> home to 30 percent of the world's poor. ... In the last two decades the
> number of the poor in Africa has grown from 150 million to 300 million,
> more than 40 percent of the region's people. Africa ... is at the bottom of
> the United Nations Development Programme's human development index,
> reflecting low levels of education, health, and economic welfare. And it is
> the only region off the required path to reach most of the Millennium
> Development Goals. (World Bank, 2005, p. 1)**

Around 200 million of Africa's 900 million people are undernourished, and 33 million
children go to bed hungry every night. More than 60% of the undernourished are
concentrated in East and Central Africa, whereas in West Africa undernutrition has
declined in recent years (InterAcademy Commission, 2005).

Over the past 45 years, per capita income in Africa has grown at only 0.5% per year,
compared to 3% in the 57 countries in the rest of the developing regions (including
North Africa). The slow growth in per capita income in Africa has meant that poverty
in Africa has not only remained the highest in the world but has failed to decline
between 1990 and 2003 (Figure 1).

Although urban poverty is increasing, more than 70% of the continent's poor still
live in rural areas. Of the 15 countries in Figure 2, the rural poor represent between

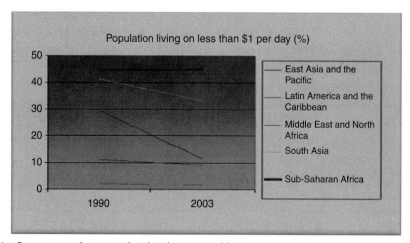

Figure 1   Poverty trends across the developing world, 1990 and 2003. Source: Pingali et al. 2007.

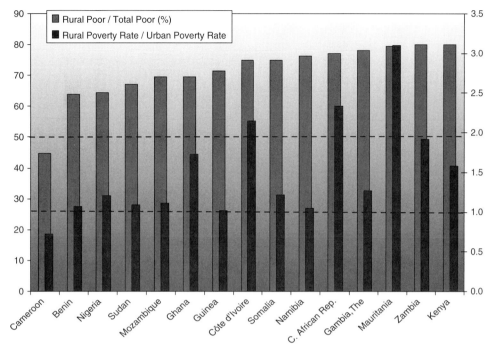

Figure 2 Poverty in SSA remains predominantly a rural phenomenon. Source: Pingali et al. 2007.

60% and 80% of all the poor. In addition, poverty rates in rural areas are still much higher than in urban areas: Of the 15 countries in the figure, nine have rural poverty rates that are at least three times as high as in urban areas. And only in Mauritania is the urban poverty rate as high as the rural one. The rural poor include small-scale farmers, nomads and herders, artisanal fishers, and wage laborers. At the same time many of them are in households headed by women and are unemployed youth, entirely landless people, or displaced persons.

Improved growth is not only critical for poverty reduction and for human development more generally: *"within SSA, an increase in the long-run growth rate of real GDP per capita by 1 percent was associated with an increase in an index of cumulative human development of nearly one-half percent."* (Ndulu, 2007, p.8). The impact of growth on poverty reduction is well illustrated by 8 SSA countries that have seen per capita growth rates of 2.9 percent on average in the 1990s and have reduced poverty at an annual rate of 1.5 percent during the period (Figure 3). On the other hand, poverty in stagnating countries has increased.

Moreover, a recent IFPRI study shows that a persistent income growth rate of 2.5% would reduce undernutrition in Africa by a range of 27–34% by 2015 (Haddad et al., 2005). And as we shall see later in this paper, economic growth also reduces

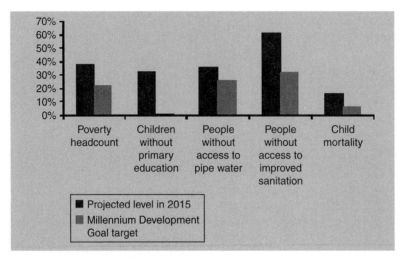

Figure 3 Growth and poverty reduction in eight SSA countries.

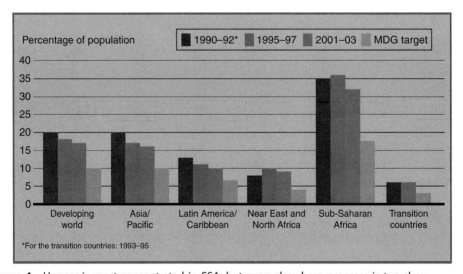

Figure 4 Hunger is most concentrated in SSA, but even elsewhere progress is too slow.

the chances of conflict. Given slow growth and high levels of poverty in SSA relative to the other developing regions, it is not surprising that the proportion of undernourished people in the population has barely declined and remains the highest in world, at above 30%. As Figure 4 shows, even in regions with much faster per capita income growth than SSA, the decline in hunger over the last two and a half decades has been disappointingly slow. Rapid per capita income growth appears to be a powerful remedy against absolute poverty, but it seems less powerful in terms of reducing hunger. It is therefore clear that, even with accelerating growth, sub-Saharan Africa will have great difficulties in reaching the Millennium Development Goal (MDG-1) of reducing hunger by half by 2015.

Economic growth has been faster in North Africa than in SSA and was close to 4% in the 10 years leading up to 2005 (ECA, 2006a). Therefore, most countries in the subregion are well on their way to reaching the 2015 millennium poverty reduction target, and Libya and Tunisia already met them in 2001. Nevertheless, in 2001 between 2% and 7% of the populations of Algeria, Egypt, Morocco, and Tunisia were still suffering from hunger. The agenda for poverty and hunger reduction in these countries is to address the remaining poverty pockets in the countries, many of which are in rural areas (ECA, 2006a).

On the other hand, economic growth and rural development have been the slowest in Eastern and Southern Africa. Of the 21 countries, no fewer than 10 have an average per capita income of less than $400. Of the 350 million people in the subregion, about 260 million live in rural areas, which account for 83% of extreme poverty, making the subregion probably the worst poverty pocket in the world. About 38% of the land base is desert, arid, or semi-arid, but these areas have relatively low population and therefore harbor only about 14% of the rural poor. The remaining 62% of the land base has medium to high potential for increased production but harbors no less than 86% of the rural poor (IFAD, 2002b). It is in this subregion that hunger is the most pronounced (Figure 5). And as a look at the map of HIV-prevalence in Chapter 8 shows

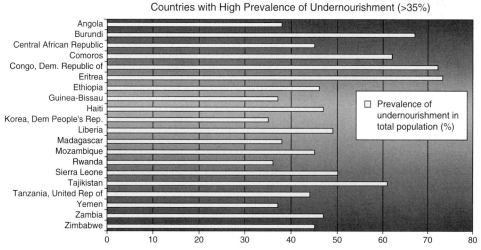

Figure 5 Poverty, and therefore hunger, are most concentrated in Central, East, and Southern Africa. Source: Pingali et al. (2007).

(Figure 39), this is combined with by far the highest HIV prevalence rates in the world. Figure 40 shows that it is now the cohort of young people between 20 and 30 who are disproportionately affected by HIV.

In West and Central Africa, for the 16 (out of 24) countries for which poverty data are available, 41% of the total population is classified as poor. Of these 125 million poor people, around three quarters live in rural areas—still very high but a bit less than in East and Southern Africa. Poverty is higher in the Northern Sahelian and Guinean areas, which are characterized by livestock, cereal, and cotton production, but there are indications that poverty might be rising in the forest zones, which suffer from highly volatile prices of tree crops. As shown in Chapter 8, HIV/AIDS prevalence rates are much lower in the subregion, except in Cameroon and the Central African Republic. (Figure 39). The FAO hunger maps show that hunger has sharply increased in the conflict-ridden Democratic Republic of the Congo. On the other hand, it is in West Africa that hunger has significantly declined.

2.3 The special role of agricultural growth in reducing poverty and hunger

It is not only how much growth occurs but whether it is based on rapid agricultural growth that counts for poverty reduction. The WDR 2008 on *Agriculture for Development* shows that today across the world, 2.1 billion people live on less than $2 a day. Most of them live in rural areas and depend on agriculture for their livelihood. The number of rural poor has increased in SSA and South Asia and has reduced in East Asia and the Pacific. The report summarizes an extremely large literature that demonstrates the great power of agricultural growth for poverty reduction. Over the past 10 years global poverty with a $2-a-day poverty line declined 8.7% in absolute numbers. *This decline was caused entirely by* rural *poverty reduction, with* agriculture *as the main source of growth.* At the same time, *urban* poverty has increased. *Migration is not the main instrument for rural (and global) poverty reduction. Improved rural conditions are the main cause.*

As Mellor and Johnston (1961) showed nearly 50 years ago, agricultural growth reduces rural poverty:
- By raising agricultural profits and labor income
- By raising rural nonfarm profits and labor income via forward, backward, and especially consumer demand linkages
- By causing lower prices of (nontradable) foods, and therefore the consumption basket of the poor gets cheaper
- Lower food prices reduce urban real wages and accelerate urban growth
- Labor-intensive agricultural growth leads to tightening labor markets and higher rural and eventually economywide unskilled wages

The WDR divides developing countries into *urbanizing countries*, mostly in Latin America (but also including South Africa), with 255 million people; *transforming countries*, mainly in East Asia and MENA, with about 2.2 billion rural people, and *agricultural countries*, mostly in SSA, with 417 million rural people.

- In the agricultural countries, the sector accounts for 32% of GDP growth and two thirds of employment. Growth in agriculture can drive economywide growth and mass poverty reduction, as it has in East and Southeast Asia and, to a lesser extent, in South Asia.
- In transforming countries, agriculture contributes 7% of growth, but 79% of all poor are still rural. The role of agriculture in these countries is to reduce poverty and confront rising rural/urban income disparities.
- In urbanizing countries, rural areas still have 39% of all the poor. Even though the share of the sector in GDP is small, it has been the fastest-growing sector in this country group for over a decade, with Brazil and Chile as the shining examples. The sector therefore provides major investment opportunities for commercial enterprises and a large number of smallholders. It is needed to reduce remaining rural poverty.

Christiansen et al. (2006) find that in low-income countries, including in Africa, the "participation effect"[3] from agricultural growth on the poverty head count on average is 2.3 times larger than the participation effect from nonagriculture. Relative to the service sector, the impact is even larger at a factor of 2.5 on average and 4.25 in sub-Saharan Africa. These differences do not primarily follow from the large share of agriculture in these economies but rather from the much larger elasticity of overall poverty to agricultural GDP than to nonagricultural GDP. The larger impact of agriculture on poverty headcounts also holds for the middle-income countries such as those in North Africa, where the participation effect of agricultural growth on head count poverty is on average 1.34 times larger than that of equal growth in the other sectors. However, the authors caution that these higher poverty reduction impacts are dependent on the use of the right technology (e.g., focused on nontradable food versus tradable export crops; land versus labor saving) and its targeting (small versus large farmers).

Figure 6 shows that since the 1960s, North Africa and to a lesser extent the "other" country group in SSA have reduced their dependence on agriculture as an economic sector and a source of employment, the Least Developed Countries in Africa have seen a virtually constant share of agriculture in GDP and only a slight decline in agriculture as a source of employment.

Although general economic growth does not necessarily reduce hunger fast, agricultural growth has a much more direct impact on hunger: Figure 7 shows how the rate of per capita agricultural growth between 1990 and 2005 has translated into hunger reduction in SSA. By and large the countries with faster agricultural growth have made more progress against hunger. Hunger increased significantly in the conflict or coup countries of Liberia, Sierra Leone, Comoros, Burundi, Guinea Bissau, and most dramatically, the DRC. Other countries with significant increases in hunger are Gambia and, surprisingly, Botswana.

Share of Agriculture in GDP				
	1969–71	1979–81	1989–91	2002–04
North Africa	19.1	14.7	16.0	13.6
Sub-Saharan Africa: LDC	40.2	40.4	37.5	38.8
Sub-Saharan Africa: Other	30.6	27.6	27.1	26.6
Africa	31.9	29.6	28.7	28.4
Share of economically active population in agriculture in total economically active population				
	1969–71	1979–81	1989–91	2002–04
North Africa	0.54	0.43	0.30	0.23
Sub-Saharan Africa: LDC	0.83	0.79	0.76	0.71
Sub-Saharan Africa: Other	0.68	0.60	0.49	0.41
Africa	0.76	0.70	0.63	0.57

Figure 6 The dependence of LDCs in Africa on agriculture has barely changed from 1969–2004. Source: Sarris et al. (2007).

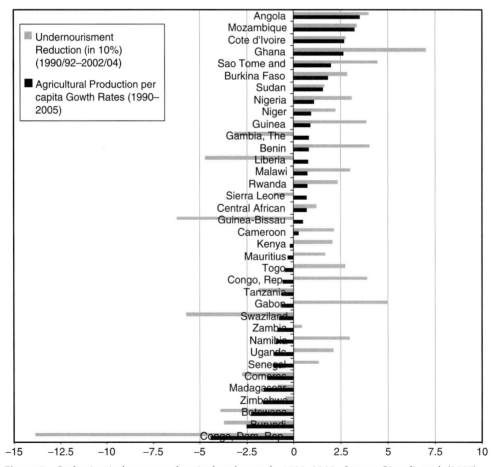

Figure 7 Reduction in hunger and agricultural growth, 1990–2005. Source: Pingali et al. (2007).

To sum up: Past failure to grow and the neglect of agriculture have dramatically increased poverty and hunger in SSA while growth has contributed to poverty reduction in North Africa. Recent economic growth on the other hand has reduced poverty and the associated agricultural growth is a powerful factor in reducing hunger.

3. THE CHANGING INTERNATIONAL LANDSCAPE OF DEVELOPMENT ASSISTANCE

3.1 The changing international and institutional landscape for ARD, 1980–2007

There have been substantial changes in the international and institutional landscape of agriculture and rural development within which agricultural development agencies have functioned historically and will implement their future rural strategies. Organizations are heavily influenced by their historical context. That context is shaped by major issues of substance and critical events that are then dominating the political, economic, and social debate. This context defines the critical questions and shapes the dominant objectives of the time. Conceptual models of how to accomplish these objectives were driven by prevailing paradigms. Paradigms need to be converted to processes and approaches—the "hows" of development. Finally, plans and policies have to be implemented by someone—governments, intergovernmental organizations, private organizations, and interest groups. These are called the *players*. Using this framework we characterize the radical changes in the ARD environment that have occurred in the period 1980–2007. We close this section with a special look at what has been happening in the nature and effectiveness of aid in the so-called new AID architecture.

3.1.1 The 1980s

The early 1980s was a period characterized by rapid inflation and slow growth, which were the fallout of the run-up in oil and commodity prices in the 1970s. This made concerns about poverty and social issues that had been raised in the late 1970s come into competition with, and be partially crowded out on the international agenda, by structural adjustment and other priorities in the 1980s. The food price run-up of the middle 1970s, coupled with the recognition that poverty was a predominantly rural phenomenon, made agriculture and rural development major items on the agenda. But they had new competitors for priority in the global context as issues of the environment, health, education, and social services emerged in the late 1980s. The Cold War continued to drive bipolar competition, including in foreign aid. New global powerhouses in China, India, and Brazil had yet to emerge.

The paradigms of development were in a state of change. By the 1980s the world trading system had evolved by substantially reducing barriers to industrial trade and trade volumes, and values increased substantially. GATT initiated the Uruguay Round of trade negotiations in 1986, which, when it concluded in 1994, brought agricultural trade under the general rules of the newly formed World Trade Organization (WTO) but with little impact on effective protection. Some nations in East Asia abandoned the inward-looking import-substitution industrialization model and succeeded in growing rapidly by expanding exports. Thus export-led growth was a new competing paradigm for general economic development. The new priority of poverty reduction necessarily focused more attention on rural areas because most poor people live in rural areas.

Despite the path-breaking academic study by Johnston and Mellor (1961), which argued that agriculture had a very positive role to play in the early stages of economic development, the sector was still discriminated against. It was seen more as a source of resources than a positive engine of growth. Rural development was approached via massive integrated rural development projects (IRDPs), which focused more on infrastructure, food production, and investment in social capital than on improving the earning potential of the commercial crops of small farmers. However, the new rural development paradigm did recognize that rural well-being depended on income and access to physical and social infrastructure.

The "how" of development was also changing. International financial institutions (IFIs), especially the World Bank, greatly expanded lending to a broader set of sectors. In the 1980s rural development represented the largest sector of lending for the World Bank. Development assistance expanded through IDA, the newly established European Union, and through competitive bilateral assistance and reached new heights. Cleaver (2007) claims that agriculture received 18% of total ODA in 1979.

The prevailing mechanisms for support of general economic development continued to evolve. Project lending focused on poverty reduction was often not sustainable after the projects ended, in part because many nations had large fiscal, monetary, and debt imbalances, and projects had not been mainstreamed into sector institutions. Often the taking on of additional commitments made matters worse. Thus poverty lending gave way to structural adjustment lending in the 1980s and then policy lending in the 1990s.

The number of players in the international agricultural scene had greatly increased. Rural development lending expanded not only for the World Bank, but the regional development banks, including AfDB, and the newly formed IFAD became major players, as did a growing number of bilateral donors.

3.1.2 The early 2000s

The *international and institutional landscape* of the early 2000s is radically different from the 1980s and can only be understood by tracing its rapid evolution over the short period of 20 years. At the turn of the century the landscape was still changing rapidly. Compared to the 1980s some major changes were as follows:

- The Cold War was over, replacing a nuclear standoff with increasing numbers of regional, national, and subnational conflicts. The end of the Cold War reduced competitive pressures to expand aid, and support levels fell.

- Severe food emergencies and large numbers of refugees emerged with increasing frequency, not only increasing needs for World Food Program (WFP) help but also placing demands on many traditional agencies for post-emergency assistance.
- Middle East conflicts continued to contribute to rising petroleum prices.
- The Millennium Assessment laid out eight Millennium Development Goals (MDGs). Several, particularly #1 on poverty and hunger, refocused attention on rural development and on SSA.
- The rise of the environment and other social sectors, especially health, radically shifted lending and assistance portfolios of IFIs and bilateral agencies. HIV/AIDS emerged as a huge health, labor, and poverty issue. Funding for agriculture and rural development hit a 25-year low in 2001. Cleaver (2007) says that agriculture's share of total ODA dropped to 3.5% by 2004.
- The molecular biology revolution was in full swing, leading to rapid privatization of agriculture research, the GMO debate, and patents on living organisms. The public/private landscape in agricultural research was fundamentally altered. Civil society organizations (CSOs) and nongovernmental organizations (NGOs) emerged as powerful forces in international development and global environmental and health issues.
- The World Bank and other development agencies are now championing good governance and have declared war on corruption.
- GATT has been transformed into the World Trade Organization (WTO). The Doha Development Round focused (so far unsuccessfully) on trade liberalization of particular benefit to developing countries.
- The world's attention to agriculture and rural development seemed to wane even though rural poverty and more than 800 million undernourished people persisted. "The Five Years After" follow-up to the World Food Conference of 1996 found very slow progress toward the goal of halving the number of undernourished by 2015. Recently, however, the rhetorical interest at least seems to be rising. The InterAcademy Council report (2005), the "Blair Report" of the Commission for Africa (2005), and the World Bank WDR of 2008 all make forceful cases for the positive role agriculture can play in SSA.

So the beginning of the new millennium was characterized by great uncertainty, rising conflicts, and increased competition for funds. The prevailing paradigms of general economic development continued to evolve. The current paradigm is open-economy, market-driven, private sector-led economic development. The role of government is to set appropriate rules, provide necessary public goods, and make sure the playing field is level, fair, and open.

Agricultural development paradigms also continued to change. Massive rural development projects and support to agricultural credit institutions had high rates of failure, and support for agriculture/rural activities in general plummeted. But rural poverty continued to be the predominant persistent poverty problem. Some countries had achieved rapid growth with agriculture exports leading that growth, and it began to be recognized that agriculture was a productive sector potentially able to contribute to poverty reduction through growth. The longstanding but artificial distinction between food crops and market/export crops disappeared when it was recognized that with improved technology and access to markets, farmers producing marketable surpluses of any commodity could improve their incomes. Further, agriculturally stimulated rural nonfarm activities in many countries provided for growth in employment and incomes. Thus the 1961 Johnston-Mellor argument finally seemed to be back in vogue, refocusing attention on the critical importance of agricultural growth, particularly in the early stages of the economic transformation. It was finally recognized that agriculture in most countries was the largest private sector activity and that farmers would respond to incentives.

Accepted processes of development—the "hows" —continued to be challenged and added to. The emergence of a wide variety and burgeoning numbers of CSOs and NGOs at the local, national, and international levels radically altered our perceptions of the players. They had many new ideas about what needed to be done. Almost all were advocates for particular sectors, groups, or causes. Many became involved in the implementation of activities, particularly in emergencies, and many have evolved to have sufficient capacity to be technical partners. Nowhere is the incredible array of involved entities more obvious than in the rural sector of many of the poor developing countries.

The concept of democratization in the design and implementation of projects necessarily required participation of potential beneficiaries. The adoption of the concept of subsidiarity—decentralizing decisions to the lowest (often community) levels—led to the concept of client ownership, a far cry from top-down, complicated, complex, expatriate-dominated, integrated rural development projects (IRDPs). Privatization, the end of central planning, and the rise of markets refocused attention on what contributed most to rural growth. For farmers it meant technology that increased productivity and profitability; access to necessary inputs; and functioning fair and open markets at home and abroad. Thus trade liberalization became part of the rural development policy mix. For the rural sector it dictated needs for education, infrastructure (especially transport), and functioning markets.

The end of the Cold War and the rash of new conflicts and disasters has changed the rationale for international assistance and focused even more attention on the short run. Thus support for long-term and continuing investments in development such as agricultural research in general, and the CGIAR in particular; institution building; and rural infrastructure are more difficult to generate.

Overall, development processes have become more complex, with larger numbers of projects (because of decentralization and local ownership) more fragmented and inevitably more heterogeneous. The numbers of players who claim a legitimate interest have, to use Homi Kharas's term, "exploded." To quote him: "Estimates suggest that there are 233 multilateral development agencies; 51 bilateral donor countries (most with multiple official agencies); several hundred international NGOs; and tens of thousands of national NGOs, not including community-based organizations which could number in the millions" (Kharas, 2007, p. 3). Many are new players who have emerged in a big way in the past few years. Kharas classifies them into two groups:

- New bilateral donors from the South, including China (US$2 billion per annum), India and Saudi Arabia (over $1 billion each), several more in the half-billion-dollar range (Korea, Turkey, Kuwait, and Taiwan), and a total of 21 more who have or are establishing aid programs. Kharas concludes that "Estimates of aid from new players equaled or exceeded official development aid from traditional donors in 2005" (p. 6). There is also an ongoing change in the architecture of aid from horizontal, multisector agencies to new specialized (vertical) agencies such as the Global Fund to Fight AIDS, Tuberculosis and Malaria.
- Private organizations such as international NGOs like World Vision International with a budget exceeding US$2 billion, four with budgets between $500 million and $900 million (Save the Children International, Care USA, Catholic Relief Services, and Plan International), and thousands of philanthropic foundations that contribute to international causes. The largest of these in 2004 were the Gates Foundation, at $1.2 billion, and the Ford Foundation, at $250+ million.

Literally thousands of NGOs/CSOs pay some attention to the rural landscape. The privatization of agricultural research and the marketing of GMO seeds by large multinationals have placed larger agribusiness firms in the mainstream, particularly in pest management in agriculture. Plant patenting has introduced many complications into international policies for preserving plant genetic resources. FAO shepherded through the International Treaty on Plant Genetic Resources (ITPGR), but the Convention on Biodiversity (CBD), the World Intellectual Property Organization (WIPO), and TRIPS/WTO, all with competing concepts, have greatly complicated the landscape.

In the United Nations sphere, other agencies such as WHO, UNICEF, UNAIDS, and FIVIMS became increasingly engaged in issues of nutrition and health. Millennium Development Goal Task Forces, particularly Task Force One, are new players. New conventions, such as the ones on desertification and the Montreal Protocol, overlap somewhat with FAO, and WFP and IFAD's roles are now more closely entwined in terms of emergencies, early warnings, and a renewed focus on Africa.

There are many new institutions and players relevant to Africa. African nations working through the African Union (AU) have identified joint action as critical and have created the New Partnership for Africa's Development (NEPAD). In NEPAD agriculture has a critical role through the AU-NEPAD Comprehensive Africa Agricultural Development Program (CAADP) (see also Section of8of this chapter on technology). Finally, it needs to be underlined that new bilateral aid players such as China, India, and Brazil are also now major commercial development players in terms of markets, inputs, technology, and finance. BBC News estimates that the most recent wave of Chinese migrants to Africa is "thought to total up to 750,000. . . . They are settling all over the continent, in rural and urban areas, are involved in agriculture, construction and trade" (BBC News, November 29, 2007).

3.2 Aid: The new architecture and the magnitude and effectiveness of ODA

Homi Kharas (2007), in his paper "The New Reality of Aid," analyzes the growth and further fragmentation of the aid landscape and the discouraging trend showing that once you account for all the things that are not really for development, aid for development has hardly grown:

> **Of the $100+ billion of official development assistance disbursed by rich countries to developing countries in 2005 only $38 billion was oriented towards long-term development projects and programs. Of this $38 billion, perhaps half reached the intended beneficiaries. The balance of the money is tied up in special purpose funds like debt relief and technical assistance, or in administrative costs incurred in both the donor and recipient country. Presumably some is lost to corruption, too. . . . Traditional donors are splintering into many specialized agencies. Large new bilaterals have emerged from the South with their own approaches to development cooperation. The number of private nonprofits is exploding and the value of their donations could already equal or exceed official aid. The new reality of aid is one of enormous fragmentation and volatility, increasing costs and potentially decreasing effectiveness. A key challenge for the new era of development assistance will be to understand how coordination, information sharing and aid delivery will work in the new aid architecture. (Kharas, p. 1)**

Kharas's analysis regarding SSA is particularly sobering as he answers the question:

> **This same story is replayed on the ground in Africa. The rhetoric is one of progress: the G8 has an Africa Action Plan, with special representatives to keep a focus on the poorest continent. But so far, sub-Saharan Africa (SSA) has hardly seen any funding increase at all. Astonishingly, our estimates suggest that only $12.1 billion of the overall official development assistance takes the form of funds that SSA countries can use to invest in social and infrastructure development programs—one cent for every $27 in rich country income. This is almost the same as the amount received by these countries twenty-two years ago in 1985 ($11.6 billion). In proportion to either Africa's needs, its population, number of poor people, or rich country income, net development aid to Africa has been falling with no signs of concrete plans to raise this in an effective fashion. Small wonder that patience with official aid is running thin. (p. 5)**

A second, even more critical paper is one by William Easterly under the provocative title, "Are Aid Agencies Improving?" Easterly uses statistical analysis of OECD DAC data to see if donors are learning to do a better job of addressing three clusters of issues:

1. Learning to resolve chronic problems of foreign aid: donor coordination, aid tying, and food aid and technical assistance
2. Learning new theories of development: responding to need, importance of government polices and importance of institutions
3. Learning from failure: structural adjustment and debt relief

His conclusions are perhaps even more pessimistic than Kharas's:

> **The record of the aid agencies over time seems to indicate weak evidence of progress due to learning or changes in political support for poverty alleviation. The positive results are an increased sensitivity to per capita income of the recipient (although it happened long ago in the 1970s), a decline in aid tying, and a decrease in food aid as a share of total aid. Most of the other evidence—increasing donor fragmentation, unchanged emphasis on technical assistance, little or no sign of increased selectivity with respect to policies and institutions, the adjustment lending-debt relief imbroglio—suggests an unchanged status quo, lack of response to new knowledge, and repetition of past mistakes. (Easterly, p. 38)**

Collier (2007) also analyzes aid and comes to somewhat more positive conclusions. Collier et al. have estimated that aid on average has added 1% to the growth rate of the "bottom billion," sometimes preventing it from becoming negative. Aid has been more successful than oil revenues in improving growth. Oil revenues are still poorly invested, and the recent rate of growth of the SSA countries benefiting from the oil bonanza has not been higher than that of the other SSA countries that suffer from the higher oil prices. The projects, conditions, and procedures associated with aid have been helpful. Aid also reduces capital flight because it makes private investment more attractive and keeps money in the country. Nevertheless, because of the fungibility of money, aid inadvertently helps finance about 40% of African military expenditures. Aid has been more successful where governance and policies are better. The allocation of aid is not poverty efficient, that is, it does not favor the poorest countries. Far too much goes to middle-income countries.

Overall these analyses are not encouraging in terms of how well the development community has learned to make more effective use of aid. It should make us all give very careful attention to how we recommend the use of aid for African agricultural development. We believe we are now much better positioned to know what is likely to work, but we must always be careful to learn from past experiences.

Of course, these discouraging trends have not gone unnoticed: The new millennium brought about a sober reassessment of world progress in improving the economic and social conditions of the global community. The agreement on goals led to calls for more harmonization and alignment of operational policies, procedures, and practices of development institutions. These were articulated in the Rome Declaration on Harmonization and Alignment of February 2003. This was followed in March 2005 by the Paris Declaration, which was an agreement to which over 100 ministers, heads of agencies, and other senior officials committed to continue efforts in harmonization, alignment, and managing aid for results with a set of monitorable actions and indicators. These continuing attempts at coordination and harmonization reflect the rapid increases in the number of actors in the aid business. Progress, however, has been slow.

Africa has also reacted to the proliferation of donors, both at the national level as well as at the Africa-wide level. The New Partnership for Africa tried to influence donor behavior to not only increase aid flows but also to harmonize them more with the priorities of African countries and their regional institutions. In the agricultural sector, NEPAD and the African Union developed the CAADP framework, which contains four pillars: (1) land and water management, (2) market access, (3) food supply and hunger, and (4) agricultural research. Under this framework, countries develop CAADP compacts that are to be translated into national agricultural development programs that are jointly funded by governments and via budget support from the donors. As of this writing most SSA countries are working on their CAADP compacts, but only one, Rwanda, has yet completed it. It remains to be seen whether this strategic coordination activity for the agricultural sector will progress to fundable programs, significant government funding, and coordinated donor support.

There are a number of issues and opportunities that flow from the proliferation of donor agencies, the slow progress in improving donor effectiveness, and the Rome and Paris Declarations. These are discussed here. We conclude this section by looking in some detail at aid flows to the agriculture/rural sector in Africa. We use official OECD DAC data as provided to us by IFAD. The data are reported commitments to agriculture and to rural development in constant 2005 U.S. dollars.

Figure 8 plots three sets of data for the period from 1975–2005. The lowest plot is the sum of bilateral and multilateral official development assistance (ODA) commitments to rural development for Africa. Except for a couple of spikes in the 1980s, this figure has been below US$500 million for most of the period. The second plot is ODA for agriculture, which is higher and is considerably more volatile. From a 1970s level of just above $1.5 billion, it doubled in the early 1980s and then spiked at $4 billion in 1988. By 1991 it had fallen by more than half, to $1.8 billion, and then trended downward to vacillate around $1.2 billion since 2001. The upper plot is the sum, which shows what has happened to overall assistance. Donors quickly tripled ODA in the 1980s, reflecting the rush into IRDP projects focused on agriculture, lending to agricultural credit institutions, and agricultural sector adjustment lending. When these programs fell out of favor, ODA plunged from above $5 billion in 1988 to below $2 billion in 1993. Since then it has fluctuated between $1.5 billion and $2.0 billion, ending in 2005 at just above $1.5 billion.

Looking further into the data, one finds no significant differences in the fluctuations of total bilateral and total multilateral aid. Over the period 1974–2005, bilateral aid totaled just over $40 billion while the full multilateral aid totaled $37.7 billion. However, there are wide fluctuations in the commitments of individual donors. The largest bilateral donor over the period was the United States, whose commitments in agriculture varied between a high of $522 million (1988) and a low of $47 million (2003). The U.S. variation in rural development occurred between $89 million and zero.

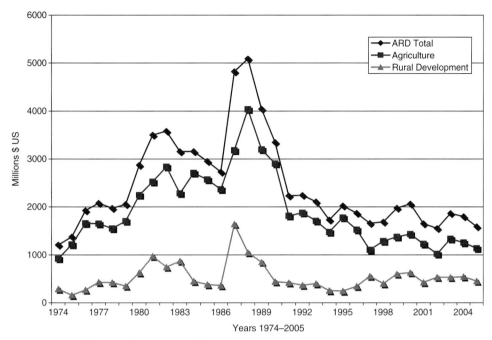

Figure 8 ODA for agriculture and rural development, 1974–2005.

Similarly, for agricultural ODA, France varied between US$280 million and $35 million, Italy between US$364 million and zero, and Japan US$341 million and $49 million. In many cases, year-to-year variations were orders of magnitude. On the multilateral side there were also wide swings. The European Community went from a high of US$949 million (1982) to a low of $65 million (2005) in agriculture, and in rural development from $969 million in 1987 to $61 million in 2005, The World Bank (IDA) went from US$845 million in 1990 to $125 million in 2005 in agriculture and from $369 million to zero in rural development.

The commitments of IFAD and AfDB are shown in Figure 9 for total ARD. Except for two peaks in the late 1980s by AfDB, each agency had a fairly stable pattern of commitments between US$100 and $300 million. If any trends are evident, it would be an overall downward trend in IFAD commitments and an upward tend in AfDB commitments from 1994–2003 before dropping sharply in 2004 and 2005. But overall the commitments of these organizations have been much less volatile than many bilateral donors and certainly more stable than for the EC and the United States.

On the bilateral side, the largest donors over the full period are the United States, accounting for 20% of total bilateral aid; France, 16%; Japan, 10%; Germany, 8.8%; Netherlands, 8.4%; Italy, 7%; and the United Kingdom and Canada, both at about 5%. Comparing these shares to the most recent period, 1998–2005, sheds light on

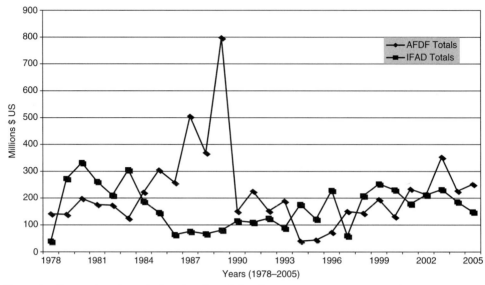

Figure 9 Fluctuations in agricultural and rural development, 1978–2005.

changing donor preferences. In this latter period, the U.S. share dropped to 17%; France to 13%; Japan, 9%; Netherlands, 7.4%; and Italy, 2.4%. On the other hand, Germany, the United Kingdom, and Canada increased their shares of a much smaller total. On the multilateral side, the IDA share dropped from 39% over the period 1974–2005 to 29% in the period 1998–2005, and the EC dropped from 30% to 20%. Offsetting these declines, AfDB's share of multilateral aid increased from 17.3% in the full period to 25.5% in the recent period. Similarly, IFAD's share increased from 12.5% in the full period to 24.1% in the recent period. Thus these two institutions now make up nearly 50% of multilateral commitments, and their share of total ARD rose from 14.5% in the long period to 23.8% in the most recent period. They have become much larger players in a contracted environment. Therefore the way they choose future strategies is critical for Africa.

4. GLOBAL WINDS OF CHANGE

Major forces continue to buffet the global agricultural/food/natural resource complex and will continue to do so for the foreseeable future. Some are sufficiently well developed that initial conclusions about their impact are possible. Others are in very early stage, which makes prediction fraught with danger. The private sector will play an even larger role in the future, being a major player in most of the issues and challenges listed here. The recent explosion in food prices created major short-run policy challenges. After settling back, somewhat higher expected prices will create significant opportunities for African agriculture. Some have identified them as irreversible structural changes. We discuss five:

- Globalization, trade liberalization, international private sector consolidation, and the changing role of the private sector
- Climate change and other transboundary issues
- Biotechnology and the privatization of agricultural research
- Biofuels—a permanent or transitory global demand factor
- Changing markets and price trends for food and agriculture

The integration of all the Africa-specific and global issues takes place on the farm and in nonfarm enterprises in the rural sector. We try to trace how the global challenges and opportunities will be perceived and how they will affect farmers, communities, farmers' associations, nonfarm enterprises, and local governments, and how these entities will react.

4.1 Globalization, trade liberalization, international private sector consolidation, and the changing roles of the private and public sectors

4.1.1 Globalization

The latest wave of globalization is only the last one of many that profoundly shaped the current situation. The first started with the transatlantic silver, sugar, and cotton trade in the 16th century, which was to fuel the terrible transatlantic slave trade that burdened SSA for over 300 years. By the first decade of the 19th century the transport revolution associated with steamships, and later railroads of the second half of the 19th century, brought all SSA into the international division of labor. It culminated in the exceptionally rapid and complete conquest of the continent by the European powers. After the interruptions of World War I, the Great Depression, and World War II, globalization started to flourish again in the second half of the 20th century but was held back by restrictive trade policies that have now been reduced, thanks to multilateral trade liberalization and unilateral dismantling of protective structures in Africa. After the discovery of the Americas, the first wave of globalization brought many benefits to Africa, including some of its major staple crops that arrived as part of the Colombian exchanges, such as maize, potatoes, sweet potatoes, cassava, and fruits and vegetables, including the ubiquitous tomato. However, successive waves of globalization also brought slavery, migrant labor systems, diseases, colonialism, unfair trade and taxation, war, and the destruction of indigenous social systems and cultures. In addition, globalization brought new modes of transport, goods, services, technologies, and institutions to Africa that are too numerous to list. Although there were many losers, there were innumerable gainers as well.

How negative or positive will the current wave of globalization be for Africa, and who will lose or gain? Clearly today, with stronger state and regional institutions, this is not just a question of what globalization will do to Africa; it is also a question of how countries and institutions will seize globalization's opportunities and shape its impact. They are no longer as helpless as they have sometimes been in the past. Over the past two decades, many African countries have clearly been benefiting from globalization via mineral exports, cheaper consumer goods, cheaper foods, agricultural market opportunities, and associated technologies but with differentiated impacts across Northern Africa and SSA. There has been considerable transfer of global chicken and other livestock technologies but less of crop technology.

The emergence of the international supply chains as a result of globalization in general and of the revolution in food retailing in particular (discussed in a moment) significantly changes farmer market opportunities both domestically and regionally. Even though globalization opens up new opportunities in agriculture, its negative side is very stiff international competition in food grains, meats, horticulture, and processed products. For particular African fresh fruits, vegetables, and horticultural products, competition from other developing countries has become more fierce.

4.1.2 Trade liberalization

Trade over the past 50 years grew much more rapidly than global GNP, so it now makes up a larger share of world economic activity. A rising share of the world's food supply is also traded and, even without further trade liberalization, agricultural trade will become an even larger share as a consequence of increased South/South trade. With the phasing out of the Multi Fiber agreement under the Uruguay Round of trade negotiations, the constraints to trade in agriculture are the last bastion of protectionism in the real trade sector. The important gains for Africa from multilateral trade liberalization with OECD and developing countries is now fully recognized. Nevertheless, the Doha Round of WTO negotiations has yet to conclude, because developing countries, led by India, China, and Brazil, are demanding that rich (OECD) countries significantly liberalize access to their agricultural markets and substantially reduce subsidies to commercial farmers, in particular the EU and the United States. Regardless of the outcome of Doha, the process of globalization seems sure to continue, driven increasingly by changes in the private sector. For example, in highly regulated sectors such as agriculture, foreign direct investment (FDI) by multinational firms has become a substitute for trade, leading to massive international food sector conglomerates and global supply chains, discussed shortly.

As we will note again in Sections 5 and 8, *African farmers clearly need more access to international, regional, and subregional markets.* But the big players in trade negotiations are the WTO, the Group of 20 developing countries (which includes only five African countries: South Africa, Nigeria, Egypt, Tanzania, and Zimbabwe), the World Bank, the United States, the EC, and UNCTAD, the latter in terms of analysis and pressure for developing countries. ECA, the AU, and NEPAD are more observers on the margins. African governments and institutions need to carefully watch how the Doha

Round turns out. It is likely to be the last major multilateral trade negotiation for some time. Unfortunately, by April 2009, when this chapter was being finalized, all attempts to conclude the Doha Round had failed, largely because of disagreements about agricultural trade. Unless agreement can still be reached, it is likely that the major trading nations will seek to gain access to closed markets and to attack "unfair" barriers to trade, using trade litigation and the WTO dispute settlement mechanism. This will further disadvantage small African nations because the process is expensive in terms of both money and intellectual capital. Another likely consequence of failure would be a further acceleration of bilateral and regional preferential trading agreements (PTAs). There are already too many regional trade agreements in Africa, and a further movement to bilateralism in Africa is clearly counterproductive.

It therefore remains clearly a major interest of African agriculture to achieve further liberalization in OECD country policies through a successful conclusion of the Doha Round. The AU and NEPAD will have to recognize the need to streamline the regional trade architecture. The AfDB appears to be giving high priority in the future to regional integration. Clearly, as part of these efforts, much needs to be done to increase regional trade integration, as we again discuss in other sections of the chapter.

4.1.3 International private sector consolidation

There continue to be radical changes in the number, size, and structure of multinationals in the global agri/food industry that have so far led to increased international consolidation and concentration of multinational companies through both vertical and horizontal integration. The implications for African agriculture are important because access to input and output markets is central to any strategy of rural poverty reduction.

If we think of the smallhold farmer in Africa as at the center of the food security and poverty challenge of the 21st century, we realize that to succeed, she requires interaction with a broad set of interfaces/markets: *for seeds and breeding stock*, increasingly supplied by the private sector and ultimately multinationals; *for inputs—fertilizer, chemicals, machinery, and feed supplements*, again supplied by the private sector; and *for markets for primary products*, again primarily private sector, including very large multinationals such as Cargill, ADM, Bunge, Louis Dreyfus, and Con Agra. Once the primary product is assembled, it has to be *processed, stored, and transported*, again most likely by major multinational firms such as Nestlé, Unilever, ADM, Cargill, Tyson, Con Agra, PepsiCo, Coca-Cola, and so on. Ultimately the food is *sold in retail stores to consumers*, and it is here that perhaps the most active "supermarket" revolution is just now unfolding. The bottom line is that globally private agri/food multinationals are driving changes in the global food economy more than ever before.

Overall the process is characterized by increasing international consolidation of firms, involving both vertical and horizontal integration. In all the markets/interfaces we've noted, this is true. Seeds, genetic improvements, and technology are dominated by six multinational firms. Many of these same firms are involved in providing agricultural pest control. Provision of fuels, fertilizers, and other chemicals also comes from industries characterized by significant economies of scale and are similarly concentrated globally. As one shifts to the marketing side, major firms such as Cargill, ADM, Bunge, Con Agra, the Conti Group, and Louis Dreyfus, generally identified as primary (grains, oilseeds) product handlers, are also variously engaged in seeds, feeds, fertilizers, food processing, sweeteners, biofuels, and, in a few cases, wholesale food distribution. Firms primarily identified with food processing, such as Nestlé, Unilever, Kraft Foods/Philip Morris, Tyson, PepsiCo, Heinz, and Sara Lee, also are integrating forward to distribution and backward to primary product handling. Of course, firms such as Cargill and ADM are also important in the processing sector.

These trends have been going on for sometime in the OECD countries and are well known, though the degree of concentration continues to increase with mergers and acquisitions. What is new is that these same firms' presence is now becoming very large in the rest of the developing world. In part this is being driven by what is called the *supermarket revolution*. It is to that phenomenon we now turn. The supermarket revolution is radically changing national, regional, and global food supply chains. "Supermarkets have spread extremely rapidly in developing countries after take-off in the early to mid 1990s" (Reardon, Henson, and Berdeque, p. 1). Reardon and colleagues postulate several hypotheses as why the take-off occurred so rapidly. First there was an "avalanche" of foreign direct investment (FDI) in developing countries reflecting major policy changes toward investment liberalization by developing countries. This, coupled with the failure of the Uruguay Round to significantly liberalize food trade, made getting behind domestic barriers the preferred approach for international expansion. Second, there were institutional and regulatory reforms in many developing countries that removed or reduced barriers to entry into the grocery business. Third, the "... modernization of the supermarket procurement system reduced costs and increased the competitiveness of super markets relative to traditional retailers" (Reardon et al., p. 3).

The spread occurred rapidly in four waves, with the first wave starting in the middle 1990s and the fourth one now under way. The supermarket revolution in SSA started in the middle 1990s in South Africa and in eastern Africa, particularly in Kenya. Unlike other parts of the world, where entry by European and North American multinationals drove the revolution, in SSA so far it has been by African firms that scaled up and proliferated. The shift from differentiated small local firms to large supermarkets occurred first in large urban areas of South Africa and Kenya. As of 2003, 55% of food retail sales in South Africa already occurred through supermarkets. The market was dominated by four firms. These same firms then spread to smaller cities and other countries. For example, Shoprite, the largest South African firm, in 2003 operated over

400 supermarkets in 14 countries (in 1979 it had eight stores in South Africa; Weatherspoon and Reardon, 2003). In their analysis they were particularly concerned about the implications for small local farmers:

> **Where medium-large growers are available in the country in which a chain is operating, the retailer draws as much as possible on these growers who are usually formed into associations that both export and sell to local supermarkets ... (ii) Where the larger growers are not available, and where small farmers cannot yet meet the standards of the supermarkets, there is some reliance on importing produce to the stores in a given country from South Africa or other countries where the needs can be met; (iii) Where projects can be put in place to "upgrade" the small farmers to meet the needs of supermarkets, the chains appear to be eager to participate in these schemes. (ibid)**

Similar developments happened in Kenya after 2000, where two leading indigenous firms first became dominant in Nairobi retails sales and then expanded to other towns in Kenya. The largest firm, Nakumatt, now has 19 stores and has announced plans to expand into Uganda, Tanzania, and Rwanda (*Global Retail Bulletin*, November 30, 2007).

There are two major issues that have been raised about this phenomenon: First, is it only for upper-income urban dwellers? And second, what happens to traditional small producers who sell in local markets? Regarding the first issue, Neven, Reardon, et al. studied the socioeconomic status of Nairobi supermarket customers and:

> **... The key finding is that contrary to the conventional image of supermarkets in developing regions—the place for the rich to shop—purchasing from supermarkets has penetrated the food markets of the poor and low income groups—in Kenya, already 56% of supermarket clientele. 60% of the Nairobi poor, buy some of their food in supermarkets each month. (Neven, Reardon et al., 2006, p. 16).**

Regarding the second question, the paper by Neven, Odera, et. al. presents a clear finding:

> **Are the rural poor excluded from supermarket channels in developing countries? We analyzed the farm-level impact of supermarket growth in Kenya's horticulture sector, which is dominated by smallholders. The analysis revealed a threshold capital vector for entrance in the supermarket channel, which hinders small, rain-fed farms. Most of the growers participating as direct suppliers to that channel are a new group of medium sized, fast-growing commercial farms managed by well educated farmers and focused on the domestic supermarket market. Their heavy reliance on hired workers benefits small farmers via the labor market. (Neven, Odera et al., p. 1)**

So far non-African multinationals have not penetrated the African market (though Weatherspoon and Reardon think they will). Their traditional model was to focus on urban areas starting with durables, flour, salt, and canned goods, often bringing with them their wholesale suppliers and sourcing from their home country. Thus to date there is limited evidence of displacing domestic supply chains. When local firms finally start selling fresh produce, they are sourced domestically at premium prices but with demanding standards in terms of quality. Some domestic producers win, others lose. They are likely to bring technology requirements and specify varieties, and they can also bring processing industries.

The challenge for SSA is that in many small countries, it might not pay outside firms to invest in local wholesale and processing facilities, and they may source outside. South African and Kenyan supermarkets are spreading in Africa. To what extent are they sourcing locally? To compete, African supply chains, from farmers to wholesale, need to adapt. Farmer organizations could play an important role, especially regional and subregional associations that could form regional cooperatives or joint venture companies. The evidence seems to suggest that African firms prefer to source locally, especially in fresh produce, so these developments offer opportunities as well as threats.

The supermarket revolution is one more major change force that, when added to the need for change arising from income and population growth and potential expansion of subregional trade, clearly requires integrated policy attention. The needs are to sharply reduce monopolies in transport; address corruption; and invest in better on-farm technology, which takes us back to rebuilding capacity in science and adaptive research.

4.2 Climate change and other transboundary issues

In this subsection we review the issues related to climate change, resource degradation, desertification, water availability, and infectious diseases.

4.2.1 Global warming and climate change are potentially large but manageable for agriculture

Africa has experienced enormous climate changes since it gave rise to mankind about 150,000 years ago. Ever since the onset of agriculture about 8000 years ago, climates have changed periodically. The most important evidence of such change is found in the records of two periods of pastoralism that have covered almost the entire Sahara desert, only to retreat again since about 4500 years ago (Reader, 1998, p. 171ff). The adaptive capacity of African agriculture to these massive climate changes in the past is well documented. It also has suffered repeated long-term droughts with devastating impacts on population size and welfare, such as the decade-long drought that afflicted West and Central Africa between 1774 and 1785 and that, *inter alia*, contributed to the peak in the transatlantic slave trade (ibid, p. 429 ff).

Except for a few diehards, there seems to be agreement that global warming caused by human activity is occurring. The basic questions now are can the process be slowed, stopped, or even reversed, and at what cost? This is the issue of *mitigation*. The second issue is *adaptation*, that is, how will the world adjust to the outcome? This debate has recently been joined by Bjorn Lomborg in his book, *Cool It: The Skeptical Environmentalist's Guide to Global Warming* (2007). Lomborg's case is that we should do a serious cost/benefit analysis comparing the benefits of spending a lot of money on minimal reductions on CO_2, or the same or less money on pressing current issues and on adaptation and adaption research. For our purposes his book is useful in highlighting that this is a real trade-off, and nowhere is this more true than in tropical and subtropical agriculture, that is, African agriculture. SSA is the continent contributing the least to global warming. It has the most urgent economic and social problems. Except for land-use changes, discussed in a moment, the case for putting less emphasis on mitigation in SSA and more on dealing with the pressing current needs and with preparations for future adaptation is stronger here than anywhere else.

For agriculture, a growing number of modeling efforts are suggesting that there will be changes not only in temperatures but also changes in the spatial and the temporal distribution of precipitation. The models suggest that the temperature impacts will be greater in the higher latitudes and that night temperatures are likely to increase more than day temperatures. Precipitation will increase in higher latitudes but will reduce in areas such as the Mediterranean and Southern Africa. Adverse agricultural consequences are likely to be negative in the lower latitudes, where temperatures are already high and precipitation is already limiting, and they could be positive in the higher latitudes, closer to the poles. The African impacts are estimated to be considerably more adverse than predictions for the developed world but less alarming than, for example, India and Mexico. The consequences for poor smallhold farmers and poor consumers could be substantial and mostly negative. There is also a growing view that frequency and amplitude of extreme weather events could be increasing. All these happenings increase risks to farmers, especially resource-poor small farmers in rain-fed agricultural areas.

This is not the place to debate in detail the magnitudes of impacts on agriculture. The more relevant issue is, how can African agriculture adapt and possibly profit from climate change? The implications of global warming for African farmers are obvious. They increase agronomic complexity and increase risks of shocks at the farm and community levels and imply additional changes in crops, cropping patterns, timing, agronomic practices, and seed needs. They reinforce the need for stronger research systems capable of improving the resistance of crops and animals to biotic stresses and investments in irrigation and water management. The critical issue is how to strengthen farmers' capacity to adjust. Again, they will be better able to do so if agriculture is highly profitable and they have the required savings to invest in these adaptations.

In addition, there could be areas that will go out of agriculture or that might switch from agro-pastoral systems to extensive pastoralism and require more outmigration.

Therefore, regional integration will become more important to provide destinations, especially from countries such as Niger or the Sudan.

African agriculture not only needs to adjust to the impacts of climate change but also take advantage of opportunities it may present. The question is how it should do this. "Climate mitigation through carbon offsets and carbon trading can increase income in rural areas in developing countries, directly improving livelihoods while enhancing adaptive capacity" (Gary Yohe et al., 2007, p. 1).

> **Land use change (18.2%) and agriculture (13.5%) together create nearly one-third of greenhouse gas emissions ... Achieving significant carbon mitigation in developing countries will require tapping carbon offsets from agriculture and land use change. While not as large as potential savings from reducing the consumption of fossil fuels, the total potential saving ... is still substantial and is achievable at a competitive cost. With as much as 13 gigatons of carbon dioxide per year at prices of US\$10–20 per ton, this represents potential financial flows of US\$130–260 billion annually, comparable to ODA of US\$100 billion, and foreign direct investment in developing countries of US\$150 billion. (ibid, p. 3)**

It is clear that to take advantage of these opportunities will require building appropriate policies and institutions at national, subregional, and regional levels.

Adaptation to climate change and the risks it brings should be part of overall development and coping strategies. Yohe et al., in a section headed "Mainstreaming Adaptation into Development Planning," conclude: "(t)he tendency has been to treat adaptation to climate change as a stand-alone activity, but it should be integrated into development projects, plans, policies, and strategies" (ibid, p. 2). Howden et al. (2007) make a similar argument: "We argue that achieving increased adaptation action will necessitate integration of climate change-related issues with other risk factors, such as climate variability and market risk, and with other policy domains, such as sustainable development."

The potential implications of climate change are still unfolding, and it is clear that it cannot be either mitigation or adaptation but some combination, hopefully influenced by realistic analysis of cost and benefits in particular circumstances. The Lomborg message should be heeded. For African agriculture it means coping, adapting, and contributing to mitigation, primarily via judicious management of land use. The three basic lessons we should take away from the literature are: First, African farmers in the past have adapted to climate change and will do so in the future. Second, dealing with climate change must be considered as one additional element in agricultural development strategies, not something apart. Both farmers and governments can proactively manage the likely changes by investing in research and irrigation and taking advantage of the promised carbon-trading opportunities. Third, managing increased climate variability should be included as an additional risk to be managed at the farm, national, and regional levels, as a part of an overall risk management strategy.

4.2.2 Infectious animal diseases and epidemic plant diseases: Old issues and new solutions

Infectious animal and plant diseases have ravaged Africa from time immemorial. Many of the known human diseases crossed over from animals to humans, the latest example being HIV and AIDS. Reader (1996) describes a rinderpest epidemic around the turn of the 19th to the 20th century that might have killed off nine tenths of Africa's livestock herds and led to catastrophic population losses as well as economic, social, and cultural decline that paved the way for the exceptionally easy conquest of Africa by the European colonizers. Earlier devastating impacts are also historically documented. What is new, however, is that modern science and appropriate management of the risks, by governments and regional organizations, can sharply mitigate, and in some cases eliminate, these risks.

According to Samuel C. Jutzi of FAO (2007):

Highly infectious diseases do not respect borders—geographical borders, political borders and often not even species borders. Infectious diseases are very diverse and dynamic in their adjustment to changing conditions of environment and management. The impacts of infectious diseases and their control on the agricultural sector, on national economies, on rural development, on livelihoods, on regional and international trade, on food security, on agricultural biodiversity and on human health are actually and potentially massive. Diseases in plants and animals importantly act as barriers to economic development and also threaten ecosystems, and it has been established that 70% of all new infectious diseases of humans stem from animals.

4.3 Biotechnology and the privatization of agricultural research

Biotechnology (BT) includes a number of techniques, the most powerful and controversial of which is the development of transgenic crops and animals. Farmers have been genetically modifying plants and animals for 5000 years or more, and agricultural scientists have joined them ever since the Gregor Mendel revolution in the 19th century. The controversial issue is only whether it is appropriate to transfer genes from one species to another. Evenson and Raney (2007) address these political and scientific issues. Among the developing countries, China and Brazil, followed by India, have invested significantly in agricultural biotechnology. On the other hand, the CGIAR system is spending less than 10% of its overall budget on BT research, perhaps because of resistance of important European donors. The great success of BT cotton and the prospects of nutritionally fortified rice and other crops have taken some of the wind out of the sails of environmental critics. BT cotton has resulted in dramatic reductions in pesticide use wherever it has penetrated, as well as higher yields and incomes of small farmers and no observable adverse environmental consequences. Biotechnologies are regulated from the point of experimentation to field trials and ultimate release.

Further regulations govern where and how the crops may be grown and how and where the products may be sold.

As part of its effort to bridge the technology divide, it appears that Africa urgently needs to take advantage of the many possibilities that biotechnology holds. Carl Eicher et al. (2006) review biotechnology development for six food crops and cotton in Africa and find unexpected scientific, legal, economic, and political barriers to the development of GM crops and long delays in developing and implementing national biosafety regulations and guidelines. They unfortunately conclude that with the exception of BT cotton, most GM crops are at least 10–15 years from reaching smallholders in Africa.

4.3.1 The acceleration phase of the molecular biology revolution

The potential of rapidly expanding knowledge of genomics and our increased capacity to modify useful plants and animals is just at its beginning and can become an important factor in adaptation to and mitigation of climate change, desertification, increasing resource scarcity, and threats from pests and diseases. Possibilities for building in stress resistance (drought, heat, and cold), immunity to pests and diseases, and improved nutritional values, as well as manufacturing pharmaceuticals in plants that 20 years ago were wild dreams, are now much closer to reality. For example, Monsanto and BASF recently announced a $1.5 billion research and development partnership using biotechnology research. "Focus of efforts will be on the development of higher yielding crops that are more tolerant to adverse environmental conditions such as drought" (*CropBiotech Update*, March 23, 2007). But will these developments occur fast enough to offset continued population and income growth and rising stresses on natural resources?

The answers will come mainly by private sector proprietary research with intellectual property protection. The fundamental question is how the benefits of biotechnology can accrue to small African farmers in a world of privatized research. But surely there remain major public goods issues. We list three:

- *Conservation of global genetic resources.* We have made significant progress on issues of preservation, conservation, access, ownership, and returns from genetic modification for the 64 plant varieties under the International Treaty on Plant Genetic Resources (ITPGR); but what about the rest of the rest of the plant kingdom, including forests, animals, fish, and critical microbial life? Who is helping developing countries deal with conflicts among TRIPS/WTO, CBD, and ITPGR? Given the large number of nontraditional, little-traded crops grown in African farming systems, this is an important issue.
- *Biosafety protocols.* These regard rules and regulations regarding the development and testing of GMOs. Although these are clearly national policy issues, competing and conflicting paradigms between North America and Europe put small developing countries at the mercy of large trading blocks when they attempt to decide whether they want to develop, import, or consume GMOs. Where is FAO as an important global provider of help to countries in developing necessary rules and decision processes?

- *Access to promising genetic materials and techniques.* Molecular biology research is expensive, and much of it now is done by private sector firms that protect their discoveries with intellectual property rights (IPRs). Current estimates suggest that six multinational firms dominate molecular genetic research on plants and animals. These firms include Monsanto, Syngenta, BASF, Bayer, Dow AgroSciences, and DuPont. The challenge is to find ways these firms can share promising technologies with developing countries without compromising their legitimate right to garner profits from their investments in discovery. The Danforth Plant Science Center may be one example. AATF, discussed earlier, is another model. But eventually, at a minimum, regional research organizations must acquire the capacity to participate as peers as the molecular biology revolution plays out.

Even where gene technology is donated, there could be slow progress, despite there being at least three biotech initiatives in Africa: NEPAD's biotech initiative, AATF, and AGRA. Can Africa afford to be left behind China, India, and Latin America? Should it adhere to complex regulations dictated by others? Rather, should it insist on more streamlined approaches? Whatever the answers to these questions, biotechnology approaches must be nested and integrated into plant breeding programs. Special attention should be given to raising public awareness of and political support for biotechnology and commitment to strengthening African capacity in biotechnology, biosafety, food safety, IPR, and the training of the next generation of African plant breeders and GM crop specialists.

4.4 Biofuels: Permanent or transitory global demand factor

A significant part of the cause of the recent food price spike, claim many, is extensive subsidies and/or mandates to substantially increase ethanol production to partially substitute for petroleum products in providing motor vehicle fuel. Many countries are seeking renewable energy sources to replace declining supplies of nonrenewable sources such as petroleum. In this section we first review the trends in biofuels and other efficiency issues. In the next section we discuss the potential impact of biofuels on the food price spike and their expected longer-term trend. The use of biological material for energy production has a long history in the use of fuel wood, charcoal, manure, biogas, agricultural wastes, and byproducts to produce energy, now labeled bioenergy. The typical approach has been to transform the material into gas or steam to be used in producing electricity or heat. However, the use of purpose-grown crops to produce liquid biofuels—ethanol and biodiesel—is of more recent vintage. Brazil has been producing ethanol from sugar cane for over 30 years, and recently the United States has embarked on a massive subsidized program to substitute ethanol produced from corn for gasoline to power autos. The United States has mandated an increase from 5% to 10% of its auto fuel supply coming from ethanol (produced mainly from corn, or maize) by 2011 and seems poised to increase it more. Some are pushing for 20%, production of which would require up to 50% of current U.S. corn acreage.

Europe has embarked on a program of promoting biodiesel as a renewable substitute for diesel using temperate oilseeds such as rape, canola, and soybeans. Brazil has been in the business the longest now, making up to more than 40% of its auto fuel supply with ethanol produced from sugar cane.

There are very serious issues related to how much net energy savings there really are from using corn produced with high fossil-fuel inputs—petrol, fertilizers, pesticides, and other petroleum-based inputs—processed into ethanol by a high-energy-using process and at very high costs. Further, there are significant differences in energy yields from different feed stocks. For example, 1 hectare of sugar cane yields 6000 liters of ethanol, compared to 3000 from corn, 2500 from wheat, and 1000 from barley. One hectare of palm oil yields 4500 liters of biodiesel, compared to 2000 from jathropha, 1100 from rapeseed, and 500 from soybeans (World Watch Institute, 2006). At some time in the future (still uncertain), a process using cellulostic feed stocks (grass, waste products, trees) to produce ethanol will become commercially feasible, which should provide a higher product yield at lower cost. The problem is in breaking down the cellulose to free the carbon; it can be done by enzymes, but it is hard to scale up. It is an engineering, not a science, problem.

These energy efficiencies translate into a ranking of inputs for biofuels in economic terms. In 2005, before the recent rise in food prices (discussed in the next section), Schmidhuber computed parity prices for oil at which biofuel production would have started to become profitable; these computations provide useful rankings, even though the prices of the foodstuffs have changed significantly. The most economical production of biofuel was from sugar-cane producers in Brazil, with a parity oil price of $35 per barrel of oil. Next was large-scale cassava-based ethanol production in Thailand at US$38/bbl, followed at US$45/bbl for palm oil-based biodiesel in Malaysia. Given crude oil prices that prevailed in 1995, these three feedstocks and locations were already profitable. Maize-based ethanol production in the United States was much less efficient, with a parity oil price of US$58/bbl. For mixed feedstocks in Europe and for biomass-to-liquid synfuel production, the parity prices rose to US$80 and US$100/bbl, respectively, requiring enormous subsidies at the time (Schmihuber, 2006).

However, these breakeven points depend sharply on the price of the feedstock used for biofuel production (Table 1). At $60 per barrel for crude oil, the breakeven price of maize, above which biofuels production is not profitable without subsidies, would be $2.01 per bushel of maize. At a $120 crude oil price, maize could cost more than 2.5 times as much, namely US$5.20 per bushel, before the breakeven point is reached, beyond which biofuels from maize become unprofitable. In June 2008 maize traded above $7 per bushel in Chicago, which meant that it was too expensive for ethanol production without subsidies. Table 1 makes clear that at a crude oil price of around US$50/barrel, which prevailed at the end of March 2009, biofuels from maize priced near US$4.00/bushel would still be unprofitable without subsidies.

Table 1   Breakeven maize prices for producing biofuels at various crude oil prices

Crude Oil Price (US$/bbl)	Breakeven Maize Price (US$/Bushel Without Subsidies)
40	0.96
60	2.01
80	3.08
100	4.14
120	5.20

Source: Tyner and Thareipour, 2008.

Except in Brazil, Thailand, and Malaysia, production of biofuels therefore had to be subsidized to be profitable. The amounts of subsidies provided have exploded: Steenblick (2007) provides estimates of total subsidy equivalents for biofuels production, which represents the total value of all government support to the biofuels industry (including the total value of consumption mandates, tax credits, import barriers, investment subsidies, and general support to the sector, such as public research investment). It does not include support to agricultural feedstock production. U.S. biofuels processors and farmers received about US$6.7 billion in 2006. Those in the European Union received about US$4.7 billion. In addition, the majority of support varies with the level of production, which means that increases in biofuels mandates will lead to much larger OECD biofuel subsidies.

Although fuel prices always had a significant impact on food prices via their impacts on the costs of running mechanized equipment, the costs of transportation to and from farms, and the costs of fertilizers, pesticides, and herbicides, increased biofuel production has created a new, much more direct link between food and energy prices, as amply demonstrated in Table 1. What are the other consequences of trade-offs of using agricultural production for energy rather than food supplies? Can world agriculture do both? And at what price? These issues are discussed extensively in FAO (2008), based on exploding recent literature on the topic. IFPRI and the CGIAR have produced a series of Issue Briefs (IFPRI, December 2006). The UN has announced the formation of an International Biofuels Forum (*CropBiotech Update*, March 9, 2007), which is aimed at promoting the sustained use and production of biofuels on an international scale. The World Watch Institute, in partnership with GTZ, published a major study on *Biofuels for Transportation* in June 2006.

For Africa these developments will have multiple, often competing impacts. Returns to small farmers rise with rising prices, but so do food costs for the urban poor and the landless. But beyond these obvious impacts are opportunities. The relative efficiency of commodities in production of biofuels, as noted, varies greatly; sugar and palm oil are the most efficient so far.

This could open opportunities for certain African countries to produce for the global market without subsidies. If Africa could produce at costs similar to those of Brazil, Thailand, and Malaysia, it could make sugar cane, cassava, and palm oil production more profitable. Production of biofuels from cellulose could open huge potential in the future, especially for the many areas of medium-quality cropland that are not yet intensively farmed and for the humid tropics. In all cases, decisions to engage in the production of biofuels should not be made on a political basis, as is often done in the developed world, but on the basis of careful benefit/cost analysis. SSA cannot afford to subsidize the production of biofuels.

4.5 Changing market and price trends for food and agriculture

During the past three years the world has experienced a major food price spike. To put it into perspective, here we first review the history of food price trends since the early 1960s, in both nominal and real terms, and then compare them to some exchange rate movements and the changes in prices of energy that also have also seen a dramatic spike. We then discuss the drivers of the rising global demand for food, followed by a discussion of the emerging demand for food crops from biofuels. Finally we discuss whether these price changes reflect a permanent shift in the global balance of agricultural supply and demand.

4.5.1 Trends and spikes in prices of food and raw materials

Figure 10 shows the long-term evolution of real commodity prices since 1980. After declining for nearly 20 years, oil prices started to rise in 1998 and in 2008 rose to about four times their previous level, only to drop sharply from their peak as a consequence of the global economic crisis to about twice their late-1990 level. Metal prices

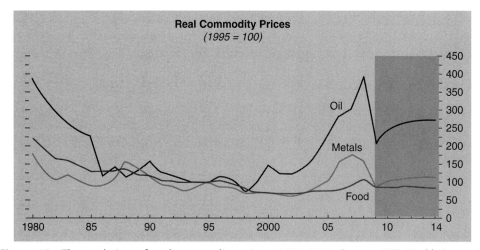

Figure 10 The evolution of real commodity prices, 1980–2014. Source: *IMF World Economic Outlook* update, January 28, 2009.

continued their decline until around 2002 and peaked at less than twice their 1980 levels in 2007. Real food prices, however, had declined steadily from 1980 to 1998. They started to rise in 2007, much later than oil and metals prices, and peaked in 2008. Using real prices reduces the food price shock since 1998–2000 to about a 65% increase. The percentage increase of the 2008 shock is significantly less than the food price shock of the early 1970s, and real prices are still lower than in 1980. Nevertheless the recent food price shock created a real crisis for food-importing countries.

The recent food price spike reflects (1) the rapidly rising food demand from accelerating global economic growth since the mid-1990s, especially concentrated in Asia and in Africa; (2) the emergence of demand for biofuel crops, especially maize, oilseeds, and sugar cane; (3) poor weather conditions in several parts of the world, especially since 2005; (4) declining rates of productivity growth in major cereals (Figure 11); and (5) declining trends in food stocks, which fell from over 600 million tons in 2000 to around 400 million tons in 2008. These stock changes are not just a consequence of bad harvests but also reflect the information revolution, new hedging mechanisms in food and financial markets, and altered storage behavior of major importers and exporters (OECD and FAO, 2008). These longer trends and weather events then have led to declines in stocks to use ratios to the same or lower levels as those that led to the food price explosion in the 1970s (ibid). The recent food price rises have triggered export restrictions in many food-exporting countries, aggravating price increases. In rice, for example, prices shot up precipitously after major players such as India and Vietnam applied export limitations. Further food subsidies and other policies that tend to dampen domestic food and agricultural price rises slow necessary adjustments in demand and truncate or eliminate domestic supply response.

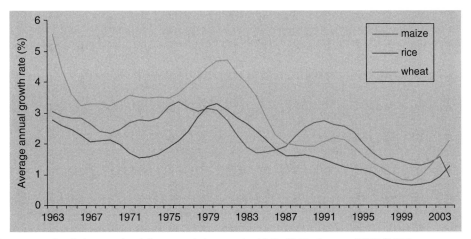

Figure 11   Declining productivity growth in cereals, 1963–2003. Source: WDR (2008).

Figure 11 also shows that from 1980 to around 2000, real food prices in U.S. dollar terms dropped steadily to about half their levels. This created huge benefits for food consumers and poor farmers who are net buyers of food but also implied large losses for those net sellers of food who were not able to adopt new and more efficient technologies to offset the price declines, many of which were in Africa. It benefitted net food-importing countries and hurt net food exporters who were not able to compensate for the falling prices with efficiency gains in production. Africa was unable to compete in many food commodities and therefore became a net importer for food.

The long-term trends in real food prices hide many factors that can drastically change the impact of aggregate world price changes on food consumers and food producers in specific countries. We look at three: exchange rates, oil and input prices, and the specific commodities involved.

4.5.2 Impacts of exchange rate movements

The real price index used in Figure 10 is in U.S. dollar terms. Table 2 shows that a typical low-income country experienced an adjustment in its real exchange rate to the U.S. dollar of 16% between 2003 and 2007, when the bulk of the food price increases happened. Further appreciations in early 2008 are not taken into account. For example, if a country experienced an appreciation of 50% against the dollar while the average exchange rate of high income appreciated only 12%, its real food costs in domestic currency would not have increased 65%, as discussed earlier, but by 42%.[4] But this is only a back-of-the-envelope calculation, and individual countries should do their own analysis using their own import mix and trading partners.

4.5.3 Impacts of energy and fertilizer prices

The spike in energy and other raw material prices also influenced the overall impact of the food prices on countries' ability to afford food imports. Although net energy and mineral exporters were able to afford the higher food prices, the net energy importers confronted a double shock from both higher energy and higher food prices.

Table 2 Average real exchange rate appreciation of domestic currencies versus the U.S. dollar, by World Bank income classification, 2003–2007

Income Class	Appreciation (%)
Low income	16
Lower middle income	14
Upper middle income	19
High income	12

Source: OECD-FAO (2008).

The energy price increases transmitted themselves to higher fertilizer and pesticide prices, higher costs of running farm machinery, and higher freight costs for inputs and outputs. For example, world fertilizer prices rose steadily from 2004 through 2006 and then exploded, as shown in Figure 12. Prices of the basic raw material for nitrogenous fertilizers almost tripled, fully reflected in the price of urea and partly in the price of calcium ammonium nitrate (CAN). However, the former two prices have come down to their levels in the mid-1990s, whereas CAN still remains high. Prices of phosphate fertilizers are not shown, but they exploded equally and have not yet come down significantly. On average, therefore, fertilizers remain significantly more expensive than they were until the mid-1990s.

During the food crisis, therefore, the costs of purchased inputs increased much more than food prices across the world and have dampened the rise in profits of food producers. This negatively impacted the supply responses from producers.

4.5.4 Prices of individual food groups

Figures 13 and 14 focus on what happened to the prices of the most important food groups that make up the overall index of food prices. Figure 13 shows that between 1961 and 2002 the real international prices of meat, dairy, and horticulture products have roughly stayed constant. On the other hand, *real* prices of cereals, oil crops, tropical beverages, agricultural raw materials, and sugar were roughly between 50% (raw materials) and 100% (oil crops) higher in the 1960s than in the five years leading

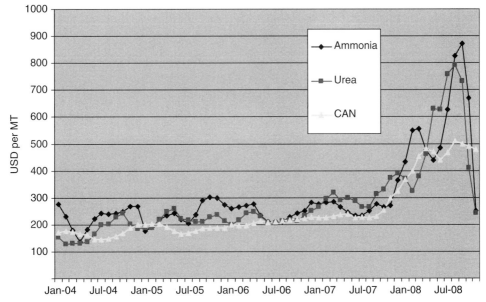

Figure 12 Recent fertilizer price trends, 2004–2008.

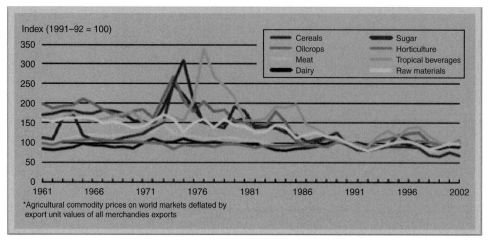

Figure 13 Real prices for agricultural commodity groups, 1961–2002. Source: FAO.

up to 2002. This means that price declines were concentrated heavily in basic staple foods, tropical beverages, agricultural raw materials, and sugar. Indeed, except for horticulture, real prices for all commodity groups stopped declining in about 1986, which means that they stayed approximately constant for 20 years before the recent price spike.

The significant erosion in these prices implies a major shift in prices relative to the former group to meat, dairy, and horticulture, which, unlike some of the staples, are higher-valued commodities. Only countries experiencing rapid technical change remain competitive in cereals, oilseeds, tropical beverages, and sugar. Another major feature of the period was high volatility in prices, with staggered sharp peaks of all prices (other than dairy and horticulture).

Figure 70 a and b look at the evolution of real food prices for since 1999 and until after the spike in early 2009. Real cereals, oils and sugar prices rose by more than 100 percent, with the peak in sugar prices occurring at the beginning of 2006, two years earlier than for the other commodities. Real diary prices barely rose above their base year level in 1998-2000. In early 2009, the prices of oils are at the same level than in the base period, while cereals and sugar prices are approximately 50 percnet higher. As a consequence the overall real food price index is only about 15 percent higher than in the base period.

To put these recent price changes into perspective, we need to review the longer history. Overall food price indices are not available, so we look at real grain prices. Since the 1870s real grain prices have declined substantially. Except for price run-ups in 1910–1914, a spike in 1972–1974, and another brief blip in 1996–1998, the long-run rate of supply increase has been greater than the rate of demand growth. Malthus is still waiting for the opposite. Thus the historical record is clear: a long-term decline with sharp peaks, followed by even lower trends. Historically farmers have always

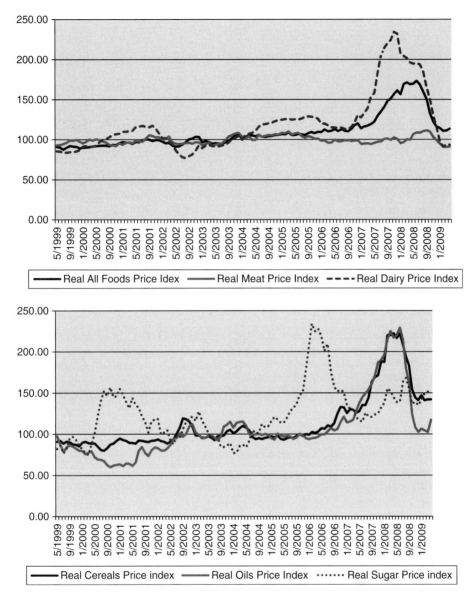

Figure 14 (a) Real Price Indices: All Foods, Meats and Dairy Products, 1999-2000. (b) Real Price indices for Cereals, Oils and Sugar, 1999-2009. Source: FAO; The deflator is the Manufactured Unit Value Series of produced by the IMF.

invested excess profits into capacity, and output has always expanded to put long-run downward pressure on peak prices. The declining trend in food prices stopped in 1998, and in cereal prices it stopped in 2000. Therefore the recent price spike may have been just another bubble. To understand better what is likely to happen, we now need to turn our attention to what has been driving the recent trends.

4.5.5 The drivers of demand for food

The drivers of food demand are *population, income growth*, and *urbanization*. The latter two change demand patterns away from cereals toward meat, dairy, fruits, and vegetables. Figure 15 shows that population growth for the world as a whole is slowing but remains around 1% per year.

Population growth remains much higher in the developing world than the developed world, where it is falling fast to zero. It remains at around slightly less than 2% in Africa and at 2% for all least developed countries (LDC). Clearly, *the main impetus of population growth on demand will come from developing countries, and among them from Africa, and least developed countries elsewhere.*

As Figure 16 shows, most population growth will be in urban areas of developing countries, including in urban Africa. Again this suggests that Asia and Africa will be the major source of changes in food demand patterns and the corresponding opportunities for African agriculture.

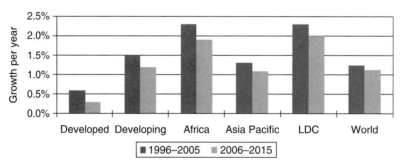

Figure 15 Population growth is slowing but remains high in the developing world, 1996–2015. Source: UN Population Prospects, 2006.

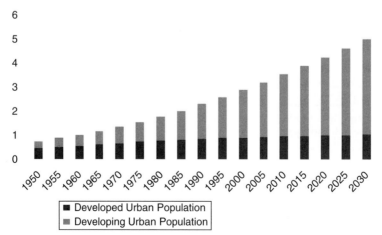

Figure 16 Most population growth will be in urban areas of developing countries, 1950–2030.

The demographic transition to longer lives and lower population growth leads to lower dependency rates and higher labor force participation. This so-called population dividend is discussed in Section 5, and coupled with the wider processes of globalization, technological change, information and financial integration, leads to prospects for global income or GDP growth that have rarely been brighter than they are now. Therefore, income growth, in addition to population growth, will be the major factor driving the demand for food and other agricultural products.

In 2007, world real GDP grew 5.2%, which translates into a 4.2% growth in per capita economic output (Table 3). World output growth then declined to 3.2% in 2008 and is projected to decline at a −1.9% rate in 2009. The IMF then projects a rebound to 1.9% and 4.3%, respectively, in 2010 and 2011. This means that global per capita output is projected to decline about 2.9% for the first time in decades, suggesting perhaps a negative change in global food demand in 2009. However, the decline in output is concentrated in the advanced economies, where income elasticity of food demand is very low. For the emergent and developing economies, where income elasticity of demand is higher on account of their lower income, the growth rate for 2009, 2010, and 2011 is projected at 1.6%, 4.0%, and 6.1%, respectively. They expected to be less hard hit by the global economic crisis, and their rising income may offset declines in food demand elsewhere in 2009 and add a positive trend to global food demand thereafter.

For Africa as a whole as well as for sub-Saharan Africa, the projected growth trends in output are similar to those for emerging and developing economies. It is particularly noteworthy that the output growth in sub-Saharan Africa in 2009, 2010, and 2011 is expected to be about 1.7%, 3.9%, and 4.5%, respectively. Since population growth is about 2% in SSA, the per capita income is only expected to decline marginally in 2009, suggesting that even in SSA, food demand may resume its growth fairly soon.

Table 3 Growth rates in GDP at constant prices, 2007–2011

Region	2007	2008	2009	2010	2011
Advanced economies	2.7	0.9	−3.7	0.0	2.6
Emerging and developing economies	8.3	6.1	1.6	4.0	6.1
Africa	6.2	5.2	2.0	3.8	5.2
Sub-Saharan Africa	6.9	5.5	1.7	3.9	5.4
World GDP	5.2	3.2	−1.9	1.9	4.3

Source: *IMF World Economic Outlook* (April 2009).

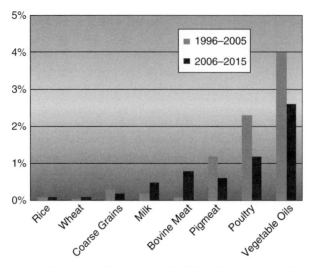

Figure 17   Projected growth in world food demand, 1996–2015. Source: FAO (2008).

Figure 17 shows the food demand growth projected in 2006, before the onset of the current economic crisis. Although the lower global per capita income growth may also reduce all these growth rates a bit, the relative growth rates will not have changed. Because of expected shifts in consumption away from rice and wheat toward more diversified diets, growth in demand for these commodities is expected to be almost zero. The higher incomes, on the other hand, will drive demand for fruits and vegetables very rapidly, followed by poultry. Pig meat, beef, and milk will grow between 1% and 0.5%.

Clearly, the secular trend in relative prices from grains to foods with higher income elasticities is likely to continue—a trend that should be accounted for in future agricultural development strategies. However, these demand projections do not yet reflect the impact of biofuels on land use, production, and commodity mixes.

4.5.6 Are higher food prices here to stay?
Predicting prices is hazardous at any time but perilous for long-term predictions. The situation now is particularly difficult. In addition to the demand factors we have already discussed, there are many factors on the supply side we have or will discuss in this chapter: little progress in reducing agricultural trade barriers and subsidies in rich countries; slowing yield growth; constraints on the use of biotechnology; little investment in irrigation; deterioration of existing irrigated areas; environmental constraints; loss of land to competing uses such as urbanization, infrastructure, and environmental set asides; and water constraints.

Though the history we reviewed earlier suggests that the the recent food price spike may well have been another major bubble, it is not clear whether food prices will settle back to the same level they were in the early years of this century or at a lower or higher level. The fact that their long-term decline has stopped for over a decade years and that demand forces are expected to be strong makes it unlikely that they will resume their secular decline.

This price spike has stimulated a good deal of writing about the nature of the price increases, their likely duration, and the nature of a return to more normal times. Within the past few months IFPRI (May 2008), IMF (March 2008), FAO (April 2008), UNCTAD (May 2008), OECD/FAO (2008), USDA/ERS (Trostle, May 2008), and Australia (Stoeckel, June 2008) have all published analysis. *The New York Times* ran a series under the general heading "The Food Chain" from January through June 2008, and *The Economist* has carried many articles in the last six months. All these analyses do not, however, agree on the causes, likely duration, and ultimate end of the spike, although all do agree prices will come down from recent levels. There are at least four competing hypotheses floating about, which we briefly review here.

Story One: Macroeconomic factors drove the price rises What we experienced was a broad commodity boom. Oil, minerals (especially gold and copper), and agricultural commodity prices all rose and fell in a similar pattern, which suggests that broad macroeconomic variables have been driving the boom. Explanations included the rapid decline in the value of the U.S. dollar. Given that all global commodity markets are denominated in dollars, the declining dollar made all commodities cheaper to the rest of the world, driving up demand and prices (Hanke and Ransom, *Wall Street Journal*, March 25, 2008). Supporting this view is the fact that when the U.S. dollar began to appreciate sharply in mid-2008, commodity prices began to fall sharply. In parallel, U.S. concerns about recession led to successive cuts in nominal and real interest rates, which reduced the price of storage and encouraged buying and holding real commodities. This phenomenon would drive up all real commodity prices (Frankel, 2008). However, this theory does not explain the subsequent fall in commodity prices.

Story Two: Speculators drove prices up and increased volatility In periods of uncertainty or recession, investors shift assets to real assets, including commodities. Further, the rise in hedge and particularly index funds led to large increases in non-traditional investments in commodity markets. These fund investors went very long (betting on continued price increases) in commodity markets. When contracts expired they liquidated their holdings, causing prices to drop. Though this phenomenon could explain increased volatility of prices, it offers little explanation for longer-term causes of the price spike. The IMF argues that speculation is unlikely to drive sustained price increases (IMF, 2008), and the subsequent price collapse has vindicated this view.

Story Three: Simultaneous and big shocks drove prices up   International commodity markets operate on a knife's edge between the rate of supply growth and demand growth. Several years of weather impacts in Europe in 2006–2007 and North America in 2006–2007 and a continuing severe drought in Australia in 2006–2009 drew stocks down to critical lows. This, coupled with the surge in biofuel demand, created a price spike that will surely end when conditions return to normal. Record low stock-to-use ratios recorded in 2007–2008 caused all players in the market to switch behavior in favor of holding supplies from the market, as clearly happened in the rice market. Record crops of wheat and rice in 2008–2009, which surely contributed to recent price declines, lend credibility to this concept, at least as a partial explanation for what has happened.

Story Four: A combination of permanent structural changes in supply and demand conditions was exacerbated by shocks   This was the predominant story in the literature. This story argues that there was a confluence of permanent and transitory factors that were driving the price spike. On the demand side, rapid growth and rising incomes in emerging economies such as India and China increased the rate of demand expansion. Urbanization and global growth mean demands for a larger and more varied food supply. Finally, at least some of the increase in biofuel demand will be around for a while. On the supply side, the rate of increase supply has slowed over the past decade because of declining rates of productivity growth and increased competition for water and land. Investments in agricultural R&D have declined globally, as has investment in agricultural development. Finally, higher petroleum prices have permanently increased the costs of agricultural production. Global grain consumption exceeded global production in six of the first eight years of the 21st century. The result was a drawdown of stocks to critically low levels. Thus when shocks such as weather and the surge in biofuel demand occurred, they caused prices to rise sharply.

The real explanation probably has elements of all four stories. However, if one favors any or all of the first three, the long run is clear: When the contributing factors revert to "normal," the bubble breaks, and we could well resume the same long-run downward path in real prices as happened in earlier episodes.

Only Story Four proposes the possibility of a different ending. Two outcomes seem possible. After the spike, nominal prices have fallen but stabilize at higher levels of real prices and continue their secular decline, likely at a slower rate. A second variant would be that the permanent structural changes are sufficiently strong that the historical pattern of declining real prices is over and real prices will rise modestly over the foreseeable future. Here we review empirical estimates that support each of these possibilities.

The first is a set of projections to 2017, jointly prepared by OECD and FAO in early 2008. Figure 18 shows the OECD-FAO price projections. The figure compares the average level of prices for the past decade (which were already higher than prices in

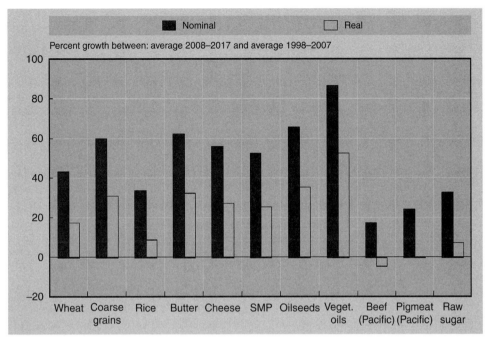

Figure 18   Expected world commodity prices for the decade until 2017.

the 1990s) with average expected nominal and real prices for the coming decade. Though nominal prices of all major food groups are likely to increase, this is not so for real prices (in real U.S. dollars), which are expected to decline slightly or stay constant for beef and pig meat. For sugar and rice they are expected to increase between 5% and 10%, reflecting in the case of rice the expected slow growth of demand in Asia and for sugar a high supply response capacity. By far the highest real price increase is expected in vegetable oils, more than 50%, whereas for the other commodities the real price increases range between 25% and 30%. Given the prices we have been seeing in the early part of 2009, this shows that a number of the high prices have dropped back significantly but still remain 40–60% higher than in the last decade.

The second study is a recent IFPRI analysis using their IMPACT Model, which makes much longer-term projections. It projects that real grain and oilseed prices will not decline from levels they reached in late 2007 and will show a modest increase through 2050. Figure 19 shows those projections for rice, wheat, maize, oilseeds, and soybeans. This is one of the first substantive analyses we have seen that seems to support the proposition that the long-term secular decline in grain and oilseed prices might be over. It should be noted that wheat and corn prices in early 2009 dropped considerably but are showing a great deal of short-run instability, around US$200/ton for wheat and US$150 for corn. These are below IFPRI's projection, especially for wheat.

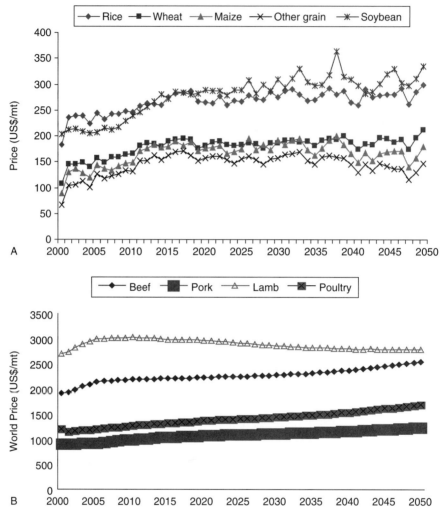

Figure 19 Long-term agricultural price projections to 2050.

4.5.7 Sensitivity of projected prices to key assumptions

Figure 20 shows how sensitive OECD-FAO projected world wheat, rice, and oilseeds prices are to key assumptions. It shows the reductions in prices from the baseline projection in 2017 that would come from five different scenarios (OECD-FAO, 2008):

Instead of rising rapidly over the next decade, biofuel production would be maintained at the level of 2007. For the two main biofuels inputs, vegetable oils and coarse grains, this would lead to a reduction of 2017 prices by between 15% and 12%, respectively, more than any other scenario change. Wheat that would be affected indirectly;

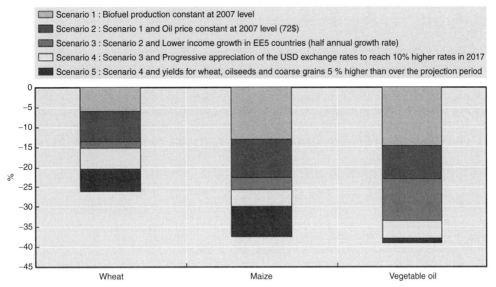

Figure 20 Sensitivity of projected world prices to changes in five key assumptions (percentage difference from baseline values), 2017.

the reduction would be around 6%. Simulations by Rosegrant using the IFPRI IMPACT model come to the same conclusion. Clearly, there is no longer any question that biofuel policy and the resulting production will have a major impact on future food prices.

Keeping oil prices constant at $72 per barrel, the average 2007 level would reduce maize and oilseed prices by around 10% and wheat prices by 7% compared to their baseline 2017 prices. This shows the very high sensitivity of food production costs and prices to energy prices.

If their rate of growth in EE5 countries (China, India, Brazil, Indonesia, and South Africa) were reduced by half relative to current high projections, this would lead to price reductions in vegetable oils that are highly income elastic, of about 10%, whereas it would reduce maize by significantly less and leave the wheat price almost unchanged.

If the U.S. dollar were to appreciate by 10% relative to the baseline scenario (which already incorporates a modest expected U.S. dollar appreciation), it would increase incentives in exporting countries to produce more and would reduce import demand elsewhere. The combined effect would reduce all three prices by about 5% relative to their baseline.

If crop yields at the end of the period would rise an additional 5%, it would reduce wheat and maize prices by 6% to 8% but leave vegetable oil prices relatively unaffected.

The OECD-FAO conclusion is worth quoting because it comes closest to our current views:

> **World reference prices in nominal terms for almost all agricultural commodities covered in this report are at or above previous record levels. This will not last and prices will gradually come down because of some of the transitory nature of some of the factors that are behind the recent hikes.** *But there is strong reason to believe that there are now also permanent factors underpinning prices that will work to keep them both at higher average levels than in the past and reduce the long-term decline in real terms.* **(p. 11 emphasis ours)**

4.6 Implications of higher food prices
4.6.1 The impact of the price spikes on the balance of trade

The food price spike was projected to have important implications for the balance of trade of countries that are summarized in Figure 21. Highly specialized net exporters of food, such as Argentina, were likely to see their trade balance improve more than 1%, whereas other food exporters such as Brazil, the United States, Russia, or Australia were likely to see their trade balances improve less than 1%. Net food importers include much of the developing world, with the exception of Thailand, Indonesia, and about half the South American countries. All of Africa was expected to be hurt, with the hardest-hit countries including all of North Africa and much of Eastern Africa. Of course, these impacts have to be seen in the context of the rising prices of energy

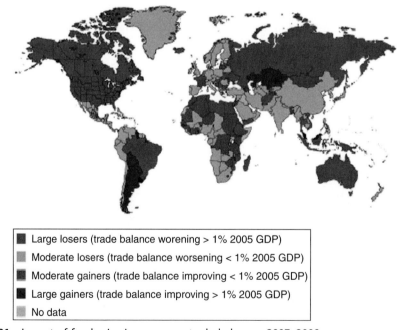

■ Large losers (trade balance worening > 1% 2005 GDP)
▦ Moderate losers (trade balance worsening < 1% 2005 GDP)
■ Moderate gainers (trade balance improving < 1% 2005 GDP)
■ Large gainers (trade balance improving > 1% 2005 GDP)
▦ No data

Figure 21   Impact of food price increases on trade balances, 2007–2008.

and other raw materials. In Algeria and Libya the higher cost of food imports was be more than offset by higher oil prices, whereas East African countries saw a double hit from higher oil and higher food prices. For this review it is striking that the East and Southern African countries that have the highest rates of poverty and unemployment as well as the highest HIV and AIDS rates were among those in this group. Special balance-of-payment support measures were therefore put in place for these and other highly affected countries.

4.6.2 Impact on domestic producer and consumer prices

Apart from exchange rate movements, policy factors determine how much of the international price rises were transferred to the domestic economy. Mundlak and Larson (1992) have shown that international food prices fully transmit to domestic prices over the medium to long run across both the developed and the developing world. However, in the short run, policy can slow this transmission considerably. Developing countries acted quickly to reduce the impact of international prices on their consumers: Almost half of 77 countries surveyed by FAO in early 2008 had reduced import taxes on food (Figure 22). Such reductions may worsen fiscal imbalances that can arise from higher food bills. For these countries, the achievable price reduction is sharply limited and cannot exceed the tax collected prior to their reduction. Therefore, even more countries (55%) resorted to food subsidies or price controls. Again, these measures might or might not be fiscally sustainable. More sustainable is dipping into domestic food reserves, which could have been accumulated precisely for episodes of scarcity

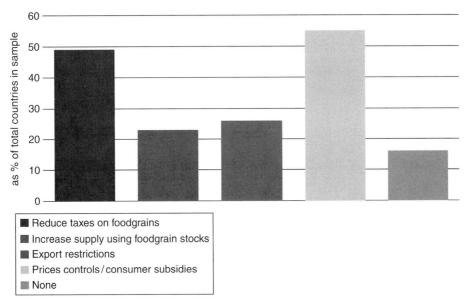

Figure 22 Policy actions to address high food prices. Source: FAO (2008).

arising from international price increases or domestic production shortfalls. Only about 25% of countries have been able to do so, however. An even lower percentage of countries, only about 17%, responded via measures to increase the food supply.

Net exporting countries had much stronger possibilities to influence food prices, either by imposing export taxes (recently done by Argentina) or export bans (recently done by India, the Philippines, and Vietnam). There are many fewer exporting countries than importing countries, and of the sample of 77 countries, about 25 countries limited exports in one way or another. However, some of them were able to affect domestic prices very significantly.

As a consequence of these policy measures, the pass-through of higher rice prices to domestic prices ranged from 6%, 9%, and 11% of the international price rises, respectively, in the Philippines, India, and Vietnam, all net food exporters. The price rises were 43%, 53%, and 64%, respectively, in Bangladesh, Indonesia, and China, which import some and export other foods. Argentina, a major wheat exporter, was able to keep the price rise of wheat to less than a third of the price rise in the international price, whereas in Chile, domestic prices almost fully reflect the rises in the international price.

In South Africa, because of weather disturbances, the price of white maize started rising in 2005, much earlier than international prices for yellow maize. White and yellow maize are substitutes in livestock feed but not in human consumption and therefore are only partially linked. For this reason the sharp rises in the international price of yellow maize have not led to further increases in the South African price for white maize. International and domestic prices thus can differ significantly in the short run, but in most countries domestic consumer and producer prices have remained closely aligned (all data from FAO, 2008).

4.6.3 The likely Impact on poverty of the food price spike

Countries unable to shield themselves from the food price spike confronted increases in poverty and hunger. Ivanic and Martin (2008) took high-quality household data from 10 countries to simulate the short-run impact of the rise in commodity prices from 2005 to 2007 on poverty incidence and depth. Longer-run impacts that arise from rural linkage effects (via forward, backward, and consumer demand linkages) that come about as a consequence of higher farm profits associated with higher output prices are not included in the analysis. The prices they took into account are for dairy (+90%), maize (+80%), poultry (+15%), rice (+25%), and wheat (+70%). They omitted edible oils and do not consider the price rises that happened in early 2008, which biases the results toward a lower poverty impact. On the other hand, they assumed that 100% of these price rises would be transmitted to domestic consumers, which biases the results toward a higher poverty impact. Ivanic and Martin present two scenarios, one in which they assume that wage rates do not respond to higher food prices, and one in which they adjust partly. (They use short-run wage elasticities derived from the general equilibrium Global Trade Analysis Project models to do so.) The impact of the adjustment of wages can be seen in Figure 23 in the all-countries comparison, shown with wage adjustments and without: Urban poverty impacts decline from 3.6% to 3.2%, whereas rural impacts decline from 2.5% to 2.2%. Overall these are small adjustments to the poverty impact, and for the countries, we show only the results, including the wage adjustments. The other overwhelming impression from Figure 23 is the significant disparities in short-term poverty impacts of identical food price rises around the globe.

On average, it is clear that urban poverty increases more than rural poverty. This is because rural households produce some of their own staple foods. However, there are some exceptions: In Zambia rural poverty increases more than urban poverty, probably because a much larger proportion of the rural population is just above the poverty line than in urban areas and therefore are pushed below the poverty line by the price changes. The same is true for Malawi and Cambodia, all countries in which few rural households are sufficiently well off that they are net sellers of food. The highest poverty impact of the price rises is on urban populations in Nicaragua, who spend a large share of their income on the foods included in the analysis, and rural populations of Zambia, who are net buyers of maize, dairy, and poultry. On the other hand, the rural poverty rate in Vietnam declines 3.1% because most of the population are net sellers of rice, maize, and poultry. In Peru, a middle-income country, rural poverty also declines because many poor people are net sellers of maize and dairy, whereas the impact of the prices of raw foods on the much richer urban population is not

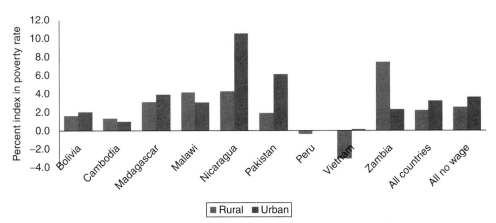

Figure 23 The short-run impact of higher food prices on rural and urban poverty by country. Source: Ivanic and Martin (2008; Table 5).

measurable. The changes in depth of poverty paint a similar picture to the changes in the poverty rates.

These estimates are a good indicator of what policymakers were up to if they wanted to mitigate adverse poverty effects of the price spike in the short run. Clearly, this was a difficult task: It was not only the additional poor people who most needed help, of those among the 2.3 billion who were poor before the food price spike. Small increases in safety net programs that rarely had significant coverage in the first place would not have been up to the task at all. No wonder, therefore, that policymakers preferred aggregate measures such as reducing taxation of food, general food subsidies or price controls, releases from stocks, and export controls. If these measures were indeed used only to mitigate the short-run impacts and then quickly phased out, they could well have been justified.

4.6.4 The longer-term poverty impact of expected rising trends in food prices

It is generally assumed that higher food prices are good for rural populations in the long run because they lead to greater investments, outputs, profits, and rural wage rates. They do so both directly and indirectly via forward, backward, and consumer demand linkages on the rural economy. For economies dominated by agricultural sectors, there could also be important positive linkage effects on urban economies as well as higher unskilled urban wages that are transmitted from rural to urban economies. The higher food prices projected for the future are therefore likely to provide important long-run benefits for many African economies, especially for rural populations that generally are poorer than urban populations. An example of the positive price effect on rural poverty reduction comes from China, where a significant share of overall poverty reduction was associated with price reforms in the 1980s that led to higher producer prices. However, these positive impacts take time to achieve, and in the short term the higher food prices tend to increase poverty.

5. ECONOMIC AND AGRICULTURAL GROWTH, THEIR SOURCES, AND THEIR CONSTRAINTS

We demonstrated in Section 2 that the absence of growth in SSA, and specifically of agricultural growth, has not only been the main reason for lack of poverty reduction; it also is the key to the deplorable rate of progress in the reduction in hunger. As discussed in Section 5, the situation in SSA has fortunately changed: Between 2004 and 2008, real growth rates for Africa as a whole have now been above 5%, and for sub-Saharan Africa rates have exceeded 5% since 2005 (ECA, 2007, and Table 3). Although the current global economic crisis is expected to depress these growth rates to about 3.5%, they are expected by the IMF to rebound to about 5% in 2010. As a consequence, real per capita income growth in Africa as a whole and in SSA between 2004 and 2008 has been above 3%. A recent report on the challenge of growth in sub-Saharan Africa sums up the rapid changes that have happened in the last decade:

> In the *2006 Doing Business Report* **(World Bank, 2006), Africa has moved from last to third among regions on the pace of reforms, ahead of the Middle East and Latin America. Africans at the grass roots level are hopeful and striving to do better for themselves. A recent Gallup poll shows that Africans are more optimistic about their future than people in many other developing regions. Following a wave of democratization in the region since early 1990s, there are now 31 young democracies in the region, representing more than two thirds of the countries.... The number of countries in conflict likewise has come down sharply from 15 in the early 2000s to 5 currently. (Ndulu et al., 2007)**

In the next sections we therefore turn to the determinants of general economic and agricultural growth, the determinants of severe underperformance of the countries of the "bottom billion," and the determinants of past agricultural underperformance and the recent recovery.

Because growth is so important, this section first summarizes the key findings of the report, *Challenges of Economic Growth in Africa* (Ndulu et al., 2007). The report is based on an impressive body of SSA growth research carried out by researchers of the African Economic Research Consortium. It includes not only analysis of macroeconomic data but also many other studies, in particular a comparative analysis of in-depth surveys of firms all over the developing world. The section includes additional information on North Africa and information from other sources that is specifically cited to distinguish it from the findings of Ndulu et al.

The general factors discussed by Ndulu et al. are, of course, also key determinants of agricultural growth. In addition, there are agriculture-specific policies and programs, which are analyzed at the end of this section. The one factor that has contributed significantly is the great improvement in agricultural price and trade policies in Africa.

Ndulu et al. shows that poor long-term growth performance lies behind the situation of low per capita income and high poverty in sub-Saharan Africa. Growth in 41 SSA countries for which data for the full 45-year period are available was only 0.5%, compared to 3% in 57 countries in the rest of the developing regions, including North Africa. The growth performance has been quite diverse: Six of 47 SSA countries have more than tripled per capita incomes between 1960 and 2005, nine countries have per capita incomes at the same level at which they started or below, and the remaining 32 have seen modest growth in per capita income but not enough to make a significant dent in poverty. As a consequence, the number of middle-income countries has risen from 2 in 1960 (Mauritius and South Africa) to 13 in the region. Seven of these acquired their middle-income status largely because of mineral wealth. The middle-income countries account for only 13% of the population but two thirds of national income.

In addition, growth in many countries has been episodic. The majority of countries experienced modest growth between 1960 and 1974, declines between 1975 and 1994, and renewed and accelerating growth since then. The prolonged period of economic decline between 1975 and 1994 was much deeper if growth rates are weighted by population numbers, which give far greater weight to the poor performance of the large countries Nigeria and Ethiopia. The period of decline started with a set of shocks to energy and tropical commodity markets and ended with a wave of democratic reforms between 1989 and 1994. During 1994–2004 there was more rapid per capita income growth, during which 20 countries grew more rapidly than the average of the rest of the developing world. New entry into this high-growth club was associated with either natural resource exploitation (Angola, Chad, Equatorial Guinea, and Sudan) or with strong reform movements (Benin, Ethiopia, Ghana, Mali, Malawi, Mozambique, Senegal, and Tanzania).

Economic growth further accelerated in all of Africa between 2004 and 2006, fueled by strong global economic growth and higher raw material and energy prices (ECA, 2007). In North Africa it accelerated from 3.8% and 4% between 1995–1999 and 2000–2004 to 5.2% and 6.4%, respectively, in 2005 and 2006 (ECA, 2007 and 2006). The only subregion that did not participate is West Africa, where growth slowed from 5.4% in 2005 to 4.6% in 2006 (ECA, 2007), perhaps associated with higher oil prices and the appreciation of the FCFA.[5]

For SSA, what is striking is that countries with similar opportunities have ended up at completely different ends of the growth spectrum: Zambia and Botswana are both landlocked and mineral rich, and Mauritius and Côte d'Ivoire are both coastal countries. Yet Botswana and Mauritius ended up in the higher middle-income group, whereas per capita incomes in Zambia and Côte d'Ivoire have barely moved in 45 years.

Over the long haul, slightly less than one half of the lower growth in SSA relative to the rest of the developing world is associated with lower growth of physical capital, and slightly more than half is associated with lower productivity growth. The share of investment in GDP has been only about half as high as elsewhere, and for given investment, SSA has achieved only about two thirds of the productivity growth.

The preceding decomposition of the differences in growth rates tells us only what has failed to happen: namely, investment and productivity growth. To understand the "why," Ndulu et al. looked in detail at constraints to investment incentives and returns on investment, or conversely, to the sources of growth that could be activated.

5.1 Poor resource endowments

Endowments partly explain the poor incentives: The more than 90% of SSA that lies between the Tropics suffers from much higher incidences of diseases that impact negatively on life expectancy, human capital, and labor force participation. This compares to 3% of OECD countries and 60% for East Asia.

SSA is highly fragmented. Its 48 small economies have a median income of only US$3 billion. On average, each country shares borders with four other countries, versus 2.9 for other developing countries.

Forty percent of the population lives in landlocked countries, compared with only 7.5% in other developing countries and none in North Africa (excluding Sudan). This combines with a road density in SSA of only 0.13 km per sq km, versus 0.41 km in other developing countries.

Twenty-six percent of the SSA countries are both landlocked and resource poor, whereas 6% are landlocked and resource rich. Coastal resource-poor countries make up 43% of the countries; coastal resource-rich ones make up 26%.

How being landlocked interacts with poverty in resources to produce poor growth performance is illustrated in Figure 24: Resource-rich landlocked countries did much better than their resource-poor landlocked counterparts, especially in the 1970s and since 2000. Coastal resource-poor and coastal resource-rich countries did about the same over the long haul, although the performance of coastal resource-rich countries dropped well below that of their resource-poor counterparts during the 1980s. Clearly, it is not just the presence of resources that counts, but the use of the money that is made from them. Contrary to conventional wisdom, landlockedness did not seem to hurt growth much: Except for the 1960s, coastal resource-poor countries fared no better than landlocked resource-poor countries. And costal resource-rich countries fared

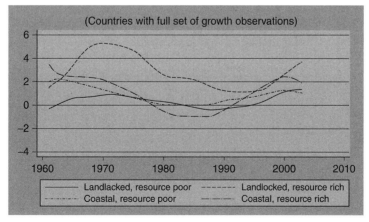

Figure 24 Growth experience according to geography and resource endowments, 1960–2010. Source: Ndulu et al. (2007).

much worse than landlocked resource-rich countries during almost the entire period. Clearly, geography is not destiny.

Geographic isolation and poor management of natural resources could explain about one third of the growth gap in SSA compared to the rest of the developing world. These adverse factors should be tackled by infrastructure investments and improved management of natural resource revenues, topics to which we will return later.

5.2 Rapid demographic change

A very important reason for poor investment incentives and returns is that the demographic transition in Africa began later than elsewhere and is slower than in the rest of the world, leading to much higher dependency rates than elsewhere and creating both household and fiscal pressures. The delayed demographic transition in SSA consistently predicts two thirds of the difference in growth performance with the rest of the developing world. Lower life expectancies are also shown to contribute to the poorer growth performance, and the AIDS epidemic has made this factor much worse, especially in Eastern and Southern Africa. The current situation results in a high level of age dependency, which reduces saving, reduces investment in human capital, and results in slower growth of the labor force. All of this reduces economic growth rates from what they might have been if the age-dependency ratio were lower. Declines in fertility rates seem to be linked to income growth, urbanization, girls' education, and reduced infant and child mortality rates, all of which have been delayed in SSA because of stagnant growth rates. Thus, as growth begins to accelerate, declining age-dependency ratios can accelerate per capita growth rates by 1% or more. Given the importance of this issue and the fact that donors have reduced their funding for family planning programs, it would be well to revisit the relative priority of investments in family planning.

5.3 Poor governance and policy

As discussed in his book on the "bottom billion" (see Section 6), Collier shows that three quarters of the bottom-billion countries have suffered from prolonged periods of poor governance and poor policies. Poor governance can ruin the most promising prospects, as, for example, in Zimbabwe. These countries are not able to provide essential services required for growth. Resources get eaten up in corruption before they reach the service providers. Poor governance and poor policies create a trap because powerful vested interests benefit from them and oppose reforms. In addition, correcting them requires skills that often have outmigrated or fled the country. Donors conditionality cannot substitute for the lack of political will or skills (Collier, 2007).

Historical, institutional, and policy-related constraints have reduced risk-adjusted returns to investment. Controlling for differences in opportunities, the impacts of poorer governance and policy contribute between 25% and 50% of the difference in growth performance between SSA and the rest of the developing world (Ndulu, 2006).

Launching a turnaround takes courage, and proponents of change take a lot of risks. Democracy has spread in Africa, but democracy alone does not seem to help a turn-around. A larger population, a higher proportion of people with secondary education, and having recently emerged from a civil war increase the chances of a turnaround. But probabilities of a turnaround in the "failing states" such as the Central African Republic, Liberia, Sudan, and Zimbabwe have been distressingly low: only 1.6% per year. Therefore, failing states have stayed in their trap for a very long time, during which huge costs accumulate: The cumulative cost of a failing state to itself and to its neighbors is about $100 billion. The benefits of helping turn around a failing state are therefore huge (Collier, 2007).

Avoiding policy distortions includes actions needed for sustained macroeconomic stability, maintaining a prudent exchange rate policy to support export-led growth, and improving market efficiency to spur private sector initiatives and enterprise. In spite of the low probabilities of past turnarounds measured by Collier et al., policies have significantly improved over the last decade: unweighted consumer price inflation persistently and sharply fell within a decade, from 27% in 1995 to about 6% by 2004. In a median SSA country, government spending as a proportion of GDP also fell sharply in the past decade, as it has in other developing countries in the world, and the average fiscal deficit was halved to 2% of GDP by 2000. Except in a few countries, black market exchange rate premiums now average just 4%. Through unilateral trade reforms, SSA countries have also compressed tariff rates; the average rate is currently 15%. As a consequence of the major policy reforms initiated in the continent since 1990, the impact of poor policies on growth may have waned (Ndulu et al., 2007).

One factor that explains better policies and governance is having the right leader: It has made a huge difference in growth outcomes across Africa since 1960 (Glaeser et al., 2004). Leaders make a difference, either directly by influencing policies or indirectly by shaping institutions (Ndulu, 2006b). Political competition, transparency, and strong domestic accountability not only raise the chances of having good leaders but also of having it sustained.

5.4 Integration into the world economy

Greater integration in the world economy consistently is associated with higher growth performance. This factor operates not only at the country level but also at the firm level. It is not just border trade policy and port capacity and efficiency that count but, increasingly, infrastructure, standards, and access to information.

5.5 Deficient infrastructure and business environment

Investment incentives and returns are also conditioned by infrastructure. We have already commented on the low road density in SSA relative to the rest of the developing world. Transport costs are among the highest in the world and can reach as high as 77% of the value of exports (Economic Commission for Africa, 2004). And SSA farmers have to pay up to three times the price for fertilizer compared to farmers in Thailand, India, or Brazil.

But it is not just the state of infrastructure that counts. Before the 1980s most transport businesses in Africa, including railways, bus and trucking companies, airports, seaports, and civil aviation, were publicly owned and managed and heavily regulated. These enterprises charged low tariffs, and their reduced viability imposed heavy costs on both users and the national economies. Since the 1990s the transport businesses have mostly been deregulated and privatized. Concessions for operating railways, ports, and airports have become common. Remaining public enterprises have been given more autonomy, and arbitrary regulation has been replaced by regulation through consensual performance contracts. In the highway sector, setting up more sustainable institutions—autonomous road agencies and dedicated road funds—has become the norm and has started to show positive results (World Bank, Africa Transport Unit website).

A serious problem in Africa is the extractions and bribes imposed by the police and others at border posts and roadblocks. "Along the West African road corridors linking the ports of Abidjan, Accra, Cotonu Dakar and Lomé to Burkina Faso, Mali, and Niger, truckers paid $322 million in undue costs at police customs and gendarmerie checkpoints in 1997, partly because the Inter-State Road Transport Convention had not been implemented" (Economic Commission for Africa, 2005). Since these extractions respond to the profitability of the commodities transported, there is therefore a real danger that if other margins of profitability improve, these extractions will go up and prevent the transmission of improvements to the farm. Well-organized producer organizations are needed to ensure that governments crack down on these practices.

Access to electricity is the most costly and unreliable in SSA, problems that stem from state monopolies and inefficient state enterprises. Energy costs are higher and power outages are more frequent than in any other region of the world, particularly compared to China (Figure 25). This generates the need for heavy investment in backup facilities.

Other components of the business environment that impact incentives and returns include rules and regulations, which are more onerous in SSA than elsewhere. Figure 26 shows the high costs of crime and security in SSA relative to Morocco and China, of unofficial payments to get things done, and of payments to secure contracts.

Firm-level data from a major cross-country study show that all the indirect costs of infrastructure, security, and unofficial payments imply that indirect production costs (other than for materials, capital, and labor) are a larger share of total costs in sub-Saharan Africa than elsewhere (Figure 27): In China, Nicaragua, Morocco, India, Senegal, and Bangladesh they are close to 15% of total production costs, whereas in a sample of SSA countries they vary between 27% and 19% (Ndulu, 2001). The higher costs reduce investment incentives and returns.

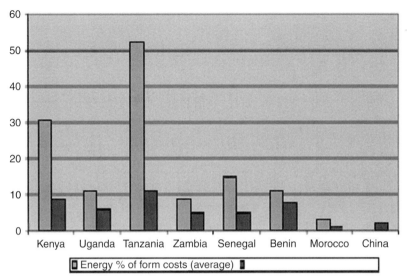

Figure 25   Energy costs and power outages by country. Source: World Bank Enterprise Surveys, 2001–2005.

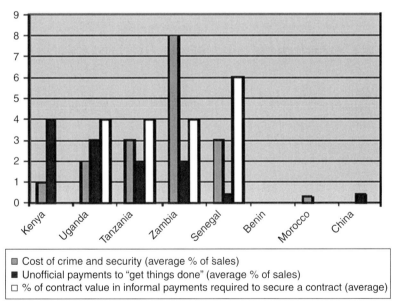

Figure 26   Cost of crime and security and unofficial payments by country. Source: World Bank Enterprise Surveys, 2001–2005.

5.6 Inadequate capacity

A World Bank report, *Building Effective States and Forging Engaged Societies* (2005), further concludes that a capable state requires an engaged society that holds governments account-able. However, only five sub-Saharan countries were rated above the global average on

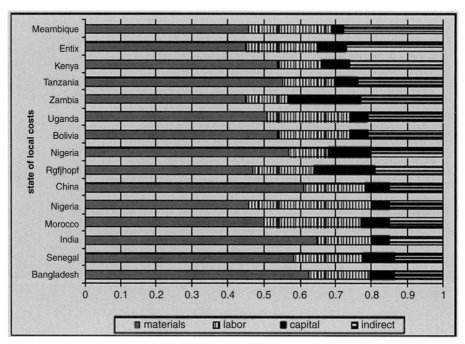

Figure 27 Indirect costs are higher in SSA than elsewhere. Source: Ndulu et al., 2007.

state effectiveness—Botswana, South Africa, Mauritius, Namibia, and Mauritania. A further seven were rated above the global average on societal engagement—Cape Verde, São Tomé and Principe, Ghana, Mali, Benin, Lesotho, and Senegal.

Capacity development is a learning process, engaging existing capacities and providing them with better incentives and checks and balances. It is a long process not amenable to shortcuts. The earlier technocratic approach ignored the links among governance, policy, and capacity development. It therefore requires effective political leadership from the highest level of government, as illustrated in the 12 countries with better state capacity that were studied by the task force that produced the 2005 report. Therefore, state capacity development (often including decentralization) is rarely amenable to a gradualist and incremental approach, but it could require large-scale, nationwide, multisectoral, and demand-driven programs of capacity development and devolution of power and resources to local governments. The countries' own systems for allocating and managing money need to be used and strengthened rather than using parallel systems, not only at the central level but at decentralized levels that are part of the intergovernmental fiscal system. Or where these systems do not exist, as in fragile states, they have to be built *de novo* with external support. The share of technical assistance funding going to capacity-building activities instead of expatriate salaries and support must increase. This is best done by pooling the fragmented financing arrangements into a basket to fund prioritized capacity development activities or filling country-identified short-term needs for achieving results. This means untying and pooling funding for technical cooperation (World Bank, 2005).

SSA has made significant progress in basic education, but success in skills development has been distressingly slow. The sheer scale of what needs to be done to achieve growth, basic health care, and improved government dwarfs the capacity on the ground. Moreover, emigration from the region occurs predominantly in terms of skilled manpower. In addition, the pandemics of AIDS, malaria, and TB add to the losses. SSA countries should expand tertiary education enrollment and achievement. After decades of decline, many SSA universities are reforming themselves, pursuing self-sufficiency in finance and improved management and partnering with the private sector. Private universities are mushrooming in both the for-profit and faith-based sectors.

5.7 Underdeveloped financial sectors

SSA financial sectors are among the least developed in the world. "The M2/GDP ratio of about 27% for the period 2001–2004 is considerably lower than the 43% for South Asia and 50% and 56.9% for Latin America and South East Asia, respectively. These comparisons are also reflected in the private sector credit averages, whereby Africa scores 16% against 26% for South Asia, 44% for Latin America, and 45% for South East Asia" (Ndulu et al., p. 117). Because of high operating costs, risks of policy instability, high concentration, and lack of competition, the median spread of interest rates is 13% in SSA, compared with between 5% and 10% for the other developing regions. The lending environment across SSA is characterized by a poor credit culture, poor contract enforcement, and lack of protection of creditor rights. Access of small firms to loans is low, and costs and collateral requirements are very high compared to China and India (Figure 28). Financial systems for a broad part of the population could be improved by innovations such as cell-phone banking, smart cards, and improved infrastructure and greater competition for the transmission of remittances.

5.8 Low savings

Savings rates in the region have stayed far below those of other developing regions. Although South Asia and SSA both had savings rates of around 10% in the 1970s, in South Asia they have climbed to more than 20%, compared to a mere 9% in SSA between 1991 and 2003. Excluding the resource-rich countries brings the average savings rate further down, to 3%. Both public and private savings rates are below those of other developing regions. Reasons include low incomes, low interest rates paid by banks on deposits, and the scarcity of savings infrastructure. In addition, a good deal of savings in the rural areas is in kind in the form of trees, livestock, and land improvements (dwellings, and investment in children's education). In rural Ghana, for example,

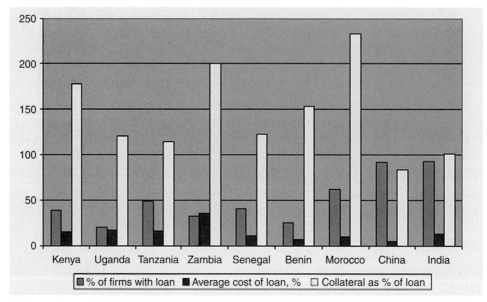

Figure 28   Access to financial capital in SSA is limited. Source: Ndulu et al., 2007.

the median household saved over 30% of its annual income. Mobilizing this savings capacity for agricultural development is both a major opportunity and a challenge. But poor people are kept out of formal financial systems by very high balance requirements, complex administrative procedures, and astronomical transactions costs in the formal banking sector. Microfinance institutions have only managed to mobilize a small pool of savings and have limited coverage and narrow areas of operations. High management costs have been the norm and lead to negative net worth and high probability of failure. For microfinance to fulfill its role as a complement to formal finance, the institutions will need to become much more efficient. At the same time, the formal sector will need to reach out to poorer segments of the population, including via technological and process innovations.

5.9 The agenda for economic growth

Countries with large populations, such as Ethiopia, the Democratic Republic of the Congo, Nigeria, and Sudan, will have to grow more rapidly. Some of these could follow the East Asian model of export-driven growth. It is not just higher levels of investment that must be achieved but greater productivity of the investment. A big push is required for infrastructure development to make up for past neglect, especially to connect the landlocked countries to their neighbors, the sea, and the international communication and data systems.

Based on the analysis in their report, Ndulu et al. propose a medium-term strategy that hinges on taking action in four areas (characterized as the four "Is"): improving the *investment* climate; a big push toward closing the *infrastructure* gap with other regions of the world; a greater focus on *innovation* as the primary motor for productivity growth and enhanced competitiveness; and *institutional* and human capacity.

5.10 Agricultural growth has accelerated

Agricultural value added in SSA has grown at an average of around 3% per year for the past 25 years, close to the average for all developing countries and the same as the Middle East and North Africa (MENA). Livestock growth was a very significant contributor to this growth all around the world, especially so in Africa. But in SSA growth per agricultural population, a crude measure of income of the rural population, has been only 0.9%, less than half that of any other developing region. Fortunately, in line with the general growth trends in SSA, agricultural growth has accelerated recently and reached 3.5% per capita in the first half of the 2000s. Unlike in Asia, the growth was primarily achieved by area expansion rather than growth in productivity (Figure 29).

Figure 30 first confirms that improving agricultural growth was very much driven by improved macroeconomic policies. In addition, we will show that agricultural policies improved tremendously over the past two decades. It is these policy factors and the general environment for growth discussed previously that have led to the agricultural recovery in Africa, not agricultural-specific interventions and programs. We can infer this from our knowledge that few African countries have as yet increased their investments in agricultural technology and services, and in many they have continued to decline. But there were two additional factors that are discussed here—namely, the continuing adverse policies of the developed world and the sharp improvements in agricultural policies in Africa itself.

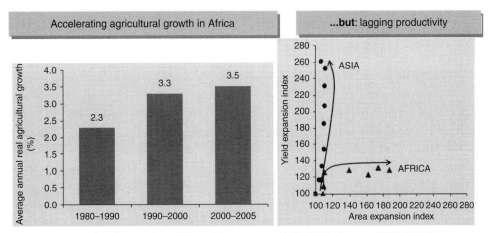

Figure 29   Agricultural growth in SSA and its sources, 1980–2005. Source: WDR (2008).

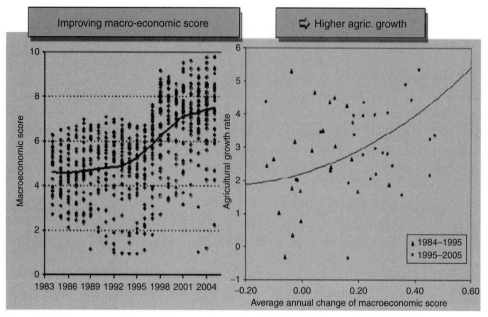

Figure 30 Macroeconomic conditions and growth, 1983–2004. Source: WDR (2006).

The same conditions that have shaped economywide growth and performance have also been key determinants of agricultural growth and performance. Furthermore, the same factors that have kept the bottom-billion countries in their traps also have prevented them from achieving success in agriculture. We therefore do not need to separately analyze the impacts on agricultural growth of the factors discussed previously, such as investment and savings levels, financial sector development, macroeconomic policies, governance, demography, infrastructure, the investment climate, natural resources, and conflict on the performance of the agricultural sector. Instead we can concentrate on agriculture-specific trends and issues.

5.11 Agriculture suffers from global agricultural trade barriers

The agricultural sector in SSA, however, continues to have to struggle against an adverse policy environment in the developed world. Average nominal rates of assistance in the developed world peaked at over 50% between 1985 and 1989. On average, they have declined only slightly, to a little less than 40%, since then (Figure 31). Among the developed economies, they declined only in Europe; they increased sharply in Japan and slightly in North America. The impact of this protection on world prices and trade shares is severe: The prices of cotton, oilseeds, dairy products, and cereals are reduced 21%, 15%, 12%, and 7%, respectively, and the trade shares of developing countries in these commodities are reduced 27%, 34%, 7%, and 5%, respectively.

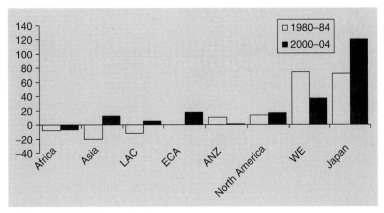

Figure 31 Nominal rates of assistance to agriculture by region (%), 1980–1984 and 2000–2004. Source: Anderson (2009).

Although price impacts on processed meats and sugar are less severe, the respective impacts on developing country trade shares are 19% and 9%, respectively (WDR, 2008). The universally common practice of tariff escalation, under which processed goods are charged higher tariffs than raw products, further aggravates the impact of these policies on the prospect of agroindustrial development in developing countries.

The impact of trade liberalization in agriculture across the world was studied by Anderson et al., 2006, using large international CGE models. With unilateral trade reform in SSA alone, African agriculture trade would change little in the aggregate, because the barriers imposed by the developed world and other developing countries would remain significant. But with globally multilateral reform of all goods, African agriculture and food exports would increase 38%, whereas imports would increase but 29%. Clearly, African agriculture stands to gain the most from multilateral trade reform. Moreover, in the absence of a breakthrough in the Doha Round of trade negotiations, China and India could follow the developed world, Korea, and Taiwan in protecting their agriculture to close the rising urban/rural income gap. This would close the major future export opportunity for SSA agriculture.

Although the international price reductions caused by developed countries now look small compared to the price changes under the current price spike, they clearly had a very adverse impact during the long period of declining and low international prices that preceded it. In addition, they would again have a significant impact if after the spike prices settle at only modestly higher levels than they had been prior to the spike.

African countries have, of course, recognized the adverse consequences of these trade restrictions in agriculture and have become active participants in the trade negotiations. The price spike should not change their policy stance.

5.12 Domestic taxation of agriculture was exceptionally high but has been reduced

After the end of colonization, African countries started to discriminate sharply against agriculture via overvalued exchange rates, industrial protection, and direct agricultural taxation. A major study now has measured the combined effects of these three interventions on the net rate of agricultural assistance and compares them across the developing and developed world. A negative rate of protection is in fact the rate of taxation. This is sometimes called *disprotection*. As shown in Figure 32 for Africa as a whole, the net protection rates have improved from about −20% in 1975–1979 to less than −10% in the first half of the present decade.

However, Asia changed from being a net disprotector of agriculture until around 1960 to a net protector of agriculture at rather high levels of between 20% and 25% since the second half of the 1980s, The same protection levels are also now applied in Eastern Europe and Central Asia (Figure 31). Similarly, Latin America, since the mid-1980s, is protecting its agriculture at a rate of about 5%. The average of the developed world, protection rates remain at close to 40%.

As Figure 32 shows, the antitrade bias against agriculture was concentrated on exportable commodities, which in the late 1970s were taxed at around 40%, whereas importables were almost always slightly protected. Although disprotection overall is now less than 10% in Africa, it remains at almost 20% for the exportables.

Within SSA, agricultural taxation remains the most severe in Zimbabwe, the Ivory Coast, Zambia, and Tanzania (Figure 33). The greatest improvements since the first

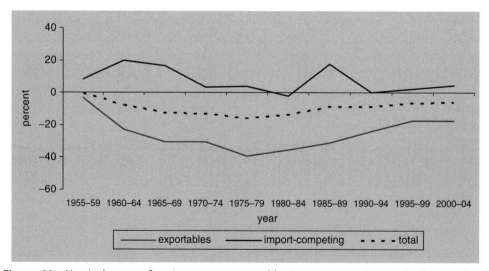

Figure 32 Nominal rates of assistance to exportable, import-competing, and all agricultural products, African region, 1955–2004.[6] Source: Anderson and Masters (2009).

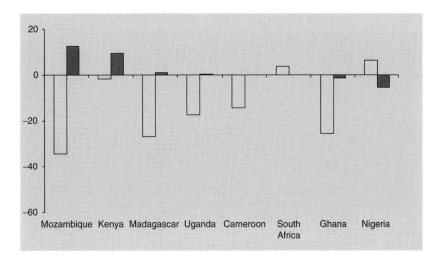

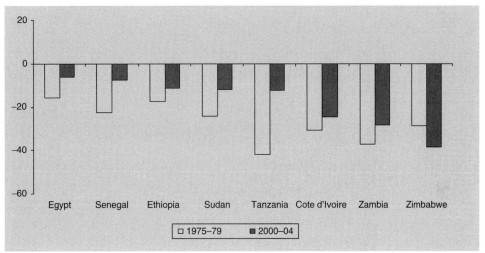

Figure 33 Nominal rates of assistance to agriculture in Africa by country (%), 1975–1979 and 2000–2004.[7] Source: Anderson and Masters (2009).

half of the 1980s were made in Mozambique, Kenya, Madagascar, Uganda, and Cameroon, where nominal rates of assistance are now positive or zero. In Egypt, the only North African country for which data are available, the NRA also remains close to −10%.

Among agricultural commodities in Africa (except for South Africa), the nominal rates of assistance (NRA) across Africa for tobacco, soybeans, groundnuts, cocoa, cotton beans, beef, tea and coffee remained at between −45% (for tobacco) and −15% for coffee (Figure 34). Clearly, across commodities and across countries there remain important opportunities for improvement in the incentive regime of SSA agriculture.

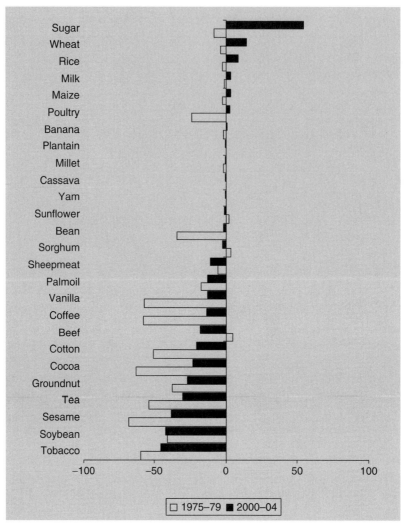

Figure 34   Nominal rates of assistance across commodities (%), 1975–2004.[8]   Source: Anderson and Masters (2009).

In terms of Africa's own agricultural trade policies, five conclusions stand out:

- On balance, protection rates (or more precisely, nominal rates of assistance to agriculture) are no longer negative; they remain below −10% in Ethiopia, Sudan, Tanzania, Zambia, Côte d'Ivoire, and Zimbabwe.
- Taxation is still concentrated on exportable commodities. However, from taxing them at extremely high rates in the 1970s and 1980s, Africa has steadily improved its incentives regime. On average it is now less than 10%. However, taxation levels of a number of individual exportable commodities remain alarmingly high.

- Despite the improvements in incentives, African farmers still face the worst agricultural incentives in the world. This is first because only Europe has reduced its nominal rates of assistance to agriculture, whereas both the United States and, especially, Japan have increased them. Second, the other developing regions have moved from disprotecting agriculture to protecting their agriculture, in the case of Asia at a level that is now getting closer to the average of the developed world.
- Progress is being made in terms of regional integration across all subregions of SSA, but agricultural incentives also still suffer from barriers to interregional trade and poor phytosanitary capacities.
- Though improving, the business climates in most countries still remain far worse than in other developing countries, holding back private sector activities upstream and downstream from the farm. There has been significant progress in incentivers' regimes, but if countries in SSA want to compete better in domestic, regional, and international markets and benefit from the likely rising trend in international agricultural prices, they must move aggressively to eliminate export taxation of agriculture and remaining barriers to regional trade.

6. THE "BOTTOM BILLION"

Despite the progress that SSA has made over the past 15 years and despite the extremely favorable international environment for growth in the past three years, seven countries (Brundi, Comoros, Eritrea, Niger, the Seychelles, Togo, and Zimbabwe) in SSA still had negative average per capita income growth between 2004 and 2006, and a further six (Benin, Central African Republic, Cote d'Ivoire, Gabon, Guinea, and Guinea Bissau) had three-year average per capita growth rates of less than 1%. These countries are stuck at the bottom; at the same time, the average three-year rate of per capita income growth for SSA was 3.2%. Clearly, these countries deserve special attention in a period of global prosperity when the rest of the world is marching on. This section summarizes the studies of Collier and his collaborators, which were recently summarized in Collier (2007).[9]

Collier and his collaborators divided the developing world into the rapidly growing countries in which the "middle 4 billion" of people live and the 58 relatively small countries in trouble, with about a billion people. Of these, 73% of people are or have recently been through civil war; 29% live in countries dominated by natural resources; 30% are landlocked, in resource-poor countries, and with bad neighbors; and 76% have gone through a prolonged period of poor governance and poor policies. (Because these countries often suffer from more than one problem, the percentages add up to more than 100%.) "As a result, while the rest of the developing world has been growing at an unprecedented rate, [these countries] have stagnated or declined. From time to time they have broken free of the traps, but the global economy is making it much harder to follow the path taken by the majority" (Collier, 2007, p. 99).

Most of the countries housing the bottom billion are in SSA, but they also include countries such as Haiti, Laos, Cambodia, Yemen, Burma, North Korea, and the Central Asian Republics. In the trapped countries, life expectancy is much lower, infant mortality is much higher, and hunger is much more prevalent. In addition, missing prospects for development shroud their populations in despair.

Collier et al. use a large cross-country data set from 1960 to the early years of this decade to statistically estimate the impacts of various conditions and variables on the likelihood of people falling into and emerging from these traps as well as the contributions to growth of resource income and policy interventions in the countries on the likelihood of achieving higher growth. For a number of those relationships, they have to overcome endogeneity issues, which could bias the estimated coefficients. They do this via instrumental variable techniques. The underlying papers have been published in peer-reviewed journals, but a number of econometricians believe that it is hard to estimate stable structural parameters from cross-country regressions and that instrumental variable techniques are a relatively ineffective tool to overcome endogeneity problems. Therefore, there is still a lively debate about the reliability of the resulting estimates, especially where subtle effects are being estimated using relatively poor data. However, the policy conclusions presented by Collier rely not only on the statistical evidence but also on other bodies of knowledge and evidence.

6.1 Conflict

Collier discusses that almost three quarters of the "bottom-billion countries" have recently been or are in civil war. Specifically for SSA, Ndulu et al. (2007) provide the following data on conflicts: Until about 1990, conflicts were about equally prevalent across SSA as in the other developing regions of the world, but in the early 1990s they peaked in SSA, whereas they started to decline elsewhere (Figure 35). Despite recent declines, over 15% of SSA countries remained in conflict at the beginning of the 21st century. The proportion of SSA's population in conflict was always much higher than the proportion of countries, reaching a much earlier peak near 60% in 1984 and another close to 50% in the early 1990s. Conflict, therefore, was a more important determinant of the collapse of growth in the 1980s than is usually recognized. Since 2000, further progress has been made with the cessation of conflicts in Angola, Sierra Leone, Liberia, and Southern Sudan. Conflicts in which a warring party was the government declined from 15 in 2003 to 5 today. Furthermore, in 2004 there were 40% fewer coup attempts than in 1960, and all of them failed.

Collier et al. have analyzed the determinants of conflicts in depth: Civil war is more likely where income is low, stagnates, or declines; in countries dependent on oil, diamonds, and other primary exports; but interestingly, not where inequality is high.

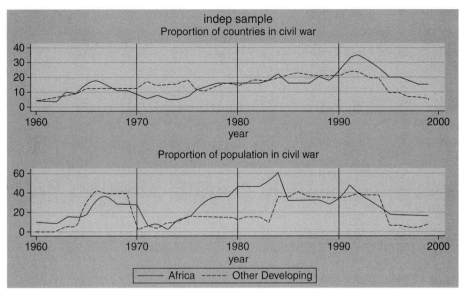

Figure 35 Countries and populations in civil war: SSA and the developing world, 1960–2000. Source: Sambani's dataset.

Civil wars last 10 times as long as international wars (which last an average of six months). Once they are over, they are alarmingly likely to restart. Civil wars reduce growth, on average, by 2.3%. They sharply increase disease incidence. The end of civil war ushers in a boom in homicides. As a consequence of these and other factors, nearly half of all costs arise after the war is over. These costs spill over to neighboring countries and the rest of the world. Collier and his collaborators estimate the overall cost per civil war, including spillovers, at $64 billion.

6.2 Natural resources

Natural resources contribute to the risk of civil war. Paradoxically, even during times of peace, natural resource exports reduce growth. The "resource curse" arises from "Dutch disease," the fact that resource exports lead to an appreciation of the exchange rate, which makes domestic products uncompetitive in international markets as exports or as import substitutes. Sharp price fluctuations of natural resources also lead to a boom-and-bust cycle. But resources also mess up politics by making it easy to finance patronage politics and reducing the restraints on political power that are so important for a functioning democracy: an independent central bank, judiciary, and press; financial transparency; competitive bidding and the like. The reason is that governments do not need to raise taxes from their people and can therefore ignore their wishes. Where restraints can nevertheless be put in place, they improve investment decisions and reduce corruption.

6.3 Landlocked, with poor neighbors

Around 30% of SSA's population lives in landlocked, resource-scarce countries. Their transport costs depend less on distance and more on how much their neighbors spent on transport infrastructure. Because they have not focused on serving neighboring markets, if their neighbors grow an extra 1%, SSA landlocked countries grow only an extra 0.2% (against 0.7% for non-SSA landlocked countries). To increase these multipliers, these countries need to focus on their own and their neighbors' transport infrastructure, including transport to the sea; on regional integration; and on reducing external trade barriers of their entire region. They must be interested in good economic policies of their neighbors. Last but not least, they need to focus on agricultural and rural development. Growing urban, subregional, and international markets can provide many opportunities for their agriculture.

6.4 Missing the boat of globalization

Developing countries have changed from exporters of raw materials to exporters of manufactures, which today constitute 80% of their exports, and service exports are mushrooming. These changes have come about only recently because trade restrictions by developed countries and developing countries themselves were removed only a few years ago. The enormous labor forces of China and India, therefore, have entered the global economy only in the last decade. Therefore it is only recently that the existing wage gap with the developed world has turned into an effective wage gap. It is also only now that these economies have been able to harness economies of scale and agglomeration, and the agglomerations in Asia have become fabulously competitive. By persisting with poor governance and poor policies, even the coastal SSA countries shot themselves in the foot and largely missed the boat, to mix metaphors a bit. Given the productivity of their Asian competitors, it is likely that it has now become more difficult to take advantage of globalization. Therefore, the benefits of globalization in trade will not easily be harnessed by the countries that house the bottom billion.

SSA is desperately short of capital, which, in principle, globalization could supply. But the biggest capital flows are not going to countries that have the least capital. The perceived risk of investment remains high, even in SSA countries that have turned around. International risk ratings take a very long time to reflect positive changes, especially if reforms are fragile. *Changing countries need better ways of signaling that they have committed to reform.* In addition, SSA has suffered from capital outflows. By 1990, *38% of its private capital was held abroad.* Africans, like the rest of the world, voted with their wallets. Migration decisions of educated Africans reflect similar economic choices.

Although globalization is helping the countries in the middle converge to the developed world, the preceding analysis suggests that it will not do it easily for the "bottom-billion" countries. One of the major opportunities for convergence that is ignored in Collier's analysis is agriculture and rural development. Globalization, rapid income growth, and urbanization in the middle 4 billion countries and biofuel subsidies in the high-income countries are sharply increasing the demand for agricultural products and the diversity of the demand, and therefore the quantity and diversity of agricultural trade. Demand growth will be concentrated in developing countries and supply growth in OECD countries will be relatively constrained. Therefore, most of the trade growth in agriculture will be in the form of South/South trade. In addition, the Africa-wide acceleration of growth and urbanization also increases demand at country and subregional levels. Most analysts predict an end to the secular decline of agricultural prices, and sustained price rises are also possible. Therefore, import substitution options, subregional trade, and export opportunities will rise rapidly. Many of the "bottom-billion" countries have very large, untapped agricultural potential that can be developed by appropriate policies and investment programs, as explained in WDR (2008).

6.5 Aid

Collier shows that aid has improved growth by about 1% per year, in contradiction with the assertion of other researchers. In some instances the additional growth could simply have just have prevented an even faster decline, however. The faster growth associated with aid would have provided modest benefits in terms of security. In post-conflict countries, the security benefits of the higher growth coming from aid imply that large aid programs are economically justified. In natural resource-rich countries, aid is pretty impotent. On the other hand, in landlocked, resource-poor countries it is there not only to improve conditions for growth but also to bring some minimum decency to standards of living. A major opportunity of aid in these countries is to improve their transport links to the coast and to urban centers in their neighbors. It can also help in developing the agricultural potential of these countries.

In addition, Collier concludes that policy conditionality has not worked in countries with poor policies. Governance conditionality might do better, since such conditionality does not shift power from the government to the donors but from the government to its own citizens.

Technical assistance (TA) does not have a positive impact on growth prior to a reform effort, but in post-conflict situations and incipient turnarounds, TA can help provide the huge number of skills needed in these situations and make up for lack of skills that have been lost. Collier et al. estimate a positive effect of TA in the first four years of an incipient reform. TA packages during these periods of time should be large and create the conditions for productive use of subsequent aid. After that, TA should progressively be phased out, since the usual objections to technical assistance reemerge when business is more usual. Technical assistance should be reorganized to look more like emergency relief, not like a pipeline of projects.

Other aid money early in a reform is counterproductive: It makes it less likely that reform will be sustained. After a few years of reform, the statistical effects of aid and technical assistance reverse themselves: Technical assistance becomes useless, whereas other aid starts reinforcing the reform process in an environment of better governance and policies. Of course, aid remains highly risky in such contexts because the chances of a reversal to conflict or bad governance and policies remain high. But given the huge cost of such reversals, the risks are well worth taking. Donors need to adapt to this high risk of operation.

In failing states, project implementation is poorer than elsewhere. However, Collier et al. showed that money spent on project supervision in these states had been differentially effective. Therefore, in the environments in which aid agencies should be increasingly operating, they should allow for higher operational costs and budgets, especially for supervision. This recommendation contradicts the conventional pressure on operational budgets of aid agencies. Low operational costs in failing states are the opposite of what the aid agencies should allow for.

Given the increasing difficulties in breaking into international markets, aid should also be concentrated on helping countries break into export markets—for example, by improving port infrastructure and roads.

6.6 Other program components

Military intervention, as in Sierra Leone and Liberia, is often necessary to maintain post-conflict peace. The military needs to be present for much longer than usually assumed to be effective. They can help in bringing down government spending on the military and free resources for economic growth. They also can help prevent coups. Of course, the military should be used selectively and not be motivated by considerations such as securing access to natural resources—in particular, oil.

International norms and standards can also be effective, such as the efforts to reduce conflicts over diamonds and to encourage transparency in the use of oil revenues. Collier argues that such norms and standards could be helpful in a wide variety of areas, since they would significantly reduce the one-on-one negotiations required in each turnaround situation and make a readily available and agreed-on menu of actions available for implementation. For example, corruption is concentrated in natural resource extraction and construction sectors. It is particularly costly for "bottom-billion" countries because it is likely to undermine any political reform process. In 1999 the OECD countries finally agreed to legislate to make bribery of foreign officials by OECD nationals and their entities a criminal offense. The issue now is how well these laws are enforced. A charter with norms and standards for natural resources would be helpful to the future of the countries in the resource trap. A charter for democracy could provide guidance on the checks and balances that are so important for the proper functioning of democracy: the independent judiciary, central bank, free press, and others. And a charter on post-conflict situations would provide a road map for the many actors involved in post-conflict support, including the government, in setting priorities and modes of operation.

Clearly, action to help the bottom billion *cannot be done by aid alone*. The overall agenda includes changes in aid policy, in military interventions, in OECD laws via the promulgation of International Standards and Charters, and changes in international trade policies. Progress on all four pillars is needed to change the fate of the bottom billion.

The analysis presented by Collier is very pessimistic in terms of probabilities of emerging from the traps in which countries find themselves. However, the recent acceleration of growth in a large number of SSA countries appears to be in conflict with this pessimism. We commented at the beginning of this section on the difficulties of estimating structural parameters using cross-country regressions. The many policy initiatives of SSA governments over the past decade and a half could have changed the structure. Given that most of the data on which the estimation was based were for the period from 1960 to the early 2000s, the estimates would not capture the changes in the underlying structure and could therefore be too pessimistic.

7. THE INSTITUTIONAL PILLARS FOR ARD

We have already discussed the process of democratization in Africa since the early 1990s, the greater space for civil society, and improvements in governance. We now turn to specific institutional issues that have in the past hampered agricultural and rural development in Africa, that have improved since the 1980s, and that were discussed in Binswanger (2008). In 1980, in a typical country in Africa, a young rural woman (or man) who wanted to help develop her community would have found herself almost completely disempowered. Three of the five pillars of the institutional environment for rural development, discussed in this section, were poorly developed: The first pillar, the private sector, was largely confined to small-scale farming and the informal sector. Much of the marketing, input supply, and agro-processing was in the hands of parastatal enterprises. The second pillar, independent civil society, community organizations, and traditional authorities, was highly constrained or suppressed. In the wake of decolonization, central governments had suppressed the third pillar, local government, or starved it of fiscal authority and resources. Since none of these three pillars was providing much opportunity for the young woman, she had to join the central government if she wanted to contribute to her community. But the central institutions failed the rural sector miserably (World Bank, 1982).

Well-structured institutions can tackle all the components of rural development, from health and education to infrastructure, agricultural services, social protection, resource management, and more. Not only does the institutional environment determine who can contribute to development and how successful that contribution will be; it also is the most important determinant of the distribution of benefits. More specifically, where institutions are disempowering, they can be used by strong individuals and groups to direct the benefits of development to themselves via elite capture.

We will see how the division of labor is changing between the private sector and the public sector. We first focus on local development, which is a core component of ARD, although the latter also involves nonlocal components such as transport, processing, and marketing activities. No institution by itself can carry the burden of local development. Instead, the new paradigm that has emerged gives equal weight to the private sector, communities and civil society, local government, and the sector institutions such as health, education, and agriculture (World Bank, 2004). This is a departure from the past, when different disciplines and sectors single-mindedly advocated approaches involving only one of the four sets of actors. A broad consensus has been reached that local development (and therefore rural development) has to be viewed as a coproduction by all these four groups of actors. They need to take account of their comparative advantage, delegate functions to the other partners in coproduction, and reform themselves to be able to function under this new paradigm. How such an integrated approach would be fostered in a particular country should depend on past history, what currently exists and can be built on, the prevailing traditions and cultures and past history, and a diagnosis of the existing capacities and disfunctionalities. Figure 36 illustrates this emerging consensus. One can think of the capacities of each of the sectors by the size of the circles in a country-specific variant of Figure 36. Various countries would have different diagrams, with some having small circles for local governments, whereas others would have small circles for their communities.

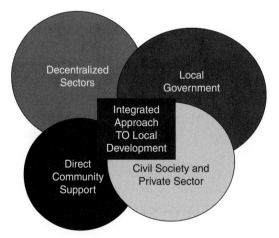

Figure 36 The integrated approach to local development.

Only country-specific analysis can reveal where the greatest weaknesses are and the best opportunities for improvements in the institutional environment. There are no universal magic bullets (Binswanger et al., 2009).

7.1 Pillar 1: The private sector

The World Bank's agricultural adjustment programs identified the suppression of the private sector, the underperformance of parastatal enterprises, and the fiscal black holes they created as the root causes of the underperformance of agriculture. Although this view was partially correct, it was too narrow. The withdrawal of the parastatals did not lead to spontaneous growth of private replacements. As we have seen, too many other problems existed in the "business environment," including corruption, overregulation, and poor infrastructure and services. Only in the last few years have cross-sector analytical work and programs addressed the business environment in a systematic way (World Bank, 2005b,c; Economic Commission for Africa, 2004, 2005a).

In Section 4 we provided a full discussion of the deep changes that are taking place in the private agricultural sector along the entire value chain and at global, regional, domestic, and local levels, many of which are associated with the supermarket revolution. Here we note that as part of these changes, the private sector is entering the standard setting and regulatory areas across countries and sectors and therefore starting to deal with public goods. The radical changes in retail markets and their supply chains greatly increase concern about food safety and quality. The food industry globally has been very active in establishing norms and standards for itself and has not waited for governments to come up with them. The two best known standards are the Hazard Analysis and Critical Control Points System (HACCP), which sets process standards for safety and quality control in food processing. It has been widely adapted by the global food industry. The second is the work of the International Organization for Standardization, which goes by the acronym ISO. It is a network of 157 national standards institutions that come together to agree on comparable international standards. Two of these are ISO #65, dealing with agriculture, and ISO #67, dealing with food technology. The ISO's most recent effort is ISO/TS 22003, which, in 2007, set standards for food safety management systems.

7.2 Pillar 2: Communities, civil society, and social capital

In the 1980s the development community woke up to the important role of communities, civil society, and social capital, which activists and academics had strongly emphasized before them. A broad range of NGOs started to sharply criticize donor-financed projects, policies, and structural adjustment programs (Mallaby, 2004).The focus on communities came from two additional sources: Sector specialists in water supply and natural resource management in the 1980s had started to involve communities systematically and found that this involvement enhanced project performance significantly (World Bank, 1996b). The other source was social funds, which quickly discovered the power of communities to assist in project design and implementation. In some of the early social funds, NGOs were used as intermediaries to substitute for the presumed lack of capacity at the community level. But this approach proved costly and has increasingly been abandoned in favor of direct empowerment of communities with knowledge and resources, whereas NGOs remain important facilitators and sources of knowledge. From letting communities participate in the design, finance, and maintenance of micro-projects, community-driven development programs have moved on to truly empower them to chose, design, and execute a large range of micro-projects by transferring both the responsibility and the cofinancing resources for these project to the communities. In countries as diverse as Mexico, Burkina Faso, and Indonesia, such programs have now successfully been scaled up to national levels, integrated into local government institutions and the intergovernmental fiscal systems, and linked to the relevant sector institutions, as illustrated in Figure 36 (Binswanger et al., 2009). At about the same time, social scientists discovered the merits of social capital and traditional institutions, and they are now often systematically assessed and integrated into policies and programs (Economic Commission for Africa, 2005a,b; World Bank, 2003b).

For agricultural development, a particularly important change is the formation and progressive development of independent farmers' organizations and microfinance institutions (World Bank, 1991). They are increasingly replacing or complementing cooperatives that were often created by the state and did not really lead to empowerment. The growth and development of communities, NGOs, and social capital are important not only for the implementation of development programs, diversity, and strength of these organizations but also as a defense against elite capture of programs and project benefits.

A recent review compared the development of producer associations in Mozambique, Nigeria, and Zambia to those in Brazil and Thailand:

> **Effective producer associations thrive in a democratic environment that provides a favorable climate for civil society organizations in general. A really active role in defending smallholder rights, including those to land and favorable contracts, has emerged in Brazil and Thailand but in Africa is still poorly developed. Although a significant start has been made, few SSA associations have been able to develop themselves and their commercial linkages sufficiently to take on a major role in service delivery. And many continue to be heavily dependent on donor support. While farmer's organizations have become significant stakeholders in discussions of agricultural policies, they have not yet been able to generate the strong political will in favor of agriculture which has propelled development of the CERRADO and of North East Thailand. Nevertheless, SSA countries today are probably more advanced in the development of producer associations than were the farmers in the Cerrado and North East Thailand in 1960, and therefore may have a more favorable starting point. (Binswanger-Mkhize, 2007)**

7.3 Pillar 3: Local government

During the late 1980s democratization in Latin America, and later in other parts of the world, led to the restoration or strengthening of local governments. Another factor was the inability of central states to deliver services in widely heterogeneous environments. But decentralization was often viewed as a dangerous development because provincial and state governments were often seen as a source of fiscal irresponsibility. Fortunately, by the mid-1990s, the negative views on decentralization had given way to a more balanced assessment, recognizing both successes and failures (Faguet, 1997; Piriou-Sall, 1997; World Bank, 1995). Equal emphasis on political, administrative, and fiscal decentralization is needed. Unsuccessful decentralization programs are almost always characterized by inadequate allocation of fiscal resources to the local level (Manor, 1999; Shah, 1994). Successful decentralization is often pursued by strong leaders in relatively strong states and puts a great deal of emphasis on accountability at all levels (Manor, 1999). Local governments can, of course, become an instrument for elite capture and corruption. To prevent that, they must be democratic institutions, but that in itself is not enough. Without strong communities and civil society and a strong private sector, local governments will not be subject to the scrutiny and the bargaining processes that are needed to make local development inclusive and efficient.

In the early 1990s, the World Bank first discovered the power of local governments in its community-driven development programs in Mexico (World Bank, 1991b) and later in Northeast Brazil. The innovation spread from there to Indonesia and East Asia, then to Africa and the rest of the world. Social funds started to build the capacity of local governments and entrust them with coordination and some implementation functions, and eventually the distinction between community-driven development and social funds disappeared. A research program on decentralization, fiscal systems, and rural development in the mid-1990s strengthened our understanding of this nexus of issues (McLean et al., 1998; Piriou-Sall, 1998). It analyzed the level of decentralization of rural service delivery in 19 countries (or provinces thereof) across the World (Figure 37).

Four SSA countries had the lowest decentralization scores, whereas Jianxi Province in China had the highest one. Latin American countries scored in the upper half; Karnataka state of India ranked ninth, and Punjab, Pakistan, ranked at 13. The recent *Governance Report of the Economic Commission for Africa* (2005) shows that not much progress has been made in the past decade and a half: Decentralization, along with corruption, still receives some of the lowest scores of a whole series of governance indicators studied in 28 countries of Africa.

There are powerful reasons for using the lowest level of local government for coordination and execution of rural development. At the local level, people have direct

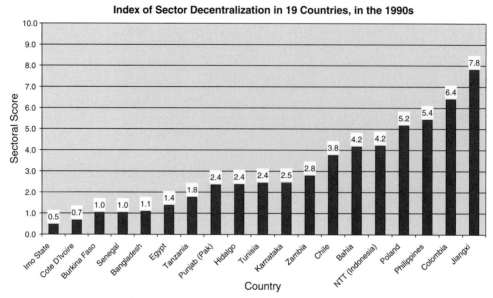

Figure 37 Decentralization of service delivery for rural development across the world by country. Source: McLean et al. (1998).

knowledge of the local conditions. Transparency is relatively easy to achieve, since people can often verify the result of expenditures, or lack thereof, with their own eyes. Given the heterogeneity of rural space, coordination of the sectors involved in rural development at the central level is almost impossible. Empowered and properly resourced local governments can mobilize latent capacities in communities and at the local level more easily than centralized systems can. Finally, local governments do exist in remote areas where neither NGOs nor the private sector tend to operate.

In most OECD countries and in high-performing China, local governments perform functions in education, health, social protection, environment, agriculture, land, local and community infrastructure, and promotion of private sector development. They are a multisector coordination tool, even though their coordination capacity is always imperfect.

7.4 Pillar 4: Sector institutions

In 1980, sector institutions were the main focus of donor financed programs, even though they again and again were unable to effectively implement programs in widely dispersed rural areas. There has been a growing realization that the sector institutions should delegate implementation to the private sector, communities, civil society organizations, and local governments, using the principles of subsidiarity[10] and comparative advantage. The other pillars of the institutional environment will not reach their full potential without fundamental change in the sector institutions. Instead of providing services and implementing programs, they should formulate policies, set standards, and enhance and control quality (World Bank, 2004).

Rural development involves almost all sectors of ministries, from the police, local government, education, and health to land, environment, agriculture, and more. The ones specifically associated with agriculture and natural resources often have poor commitment to smallholder services and/or poor capacity to provide them. Agricultural credit institutions and insurance systems not only achieved little for small and poor farmers, they also were fiscal black holes, benefiting primarily the wealthy. Ministries of lands have lacked an effective constituency to ensure proper budgets for them and are often highly centralized and corrupt. Ministries of agriculture are notoriously weak and politicized. In addition, they are poor at collecting the necessary data, monitoring sector developments, analyzing sector policy issues, and designing and implementing appropriate agricultural policy regimes and programs. Worst of all, they are often captured by large farmer elites and function more like pressure groups for them. Efforts to reform individual sectors one by one have had little success. Transformation and deconcentration of the sector institutions are probably better done via cross-sector governance and public sector reforms.

7.5 Pillar 5: The central government and other central institutions

Today the functions of central governments that are considered important for development are very different from the roles they saw for themselves in the 1960s and 1970s. The central government still has the ultimate design, oversight, and coordination role of national development programs, including those for rural development. But central government is less and less in a direct service delivery and executing role, except in defense, taxation, management of expenditures and of the intergovernmental fiscal system, and the electoral processes. However, the central government has a particularly important role to play in bringing about the changes needed for successful coproduction among the four institutional pillars we've discussed. It has to drive forward the process of decentralization of functions, resources, and accountability mechanisms to local governments and to the end users and to ensure that the sector institutions transform themselves. It has to ensure that the business climate for the private sector improves and that communities and civil society are free to take on their coproduction functions.

Other specific central institutions, such as the judiciary, parliament, the press, and national civil society organizations, are today recognized as important for rural development as well in areas of contract enforcement, resource allocation to development programs, and provision of information. In addition, they should be the guardians of good governance. They also need to press for further devolution of power and resources to local levels and communities.

Institutional environments in rural Africa have in many cases significantly improved. Today the young woman about whom we spoke at the beginning of this section can operate much more freely in the private sector in a steadily improving business environment. In most countries and commodities she can join a producer association. She can also help her community by engaging in a wide variety of community-driven initiatives for which funding is becoming available more systematically. She can work for one of many NGOs and either use her technical skills in NGO-facilitated development programs or her advocacy skills in advocacy NGOs. In countries such as Senegal or Uganda, a number of former functions of ministries of agriculture are either being privatized or performed by producer associations, often partially financed by the state, and the young woman can operate in one of these services. Finally, most countries have pursued decentralization initiatives, and the young woman can work for her locality as either a staff member of a local government or an elected counselor. Unfortunately, however, progress in decentralization has been slow in most countries other than Uganda, South Africa, Burkina, and a few more. Elsewhere the process of administrative decentralization, that is, transferring functions to local governments, has been slow. Even where it has proceeded more rapidly, fiscal decentralization has been lagging badly, leaving most local governments with few resources to execute their mandated functions, let alone take a leadership role in local development.

Nevertheless, compared to 1980, today's institutional environment for agricultural and rural development has improved. Although there are no studies that measure the impact of the improved institutions on agricultural growth, there is little doubt that these improvements, in addition to macroeconomic stability and improved price incentives, are among the factors explaining the recent acceleration of agricultural growth.

7.6 The capacity of agricultural and rural institutions

The general approach to capacity development has already been discussed in Section 5 and 7, emphasizing the broad-based process and the patience that is required to achieve it. Capacity development of agricultural and rural institutions would therefore flourish best in the context of a broader, national capacity development strategy and program. More specifically, capacity development for local rural and agricultural institutions must build on the considerable latent capacities that are found in rural areas all over the world. To do so, rules and regulations for program execution must become much more participatory and empowering and eliminate complex features that destroy latent capacity or hinder its mobilization and further development (Binswanger and Nguyen, 2005). As far as possible, the institutions and organizations of rural communities, agricultural producers, and accountable local governments should be relied on for program execution and service delivery. Agricultural and rural capacity building cannot be done as a top-down provision of capacity development services. Instead, it involves the following processes: learning by doing, in which communities, local governments, farmer's organizations, and private sector actors are given opportunities and resources to actually exercise control over their own development processes, graduating from smaller to larger initiatives and responsibilities. As part of learning by doing, these actors could be provided with mandatory training, in particular in diagnosis and planning, financial management and reporting, procurement, and monitoring and evaluation. Other training should be provided largely on a demand-driven basis. Finally, as emphasized in the WDR of 2005 on service delivery, the broader-sector institutions involved in ARD need to become much more accountable to their clients.

8. CURRENT OPPORTUNITIES AND CHALLENGES FOR AFRICAN ARD

The Inter-Academy Council (2005) cites the following unique features of SSA agriculture that represent special challenges to agricultural performance: (1) dominance of weathered soils of poor inherent fertility; (2) predominance of rain-fed agriculture, little irrigation, and very limited mechanization; (3) heterogeneity and diversity of farming systems; (4) key roles of women in agriculture and in ensuring household food security; (5) poorly functioning markets for inputs and outputs; and (6) large and growing impact of human health on agriculture. Unlike in Asia, the growth was primarily achieved by area expansion rather than growth in productivity. But these challenges have to be seen against the great opportunities arising from unused and underused arable land, from higher commodity prices, and from the generally improved growth environment in Africa that we have reviewed in previous sections.

In this section we first look at where the major new market opportunities for African agriculture lie. We then look at the challenges under five broad headings: demographic, social, and health; agro-climatic and biophysical resources; economic incentives and investments; agricultural technology; and the imperative of regionalization.

8.1 Where are the short- and medium-term market opportunities for Africa?

In Section 4 we carefully analyzed the drivers of the change in international prices of agricultural commodities. Although the current price spike creates significant short-run policy challenges for countries, the international market outlook for agriculture appears to be very positive in general. Where will the next market opportunities for African farmers lie? Recent studies of the history and prospects of commercial agriculture in SSA suggest that domestic and subregional markets will represent the main opportunities for SSA producers in the short to medium run (Poulton et al., 2007; World Bank, forthcoming). Since SSA is an importer of many agricultural commodities, SSA producers compete in these markets at the import parity price rather than the lower export parity price. In addition, quality standards are not as high and phytosanitary barriers are much lower than in international markets. Bottlenecks in road and export infrastructure in SSA are likely to be removed only gradually, reinforcing these conclusions. Of course, with appropriate policies and investments, including in transport infrastructure and technology, positive international market trends in agriculture could eventually be captured by SSA as well.

On the demand side, the trends are favorable for domestic and subregional markets: The combined value of domestic and regional markets for food staples within SSA is considerably in excess of its total international agricultural exports (Diao et al., 2003) and will grow significantly with both population and income over time. SSA's demand for food staples is projected to approximately double by 2020. Moreover, an increasing share of output will become commercialized as the continent becomes more urbanized. This offers considerable growth in national and regional markets for food staples that in value terms could far exceed the potential growth of all high-value agricultural products, at least for the next decades.

The fact that domestic and subregional markets for food crops present the best opportunities does not mean that there are no opportunities in international markets. However, all notable cases of SSA agricultural export success, with the exception of sugar, have so far occurred in high-value commodities (a basic commodity value of US$500 per ton or more: tobacco, tea, groundnuts, cashews, seed cotton, coffee; Poulton et al., 2007). They are high value because "ideal" agro-ecological conditions or low labor costs are necessary for their production, which limits global supply and provides advantage to SSA producers. Their high value in turn allows SSA supply systems to recoup their inherently high costs. By contrast, SSA has yet to record any significant export success in low-value commodities (e.g., cereals, cassava, soybeans) that can be grown in a wide range of locations, including by mechanization. To cross the threshold from import substitution to competitiveness as an international exporter, the cereal case study suggests that continued public investment in both research and infrastructure is needed. Finally, because food staples are grown by small farms across SSA, broad-based productivity gains in these crops can have far-reaching impacts on the rural poor.

Although most countries grow many of the same food crops, especially maize, there are latent differences in their comparative advantages, even within the same subregions (Diao et al., 2003), leading to subregional trade opportunities. Subregional trade could therefore be a relatively efficient way of smoothing out the impacts of droughts on production and prices at country and subregional levels. There are many physical and institutional impediments to cross-border trade within SSA, including differences in food safety requirements, rules of origin, and quality and product standards. More important, trade in food staples was for long discouraged by national food policies that placed a high priority on self-sufficiency, and vestiges of these policies still prevail in many countries. One of the biggest impediments to large-scale private investment in cross-border trading capability, particularly in Southern and Eastern Africa, is the unpredictable behavior of governments in imposing export bans whenever they fear food shortages in their own markets.

In its analysis of growth strategies in East and Central Africa, IFPRI reaches the same conclusions: "First, the analysis indicates that the greatest potential for agriculture-led growth and poverty reduction in the region lies in agricultural subsectors serving domestic and regional markets—not those directed at overseas markets. Export commodities will continue to be crucial income earners in key parts of ECA, but they will not be the answer to the problem of widespread poverty and hunger in the region. Second, the analysis indicates that among agricultural subsectors for which there is large and growing domestic and regional demand, staples loom large as a group. Production and sale of these 'poor man' crops can be pathways out of poverty for millions of citizens of ECA" (Omamo et al., 2006).

How likely is sub-Saharan Africa to improve its growth and commercialization performance in food crops? Total cereal production for Africa increased 74.5% between 1979–1981 and 2003–2005, driven primarily by area expansion rather than yield increases, a trend reminiscent of Northeast Thailand and the Cerrado of Brazil until the late 1970s. Production of roots and tubers increased much more sharply in the same period, by 165.3%, driven largely by cassava production. Yield growth for roots and tubers played a much bigger role than with cereals, increasing 40% over the period.

The livestock sector has been a successful export sector in parts of Africa, but exports have stagnated in recent years and there is little sign that SSA is able to maintain, let alone increase, its share of the explosive growth in world market demand for livestock products. Moreover, imports of poultry meat are growing rapidly. Again, in this sector import substitution and subregional trade opportunities are more important than export opportunities.

That domestic and regional markets are the most promising areas for agricultural growth means that small farmers, despite the supermarket revolution and rising international quality standards, will be better placed to seize them than if the best opportunities were in global markets, where quality standards are much more demanding.

8.2 Demographic, social, and health challenges
8.2.1 Demography

In Section 4 we discussed general population trends, which will still be around 2% per year for Africa as a whole. The gradual slowdown of population growth associated with economic growth and the demographic transition will reduce dependency rates and therefore open up the opportunity of per capita growth dividends in Africa. These will be higher in North Africa, where the demographic transition is more advanced than in SSA. Despite rapid rural/urban migration, the high population growth rates mean that the absolute number of rural people will continue to grow in SSA and poverty will remain concentrated in rural areas for a long time.

In the Middle East and North Africa the absolute number of youth will peak in the next 25 years. As in all regions, unemployment is concentrated among the young.

In most countries, the share of unemployment of youth is more than 50%, and employment is the key concern among them (WDR, 2007). Among women, including the young ones, a low labor force participation rate persists. Schooling for both young men and women has increased but is yet insufficient to ensure gainful employment of the young generation.

SSA is home to over 200 million young people who are between 12 and 24 years old. The demographic transition to reduce the proportion of young people in the population has barely started, and a decline in absolute numbers will only come in the distant future. The poor quality of primary education severely limits their opportunities: In many countries, fewer than half of women aged 15–24 can even read a simple sentence, and their dropout rates are very high. Young adults are at greatest risk of HIV/AIDS, and the more so, the less they stay in school. In Kenya the probability that a 20-year-old will die before age 40 is 36%, whereas it would be only 8% in the absence of HIV/AIDS. Many young people become combatants and lose future opportunities as a consequence; they number 100,000 in Sudan alone (WDR, 2007).

8.2.2 Migration, remittances, and the brain drain

According to IFAD et al. (2007), Africa has over 30 million people in the Diaspora. However, its most predominant migrant flows are within the region, usually from poorer countries to less poor countries. As a consequence, the average share of migrants in total population is 7%, a share that rises to 20% in countries with populations of less than 1 million. There is also significant international migration to former European colonial powers such as France, England, the Netherlands, and Italy.

"Remittance flows to and within Africa approach US$40 billion, North African countries such as Morocco and Egypt are the continent's major recipients. East African countries depend heavily on these flows … For the entire Region, these transfers are 13% of per capita income …" (ibid, p. 9). Annual average remittances are $83 per capita, and remittances per migrant are $1358. Clearly, remittances are a major opportunity for Africa.

"Rural remittances are significant and predominantly related to intraregional migration, particularly in Western and Southern Africa …" (ibid, p. 9). Transfer costs are higher than for other regions of the world, partly because of financial restrictions imposed by most African governments. As a result there is both the emergence of informality in money transfers as well as the emergence of monopolies. "In West Africa, for example, 70% of payments are handled by one money transfer operator" (ibid).

Over the past 10 years, developed countries have selectively dismantled barriers to immigration of the highly skilled. Therefore, the proportion of educated people has increased among migrants across the world (Kapur and McHale, 2007). In Eastern

Africa the percentage of skilled workers living in OECD countries has risen from around 18% in 1990 to around 20% in 2000; for West Africa the corresponding numbers are 20% and over 25%. Other long-term trends that fuel these changes are the increased skills intensity of economic growth, the aging populations of rich countries, and the broader globalization of production and trade. But countries are very unevenly affected, as Figure 38 shows.

Although the effect on the welfare of migrants will generally be positive, Kapur and McHale distinguish four effects of migration on the welfare of those left behind in the origin countries. The *prospect channel* of migration increases the incentives of those left behind to get more education and in areas that will increase their prospects for migration such as nursing or accounting. The *absence channel* measures the economic loss to the country of the person actually leaving—the difference between what the emigrant was adding to the economy and what he or she was being paid. In addition, absence might reduce a country's capacity to reform and build its own institutions. The *Diaspora channel* focuses on the impact of the Diaspora. Many SSA countries, including South Africa and Senegal, are both host to Diasporas from other countries as well as contributors to diasporas in more advanced countries. They could therefore both benefit from remittances as well as be a source of them. And they might receive skills as well as sending them. Finally, the *return channel* looks at how emigrants returning with enhanced human and financial capital are contributing to their home countries. Clearly, the impacts of the brain drain are not all negative and can be improved by judicious policies and actions. Kapur and McHale show that solutions to brain-drain

Percentage of nationals with university education living abroad, 2000	
>50	Cape Verde, Gambia, Seychelles, Somalia
25–50	Angola, Equatorial Guinea, Eritrea, Ghana, Guinea Bissau, Kenya, Liberia, Madagascar, Mauritius, Mozambique, Nigeria, Sao Tome and Principe, Sierra Leone
5–25	Algeria, Benin, Burundi, Côte d'ivotre, Cameroon, Chad, Comores, Congo, DRC (formerly Zaire), Djibouti, Ethiopia, Gabon, Guinea, Malawi, Mali, Mauritania, Niger, Morocco, Rwanda, South Africa, Senegal, Sudan, Swaziland, Tanzania, Togo, Tunisia, Uganda, Zambia, Zimbabwe
<5	Botswana, Lesotho, Burkina Faso, Central African Republic, Egypt, Libya, Namibia

Figure 38 Brain drain from SSA: Emigration rates for the tertiary educated, 2000. Source: Kapur and McHale (2005).

problems involve actions on the part of both the developed as well as the developing countries: For example, in developed countries, improved human capital planning should help avoid skills shortages in health and education, whereas higher education reforms in developing countries would enable private sector higher education institutions to offer more education in the skills in high international demand. Other possible measures focus on controls and on compensation.

8.2.3 Gender equity

In many parts of the developing world, women are a majority of the agricultural labor force, and in sub-Saharan Africa they are the majority of the farmers. Yet their rights over land are often poorly developed, and they face disadvantages in education and health care and in access to information, markets, and capital. These restrictions have a negative impact on the efficiency of both men and women and of agriculture as a whole (Economic Commission for Africa, 2005c). Over the last decades, OECD countries have become major advocates for women's rights in the developing world, but entrenched social attitudes constrain the progress that has been achieved.

Ambler et al. argue that:

> **Poverty and hunger cannot be conquered without meeting the specific needs of poor women. Like poor men, they lack the assets and income necessary to exit poverty, but poor women and girls are also subject to a confluence of gender-based vulnerabilities that keep them trapped in poverty. Women have fewer benefits and protections under customary or statutory legal systems than men; they lack decision making authority and control of financial resources; and they suffer under greater time burdens, social isolation, and threats or acts of violence.**

The issues of gender inequalities seem better understood now, but the international establishment still seems slow in responding. Holmes and Slater compare the 2008 World Bank WDR, *Agriculture for Development* to the last Bank WDR, **A**griculture *and Economic Development*, published in 1982, and conclude:

> **Comparing how gender equality is analyzed in the recently published 2008 report to the 1982 report indicates that much progress has been made. Nevertheless, significant gaps remain in the 2008 report, clearly showing that there is still much work to do to ensure that rigorous gender analysis becomes central to rural development policy making ... For all its merits, there are also substantial areas in the 2008 report that lack important gender analysis. The report focuses very little on the impacts and implications for the global economy, such as the impact of deregulated and liberalized economic policies, and global agricultural trade markets, on gender equality and subsequently, for growth and poverty reduction. ... The report also lacks a rigorous analysis of some key gender-specific constraints—for example, women's reproductive responsibilities or cultural barriers—when identifying mechanisms for increasing the role of efficient and equitable labour markets in enabling agricultural growth and poverty reduction.**

Furthermore, at both the household and community level, the 2008 report does not discuss the economic constraints to improving women's participation in farmers' organizations or community committees. (Holmes and Slater, 2007, pp. 1–2)

The *Independent External Review of FAO* (2007) finds that although gender is given greater prominence at high levels, it has not yet been fully mainstreamed at the program and country levels. Johanson and Saint, in their analysis of agricultural education in SSA, conclude that

Although women play multiple roles in agriculture and account for more than half of agricultural output in the continent (and three-quarters of food production) they have continuously received a less-than proportionate share of investment in agriculture, particularly in terms of interventions relating to education, extension, capacity strengthening, empowerment, and market access. (Johanson and Saint, p. 26)

Finally, the Commonwealth Secretariat notes that regarding climate change:

It is clearly evident that there has been very little attention to gender issues in the international processes concerning the development of climate change, whether in protocols, treaties or debates around them. ... Gender differences in property rights and in issues related to access to information and the different cultural, social and economic roles for men and women means that climate change is likely to affect them differentially (Commonwealth Secretariat, 2007).

Changing gender norms in a society is a difficult historic process that is far from complete in the developed world. Growth and economic opportunities for women have been a main factor in driving such change, again putting the emphasis back onto achieving higher growth. We noted earlier that in many countries, fewer than half of women aged 15–24 can even read a simple sentence, and their dropout rates are very high. Thus the basic challenge of gender equity in terms of access to education and health care remains huge. Proactive fostering of change in gender norms and opportunities requires mainstreaming of the gender agenda into all the activities of domestic and external development actors. Since there is no magic bullet, this is the only way to make progress.

8.2.4 Security of access to resources

Farmers will rarely invest in fixed assets unless they have secure land rights. Though traditional tenure systems have often provided secure inheritable usufruct rights, in many parts of SSA they have come under pressure from rising population density and increased market access (World Bank, 2004; Economic Commission for Africa, 2005c). They also often failed to provide secure tenure rights to women, and to manage the potential conflicts that arise when immigrants need to be accommodated and enclosure of pasture threatens the livelihood of herders. Assisting these systems to evolve is therefore an important priority. This has been a topic of intense interest in

SSA in recent years. DFID sponsored a workshop in 1999 that resulted in a valuable compendium of information, published as *Evolving Land Rights, Policy, and Tenure in Africa* (Camilla Toulmin, ed., 2000). Deininger's recent book, *Land Policies for Growth and Poverty Reduction* (2003), contains a major section on Africa, and most recently the CGIAR's Systemwide Program on Collective Action and Property Rights (CAPRi) has released a set of 12 policy briefs in a volume, *Land Rights for African Development: From Knowledge to Action* (2006). Ngaido argues that "... ensuring access to and control over land for poor and marginalized rural households, women, and groups (equity) are critical policy objectives for promoting agricultural growth and combating poverty in Africa" (Ngaido, 2004).

Excessive inequality of land ownership tends to reduce access to land and efficiency of its use (Binswanger, Deininger, and Feder, 1995). Large-scale farms from Brazil to the Philippines and Zimbabwe and Namibia have underutilized their land and have depended on subsidies to reduce their dependence on hired labor via mechanization. Small farms, on the other hand, have inadequate access to capital to make their operations more efficient and improve their profits. As a consequence, both farm sectors suffer an efficiency loss. For these reasons, the World Bank has become a major player in land reform programs in the countries that still have important land reform agendas (Binswanger and Deininger, 1995). However, a lot of controversy still surrounds the best way of implementing land reform, slowing progress in the countries most in need of it (van den Brink et al., 2006; Binswanger et al., 2009b).

8.2.5 Rural HIV and AIDS and agriculture

Following the wave of infections by around a decade, the wave of deaths from HIV and AIDS is now fully upon us, leading in a number of countries to a stabilization or slight decline of HIV prevalence rates. The third wave of orphans has also started but is still far from its peak, with predictions that the number could reach 20 million in SSA in the next decade. Rural areas are now suffering almost as much as urban areas, and maybe even more, from the orphan crisis as many orphaned urban children are returned to rural homes.

Prevalence of HIV and AIDS varies widely across countries of SSA for reasons that are still poorly understood (Figure 39). Four countries in SSA have prevalence rates above 20%, another seven have prevalence rates between 10% and 20%, seven have rates between 5% and 10%, and 26 have rates below 5%. The nine countries of Southern Africa and the Central African Republic will experience the biggest demographic impact. Deaths are concentrated among prime-age adults. Therefore, the impact on the age structure of these countries is very adverse (Figure 40). In 10 years, Southern Africa went from having one third to two thirds of annual deaths in the working-age population. It is unclear whether fertility will increase or decrease, but age-dependency rates will increase and thus reduce economic growth rates.

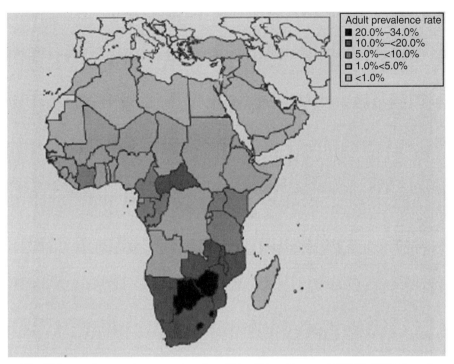

Figure 39 HIV prevalence rates vary sharply within Africa. Source: UNAIDS, 2006 Report on the Global AIDS Epidemic.

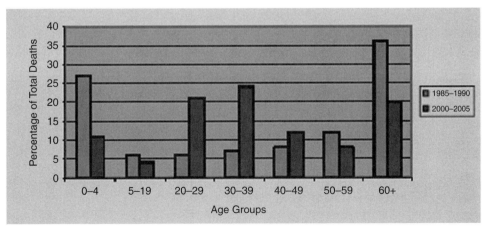

Figure 40 Age distribution of deaths in Southern Africa, 1985–2005. Source: World Bank, World Development Indicators (2006).

In this section we will not further review the evidence of the economic impact of HIV/AIDS in general but instead focus on the various interactions among HIV/AIDS, food and nutrition, and agriculture. We summarize the findings from a literature review by Binswanger (2006).

Nutrition status, the risk of HIV infection, and survival rates after infection   A significant body of indirect biomedical evidence suggests that poor nutrition and parasitic infections should make a person more vulnerable to HIV infection, but major epidemiological studies cast doubt on this conventional wisdom. In multidisciplinary surveys across cities, the factors that determined differences in prevalence rates included circumcision; the prevalence of SIV-1 (herpes simplex); being married, having been married, or marrying early (all increasing prevalence); and for men, being employed. Across villages what counted was the level of economic activity and proximity of the rural communities to cities. Individual income did not figure as a major determinant, which suggests that food intake and nutrition are not major determinant of differences in prevalence rates.

In longitudinal studies in SSA, the median survival rate after HIV infection was estimated at between eight and nine years in the absence of antiretroviral treatment. These survival rates are only about 20% lower than the survival rates in OECD countries before the advent of powerful antiretroviral therapy (ART). Just the differences in background mortality and in the prevalence of infectious diseases and parasites are likely to account for the measured difference in survival rates, leaving little room for food intake and nutrition to be important determinants. Clearly, therefore, ART, not food and nutrition interventions, is the only way that survival rates can be significantly increased.

The impact of AIDS on agriculture, food, and nutrition   Although the main welfare loss associated with AIDS is the loss of life of the person affected, the economic literature is primarily concerned with the welfare impacts on surviving family members, orphans, communities, and countries. Mahter et al. (2005) concluded that AIDS will result in a roughly constant number of working-age adults. Many affected agricultural households quickly recruit new adults, and the agricultural labor shortages are likely to induce urban/rural labor migration. Therefore, for poorer smallhold households, land is likely to remain the primary constraint on income growth. HIV/AIDS is likely to progressively decapitalize highly affected rural communities, and increasing scarcity of capital (savings, cattle, draft animals) could come to pose the greatest limit on rural productivity and livelihoods. IFAD's focus on all the assets of the rural poor is therefore as applicable to households that have experienced a death, from HIV or any other cause, as to any other household affected by a negative shock.

Orphans usually face serious psychosocial consequences of the loss of one or both of their parents. The consequences for their food intake and nutrition, their growth, and their school attendance depend on the households within which they are placed.

Extended families are most likely to choose better-off members as the fostering parents. As a consequence, studies have shown that orphan-fostering households are not necessarily the poorest and most vulnerable ones. Rivers et al. (2005) showed that orphaned children, regardless of the way they were defined, were not consistently more malnourished than nonorphaned children. On the other hand, households with more than one orphan reported significantly more food insecurity and hunger than households with no or only one orphan.

The longitudinal data set in Kenya (Yamano and Jayne, 2004) shows that the death of an adult male household head is associated with a larger negative impact on household crop production, nonfarmer income, and crop production than any other kind of adult death. In addition, the Kenya data show that the impact of adult mortality on household welfare is more severe for households in the lower half of the per capita income distribution.

Interventions against HIV/AIDS in rural areas   We have seen that agricultural and food and nutrition interventions are not likely to be powerful interventions against the spread of the disease or the progression of an infected individual from infection to death. Instead, direct prevention and intervention are required, as is making ART widely available in rural areas. On the other hand, agricultural, food, and nutrition interventions are likely to be important in mitigating the impact of the disease on affected households, especially those with more than one orphan, households headed by women and grandmothers, and children-headed households. Better and more food could also help the adherence of patients to ART.

A major difficulty for HIV/AIDS interventions in rural areas is that in each of the areas of prevention, care and treatment, and mitigation, a number of activities are required. This means that intervention programs are complex and involve several sectors and actors. Where interventions must become available to all populations, service delivery approaches relying on specialized government implementing agencies or NGOs, which each focus on a one or a small subset of components of the required interventions, will not be scalable in rural areas. The main reasons for this are that (1) delivering a multiplicity of services via specialized providers in separate programs would lead to very high overhead and transport costs, and (2) in widely dispersed rural areas, holistic, multisector interventions can be coordinated only at local levels and implemented by communities themselves, supported by local actors, as we have learned over time through our integrated rural development programs.

- *Prevention.* If people can be convinced to change their behaviors and abstain from sex, be faithful, or use condoms, they will be protected from infection. This is so regardless of the factors determining prevalence in any given environment and regardless of the fact that it is not differences in behavior that determine prevalence rates. In rural areas of Africa, interventions require not only interpersonal communication but participatory involvement of whole communities, such as the model of

TANESA, which was scaled up to all villages in an entire district. Therefore, all rural development interventions should be designed to contribute to mainstreaming HIV and AIDS prevention efforts. This does not necessarily have to be a costly effort, since the operations already strengthen community institutions that can be entrusted with the task. Mainstreaming HIV and AIDS prevention certainly should receive emphasis equal to other mainstreamed agendas, such as improving gender relations and the management of natural resources.

- *Treatment.* The WHO guidelines for HIV/AIDS treatment, including ART (WHO, 2004), have been designed in such a way that a nurse in a rural health post, without laboratory equipment, can use syndromic management (i.e., diagnosis based solely on observable symptoms) to diagnose advanced HIV disease and prescribe a standard first-line treatment to adults. The WHO guidelines recommend the strong involvement of communities in the provision of the other components, such as training in healthy living and survival skills, provision of food and nutrition, and adherence support.

- *Care and support.* Care and support involve psychosocial support, health care, home-based care, education, food and nutrition interventions, and livelihood support. The consensus of the literature is that care and support should take a holistic approach to the needs of affected families and individuals rather than dealing with sector-specific interventions one at a time. However, very few holistic and community-based care and support initiatives have been scaled up beyond the level of small boutiques. We have seen that HIV/AIDS impacts are highly differentiated according to who is sick or dies in a family, how well off the household was before experiencing an HIV/AIDS impact, and how large and well off its extended family network. Therefore, only a fraction of the affected households and individuals need care and support interventions from the outside. A better way to provide care and support in a holistic and multisectoral way in rural areas would therefore be to design and financially support more general social safety nets on all highly vulnerable households and individuals, irrespective of the source of their vulnerability.

The high prevalence of AIDS stigma means that it is rarely possible to provide care and support interventions only to families and individuals affected by HIV/AIDS. And why would one want to direct support only to families who have chronically ill HIV/AIDS patients, rather than all families with chronically ill patients, or only HIV/AIDS orphans, rather than all orphans? Care and support to HIV/AIDS orphans should therefore be approached within broad, community-driven social protection programs.

8.3 Agro-climate, biophysical resources, and natural resources management

At the global level there is increasing competition for land and water. Global population passed 6 billion in 1999 and will likely approach 9 billion by 2050. This will put increased pressure on two nonrenewable resources critical to agriculture: land and water. Feeding 9 billion people might be doable on the same land area through productivity improvements, but it will surely require more water. However, additional population increases competition for land in many ways: space for housing, recreation, infrastructure, and waste disposal. Similarly, more people, most living in urban settings, will demand more water and will produce more liquid and solid waste. Intensification of agriculture can cause water pollution, erosion, and salinization. We might understand these pressures individually, but the collective regional and global impacts receive less attention.

Water, for example, is essential for life, but who ensures all people have access? Developing and managing water supplies costs money, but some people see access to water as a right, and we know people overuse a free good. In both developed and developing countries, water use in agriculture is often highly wasteful, a consequence of past subsidies for the development of irrigation and low water and electricity tariffs. Powerful vested interests defend these privileges. As a consequence, improved water-use efficiency, so necessary for managing the competition for water, is rarely achieved. If these issues are not addressed in the rest of the world, Africa could once more be hit with rising food prices on account of increasing global water "scarcity."

Africa is the world's oldest and most enduring land mass, containing 22% of the earth's land surface (Reader, p. 9). It was characterized by the InterAcademy Council's path-breaking study, *Realizing the Promise and Potential of African Agriculture* (2005), as having a "dominance of weathered soils of poor inherent fertility; predominance of rain-fed agriculture, little irrigation, and very limited mechanization; and heterogeneity and diversity of farming systems." Thus the natural endowments of the continent deserve careful attention.

In this section we address issues of land, water, forest, and fisheries.

8.3.1 Africa's land resource

Of Africa's most valuable resource, the *2007 African Development Report* said it best: "Land is a critical natural resource in Africa and the basis of survival for the majority of Africans. ... If sustainably managed, the African landscape, a rich and dynamic mosaic of resources, holds vast opportunities for the development of human well being" (p. xvi). Yet it is frequently argued that this valuable resource is being severely degraded. Land degradations caused by nutrient depletion, soil erosion, salinization, pollution, overgrazing, and deforestation are clearly major issues in African agriculture. Many observers are of the view that low and declining soil fertility is a critical problem in Africa. The InterAcademy study says: "Depletion of soil fertility is a major biophysical cause of low per capita food production in Africa .... Small holders have removed large quantities of nutrients from their soils without applying sufficient quantities of manure or fertilizers to replenish the soil" (InterAcademy Council, p. 47). The World Bank IEG Review agrees, using different references: "Low soil fertility is a major contributor to the low productivity of African production systems ... Only 6 percent of the land in the Region has high agricultural potential" (p. 14). The new Gates/Rockefeller Foundations initiative, Alliance for a Green Revolution for Africa (AGRA), has identified soil health as one of its priority program areas.

However, it is troubling that most of the evidence is anecdotal, based on local soil surveys and multitudes of plot studies (Stocking, 1996). As far as we can determine, there has never been a comprehensive soil survey for most of Africa and, beyond soil vulnerability maps, there are no current or historical soil degradation maps. Fortunately, the Global Environmental Facility has recently funded a global Land Degradation Assessment for Drylands (LADA) that is executed by FAO, UNEP, and a number of collaborating institutions. It is based on worldwide satellite measurement of vegetation covers in 8 km × 8 km grids with national and local follow-up. The local follow-up focuses both on hotspots, that is, the areas with the most land degradation, as well as bright spots, where degradation has been reversed. It appears that globally and in most places, vegetation cover has increased over the past 25 years, except in a number of hotspots, such as the former homelands of South Africa (personal communication, Freddy Nachtergaele). A full analysis of the results has not yet been published, however.

Neither higher population nor poverty necessarily leads to land degradation.[11] In the transition from long-fallow systems to permanent agriculture, soil fertility declines and farmers eventually have to introduce new techniques to stem and reverse this decline. This they tend to do during the evolution of the farming system to higher land-use intensity, as discussed so well by Ester Boserup (1965) and Hans Ruthenberg (1973). Their theories are consistent with an increasing number of studies that have shown that the normal processes of land improvement associated with agricultural intensification are taking place in many countries (Pingali, Bigot, and Binswanger, 1987; Tiffen, Mortimore, and Gichuki, 1994). Significant cases of soil degradation, on the other hand, are usually associated with open access regimes, insecurity of tenure, and other policy failure, which implies that the normal investment responses of individuals are impeded and the necessary soil investments are not made (Heath and Binswanger, 1996).

Clearly, the alarmist view that in many parts of the developing world, land is being rapidly and irreversibly degraded might be exaggerated. Thirty years ago a World Bank sector report estimated that land losses in Burkina Faso amounted to something like 2% of GDP per year. Today the land supports nearly twice the population as in 1980, and Kabore and Reij (2004) have documented how this was achieved. The change is visible to the naked eye: On a recent visit crops looked greener and healthier than the visitor had ever seen them before, crop livestock integration had happened in many locations, degraded arid lands were being recuperated via traditional and new techniques, a number of new crop varieties had been introduced, and there were more trees on the land.

This does not mean that desertification and soil erosion are not problems worthy of attention, only that we can be more optimistic than the usual rhetoric implies. Indeed, the World Bank, in its *News & Broadcast* of November 7, 2007, article, "Desertification and Land Degradation Threaten Africa's Livelihoods," defines the issues and describes what action it is taking:

> **Desertification is a very severe form of land degradation, involving the steady but gradual loss of agricultural productivity and distinct decline of ecological health. The phenomenon matters for Africa's environmental future, more so for the brake it puts on economic activities directly tied to healthy ecosystems. Take the case of farming. Desertification, drought and lately, climate change are all adversely impacting farming, threatening the principal source of livelihood—and exports—for millions of poor people. To tackle the problem of land degradation more forcefully in Sub-Saharan Africa, in 2005 the World Bank and its partners, including the New Partnership for Africa's Development (NEPAD), launched the TerrAfrica initiative tasked with promoting sustainable land management practices by mobilizing coalitions, knowledge, and scale up financing.**

Global attempts at dealing with the issues of desertification and the related issue of biodiversity loss are handled in various international accords, including the Conventions on Desertification and Biodiversity.

Climate change, desertification, and biodiversity losses really come together in the local government arena, in communities, and on farms, requiring management and adjustment capacities. Conventions in all three areas provide financing opportunities. These also require capacities to harvest the funds at the level of producers, local and national governments, and subregional organizations and therefore provide capacity development opportunities for many development agencies.

8.3.2 Water resource issues

Water is crucial to Africa's development but it is becoming increasingly scarce. To quote the *Africa Development Report, 2007*:

> **Available statistics reveal that nine African countries already face "water scarcity" on a national scale (less than 1,00m3 of water per person annually), eight countries face "water stress" (less than 1,700m3), while at least another six countries are likely to join the list in the coming decades. More than 300 million people in Africa still lack access to safe water and adequate sanitation. The majority of these people are in sub-Saharan Africa, where only 51% of the population has access to safe water and 45% to sanitation. By 2025, almost 50% of Africans will be living in an area of water scarcity or water stress. (p. 12)**

Although in the aggregate Africa would seem well endowed with water, having 17 major rivers and 160 lakes, the distribution of these endowments spatially and temporally is very uneven. For example, the Congo River basin, which receives over 35% of annual African rainfall, is home to just 10% of Africa's population. This means that in some areas (North Africa and Southern Africa) there is high dependence on groundwater; in others, major rivers routinely dry up for several months a year. Further, the major rivers cross several national boundaries, making water development more complicated. Despite limited irrigation development, agriculture is responsible for 86% of water withdrawals. Given Africa's still rapid population growth and an expected increase in urbanization, water is sure to become a larger regional issue. This is compounded by the fact that the many small countries in Africa cannot go it alone on water issues. (For interested readers, the *2007 Development Report* contains more detailed analysis of African water issues.)

The InterAcademy Council Report provides further useful analysis: "The vast majority of farming systems in Africa are rain-fed and only a small area is irrigated. The possibilities for full and supplementary irrigation are limited. In 1995, 96% of cereals in sub-Saharan Africa were sown in rain-fed agricultural systems" (p. 46–47). Further:

> **The implication of water scarcity for much of Africa, especially in semi-arid farming systems, is that more water-efficient farm management systems will be needed. They will incorporate drought-tolerant varieties, choose species with higher water use efficiencies, and use crop and simulation modeling for increased water use efficiency, but they still will not be sufficient. Countries will need to devote more resources to increasing the supply of water. ... Most of the additional investment should not be in classic large-scale irrigation systems. There is considerable potential for capturing rainfall through improved soil surface management practices, small water harvesting systems and small-scale irrigation systems, enabling intensification of farming and crop diversification in inland valleys, and in upland systems using supplementary irrigation of high-value rain-fed crops. (p. 51)**

8.3.3 Irrigation and drainage

The Green Revolution has shown the importance of water control in making high levels of input use profitable. In India the new varieties and higher input use spread first to those areas with the best water control in the northwest and south, and moved east and to the center later, partly as a consequence of farmer investment in irrigation and drainage and partly because research made high-yielding varieties available for dry-land crops. Sub-Saharan Africa is lagging badly in irrigation and drainage: Less than 7% of crop area in SSA is irrigated, compared to 33% in Asia (Gelb et al., 2000). Large-scale irrigation has suffered from unaffordable costs and centralized bureaucratic institutions. Although models for changing these institutions into autonomous entities partially or fully controlled by the farmers have been successful in some countries such as Mexico or the Office du Niger, this approach has not yet been replicated in many countries, and therefore even rehabilitation is often not yet a viable option. Small-scale irrigation is a more promising option, but investments are constrained by low profitability of agriculture and therefore low investment capacities of the farmers. Thus future development of irrigation capacity will need to be carefully planned in the context of increasing competition for water.

8.3.4 Forests

Forests cover 22% of Africa's land area, and African forests make up 17% of global forest cover. In contrast, extreme desert covers 43% of Africa's land area. African forests range from open savannahs to closed tropical rainforests. FAO (2006) produces an assessment of the world's forests every 5–10 years. Based on figures and assessments, FAO concluded that the situation at the global level had remained relatively stable, but the trend for Africa was of particular concern. There appears to have been very limited progress toward sustainable forest management. Although there were some positive indicators that the net loss had slowed, overall the continued rapid loss of total forest area (4 million ha annually) is "disconcerting." The ADB's *African Development Report 2007* concludes that "... deforestation, forest degradation, and the associated loss of forest products and environmental services are serious challenges facing African countries. The size of natural forests and woodlands in Africa has been drastically reduced over the last century" (p. 25). Degradation not only reduces economic returns from forest products but also contributes to losses of biodiversity, increases the rate of erosion, reduces water quality, and increases the risks of flooding in surrounding areas. Though the particular issues pertaining to forests are very different among regions in Africa, there is obviously a strong need for all development programs to be sensitive to potential impacts on forest resources. This would include expanded forested areas brought under agricultural production. Again, as with water, transboundary issues are very significant. (For more detail on forestry issues, the reader should refer to the *2007 African Development Report*.)

8.3.5 Fisheries

Africa is a marginal and declining player in the world fish scene. Worldwide production in 2005 was 141.6 million tonnes: 84.2 marine capture, 9.6 inland capture, and 47.8 million tonnes of aquaculture production. Africa's total production was just less than 8 million tonnes (5.6% of global): 4.8 from marine capture (5.7% of global), 2.5 tonnes inland capture (26% of global), and 0.7 tonnes from aquaculture (1% of global). Two countries, Egypt (82%) and Nigeria (8.6%), account for over 90% of aquaculture production. Globally overall production is growing almost exclusively, from growth in aquaculture output, which increased from 35.5 million tonnes in 2000 to 47.8 million tonnes in 2005, while capture tonnage declined slightly. African production was basically stagnant (FAO-SOFIA, 2006).

Per capita fish consumption in Africa is less than the global average per capita availability and is declining. In 2004, per capita global availability was 16.6 kg/cap, whereas Africa consumption in 2003 was 7.6 kg/cap, down from 9.9 kg/cap in 1982.

Despite Africa's small role globally, fish are important as both a source of income for fisherpersons and as a source of protein. NEPAD convened a "FISH for ALL" summit in 2005 that approved an action plan. NEPAD's analysis in advance of the summit is instructive, and we quote at length here:

> African fisheries and aquaculture are at a turning point. The fish sector makes vital contributions to food and nutrition security of 200 million Africans and provides income for over 10 million engaged in fish production, processing and trade. Moreover, fish has become a leading export commodity for Africa, with an annual export value of US$2.7 billion. Yet these benefits are at risk as the exploitation of natural fish stocks is reaching their limits and aquaculture production has not yet fulfilled its potential. (NEPAD, 2005, p. 4)

A growing part of the trade value is highly valued fresh Nile perch exports to Europe from Uganda and Kenya.

> Strategic investments are needed urgently to safeguard the future contribution of Africa's fish sector to poverty alleviation and regional economic development. Broadly, investment is needed: (i) to improve the management of natural fish stocks; (ii) to develop aquaculture production; and (iii) to enhance fish trade in domestic, regional and global markets. In support of this investment, capacity needs to be strengthened at regional and national levels for research, technology transfer and policy development.
>
> As a first step, stakeholders in the region need to build a common and strategic understanding of the importance of fisheries and aquaculture for Africa's development and the challenges being faced by the sector. (ibid. p. 4)
>
> Africa currently produces 7.31 million t of fish each year. Of these, 4.81 million t come from marine fisheries, and 2.5 million t from inland fisheries. While capture fisheries rose steadily throughout the 1980s and 1990s, they have stagnated since then, reaching about 6.85 million t in 2002. Aquaculture on the other hand has risen, but slowly, and only in Egypt has growth achieved rates of increase seen in other parts of the world, rising from 85,000 t in 1997 to over 400,000 t in 2004. These trends combined with population growth mean that per capita consumption of fish in Africa is low and stagnating, and in sub-Saharan Africa specifically per capita consumption has fallen in the past 20 years. In a recent study by the International Food Policy Research Institute (IFPRI) and the WorldFish Center analysis of future demand and supply of fish suggested that if per capita consumption is to be maintained at present levels up to the year 2020, capture fisheries will need to be sustained and where possible enhanced, and aquaculture developed rapidly, with an increase of over 260% in sub-Saharan Africa alone over the course of the next 15 years. (ibid, p. 5)

Current concerns revolve around three sets of issues. The first is the continuing decline of coastal fisheries, alleged to be caused by foreign fishing fleets and the consequent impacts on the income of traditional artisanal fishers. Two recent news releases highlight the issue in rather stark terms. The Institute for Security Studies' October 2, 2007, release defines the issue in its title: "The Crisis of Marine Plunder in Africa." The Gristmill blog's headline of July 18, 2007, is "West African fisheries being destroyed."

The second set of issues is improved management of inland capture fisheries, which are comparatively more important in Africa. The third set of issues is to rapidly expand aquacultural production. The NEPAD plan of action lays out an ambitious set of investment proposals. Progress to date appears to be mainly on the side of capacity building and research (NEPAD, October 2007).

All these natural resource management issues—land, water, forest, and fisheries— are highly interdependent and will become more so with increased population pressure and rapid urbanization. The challenges are to find ways to incorporate sustainable NRM into programs of growth and poverty reduction.

We close this section with brief discussions of two issues that are frequently raised as strategic issues.

8.3.6 Are poor natural conditions a constraint to agricultural growth and commercialization in Africa?

Some of the past successes in commercialization in sub-Saharan Africa depended on agro-ecological conditions that were "ideal" for cocoa, tea, coffee, sugar, and some other commodities. In some of these (e.g., tea and coffee), the market pays high-quality differentials and the desired quality attributes can only be obtained where particular growing requirements are fulfilled. Therefore, the global players (either traders or processors) have to access supplies from certain African countries to be able to satisfy their customers. Success in these commodities has therefore taken place despite the fact that many of the best regions were landlocked and remote. On the other hand, ideal agricultural conditions are not sufficient for success, shown by the example of the slow-growing Zambian sugar sector, which enjoys some of the best growing conditions in the world. There is a major sugar factory in Zambia, but it has been unable to export sugar except into the protected European market. Other success stories in Africa, such as cotton and cassava in West Africa, occurred under favorable, but not ideal, climatic and soil conditions. These successes depend on highly labor-intensive production processes that are difficult to mechanize and therefore benefit from low labor cost in Africa (Poulton et al., 2007). Beyond Africa, as discussed in Box 1, agricultural success was achieved in a spectacular manner in landlocked areas of at best moderate agro-climatic potential in the Cerrado of Brazil and in Northeast Thailand.

8.3.7 Marginal versus favored areas

With the accumulation of more experience and knowledge, the debate about this topic has come to the conclusion that this could be a false dichotomy. Investments in both areas are necessary, and both pay under many circumstances. The WDR defines less favored areas as ones constrained by poor market access and/or limited by rainfall. Using mapping overlays of both factors, the WDR attempts to define where these areas exist (WDR, pp. 55–57). The WDR (2008) clearly lays out possible strategies for less favored areas, arguing that public policy interventions to reduce poverty and preserve

Box 1   Success is possible in landlocked areas where agricultural conditions are far from ideal

Decades of disappointing growth, continuing erosion of the competitiveness of traditional export crops, and increasing reliance on food imports have led many to conclude that African agriculture is condemned to perpetual stagnation. Yet over the same period, two landlocked agricultural regions in the developing world have developed at a rapid pace and conquered important world markets: Northeastern Thailand and the Cerrado region of Brazil. Northeastern Thailand is characterized by relatively abundant but highly unreliable rainfall, combined with poor soils and a high population density. The Cerrado, in contrast, is characterized by its remoteness, problematic soils prone to acidification and toxicities, and low population density. The paths along which commercial agriculture developed were very different in the two regions. In Northeast Thailand, smallhold production systems dominate; export success was led by cassava chips, soybeans, and sugar. In the Cerrado, large-scale mechanized production systems dominate; Brazil became a world export leader in soybeans, sugar, and cotton.

The success achieved by Thailand and Brazil suggests that the pessimism found in Africa today could be exaggerated. A major study carried out by FAO in 2001 identified the vast Guinea savannah zone as one of the zones in Africa with the highest potential for agricultural development. The Guinea savannah shares a number of similarities with Northeast Thailand and the Brazilian Cerrado. The cereal/root crop mixed farming system of the Guinea savannah zone extends from Guinea through Northern Côte d'Ivoire to Ghana, Togo, Benin, and the midbelt states of Nigeria to Northern Cameroon and into the Sudan; there is a similar zone in Central and Southern Africa, in Angola, Southern Zambia, and Mozambique. It accounts for 13% of the agricultural area of Africa and 18% of the cultivated area and supports 15% of the region's agricultural population. It is about four times as large as the immense Cerrado area of Brazil. Onchocerciasis, or river blindness, control efforts have freed up an estimated 25 million ha of cultivated land for agricultural development. However, in some areas tsetse-transmitted African animal trypanosomosis is still a significant constraint. A number of characteristics set this zone apart from other farming systems, namely low altitude, high temperatures, low population density, abundant cultivated land, high livestock numbers per household, the presence of a tsetse challenge in some areas, and poorer transport and communications infrastructure. Crops include maize and sorghum, millet in the drier parts, cotton, cassava, soybeans, and cowpeas; yams near the border of the root crop zone; and wetland rice in parts of the river plains and valley areas. The main source of vulnerability is drought. Agricultural growth prospects are excellent, and this system could become the bread basket of Africa and an important source of export earnings (FAO, 2001).

While the Cerrado in Brazil and Northeast Thailand share important agro-climatic features with the Guinea savannah of Africa, significant differences exist in terms of history, culture, social systems, political structures, and institutions that make it unlikely that any development model, however successful, can be gained. This is what the large-scale study of the World Bank, entitled *Towards Competitive Commercial Agriculture in Africa* (CCAA study, forthcoming), has attempted to do. In addition to Northeast Thailand and the Cerrado of Brazil, it studied the history of commercial agriculture in Africa (Poulter et al., 2007) that was previously cited, as well as conditions and the history of commercialization in Nigeria, Mozambique, and Thailand. It used a comparative value chain methodology to quantify the relative international competitiveness of cassava, rice, soybeans, soybean oil, seed cotton, cotton lint, granulated sugar, maize, and beef cattle across the five countries and quantified the bottlenecks to international competitiveness in Africa. The findings of the study are referred to in the relevant sections of this chapter.

Source: World Bank (2009).

the environment are warranted in many of these regions. Despite past arguments that these investments don't pay, there is now analysis to support the conclusion that "... public investments in roads, education, irrigation, and some types of research and development can produce competitive rates of return" (Fan and Hazell, 2001) and "positive outcomes for poverty and the environment in less favored areas" (WDR, 2007, p. 192). The strategies recommended are "... based on two key interventions: (1) improving technologies for sustainable management of land, water, and biodiversity resources and (2) putting local communities in the driver's seat to manage natural resources" (ibid., p. 193).

Absolute numbers of people living in marginal areas do not decline until a very advanced stage of urbanization is reached. Outmigration is not a solution to the marginal areas problems. What is needed is to harness all economic opportunities. If they have been relatively neglected, as in India, rates of returns to investments could be as good as in better-endowed areas. For example, Ethiopia still has a huge backlog in small-scale irrigation.

Nevertheless, a development approach to these areas has to empower the local populations with the authority and sufficient fiscal resources to provide the necessary human development and social services so that new generations have the needed human capital if they choose to migrate. Those who choose to stay behind can then combine remittances and social assistance with locally earned income for a decent living standard. As Foster and Rosenzweig (2003) have shown, such areas may also be able to attract some industrialization based on their lower labor costs.[12]

8.3.8 The future of small farmers

Recently there have been many media reports about the scramble for agricultural land in Africa that was first triggered by the biofuels boom and later stimulated even further by the global food price explosion. Investor interest is driven mainly by biofuels speculators (Cotula, Dyer, and Vermeulen, 2008) and by the desire to invest in land for food production (*Grain Briefing*, 2008). The debate over the relative advantages and disadvantages in Africa of large-scale versus small-scale farming models has been further stimulated by leading development economist Paul Collier (2008). Information and analysis presented at the World Bank (2009) make it clear that there is enormous potential for competitive commercial agriculture in Africa and that the more favorable prices expected to prevail over the longer term are likely to make investments in African agriculture even more attractive in future. What is not clear, however, is whether the large-scale farm models contemplated for such investments have been fully thought through.

Past experience is not very encouraging. For decades, empirical data from all over the world have consistently shown that large farms dependent on hired managers and workers are less productive and less profitable (per hectare) than small farms managed by families and operated primarily with family labor. The results were presented by the World Bank (2009). What this means is that farm-level agricultural production (primary production) is normally subject to diseconomies of scale. This finding is admittedly counterintuitive: One would assume there are scale economies associated with use of large machines, better access to capital and credit, increased power to negotiate favorable prices for inputs and outputs, stronger incentives to stay abreast of rapid technical change, and the ability to self-provide infrastructure and services.

Probably because the finding is so counterintuitive, an enormous amount of work has focused on examining the decreasing scale economies in agriculture and exposing the reasons for the relative efficiency of the family farm. (For a summary of the literature, see Binswanger et al., 1995.) The theoretical literature shows that the main source of the superior productive efficiency of small farms derives from the greater incentives felt by family labor to work hard. In addition, the heterogeneity of land quality, even within small farms, and the fact that production occurs under highly variable weather conditions put a premium on close management and supervision of farm operations by family members, who have a strong incentive to maximize returns. The productivity advantage is therefore not so much associated with smaller farm size per se but with the incentives felt by management and labor. The recurring empirical finding that primary agricultural production is usually characterized by decreasing economies of scale shows that the advantage conferred by these greater incentives are, in practice, rarely offset by the lower information, financing, and marketing costs and other advantages typically enjoyed by larger-scale operations.

Exceptions to the lack of economies of scale arise in the so called "plantation crops," such as sugar, oil palm, tea, or bananas, and horticultural crops grown for export. After harvest, these crops need to be processed very quickly and/or transferred to a cold storage facility; otherwise they experience rapid declines in quality and hence value. Assuming the farm operations of planting and harvesting can be successfully coordinated with the off-farm operations of processing and shipping, the economies of scale associated with the processing and/or shipping of these crops are transmitted to the farm level (Binswanger and Rosenzweig, 1986). The coordination problem associated with plantation crops is typically solved using one of three organizational models: (1) production takes place on a large-scale farm or plantation over which the processing firm has direct control, (2) production is assured by small-scale family farmers working under contract with the processor; or (3) production is assured by a mix of the two farm types, usually constituted as a nucleus estate surrounded by family farmers. In Thailand, the contract farming model is universally practiced for plantation crops. The economies of scale that can be realized through the use of agricultural machinery are realized in Thailand and in many other parts of the developing world through the use of contract hire services for machinery. In Thailand and elsewhere, access to information and credit is provided by specialized institutions that cater to smallholds, and infrastructure is provided by the public sector. All three modes of organization also can be found in African sugar, oil palm, and tea production.

Some proponents of large-scale farming model have argued that even if large-scale farming is not more productive, it is easier to introduce and easier to scale up rapidly, making it more suitable for jump-starting agricultural growth. This argument is not supported by empirical evidence, however. Over the past 15 years and more, rapid growth in agriculture has not been positively correlated with large-scale farming models. Over this period, Brazil's agricultural growth rate of about 4% has been exceeded by China, Vietnam, and no fewer than eight sub-Saharan African countries (Angola, Benin, Burkina Faso, Côte d'Ivoire, Ghana, Liberia, Mozambique, and Nigeria), all of which feature agricultural sectors dominated by small-scale farming (Wiggins, 2008).

Yet if large-scale agriculture is less efficient, why are there such apparently successful large-scale farming sectors in eastern and southern Africa and in other parts of the developing world, most notably Latin America? Should small-scale family operations not have driven the large operations out of business, thanks to their greater productive efficiency? Binswanger et al. (1995) showed that the early spread of commercial agriculture in Latin America and in the settler economies of South Africa, Kenya, and Zimbabwe involved the systematic appropriation of high-quality land by settlers, combined with displacement of indigenous populations to areas with typically lower soil fertility and locational disadvantages. To further undermine the competition from indigenous farmers, smallholders were often prohibited from producing cash crops or excluded from marketing cash crops via monopolistic marketing boards. In addition, public infrastructure, research and extension services, and subsidized credit were focused on the large-scale farms. Finally, to help the large-scale farms attract labor, taxes were imposed on the indigenous population, which, in the absence of a commercial crop, they could pay only by selling their labor to the large-scale farms as workers or tenants. It was only thanks to discriminatory rules of the game that conferred settler farms with extreme privileges that the large-scale commercial farms of Africa and Latin America were able to prosper.

The paper on the experience of the Commonwealth Development Corporation (CDC) shows a 50-year history of support to the introduction of large-scale farming all over Africa. Of all the ventures studied, about one-half failed outright—for technical reasons, economic reasons, or both. Not surprisingly, most of the successes involved plantation crops (including timber and wood products). Some of the successful ventures used the contract farming or nucleus estate models. The CDC considered food crop production to be better done by the smallhold sector and only rarely ventured into food crops, recording a few rare successes and many failures. No large-scale venture supported by the CDC ever managed to achieve export competitiveness in food crops. High costs of machinery and high overhead costs associated with expatriate management were usually the main obstacles. The only large-scale farming ventures that have ever managed to produce food crops for export have been the large-scale commercial farms that were created with extremely high levels of state support under colonialism or apartheid.

However, previous chapters described how agricultural production and marketing conditions are changing rapidly, often in ways that apparently provide advantages to larger-scale operations. Examples of where these changing conditions are encouraging the emergence of large-scale farming are beginning to appear in Africa. Maertens and Swinnen (2006), Maertens (2008), and Tyler (2008) describe how tightening phytosanitary requirements have caused production for export of fruits and vegetables to shift toward larger farms in Senegal and Kenya. Another example of successful large-scale commercial farming in Africa involves irrigated production of sugar (Tyler, 2008b). In contrast, rain-fed sugar production continues to be dominated by smallholders, who often work under contract to a centralized processing facility. The higher incomes associated with these crops have significantly reduced poverty in surrounding communities. However, these success stories represent special cases of highly perishable products produced for export into markets characterized by very demanding quality standards or that have to be processed quickly in a large sugar factory. They therefore fit the case of "plantation crops" discussed earlier.

If past experience with large-scale commercial agriculture in Africa has been mixed, the same can be said for small-scale commercial agriculture (Poulten et al., 2007). Clearly, there have been some unequivocal success stories, cases in which growth in smallhold agriculture has generated important economic and social benefits and has served as a powerful source of poverty reduction. Some of the best-known examples have been in the cotton production systems of Francophone West Africa (Grimm and Gunther, 2004; Tefft et al., 1997).

Experience from throughout the world suggests that the development of smallhold-led commercial agriculture is much more likely to succeed when smallhold farmers have ready access to technology, inputs (including credit), market information, and marketing services. Under contract farming, some of these services are provided by the contractor, and their costs are privately financed. In the absence of contract farming, they have to be financed partly or entirely by the state, either at the national level or at the local level. Many different models exist for the provision of these services: via farmer's organizations, NGOs, private sector providers contracted by government, or government services of local or national governments.

Based on this review, there is little to suggest that the large-scale farming model is either necessary or even particularly promising for Africa. The argument in favor of large-scale agriculture is further undermined by the finding of this study that the most promising markets for Africa's farmers are domestic and regional markets for basic food crops and livestock products, which do not fall into the category of plantation crops.

That large-scale farming is in most cases unlikely to be the most appropriate avenue for the commercialization of African agriculture does not mean that there are not important investment opportunities awaiting in the sector. However, for the foreseeable future, the main opportunities for private investors, domestic or foreign, will remain in seed development, input supply, marketing, and processing. At the same time, many opportunities exist for engaging family farmers in agribusiness ventures through contract farming arrangements or via organizations of small farmers. For this reason, the future of smallhold production remains bright.

Hazell et al. (2007) make a very good case for policy support for small farmers:

In conclusion, the case for smallholder development as one of the main ways to reduce poverty remains compelling. The policy agenda, however, has changed. The challenge is to improve the workings of markets for outputs, inputs, and financial services to overcome market failures. Meeting this challenge calls for innovations in institutions, joint work between farmers, private companies, and NGOs, and for a new, more facilitating role for ministries of agriculture and other public agencies. New thinking on the role of the state in agricultural development, wider changes in democratization, decentralization, and participatory policy processes, and a renewed interest in agriculture among major international donors do present opportunities for greater support to small-farm development. But unless key policymakers adopt a more assertive agenda toward small-farm agriculture, there is a growing risk that rural poverty could increase dramatically and waves of migrants to urban areas could overwhelm available job opportunities, urban infrastructure, and support services. (p. 32)

8.3.9 Enhancing agricultural profits and rural investment

Once a well-developed institutional environment is in place and except for marginal agricultural areas, rural development can be viewed as primarily a multifaceted agricultural investment issue. Few of the needed investments will occur if agriculture is not profitable. This is obvious for the on-farm investments, but none of the other institutional pillars are in a position to invest unless agriculture and agro-industry are profitable. Unless they can save, communities will not have the means to finance or cofinance their investments. Independent civil society organizations (rather than creations from the outside) must finance a share of their costs from local sources, and these, again, depend directly or indirectly on profits from agriculture and other natural resources. Local governments that do not mobilize part of their own resources tend not to be accountable to their constituencies (Manor, 1999) and instead they will be vulnerable to elite capture. The local tax base in turn depends on agricultural and natural resource profits.

It is sometimes assumed that private agricultural investments can be financed via credit. Unfortunately, as we see in the section on rural finance, SSA provides some of the most inhospitable environments for rural finance in the world: low population density, high and covariant risk, little irrigation. In other regions of the world where rural finance has been more successful, regions with such characteristics have defied rural financial intermediation as well. But even if institutions for rural finance could be built, their success would depend on farmers' borrowing and repayment capacity, both of which depend critically on agricultural profitability. There is therefore no shortcut to capital accumulation in agriculture except via higher profits and ultimately higher savings and investments out of these profits.

It is often assumed that rural nonfarm activities can be an independent engine of growth for rural development. But most rural nonfarm activities produce goods and services that are linked to agriculture via forward, backward, and consumer demand linkages (Hazell and Hagbladde, 1993; World Bank, 1983). Some industrial activities producing for the economy at large sometimes locate in rural areas because of low wages (Foster and Rosenzweig, 2003). But the advantage of lower rural wages is frequently offset by other disadvantages of a rural location. Therefore the potential for rural industrialization is usually overestimated. Agricultural growth, therefore, remains the single most important driver of the rural nonfarm sector.

In areas with limited agricultural potential, investment opportunities will be limited even if the institutional environment is properly developed and agriculture in general is profitable. Although these favorable conditions will enable the limited potential to be fully developed, that is not enough to provide for income growth of the populations of these areas. A development approach to these areas has to empower the local populations with the authority and sufficient fiscal resources to provide the necessary human development and social services so that new generations have the human capital needed if they choose to migrate. Those who choose to stay behind can then combine remittances and social assistance with locally earned income for a decent living standard. As Foster and Rosenzweig (2003) have shown, such areas might also be able to attract some industrialization based on their lower labor costs.[13]

Based on this discussion and the analysis in other sections of this chapter, next we summarize the remaining challenges to improving agricultural incentives.

8.3.10 Protection of importables and subsidies for exportables: Not a good idea!

SSA countries have already altered their own policies and eliminated overall disprotection of the sector (Section 5). However, we have also seen that their incentives are still below those of the other regions of the world, especially OECD countries. It would be tempting for African policymakers to attempt to further improve agricultural incentives by following the example of OECD countries and subsidizing their agricultural exports or restricting imports to protect their producers. However, as shown in Section 5, on average African countries already provide protection to their agricultural importables. Raising these protection levels further would in many instances tax poor consumers and increase poverty, rather than reducing it. In the context of the recent agricultural price boom, it would be more appropriate to lower the protection levels than increase them. Increases in the protection of agricultural importables would also often lead to higher protection levels than for industrial goods and indirectly disprotect them. Subsidizing agricultural exports is constrained by the poverty of the countries and is a very inefficient way of supporting the agricultural sector compared to the use of scarce fiscal resources for infrastructure, technology development, and smallholder services. Furthermore, such subsidies would become contrary to WTO rules if the Doha Round of negotiations succeeds.

8.3.11 Input markets

Access to markets for both inputs and outputs is critical to the commercialization of small-scale African farmers. The WDR (2008) argues that developing efficient input markets is a necessary prerequisite to expanded use of improved seeds and fertilizer. Yet these markets are marked by highly seasonal demand for small quantities that are dispersed over wide geographic areas. Furthermore, farmer demand is subject to change because of rain/climate variability. Finally, as is obvious, rural infrastructure is essential. The WDR shows that domestic port and transport costs make up to 50% of farm-gate fertilizer costs in Nigeria, Malawi, and Zambia compared to slightly over 25% for the United States. Scale economies in fertilizer production are substantial, so for the vast majority of small SSA countries, domestic production is infeasible and, in fact, as noted by the WDR, cost-effective minimum import lots of 25,000 tons are "...considerably above the annual demand in most sub-Saharan African countries" (WDR, 2007, p. 150). Again, this underlines the need for regional approaches.

It also raises the perennial issue of fertilizer subsidies, addressed in detail in the WDR (WDR, Box 6.7, p. 152) with a proposal for what they call "market smart" subsidies targeted at poor farmers to encourage initial use of incremental amounts of fertilizer. They also note that widespread use of fertilizer subsidies is expensive. Zambia spent 37% of its public budget for agriculture in 2004–2005 on its fertilizer support program. Of course, other inputs will become important in the commercialization process as needs for tools, machinery, pest management, and possibly irrigation equipment emerge. A market-oriented agriculture requires access to functioning input markets. The challenge is how to encourage and support their development.

8.3.12 Rural finance

One critical input market is rural finance. The macroeconomic instability that characterized Africa well into the 1990s has resulted in exceptionally high real interest rates. Agriculture is rarely so profitable that it can compete with urban investments in such environments. In addition, rural areas in general, and small farmers in particular, face significant disadvantages in financial markets. Clients are usually small and widely dispersed, and seasonality and covariant risk make financial intermediation difficult (Binswanger and Rosenzweig, 1986). Cooperative institutions have been a success for larger farmers in middle-income countries such as Brazil, but specialized agricultural financial institutions have been a failure all over the world (World Bank, 1996b). The microfinance movement can make a modest contribution, but it has found it difficult to overcome the rural disadvantages and emerge as an important agricultural lender (Gine, 2004).

Successful approaches to improving rural financial intermediation have been focused on savings mobilization, postal systems, and improving access to finance by the rural nonfarm sector, input suppliers, marketing systems, and contract farming (Yaron et al., 1998).

The government of India has forced commercial banks to open rural branches and reserve a proportion of their lending to agriculture and agro-industry. Two separate studies have shown significant impact on agricultural growth and the rural wage (Binswanger and Khandker, 1996).

In light of this analysis, it is not surprising that African-focused development institutions such as IFAD and the AfDB have found it difficult to achieve more than spotty success in rural finance in SSA. Yet both put rural finance high on their agenda in their agricultural programs. An alternative approach to fostering rural investment is to focus on agricultural profitability in general and support for effective, easily accessible, and low-cost savings mechanisms such as postal savings systems linked to rural savings clubs. A complementary approach would be to finance more agricultural and rural investments via matching grants, with the matches coming from both community contributions in kind as well as individual savings.

8.3.13 Output markets

The same problems that negatively affect input markets also impede the development of output markets, and most of them have already been discussed: low population density, landlockedness, poor road and port infrastructure, high transport costs for given infrastructure, illegal extractions along the road, inadequate competition, poor financial markets and the resulting high costs of finance, and a business environment that is only slowly improving. Market development in food crops is also impeded by frequent and unpredictable government interventions in the markets. Fortunately, farmers associations are increasingly entering input and output markets, but much more support will be needed for them to achieve the kind of prominence they have in East Asian countries or Brazil, for example. The WDR of 2008 provides a comprehensive analysis of how to foster output markets in general and the participation of producer organizations in particular. Intraregional trade in basic commodities offers real possibilities for African agriculture but is constrained by serious barriers to trade.

8.3.14 Barriers to intraregional trade

In addition to domestic and global markets, intraregional trade offers major opportunities for SSA agriculture. It also helps avoid unwanted price declines. Domestic demand for most agricultural commodities is price and income inelastic; therefore rapid gains in production will inevitably lead to lower domestic prices and quickly reduce gains in farm profits. Moreover, high production volatility translates into high price variability and risk. Opening subregional trade can reduce the impacts of these factors and increase regional food security.

Africa is a net agricultural and food importer, and that trade imbalance is growing. As Table 4 shows, African agricultural imports grew from $16.3 billion in 1990–1992 to $24.6 billion in 2002–2004 (3.2% per year); exports grew from $11.5 billion to $17.2 billion (3% per year) over the same period. The deficit grew in total agricultural trade but declined in food. As Figure 41 shows, intra-Africa trade in agriculture was a small share of the total, but that share rose from 11–18% over the period. The largest deficits are in cereals, followed by oils and fats, dairy products, and meats. Thus on the surface at least it seems that there is substantial potential to expand intra-Africa trade in agricultural and food products.

Of course, there are barriers that have to be overcome, including transport and handling costs, sanitary and phytosanitary issues, tariff and nontariff barriers to trade, and market information. Lynam has argued that there are real possibilities and real challenges in developing profitable access by African smallholders to growing African urban markets (private communication).

Nevertheless, regional integration in agriculture has been slow. The Economic Commission for Africa has shown that

> **there have been some strides in trade, communications, macroeconomic policy and transport. Some regional economic communities have made significant strides in trade liberalization and facilitation ... in free movement of people ... in infrastructure ... and in peace and security. ... Overall, however, there are substantial gaps between the goals and achievements of most regional economic communities, particularly in greater internal trade, macroeconomic convergence, production and physical connectivity. (Economic Commission for Africa, 2004, p. 1)**

8.3.15 Phytosanitary rules and regulations

These rules and regulations are steadily emerging as more important barriers for developing country agricultural and agro-industrial exports. Their increasing stringency is driven by consumer demand factors as well as by their potential to replace tariff barriers as a protection against imports (World Bank, 2005a). Developing countries have little choice but to insert themselves into the standard-setting processes and bodies and to build up their capacity to comply with these regulations (Ingco and Nash, 2004). Small countries are at a particular disadvantage; they will have difficulties providing the necessary services. Regional collaboration and integration will be necessary to enable compliance at an affordable cost.

Functioning input and output markets, reductions of barriers to trade, and rural investment are all crucial to enhancing the profitability of African farmers. Getting incentives right is a necessary prerequisite to adopting appropriate technology, the topic to which we now turn.

3694 Hans Binswanger-Mkhize and Alex F. McCalla

Table 4 Overview of the trends in Africa's food and agricultural trade, 1990–2004

	1990-92		2002-04		Growth Rate % per year[1]
	Value ($ million)	%	Value ($ million)	%	
Agricultural Imports					
Agricultural products (total)	16341	–	24650	–	3.2
Total food (excluding fish)	13082	100.0	19976	100.0	3.2
Cereals and preparations	5775	44.1	9142	45.8	3.6
Vegetable oils	1405	10.7	2440	12.2	4.1
Milk and dairy products	1524	11.6	1804	9.0	1.0
Fruits and vegetables	985	7.5	1625	8.1	3.9
Sugar	1264	9.7	1504	7.5	1.3
Meat and meat products	789	6.0	1030	5.2	1.4
Other foods	1339	10.2	2431	12.2	4.7
Non-food agriculture	3259	–	4674	–	2.9
	%		%		
Total food as % of agriculture	80		81		0.1
Agricultural Exports					
Agricultural products (total)	11487	–	17220	–	3.0
Total food (excluding fish)	6692	100.0	10946	100.0	3.6
Cereals and preparations	420	6.3	696	6.4	2.6
Vegetable oils	464	6.9	540	4.9	0.6
Milk and dairy products	55	0.8	146	1.3	7.4
Fruits and vegetables	2013	30.1	3314	30.3	3.8
Sugar	999	14.9	935	8.5	−0.1
Meat and meat products	208	3.1	207	1.9	−0.6
Other foods	2532	37.8	5108	46.7	5.2
Non-food agriculture	4795	–	6274	–	2.0
	%		%		
Total food as % of agriculture	58		64		0.6

[1]Growth rate was estimated as the slope b (times 100 for percentage) of the trend line log $(Y) = a + b\,t$, where Y is the variable in question and t is time period (1990 to 2004).

Source: Based on FAOSTAT data (accessed September 2006).

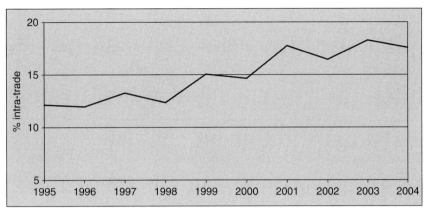

Figure 41   Trends in intratrade in agriculture; Africa's imports from Africa as a percentage of Africa's total imports, 1994–2005. Source: FAO, based on the WTO annual trade statistics.

8.4 The ultimate source of growth: Agricultural technology

Despite the enormous growth in human population and incomes, for more than 150 years agricultural commodity prices have followed a declining trend. This astonishing phenomenon has been caused by the combination of increasing international trade and sustained technical change in agriculture (Mundlak, 2001). Adaptation of the stock of scientific and technical knowledge to local conditions and implementation of new technology are most impressive in OECD countries, where the necessary investments have benefited from the distortions in favor of agriculture. Asia and parts of Latin America have also done well. In particular, India and China have had some of the most impressive agricultural performances, and therefore over a third of humanity has escaped the threat of famine during the past 30 to 40 years.

Eventually, most if not all benefits from technical change in agriculture elude farmers and are transferred to consumers in the form of lower commodity prices, the famous agricultural treadmill. Evenson and Collin (2003) show this once again for the Green Revolution from 1996 to 2000. It is therefore not sufficient to improve the institutional environment and eliminate the barriers to profitability in the low-income countries so that they can adopt the already available technology. In a global agricultural system, agricultural profits will go to those who are ahead of the curve in terms of implemented technology, human capital, and institutions. The underperforming countries will need to produce a steady stream of new technology by strengthening and rebuilding their agricultural research and technology adoption systems.

8.4.1 The growing technology divide

However, SSA has not participated much in technical change and the associated growth in yields. Figure 42 for maize shows these adverse trends, which are similar for other cereals. Only in North Africa and, to a lesser extent, in South Africa have

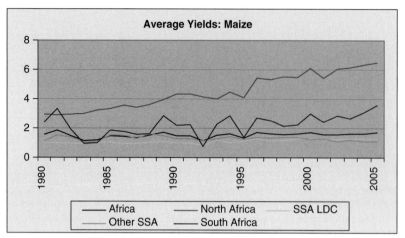

Figure 42   Average maize yields since 1980.

maize yields increased in the last 25 years. We have already reviewed a number of factors behind this dismal trend, including poor infrastructure, lack of competition in input and output markets, and therefore low use of purchased inputs. However, low expenditures on agricultural research and institutional weaknesses in research are major causes as well.

Recall that SSA agriculture is characterized by a multitude and diversity of farming systems, heterogeneity within farming systems (rather than dominance by one or two crops), the presence of many endemic plant and animal diseases, weathered soils with low fertility, and erratic rainfall. In terms of its resource endowments and production mixes, SSA agriculture differs more sharply from the developed world than other developing regions of the world (Pardey et al., 2006), therefore limiting the ability of SSA to benefit from direct technology transfer or spillover of scientific and research findings. Moreover, the heterogeneity of climate, soils, and farming systems within SSA limits transfers of technology and research findings within SSA. These features therefore imply that a greater scientific and adaptive research effort is required to increase agricultural productivity in SSA than elsewhere in the world.

Around 1961, average cereal yields were around 1 ton per ha in the developing world; they rose to nearly 3 tons per ha by 2005. They increased to around 4.5 tons in East Asia and the Pacific (EAP) and to around 2.3 tons in the Middle East and North Africa (MENA), whereas they stagnated around 1 ton in sub-Saharan Africa (SSA) (WDR, 2008, Figure 2.1). In the other regions, the yield gains were driven by increases in irrigation, new varieties, and fertilizers. By 2002, irrigation covered 39% of arable and permanent cropland in South Asia, 29% in MENA, and 11% in Latin America and the Caribbean (LAC), but it covered only 4% in SSA. In 2000, improved crop varieties covered 84% of the cereal area in EAP and 61% in MENA and LAC, but they covered only 22% in SSA. In 2002, fertilizer consumption had reached a staggering 190 kg per ha of arable and permanent crop land in East Asia and the Pacific and 73 kg in MENA but only 13 kg in SSA. As a consequence, even the significant penetration of high-yielding varieties led to only very limited yield growth in SSA.

In 2000, global agricultural R&D spending (including pre-, on-, and post-farm-oriented R&D) was $36.3 billion, of which 37% was conducted by the private sector while 63%, or about $23 billion, was conducted by public entities. Ninety-three percent of the private research was conducted in developed countries, where for the first time in 2000 private agricultural R&D exceeded public R&D (all figures from Pardey et al., 2006). On the other hand, public agricultural R&D grew faster in the developing world and is increasingly concentrated in China, India, and Brazil, whose combined share in spending rose from 33% of developing country expenditures in 1981 to 47% in 2000. In stark contrast, public agricultural research in SSA grew at only about 1% per annum in the 1990s and in 2000 was around $1.6 billion, of which only slightly more than 10% was spent by the CGIAR. Therefore the CGIAR can play only a minor role in catching up public research funding to international levels. Sub-Saharan Africa has the lowest share of private agricultural R&D spending in the world, only 1.7% of already low public spending (ibid.). Of total agricultural research spending, donors provide about 40%, and in some countries this rises to 60%. Only five African countries—Nigeria, South Africa, Botswana, Ethiopia, and Mauritius—are paying the recurrent budget of their NARS from national sources.

Pardey et al. summarize these data as follows:

> **Collectively these data point to a disturbing development—a growing divide regarding the conduct of (agricultural) R&D—and, most likely, a consequent growing technological divide in agriculture. ... The measures also underscore the need to raise current levels of funding for agricultural R&D throughout the region while also developing the policy and infrastructure needed to accelerate the rate of knowledge creation and accumulation in Africa over the long haul" (ibid., p. 68)**

8.4.2 The changing nature of technology discovery

All around the world, innovation is shifting away from a linear pattern that starts with scientific discovery and moves successively to technology development, adaptation to local conditions, and dissemination to farmers. In its place comes a broader and more circular paradigm; it is broader in the sense that innovations no longer concentrate on basic food or industrial agricultural outputs but instead include the entire value chain, from farm production, natural resource management, assembly, processing, marketing, and retail to consumers. Driven by consumer demand changes, attributes of appearance, convenience, nature of the production process (organic, environmentally friendly, genetic and location origin) are assuming importance, most strongly so in developed countries but increasingly in middle- and low-income countries.

The growth in information and communications technology has transformed the ability to take advantage of knowledge developed in other places or for other purposes. Within this broader paradigm, private research and development play an increasing role, facilitated by the development of broader intellectual property rights in agricultural technology, which provide many promises but also induce high levels of anxiety about exclusion and high transactions costs for developing country agricultural innovation.

The trends in intellectual property rights in agriculture and their impacts on technology discovery are ably reviewed in Pardey et al. (2006). A number of larger developing countries are taking advantage of greater private sector involvement, including, most recently, India, which now boasts over 100 private domestic and multinational seed companies. The private seed sector is also growing in SSA, with Kenya perhaps the most advanced. Pardey et al. conclude that developing countries would be well advised to strengthen their own intellectual property rights systems for agriculture, in line with commitments that many have already made under WTO rules.

The last major change is the emergence of biotechnology, which we discussed in Section 4. Some of the needed institutional responses have already been initiated, as discussed in the next subsection.

8.4.3 The institutional framework for agricultural technology generation

Sub-Saharan Africa has over 400 public and private entities engaged in agricultural research, of which nearly 200 are public research institutions and another 200 are universities (compared to 20 in 1960). However, 40% of them have fewer than five researchers and 93% have fewer than 50 full-time researchers (Beintema and Stads, 2004). Sub-Saharan Africa has nearly 50% more agricultural scientists than India and about a third more than the United States, but all of sub-Saharan Africa spends only about half of what India spends and less than a quarter of what the United States spends. Only a quarter of African scientists have Ph.D. degrees compared with all or most scientists in India and the United States.

All institutions engaged in research within each country are collectively aggregated into national agricultural research systems" (NARS). In the various subregions of Africa the NARS have created subregional organizations (SROs), the strongest of which are CORAF/WECARD for West and Central Africa and ASARECA for Eastern and Central Africa. The SRO for Southern Africa is the SADC Food Agriculture and Natural Resource Directorate (SADC/FANR), and a North Africa SRO, initially comprising Morocco, Algeria, Tunisia, and Libya, is also under development. The SROs foster research collaboration in their subregions, and ASARECA and CORAF/WECARD have established research grant-funding mechanisms of their own, with significant support from the European Union (according to the FARA website and websites of the individual SROs).

In 2001 the three SROs for sub-Saharan Africa established the Forum for African Agricultural Research (FARA), which has its secretariat at the regional FAO office in Ghana. FARA has been entrusted by the African Union and NEPAD to coordinate Pillar 4 of its Comprehensive African Agricultural Development Program (CAADP). which focuses on agricultural research and technology dissemination (Figure 43).

To strengthen biotechnology research, four regional biosciences network initiatives were established under the auspices of the New Partnership for African Development (NEPAD). The Biosciences Eastern and Central Africa Network (BecANet) facility was established in 2004. BecANet consists of a secretariat and hub located on the campus of the International Livestock Research Institute (ILRI) in Nairobi, Kenya (which should provide a common biosciences research platform, research-related services, capacity building and training opportunities), regional nodes, and other laboratories distributed throughout Eastern and Central Africa for the conduct of research on priority issues affecting Africa's development. In addition, NEPAD has initiated three other African biosciences initiatives, which are networks of leading centers and consist of hubs and nodes in Northern, Southern, and Western African, i.e., the Southern African Network for Biosciences (SANBio), with its hub at the Council for Scientific and Industrial Research (CSIR), Pretoria, South Africa; the West African Biosciences Network (WABNet), with the hub at Institute Senegalais de Recherches Agricoles (ISRA) in Dakar, Senegal; and the Northern Africa Biosciences Network (NABNet), with the hub at National Research Centre (NRC) of Cairo, Egypt. These hubs possess

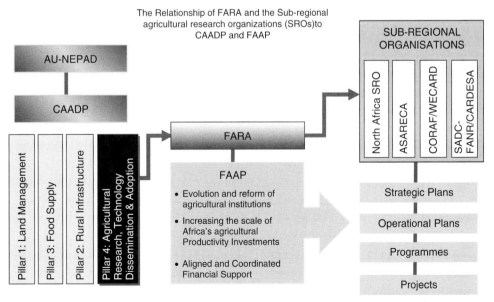

Figure 43   FARA and its institutional and operational links. Source: FARA Strategic Plan, 2007.

and are strengthening the necessary physical infrastructure to develop and implement regional and continental biosciences projects (NEPAD, 2007).

In the early 2000s a public/private sector partnership to foster access to proprietary research was created, funded by the Rockefeller Foundation. The African Agricultural Technology Foundation (AATF) is an international not-for-profit organization designed to facilitate and promote public/private partnerships for access and delivery of proprietary technologies that meet the needs of resource-poor smallhold farmers in SSA. Through a catalytic and facilitative role, AATF tries to serve as an honest broker between owners and/or holders of proprietary technologies and those that need them to promote food security and improve livelihoods for smallhold farmers in SSA. AATF was incorporated in the United Kingdom in January 2003 and in Kenya in April 2003.

The Consultative Group on International Agricultural Research (CGIAR) supports the research of 15 international centers, of which 13 are located in developing countries. In 2006 the CGIAR consisted of 1115 internationally recruited scientists and a total staff of 8154 working in over 100 countries. A strategic component of the system is the *ex-situ* germplasm collections of 11 of the International Agricultural Research Centers (IARCs). Building on earlier independent initiatives, the CGIAR since the early 1990s has rapidly broadened its focus from crop genetic improvement toward natural resource management (NRM), environmental issues, and policy research.

In 2006, of total CGIAR expenditures of $458 million, around $220 million, or 48%, went to SSA. Africa also benefited from the share of 9% share of CGIAR expenditures that went to North Africa and Central and West Asia. All centers currently have programs in SSA. Two centers are located in West Africa (IITA and WARDA); two are in Eastern Africa (ILRI and ICRAF-World Agroforestry Center). In 2003 there were a total of 70 center offices/sites in SSA, distributed in 21 countries. Thirteen centers operated in Kenya alone. There were a total of 162 CGIAR Centers' programs/projects in SSA, of which 82 were conducted by the SSA-based centers. To implement these programs/projects, the centers engaged a total of 389 internationally recruited staff (IRS), 121 regionally recruited staff (RRS), and 2607 local staff (LS).

However, as discussed previously, the CGIAR spends less than 10% of its overall resources on biotechnology research, and little of that is likely to be spent in or for Africa. The establishment of the BecANet facility in 2004 was seen as a partial remedy to this situation.

CGIAR research has made significant contributions to SSA agriculture. Many previous studies highlight successes, such as the high-yielding cassava varieties that include resistance to mites, mealy bugs, cassava bacterial blight, tolerance to drought, low cyanogens potential, and good cooking quality; the famous biological pest control, especially in cassava but also in other crops; biological pest control in potatoes, including via pest-resistant cultivars; improved hybrids and open-pollinated varieties of maize in Western, Eastern and Southern Africa; higher-yielding wheat in Eastern and Southern Africa; hybrid sorghum in Sudan; semi-dwarf rice for irrigated regions in West Africa; early maturing cowpeas in West Africa; and disease-resistant potatoes in the Eastern and Central African highlands.

The CGIAR is not the only set of advanced research institutes (ARIs) operating in or for Africa. France's Centre de Coopération Internationale en Recherche Agronomique pour le Développement (CIRAD) and the Institut de Recherche pour le Développement (IRD), formerly Office de la Recherche Scientifique et Technique Outre-mer (ORSTOM), also operate on the continent. The combined budgets of these two institutes are as large as the entire CGIAR budget (NEPAD, 2007).

8.4.4 Returns to agricultural research

The adoption of new crop varieties in SSA has been significant. In the late 1990s the adoption rate of improved varieties of all crops was 22% of total area planted, and of this 11% was planted to CGIAR-related varieties, usually produced in collaboration with the NARS (Pardey et al., Table 6). Data from between 2000 and 2005 show overall adoption rates for wheat, slightly above 70%; for maize, around 45%; rice at 26%, cassava, 19%; sorghum, 15%; and potatoes at 12%. In Eastern, Central and Southern Africa, 10 million farmers are reported to plant and consume improved varieties of beans.

Alston et al. (2000) assembled more than 1500 rate-of-return estimates to agricultural research and extension (Box 2). The median of the rate-of-return estimates was 48.0% per year for research, 62.9% for extension studies, 37% for studies that estimated the returns to research and extension jointly, and 44.3% for all studies combined. Box 2 shows that the median return in the developing world is about the same as in the developed world and that the median rate of return in Africa is slightly lower than elsewhere but still very high, at 34%.

Box 2   Estimated rates of return to investment in agricultural research, 2000

Region	Number of Estimates	Median Rate of Return
Africa	188	34
Asia	222	50
Latin America	262	43
Middle East/North Africa	11	36
All developing countries	683	43
All developed countries	990	46

Source: Alston et al. (2000).

Evenson (2003) estimates CGIAR contributions to yield growth due to CGIAR research in SSA to be in the range of 0.11–0.13% per year. This range is much smaller than the 0.30–0.33% per-year average yield growth across all developing regions (Evenson, 2003). Despite substantial introduction of new varieties, there has not been a great aggregate impact on yields compared with other regions, partly because of the much lower adoption rates and partly because of lack of irrigation, fertilizer, and inappropriate policies.

Evenson and Rosegrant (2003) tried to estimate the aggregate effects of CGIAR research on crop genetic improvement in various regions of the world. They show that in the absence of the global CGIAR research, the area planted to major food crops in SSA would have been 0.6–1.0% more, whereas total food production would have been reduced 1–2%. In addition, the number of malnourished children would have increased 1%, and the availability of calories to the general population would have declined 3–4%. All these estimated effects are more modest than the effects estimated for other regions of the developing world.

The upshot of this returns discussion is that the underinvestment in agricultural research in Africa is not warranted by either low returns or low adoption rates. In the aggregate, the main problem is not the quality or impact of the research but that so little has been done compared to the enormous diversity of climates, soils, and agricultural production systems and the limited opportunities for borrowing from elsewhere in the world.

8.4.5 The most urgent need for action

FARA has developed the Framework for African Agricultural Productivity (FAAP, 2006) that sets out guiding principles for how research is to be fostered, institutionalized, and financed in Africa. Under FAAP, FARA, the SROs, and the NARS will collectively guide the evolution and reform of agricultural institutions and services, foster an increase in the scale of Africa's agricultural productivity investments, and help align and coordinate financial support.

Figure 44 shows existing and proposed expenditure levels and breaks them down into global, regional, and national components. Subregional expenditures are the ones that will have to grow the fastest to reach $500 million per year.

A joint donor evaluation analyzed FARA and its programs as follows:

> **FARA is a young organization. . . . it has developed a strong organizational framework in its first three years of full existence. . . . The Secretariat has demonstrated that it is both efficient and effective in its operations . . . with increasingly significant tasks being assigned to the FARA Secretariat and the various FARA constituencies, these . . . urgently need to increase their human resource capacity. . . . JEE believes that the FAAP provides a framework for harmonizing donor support, and that committing to consolidated funding of the FARA Rolling Work Programme & Business Plan [RWPBP] is the best means of pooling resources. (JEE report, 2007, p. 11).**

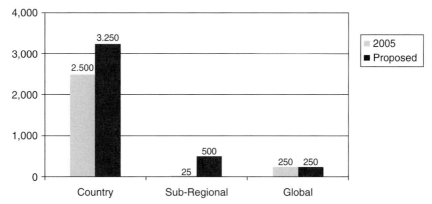

Figure 44   Actual and proposed agricultural research and extension expenditures, 2005. Source: FARA Strategic Plan (2007).

Despite these favorable developments and external assessments, the work programs of FARA, of the SROs, and of the NARS remain seriously underfunded.

8.4.6 Agricultural science and education institutions

> Africa now houses roughly 300 universities. Three quarters of African countries offer some tertiary level training in agricultural sciences. At least 96 public universities teach agriculture and natural resources management. Of these, 26 are in Nigeria, 10 in South Africa, six in Sudan, five in Kenya and three in Ghana. Nineteen separate faculties of veterinary science exist in 13 countries, five of them in Nigeria alone. (Johanson and Saint, p. 15)

Despite these many facilities, agricultural aid funding "has dropped precipitously. ... agriculture received a diminishing portion of a shrinking development assistance pie" (ibid.). Country expenditure has paralleled the drop in donor assistance, resulting in huge deficits in human capital and research support. What is left is a proliferation of institutions that have limited staff and virtually no research support money. The sad part is that now the need for agricultural technology development has regained high priority for SSA, the continent is left with a deteriorating, oversized, and fragmented infrastructure. Many vacant positions, an aging staff (FARA, 2006, estimates that 60% of agricultural professionals currently employed in the public sector will reach retirement age in five to eight years; Johanson and Saint, p. 34), outdated equipment, and no operating funds.

Johanson and Saint's conclusion is poignant: "Agricultural education and training has been demonstrated to be a vital, but much neglected, component of agricultural development in Africa. It is under-valued, under-resourced and under-provided. Human capital in agriculture has been depleted by long neglect" (p. 67). The

InterAcademy Study states that "[i]t is the conviction of this study panel that much of what would be necessary to improve agricultural productivity and food security in Africa hinges on strengthening agricultural educational systems, more specifically the coverage and quality of higher education" (p. 184).

However, there are hopeful signs. "Seven American foundations have formed the Partnership for Higher Education in Africa and pledged to invest at least USD 200 million over the next five years ... and ... the Gates and Rockefeller Foundations recently formed a separate partnership, called the Alliance for a Green Revolution in Africa (AGRA)" (ibid). UNDP is supporting a community of practice called SEMCA, Sustainability, Education and the Management of Change in Africa, focusing on agricultural education.

In conclusion, it is clear that African regional and national institutions for agricultural science, technology, and agricultural science education have started to respond to the huge scientific and technological challenges the continent faces. The challenges are intensified by increasing competition for resources, climate change, and rising international agricultural prices. These responses are occurring in a rapidly changing global research system that includes biotechnology, intellectual property rights, and patent systems as well as a growing range of players, especially the private sector. The significant institutional responses have not so far been matched by adequate funding from international donors and national governments, especially in the areas of biotechnology and science education.

8.5. The imperative of regionalization

Throughout this paper there have been many critical issues that can best or only be solved by regional action, and more are yet to come. Let's recall a sampling:
- Small countries dominate the African scene, often lacking financial capacity for public goods investments.
- Small landlocked countries generally do worse and depend on regional integration to be able to do better.
- Expanded regional trade in agriculture and food products is good for growth, farmers' incomes, and regional food security; the short-run management challenges of the recent food price spike and the long-run opportunities arising from prices that are expected to settle at higher than past levels only add to this imperative.
- Expanded regional trade and food security will be helped by the harmonization of standards and sanitary measures and subregional and regional capacities to implement them.
- Freer borders and internal infrastructure should encourage private sector traders.
- For small countries, regional infrastructure—roads, communications, ports—are critical for access to each other and external markets.
- Reversing land degradation and desertification and preserving biodiversity require transboundary collective action.

- Managing crucial but threatened forestry and fisheries resources must be approached on a transnational basis.
- Defense against plant and animal disease epidemics requires collective responses at subregional and regional levels.
- Success in agriculture crucially depends on indigenous scientific capacity to generate new technology; given small and poor countries, this is far better done on a regional or subregional basis. FARA and the SROs are on the right track, but the effort needs to be greatly expanded.
- Biotechnology research is expensive and has a large critical mass; therefore, two or three regional institutes are far superior to 48 or 24 underfunded, under-resourced national institutions.
- Indigenous scientific capacity requires trained people, again better done by regional institutions that have critical mass and necessary financial support.
- Regional approaches to rural financial architecture could increase potential deposits and loanable funds and spread risk.

These examples are hopefully enough to illustrate that the potential for regional approaches and an overall regional strategy for rural Africa are significant. Yet in most of these areas institutional development programs remain massively underfunded. The main reason for this is that the regional efforts produce regional and subregional public goods; therefore their financing is subject to the familiar free-rider problem of financing public goods. Except for the largest countries, which have an incentive to supply themselves with these regional public goods, countries will seek to benefit from the investment of others. It is precisely here that a regional development finance institution such as the African Development Bank has a major opportunity to step in, since it can both coordinate as well as contribute to the financing of these essential regional capacities.

End Notes

1. The authors gratefully acknowledge that information included in this paper was obtained under a consultancy contract with the International Fund for Agricultural Development (IFAD), who owns all the intellectual property related to the material produced under the contract, and which is publishing a shorter version of the paper. Furthermore, the authors wish to emphasize that the that views and judgements expressed in this paper, if not attributed specifically to the authors of the references consulted, are exclusively their own and cannot be attributed in any way to IFAD or the African Development Bank.
2. Hans P. Binswanger is an Honorary Professor at the Institute for Economic Research of Innovation at Tshwane University of Technology, Pretoria, South Africa; and Alex F. McCalla is Professor Emeritus, Agricultural and Resource Economics, University of California, Davis.
3. The participation effect includes all impacts on the agricultural growth rates in the preceding list of effects.
4. The additional appreciation of the country is $50 - 12 = 38\%$. But this translates into a 23% reduction of the new food price level of 165%.
5. The strong impact of the exchange value of the FCFA on agriculture and poverty rates in West Africa is discussed in the context of an earlier devaluation by Tefft et al. (1997).

6. Unweighted average across 16 countries.
7. Ethiopia data for the first period refer to 1981–1984; 1975–1979 data are unavailable.
8. Unweighted average across 21 countries.
9. Collier's book summarizes the results of a large number of studies that have appeared or are about to appear in peer-reviewed journals. Readers interested in the data and econometrics used are referred to the original articles.
10. The principle of subsidiarity states that functions should be allocated to the lowest level capable of effectively performing them, at the same time minimizing adverse spillover effects to neighboring units at the same or higher levels.
11. The CGIAR has summarized the literature on this topic in an easily accessible website (CGIAR, 2005).
12. Foster and Rosenzweig showed that in India, rural industries have located preferably in areas that benefited relatively little from the Green Revolution and the subsequent agricultural development and where rural wages were generally lower. Rural industrialization has therefore reduced rural poverty and inequality among and within rural areas. Rapid growth of rural industries in the 1990s followed an increase in the overall growth rate of the economy, which was itself partly a consequence of improved agricultural development and might have been aided by restrictive labor laws, the impact and enforcement of which might be less in rural areas than in urban areas. It is not clear how much these lessons apply to the underperforming countries that are suffering from low overall and low agricultural growth.
13. Foster and Rosenzweig showed that in India, rural industries have located preferably in areas which benefited relatively little from the green revolution and the subsequent agricultural development and where rural wages were generally lower. Rural industrialization has therefore reduced rural poverty and inequality among and within rural areas. Rapid growth of rural industries in the 1990s followed an increase in the overall growth rate of the economy, which was itself partly a consequence of improved agricultural development, and may have been aided by restrictive labor laws whose impact and enforcement may be less in rural areas than urban areas. It is not clear how much these lessons apply to the underperforming countries which are suffering from low overall and low agricultural growth.

References

AfDB. (2007, August 3). *Agriculture and Agro-Industry Department (OSAN) Draft-Agric-Sector-Strategy* (Rev.).

Alston, J. M., Chan-Kang, C., Marra, M. C., Pardey, P. G., & Wyatt, T. J. (2000). *A Meta-Analysis of Rates of Return to Agricultural R&D: Ex Pede Herculem?* Washington, DC: IFPRI, Research Report 113.

Ambler, J., Pandolfelli, L., Kramer, A., & Meinzen-Dick, R. (2007, October). *Strengthening Women's Assets and Status.* IFPRI *2020 Focus Brief.*

Anderson, K., & Masters, W. (2009). Five Decades of Distortions to Agricultural Incentives. In K. Anderson, & W. Masters (Eds.), *Distortions to Agricultural Incentives: A Global Perspective, 1955–2007* (Ch. 1). London: Palgrave Macmillan, and Washington, DC: World Bank.

Anderson, K., & Martin, W. (Ed.). (2006). *Agricultural Trade Reform and the Doha Development Agenda.* London: Palgrave Macmillan, and Washington, D.C.: World Bank.

Anderson, K., & Valenzuala, E. (2007). Do Global Trade Distortions Still Harm Developing Country Farmers? *Review of World Economics, 143*, 108–139.

Beintema, N. M., & Stads, G. J. (2004). *Investing in Sub-Saharan African Agricultural Research: Recent Trends. 2020 Africa Conference Brief No. 8.* Washington, DC: IFPRI.

Binswanger, H. P., & Rosenzweig, M. R. (1986). Behavioural and Material Determinants of Production Relations in Agriculture. *Journal of Development Studies, 22*(3), 503–539.

Binswanger, H. P., Deininger, K., & Feder, G. (1995). Power Distortions Revolt and Reform in Agricultural Land Relations. In J. Behrman T. N. Srinivasan (Eds.), *Handbook of Development Economics* (Vol. 3). Amsterdam: Elsevier Science B.V.

Binswanger, H. P., & Khandker, S. R. (1995). The Impact of Formal Finance on the Rural Economy of India. *Journal of Development Studies*, *32*(2).

Binswanger, H. P., & Swaminathan, A. (2003, May). *Scaling Up Community-Driven Development: Theoretical Underpinnings and Program Design Implications*. Policy Research Working Paper 3 03 9. World Bank.

Binswanger, H. P., & Brink, R. (2005). *Credit for Small Farmers in Africa Revisited: Pathologies and Remedies*. Savings for Development, No 3.

Binswanger, H. P., & Nguyen, T. V. (2006). *Scaling Up Community-Driven Development: A Step-By-Step-Guide*. World Bank, CDD website.

Binswanger, H. P. (2006). *Food and Agricultural Policy to Mitigate the Impact of HIV/AIDS*. Paper presented at the AAEA session on "Agriculture, Nutrition, and Health in High- and Low-Income Countries: Policy Issues" at the IAAE Conference in Brisbane, Australia, August 13–18.

Binswanger, H. P. (2008). Empowering Rural People for their Own Development. In Otsuka, Keijiro, et al. (Eds.), *Contributions of Agricultural Economics to Critical Policy Issues*, Proceedings of the Twenty-Sith Conference of the International Association of Agricultural Economists, Blackwell Synergy.

Binswanger-Mkhize, H. P., & McCalla, A. (2009). *The Changing Context and Prospects for African Agricultural Development*. Rome and Tunis: International Fund for Agricultural Development and African Development Bank.

Binswanger-Mkhize, H. P., de Regt, J. P., & Spector, S. (Eds.). (2009). *Scaling Up Local & Community-Driven Development (LCDD): A Real World Guide to Its Theory and Practice*. World Bank.

Binswanger-Mkhize, H. P., Bourguignon, C., & van den Brink, R. (Eds.). *Agricultural land Redistribution: Toward a Common Vision*. Washington, DC: World Bank, forthcoming.

Boserup, E. (1965). *Conditions of Agricultural Growth: The Economics of Agrarian Change under Population Pressure*. New York: Aldine Publishing.

Brink, V. D., Rogier, G. T., Binswanger, H. P., Bruce, J., & Byamugisha, F. (2006). *Consensus, Confusion, and Controversy: Selected Land Reform Issues in Sub-Saharan Africa*.

Bristow, M. (2007). *China's long march to Africa*. Story from BBC News (http://news.bbc.co.uk/go/pr/fr/-/2/hi/africa/7118941.stm)

Byerlee, D., & Anderson, K. (2007). Agriculture for Development: Focus on Sub-Saharan Africa. Presentation about the *World Development Report* 2008, made at the OECD, FAO, World Bank IFAD Global Forum on Agriculture, Rome, November 12–13.

Christiaensen, L., Demery, L., & Kuhl, J. (2006). *The Role of Agriculture in Poverty Reduction: And Empirical Perspective*. Washington, DC: World Bank Policy Research. Working Paper No. 4013.

Cleaver, K. (2007). *Contemporary Issues of Agriculture and Rural Development in Africa and IFAD's Approach*. Presentation at the OECD, FAO, World Bank IFAD Global Forum on Agriculture, Rome, November 12–13.

Cliffe, S., Guggenheim, S., & Kostner, M. (2003). *Community-Driven Reconstruction as an Instrument in War-to Peace Transitions*. CPR working paper 7. Social Development Department, World Bank.

Cline, W. R. (2007). *Global Warming and Agriculture: Impact Estimates by Country*. Washington, DC: Center for Global Development and the Peterson Institute for International Economics.

Collier, P. (2007). *The Bottom Billion: Why the Poorest Countries Are Failing and What Can Be Done About It*. Oxford: Oxford University Press.

Commonwealth Secretariat. (2007). Gender and Climate Change. *CropBiotech Update*. A weekly summary of world developments in agri-biotech for developing countries, produced by the Global Knowledge Center on Crop Biotechnology, International Service for the Acquisition of Agri-biotech Applications SEAsiaCenter (ISAAA), and AgBiotechNet.

Cotula, L., Dyer, N., & Vermeulen, S. (2008). *Fueling Exclusion, "The Biofuel Boom and Poor People's Access to Land"*. International Institute for Environment and Development, and Food and Agriculture Organization of the United Nations.

Deininger, K. W. (2003). *Land Policies for Growth and Poverty Reduction*. Oxford University Press.

DFID. (2007). *The Forum for Agricultural Research in Africa: Joint External Evaluation Central Research Department*. Programme of Advisory Support Services for Rural Livelihoods. London: Department for International Development, PASS Project Code CR0380.

Diao, X., Hazell, P., Resnick, D., & Thurlow, J. (2006). *The Role of Agriculture in Development: Implications for Sub-Saharan Africa*. Washington, DC: IFPRI Discussion Paper.

Easterly, W. (2007). *Are Aid Agencies Improving?*. Washington, DC: Center for Global Development.

Economic Commission for Africa. (2004). *Assessing Regional Integration in Africa: A Policy Research Report*. Addis Ababa.

Economic Commission for Africa (ECA). (2005). *Striving for Good Governance in Africa*. Addis Ababa.

ECA. (2006a). *Economic and Social Conditions in North Africa: A Mid-Decade Assessment*. Addis Ababa.

ECA. (2006b). *Assessing Regional Integration in Africa II*. Addis Ababa.

ECA. (2007). *Recent Economic Performance in Africa and Prospects for 2007*. Addis Ababa.

Eicher, C. K., Maredia, K., & Sithole-Niang, I. (2006). Crop Biotechnology and the African Farmer, Amsterdam. *Food Policy*, *31*, 504–527.

Eicher, C. K. (2006). *The Evolution of Agricultural Education and Training: Global Insights of Relevance for Africa*. Department of Agricultural Economics Staff Paper 26. East Lansing: Michigan State University.

Evenson, R. E., & Collin, D. (2003). Assessing the Impact of the Green Revolution. *Science*, *300*(2 May), 758–762.

Evenson, R. E., & Rosegrant, M. (2003). The Economic Consequences of CGIAR Programs. In R. E. Evenson & D. Gollin (Eds.), *Crop Variety Improvement and its Effect on Productivity: The Impact of International Agricultural Research*. Oxon, UK: CABI.

Evenson, R. E., & Raney, T. (Eds.). (2007, June). *The Political Economy of Genetically Modified Foods*. Edward Elgar Publishing.

Faguet, J. P. (1997). *Decentralization and Local Government Performance Improving Public Service Provision in Bolivia*. www.urosario.edu.co/FASE1/economia/documentos/v3n1Faguet(2000).pdf.

Fan, S., & Hazell, P. (2001). Returns to Public Investments in the Less-Favored Areas of India and China. *AJAE*, *83*(5), 1217–1223.

FAO. (2006). *Global Forest Resources Assessment 2005*. Rome: FAO.

FAO. (2006). *The State of World Fisheries and Aquaculture (SOFIA)*. Rome: FAO.

FAO. (2006). *Enhancing Intra-African Trade in Food and Agriculture*. Background paper prepared for African Union/FAO meeting Libreville, Gabon, 27 November–1 December.

FAO. (2007). *Independent External Evaluation: The Challenge of Renewal*. Rome.

FAO. (2008). *Soaring Food Prices: Facts, Perspectives, Impacts and Actions Required*. High-Level Conference on World Food Security: The Challenges of Climate Change and Bioenergy, Rome, 3–5 June.

FARA. (2006). *Framework for African Agricultural Productivity*. Accra.

FARA. (2007). *FARA 2007–2016 Strategic Plan: Enhancing African Agricultural Innovation Capacity*. Accra.

Foster, A. D., & Rosenzweig, M. R. (2003). *Agricultural Development, Industrialization and Rural Inequality*. Mimeo. Harvard University.

Gelb, A., Ali, A. A. G., Dinka, T., Elbadawi, I., Soludo, C., & Tidrick, G. (2000). *Can Africa Claim the 21st Century?* Washington, DC: World Bank.

Gine, X. (2004). *Literature Review on Access to Finance for SME and Low-income Households*. mimeo. World Bank.

Glaeser, E., Porta, R. L., Lopez-de-Silanes, F., & Shleifer, A. (2004). *Explaining Growth: Institutions, Human Capital, and Leaders*. Washington, DC: Brookings Papers on Economic Activity.

Global Retail Bulletin. (2007, November 30, Friday).

Grain Briefing. (2008, October). Seized: The 2008 land grab for food and financial security, www.grain.org/go/landgrab

GRISTMILL. (2007, July 18). *West African Fisheries Being Destroyed: Unsustainability in the Water*. http://gristmill.grist.org

Haddad, L., Alderman, H., Appleton, S., Song, L., & Yohannes, Y. (2005). *Reducing Child Undernutrition: How Far Does Income Growth Take Us*. Washington, DC: IFPRI Discussion Paper 137.

Hazell, P., & Pachauri, R. K. (Eds.). (2006). *Bioenergy and Agriculture: Promises and Challenges*. Washington, DC: IFPRI 2020 Focus 14, December.

Hazell, P., Poulton, C., Wiggins, S., & Dorward, A. (2007). *The Future of Small Farms for Poverty Reduction and Growth*. IFPRI 2020 Discussion Paper 42 May.

Hazell, P., & Hagbladde, S. (1993). Farm-Nonfarm Growth Linkages and the Welfare of the Poor. In M. Lipton, & J. Gaag (Eds.), *Including the Poor* (pp. 190–204). Washington, DC: the World Bank.

Heath, J., & Binswanger, H. P. (1996). Natural resource degradation effects of poverty are largely policy-induced: The case of Colombia. *Envir. and Development Economics*, *1*, 65–84.

Holmes, R., & Slater, R. (2007). Realising gender in agricultural policies: The fight for equality is not over (ODI Opinion 91, December, p. 1).

Howden, S. M., Soussana, J. F., Tubiello, F. N., Chhetri, N., Dunlop, M., & Meinke H. (2007, December 11). Adapting agriculture to climate change. *PNAS*, *104*(50), 19691.

IFAD. (2001). *Rural Poverty Report 2001: The Challenge of Ending Rural Poverty*. Rome.

IFAD. (2007a). *IFAD Strategic Framework 2007–2010: Enabling the Rural Poor to Overcome Poverty*. Rome.

IFAD. (2007). *Innovation Strategy*. Rome.

IFAD, et al. (2007). *Sending Money Home: Worldwide Remittance Flows to Developing Countries*. Rome.

IFPRI. (2008, May). *High Food Prices: The What, Who, and How of Proposed Policy Actions*. Washington, DC: Policy Brief.

Ingco, M., & Nash, J. (2004). *Agriculture and the WTO: Creating a Trading System for Development*. World Bank.

IMF. (2008, March). Riding a Wave: Soaring commodity prices may have a lasting impact. *Finance and Development*, *45*(1).

IMF. (2009). *World Economic Outlook Update*. January 28, Institute for Security Studies, 2007. The Crisis of Marine Plunder in Africa. www.issafrica.org 2 October.

InterAcademy Council (IAC). (2005). *Realizing the promise and potential of African agriculture*.

Ivanic, M., & Martin, W. (2008). *Implications of Higher Global Food Prices for Poverty in Low-Income Countries*. Washington, DC: World Bank, Policy Research Working Paper 4594.

Jayne, et al. (2005). on constraints to food trade in Africa.

Johanson, R., & Saint, W. (2007, June). *Cultivating Knowledge and Skills to Grow African Agriculture*. Washington, DC: World Bank (AFTHD).

Johnston, B. F., & Mellor, J. W. (1961). The Role of Agriculture in Economic Development. *American Economic Review*, *51*(4), 566–593.

Jones, M., Kaufmann, R., & Wopereis, M. (2007). *Advancing the African Agenda Through CAADP Pillar 4: Agricultural Research, Dissemination and Adoption and FAAP: Framework for African Agricultural Productivity*. Accra: FARA, mimeo.

Kaboré, D. X. X. , & Reij, C. (2004). *The emergence and spreading of an improved traditional soil and water conservation practice in Burkina Faso*. EPTD Discussion Paper No. 114. Washington, DC: IFPRI.

Kapur, D., & McHale, J. (2005). *The Global Migration of Talent. What Does It Mean for Developing Countries?* Washington, DC: Center for Global Development, CGD Brief.

Kaufmann, D., Kraay, A., & Mastruzzi, M. (2007, July). *Governance Matters IV: Governance Indicators 1996–2006*. World Bank Policy Research Working Paper No. 4284.

Katito, G. (2007, December 24). Africa in 2007: Trends Towards Democracy. *Business Day*. Johannesburg.

Kharas, H. (2007). *The New Reality of Aid*. Washington, DC: Center for Global Development.

Leach, M., & Mearns, R. (Eds.). (1996). *The Lie of the Land: Challenging Received Wisdom on the African Environment*. Oxford: The International African Institute.

Lomberg, B. (2007). *Cool It: The Skeptical Environmentalist's Guide to Global Warming*. New York: Alfred A. Knopf.

Mallaby, S. (2004). *The World's Banker: A Story of Failed States, Financial Crises, and the Wealth and Poverty of Nations*. Council on Foreign Relations Books (Penguin Press).

Manor, J. (1999). *The Political Economy of Democratic Decentralization. Directions in Development*. Washington, DC: World Bank.

Mather, D., Donovan, C., Jayne, T. S., Weber, M., Mazhangara, E., Bailey, L., et al. (2004). *A cross-country analysis of household responses to adult mortality in rural sub-Saharan Africa: Implications for HIV/AIDS mitigation and rural development policies*. Paper prepared for the International AIDS Economics Network Pre-Conference, Bangkok, Thailand, 9–10 July.

McLean, K., Kerr G., & Williams, M. (1998). *Decentralization and Rural Development: Characterizing Efforts of 19 Countries*. World Bank Working Paper. Washington, DC.

Morton, J. F. (2007, December 11). The impact of climate change on smallholder and subsistence agriculture. *PNAS*, *104*(50), 19680–19685.

Mundlak, Y., & Larson, D. (1992). On the transmission of world agricultural prices. Washington, D.C., *World Bank Economic Review*, *6*(3), 399–422.

Mundlak, Y. (2001). Explaining Economic Growth. *American Journal of Agricultural Economics*, *83*(5), 1154–67.

Mwangi, E. (Ed.). (2006). *Land Rights for African Development: From Knowledge to Action*. Washington, DC: IFPRI.

Mywish, K. M., & Raitzer, D. A. (2006). *CGIAR and NARS partner research in sub-Saharan Africa: evidence of impact to date*. Rome: Science Council of the CGIAR, Standing Panel on Impact Assessment.

NEPAD. (2005, August). *Fish for All: The NEPAD Action Plan for the Development of African Fisheries and Aquaculture*. Abuja.

NEPAD. (2007, October). NEPAD Agricultural Unit, CAADP. *July–September 2007 Quarterly Report*.

Neven, D., Reardon, T., Chege, J., & Wang, H. (2006). Supermarkets and Consumers in Africa: The case of Nairobi, Kenya. *International Food and Agribusiness Marketing*, *18*(1/2), 103–123.

Neven, D., Odera, M., Reardon, T., & Wang, H. (2007). Domestic Supermarkets and Horticulture in Kenya. *World Development*, forthcoming.

New Partnership for Africa's Development (NEPAD). (2007). *Consultation on the Roles and Productivity of International Centers in Africa's Agricultural Research System*. Concept paper for AMCOST, Pretoria.

Ndulu, B., Chakraborti, L., Lijane, L., Ramachandran, V., & Wolgin, J. (2007). *Challenges of African Growth: Opportunities, Constraints and Strategic Directions*. Washington, DC: World Bank.

Ngaido, T. (2004). *Reforming Land rights in Africa*. Washington, DC: IFPRI 2020 Africa Conference Brief 15.

OECD-FAO. (2008). *Agricultural Outlook: 2008–2017: Highlights*. Paris and Rome.

Omamo, S. W., Diao, X., Wood, S., Chamberlin, J., You, L., Benin, S., et al. (2006). Strategic priorities for agricultural development in Eastern and Central Africa. (Research Report 150). Washington, DC: International Food Policy Research, (IFPRI). [Language: EN].

Pardey, P., James, J., Alston, J., Wood, S., Koo, B., Binenbaum, E., et al. (2006). *Science, Technology and Skills*. Rome: mimeo, Science Council.

Pingali, P., Stamoulis, K., & Anriquez, G. (2007). *Poverty, Hunger, and Agriculture in Sub-Saharan Africa: Opportunities and Challenges*. Presentation at the OECD, FAO, World Bank IFAD Global Forum on Agriculture, Rome, November 12–13.

Piriou-Sall, S. (2007). *Decentralization and Rural Development: A Review of Evidence*. Washington, DC: World Bank.

Piwoz, E., & Preble, E. (2000). *HIV/AIDS and nutrition: A review of the literature and recommendations for nutritional care and support in sub-Saharan Africa*. SARA Project. Washington, DC: U.S. Agency for International Development.

Poulton, C., Tyler, G., Dorward, A., Hazell, P., Kydd, J., & Stockbridge, M. (2007). *All-Africa Review of Experiences with Commercial Agriculture: Summary report*. Background study to World Bank, 2009, Awakening Africa's sleeping giant: Prospects for commercial agriculture in the Guinea Savannah zone and beyond. Washington, DC: World Bank, 2009.

Rashid, S. (2002). *Dynamics of agricultural wage and rice price in Bangladesh: a re-examination. Markets and Structural Studies Division Discussion Paper No. 44*. Washington, DC: International Food Policy Research Institute.

Raitzer, D. A. (2003). *Benefit-Cost Meta-Analysis of Investment in the International Agricultural Research Centres of the CGIAR*. Rome: Science Council of the CGIAR, Standing Panel on Impact Assessment.

Ravallion, M. (1990). Rural welfare effects of food price changes under induced wage responses: theory and evidence for Bangladesh. *Oxford Economic Papers*, *42*(3), 574–585.

Reader, J. (1998). *Africa: A Biography of the Continent*. New York: First Vintage Books.

Reardon, T., Henson, S., & Berdegué, J. (2007). Proactive fast-tracking diffusion of supermarkets in developing countries: Implications for market institutions and trade. *Journal of Economic Geography*, 7(4), 1–33.

Rivers, J., Silvestre, E., & Mason, J. (2004). *Nutritional and Food Security Status of Orphans and Vulnerable Children*. A report of a research project supported by UNICEF, IFPRI, and WFP. New Orleans, LA: Department of International Health and Development, Tulane University School of Public Health and Tropical Medicine.

Rosegrant, M. W. (2008, May 7). *Biofuels and Grain Prices: Impacts and Policy Responses*. Washington, DC: International Food Policy Research Institute: Testimony for the U.S. Senate Committee on Homeland Security and Governmental Affairs.

Ruthenberg, H. (1976). *Farming Systems in the Tropics* (2nd ed.). Oxford: Clarendon.

Sarris, A. (2007). *Outlook, Opportunities and Constraints for African Agricultural Markets and Trade*. Presentation at the OECD, FAO, World Bank IFAD Global Forum on Agriculture, Rome, November 12–13.

Schmidhuber, J. (2006). *Impact of an increased biomass use on agricultural markets, prices and food security: A longer-term perspective*. Rome: FAO.

Serrano-Berthet, R., Helling, L., van Domelen, J., & van Wicklin, W. (2008). *Making Sense of the Rationales, Evolution and Future Options for Social and Local Development Funds in the Africa Region*. World Bank. mimeo.

Shah, A. (1994). The Reform of Intergovernmental Fiscal Relations in Developing and Emerging Market Economies. *Policy and Research Series*, *23*, World Bank.

Steenblik, R. (2007). Biofuels: at what cost? Government support for ethanol and biodiesel in selected OECD countries. Global Subsidies Initiative.

Stillwagon, E. (2005). *The Ecology of Poverty: Nutrition, Parasites, and Vulnerability to HIV/AIDS*.

Stocking, M. (1996). Soil Erosion: Breaking New Ground. In Leach, & Mearns (Eds.), *The Lie of the Land: Challenging Received Wisdom on the African Environment*. Oxford: International African Institute.

Stoeckel, A. (2008, June). *High Food Prices: Causes, Implications and Solutions*. Australian Government, Rural Industries Research and Develpoment Corporation. RIRDC Publication No 08/100.

Tefft, J., Staatz, J., & Dioné, J. (1997, September). *Impact of the CFA Devaluation on Sustainable Growth for Poverty Alleviation: Preliminary Results*. Bamako: INSAH/PRISAS.

The Worldwatch Institute and GTZ. (2006). *Biofuels for Transportation*. Washington, DC: Bonn.

Tiffen, M., Mortimore, M., & Gichuki, F. (1994). *More people, less erosion: environmental recovery in Kenya*. Chichester, UK: John Wiley & Sons.

Toulmin, C. (Ed.). (2000). *Evolving Land Rights, Policy, and Tenure in Africa*. London: IIED.

Trostle, R. (2008, May). *Global Agricultural Supply and Demand: Factors Contributing to the Recent Increase in Food Commodity Prices*. Washington, DC: ERS/USDA WRS-0801.

Tyler, G. (2007). The Fall and Rise of the Colonial Development Corporation. In *Awakening Africa's sleeping giant: Prospects for commercial agriculture in the Guinea Savannah zone and beyond*. Washington, DC: World Bank, 2009.

Tyner, W. E., & Taheripour, F. (2008). *Policy Options for Integrated Energy and Agricultural Markets*. Paper presented at the Transition to a Bio-Economy: Integration of Agricultural and energy Systems conference on February 12–13, 2008, at the Westin Atlanta Airport; planned by the Farm Foundation.

UNAIDS. (2004b). Bringing comprehensive HIV prevention to scale. In *2004 Report on the global AIDS Epidemic* (Chapter 4). Geneva.

UNAIDS. (2006). *Report on the Global AIDS Epidemic*. Geneva.

UNCTAD. (2008, May). *Assessing the Global Food Crisis: Key trade, investment and commodity policies in ensuring sustainable food security and alleviating poverty*. Geneva: UNCTAD/OSG/2008/1.

United Nations. (2006). World Population Prospects: 2006 Revision, Department of Social and Economic Affairs, Population Division, New York.

Weatherspoon, D. D., & Reardon, T. (2003). The Rise of Supermarkets in Africa: Implications for Agrifood Systems and the Rural Poor. *Development Policy Review*, *21*(3), 333–355.

WHO. (2004). *Scaling up antiretroviral therapy in resource-limited settings: Treatment guidelines for a public health approach*. Geneva.

World Bank. (1994). *Farmer Empowerment in Africa through Farmer Organizations: Best Practices*. AFTES Working Paper No. 14. Africa Region: Agricultural Policy and Production. Technical Department.

World Bank. (1995). *The World Bank and Irrigation*. Report Number 14908. Washington, DC: *Independent Evaluation Group*.

World Bank. (1996a). *A Review of World Bank Lending for Agricultural Credit and Rural Finance (1948-1992): A follow up*. Rep. number 15221. Washington, DC: Oper. Eval. Dep.

World Bank. (2003). *Land Policies for Poverty Reduction*. A World Bank Policy Research Report. Oxford University Press.

World Bank. (2004). *World Development Report 2004: Making Services Work for Poor People*. Washington, DC, 2003.

World Bank. (2004). *Agricultural Investment Sourcebook*. Washington, DC.

World Bank. (2005a). *Building Effective States, Forging Engaged Societies*. Report of the World Bank Task Force on Capacity Development in Africa, Washington, DC.

World Bank. (2005b). *Global Agricultural Trade and the Developing Countries*. Washington, DC.

World Bank. (2005c). *World Development Report 2005: A Better Investment Climate for Everyone*. Washington, DC, 2004.

World Bank. (2006). *Enterprise Surveys 2001-2005*, http://www.enterprisesurveys.org/

World Bank. (2006). *World Development Indicators*, Washington DC.

World Bank. (2006). *Enhancing Agricultural Innovation: How to Go Beyond the Strengthening of Research Systems*. Washington, DC: Agriculture and Rural Development Department.

World Bank and IFC. (2006a). *Doing Business in 2006: Creating Jobs*. Washington, DC.

World Bank. (2007a). *World Development Report 2007: Development and the Next Generation*. Washington, DC, 2006.

World Bank. (2007b). *World Development Report 2008: Agriculture for Development*. Washington, DC.

World Bank. (2009). *Awakening Africa's sleeping giant: Prospects for commercial agriculture in the Guinea Savannah zone and beyond*. Washington, DC.

World Bank. (2007c). *Cultivating Knowledge and Skills to Grow African Agriculture*. Report No. 40997-AF.

World Bank. (2008, July 2). *Double Jeopardy: Responding to High Food and Fuel Prices*. G8 Hokkaido-Toyako Summit.

Worldwatch Institute. (2006, June). *Biofuels for Transportation: Global Potential and Implications for Sustainable Agriculture and Energy in the 21st Century*. Washington, DC: Worldwatch Institute.

Wright, B., Pardey, P., Nottenburg, C., & Koo, B. Agricultural Innovation: Economic Incentives and Institutions. In R. E. Evenson & P. Pingali (Eds.), *Handbook of Agricultural Economics* (Chapter).

Yamano, T., & Jayne, T. S. 2004. Measuring the Impacts of Working-Age Mortality on Small-Scale Farm House-holds in Kenya. World Development, *32*(1), 91–119.

Yaron, J., Benjamin M., & Charitonenko, S. (1998). Promoting Efficient Rural Financial Intermediation. *World Bank Research Observer, 13*, 147–170.

Yohe, G., Burton, I., Huq, S., & Rosegrant, M. W. (October 2007). *Climate Change: Pro-poor Adaptation, Risk Management, and Mitigation Strategies*. IFPRI 2020 Focus Brief.

CHAPTER 71

Agricultural Productivity in Latin America and the Caribbean and Sources of Growth

Antonio Flavio Dias Avila
Agricultural Economist, Ph.D., Embrapa, Brazil

Luis Romano
Agricultural Economist, Ph. D., Bogotá, Colombia

Fernando Garagorry
Operations Research, Ph.D., Embrapa, Brazil

Contents

Handbook of Agricultural Economics, Volume 4
© 20010 Elsevier BV. All rights reserved.

doi: 10.1016/S1574-0072(09)04071-7

Abstract

Agricultural productivity in the Latin American and Caribbean (LAC) countries between 1961
and 2001 increased due to market regulation, economic openness, and estate reduction.
In the six major sections of this chapter, we analyze the evolution of this productivity as well
as the output and input growth for the agricultural and livestock sectors. We look closely at economic indicators related to food demand and population growth as well as total factor productivity growth for the region, with an emphasis on the Brazilian and Colombian agricultural
sectors. We also discuss some sources of productivity growth, highlighting agricultural research,
rural extension, schooling, and nutrition, and ultimately review income improvement and
poverty reduction studies.
JEL classifications: Q15, Q18, J43, E61

Keywords

agricultural productivity
food demand
population growth
poverty reduction

1. INTRODUCTION

To face secular problems concerning inflation, underemployment, poverty, and fiscal
deficits, during recent decades Latin American and Caribbean (LAC) countries implemented "structural adjustment" policies such as market deregulation, economic openness, and estate reduction. Consequently, the region experienced considerable
economic and institutional transformation in its agricultural sector in terms of production, productivity, competitiveness, and profitability. In addition, the structural
adjustment processes that have been carried out have led to a reallocation of fiscal
resources, since they are now focused to provide basic services (health, education,
and security, among others). The remaining resources to support agricultural activities
such as science and technology, irrigation, price support, and subsidies to credit have
decreased, especially in the Andean countries (IICA, 1999).

In this chapter, we analyze this evolution of agricultural productivity from 1961 to
2001, calculating partial and total productivity indexes by region (Southern Cone,
Andean, Central America, and Caribbean) and their countries and for the LAC as a whole.

In Section 2 we analyze the output and input growth for the agricultural and
livestock sectors. The section also includes an analysis of some regional productivity

indicators based on the World Bank database. This section is completed with an analysis of some partial productivity indexes such as labor and land productivity, fertilizer, and machinery per hectare and agricultural capital per worker.

Section 3 presents some economic indicators related to food demand and population growth according to IFPRI projections, average and rate of growth of GDP per capita, birth, mortality, and child mortality based on Economic Commission for Latin America and the Caribbean (ECLAC) estimations.

Total factor productivity growth for the LAC region is analyzed in Section 4, with emphasis on the Brazilian and Colombian agricultural sectors. A synthesis of the other TFP studies developed in the region is presented in the same section. In the analysis we compare these results with the recent estimations of TFP for the region developed by Evenson and Avila (2003) based on the FAO statistical database. The paper also presents an analysis of the regional diversity in terms of agroecological zones.

In Section 5 we discuss some sources of productivity growth, with emphasis on agricultural research, rural extension, schooling, and nutrition. The LAC research intensity is analyzed by country and subregion and is compared with research indicators from other world regions. We also include an analysis of the determinants of TFP in LAC.

Section 6 is concerned with income improvement and poverty reduction studies based on several ECLAC documents.

Finally, Section 7 is devoted to conclusions.

2. AGRICULTURAL INDICATORS

2.1 Crop area yield accounting

Table 1 presents the rates of growth for LAC and by each one of its regions and their countries for two periods: 1962–1981 and 1982–2001. In general, only the Caribbean region presents a poor performance of the agricultural sector in terms of annual growth, with 0.60% in the period. The other three LAC regions experienced annual rates of growth superior to 2.5%. The annual average rate of output growth for the entire region was 2.31%.

If we analyze the LAC countries individually, Costa Rica, Bolivia, and Brazil present the highest rates of growth in output during the period. At the other extreme, we have all the Caribbean countries with poor rates of growth in agriculture. The poorest performance was in Cuba, where the agricultural output decreased substantially in the recent period (1982–2001). Uruguay had also a low rate of growth, but it was basically influenced by poor performance of the livestock sector.

The rates of growth for land for the LAC regions are presented in Table 2. The table includes rates of growth for cropland and permanent pastureland and for the aggregate. Comparing the two periods of analysis, the rates of growth for agricultural land (crops and livestock) are decreasing in the Southern Cone, Andean, and Caribbean regions

Table 1 Latin American and Caribbean agricultural output growth rates (%), 1962–2001

Regions/ Countries	Crops			Livestock			Average Growth		
	1962–1981	1982–2001	Average	1962–1981	1982–2001	Average	1962–1981	1982–2001	Average
Southern Cone	2.79	2.98	2.89	1.74	2.95	2.34	2.27	2.96	2.62
Andean	2.43	2.65	2.54	3.95	2.92	3.44	3.19	2.79	2.99
Central America	3.60	1.32	2.46	4.35	2.84	3.59	3.97	2.08	3.03
Caribbean	1.20	−0.71	0.24	2.78	0.77	1.78	1.99	0.03	0.60
Average rate	2.55	1.57	2.06	3.56	2.38	2.97	3.05	1.98	2.51

Source: FAO agricultural data; FAOSTAT (agricultural production indices).

Table 2 Latin American and Caribbean agricultural land growth rates (%), 1961–2000

Regions/ Countries	Crop Land			Permanent Pastures			Average Growth		
	1961–1980	1981–2000	Average	1961–1980	1981–2000	Average	1961–1980	1981–2000	Average
Southern Cone	1.79	−0.14	0.82	0.81	0.39	0.60	1.30	0.12	0.71
Andean	1.04	−0.06	0.49	0.92	0.30	0.61	0.98	0.12	0.55
Central America	0.47	0.90	0.68	1.08	0.95	1.02	0.77	0.92	0.85
Caribbean	1.43	0.78	1.10	−0.02	−0.47	−0.24	0.71	0.15	0.43
LAC average	1.18	0.43	0.80	0.92	0.35	0.64	1.05	0.39	0.72

but are increasing in Central America. At the country level, the reduction in the cropped area was more important in Chile, Uruguay, Colombia, and Jamaica, which presented an average negative rate of growth. On the contrary, we see Brazil, Paraguay, Ecuador, Costa Rica, Nicaragua, Guatemala, and Trinidad and Tobago presenting higher rates of growth (more than 1%).

Using the rates of growth for the crops and livestock output and for land, we calculated the yield accounting for crops, livestock, and aggregate, presented in Table 3. The yield accounting results also indicate that in the Caribbean region the productivity of the agricultural sector is decreasing. The other LAC regions perform very well, especially the Andean region and the Southern Cone.

At the country level, we had good performance in the first period (1961–1980) in the case of Bolivia, Venezuela, Mexico, Guatemala, Honduras, and Panama. However, these rates of growth were not uniform, considering the two sectors analyzed (crops and livestock). In general, this good performance was due to the livestock sector, except for Guatemala.

During the 1980s and 1990s, the productivity growth rates were again good for Bolivia and Honduras but also high for other countries (Chile, Brazil, Argentina, Ecuador, and Costa Rica). The rate of growth for crops was better for Chile, Bolivia, Argentina, and Costa Rica and good for livestock in Brazil, Ecuador, Peru, Dominican Republic, and Honduras. Chile also performed very well in livestock.

2.2 Input productivity and cereal yields

Based on some World Bank indicators for the agricultural sector, presented in Table 4, we can verify that the LAC regions, except the Caribbean, improved the performance in cereal yields, agricultural productivity, and fertilizer consumption from the final years of the 1970s and beginning of the 1980s to recent years. These results are consistent with all the calculations shown previously.

Table 3 Latin American and Caribbean agricultural area yield accounting (%), 1962–2001

Regions/ Countries	Crops			Livestock			Aggregate		
	1962–1981	1982–2001	Average	1962–1981	1982–2001	Average	1962–1981	1982–2001	Average
Southern Cone	1.01	3.12	2.06	0.93	2.56	1.74	0.97	2.84	1.90
Andean	1.39	2.71	2.05	3.03	2.63	2.83	2.21	2.67	2.44
Central America	3.13	0.42	1.78	3.27	1.89	2.58	3.20	1.16	2.18
Caribbean	−0.23	−1.49	−0.86	2.80	1.24	2.02	1.28	−0.12	0.58
LAC average	1.37	1.15	1.26	2.64	2.03	2.33	2.00	1.59	1.80

Table 4   Latin American and Caribbean World Bank agricultural indicators by region, 1979–2000

Regions/ Countries	Cereal Yield (kg/Ha)		Agricultural Productivity (Agricultural Value Added/Wk)		Fertilizer Consumption (100 kg/Ha Arable Land)	
	1979–1981	1998–2000	1979–1981	1998–2000	1979–1981	1997–1999
Southern Cone	1797	3264	4138	6494	381	1016
Andean	1824	2533	2362	2618	480	1088
Central America	1730	2146	1864	2319	938	2008
Caribbean	2265	2205	1723	1737	991	806
LAC average	1904	2537	2522	3292	698	1230

2.3 Agricultural technology adoption

According to Evenson (2003), in Latin America the rate of growth in the adoption of modern varieties was very high during the last 30 years (Table 5). This rate of growth was more impressive during the 1980s, especially in the case of wheat, maize, rice, and potatoes. For beans and cassava these rates of growth are still relatively small.

Table 5   Adoption of modern varieties in the main crops cultivated in Latin America (% of area planted to modern varieties), 1970–2000

Crop	1970	1980	1990	2000
Wheat	11	46	82	90
Rice	2	22	52	65
Maize	10	20	30	46
Beans	1	2	15	20
Cassava	0	1	2	7
Potatoes	25	54	69	84
All crops	8	23	39	52

Source: Evenson, R. E., "Production Impacts of Crop Genetic Improvement." In: Evenson, R. E., and Gollin, D. (eds.), *Crop Variety Improvement and Its Effect on Productivity: The Impact of International Agricultural Research*, CABI Publishing, Wallingford, U.K., Chapter 20, pp. 409–25.

The aggregated rate of adoption considering all Latin American crops also presented a high rate of growth (from 8–52% of the cropped area). When we desegregate these adoption rates by LAC subregion, the Southern Cone presents better performance. For this subregion it is estimated that 75% of the agricultural cropped area uses modern varieties. This rate of adoption is 64% in the Andean region and 45% in Central America. In the Caribbean this adoption rate is around 40%.

3. ECONOMIC INDICATORS

3.1 Food demand and population growth

According to the International Model of Policy Analysis of Commodities and Trade (IFPRI), under the most likely scenario global demand for cereal will increase 39% from 1995–2020, reaching 2466 millions tons; demand for meat is expected to increase 58%, and demand for roots and tubers, 37% (Pinstrup-Andersen et al., 1999).

Almost all the increase in food demand will take place in developing countries, since they will account for about 85% of the 690 million tons of increase in global demand for cereals between 1995 and 2020. Of this amount, LAC will represent 10.6%. In the case of meat products, LAC will participate with 16.4% of the total demand, and roots and tubers with 9.9% (Pinstrup-Andersen et al., 1999).

These large increases in food demand will result from population growth as well as urbanization, income growth, and changes in lifestyles and food preferences.

Regarding population and based on the "World Population Prospect" (UN, 1999), the world's population will grow by 1836 million from 1995–2020 (see Table 1), an increase of 32.4%. In this picture, LAC countries will increase their population levels from 480 million to 665 million in 25 years, an increase of 38.5%. LAC countries will contribute 10% of the world's population increase during this period. Table 6 reports population estimates for 1995 and 2020.

In addition, by 2020 about 52% of the developing countries' population will be living in urban areas, up from 38% in 1995 (UN, *op. cit.*). In the case of LAC, the population living in urban areas will represent 83% of the total population (Sànchez-Griñan, 1998). This rapid urbanization will have significant effects on food preferences and hence on demand, since people in urban areas tend to consume more livestock products, fruits, vegetables, and processed foods and lesser amounts of coarse grains.

From the demand side, even though most LAC people get enough food to meet their caloric requirements, 15% of the population is still underfed (Garret, 1995). Related to the supply side, urbanization, as mentioned, is carrying significant changes in the structure of food demand, but this in turn will have important effects on the structure of agricultural production and technology development to face these mentioned changes (Trigo, 1995). As an example of the challenges to come, according to

Table 6 World population (M), 1995 and 2020

World Regions	Population Level		Population increase		Share of Pop. increase
	1995	2020	1995–2020		
	Millions		Millions	Percent	Percent
Latin America and the Caribbean	480	665	185	38.5	10.1
Africa	697	1187	490	70.3	26.7
Asia, excluding Japan	3311	4421	1110	33.5	60.5
China	1221	1454	233	19.1	12.7
India	934	1272	338	36.2	18.4
Developed countries	1172	1217	45	3.8	2.5
Developing countries	4495	6285	1790	39.8	97.5
World	5666	7502	1836	32.4	100.0

Source: United Nations, *World Population Prospect: The 1998 Revision*. New York: UN, 1999.

the estimations of IFPRI, a modest expansion in cereal area is forecast in LAC, so important crop yield will be required to obtain the necessary production increase.

On the other hand, the population figures of each LAC country presented in Appendix 1 for the years 1980 and 2000 show different patterns of growth: Although the representative countries of the Caribbean (Jamaica, Trinidad and Tobago, and Cuba) and the Southern Cone, with the exception of Paraguay, had the lowest population growth rates from 1980 to 2000, the highest correspond to Andean and Central America countries.

3.2 LAC GDP per capita

Table 7 presents the annual growth of GDP per capita by region of Latin America and the Caribbean, by period of analysis.

The best performance is presented by the Southern Cone region in the two periods. In general, overall the LAC regions had a good GDP per capita performance during the first period (2.6%) but very poor results during the 1980–2001 period. In the second period, only the Southern Cone presented a good rate, but it was basically due to the excellent performance of the Chilean economy, with a GDP growth rate of 4.72%.

Table 7   Latin America and the Caribbean GDP per capita and growth rate (*), 1961–2001

Region/ Countries	Average GDP, 1961–1980**	Rate of Growth, 1961–1980 (%)	Average GDP, 1981–2001	Rate of Growth, 1981–2001 (%)
Southern Cone	3389	3.17	4440	2.11
Argentina	6619	1.98	7151	1.04
Brazil	2751	5.10	4235	0.86
Chile	2268	0.74	3750	4.72
Paraguay	1186	3.46	1794	−0.13
Uruguay	4121	1.39	5271	1.96
Andean	1995	2.50	2059	0.29
Bolivia	951	1.02	887	0.45
Colombia	1439	2.84	2134	1.47
Ecuador	1065	4.25	1506	0.02
Peru	2361	1.36	2266	−0.48
Venezuela	4159	0.55	3501	−0.28
Central America	1638	2.30	1932	0.49
Costa Rica	2465	3.09	3165	2.02
El Salvador	1657	1.40	1500	1.74
Guatemala	1244	2.92	1432	0.54
Honduras	613	1.98	699	0.22
Mexico	2355	3.23	3320	0.62
Nicaragua	860	0.61	497	−2.52
Panama	2270	2.91	2911	0.82
Caribbean	1663	2.43	2161	0.12
Dominican Republic	956	4.13	1543	2.14
Haiti	517	0.47	451	−2.71
Jamaica	2169	1.22	2107	0.87

Continued

Table 7 Latin America and the Caribbean GDP per capita and growth rate (*), 1961–2001—Cont'd

Region/ Countries	Average GDP, 1961–1980**	Rate of Growth, 1961–1980 (%)	Average GDP, 1981–2001	Rate of Growth, 1981–2001 (%)
Trinidad and Tobago	3008	3.91	4542	0.17
LAC	2144	2.60	2603	0.75

*Weighted by cropped area.
**Constant 1995 US$ prices.

3.3 Birth and death rates

In the following sections we analyze the evolution of the death and birth rates during the 1960–2005 period in the LAC subregions: Southern Cone, Andean, Central America, and the Caribbean. The information was taken from ECLAC-CELADE (2004).

3.3.1 Birth rates

Figure 1 shows a strong decrease in the crude birth rates (per thousand) in all the four subregions and for LAC as a whole. The average birth rates reduced from 41.1 in the 1960–1965 period to 22.0 in 2000–2005. Actually, these rates are very similar in the Southern Cone, Central America, and the Caribbean (around 20) and a little higher in the Andean region. The worst performances in this indicator are those of Bolivia, Guatemala, Honduras, Nicaragua, and Haiti, with indexes superior to 30. The best performance is observed in Chile, Uruguay, Cuba, and Trinidad and Tobago.

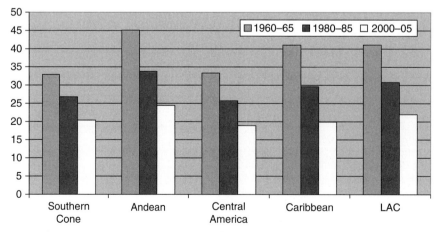

Figure 1 Birth rates in Latin American and Caribbean countries, 1960–2005.

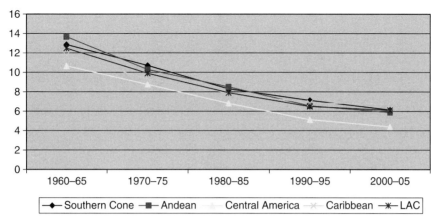

Figure 2   Mortality rates in Latin America and the Caribbean region, 1960–2005.

3.3.2 Mortality rates

The situation of the LAC countries in regard to the crude mortality rates are also decreasing. The crude mortality rates per thousand were reduced more than 50% during the last 40 years. The average rate was 12.5% in 1960–1965 and now is close to 6%. Uruguay is also the leader in this indicator. The worst indexes are observed in Brazil, Argentina, Bolivia, Costa Rica, Jamaica, and the Dominican Republic.

3.4 Infant mortality rates

The infant mortality rates for Latin America are shown in Figure 3. This indicator presented excellent performance during the period of analysis, with a decrease of more than three times (108 in 1960–1965 against 28 in 2000–2005).

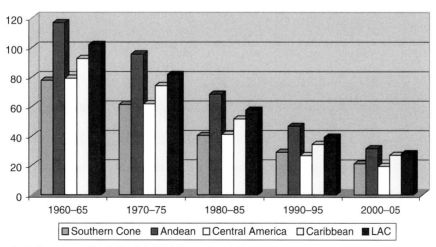

Figure 3   Infant mortality in LAC (per thousand), 1960–2005.

4. AGRICULTURAL TFP MEASURES IN LAC

This section presents an overview of the agricultural TFP studies in Latin America and the Caribbean, with emphasis on two countries, Brazil and Colombia, one located in the Southern Cone and other in the Andean region but both with an agricultural sector very important to the economy. The new agricultural TFP calculations presented in this section are an update of previous studies developed by Avila and Evenson (1995) and Romano (1987), respectively, for Brazil and Colombia. The section is completed with regional TFP indexes using FAO data (Evenson and Avila, 2004) and a review of the main TFP studies developed in Latin America.

4.1 TFP measures: Country studies
4.1.1 Brazil
Methodology The Brazilian study is based on the definition of TFP that is derived from a cost-accounting framework, which allows us to define a change in TFP from period $t-1$ to period t. Changes from period to period can then be summed up to create TFP measures when we have more than two periods. If no extraordinary profits exist and returns to all factors are properly measured, the

$$\sum_i P_i Y_i = \sum_j R_j X_j \tag{1}$$

values of all outputs (Y_i) will equal the value of all inputs (X_i).

Expression (1) does not impose strict efficiency by all farmers. It is based on an accounting condition that holds in a competitive sector.

Differentiating (1) totally with respect to time, we obtain the following expression:

$$\sum_i P_i \frac{\partial Y_i}{\partial t} dt + \sum_i Y_i \frac{\partial P_i}{\partial t} dt = \sum_J R_J \frac{\partial X_J}{\partial t} dt + \sum_J X_J \frac{\partial R_J}{\partial t} dt \tag{2}$$

For small changes, (2) expresses the relationship between changes in output and input quantities and output and input prices.

As demonstrated by Avila and Evenson (1995), the Tornqvist-Theil TFP index for multiple periods in logarithmic form is:

$$\ln\left(TFP_t / TFP_{t-1}\right) = \frac{1}{2} \sum_i \left(S_{it} + S_{it-1}\right) \ln\left(Y_{it} + Y_{it-1}\right) - \frac{1}{2} \sum_j \left(C_{jt} + C_{jt-1}\right) \ln\left(X_{jt} + X_{jt-1}\right)$$

We construct TFP indexes for each census micro-region based on data from the 1970, 1975, 1985, and 1995 Censuses of Agriculture for Brazil. For each micro-region, the Tornqvist-Theil index is computed for the three-period changes 1975–1970, 1985–1975, and 1995–1985. These are normalized to an index = 100 for the 1970–1975 averages period.

Output index   The output index was constructed using the following products: (1) temporary crops: wheat, rice, beans, maize, soybeans, cotton, manioc, onion, and tomato; (2) permanent crops: cocoa, coffee, sugar cane, apples, guaraná, cashew, rubber, banana, citrus, and grapes; and (3) livestock: beef cattle, milk, poultry, swine, wool, and eggs.

Input index   The input index was constructed using the following agricultural production factors: (1) crops: cultivated area, labor force (permanent, family, and temporary), tractors, animal power, fertilizer, and chemicals; and (2) livestock: natural and artificial pastures, labor force (permanent, family, and temporary), tractors, fertilizers, chemicals, feed, and animal medicines. In both cases, the prices used were collected from each one of the agricultural census years or from secondary sources.

Total factor productivity: Brazil and regions   Table 8 presents the TFP index for each of the five geographical Brazilian regions and for the country as a whole. These estimates were calculated based on the agricultural census data for the 1970, 1975, 1985, and 1995 periods.

The results presented in Table 8 are very consistent with the recent developments in Brazilian agriculture for the two sectors (crops and livestock) and for the aggregate. These results are also consistent with those obtained for other authors, such as Avila and Evenson (1995) and Gasquez and Conceição (2001).

The annual rates of growth in the period 1970–1995, not only for crops and livestock but for Brazil as a whole, increased 3.5% per year.

The results by region also show consistent rates of growth, with bigger TFP rates in the Center-West region, exactly the region where new arable and permanent pastures were incorporated into the production system in the last two decades. In this region the state with the best rate of growth in TFP was Mato Grosso.

Table 8 shows that besides the Center-West, the North and Northeast regions present a good performance on for crops due to the expansion of the agricultural frontier in these two regions, especially in Rondônia's State (North) and Maranhão and Piauí's States (Northeast). However, is important to note that the traditional Brazilian regions located in the Southeast and South of the country also presented good rates of growth in TFP for crops. For livestock, the better performance is again in the Center-West region, followed by the Southeast. Northeast, the poorest Brazilian region, and South,

Table 8 Agricultural TFP index and rates of growth (%) by Brazilian region, 1970–1995

Region	Sector	1970 Index	1995 Index	Growth Rate (%)
North	Crops	101.35	179.00	4.72
	Livestock	86.71	135.84	−1.33
	Aggregate	95.70	168.10	0.89
Northeast	Crops	95.60	202.08	3.04
	Livestock	80.41	77,01	−0.16
	Aggregate	86.47	130.56	1.66
Southeast	Crops	100.88	169.88	2.11
	Livestock	74.27	116.58	1.82
	Aggregate	83.91	166.06	2.77
South	Crops	86.24	157.14	2.43
	Livestock	83.79	93.48	0.44
	Aggregate	85.43	140.84	2.02
Center-West	Crops	101.99	293.89	4.32
	Livestock	82.24	158.52	2.66
	Aggregate	87.22	215.83	3.69
Brazil	Crops	94.32	269.68	4.29
	Livestock	81.46	115.74	1.41
	Aggregate	87.89	209.54	3.54

a traditional beef cattle producer, presented the lowest rates of growth in TFP for livestock. The rates of growth in the TFP for livestock in the South were not worst because in this region we had in the last decades a very good development of the swine and poultry production.

TFP by Brazilian agroecological zones   Figure 4 presents the main Brazilian agroecological zones, elaborated by the Embrapa Soil Research Center. In this figure four macro zones—crops (yellow), extractive (brown), livestock (red), and preservation (green)—are shown. Table 9 presents TFP growth rates for these macro agroecological zones.

As expected, in the estimates the macro zones more oriented for crops perform better (at an aggregate TFP annual growth rate of 2.28%) than the other macro zones (livestock and extractive). This macro zone includes the majority Center-South of Brazil and the Cerrados region, the new agricultural frontier of the country. At the

Figure 4 Brazilian agroecological zones (Embrapa Soil), 1993.

Table 9 TFP by Brazilian macro agroecological zones, 1970–1995

Agroecological Zone	Aggregated Index				Rate of Growth (%)
	1970	1975	1985	1995	
Crops	85.85	114.14	134.17	150.84	2.28
Extractive	95.90	104.10	112.40	141.26	1.56
Livestock	85.66	114.34	125.26	127.59	1.61
Preservation	91.55	108.45	104.99	119.16	1.06

other extreme, the macro zone classified by Embrapa as preservation, involving the majority of the municipalities in the Amazon, semi-arid, "pantanal," and coastal tablelands regions, presented the smaller aggregate TFP index (1.06%).

4.1.2 Colombia

Methodology   In the Colombian TFP study developed for the 1960–2001 period (Romano, 2003), we used a chain-linked variable weight (Divisia type index) with a Tornquist approximation; current prices are used as a base for each year in succession, and the year-to-year rates of growth are linked with a chain index. All calculations are performed in real terms (1970 = 100).

The variables used to calculate the TFP are the following:

O = Gross value of crops and livestock in each year.
L = Labor; the total number of man-days employed in crop and livestock production per year.

instead of working with an aggregate capital variable. The capital variable is divided into selected categories as follows:

A = Land as hectares of cropped and pasture land per year.
I = Intermediate purchased inputs used in production of crops and livestock (seed, fertilizers, concentrates, pesticides, etc.) measured in monetary value per year.
S = Stock of inventory of machinery, livestock, and land improvements.

Partial Productivities

Input Growth   According to Table 10, during the period 1991–2001 the cropland decreased 1.56% annually, with a fall in temporary crops of 3% and a rise of 0.3% in perennial crops. In contrast, pastureland increased 1.0% annually. This situation reflects a structural transformation in Colombian agriculture during that period, when the Colombian government carried out several free-market reforms. It is necessary to mention that such changes began during the 1981–2001 period, when cropland decreased 0.20% and pastureland increased 0.91%; previously, during 1961–1980, cropland increased 1.50% and pastureland, 1.68%.

In addition, during the 1991–2001 period, everything decreased in the Colombian agricultural sector: labor decreased 0.09%, fertilizer, 0.28%; and machinery, 3.82%. In relation to labor, it decreased in most of the periods, but surprisingly it increased during the 1981–2001 period; in contrast, fertilizer, with the above exception (1991–2001), increased during the rest of the periods.

Machinery shows a steady trend toward decreasing, and this fact is an indication of a less favorable situation for investing in agriculture, probably because of the sharp social

Table 10   Annual growth rates of agricultural production factors (%), 1961–2001

Production Factor	Selected Years					
	1961–1970	1971–1980	1981–1990	1991–2001	1961–1980	1981–2001
Cropland (ha)	1.40	2.50	1.00	−1.60	1.50	−0.20
Pastureland (ha)	1.88	1.56	0.84	1.01	1.68	0.91
Labor (thousands)	1.37	−2.22	0.66	−0.31	−0.20	0.72
Fertilizers (tons)	9.56	4.67	8.47	−0.28	6.65	4.54
Machinery (H.P.)	5.00	2.02	1.00	−4.00	4.00	−1.00

and political conflict in rural Colombia. Furthermore, because Colombia does not produce heavy rural machinery and because the importation of some items such as tractors in the past incurred high tariffs, especially in years previous to the 1990s.

Productivity ratios   Labor productivity increased at a good pace during the major part of the analysis period, but it began to decrease from 1981–2001 (Table 11). The trend of the components of this ratio (O/L), that is, land productivity (O/A) and land per worker (A/L), shown in Figure 1, indicates that land productivity has exhibited more dynamic behavior than land per worker.

According to theory (Hayami and Ruttan, 1985), that means that biological innovations (improved varieties, pest management, etc.) have been adopted by farmers, and those innovations have been more important than mechanical innovation, as indicated by the land-per-worker ratios. It is a matter of worry that the labor and land

Table 11   Annual growth rates in labor and land productivity (%), 1961–2001

Input	1961–1970	1971–1980	1981–1990	1991–2001	1961–1980	1981–2001
Labor productivity (O/L)	2.01	7.06	2.31	0.07	4.15	1.87
Area/labor (A/L)★	0.43	3.91	0.20	0.97	1.92	0.99
Land productivity (O/A)★★	1.57	3.15	2.11	−0.90	2.13	0.88

Note: O/L = (A/L) (O/A).
★Mechanical technology.
★★Biological technology.

productivities and the A/L ratio decreased from 1961–1980 to the 1981–2001 period, since this situation is very inconvenient for facing more competitiveness in national and international markets (Figure 5).

Another way to view Colombian technological development is by analyzing the proxy index for factors substituting for land (F/A) and the proxy index for factors substituting for labor (M/A), where fertilizers = F, machinery = M, area = A, and workers = L. As shown in Table 12, the F/A ratio has a more dynamic trend than M/A during the whole period of analysis, even during the 1991–2001 period, which means that agricultural technological development in Colombia has saved relatively more land than labor.

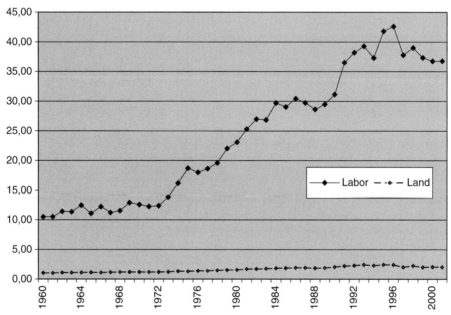

Figure 5   Land and labor productivity in Colombia (Colombian pesos), 1960–2001.

Table 12   Annual growth rates in fertilizer and HP/ha and capital stock/worker (%), 1961–2001

Input	1961–1970	1971–1980	1981–1990	1991–2001	1961–1980	1981–2001
Fertilizer (F.)/ha	8.19	2.18	7.44	1.29	5.88	4.70
HP tractor (M)/ha	3.21	0.00	−2.60	−2.32	2.07	−1.34
Capital stock (K)/worker	−0.68	6.41	−1.56	−0.42	2.76	−0.56

During the 1990s this tendency lost much of its dynamism in Colombian agriculture, as shown in Figure 6. Note that fertilizer is still an important source of productivity in Colombia.

To complete our analysis, the ratio of capital stock (K) per worker (L) was estimated. It is difficult to measure the contribution of work capital assets in the improvement productivity in the Colombian agricultural sector.

Total factor productivity   The evolution of the input cost shares for Colombia is presented in Table 13. Note that labor (wage bill) shows a natural and expected decreasing tendency from 1960–1990 but recovers its importance in 2001; on average, for 1961–1980 and 1981–2001, labor maintains high participation as a cost of production.

It is necessary to mention that during the last period, Colombia carried out a decentralization process, transferring important resources to small cities and providing some employment opportunities to the farmer; in some ways this fact helps retain some of the people migrating from the rural sector.

In contrast, intermediate consumption of modern inputs increased participation in factor cost shares, from 1960–1990 and 2001. In spite of the Colombian agriculture crisis, these inputs remained with high participation during 1981–2001 (29%). This trend is probably a consequence of the technological package coming from the Green Revolution and still in wide use in Colombian agriculture.

Land and capital, represented by their rental values, show a steady tendency to decrease over the whole period of analysis. These trends confirm the results from the

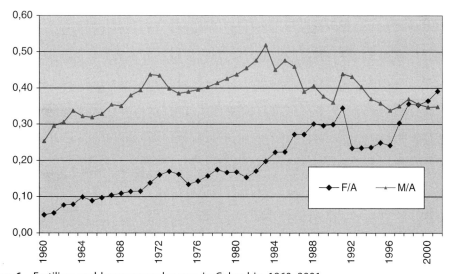

Figure 6   Fertilizer and horsepower by area in Colombia, 1960–2001.

Table 13   Colombian input costs shares (%), 1960–2001

Year	Labor (Wage Bill)	Modern Inputs	Land (Rental Value)	Capital (Rental Value)
1960	46	14	20	20
1970	41	22	18	19
1980	40	24	21	15
1990	34	34	17	15
2001	43	34	11	12
1961–1981	43	20	20	17
1981–2001	41	29	16	14

partial productivity analysis, that is, the loss of importance of the capital as a source of growth in the agricultural sector in Colombia. As mentioned before, capital is defined here as machinery, livestock, and land improvements.

Finally, we obtained TFP indexes (output, inputs, and multifactorial), as shown in Figure 7, based on the information shown in Appendix 2.

The analysis of the TFP evolution by annual rate of growth allows us to perform some kind of source-of-growth analysis. In Table 14 we observe that during the

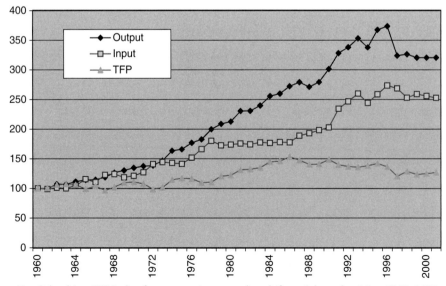

Figure 7   Colombian TFP index for output, input, and multifactorial productivity, 1960–2001.

Table 14 TFP average annual growth rates for Colombia (%), 1961–2001

	1961–1970	1971–1980	1981–1990	1990–2001	1961–1980	1981–2001
Output	3.38	4.84	2.97	−0.23	4.00	1.64
Inputs	2.26	3.45	1.49	0.93	2.95	1.79
Labor	0.51	1.16	−0.06	1.16	0.94	0.80
Modern inputs	1.11	1.10	1.60	−0.14	1.07	1.13
Capital	0.31	0.92	−0.18	−0.24	0.64	−0.24
Land	0.33	0.27	0.13	0.16	0.30	0.10
Productivity	1.12	1.51	1.48	−1.18	1.05	−0.19

1961–1980 and 1981–2001 periods, the contribution of the multifactorial productivity is less than the contribution of inputs to the output annual growth rate. In addition, during the 1990–2001 period, this TFP index decreased at a rate of 1.18% annually; the output growth also decreased (−0.23%). The rate of growth in inputs was positive and rather low at the total.

Observing the four decades, we can characterize each as follows: 1961–1970 as the "take-off" period, when the national agricultural research institute was created and it developed many improved varieties and some other technological products; 1971–1980 as the acceleration period, when the product or research were diffused and adopted by farmers and the Colombian government assigned important financial resources to agricultural research and extension; 1981–1990 as the stagnation period; and 1990–2001 as the decreasing period, related to less support from the government and institutional change concerning agricultural research.

4.1.3 Other LAC TFP studies

The TFP for the Argentinean agricultural sector was recently calculated by Lema and Parellada (2001). The results showed that agricultural TFP growth rates in this country were positive during all of the periods of analysis. The TFP estimated for the entire period of analysis, 1970–1997, was 1.55%. The best performance was found in 1970–1980, with 2.21%; the worst occurred during 1980–1990, when growth was only 0.34%.

Arias and Rodríguez (2002), in their paper on the evolution and performance of the agricultural sector in Costa Rica, estimated the total factor productivity for the 1977–2000 period. The rate of growth for the Costa Rican agricultural sector was strongly positive in the beginning of the period of analysis and relatively modest for the rest of the period. The estimated TFP growth rate for the entire period was 0.45%.

Madrid-Aris (1997) estimated the total factor productivity for the Cuban agricultural sector during the 1963–1988 period. The author estimated a negative rate of growth for the agricultural sector for the period of analysis (−1.5%) and for all the three desegregated periods (1963–1970, 1971–1980, and 1981–1988). The paper also includes TFP indexes for the rest of the Cuban economy.

Avila and Evenson (1995) estimated Tornqvist-Theil TFP indexes for the Brazilian agricultural sector and by subsector (crops and livestock) for the 1970–1985 period based on the agricultural census data. Their study also included TFP indexes by each one of the five Brazilian macro regions (North, Northeast, Southeast, South, and Center-West) and by agroecological zones.

The Avila and Evenson results were higher in the Southeast and Center-West regions (3.1% and 3.8%, respectively), where the Cerrados, the new agriculture frontier in Brazil, is located. The annual rate of growth for the entire Brazilian agricultural sector was estimated at 2.45%, whereas by subsector the higher value was found for crops (3.63%). The annual TFP growth rate at the livestock subsector was 2.12%.

Another Brazilian TFP study was developed by Gasques and Conceição (2001), also based on the agricultural census data and using the Tornqvist-Theil formula. The authors estimated TFP indexes for the entire country and by Brazilian state but only for the agricultural sector as a whole (aggregate). The aggregated annual growth rate estimate was 2.33%. The desegregated TFP results showed that only two of the 27 Brazilian states posted negative productivity growth. The higher annual TFP growth rates were found in states located in the central regions, consistent with the results shown earlier. The poorest performance was verified as the states located in the Amazon region, a non-traditional region for agricultural and livestock production and not directed affected by the recent technological boom of the agricultural sector in the South and Center of Brazil.

Araujo et al. (2002) estimated TFP growth rates of the agricultural sector in the state of São Paulo, one of the more developed Brazilian states. The TFP rates estimated by the authors for the 1960/1999 period showed an average annual growth rate of 1.71%. During the first decade (1960/70) the annual rate of agricultural TFP was very low but for the 1970/99 period the authors found an annual rate greater than 2% per year.

Finally, is important to highlight the results obtained by Gasques et al. (2004). The Tornqvist indexes estimated by these authors for the 1974/2002 period and sub-periods are presented in the Table 15. All the TFP growth rates estimated by Gasques et al. (2004) are very high but consistent with the results presented above.

The overall TFP growth rates of the Brazilian agricultural sector estimated by Avila and Evenson (1995), Gasques and Conceição (2001), Gasques et al.(2004) or those presented early in this section show rates that are relatively high, according to the LAC studies presented earlier. These results are also high compared with TFP index estimates in other world regions or those estimated in developed countries, such as the United States (around 1.5%).

Table 15 Brazilian agricultural TFP growth rates by decade

Period	Output index	Input index	TFP index
1975-2002	3.28	−0.02	3.30
1975-1979	4.37	−0.10	3.62
1980-1989	3.38	0.19	1.52
1990-1999	2.99	−0.17	4.88
2000-2002	5.89	−0.53	6.04

Source: Gasques et al., 2004.

4.2 LAC TFP using FAO databases

Table 16 shows the results of the recent estimates of TFP growth rates for LAC and all its four subregions and countries according to methodology developed by Evenson and Avila (2004). In the aggregate, the LAC performance was very good for both periods (1962–1981 and 1982–2001).

The results by subregion show us that the Caribbean region presents the poorest performance, especially in Cuba and Trinidad and Tobago. The table also includes estimates for the agricultural and livestock sectors, where we found that livestock performs better than the crop sector in the first period. The crop sector presents a better performance in the second period, especially in the Southern Cone (Brazil, Argentina, and Chile) and Andean regions.

During 1980–2001 the majority of the countries in Central America presented a poor performance in productivity growth in agriculture. The Caribbean countries continued with negative or small rates of growth in TFP.

5. SOURCES OF PRODUCTIVITY GROWTH

5.1 Agricultural research

According to Figure 8, public research expenditure in LAC remained almost the same proportion of total world expenditure from 1976 (9.22%) to 1995 (9.00%). In this same period, China and other Asian and Pacific countries increased their participation in the total of agricultural research expenditures (17.21% to 30.89%).

As shown in Table 17, in average, Latin America spent 1.12% of its agricultural GDP in 1996, almost double that spent in 1976. Intensities in 1996 varied, from 0.13% for Guatemala to 1.73% for Brazil. In the LAC region the majority of the countries increased their participation from 1976 to 1996, with the exception of Chile and Guatemala.

Table 16 TFP growth rates for LAC regions (%), 1961–2001

Regions and Countries	Agricultural TFP Growth Rates (%)						
	Crops		Livestock		Aggregate		
	1961–1980	1981–2001	1961–1980	1981–2001	1961–1980	1981–2001	Average
Southern Cone	1.49	3.14	0.72	2.51	1.02	2.81	1.92
Argentina	3.08	3.93	0.90	0.43	1.83	2.35	2.09
Brazil	0.38	3.00	0.71	3.61	0.49	3.22	1.86
Chile	1.08	2.22	0.24	1.87	0.69	2.05	1.37
Paraguay	3.97	−1.01	−0.36	1.29	2.63	−0.30	1.17
Uruguay	1.29	2.02	−0.32	0.53	0.01	0.87	0.44
Andean	1.11	1.71	1.73	1.92	1.41	1.81	1.61
Bolivia	1.73	3.14	2.81	1.39	2.30	2.33	2.31
Colombia	2.01	1.27	0.49	2.24	1.37	1.73	1.55
Ecuador	−0.74	2.24	0.98	2.51	−0.16	2.34	1.09
Peru	−0.83	1.86	1.86	2.14	0.36	1.98	1.17
Venezuela	2.42	0.87	3.41	1.07	3.03	0.99	2.01
Central America	1.65	1.05	2.77	1.53	2.17	1.32	1.74
Costa Rica	2.86	2.09	1.10	0.75	1.74	1.19	1.47
El Salvador	1.22	−0.87	1.99	1.00	1.77	0.32	1.05
Guatemala	3.31	0.53	0.90	−0.28	1.38	−0.08	0.65
Honduras	1.54	−0.39	2.07	1.91	1.91	1.25	1.58
Mexico	1.53	1.43	3.02	1.63	2.26	1.51	1.89
Nicaragua	1.33	−0.70	2.94	1.92	2.25	0.99	1.62
Panama	2.29	−1.33	1.61	1.49	1.93	0.02	0.97
Caribbean	0.74	−2.05	1.20	0.64	0.98	0.29	0.64
Cuba	0.88	−2.88	−0.26	−1.03	0.12	−1.69	−0.78

Continued

Table 16   TFP growth rates for LAC regions (%), 1961–2001—Cont'd

| Regions and Countries | Agricultural TFP Growth Rates (%) | | | | | | |
| | Crops | | Livestock | | Aggregate | | |
	1961–1980	1981–2001	1961–1980	1981–2001	1961–1980	1981–2001	Average
Dominican Rep.	0.99	−1.15	1.88	2.60	1.62	0.89	1.25
Haiti	0.60	−1.04	3.44	1.80	2.73	1.00	1.87
Jamaica	−0.65	1.32	3.28	−0.35	2.07	0.29	1.18
Trinidad and Tobago	−0.88	0.16	3.00	−1.39	1.80	−0.80	0.50
Average rate	*1.45*	*2.26*	*1.39*	*2.13*	*1.36*	*2.24*	1.80

Source: Evenson and Avila (2004).

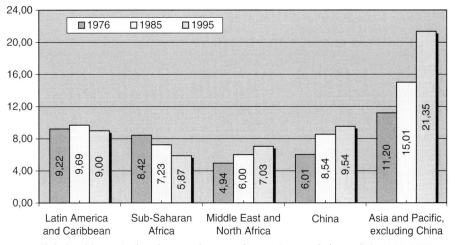

Figure 8   Global public agricultural research expenditures: Regional shares (%), 1976–1995.

The government remains the principal source of resources for agricultural research in the LAC region, with 71% of the total in 1996, even though government spending ranged from 82% in Brazil to 13% in Honduras. Nonprofit organizations represent a small part of the total, but this means a significant share in Colombia and some Central American countries. Higher-education institutions are a very important source of agricultural research in countries such as Argentina (42%), Mexico (45%), and Uruguay (39%). Table 18 shows these ratios for selected LAC countries.

Table 17　LAC public agricultural research expenditures as a share of the agricultural GDP, 1976–1996

LAC Country	1976	1986	1996
Argentina	0.79	0.95	1.12
Brazil	0.75	1.00	1.73
Chile	1.92	1.64	1.43
Colombia	0.25	0.48	0.53
Costa Rica	0.53	0.72	0.56
Guatemala	0.22	0.31	0.13
Honduras	0.17	0.71	0.34
Mexico	0.48	0.61	0.88
Panama	0.64	1.35	1.07
Paraguay	0.06	0.13	0.18
Uruguay	0.52	0.77	1.70
Average	**0.59**	**0.79**	**1.12**

Source: Beintema and Pardey (2001).

Table 18　Composition of the agricultural research expenditures in LAC, 1996

LAC Country	Government Principal	Other	Nonprofit Organizations	Higher Education
Argentina	51	7	—	42
Brazil	59	23	3	15
Chile	49	18	—	33
Colombia	57	10	24	9
Costa Rica	33	4	28	35
Guatemala	57	—	41	2
Honduras	13	—	84	3
Mexico	44	9	2	45
Panama	81	8	—	11

Continued

Table 18 Composition of the agricultural research expenditures in LAC, 1996—Cont'd

LAC	Government		Nonprofit Organizations	Higher Education
Country	Principal	Other		
Paraguay	75	—	0	25
Uruguay	47	14	0	39
Average	**54**	**17**	**4**	**25**

Source: Beintema and Pardey (2001).

5.2 Studies of rates of return

Table 19 shows that in developing countries the median of the estimated rates of return is lower in Africa and Middle East/North Africa than in LAC or Asia. Similarly, the median of the estimates is higher in Europe and North America than in Australia, New Zealand, Japan, and Israel. However, the table also indicates that on average, the developing and developed countries and the CGIAR centers have high and similar rates of return for agricultural research.

Table 19 Median of rates of return for agricultural research by world region, 1996

Geographical Region	Rate of Return (%)
Developed countries	46.0
United States and Canada	46.5
Europe	62.2
Australia and New Zealand	28.7
Japan and Israel	37.4
Developing countries	43.0
Africa	34.3
Asia/Pacific	49.5
Middle East/North Africa	36.0
Latin America	41.0
CGIAR centers	40.0

Source: Alston et al. (2000) and Avila (2002), updated by the authors.

The results presented are a strong indicator that agricultural research is playing an important role in the progress of the agricultural sector in the world and certainly was responsible for a large part of the agricultural productivity growth observed in recent decades.

In LAC more than 130 economic studies were developed to evaluate the impact of agricultural research. As shown on Table 20, Brazil is the leader in the development of this kind of study and was responsible for almost 50% of them. Some other countries also have performed a significant number of studies and calculations on this matter, as in the case of Ecuador, Colombia, Argentina, Peru, and Mexico.

By subregion, the Southern Cone presents the major number of calculations, followed by the Andean region; the Caribbean has no studies about impact evaluation. Appendix 3 presents an updated list of the main studies developed in the region.

Particularly in the case of Brazil, it is important to note that the majority of these studies (75%) were developed or directly supported by Embrapa, the Brazilian Corporation for Agricultural Research. The continuous development of impact assessment studies at Embrapa, by their own researchers or by invited experts, are an institutional priority (Avila, 2002). If we focus the LAC by sector, we note the absence of estimations concerning fishery, forestry, and soil and water, since there is now a great deal of interest in investment of this kind and the necessity to evaluate its social and economic value.

The majority of the studies (98) are related to crops; 20% are aggregated and only five are from livestock. This is also a surprisingly low number, which does not correspond with the importance of this activity within the region. When we analyze the 130 LAC studies by commodity, soybeans and rice show the major number of estimations in Brazil, and wheat, maize, potato, and rice are the dominants in the rest of LAC.

Table 20   Regional frequency of agricultural research impact studies

Southern Cone		Andean		Central America	
Brazil	61	Colombia	13	Mexico	7
Argentina	12	Ecuador	14	Panama	1
Chile	3	Peru	9	Honduras	2
Uruguay	1	Bolivia	0	Others	0
Paraguay	0	Venezuela	0	Caribbean	0
—	—	Peru/Colombia	1	—	
PROCISUR	3	PROCIANDINO	1	—	
Subtotal	**80**	**Subtotal**	**38**	**Subtotal**	**10**
Latin America			**2**	**Total LAC**	**130**

The results show us that in all countries the returns were superior to other economic activities. This means that agricultural development depends on investments in science and technology generation.

5.3 Rural extension services

In the last three decades, the rural extension services in Latin America have been undergoing important transformations. The public extension workers, very important during the 1960s and 1970s, are gradually being replaced by the private sector. The majority of commercial farmers, especially in the Southern Cone, are now assisted by private extension workers paid by their own rural extension service. Actually, the public extension workers are more concentrated in the technical and social assistance of small farmers. Table 21 presents a small picture of the situation of the rural extension service in Latin America during the 1980s, according to FAO databases.

Table 21   Public extension workers in Latin America by subregion and country, 1985

Country	Number of Public Extension Workers	Country	Number of Public Extension Workers
Argentina	400	Costa Rica	233
Brazil	1407	El Salvador	90
Chile	450	Guatemala	363
Paraguay	136	Honduras	280
Uruguay	20	Mexico	680
Southern Cone	2413	Nicaragua	85
Bolivia	80	Panama	1124
Colombia	1832	Central America	2855
Ecuador	150	Dominican Rep	70
Peru	650	Haiti	360
Venezuela	1271	Jamaica	475
Andean	3983	Caribbean	4884

Source: FAO (1985).

Although the numbers of extension workers have changed in the past two decades, this service (public and private) continues to be an important source of agricultural productivity growth.

The difficulties experienced by extension work in LAC are present in all countries. The general feeling is that extension should be serviced by private sector and the public extension should be strictly oriented to small farmers. The future agricultural policy should consider the access of large, medium-sized, and small farmers to extension services (whether public or private); otherwise many new technologies will not be diffused among the potential producers.

5.4 Schooling

Schooling is one the most important sources of growth in agricultural productivity. Figure 9 presents the evolution of the number of years of education for adult males from 1970–2000, according to the World Bank. This variable, from the Barro-Lee database of the World Bank, is not specific to agricultural workers.

It is probably the case that the average schooling of agricultural workers is lower than the average schooling for all workers. But for our purposes, it is the growth rate in schooling that is important. Again, in this case the Southern Cone is the subregion of Latin America with better indexes, followed by the Andean region.

5.5 Nutrition

Another source of productivity growth is the Dietary Energy Sufficiency (DES). Figure 10 presents the DES index published by the FAO for the 1970–2000 period. This index is based on consumption data and effectively is an average calories per capita measure. Both measures are reported by developing country regions to show the diversity in changes in these indexes.

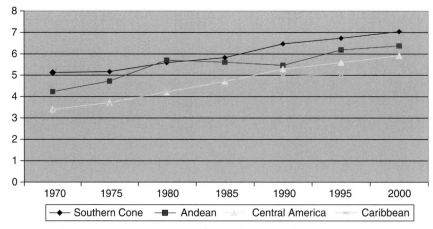

Figure 9   Schooling in Latin America (years of schooling in adult males), 1970–2000.

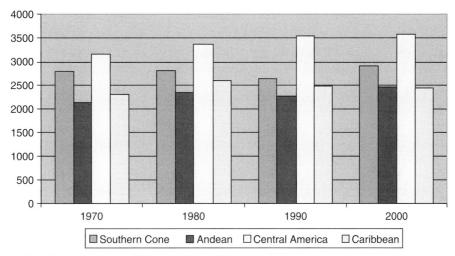

Figure 10 Dietary energy sufficiency index, 1970–2000.

The data show that in Latin America, the countries located in the Central America subregion are those with better dietary energy indexes. This index is also growing faster there than in other LAC subregions.

6. ANALYSIS OF THE DETERMINANTS OF TFP GROWTH IN LAC

In this section we analyze the relationship between the sources of productivity growth discussed in the previous section and the estimated TFP of the agricultural sector of Latin America and the Caribbean. The analysis of the determinants of the agricultural TFP growth included 20 LAC countries and two periods (1961–1980 and 1981–2001). In this analysis we used the same TFP decomposition framework adopted by Avila and Evenson (2004) to evaluate the determinants of agricultural TFP growth in the developing countries. This model, adapted for the LAC case, is a three-equation model as described here:

AdopMV: Instruments
GrDES: Instruments
Aggregate TFP: AdopMV, GrDES, GrASch, Lac1, Lac2, Lac3

where

TFP_{ct} is the TFP index value for each LAC country c for period t.
$AdopMV_{ct}$ is the adoption rate of modern varieties weighted by crop area.
$GrASch_c$ is the growth rate of average years of schooling of adult males between
   periods.

GrDES$_c$ is the growth rate on the Dietary Energy Sufficiency (DES) index (published by the FAO) between periods.

Lac1, Lac2, and Lac3 are dummy variables for each LAC subregion (Southern Cone, Andean, and Central America, with the Caribbean region left out).

The instruments for AdopMV and GrDES include the exogenous variables in the aggregate TFP equation, Lac1, Lac2, Lac3, and GrASch, plus innovation classes dummy variables IrrigLand, Extwork, and Rurpopden. These other variables mean the following:

RurpopDen is the rural population density by country for period t.

Extwork is the number of extension workers in each country for period t.

In Class2 to InClass6 are dummies for innovation class variables (explanation below).

These innovation classes, according to Avila and Evenson (2004), measure the research capacity of each country. They were constructed using the ratio of agricultural researchers by cultivated area and the percentage of GDP applied in R&D. The distribution of Latin American countries by innovation classes is as follows:

Innovation class D24: Nicaragua, Ecuador, and Dominican Republic
Innovation class D32: Honduras
Innovation class D33: Haiti and Paraguay
Innovation class D34: Uruguay
Innovation class D35: Guatemala, Panama, Peru, and Venezuela
Innovation class D44: Bolivia, Colombia, and Jamaica
Innovation class D45: Argentina and Mexico
Innovation class D55: Costa Rica
Innovation class D56: Chile, El Salvador, and Brazil

The numbers represent classes during each period of analysis (1961–1980 and 1981–2001). For estimation purposes, we grouped the countries in five classes (2 through 6) and according to the classification by period. This aggregation was based on the innovation index for the first period, except in case of the Group 3, which was split into two subgroups, $-32 + 33$ and $34 + 35$. It is important to note that a low number, D24, for example, means a low grade of innovation, whereas D56 represents the highest grade of science and technology development. That leaves four innovation classes (InClass2, InClass3, InClass4, and InClass5) in the econometric model and one class left out (InClass6) for estimation purposes.

Two of the three variables (AdMV and GrDES) are treated as endogenous in the TFP model. The method used to deal with this fact is to use instrumental variables.

The instruments for AdopMV and GrDES include the exogenous variables in the aggregate TFP equation, Lac1, Lac2, and Lac3, and GrASch, plus the innovation class dummies (2 through 5), extension workers, and rural population density.

Table 22 reports the estimates for both the first-stage instrumented variables, AdoptMV and GrDES, and the second-stage aggregate TFP equations. Adoption of modern varieties, the growth in schooling, and improved dietary nutrition had positive and significant effects on agricultural TFP growth in LAC countries.

These results confirm those obtained by Avila and Evenson (2004) for all the developing countries in which the adoption of Green Revolution modern varieties, increases in schooling of the labor force, and increases in dietary energy were identified as sources of TFP growth.

7. INCOME IMPROVEMENT: POVERTY REDUCTION STUDIES

The information given in this section is based on studies and publications from the Economic Commission for Latin America and the Caribbean (ECLAC), which has the basic function of monitoring the economic and social situation of the LAC countries and analyzing the public policies carried out to reach some important development goals.

The information presented here is heavily based on ECLAC publications such as *A Decade of Social Development in Latin America, 1990–1999* (2000), *Social Panorama of Latin America, 2002–2003* (2004), and *Meeting the Millennium Poverty Reduction Targets in Latin America and the Caribbean* (2002). This information has to do with the magnitude and profile of poverty, factors related to poverty reduction, income distribution, and the millennium poverty reduction targets.

7.1 Poverty magnitude

According to Table 23, although the percentage of poor people out of the total population decreased in most LAC countries in the 1990s, the number of poor rose from 200 million to 211 million. In addition, the poor population represented 40.5% of the total in 1980, 48.3% in 1990, and 43.5% in 1999.

In terms of indigent people (extreme poverty), the figures were 18.6% for 1980, 22.5% for 1990, and 18.5% for 1999. So, comparing 1980 with 1999, the region made no progress in this matter in two decades (ECLAC, 2000). For 2002, the percentage of poor were estimated to be 44% and those in indigence or extreme poverty, 19.4% (ECLAC, 2004).

Table 24 presents the situation of poverty and indigence by country (18). According to the table, poverty rates fell in 11 countries in the region, representing the bulk of the population: Brazil, Chile, and Panama hold the best performance, followed by Costa Rica, Guatemala, and Uruguay. In contrast, Bolivia, Ecuador, Paraguay, and Venezuela failed to make progress reducing poverty in the last decade. Colombia made very little progress. In the case of indigence, the picture is almost identical. In addition, it is worth noting that Uruguay shows the smallest rates of poverty and indigence in all the region.

Table 22   Determinants of the TFP growth in Latin America and the Caribbean

	First-Stage Instrumented Variables		Second-Stage Estimates
	Adopt MV	Dietary Nutrition/ Share Labor	Aggregate TFP
Growth rate Schooling × Labor Force	−5.81 (−2.51)	4.29 (1.57)	0.3994 (2.27)
Lac 1: Southern Cone	46.08 (3.11)	−5.73 (−0.33)	−0.61 (−0.46)
Lac 2: Andean	19.28 (1.25)	2.98 (0.16)	−0.147 (−0.12)
Lac 3: Central America	20.74 (1.37)	−11.25 (−0.63)	0.280 (0.27)
Innovation class2	−29.13 (−1.77)	11.97 (0.61)	
Innovation class3	−32.50 (−2.66)	7.57 (0.52)	
Innovation class4	−29.67 (−3.33)	19.99 (1.90)	
Innovation class5	−15.36 (−2.82)	2.77 (0.43)	
Extension workers	−0.003 (−5.03)	0.004 (4.92)	
Rural population density	−2.77 (−1.58)	6.05 (2.93)	
Adoption rate, modern varieties			0.0662 (2.88)
Dietary Nutrition x Labor Force			0.0377 (1.94)
# obs	40	40	40
R-*squared*	0.77	0.57	0.58
Prob > F	0.0000	0.0022	0.0023

Table 23 Latin America: Poor and indigent households and individuals, 1980–1999 (M households and individuals and %)*

Year	Poor**						Indigent***					
	Total		Urban		Rural		Total		Urban		Rural	
	M	%	M	%	M	%	M	%	M	%	M	%
						Households						
1980	24.2	34.7	11.8	25.3	12.4	53.9	10.4	15.0	4.1	8.8	6.3	27.5
1990	39.1	41.0	24.7	35.0	14.4	58.2	16.9	17.7	8.5	12.0	8.4	34.1
1999	41.3	35.3	27.1	29.8	14.2	54.3	16.3	13.9	8.3	9.1	8.0	30.7
						Individuals						
1980	135.9	40.5	62.9	29.8	73.0	59.9	62.4	18.6	22.5	10.6	39.9	32.7
1990	200.2	48.3	121.7	41.4	78.5	65.4	93.4	22.5	45.0	15.3	48.4	40.4
1999	211.4	43.8	134.2	37.1	77.2	63.7	89.4	18.5	43.0	11.9	48.4	38.3

*Estimates corresponding to 19 countries of the region.
**Households and population living in poverty. Includes indigent households (population).
***Indigent households and population.
Source: ECLAC, on the basis of special tabulations of data from household surveys conducted in the respective countries.

Table 24 Latin America: Poverty and indigence indicators (%), 1990–1999

Country	Year	Households and Population Below the Poverty Line*		Households and Population Below the Indigence Line	
		Households	Population	Households	Population
Argentina**	1990	16.2	21.2	16.2	21.2
	1999	13.1	19.7	13.1	19.7
Bolivia	1989***	49.4	53.1	49.4	53.1
	1999	54.7	60.6	54.7	60.6
Brazil	1990	41.4	48.0	41.4	48.0
	1999	29.9	37.5	29.9	37.5
Chile	1990	33.3	38.6	33.3	38.6
	2000	16.6	20.6	16.6	20.6

Continued

Table 24 Latin America: Poverty and indigence indicators (%), 1990–1999—Cont'd

Country	Year	Households and Population Below the Poverty Line*		Households and Population Below the Indigence Line	
		Households	Population	Households	Population
Colombia	1991	50.5	56.1	50.5	56.1
	1999	48.7	54.9	48.7	54.9
Costa Rica	1990	23.7	26.2	23.7	26.2
	1999	18.2	20.3	18.2	20.3
Ecuador★★★★	1990	55.8	62.1	55.8	62.1
	1999	58.0	63.6	58.0	63.6
El Salvador	1999	43.5	49.8	43.5	49.8
Guatemala	1989	63.0	69.1	63.0	69.1
	1998	53.5	60.5	53.5	60.5
Honduras	1990	75.2	80.5	75.2	80.5
	1999	74.3	79.7	74.3	79.7
México	1989	39.0	47.8	39.0	47.8
	2000	33.3	41.1	33.3	41.1
Nicaragua	1993	68.1	73.6	68.1	73.6
	1998	65.1	69.9	65.1	69.9
Panamá	1991	36.3	42.8	36.3	42.8
	1999	24.2	30.2	24.2	30.2
Paraguay	1990★★★★★	36.8	42.2	36.8	42.2
	1999	51.7	60.6	51.7	60.6
Peru	1999	42.3	48.6	42.3	48.6
Dominican Republic	1998	25.7	30.2	25.7	30.2
Uruguay★★★★	1990	11.8	17.8	11.8	17.8
	1999	5.6	9.4	5.6	9.4
Venezuela	1990	34.2	40.0	34.2	40.0
	1999	44.0	49.4	44.0	49.4

Continued

Table 24 Latin America: Poverty and indigence indicators (%), 1990–1999—Cont'd

Country	Year	Households and Population Below the Poverty Line*		Households and Population Below the Indigence Line	
		Households	Population	Households	Population
Latin America	1990	41.0	48.3	41.0	48.3
(19 countries)	1999	35.3	43.8	35.3	43.8

*Includes households (individuals) living in indigence or extreme poverty.
**Greater Buenos Aires.
***Eight departmental capitals plus the city of El Alto.
****Urban areas.
*****Asunción Metropolitan.
Source: ECLAC, on the basis of special tabulations of data from household surveys conducted in the respective countries. For a definition of each indicator, see ECLAC (2004).

Concerning the spatial distribution of poverty, the relative importance of urban poverty continued to increase during the decade; by 1999, 134 million of 211 million poor people lived in urban areas and 77 million in rural areas. One of the most important factors explaining this situation has to do with migration from rural areas to the cities, since the urban economy faces the challenge of absorbing a larger proportion of the working-age population and, consequently, the increased demand for social services, not always with success (ECLAC, 2000).

However, the incidence of poverty is higher in rural areas than in cities, since almost 64% of people are poor and rural compared to 37% in cities. In addition, poverty is more extreme in rural areas, since most of the people there are indigent (46 million of 89 million). In addition, in Bolivia, Costa Rica, El Salvador, Guatemala, Honduras, Nicaragua, Paraguay, and Peru, poverty is still a rural situation, whereas in Colombia, Mèxico, and Dominican Republic, almost 45% of the poor reside in rural areas (Table 25).

7.2 Factors related to poverty

Several studies carried by ECLAC have stablished that poverty levels are affected by economic, demographic, and social factors. The economic factors include economic growth, public transfers, and relative prices. Demographic aand social factors include the size, composition, and geographical location of households as well as the level of education of household members and the labor market (ECLAC, 2000; ECLAC, 2002). Some findings concerning these topics are as follows:

Table 25   Latin America: Magnitude and relative share of rural poverty (%), 1999

Rural Households Below the Poverty Line	Poor Rural Households in Relation to Total Poor Households		
	Less Than 35%	Between 35% and 49%	50% or More
Over 65%			Guatemala Honduras Nicaragua
Between 51% and 65%		Colombia Ecuador México	Bolivia El Salvador Paraguay Peru
Between 31% and 50%	Brazil Panama Venezuela	Dominic Republic	
Up to 30%	Argentina Chile Uruguay		Costa Rica

Source: Prepared on the basis of ECLAC, Social Panorama of Latin America, 1998 (LC/G.2050-P), Santiago, Chile, May 1999. United Nations publication, Sales No. E.99II.G.4, Table 16 of the statistical.

Throughout the decade the ups and downs in per capita income were closely correlated to decreases or increases in poverty, especially in extreme cases—for example, Chile and Venezuela. But similar growth rates have different effects on poverty levels. In Chile, for example, per capita GDP increased 55% from 1990 to 1999; at the same time, poverty fell 50%. Meanwhile, in Uruguay, a much smaller increase in per capita GDP (28%) correlated with a larger decrease in poverty (53%). In Bolivia and Panama, per capita GDP grew at similar rates over the period (16% and 20%), but the decline of urban poverty in both countries was very different: 14% and 25%, respectively (Table 26).

The growth of labor productivity was uneven across various sectors and firms; growth in labor productivity was typical of big companies linked with the international market, although these firms generated few new jobs. In contrast, low-productivity employment, mostly in the informal sector, expanded in nearly all the countries.

On the other hand, public transfers were very important in reducing the incidence of poverty. In Argentina, Costa Rica, Panama, and Uruguay, such transfers represented

Table 26   Latin America (14 countries): Per capita GDP and percentage of the population living in poverty and indigence, 1990–1999

Country	Year	Per Capita GDP (1995 Dollars)	Percentage of the Population		Variation Over the Period (Annual Average)		
			Poor	Indigent	GDP*	Coefficient of	
						Poverty (P)	Indigence (I)
Argentina★	1990	5.545	21.2	5.2			
	1999	7435	19.7	4.8	3.3	−0.8	−0.9
Brazil	1990	3859	48.0	23.4			
	1999	4.204	37.5	12.9	1.0	−2.7	−6.4
Chile	1990	3.425	38.6	12.9			
	2000	5.309	20.6	5.7	4.5	−6.1	−7.8
Colombia	1991	2.158	56.1	26.1			
	1999	2.271	54.9	26.8	0.6	−0.3	0.3
Costa Rica	1990	2.994	26.2	9.8			
	1999	3.693	20.4	7.8	2.4	−2.7	−2.5
Ecuador ★★	1990	1.472	62.1	26.2			
	1999	1.404	63.5	31.3	−0.5	0.2	2.0
El Salvador	1995	1.675	54.2	21.7			
	1999	1.750	49.8	21.9	1.1	−2.1	0.2
Guatemala	1989	1.347	69.1	41.8			
	1998	1.534	60.5	4.1	1.5	−1.5	−2.2
Honduras	1990	686	80.5	60.6			
	1999	694	79.7	56.8	0.1	−0.1	−0.7
Mexico	1989	3.925	47.8	18.8			
	1998	4.489	46.9	18.5	1.5	−0.2	−0.2
Nicaragua	1993	416	73.6	48.4			
	1998	453	69.9	44.6	1.7	−1.0	−1.6
Panama	1991	2.700	42.8	19.2			
	1999	3.264	30.2	10.7	2.4	−4.3	−7.0
Uruguay★★	1990	4.707	17.8	3.4			
	1999	5.982	9.4	1.8	2.7	−6.8	−6.8

Continued

Table 26 Latin America (14 countries): Per capita GDP and percentage of the population living in poverty and indigence, 1990–1999—Cont'd

Country	Year	Per Capita GDP (1995 Dollars)	Percentage of the Population		Variation Over the Period (Annual Average)		
			Poor	Indigent	GDP*	Coefficient of	
						Poverty (P)	Indigence (I)
Venezuela	1990	3.030	40.0	14.6			
	1999	30.37	49.4	21.7	0.0	2.4	4.5
Latin America	1990	3.349	48.3	22.5			
	1999	3804	43.8	18.5	1.4	−1.1	−2.2

*Greater Buenos Aires.
**Total for urban areas.
Source: ECLAC, on the basis of official figures and special tabulations of data from household surveys conducted in the respective countries.

more than 20% of total urban household income and about 10% in Brazil, Chile, Colombia, Ecuador, Mexico, and Venezuela.

7.3 Income distribution

The highly uneven income distribution that has been typical of LAC remained the same or worsened in most of the countries in the 1990s. According to Table 27, the major share of the population (70% and more) in each country were below the average per capita income; also, the high degree of income concentration in Latin America can be inferred from the Gini coefficient.

According to this coefficient, Brazil presents the highest concentration with a Gini index of almost 0.64, followed by Bolivia, Colombia, Nicaragua, Guatemala, and Honduras. By contrast, Uruguay presents the lowest income concentration. Additionally, 11 out of 17 countries showed an increment in income concentration from 1990 to 1999; the rest of the countries made very little progress in this area during the same period (ECLAC, 2000).

Table 28 illustrates another feature of income distribution in Latin America, that is, income distribution is not clearly related to the countries' level of development. For each category of per capita income (high, intermediate, and low) there is high, intermediate, and low income concentration. For example, Argentina and Uruguay, which both have high income levels in regional terms, have very different income distribution structures.

Table 27   Latin America: Indicators of income concentration by country,* 1990–1999

Country	People (%) with Per Capita Incomes Below:			Gini
	Year	Average	50% of Average	Coefficient*
Argentina	1990	70.6	39.1	0.501
	1999	72.5	44.2	0.542
Bolivia	1989★	71.9	44.1	0.538
	1999	70.4	45.5	0.586
Brazil	1990	75.2	53.9	0.627
	1999	77.1	54.8	0.640
Chile	1990	74.6	46.5	0.554
	2000	75.0	48.4	0.559
Colombia	1994	73.6	48.9	0.601
	1999	74.5	46.6	0.572
Costa Rica	1990	65.0	31.6	0.438
	1999	67.6	36.1	0.473
Ecuador★	1990	69.6	33.8	0.461
	1999	72.1	42.0	0.521
El Salvador	1995	69.7	38.4	0.507
	1999	68.5	40.6	0.518
Guatemala	1989	74.9	47.9	0.582
	1998	75.0	49.5	0.582
Honduras	1990	75.1	52.3	0.615
	1999	71.8	46.4	0.564
Mexico	1989	74.2	43.5	0.536
	1998	72.8	43.1	0.539
Nicaragua	1993	71.5	45.9	0.582
	1998	73.1	45.9	0.584
Panama	1991	71.3	46.4	0.560
	1999	72.1	46.4	0.557
Paraguay	1990	69.2	33.4	0.447
	1999	72.3	46.3	0.565
Dominican Republic	1997	71.4	39.8	0.517

Continued

Table 27   Latin America: Indicators of income concentration by country,* 1990–1999—Cont'd

Country	People (%) with Per Capita Incomes Below:			Gini
	Year	Average	50% of Average	Coefficient*
Uruguay★	1990	73.2	36.8	0.492
	1999	67.1	32.2	0.440
Venezuela	1990	68.0	35.5	0.471
	1999	69.4	38.6	0.498

*Low (under 0.48), intermediate (between 0.48 and 0.54), and high (over 0.54) Gini coefficient.

Table 28   Latin America (17 countries): Per capita income and degree of income concentration in urban areas by country, 1999

Per Capita Income	Country	Income Concentration*
High (More than US$4,000)	Argentina	High
	Uruguay	Low
	Chile	High
	Mexico	Intermediate
	Brazil	High
Intermediate (Between US$2,000 and US$4,000)	Costa Rica	Low
	Panama	Intermediate
	Venezuela	Low
	Dominican Republic	Intermediate
	Colombia	High
Low (Less than US$2,000)	El Salvador	Low
	Paraguay	Intermediate
	Guatemala	High
	Ecuador	Intermediate
	Bolivia	Intermediate
	Honduras	High
	Nicaragua	High

Source: ECLAC, based on special tabulations from household surveys in the countries concerned.

7.4 Millenium poverty reduction target

The report *Meeting the Millennium Poverty Reduction Target in Latin America and the Caribbean* (ECLAC, IPEA, and PNUD, 2002) looks at the conditions under which 18 LAC countries would be able to meet the extreme poverty reduction target established by the Millennium Declaration as one of the United Nations Millennium Development Targets.[1] The question that the report seeks to answer is wheather or not each country will succeed in decreasing its 1999 extreme poverty rate by 2015.

For each country, two scenarios were considered: the "historical" one, which extrapolates the countries' growth and inequality dynamics of the 1990s into the future, and the "alternative" one (in comparisson with a "regional ideal"). As expected, the report's findings give reasons for both concern and moderate optimism.

According to the "historical" scenario, if the countries in the sample continue to perform as they did in the 1990s, only seven of them will reach the extreme poverty reduction target; these countries are Argentina, Chile, Colombia, Dominican Republic, Honduras, Panama, and Uruguay. Another six countries would continue to reduce poverty but at a very slow pace: Brazil, Costa Rica, El Salvador, Guatemala, Mexico, and Nicaragua. The rest of the countries—Bolivia, Ecuador, Paraguay, Peru, and Venezuela—would see higher levels of extreme poverty because of increases in inequalities, per capita income, or both.

Concerning the "alternative" scenario and with respect to the international poverty line (which corresponds to a $1-a-day line), it was found that 16 countries could meet the target by combining average annual growth rates of per capita GDP of 3% with cumulative reductions in inequality of 4% or less. The exceptions are Bolivia and El Salvador. The findings appear to indicate that even very small reductions in inequality can have very large positive impacts in terms of poverty reduction, and this effect is more important than the reduction in poverty due to economic growth.

8. CONCLUSION

The partial agricultural productivity indexes and the TFP growth rates analyzed in this chapter show that the Latin American and Caribbean region presents a very diverse situation. In general, the Southern Cone and the Andean regions present more positive indicators. In contrast, the Caribbean region presented the worst productivity indicators.

In general, the countries' TFP results discussed in this chapter indicate a better performance for the LAC countries in the last two decades. This results are compatible with other indicators and sources of productivity growth analyzed in the chapter.

The information concerning the R&D intensities suggests that the results are positive for the region. The share of research expenditure and agricultural GDP is increasing in the majority of the countries, the government continues to present strong sources of funding for agricultural research, and the rates-of-return estimates in the region are comparable to those calculated in developed countries and CGIAR centers.

Brazil is the leader in the development of impact studies, followed by Ecuador, Colombia, Argentina, Peru, and Mexico. By LAC subregion, the Southern Cone presents the major number of calculations, followed by the Andean region; the Caribbean has no studies covering impact evaluation of agricultural research programs.

Schooling and nutrition are three other important sources of productivity growth. In general, the data show good performance by the Latin American countries in these regards. The Southern Cone is again the leader for schooling, but Central American countries present the best indexes for dietary energy sufficiency (DES).

The TFP decomposition exercise confirmed results obtained by other authors in this same kind of study and cited in the economic literature. The adoption of Green Revolution modern varieties, increases in schooling of the labor force, and increases in dietary energy were very important sources of agricultural TFP growth in the Latin American and the Caribbean countries during the last four decades.

End Note

1. The United Nations Millennium Declaration stipulates that the target is to halve the proportion of extreme poverty that existed in 1990; 1999 was chosen as the reference point because of data availability.

References

Alston, J., Chan-Kang, C., Marra, M. C., Pardey, P., & Wyatt, T. J. (2000). *A Meta Analysis of Rates of Return to Agricultural R&D: Ex Pede Herculem?* Research Report, 113. Washington: IFPRI.

Amores, P. F. (1999). *Impacto de la Investigación agrícola en Cacao.* MSc. thesis. Quito, Ecuador: Universidad Internacional SEK del Ecuador, Facultad de Ciencias Económicas y Administrativas.

Aragón, J., & Forero, F. (1976). Estudio Socioeconómico de las Inversiones realizadas en Investigación y Fomento de la Palma Africana en Colombia. *Revista ICA, 11*(3), 243–256.

Araujo, P. F. C., Schuh, G. E., Barros, A. L. M., Shirota, R., & Nicolella, A. C. O. (2002, Dezembro). *Crescimento da Agricultura paulista e as Instituições de Ensino, Pesquisa e Extensão numa Perspectiva de Longo Prazo: Relatório Final do Projeto.* São Paulo: FAPESP.

Ardila, J. (1973). *Rentabilidad Social de las Inversiones en Investigaciones de Arroz en Colombia.* MSc. thesis. Bogotá: PEG UN-ICA.

Arias, J., & Rodriguez, S. (2002, mayo). *Evolución y Desempeno del Sector Agroelimentario Costaricense: 1960–2000.* San José: IICA.

Avila, A. F. D., & Evenson, R. E. (1995). Total Factor Productivity Growth in Brazilian Agriculture and the Role of Agricultural Research. In *Anais do XXXIII Congresso Brasileiro de Economia e Sociologia Rural* (Vol. I, pp. 631–657). Curitiba, 31/07 a 03/08/95.

Avila, A. F. D., & Souza, G. S. (2002, February 4–7). *The Importance of Impact Assessment Studies for the Brazilian Agricultural Research System in Brazil.* Paper presented at the "International Conference on

Impacts of Agricultural Research and Development: Why has impact assessment research not made more a difference?" San José (Costa Rica).

Avila, A. F. D., & Evenson, R. E., (2004, March). Total Factor Productivity Growth in Agriculture: The Role of Technological Capital Paper presented in the Fontagro Seminar, "Competitividad rural: Retos, Oportunidades y Recursos para la Innovación Tecnológica Agrícola en América Latina y el Caribe," held in Lima (Peru). 39 p.

Beintema, N., & Pardey, P. (2001, November 7–9). *Recent Developments in the Conduct of Latin American Agricultural Research*. Paper presented for the ICAST Conference on Agricultural Science & Technology, Beijing.

ECLAC. (2000). *A Decade of Social Development in Latin America, 1990–1999*. Santiago, Chile: CEPAL.

ECLAC/IPEA/PNUD. (December 2002). *Meeting the Millennium Poverty Reduction Targets in Latin America and the Caribbean*. Santiago, Chile.

ECLAC. (May 2004). *Social Panorama of Latin America, 2002–2003*. Santiago, Chile: CEPAL.

ECLAC-CELADE. (2004, Jan.). Population Estimates and Projections, 1950–2050. In *Demographic Bulletin of LAC*. Santiago, Chile: CEPAL.

Embrapa. (1993). Ministério da Agricultura e reforma Agrária. Serviço Nacional de Levantamento e Conservação de Solos. In *Delineamento Macroagroecológico do Brasil*. Rio de Janeiro: Embrapa.

Evenson, R. E. (2003). *Agricultural Research and Intellectual Property Rights*. Yale University.

Farfán, M. L. (1999). *Impacto Económico de la Investigación en Café en Colombia: el caso de la Variedad Colombia*. Documento CEDE 99–03. Bogotá: Centro de Estudios sobre el Desarrollo Económico. CEDE. Universidad de los Andes.

FAO, Annual report 1985. Rome, Italy, UN FAO, 1987.

Garrett, J. L. A. (1995, October). *A 2020 Vision for Food, Agriculture and the Environment in Latin America*. Washington: IFPRI. 2020 Vision, Discussion paper 6.

Gasques, J. G., & Conceição, J. C. P. R. (2001). Transformações Estruturais da Agricultura e Produtividade Total dos Fatores. In: *Transformações da Agricultura e Políticas Públicas* (pp. 17–92). Brasília: IPEA.

Gasques, J. G., Bastos, E. T., Bacchi, M. P. R., & Conceição, J. C. P. R. (2004). *Condicionantes da Produtividade da Agropecuária Brasileira*. Brasília: IPEA (Texto para Discussão, 1017).

Hayami, Y., & Ruttan, V. (1985). *Agricultural Development: An International Perspective* (2nd ed.). Baltimore: The John Hopkins University Press.

IICA. (1999). *Limitaciones y Desafíos del Sector Agroalimentario Andino*. Lima, Perú: Centro Regional Andino.

Jaramillo, F. (1976). *Evaluación Económica de las Inversiones en la Investigación sobre el Cultivo de la Cebada*. Boletín de Investigación No 42. Bogotá: ICA.

Lema, D., & Parellada, G. (2001). *Productivity and Competitive Advantage of the Argentinean Agriculture*. Buenos Aires: Instituto de Economia y Sociología. INTA.

Madrid-Aris, M. (1997). *Growth and technological change in Cuba*. ASCE: Cuba in Transition.

Manzano, B. (1999). *La inversión en Investigación y Transferencia de Tecnología ha Contribuido al Desarrollo del Sector Arrocero, Generando Beneficios Económicos que se Distribuyeron entre Consumidores y Productores*. BSc. thesis. Quito, Ecuador: Universidad Internacional SEK del Ecuador, Facultad de Ciencias Económicas y Administrativas.

Mendoza, C. L. (1987). *Estimación del Impacto Económico de los Resultados de la investigación del Instituto Nacional de Investigaciones Agropecuarias (INIAP)*. BSc. thesis. Quito, Ecuador: Universidad Central del Ecuador, Facultad de Ciencias Económicas.

Montes, G. (1973). *Evaluación de un Programa de Investigación Agrícola: el Caso de la Soya*. MSc. thesis. Bogotá: Universidad de los Andes.

Palomino, J., & Echeverría, R. (1991). *Impacto de la Investigación Agrícola en el Ecuador; El caso del Arroz*. Quito, Ecuador: INIAP, ISNAR, FUNDAGRO.

Palomino, J., & Norton, G. (1992). *Impacto de la Investigación Agrícola en el Ecuador; El caso del Maíz Duro*. Quito, Ecuador: INIAP, ISNAR, FUNDAGRO.

Pardey, P., & Beintema, N. (2001). *Slow Magic: Agricultural R&D a century after Mendel*. Washington: IFPRI and ASTI (Food Policy Research).

Peña, M. (1976). *Evaluación Económica de las Inversiones Estatales en Investigación sobre el Cultivo de la Papa*. MSc. thesis. Bogotá: Universidad La Gran Colombia.

Pino, P. S. (1991). *Evaluación del Impacto Económico de las Inversiones en Investigación Agrícola*. BSc. thesis. Quito, Ecuador: Universidad Central del Ecuador, Facultad de Ciencias Económicas.

Pinstrup-Andersen, P., Pandya-Lorch, R., & Rosegrant, M. W. (1999). *World Food Prospects: Critical Issues for the Early Twenty-First Century*. Washington: IFPRI (Food Policy Report).

Racines, J. M. (1992). *Evaluación del Impacto Económico de la Investigación y Transferencia de Tecnología en los cultivos de Palma Africana y Soya*. BSc. thesis. Quito, Ecuador: Universidad Central del Ecuador, Facultad de Ciencias Agropecuarias.

Romano, L. (1987). *Economic Evaluation of the Colombian Agricultural Research System*. Ph.D. thesis. Stillwater, OK: Oklahoma State University.

Romano, L., Bermeo, A., Torregrosa, Y. M. (1994). *Impacto Socioeconómico de la Investigación del ICA en el cultivo del Sorgo*. ICA, Boletín Técnico.

Romano, L. (2003). *Indicadores de la Productividad Agropecuaria en Colombia*. Bogotá, Colombia: ICA.

Sànchez-Griñan, M. (1998, Enero). *Seguridad Alimentaria y Estrategias Sociales. Su contribución a la Seguridad Nutricional en Areas Urbanas de América Latina*. Washington: IFPRI (2020 Vision, Discusión Paper 23).

Scobie, G., & Posada, R. (1977). *The Impact of Rice Varieties in Latin America, with special emphasis in Colombia*. Series JE–01, Cali: CIAT.

Trigo, E. (1995, December). *Agriculture, Technological Change and the Environment in Latin America: A 2020 Perspective*. Washington: IFPRI (2020 Vision, Discussion paper 9).

Trujillo, C. (1974). *Rendimiento Económico de la Investigación en Trigo en Colombia*. MSc. thesis. Bogotá: PEG, UN-ICA.

United Nations. (1999). *World Population Prospect: The 1998 Revision*. New York: UN.

Vivas, L., Zuluaga, J., & Castro, H. (1992). *Las Nuevas Variedades de Caña y su Impacto Económico en el Sector Azucarero del Valle del Cauca*. MSc. thesis. Cali: Universidad del Valle.

APPENDIX 1

Table A.1   LAC country population, 1980–2000

Country	Population (Thousands)		Growth Rate (%)
	1980	2000	
Argentina	28.094	37.032	31.82
Bolivia	5.355	8.329	55.53
Brazil	121.672	170.693	40.29
Colombia	28.447	42.321	48.77
Costa Rica	2.284	4.023	76.10
Cuba	9.710	11.199	15.35
Chile	11.147	15.211	36.46
Ecuador	7.861	12.646	58.84
El Salvador	4.586	6.397	36.85
Guatemala	6.920	11.385	66.94
Haiti	5.454	8.357	53.23
Honduras	3.569	6.483	81.73
Jamaica	2.133	2.576	21.10
Mexico	67.570	98.881	46.34
Nicaragua	2.921	5.071	73.71
Panama	1.950	2.856	46.47
Paraguay	3.114	5.496	76.52
Peru	17.324	25.939	48.13
Dominican Republic	5.697	8.396	49.12
Trinidad y Tobago	1.082	1.294	20.06
Uruguay	2.814	3.337	14,54
Venezuela	15.091	24.170	60.16

Source: *Economic Commission for Latin America and the Caribbean 2002 Yearbook*, Santiago de Chile (2003; www.eclac.org).

APPENDIX 2

Table A.2   Colombian agricultural TFP: Input, output, and multifactorial indexes, 1960–2001

Year	Input	Output	Productivity
1960	100	100	100
1961	98.92	99.40	100.49
1962	101.16	107.51	106.27
1963	99.93	107.12	107.19
1964	104.99	111.57	106.27
1965	115.61	114.33	98.90
1966	110.69	114.83	103.75
1967	122.99	118.83	96.61
1968	124.17	126.68	102.02
1969	118.92	130.56	109.79
1970	121.46	134.74	110.93
1971	127.17	137.50	108.13
1972	141.07	138.72	98.33
1973	144.36	146.72	101.64
1974	142.91	163.63	114.50
1975	141.51	165.93	117.25
1976	152.03	176.93	116.38
1977	166.28	182.61	109.82
1978	180.43	199.64	110.65
1979	172.66	208.72	120.88
1980	173.94	212.61	122.23
1981	175.72	230.67	131.27
1982	174.27	230.87	132.48
1983	177.63	239.90	135.06
1984	176.69	255.87	144.81

Continued

Table A.2 Colombian agricultural TFP: Input, output, and multifactorial indexes, 1960–2001—Cont'd

Year	Input	Output	Productivity
1985	177.99	259.77	145.94
1986	177.65	272.34	153.30
1987	189.02	279.11	147.66
1988	193.00	271.18	140.51
1989	198.13	279.36	141.00
1990	202.75	301.44	148.68
1991	234.42	328.04	139.94
1992	246.82	338.14	136.99
1993	260.15	353.18	135.76
1994	244.36	337.94	138.30
1995	258.76	367.48	142.01
1996	273.59	373.49	136.51
1997	268.74	323.97	120.55
1998	253.22	326.27	128.85
1999	259.23	320.43	123.61
2000	256.06	320.43	125.14
2001	252.67	320.43	126.82

APPENDIX 3

Table A.3 The Brazilian experience on agricultural research impact evaluation (IRR)

Authors and Year	Location (Country, State, Center, etc.)	Commodity/Level	IRR (*)
1. Ayer and Schuh (1972)	State of São Paulo	Cotton	77
2. Monteiro (1975)	Brazil	Cocoa	16–18
3. Fonseca (1976)	Brazil	Coffee	23–26
4. Moricochi (1980)	State of São Paulo	Citrus	28–78
5. Avila (1981)	State of Rio Grande do Sul	Irrigated rice	87–119
6. Cruz, Palma, and Avila (1982)	Embrapa research	Aggregate	22–43
7. Ribeiro (1982)	State of Minas Gerais	Rice Cotton Soybeans	69 48 36
8. Cruz and Avila (1983)	World Bank Project: Embrapa research	Aggregate	20–38
9. Avila, Borges, Irias, and Quirino (1984)	Embrapa Human Capital	Training program	22–30
10. Roessing (1984)	Soybeans Research Center, Embrapa	Soybeans	45–62
11. Ambrosi and Cruz (1984)	Wheat Research Center, Embrapa	1974–1982	59–74
12. Avila, Irias, and Veloso (1985)	IDB Agricultural Research Project I: Embrapa research South research system	 Aggregate Aggregate	 27 38
13. Monteiro (1985)	Minas Gerais and Espirito Santo states	Cocoa	61–79
14. Barbosa, Cruz, and Avila (1988)	Embrapa research	Aggregate	34–41
15. Barbosa, Avila, and Motta (1988)	World Bank Project II: Embrapa research	Aggregate	43
16. Kitamura et al. (1989)	Embrapa research: North region	Aggregate	24

Continued

Table A.3   The Brazilian experience on agricultural research impact evaluation (IRR)—Cont'd

Authors and Year	Location (Country, State, Center, etc.)	Commodity/Level	IRR (*)
17. Santos et al. (1989)	Embrapa research: Northeast region	Aggregate	25
18. Teixeira et al. (1989)	Embrapa research: Center/West region	Aggregate	43
19. Lanzer et al. (1989)	Embrapa research: South region	Aggregate	45
20. Santos and Barros (1989)	Cotton Research Center, Embrapa	Aggregate	24–37
21. Gonçalves, Souza, and Rezende (1989)	São Paulo state	Rice	85–95
22. Kahn and Souza (1991)	Cassava and Fruit Research Center, Embrapa	Cassava and cow-pea crop system	29–46
23. Barbosa and Cruz (1993)	IDB Project II: Embrapa research	Aggregate	43
24. Dossa and Contini (1994)	Soybeans Research Center: a reevaluation	Soybeans	65
25. Avila and Evenson (1995)	a1) Embrapa national programs	Aggregate (1)	56
	b1) Embrapa regional centers		46
	c1) State research		19
	a2) Embrapa national programs	Livestock (2)	90
	b2) Embrapa regional centers		25
	c2) State research		63
	a3) Embrapa national programs	Crops (3)	38
	b3) Embrapa regional centers		75
	c3) State research		29

Continued

Table A.3 The Brazilian experience on agricultural research impact evaluation (IRR)—Cont'd

Authors and Year	Location (Country, State, Center, etc.)	Commodity/Level	IRR (*)
26. Avila & Evenson (1995)	Embrapa Grain Research	Wheat Soybeans Maize Rice	40 58 37 40
27. Oliveira and Santos (1997)	Goat Research Center, Embrapa	Aggregate	24
28. Vilela, Morelli, and Makishima (1997)	Vegetables Research Center, Embrapa	Carrots research	36
29. Pereira and Santos (1998)	Cotton Research Center, Embrapa	Aggregate	15
30. Cançado Júnior, Lima, and Rufino (2000)	State Minas Gerais	Aggregate	32
31. Almeida, Avila, and Wetzel (2000)	Embrapa Research	Soybeans breeding program	69
32. Ambrosi (2000)	Wheat Research Center, Embrapa	Aggregate	88–143
33. Almeida and Yokoyama (2001)	Rice and Beans Research Center, Embrapa	Upland rice breeding program	93–115

*Estimations of average internal rate of return (IRR).
Source: Avila (2002).

Table A.4 Other Brazilian agricultural research impact evaluations (MIRR)

Authors and Year	Location (Country, Region, Center, Project ...)	Commodity or Level	MIRR (*)
34. Evenson (1982)	Brazil	Aggregated	69
35. Silva (1984)	Brazil	Aggregated	60
36. Pinazza et al. (1984)	State of São Paulo, Brazil	Sugar cane	35
37. Ayres (1985)	Brazil	Soybeans	46
	State of Paraná		51
	State of São Paulo		23
	State of Santa Catarina		31
	State of Rio Grande Sul		53
38. Evenson and Cruz (1989a)	Brazil	Wheat	39
		Maize	30
		Soybeans	50
39. Evenson (1990a)	Brazil: Field crops	Field crops	41–141
40. Evenson (1990b)	Brazil: Center/South	Field crops	68–75
		Perennial crops	71–78

*Estimations of marginal internal rate of return (MIRR).
Source: Avila (2002).

Table A.5 The agricultural research impact in Hispanic countries in LAC

Authors	Country	Commodity/Level	Rates of Return (%)
41. Barletta (1971)	Mexico	Wheat	74–104
		Potato	69
		Maize	26–59
		Other crops	54–82
42. Himes (1972)	Peru	Maize	65
43. Ardila (1973)	Colombia	Rice	58
44. Montes (1973)	Colombia	Soybean	79
45. Trujillo (1974)	Colombia	Wheat	12
46. Jaramillo (1976)	Colombia	Barley	53
47. Pena (1976)	Colombia	Potato	68
48. Aragón and Forero (1976)	Colombia	Oil palm	30
49. Scobie and Posada (1977)	Colombia	Rice	87
50. Pazols (1981)	Chile	Rice	16–94
51. Yarrazaval R. (1982)	Chile	Wheat	21–28
		Maize	36–34
52. Martinez (1983)	Panama	Maize	47–325
53. Norton (1987)	Peru	Beans	14–24
		Maize	10–31
		Potato	22–48
		Rice	17–44
		Wheat	18–36
		Other crops	17–38
54. Mendoza (1987)	Ecuador	Potato	28
		Rice	44
		Soybeans	17
		Oil palm	32
55. Romano (1988)	Colombia	Crops and livestock**	72–85
		Crops and livestock	141

Continued

Table A.5 The agricultural research impact in Hispanic countries in LAC—Cont'd

Authors	Country	Commodity/Level	Rates of Return (%)
56. Scobie (1988)	Honduras	Fruit, nut Other crops	16–93 17–76
57. Cordomi (1989)★★	Argentina	Aggregated Other crops	41 33–38
58. Echeverría (1989)	Uruguay	Rice	52
59. Evenson and Cruz (1989b)	PROCISUR Region: Southern Cone of South America	Wheat Maize Soybeans	110 191 179
60. Ruiz de Londono (1990)	Peru / Colombia	Beans	15–29
61. Traxler (1990)	Mexico	Wheat	22–24
62. Pino (1991)	Ecuador	Wheat Potato Soft Maize Beans	29 29 3 5
63. Palomino and Echeverría (1991)	Ecuador	Rice	34
64. Taxler (1992)	Mexico	Wheat	15–23
65. Cruz and Avila (1992)	Andean region	Aggregated	24
66. Vivas, Zuluaga, and Castro (1992)	Colombia	Sugar cane	13
67. Racines (1992)	Ecuador	Oil Palm Soybeans	32 35
68. Palomino and Norton (1992)	Ecuador	Flint maize	54
69. Byerlee (1994)	Latin America/ Caribbean Mexico	Wheat Wheat	81 53

Continued

Table A.5 The agricultural research impact in Hispanic countries in LAC—Cont'd

Authors	Country	Commodity/Level	Rates of Return (%)
70. Cap (1994)	Argentina	Beef	74
		Dairy	55
		Maize	77
		Potato	69
		Wheat	67
		Other crops	54–59
71. Macagno (1994)	Argentina	Maize	47
		Wheat	32
		Other crops	34
72. Penna (1994)	Argentina	Potato	53–61
73. Romano, Bermeo, and Torregrosa (1994)	Colombia	Sorghum	70
74. Byerlee (1995)	Latin America	Wheat	82
75. Fonseca (1996)	Peru	Potato	26
76. Ortiz (1996)	Peru	Potato	30
77. Farfán (1999)	Colombia	Coffee	21–31
78. Manzano (1999)	Ecuador	Rice	58
79. Amores (1999)	Ecuador	Cocoa	31
80. Goméz (2001)	Colombia	Oil palm	—

*Average internal rate of return.
**Estimations of marginal internal rate of return (MIRR).
Source: Colombia and Ecuador, authors; other countries, Alston et al. (2000).

CHAPTER 72

Total Factor Productivity Growth in Agriculture: The Role of Technological Capital

Antonio Flavio Dias Avila
Agricultural Economist, Ph.D., Embrapa Brazil, and Postdoctoral Fellow at the Economic Growth Center, Yale University

Robert E. Evenson
Professor of Economics, Economic Growth Center, Yale University

Contents

Abstract

In this chapter we compute measures of total factor productivity (TFP) growth for developing countries and then contrast TFP growth with technological capital indexes. In developing these indexes, we incorporate schooling capital to yield two new indexes: Invention-Innovation Capital and Technology Mastery. We find that TFP performance is strongly related to technological capital and that technological capital is required for TFP and cost reduction growth. Investments

Handbook of Agricultural Economics, Volume 4
doi: 10.1016/S1574-0072(09)04072-9

in technological capital require long-term (20- to 40-year) investments, which are typically made by governments and aid agencies and are the only viable escape route from mass poverty. *JEL classifications:* Q16, Q18, Q11, O13, O47

Keywords

total factor productivity
technological capital
crop production
livestock production
aggregate production

1. INTRODUCTION

This chapter has two objectives: The first is to compute measures of total factor productivity (TFP) growth for developing countries utilizing data from the Food and Agricultural Organization (FAO) of the UN. The second is to define and contrast indexes of technological capital for agriculture in developing countries and to relate these indexes to TFP growth and other indicators of economic performance in agriculture.

FAO publishes data on production of crops and livestock. FAO also publishes data on cropland, pastureland, labor used in agriculture, fertilizer, seeds, tractors and combine harvesters, and animal stocks. We utilize these data to calculate rates of change in TFP for crop production, livestock production, and aggregate agricultural production for two periods, 1961–1980 and 1981–2001.

These calculations have clear limitations, given the nature of the data on which they are based. The first limitation is that we only compute rates of change in TFP. TFP "levels" cannot be compared across countries. The second and most important limitation is that we do not make adjustments for input "quality" changes. Although in section 7 we did some adjustments for labor quality indirectly in the analysis of the determinants of TFP changes using schooling and nutrition indices applied to the labor force data (Table 10).

There is one merit, however, to these raw TFP growth calculations relative to calculations in the literature, and that is that these calculations have a "standardized" quality. A common methodology is applied in the calculation of share weights for all countries. A common time period is utilized for all countries. The fact that we have not attempted input quality adjustments also contributes to the standardized nature of the calculations.

Our second objective in this work is to develop indexes measuring technological capital. Two forms of human capital in economics have been in use for some time. We are proposing a third. The oldest form of human capital is *schooling capital*. We incorporate schooling capital in one of the technological capital indexes. In recent years, the term *social capital* has begun to be used to measure membership in social and political organization and activities associated with such memberships, including communication networks. We do not make use of this concept in this chapter.

We introduce two new indexes of technological capital. The first is Invention-Innovation Capital (II). This index is designed to measure the capacity to invent and innovate. The term *invention* includes "adaptive" inventions. The term *innovation* is used to describe activities required to "commercialize" an invention by producing products embodying the invention.

Our second technological capital index is a Technology Mastery (TM) index. This index is motivated by activities associated with technology mastery, where a producer masters techniques of production first developed by others.

Section 2 of this chapter discusses the methods used to construct estimates of TFP growth. Section 3 summarizes TFP estimates by country and region. Section 4 introduces and defines the Invention-Innovation Capital and Technology Mastery Capital Indexes. Section 5 reports an analysis of changes in technology capital. Section 6 reports relationships between technological capital and TFP growth. Section 7 reports more general "TFP decomposition" estimates. Section 8 discusses technology policy issues.

2. METHODS FOR TFP MEASUREMENT

TFP indexes can be derived in several comparable ways. The least restrictive derivation is from an accounting relationship in which the value of products is equal to the value of factors used to produce these products.

2.1 The accounting relationship derivation

Consider:

$$\sum_i P_i Q_i = \sum_j R_j I_j, PQ = RI \tag{1}$$

where P_i are product prices, Q_i product quantities, R_j input prices and I_j input quantities. P and R are price vectors, Q and I product and input vectors.

This accounting relationship simply requires that inputs, I_j, receive payments, R_j, that exhaust the total value of production $(\sum P_i Q_i)$. It does not require that all producers be technically efficient in the sense that they produce on a production function. Nor does it require that producers are allocatively efficient.

When Eq. (1) is expressed in a "rate of change" form, the resultant expression is:

$$\sum_i Q_i \frac{\partial P_i}{\partial t} dt + \sum_i P_i \frac{\partial Q_i}{\partial t} dt = \sum_j I_j \frac{\partial R_j}{\partial t} dt + \sum_j R_j \frac{\partial I_j}{\partial t} dt \tag{2}$$

Now divide both sides of Eq. (2) by $\sum_i P_i Q_i$ and multiply the two right-side terms by R_j/R_j and I_j/I_j . Note that $\frac{I_j R_j}{\sum I_j R_j} = C_j$, the cost share of factor j.

The rate of change in a variable is defined as:

$$\hat{I}_j = \frac{1}{I_j}\frac{\partial I_j}{\partial t}\, dt$$

Thus, $\hat{P} + \hat{Q} = \sum_j C_j \hat{R}_j + \sum_j C_j \hat{I}_j = \hat{R} + \hat{I}$ when TFP is constant.

The residual TFP growth then can be measured in two equivalent ways in a closed economy in competitive equilibrium:

$$G_{TFP} = \hat{R} - \hat{P} \tag{3}$$

and

$$G_{TFP} = \hat{Q} - \hat{I} \tag{4}$$

With international trade, the price relationship will not necessarily hold, but the $\hat{Q} - \hat{I}$ relationship holds in all economies.

Note that:

$$\hat{Q} = \sum_i S_i \hat{Q}_i \tag{5}$$

where S_i is the share of product i in total output, and

$$\hat{I} = \sum_j C_j \hat{I}_j$$

where C_j is the cost share of input j in total costs.

This relationship can also be derived from a minimized cost function, and as a result, G_{TFP} is also a measure of cost reduction at constant factor prices.

2.2 Production growth rates

For calculations from FAO data, we make an approximation for estimating $\hat{Q}$. FAO publishes "indexes" of crop (I_C), livestock (I_L), and aggregate (I_A) production for each country for the 1961–2001 period. Because production is affected by weather, we first form three-year moving averages of each index and then estimate the following for two periods, 1961–1980 and 1980–2001:

$$\begin{aligned} \text{Ln}(I_C) &= a + b_C \text{Year} \\ \text{Ln}(I_L) &= a + b_L \text{Year} \\ \text{Ln}(I_A) &= a + b_A \text{Year} \end{aligned} \tag{6}$$

The coefficients b_C, b_L, and b_A are geometric rates of change in the indexes. Note, however, that the indexes are actually Laspayres indexes using FAO dollar prices. Given the complexities of the number of commodities and the year-to-year variability, we argue that this approximation is not a serious departure from the accounting framework. Output growth rates for 20 Latin American, 21 Asian, and 37 African countries are reported in Appendix 1.

2.3 Input growth rates

For inputs, the same procedure was used to estimate growth rates for the two periods. The inputs for crop and livestock production were:

Crops: Cropland, labor, fertilizer, animal power, machine services (tractors plus harvesters)
Livestock: Pastureland, labor, fertilizer, animal capital, feed

FAO reports data series for cropland, pastureland, labor, and fertilizer. For animal power, the total of horses and mules was the series used. For machine services, tractors plus combine harvesters formed the series. Animal capital was based on cattle numbers.

Feed estimates are from Nin, Arndt, Hertel, and Preckel (2003). These authors transformed the total of feed consumed by animals (for all products) from the FAO database in terms of Mcal of metabolizable energy for ruminants per kg of feed (not on a dry-matter basis) based on the *United States-Canadian Tables of Feed Composition: Nutritional Data for United States and Canadian Feeds* (1982). In a second step, they transformed the total feed for each country in tons of corn equivalent, dividing the total of energy by the content of energy in a kilogram of corn. In our study we used this total of feed to estimate the annual growth rate for feed in each of the 78 developing countries and for each of the two periods of analysis.

Input growth rates are reported in Appendix 2.

2.4 Input cost shares

The starting point for establishing input cost shares was that studies for Brazil (Avila and Evenson, 1995) and India (Evenson and Kislev, 1975) reported carefully measured share calculations. For India, share calculations for crop production are available for 1970 and 1985. For Brazil, share calculations are available for both crop and livestock production for 1970 and 1990 based on Agricultural Census data.

For crop production shares, "adjusted" India shares were applied to Asian and African countries. Adjusted Brazil shares were applied to Latin American countries. The adjustment process requires computing quantity cropland ratios for fertilizer quantities, seed quantities, number of work animals, and number of tractors and harvesters. These quantity/cropland ratios were then expressed relative to Brazil or India ratios. Cost shares to Brazil were as measured in Brazil studies. For other Latin American countries, the cost shares for fertilizer, seed, work animals, and machine services were scaled using the country/Brazil comparisons. The shares of cropland and labor were adjusted proportionately so that the sum of shares equaled 1.

The same procedure was applied to obtain African and Asian shares, using Indian shares as the comparison.

For livestock shares, only Brazilian shares were carefully measured. The adjustment process called for creating quantity/value ratios in real U.S. dollars for fertilizer, animal capital, and feed. The shares for fertilizer, animal capital, and feed were adjusted by comparing these quantity/value ratios to Brazil shares. The pastureland and labor shares were adjusted proportionately so as to sum to 1.

For inputs with exceptionally high growth rates (see Appendix 2)m a further adjustment was required to reflect the fact that over a 20-year period the midpoint share overstates the average geometric shares. Input growth rates were compared to production growth shares for this adjustment.[1]

All input shares are reported in Appendix 3.

For aggregate TFP growth, livestock and crop shares in aggregate value were used to weight crop and livestock TFP growth (Prasad Rao and T. Coelli, 2003).

3. TFP ESTIMATES BY REGION AND COUNTRY

3.1 Latin America and the Caribbean

Table 1 reports TFP growth estimates for Latin American and the Caribbean countries for crop, livestock, and aggregate TFP growth. The average TFP growth for both periods is also reported. Regional TFP growth rates are weighted by cropped area.

For the 1961–2001 period, only three Latin American countries—Uruguay, Guatemala, and Panama—experienced TFP growth rates below 1%. (This is roughly the rate of decline in the real prices of farm commodities; see Figure 1.)

Table 1   TFP Index growth rates for Latin America and Caribbean Countries, 1961–1980 and 1981–2001

| Region/Country | Agricultural TFP Growth Rates (%) | | | | | | |
| | Crops | | Livestock | | Aggregate | | |
	1961–1980	1981–2001	1961–1980	1981–2001	1961–1980	1981–2001	Average
Southern Cone	1.49	3.14	0.72	2.51	1.02	2.81	1.92
Argentina	3.08	3.93	0.90	0.43	1.83	2.35	2.09
Brazil	0.38	3.00	0.71	3.61	0.49	3.22	1.86
Chile	1.08	2.22	0.24	1.87	0.69	2.05	1.37
Paraguay	3.97	−1.01	−0.36	1.29	2.63	−0.30	1.17
Uruguay	1.29	2.02	−0.32	0.53	0.01	0.87	0.44

Continued

Table 1   TFP Index growth rates for Latin America and Caribbean Countries, 1961–1980 and 1981–2001—Cont'd

| Region/Country | Agricultural TFP Growth Rates (%) | | | | | | |
| | Crops | | Livestock | | Aggregate | | |
	1961–1980	1981–2001	1961–1980	1981–2001	1961–1980	1981–2001	Average
Andean	1.11	1.71	1.73	1.92	1.41	1.81	1.61
Bolivia	1.73	3.14	2.81	1.39	2.30	2.33	2.31
Colombia	2.01	1.27	0.49	2.24	1.37	1.73	1.55
Ecuador	−0.74	2.24	0.98	2.51	−0.16	2.34	1.09
Peru	−0.83	1.86	1.86	2.14	0.36	1.98	1.17
Venezuela	2.42	0.87	3.41	1.07	3.03	0.99	2.01
Central America	1.65	1.05	2.77	1.53	2.17	1.32	1.74
Costa Rica	2.86	2.09	1.10	0.75	1.74	1.19	1.47
El Salvador	1.22	−0.87	1.99	1.00	1.77	0.32	1.05
Guatemala	3.31	0.53	0.90	−0.28	1.38	−0.08	0.65
Honduras	1.54	−0.39	2.07	1.91	1.91	1.25	1.58
Mexico	1.53	1.43	3.02	1.63	2.26	1.51	1.89
Nicaragua	1.33	−0.70	2.94	1.92	2.25	0.99	1.62
Panama	2.29	−1.33	1.61	1.49	1.93	0.02	0.97
Caribbean	0.66	−0.89	2.60	2.06	2.07	0.87	1.47
Dominican Rep.	0.99	−1.15	1.88	2.60	1.62	0.89	1.25
Haiti	0.60	−1.04	3.44	1.80	2.73	1	1.87
Jamaica	−0.65	1.32	3.28	−0.35	2.07	0.29	1.18
Average rate	1.46	2.40	1.42	2.21	1.39	2.31	1.85

The Southern Cone countries had the best TFP performance; the Caribbean countries had the worst (largely because of poor crop productivity performance in the 1981–2001 period). Aggregate TFP performance as well as crop and livestock TFP performance was better in the 1981–2001 period for countries in the Southern Cone and Andean regions. For Central America and the Caribbean, the 1981–2001 period showed slower TFP rates than the 1961–1980 period.

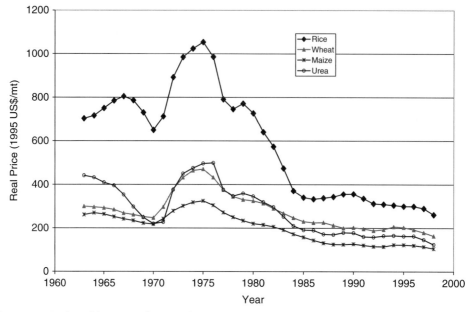

Figure 1 Real-world prices of rice, wheat, maize, and urea (five-year moving average), 1961–2000. Source: IFPRI.

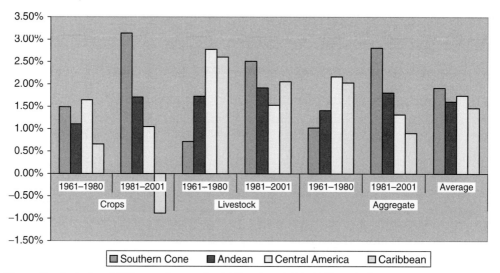

Figure 2 Agricultural TFP growth rates for LAC region, 1961–1980 and 1981–2001.

These results, in general, are very similar to those obtained by other authors for Latin American countries, e.g., Avila and Evenson (1995) and Gasquez and Conceição (2001) for Brazil, Lema and Parrellada (2000) for Argentina, and Romano (1993) for Colombia.

TFP growth rates for LAC subregions are also shown graphically in Figure 2.

3.2 Asia

Table 2 shows the TFP growth rates for the Asian countries calculated for the two periods of analysis, 1961–1980 and 1981–2001, and for crops, livestock, and the aggregate.

The TFP results are also similar to those calculated for Asian countries such as India (Evenson, Pray, and Rosegrant, 1999), Thailand (Krasachat, 2002), Malaysia (Shamsudin, Rhadam, and Abdlatif, 1999), and Vietnam (Ngoc Qu and Goletti, 2001).

Table 2   TFP Index growth rates for Asia, 1962–1981 and 1981–2001

Region/ Country	Agricultural TFP Growth Rates (%)						
	Crops		Livestock		Aggregate		
	1961– 1980	1981– 2001	1961– 1980	1981– 2001	1961– 1980	1981– 2001	Average
Middle East	2.68	0.79	1.76	1.23	2.39	0.98	1.68
Afghanistan	0.63	−0.94	0.94	2.54	0.71	−0.05	0.33
Iran	3.32	2.32	2.37	5.00	2.71	3.17	2.94
Iraq	2.53	−0.06	1.25	−5.81	2.00	−1.24	0.38
Saudi Arabia	4.54	1.22	5.05	3.41	3.58	2.16	2.87
Syria	0.55	2.45	2.62	0.67	1.10	1.94	1.52
Turkey	3.40	0.12	1.43	−0.07	3.06	0.08	1.57
Yemen	1.07	2.50	0.53	2.21	0.93	2.43	1.68
South Asia	1.42	2.14	2.34	2.76	1.71	2.34	2.03
Bangladesh	−0.23	1.06	0.75	2.65	−0.01	1.30	0.65
India	1.54	2.33	2.63	2.66	1.92	2.41	2.16
Nepal	0.20	2.42	1.36	1.11	0.50	2.10	1.30
Pakistan	1.48	1.32	1.17	3.98	1.18	2.54	1.86
Sri Lanka	−0.39	−1.21	−2.19	1.30	−0.93	−0.92	−0.93
South East Asia	2.16	0.34	1.61	2.13	2.37	0.61	1.49
Cambodia	−6.14	2.27	−0.66	0.54	−5.75	1.96	−1.89
Indonesia	3.95	−0.78	3.08	2.41	4.43	−0.39	2.02

Continued

Table 2   TFP Index growth rates for Asia, 1962–1981 and 1981–2001—Cont'd

Region/ Country	Agricultural TFP Growth Rates (%)						
	Crops		Livestock		Aggregate		
	1961– 1980	1981– 2001	1961– 1980	1981– 2001	1961– 1980	1981– 2001	Average
Laos	1.74	1.95	−0.01	3.43	1.20	2.52	1.86
Malaysia	2.95	0.67	3.80	3.70	3.62	1.39	2.51
Philippines	1.62	−1.13	1.87	3.29	1.89	−0.30	0.79
Thailand	1.61	1.04	−0.76	1.26	1.18	1.08	1.13
Vietnam	−0.52	3.94	0.22	0.76	−0.37	3.26	1.45
East Asia	1.39	3.49	2.56	6.52	1.75	4.70	3.22
China	1.39	3.63	2.58	6.59	1.76	4.76	3.26
Mongolia	0.37	−9.48	1.09	−0.02	0.31	−0.54	−0.12
Average rate	1.71	2.02	2.20	3.45	1.92	2.50	2.21

TFP rates for Asian economies over the 1961–2001 period are higher than those observed in Latin America. This is primarily because of the excellent TFP performance of China. The South Asia economies had TFP performance similar to that of the Southern Cone countries in Latin America.

TFP performance varied by period. The Middle East had an excellent performance in the 1961–1980 period but a poor performance in the 1981–2001 period. The same was true for Southeast Asian countries.

Seven countries (Afghanistan, Iraq, Bangladesh, Sri Lanka, Cambodia, the Philippines, and Mongolia) had TFP growth rates below 1%. All were subject to civil strife.

Figure 3 depicts subregional TFP growth rates for Asia.

3.3 Africa

The agricultural TFP growth rates for five African subregions are presented in Table 3.

For Africa as a region, crop and livestock TFP rates were similar. TFP performance was better in the 1981–2001 period, particularly in North Africa and West Africa.

Sixteen of the 37 countries in Africa had TFP growth rates for the 1961–2001 period that were below 1%. Seven had negative growth rates. Both East and Central Africa had regional growth rates below 1%. The results are consistent with those obtained in other studies dealing with Africa such as: Wiebe, Soule & Schimmelpfennig (2002) and Piese, Lusigi, Suhariyanto & Thirtle (2001).

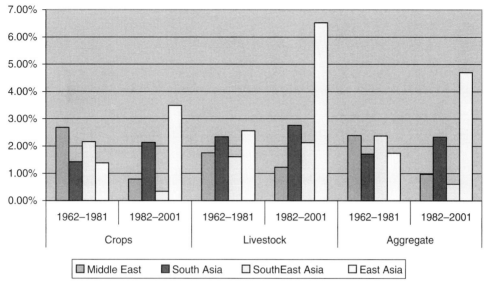

Figure 3   Agricultural TFP growth rates for Asia, 1961–1980 and 1981–2001.

Figure 4 shows African TFP growth by region.

The average TFP index growth for all three world regions for agriculture, livestock, and the aggregate are presented in Figure 5.

A synthesis of the results obtained for all the regions is presented in Table 4, classified by range.

Table 4 shows the poor performance of the African countries; more than 20% of the countries had negative growth in TFP and another 20% had TFP growth rates below 1%. The countries in Asia demonstrated the best performance (30% of the countries had TFP of more than 2%). In the aggregate, Latin American and Caribbean countries also had a good performance, with no negative TFP rates and more than 85% of the countries with TFP growth rates above 1%.

4. DEFINING TECHNOLOGICAL CAPITAL

At least three distinctive types of human resource capital have been used in the context of understanding agricultural TFP performance in developing countries:

- *Human capital* is a term that has been in use for many years. It is generally measured in years of schooling attained by workers in the labor force.
- *Social capital* is a term introduced more recently to capture social relationships in communities and countries. The measurement of social capital is not standardized but must be done in terms of organization, membership, and participation.
- *Technological capital* is a term in limited use to describe the capacity of a region or country to invent new technology and to innovate or commercialize that technology (we call this Invention-Innovation Capital, or II). It is also used to describe the

Table 3   TFP Index growth rates for Africa, 1961–1980 and 1981–2001

| Region/ Country | Agricultural TFP Growth Rates (%) | | | | | | |
| | Crops | | Livestock | | Aggregate | | |
	1961– 1980	1981– 2001	1961– 1980	1981– 2001	1961– 1980	1981– 2001	Average
North	0.78	1.88	2.20	2.12	1.29	1.98	1.63
Algeria	−1.76	2.86	4.08	2.49	0.27	2.69	1.48
Egypt	1.26	3.07	1.54	2.89	1.33	3.03	2.18
Libya	5.86	1.31	3.15	−0.38	5.13	0.76	2.95
Morocco	0.64	0.83	0.36	1.56	0.56	1.10	0.83
Tunisia	2.40	1.84	2.29	3.21	2.37	2.40	2.39
East	0.35	0.62	0.75	0.97	0.68	0.95	0.82
Ethiopia	0.14	1.95	−0.37	0.74	−0.06	1.52	0.73
Sudan	1.47	0.75	1.31	1.24	1.38	1.07	1.22
Uganda	−0.09	0.53	1.76	1.43	0.26	0.67	0.46
Kenya	1.96	−0.16	1.64	1.09	1.80	0.50	1.15
Madagascar	0.29	−0.92	0.62	0.59	0.41	−0.37	0.02
Central	0.97	0.54	1.18	1.32	1.09	0.68	0.89
Cameron	2.09	1.74	2.50	1.80	2.17	1.75	1.96
Chad	−1.41	3.85	0.84	2.48	−0.26	3.39	1.56
Dem. Rep. Congo	0.85	−1.41	−0.56	0.32	0.52	−1.00	−0.24
Rep. Congo	−0.87	−0.41	1.83	1.12	−0.24	−0.05	−0.14
Rep. Central Africa	1.42	0.76	2.98	2.36	1.78	1.14	1.46
Rwanda	1.54	−3.57	3.90	−0.14	1.76	−3.18	−0.71
Western	0.99	3.22	1.73	1.13	1.19	2.93	2.06
Benin	0.51	5.25	3.50	1.99	1.25	4.68	2.96

Continued

Table 3   TFP Index growth rates for Africa, 1961–1980 and 1981–2001—Cont'd

Region/ Country	Agricultural TFP Growth Rates (%)						
	Crops		Livestock		Aggregate		
	1961– 1980	1981– 2001	1961– 1980	1981– 2001	1961– 1980	1981– 2001	Average
Guinea	0.51	2.56	1.05	2.63	0.63	2.58	1.60
Ghana	−1.34	4.32	2.31	−0.14	−0.84	3.93	1.54
Togo	−0.15	2.82	1.09	2.14	0.16	2.70	1.43
Mauritania	−0.56	5.67	0.69	1.33	−0.25	4.90	2.32
Niger	−2.27	1.13	0.73	1.62	−1.13	1.30	0.09
Burkina Faso	0.35	2.42	−0.89	3.49	−0.02	2.73	1.35
Ivory Coast	1.85	0.62	2.81	0.82	1.91	0.63	1.27
Mali	1.47	−2.99	3.14	0.35	2.45	−1.45	0.50
Nigeria	1.83	4.31	1.58	0.94	1.76	3.75	2.75
Senegal	−1.52	4.98	3.98	0.65	0.19	3.46	1.83
Sierra Leone	−1.71	0.34	1.37	3.58	−0.95	0.91	−0.02
Southern	2.06	1.12	1.60	0.26	1.80	0.79	1.30
Angola	1.03	0.82	−0.05	−1.08	0.66	0.23	0.44
Botswana	−3.90	2.13	0.78	0.65	−2.25	1.58	−0.34
Malawi	0.64	−1.21	−0.29	−1.50	0.54	−1.24	−0.35
Mozambique	1.56	1.07	4.07	0.87	1.92	1.04	1.48
Zimbabwe	−1.75	−0.06	0.40	−1.19	−1.16	−0.40	−0.78
South Africa	4.11	2.74	3.05	1.91	3.61	2.32	2.96
Zambia	1.95	−0.28	−0.42	−1.41	1.12	−0.70	0.21
Namibia	2.00	0.56	3.81	2.21	2.64	1.18	1.91
Tanzania	−0.59	−0.40	−0.55	−1.23	−0.58	−0.63	−0.61
Average rate	1.03	1.74	1.49	1.09	1.20	1.68	1.44

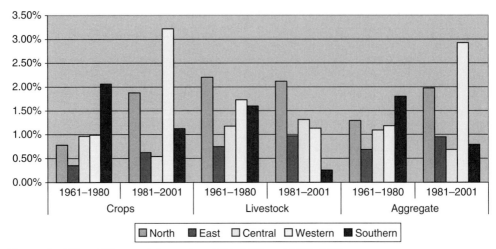

Figure 4 African TFP growth by region, 1961–1980 and 1981–2001.

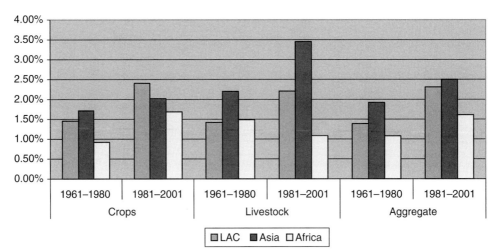

Figure 5 World TFP growth rates, 1961–1980 and 1981–2001.

Table 4 Regional aggregate TFP calculations classified by region

Region	0% > TFP	0%< TFP < 1%	1% < TFP < 2%	TFP + 2%	Total
LAC	—	3	14	3	20
Asia	3	4	8	6	21
Africa	8	8	14	7	37
Total	11	15	36	16	78

capacity to "master" technology produced outside the region or country (we call this capacity Technology Mastery Capital, or TM).

For the agricultural sector, it is well known that crop varieties developed by international Agricultural Research Centers (IARCs) and National Agricultural Research System (NARS) plant-breeding programs have a high degree of location specificity. The field performance of a crop variety depends on soil, climate, and market conditions. The Green Revolution modern crop varieties (MVs), for example, showed a high degree of sensitivity to soil and climate conditions. IARC-crossed MVs were typically released in several countries served by IARC mandates. NARS-crossed MVs, on the other hand, had limited value outside the region for which they were targeted; Evenson and Gollin (2000) report that only 6% of NARS-crossed rice MVs were released in a second country. IRRI-crossed rice varieties were typically released in several Asian countries but had little adoption in Latin America and Africa.

Yet it remains the case that many development programs in agriculture are designed to achieve TFP-based cost reductions through TM. Agricultural extension programs, in particular, are not designed to produce innovations; they are designed to facilitate improved mastery of technology already available to farmers.

In considering mechanical and chemical inventions, however, economists have differing perspectives on "spill-in" potential. Some argue that little investment is required for spill-in. Others argue that a threshold level of R&D in producing firms in a country is required for the development of the capacity to absorb technology from abroad.

Most economists also consider a distinction between domestic goods and international goods. In addition, most economists note that production for the domestic market tends to precede production of international goods for international markets. Most agree that domestic market goods are sensitive to wage rates in the country. Thus, rice harvesting has been undertaken mechanically in the United States for most of the past century. Hundreds of machines have been developed and sold by a number of farm machinery manufacturers. Brazil has realized falling costs of rice harvesting for the past 60 years because of the R&D of these firms. Bangladesh has not, because wages there are low and hand harvesting is still the minimum-cost technique for rice harvesting in Bangladesh. The TM required for effective technology spill-in is almost certainly subject to a threshold investment effect.

Ninety-two developing countries are classified by our two Technological Capital Indexes (78 have TFP estimates). Twenty-five developing countries report no R&D expenditures to UNESCO. An additional 13 countries have the lowest index value, thus at least 25 developing countries, and as many as 38, are simply not investing enough to realize industrial technology spill-in.

The appendix reports all data used for classifying criteria. The classification is done for two periods, 1970 and 1990.

4.1 The Invention-Innovation (II) Capital Index

The II Index is based on two indicators: agricultural scientists per unit of cropland and R&D as a percentage of GDP. Data for the first index are from several studies conducted by the International Service for National Agricultural Research (ISNAR) on International Agricultural Research Center. The second index is reported by UNESCO. UNESCO data may include some agricultural research, but they are interpreted here as primarily related to industrial activities. Countries are given II index values of 1, 2, or 3 based on the following:

Agricultural scientists/cropland (million ha):

$$
\begin{aligned}
\text{Index} \quad &= \quad 1 \text{ if value is } 0.02 \text{ or lower} \\
&= \quad 2 \text{ if value is } 0.021 \text{ to } 0.06 \\
&= \quad 3 \text{ if value is greater than } 0.06
\end{aligned}
$$

R&D/GDP

$$
\begin{aligned}
\text{Index} \quad &= \quad 1 \text{ if value is } 0.002 \text{ or lower} \\
&= \quad 2 \text{ if value is between } 0.002 \text{ and } 0.006 \\
&= \quad 3 \text{ if value is greater than } 0.006
\end{aligned}
$$

The sum of the two index values for 1970 and 1990 is the II for these two periods.

4.2 The Technology Mastery (TM) Index

The TM Index is also based on two indicators. The first is the number of extensive workers per unit of cropland. The second is the schooling levels of males over age 25. Agricultural extension programs have been widely utilized to provide advice on technological practices to farmers. Schooling is also a factor in technology mastery.

Countries are given TM index values of 1, 2, or 3 based on the following:

Extension workers/cropland (million ha):

$$
\begin{aligned}
\text{Index} \quad &= \quad 1 \text{ if value is } 0.2 \text{ or lower} \\
&= \quad 2 \text{ if value is } 0.2 \text{ to } 0.6 \\
&= \quad 3 \text{ if value is greater than } 0.6
\end{aligned}
$$

Average schooling of males over 25:

$$
\begin{aligned}
\text{Index} \quad &= \quad 1 \text{ if value is less than } 4 \text{ years} \\
&= \quad 2 \text{ if value is between } 4 \text{ and } 6 \text{ years} \\
&= \quad 3 \text{ if value is greater than } 6 \text{ years}
\end{aligned}
$$

The appendix table provides data on these indexes. The TM Index is the sum of the values for 1970 and 1990.

4.3 Country classification

Figure 6 reports the classification of countries for two periods, 1970 and 1990. The index values are organized by II index values. Thus, II 22 means that the countries

II Classes 2 and 3 in 1970

22	23	24	32	33	34	35
Afghanistan (22)	Benin (34)	Dominican Republic (24)	Guinea Bissau (22)	Chad (22)	Algeria (34)	Guatemala (33)
Angola (22)	Burkina Faso (43)	Ecuador (23)	Sudan (22)	Gabon (32)	Cameroon (34)	Kenya (45)
Cambodia (22)	Burundi (22)	Guinea (33)		Haiti (33)	Guyana (44)	Malawi (44)
Congo (Zaire) (23)	Central African Republic (33)	Mali (34)	Honduras (34)	Laos (33)	Indonesia (25)	Panama (56)
Ethiopia (23)	Morocco (44)	Nicaragua (34)		Madagascar (22)	Iran (23)	Peru (45)
Mongolia (44)	Rwanda (44)	Togo (23)		Mauritania (33)	Lybia (33)	Venezuela (33)
Mozambique (22)	Somalia (22)	Tunisia (24)		Morocco (33)	Nepal (34)	
Namibia (22)				Myanmar (33)	Nigeria (34)	
Niger (22)				Paraguay (24)	Senegal (33)	
				Zambia (34)	Syria (35)	
					Tanzania (34)	
					Uganda (34)	
					Uruguay (34)	
					Vietnam (33)	
					Yemen (23)	

Figure 6   Country classifications, 1970 (II Classes in Headings, TM Classes in Parentheses)

II Classes 4 and 5 in 1970

43	44	45	46	55	56
Saudi Arabia (23)	Bangladesh (33)	Argentina (44)	Turkey (25)	Cuba (44)	Brazil (46)
Zimbabwe (45)	Bolivia (33)	Botswana (45)	India (24)	Costa Rica (44)	Chile (35)
	Colombia (44)	Egypt (35)		Philippines (46)	China (56)
	Côte d'Ivoire (23)	Iraq (22)		South Africa (46)	El Salvador (25)
	Gambia (22)	Malaysia (35)			Pakistan (24)
	Ghana (34)	Mauritius (56)			
	Honduras (24)	Mexico (35)			
	Jamaica (45)	Sri Lanka (56)			
	Jordan (45)	Thailand (45)			
	North Korea (22)				
	Sierra Leone (44)				
	Surinam (22)				
	Trinidad-Tobago (45)				

Figure 6,   Cont'd

were II Class 2 in both 1970 and 1990. II 23 means that the country moved to Innovation Class 3 in 1990.

TM Class values for all countries are reported in parentheses. An asterisk means that the R&D/GDP component of the Innovation Index was actually reported to be zero.

Consider the countries that started in II Class 2. Nine countries were in Class 2 in both periods, six moved to Class 3 in 1990, and seven moved to Class 4 in 1990. Seven of the nine 22 countries also had TM 22 indexes, as did two of the six 23 countries. Only two of the 22 countries had R&D/GDP indexes of 2. Fourteen of the 22 countries reported R&D ratios of zero. Two countries, Guinea Bissau and Sudan, actually lost II ranking, reverting to level 2 status in 1990. Of the 24 countries either starting in II Class 2 or ending in that class, none would be considered to be host to competitive industries producing international goods. None are ranked as industrially competitive by UNIDO. Most are in sub-Saharan Africa, where the end of the colonial period dates from 1960. These countries inherited virtually nothing from their colonial masters (not all were in colonial relationships, however).

Next, consider the 33 countries starting in II Class 3. Two reverted to Class 2. Ten remained in II Class 3 in both periods. Sixteen improved to Class 4 and five improved to Class 5. Of the 10 countries remaining in Class 3, only 2 were in Class 3 because of industrial R&D. Six of these countries reported zero R&D. Eight of these countries were in Class 3 because of public sector investment in agricultural research. Of the 16 countries moving to Class 4, nine moved on the strength of R&D/GDP ratios. Seven countries moved to Class 4 on the strength of public sector investment in agricultural research. Of the five countries moving to Class 5, all had agricultural research investment indexes of 3 and all invested in industrial R&D.

Twenty-six countries had II index scores of 4 in 1970. Two, Saudi Arabia and Zimbabwe, reverted to Class 3 in 1990. Thirteen remained in Class 4. Nine moved to Class 5, and two moved to Class 6. Of the 13 countries remaining in Class 4, eight had agricultural research indicators of 3. Four reported zero R&D levels to UNESCO. All the countries improving to II Classes 5 and 6, of course, have significant R&D capacity.

Nine countries began in II Class 5. Five of these moved to II Class 6.

But it is clear that the 30 countries in II Class 5 or 6 in 1990 have good to excellent economic performance. Conversely, the 27 countries in II Classes 2 or 3 in 1990 have poor economic performance. All are countries in "mass poverty." The 29 countries in II Class 4 in 1990 have had mixed economic success. In general, the countries in Class 4 in 1990 with R&D capacity have tended to do a little better than the countries without such capacities.

5. CHANGES IN TECHNOLOGICAL CAPITAL

Was improvement in II Class closely related to improvements in TM Class? Was improvement related to the first-period II Class levels?

In addition to the II and TM Classes, there are two other indicator variables available for two periods. One of these is the index of industrial competitiveness constructed by the United Nations Industrial Development Office (UNIDO). The second is a ranking of an important institutional index, the Patent Effectiveness indicator of Park and Ginnarte.

Table 5 reports Tobit estimates of changes in each of the four indexes as they relate to Period 1 levels of the four indexes. These estimates indicate the following:
- Improvements in all indexes, except patent rights, are subject to diminishing returns. High Period 1 values are associated with lower improvement values.
- TM Class improvements are associated with high II Classes but not to high levels of industrial competitiveness or patent rights.
- II Class improvements are not closely related to levels of other indexes.
- Industrial competitiveness improvements and patent rights are related to TM Class levels. This appears to be primarily a schooling effect.

6. TFP GROWTH AND OTHER ECONOMIC INDICATORS AND TECHNOLOGICAL CAPITAL

Table 6 provides cross-tabulations (weighted by the value of agricultural production) of TFP growth for II Class and TM Class. These tabulations are for each period and suggest that TM class improvement does not add to II Class.

To test for this further, Table 7 reports two regressions (weighted by value of production). The first is based on II Class dummy variables plus a variable measuring the difference between TM class and II class. The second is based on TM Class dummy variables plus the II–TM Class difference.

Table 8 shows the relationship between II Class and four agricultural indicators. Countries in II Classes 22 and 23 have very low levels of Green Revolution varietal adoption and very low cereal yields. They use very little fertilizer. The 15 countries in these two classes remain in traditional agriculture. Farmers in these countries have little access to "modern" crop varieties. The Green Revolution has not reached most farmers. They also have very poor import markets.

Table 9 shows that they have low per capita incomes and that incomes have not grown significantly since 1962. All these countries are in mass poverty.

Table 5 Tobit estimates: Technology capital improvements from Period 1 to Period 2

	TM Class		II Class		Industrial Competitiveness	Patent Rights
Period 1	(1)	(2)	(1)	(2)	(2)	(2)
TM Class	−.862 (4.17)	−.871 (2.71)	−.153 (1.56)	−.116 (.81)	.04 (4.23)	.204 (2.54)
Period 2 Class	.688 (4.47)	.631 (2.43)	−.154 (2.03)	−.217 (1.87)	−.002 (.26)	−.063 (.96)
Industrial Competitiveness		−.336 (.07)		−.338 (.15)	−.047 (.29)	8.091 (5.73)
Patent rights Index		−.329 (1.26)		−.069 (.43)	−.006 (.60)	−.380 (4.22)
Constant	1.309 (2.22)	2.506 (1.98)	1.835 (5.46)	2.319 (3.31)	−.094 (2.03)	.201 (.51)
#obs	77	47	77	47	47	47
Prob> $Chi2$	.0000	.0003	.004	.1192	.0016	.0000
Pseudo−$R2$	.1090	.1464	.0605	.0514	−.1818	.3438

Table 6 TFP Growth: II Class vs. TM Class

II Class	TM Class			
	2	3	4	5, 6
2	0.775	0.394	1.172	
3	2.466	1.459	0.131	0.955
4	2.310	1.270	1.665	−0.187
5, 6	0.758	0.687	2.582	3.216

Table 7 Agricultural indicators by innovation class

II Class	Growth in TFP	Adoption of Green Revolution Varieties (%)	Cereal Yields (kg)	Fertilizer per Hectare (kg)
22	0.55	14	960	6
23	1.84	21	928	9
24	1.26	45	1733	48
33	0.78	44	1393	16
34	1.33	62	2368	81
45	1.83	79	2922	91
56	3.86	81	3760	210

Table 8 Agricultural indicators by II Class

II Class	Growth in TFP	Adoption of Green Revolution Varieties (%)	Cereal Yields (kg)	Fertilizer per Hectare (kg)
22	0.55	14	960	6
23	1.84	21	928	9
24	1.26	45	1733	48
33	0.78	44	1393	15
34	1.33	62	2368	81
45	1.83	79	2922	91
56	3.86	81	3760	210

Table 9   Economic growth by II Class

II Class	GDP Per Capita PPP$ (1998)	Growth in GDP Per Capita PPP$ (1962–1992)
22	1160	−1.08
23	930	1.04
24	3203	2.14
33	2291	0.60
34	2881	2.49
45	8430	3.49
56	4156	3.67

7. DETERMINANTS OF TFP GROWTH: A STATISTICAL DECOMPOSITION

The previous section of this paper showed that TFP growth was associated with technological capital. In this section, we refine this analysis further in a TFP decomposition framework. We consider two "adjustments" for labor quality in this section. We also consider proxy variables for general technological progress.

Consider the following TFP derivation from a production function.

$$Y = A_{(t)}(LQ_L)^\alpha H^\beta K^{1-\alpha-\beta} \tag{7}$$

where:

Y is aggregate production
$A_{(t)}$ is a shifter of the production function
L is unadjusted labor
Q_L is a labor quality index
H is land
K is machine and animal capital

When transformed to TFP form, this production function yields:

$$G_{TFP} = G_Y - C_L(G_L + G_{QL}) - C_H G_H - S_K G_K - G_A \tag{8}$$

where G represents growth rates in variables.

The actual "unadjusted" TFP calculations reported in Tables 1, 2, and 3 are based on:

$$G^*_{TFP} = G_Y - C_L G_L - C_H G_H - C_K G_K \tag{9}$$

The difference is:

$$G_{TFP} - G^*_{TFP} = C_L G_{QL} + G_A \tag{10}$$

This suggests that variables measuring labor quality and the shift in A could be used to "explain" TFP growth.

We have two measures of labor quality. The first is associated with increased schooling of the workforce. The second is associated with increased nutrition of the workforce.

The first is the average schooling of adult males in the workforce. This variable (from the Barro-Lee database of the World Bank) is not specific to agricultural workers. It is probably the case that the average schooling of agricultural workers is lower than the average schooling for all workers. But for our purposes, it is the growth rate in schooling that is important.

The second index is the Dietary Energy Sufficiency (DES) index published by the FAO. This index is based on consumption data and effectively is an average calorie per capita measure. Both measures are reported by developing country region to show the diversity in changes in these indexes.

The measure of G_A that we use is the adoption of Green Revolution modern crop varieties in the country for the 1961–1980 and 1980–2000 periods. This is weighted by the crop shown in total agricultural production. Two of the three variables are treated as endogenous in the TFP model. The method used to deal with this is instrumental variables.

The instruments for S_CGRMVA and DES X SHL include the exogenous variables in the $G_{TFP}(A)$ equation, Reg1, Reg2 and GSCH X SHL, plus the Innovation Class variables.

Table 10 reports the estimates for both the first stage instrumented variables, S_CGRMVA and DES X SHL, and the second-stage $G_{TFP}(A)$ equations. In the TFP decomposition estimates, we find that the adoption of Green Revolution modern varieties, the growth in schooling, and improved nutrition all contribute significantly to TFP growth.

Table 10 reports a "growth accounting" exercise attributing growth to Green Revolution MVs, increases in schooling, and increases in nutrition.

8. POLICY IMPLICATIONS

In this chapter, we develop estimates of growth in TFP for two periods and for crop, livestock, and aggregate production. These growth rates bear the interpretation of rates of cost reduction at constant factor prices.

Although these growth rates are subject to errors of measurement, they are broadly consistent with our understanding of productivity growth. Highest TFP growth rates

Table 10   Determinants of TFP (Aggregate) growth: Instrumental variables

	Share Labor × Growth in Calories (Per Capita)	Share Crops × MV Adoption	TFP Growth (Aggregate)	
Constant	−10.55 (0.9)	6.73 (1.2)		−1.31 (1.5)
Din 3	27.4 (2.2)	11.2 (2.0)	Share labor × Growth in Calories	0.061 (4.0)
Din 4	31.5 (2.7)	25.6 (4.6)	Share labor × Growth schooling	
Din 5	33.9 (2.9)	30.5 (5.5)		1.5
Din 6	43.5 (3.6)	40.8 (7.2)	Share crops × MV adoption	0.029 (2.2)
OBS	15.6	15.6		15.6
R^2	0.17	0.59		—

were achieved in East Asia, followed by South Asia and the Southern Cone countries in Latin America. Lowest TFP growth rates were in East and Central Africa.

International prices for agricultural commodities have been declining in real terms over most of the second half of the 20th century (see Figure 1). All OECD countries have realized more rapid TFP gains for the agricultural production sector than for the rest of the economy. These differences average about 1% per year. Developing countries have realized Green Revolution gains at different rates. Many developing countries with slow TFP growth have realized few Green Revolution gains. Others have realized high Green Revolution gains.

Countries with low TFP gains in agriculture have fared poorly in a world where they are delivered falling real prices in an increasingly globalized economy.

Two Technological Capital Indicators were developed. The Imitation indicator was based on extension programs and on schooling levels. The Innovation indicator was based on investments in agricultural research, largely in the public sector, and industrial R&D, largely in the private sector.

Perhaps the dominant message of this chapter is that TFP performance is strongly related to technological capital. These relationships (Table 6) show that countries with minimal II or TM capital (Figure 5) are "trapped" in a price/cost squeeze. Real prices are falling more rapidly than costs are falling.

Table 11   Growth accounting, 1960–2000

Region	Actual TFP Growth	Proportion Due to:		
		Increased Schooling	Increased Nutrition	Green Revolution MVs
Latin America				
Southern Cone	2.24	0.19	0.24	0.57
Andean	1.63	0.30	0.22	0.48
Central America	1.72	0.35	0.19	0.46
Caribbean	1.58	0.39	0.26	0.35
Middle East–North Africa				
Middle East	1.63	0.19	0.23	0.58
North Africa	2.29	0.28	0.20	0.52
Asia				
South Asia	1.96	0.22	0.14	0.64
Southeast Asia	1.05	0.17	0.21	0.62
East Asia	3.24	0.13	0.33	0.54
Sub-Saharan Africa				
East Africa	0.78	0.51	0.02	0.47
Central Africa	0.87	0.62	0.00	0.38
West Africa	2.05	0.29	0.35	0.36
Southern Africa	1.29	0.39	0.03	0.58

Countries with minimal technological capital have cereal yields that are only one fourth the yields of countries with technological capital. They use only 5% as much fertilizer per hectare. They have low levels of adoption of Green Revolution modern varieties. Value added per agricultural worker is one quarter that of countries with technological capital. Growth rates in GDP per capita, though positive, are only one third those of countries with technological capital.

An effort to distinguish between the importance of innovation and imitation capital was made. It is difficult to establish this difference because the two indexes are highly correlated. It does appear that higher innovation capital, given imitation capital, contributes more to TFP growth than higher imitation capital, given innovation capital.

This chapter also reports a TFP decomposition exercise. This exercise identified the adoption of Green Revolution modern varieties, increases in schooling of the labor force, and increases in dietary energy as sources of TFP growth.

As noted, however, the major conclusion of this chapter is that technological capital is required for TFP and cost reduction growth, and this means investment in agricultural research systems. It also means investment in industrial R&D as well as in private and public extension systems and in the schooling of farmers.

Investments in technological capital require long-term commitments to investments by national governments and by aid agencies. These investments are typically not made by NGOs. Many aid agencies have backed away from long-term (20- to 30- or 40-year) technological capital development programs. Tragically, many countries in Africa today are not receiving national government support to build the technological capital that is their only escape route from mass poverty.

End Note

1. For input/output growth differences, the adjustment was:

    2% 0.91

    3% 0.83

    4% 0.75

    5% 0.68

References

Avila, A. F. D., & Evenson, R. E. (1995). Total factor productivity growth in brazilian agriculture and the role of agricultural research. In *Anais do XXXIII Congresso Brasileiro de Economia e Sociologia Rural* (Vol. I, pp. 631–657). Curitiba, 31/07 a 03/08/95.

Evenson, R. E., & Kislev, Y. (1975). *Agricultural research and productivity*. New Haven and London: Yale University Press.

Evenson, R. E. (2003). *Agricultural research and intellectual property rights*. Yale University.

Evenson, R. E., Pray, C. E., & Rosegrant, M. W. (1999). *Agricultural research and productivity growth in india* (Research Report, 109). Washington: IFPRI.

Gasquez, J. G., & Conceição, J. C. P. R. (2001). Transformações estruturais da agricultura e produtividade total dos fatores. In *Transformações da Agricultura e Políticas Públicas*. Brasília: IPEA.

Huffman, W. E., & Evenson, R. E. (1993). *Science for agriculture: a long-term perspective*. Ames, Iowa: Iowa University Press.

Krasachat, W. (2002). *Deforestation and productivity growth in thai agriculture*. Paper presented in the International Symposium on Sustaining Food Security and Managing Natural resources in South East Asia. Challenges for the 21st century. Thailand: Chiang Mai.

Lema, D., & Parellada, G. (2000). *Productivity and competitive advantage of the argentinean agriculture*. INTA. Buenos Aires: Instituto de Economia y Sociología.

Madrid-aris, M. (1997). Growth and technological change in cuba. In *Cuba in transition*. ACSE.

Ngoc qe, N., & Goletti, F. (2001, June). *Explaining Agricultural Growth in Vietnam*. Agrifood Consulting International.

Nin, A., Arndt, C., Hertel, T. W., & Preckel, P. V. (2003). Bridging the gap between partial and total factor productivity measures using directional distance functions. *American Journal of Agricultural Economics*.

Piese, J., Lusige, A., Suharihanto, Q., & Thirtle, C. (2001). *Multi-factor agricultural productivity and convergence in botswana, 1981–96*. Oxford Policy Management.

Prasada rao, D. S., & Coelli, T. J. (2003). *Catch-up and Convergence in Global Agricultural Productivity*. Brisbane: Center for Efficiency and Productivity Analysis. University of Queensland. (unpublished).

Romano, L. O. (1993). *Productividad Agropecuaria: Evolución, Estado Actual y Tendencias Futuras*. Boletín Técnico. ICA, División Planeación Estratégica.

Shamsudin, M. N., Radam, A., & Abdlatif, I. (1999, July). *Productivity in the Malaysian Agriculture Sector.* Paper presented at the "Seminar on Repositioning the Agriculture Industry in the Next Millennium," (pp. 13–14). UPM Department of Agribusiness and Information System, Faculty of Agriculture, UPM.

Weibe, K. D., Soule, M. J., & Scimmelpfenning, D. E. (2001). Agricultural Productivity for Sustainable Food Security in Sub-Saharan Africa. In L. Zepeda (Ed.), *Agricultural Investments and Productivity in Developing Countries.* University of Wisconsin-Madison and FAO (FAO Economic and Social Development, Paper 148).

APPENDIX 1

OUTPUT GROWTH RATES

Table A.1a Latin America and Caribbean: Growth Rates on Agricultural Production, 1962–1981 and 1981–2001

| Region/Country | Agricultural Output Growth Rates (%) | | | | | |
| | Crops | | Livestock | | Aggregate | |
	1961–1980	1981–2001	1961–1980	1981–2001	1961–1980	1981–2001
Southern Cone	2.79	2.98	1.74	2.95	2.16	2.80
Argentina	2.86	4.43	1.24	0.92	1.86	2.18
Brazil	3.20	3.60	4.28	4.58	3.72	3.41
Chile	1.40	2.99	1.92	3.92	1.53	3.67
Paraguay	5.35	1.31	1.26	4.17	3.53	3.27
Uruguay	1.16	2.58	0.00	1.16	0.18	1.48
Andean	2.43	2.65	3.95	2.92	3.00	3.09
Bolivia	4.01	4.36	4.72	2.77	4.45	3.83
Colombia	3.77	1.19	2.81	3.02	3.22	2.18
Ecuador	0.67	3.65	3.81	4.18	1.72	4.05
Peru	0.87	3.18	2.79	3.38	1.49	3.53
Venezuela	2.83	0.87	5.61	1.26	4.10	1.86
Central America	3.60	1.32	4.35	2.84	3.87	1.89
Costa Rica	4.76	4.26	5.74	3.14	5.15	3.77
El Salvador	2.95	−0.17	3.64	2.48	3.04	0.69
Guatemala	4.85	2.51	3.17	2.92	4.36	2.63
Honduras	3.26	1.32	3.73	4.14	3.40	2.28
Mexico	3.10	1.71	4.76	2.35	3.53	1.96
Nicaragua	2.92	0.30	5.39	2.13	3.95	1.09
Panama	3.39	−0.71	3.98	2.73	3.64	0.80
Caribbean	1.20	−0.71	2.78	0.77	1.48	−0.28

Continued

Table A.1a Latin America and Caribbean: Growth Rates on Agricultural Production, 1962–1981 and 1981–2001—Cont'd

Region/Country	Agricultural Output Growth Rates (%)					
	Crops		Livestock		Aggregate	
	1961–1980	1981–2001	1961–1980	1981–2001	1961–1980	1981–2001
Cuba	2.51	−3.11	2.25	−3.00	2.09	−3.09
Dominican Republic	2.32	−0.97	4.44	3.59	2.79	0.55
Haiti	1.68	−1.34	2.75	1.60	2.05	−0.67
Jamaica	−0.51	1.84	4.45	1.68	0.48	1.80
Trinidad and Tobago	−1.33	0.82	5.46	−0.70	0.06	0.26
Average growth rate	2.55	1.57	3.56	2.38	2.74	1.89

Table A.1b Asia: Growth rates on agricultural production, 1962–1981 and 1981–2001

Region/Country	Agricultural Output Growth Rates (%)					
	Crops		Livestock		Aggregate	
	1961–1980	1981–2001	1961–1980	1981–2001	1961–1980	1981–2001
Middle East	2.56	2.38	3.04	2.82	2.42	2.71
Afghanistan	1.64	0.01	1.92	3.82	1.81	2.15
Iran	4.74	4.16	3.26	4.30	4.06	4.15
Iraq	2.93	0.07	1.79	−3.42	2.18	−0.66
Jordan	−3.67	3.61	3.09	5.81	−2.17	3.88
Saudi Arabia	4.62	3.20	6.76	5.09	4.17	4.46
Syria	4.25	2.72	3.92	2.52	4.08	2.66
Turkey	3.41	2.01	2.19	1.03	3.09	1.81

Continued

Table A.1b   Asia: Growth rates on agricultural production, 1962–1981 and 1981–2001—Cont'd

Region/ Country	Agricultural Output Growth Rates (%)					
	Crops		Livestock		Aggregate	
	1961–1980	1981–2001	1961–1980	1981–2001	1961–1980	1981–2001
Yemen	2.54	3.24	1.39	3.44	2.13	3.27
South Asia	2.18	2.46	2.29	3.68	2.21	2.80
Bangladesh	1.52	2.15	1.75	3.69	1.56	2.37
India	2.26	2.72	2.84	3.84	2.44	3.00
Nepal	1.51	3.66	2.65	2.29	1.85	3.26
Pakistan	3.63	3.13	2.75	6.00	3.29	4.47
Sri Lanka	2.01	0.62	1.45	2.58	1.91	0.89
South East Asia	2.28	3.00	2.41	5.32	2.27	3.47
Cambodia	−4.73	4.12	−1.96	6.20	−4.31	4.56
Indonesia	3.31	2.78	3.81	3.98	3.36	2.92
Laos DPR	2.37	3.65	0.68	5.74	2.12	4.03
Malaysia	4.68	2.15	6.23	7.00	4.84	3.44
Philippines	3.88	1.62	3.84	4.97	3.80	2.30
Thailand	4.34	1.91	3.32	4.09	4.15	2.20
Vietnam	2.14	4.80	0.96	5.27	1.90	4.84
East Asia	2.85	−1.52	4.08	1.88	2.92	1.61
China	3.14	3.74	5.31	8.28	3.25	5.20
Mongolia	1.80	−8.10	1.70	0.24	1.63	−0.13
North Korea	3.60	−0.20	5.25	−2.87	3.88	−0.23
Average growth rate	**2.38**	**2.15**	**2.96**	**3.55**	**2.40**	**2.80**

Table A.1c   Africa: Growth rates on agricultural production, 1962–1981 and 1981–2001

| Region/Country | Agricultural Output Growth Rates (%) | | | | | |
| | Crops | | Livestock | | Aggregate | |
	1961–1980	1981–2001	1961–1980	1981–2001	1961–1980	1981–2001
East Africa	2.48	1.47	2.36	2.03	2.42	1.99
Ethiopia	1.69	3.50	0.32	1.43	1.11	2.67
Somalia	2.11	−2.32	2.58	0.43	2.52	0.06
Sudan	2.80	2.08	3.68	3.60	3.23	2.94
Uganda	2.29	2.90	3.20	2.86	2.29	2.96
Kenya	3.84	1.72	3.02	2.47	3.45	2.10
Madagascar	2.16	0.95	1.39	1.36	1.90	1.20
Central Africa	2.25	1.74	2.74	2.31	2.29	1.80
Cameroon	2.73	2.38	3.84	3.14	2.99	2.54
Chad	−0.38	4.88	0.67	2.31	0.09	3.86
Dem. Rep. Congo	2.31	0.05	0.50	1.38	2.08	0.21
Republic of Congo	1.10	1.56	2.88	2.17	1.39	1.68
Rep. Central African	2.40	1.74	5.00	4.38	2.94	2.71
Gabon	3.24	2.31	1.22	1.77	2.12	2.12
Rwanda	4.37	−0.74	5.05	1.02	4.44	−0.52
Western Africa	1.15	3.38	2.55	2.22	1.45	2.93
Benin	2.25	6.99	4.14	2.63	2.61	6.23
Gambia	−0.94	0.07	2.34	0.71	−0.46	0.20
Guinea	1.45	3.50	1.47	3.04	1.45	3.43
Ghana	0.24	5.90	3.76	1.31	0.63	5.33
Togo	1.09	4.06	2.01	3.05	1.20	3.82

Continued

Table A.1c   Africa: Growth rates on agricultural production, 1962–1981 and 1981–2001—Cont'd

| Region/Country | Agricultural Output Growth Rates (%) | | | | | |
| | Crops | | Livestock | | Aggregate | |
	1961–1980	1981–2001	1961–1980	1981–2001	1961–1980	1981–2001
Mauritania	−1.76	4.48	0.43	1.08	0.23	1.51
Niger	0.52	3.92	1.00	1.89	0.71	3.15
Burkina Faso	2.14	4.21	0.02	4.40	1.41	4.26
Ivory Coast	4.63	3.40	4.57	2.59	4.63	3.36
Liberia	3.27	−1.19	3.80	1.01	3.32	−1.06
Mali	2.31	4.79	2.16	1.52	2.25	3.21
Nigeria	−0.09	6.42	5.11	1.79	0.70	5.60
Senegal	−0.61	1.44	2.20	4.41	−0.07	2.34
Sierra Leone	1.57	−0.65	2.63	1.71	1.69	−0.28
Southern Africa	2.00	1.79	2.43	1.41	1.90	1.52
Angola	−2.52	3.51	2.54	2.42	−1.01	3.00
Botswana	2.82	0.98	1.34	0.13	1.51	0.24
Malawi	3.58	3.09	5.28	2.07	3.74	2.91
Mozambique	0.68	2.37	2.32	0.73	0.91	1.92
Zimbabwe	3.51	2.14	3.48	2.34	3.45	1.85
South Africa	3.80	1.57	1.55	0.56	2.50	1.14
Zambia	3.17	1.72	3.94	2.34	3.50	2.00
Namibia	1.72	1.92	1.45	0.77	1.48	0.95
Tanzania	3.22	0.61	2.44	2.69	2.97	1.23
Average growth rate	1.76	2.24	2.51	1.95	1.86	2.11

INPUT GROWTH RATES

Table A.2a Latin America and Caribbean growth rates of selected agricultural inputs, 1960–1981 and 1981–2000

Region/Country	Cropland		Labor(*)		Fertilizer + Pest.(**)		Seeds		Mechanization***		Permanent Pastures		Feec****		Animal Power*****	
	1961–1980	1981–2000	1961–1980	1981–2000	1961–1980	1981–2000	1961–1980	1981–2000	1961–1980	1981–2000	1961–1980	1981–2000	1961–1980	1981–2000	1961–1980	1981–2000
Southern Cone	1.79	−0.14	0.05	0.25	8.38	8.28	1.66	0.48	2.51	2.02	0.81	0.39	3.42	3.60	−0.53	0.93
Argentina	1.70	0.00	−0.93	0.22	9.29	12.36	−0.60	1.02	1.53	1.39	−0.14	−0.04	3.57	1.35	−1.69	0.91
Brazil	2.83	1.65	1.13	−1.54	16.98	4.63	3.82	−1.59	7.06	2.01	1.78	0.37	3.41	3.35	0.54	−0.01
Chile	0.60	−3.38	0.16	0.97	3.73	7.43	−1.10	−1.69	0.77	1.49	1.72	0.06	4.02	5.89	−0.88	1.63
Paraguay	3.57	1.24	0.64	1.68	6.35	11.62	7.46	3.41	2.80	3.68	0.75	1.57	5.09	3.82	−0.84	1.55
Uruguay	0.24	−0.23	−0.75	−0.06	5.58	5.36	−1.28	1.24	0.40	1.52	−0.07	−0.01	1.00	3.60	0.23	0.58
Andean	1.04	−0.06	1.04	0.85	8.20	2.76	0.74	1.62	5.79	0.29	0.92	0.30	4.93	2.73	1.92	1.04
Bolivia	2.04	−0.31	1.87	1.79	8.02	1.03	1.03	2.62	6.55	1.04	0.61	0.33	3.92	2.63	3.47	0.21
Colombia	0.23	−1.32	1.51	−0.14	6.40	3.41	0.82	−0.20	3.13	−0.43	0.66	0.13	7.00	4.38	3.35	1.73
Ecuador	0.01	0.93	0.64	1.06	10.00	4.98	−3.33	4.68	7.87	1.46	3.00	0.85	−0.30	3.97	1.52	2.88
Peru	2.69	0.88	1.38	1.39	2.51	4.30	0.67	1.93	2.81	−1.22	−0.19	−0.01	3.92	3.50	0.79	0.32
Venezuela	0.25	−0.47	−0.21	0.16	14.05	0.10	4.53	−0.94	8.58	0.59	0.50	0.18	10.09	−0.83	0.50	0.07
Central America	0.47	0.90	1.35	0.78	8.58	2.86	0.08	−0.71	8.90	0.85	1.08	0.95	6.92	3.83	0.11	0.68
Costa Rica	0.22	−0.13	1.68	0.87	6.89	5.18	0.78	−1.98	2.79	0.96	4.31	0.44	9.04	7.70	−0.04	1.89
El Salvador	0.96	0.66	1.61	0.73	6.63	0.72	2.31	0.52	4.24	0.94	0.04	1.71	8.54	2.76	0.57	0.40
Guatemala	0.72	0.49	1.70	2.07	10.82	5.67	−0.42	−1.01	6.25	0.64	0.83	3.41	8.53	3.69	−2.91	0.84

	*	**	***	****								*****				
Honduras	0.97	0.10	1.74	0.55	7.66	10.31	1.70	1.16	15.03	2.25	0.00	0.08	6.16	4.85	−1.27	0.31
Mexico	0.18	0.63	1.44	0.36	9.91	−0.02	0.40	−7.46	4.29	1.57	0.00	0.47	8.54	2.18	3.06	0.18
Nicaragua	0.38	3.68	1.14	−0.06	10.18	−3.23	1.06	−0.11	15.02	0.98	1.14	0.00	4.85	0.20	2.59	−0.41
Panama	−0.14	0.83	0.14	0.94	7.96	1.38	−5.31	3.94	14.66	−1.40	1.23	0.55	2.79	5.41	−1.20	1.53
Caribbean	0.55	0.42	0.32	−0.43	6.32	2.63	0.06	0.32	1.27	−0.56	−0.02	−0.47	6.55	0.79	0.33	0.25
Dominican Rep.	1.92	0.58	0.53	−0.72	12.25	3.76	2.68	0.44	1.02	−0.83	0.00	0.00	15.64	5.88	0.96	0.27
Haiti	1.53	0.08	0.53	−0.72	19.22	6.94	0.10	−0.19	4.05	−2.30	−0.90	−0.21	−2.72	0.07	2.21	0.87
Jamaica	−0.69	1.42	0.53	−0.72	0.13	2.46	−2.49	1.38	1.29	0.34	0.01	−0.85	13.25	1.40	−1.54	0.09
Average rate	1.01	0.37	0.82	0.44	8.73	4.42	0.64	0.36	5.51	0.73	0.76	0.45	5.82	3.29	0.47	0.79

*Population economically active in agriculture.
**Fertilizers + Pesticides = growth rates of fertilizers.
***Growth rate of tractors + harv. mach.
****Total consumption of feed (energy) in tons of corn equivalent.
*****Animal power − stock of mules, horses and camels.

Table A.2b Asia: Growth rates of selected agricultural inputs, 1960–1981 and 1981–2000

Agricultural Input Growth Rates (%)

Region/Country	Cropland		Labor*		Fert. +Pest.**		Seeds		Mechanization***		Perm. Pastures		Feed****		Anim. Power*****	
	1961–1980	1981–2000	1961–1980	1981–2000	1961–1980	1981–2000	1961–1980	1981–2001	1961–1980	1981–2000	1961–1980	1981–2000	1961–1980	1981–2000	1961–1980	1981–2000
Middle East	0.60	0.78	0.37	0.78	20.20	1.03	-0.28	0.32	8.44	3.12	-0.07	0.72	7.48	3.41	-1.16	-1.99
Afghanistan	0.21	0.00	1.50	2.26	24.72	-16.74	-0.56	0.60	8.85	0.35	0.00	0.00	4.68	2.13	1.21	-4.09
Iran	0.05	1.25	0.56	1.44	19.68	2.16	1.86	-0.64	9.14	4.32	0.00	0.00	6.29	4.02	-2.45	-1.44
Iraq	0.75	0.07	-0.94	-2.30	21.47	8.40	-1.77	-0.06	8.71	2.62	-0.09	0.00	5.03	-4.97	-6.01	-5.68
Jordan	0.72	0.77	-1.11	3.35	8.07	3.27	-3.82	1.18	4.44	1.02	0.00	0.00	3.38	8.94	-2.45	-1.44
Saudi Arabia	2.85	3.37	2.09	-4.25	8.70	4.51	0.70	-2.24	11.44	8.92	0.00	4.55	4.68	2.13	7.92	1.20
Syria	-0.89	-0.28	0.43	2.03	12.87	4.55	2.25	4.40	6.15	5.13	0.27	-0.02	5.79	2.12	-7.89	-3.27
Turkey	0.63	-0.01	0.19	1.16	16.82	1.99	0.69	0.40	9.21	1.55	-0.73	1.25	2.88	0.55	2.42	-2.72
Yemen	0.49	1.06	0.22	2.56	49.26	0.08	-1.57	-1.09	9.59	1.06	0.00	0.00	4.68	2.13	-1.98	1.55
South Asia	0.70	0.30	1.61	1.45	14.12	5.00	2.09	1.12	10.99	2.70	0.83	-0.25	2.57	4.15	-0.02	-1.22
Bangladesh	0.16	-0.74	1.20	1.23	14.22	5.97	1.05	0.39	10.09	0.95	0.00	0.00	2.02	2.59	-0.65	-0.09
India	0.26	0.03	1.63	1.21	13.88	5.30	3.07	1.87	8.28	5.03	-1.00	-0.62	1.56	3.50	-0.65	-0.09
Nepal	1.71	1.66	1.40	1.98	23.30	6.81	2.32	1.46	15.18	3.62	0.57	-0.64	2.57	4.15	1.62	-2.31
Pakistan	0.74	0.44	2.10	1.29	17.26	4.94	3.15	2.20	16.64	6.03	0.00	0.00	4.47	5.28	1.10	0.41
Sri Lanka	0.63	0.08	1.75	1.52	1.96	1.97	0.88	-0.30	4.74	-2.10	4.59	0.02	2.23	5.25	-1.55	-4.04
South East Asia	0.59	1.26	1.41	1.36	6.91	8.45	0.74	2.03	8.21	7.46	0.87	1.71	3.55	5.80	2.24	-0.59
Cambodia	-3.06	3.65	0.65	2.72	-4.86	9.49	-5.88	4.74	8.18	0.65	0.00	5.51	-4.55	5.54	5.43	5.65

Indonesia	0.00	1.15	1.14	1.68	12.45	2.72	1.96	1.03	4.34	15.44	−0.27	−0.43	4.60	5.20	−0.56	−1.65
Laos	1.37	0.86	1.72	2.20	0.42	15.06	2.08	3.00	16.18	2.65	−0.39	0.30	3.55	5.80	3.00	−2.19
Malaysia	1.04	2.51	0.93	−1.12	10.00	6.29	1.22	0.31	8.56	10.28	0.84	0.60	8.67	5.42	0.67	−0.91
Philippines	1.65	0.20	2.00	1.26	8.25	5.12	1.65	0.39	6.78	1.99	1.13	0.94	5.75	4.03	9.45	−0.16
Thailand	2.62	−0.22	2.08	0.90	14.69	9.26	2.65	0.12	4.33	10.33	4.64	0.93	4.37	7.33	−2.77	−4.89
Vietnam	0.51	0.68	1.36	1.90	7.41	11.19	1.52	4.63	9.10	10.91	0.12	4.16	2.45	7.30	0.44	0.00
East Asia	0.89	0.45	0.85	0.24	15.16	−5.86	1.62	−2.09	7.40	0.65	0.38	0.22	4.85	5.19	0.83	0.79
China	−0.29	1.26	1.90	1.06	13.72	4.82	0.53	0.00	10.83	4.70	1.80	0.76	7.45	3.97	4.10	−0.80
Mongolia	2.32	−0.13	0.51	0.10	21.73	−13.05	3.02	−6.61	4.13	−4.12	−0.68	−0.11	3.55	5.80	−0.80	1.59
North Korea	0.62	0.22	0.13	−0.43	10.03	−9.36	1.31	0.33	7.23	1.38	0.00	0.00	3.55	5.80	−0.80	1.59
Average rate	0.66	0.78	1.02	1.03	14.18	3.25	0.80	0.70	8.79	4.03	0.47	0.75	3.90	4.09	0.38	−1.03

Table A.2c Africa: Growth rates of selected agricultural inputs, 1960–1981 and 1981–2000

Agricultural Input Growth Rates (%)

Region/Country	Cropland		Labor*		Fert. + Pest.**		Seeds		Mechanization***		Permanent Pastures		Feed****		Animal Power*****	
	1961–1980	1981–2000	1961–1980	1981–2000	1961–1980	1981–2000	1961–1980	1981–2000	1961–1980	1981–2000	1961–1980	1981–2000	1962–1981	1982–2001	1961–1980	1981–2000
North Africa	0.55	0.83	0.16	−0.30	9.46	−0.51	1.39	0.24	4.53	1.88	0.57	0.67	14.09	4.58	−2.49	−0.88
Algeria	0.65	0.61	−1.34	1.99	9.11	−5.73	1.22	−0.13	2.25	3.30	−0.25	−0.03	22.62	4.88	0.82	−2.51
Egypt	0.02	1.96	1.38	−0.03	5.08	2.04	1.80	0.85	3.87	2.62	0.02	1.96	3.74	4.51	−5.16	0.17
Libya	0.28	0.34	−0.56	−4.41	15.89	−1.57	2.80	0.33	9.82	1.43	1.81	0.03	20.19	1.79	−7.27	−3.25
Morocco	0.78	1.14	1.21	0.39	10.23	1.61	0.51	0.74	3.67	0.77	1.14	0.03	1.67	5.92	−0.71	−0.01
Tunisia	1.03	0.10	0.10	0.56	7.01	1.12	0.61	−0.60	3.03	1.31	0.15	1.36	22.24	5.81	−0.14	1.19
East Africa	0.96	0.35	1.79	1.89	5.33	5.86	1.15	−1.07	6.37	1.03	−0.11	−11.23	2.84	3.00	0.75	−0.63
Ethiopia	0.91	−1.38	1.89	1.90	21.17	9.61	−2.12	2.10	16.57	−2.45	−0.11	−5.89	2.92	4.51	0.15	−3.63
Sudan	0.78	1.86	1.57	1.69	4.10	−1.38	7.06	5.33	12.17	−0.40	−0.11	1.09	5.70	3.98	1.54	0.66
Uganda	1.57	0.69	2.39	2.43	−7.55	13.11	−1.65	−0.02	6.89	2.29	−0.11	−5.89	5.04	6.89	2.92	0.88
Kenya	0.58	0.28	2.73	3.13	7.57	2.76	1.98	−0.57	5.24	5.41	−0.11	−5.89	3.57	1.29	2.92	0.88
Madagascar	1.91	0.64	2.17	2.19	6.68	11.07	1.63	−13.24	−2.65	1.35	−0.11	−5.89	−0.21	1.31	−3.03	−2.57
Central Africa	0.99	0.30	1.27	1.24	7.31	−0.97	1.74	5.66	8.10	0.70	−2.70	−0.28	3.42	2.94	0.03	0.39
Cameroon	1.18	0.08	0.76	1.52	10.35	−0.78	1.75	0.52	16.77	−1.39	−0.45	−0.05	1.19	4.26	−7.47	−1.23
Chad	0.47	0.77	1.25	1.86	22.22	5.99	−1.59	5.49	12.34	−0.12	−0.45	−0.05	2.90	8.58	1.54	2.18
Dem. Rep. Congo	0.51	0.14	1.88	2.22	15.38	−7.92	2.87	2.62	6.25	3.15	−0.45	−0.05	4.47	2.30	1.54	−1.59

Rep. Congo	1.23	1.18	1.48	1.04	-8.35	6.65	3.40	1.23	6.79	0.22	-0.45	-0.05	7.82	-2.57	1.54	-1.59
Rep. Cent. African	0.59	0.17	0.86	1.04	5.09	-4.89	2.36	0.74	7.22	2.58	-0.45	-0.05	2.09	4.69	1.54	2.18
Rwanda	2.95	-0.23	2.67	0.99	6.49	-5.85	3.38	29.01	7.33	0.45	-0.45	-0.05	5.51	3.36	1.54	2.76
Western Africa	0.73	1.61	1.26	1.48	14.20	3.52	0.51	1.87	7.80	2.98	-0.48	10.19	2.82	2.02	0.85	0.99
Benin	2.62	1.54	0.23	1.62	5.37	13.80	-0.21	3.12	2.69	2.77	-0.48	1.86	1.55	4.79	4.03	-12.48
Guinea	0.37	1.67	1.48	2.31	-6.22	12.46	2.49	1.34	7.93	7.09	-0.48	1.86	0.68	0.72	-0.52	5.73
Ghana	0.44	2.18	2.07	2.65	18.75	-1.41	4.52	-3.03	11.25	-7.15	-0.48	-0.03	3.02	4.74	1.41	-0.17
Togo	0.30	1.36	1.76	2.02	26.58	8.93	-1.71	13.24	5.04	-0.61	-0.48	1.86	3.43	6.30	2.39	4.04
Mauritania	-2.18	4.16	0.50	0.91	23.97	20.24	-5.32	23.22	10.58	6.06	-0.48	1.86	1.82	3.21	1.27	2.87
Niger	2.11	1.48	2.39	2.89	19.94	-0.47	2.57	-9.03	16.81	0.16	-0.48	1.86	12.65	4.77	0.98	-0.73
Burkina Faso	1.45	1.50	1.56	1.98	28.97	7.46	0.09	2.03	7.50	19.11	-0.48	1.86	9.48	-7.72	-0.41	1.45
Ivory Coast	2.31	2.95	2.34	1.65	11.34	5.25	3.39	0.98	14.45	2.04	-0.48	1.86	3.98	2.63	1.41	-0.17
Mali	1.24	5.34	1.71	1.79	24.50	-11.95	0.35	-0.04	11.00	6.07	-0.48	1.86	-0.12	5.14	0.80	3.88
Nigeria	0.28	0.10	0.78	0.27	24.34	-1.67	-3.80	-0.20	17.44	5.27	-0.48	1.86	-2.06	6.94	-1.55	-0.48
Senegal	0.00	-0.06	2.31	2.03	8.16	2.41	2.68	-4.96	4.92	1.17	-0.48	1.86	2.57	-0.06	2.60	4.21
Sierra Leone	1.21	0.30	0.55	0.58	13.04	-5.77	2.08	-0.49	-0.35	-0.23	-0.48	1.86	2.43	-3.22	-0.52	5.73
Southern Africa	0.62	0.70	1.18	1.55	8.47	-3.39	1.81	0.81	5.70	0.07	-0.41	0.86	3.03	2.92	3.34	0.59
Angola	0.35	0.10	1.15	2.32	13.56	-7.64	0.25	1.24	11.21	0.03	-0.41	0.21	2.45	2.95	0.47	0.42
Botswana	0.04	-0.92	0.63	1.03	1.32	7.93	4.25	2.90	8.42	3.41	-0.41	0.21	-0.91	7.62	4.97	1.74
Malawi	1.34	1.25	2.10	2.49	11.91	0.49	1.26	5.54	10.04	0.68	-0.41	0.21	2.69	2.96	3.52	-4.69

Continued

Table A.2c Africa: Growth rates of selected agricultural inputs, 1960–1981 and 1981–2000—Cont'd

Agricultural Input Growth Rates (%)

Region/Country	Cropland		Labor*		Fert. + Pest.**		Seeds		Mechanization***		Permanent Pastures		Feed****		Animal Power*****	
	1961–1980	1981–2000	1961–1980	1981–2000	1961–1980	1981–2000	1961–1980	1981–2000	1961–1980	1981–2000	1961–1980	1981–2000	1962–1981	1982–2001	1961–1980	1981–2000
Mozambique	1.05	1.52	1.82	1.79	9.03	−25.08	1.74	−6.24	5.70	0.00	−0.41	0.21	1.16	5.66	5.85	1.48
Zimbabwe	1.43	1.35	2.25	1.99	6.18	0.48	2.38	−4.82	4.54	1.24	−0.41	0.04	4.51	−0.13	5.85	1.48
South Africa	0.19	1.25	−1.34	−0.50	7.63	−1.65	0.90	−13.99	3.34	−5.71	−0.41	0.21	3.94	1.88	−4.29	0.82
Zambia	0.30	0.15	2.27	2.22	12.79	−4.14	−1.97	4.91	8.23	0.88	−0.41	0.21	4.83	−1.33	5.85	1.48
Namibia	0.12	1.46	0.54	1.27	7.70	−3.08	3.53	15.58	2.41	1.05	−0.41	0.21	2.53	5.36	4.97	1.74
Tanzania	1.34	0.87	2.34	2.85	14.54	−1.24	3.96	2.13	−2.62	−0.97	−0.41	0.21	6.05	1.33	2.92	0.88
Average rate	0.86	1.02	1.35	1.48	11.19	1.11	1.34	1.83	7.52	1.70	−0.26	0.07	4.81	3.14	0.93	0.37

APPENDIX 3

INPUT COST SHARES

Table A.3a   Latin America and Caribbean: Crop input cost shares, 1960–1981 and 1981–2000

Region/ Country	Crop Input Cost Shares (%)											
	Cropland		Labor*		Fert. + Chemicals*		Seeds		Mechanization*		Animal Power	
	1961– 1980	1981– 2001	1961– 1980	1981– 2001	1961– 1980	1981– 2001	1961– 1980	1981– 2001	1961– 1980	1981– 2001	1961– 1880	1981– 2001
Southern Cone	22.61	23.60	60.92	47.28	1.87	6.14	2.01	4.37	10.65	18.69	6.86	3.28
Argentina	26.59	30.45	66.65	55.98	0.15	1.34	1.62	4.67	4.71	9.36	7.50	3.84
Brazil	30.22	17.26	62.22	43.78	2.78	12.33	1.89	3.21	9.49	23.41	7.01	3.21
Chile	18.53	20.24	58.79	41.08	3.07	10.02	2.65	3.87	11.57	22.69	6.61	2.81
Paraguay	18.32	29.49	63.38	47.66	0.50	2.23	1.69	6.05	8.17	17.34	7.13	3.27
Uruguay	19.35	20.57	53.55	47.88	2.85	4.76	2.17	4.07	19.34	20.66	6.02	3.28
Andean	23.20	21.98	62.81	52.84	2.98	7.46	1.45	4.59	5.10	9.10	7.07	3.62
Bolivia	24.09	26.72	66.65	57.93	0.23	0.35	2.07	7.16	3.83	6.37	7.50	3.97
Colombia	19.37	22.82	61.45	53.11	5.37	8.06	1.78	6.37	6.20	7.09	6.91	3.64
Ecuador	24.36	17.98	56.92	45.62	3.15	5.61	0.74	1.25	8.32	22.34	6.40	3.13
Peru	18.26	22.17	63.14	56.23	4.35	7.02	1.64	4.64	5.51	4.57	7.10	3.85
Venezuela	29.92	20.23	65.90	51.33	1.82	16.29	1.03	3.50	1.61	5.13	7.41	3.52
Central America	23.29	23.59	63.62	48.30	3.91	12.55	0.92	3.19	4.04	10.23	7.16	3.31
Costa Rica	17.84	12.32	56.60	31.25	9.00	34.04	0.75	1.66	10.02	15.42	6.37	2.14
El Salvador	22.01	21.94	65.05	55.65	4.51	10.30	0.54	1.95	2.84	6.34	7.32	3.81

Continued

Table A.3a Latin America and Caribbean: Crop input cost shares, 1960–1981 and 1981–2000—Cont'd

Crop Input Cost Shares (%)

Region/Country	Cropland		Labor*		Fert. + Chemicals*		Seeds		Mechanization*		Animal Power	
	1961–1980	1981–2001	1961–1980	1981–2001	1961–1980	1981–2001	1961–1980	1981–2001	1961–1980	1981–2001	1961–1380	1981–2001
Guatemala	25.15	26.71	65.90	51.33	2.88	13.52	1.03	3.50	2.37	5.13	7.41	3.52
Honduras	23.79	21.86	65.81	44.36	1.83	11.31	0.96	2.85	1.87	10.51	7.40	3.04
Mexico	26.12	29.97	65.46	55.10	1.87	6.28	1.31	3.57	3.93	9.55	7.36	3.78
Nicaragua	25.66	30.79	64.31	56.59	3.27	4.47	1.12	5.51	1.49	6.32	7.23	3.88
Panama	22.49	21.57	62.22	43.78	4.05	7.95	0.70	3.31	5.72	18.34	7.00	3.00
Caribbean	15.65	15.77	38.56	31.53	2.54	6.53	0.92	3.16	1.70	3.17	4.34	2.16
Dominican Rep.	27.24	25.74	63.65	52.24	2.78	11.12	1.29	4.18	3.04	4.58	7.16	3.58
Haiti	33.79	35.63	69.56	61.08	0.11	1.50	1.89	7.23	0.26	0.54	7.83	4.19
Jamaica	17.23	17.47	59.59	44.33	9.84	20.04	1.41	4.39	5.22	10.73	6.70	3.04

*Input costs ratio adjusted for geometric as explained in Section 2.3.

Table A.3b Latin America and Caribbean: Livestock input cost shares, 1960–1981 and 1981–2000

Region/ Country	Livestock Input Cost Shares (%)											
	Permanent Pastures		Labor*		Fert. + Chem. + Medic.		Feed		Mechanization		Animal Stock	
	1961– 1980	1981– 2001	1961– 1980	1981– 2001	1961– 1980	1981– 2001	1961– 1980	1981– 2001	1961– 1980	1981– 2001	1961– 1980	1981– 2001
Southern Cone	59.95	40.47	22.72	28.76	1.74	4.42	11.21	13.91	4.38	12.44	13.42	10.78
Argentina	62.34	44.76	23.62	31.82	0.15	1.17	11.66	15.39	2.24	6.87	9.97	9.25
Brazil	58.32	38.55	22.10	27.40	3.62	6.63	10.91	13.25	5.05	14.17	19.40	15.36
Chile	59.19	37.85	22.43	26.90	2.18	8.32	11.07	13.01	5.13	13.91	6.29	3.74
Paraguay	60.86	41.11	23.06	29.22	0.31	3.02	11.39	14.13	4.38	12.51	17.39	15.87
Uruguay	59.04	40.07	22.37	28.48	2.43	2.96	11.04	13.77	5.11	14.73	14.06	9.71
Andean	60.42	43.50	22.89	30.92	2.61	4.50	11.30	14.95	2.78	6.12	13.42	10.78
Bolivia	62.46	46.29	23.67	32.90	0.18	0.23	11.68	15.91	2.01	4.67	9.97	9.25
Colombia	59.56	44.08	22.57	31.33	3.67	4.97	11.14	15.15	3.05	4.48	19.40	15.36
Ecuador	58.11	39.48	22.02	28.06	3.97	4.37	10.87	13.57	5.03	14.51	6.29	3.74
Peru	60.44	45.02	22.90	32.00	2.68	3.80	11.31	15.47	2.68	3.71	17.39	15.87
Venezuela	61.52	42.64	23.31	30.31	2.54	9.15	11.51	14.66	1.12	3.24	14.06	9.71

Continued

Table A.3b Latin America and Caribbean: Livestock input cost shares, 1960–1981 and 1981–2000—Cont'd

Livestock Input Cost Shares (%)

Region/Country	Permanent Pastures		Labor*		Fert. + Chem. + Medic.		Feed		Mechanization		Animal Stock	
	1961–1980	1981–2001	1961–1980	1981–2001	1961–1980	1981–2001	1961–1980	1981–2001	1961–1980	1981–2001	1961–1980	1981–2001
Central America	60.10	40.98	22.78	29.12	3.13	8.94	11.24	14.08	2.75	6.87	7.30	5.72
Costa Rica	56.66	31.66	21.47	22.50	6.37	23.31	10.60	10.88	4.91	11.64	8.28	3.40
El Salvador	60.91	44.12	23.08	31.36	3.27	5.52	11.39	15.17	1.35	3.83	3.72	3.99
Guatemala	61.52	42.64	23.31	30.31	2.54	9.15	11.51	14.66	1.12	3.24	3.92	3.95
Honduras	61.60	38.97	23.34	27.70	1.47	12.91	11.52	13.39	2.07	7.02	6.59	5.93
Mexico	61.50	44.18	23.30	31.40	1.82	3.41	11.50	15.19	1.88	5.83	6.84	6.37
Nicaragua	60.75	45.38	23.02	32.25	3.20	2.92	11.36	15.60	1.66	3.86	13.46	12.98
Panama	57.79	39.87	21.90	28.34	3.22	5.38	10.81	13.70	6.27	12.71	8.28	3.40
Caribbean	32.60	19.47	12.35	13.84	7.96	18.90	6.10	6.69	0.99	1.11		
Dominican Rep.	60.40	43.23	22.89	30.73	3.94	8.29	11.30	14.86	1.47	2.89	4.42	5.47
Haiti	63.65	47.77	24.12	33.96	0.20	1.53	11.91	16.42	0.13	0.32	3.14	4.89
Jamaica	38.93	6.33	14.75	4.50	35.66	84.66	7.28	2.18	3.37	2.33	3.14	4.89
LAC Average rate	59.28	40.20	22.46	28.57	4.17	10.08	11.09	13.82	3.00	7.32	9.80	8.16

Table A.3c   Asia: Crop input cost shares, 1960–1981 and 1981–2000

Region/ Country	Crop Input Cost Shares (%)											
	Cropland (*)		Labor		Fert. + Pest.*		Seeds		Mechanization*		Animal Power	
	1961–1980	1981–2001	1961–1980	1981–2001	1961–1980	1981–2001	1961–1980	1981–2001	1961–1980	1981–2001	1961–1980	1981–2001
Middle East	58.29	38.71	41.02	38.75	1.23	6.19	2.64	4.05	6.96	13.01	6.53	3.60
Afghanistan	71.51	69.74	46.82	49.58	0.23	0.04	2.00	3.77	0.28	0.40	7.45	4.61
Iran	54.63	34.26	38.27	37.55	1.02	4.45	2.76	2.65	11.78	19.51	6.09	3.49
Iraq	61.73	39.56	40.42	31.93	0.70	7.05	3.71	7.42	7.14	15.82	6.43	2.97
Jordan	54.85	25.63	38.43	30.62	2.58	16.94	4.53	7.28	5.19	15.17	6.11	2.85
Saudi Arabia	45.78	35.51	40.29	42.41	2.89	11.05	1.72	1.14	6.88	4.04	6.41	3.95
Syria	55.16	30.76	41.00	36.75	1.01	4.43	2.61	4.63	10.65	18.21	6.52	3.42
Turkey	57.93	31.20	40.59	37.27	1.18	4.14	2.77	3.64	7.17	20.29	6.46	3.47
Yemen	64.73	43.01	42.38	43.91	0.23	1.41	1.00	1.83	6.59	10.67	6.74	4.08
South Asia	59.30	41.70	43.82	45.64	1.13	4.03	1.33	1.87	4.04	5.29	6.97	4.25
Bangladesh	67.36	48.79	47.19	49.81	0.45	2.20	0.90	0.97	0.23	0.23	7.51	4.63
India	62.18	39.24	43.56	43.00	0.85	4.55	1.98	3.00	3.68	8.19	6.93	4.00
Nepal	71.74	48.94	46.97	49.96	0.10	0.88	1.07	1.45	0.63	1.06	7.47	4.65
Pakistan	58.58	33.38	41.04	39.87	1.21	6.22	1.51	2.22	4.64	13.28	6.53	3.71

Continued

Table A.3c Asia: Crop input cost shares, 1960–1981 and 1981–2000—Cont'd

Crop Input Cost Shares (%)

Region/Country	Cropland (*)		Labor		Fert. + Pest.*		Seeds		Mechanization*		Animal Power	
	1961–1980	1981–2001	1961–1980	1981–2001	1961–1980	1981–2001	1961–1980	1981–2001	1961–1980	1981–2001	1961–1980	1981–2001
Sri Lanka	36.64	38.15	40.31	45.57	3.06	6.28	1.20	1.70	10.99	3.69	6.41	4.24
South East Asia	52.58	48.14	45.32	44.90	1.40	4.73	1.06	1.78	2.37	2.95	7.21	4.18
Cambodia	42.10	48.08	46.31	49.09	0.10	0.10	2.06	4.43	0.89	0.56	7.37	4.57
Indonesia	63.36	64.17	47.09	48.82	0.81	3.35	0.38	0.58	0.67	0.79	7.49	4.54
Laos	42.69	41.56	46.96	49.64	0.08	0.12	1.74	3.16	0.46	0.76	7.47	4.62
Malaysia	46.40	35.36	38.67	28.54	6.60	21.80	0.28	0.31	8.34	8.08	6.15	2.65
Philippines	52.20	40.91	45.93	48.87	1.23	2.75	1.02	1.25	2.13	1.11	7.31	4.55
Thailand	66.48	54.31	46.58	43.83	0.33	2.36	1.03	1.19	1.87	5.41	7.41	4.08
Vietnam	54.82	52.61	45.68	45.54	0.66	2.62	0.92	1.55	2.25	3.92	7.27	4.24
East Asia	58.18	35.48	41.44	40.30	1.71	3.16	2.42	3.77	7.13	13.34	6.59	3.75
China	62.90	38.80	44.07	46.35	1.02	6.22	1.24	1.48	3.24	2.83	7.01	4.31
Mongolia	61.40	35.98	40.20	36.73	0.35	0.99	5.34	7.78	9.50	16.60	6.40	3.42
North Korea	50.25	31.66	40.06	37.81	3.75	2.28	0.69	2.04	8.64	20.59	6.37	3.52
Average rate	56.76	41.81	42.99	42.32	1.32	4.88	1.85	2.85	4.95	8.31	6.84	3.94

*Input costs ratio adjusted for geometric as explained in Section 2.3.

Table A.3d   Asia: Livestock input cost shares, 1960–1981 and 1981–2000

Region/Country	Permanent Pastures		Labor		Livestock Input Cost Shares (%) Fert. + Ch. + Med.		Feed		Mechanization		Animal Stock	
	1961–1980	1981–2001	1961–1980	1981–2001	1961–1980	1981–2001	1961–1980	1981–2001	1961–1980	1981–2001	1961–1980	1981–2001
Middle East	53.69	36.40	20.35	25.87	1.10	4.11	3.84	13.27	2.32	8.61	4.91	3.00
Afghanistan	63.57	48.51	24.09	34.48	0.38	0.10	11.89	16.67	0.06	0.25	6.90	3.72
Iran	61.33	40.17	23.24	28.55	1.52	4.35	11.47	13.81	2.44	13.12	5.07	4.24
Iraq	59.72	36.44	22.63	25.90	1.30	11.75	11.17	12.52	5.17	13.39	6.88	6.77
Saudi Arabia	61.31	42.73	23.23	30.37	2.36	8.45	11.47	14.69	1.63	3.76	3.92	0.77
Syria	61.45	39.04	23.28	27.75	1.17	3.57	11.49	13.42	2.60	16.23	2.34	1.59
Turkey	59.53	39.90	22.56	28.36	1.62	3.36	11.14	13.71	5.15	14.67	10.24	6.15
Yemen	62.62	44.41	23.73	31.57	0.42	1.30	11.71	15.26	1.52	7.46	3.92	0.77
South Asia	62.57	45.28	23.71	32.18	1.13	3.25	1.80	4.94	0.89	3.73	17.63	11.49
Bangladesh	63.46	47.67	24.05	33.88	0.56	1.93	11.87	16.38	0.06	0.14	27.36	17.70
India	62.60	43.97	23.72	31.25	1.14	3.88	11.71	15.11	0.83	5.79	15.02	8.73
Nepal	63.62	47.99	24.11	34.11	0.17	0.77	11.90	16.49	0.19	0.64	21.65	14.68
Pakistan	61.77	41.61	23.41	29.58	1.70	4.93	11.55	14.30	1.57	9.58	6.90	3.72

Continued

Table A.3d Asia: Livestock input cost shares, 1960–1981 and 1981–2000—Cont'd

	Livestock Input Cost Shares (%)											
Region/Country	Permanent Pastures		Labor		Fert. + Ch. + Med.		Feed		Mechanization		Animal Stock	
	1961–1980	1981–2001	1961–1980	1981–2001	1961–1980	1981–2001	1961–1980	1981–2001	1961–1980	1981–2001	1961–1980	1981–2001
Sri Lanka	61.41	45.14	23.27	32.09	2.06	4.72	11.49	15.52	1.78	2.53	17.20	12.64
South East Asia		44.45	23.80	31.59	1.25	5.03	1.35	4.39	0.38	3.64	7.52	6.65
Cambodia	63.64	48.42	24.12	34.41	0.06	0.11	11.91	16.64	0.27	0.42	23.65	21.76
Indonesia	63.27	46.94	23.97	33.37	0.84	2.44	11.84	16.13	0.09	1.11	8.81	5.93
Laos DPR	63.74	48.35	24.15	34.37	0.04	0.20	11.92	16.62	0.14	0.47	6.29	8.02
Malaysia	59.31	31.02	22.47	22.04	5.98	23.97	11.09	10.66	1.15	12.31	2.36	0.90
Philippines	63.08	47.16	23.90	33.52	0.91	2.43	11.80	16.21	0.31	0.67	2.53	1.53
Thailand	63.43	44.06	24.04	31.32	0.42	2.90	11.87	15.14	0.25	6.57	5.72	5.52
Vietnam	63.20	45.20	23.95	32.13	0.54	3.19	11.82	15.54	0.49	3.94	3.27	2.87
East Asia	40.88	28.80	15.49	20.47	0.67	1.92	3.48	11.59	1.97	5.59	3.82	3.82
China	62.53	45.56	23.70	32.38	1.36	4.64	11.70	15.66	0.72	1.75	4.35	2.11
Mongolia	60.12	40.83	22.78	29.02	0.65	1.11	11.25	14.03	5.21	15.01	7.12	9.36
Average rate	62.13	43.58	23.54	30.97	1.20	4.29	11.62	14.98	1.51	6.18	9.12	6.64

Table A.3e   Africa crop input cost shares, 1960–1981 and 1981–2000

Region/ Country	Cropland 1961– 1980	Cropland 1981– 2001	Labor 1961– 1980	Labor 1981– 2001	Fert. + Pest. 1961– 1980	Fert. + Pest. 1981– 2001	Seeds 1961– 1980	Seeds 1981– 2001	Mechanization 1961– 1980	Mechanization 1981– 2001	Animal Power 1961– 1980	Animal Power 1981– 2001
North Africa	49.48	31.65	39.75	37.80	2.64	4.14	3.04	4.99	9.74	15.51	6.32	3.52
Algeria	56.10	30.89	39.30	36.90	2.04	1.51	3.76	5.78	8.47	20.09	6.25	3.43
Egypt	44.46	38.20	41.80	45.63	3.10	4.51	1.12	0.89	8.69	6.53	6.65	4.24
Libya	49.73	25.83	36.96	30.86	4.76	7.67	4.80	8.89	8.74	16.80	5.88	2.87
Morocco	53.85	32.44	40.03	38.74	1.21	2.88	2.65	5.63	12.24	14.04	6.37	3.60
Tunisia	43.24	30.87	40.66	36.87	2.07	4.12	2.86	3.79	10.56	20.07	6.47	3.43
East Africa	38.33	31.79	31.63	33.24	0.28	1.03	0.84	0.90	0.04	0.16	5.03	3.09
Ethiopia	72.34	53.03	47.36	47.98	0.10	3.33	1.68	1.26	0.01	0.51	7.54	4.46
Sudan	42.96	46.14	47.26	50.57	0.73	0.40	1.37	1.77	0.09	0.13	7.52	4.70
Uganda	64.51	42.85	47.95	51.19	0.05	0.01	0.64	1.09	0.08	0.09	7.63	4.76
Kenya	50.19	48.71	47.19	49.73	0.78	2.47	1.35	1.28	0.07	0.21	7.51	4.63
Madagascar	53.64	42.81	47.20	51.13	0.14	0.37	2.13	0.38	0.05	0.07	7.51	4.76
Central Africa	57.62	45.66	38.65	35.95	0.34	2.04	5.06	13.54	0.20	0.36	7.17	3.90
Cameroon	57.92	48.97	46.17	50.00	1.06	1.40	2.79	1.80	0.01	0.02	7.34	4.65
Chad	72.32	52.53	47.35	50.19	0.07	0.75	1.84	2.36	0.01	0.01	7.53	4.67

Continued

Table A.3e Africa crop input cost shares, 1960–1981 and 1981–2000—Cont'd

Region/Country	Cropland		Labor		Fert. + Pest.		Seeds		Mechanization		Animal Power	
	1961–1980	1981–2001	1961–1980	1981–2001	1961–1980	1981–2001	1961–1980	1981–2001	1961–1980	1981–2001	1961–1980	1981–2001
Dem. Rep. Congo	66.39	57.77	46.52	50.00	0.19	0.03	3.26	3.36	0.08	0.06	7.40	4.65
Rep. Congo	44.29	27.81	36.91	25.17	0.25	9.91	21.59	34.80	1.08	2.04	5.87	2.34
Rep. Central African	57.44	58.20	45.78	50.37	0.45	0.11	4.81	2.58	0.01	0.01	7.28	4.69
Rwanda	47.36	28.68	47.80	25.95	0.04	0.03	1.09	49.86	0.01	0.01	7.60	2.41
Western Africa	56.82	47.51	40.01	42.27	0.30	0.56	2.21	3.26	0.04	0.03	6.37	3.93
Benin	50.50	57.72	47.48	49.96	0.14	1.41	1.63	1.28	0.01	0.01	7.55	4.65
Guinea	59.15	62.84	47.14	50.71	0.05	0.08	2.40	1.92	0.01	0.02	7.50	4.72
Ghana	70.55	59.01	46.20	51.08	0.36	0.26	3.09	0.89	0.10	0.05	7.35	4.75
Togo	72.32	50.21	47.35	47.98	0.13	0.91	1.67	6.17	0.01	0.00	7.53	4.46
Mauritania	69.93	55.92	45.79	39.76	0.62	0.74	3.07	20.86	0.24	0.09	7.28	3.70
Niger	72.42	53.92	47.42	51.52	0.02	0.04	1.87	0.49	0.00	0.00	7.54	4.79
Burkina Faso	72.44	49.71	47.43	50.75	0.09	0.70	1.61	1.15	0.00	0.02	7.55	4.72
Ivory Coast	56.78	41.39	45.26	49.44	1.52	1.91	3.78	2.57	0.08	0.09	7.20	4.60

Mali	71.68	67.11	46.93	51.06	0.18	0.01	2.33	1.37	0.02	0.03	7.47	4.75
Nigeria	72.43	59.23	47.43	51.27	0.26	0.26	1.05	0.56	0.02	0.07	7.54	4.77
Senegal	60.65	51.99	45.08	49.68	0.82	1.46	5.18	2.13	0.02	0.02	7.17	4.62
Sierra Leone	66.64	56.09	46.69	48.55	0.06	0.02	3.28	6.25	0.01	0.01	7.43	4.52
Southern Africa	56.89	49.23	45.18	46.66	1.75	2.14	3.17	5.74	0.53	1.53	7.19	4.34
Angola	65.60	62.07	45.96	50.09	0.82	0.13	1.97	2.16	0.56	0.91	7.31	4.66
Botswana	40.57	31.63	38.15	30.22	1.69	5.65	16.33	24.05	1.18	10.08	6.07	2.81
Malawi	63.49	41.99	47.19	50.15	0.49	1.03	1.43	2.14	0.02	0.03	7.51	4.67
Mozambique	55.44	72.37	46.20	51.46	1.13	0.00	2.40	0.49	0.36	0.15	7.35	4.79
Zimbabwe	55.23	41.09	46.02	49.08	2.16	4.07	1.24	0.65	0.33	0.55	7.32	4.57
South Africa	52.26	48.82	45.99	49.84	2.66	2.76	0.73	0.13	0.62	0.21	7.32	4.64
Zambia	62.79	54.73	46.67	49.52	1.30	1.17	0.80	2.37	0.14	0.31	7.42	4.61
Namibia	48.90	40.44	43.03	38.64	5.30	4.19	2.47	18.38	1.48	1.44	6.85	3.59
Tanzania	67.74	49.90	47.46	50.94	0.21	0.25	1.18	1.27	0.12	0.09	7.55	4.74
Average rate	59.03	47.94	45.22	46.03	1.00	1.80	3.17	6.02	1.50	2.56	7.19	4.28

*Input costs ratio were adjusted for geometric as explained in Section 2.3.

Table A.3f　Africa livestock input cost shares, 1961–1980 and 1981–2001

Region/Country	Permanent Pastures		Labor		Fert. + Chem. + Medic.		Feed		Mechanization		Animal Stock	
	1961–1980	1981–2001	1961–1980	1981–2001	1961–1980	1981–2001	1961–1980	1981–2001	1961–1980	1981–2001	1961–1980	1981–1901
North Africa	49.58	33.09	18.79	23.52	1.99	4.15	9.27	11.37	3.71	11.19	4.32	2.20
Algeria	58.79	40.30	22.28	28.64	2.85	2.40	11.00	13.85	5.09	14.81	5.41	2.36
Egypt	60.22	40.91	22.82	29.08	0.48	0.91	11.27	14.06	5.21	15.04	2.57	2.34
Libya	57.07	35.91	21.63	25.52	5.68	13.02	10.68	12.34	4.94	13.20	3.93	2.22
Morocco	61.77	41.82	23.41	29.73	1.45	4.54	11.55	14.38	1.83	9.53	10.04	4.04
Tunisia	59.62	39.62	22.59	28.16	1.47	4.05	11.15	13.62	5.16	14.56	3.93	2.22
East Africa	42.12	29.97	15.96	21.30	0.23	1.44	7.88	10.30	0.49	3.65	12.69	12.38
Ethiopia	63.57	39.87	24.09	28.34	0.21	5.38	11.89	13.70	0.24	12.71	23.71	23.42
Sudan	62.82	47.11	23.81	33.49	0.48	0.54	11.75	16.19	1.14	2.67	19.20	24.36
Uganda	63.37	47.79	24.01	33.97	0.06	0.02	11.85	16.43	0.70	1.80	16.09	13.01
Kenya	62.94	45.06	23.85	32.03	0.61	2.70	11.77	15.49	0.83	4.72	17.13	13.49
Madagascar	63.53	47.57	24.07	33.81	0.13	0.96	11.88	16.35	0.39	1.31	18.19	15.71
Central Africa	53.94	38.95	20.44	27.68	0.33	3.65	10.70	250.99	1.06	2.39	22.33	18.97
Cameroon	63.02	47.56	23.88	33.80	1.14	1.93	11.79	16.35	0.17	0.36	22.76	16.52

Chad	63.72	48.18	24.14	34.25	0.14	0.87	11.92	16.56	0.08	0.15	24.81	31.73
Dem. Rep. Congo	63.24	47.95	23.96	34.08	0.29	0.05	11.83	16.48	0.68	1.44	25.78	21.79
Rep. Congo	60.28	32.05	22.84	22.78	0.38	22.38	11.28	11.02	5.22	11.78	22.76	16.52
Rep. Central African	63.57	48.49	24.09	34.46	0.33	0.21	11.89	16.67	0.12	0.18	22.76	16.52
Rwanda	63.78	48.42	24.17	34.42	0.03	0.09	11.93	16.64	0.10	0.43	15.13	10.74
Western Africa	54.17	40.86	20.53	29.04	0.46	0.99	2.41	13.69	0.43	0.77	13.37	12.53
Benin	63.73	47.32	24.15	33.63	0.11	2.60	11.92	16.26	0.08	0.19	12.88	11.73
Guinea	63.78	48.33	24.17	34.35	0.06	0.19	11.93	16.61	0.07	0.53	21.35	28.69
Ghana	62.31	47.47	23.61	33.74	0.74	0.47	11.66	16.32	1.69	2.00	7.94	9.38
Togo	63.64	47.91	24.11	34.05	0.26	1.47	11.90	16.47	0.09	0.11	12.88	11.73
Mauritania	61.77	46.10	23.41	32.77	1.28	3.23	11.55	15.84	1.99	2.06	10.04	10.04
Niger	63.82	48.62	24.18	34.56	0.04	0.07	11.94	16.71	0.02	0.05	19.04	11.07
Burkina Faso	63.71	47.83	24.14	34.00	0.19	0.96	11.92	16.44	0.03	0.76	23.70	18.64
Ivory Coast	62.12	46.74	23.54	33.22	1.65	2.17	11.62	16.07	1.07	1.80	8.75	10.61
Mali	63.46	48.18	24.05	34.24	0.37	0.03	11.87	16.56	0.25	0.99	15.37	12.41
Nigeria	63.27	47.80	23.97	33.97	0.53	0.47	11.84	16.43	0.40	1.33	12.88	11.73
Senegal	63.06	47.28	23.90	33.60	1.07	2.24	11.80	16.25	0.18	0.63	21.05	10.67
Sierra Leone	63.73	48.52	24.15	34.49	0.10	0.04	11.92	16.68	0.10	0.28	21.35	28.69

Continued

Table A.3f Africa livestock input cost shares, 1961–1980 and 1981–2001—Cont'd

Region/Country	Permanent Pastures		Labor		Fert. + Chem. + Medic.		Feed		Mechanization		Animal Stock	
	1961–1980	1981–2001	1961–1980	1981–2001	1961–1980	1981–2001	1961–1980	1981–2001	1961–1980	1981–2001	1961–1980	1981–1901
Southern Africa	60.69	43.31	23.00	30.78	1.70	3.24	3.26	22.49	3.26	7.79	20.29	15.91
Angola	58.61	41.10	22.21	29.21	1.19	0.24	10.96	14.13	7.04	15.31	25.78	21.79
Botswana	59.57	36.73	22.57	26.11	1.55	11.04	11.14	12.62	5.16	13.50	22.15	16.55
Malawi	63.30	47.81	23.99	33.99	0.62	1.19	11.84	16.43	0.26	0.58	18.88	13.75
Mozambique	61.46	47.05	23.29	33.44	1.08	0.01	11.50	16.17	2.68	3.32	17.41	13.42
Zimbabwe	60.82	41.96	23.05	29.83	2.05	4.19	11.38	14.42	2.70	9.59	22.15	16.55
South Africa	59.76	43.99	22.64	31.26	2.25	3.54	11.18	15.12	4.17	6.09	8.05	7.40
Zambia	62.02	44.98	23.50	31.97	1.63	1.89	11.60	15.46	1.24	5.70	25.78	21.79
Namibia	57.71	38.51	21.87	27.37	4.63	6.72	10.80	13.24	5.00	14.16	22.15	16.55
Tanzania	62.94	47.63	23.85	33.85	0.32	0.34	11.77	16.37	1.12	1.81	20.25	15.36
Average rate	62.05	44.88	23.51	31.90	1.01	2.79	11.61	15.42	1.82	5.01	16.87	14.47

PART Three

Agriculture Growth and Development

CHAPTER 73

Agricultural Productivity and Economic Growth

Douglas Gollin*

Williams College

Contents

Abstract

In most poor countries, large majorities of the population live in rural areas and earn their livelihoods primarily from agriculture. Many rural people in the developing world are poor, and conversely, most of the world's poor people inhabit rural areas. Agriculture also accounts for a significant fraction of the economic activity in the developing world, with some 25% of value added in poor countries coming from this sector. The sheer size of the agricultural sector implies that changes affecting agriculture have large aggregate effects. Thus, it seems reasonable that agricultural productivity growth should have significant effects on macro variables, including economic growth.

But these effects can be complicated. The large size of the agricultural sector does not necessarily imply that it must be a leading sector for economic growth. In fact, agriculture in most developing countries has very low productivity relative to the rest of the economy. Expanding a low-productivity sector might not be unambiguously good for growth. Moreover, there are issues of reverse causation. Economies that experience growth in aggregate output could be the beneficiaries of good institutions or good fortune that also helps the agricultural sector. Thus, even after 50 years of research on agricultural development, there is abundant evidence for correlations between agricultural productivity increases and economic growth but little definitive evidence for a causal connection.

Handbook of Agricultural Economics, Volume 4   doi: 10.1016/S1574-0072(09)04073-0

This chapter reviews theoretical arguments and empirical evidence for the hypothesis that agricultural productivity improvements lead to economic growth in developing countries. For countries with large interior populations and limited access to international markets, agricultural development is essential for economic growth. For other countries, the importance of agriculture-led growth will depend on the relative feasibility and cost of importing food.
JEL classifications: O11, O13, O41, O47, Q1

Keywords

agricultural productivity
economic growth
economic development
structural transformation
agriculture

1. INTRODUCTION

In most poor countries, large majorities of the population live in rural areas and earn their livelihoods primarily from agriculture. In sub-Saharan Africa and some parts of Asia, as much as 60% of the economically active population works primarily in agriculture, and approximately the same fraction resides in rural areas. Many of the people living in the rural areas of the developing world are poor, and conversely, most of the world's poor people inhabit rural areas—as much as 70–75%, according to Ravallion et al. (2007).

Agriculture also accounts for a significant fraction of the economic activity in the developing world, with some 25% of value added in poor countries coming from this sector (World Development Indicators, 2009). Agriculture also makes up a large fraction of the exports of developing countries, with both food and nonfood crops playing important roles. In a few countries, exports of raw agricultural commodities total 15–30% of GDP.

The sheer size of the agricultural sector implies that changes affecting agriculture have large aggregate effects. But these effects might be complicated. The large size of the agricultural sector does not necessarily imply that it must be a leading sector for economic growth. In fact, the agricultural sector in most developing countries has very low productivity relative to the rest of the economy. Expanding a low-productivity sector might not be unambiguously good for growth. In fact, a skeptical line of thought in development economics has long argued that the agricultural sector is at best a limited source of growth; this "agro-pessimist" viewpoint, expressed in recent writings such as Dercon (2009), is discussed here.

Economic theories and models dating back to the work of Mellor, Gardner, and Johnston in the 1960s offer insights into the mechanisms through which agricultural productivity growth might drive overall economic growth, but the assumptions invoked by some models are strong. Under alternative assumptions, some researchers (e.g., Matsuyama, 1992) find exactly the opposite: that agricultural productivity gains may be negatively related to economic growth.

Many empirical analyses have also attempted to use time series or cross–country studies to demonstrate a causal link from agricultural productivity levels or growth rates to the broader economy. But although this work draws on a plethora of different methodological approaches and data types, there is little that meets contemporary standards of econometric identification. As a result, the correlations between agricultural productivity growth and economic growth are empirically well demonstrated, but the causal relationships are less clear.

This chapter selectively reviews the literature on agricultural productivity and its contributions to economic growth. It argues that agricultural productivity growth is neither a necessary nor sufficient condition for economic growth—but that in many developing countries, agricultural productivity growth is nevertheless the first and most important source of economic growth. Recent research has offered a vast amount of evidence documenting the links between agricultural development and economic growth (including the World Bank's *World Development Report 2008* and the associated background papers), and recent work in the growth literature has helped clarify agriculture's role. The chapter argues that we now understand fairly clearly the circumstances in which agricultural productivity can and must play a central role in economic growth—as well as those circumstances in which it will not.

Some specific questions addressed here include these:

• How convincing are the empirical claims that increasing agricultural productivity leads to economic growth? What lessons can we draw from historical episodes, and what do recent country experiences tell us?
• What underlying rationales or models support these claims?
• What assumptions are critical to these models? Could alternative models also apply?
• What empirical evidence can allow us to distinguish between models? Under what conditions might one model be more useful than others?

The chapter proceeds as follows: Section 2 sets out some central facts about agricultural productivity and economic growth. Section 3 reviews some of the theories that might provide guidance in thinking about causal mechanisms. Section 4 reviews some of the empirical literature that documents links between agricultural productivity and economic growth. Section 5 considers skeptical views of the relationship between agricultural productivity and growth and concludes by offering a summary and interpretation of the evidence.

The literature in this field is too vast for any review article to be comprehensive or exhaustive. This chapter instead tries to cover a somewhat representative assortment of the literature, focusing in particular on some writings from the growth field that might be unfamiliar to many agricultural economists. Readers in search of other recent literature reviews might want to consult such previous efforts as Byerlee et al. (2009), Diao et al. (2004), Irz et al. (2001), Mellor (1999), Mundlak (2000), Staatz and Dembélé (2007), Thirtle et al. (2001), Timmer (2003), and of course, the comprehensive effort represented by the World Bank's *World Development Report 2008*. In addition, no fewer than three previous chapters in various *Handbook* volumes have addressed similar questions: Timmer's piece on "The Agricultural Transformation" in the *Handbook of Development Economics* (1988); Timmer's piece on "Agriculture and Economic Development" in the *Handbook of Agricultural Economics* (2002); and Foster and Rosenzweig's article on "Economic Development and the Decline of Agricultural Employment" in the *Handbook of Development Economics* (2008). Many of the issues addressed in the current chapter have been covered previously in these excellent surveys, among others.

2. BACKGROUND: WHY FOCUS ON AGRICULTURE?

As noted, a large fraction of the developing world's labor force works in agriculture. For the world as a whole, about 40% of workers earn their living primarily from agriculture. For the poorest countries in the world, the fraction is much higher: In those countries classified by the United Nations as least developed, 65% of the labor force is employed in agriculture. More than a dozen countries have agriculture shares of employment that exceed 75%, and the East African region as a whole approaches this level. Table 1 offers a breakdown for a number of regional aggregates; Figure 1 shows a scatter plot of the data for individual countries.

These numbers are necessarily imprecise. In principle, the data report the share of individuals who earn their living primarily from agriculture, but this could overstate the actual fraction of hours worked in agriculture. Many people who are counted as working in agriculture also supply labor for other market and nonmarket activities. The numbers understate, however, the fraction of individuals whose livelihoods are linked closely to the agricultural sector, such as those employed in transporting or processing agricultural goods. One crude way to measure the number of people in this category is to look at rural populations. For the world as a whole, the UN Food and Agriculture Organization (FAO) reports that approximately half of the world's people live in rural areas, and in the least developed countries, the figure is about three fourths (see Table 2).

Agriculture also accounts for large fractions of economic activity, measured in value terms. In many developing countries, 25–30% of GDP comes from agriculture; in a few poor countries, primarily in Africa and Southern Asia, agriculture's share of output exceeds 40%. (See Table 3 for regional aggregates.) In general, there is a strong and negative relationship between a country's level of income per capita and the fraction of agriculture in output. This relationship, one of the oldest stylized facts in the growth

Table 1 Agricultural population and economically active population, as share of total, 2010

Region	Total Population	Agricultural Population as Fraction of Total	Total Economically Active Population (1000)	Fraction of Economically Active Population in Agriculture
Africa	1,032,014	0.508	459,461	0.524
−Eastern Africa	332,106	0.732	160,585	0.744
−Middle Africa	129,582	0.569	55,510	0.580
−Northern Africa	206,295	0.314	86,267	0.301
−Southern Africa	56,592	0.138	24,269	0.107
−Western Africa	307,439	0.440	132,830	0.457
Americas				
−Northern America	348,573	0.017	182,535	0.016
−Central America	153,658	0.208	67,758	0.185
−Caribbean	42,300	0.217	19,980	0.208
−South America	397,742	0.138	180,736	0.135
Asia				
−Central Asia	62,061	0.213	30,441	0.206
−Eastern Asia	1,562,575	0.536	937,594	0.544
−Southern Asia	1,715,319	0.481	784,158	0.520
−South-Eastern Asia	594,214	0.434	313,463	0.469
−Western Asia	232,140	0.183	99,233	0.241
Europe	719,955	0.058	365,121	0.060
Australia and New Zealand	25,647	0.045	13,197	0.046
Other Oceania	9,842	0.606	4,699	0.588
Least Developed Countries	862,829	0.645	414,307	0.650
World	6,896,040	0.384	3,458,376	0.406

Source: FAOSTAT 2009.

literature, is illustrated in Figure 2, which uses PPP measures of real per capita income from the Penn World Tables (Heston et al., 2006) for the year 2005.

The cross-section data on agriculture's share of employment and output echo the time-series data for countries that are currently rich. Figures 3 and 4 show agriculture's share of employment and output for 15 of today's industrial countries at moments in

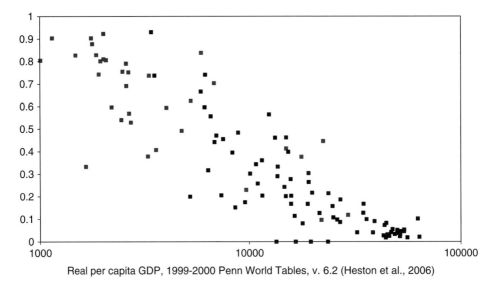

Real per capita GDP, 1999-2000 Penn World Tables, v. 6.2 (Heston et al., 2006)

Figure 1   Agriculture Share of Workforce, Cross-Section Data, 2000.

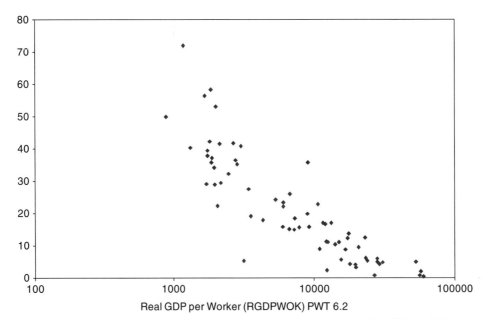

Real GDP per Worker (RGDPWOK) PWT 6.2

Figure 2   Agriculture's Share of GDP, Cross-Section Data. Sources: Data on Real GDP per Worker are taken from Penn World Tables, v. 6.2 (series RGDPWOK) for 2000; data on agriculture's share of GDP are from the World Bank's *World Development Indicators* accessed April 2009.

Table 2 Total population and fraction rural, 1950-2010

Region	1950 Total	1950 Rural	1960 Total	1960 Rural	1970 Total	1970 Rural	1980 Total	1980 Rural	1990 Total	1990 Rural	2000 Total	2000 Rural
Africa	224,203	0.855	282,238	0.813	364,135	0.764	479,786	0.721	637,420	0.680	820,960	0.641
–Eastern Africa	65,071	0.947	82,758	0.926	109,021	0.896	145,950	0.853	197,244	0.821	257,293	0.793
–Middle Africa	26,104	0.860	32,173	0.823	41,289	0.751	54,715	0.710	73,632	0.675	97,765	0.628
–Northern Africa	53,303	0.752	67,308	0.696	85,939	0.637	111,364	0.597	143,965	0.553	174,436	0.516
–Southern Africa	15,591	0.624	19,731	0.581	25,462	0.563	32,974	0.553	41,827	0.512	51,950	0.461
–Western Africa	64,134	0.901	80,268	0.848	102,424	0.786	134,783	0.727	180,752	0.668	239,516	0.612
Americas	339,241	0.472	424,319	0.410	519,473	0.355	619,924	0.314	728,198	0.275	838,719	0.232
–Northern America	171,615	0.361	204,150	0.301	231,931	0.262	255,545	0.261	283,921	0.246	315,671	0.209
–Central America	37,515	0.608	50,916	0.536	69,581	0.462	92,254	0.397	112,725	0.350	135,587	0.313
–Caribbean	17,132	0.632	20,773	0.599	25,421	0.545	29,855	0.483	34,356	0.440	38,616	0.384
–South America	112,979	0.573	148,480	0.490	192,540	0.403	242,270	0.317	297,196	0.255	348,845	0.205
Asia	1,384,367	0.836	1,668,862	0.806	2,092,096	0.778	2,578,620	0.742	3,112,431	0.685	3,704,836	0.629
–Eastern Asia	669,906	0.835	791,743	0.798	986,627	0.772	1,178,001	0.743	1,343,911	0.670	1,476,295	0.596
–Southern Asia	493,949	0.842	597,904	0.828	744,255	0.806	940,609	0.766	1,192,559	0.735	1,460,856	0.710
–South-Eastern Asia	178,149	0.846	223,127	0.815	286,762	0.786	359,107	0.745	440,574	0.684	519,997	0.603
–Western Asia	42,363	0.737	56,088	0.659	74,452	0.566	100,903	0.488	135,387	0.386	192,389	0.363
Europe	566,339	0.491	631,477	0.436	693,553	0.381	739,288	0.332	777,792	0.312	717,700	0.290
Australia/New Zealand	10,127	0.238	12,648	0.195	15,548	0.155	17,751	0.146	20,284	0.147	22,993	0.131
Other Oceania	2,680	0.915	3,234	0.878	4,089	0.813	5,102	0.776	6,449	0.756	8,112	0.764
Least Developed	200,175	0.927	247,118	0.905	315,603	0.869	405,528	0.827	525,118	0.790	678,997	0.752
World	2,526,957	0.709	3,022,778	0.671	3,688,894	0.640	4,440,471	0.609	5,282,574	0.571	6,113,320	0.535

Source: FAOSTAT 2009.

Table 3 Agriculture's share of GDP (%), selected regional aggregates

Region	1965	1970	1980	1990	2000	2006
High income	..	..	4.0	2.8	1.9	1.4
Middle income	27.0	25.0	20.1	16.8	10.8	9.2
Low income	..	..	..	34.2	30.4	25.9
East Asia & Pacific	37.8	34.6	28.6	25.0	14.6	11.8
Europe & Central Asia	..	..	..	15.4	9.5	7.4
Latin America & Caribbean	16.1	12.9	10.1	8.9	5.9	5.9
Middle East & North Africa	..	..	15.6	18.1	12.6	11.7
South Asia	41.0	41.5	34.7	29.1	23.9	18.5
Sub-Saharan Africa	21.9	19.6	18.5	18.8	16.5	16.3
World	..	..	6.6	5.4	3.6	3.0

Source: World Bank, World Development Indicators, accessed 4-30-09.

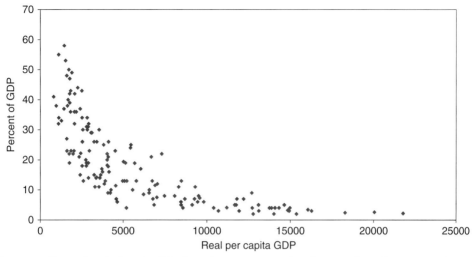

Figure 3   Share of agriculture in GDP, based on time series data for 15 industrial countries. Sources: Mitchell 1992, pp. 912-917; Kurian 1994, p. 93-94; Mitchell 1993, pp. 775-77; Mitchell 1995, pp. 1027-31. Data on real per capita GDP are taken from Penn World Tables, v. 5.6, for the available years of coverage; historical data are taken from Maddison 1995, pp. 194-206.

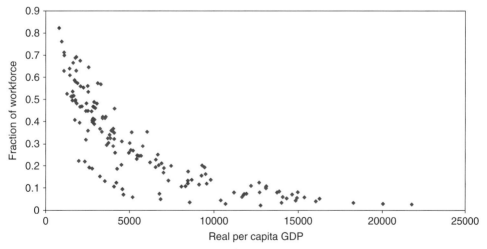

Figure 4   Employment in agriculture as share of total employment, based on time series data for 15 industrial countries. Sources: Mitchell 1992, pp. 141-58; Kurian 1994, p. 78; Mitchell 1993, pp. 99-103; Mitchell 1995, pp. 95-103. Data on real per capita GDP are taken from Penn World Tables, v. 5.6, for the available years of coverage; historical data are taken from Maddison 1995, pp. 194-206.

the historical past when they were relatively poor. It is striking that the historical data display the same patterns as the cross-section data.

As the preceding paragraphs make clear, agriculture's shares in both employment and output are higher in poor countries than in rich ones; but the employment shares are substantially higher than the output shares in most developing countries. This fact is somewhat underappreciated, but it has important implications. As an arithmetic matter, if agriculture accounts for a higher share of employment than of value added, output per worker in agriculture must be lower than in nonagriculture. In fact, the implied differences in output per worker are large.

Table 4 reports calculations of output per worker in agriculture and nonagriculture for a relatively small set of countries. These are calculated somewhat crudely from the aggregate data on agriculture's shares of value added and employment. As such, they should not be taken as careful micro estimates of differences in labor productivity. For that purpose, ideally, we would have firm-level data or wage data from competitive labor markets. Nevertheless, the productivity differences suggested by these calculations are striking. They point to a sharp difference in average labor productivity between sectors. To the extent that average products may be indicative of marginal products or wages, the data offer a clear suggestion that rural areas are poor and that agricultural labor offers low returns.

Table 4 offers additional information on rural poverty. If we take these numbers literally, a number of developing countries have *average* agricultural output per worker that is less than $1000. With the dependency ratios typical in most developing countries, this corresponds to levels of income per capita substantially below $1/day. For many countries, agricultural output per capita is less than $2/day. By contrast, very few countries in the data have nonagricultural output per capita of less than $2/day.[1]

Using a different data set and different PPP exchange rates, the World Bank reports its own data on output per worker in agriculture. In their data, for those countries designated as low income, agricultural value added per worker in 2005 averaged $330, below the $1/day poverty line. For the least developed countries, the corresponding figure was $254. Although we cannot rely too much on these aggregate data for measures of poverty, the data point strongly toward the conclusion that the problem of poverty in the developing world is, at least in a proximate sense, related to a problem of low productivity in agriculture.

There are many possible reasons for the productivity differences across sectors. One possibility is that the sectoral disparity is simply an illusion—an artifact of measurement problems with both labor and output. The labor figures used here do not measure hours worked in agriculture; they instead represent the fraction of the economically active population who report that agriculture is their primary source of income. To the extent that rural people are counted, by default, as working in agriculture, we may overestimate the labor used in agriculture.[2] Similarly, the data might do a poor job of accounting for the value of agricultural output. National income and product accounts in principle include home-consumed agricultural goods, so the problem is not one of theory. Implementation, however, can be tricky. Sectoral output is usually estimated from area and yield data rather than from market sales, but it is not always straightforward to quantify the volume of output, nor is it obvious what prices should be used for valuing agricultural production.

Ultimately, however, it seems difficult to make the case that the sectoral differences are primarily due to mismeasurement. Living standards in rural areas are visibly lower in much of the developing world; this is borne out in household survey data, anthropometric studies, and other empirical research.[3] Although measurement problems might be real, it is simply implausible to argue that the sectoral gap does not have a real origin.

Among other possible explanations, it might be the case that agricultural labor is disproportionately low-skilled or that agricultural firms are poorly managed. Perhaps many poor countries are simply and irremediably very poor at agriculture—a result, possibly, of adverse climate and geography. Technologies (such as crop varieties and agronomic practices) could be less well developed in the tropics than in other regions (as argued, for example, by Gallup and Sachs 2000 or Masters and McMillan 2001). Any or all of these explanations might help to account for the low measured productivity levels in developing countries' agriculture.

Beyond productivity and agriculture's role as a productive sector, there are other reasons to focus on agriculture as a sector that has important economywide impacts on growth. One particularly important issue is the sector's central role in providing food for poor populations. The relationship between agricultural production and food consumption is too obvious to require any elaboration. Clearly, agriculture produces nonfood goods, but in most developing countries, a large fraction of agricultural land is devoted to food production.

The converse is also true. Although some middle-income countries rely on food imports, much of the food consumed in low-income countries is produced domestically. Few developing countries import more than 10% of their calorie consumption. In sub-Saharan Africa, for example, approximately 90% of all calories consumed as food are produced within the region; most food is in fact produced within the countries where it is consumed. A few coastal cities import significant quantities of grain and meat, but much of the continent consumes virtually no imported food. Many interior countries are almost entirely self-sufficient, except for a few luxury goods consumed by urban elites. Uganda, for example, imports less than 2% of its total calorie consumption.

With low productivity in agriculture, relatively few imports, and low incomes, people in developing countries face high food costs relative to incomes. An equivalent statement is that the real wage is low. In many developing countries, it is common for households to spend half of their incomes on food. In a number of surveys, food accounts for two thirds, three quarters, or even 80% of household expenditure, with higher numbers in rural areas than in urban areas. Numbers like these almost necessarily imply deep poverty, closely related to low agricultural income and output.

Food production thus has importance in the developing world because of its impacts on the poor. It also has particular significance because of its importance for

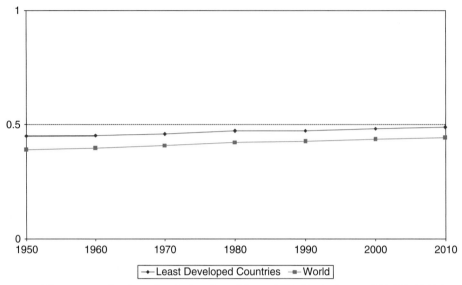

Figure 5   Women as a fraction of agricultural workforce, 1950-2010. Source: FAOSTAT 2009.

women. For the world as a whole, women make up about 45% of the agricultural workforce; in the least developed countries, the fraction is very nearly half (see Figure 5). Perhaps more strikingly, of the world's economically active women, approximately half work in agriculture—a significantly higher fraction than for men. This is particularly true in the least developed countries, where 73% of economically active women work in agriculture, compared with 59% of economically active men. Thus, where women are economically active, especially in the poorest countries, they work in farming. Although this fraction is falling as economies move out of agriculture and opportunities open up for women in other sectors, Figure 6 shows that the transition has not been rapid. These data suggest that, since women disproportionately work in agriculture and since women tend to be disproportionately represented among the poor, agricultural development could have particular relevance from a gender perspective.

Taken together, the facts presented here suggest that if our goal is to understand economic growth in the developing world, we should begin with a careful examination of the agricultural sector. In a proximate sense, it is clear that a major cause of low incomes and slow growth in the developing world is the low level and the slow growth of agricultural productivity. This does not necessarily imply that agriculture should be targeted for remedial investments; after all, perhaps a better strategy is to import larger quantities of food or even to provide food aid on a more systematic basis. But it appears essential to look at developing economies in ways that disaggregate by sector.

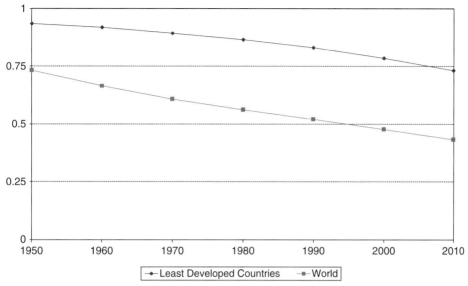

Figure 6 Fraction of economically active women who work in agriculture, 1950-2010. Source: FAOSTAT 2009.

The agricultural situation described here raises a number of questions. Why are so many people in the developing world "stuck" in the subsistence agricultural sector, using little improved technology and essentially unable to benefit from the division of labor? Given the income and productivity differences across sectors, why do we not observe more people migrating out of subsistence agriculture and moving to cities? To address these questions, it is useful to look at previous theories and empirical studies.

3. THEORIES OF STRUCTURAL TRANSFORMATION

As early as Adam Smith, economists recognized that economic growth is accompanied by a sectoral transformation that leads to the movement of labor and other resources out of agriculture and into other activities.[4] The nature of this transition—and the direction of causation—have attracted much discussion and generated a surprising degree of controversy. For example, economic historians have debated whether or not agricultural productivity improvements preceded the Industrial Revolution, and development economists have argued over whether foreign assistance should give priority to agricultural development or industrial development. The stylized facts, however, are not in dispute. Kuznets (1966) initially documented the nature of the structural transformation in both time-series and cross-section data; other early empirical work includes Chenery and Syrquin (1975), Syrquin (1988), and similar studies that documented patterns of sectoral change within and across countries.

The structural transformation—the movement of workers and other resources out of agriculture and into other sectors—has important implications for income levels and growth rates. Since there are large differences in output per worker between agriculture and nonagriculture in the developing world, the movement of workers out of agriculture is, on average, an important source of growth. To see this, consider again the data in Table 4. The right-hand column for each country shows the ratio of labor productivity in nonagriculture relative to agriculture. For a number of countries in the data, nonagricultural labor productivity is far higher than agricultural labor productivity, with tenfold and twentyfold differences not infrequent. In these countries, a marginal worker who moves from agriculture into the nonagricultural sector will drive up the average product of labor for the economy as a whole. Looking back over the past 50 years, the sectoral reallocation of labor has been an important source of income growth in many countries.

Table 5 shows a decomposition of growth in output per worker for those developing countries with available data. The first column in this table shows the average annual compound growth rate for output per worker, as reported in the PWT 6.2 data (Heston et al., 2006). Country observations are sorted in descending order by this variable. The next two columns show the contributions to overall growth in output per worker that come from productivity growth within agriculture and nonagriculture. Figure 7 shows a scatter plot of growth in output per worker in agriculture and for the aggregate economy. To derive these numbers, the growth rates of agricultural output per worker and nonagricultural output per worker are calculated, based on analysis comparable to that in Table 4 but going back to previous years. Growth rates within each sector are then weighted by the share of each sector in output in 1980 (approximately the midpoint of the data). The weighted sector growth rates are shown in the second and third columns of Table 5. The residual unexplained growth in output per worker is then due to sectoral reallocation, and it is shown in the rightmost column of the table.

A striking result is that for many of the countries in the data, sectoral reallocation is a major source of growth in output per worker. China, which is the country in the data with the most rapid growth in output per worker, appears to have gotten almost all of its growth from the reallocation of workers out of agriculture. Other countries with large fractions of their growth coming from sectoral reallocation include Egypt, Turkey, Brazil, Mexico, and Kenya. In total, about 30 of the countries in the data received more of their growth from sectoral reallocation than from productivity growth within either sector.

Another striking result is that for almost 30 countries, average labor productivity grew faster in agriculture than in nonagriculture. This of course reflects changes in inputs as well as in technology; it is not a measure of TFP growth. For many countries, agricultural labor productivity rises at least in part because of the severe diminishing marginal returns to labor in agriculture. Where marginal product is low, the movement

Table 4   Sectoral labor productivity, agriculture and non-agriculture, 1999-2000

Country	Real per capita GDP per worker (PWT 6.2)	Agricultural output per worker	Non-agricultural output per worker	Ratio	Country	Real per capita GDP per worker (PWT 6.2)	Agricultural output per worker	Non-agricultural output per worker	Ratio
Liberia	1,174	1,250	1,016	0.81	Suriname	12,453	7,310	13,661	1.87
Congo, DR	885	699	1,205	1.72	Egypt	11,940	5,972	14,941	2.50
Sierra Leone	1,846	1,734	2,030	1.17	Guatemala	10,609	5,341	14,977	2.80
Togo	1,947	1,116	3,180	2.85	Colombia	14,054	7,139	15,825	2.22
Central African Rep.	2,005	1,467	3,438	2.34	Fiji	11,482	4,897	15,871	3.24
Benin	2,769	1,874	3,819	2.04	Zimbabwe	7,302	2,152	15,978	7.43
Sudan	2,669	1,822	3,996	2.19	Dominican Republic	15,009	10,029	16,001	1.60
Chad	1,810	1,018	4,211	4.13	Paraguay	13,150	6,493	16,649	2.56
Guinea-Bissau	1,667	1,135	4,236	3.73	China	6,689	1,512	17,018	11.25
Ghana	2,827	1,750	4,252	2.43	Brazil	15,470	5,196	17,527	3.37
Madagascar	1,722	677	4,733	6.99	Burkina Faso	1,962	617	17,931	29.07
Congo, Rep.	3,150	413	5,011	12.14	Venezuela	17,913	9,306	18,672	2.01
Zambia	2,051	661	5,184	7.84	Algeria	16,661	6,058	20,087	3.32
Mauritania	3,436	1,800	5,266	2.93	Tunisia	17,289	8,658	20,111	2.32
Gambia	1,859	845	5,620	6.65	Turkey	12,205	2,986	20,132	6.74
Lesotho	4,317	1,976	5,824	2.95	Iran	17,595	9,081	20,679	2.28
Malawi	1,742	831	6,166	7.42	South Africa	19,760	6,761	21,136	3.13
Mali	2,138	1,097	6,587	6.01	Papua New Guinea	9,055	4,355	22,702	5.21
Kenya	2,458	1,054	6,775	6.43	Thailand	10,876	1,738	22,724	13.07
Honduras	5,976	3,008	7,343	2.44	Costa Rica	20,596	9,678	23,347	2.41
Uganda	2,163	798	7,664	9.60	Mexico	19,621	3,810	23,943	6.28

Continued

Table 4 Sectoral labor productivity, agriculture and non-agriculture, 1999-2000—Cont'd

Country	Real per capita GDP per worker (PWT 6.2)	Agricultural output per worker	Non-agricultural output per worker	Ratio
Côte d'Ivoire	5,325	2,622	7,940	3.03
Burundi	1,328	594	8,256	13.91
Niger	1,749	755	8,841	11.72
Pakistan	6,719	3,701	9,401	2.54
Senegal	3,542	920	10,884	11.83
Bolivia	7,195	2,445	10,953	4.48
India	6,033	2,363	11,456	4.85
Cameroon	6,023	2,244	11,552	5.15
Rwanda	1,874	768	12,629	16.43
Indonesia	7,800	2,516	12,748	5.07
Philippines	9,229	3,680	12,857	3.49
Sri Lanka	8,967	3,920	13,182	3.36
Jordan	12,239	2,489	13,511	5.43

Country	Real per capita GDP per worker (PWT 6.2)	Agricultural output per worker	Non-agricultural output per worker	Ratio
Hungary	23,789	11,958	25,202	2.11
Nepal	3,012	1,319	26,132	19.81
Barbados	29,178	29,165	29,179	1.00
Argentina	27,980	14,289	29,457	2.06
Swaziland	23,044	8,456	30,544	3.61
Chile	27,995	10,870	31,194	2.87
Korea, Rep.	30,621	14,971	32,352	2.16
Malaysia	26,868	1,235	32,766	26.53
Gabon	23,141	3,809	34,864	9.15
Saudi Arabia	52,825	26,304	55,752	2.12
Puerto Rico	55,981	21,074	56,800	2.70
Kuwait	59,647	19,607	60,085	3.06
Oman	57,038	3,018	88,695	29.39

Source: Author's calculations from PWT 6.2 (Heston et al., 2006) and FAOSTAT.

Table 5 Growth Decomposition, 1960-2000 unless otherwise indicated

Country	Growth of Output per Worker (PWT v. 6.2)	Growth from Agriculture	Growth from Non-Agriculture	Growth from Sectoral Shifts	Remarks
China	0.053	0.014	-0.015	0.054	
Korea, Rep.	0.051	0.007	0.030	0.014	
Thailand	0.043	0.004	0.007	0.032	
Malaysia	0.042	-0.002	0.030	0.014	
Swaziland	0.038	0.005	0.117	-0.084	1970-2000
Sri Lanka	0.034	0.008	0.021	0.005	
Lesotho	0.032	-0.001	0.075	-0.042	
Pakistan	0.030	0.007	0.005	0.018	
Indonesia	0.028	0.001	-0.001	0.027	
India	0.028	0.006	-0.014	0.036	
Egypt	0.028	0.006	-0.011	0.032	1970-2000
Hungary	0.026	0.002	0.038	-0.014	1970-2000
Turkey	0.026	-0.003	-0.009	0.037	1970-2000
Ghana	0.025	0.014	0.007	0.004	
Puerto Rico	0.022	0.001	0.132	-0.110	1970-2000
Papua New Guinea	0.022	0.008	0.026	-0.012	1970-2000
Tunisia	0.021	0.005	0.055	-0.039	1970-2000
Dominican Rep.	0.019	0.005	0.048	-0.034	1970-2000
Malawi	0.019	0.007	-0.006	0.018	
Oman	0.018	-0.001	0.180	-0.161	1970-2000
Nepal	0.018	0.003	-0.002	0.018	1970-2000
Paraguay	0.017	0.003	0.027	-0.013	
Brazil	0.017	0.002	-0.005	0.021	
Congo, Rep.	0.015	-0.001	0.017	-0.002	
Côte d'Ivoire	0.014	0.004	0.000	0.010	
Gabon	0.014	-0.001	0.028	-0.013	
Philippines	0.013	0.003	-0.003	0.013	
Cameroon	0.013	0.003	-0.003	0.013	1970-2000
Burkina Faso	0.013	0.002	0.006	0.006	
Chile	0.012	0.002	0.025	-0.015	
Colombia	0.011	0.001	0.011	-0.001	1970-2000
Benin	0.011	0.006	-0.007	0.012	
Guinea-Bissau	0.011	0.009	0.017	-0.015	1970-2000
Zimbabwe	0.011	0.002	0.015	-0.007	1970-2000
Mali	0.010	0.003	-0.010	0.017	1970-2000
Mexico	0.010	-0.001	-0.002	0.013	1970-2000
Mauritania	0.010	0.007	0.013	-0.010	1970-2000

Continued

Table 5 Growth Decomposition, 1960-2000 unless otherwise indicated—Cont'd

Country	Growth of Output per Worker (PWT v. 6.2)	Growth from Agriculture	Growth from Non-Agriculture	Growth from Sectoral Shifts	Remarks
Barbados	0.010	0.002	0.061	-0.053	
South Africa	0.009	0.001	0.009	0.000	
Iran	0.009	0.001	0.007	0.001	1970-2000
Guatemala	0.009	0.002	0.032	-0.025	1970-2000
Gambia	0.008	0.002	0.031	-0.026	1970-2000
Algeria	0.007	0.003	0.027	-0.022	1970-2000
Costa Rica	0.006	0.000	0.028	-0.022	
Honduras	0.006	0.002	0.005	-0.001	
Argentina	0.005	0.000	0.028	-0.022	1970-2000
Burundi	0.005	-0.011	0.000	0.016	1970-2000
Kenya	0.003	0.001	-0.014	0.016	
Bolivia	0.003	-0.001	0.031	-0.028	1970-2000
Fiji	0.003	-0.001	0.106	-0.102	1970-2000
Uganda	0.003	-0.003	-0.007	0.013	
Central African Rep.	0.000	0.008	-0.013	0.005	1970-2000
Rwanda	0.000	-0.010	0.000	0.010	1970-2000
Zambia	0.000	0.002	-0.014	0.011	1970-2000
Sudan	0.000	0.003	-0.027	0.024	1970-2000
Senegal	0.000	-0.001	-0.005	0.006	
Togo	-0.002	-0.001	0.000	-0.001	
Jordan	-0.004	-0.002	0.088	-0.090	1970-2000
Venezuela	-0.005	0.001	0.008	-0.014	
Chad	-0.005	-0.001	-0.024	0.020	
Niger	-0.006	-0.010	0.000	0.004	
Suriname	-0.006	0.002	0.136	-0.144	1970-2000
Saudi Arabia	-0.007	0.001	0.068	-0.076	1970-2000
Madagascar	-0.011	-0.002	-0.028	0.020	1970-2000
Sierra Leone	-0.018	0.004	-0.012	-0.011	1970-2000
Congo, DR	-0.037	0.001	-0.071	0.033	1970-2000
Kuwait	-0.042	0.000	0.170	-0.212	1970-2000
Liberia	-0.050	-0.001	-0.027	-0.021	1970-2000

Source: Author's calculations from PWT 6.2 (Heston et al., 2006), FAOSTAT, and World Development Indicators.

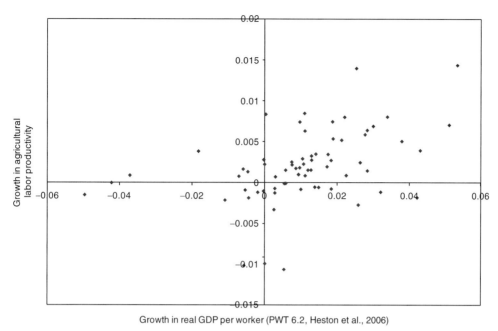

Growth in real GDP per worker (PWT 6.2, Heston et al., 2006)

Figure 7   Growth in output per worker and growth in agricultural labor productivity, 1960-2000.

of workers out of agriculture should drive up the average product of the labor that remains. We see this phenomenon in Pakistan, India, and Indonesia—all countries that had relatively strong growth in agricultural TFP over the period 1960–2000.

These empirical observations are consistent with a number of longstanding theories of economic development. The role of structural transformation has been a major theme in the development and growth literature, as will be explored in the following section.

3.1 Theories of agriculture's role

The early development literature offered two different views of the structural transformation—and more generally of the role of agriculture in development. One influential early view was that of Lewis, who, along with influential scholars such as Rosenstein-Rodan (1943) and Rostow (1960), viewed modern economic growth as essentially identifiable with industrialization. These authors, like most of the early growth and development economists, tended to view subsistence agriculture as a default source of employment and as a pool of reserve labor. The challenge of development, in their view, was to create and expand employment in the modern industrial sector. This sector was seen as having high potential for growth, and it was assumed that industry (and, to a lesser extent, services) would gradually absorb workers from agriculture. Lewis

(1955) and Fei and Ranis (1964) viewed the agricultural sector essentially as a pool of surplus labor, with a very low shadow wage.

In many dual-economy models, such as those of Lewis, the labor market dynamics were somewhat ill defined. It was assumed that wage differences could and would arise between the modern sector and the traditional sector, with some kind of efficiency wage story (or, alternatively, a price-distorting minimum wage) accounting for the high wages paid in the modern sector. Harris and Todaro (1970), among others, recognized that incentives would arise for rural-to-urban migration in this model, but they maintained the assumption that the modern sector would provide a limited number of jobs, with wages above the market-clearing level.

An alternative view, also present in the early development literature, was that many poor economies suffered from what T. W. Schultz (1953) characterized as the "food problem." Simply put, Schultz argued that many poor countries are in a situation of "high food drain," in which they have "a level of income so low that a critically large proportion of the income is required for food." Schultz took it as given that countries in this situation must produce the bulk of their own food to satisfy subsistence needs, presumably because imports are prohibitively costly and because these countries have few goods or resources to exchange for food. Until they can meet their subsistence needs, Schultz said, they are unable to begin the process of modern economic growth.

Schultz's view was later echoed in a large literature on development, which held that an agricultural surplus is a necessary condition for a country to begin the development process. The hypothesis was a central argument of Johnston and Mellor (1961), Johnston (1970), Johnston and Kilby (1975), Timmer (1988), and Johnson (1997), and it continued to figure prominently in the later works of Mellor (1995, 1996) and the analyses of many other scholars (e.g., Eswaran and Kotwal, 1993; Mundlak, 2000).

A view that can be characterized as the *Mellor hypothesis* took hold in the agricultural development literature. This hypothesis was typically stated as a narrative model that outlined a set of general equilibrium impacts that were claimed to result from agricultural productivity growth. The Mellor hypothesis held that agricultural productivity growth resulted in a linked set of impacts, including:

- Increases in farm income and profitability, resulting in improved welfare of farmers and the rural poor
- Declining food prices, benefiting poor rural and urban consumers, including small farmers who might be net purchasers of food
- Reductions in the nominal wage, consistent with increases in the real wage, allowing the industrial sector to reduce costs
- Increases in the domestic demand for industrial output
- Increasing competitiveness of both agricultural and industrial exports, with positive impact on hard currency earnings
- Expansion of the domestic industrial sector, pulling labor and investment resources out of agriculture

This framework has been spelled out in various forms in many places (e.g., Mellor, 1995, 1996), but with little effort to model it formally or to test it empirically. Various authors provided empirical support for particular elements of the argument, but there was little effort to test the Mellor hypothesis as a unified theory. In recent years, however, a number of authors have offered explicit two-sector models in which some parts of the Mellor hypothesis can be explored formally.

3.2 Two-sector models

Following a brief flurry of interest in multisector models in the early 1960s (e.g., Uzawa, 1961, 1963), little was written on the subject of structural transformation until perhaps the mid-1990s. Since then, however, a number of researchers have sought to examine the importance of structural change in the growth process. Many recent papers have attempted to offer formal models of structural change, industrialization, and growth. Some have focused on long-run growth processes; others have sought to explain cross-section differences among countries.

One distinction in this literature is whether the models allow for *dualism*, which is often interpreted as simply meaning that markets do not fully clear across sectors or that there are some kinds of barriers or transaction costs that constrain the equilibrium. Dual-economy models are contrasted with fully neoclassical models, in which labor, capital, and goods markets clear across sectors. The distinction has not proven entirely useful, since recent papers have blurred the line by providing various microfoundations for dualism.

Among the first papers in this two-sector literature were some that sought to reproduce the structural transformation. These included Echevarria (1995, 1997); Kogel and Prskawetz (2001); Irz and Roe (2001), and Kongsamut, Rebelo, and Xie (2001). A related set of papers sought to model the structural transformation from a traditional (implicitly agricultural) economy to a modern (largely non-agricultural) economy, focusing primarily on long-run growth issues. Among these papers were King and Rebelo (1993); Goodfriend and McDermott (1998); Laitner (2002); Hansen and Prescott (2002); Ngai (2004); and Ngai and Pissarides (2007).

Several papers have explicitly tried to reproduce the dualism of Harris and Todaro (1970) while bringing a new level of formalism and explicit general equilibrium analysis. For example, Temple (2005), Vollrath (2004), and Vollrath (2008), among others, have explored multisector models in which unemployment or underemployment is possible. In these papers, there may be fixed urban wages or other rigidities that prevent the urban labor market from clearing; other papers (e.g., Caselli and Coleman, 2001) rely on transaction cost wedges that prevent the labor market from equalizing marginal products across sectors. These papers often have the feature that the allocation of resources across sectors is inefficient; the social planner would allocate labor and capital differently.

A stylized implication of this class of models is that policies should focus on removing or reducing the rigidities that lead to inefficient outcomes and overallocation of resources to agriculture.

Another set of growth papers, including Gollin et al. (2002, 2007), follow Schultz in assuming that many poor countries are hindered in their growth processes by the need to tie down large amounts of labor and other resources in food production. These papers show that the transition to modern "Solow"-type growth can be slowed dramatically when countries must feed themselves. Countries that have low agricultural productivity—which could be due to poor technology, geography, or institutions—will trail far behind the leaders, even though in the long run the agricultural sector will be unimportant as a source of cross-country income differences. A stylized policy implication of this line of argument is that efforts to boost agricultural productivity may have a large payoff in terms of growth—a view argued forcefully in Schultz (1964), anticipating much of the subsequent literature. A model based on Gollin et al. (2002) is presented in this chapter.

A key assumption in these papers is that the economies are closed to food imports. If food is essential for consumption and if there is no effective alternative to countries producing this food domestically, development must begin with a focus on agriculture and agricultural productivity—and specifically with food production.

In an open economy world, different results obtain. Matsuyama (1992) offers an example of a model economy in which the importance of the closed economy assumption is made clear. Matsuyama offers a two-sector model with an agricultural sector and a manufacturing sector. In the closed economy version, countries that are good at agricultural production have an advantage in that fewer resources need to be allocated to producing food. However, when the economy is open, a country that has a comparative advantage in agricultural production can become locked into a sector with low levels of technological progress, leaving it doomed to fall farther behind countries that have a comparative advantage in industry. This result is mirrored in a dynamic setting in the one-sector environment explored by Hansen and Prescott (2002). Hansen and Prescott model an economy with a single sector that undergoes a conversion from a Malthusian traditional economy to a modern Solow economy at some point in its development. In this framework, economies that have high productivity levels in the traditional sector will undergo this structural transformation later in history, resulting in lagging long-run levels of output per capita.

In Matsuyama's framework, the availability of imported food allows countries to move resources into the manufacturing sector, where there is more rapid growth. This basic observation, which is echoed to a degree by many more recent critics of agricultural-based development strategies (e.g., Dercon 2009), will be addressed later in this chapter.

Vollrath (2008) offers a different channel through which it could be dynamically disadvantageous for countries to have high agricultural productivity levels. In his model, traditional sector work (which might be assumed to correspond to agriculture) has production complementarities with fertility and the production of children. Because childrearing is time consuming, countries that experience an increase in the productivity of the traditional sector will see increases in the share of people in the traditional sector, along with rising levels of fertility and increases in population growth rates. Measured output per person will fall, although utility will rise. In this model, agricultural productivity gains will reduce measured output levels but will be efficient from the vantage point of a utility-maximizing social planner. In a sense, this paper is related to Gollin et al. (2004), in which agricultural production has similar complementarities with home production.

Overall, the theoretical literature offers a number of perspectives on the role of agricultural productivity as a source of modern economic growth. The Mellor hypothesis, in which agricultural productivity is necessarily the source of long-run economic growth, does not necessarily hold in all growth models. The hypothesis is most likely to hold in a closed economy in which the agricultural sector is producing food staples that cannot easily be supplanted with imports. Is this the relevant case? Over a number of years, an empirical literature has attempted to ask whether agricultural productivity is linked causally with economic growth. The following section surveys this literature and explains why the literature has struggled to offer cleanly identified causal links.

4. EMPIRICAL EVIDENCE FOR AGRICULTURE'S ROLE

A voluminous literature, dating back to the work of Chinery, Syrquin, and others referenced earlier, has attempted to uncover causation in the (undisputed) correlations between agricultural growth and economic growth. This literature takes a number of different forms. Some studies have sought to use cross-country or cross-section studies that compare agricultural productivity growth rates with GDP growth rates; others have looked at returns to research. Still other papers have used the techniques of growth accounting, or *levels accounting*, to arrive at estimates of agriculture's role in generating economic growth. A recurring problem in the empirical literature is establishing any convincing identification of a causal relationship.

4.1 The difficulty of identification

To understand why identification has been so elusive, consider the following thought experiment: What would be the *ideal* experiment needed to provide clear and unambiguous evidence of the effects of agriculture on overall growth and poverty reduction? For obvious reasons, this can only be a thought experiment rather than a real one. The thought experiment is useful, however: It provides a benchmark against which to measure the other empirical and theoretical evidence that is actually available.

There are many possible variants on the experimental design, but essentially they would all have the following elements. First, take a large number of otherwise identical versions of the world as it currently exists. In each version of the world, identify a single developing country at random to take part in a "treatment." Other countries will be left unchanged. With enough replicates of the world, we will have a large number of treatment countries; indeed, for each country we will have a large number of treatment experiences and control experiences. For the most effective control, we should also include a number of replicates of the existing world in which no country receives a treatment.

The treatment will consist of a fully funded program that will spur agricultural development, perhaps by achieving a given rate of growth in agricultural productivity. Control countries will receive no development programs, or possibly they will receive comparably sized development programs that target some other sector or sectors. The correct control is unclear.

As part of the experiment, we will observe these economies growing over time. Because the impacts of their development programs could take a long time to come online, we will follow these worlds over a period of several decades at least.

At the conclusion of this time period, we will compare treatment countries with nontreatment versions of themselves and with nontreatment versions of other developing countries. If we collect our data carefully, this comparison will allow us to identify (in a causal sense) the effects of agricultural development programs on growth and poverty reduction. We will be able to infer (with sufficient replications) that differences between the treatment and control versions of the same country are in fact due to the agricultural development treatment.

Obviously this thought experiment is an unattainable ideal. But it serves as a useful benchmark in evaluating the actual comparisons that economists have made in looking at the data. Both supporters and opponents of agriculture-centered approaches to development have tended to focus on the limited cross-country data, either in regression analyses or in more anecdotal accounts and case studies. The usual idea is to look at countries that have implemented a set of policies (e.g., agricultural development policies) and to compare them with those that have not. But these cross-country comparisons are almost certainly flawed because there is no randomness in the "assignment" of countries to treatment or control. Moreover, countries may differ in ways that are correlated with the assignment and that directly affect their outcomes. For example, many of the poorest countries could have weak institutions, low productivity, poor geography, and little access to international markets. These countries are almost certainly agricultural, and many might have pursued agricultural development strategies—which in turn are likely to have proven ineffective.

Supporters of agricultural development generally look at successful countries and argue that they have almost all experienced significant agricultural development. This is a specious argument. Almost by definition, any country that has developed has undergone a structural transformation that involves some growth in the agricultural sector. As a result, these countries appear to show a positive relationship between agricultural development and growth; but this relationship could be spurious.

Opponents of a focus on agriculture, especially in sub-Saharan Africa, tend to argue that previous efforts have achieved little; they infer from this that it would be futile to pursue agricultural development efforts—or at least that it might be more productive to invest in other sectors. But this argument suffers from the opposite fallacy. If African development has been hampered by other barriers (e.g., civil conflict, poor institutions), any development efforts, not just agricultural programs, will have failed. It would be erroneous on this basis to arrive at the conclusion that agricultural development is futile.

We might seek evidence from "before" and "after" comparisons of individual countries that institute pro-agriculture reforms. But these reforms are seldom random in their timing; they typically accompany other policy changes that may have a greater direct effect on outcomes. Any inference about the impact of the agricultural policy changes on outcomes will be "contaminated," in a statistical sense, by the impact of the other reforms.

Essentially the same problem holds with any of the real-world experiences on which we might be tempted to base our analysis. None of these really approximates the benchmark experiment. As a result, we will have great difficulty in interpreting the cross-country or time-series data as offering any conclusive or clear evidence on the impact of agriculture on growth and poverty.

Nevertheless, a number of recent studies have taken aim at the relationship between agricultural growth and economic growth, making use of the best available econometric tools.

4.2 Cross-section and panel studies

A number of recent papers nevertheless have attempted to find relationships between agricultural productivity growth and economic growth using cross-section or panel data, drawing on a variety of econometric techniques.

In a recent paper, Self and Grabowski (2007) report a set of results in which economic growth rates are regressed on a number of right-hand variables, including a variety of direct and indirect measures of agricultural productivity. The results support strong correlations between their productivity measures and growth rates of per capita income. They also find agricultural productivity levels correlated with the growth in the human development index (HDI) achieved by countries. A weakness of their approach, which is acknowledged by the authors, is that the right-hand variables in their regressions could be endogenously determined. The authors admit that their results might not be cleanly identified for this reason, but they note the lack of any obvious instruments that would allow them to bypass this problem.

In an earlier paper along the same lines, Humphries and Knowles (1998) estimate a Solow-type growth model, in the spirit of Mankiw, Romer, and Weil (1992), using as a right-hand variable the proportion of the labor force working outside the agricultural sector. They interpret the coefficient supporting a positive association between the fraction of the workforce outside agriculture and the growth of income per capita from 1960–1985. Recognizing the possible endogeneity of the labor force variable, the authors also report results based on estimations using instrumental variables. Their preferred instruments are climate variables that are presumed to affect the magnitude of the agricultural sector but not the overall growth rate. They report results that seem consistent with their OLS results.

In an earlier paper, Dowrick and Gemmell (1991) ask how the size of the agricultural sector affects countries' ability to achieve convergent growth. This paper finds that agricultural productivity for the poorest countries in their sample is converging toward the levels of the world leaders, at least after 1973, but it finds that the convergence in agricultural technology is not sufficient to achieve overall convergence in income levels.

A different approach is to ask whether changes in agricultural output (rather than TFP) are causally related to changes in GDP. For example, Tiffin and Irz (2006) use Granger causality tests to argue that the correlation between these two variables takes a form that implies a causal direction from agriculture to the aggregate economy rather than the converse. Bravo-Ortega and Lederman (2005) also rely on Granger causality tests in an attempt to trace causal links from agricultural productivity growth to a variety of aggregate welfare measures.

Perhaps more common in the literature are studies that seek to trace causal links from agricultural productivity to poverty reduction (for example, Datt and Ravallion, 1996; Thirtle et al., 2001; Irz et al., 2002; Fan et al., 2000). Much of this literature argues that agriculture-based growth is more effective than other forms of growth at reducing poverty. Mellor (2000) expressed this view most forcefully, in a view characterized critically by Hasan and Quibria (2004) as "agricultural fundamentalism." Mellor specifically makes the claim: "There has been a tendency to generalize that economic growth reduces poverty when in fact it is the direct and indirect effect of agricultural growth that accounts for virtually all the poverty decline." Because this chapter focuses on the links to economic growth, the literature on agriculture and poverty reduction lies largely beyond our scope.

To sum up, the empirical evidence linking agricultural development to economic growth in the cross-country data is highly suggestive but offers few examples of convincingly identified causal links. Reviewing this literature, Gardner (2003) and Tsakok and Gardner (2007) found little well-identified empirical evidence. Gardner and Tsakok conclude in fact that "this approach is fraught with difficulties that have so far precluded definitive findings" (p. 1145). They add the somewhat damning conclusion that "our view is that economists will simply have to face the fact that econometric studies of country data will not be able to establish causality."

4.2.1 Growth accounting and productivity measurement

As an alternative to running regressions on cross-section or panel data, a number of scholars have turned to other strategies for looking at agriculture's impact on overall economic growth. One alternative strategy is to carry out a sectoral growth accounting exercise, based on methodology introduced initially by Solow (1957). This kind of analysis can indicate whether productivity growth in agriculture has been more rapid than in other sectors; if so, it seems reasonable to argue that the sector plays a key role in generating economic growth.

Growth accounting exercises conducted for the agricultural sector itself can also show the importance of productivity growth—as opposed to intensification of input use—as a source of output increases.

Several papers in this literature argue that productivity growth has been higher in agriculture than in manufacturing. This result was obtained in Jorgenson, Gollop, and Fraumeni for the U.S. time series (1987) and Jorgenson and Gollop (1992); Jorgenson and Stiroh (2000) found a similar result for a more recent data period, with agriculture among the sectors with the highest TFP growth. Mundlak (2005) similarly finds that TFP growth accounts for essentially all of agriculture's productivity growth in the period 1940–90 in the US.

Looking at a broader set of countries, including a number of developing countries, Martin and Mitra (2001) find that TFP growth in agriculture exceeds that in manufacturing. Bernard and Jones (1996) find that agricultural TFP growth is higher than nonagricultural TFP growth in a sample of 14 OECD countries for the period from 1970–1987.

In a recent study focusing on two rapidly growing large economies, Bosworth and Collins (2008) find that agricultural TFP growth has been a major source of economic growth for both India and China during the past 25 years, though not so important as industrial growth in China or growth in services in India. This study also notes the important role that has been played in both countries by sectoral reallocations of labor out of (low productivity) agriculture into higher productivity industry and services. The results of this paper are echoed to a large extent in Gulati et al. (2005), who find that China's growth was heavily influenced by agricultural reforms, with strong accompanying effects on poverty reduction. Gulati and his coauthors argue that China has been more successful than India at reducing the poverty headcount, and they attribute this performance to the agricultural roots of Chinese reforms.[5]

A widely recognized difficulty in the growth accounting literature is that the technique only provides a decomposition of the immediate sources of growth—into inputs and TFP. To the extent that increases in TFP stimulate increased input use (or to the extent that new inputs such as machinery may embody new technologies), the methodology cannot disentangle the underlying causation.

There are also conceptual problems in interpreting comparisons of TFP growth rates across sectors. Theories of structural transformation suggest that growth in other sectors of the economy may pull underutilized resources out of agriculture. We observe this as increases in agricultural TFP, if output remains constant while inputs are falling. But it would be misleading to infer that agricultural productivity growth is therefore the source of overall economic growth.

An interesting and relevant illustration of the ways in which growth accounting can obscure the underlying causal mechanisms is given by Landon-Lane and Robertson (2003), who show that in a two-sector model, factor accumulation can lead to sectoral reallocations, which in turn lead to increases in aggregate output. Without accounting carefully for these sectoral changes, an observer might treat the sectoral reallocation as a manifestation of TFP growth within the two sectors. Properly speaking, however, it should be viewed as a result of the factor accumulation. Landon-Lane and Robertson show that this channel of impact is quantitatively important in a panel data study of 78 countries. An implication is that growth accounting exercises that find high impact from agricultural TFP growth might be overstating the importance of within-sector changes and understating the importance of across-sector reallocations.

4.3 Development accounting

In recent years, a number of papers have sought to explore a different approach in attempting to assess agriculture's contributions to overall economic growth. These papers have used models to provide an accounting framework with which to analyze the sources of cross-country disparities in income per capita. Characterizing this literature as *development accounting,* or *levels accounting,* these papers follow the techniques explored first by Klenow and Rodríguez-Clare (1997) and Hall and Jones (1999). The goal of papers in this literature is to understand whether the gaps between rich and poor countries are primarily due to differences in accumulated factors of production or to actual differences in efficiency or TFP.

The initial papers using this technique used single-sector models, but a number of recent papers have used multisector models to look at the impact of sectoral issues. Possibly the first of these was Caselli's paper (2005) in the *Handbook of Economic Growth.* In this paper, Caselli finds that efficiency differences *within* the agricultural sector are very important as a source of cross-country income differences. He argues that income differences between poor and rich countries do not simply reflect differences in the sectoral composition of output, with poor countries devoting more resources to a low productivity sector; he suggests that in fact the low levels of efficiency within agriculture are important for the low income levels of developing countries.

A different conclusion emerges from a related paper by Cordoba and Ripoll (2007), in which the authors extend the accounting analysis by adding a measure of human capital in different sectors. They find that a large fraction of the disparity in output per worker within the agricultural sector is traceable to differences in human capital levels between rural and urban workers. This implies that increasing productivity in developing country agriculture might not lead to large increases in national income, since these countries will still lag far behind in human capital in the agricultural sector.

Several other development accounting papers offer insights into the "factors or efficiency" debate. Restuccia et al. (2008) offer another accounting analysis, in a model that incorporates intermediate inputs. They show that agricultural inputs appear to be unusually expensive in poor countries, so they are used in relatively low quantities. This reduces the overall efficiency of the agricultural sector. They also find that the allocation of workers to the agricultural sector appears to be inefficiently high, which they interpret as suggesting that some transaction cost or barrier prevents the intersectoral mobility of labor. In a sense, this paper draws less on the development accounting literature than on the "business cycle accounting" techniques introduced by Chari, Kehoe, and McGrattan (2007).

Related to this work, a number of recent accounting papers consider the impact of factor misallocations. Vollrath (2009) considers misallocations of labor as a possible cause of low efficiency in developing country agriculture. This paper argues that misallocation of factors—which he characterizes as "dual economy" effects—explain a large fraction of the differences in income per capita across countries and an even large fraction of the measured differences in TFP. In this respect, Vollrath echoes a theme emphasized in Chanda and Dalgaard (2008) and Temple (2004, 2005).

The dual-economy versions of the development accounting literature tend to argue that neither technology improvements nor factor accumulation will bring about dramatic output gains in developing country agriculture. These papers collectively suggest that there could be significant allocative inefficiency in developing country agriculture, due either to policy barriers or transaction costs of some kind.

4.4 Other approaches

Several other empirical approaches have been used, to varying degrees, by researchers studying contemporary links between agricultural productivity and economic growth. This chapter does not devote much space to these methods. Some have been adequately (or even exhaustively) covered elsewhere; others have been used less extensively in the literature. Nevertheless, it is worth touching on them briefly here.

4.4.1 CGE models and growth multipliers

One way to assess the growth impacts of agricultural productivity improvements is to use computable general equilibrium models (CGEs) or other structural frameworks in which estimated elasticities are applied in the context of formal models. A related approach involves calculating growth multipliers, as in Block (1999). Because this material has been covered extensively elsewhere in the *Handbook of Agricultural Economics* (Volume 2A, Part 4, contains three chapters on applied macroeconomic analysis of the agricultural sector), the current chapter considers this literature only in passing.

A standard workhorse CGE model with an agricultural sector is presented in detail in Löfgren et al. (2001). This model and its variants have been used in an extensive policy analysis literature that focuses primarily on the impact of trade, price, and policy reforms. The model also allows for analysis of the effects of agricultural productivity growth, although it offers only a comparative static measure rather than long-run dynamics. For many purposes, however, the simple comparative static measure might be sufficient.

Several other larger-scale models of global agriculture also offer the potential to analyze productivity impacts at the national or global level. These include the IMPACT model at the International Food Policy Research Institute (IFPRI), which is described in Rosegrant et al. (2008), and the GTAP model, described in part in Powell (2007).

A number of analyses of agricultural research impacts, including Evenson et al. 1999 and Evenson and Gollin (2003b), have drawn on the IMPACT and GTAP models for their estimates of impacts.

Models of this kind offer the advantages of clean causal identification—at least relative to the econometric approaches described earlier. However, CGE models depend fundamentally on the underlying elasticity estimates, functional specifications, and coefficients. For this reason, their results are sometimes accused of lacking transparency. Nevertheless, a number of CGE models have been developed that offer the best available estimates of specific productivity improvements—for example, for the introduction of improved sweet potatoes in Uganda. For further discussion of these models and their usefulness in analyzing agricultural productivity changes, see Hertel (2002).

4.4.2 Returns to research

An abundant literature examines the economic returns to agricultural research. This literature often measures internal rates of return or benefit/cost ratios. Some studies report elasticities of various welfare measures to investments in research. A few report growth effects—or economywide benefits—of investments in agricultural research.

This chapter does not devote much space to summarizing the research, since an entire previous section of the *Handbook of Agricultural Economics* addresses issues of invention and innovation (Part 3 of Volume 3, consisting of six chapters). In addition, Evenson's contribution to Volume 1A of the *Handbook* (2001) specifically focused on the economic impacts of agricultural research and extension. A separate and remarkably comprehensive study by Alston et al. (2000) examined nearly the entire literature to that point on the returns to research, casting a skeptical eye on some of the commonly reported claims of impact. Even this critical meta-analysis concluded that rates of return to research are extremely high—although it posed the question of why such high rates of return have not been manifested either in rapid rates of agricultural growth or in massive public investments in research.

The high rates of return do provide evidence, of a limited kind, for agricultural productivity contributions to economic growth. After all, research generates improvements in TFP, which in turn should translate into economic growth. In practice, however, it might be difficult to identify these impacts. In many studies, the research benefits are narrowly defined to consist of partial equilibrium impacts on producers of a specific crop in a narrowly specified area. Some studies cover larger geographic areas and longer time scales—although typically the econometric identification problems become more acute as the area broadens and the duration lengthens.

The identification problems matter because many of the growth impacts of agricultural research are expected to be diffuse and could involve long time scales. For example, if research contributes to growth of grain yields, the long-term growth impact will most likely not be improved profits or incomes for farmers. Instead, the main impact may be on rates of urbanization and subsequent industrial growth. The impacts of agricultural research on industrial growth will surely be difficult to untangle on a national scale using econometric techniques.

Nevertheless, a number of papers report evidence of research impacts on economic growth and other welfare measures. These include impacts at the global level (e.g., Evenson and Gollin, 2003b); and at the national level (e.g., Fan and Pardey, 1997, for China; Evenson et al., 1999, for India). A recurring finding in this literature is that agricultural research investments are correlated with strong productivity gains in agriculture and improvements in a variety of welfare measures. A potential identification problem arises because research investments are not randomly distributed, either across countries or within them. Research tends systematically to take place in (and therefore to target) countries, states, or regions with effective governance and institutions. If growth and welfare gains occur subsequent to the research investments, we face an attribution problem: How much of the gains are due to research, and how much are due to other institutional characteristics or to changes that are related to the research? This problem makes it difficult to reach convincing conclusions about the relationship between research-induced productivity gains and economic growth.

4.4.3 Lessons from economic history

If the recent cross-country experience offers little cleanly identified evidence for the growth impacts of agricultural productivity, what can we learn from the historical record? A lively debate in the economic history literature concerns the role of agricultural productivity growth in the Industrial Revolution in Europe.

One view is that agricultural productivity gains preceded the Industrial Revolution (e.g., Crafts, 1985). The additional argument is sometimes made that essentially *all* countries experiencing rapid industrial growth have first undergone significant growth in agricultural productivity. Versions of this argument are presented in Huffman and Orazem's chapter (2007) in this *Handbook,* and a number of references are offered in a paper by Bezemer and Headey (2008).

An opposing view holds that agricultural productivity growth was not coincident with the Industrial Revolution in Britain and that agricultural productivity *levels* were higher in other parts of the world than in Britain (begging the question of why the

Industrial Revolution did not happen first elsewhere). This view is summarized in Dercon (2009) and reflects recent work by a number of economic historians, including Allen (1999) and Clark (1998, 2002).

Although this debate focuses on events that took place several centuries ago, the implications for current thinking about agricultural development could be significant. If agricultural productivity growth was not an essential part of the Industrial Revolution, perhaps it is even less necessary for today's developing economies, which after all have access to robust international markets for most agricultural goods.

Interestingly, however, none of the researchers looking at the Industrial Revolution in Britain argues that improvements in agricultural productivity were entirely irrelevant to urbanization and industrial growth. As the Industrial Revolution proceeded and urban populations grew, the farming sector needed to produce most of the food needed in cities. If agricultural productivity growth did not come prior to the Industrial Revolution, it was nevertheless an important concurrent event in most countries. Whether or not it came first, the agricultural revolution seems to have made a significant contribution in determining the pace of modern economic growth.

5. AGRO-PESSIMISM

The previous section suggests that there is no clearly identified empirical evidence that unambiguously demonstrates a channel from agricultural development to economic growth. Some skeptics have gone farther and argued that in fact agriculture plays a trailing role, if any, in the development trajectories of many countries. These "agro-pessimists" argue that development policy has suffered from an overemphasis on agriculture, driven by underlying confusion about the causal relationship between agriculture and development.

Although the agro-pessimists acknowledge that the agricultural sector accounts for large fractions of employment and economic activity in poor countries, they also argue that in some countries it might have relatively low growth potential. The East Asian miracle is viewed by some as evidence that growth does not necessarily require broad agriculture-based development. Instead, many Asian countries appear to have developed through export-oriented manufacturing. For example, Amsden (1989) made the case that Korea industrialized without any preceding agricultural revolution, and a number of scholars have argued that China's recent growth miracle was driven only in its earliest stages by agricultural policy reforms.[6]

Dercon (2009) proposes that causation might in fact run from economic growth to improvements in agricultural productivity. He notes that efforts to support smallholder agriculture could be supporting the least productive activities in the entire economy. Better prospects for reducing rural poverty and stimulating growth might come from nonagriculture, creating additional opportunities for people to exit farming. A strategy of exporting nonagricultural goods or cash crops and importing food might prove better than a development strategy based on agriculture. To the extent that policies target rural areas, he suggests, the focus should be on health and education investments that make it easier and cheaper for individuals to leave agriculture in due course. In the long run, those who succeed in leaving behind smallhold agriculture are likely to be the best off.

Dercon notes that there is considerable heterogeneity within developing countries, and he acknowledges that agriculture-based growth might be necessary in some land-locked and resource-poor countries. In coastal countries and those with richer endowments of natural resources, however, he argues that countries might do better to export other goods and to import food. In these economies, he says, "agriculture is not the crucial constraint." Some other researchers arrive at similar conclusions. Ellis and Harris (2004) write that policies facilitating rural-to-urban migration could be more sensible than policies to support agriculture.

This view is echoed by a number of influential figures in the development policy arena, such as Paul Collier (2008), who dismisses visions of smallholder agricultural development as a form of "romantic populism," part of the "middle- and upper-class love affair with peasant agriculture" (Collier 2008, p. 71). Collier suggests that "urban dynamism" is the key to solving agriculture's problems.[7] He takes particular issue with the notion that smallholder agriculture must be the target of development efforts. Although the poor do primarily earn their livings from smallholder systems, he notes, there is little evidence that productivity can increase sufficiently within these systems to generate growth. By contrast, a development strategy that focuses on large-scale commercial farms and on the nonagriculture sector could ultimately provide greater benefits for the poor by expanding the livelihood opportunities available to them.

6. RECONCILING COMPETING VIEWS

How can we reconcile the views of the agro-pessimists with the Mellor hypothesis presented earlier? And how can we interpret the vast amounts of not-quite-definitive empirical evidence that agriculture plays a key role in development?

Given the differing views in the literature, it is useful to write down a simple model as a heuristic device for considering the ways in which agricultural development could generate differing impacts under different circumstances.

Consider the following simple static model economy, drawn from Gollin and Rogerson (2009) and similar in spirit to Gollin, Parente, and Rogerson (2007) or, in fact, to Eswaran and Kotwal (1993).

In this model economy, each individual has preferences over two goods, which we label as agriculture (a) and manufacturing (m), given by:

$$u(a - \bar{a}) + v(m + \bar{m}) \tag{1}$$

where u and v are defined for non-negative values. We assume that both functions are increasing and strictly concave. The parameters $\bar{a}$ and $\bar{m}$ are both strictly positive.[8] The key feature of these preferences is the presence of the $\bar{a}$ and $\bar{m}$ terms, which serve to make the income elasticity of the agricultural good less than one and that of the manufactured good greater than one.[9] An extreme version of these preferences is the special case where:

$$u(a - \bar{a}) = \begin{cases} -\infty & \text{if } (a - \bar{a}) < 0 \\ \omega & \text{if } (a - \bar{a}) \geq 0 \end{cases}$$

This utility function gives rise to an extreme Engel curve in which utility is flat once the economy has satisfied its food needs. A slight relaxation of this assumption gives the utility function in Gollin, Parente, and Rogerson (2007)—that is,

$$u(a - \bar{a}) = \begin{cases} a & \text{if } (a - \bar{a}) < 0 \\ \bar{a} & \text{if } (a - \bar{a}) \geq 0 \end{cases}$$

The economy is endowed with one unit of land and each individual is endowed with one unit of time.

The technology for producing the manufactured good is given by:

$$m = A_m n_m \tag{2}$$

where n_m is the number of workers that work in the manufacturing sector, and the technology for producing the agricultural good is given by:

$$a = A_a L^\theta n_a^{1-\theta} \tag{3}$$

where n_a is the number of workers that work in the agricultural sector and L is land.

Given the extreme version of the preferences used here, we simply assume that the economy is able to produce sufficient amounts of a so as to provide all individuals with at least $\bar{a}$ units of the agricultural good. A sufficient condition for this is that $A_a > \bar{a}$. We assume that land ownership is equally distributed across the population.

The social planner's problem in this model economy is to maximize the utility of a representative household subject to the feasibility constraints. This turns out to be somewhat trivial given the extreme form of preferences that we have assumed. In particular, given that everyone needs to consume exactly $\bar{a}$ units of the agricultural good but receives no benefit from consuming any additional amount, the optimal allocation is to place enough workers in the agricultural sector so as to produce $\bar{a}$ for each individual in the economy and then to allocate all remaining workers to the manufacturing sector. It follows that the optimal value for n_a is given by:

$$n_a = [\frac{\bar{a}}{A_a}]^{1/(1-\theta)}. \tag{4}$$

The key implication of this model is that in a closed economy in which food is a necessity, there is a powerful negative relationship between agricultural TFP and employment in agriculture. In particular, a 1% decrease in agricultural TFP A_a will lead to an even larger percentage increase in employment in agriculture, equal to $1/(1-\theta)$.

This basic result holds robustly so long as the economy is closed. The model sharply underscores the somewhat obvious point that in a relatively closed economy in which food is an essential consumption good (and in which food must be produced domestically), agricultural productivity is linked directly to the fraction of the population working in the agricultural sector. If we observe a large number of people in this sector, with low productivity levels, we should not view the result as a paradox; instead, it is a natural implication of a simple model with subsistence food production.

Gollin and Rogerson (2009) show that the same result holds for more general specification of preferences and for situations in which the nonagricultural good is used as an input into agriculture. They also show that high transportation costs can exacerbate the effects of low agricultural productivity. In an economy where it is costly both to produce and to transport food, we should expect to find lots of people living in rural areas and producing their own food.

Although this simple sketch of a model is not intended to be taken as a literal representation of a poor developing economy, the point is that a rudimentary model of this type makes it unsurprising that large fractions of the population in developing countries are engaged in agriculture, even while they have relatively low productivity and live in isolated rural areas. This is a predictable equilibrium outcome, so long as productivity is low and there are few alternative sources of food.

The closed economy assumption is restrictive but also revealing. Countries have a growth advantage if they are in a position to import significant quantities of food in exchange for exports of nonfood goods or services. Trade can be a substitute for the long, slow business of increasing agricultural productivity. But for many countries with large populations in remote areas, it is difficult to see how food imports will plausibly replace domestic production. Although people will continue to move to the coastal cities of the world, these migrations entail significant transaction costs in the short and medium term. As a result, in these countries a trade-based food strategy will be difficult to implement.

In other countries or under different circumstances, however, the link between agricultural productivity and economic growth might be less clear. Increasing the productivity of nonfood cash crops could be more important for some countries than increasing the productivity of food crops; some countries might be better off relying on nonagricultural production altogether. Agro-pessimism might be warranted in those countries that have the human capital and institutional capability such that they can move into world markets as producers of manufactured goods or other tradables.

7. CONCLUSION

A model in which countries must attain a high degree of food self-sufficiency seems appropriate at present for those parts of the developing world that are landlocked, predominantly rural, and have large fractions of their population living at a considerable distance from coastal cities, where they might have access to inexpensive food imports. This might include, for example, a number of African countries: Uganda, Congo, Mali, Niger, Ethiopia, and Burkina Faso. It might also include a number of countries in South America and Asia: Peru, Bolivia, Mongolia, Cambodia, and others.

Some other countries, however, might be able to rely much more on imported food. Small island economies (e.g., Mauritius or Fiji), along with coastal economies with well-developed port infrastructure and good access to international markets (e.g., South Africa, much of North Africa, and some countries in Central America and the Caribbean), might be able to feed themselves more efficiently from imports than through domestic production.

Recent debates between agro-pessimists and agricultural fundamentalists paint an excessively stark choice between development strategies that focus exclusively on agriculture and those that largely ignore the sector. This is unfortunate. Given that many or most developing countries have at least one quarter of their workforce in agriculture and given the importance of agricultural output in the consumption baskets of the poor, it is hard to imagine that significant growth or poverty reduction will arrive in the absence of agricultural productivity growth.

A few countries might be able to substitute agricultural imports for productivity growth; these countries will be at a considerable advantage relative to their neighbors. But many countries, including some very large and very poor countries, will be unable to feed their populations with imports. A country such as Congo, for example, will continue to depend heavily on domestic production for its food needs.

In the long run, nonagricultural productivity growth will be crucial for the developing world, as it has been in every other region. The nonagricultural sector will eventually become the primary source of employment, and a smaller number of people (presumably operating larger farms) will produce food for urban markets. This general story—told convincingly in the early agricultural development literature—seems in large measure to be right.

What is the role of government and the international community? The structural transformation will take place in today's developing countries—as it did previously in today's rich countries—because of the low income elasticities of agricultural goods combined with improvements in agricultural technologies. Governments have little direct role to play in managing this transformation or hindering it. However, government certainly has a role in supplying public goods that could affect the speed of the transformation.

For example, agricultural research is almost always a public sector activity because the replicability of seeds makes it difficult for private firms to recoup the benefits of genetic improvement research.[10] Transportation infrastructure also has a public good aspect, since private actors are likely to under-provide and under-maintain roads.[11] Governments (or perhaps farmer organizations) also have a role to play in managing quality and setting standards (for domestic as well as export markets). Governments also have a role to play in providing pubic goods for the nonagricultural sector, including a variety of legal and regulatory functions.

Perhaps it is useful in closing to recall Adam Smith's admonition to remember the interdependence of the agricultural sector and the nonagricultural sector (1986; Book III, Chapter 1):

> **The great commerce of every civilised society is that carried on between the inhabitants of the town and those of the country. It consists in the exchange of rude for manufactured produce, either immediately, or by the intervention of money, or of some sort of paper which represents money. The country supplies the town with the means of subsistence and the materials of manufacture. The town repays this supply by sending back a part of the manufactured produce to the inhabitants of the country. The town, in which there neither is nor can be any reproduction of substances, may very properly be said to gain its whole wealth and subsistence from the country. We must not, however, upon this account, imagine that the gain of the town is the loss of the country. The gains of both are mutual and reciprocal, and the division of labour is in this, as in all other cases, advantageous to all the different persons employed in the various occupations into which it is subdivided.**

End Notes

*. Much of the content of this chapter reflects the author's long-term collaborations with Robert Evenson and with Richard Rogerson and Stephen Parente. However, the views presented in this chapter are the author's own and do not implicate any of these coauthors. The author has also benefited from many years of discussions about agriculture's role in development—and about development economics in general—with Anand Swamy and especially Cheryl Doss.

1. Note that the table shows levels of output per worker, which is a useful measure of productivity. The data on output per capita can be obtained simply from these data, but for conciseness, they are not presented here.

2. This is not, however, a problem unique to poor countries. In many rich countries, farmers may work in off-farm activities (e.g., holding a steady job "in town"), and it is not clear whether we are likely to overestimate agricultural labor more severely in rich countries or in poor ones.

3. See Ravallion et al. (2007) for a detailed analysis, based on household survey data, of rural versus urban living standards.

4. Smith even seemed to recognize the fact that productivity differences across countries were greater in agriculture than in nonagriculture. He wrote (1986, p. 111), "The most opulent nations, indeed, generally excel all their neighbors in agriculture as well as in manufactures; but they are commonly more distinguished by their superiority in the latter than in the former." He also seemed to argue (p. 483) that agricultural productivity growth would normally precede industrial growth: "According to the natural course of things, therefore, the greater part of the capital of every growing society is, first, directed to agriculture, afterwards to manufactures, and last of all to foreign commerce. This order of things is so very natural that in every society that had any territory it has always, I believe, been in some degree observed.

5. China was also the subject of a related study by Fan et al. (2003) that found similarly high rates of return to investment in rural areas.

6. Amsden's view has been challenged by Kang and Ramachandran (1999), among others.

7. Collier has pressed this argument vociferously in nonacademic forums, including the opinion pages of various newspapers; in a speech before the British All Party Parliamentary Group on Overseas Development, among other places, he has explicitly argued that the agricultural sector is unlikely to play a key role in generating growth or reducing poverty in Africa. He has called instead for more resource-based activities and low-tech manufacturing. (A podcast of his APPGOD speech is available at www.odi.org.uk/events/apgood/Agric_in_Africa_05/apgood_oct17/audio/PCollier.wma.)

8. Although we refer to the nonagricultural good as the manufacturing good, it should be interpreted as representing both the manufacturing and the service sectors.

9. It is sufficient that at least one of $\bar{a}$ or $\bar{m}$ be greater than zero for this property to hold. Having both positive allows for the possibility of a corner solution in which $m = 0$.

10. The few exceptions to this pattern involve hybrid seeds, where heterosis effects make it worthwhile for farmers to purchase fresh seed each season, and a few other crops in countries where intellectual property rights allow breeders to collect rents from their research.

11. The need for public involvement here is somewhat less clear; history provides many examples of privately funded road construction and maintenance, with toll collection offering a mechanism for cost recovery. However, it is telling that most countries have opted for a strong public role in road construction. One concern is that privatized roads are often natural monopolies, so that a public role could be needed from a regulatory standpoint, even if it is not required for construction or maintenance.

References

Allen, R. C. (1999). Tracking the agricultural revolution in England. *Economic History Review*, *52*(2), 209–235.

Alston, J., Wyatt, T. J., Pardey, P. G., Marra, M. C., & Chan-Kang, C. (2000). *A meta-analysis of rates of return to agricultural R & D: ex pede Herculem?* (Research Report 113). Washington, DC: International Food Policy Research Institute (IFPRI).

Amsden, A. (1989). *Asia's Next Giant: South Korea and Late Industrialization*. London: Oxford University Press.

Bernard, A. B., & Jones, C. I. (1996). Comparing Apples to Oranges: Productivity Convergence and Measurement across Industries and Countries. *American Economic Review*, *86*(5), 1216–1252.

Bezemer, D., & Headey, D. (2008). Agriculture, development, and urban bias. *World Development*, *36*(8), 1342–1364.

Block, S. (1999). Agriculture and economic growth in Ethiopia: Growth multipliers from a four-sector simulation model. *Agricultural Economics*, *20*(3), 241–252.

Bosworth, B., & Collins, S. M. (2008). Accounting for growth: Comparing China and India. *Journal of Economic Perspectives, 22*(1), 45–66.

Bravo-Ortega, C., & Lederman, D. (2005). *Agriculture and national welfare around the world: Causality and international heterogeneity since 1960.* World Bank Policy Research Working Paper #3499. Washington, DC: The World Bank.

Byerlee, D., de Janvery, A., & Sadoulet, E. (2009). Agriculture for development: Towards a new paradigm. *Annual Review of Resource Economics*, forthcoming.

Caselli, F., & Wilbur John Coleman I. I. (2001). The U.S. Structural Transformation and Regional Convergence: A Reinterpretation. *Journal of Political Economy, 109*(3), 584–616.

Chanda, A., & Dalgaard, C. J. (2008). Dual economies and international Total Factor Productivity differences: Channelling the impact from institutions, trade, and geography. *Economica, 75*(300), 629–661.

Chari, V. V., Kehoe, P. J., & McGrattan, E. R. (2007). Business cycle accounting. *Econometrica, 75*(3), 781–836.

Chenery, H. B., & Syrquin, M. (1975). *Patterns of Development, 1950–1970.* London: Oxford University Press.

Clark, G. (1998). Renting the revolution. *Journal of Economic History, 58*, 206–210.

Clark, G. (2002). The agricultural revolution and the Industrial Revolution: England. *1500–1912.* Unpublished working paper. Davis: Department of Economics, University of California.

Collier, P. (2008). The politics of hunger: How illusion and greed fan the food crisis. *Foreign Affairs, 87*(6), 67–79.

Crafts, N. (1985). *British Economic Growth during the Industrial Revolution.* Oxford: Clarendon Press.

Datt, G., & Ravallion, M. (1996). How important to India's poor is the sectoral composition of economic growth? *The World Bank Economic Review, 10*(1), 1–25.

Diao, X., Hazell, P., Resnick, D., & Thurlow, J. (2006). *The role of agriculture in development: Implications for sub-Saharan Africa.* DSGC Discussion Paper #29. Washington, DC: International Food Policy Research Institute.

Dowrick, S., & Gemmell, N. (1991). Industrialisation, catching up and economic growth: A comparative study across the world's capitalist economies. *Economic Journal, 101*(405), 263–275.

Echevarria, C. (1995). Agricultural development vs. industrialization: Effects of trade. *Canadian Journal of Economics, 28*(3), 631–647.

Echevarria, C. (1997). Changes in sectoral composition associated with economic growth. *International Economic Review, 38*(2), 431–452.

Ellis, F., & Harris, N. (2004). *New thinking about urban and rural development.* Keynote Paper for DFID Sustainable Development Retreat.

Eswaran, M., & Kotwal, A. (1993). A theory of real wage growth in LDCs. *Journal of Development Economics, 42*(2), 243–269.

Evenson, R. E. (2001). Economic impacts of agricultural research and extension. In B. Gardner, & G. Rausser (Eds.), *Handbook of Agricultural Economics* (Vol. 1A, Chapter 11, pp. 574–616). Amsterdam: Elsevier Science.

Evenson, R. E., & Gollin, D. (Eds.). (2003). *Crop Variety Improvement and Its Effect on Productivity: The Impact of International Agricultural Research.* Wallingford, UK: CAB International.

Evenson, R. E., & Gollin, D. (2003b). Assessing the impact of the Green Revolution, 1960–2000. *Science, 300*(5620), 758–762.

Evenson, R. E., Pray, C. E., & Rosegrant, M. W. (1999). *Agricultural research and productivity growth in India.* Research Report # 109. International Food Policy Research Institute (IFPRI).

Fan, S., Hazell, P., & Thorat, S. (2000). Government spending, growth and poverty in rural India. *American Journal of Agricultural Economics, 82*(4), 1038–1051.

Fan, S., & Pardey, P. G. (1997). Research, productivity, and output growth in Chinese agriculture. *Journal of Development Economics, 53*(1), 115–137.

Fan, S., Zhang, X., & Robinson, S. (2003). Structural change and economic growth in China. *Review of Development Economics, 7*(3), 360–377.

Fei, J. C. H., & G, Ranis. (1964). *Development of the Labor Surplus Economy: Theory and Policy.* A Publication of the Economic Growth Center, Yale University. Homewood, Illinois: Richard D. Irwin, Inc.

Gallup, J. L., & Sachs, J. D. (2000). Agriculture, climate, and technology: Why are the tropics falling behind? *American Journal of Agricultural Economics*, *82*(3), 731–737.

Gardner, B., & Tsakok, I. (2007). Agriculture in economic development: Primary engine of growth or chicken and egg. *American Journal of Agricultural Economics*, *89*(5), 1145–1151.

Gollin, D., Parente, S. L. & Rogerson, R. (2002). The role of agriculture in development. *American Economic Review: Papers and Proceedings*, *92*(2), 160–164.

Gollin, D., Parente, S. L., & Rogerson, R. (2004). Farm work, home work, and international productivity differences. *Review of Economic Dynamics*, *7*(4), 827–850.

Gollin, D., Parente, S. L., & Rogerson, R. (2007). The food problem and the evolution of international income levels. *Journal of Monetary Economics*, *54*(4), 1230–1255.

Gollin, D., & Rogerson, R. (2009). *The Greatest of All Improvements: Roads, Agriculture, and Economic Development in Africa*. Mimeo: Williams College Department of Economics.

Goodfriend, M., & McDermott, J. (1998). Industrial development and the convergence question. *American Economic Review*, *88*(5), 1277–1289.

Gulati, A.; Fan, S., & Dalafi, S. (2005). The dragon and the elephant. MTID discussion papers 87. Washington, DC: International Food Policy Research Institute (IFPRI).

Hansen, G., & Prescott, E. C. (2002). Malthus to Solow. *American Economic Review*, *92*(4), 1205–1217.

Harris, J., & Todaro, M. (1970). Migration, unemployment and development: A two-sector analysis. *American Economic Review*, *60*(1), 126–142.

Hasan, R., & Quibria, M. G. (2004). Industry matters for poverty: A critique of agricultural fundamentalism. *Kyklos*, *57*(2), 253–264.

Hertel, T. W. (2002). Applied general equilibrium analysis of agricultural and resource policies. In B. L. Gardner, & G. C. Rausser (Eds.), *Handbook of Agricultural Economics* (Vol. 2, Chapter 26, pp. 1373–1419). Amsterdam: Elsevier.

Heston, A., Summers, R., & Aten, B. (2006). Penn World Table Version 6.2, Center for International Comparisons of Production, Income and Prices at the University of Pennsylvania. Online at http://pwt.econ.upenn.edu/php_site/pwt62/pwt62_form.php. Last accessed April 2, 2009.

Humphries, H., & Knowles, S. (1998). Does agriculture contribute to economic growth? Some empirical evidence. *Applied Economics*, *30*(6), 775–781.

Irz, X., Lin, L., Thirtle, C., & Wiggins, S. (2002). Agricultural growth and poverty alleviation. *Development Policy Review*, *19*(4).

Irz, X., & Roe, T. (2001). *Agricultural productivity and economy-wide growth: investigation in a Ramsey framework*. Manuscript. University of Reading, Department of Agricultural and Food Economics.

Johnson, D. G. (1997). Agriculture and the Wealth of Nations. Richard T. Ely Lecture. *American Economic Review*, *87*(2), 1–12.

Johnston, B. F., & Mellor, J. W. (1961). The role of agriculture in economic development. *American Economic Review*, *51*(4), 566–593.

Johnston, B. F., & Kilby, P. (1975). *Agriculture and Structural Transformation: Economic Strategies in Late-Developing Countries*. New York: Oxford University Press.

Jorgenson, D. W., & Gollop, F. M. (1992). Productivity growth in U.S. agriculture: A postwar perspective. *American Journal of Agricultural Economics*, *74*(3), 745–750.

Kang, K., & Ramachandran, V. (1999). Economic transformation in Korea: Rapid growth without an agricultural revolution? *Economic Development and Cultural Change*, *47*(4), 783–801.

King, R. G., & Rebelo, S. T. (1993). Transitional dynamics and economic growth in the neoclassical model. *American Economic Review*, *83*(4), 908–931.

Kogel, T., & Prskawetz, A. (2001). Agricultural productivity growth and escape from the Malthusian Trap. *Journal of Economic Growth*, *6*, 337–357.

Kongsamut, P., Rebelo, S., & Xie, D. (2001). Beyond Balanced Growth. *Review of Economic Studies*, *68*(4), 869–882.

Kuznets, S. (1966). *Modern Economic Growth*. New Haven: Yale University Press.

Landon-Lane, J., & Robertson, P. (2003). *Accumulation and productivity growth in industrializing economies*. Departmental Working Paper 2003–05. Rutgers University, Department of Economics.

Lewis, W. A. (1955). *The Theory of Economic Growth*. London: George Allen & Unwin.

Löfgren, H., Harris, R. L., & Robinson, S. (2001). *A standard computable general equilibrium (CGE) model in GAMS.* TMD Discussion Paper #75. Washington, DC: International Food Policy Research Institute (IFPRI).

Mankiw, N. G., Romer, D., & Weil, D. N. (1992). A contribution to the empirics of economic growth. *Quarterly Journal of Economics, 107,* 407–437.

Martin, W., & Mitra, D. (2001). Productivity Growth and Convergence in Agriculture versus Manufacturing. *Economic Development and Cultural Change, 49*(2), 403–422.

Masters, W. A., & McMillan, M. S. (2001). Climate and scale in economic growth. *Journal of Economic Growth, 6*(3), 167–186.

Matsuyama, K. (1992). Agricultural productivity, comparative advantage, and economic growth. *Journal of Economic Theory, 58,* (2): 317–334.

Mellor, J. W. (1995). Introduction. In J. W. Mellor (Eds.), *Agriculture on the Road to Industrialization.* Baltimore: Johns Hopkins University Press for the International Food Policy Research Institute (IFPRI).

Mellor, J. W. (1996). Agriculture on the road to industrialization. In J. P. Lewis, & V. Kallab (Eds.), *Development Strategies Reconsidered.* New Brunswick, NJ: Transaction Books for the Overseas Development Council.

Mellor, J. (1999). Faster, more equitable growth: The relation between growth in agriculture and poverty reduction. Research Report No. 4. *Agricultural Policy Development Project.* Washington, DC: International Food Policy Research Institute.

Mellor, J. (2000). Faster more equitable growth: The relation between growth in agriculture and poverty reduction. CAER II Discussion Paper #70. Cambridge, Mass.: Harvard Institute for International Development.

Mundlak, Y. (2000). *Agriculture and Economic Growth: Theory and Measurement.* Cambridge, Mass.: Harvard University Press.

Mundlak, Y. (2005). Economic growth: lessons from two centuries of American agriculture. *Journal of Economic Literature, 43*(4), 989–1024.

Powell, A. (2007). *Why, How, and When Did GTAP Happen? What Has It Achieved? Where Is It Heading?* GTAP Working Paper No. 38; Presented at the 10th Annual Conference on Global Economic Analysis, Purdue University.

Ravallion, M., Chen, S., & Sangraula, P. (2007). *New Evidence on the Urbanization of Global Poverty.* World Bank Policy Research Working Paper 4199. Washington, DC: The World Bank.

Restuccia, D., Yang, D. T., & Zhu, X. (2008). Agriculture and aggregate productivity: A quantitative cross-country analysis. *Journal of Monetary Economics, 55*(2), 234–250.

Ripoll, M., & Cordoba, J. C. (2007). *Agriculture, aggregation, and development accounting.* Working paper. University of Pittsburgh Department of Economics.

Rosegrant, M. W., Ringler, C., Msangi, S., Sulser, T. B., Zhu, T., & Cline, S. A. (2008). *International Model for Policy Analysis of Agricultural Commodities and Trade (IMPACT): Model Description.* Unpublished paper. Washington, DC: International Food Policy Research Institute.

Rosenstein-Rodan, P. N. (1943). Problems of industrialization of Eastern and South-Eastern Europe. *Economic Journal,* (June–September) 204-07. Reprinted in Meier, G. M. (1995). *Leading Issues in Economic Development* (6th ed.). New York: Oxford University Press.

Rostow, W. W. (1960). *The Stages of Economic Growth.* Cambridge: Cambridge University Press.

Schultz, T. W. (1953). *The Economic Organization of Agriculture.* New York: McGraw-Hill.

Schultz, T. W. (1964). *Transforming Traditional Agriculture.* New Haven: Yale University Press.

Self, S., & Grabowski, R. (2007). Economic development and the role of agricultural technology. *Agricultural Economics, 36*(3), 395–404.

Smith, A. (1986). *The Wealth of Nations: Books I–III.* Originally published 1776. New York: Penguin Books.

Solow , R. (1957). Technical change and the aggregate production function. *Review of Economics and Statistics, 39,* 312–320.

Staatz, J. M., & Dembélé, N. N. (2007). *Agriculture for development in sub-Saharan Africa.* Background paper for the *World Development Report 2008.* Washington, DC: World Bank.

Syrquin, M. (1988). Patterns of structural change. In H. Chenery, & T. N. Srinivasan (Eds.), *Handbook of Development Economics* (Vol. I, Chapter 7). Amsterdam: Elsevier Science Publishers.

Temple, J. (2004). *Dualism and aggregate productivity.* London. CEPR Discussion Papers, No. 4387.

Temple, J. (2005). Dual economy models: A primer for growth economists. *The Manchester School, 73*(4), 435–478.

Thirtle, C., Irz, I., Lin, L., McKenzie-Hill, V., & Wiggins, S. (2001). *Relationship between changes in agricultural productivity and the incidence of poverty in developing countries*. Department for International Development Report No. 7946. London: DFID.

Timmer, C. P. (2003). *Agriculture and pro-poor growth: What the literature says*. USAID Pro-Poor Economic Growth Research Studies: Contract No. PCE-I-02-00-00015-00.

Vollrath, D. (2009). How important are dual economy effects for aggregate productivity? *Journal of Development Economics, 88*(2), 325–334.

World Bank. (2008). *World Development Report 2008: Agriculture for Development*. Washington, DC: The World Bank.

CHAPTER 74

Agriculture Renaissance: Making "Agriculture for Development" Work in the 21st Century

Prabhu Pingali[1]

Bill and Melinda Gates Foundation

Contents

Handbook of Agricultural Economics, Volume 4
doi: 10.1016/S1574-0072(09)04074-2

Abstract

Agriculture renaissance means the renewed understanding and recommitment to the fundamental role of agriculture in the development process. Operationally it implies different approaches at the country level based on the stage of development. For the least developed countries of the world, it could mean re-engaging agriculture's potential as a driver of overall economic development. While for the emerging economies, it could be small holder inclusion in agricultural commercialization and/or reducing rural-urban income gaps. Food sectors in developing countries are witnessing profound changes driven by: rapid income growth; urbanization; global inter-connectedness; technology access; and climate change. Country typologies, by stage of agricultural transformation, are used to discuss the implications of the changes and the public policy options for the way forward.
JEL Codes: O13, Q1, Q10, Q18

Key Words

Agriculture
development
commercialization
structural transformation
renaissance
change
drivers

INTRODUCTION

Not since the late 1960s has there been as much attention paid to agriculture as there is today. Agriculture's crucial role in economic development is being re-discovered by developing country policy makers as well as by managers of foreign assistance in OECD countries and multi-lateral agencies. Small holder lead productivity growth is once again being touted as the vehicle for poverty reduction in the least developed countries, particularly those in Sub-Saharan Africa. For emerging economies, such as China and India, strategies for small holder inclusion in the process of agricultural commercialization and for reducing the growing gaps between urban and rural incomes have motivated the renewed interest in agriculture development. Industrialized countries are examining ways of promoting agriculture's multiple roles, especially its role in providing biofuel feed stock and its ability to economically sequester carbon.

Renewed attention to agriculture may have been triggered by the sharp rise in food prices in 2008, but its persistence in global and national debates points to the growing realization that the problem is not transitory. Developing country agriculture is faced with a growing set of challenges: meeting the demands of diet diversity resulting from rapidly rising incomes; feeding rapidly growing urban populations; dealing with the challenges and opportunities of an increasingly globalised food sector; accessing technologies that are under the purview of proprietary protection; and gearing up for the projected negative consequences of climate change. Even as it absorbs the "new" challenges, the food policymaking community continues to grapple with its traditional pre-occupation of the persistence of hunger and poverty in the developing world.

Agriculture renaissance means the renewed understanding and recommitment to the fundamental role of agriculture in the development process. Operationally it implies different approaches at the country level based on the stage of development it's in. For the least developed countries of the world, it could mean re-engaging agriculture's potential as a driver of overall economic development. While for the emerging economies, it could imply policies and strategies that help sustain past productivity gains and focussed efforts on addressing the needs of marginal regions and populations left behind.

The first part of this chapter presents a brief review of the state of knowledge on the role of agriculture in economic development, with particular attention to poverty reduction. The crucial role played by productivity growth in improving food supplies, reducing food prices and reducing poverty is highlighted. The second part of the chapter discusses the profound changes that the food sectors in developing countries are witnessing today and the drivers of these changes, such as rapid income growth, urbanization, global inter-connectedness, technology access, and climate change. Part three describes the implications of the changes presented earlier for the modernization and transformation of the agriculture sector. Country typologies by stage of agricultural transformation are used to organize the discussion in part three. The final part of the paper presents a detailed discussion on the public policy options for the way forward in successfully managing an agricultural renaissance.

1. AGRICULTURAL GROWTH AND ECONOMIC DEVELOPMENT

Development economists in general and agricultural economists in particular have long focused on how agriculture can best contribute to overall economic growth and modernization. Many early analysts (Rosenstein-Rodan, 1943; Lewis, 1954; Scitovsky, 1954; Hirschman, 1958; Jorgenson, 1961; Fei and Ranis, 1961) highlighted agriculture because of its abundance of resources and its ability to transfer surpluses to the more important industrial sector. The conventional approach to the roles of agriculture in development concentrated on agriculture's important market-mediated linkages: (i) providing labor for an urbanized industrial work force; (ii) producing food for expanding populations with higher incomes; (iii) supplying savings for investment in industry; (iv) enlarging markets for industrial output; (v) providing export earnings to pay for imported capital goods; and (vi) producing primary materials for agro-processing industries (Johnston and Mellor, 1961; Ranis et al., 1990; Delgado et al., 1994; Timmer, 2002).

There are good reasons for why these early approaches focused on agriculture's economic roles as a one-way path involving the flow of resources towards the industrial sector and urban centers. In agrarian societies with few trading opportunities, most resources are devoted to the provision of food. As national incomes rise, the demand for food increases much more slowly than other goods and services. As a result, value added from the farm household's own labour, land and capital, as a share of the gross value of agricultural output falls over time. Farmers' increasing use of purchased intermediate inputs and off-farm services adds to the relative decline of the producing agriculture sector, per se, in terms of overall GDP and employment (Timmer, 1988, 1997; Pingali, 1997).

Less well understood is agriculture's multiple contributions to pro-poor economic development (Byerlee, et. al., Valdes, et al., etc). These include the contributions of a vibrant agricultural sector to: income growth, food security and poverty alleviation; gender empowerment; and the supply of environmental services (FAO, 2004a). While agriculture's direct, private contributions to farm households (such as farm incomes) are tangible, easy to understand and simple to quantify, it's numerous in-direct benefits (such as, contributions to improved child nutrition and education) tend to be overlooked in assessing rates of returns. Ignoring the whole range of economic and social contributions of agriculture underestimates the returns to investment in the sector (Valdes and Foster, 2005).

Agriculture productivity growth and poverty reduction

Past experience from Asia and elsewhere indicates that productivity growth that resulted from agricultural R&D has had an enormous impact on food supplies and food prices, and consequent beneficial impacts on food security and poverty reduction (Hayami and Herdt, 1977; Pinstrup-Andersen et al., 1976; Binswanger, 1980; Hazell and Haggblade, 1993).

> **"Because a relatively high proportion of any income gain made by the poor is spent on food, the income effects of research-induced supply shifts can have major nutritional implications, particularly if those shifts result from technologies aimed at the poorest producers".** (Alston et al., 1995, p. 85)

There is a large econometric literature that uses cross-country or time-series data to estimate the relationship between agricultural productivity growth and poverty. These studies generally find high poverty reduction elasticities for agricultural productivity growth (Hazell, this volume). Thirtle, Lin, and Piesse (2002) estimate that each 1% increase in crop productivity reduces the number of poor people by 0.48% in Asia. For India, Ravallion and Datt (1996) estimate that a 1% increase in agricultural value added per hectare leads to a 0.4% reduction in poverty in the short run and 1.9% in the long run, the latter arising through the indirect effects of lower food prices and higher wages. Fan, Hazell and Thorat (2000) estimated that each 1%

increase in agricultural production in India reduces the number of rural poor by 0.24%. For South Asia, these poverty elasticities are still much higher for agriculture than for other sectors of the economy (World Bank, 2007; Hasan and Quibria, 2004). Christiaensen et al. (2006) find that, for low income countries, the impact on poverty headcount to be larger from agriculture growth relative to equivalent growth in the non-agriculture sector at a factor of 2.3 times. In the case of sub-Saharan Africa agriculture's contribution to poverty reduction was estimated to be 4.25 times that of equivalent investment in the service sector. The larger impact of agriculture on poverty headcounts also holds for the middle income countries such as those in North Africa, where the participation effect of agricultural growth on head count poverty is on average 1.34 times larger than that of equal growth in the other sectors.

Agriculture research and development makes a difference

It is important for us to recognize that the relatively higher poverty reduction impacts of agriculture growth discussed above are dependent on the use of the right technology, (e.g. focused on non tradable food versus tradable export crops; land versus labor saving) and its targeting (small versus large farmers) (Christiaensen et al, 2006; Binswanger and McCalla, this volume). Fan *et al.* (1999) find that agricultural R&D investments in India have not only given the highest productivity returns in recent decades, but have also lifted more people out of poverty per unit of expenditure than most other types of public investment. Investments in agricultural R&D and rural roads dominate all others in terms of the size of their impacts, and can be considered the best "win-win" strategies for achieving growth and poverty alleviation in India. Fan and Brzeska (this volume) report similar results for China although the ranking was different. The poverty-reduction effect of education investment ranked first, followed by investment in agricultural research.

Long-term investments in research, extension, rural infrastructure and irrigation have a large impact on agricultural production (Fan and Brzeska, this volume; Fan and Pardey 1998). Fan and Rao (2003), analysis of 43 developing countries showed that agricultural research spending has a much greater impact on productivity than other forms of public (non-research) spending. Moreover, properly managed public investments could also stimulate private investments, thereby generating further production and productivity growth (Fan and Pardey 1998). Herdt (this volume) provides an extensive and historic review of aid based public investments in agriculture and their returns and impact.

Gender and Agriculture productivity growth

Gollin (this volume) argues that agriculture productivity growth (particularly that of food crops) has particular significance because of its importance for women. Of the world's economically active women, approximately half work in agriculture – a significantly higher fraction than for men. This is particularly true in the least developed countries (mostly sub-Saharan African countries), where 73 percent of economically active women work in agriculture, compared with 59 percent of economically active men. Since women disproportionately work in agriculture, and since women tend to be disproportionately represented among the poor, agricultural development has particular relevance from a gender perspective.

Urban and economy wide impacts of agriculture growth

The poverty reduction impact of public investment for agriculture productivity growth goes beyond rural areas (Fan and Brzeska, this volume). Fan, Fang and Zhang (2001) examined the effect of agricultural R&D investments and of subsequent increases in agricultural production on food prices and the incidence of urban poverty in China. According to the study, increased investment in agricultural R&D lowers food prices through increased agricultural production, which, in turn, benefits the urban poor, who spend more than 60 percent of their income of food. Agricultural research investments are thus an effective tool in helping the urban poor rise above the poverty line, with such investments accounting for 18-30 percent of the urban poverty reduction between 1992 and 1998. The results show that agricultural research has played an important role in reducing not only rural but also urban poverty in China. Although the impact has weakened in recent years due to increasing incomes and the devolution of food items in most households' budgets, the ongoing urbanization within China makes this price-effect a relevant issue. The results of this study are consistent with later findings by Fan (2002), in which agricultural research in India was found to have the largest impact on urban poverty reduction among all the rural investments considered through similar food price channels.

The powerful economy-wide benefits emanating from technologically-driven agricultural growth were amply demonstrated during the GR era in South Asia (Mellor, 1976). In India, the fact that non-agriculture's share of total national employment did not change for over a century, until the full force of the green revolution was underway in the 1970s, provided strong circumstantial evidence of the importance of agricultural growth as a motor for the Indian economy (Hazell, this volume). This was also confirmed by Rangarajan (1982) who estimated that a one percentage point addition to the agricultural growth rate stimulated a 0.5 percent addition to the growth rate of industrial output, and a 0.7 percent addition to the growth rate of national income.

2. AGRICULTURE'S CONTRIBUTION TO DEVELOPMENT IN A CHANGING WORLD

The transformation of agriculture from its traditional subsistence roots, induced by technical change, to a modernizing and eventually industrialized agriculture sector is a phenomenon observed across the developing world. However, there are also a large number of countries that have stalled in the transformation process or have yet to "get agriculture moving". These are almost always countries that are classified as the "least developed". Even within countries that are well on the pathway towards agricultural transformation there are significant inter-regional differences (Eastern India, for example). Pingali (2006) provides the following reasons for the poor performance of their agriculture:

i) low and inelastic demand for agricultural output due to low population density and poor market access conditions;
ii) poor provision of public good investments in rural areas;
iii) lack of technology R&D on commodities and environments important to the poor;
iv) high share of agro-climatically constrained land resources; and
v) institutional barriers to enhancing productivity growth.

Food markets in developing countries are undergoing profound changes that are fuelled by rapid income growth, urbanization, globalization and trade integration, technology access and the emerging threat of climate change (Pingali 2006; Byerlee et al. 2009; Binswanger and McCalla, this volume; Pingali and McCullough 2009; and McCullough et al, 2008). Will these changes offer new opportunities for agriculture led growth, or will they further marginalize excluded countries, regions and groups?

Income growth and diet diversification

Per capita incomes have risen substantially in many parts of the developing world over the past few decades. In developing countries, per capita income growth averaged around 1% per year in the 1980s and 1990s but jumped to 3.7% between 2001 and 2005 (World Bank 2006b). East Asia has led the world with sustained per capita growth of 6% per year in real terms since the 1980s. In South Asia, growth rates have been consistently positive since the 1980s although not as spectacular. Eastern Europe and Central Asia experienced economic decline in the 1990s but have since obtained per capita growth rates of 5% per year. Latin America and Sub-Saharan Africa have also experienced negative growth rates which reversed themselves in the 1990s in Latin America and since 2000 in Sub-Saharan Africa. Income growth is closely linked with higher expenditure on food items and with diet diversification out of staples (Bennett's Law). Consumers diversify their diets towards food groups with positive income elasticities of demand, such as fruit and vegetables, meat and livestock products. The trend towards diet diversification has been documented at the household level in poor and middle income countries in Asia, Africa, and Latin America (Pingali 2007; Mendez and Popkin, 2004; Hoddinott and Yohannes, 2002; Huang and Bouis, 1996). The effect of per capita income growth on food consumption is most profound for poorer consumers who spend a large portion of their budget on food items (Engel's Law).

Urbanization and feeding the cities

Demographic transformation is comprised of urbanization and rising female employment across the developing world. Urban dwellers outnumbered rural populations for the first time in 2007 (Population Division of UN 2006). Female employment has at least kept pace with population growth in developing countries since 1980 (World Bank 2006a). Female employment rates have risen substantially in Latin America, East Asia, and the Middle East and North Africa since the 1980s. Both urbanization and rising female employment have contributed to rising incomes for many families in developing countries. As wages increase, urban consumers are willing to pay for more convenience, which frees up their time for income-earning activities or leisure. This results in a growing demand for more processed foods with shorter preparation times. Higher rates of female participation in the work force have been linked to greater demand for processed foods (Pingali 2006, Popkin 1999, Regmi and Dyck 2001). Consumers in large, urban centres are more exposed to non-traditional foods as a result of their access to food retail outlets and marketing campaigns (Reardon, Timmer, et al., 2003). Large urban markets create the scope for the establishment of large supermarket chains, and they attract foreign investments and advertising from global corporations. Non-traditional foods are more accessible as a result of trade liberalization and declining costs of transportation and communication (Chopra, Galbraith and Darnton-Hill, 2002).

Globalization and trade integration

"Globalization" is marked by liberalization of trade as well as of foreign direct investment in retail and in agribusiness. Trade has matched, but not outpaced, worldwide growth in food consumption. However, trade has shifted towards higher value and more processed products and away from bulk commodities (Regmi and Dyck 2001). Foreign direct investment in agriculture and the food industry grew substantially in Latin America and in Asia between the mid-1980s and mid-1990s, although investment remained very low in sub-Saharan Africa (FAO 2004). In Asia, FDI in the food industry nearly tripled, from $750 million to $2.1 billion between 1988 and 1997. During that same period, food industry investment exploded in Latin America, from around $200 million to $3.3 billion. McCullough et al (2008) report that economy-wide data through 2005 show a similar pattern: with long term increases in developing countries in Asia and Latin America. FDI flows into in Africa have lagged behind those of Asia and Latin America because of structural and institutional constraints. The world's least developed countries receive only 2 per cent of global foreign direct investment.

Technology change and access

Over the past decade the locus of agricultural research and development has shifted dramatically from the public to the private multinational sector. Three interrelated forces are transforming the system for supplying improved agricultural technologies to the world's farmers. The first is the strengthened and evolving environment for protecting intellectual property in plant innovations. The second is the rapid pace of discovery and growth in importance of molecular biology and genetic engineering. Finally, agricultural input and output trade is becoming more open in nearly all countries. These developments have created a powerful new set of incentives for private research investment, altering the structure of the public/private agricultural research endeavour, particularly with respect to crop improvement (Pingali and Traxler, 2002).

Unlike the green revolution technologies, transgenic technologies are transferred internationally primarily through market mechanisms, often through commercial relationships between the multinational bio-science firms and national seed companies. This system of technology transfer works well for commercially viable innovations in well-developed markets, but perhaps not for the types of innovations needed in developing countries: crops and traits aimed at poor farmers in marginal production environments. These "orphan" technologies have traditionally been the province of public sector research. Given the dominance of private sector research in transgenic crop research and meagre resources being devoted to public sector research in most developing countries, it is unlikely that public sector research can play this role for transgenic crops (Pingali and Raney, 2007).

At the same time innovations in information and communications technology have allowed supply chains to become more responsive, innovations in processing and transport have made products more suitable for global supply chains. Meanwhile, a downward trend in transportation costs and widespread availability of atmosphere-controlled storage infrastructure have made it cost effective to transport products over longer distances. Raw materials have been engineered to meet processing standards and improve shelf life through conventional breeding, and, more recently, genetic engineering. The technical changes across the value chain, described above, are contributing to the emerging transformation of food systems in the developing world but with significant asymmetries in terms of access and benefits between countries and within societies in a particular country.

Climate change and agriculture development

Agriculture production is particularly sensitive to climate change, since crop yields depend in large part on climate conditions such as temperature and rainfall patterns. There are still large uncertainties as to when, how and where climate change will affect agriculture production and food security. But recent research has suggested that the impacts will be more adverse in tropical areas than in temperate areas (Stern 2007, IPCC 2007, Parry et al 2004, Parry et al 2005, Fischer et al 2005), and that climate change effects will likely widen the gap between developed and developing countries. The effects of climate change on agriculture will also, of course, depend on the degree of adaptation, which will be determined by income levels, market structure, farming type, etc (Stern 2006).

The projected number of people affected by climate change, in terms of hunger and poverty, depends to a large degree upon the development pathway. In a pathway characterized by relatively low per capita income and large population growth, the projected number of people affected is considerably greater than under pathways with higher per capita income and lower population growth (Parry *et al* 2005, IPCC 2007). This difference is largely explained by differences in vulnerability, and not by differences in changes of climate. *"The poorest countries and people will suffer earliest and most"* (Stern 2007).

3. IMPLICATIONS FOR THE TRANSFORMATION OF AGRICULTURE

The emerging trends discussed above have enormous implications for the conduct of agriculture in developing countries. Whether countries benefit from these trends and move their agriculture productivity growth to higher plateaus or whether they lose out in the process and become further vulnerable and impoverished depends on the stage of agricultural transformation that they are in. This section describes the process of adjustment that countries face relative to their stage of agriculture development.

Countries at the low end of the agricultural transformation process

Countries in this category are invariably low income, least developed countries, the vast majority of whom are in Sub-Saharan Africa. Most of them are in the bottom half of the UNDP's Human Development Index. The World Development Report 2008 classifies them as "Agriculture based countries". They face low prospects for meeting the Millennium Development Goals of hunger and poverty reduction.

In 2007 Sub-Saharan Africa accounted for less than 2 percent of global gross domestic product (GDP) and exports and just 5% of the agricultural GDP but it also accounted for 12 percent of the world's farmers, 16 percent of the agricultural land, and 28 percent of those living on less than $1.25 a day (World Bank and the FAO 2009). Sixteen of the 37 countries in Africa had TFP growth rates for the 1961-2001 period below one percent. Seven had negative growth rates. Both East and Central Africa had regional growth rates below one percent (Avila and Evenson, this volume). Growth in agricultural value added per capita, a crude measure of income of rural population has only been 0.9 percent for the past 25 years, less than half that of any other developing Region (Binswanger and McCalla, this volume).

However, it's not all bad news. Binswanger and McCalla (this volume) report that Africa is witnessing positive trends in its agriculture sector. In line with the general growth trends in SSA, agricultural growth has accelerated recently and reached 3.5 percent per capita in the first half of this decade. Unlike in Asia, the growth was primarily achieved by area expansion rather than growth in productivity. Binswanger and McCalla argue that agricultural recovery in Africa was driven by improved macro-economic and agricultural policies rather than specific interventions and programs. Masters and Anderson (this volume) provide detailed evidence to indicate that African governments have removed much of their earlier anti-farm and anti-trade policy biases. Government policy biases against agriculture had worsened in the late 1960s and 1970s, primarily through increased taxation of exportable products. Reforms of the 1980s and 1990s reversed that trend, and average rates of agricultural taxation are back to, or below the levels of the early 1960s.

However, substantial distortions remain, and still impose a large tax burden on Africa's poor. In constant (2000) US dollar terms, the transfers paid by African farmers peaked in the late 1970s, at over $10 billion per year or $134 per farm worker. In 2000-04 the burden of taxation averaged $6 billion per year, or $41 per person working in agriculture. However, even this lower amount is appreciably larger than public investment or foreign aid into the sector (Masters and Anderson 2009).

The continuing taxation in Africa contrasts with both Asia and Latin America, where the average agricultural NRAs and RRAs had risen all the way to zero by the early 21st century, and from lower levels than in Africa (Anderson, this volume). Within SSA, agricultural taxation remains the most severe in Zimbabwe, the Ivory Coast, Zambia and Tanzania. The greatest improvements since the first half of the 1980s were made in Mozambique, Kenya and Madagascar, where nominal rates of assistance are now positive. In Egypt, the only North African country for which data is available, the NRA also remains close to -10% (Masters and Anderson, 2009). *While there has been significant progress in incentives regimes, if countries in SSA want to compete better in domestic, regional, and international markets, and benefit from the likely rising trend in international agricultural prices, they must move aggressively to eliminate export taxation of agriculture and remaining barriers to regional trade. (Binswanger and McCalla, this volume).*

The agricultural sector in SSA, however, continues to have to struggle against an adverse policy environment in the developed world. Anderson (this volume) reports that, the average nominal rates of assistance in the developed World peaked at over 50 percent between 1985 and 1989. On average they have declined only slightly, to a little less than 40 percent since then. Among the developed economies they only declined in Europe, but increased sharply in Japan, and slightly in North America. The impact of this protection on world prices and trade shares are severe: The prices of cotton, oilseeds, dairy products and cereals are reduced by 21, 15, 12, and 7 percent respectively, and the trade shares of developing countries in these commodities by 27, 34, 7 and 5 percent respectively. While price impacts on processed meats and sugar are less severe, the impacts on developing country trade shares are 19 and 9 percent respectively (WDR 2007). The universally common practice of tariff escalation, under which processed goods are charged higher tariffs than raw products, further aggravates the impact of these policies on the prospect of agro-industrial development in developing countries.

The impact of trade liberalization in agriculture across the World was studied by Anderson et al, 2006, using large international CGE models. With unilateral trade reform in SSA alone, African agriculture trade would change little in the aggregate, as the barriers imposed by the developed World and other developing countries would remain significant. But with multilateral reform of all goods globally, African agriculture and food exports would increase by 38 percent while imports would increase by 29 percent. Clearly African agriculture stands to gain the most from multilateral trade reform (Binswanger and McCalla, this volume).

The prospects for a renaissance in African agriculture over the next two decades are very promising. On the demand side the trends are favourable, for domestic and sub-regional markets. The combined value of domestic and regional markets for food staples within SSA is considerably in excess of its total international agricultural exports (Diao et al., 2003) and will grow significantly with both population and income over time. SSA's demand for food staples is projected to about double by 2020. Moreover, an increasing share of output will become commercialized as the continent becomes more urbanized. This offers considerable growth in national and regional markets for food staples which in value terms may far exceed the potential growth of all high value agricultural products, at least for the next decades. Moreover, sub-regional trade can be a relatively efficient way of smoothing out the impacts of droughts on production and prices at the country and sub-regional levels. Because food staples are grown by small farmers across SSA, broad based productivity gains in these crops can have far reaching impacts on the rural poor (Binswanger and McCalla, this volume).

We are also starting to see some new enthusiasm for enhancing agriculture productivity in sub-Saharan Africa from national governments as well as outside agencies, as evidenced by increased budgets and ODA flows for public good investments. The CGIAR system is increasingly targeting its resources towards Sub-Saharan Africa. The emergence of democracies and the consequent improvements in governance bode well for the future. Finally, the prospects for commercial production of bio-fuels and utilizing under used lands for carbon sequestration provide new opportunities for income growth for rural communities.

Countries in the process of agricultural modernization

In modernizing economies, the agriculture sector accounts for a 10 to 30 per cent share of the economy and a 15 to 50 per cent share of the work force (McCullough et al, 2008). Countries in this category have successfully used agriculture as an engine of overall growth and are experiencing a steady decline in the share of agriculture in GDP and the share of agriculture in total labour force. Rapidly growing Asian and Latin American economies, mostly in the middle income level, are examples of countries that fall into this category. Small farm led staple food productivity growth, such as for rice and wheat, drove the process of agricultural transformation (See chapters by Hazell; Estudillo and Otsuka; and Avila and Romano this volume). Rising productivity in the agricultural sector has also stimulated growth in the non-agricultural sectors through forward and backward linkages. Agricultural sectors while continuing to grow, in terms of output and total factor productivity growth, are now lagging behind the manufacturing and service sectors. *Revitalization of the agriculture sector in modernizing economies is likely to be induced by: commercializing smallholder agriculture; enhancing productivity and competitiveness of traditional staple crop systems; and boosting productivity growth in the lagging regions.*

Smallholder Commercialization: Rising incomes and urbanization are leading to rapid diversification of national diets with high growth rates in demand for many high-value foods, particularly livestock products and fruits and vegetables (Pingali, 2007; Joshi *et al.*, 2007; Dorjee *et al.*, 2003). Trends in consumption pave the way for consolidation in the retail sector, which then reinforces dietary changes. Demand for safe food and for processed food products provides an entry point for organized, large scale retail outlets in urban areas (McCullough et al, 2008). The spread of supermarkets has been documented for specific countries and regions (Reardon and Timmer, 2007; Reardon and Berdegue, 2002; Dries et al, 2004; Weatherspoon and Reardon, 2003; and Hu et al, 2004). Meeting the growing urban demand for increased quantity, quality and diversity of food and agricultural products could be the new source agriculture sector growth. Will smallholders benefit from this trend?

The issue of agricultural commercialization and the small farmer is by no means new. Most developing countries have witnessed agriculture "moving away from traditional self-sufficiency" to an activity where "farm output is more responsive to market trends" (Pingali and Rosegrant, 1995). It has long been understood that with increasing economic growth, small farm production systems could not remain static and would need to gear themselves to some degree of commercialization for their survival. The commercialization process today has a very different face from even that of 10 years ago. What is new in the story of commercialization is the focus on agribusiness, and the scale at which agribusiness is influencing the process of change. There is a much greater degree of integration between producers and the output market, with a strong emphasis on standards in relation to quality and safety (Pingali 2007).

Small farmers find an increasingly skewed structure in the food system, facing on the one hand a small and reducing number of large food companies and food retailers. On the other hand, at the point of input supply to farmers, large chemical and seed companies are creating patented input supply systems controlled by a small number of companies (Napier, 2001). Facing this structure, small agricultural producers will find it increasingly difficult to negotiate favourable terms of the contract (Pingali, Khwaja, and Meijer, 2007).

Thus, entering the food system on a competitive basis is problematic for small farmers because of physical investments needed to enter but also because of the transactions costs associated with the new agricultural market (Pingali et al., 2007). The increasing disconnection between the modern food system and the established social networks and traditional institutions tends to aggravate the costs of market participation. Farmers will not enter markets when the value of participating is outweighed by the costs of undertaking the transaction (Sadoulet and de Janvry, 1995).

McCullough et al (2008) provide a detailed evaluation of developing country experiences of small holders integrating into modern retail chains. They argue that as long as there are entities or intermediaries that can buffer the scale specific needs of buyers against the capabilities of the small-scale producer, and cover their costs by adding value, there is no reason why smallholders should be excluded in a world where organized retail is expanding rapidly.

Enhancing competitivenes: Past investments in rural infrastructure, productivity enhancing technologies, as well as market institutions, make modernizing societies more responsive to global market signals. The reduction in anti-agriculture and anti-trade biases of policies of many modernizing countries has contributed to opening up of the food and agriculture sectors of these countries. Although, some of them are now moving towards protecting their agriculture sectors following the historical path of high income countries (Anderson, this volume).

Over the past four decades the net flow of agricultural commodities between developed and developing countries, has reversed direction. In the early 1960s, developing countries had an overall agricultural trade surplus of almost US$ 7 billion per year. By the end of the 1980s, however, this surplus had disappeared. During most of the 1990s and early 2000s, developing countries were net importers of agricultural products. The outlook to 2030 suggests that the agricultural trade deficit of developing countries will widen markedly, reaching an overall net import level of US$31 billion (FAO, 2002).

Increased developing country imports of cereals and livestock products are due to increased demand combined with the low competitiveness of their domestic agriculture, though the relative weight of these factors varies across countries. Low competitiveness is often the result of insufficient resource mobilisation for the enhanced competitiveness of poor rural communities, the sustainable use of natural resources, the provision of market infrastructure and research. Growing food imports are also the result of inflows of lower priced food from subsidised agriculture in developed countries. Rapid urbanisation, especially the growth of mega-cities on the coast, has added to the competitiveness of food imports relative to transporting it from the hinterlands.

With regard to agricultural exports, markets for traditional exports are generally saturated, but there is potential for significant gains by developing countries if the processing and marketing of value-added tropical products is moved from consumer to producer countries (FAO 2004b). However, lack of capacity on the part of the exporters and the presence of tariff escalation in the importing countries both contribute to the loss of potential export revenue. Capacity limitations are particularly felt in markets where access depends on increasingly strict sanitary and phyto-sanitary standards.

Some emerging economies have been able to diversify from their traditional agriculture export base into non-traditional agricultural exports, including fruits, vegetables and selected speciality and processed products (excluding trade in bananas and citrus). Hallam *et al*, (2004) estimate that such exports are currently worth more than US $ 30 billion annually. Developing countries held a 56 percent share of world trade in non-traditional fruit and vegetables in 2001. In the same year, developing countries also accounted for two-thirds of trade in selected speciality products, such as chillies, ginger and garlic. The non-traditional agricultural export market is, however, dominated by just a handful of countries. Some of these, such as Mexico, Chile, Argentina, Brazil and Costa Rica are leading developing country exporters of more than one product. Other countries are dominant in the market for only one product: for example; Kenya for green beans, Malaysia for minor tropical fruits, Thailand for minor fresh fruits and Zimbabwe for green peas.

Globalization and trade integration lead to both an improvement in the competitiveness of the staple food sector as well as a move towards diversification out of staples even where the production is primarily for domestic consumption. Reducing unit production cost through efficiency improvements is the primary means by which the staple food systems sustain their competitiveness. For instance, the switch to conservation tillage reduced production costs by as much as 30% per ton of wheat and soybean in Argentina and Brazil (Ekboir 2003). At the same time, the staple food sector is re-orientated towards supplying the diversified urban diets and towards high value exports. The returns to diversification are, however, conditional on investments in post harvest technologies for processing, quality and food safety. The benefits from a global orientation of the agricultural sector can be pro-poor where the production and post-harvest activities continue to be labour intensive (Pingali 2006).

Reducing inter-regional differences Significant inter-regional differences are observed even within countries well on the path towards agricultural transformation, in terms of agricultural productivity and responsiveness to urban and global market signals. Eastern India, Western China, and Northeast Brazil are examples of regions that get left behind even as these countries are making rapid economic progress. Relatively higher levels of poverty and food insecurity persist in these regions. Many of these regions have a disproportionately higher amount of land of poorer agro-climatic potential or suffer from a higher incidence of agriculture related stresses, such as drought.

These so-called marginal production environments face declining competitiveness in an increasingly integrated global food economy. However, we ought to note that an area might be marginal or less-favored for use as a crop production area under a specific production system, either for example due to water scarcity or lack of market access. The same area though could nevertheless become more favorable, if either new water-saving technologies or new marketing routes became available. For example, the availability of drought tolerant varieties may make maize production profitable in some parts of Eastern India. Hazell (this volume) argues that the marginal returns to research investments are relatively higher in these more marginal production environments than in the higher potential environments.

Lipper et al (2006) provide a framework for mapping development strategies for marginal production environments. In land abundant areas, including areas where rising off-farm employment opportunities have drawn populations out of rural areas, the potential for setting aside land for non-agricultural uses is high. Conversion of agricultural lands to forests contributes to carbon sequestration, watershed protection and biodiversity conservation. An example of this kind of conversion is China's Sloping Lands Program, in which the Chinese government has to goal of converting 14.6 million hectares of cropland on slopes into forest to stop soil erosion and improve water retention. Given the low opportunity cost of land, the trade-off with food and fiber production is small in these areas, particularly where transport infrastructure is a limiting factor for competitive agricultural production. On the other hand, in land scarce environments the trade-off between agricultural and nonagricultural services is high. The returns to agriculture R&D are high when targeted towards stress tolerant varieties of staple crops, and improved resource management technologies, such as water harvesting, agro-forestry and silvo-pastoral systems. Biofuel crop production is also worth examining, especially in areas that are better connected to markets.

Migration to urban areas or to regions of higher agricultural productivity (such as the Indian Punjab) is one of the few viable options for small farm and landless labour populations in these areas. Estudillo and Otsuka (this volume) provide evidence from Southeast Asia that shows that rural households in marginal environments benefitted from the Green Revolution through seasonal migration to higher potential areas. Investments in children's education paid for by migrants incomes helped create long term pathways out of poverty. When migration out of rural areas occurs faster than the growth in non-agricultural employment opportunities it results in a transfer of poverty rather than true poverty reduction associated with agricultural transformation (Ravallion et al., 2007). Hence macroeconomic policies that promote overall economic growth are absolutely crucial, if the poverty reduction gains made by agriculture productivity growth are to be sustained over the long term. It's only in these conditions that we begin to see a drop in rural labour force that is commiserate with the declining share of agriculture in GDP.

Countries at the high end of the transformation process

These are mainly high income countries with relatively small rural populations, such as the USA, the EU countries, Australia, New Zealand, Japan, South Korea, etc. Agriculture typically accounts for less than 10 per cent of GDP and less than 15 per cent of the work force. Agriculture sectors in Industrial economies are highly commercialized, vertically integrated and globalized. For these countries the big challenge will be to create new opportunities for rural incomes while liberalizing trade and reducing current levels of protection on commodities that developing countries have a unique comparative advantage in, such as: cotton, rice, & sugar. In this context the non-commodity roles of agriculture, such as biodiversity conservation, agro-tourism, carbon sequestration, provide opportunities for the emergence of markets.

Preserving rural societies and landscapes becomes important not only for political and nostalgic reasons, but also as a matter of economics. This could become an increasingly important trend in middle income countries as they reach the end of the transformation process. Public policy needs to create an enabling environment for the emergence of markets for environmental services. Direct public support for sustaining the non-commodity roles of agriculture would only be necessary under market failure conditions. Fortunately the OECD countries have the income to pay for this support, if necessary.

4. PUBLIC POLICY FOR MANAGING AGRICULTURAL RENAISSANCE

Designing food and agriculture policy is substantially more complex in today's world than it was in the past when relatively closed food economies were the norm. While, chronic hunger and poverty continue to be daunting problems in much of the developing world, income growth, urbanization and global inter-connectedness bring about new policy challenges both for countries well into the process of agricultural transformation and for countries at the lower end of the transformation process. Climate change adds to and/or intensifies the stresses faced by poor farm households, particularly those in the least developed countries and the dollar poor in the emerging economies. The food policy needs to be redesigned and adapted to the emerging trends that developing countries are facing while at the same time ensuring that it reflects the stage of the transformation process that the country is in. The following are some of the areas of policy focus and re-direction.

Continued emphasis on promoting agriculture as an "engine of growth"

For countries at the low end of the transformation process, concerted action towards enhancing food security especially through agricultural productivity growth is crucial in the quest for income growth and economic development. The same is true for low productivity regions in countries that are well into the process of agricultural modernization. While "trickle down" from globalization induced income growth can to some extent help alleviate poverty and food insecurity it will not be adequate without concerted efforts targeted at the neediest populations. Productivity-induced agricultural growth has a wider impact on rural areas through the strengthening of off-farm activities, rural employment and wages. Thereby, moving the society, region and country, onto the agricultural transformation trajectory.

Some argue that the benefits of low food prices are as easily accessed by trade as by investing in domestic agriculture (Sachs, 1997). This argument ignores the strong historical connection between domestic food production and consumption because of the difficulty and expense of transporting and marketing food staples in rural areas, far from ports and efficient transport links (Timmer, 2002). "For both microeconomic and macroeconomic reasons, no country has ever sustained the process of rapid economic growth without first solving the problem of food security" (Timmer, 2002).

Enhancing food security in the rural areas entails improvements in the productivity of smallholder agriculture. In the first instance, enhancing local food supplies contributes to improved household nutrition and thereby contributes to labor performance improvements. In the long term it broadens participation in market-led growth. Promoting sustainable use of natural resources, improving rural infrastructure, research and communications, facilitating the functioning of markets and enhancing rural institutions are integral parts of the strategy.

Recent interest in fertilizer subsidies as an instrument for jumpstarting agricultural productivity growth ought to be viewed with caution. An across-the-board fertilizer subsidy is unlikely to benefit many smallholders, especially in African, given poor infrastructure and under developed agro-dealer networks. A focus on alleviating infrastructure and input supply constraints as well as improving procurement efficiency (joint procurement arrangements and regional procurement hubs) could achieve the goal of enhancing farm level fertilizer supplies at a lower price. Facilitating the movement of fertilizers across borders (removing customs duties and export taxes) will contribute to overall improvements in supply efficiency. A carefully targeted and time bound fertilizer subsidy program may be defensible when introduced as part of a balanced pro-poor growth strategy. Complementary investments in infrastructure, extension, credit, and enabling market oriented policies must also be part of the strategy. Underwriting the risks of agro-dealer network penetration into lower potential production environments may be an important element of the above strategy. Even where targeted fertilizer subsidies are justifiable on pro-poor grounds, it ought to be recognized that the costs associated with these programs can be very high, in operational terms (how targeting is done) as well as in terms of the opportunity cost of foregone alternatives.

Re-orienting agricultural research and development priorities

Harnessing the best of scientific knowledge and technological breakthroughs is crucial as we attempt to "retool" agriculture to face the challenges of an increasingly commercialised and globalised agriculture sector. The primary objective of the research system remains to generate new technologies that sustainably improve productivity and farmers' income. Governments have a difficult task to perform: on one hand, continued food security needs to be assured for populations that are growing in absolute terms; on the other hand, research and infrastructural investments need to be made for diversification out of the primary staples. In responding to diversification trends, the research should not abruptly shift from an exclusive focus on one set of commodities to another set of commodities. The focus of research should be to provide farmers the flexibility to make crop choice decisions and to move relatively freely between crops and other agricultural enterprises (Pingali and Rosegrant, 1995).

For countries at the early stages of the transformation process, modern science and technology can help provide new impetus for addressing the age-old problems of yield improvement, production variability and food insecurity especially for rural populations living in marginal production environments. Whilst the real and potential gains from science and technology are apparent, it is also necessary to take into consideration the fact that research and technology development are more and more in the private domain: biotechnology is a prime example.

For commercial crops in favourable production environments private sector generated transgenic crops have reduced yield variability, and reduced unit production costs, the latter due to the diminished need for insecticides. An enabling policy environment that includes intellectual property protection, reduced trade barriers, and a transparent bio-safety procedure will lead to further private sector research investments for commercial production systems in the countries that are well into the transformation process. However, large areas of the developing world, especially sub-Saharan Africa, remain outside the orbit of private sector interest. The private sector is also unlikely to invest in research for difficult growing environments, such as drought prone or high temperature environments. Public sector research investments ought to be partnered with the rapid progress being made by the private sector in order to meet the needs of the poor (FAO, 2004c).

Creating an enabling environment for smallholder transformation

The challenges faced by smallholder agriculture should be seen in the context of the general trends that will influence the structure of agricultural production. Namely, the transformation of diets and rising import competition will contribute to the increasing commercialization of the small farm sector. Governments ought to help create an enabling environment for smallholder commercialization through infrastructure investments and institutional reform.

Rural infrastructure investments play a crucial role in inducing farmers to move toward a commercial agricultural system. The emphasis for public investments should be on improving general transport, communications, and market infrastructure, while allowing the private sector to invest in commodity-specific processing, storage, and marketing facilities. Accessible and cost-effective communication systems such as mobile telephones can help generate information and other market-related services. The Internet explosion and related technologies have drastically reduced exchange and search costs in many Organisation for Economic Co-operation and Development countries and may be highly indicative of the potential benefits to developing countries (Bussolo and Whalley, 2003).

Efficient land markets and secure property rights are essential to capture agricultural growth (Binswanger et. al., 1993). Where land rights are secure, farmers have the greater incentive needed to invest in land improvements. Moreover, land ownership is an important source of collateral that can improve the credit status of farmers, leading to easier access to funding for inputs and so forth (Feder et al., 1988). Individual farmers and households need to be assured "stable engagement" with other resources, such as water, water use rights that are flexible enough to promote comparative advantage in food staples and cash crops. Those rights must be matched by access to rural credit and finance and the dissemination of technology and good practices in water use (De Haen et al., 2003).

Reducing small farm transactions costs

Smallholder participation in commercial and vertically integrated markets is becoming an issue of major concern, especially in countries with rapidly modernizing agricultural systems. Because transaction costs vary over households and enterprises, commodities and regions, there is no single innovation or intervention, public or private, which can reduce them. However, there are a number of ways in which market entry by small farmers can be developed. These include contract farming, the development of farmer organizations for marketing, development of the supply chain for high value exports produced by smallholders through an appropriate mix of *private* and *public* sector initiatives and facilitating private sector provision of market information via improved telecommunications (Kydd et al., 2000; MCCullough et al. 2008). Hayami (this volume) argues that the scale economies associated with plantation agriculture can be recreated through contract farming arrangements that tie together the activities of a large number of small farmers in a particular area. Lipton (this volume) suggests that the emergence of intermediaries between small farmers and large buyers is crucial to ensure positive welfare benefits. Lipton indicates that some initial subsidy to administrative cost of (rather than to prices paid or charged by) intermediaries may be necessary.

The role of government is crucial in specifying property rights and enforcing contracts in order to promote specialization and reduce the costs of market exchange

(North, 2000). Moreover, government policy needs to create incentives and send signals that encourage private sector participation in developing rural economies. Investing in market and transport infrastructure, as well as transport services, will reduce transactions costs associated with negotiation as marketing costs are lowered and more marketing channels become available. Improving the legal and institutional environment surrounding contract formulation and arbitration will reduce smallholders' costs of entering into more formal agreements by making them more available. Public investments in specific chains and projects should be carefully considered. Picking "winners" is problematic (McCullough et al, 2008). The bottom line is that public sector interventions are best left for public good provision and institutional reforms to correct incomplete or absent markets and improve the rural business climate. The reduction of transaction costs associated with particular commodity production and processing systems is best left in the hands of the private sector.

Seeking complementarity between trade and domestic policy

Trade liberalization can be a powerful tool to promote economic growth, however, low income countries, in order to benefit from trade reform, will need to enhance domestic competitiveness through policy and institutional reform (FAO 2005). Liberalization of domestic markets, through removal of quantitative restrictions on trade, and opening up of economies to internal trade opportunities is often a key step in starting or accelerating the process of commercialization. Anderson (this volume) argues for a strategy that would treat agriculture in the same way that the non-farm tradable sectors are treated. That would involve opening the sector to international competition, and relying on more-efficient domestic policy measures for raising government revenue (e.g., sales tax or value added tax).

While OECD countries have made significant progress in reducing trade distorting policies in proportional terms, support to farmers in dollar terms continues to grow because of growth in the value of farm output (Anderson, this volume). Moreover, domestic support continues to be high for commodities such as, rice, milk, sugar, and cotton, where developing countries are more efficient producers and could compete effectively. OECD farm policy reform can have direct and beneficial impact on developing country agriculture, particularly for countries in the early stages of the transformation process.

Trade liberalization, for countries at the low end of the transformation process, could have adverse effects, particularly in the short run as productive sectors and labour markets adjust. To minimize the adverse effects and to take better advantage of emerging opportunities, such as those arising from agriculture diversification to bioenergy and other non-food products, governments need to understand better how trade policy fits into the national strategy to promote poverty reduction and food security. Trade liberalization should go hand in hand with public support for improving agriculture productivity and competitiveness.

Establishing safety standards and regulations

Globalization increases the "effective demand" for safe and healthy food. Government schemes to certify quality and safe food according to public regulations are required. This is important for domestic consumption and food safety, and even more so if a country wants to access foreign markets. If a country wants to export, it is necessary that an independent body will guarantee that the produce adheres to the required quality and safety standards, such as *Codex Alimentarius* that is jointly serviced by FAO and WHO (De haen, et al, 2003). However, public systems to ensure food quality and safety suffer from lack of organization and adequate funding. To the extent that developing country governments do not impose international-level standards, private standards are being implemented by the leading players in retail and food processing (Reardon and Farina, 2001).

Enhancing incentives for sustainable resource use

Public policy can play an important role in encouraging the sustainable use of natural resources. First, by correcting incentive-distorting policies which encourage unsustainable use of the resource base (Pingali, 2001). Second, by identifying market based instruments for promoting the supply of environmental services through appropriate changes in agricultural production systems and land use.

Governments have a role to play in stimulating desirable land use change as well. In the process of economic development, as agricultural populations shrink and non-agricultural sectors grow, the potential for setting aside land for non-agricultural uses is high. Conversion of marginal agricultural lands to forests contributes to carbon sequestration, watershed protection and biodiversity conservation. OECD countries are going through this process of land use change supported by public polices such as the Conservation Reserve Program in the U.S. For developing countries with similar conditions in the agricultural sector, national and international public sector support for land use changes that generate global environmental goods and services can be an important means of attaining sustainable resource use. However, the successful incorporation of environmental services into the livelihoods of the poor via changes in either agricultural production systems or land use is dependent on the presence of enabling conditions such as property rights, food security and low transactions costs, as well as local and global recognition and willingness to pay for environmental goods and services.

Enabling income and livelihood diversification

It is important to start by recognizing that rural households, at all stages of development, rely on a diverse set of non-farm opportunities for earning incomes and sustaining food security and livelihoods. Higher agricultural productivity has contributed to the growth in rural non-farm and off-farm income earning opportunities through backward and forward linkages. Surveys of the rural non-farm literature indicate rural non-farm income represents on average 42% of rural income in Africa, 32% in Asia, 40% in Latin America and 44% in Eastern Europe and CIS countries (Davis, 2004; FAO 1998). The diversity of income generating activities in the rural areas calls for policies with wider impact as opposed to sector specific policies: education and rural infrastructure such as communications, roads and electrification will have beneficial effects to a wide spectrum of rural activities (Winters et al, 2006). Public investments ought to be accompanied by policies that induce complementary flows of private investment. Finally, public investments made to create an enabling environment for non-farm employment will also be useful in preparing populations for exits from rural areas as economic development proceeds.

End Note

1. Deputy Director, Agriculture Development Division, at the Bill & Melinda Gates Foundation. Views expressed in this chapter are personal and should not be attributed to the Foundation. This chapter builds on my Presidential Address to the International Association of Agricultural Economists in August 2006. While this is the closing chapter of the Handbook it does not try to provide a comprehensive synthesis of all the chapters in the volume, but it highlights some of the material selectively in making the case for an agricultural renaissance.

References

Alston, J. M., Norton, G. W., & Pardey, P. G. (1995). *Science Under Scarcity: Principles and Practices for Agricultural Research Evaluation and Priority Setting*. Ithaca, New York: Cornell University.

Anderson, K. (2006). Subsidies and Trade Barriers. In: B. Lomborg (Ed.), *Solutions for the World's Biggest Problems*. Cambridge University Press.

Anderson, K., Martin, W., & van der Mensbrugghe, D. (2006). 'Distortions to World Trade: Impacts on Agricultural Markets and Farm Incomes'. *Review of Agricultural Economics*, 28(2), 168–194, Summar.

Binswanger, H. P. (1980). Income distribution effects of technical change: Some analytical issues. *South East Asian Economic Review*, 1, 179–218.

Binswanger, H. P., Deininger, K., & Feder, G. (1993). Agricultural land relations in the developing world. *American Journal of Agricultural Economics*, 75, 1242–1248.

Binswanger, H. P., & McCalla (this volume)

Boehlje, M. (1999). Structural changes in the agricultural industries: how do we measure, analyze and understand them? *American Journal of Agricultural Economics*, 81, 1028–1041.

Bussolo, M., & Whalley, J. (2003). *Globalization in developing countries: the role of transaction costs in explaining economic performance in India*. Development Centre Working Papers. Paris: OECD Development Centre.

Byerlee, D., de Janvry, A., & Sadoulet, E. (2009). Agriculture for Development: Toward a New Paradigm. *Annual Review of Resources Economics*.

Chopra, M., Galbraith, S., & Darnton-Hill, I. (2002). A global response to a global problem: the epidemic of overnutrition. *Bulletin of the World Health Organization*, 80, 952–958.

Christiaensen, L., Demery, L., & Kuhl, J. (2006). *The Role of Agriculture in Poverty Reduction: And Empirical Perspective*. Policy Research Working Paper No. 4013.Washington DC: World Bank.

Davis, J. (2004). *The Rural Non-Farm Ecnomy, Livelihoods and their Diversification: Issues and Options*. Chatham, UK: Natural Resource Institute.

De Haen, H., Stamoulis, K., Shetty, P., & Pingali, P. (2003). The world food economy in the twenty-first century: Challenges for international co-operation. *Development Policy Review*, 21, 683–696.

de Janvry, A. (1984). *Searching for styles of development: lessons from Latin America and implications for India.* Working Paper No. 357. Berkeley, California: University of California.

Delgado, C. L., Hopkins, J., Kelly, V. A., Hazell, P., McKenna, A. A., Gruhn, P., et al. (1994). *Agricultural growth linkages in Sub-Saharan Africa.* Washington, DC: US Agency for International Development.

Diao, X. S., et al. (2006). *Market opportunities for African agriculture: an examination of demand-side constraints on agricultural growth.* Washington DC: International Food Policy Research Institute.

Diao, Xinshen, Peter Hazell, Danielle Resnick, & James Thurlow (2006). "The Role of Agriculture in Development: Implications for Sub-Saharan Africa." Washington DC, IFPRI Discussion Paper.

Dixon, J., Gulliver, A., & Gibbon, D. (2001). *Farming Systems and Poverty: Improving Farmers' Livelihoods in a Changing World.* Rome, Italy and Washington, DC: FAO and the World Bank.

Dolan, C., & Humphrey, J. (2001). Governance and trade in fresh vegetables: the impact of UK supermarkets on the African horticultural industry. *Journal of Development Studies, 37,* 147–176.

Dorjee, Kinlay, Broca, Sumter, & Pingali, Prabhu (2007). "Diversification in South Asian Agriculture; Trends and Constraints." In Joshi, P.K., Gulati, Ashok, & Cummings, Ralph, Jr. (eds). Agricultural Diversification and Smallholders in South Asia. New Delhi: Academic Press, pp. 129-150.

Dries, L., Reardon, T., & Swinnen, J. (2004). 'The rapid rise of supermarkets in central and eastern Europe: implications for the agrifood sector and rural development,' *Development Policy Review,* vol 22, no 5, pp. 525–556, 2004.

Eastwood, R., Lipton, M., & Newell, A. (2005). Farm Size. In R. Evenson, & P. L. Pingali (Eds.), *Handbook of Agricultural Economics.* Amsterdam: North Holland press.

Ekboir, J. M. (2003). Adoption of no-till by small farmers: Understanding the generation of complex technologies. In L. Garcia-Torres, J. Benites, A. Martinez-Vilela, & A. Holgado-Cabrera (Eds.), *Conservation Agriculture: Environment, Farmers Experiences, Innovations, Socio-Economy, Policy.* The Netherlands: Kluwer Academic Publishers.

Fan, S., & Pardey, P. (1998). Government Spending on Asian Agriculture: Trends and Production Consequence. In *Agricultural Public Finance Policy in Asia.* Tokyo: Asian Productivity Organization.

Fan, S., Hazell, P., & Thorat, S. (1999). *Linkages between government spending, growth and poverty in rural India.* Research Report 110. Washington DC: IFPRI.

Fan, S., Hazell, P., & Thorat, S. (2000). Government Spending, Growth and Poverty in India. *American Journal of Agricultural Economics, 82*(4), 1038–1051.

Fan, S., Fang, C., & Zhang, X. (2001). "How agricultural research affects urban poverty in developing countries: The case of China." EPT Discussion Paper No. 83. Washington, DC: International Food Policy Research Institute.

Fan, S. (2002). *Agricultural Research and Urban Poverty in India.* Environment and Production Technology Division. Discussion Paper, September, 2002.

Fan, S., & Rao, N. (2003). *Public spending in developing countries: Trends, determination, and impact.* Environment, Production and Technology Division Discussion Paper 99. Washington, DC: International Food Policy Research Institute.

Fan, & Brzeska (this volume)

FAO. 1998. *The State of Food and Agriculture 1998: Rural non-farm income in developing countries.* Rome, Italy: Food and Agriculture Organization.

FAO. (2002). *World agriculture: towards 2015/2030.* Rome: FAO.

FAO. (2004). *The state of food insecurity in the world.* Rome: FAO.

FAO. (2004a). *Socio-economic analysis and policy implications of the roles of agriculture in developing countries.* Research Programme Summary Report. Rome, Italy: Roles of Agriculture Project, FAO.

FAO. (2004b). *The state of agricultural commodity markets.* Rome, Italy: Food and Agriculture Organization.

FAO. (2004c). *The State of Food and Agriculture 2003–2004: Agricultural biotechnology, meeting the needs of the poor?* Rome, Italy: Food and Agriculture Organization.

FAO. 2005. *The State of Food and Agriculture 2005: Making trade work for the poor.* Rome, Italy: Food and Agriculture Organization.

Feder, G., Onchan, Y., Chalamwong, Y., & Hongladarom, C. (1988). *Land policies and farm productivity in Thailand.* London: Johns Hopkins University Press.

Fei, J. C., & Ranis, G. (1961). A theory of economic development. *American Economic Review, 514*, 533–565.

Fischer, G., et al. (2005). Socio-economic and climate change impacts on agriculture: an integrated assessment. *Philosophical Transactions of the Royal Biological Sciences Society, 360*, 2067–2083.

Fuller, F., Tuan, F., & Wailes, E. (2001). Rising demand for meat: who will feed China's hogs? In USDA (Ed.), *China's Food and Agriculture: Issues for the 21st Century. AIB-775*. Washington DC: Economic Research Service, United States Department of Agriculture.

Gollin (2009). (this volume)

Hallam, D., Liu, P., Lavers, G., Pilkauskas, P., Rapsomanikis, G., & Claro, J. (2004). 'The market for non-traditional agricultural exports,' FAO Commodities and Trade Technical Paper, FAO, Rome.

Hallum, et al. (2004). *The market for non-traditional agricultural exports.* FAO Commodities and Trade Technical Paper.

Hasan, R., & Quibria, M. G. (2004). Industry matters for poverty: A critique of agricultural fundamentalism. *Kyklos, 57*, 253–264.

Hayami, Y., & Herdt, R. W. (1977). Market price effects of technological change on income distribution in semi-subsistence agriculture. *American Journal of Agricultural Economics, 59*, 245–256.

Hazell, P., & Haggeblade, S. (1993). Farm-nonfarm growth linkages and the welfare of the poor. In M. Lipton, & J. van de Gaag (Eds.), *Including the poor*. Washington, DC: The World Bank.

Hazell, P. (2009). (this volume)

Herdt (2009). (this volume)

Hirschman, A. O. (1958). *The Strategy of Economic Development in Developing Countries*. New Haven, Connecticut, USA: Yale University Press.

Hoddinott, J., & Yohannes, Y. (2002). *Dietary Diversity as a Food Security Indicator*. Food Consumption and Nutrition Division Discussion Paper No. 136. Washington DC: International Food and Policy Research Institute.

Huang, J., & Bouis, H. (1996). *Structural Changes in the Demand for Food in Asia*. 2020 Brief 41. International Food Policy Research Institute.

Hu, D., Reardon, T., Rozelle, S., Timmer, C., & Wang, H. (2004). 'The emergence of supermarkets with Chinese characteristics: challenges and opportunities for China's agricultural development,' *Development Policy Review*, vol 22, no 4, pp. 557–586, September 2006.

IPCC (2007). Fourth Assessment Report. Climate Change 2007: Synthesis Report.

Johnston, B. F., & Mellor, J. W. (1961). The role of agriculture in economic development. *American Economic Review, 51*, 566–593.

Jorgenson, D. G. (1961). The development of a dual economy. *Economic Journal, 71*, 309–334.

Joshi, P.K., Gulati, Ashok, & Cummings, Ralph, Jr. (eds). Agricultural Diversification and Smallholders in South Asia. New Delhi: Academic Press, 2007.

Kydd, J., Poulton, C., et al. (2000). *Globalisation, agricultural liberalisation, and market access for the rural poor*. Kent, UK: Wye College.

Lewis, W. A. (1954). Economic development with unlimited supplies of labour. *Manchester School of Economics, 20*, 139–191.

Lippor Lipper, L., Pingali, P., & Zurek, M. (2006). Less-favoured areas: looking beyond agriculture towards ecosystem services. In R. Ruben, J. Pender, & A. Kuyvenhoven (Eds.), *Sustainable Poverty Reduction in Less-Favoured Areas: Problems, Options and Strategies*. (pp. 442–460). Wallingford, UK: CABI.

Masters, W. & Anderson, K., (Eds.). (2009). *Distortions to Agricultural Incentives in Africa*. Washington DC: World Bank.

McCullough, E., Pingali, P., & Stamoulis, K. (2008). In E. McCullough, Pingali, & Stamoulis, P. (Eds.), *The Transformation of Agri-Food Systems: Globalization, Supply Chains, and Smallholder Farmers*. Rome, Italy: Food and Agriculture Organization.

Mellor, J. W. (1976). *The New Economics of Growth: A Strategy for India and the Developing World*. Ithaca, NY: Cornell University Press.

Mendez, M., & Popkin, B. (2004). Globalization, Urbanization and Nutritional Change in the Developing World. *Journal of Agricultural and Development Economics, 1*(4), 220–241.

Murgai, R., Ali, M., & Byerlee, D. (2001). Productivity growth and sustainability in post-Green Revolution agriculture: the case of the Indian and Pakistan Punjabs. *World Bank Research Observer, 16*(2), 199–218.

Napier, R. (2001). *Global trends impacting farmers: implications for family farm management, Paper presented at Pulse Days, 2001.* Australia: Saskatoon. New South Whales.

North, D. C. (2000). Revolution in economics. In C. Menard (Eds.), *Institutions, Contracts, and Organisations: Perspectives from New Institutional Economics.* Cheltenham, UK: Edward Elgar.

Parry, et al. (2004). Effects of climate change on global food production under SRES emissions and socio-economic scenarios. *Global Environmental Change, 14*(1), 53–67.

Parry, et al. (2005). Climate change, global food supply and risk of hunger. *Philosophical Transactions of the Royal Society, 360,* 2125–2138.

Pingali, P. L., & Rosegrant, M. (1995). Agricultural commercialization and diversification: Processes and policies. *Food Policy, 20,* 171–185.

Pingali, P. L. (1997). From subsistence to commercial production systems: the transformation of Asian agriculture. *American Journal of Agricultural Economics, 79*(2), 628–634.

Pingali, P. L., Hossain, M., & Gerpacio, R. V. (1997). *Asian rice bowls: the returning crisis?* Wallingford, UK: CAB International.

Pingali, P. L. (1998). Confronting the ecological consequences of the rice Green Revolution in tropical Asia. In C. K. Eicher, & J. M. Staatz (Eds.), *International Agricultural Development* Baltimore: Johns Hopkins University Press.

Pingali, P. L. (2001). Policy re-directions for sustainable resource use: the rice-wheat cropping system of the Indo-Gangetic Plains. *Journal of Crop Production, 3*(2), 103–118.

Pingali, P. L., & Rosegrant, M. (2001). Intensive food systems in Asia: Can the degradation problems be reversed? In D. R. Lee, & C. B. Barrett (Eds.), *Tradeoffs or Synergies? Agricultural intensification, economic development and the environment.* Wallingford, UK: CABI.

Pingali, P., & Traxler, G. (2002). Changing locus of agricultural research: will the poor benefit from biotechnology and privatization trends? *Food Policy, 27*(2), 223–238.

Pingali, P., & Stringer, R. (2004). Agriculture's contributions to economic and social development. *Electronic Journal of Agricultural and Development Economics, 1,* 1–5.

Pingali, P. L. (2006). Agricultural growth and economic development: a view through the globalization lens. Presidential Address to the 26th International Conference of Agricultural Economists, Gold Coast, Australia, 12–18 August, 2006.

Pingali, P. L., & Khwaja, Y. (2004). *Globalisation of Indian diets and the transformation of food supply systems.* ESA Working Paper No. 04-05. Rome, Italy: FAO.

Pingali, P. L., Khwaja, Y., & Meijer, M. (2007). The role of the public and private sector in commercializing small farms and reducing transaction costs. In J. F. M. Swinnen (Eds.), *Global Supply Chains, Standards, and the Poor.* Wallingford, UK: CABI Publications.

Pingali, P. L. (2007). Westernization of Asian diets and the transformation of food systems: Implications for research and policy. *Food Policy, 32*(3), 281–298.

Pingali, P., & Raney, T. (2007). Sowing a Gene Revolution. *Scientific American,* September.

Pingali, P., & McCullough, E. (in press) (2009). Drivers of Change in Global Agriculture and Livestock Systems. In H. Steinfeld, H. Mooney, & F. Schneider (Eds.), *Livestock in a Changing Landscape.*

Pinstrup-Andersen, P., Ruiz de Londaño, N., & Hoover, E. (1976). The impact of increasing food supply on human nutrition: Implications for commodity priorities in agricultural research. *American Journal of Agricultural Economics, 58,* 131–142.

Popkin, B. (1999). Urbanization, lifestyle changes and nutrition transition. *World Development, 27*(11), 1905–1916.

Population Division of the Department of Economic and Social Affairs of the United Nations Secretariat (2006) *World Population Prospects: The 2006 Revision and World Urbanization Prospects: The 2005 Revision,* [online] http://esa.un.org/unpp.

Rangarajan, C. (1982). *Agricultural growth and industrial performance in India.* Research Report 33. Washington DC: IFPRI.

Ranis, G., Stewart, F., & Angeles-Reyes, E. (1990). *Linkages in Developing Economies: A Philippine Study*. San Francisco: ICS Press.

Ravillion, & Datt (1996). How important to India's poor is the sectoral composition of economic growth? *World Bank Economic Review*, *10*(1), 1–26.

Ravillion, M., Chen, S., & Sangraula, P. (2007). New evidence on the urbanization of global poverty. Background Paper for the WDR 2008.

Reardon, T., & Farina, E. M. (2001). The rise of private food quality and safety standards: Illustrations from Brazil. *International Food and Agribusiness Management Review*, *4*, 413–421.

Reardon, T., Berdegue, J., & Farrington, J. (2002). *Supermarkets and farming in Latin America: Pointing directions for elsewhere?* Natural Resource Perspectives No. 81. London: Overseas Development Institute.

Reardon, T., & Berdegue, J. (2002a). The rapid rise of supermarkets in Latin America: Challenges and opportunities for development. *Development Policy Review*, *20*(4), 371–388.

Reardon, T., & Berdegue, J. (2002b). Supermarkets and agrifood systems: Latin American challenges. *Development Policy Review*, *20*, Theme Issue.

Reardon, T., Timmer, C. P., Barrett, C., & Berdegue, J. (2003). The rise of supermarkets in Africa, Asia, and Latin America. *American Journal of Agricultural Economics*, *85*, 1140–1146.

Reardon, T., Stamoulis, K., & Pingali, P. (2007). Rural Nonfarm Employment in Developing Countries in an era of Globalization. In K. Otsuka, & K. Kalirajan (Eds.), *Contributions of Agricultural Economics to Critical Policy Issues: Proceedings of the Twenty-Sixth Conference of the International Association of Agricultural Economists, 12–18 August, 2006*. Brisbane, Australia: Blackwell Publishing, Malden.

Regmi, A., & Dyck, J. (2001). Effects of urbanization on global food demand. In: A. Regmi (Eds.), *Changing Structures of Global Food Consumption and Trade*. ERS WRS 01-1. Washington, DC: Economic Research Service, United States Department of Agriculture.

Rondot, P., Bienabe, E., & Collion, M. (2004). *Rural economic organization and market restructuring: What challenges, what opportunities for small holders?* A global issue paper. Paris, France: CIRAD.

Rosegrant, M., Ageaoili-Sombilaa, M., & Perez, N. (1995). *Food projections to 2020: Implications for investment*. Washington, DC: International Food Policy Research Institute.

Rosenstein-Rodan, P. N. (1943). Problems of industrialization of Eastern and South-Eastern Europe. *Economic Journal*, *53*, 202–211.

Ruel, M. T., Garrett, J. L., Morris, S. M., Maxwell, D., Oshaug, A., Engle, P., et al. (1998). *Urban challenges to food and nutrition security: A review of food security, health, and caregiving in the cities*. IFPRI FCND Discussion Paper No. 51. Washington, DC: International Food Policy Research Institute.

Sachs, J. (1997). Nature, nurture, and growth. *Economist June*, *14*, 9–27.

Sadoulet, E., & de Janvry, A. (1995). *Quantitative Development Policy Analysis*. Baltimore, Maryland: John Hopkins University Press.

Scitovsky, T. (1954). Two concepts of external economies. *Journal of Political Economy*, *62*, 143–151.

Stern, N. (2007). *The Economics of Climate Change. The Stern review*. Cambridge University Press, Cambridge, UK.

Thirtle, C., Lin, L., & Piesse, J. (2003). The Impact of Research-Led Agricultural Productivity Growth on Poverty Reduction in Africa, Asia, and Latin America. *World Development*, *31*(12), 1959–1975.

Timmer, C. P. (1988). The agricultural transformation. In H. Chenery, & T. N. Srinivasan (Eds.), *Handbook of Development Economics* Amsterdam: North Holland.

Timmer, C. P. (1997). Farmers and markets: the political economy of new paradigms. *American Journal of Agricultural Economics*, *79*, 621–627.

Timmer, C. P. (2002). Agriculture and economic development. In B. Gardner, & G. Rausser (Eds.), *Handbook of Agricultural Economics*. Amsterdam, North Holland: Elsevier Science.

Timmer, C. P. (2008). Food policy in the era of supermarkets: What's different. In E. McCullough, Pingali, & P. Stamoulis (Eds.), *The Transformation of Agri-Food Systems: Globalization, Supply Chains, and Smallholder Farmers*. Rome, Italy: Food and Agriculture Organization.

Valdes, A., & Foster, W. (2005). *Reflections on the role of agriculture in pro-poor growth*. Paper prepared for the research workshop: the future of small farms. Kent: Wye College.

Weatherspoon, D., & Reardon, T. (2003). 'The rise of supermarkets in Africa: implications for agrifood systems and the rural poor,' *Development Policy Review*, vol 21, no 3, pp. 333–355.

Winters, P., Carletto, G., Davis, B., Stamoulis, K., & Zezza, A. (2006). *Rural income-generating activities in developing countries: a multi-country analysis.* Paper prepared for the conference "Beyond Agriculture: the Promise of the Rural Economy for Growth and Poverty Reduction," January 16–18, 2006. Rome, Italy: Food and Agriculture Organization.

World Bank. (2006a). *World Development Indicators*, Washington, DC: World Bank.

World Bank. (2006b). *Global Economic Prospects: Economic implications of remittances and migration.* Washington, DC: International Bank for Reconstruction and Development.

World Bank. (2007). *World Development Report 2008: Agriculture for Development.* World Bank: Washington DC.

World Bank. (2008). *World Development Indicators.* Washington DC: World Bank.

World Bank. (2009). *"Awakening Africa's sleeping giant: Prospects for commercial agriculture in the Guinea Savannah zone and beyond,"* Washington DC, 2009.

Page numbers followed by *b*, *f*, or *t* indicates boxes, figures or tables, respectively.